Object-Oriented Programming with Java™

An Introduction

David J. Barnes

Department of Computer Science
University of Kent at Canterbury

Prentice Hall
Upper Saddle River, New Jersey 07458
www.prenhall.com

An Alan R. Apt Book

Library of Congress Cataloging-in-Publication Data

Barnes, D. (David J.)
    Object oriented programming with Java: an introduction/David J. Barnes
      p. cm.
    Includes bibliographical references and index.
    ISBN 0-13-086900-7
      1. Object-oriented programming (Computer science)   2. Java (Computer
program language) I. Title

QA76.64 B38 2000
005.13′3—dc21   99-057040
                                                CIP

Vice president and editorial director: *Marcia Horton*
Publisher: *Alan R. Apt*
Editorial assistant: *Toni Holm*
Marketing manager: *Jennie Burger*
Production editor: *Interactive Composition Corporation*
Executive managing editor: *Vince O'Brien*
Managing editor: *David A. George*
Art director: *Heather Scott*
Interior design: *Liah Rose*
Cover design: *John Christiana*
Cover image: *"sense" by snail snail ©1999 John Barnes*
Manufacturing manager: *Trudy Pisciotti*
Manufacturing buyer: *Beth Sturla*
Assistant vice president of production and manufacturing: *David W. Riccardi*

© 2000 by Prentice-Hall, Inc.
Upper Saddle River, New Jersey

The author and publisher of this book have used their best efforts in preparing this book. These efforts
include the development, research, and testing of the theories to determine their effectiveness.

Printed in the United States of America
10   9   8   7   6   5   4   3   2   1

ISBN 0-13-086900-7

Prentice-Hall International (UK) Limited, *London*
Prentice-Hall of Australia Pty. Limited, *Sydney*
Prentice-Hall Canada Inc., *Toronto*
Prentice-Hall Hispanoamericana, S.A., *Mexico*
Prentice-Hall of India Private Limited, *New Delhi*
Prentice-Hall of Japan, Inc., *Tokyo*
Pearson Education Asia Pte. Ltd., *Singapore*
Editora Prentice-Hall do Brasil, Ltda., *Rio de Janeiro*

This book is dedicated to

Helen,

John, Hannah, Ben, and Sarah

With thanks for being a loving family

$\Delta O \Xi A E N \Upsilon \Psi I \Sigma T O I \Sigma \Theta E \Omega$

Contents

List of Tables

Preface

Introduction

This book is designed for those readers who wish to start learning to program in an object-oriented programming language. It has been designed primarily as a first programming text. It is also suitable for those who already have some experience with another programming language, and who now wish to move on to an object-oriented one. Indeed, much of the material is based on courses delivered by the author to students with a wide range of both non-programming and programming backgrounds. The language we use to teach object-oriented programming is Java.

Since its arrival on the scene in 1995, the adoption of Java as a primary programming language has been amazing. In its favor at the time of its arrival were the facts that it was an object-oriented language, and that it offered a safer and more portable alternative to other languages. It also rode the wave of interest in the World Wide Web, with which it integrated well in its provision of applets. Since then, however, Java has come to be regarded as a genuine mainstream programming language.

Our approach in this book is to regard Java as a language that readers will want to use as a primary tool in many different areas of their programming work—not just for creating programs with graphical content within Web pages. For this reason, in the early chapters we have avoided an emphasis on creating applets and GUI-based programs. While being able to create GUI-based programs is superficially attractive, the language concepts required to create them properly are, in fact, quite advanced. Nevertheless, we recognize that visual examples are much more fun to create and work with. To this end, many of our early examples and exercises are enhanced by the provision of visual material that makes them more interesting to experiment with. An object-oriented language makes this approach relatively easy, without the reader needing to become enmeshed in the details of how they are implemented.

Key Features

The following are key features of this book:

- An 'objects-early' approach; showing how to interact with fully-fledged objects, before moving on, in Chapter 4, to define classes from scratch.
- Frequent in-place exercises and reviews.

- A thorough glossary, explaining many of the highlighted items of terminology found in the text.
- An accessible introduction to the fundamental object-oriented topics of *polymorphism* and *inheritance*.
- Significant coverage of the many GUI classes belonging to both the Abstract Windowing Toolkit (AWT) and Swing (JFC), which support both *standalone applications* and *applets*.
- Up-to-date coverage of the Java 2 Platform API.
- How to use the power of *threads* for multi-threaded programs, while avoiding hazards such as deadlock, livelock, and thread starvation.
- Timely coverage of networking, via TCP/IP, to interact with non-Java programs.
- A unique chapter on event-driven simulation.

Chapter Outlines

In Chapter 2 through Chapter 15, we cover the most important features of object-oriented programming and the Java language. Within those chapters, exercises have been deliberately positioned between sections, rather than grouped at the end. We recommend that these exercises are attempted at the point they are reached, because many of them are designed to reinforce important concepts that you should feel confident with before moving forward. Each of these chapters also includes periodic reviews to reprise and reinforce the main points of the material covered in the preceding sections. From time to time, case studies are used in order to reinforce or bring out further points that are best made in looking at the design and implementation of a larger problem.

In the remaining chapters, we describe in detail how to use many of the GUI components provided by the AWT and Swing classes, how to write multi-threaded programs, and how to interact with programs across a network. We conclude with a chapter on simulation—a common application area for object-oriented programs. Throughout the book, there is an emphasis on the importance of good programming style; particularly the need to maintain an object's integrity from outside interference.

The individual chapters are organized as follows:

- Chapter 1 provides an introduction to the basics of computer systems, for those with little or no experience of using a computer to write programs. We present a simple model of a computer and its components, in order to provide a foundation for the ways in which the design of most programming languages is shaped by them. Experienced programmers will find that they can skip this chapter.
- In Chapter 2, we describe the fundamental elements of the Java language, and show how to compile and run a simple program.
- In Chapter 3, we provide an introduction to basic object-oriented concepts, such as classes and objects. The approach taken in this chapter is fundamental to that taken in the rest of the book: *objects are important*. We believe that an 'objects-early' approach is the best way to learn an object-oriented language. At this stage, the emphasis is on *using* existing classes rather than defining them. This approach helps to emphasize that objects communicate by *passing messages* to one another.

- In Chapter 4, we begin to show how simple classes may be defined from scratch. We discuss the ways in which objects use attributes to maintain their state and the importance of protecting those attributes from inappropriate modification. It is at this early stage that the concepts of *accessors*, *mutators*, and *encapsulation* are introduced.
- In Chapter 5, we start to introduce the core features of Java that enable behavior to be added to class definitions. We concentrate on straight-line sequences of statements, and discuss arithmetic expressions.
- In Chapter 6, we continue to add behavior to classes but introduce statements that allow objects to perform alternative sequences of statements. We include a discussion of Boolean expressions, which are used to control this behavior.
- In Chapter 7, the ability to repeat statements is added to class definitions. By the end of this chapter, we are able to use the three fundamental elements of behavior—sequence, choice, and repetition.
- In Chapter 8, we introduce *packages*—Java's means of grouping related classes. We include a description of several pre-defined classes that are used over and over again in programs: `Math`, `String`, and `StringBuffer`.
- In Chapter 9, we describe *array objects*, which make it possible to group related objects or items of data into fixed-sized collections.
- In Chapter 10, we introduce classes that support arbitrary-sized collections of objects. While most programming languages provide array facilities, Java adds standard collection classes that other languages often leave to programmers to create for themselves.
- In Chapter 11, we explore Java's exception-handling mechanism. This provides a way for objects to indicate when an unexpected situation has arisen with which they do not know how to deal. Complementary to this is the ability to 'catch' exceptions and develop work-arounds for the problems encountered.
- In Chapter 12, we look at some of the many ways in which a program can interact with the external file system, via pre-defined input-output classes.
- In Chapter 13, we investigate Java's `interface` facility. In earlier chapters we use the term 'public interface' informally, but this chapter explores the issue in more depth. Central to it is the concept of *polymorphism*. Since polymorphism is such a fundamental concept in any object-oriented language, we continue our discussion of it in the next chapter.
- In Chapter 14, we take the discussion of polymorphism one stage further by describing Java's `extends` facility for class inheritance. Inheritance provides the ability to derive new classes that inherit much of their code and functionality from existing classes. Among other things, this permits code reuse. As part of the material in this chapter, we discuss alternatives to inheritance and inappropriate inheritance.
- In Chapter 15, we look at abstract classes, nested classes, and nested interfaces. By the end of this chapter, we have covered most of the main features of the Java language. Apart from Chapter 18, therefore, the remaining chapters are largely concerned with using these features in different applications; such as graphical programming, networking, and simulation.
- In Chapter 16, we describe the classes of the *Abstract Windowing Toolkit (AWT)*. The AWT provides a powerful collection of classes that simplify the

creation of applications with graphical user interfaces. They free a programmer from a need to know details of the windowing environment in which their
programs will be run. For the sake of generality, we concentrate on standalone
applications, rather than applets. Applets are covered, separately, in Chapter 20.

- In Chapter 17, we continue the description of Java's graphical features. This
chapter covers the Swing classes, which build on the AWT facilities to provide
a more complex set of classes, and greater programmer control over the look-
and-feel of a program.

- In Chapter 18, we introduce the final major language feature: *threads*. Threads
are a powerful feature that make it possible to create objects that run concurrently, sharing the available processor time between them. However, the power
of threads brings with it a number of new problems of which the designer of
multi-threaded programs needs to be aware. We discuss problems such as race
hazards, starvation, livelock, and deadlock, and how to avoid them.

- In Chapter 19, we introduce the classes that allow a program to interact with
other programs across a network. We discuss use of the reliable TCP protocol
and the unreliable UDP protocol, both of which are well supported by Java's
socket classes.

- In Chapter 20, we return to features of graphical programming, with a description of applets. Applets are largely restricted forms of the stand-alone
applications described in Chapter 16. They are provided with a secure environment which prevents them from directly accessing the host machine on which
they are run. These restrictions apply so that they can be run within browsers,
providing the familiar active content of Web pages.

- Chapter 21 concludes the main content of the book with a description of the
basic elements of event-driven (discrete) simulation. Simulations represent an
important set of object-oriented programs and we describe them through the
presentation of two case studies.

- The Appendices provide additional background material on primitive data
types, number representations, operators, and a list of Java's reserved words.
Some recurring design patterns are discussed in Appendix E, and our main
stylistic conventions are summarized in Appendix F. The book concludes with
a comprehensive glossary of terminology.

The Java API continues to grow, and it is impossible to cover it all in detail
within the scope of a teaching text such as this. In Chapter 16 through Chapter 20,
therefore, we only attempt to sample the riches of the classes it defines, and provide
illustrations of something of what is possible with them. By that stage, our hope is
that the reader will be able to harness the power that object-oriented programming
in Java permits, and be able to create their own interesting and practical everyday
programs.

Supporting Materials

The examples we use have been developed using the Java 2 SDK, which is freely available from the JavaSoft Web site (http://www.javasoft.com). You are strongly
recommended to obtain a copy of the documentation on the Java API which is

available from the JavaSoft site. The source code for the examples in this book is available from the Companion Website:

```
http://www.prenhall.com/barnes
```

Acknowledgements

I have the privilege of working in a Computer Science Department in which excellent teaching is both encouraged and practiced. I have benefited enormously from working with many talented colleagues. I have probably received help and picked up ideas from most of them over the years, but I would like to thank a few by name for the particular help and support that they have given to me while putting this book together.

David Bateman—a legendary source of good teaching and great ideas for assignments. Thanks to him for allowing me to use his chess program idea. Tim Hopkins, for being a constant source of books and sink of videos (neither of which seem to get returned by either of us), for his willingness to proofread, and for his good humour [sic!]. Janet Linington, for many discussions about the best ways to teach introductory programming, and for the gas station idea that ultimately led to the chapter on simulation. Simon Thompson, who is also an excellent teacher. Thanks to him for encouraging me to start this project in the first place, and for his introducing me to Jackie Harbor (now at Macmillan) that made it happen. Ian Utting, who pioneered the teaching of object-oriented software engineering at UKC and who currently shares the teaching of the first-year course with me. He remains a constant source of wisdom in this area and contributed important ideas to the chess program.

I would also like to thank David Till of City University, for being willing to let me use his and the late Michael Bell's 'soup salting' analogy as the basis of some of my early examples. At Pearson, thanks to my publisher, Alan Apt, and his editorial assistant, Toni Holm, both of whom have been extremely efficient at making this book happen. They provided superb support at the other end of a stream of email messages from me, and were always patient when deadlines were missed! To the several reviewers of this book, I also owe a debt of thanks. Their diligence and thoroughness were remarkable, and much appreciated. During the production stages, Amy Ryan and her team at Interactive Composition Corporation did an amazing job, accommodating my frequent changes, and yet keeping us ahead of schedule.

Finally, to my immediate family, for putting up with the extreme working hours that creating a book seems to require, and to the Scottish contingent for accommodating an antisocial me and my laptop over Christmas!

David Barnes
December 1999

PART

I

Java Fundamentals

CHAPTER

1

Bits, Bytes, and Java™

In this chapter, we describe why 'high level programming languages' such as Java™ are an important aid to writing computer programs and how particular features of Java make it easy to write programs that can be run on many different types of computers. In order to do this, we provide some background on hardware and software by presenting a simple model of a computer's Central Processing Unit (CPU) and its memory. We introduce the use of binary data to model the state of objects and describe how the meaning of a particular data value depends upon the context in which it is being used.

1.1 The Challenge

Writing programs is easy, but writing them well is far harder; it would be unwise of any teacher to pretend otherwise. However, this is one of the things that make programming an exciting and challenging experience which we hope that you will discover as you work through this book. An acknowledgement of the skill required to write programs well is reflected in the way in which the names for people who write programs have changed over the years, from *coder* and *programmer* to *software engineer* and *software architect*. The more recent titles place them on a par with the skilled practitioners of other, more-established, engineering disciplines. Part of the difficulty inherent in writing programs comes from the enormous gap that now exists between the user-level simplicity of most computers and the complexity of the programs we wish to run on them. In this chapter we start to look at that gap by exploring some of the underlying details of computer hardware and software and the way in which Java helps to bridge that gap.

1.2 A Simple Model of a Computer

It is not necessary to have a detailed knowledge of the internal workings of a computer in order to be able to write programs. However, an understanding of the main elements of a computer system can make it easier to understand why a programming language such as Java is like it is. In this chapter, we shall try to help you build a simple *mental model* of the elements of a modern computer that will hopefully provide some context for the basic elements of the language that we introduce in subsequent chapters. We shall look at the main hardware and software elements of a simple computer and some background to the Java language. While you will not be learning any Java in this chapter, it should provide some useful background if you are coming to serious programming for the first time.

1.2.1 Hardware

Most people are familiar with the external features of a typical personal computer (PC): keyboard, screen, mouse, printer, and audio speakers, plus the 'box' that contains the memory and processing devices that represent the heart of a computer. You are probably also aware that computers are built from *micro-chips* and that the box contains various *disk drives* for hard disks, floppy disks, and compact disks. A typical computer might also contain a *sound card* for producing audio output through its speakers, and perhaps also a *modem* for connecting the computer to the Internet via the telephone network. All of these chips and various devices are referred to as the *hardware* of a typical PC system; that is, the physical components that go together to make up a computer.

The main chips that will be of interest to us in building this simple model are the *Central Processing Unit (CPU)* and the *Random Access Memory (RAM)*. These two elements, in particular, have a strong influence on the performance of a computer— how fast a program will run and how big a program it can run. On most computers, it is possible to change one or more parts of the hardware (a process known as *upgrading*) in order to improve its overall performance or increase its facilities in some way. This often involves adding more memory, a faster CD drive, or a higher capacity hard disk that can hold more data. Regular improvements in hardware design and manufacture mean that today's personal computers are enormously more powerful than those available ten or twenty years ago, and the pace of change means that today's computers will quickly seem relatively slow in comparison with tomorrow's.

1.2.2 Look-and-Feel Software

In order to use the hardware of a computer, it is necessary to combine it with some software. The most important pieces of software, from a computer user's point of view, are the *operating system* and *window manager*. Together, these give a collection of hardware components a particular *look-and-feel*. There are currently three predominant styles of look-and-feel that you are likely to encounter in a PC environment: Microsoft®'s Windows® (Figure 1.1), X Windows running over UNIX™ (Figure 1.2), and Apple®'s Macintosh®. The window manager provides a computer user with a *virtual desktop* containing one or more windows and working areas in which individual programs, such as editors, games, and spreadsheets, may be run. In addition, the operating system makes it possible to run several programs at the same time, and for the various hardware devices to be used. The operating system and window manager must work closely together to provide a user's working environment. For instance, the operating system must inform the window manager of movements of the mouse, so that these may be interpreted appropriately to draw a *cursor* or produce a *popup menu* at the appropriate place on the screen. The

Figure 1.1   A sample Microsoft Windows desktop

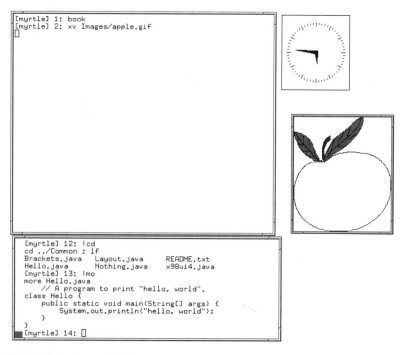

Figure 1.2   A sample X Windows desktop

operating system also enables data to be stored and retrieved from the various disk drives by providing a *file system*. Each of the look-and-feel styles mentioned above provides these facilities in its own distinctive way. This typically means that it is not possible to run a program for one windowing environment in a completely different environment, even though the hardware in both cases might be identical.[1] As we shall see in Section 1.7, however, one of the significant features of the Java programming language is that we can use it to write programs that are *portable*; that is, the same program can be run unchanged under different operating system and window manager combinations. This is a powerful concept.

1.3   Bits and Bytes

In building this simple mental model of a computer, it will help to have at least an appreciation of how the underlying hardware works, because this will make it easier to understand several features of the Java language. In this section, we describe some of the main hardware elements—the processor and the memory—together with a description of the data that is held on a computer's disks. It is important to appreciate that these descriptions are necessarily abstractions—convenient simplifications of reality—and for a more detailed overview of computer hardware you should consult a specialist book on computer architecture[TG98].

1.3.1   Bits

Most people with at least some familiarity with computers are aware that computers store and manipulate data in the form of *bits* (**bi**nary dig**its**). In reality, there are many ways in which binary digits might be represented at the hardware level: as an electrical voltage in a wire, a beam of light in a fiber optic cable, a microwave signal from a satellite, a magnetic field on a disk, and so on. Irrespective of how it is actually represented at the physical level, it is convenient to think of a single binary digit having one of only two possible values: 0 or 1. We call this decision to hide the exact details, *abstraction*. We often use abstraction when it is not necessary to know the exact details of how something works or is represented, because we can still make use of it in its simplified form. Getting involved with the detail often tends to obscure what we are trying to understand, rather than illuminate it. As we shall see, abstraction plays a very important role in programming because we often want to model, in software, simplified versions of things that exist in the real world—light bulbs, ships, banks, etc.—without having to build the real things.

1.3.2   Using Bits to Model Real-Life Objects

A bit is the fundamental unit of data from which we can build all manner of different data items, from a simple on/off light switch to an air traffic control system and beyond! A single binary digit allows us to model a range of real-life data items that

---

[1] It is common to include *multiple-boot options* that allow different windowing environments to be used on the same PC, for instance. Each environment is usually completely separate from the others.

can take on two different values. For instance, we might use the value 0 in a car engine management system to mean that the engine is turned off and the value 1 to mean that it is turned on. In another application, a 0 bit might be used to signify that an electronic security door is currently closed, while 1 means that it is open. In both of these examples, we are using an item of data (in this case a single bit) to model the *states* of an object that is part of an application or system. As long as the object to be modeled has only two possible states (on/off, open/closed, etc.), then a single binary digit is sufficient to represent the current state of that object.

In practice, we shall find that many things we want to model have more complex states, for which a single bit is insufficient. Take the case of the electronic security door mentioned above; suppose that we want to know not just whether the door is open or closed but also whether it is in the process of opening or closing. This means that there are four possible states for the door: fully closed, fully open, being closed, being opened. For these four states, 2 bits are sufficient to model the door, because there are four distinct ways in which we can arrange 2 bits: 00, 01, 10 and 11. We might associate each of these values with one of the door's states as shown in Table 1.1. The association between a particular pattern and its meaning could be chosen either arbitrarily or so that the pattern encodes a particular meaning. For instance, the left-most bit of the patterns in Table 1.1 might be used to tell whether the door is stationary (0) or moving (1). In the latter case, the right-most bit can be used to tell whether the door is moving to the closed position (0) or the open position (1)—values which match the state encoded in the right-most bit of the first two patterns. Such a detailed analysis of the individual bits within a multi-bit pattern is not always necessary.

We can represent more complex objects which have larger numbers of possible states simply by using further bits, which allow us to create more patterns. We can represent the color of an object, drawn from the seven colors of the rainbow, with the 3-bit sequences shown in Table 1.2. If the object is colored green, for instance, then the pattern 011 stored somewhere in the computer's memory could represent the fact that it is currently in that state.

Note that 3 bits actually allow us to create eight distinct patterns and the pattern 111 is unused in Table 1.2 because we only need to represent seven distinct states. We say that this pattern has a *redundant value* in this context. We might also say that an object having the pattern 111 for its color is in an *inconsistent state*: a state it should not be in because we have not designated a color for that pattern. Examples of real-life objects in an inconsistent state might be an aircraft on the ground with its undercarriage retracted, or an X-ray machine emitting radiation but whose user

Table 1.1 Using 2 bits to represent four door states

Bits	Door State
00	Fully closed
01	Fully open
10	Being closed
11	Being opened

Table 1.2 Using 3 bits to represent the colors of the rainbow	
Bits	*Color*
000	red
001	orange
010	yellow
011	green
100	blue
101	indigo
110	violet
111	(unused)

interface indicates that it is turned off. Whenever we model objects, it will be important to ensure that they can never get into inconsistent states, as this could have catastrophic consequences for the behavior of any programs of which they are a part. However, in some applications, a redundant pattern can serve a useful purpose in that it can be used explicitly as *out-of-bounds value* or *escape value*—an indicator that a different action from the norm is required at some point. We shall explore more about these issues of object state in Chapter 3.

Before reading further, try the following exercises which will help you to understand some of the features of binary digit patterns.

Exercise 1.1   How many separate 4-digit patterns can be created using 4 binary digits? Write them out.

Exercise 1.2   We have seen that 1 bit allows 2 single-bit patterns, 2 bits allow 4 patterns of length 2, 3 bits allow 8 patterns of length 3, and your answer to Exercise 1.1 should tell you how many 4-digit patterns are possible with 4 bits. Can you devise a rule for the number of patterns of length N it is possible to make with N bits, where N is any whole number greater than zero? Write out the patterns for 5 bits as a check to see if you are on the right lines.

Exercise 1.3   Notice the way in which the bits in each column of Table 1.2 alternate between the values 0 and 1. The right-most bit changes every row, the middle bit changes every second row, and the left-most bit changes every fourth row. Can you see a pattern here that relates to Exercise 1.2? Check your 4-bit and 5-bit patterns to see if they can be arranged in similar ways.

1.3.3   Bytes

In a computer program, each time we need to represent an object with a particular number of states, we could arrange to use the fewest number of bits that provide the right number of unique patterns to make this possible. In practice, this approach turns out to be relatively inefficient for a computer's hardware to support. As a result, hardware and programming language designers generally compromise on using 8-bit patterns as the smallest unit of data to be manipulated. An 8-bit quantity of data is commonly known as a *byte*. We can think of a byte as being the computer equivalent of an atom in the physical world. It is the smallest amount of data with which we usually concern ourselves, although we can split it further (into its separate bits) if necessary.

The word byte is in common usage when describing the amount of memory a computer has: 64 Megabytes, or the capacity of a hard disk: 8 Gigabytes. If you completed Exercise 1.2, you can probably work out that a byte of data allows 256 distinct 8-bit patterns to be represented. The first and last few of these are shown in Table 1.3. The fact that 8 bits will provide more patterns than we need to represent a full set of states in some circumstances (a car engine, an electronic door, the colors of the rainbow) means that there will sometimes be redundancy in the set of available bit patterns. However, a few wasted bits is largely irrelevant in the context of the large amount of memory available in most modern computers, and there is rarely a need to worry about such wastage. Of more significance is the fact that even 256 patterns will be insufficient to represent the full range of values required by most applications. Consider the need to give a unique identifying value to each student in a university, or each vehicle in a country. Such circumstances require multi-byte representations. Two bytes of data (16 bits) provide for 65,536 separate patterns—probably enough to identify the inhabitants of a medium-sized town—and 4 bytes of data (32 bits) provide over four billion separate patterns—enough for country-wide vehicle ownership, but not enough to uniquely identify each individual on the planet. Unlike the term byte, there is no commonly agreed term for 2- and 4-byte units of data, although they are often called 16-bit words and 32-bit words, respectively. As we shall see in Chapter 5, the designers of Java use terms such as `short` and `char` for 16-bit words, `int` and `float` for 32-bit words, and `long` and `double` for 64-bit words.

As you might have worked out if you attempted Exercise 1.2, the number of distinct patterns of length N possible using N bits is 2^N, which means 2 raised to the power of N or 2 multiplied by itself N times. Table 1.4 shows some common powers

Table 1.3 A few of the 256 patterns possible with 8 bits

00000000
00000001
00000010
00000011
00000100
...
11111000
11111001
11111010
11111011
11111100
11111101
11111110
11111111

Table 1.4	Common powers of 2	
Power	*Number of Patterns*	*Name*
2^0	1	
2^1	2	
2^2	4	
2^3	8	
2^4	16	
2^5	32	
2^6	64	
2^7	128	
2^8	256	
2^{10}	1,024	Kilo
2^{16}	65,536	
2^{20}	1,048,576	Mega
2^{30}	1,073,741,824	Giga
2^{32}	4,294,967,296	
2^{40}	1,099,511,627,776	Tera
2^{64}	18,446,744,073,709,551,616	

of 2. It is worth trying to remember the values of 2^1 through 2^8 and 2^{16}, as these arise quite often in computer applications. Note that 2^{10} is just over one thousand. This is the number used for the term Kilo in Kilobyte, which means that a Kilobyte is really 1,024 bytes rather than one thousand. Similarly, note the values for Mega (2^{20}), Giga (2^{30}), and Tera (2^{40}) which are rough equivalents of one million, one billion, and one trillion, respectively. Do not worry about *why* the entry for 2^0 suggests that it has one distinct pattern; any number to the power of zero is always 1 and you can easily remember it as being half of 2^1.

1.3.4   The Meaning of Data

As we have discussed in the previous sections, bits and bytes are the fundamental building blocks used to represent data in a program. In the simplified mental model of a computer that we are building, we can think of the main memory of the computer as consisting of a collection of many millions of locations, each of which is able to hold a single 8-bit pattern for a single byte of data. The meaning of a particular byte of data will always depend upon the context in which it is being used. For instance, the bit-pattern 00000010 could stand for the color yellow in one program, or the fact that an electronic door is being closed in another. An important point to recognize, therefore, is that the hardware of a computer provides a method for storing data electronically, but the software supplies an interpretation of the data. It is not possible to look at the contents of any particular bit-pattern in the computer's memory and know what it means without a software context. In a similar way, a hard disk or compact disk (CD) provides the capacity to store Gigabytes or Megabytes of data. These seemingly random collections of bytes are given structure by the software of the operating system which organizes the total collection into individual data files. An individual file might be small—a few tens or hundreds of bytes representing the contents of an email message—or very large—representing a graphical image, an audio sound track, or a multimedia presentation. The meaning of the content is imposed by the program that stores the data or uses it to perform a particular task. Without an appropriate program to interpret a particular file of data, that data is effectively meaningless.

1.4   The Central Processing Unit

The most important piece of hardware in a computer is its *Central Processing Unit (CPU)*. The CPU is the heart of a computer as it is the part that contains the computer's ability to obey instructions. Each type of CPU has its own set of instructions that it is able to obey, and this is known as its *instruction set*. Processors used to control simple devices, such as a washing machines or smart cards, will probably have smaller and simpler instruction sets than those used in an air traffic control computer, for instance. The variety in different instruction sets for different processors is rather like the variety in human languages; they are able to express essentially similar concepts and actions, but they do so in largely incompatible ways. This is one reason why it is usually very difficult to take a program written for one computer and run it on a different one.

The instructions in most instruction sets are very simple, so much of a computer's power lies in its ability to perform each instruction of a program very quickly. This makes it possible to execute many millions or billions of instructions per second. The combined effect of billions of simple instructions enables highly complex tasks to be performed within a reasonable time. The drawback of an instruction set's simplicity, however, is that it is very difficult for a person to write programs using just a CPU's basic instructions in order to accomplish even simple tasks. For this reason, most modern programs are written using a *high level programming language*, of which Java is one of very many. It is typically much easier to write a program in a higher level language than it is in a lower level language. For instance, a program written in a low level language to perform the simplest of tasks is likely to require many hundreds of instructions, whereas an equivalent high level language program might be written in just a few lines of text. The trade-off is that a program written in a higher level language cannot be run directly on a computer but must undergo a process of translation first. This translation process is known as *compilation*. We discuss this process, as it relates to Java, in Section 1.7.

High level languages mean that it is not usually necessary to know anything about the instruction set of the computer for which you intend to write programs. However, it is helpful to have a general idea of how most processors operate. This will provide some further background that will help you to understand the Java language.

1.4.1   The Fetch-Execute Cycle

Hardware manufacturers are constantly striving to make computers run faster. The more instructions that can be performed every second, the quicker programs will run, and the more work that can be handled by them. One of the things that serves to make instruction execution fast is the essentially simple set of steps that lies at the heart of the central processing unit's operation; these steps are known as the *fetch-execute cycle*. From the time it is switched on to the time it is switched off, a CPU endlessly repeats the following two main steps: *Fetch the next instruction* and *Execute the instruction just fetched.* The instructions to be executed constitute the program that the processor is running at any particular time. These instructions are stored in some part of the computer's memory that the processor is able to access at very high speed. Each instruction is fetched from the memory to the processing unit as the first step, and then executed as the second step. An individual instruction might do one of many possible operations defined by the instruction set: add two numbers together, set a pixel on the screen to a particular color, send some data to the disk drive, read a byte from the memory, and so on. A program's instructions are stored one after another in consecutive addresses within the computer's memory, and fetched in turn by repetitions of the fetch-execute cycle. The location of the next instruction to be fetched is kept track of in a part of the CPU called the *program counter* (Figure 1.3). Part of the fetch-execute cycle involves making sure that the value in the program counter is updated each time its value has been used, so that it is ready with the address of the next instruction at the start of the next cycle. This incrementing step comes directly between the two main steps, so Figure 1.4 shows the full fetch-execute cycle.

1.4.2   Skipping and Repeating Instructions

As described so far, the fetch-execute cycle would cause a contiguous sequence of instructions (occupying consecutive memory locations) to be executed one after the other. In practice, simply performing a straight-line sequence of instructions is rather limiting. Sometimes, a portion of a program's instructions needs to be executed more

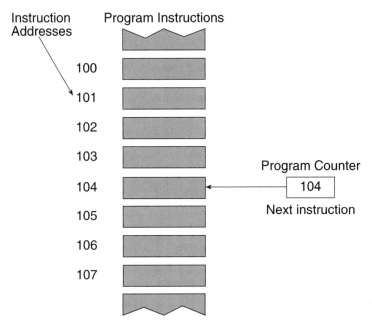

Figure 1.3   The program counter refers to the next instruction to be fetched

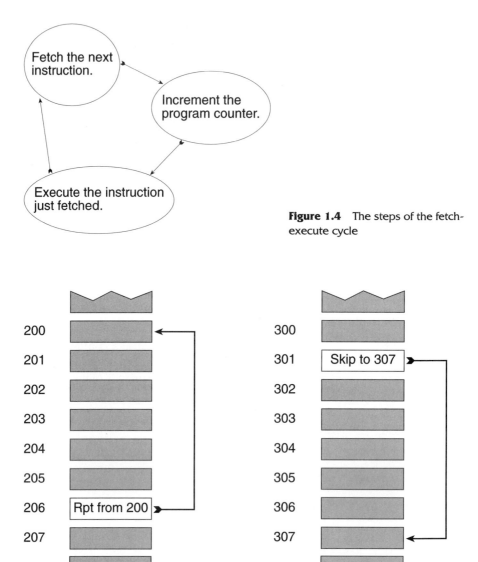

Figure 1.4 The steps of the fetch-execute cycle

Figure 1.5 Repeating a sequence of instructions

Figure 1.6 Skipping a sequence of instructions

than once, or a particular sequence might be irrelevant in some circumstances and need to be skipped over. Figure 1.5 illustrates repetition of part of a sequence of instructions and Figure 1.6 shows skipping part of the sequence. In order to achieve these variations on the normal order of execution, we have to find some way of changing which instruction is the next to be performed. In both cases, the principle is the same: we want to arrange for an instruction to be fetched next that is not the one whose address is in the program counter ready for the next repetition of the fetch-execute cycle. The ingenious method used to achieve this effect is to arrange for the

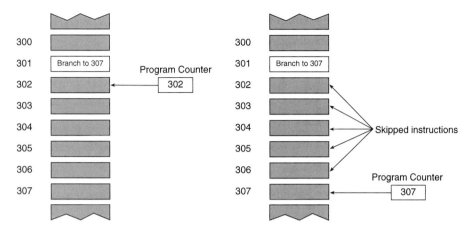

Figure 1.7 Before and after: a branch instruction alters the contents of the program counter

current instruction being executed to change the address held in the program counter, so that it contains the address of the desired next instruction, rather than the next natural instruction in the sequence. This process is known as *branching*, and part of its beauty lies in the fact that the normal fetch-execute cycle requires no modification at all in order to accommodate both repetition and skipping of instructions (Figure 1.7). Starting in Chapter 5, we shall see how these three styles of instruction execution—sequence, selective execution, and repetition—are reflected in the design of typical high level programming languages, such as Java.

1.5   Review

Here are the main points that we have covered in the preceding sections:

- Writing programs well is a skilled occupation.
- Window managers and operating systems are software programs that make computer hardware usable by people.
- It is the combination of a window manager and operating system, rather than its hardware components, that gives a particular look-and-feel to how a computer is used.
- A binary digit (bit) has a value of either 0 or 1.
- We use single bits as the fundamental building blocks for modeling data.
- By using an appropriate number of bits, we can model the different states of real-world objects.
- N bits provides 2^N different binary patterns of length N.
- Redundant binary patterns represent impossible states of an object.
- Care must be taken not to allow objects to be in an impossible or inconsistent state.
- Eight bits of data are known as a byte.

- The meaning of a particular pattern of data can only be determined from the context in which it is being used.
- The Central Processing Unit is the computational heart of a computer.
- A CPU endlessly repeats the fetch-execute cycle.
- The program counter is used to hold the memory address of the next instruction to be fetched.
- Instructions stored in consecutive memory addresses are usually executed in sequence.
- Branch instructions allow a sequence of instructions to be skipped or repeated.
- Branch instructions work by modifying the contents of the program counter.

Exercise 1.4   A Megabyte is 1,000,000 bytes; true or false?

Exercise 1.5   The bit-pattern `00000010` stored in a computer's memory always means the color yellow; true or false?

Exercise 1.6   What does *CPU* stand for?

Exercise 1.7   What is meant by the term, *instruction set*?

Exercise 1.8   What are the steps of the *fetch-execute cycle*?

Exercise 1.9   How does *branching* make it possible for instructions to be skipped or repeated?

1.6   High Level Programming Languages

The history of computing is littered with the remains of many thousands of programming languages. Of these, only a handful have had a significant impact on that history and current day practice. Java is one such language, whose impact and widespread acceptance occurred relatively rapidly, in part, because it found a particular synergy with the rapidly expanding *World Wide Web (WWW)*. Java arose formally on the scene in 1995, but its history and antecedents go back quite a long way. Many of the current day programming languages have their roots in those that arose in the late 1950s and early 1960s, such as *Algol*[Col78], *BASIC*[KK67], *COBOL*[Gra98], and *FORTRAN*[NL98]. These were among the early high level programming languages whose designers sought to find an alternative to programming in low level *assembly languages*—symbolic languages corresponding to CPU instruction sets. Writing and maintaining programs written in assembly language was a complex and error-prone task but, given the relatively slow speeds and small memory sizes of the computers of the time, it was felt to be the best way to keep both programs small and fast-running. High level languages offered the advantages of both making programs easier to write and being runnable on different computers—something not always possible with programs written in assembly languages.

    In the 1970s and early 1980s, the new languages *Pascal*[JW78], *C*[KR78], and *Ada*[Cul96] emerged as dominant, largely displacing Algol and BASIC, for instance. Other languages, such as COBOL and FORTRAN, underwent major revisions over the years to keep them up-to-date with current thinking in programming language design. The designers of new languages commonly took elements of existing languages as a starting point and variously added or removed aspects to produce something more suited to the particular purposes they had in mind. In the case of Pascal, one of its designers' goals was to create a language that would serve as a tool for teaching programming; in the case of C, the language was designed to support the development of an operating system. Both languages took off in a big way, probably far exceeding the expectations of their designers.

All of the languages described above belong to a style of programming often referred to as *imperative programming languages* or *structured programming languages*. In parallel with the development of languages in this style has been a development of languages and ideas in two other major styles: *functional programming* (of which *Haskell*[Tho99] is a modern example) and *object-oriented programming*, to which family Java belongs. Early object-oriented programming languages include *Smalltalk*[SKT96] and *SIMULA*[BDMN79]. Simula took one of the Algol languages as its core and added some major new concepts, one of which—the *class*—is a now fundamental part of the Java language. In the early 1980s, Bjarne Stroustrup created a major new programming language that was to have a very strong influence on the development of Java. He took the C programming language and added object-oriented features (among other things) to create *C++*[Str97]. The widespread availability of efficient implementations of this language helped to fuel a revolution in thinking about program and system design that has promoted the object-oriented approach as a serious alternative to the more traditional structured approaches.

In the early 1990s, James Gosling was working on a reimplementation of C++ in the context of providing a programming language for intelligent consumer devices. Originally called *Oak*, this is the language that emerged as Java in 1995. As so many language designers had done before, Gosling borrowed what he liked from existing languages, left out what he did not like or think necessary, and added his own ideas. While not initially designed with the World Wide Web in mind, Java's strong emphasis on *portability* and security made it an ideal language to incorporate in Web browsers to allow them to download programs from remote sites and run them locally. Following its initial release, Java underwent a revision in 1997 as version 1.1 and in 1998 as version 1.2.

1.7   Program Translation

High level programming languages were devised, primarily, to overcome two significant problems that arise from the use of low level languages:

- Writing programs in low level languages is difficult and error prone.
- A program written in the instruction set of one CPU cannot be run on a different CPU.

High level languages seek to overcome the first problem by providing features, such as *data types*, *methods*, and *control structures*, which make it easier to express the solution to a programming task than in a low level language. Of course the terms high level and low level are relative terms rather than absolute terms and some high level languages can be said to be at a higher level than others; for instance, Java is a higher level language than C. What this means, in part, is that Java provides

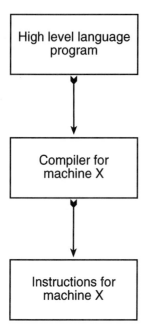

Figure 1.8   A compiler translates from a high level language to a target instruction set

a higher level of abstraction from the underlying computer than C does. 'Higher level' also expresses the notion that a language is closer, in expressive terms, to the problem area to be tackled. Furthermore, advocates of high level object-oriented languages maintain that they make it easier to express a program solution in terms of the problem domain than it is with traditional high level structured programming languages.

1.7.1   Program Portability

One of the costs of using a high level language is that the program code must be translated into the low level language of the target CPU before it can be run. This process is called *compilation* (Figure 1.8). This cost is offset by the *portability* that results from using a high level language; as long as suitable compilers exist, a high level program may be run on machines with different instruction sets (Figure 1.9).

1.7.2   Java's Approach to Portability

While language portability, in principle, is simply a matter of providing a suitable compiler for the source language and target machine, true portability is much harder to achieve in practice. It is very easy for a programmer to make assumptions about the underlying machine that do not hold true in all cases. For instance, a common difference between machines is the order in which they store the individual bytes

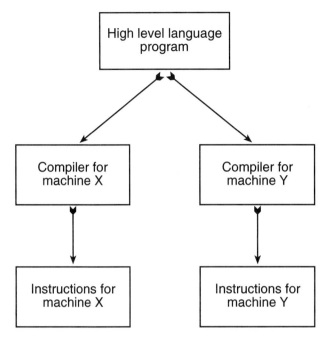

Figure 1.9   The same program may be run on different machines using separate compilers

of multi-byte numerical data.[2] A programmer making assumptions that do not hold true in all cases is likely to find that their program behaves differently on different machines.

Java seeks to address the difficulties of making programs truly portable in two main ways:

- It has rigidly defined rules for how it must be implemented on all machines.
- It is defined to be run on a well-defined *virtual machine*, rather than a real processor.

Java's approach to portability means that the phrase "write once, run anywhere" is often applied to its programs.

1.7.3   The Java Virtual Machine

Java programs are translated into *bytecodes* rather than the instruction set of any particular central processing unit. Bytecodes are like the instruction set of a pseudo-CPU or, as Java calls it, the *Java Virtual Machine (JVM)*. In order to run a Java program, therefore, the bytecodes must be executed by something (typically a program) that implements the JVM. Such a program is called a *bytecode interpreter*.

---

[2] Some machines are *big-endian*, storing the higher-order bytes before the lower-order bytes, while others are *little-endian* in which the order is reversed.

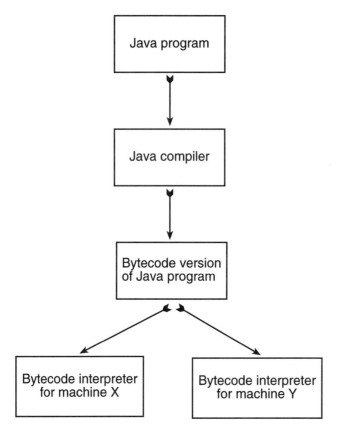

Figure 1.10   A Java program can be run on different machines after a single translation

A bytecode interpreter program must be written for each machine on which it is desired to run Java programs. Figure 1.10 illustrates the steps involved in Java compilation and interpretation. Java is often referred to as an interpreted language, therefore, because its programs are run by an interpreter program, rather than directly by a CPU.

Java's approach to compilation and interpreted execution involves a significant modification to what is normally meant by programming language portability. In order to port a Java program from one machine to another, it is not necessary to copy the Java source code of the program to the second machine and translate it there. Rather, the bytecodes generated from compilation on one machine can be transferred to a second machine and run there *without the need for a second compilation*. This is because the binary format of bytecodes is defined independently of any real machine constraints and is the same for all machines. A genuine bytecode interpreter that accurately implements the JVM will always be able to execute the bytecodes of a program, no matter where the original program was compiled. This is precisely one of the features that makes Java so easy to use over the World Wide Web in the form of *applets*; as long as you have a suitable Web browser that implements the JVM, you can download Java bytecodes from anywhere and run them locally. See Chapter 20 for more details of applets. A drawback of interpreted execution is that interpreted programs often run slower than equivalent fully compiled programs, because they are not being run directly by the CPU.

1.8 Review

Here are the main points that we have covered in the preceding sections:

- High level languages are designed to make it easier to write programs than it is in low level languages.
- There are many different high level programming languages, each with its own features and specialities.
- Programs written in high level languages are typically easier to port to different machines than those written in low level languages.
- Programs written in high level languages must be translated by a compiler before they can be run on a particular machine.
- With most programming languages, a compiler is required for each machine on which you wish to run programs written in a particular language.
- Java is designed to be a particularly portable language.
- Java achieves its portability through rigid definition of its features and its implementation in terms of a virtual machine.
- Java programs are translated to bytecodes.
- A translated Java program is executed by a bytecode interpreter, which implements the Java Virtual Machine.
- In order to port a Java program from one machine to another, it is only necessary to transfer the bytecode version; no recompilation is necessary.
- Java's approach to portability makes it an ideal language for use over the World Wide Web.

Exercise 1.10   What advantages do high level languages offer over low level languages?

Exercise 1.11   Programs written in low level languages are usually more portable than those written in high level languages; true or false?

Exercise 1.12   In what two ways does the design of Java make it more portable than most other high level languages?

Exercise 1.13   A compiled Java program can be run on any machine with a JVM without having to be recompiled; true or false?

Exercise 1.14   Try to find out the name for another high level language that is usually interpreted.

In the next chapter, we shall begin our look at the Java language, and explore what is involved in translating a Java program into bytecodes that can be executed on any bytecode interpreter.

Common Program Components

In this chapter, we describe some of the fundamental elements of the Java language that all Java programs have. We also show the way in which a program is translated by a Java compiler into its *bytecode* form, and how a translated program is run with a suitable bytecode interpreter. By the end of this chapter you should be able to compile and run a simple Java program.

2.1 Getting Past the Compiler

Flying out of the country can be a nerve-wracking and time-consuming process—making sure you have your ticket, passport, and money; check-in desk, baggage examination, and passport control before you get anywhere near the airplane. Getting your first program to run can seem just as fraught with obstacles. Modern programs are written in programming languages that often make them look like a cross between English, mathematics, and a monkey's typing efforts! Before you can run a program, it has to be thoroughly checked and then *translated* into another language that a computer or interpreter can understand. This process is called *compilation* and is performed by a program called a *compiler*. As well as the task of translation, the compiler's job is to apply a stringent series of checks to your programs before they can be approved as ready to run. Putting it another way, a compiler is a bit like the most strict English-language teacher you could ever meet. Instead of checking for full-stops, capital letters, quotation marks, and so on, the compiler is going to be checking for balanced parentheses, matching curly brackets, and various other *syntax errors* and *semantic errors*—scary stuff! Getting nine out of ten is not good enough for the compiler because it is a perfectionist. If anything is out of place, then it will tell you and it will not allow your program to be run. The compiler acts like a minder because it will only be safe to run your programs if you have made it completely clear what you want done. However, even when the compiler is satisfied, that is not the end of the story. Your program may still contain *logical errors* that the compiler is unable to spot. A logical error will result in your program not running as you planned, and it might even stop prematurely with a *runtime error* or *exception*.

In these early stages, a lot of what you will be learning will be how to get things right so that the compiler will let you run your programs. To help you in this process, you will be given a lot of small examples to study. We will also use these examples to explain details of the Java language that you will be using in just about every program you will write. Even experienced programmers make errors all the time, so mistakes are nothing to worry about and you should quickly find that most of them can be corrected very easily with a bit of thought and comparison with examples in this book.

2.2   Fundamental Language Elements

Code 2.1 shows our first example of a Java program. It is close to the shortest Java program that can be written while still keeping the compiler happy.

We have indicated in the caption that a version of this program may be found with the materials that accompany this book, stored in the file 'Nothing.java'. The program does not do anything useful but it shows the basic Java elements that will be present in most of the programs that you will write. In the next few sections, we shall explain each of its elements.

2.2.1   Reserved Words and Identifiers

All programs are made up of different *symbols*, each of which is classified by a particular technical term. Some symbols are classified as *reserved words*, others as *identifiers*, *punctuation*, *white space*, and *operators*. You can find explanations of terms such as these in the glossary in Appendix I. Reserved words are a special set of symbols, chosen by a language's designers, that are part of that language's definition. Each programming language has its own set of reserved words that reflect its features. In the example in Code 2.1, `class`, `public`, `static`, and `void` are the reserved words. There are over forty reserved words, and you will soon get to know most of them because you will find yourself needing to use them over and over again in each program you write. A list may be found in Appendix D.

The identifiers in the example in Code 2.1 are `Nothing`, `main`, `String`, and `args`. Just by looking at them, it is impossible to tell the difference between reserved words and identifiers—this only comes with familiarity. Identifiers are usually names made up by the programmer and are particular to each program. There is no practical limit to the number of possible identifiers you can make up, although you will probably find yourself reusing familiar ones in different programs. It is best to view the purpose of identifiers as being to make a program comprehensible to a human reader, so the names you use should be easy to read and easily related to the purpose of the program. Java identifiers must have either a letter, underscore (_),

Code 2.1   A do-nothing program (`Nothing.java`)

```
class Nothing {
    public static void main(String[] args) {
    }
}
```

Code 2.2 A do-nothing program with poorly chosen identifiers (`x98ui4.java`)

```
class x98ui4 {
    public static void main(String[] $1a_z$) {
    }
}
```

or dollar ($) as their first character. Thereafter, they may be made up from letters, underscores, dollars, and digits.[1] There is no limit to the number of characters in an identifier, so there is plenty of scope for choosing good names. Unfortunately, the Java compiler will not reject a program containing incomprehensible names, so the program in Code 2.2 is actually viewed in exactly the same way by the compiler as the one in Code 2.1.

Notice that, although we changed the identifiers `Nothing` and `args` in this example, we did not change `main` and `String`. This is because both of these identifiers have special meanings—they are almost, but not quite, reserved words. All Java programs must have a method called `main` in them somewhere, because this represents the point from which the program will start to run. We will say more about this in Section 2.2.4.

2.2.2 Curly Brackets

Two of the most important punctuation symbols in Java are the opening and closing *curly brackets* (or *braces*)—"{" and "}". They are a way of *grouping* parts of a program to show where something starts and where it ends. Java's technical term for anything grouped between a pair of curly brackets is a *block*. Some other programming languages use the words `begin` and `end` to enclose a block.

The first opening curly bracket in the example in Code 2.1 marks the start of a block which is called a *class body*. It is the second closing curly bracket in the example that marks the limit of the class body. The class body is preceded by a *class header* (`class Nothing`). The class header and body together make up a *class definition*. The purpose of the header is to give the class a name, in this case `Nothing`. A class body is the part that defines what a class is all about, and class definitions may become very large. Classes are a crucial concept in Java, and we shall deal with them in detail as we move through this book.

All class definitions have a very similar structure; they start with the reserved word `class`, and this is followed by an identifier chosen by the programmer, then an opening curly bracket, and after this comes the body of the class. The end of the body is always marked by a closing curly bracket. One of the things that a compiler checks is to ensure that these rules have been followed. Here is the sort of message

---

[1] Because Java uses the *Unicode* character set (see Section 12.11), letter and digit in this context refer to their characterization as such in the full Unicode character set. Effectively, this allows Java programs to be written naturally in languages other than English, so $\iota\chi\theta\upsilon\varsigma$ is just one example of a valid non-English identifier.

we might see from the compiler if we forget to put in the closing curly bracket, for instance,

```
'}' expected
```

2.2.3   The Simple Structure of a Method

The inner pair of curly brackets of the example in Code 2.1 marks the start and end of a block called a *method body*. A method body usually contains *declarations* and *statements* that enable it to perform a particular task in the context of a program. We shall soon see an example in this chapter in which the method body contains a statement that will make a program do something rather than nothing. In later chapters, we shall see many examples of methods which will help to reinforce their main features.

As we see here, it is common for one block to be nested inside another and, at times, such nesting might be quite deep. This example serves to illustrate an important principle: blocks can be nested but they cannot overlap. A block started by an opening curly bracket always completely encloses all further blocks started within it, up to its matching closing curly bracket.

A method body is preceded by a *method header* which, in Code 2.1, gives the method the name `main`.

```
public static void main(String[] args)
```

All method bodies have an associated method header, but a method named `main` always has a special meaning, so we leave further discussion of method headers until Section 2.2.4.

2.2.4   The Main Method

The example in Code 2.1 contains a method named `main`. Any method named `main` (and which looks similar to that one) has a special significance within a Java program. The *main method* of a program is taken by a bytecode interpreter to be a program's starting point when it is run. This means that most Java programs you will write will have a main method. Most Java programs contain more than one class definition and many beginning programmers make the mistake of thinking that *every class* they write will have a main method, instead of *every program*. Having more than one class with a main method might be a sign that something is wrong. The need for only a single main method should become clear as we look at multi-class programs in Chapter 3.

The header of the main method should always look like this:

```
public static void main(String[] args)
```

For the time being, it is safe to regard the `public static void` part as a bit of magic that the compiler insists on being there.[2] Its full meaning will not become clear

---

[2] If you find it hard to remember which order these three words come in, try making up a mnemonic to help you, like "*p*ublic *s*ervice *v*ehicle", or "*p*eas (are) *s*mall *v*egetables"!

until quite a lot later, and it is not important to understand it at this point. As each program we write will have a main method, there will be a lot of opportunities to revise the details we are introducing here.

The opening and closing parentheses, (and), mark the start and end of a method's *formal arguments*. Arguments represent information passed into a method to help it perform its task. Because the `main` method is the starting point of the whole program, information it might need is passed to it from the outside world—typically by whoever runs the program once it has been compiled. The argument to `main` always consists of an *array* of *strings*, which is commonly given the name `args`.[3]

```
String[] args
```

We can briefly explain this part by saying that strings are bits of text surrounded by a pair of double-quote characters (`"..."`). Between these you can write any characters you like—`"David"`, `"Walk the plank!"`, `"Do you take sugar?"`. The only restriction is that you must not break a string over more than one line.

An array is one of Java's collection types, that is, something that can hold several things at once—in this case some number of strings. How many strings are in the array will depend on how many the person running the program put there. We will deal with strings in more detail in Section 8.3 and arrays in Chapter 9. Even though our early example programs will not use the `main` method's argument at all, the compiler will insist on its being there nonetheless. If it is not there, then attempting to run a program will result in an error message such as

```
void main(String[] args) is not defined
```

from the bytecode interpreter.

2.2.5 White Space

The term *white space* is given to characters used in formatting a program neatly. These are usually spaces, end-of-line characters, and *tab characters*. Compilers do not care much about where you put them, but people reading your programs will care a great deal. For instance, suppose we had written the program in Code 2.1 like that in Code 2.3 (space characters have been shown explicitly).

Although the compiler would have been quite happy, this is a lot harder for people to read. The main places that the compiler *will* want you to use white space are between consecutive reserved words and identifiers. As we noted above, it is difficult to tell the difference between reserved words and identifiers just by looking at them, so the compiler needs them to be kept separate from one another. In Code 2.4 it would think that `classNothing` and `publicstaticvoidmain` are both user-defined identifiers. A compiler would reject that example, therefore, because it does not conform to the correct form of class structure.

Throughout this book we shall try to be consistent in the way that white space is used to lay out programs. Consistency is much more important than any particular

---

[3] As we saw in Code 2.2, the array does not have to be called `args`, but most people give it this name (or something similar, like `argv`), by a convention adopted in other languages.

Code 2.3   An example of bad program layout

```
class␣Nothing{public␣static␣void␣main(String[]args){}}
```

Code 2.4   Illegal layout: reserved words and identifier must be separated

```
classNothing{publicstaticvoidmain(String[]args){}}
```

---

style that you adopt because your eyes are able to take things in much more quickly when they know what to expect. This both aids in understanding a program and in spotting mistakes. Notice, for instance, the way in which white space indentation can be used to suggest that one block is nested inside another in Code 2.1. In addition, we have adopted a style that puts the class header at the beginning of a line, places the class header and the opening curly bracket on the same line, indents the methods of a class by four spaces underneath the `class` reserved word, and puts the closing curly bracket of the class definition at the beginning of its own line. You can find many of our stylistic conventions listed in Appendix F.

2.2.6   Comments

Because readability is an important characteristic of programs, most programming languages provide for the addition of *comments*, whose sole purpose is to inform the human reader about some aspect of a program. When a compiler reaches a special combination of symbols that indicates a comment, it suspends its normal checking rules and simply skips over the commentary. The significance of reserved words, identifiers, punctuation, and any other type of symbol is turned off for the full extent of a comment. So far, there have been no comments in the program examples we have seen, but there are several ways of introducing them in Java. The first type are *single-line comments* and this is the form that we shall use most of the time, particularly in the early examples. These are introduced with two *forward slash-characters* (//), which must have no white space between them. Everything from these characters up to the end of the line on which they appear is skipped over by the compiler and not checked at all, so

```
// This text would be ignored by a compiler.
```

The second type are *multi-line comments*. A multi-line comment is introduced with the character pair (/*) and its end is marked with the same pair reversed (*/), like so:

```
/* The text of these
   three lines
   would be ignored by a compiler.
*/
```

It is a good idea to make it easy for a person reading your program to spot where the end of a multi-line comment is. This is usually done by placing the closing comment symbol on a line by itself indented to the same level as the opening symbol, and indenting all the text of the comment so that it appears to the right of the opening and closing symbols. Some people like to draw attention to the presence of a comment by including a line of star characters (*) down the left edge, for instance,

```
/* The text of these
 * three lines
 * would be ignored by a compiler.
 */
```

This is just a stylistic preference and these extra stars have no significance to the compiler. There is no requirement to make a multi-line comment span more than one line. Some programmers will use the following form even for single-line comments, although there is no compelling reason to do so.[4]

```
/* This text would be ignored by a compiler. */
```

The third type of comment is simply a variation on the standard multi-line comment and is not really part of the language as such. It is characterized by an additional star character as part of the opening comment symbol (/**). This is a convention used in conjunction with the javadoc tool, which is used to automatically generate program documentation. More details may be found in Appendix H.

We will use comments quite often in our examples to add detail. Our stylistic guidelines give more information on when you should use comments, and what form they should take. As a general guideline, it is good practice to precede program text with a comment in order to give an overview or to explain anything that is not immediately obvious from a direct reading of the code.

2.3   Review

Here are the main points that we have covered in these sections:

- In order to run a program, you must first get it past the compiler.
- The compiler will check very carefully that you have obeyed the rules of the Java language.
- If you have not obeyed the rules, you will not be able to run your program.
- Java programs consist of many different types of symbols.
- Reserved words and identifiers look similar.
- You have a lot of freedom in your choice of identifiers, as long as they are not the same as reserved words. You should try to use names that will help human readers understand your programs.
- Curly brackets and parentheses always come in pairs to mark the start and end of something.
- Curly brackets mark the start and end of a block, such as class and method bodies.

---

[4] This form is often used by those who have programmed in languages that lack single-line comments, because it is more familiar to them.

- All programs start running from their main method. They must have one of these.
- The header of the main method must strictly adhere to a fixed set of symbols.
- Most programs will have just a single main method.
- Reserved words and identifiers must be separated by white space when placed next to each other.
- White space is an important aid in helping people to understand programs, although the compiler does not usually pay much attention to it.
- Java has both single-line and multi-line comments.
- Comments should be used to make it easier for people to understand your programs.

2.4   Compiling and Running Simple Programs

We have probably spent more than enough time discussing the various components of a do-nothing program and the time has come to compile and run something for real. Clearly, you will need to have access to a Java compiler and bytecode interpreter. There are many commercially available Java programming environments, each with its own specialized capabilities and features. In this book we shall not assume that you are using any particular one of these, but base our examples on the *Java 2 SDK*[5] which *JavaSoft*[TM] makes available for free from its Web site at `http://www.javasoft.com`. This provides a full Java implementation, although the user interface to the programs is command-line driven. Whichever programming environment you have, you should follow its setup instructions, or those provided as part of your computing environment. See Appendix G for further details about how to obtain, install, and setup the Java 2 platform.

2.4.1   Compiling a Java Program

If you have a copy of the materials that accompany this book, take a copy of the file `Nothing.java` to one of your own working directories or folders. If you do not have these materials, use a text editor[6] and create a file, called `Nothing.java`, that contains exactly the text shown in Code 2.1. Once you have done either of these things, ask the compiler to check the program for you by typing

```
javac Nothing.java
```

(Make sure you type a capital N in Nothing, and that the file has the full .java suffix, rather than something shorter like .jav.) After a short pause, you should see the command prompt again; if the compiler is happy with the program you give to it then it says nothing—silence is golden. If, instead, you see something like

```
The name specified is not recognized as an
internal or external command, operable program or batch file.
```

---

[5] Formerly known as the Java Development Kit (JDK).

[6] Word processors are not usually suitable for creating program files because they add extra material that the compiler will not recognize.

or

```
javac: Command not found
```

then you have either typed javac incorrectly, or you have not set up your environment properly. In the latter case, check the setup instructions for your Java environment and then try again.

If the compiler finds errors in a program, then it will try to give you information about where it thinks the errors are, and what those errors might be. It is actually quite hard to write compilers that tell you what is *really* wrong, so compiler error messages need to be treated with caution, but an error message is a certain indication that something needs fixing and the line number information given should be close to where the problem lies. For instance, Code 2.5 shows what the compiler might say if static had been misspelled as statc in Nothing.java.

The line number is correct, but the diagnosis is incorrect.

2.4.2 Running a Program

Our example program does nothing, so we will not bother to run it. Instead, we will look at a similar program that includes a little more, and so will be worth running; see Code 2.6, a copy of which can be found in the file Hello.java amongst the materials that accompany this book.

It is a long-standing tradition that first programs should print out the message, "hello, world"; in fact, you might have heard people talk about the hello-world program in various programming languages. This time, the main method is enclosed within a class named Hello, but its header still has the required form. Take a copy of Hello.java (or create it using an editor) and compile it by typing

```
javac Hello.java
```

just as you did with Nothing.java.

Code 2.5 Misspelled reserved word, incorrectly diagnosed

```
Nothing.java:2: Identifier expected.
    public statc void main(String[] args) {
                 ^
```

Code 2.6 A Java hello-world program (Hello.java)

```
    // A program to print "hello, world".
class Hello {
    public static void main(String[] args) {
        System.out.println("hello, world");
    }
}
```

Compiling a program stored in a file with a `.java` suffix will produce one or more files with a `.class` suffix if the compiler is satisfied. A `.class` file is produced for each class defined in a `.java` file. As a result of this compilation, we should get a single file called `Hello.class`. The `.class` file contains the bytecodes representing the translated version of the Java source. As we discussed in Chapter 1, these bytecodes may be run on any machine for which we have a bytecode interpreter. Furthermore, once a program has been successfully compiled, we may run it with an interpreter as many times as we like without having to recompile it each time.

Our program can be run by using the Java platform bytecode interpreter, which is just called `java`, as follows:

```
java Hello
```

Notice that we do not type:

```
java Hello.class
```

If we do this then the interpreter reports something like

```
Exception in thread "main" java.lang.NoClassDefFoundError: Hello.class
```

The name we give to the interpreter must always be the name of the class that contains the main method, because this is the starting point for the whole program. That is why there is usually only a single main method per program, because most programs will have a unique starting point. The interpreter is sensitive to the difference between upper- and lower-case letters, so the name of the class we give it must exactly match the case of the name in the .java file. Similarly, the prefix of the .java filename should also match the class name (`Hello.java`).

Figure 2.1 shows the relationship between `.java` and `.class` files and the `javac` and `java` programs used to translate and run them. Rather unsurprisingly, when we run the `Hello` program we should see the output

```
hello, world
```

in the window from which the program was run. This output clearly results from the extra statement that was not present in the do-nothing program

```
System.out.println("hello, world");
```

A detailed explanation of this statement is that it is a request to the `println` method of the `out` object of the `System` class to print the `String` object, `"hello, world"`! There are rather too many concepts bundled up in that description to be explained here, but they will be gradually unraveled in the succeeding sections. For the moment, it is best to regard `System.out.println` as another bit of magic for printing strings on the screen.

Worth noting is the semicolon symbol (';') at the end of the statement, as this is the first time we have met one. This is one of Java's most commonly used punctuation symbols. It is known as a *statement terminator*; that is, it tells the compiler where the

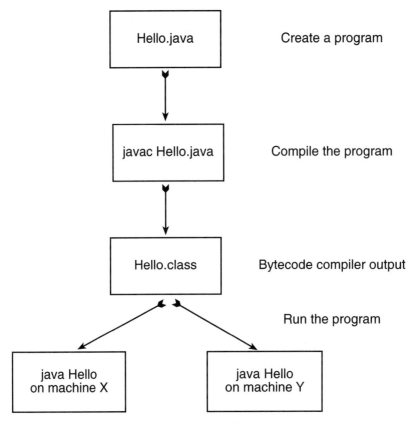

Figure 2.1 The stages involved in compiling and running a Java program with the Java platform

end of the statement is. It acts just like the full stop at the end of an English sentence. It is a common error to forget to include the semicolon at the end of a statement, and the compiler would have given an error message such as

```
Hello.java:4: ';' expected.
        System.out.println("hello, world")
                                          ^
```

had we omitted it. This time it has both the correct line and a correct diagnosis. Also worth noting is the way in which we have used white space characters to show that this statement belongs within the body of the main method.

Now try the following exercises to give yourself confidence in compiling and running programs.

Exercise 2.1   Use a text editor to modify the file `Hello.java` so that it prints out your name instead of `world`. For instance, my version would print

```
hello, David
```

Exercise 2.2   Make a copy of the file `Hello.java` and rename it so that it is called `Goodbye.java`. Now make any necessary changes to `Goodbye.java` so that it compiles and, when run, prints

    goodbye, world

If your program compiles but the interpreter prints something like

`Exception in thread "main" java.lang.NoClassDefFoundError: Goodbye`

make sure that you have changed the name of the class, as well as the string to be printed.

Exercise 2.3   Satisfy yourself that a program can be run several times over with the bytecode interpreter without having to recompile it each time.

2.4.3   The Edit-Compile-Run Cycle

When creating a new program, it is easy to make errors. These will often be simple typing errors that result in the compiler reporting syntax errors. Once your program has passed the compiler, there will often be further logical errors to correct in the light of experience, or enhancements to be made. Any changes you make might require further syntax errors to be corrected before the program can be run again. Figure 2.2 illustrates this repetitive process, which is commonly referred to as the *edit-compile-run cycle*. When developing a large program, we would encourage you to plan to go through the edit-compile-run several times over. This will be inevitable as you correct elementary syntax errors, but it is also useful to develop a large program in small stages rather than tackling it all in one go. This will help you to keep the logical errors more manageable, as well. When you make a small addition to a program that

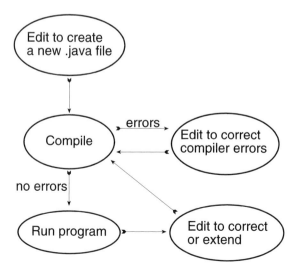

Figure 2.2   The edit-compile-run cycle

already compiles, and it then fails to compile, you should have a pretty good idea about where to look to correct the syntax errors. Similarly, if an enhancement to a working program causes it to work no longer, you have a head start in finding the probable cause.[7]

2.5 Review

Here are the main points that we have covered in the preceding sections:

- The Java platform Java compiler is called `javac`.
- A java program is stored in a `.java` file.
- The name of the file in which a class is stored should match the name of the class, with `.java` as its suffix.
- Compiling a `.java` file produces a `.class` file for each class in the file.
- Once a program has been compiled successfully, it can be given to a bytecode interpreter to be run.
- The Java platform bytecode interpreter is called `java`.
- A program is run by passing the name of the class containing the main method to the interpreter.
- A program that compiles may be run over and over without recompilation.
- The bytecode version of a program compiled on one machine may be run on any machine with a bytecode interpreter.

Exercise 2.4   Which of the following are reserved words and which are identifiers? `String`, `public`, `void`, `main`, `Hello`, `args`, `int`, `double`, `method`? (You might find it useful to refer to the list of reserved words in Appendix D.)

Exercise 2.5   Which of the following statements are true and which are false?

- It is possible to use an underscore character ("_") in an identifier.
- Every class must have a main method.
- Curly brackets ("{" and "}") mark the start and end of a block.
- It is not possible to nest blocks.
- White space characters must be used to separate reserved words and identifiers.

Exercise 2.6   Add curly brackets to the program in Code 2.7 in order to make it compile. Run the corrected program.

Exercise 2.7   Will the program shown in Code 2.8 compile and run?

Exercise 2.8   Improve the layout of the program shown in Code 2.8. Make sure that it compiles after you have made the changes.

Exercise 2.9   What should be the name of the file that holds the program shown in Code 2.9?
   What do you think will be the result of compiling and running this program? Test your answers by typing it in and running it.

---

[7] Of course, the enhancement *might* have triggered a latent failure in the original program, but the changes the new code has introduced should give valuable clues as to the underlying problem.

Code 2.7   Restore the missing curly brackets (`Brackets.java`)

```
    // Add curly brackets to this file to make it compile.
class Brackets
    public static void main(String[] args)
        System.out.println("Brackets, brackets, brackets!");
```

Code 2.8   An example of poor program layout (`Layout.java`)

```
    // Improve the layout of this program.
class Layout { public
static void
                 main(String[] args)
{
System.out.println("I need more space!");
}
}
```

Code 2.9   What file should this program be stored in?

```
class TwoPrints {
    public static void main(String[] args){
        System.out.println("One step forward, two steps back.");
        System.out.println("Two heads are better than one.");
    }
}
```

Exercise 2.10   Add further `println` statements to your solution to Exercise 2.9.

In the next chapter, we start to look at the basics of classes and objects in more detail.

3

Creating and Using Objects

In this chapter, we begin to look at how classes, objects, and the interactions between them are identified from the statement of a problem. We introduce parts of Java that allow objects to be created. We also show the way in which messages are used to request objects to perform particular tasks.

3.1 Why So Much for So Little?

In Chapter 2, we began to introduce the Java programming language by showing a very simple program to print two words on a computer screen. Even such a small example illustrates the enormous gulf there is between the things we want to do and the lengths we have to go to in order to achieve them. It would be quite reasonable to ask, "Why can't we just write

```
print hello, world
```

and have the computer do just that?"

If all we ever wanted to do was to write simple programs that performed simple tasks, then designing a programming language to accomplish that without the need for curly brackets, semicolons, and class names would be perfectly possible. Indeed, the early versions of the BASIC programming language [KK67] were very much like this. Nowadays, we tend to have big goals in mind for the programs we want to write—a chess program that can beat the world champion, air traffic control systems that will move us safely in and out of ever busier airports, banking systems that allow fast access to our accounts but keep our money secure, and so on. The need to be able to program such complex tasks, and the need to educate sufficient people to be able to program them, tend to make for bigger and more complex languages that are general purpose programming languages—that is, they allow a wide range of problems to be solved. One consequence of this is to make some simple tasks look more complicated than they ought to be, but, hopefully, it also makes the more complex tasks easier to solve.

3.2 What are Object-Oriented Languages?

Java is an object-oriented programming language; that is, it contains features that support an object-oriented view of problem solving[Boo94], [Bud97]. Another closely related programming language is C++ [Str97], which is also object-oriented.

In contrast, languages such as Pascal [JW78] and C [KR78] (the direct predecessor of C++) are not object-oriented languages. So, what is the object-oriented view of problem solving? Put fairly simply, the object-oriented view considers a problem to consist of collections of *objects* and the various interactions between them. These objects often model artifacts that are present in the real world. Objects are categorized into *classes*—groups of objects which have similar characteristics and exhibit similar behavior. A defining characteristic of an object is that it has both *state* and *behavior* and these are intimately related. An object's behavior is influenced by its state and its state may be changed by its behavior.

Object-oriented design is felt by many to be a more natural way of looking at problems than the older *structured programming* approaches [Wir71] (such as Pascal and C support). The reason for this is that an object-oriented design is carried out in terms of the very objects that comprise the problem—that is, that exist within the problem domain. An object-oriented programming language enables the overall object-oriented view of design to be carried right on through to the implementation of the problem's solution—there is no significant mid-course shift in the way the problem is looked at through the analysis, design, and implementation stages. An object-oriented language will contain features that support the direct representation of the objects that were identified at the analysis stage, as well as the interactions between those objects. A further advantage of object-oriented languages is that they often facilitate *software reuse*; the self-contained nature of classes often makes it possible to use them in many different contexts.

In the next section, we use an example to put some real-life detail onto this overview. The problem area being discussed would be a relatively large problem in real life. The scope of this book means that we can only examine it superficially in this chapter, but we shall repeatedly use parts of the overall problem in order to introduce other features of Java in various parts of this book.

3.3   Modeling the Operation of a Port

Suppose we wished to model a busy seaport in order to determine whether ship movements in and out could be performed more quickly than is happening at present, but without jeopardizing current levels of safety. In reality, this would be a very big project, requiring a detailed description of the port's current workings to be prepared before proper analysis and design could begin. However, we can use it to help us think about what objects might be involved in the model, and the classes into which they fit.

The most obvious objects in the real-life version of this scenario are the ships and the port itself. As we analyze those aspects of the port that relate to ship movements, we might recognize that the turn-around time of the ships depends upon the loading and unloading of their cargo; so we will need to consider including objects to represent cargo and the lorries used to transport it in any model that we build. If the port has passenger ferries, we will want to model passengers and their vehicles—maybe even car parks. We might model the movements of individuals, such as pilots and customs officers. A full model might also require us to understand how the port interacts with connecting road and rail networks—further sources of objects. In addition, a port's operations depend upon the weather and the tides, and objects would be used to represent these aspects of the external environment.

In identifying the objects in the problem, we have begun to notice interactions between them and can add further examples:

- Transfer of cargo between a ship and the docks.
- Passengers embarking and disembarking.
- A pilot joining and leaving a ship.
- A ship requesting permission to enter or leave the port.
- The weather causing ships to remain in port.

You can probably think of other objects and interactions, too. In a full object-oriented design, we would repeatedly explore the problem area, identifying potential objects and interactions, until we feel that we have a sound basis for more detailed design and specification, leading on to implementation. As a result of taking an object-oriented view of the problem, the objects that can be identified directly from the problem domain, and the interactions between them, will be evident from the earliest stages of the problem's analysis. These will be followed through from the design to the final implementation where objects exist within the running program for all of these components.

3.4   Classes and Objects

In thinking informally about the port simulation we have, in effect, thought about the typical objects that exist in this situation in the real world, and how they behave and interact with one another. A typical cargo ship carries cargo, which must be loaded and unloaded. A typical passenger ferry carries passengers and vehicles, which embark and disembark. In the language of object-oriented design, when we describe *typical objects*, we usually use the term *class definition*, and we say that each object belongs to a particular class. A class definition provides a general description for objects that behave like a typical member of that class. We say that:

> A class definition describes the *behavior* and *attributes* of typical *instances* of that class. The attributes are used to store the *state values* of its instances.

For example, we might have classes called `CargoShip` and `PassengerFerry`, which describe the typical behaviors of cargo ships and passenger ferries. While one cargo ship might differ from another in various ways, both will behave in broadly similar ways and have a similar set of attributes, such as cargo holds and carrying capacity. An object is an instance of a class; the *RMS Titanic*, for example, might be an instance of a class of ship we could call `Liner`. Her sister ships, *RMS Olympic* and *HMHS Britannic*, would belong to the same class. Many other ships with liner-like attributes and behavior will also belong to this same class. Within a program modeling the behavior of ships around a port, at any one time we might have many Liner, CargoShip, and PassengerFerry objects in existence. Each belongs to its own particular class which describes the general behavior and characteristics of that type of ship. Those new to object-oriented programming often find it difficult to tell the difference between classes and objects. One way to think of classes is as blueprints or templates. Objects are the items that are manufactured from these. The blueprint for a piece of equipment describes its structure, dimensions, the material it should be made from, and so on; but the blueprint is not, itself, the equipment. Many items of equipment may be manufactured from the same blueprint. Each will be essentially identical, but might have slight variations that identify it as an individual item—a serial number, or particular color, for instance. In the same way, a class definition lays down the attributes that object of the class will possess, and the way all will behave; but each object may have its own slightly different settings of those attributes to make it unique.

Classes are an essential concept in object-oriented programming. They allow us to abstract away from the exact details of any particular object and, instead, look for general characteristics possessed by objects in the system being modeled. After all, experience suggests that individual objects do tend to behave according to broadly classifiable patterns—consider the way in which market-researchers use this fact with human populations. Effectively, this principle of describing a general class of behavior and attributes frees us from having to individually identify every single ship that might ever enter the port—something which is practically impossible, anyway—and just concentrate on identifying different classes of ship. The degree of difference between objects only needs to be taken into account at the class level when it is evident in the problem being solved; a difference in the number of deck chairs on the *Titanic* and the *Olympic* would not require that they be described by different classes in the context of a port simulation. Some of the important similarities between ships in the context of the simulation might be the fact that they have state representing their position, speed and course (heading), and that they have behavior that allows them to respond to requests to change their course and speed, for instance.

3.5   Review

Here are the main points that we have covered in the preceding sections:

- Solving complex programming problems requires powerful programming languages, but these require more effort to learn how to use them properly.
- Object-oriented problem solving involves looking for classes and objects in the problem domain.
- A class description captures the behavior and attributes of typical objects belonging to that class.
- An object has both behavior (as defined by its class) and state (as captured in its attributes).
- An object's behavior is influenced by its state, and its state may be changed by its behavior.
- Some programming languages support an object-oriented view of problem solving; Java is one of these languages.
- Object-oriented programming languages support the analysis and design stages of problem solving by allowing the description of classes and objects to be carried through to the implementation stage.
- Object-oriented analysis and design also involve identifying interactions between the different classes and objects in the problem domain.

- Classes provide an abstraction from real-life objects, which should be described at a level of detail appropriate to the problem being solved.

In the next sections we look at how to create and use objects in Java.

3.6   Creating and Using Objects

In the next few sections, we shall describe the language features of Java that allow us to create and use objects. At this stage we will not be showing you how to define your own classes; instead, we have supplied some ready-made classes in the material accompanying this book. Much of this description will make use of an imaginary `Ship` class which, for the sake of simplicity, does not try to accurately describe any particular class of real-life ship. To help you visualize the way in which these ship objects behave, we have provided a graphical user interface (GUI) for an application. The GUI depicts an imaginary ocean in which ships move; Figure 3.1 illustrates what this looks like. A ship is represented in the upper area by a small circle which has a line radiating from its center, indicating the course which the ship is following. A course of zero degrees moves the ship from left to right across the ocean and a course of ninety degrees moves it from top to bottom. The top left corner of the ocean is described by the `(x,y)` coordinate position `(0,0)`. As a ship moves, it will leave a fine trail behind it. The middle text area (initially empty but with two scroll bars) is provided for the ship to report information on its course, speed and position as it moves. A button at the bottom allows the application window to be closed.

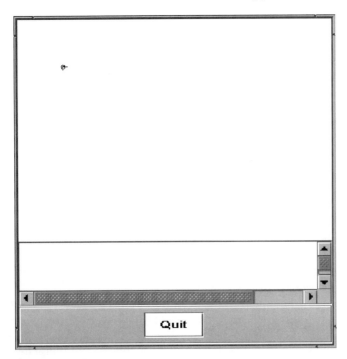

Figure 3.1   The GUI for a Ship within an ocean
(`ShipMain1.java`)

Code 3.1   Creating a `Ship` object (`ShipMain1.java`)

```
        // An illustration of object creation.
class ShipMain1 {
    public static void main(String[] args){
        // Define a method variable to refer to a Ship object.
        Ship argo;

        // Construct a new Ship object.
        argo = new Ship();
    }
}
```

3.6.1   Creating an Object

Code 3.1 shows the main method for part of the program that produces the window shown in Figure 3.1. We have deliberately hidden the details of how the graphical display is provided, because they are beyond the scope of this chapter and are not relevant to the basic ideas of objects and classes that we wish to introduce here.

This example is similar in many respects to the programs we saw in Chapter 2. It consists entirely of a class definition (`ShipMain1`) with a main method where the program starts. Inside the body of the main method there are two statements that we have not seen before. The first is a *variable declaration*:

```
    Ship argo;
```

The various symbols that make it up are:

- A class name—`Ship`.
- An identifier—`argo`.
- A terminating semicolon.

A variable declaration defines a variable, which is something that is always used to store some information. A variable defined inside a method is called a *method variable*. A variable always has a name, and the one defined here is called `argo`.[1] The information that can be stored in a variable is determined by the variable's *type*, which is always written immediately before its name in its declaration. So the type of the `argo` variable is `Ship`. Some variables can store an item of numerical data, while others store an *object reference*. Java is very strict about what sort of data can be stored in what type of variables, and the compiler will tell us we have used 'incompatible types' if we try to store something of the wrong type in a variable—the equivalent of trying to place a square peg into a round hole. What the declaration of `argo` in Code 3.1 means, therefore, is that we can use it to store a reference to a `Ship` object. In effect, a variable gives us a convenient name by which we can refer to a ship object once we have created one.

It is important to note that `argo` *is not a Ship object*; neither does defining a variable automatically create an object. Object creation is a separate operation and

---

[1] The name comes from the ship in the legend of *Jason and the Argonauts*.

is performed, for this example, in the second statement of Code 3.1:

```
// Construct a new Ship object.
argo = new Ship();
```

From the accompanying comment we can see that object creation is also called *object construction*. This statement is a Java *assignment statement*. An assignment statement is used to store something into a variable. It takes what is on the right of the *assignment operator* (=) and stores it into the variable whose name is given on the left of the assignment operator. So what is produced on the right-hand side?

```
...= new Ship();
```

The right-hand side contains the reserved word new, the Ship class name again, a pair of empty parentheses and the customary terminating semicolon. The empty parentheses after Ship look odd, but if you leave them out the compiler will report

```
'(' expected
```

Using new is the way in which an object of a particular class is constructed. Because an object is also known as an instance, object construction is also known as *instantiation*. Use of new to construct an object results in an *object reference* value for the new object on the right-hand side of the assignment. This value can be stored in the argo variable because the type of argo matches the type of the object that has just been created. Figure 3.2 shows the variable argo symbolically referring to the newly created Ship object (represented by a circle) immediately following the assignment statement.

Once the assignment statement is complete, we can use the name argo to refer to the newly created object in the remainder of the method. Although there are no further statements in this particular example, future examples will add statements that use argo to interact with the Ship object.

Exercise 3.1   Find out what the compiler says if you try to store something of an inappropriate type into the argo variable. Take a copy of the ShipMain1.java file, shown in Code 3.1, and separately try the following two variations on the assignment statement

```
// Try to store a number into a Ship variable.
argo = 3;
```

and

```
// Try to store a String object reference into a Ship variable.
argo = new String();
```

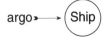

Figure 3.2 The variable argo contains a reference to a Ship object

3.6.2   Object Interactions—Message Passing

In everyday life, communication takes place between two people—a speaker and a hearer—in one of three main forms:

- The speaker communicates information to the listener: "I am going to a party tonight."
- The speaker asks the listener for information: "What is the time?"
- The speaker asks the listener to do something: "Please buy me some gum."

An object-oriented program will contain many different objects collaborating together to solve a particular problem, and these same forms of interaction are used between those objects. Objects within a program interact via a mechanism called *message passing*—that is, the passing of messages to one another. Instead of speaker and hearer, however, we often talk about *actor* and *agent*, or *client* and *server*. In object-oriented programming languages, messages are passed between objects through the use of *methods* defined in the class of the object receiving the message. Methods are always defined inside the body of a class. They implement the behavior that objects of that particular class are meant to display. They represent, therefore, the ability of objects of that class to receive particular sorts of message. An important principle to remember is that it is the class of the *receiving object* that determines whether that object is able to receive a message being sent to it. For example, if a Harbor Master object in a port simulation sends a message to a ship to alter course, it will be the ship's class that defines a method to change course. If the ship does not have such a method, then it cannot receive such a message. This is an important principle because it helps us to appreciate that you cannot ask an object to do something unless it has a method that will accept that particular message. You would not ask a chess program to forecast the weather and you would not ask a ship to leave a railway station. If an object's class contains a method to receive a particular message, then it is up to the individual object to decide how to respond to that message. This is something that the compiler will check as part of the compilation process.

3.6.3   Sending Messages to a Ship Object

In this section, we shall see how to send appropriate messages to an object once it has been created. Code 3.2 shows a main method that is similar to that shown in Code 3.1, but also has some important differences and additions.

The first difference to note is that we have rewritten the two statements concerned with the declaration of `argo` and assignment to it. It is so common to define a variable and give it an initial value immediately afterwards, that these two steps can be combined into a single *declaration and initialization statement*. The second difference is the following statement:

```
// Ask the ship to report its initial position, course and speed.
argo.report();
```

This shows the way in which a simple message may be sent to an object. The name of the message is `report`. A simple message is sent to an object by writing the name of a variable that refers to it, followed by a period, then the name of the message and

Code 3.2   Sending a message to a Ship object (`ShipMain2.java`)

```
        // An illustration of message sending.
class ShipMain2 {
    public static void main(String[] args){
        // Define a method variable and make it refer to a
        // newly constructed Ship object.
        Ship argo = new Ship();

        // Ask the ship to report its initial position, course and speed.
        argo.report();
    }
}
```

a pair of empty parentheses. The statement is terminated by a semicolon. From our earlier discussion, we can infer from this statement that the Ship class must define a method whose name is `report`, which is able to receive and act upon this particular message. We might visualize the sending of this message, and its receipt by a method inside the object as shown in Figure 3.3.

All Ship objects have a number of *attributes* which enable them to implement their ship-like behavior. These include the ship's current position, course, and speed. When a Ship object receives a `report` message, it prints values for these attributes in the text area of the graphical display shown in Figure 3.1. Compiling and running `ShipMain2.java` with the accompanying `.class` files should produce the output

```
    Position is (25,25), Course is 0.0, Speed is 5.0
```

in the text area. This shows the default initial values that all ships have for these three attributes.

The example in Code 3.2 illustrates two further points that it are worth emphasizing:

- When sending a message to an object, we write the name of a variable before the period, rather than the name of a class. If we had written by mistake

```
    Ship.report();
```

then the compiler would have given the error

```
Can't make static reference to method void report() in class Ship.
```

Hmm!

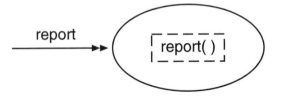

Figure 3.3 Sending and receiving a `report` message

- It must be clear which object is intended to receive a message. When inside the main method, we cannot just write the name of the message in isolation, thus

```
report();
```

In this case, the compiler would have given the error

```
Method report() not found in class ShipMain2.
```

Exercise 3.2   Compile and run the program whose main method is defined in the file `ShipMain2.java`.

3.6.4   Moving a Ship

Another simple message we can send to a Ship object is `move`. The program in Code 3.3 will create a ship and ask it to move from its initial position.

We have simply changed the message sent to the ship from `report` to `move`. Figure 3.4 shows the effect in the graphical display. Note the trail that is left behind the ship showing how it has moved. There is no output in the text area because we have not asked the ship to report its details. As with the `report` method, `move` messages can be sent to Ship objects because the Ship class defines a method with that name. In later chapters, we shall see how these methods can be implemented.

In order to obey a `move` message, a ship consults its position, course, and speed attributes and calculates its next position. As a result, the value of its position attribute will be modified, although its course and speed attributes will remain the same. The exercises below demonstrate this fact, which serves to illustrate an important principle:

> An object's response to a message depends on an interaction between the methods defined in its class and the current values of its attributes (which define its state). As a result of responding to a message, the values of some of its attributes might be changed.

Code 3.3   Moving a ship (`ShipMain3.java`)

```java
        // An illustration of ship movement.
class ShipMain3 {
    public static void main(String[] args){
        // Define a method variable and make it refer to a
        // newly constructed Ship object.
        Ship argo = new Ship();

        // Ask the ship to move from its initial position.
        argo.move();
    }
}
```

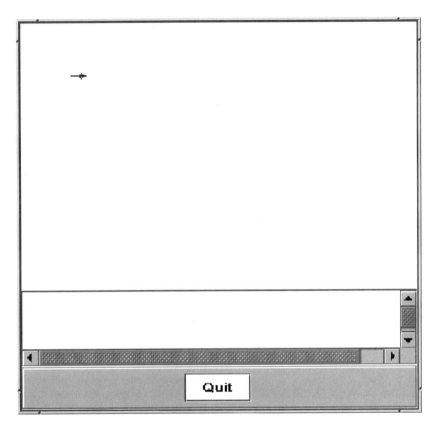

Figure 3.4 The ship after receiving a single move message (ShipMain3.java)

Exercise 3.3 Compile and run the program in ShipMain3.java. You can use the normal window manager controls to increase the size of the window, and hence the amount of space available in the ocean and text areas once it is running.

Exercise 3.4 Add two statements to the program in ShipMain3.java to request argo to report its position, both before and after it has been moved. You should see the following output in the text area:

```
Position is (25,25), Course is 0.0, Speed is 5.0
Position is (30,25), Course is 0.0, Speed is 5.0
```

Exercise 3.5 Make further additions to your solutions to Exercise 3.4 so that argo is made to move twice more before reporting for a third time. What is its position after the third move?

We have described report and move as simple messages because they do not require any extra information to be supplied along with them in order for a ship to be able to act on them. Furthermore, neither involves receiving a reply from the ship—it simply gets on with moving or printing to the text area. As we shall see in the next section, interacting with objects can be more complex, involving both passing extra information as part of the message, and receiving back a reply.

3.6.5 Passing Arguments with Messages

As we saw in Section 3.6.3, when sending a `report` message to an object, no extra information needs to be supplied with the message name in order for the object to be able to respond to it. If a ship is ordered to go, "Full steam ahead," then the speed is implicit in the message. Similarly, if a Ship object is asked to `move`, it will use the information stored in its current speed and course attributes to calculate its next position. For other types of messages, however, it is necessary to supply extra information in order for the receiving object to do its job. If a ship is asked to, "Change course," what should the new course be? Or, "Slow down," to what speed? When such messages are sent, the sender must supply the extra information that is needed in the form of *arguments*.

In addition to its simple `report` and `move` methods, the Ship class has more complex methods that allow us to request a ship to change its speed or course. Both of these further methods need to be passed arguments that tell the ship what the altered speed or course should be. Code 3.4 contains a main method as an example of how to set a ship's course to 90 degrees using its `setCourse` method.

Figure 3.5 shows the result of running this program. The first part of the ship's movement takes it on its default course of zero degrees, before the second part moves it on its new course. Figure 3.6 shows how we might visualize the sending of a `setCourse` message with an argument. The `setCourse` method inside the object defines a variable (`newCourse`) to receive the argument value, before storing this value into its `course` attribute. We shall explore this mechanism in more detail in Chapter 4.

Code 3.4 Setting a ship's course (`ShipMain4.java`)

```java
        // An illustration of using arguments with methods.
class ShipMain4 {
    public static void main(String[] args){
        // Define a method variable and make it refer to a
        // newly constructed Ship object.
        Ship argo = new Ship();

        // Ask the ship to report its initial position, course and speed.
        argo.report();
        // Ask the ship to move from its initial position.
        argo.move();
        // Ask it to change course, move and report its new settings.
        argo.setCourse(90);
        argo.move();
        argo.report();
    }
}
```

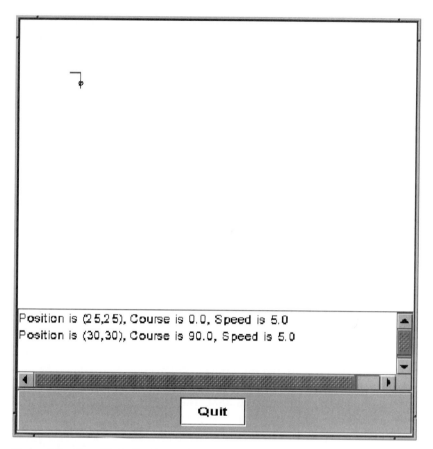

Figure 3.5   The effect of asking a ship to change course

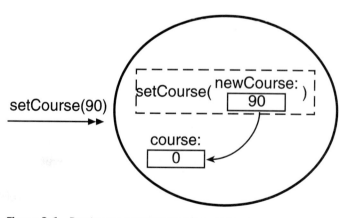

Figure 3.6   Passing an argument with a message

Exercise 3.6   Take a copy of `ShipMain4.java` and modify it with the addition of three more statements at the end of the main method:

- The argument of `setCourse` is an absolute heading rather than a relative heading. Set `argo`'s course to 180 degrees. Be careful to spell the `setCourse` method correctly (with an upper case `C`) otherwise the compiler will report:

  ```
  Method setcourse(double) not found in class Ship.
  ```

- Ask it to move.
- Ask it to report its position.

You should now see the following output:

```
Position is (25,25), Course is 0.0, Speed is 5.0
Position is (30,30), Course is 90.0, Speed is 5.0
Position is (25,30), Course is 180.0, Speed is 5.0
```

Exercise 3.7   Can you add some statements to your solution to Exercise 3.6 to get `argo` back to its original position? Ask it to report its position after it has moved each time, to help you see whether you have the right idea.

Exercise 3.8   Start with an empty main method containing just the creation of a Ship object and experiment with sending different combinations of `move`, `report` `setSpeed`, and `setCourse` messages to it.

Exercise 3.9   What happens if you try to set a negative speed, or a course that is outside the normal 0...360 range?

3.6.6   Receiving Replies from Messages

When someone asks a question of another person, they usually expect to receive a reply of some sort. The same principle can be applied to the interaction between two objects—an actor object might send a message that requires a reply from an agent object.

- "What is the time?"
- "Are there any free berths in the port?"
- "What is the square-root of 2?"

Once again, the method used to return the reply is defined in the class receiving the message. For instance, the Ship class defines the method `getSpeed` that returns its current speed to any object that wishes to know this. It might take an agent a significant period of time to respond to the message and formulate a reply, but the actor must wait for the reply. The actor cannot get on with something else while the agent is busy.[2] A reply is called a *method result* or *return value*, and it will either take the form of a simple value, such as a number, or a reference to an object. As such, it may be used as any other value or object reference. The actor will often need to store

---

[2] In Chapter 18, we look at some of the special features of the language that do allow two objects to pursue different tasks independently.

Code 3.5 Asking a ship to return its speed with `getSpeed` (`ShipMain5.java`)

```
            // An illustration of using a method that returns a result.
class ShipMain5 {
    public static void main(String[] args){
        // Define a method variable and make it refer to a
        // newly constructed Ship object.
        Ship argo = new Ship();

        // Ask the ship to report its initial position, course and speed.
        argo.report();

        // Define a variable to hold the ship's current speed.
        double currentSpeed;
        // Ask the ship what its current speed is.
        currentSpeed = argo.getSpeed();
        // Increase the ship's speed.
        argo.setSpeed(currentSpeed+1);

        // Ask the ship to move and report.
        argo.move();
        argo.report();
    }
}
```

the method result for later use. A suitable variable for storing the result is one whose type matches the type of the result. The type of the value Ship's `getSpeed` method returns, for instance, is `double`[3] (another of Java's reserved words). Code 3.5 shows a program to ask a ship its current speed and then use the value it returns to increase the speed.

The following three statements show new aspects of Java:

```
        // Define a variable to hold the ship's current speed.
        double currentSpeed;
        // Ask the ship what its current speed is.
        currentSpeed = argo.getSpeed();
        // Increase the ship's speed.
        argo.setSpeed(currentSpeed+1);
```

In the first of these, a variable called `currentSpeed` is declared. Just as the declaration of `argo` includes a type, so the reserved word `double` indicates the type of values that may be stored into `currentSpeed`. Being of type `double`, we can store *real numbers* (numbers with decimal points) into `currentSpeed`.[4] The second statement is an assignment statement, indicating that a value is being stored into `currentSpeed`. On the right-hand side of the assignment we are sending a `getSpeed` message to `argo`, indicating that we expect to receive a reply to this message. The reply will return the value `5.0` because this is the default initial speed of a ship when it is created. Note that we could have combined these two statements

---

[3] This type name is shorthand for double precision floating point number.

[4] We explain more about types such as this in Chapter 5.

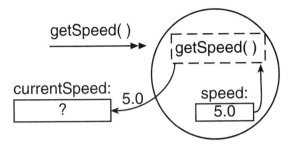

Figure 3.7   Returning a result from a method

in the following single declaration and initialization statement, as we saw previously:

```
double currentSpeed = argo.getSpeed();
```

Figure 3.7 shows how we might visualize the return of a value from a method. The `getSpeed` method retrieves the value to be returned from its `speed` attribute.

The third statement sends a `setSpeed` message to `argo` using a slightly more complicated argument than we have seen so far. This involves an *arithmetic expression* in which the value stored in `currentSpeed` is added to the number 1 before the whole result (`5.0+1`) is passed as an argument to `setSpeed`. The result of this expression is that the ship's speed will be set to `6.0`. Running the program shown in Code 3.5 produces the following output in the text area.

```
Position is (25,25), Course is 0.0, Speed is 5.0
Position is (31,25), Course is 0.0, Speed is 6.0
```

This example also serves to illustrate that variables may be defined anywhere within a method. This differs from the practice in some languages which only allow them to be defined at the start of a method.

Exercise 3.10   Modify the declaration of `currentSpeed` in the main method of ShipMain5 so that it is defined to be of type `int` instead of type `double`. What error message does the compiler give when you recompile `ShipMain5.java`?

Exercise 3.11   The Ship class has a `getCourse` method that also returns a `double` value as its result. Write statements in a main method that ask a ship its current course and then change that course by several degrees. Use the ship's `report` method to check that this is successful.

3.6.7   Variables and Objects

It is always important to distinguish between a variable and the object to which it currently refers. Throughout the life of a program, a single variable might refer to many different objects, although it can only refer to one at a time. It is also perfectly possible to have two different variables referring to the same object and this reflects what happens in real life. There might be more than one way of talking about the same ship: "Lively Lady" and "That old rust-bucket." It is also worth noting that two similarly named variables can refer to quite different objects, and this also has a real-life counterpart: there are two cities called "Canterbury," one in England and one in New Zealand. This is often a source of confusion for programmers, and Java has *scope rules* to help remove the potential ambiguity from such situations (see Section 7.7).

A common mistake made by people starting to learn about programming is that a variable can hold more than one item of information at once—rather like a box. In Java, this is not the case; whenever anything is stored into a variable via an assignment statement, any previous contents of the variable are lost and cannot be recovered. If a variable's original contents must not be lost, it is first necessary to copy those contents into another variable with an assignment statement. If we need to store multiple items of data simultaneously, then we need to use a collection object designed for this purpose (see Chapter 10).

3.6.8 Uninitialized Variables

In the example shown in Code 3.1, the `argo` variable does not refer to a Ship object until after the assignment in the statement immediately following. Similarly, in Code 3.5, a value is not stored into the variable `currentSpeed` until the statement following its declaration. It would be reasonable to ask what a variable contains before it is used on the left-hand side of an assignment statement. A method variable that has not been the subject of an assignment is said to be an *uninitialized variable*—the value it contains is not defined. It is important to appreciate that `currentSpeed` *does not* contain the value zero before its explicit initialization. The compiler will warn you if you attempt to use the contents of such a variable before it has been assigned to, as this is considered to be a logical error. Variables whose purpose is to refer to objects can be explicitly initialized with the special value `null`—a reserved word meaning 'no object'—from their point of declaration until they are made to refer to an object by an assignment. For instance,

```
// Argo does not yet refer to a Ship.
Ship argo = null;
...
// Make argo refer to a new Ship object.
argo = new Ship();
```

However, it is usually possible to defer declaring a variable until its initial value is known, so we do not often use null-initialization. For instance,

```
// Create a new ship.
Ship argo = new Ship();
argo.report();
// Find out argo's current speed.
double currentSpeed = argo.getSpeed();
...
```

3.7 Review

Here are the main points that we have covered in the preceding sections:

- Variables are used to store information, such as numbers or object references.
- An assignment statement is used to store information in a variable.

- A variable is only able to hold a single piece of information at a time.
- The type of the information stored in a variable must be compatible with the variable's declared type.
- An object is created by using the `new` reserved word followed by the class of the object.
- Objects communicate by sending messages to each other.
- The messages an object may receive are determined by the methods defined in its class.
- Simple methods do not require any arguments—the action is implicit in the method name.
- One or more arguments may be included with a message by enclosing them in the parentheses written after the method name.
- A method result may be used to return a reply from a message.

In the next sections, we reinforce these ideas with some further examples.

3.8   Further Examples of Using Objects

The previous sections have introduced you to the basics of variable declaration, object creation, sending messages to objects, and receiving replies from them. In the following sections, we want to reinforce and extend those ideas because they are fundamental to all the object-oriented programming tasks you will undertake. To avoid the ship scenario from becoming too repetitive, we will present the new examples through use of classes that represent a bank and accounts within the bank. The model that we build of the bank will be particularly simple and should not be taken as a close representation of how real banks work. Nevertheless, these classes will allow us to create accounts, make credits and debits, and produce statements, for instance.

3.8.1   The SimpleBank Class

The bank examples are based upon the `SimpleBank` class. Code 3.6 shows a main method that creates a SimpleBank object and sends it a `listAccounts` message to output a list of the current set of bank accounts (of which there are none initially).

Associated with this program is the GUI shown in Figure 3.8. Once again, for the sake of simplicity we have hidden all of the details of how this user interface is

---

Code 3.6   Creating a SimpleBank object (`SimpleBankMain1.java`)

```
        // Demonstrate the GUI for SimpleBank applications.
class SimpleBankMain1 {
    public static void main(String[] args){
        SimpleBank localBank = new SimpleBank();

        // List the full set of accounts (of which there are none so far).
        localBank.listAccounts();
    }
}
```

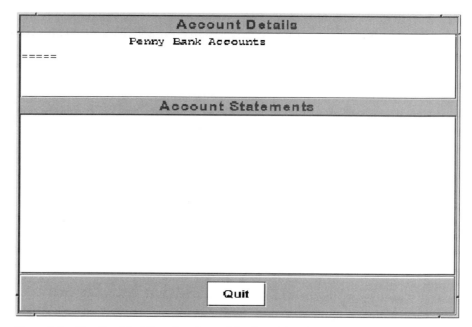

Figure 3.8   The Graphical User Interface of the SimpleBank application

created. Sending a bank object a `listAccounts` message causes it to output to the upper text area of the GUI. The lower text area is used by individual bank account objects to print account statements, as we shall see shortly.

In real life, a bank account always belongs to a particular bank. You approach a bank and ask them to set up an account for you. It is not possible to set up a bank account independently and then offer it to various banks to see if any is willing to take it! We reflect this aspect of reality in these examples by making account creation the responsibility of the SimpleBank class. If you want to create an account, you must send a `createAccount` message to a SimpleBank object. This message takes an argument, which is the name of the account, and the bank object will arrange for an appropriate account object to be created. A reference to the object it creates is returned as the result of the `createAccount` method. The class of the object it creates is `PennyBankAccount`, reflecting the fact that the amount stored in an account is always held as an integer number of pennies (cents), rather than dollars. Code 3.7 shows the addition of a statement to the previous example in order to create an account.

Running the program in Code 3.7 should produce the following output in the upper text area of the application:

```
            Penny Bank Accounts
djb             A/C#:           1
=====
```

Notice that we now have two different objects existing in the program at the same time. One is referred to by the variable `localBank` and the other by the variable `myAccount` (Figure 3.9).

Code 3.7   Asking the bank object to create a new account (`SimpleBankMain2.java`)

```
       // An example of using classes.
       // Create a bank and ask it to create a bank account.
class SimpleBankMain2 {
    public static void main(String[] args){
        SimpleBank localBank = new SimpleBank();
        // Request an account for djb.
        PennyBankAccount myAccount = localBank.createAccount("djb");

        // List the full set of accounts.
        localBank.listAccounts();
    }
}
```

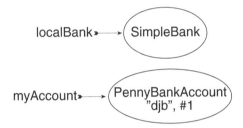

Figure 3.9   The `localBank` and `myAccount` variables refer to different objects

Exercise 3.12   Take a copy of `SimpleBankMain2.java` and add two further statements.

- After the last statement in the main method, define a new PennyBankAccount variable. Initialize this variable with a reference to another new account created for you by the bank.
- Ask the bank to list the accounts again. What is the account number of your new account?

3.8.2   The PennyBankAccount Class

A PennyBankAccount object is responsible for keeping track of the amount of money in an account—the account's balance. This is held as a whole number of cents, which could be either positive or negative. When an account is created, the balance is zero. A fictitious positive amount of money may be added to the balance by sending an account object a `credit` message, whose argument indicates how many cents to add. Similarly, money may be removed from the balance by sending a `debit` message with a positive argument. The example in Code 3.8 contains an example illustrating use of these methods.

Sending a `printStatement` message to an account object causes it to print a statement of the account to the lower text area of the applications GUI (see Figure 3.10). In the statement, all amounts are converted to dollars and cents

Code 3.8   Using the methods of a PennyBankAccount (`SimpleBankMain3.java`)

```
            // An example of using classes.
            // Create and manipulate a bank account.
class SimpleBankMain3 {
    public static void main(String[] args){
        SimpleBank localBank = new SimpleBank();
        PennyBankAccount myAccount = localBank.createAccount("djb");

        // List the full set of accounts.
        localBank.listAccounts();

        // Make some transactions on the djb account.
        myAccount.credit(1000);
        myAccount.debit(575);
        myAccount.debit(300);
        myAccount.credit(1000);
        // Print a statement for djb.
        myAccount.printStatement();
    }
}
```

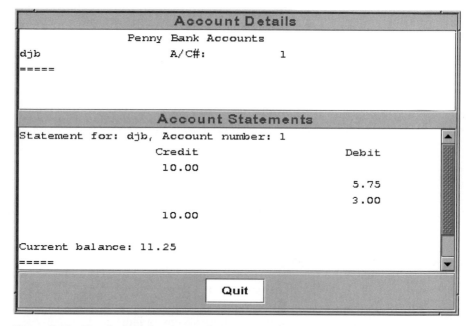

Figure 3.10   The display of an account's statement (`SimpleBankMain3.java`)

separated by a decimal point. In addition to the methods illustrated above, a PennyBankAccount has methods that return as results the account's name as a String (`getName`), the account's number as a `long` (`getNumber`), and the account's balance as a `long` (`getBalance`). None of these takes an argument.

Exercise 3.13   Using your solution to Exercise 3.12, send `credit` and `debit` messages to the second account object you created. Use the account's `printStatement` method to show the list of transactions and the balance of the account afterwards.

Exercise 3.14   What happens if you try to credit or debit a negative amount from an account?

Exercise 3.15   What happens if you debit more money from an account than is currently in its balance?

Exercise 3.16   Use PennyBankAccount's `getName` method to print the names of your two account objects on your terminal window (as opposed to the application's GUI) using `System.out.println`.

3.8.3   Aliases for Objects

The SimpleBank class has a `getAccount` method that allows us to find a particular account object from the account number. Code 3.9 illustrates this.

It is important to appreciate that looking up a bank account in this way does not result in a new PennyBankAccount object being created. There is still only one account in the bank, as the output of the `listAccounts` method will show if you run the program. When a bank receives a `getAccount` message, it finds an object in its internal list of accounts (previously stored there when the account was created) and returns a reference to that object. All objects have a unique reference that they keep from the time they are created—like an unchangeable personal identification number. The object reference returned by `getAccount` in Code 3.9, therefore, is the same as the reference returned earlier by `createAccount`. This means that the variables `myAccount` and `djbAccount` both refer to *the same object*. This is illustrated in Figure 3.11. We say that these variables are *aliases* for the same object. Figure 3.11 also helps to reinforce the point made earlier about the need to distinguish between a variable and the object to which it refers. Neither `myAccount`

Code 3.9   Looking up a bank account object (`SimpleBankMain4.java`)

```
        // Use two different variables to access the same account.
class SimpleBankMain4 {
    public static void main(String[] args){
        SimpleBank localBank = new SimpleBank();
        PennyBankAccount myAccount = localBank.createAccount("djb");

        // Lookup account number 1 (djb's account).
        PennyBankAccount djbAccount = localBank.getAccount(1);

        // List the full set of accounts.
        localBank.listAccounts();
    }
}
```

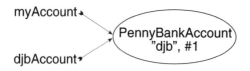

Figure 3.11   Alias variables refer to the same object

Code 3.10   Illustrating the effect of aliases (`SimpleBankMain5.java`)

```
        // Use two different variables to manipulate the same account.
class SimpleBankMain5 {
    public static void main(String[] args){
        SimpleBank localBank = new SimpleBank();
        PennyBankAccount myAccount = localBank.createAccount("djb");

        // Lookup account number 1 (djb's account).
        PennyBankAccount djbAccount = localBank.getAccount(1);

        // Show the initial details of the account through both
        // variables.
        myAccount.printStatement();
        djbAccount.printStatement();

        // Credit the account through one reference.
        myAccount.credit(1000);
        // Show the effect through the other.
        djbAccount.printStatement();
    }
}
```

---

nor djbAccount is, itself, an object; both are variables, each of which can hold a reference to an object. At this point, both contain a reference to the same object, but they could contain references to distinct objects at a later point within the same program.

One side effect of aliases is that any change we make to the account object using one of the variables will be noticeable via the other variable. This can be clearly seen in the output that is produced by the example shown in Code 3.10 and illustrated in Figure 3.12.

Printing a statement of the account using both variables produces the same result. If a credit is then made through the reference held in myAccount, the effect is seen in the statement printed through the reference held in djbAccount. This is because all messages sent via either variable are received and dealt with by the same object.

The importance of aliases will become apparent when we consider the way in which objects sometimes allow access to their attributes via *accessor methods* (see Section 4.7.1).

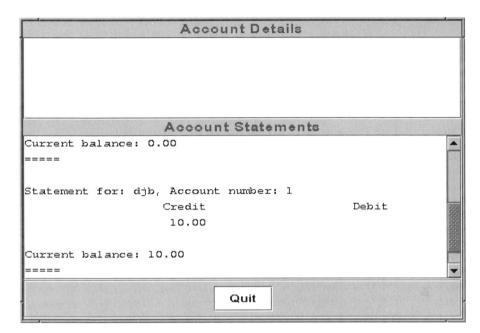

Figure 3.12   The final balance of the single account `"djb"`, `#1`

3.9   The Main Method's Class

Before we discuss in the next chapter how classes are defined, it is worth pointing out the way in which we treat classes that contain a main method—the starting point for all Java applications. You might have noticed that, although we created objects of classes such as Ship, SimpleBank, and PennyBankAccount, we have never created an object of the class containing a main method. This will be a principle that we will follow throughout this book. We treat classes containing a main method purely as the entry point for a program, and rarely define anything within such a class outside the body of the main method. On the whole, we only use a class containing a main method to perform small amounts of application initialization, application demonstration, or testing of classes as they are developed. One reason for our doing this is that the main method always has `static` in its header, which makes it a *static method*. Static methods are rather unusual in that they do not belong to objects and are slightly restricted in the way that they may be used. As you will see in the next chapter, most of the methods that are defined in a proper object-oriented program are not static methods. Having said that, static methods do have an important role to play, and they cannot be ignored. We will leave further discussion of static methods until Section 7.10.

Exercise 3.17   This exercise is designed to illustrate that the `myAccount` variable in Code 3.10 is not permanently tied to the same object as the `djbAccount` variable. Add additional statements to the end of the main method in `SimpleBank-Main5.java` that create a second account, and store a reference to this account in `myAccount`. Add further statements to print statements for the accounts now referenced by the `myAccount` and `djbAccount` variables.

3.10   Review

Here are the main points that we have covered in the preceding sections:

- Objects belonging to different classes may exist within the same program.
- Multiple instances of the same class may exist within the same program. Each instance has its own (independent) set of attributes.
- Objects of one class can be made responsible for creating objects of another class. This is commonly done when the existence of an object only makes sense in the context of another object.
- When an object is created, it is given a unique reference value.
- Two (or more) variables will refer to the same object if they contain the same object reference value.
- Multiple variables containing a reference to the same object are known as aliases for the object.
- Changing an object through one of its aliases will be detectable via any of its other aliases.
- Our practice is to never create an object of a class containing a main method.

Exercise 3.18   Which of the following statements are true and which are false?

- An object may be referred to by more than one variable.
- Classes and objects are the same thing.
- The following variable declaration creates a Ship object.

```
Ship enterprise;
```

- An object variable may refer to different objects from time to time.

Exercise 3.19   Define a class containing a main method. Inside the main method, create two Ship objects. Set different speeds and courses for the two ships and send several `move` messages to the ships. Do the ships move independently? What does this tell you about values of the attributes in the two objects?

In this chapter, we have introduced basic terminology relating to classes and objects. We have also shown how objects may be created, messages sent to them, and replies received. In the next chapter, we shall begin to look at how classes are defined.

CHAPTER 4

Defining Classes

In this chapter, we start to look at how classes are defined in terms of methods and attributes. We discuss the ways in which objects use attributes to maintain their state, and the importance of protecting those attributes from inappropriate modification. We introduce the concept of accessors and mutators to provide controlled access to private attributes, and constructors to enable an object to initialize its initial state.

4.1 Object State and Complexity

We saw in Chapter 3 that we typically send a message to an object in order either to ask it to do something or to provide some information via a method result. For instance, we might ask a ship to alter its course or tell us its current speed. In order to act on the messages it receives, an object usually maintains a set of *attributes*. For a ship, these will be things like position, course, and speed, whereas a bank account object might have attributes for an account's name and number and the balance of money it holds. The set of values contained in the attributes of an object at any one time is known as its current *state*. Some objects have a very simple state, and others have a very complex one. The following are examples of objects with simple state:

- A switch that is on or off (a `true` or `false` value).
- A television set that is on or off and has a current channel selection (a small positive integer).
- A radio that is on or off, has a wave band that is selected, and a frequency it is tuned to (a positive real number).
- A playing card that has a suit and value.

The following objects require more complex state to be maintained:

- A port simulation.
- A chess program.
- A fly-by-wire aircraft.
- A bank.

As a general principle, the more complex an object's state can be, the more attributes it will have and the harder it will be to ensure that the class has been

59

programmed correctly. Part of the reason for this is that the number of possible interdependencies between the attributes increases dramatically as the number of attributes increases. Modification of the value of any one attribute could require several others to be modified, too, or the validity of an attempt to change the value of one could be dependent upon the values of others.

It follows that one of our goals in class design should be to keep them as simple as possible, while still meeting the requirements of the problem to be solved. The complexity of a class will be related to both the object behavior it attempts to describe and the number of attributes it defines. These goals of simplicity and fidelity to the world being modeled will sometimes be in conflict. A couple of ways in which we can try to achieve them both are to:

- Divide up complex classes into several separate simpler classes, which cooperate together to achieve the overall task.
- Ensure that attributes are only defined if they clearly represent information that is needed by the whole class.

By breaking up complex classes into simpler ones, we will often find that we can gain much greater confidence in the correct working of the smaller components as individual objects—and hence the overall working of the whole system—than we ever could have had in the one larger object. One indicator of the need to divide up a class is that it contains an unusually large number of attributes, with complex interrelationships.

4.2   The Outline of a Class Definition

Before we start to define classes that we shall use to create objects, we need to review the structure of class definitions, and some of the terminology associated with them. So far all of the class definitions we have seen have been very simple. They have consisted of a *class header* (giving the class a name) and a *class body* containing a main method. Most of the classes we define from now on will not contain a main method, since only one is required per program. A class body consists of definitions of the class's *members*. There are three different sorts of member: *fields*, *methods*, and *nested classes*.[1] An outline for the placement of these members within a class definition that we shall use in this book is shown in Code 4.1.

In fact, Java allows methods and fields to be arranged in any order—fields before, after, or in between methods. In general, however, we will tend to group methods at the beginning of a class definition and fields at the end, rather than mixing them up.

We have seen that methods are used to implement the behavior of objects. The fields of a class are variables. Fields play two distinct roles within the context of a class or an instance of a class. To distinguish between these roles, we call fields either *class variables* or *instance variables*.

- The term *class variable* is used for a field that belongs to the class as a whole, and is, therefore, shared by all instances of the class. We often use the term

---

[1] We shall defer further consideration of nested classes until Chapter 15.

> **Code 4.1**   Suggested placement of method and field definitions within a class body

```
    // Define a class called 'ClassName'.
class ClassName {
    // Method definitions go here.
    ...
    // Field definitions go here.
    ...
}
```

static variable for a class variable, because of the way in which class variables are defined.

- The term *instance variable* is used for a field of which each instance of a class *has its own independent copy*. Instance variables are used to implement the attributes of an object.

We can use characteristics of the Ship class to illustrate the difference between class variables and instance variables. Each Ship object will have an attribute representing its current speed; such an attribute would be held in an instance variable because the value held in one ship's speed variable should be completely independent of that held in another ship's. Sending a `setSpeed` message to one ship will only change that particular ship's speed instance variable. In contrast, when a new Ship object is created, it is given default initial values for its speed, course, and position. These default values are the same for each new Ship, which means that they are appropriate to be held in class variables—the information they hold is common to all objects of the Ship class. Since instance variables are far more common than class variables, we shall defer further discussion of class variables until Section 7.9.

A point to note is that fields are variables that are defined *outside* the method bodies. They have some significant differences from *method variables*, therefore, which are defined inside method bodies. The most important difference is that an object's instance variables exist throughout the whole life of the object, but a method variable only exists when its containing method is responding to a message. Each time a method is called, its method variables are created afresh—they do not retain their values from one call to the next. In contrast, instance variables are only created once—when their containing object is created. A mistake often made is defining variables as instance variables when they should properly be method variables. This usually comes about when several methods use one or more variables for similar (but independent) purposes. As a general rule to follow in the early stages, a variable should only be defined as an instance variable if it is properly an attribute of the class. Variables simply to help a method perform its task should be defined as method variables.

4.3   The SimpleNote Class

Now that we have introduced the basics of class layout and terminology, we can begin to create a full class definition. The example we shall use is a class that is designed

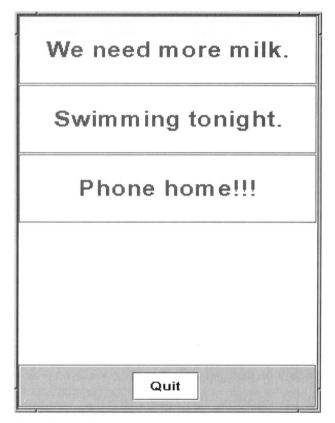

Figure 4.1   A GUI for sticky notes on a refrigerator

to model sticky reminder notes that might be stuck to a refrigerator, a notice board, and so on. Figure 4.1 shows a GUI for an application that makes use of the class we shall define. The figure shows messages stored on three separate notes.

For the sake of simplicity, we shall start by defining a version of the note class (`SimpleNote`) that stores a message but does not include a GUI. Later, we shall elaborate on SimpleNote to create the `Note` class, whose objects interact with a GUI to display their messages. Code 4.2 shows a main method that creates two SimpleNote objects.

After creating the note objects, we write a reminder on the first via its `setMessage` method, and then ask it what the message is via its `getMessage` method. The methods of SimpleNote objects are very similar in usage to methods such as `setSpeed` and `getSpeed` that we saw in Chapter 3. The final statement of the main method sends a `println` message to the `System.out` object to print the result of `getMessage`. We saw string printing in our original "hello-world program" in Section 2.4.2.

This main method illustrates that it is possible to define multiple variables in the same variable declaration statement—`milk` and `swimming`. Each declaration (and associated initialization) is separated from the next by a comma symbol. Notice that two `new` expressions must be used to make it clear that both variables are to be

---

Code 4.2   Creating two SimpleNote objects (`NoteMain1.java`)

```
        // A test rig for the SimpleNote class.
class NoteMain1 {
    public static void main(String[] args){
        // Create two new SimpleNote objects ready for messages.
        SimpleNote milk = new SimpleNote(),
                   swimming = new SimpleNote();

        // 'Write' a message on one note.
        milk.setMessage("We need more milk.");
        // Check the message.
        System.out.println(milk.getMessage());
    }
}
```

---

initialized, with references to two different objects. The result of running the program in Code 4.2 is the following line of output:

```
We need more milk.
```

Exercise 4.1   Take a copy of the file `NoteMain1` and run it to produce the "We need more milk." message.

Exercise 4.2   Set the message, "Swimming tonight.", on the object referred to by the `swimming` variable, and print it out by asking the object for it.

Exercise 4.3   Define a third variable and create an associated SimpleNote object. Set and get a message on it in a similar way.

Exercise 4.4   Is it possible to write a different message on one of the existing notes? What does `getMessage` return from that object when you do this?

4.3.1   Defining Attributes

A SimpleNote object needs to store the text of a message, which means that we need to define a suitable attribute within the SimpleNote class. The most appropriate Java type for this attribute is `String`. Having made this decision, we can start to build the SimpleNote class definition, and Code 4.3 shows this beginning. (In this example we use ellipsis—"..."—to indicate that part of the class has been omitted for the sake of simplicity.)

The attribute is an instance variable whose name is `message`. The name of the variable is immediately preceded by `String` to indicate its type. For the moment, we will defer explaining what `private` means until Section 4.7, but note that we *always* include it in the declaration of instance variables.[2] The attribute's declaration

---

[2] You might like to compare the use of `private` here with the use of `public` in the header of main methods. The relationship between the two will be revealed in due course.

Code 4.3   The attribute definition for the SimpleNote class

```
    // A class to represent a sticky note, that could
    // be stuck to a wall, door, refrigerator, etc.
    // This simplified version just stores the message and
    // provides access to it.
class SimpleNote {
    // Omit the methods for simplicity.
    ...
    // The variable used to store the text of the message.
    // The note is blank to start with.
    private String message = "";
}
```

includes an explicit initialization of the value it should have when a SimpleNote object is created. Unlike method variables (see Section 3.6.8), instance variables are always given a default initial value. The default value for a String instance variable is `null`, which represents no String. We want a new note to be blank, so the empty string (`""`) is a more appropriate representation for this than `null`. As a matter of good style, we often prefer to make it clear that we have thought about the initial value an attribute should take, and set it explicitly, rather than relying on a default value. We have preceded the declaration with two *single-line comments* to explain the variable's purpose within the context of the class.

Having defined an attribute, we now need to provide some methods that will allow other objects to interact with a note and discover or alter its state.

4.3.2   Methods of the SimpleNote Class

The main method in Code 4.2 shows that the SimpleNote class must define at least two methods—`setMessage` and `getMessage`. Code 4.4 shows the full class definition that includes these.

We explain the definition of these two methods in the next few sections.

4.3.3   Method Headers

The `getMessage` method in Code 4.4 is called an *accessor* method and `setMessage` is called a *mutator* method. Accessors and mutators fulfill the quite specific roles of returning the value and setting the value of an attribute, respectively. We make a lot of use of accessor and mutator methods in this book, and so we shall expand in detail upon the reasons for defining them in Sections 4.7 and 4.7.2. Both methods have a similar syntactic structure to the main method, which is the only other method definition we have seen so far. They have a header and a body enclosed by pair of curly brackets. The different way in which these methods are used is reflected in slight differences between their headers.

Code 4.4   The full definition of the SimpleNote class (`SimpleNote.java`)

```
// A class to represent a sticky note, that could
// be stuck to a wall, door, refrigerator, etc.
// This simplified version just stores the message and
// provides access to it.
class SimpleNote {
      // Return what the message is.
    public String getMessage(){
        return message;
    }
      // Change the message.
    public void setMessage(String m){
        message = m;
    }

    // The variable used to store the text of the message.
    // The note is blank to start with.
    private String message = "";
}
```

- `setMessage` is used to tell the object to do something, and no result or reply is expected from it. Hence the reserved word `void` immediately precedes its name.
- `getMessage` is expected to return an answer, and it does so in the form of a `String` value; hence, this method has a `String` *return type* indicated in its header.

In contrast to the main method, neither of these methods includes `static` in its header. Section 3.9 pointed out that static methods are relatively rare in object-oriented programs, so you should not normally expect to include `static` in a method header, except for the main method.

Note, too, the difference between `getMessage` and `setMessage` in terms of what is written between the parentheses in their respective headers.

- `getMessage` does not expect to receive any arguments; hence its parentheses are empty.
- `setMessage` expects to receive the message to be set (written) on the note. Hence it includes the name of a variable to receive the value of this argument.

An argument represents information passed into a method to enable it to perform its task. In this case, `setMessage` needs to know what value to store into the `message` attribute. The declaration of an argument in the header of a method is called a *formal argument* declaration or *formal parameter* declaration.[3] The value passed in from outside the method is called an *actual argument* or *actual parameter*

---

[3] The terms "argument" and "parameter" are often used interchangeably, and there is no difference between them.

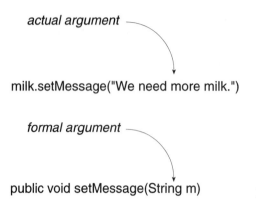

actual argument

milk.setMessage("We need more milk.")

formal argument

public void setMessage(String m)   **Figure 4.2**   Formal and actual argument

(Figure 4.2). When a method with an argument is called, a copy of the actual argument's value is taken from its original location and placed into the distinct memory location represented by the formal argument name. The name given to this process is *call-by-value* argument passing. It ensures that the two sets of argument memory locations are completely different. The most significant result of this process is that making an assignment to a formal parameter inside a method can have no effect upon the corresponding value stored in the actual parameter.

The declaration of an argument looks similar to the definition of a method variable or attribute in that it has a name and a type. There are two important differences:

- A formal argument declaration never contains a `public` or `private` reserved word. In this respect, argument declarations are closer to method variable declarations than attribute declarations.
- A formal argument declaration is not terminated by a semicolon. The end of the declaration is marked by the closing parenthesis of the method header. In the case of several arguments declared together, each is separated from the others by a comma and each must be preceded by its type, for instance,

```
public void addPoint(int x, int y) ...
```

4.3.4 Method Results

The `getMessage` method is used to return the text of the message stored in the note to anything that wants to know what it is. A method with a non-void return type must always have a *return statement* within its body that passes back the *method result* to whatever sent the message. This return statement consists of the reserved word `return` followed by an *expression*. An expression is anything that produces a value—it could be a simple number, an arithmetic expression, an object reference, or the result returned from another method call. The important feature of the expression used in a return statement is that the type of the expression must match the return type that has been declared in the containing method's header. In this case, the value returned from the method is the value stored in the `message` variable. Since this variable is defined to be of type String, the return type in the method header is also of type String. A method, such as setMessage, with a void return type is not allowed to include a return statement with an expression in its body. The compiler will check for compliance with these rules.

The role of the setMessage mutator method in the SimpleNote class is simply to copy the value stored in the formal argument into the memory location represented by the object's attribute, message. The assignment is allowed because the types of the formal parameter and the attribute are identical. Once again, this method is allowed to access the attribute, even though the attribute does not appear until later in the class body.

4.3.5   Scope

Both of these methods illustrate an important point about the accessibility of fields within a class body:

> The fields of a class definition are accessible from all methods within that class.

We say that the members of a class have, at the very least, *class scope*.[4] As a result of class scope, both getMessage and setMessage are freely able to use the message variable, even though the latter is defined after them in the class—Java allows forward references to fields within a class. This has the effect of making fields *global variables* within a class. In order to overcome some of the traditional problems associated with global variables, we prefer to limit direct access to the accessor and mutator methods of a class.

A common error when creating a mutator is to use the same name for the formal parameter as the attribute being mutated, as follows:

```
        // Incorrect mutator for message.
public void setMessage(String message){
    message = message;
}
```

The problem with this is that the formal argument "hides" the attribute within the body of the method, so the assignment just stores the value of the formal argument back into itself! There are two solutions to this problem:

- The simplest is to choose a different name for the formal parameter, as we did originally.

```
        public void setMessage(String m){
            message = m;
        }
```

- Alternatively, inside the body of a class there is a reserved word for the current object—this—which allows us to write the following:

```
        public void setMessage(String message){
            this.message = message;
        }
```

---

[4] There are several different sorts of scope available in Java, and Section 7.7 discusses some of them.

This form makes it absolutely clear that the value of the actual parameter is to be stored into the instance variable belonging to the current object. This has the effect of removing the ambiguity.

Either solution is acceptable, although we usually use the former in mutators. The latter form is useful when you want to be clear from the names of the formal arguments to a method what the arguments will be used for inside the method. We often use the latter form within *constructors* (see Section 4.8).

4.3.6 Types

In the preceding sections, we have alluded to the need to use appropriate *types* in different contexts:

- The expression type in a return statement must match the return type of its method.
- The type of an actual argument value must match the declared type of its corresponding formal argument.
- The expression type in an assignment statement must match the variable type on the left-hand side.

Whenever we define a variable, we need to decide on the type it should be. Most of our effort will go into deciding the best type for attributes. The return type of an accessor, and the formal argument type of a mutator, can be derived directly from the associated attribute's declaration. Java defines several *primitive types* that are commonly used to support the efficient representation of simple attribute values. Each type has its own reserved word, illustrated in Table 4.1. We have informally divided these into two categories—major and minor—which reflect the usage we make of them. Note that all primitive type names start with a lower-case letter. For the most part, we will limit ourselves to using just the major types: `boolean` for truth values, `char` for single characters such as keystrokes, `double` for numbers with a fractional (decimal) part, and `int` for whole numbers. We saw in Section 3.6.6, for instance, that a Ship's `getSpeed` method returns a value of type `double`.

Table 4.1 The primitive type names	
Major Primitive Types	
`boolean`	true and false values
`char`	single character values
`double`	positive and negative floating-point numbers
`int`	positive and negative integers
Minor Primitive Types	
`byte`	byte values
`float`	positive and negative floating-point numbers
`long`	positive and negative integers
`short`	positive and negative integers

Code 4.5 Outline of a class to store a population count (`Population.java`)

```
// A class designed to hold the population size of a town.
// Exercise: Complete the body of this class with an accessor
// and mutator methods.

class Population {
    // Add the accessor and mutator methods here ...

    // The attribute used to record the current size of the population.
    private int count = 0;
}
```

It is worth noting that the `String` type we used in the SimpleNote example is a commonly used type that is not actually a primitive type but a class type.[5] We discuss the String class in Section 8.3. Great care needs to be exercised in distinguishing between variables which are of a primitive type and variables which are of a class type. A variable of type `int`, for instance, is not the same as a variable of a class type. A primitive-type variable will have an associated *value* but no methods—you cannot send a message via a primitive-type variable, all you can do is examine its contents and change the value it stores.

Exercise 4.5   Code 4.5 shows the start of the `Population` class that is used to record the number of people living in a town. Complete the body of Population by defining an accessor and mutator for its `count` attribute.

The number of people living in the town is held in an attribute of type `int`, which is able to store a single integer (whole number) value. Complete the body of the Population class by defining an appropriate accessor and mutator method to go with the `count` attribute. Code 4.6 shows a main method that can be used to test your implementation of the Population class.

The main method creates two Population objects, uses their mutator methods to set values for the `count` attributes, and then prints out their values to check that they have been set properly.

4.3.7 The Note Class

We can make the SimpleNote example slightly more interesting by defining a similar class that drives the GUI illustrated in Figure 4.1. The GUI suggests the door, refrigerator, etc., on which the notes are displayed. Code 4.7 defines the `Note` class to this end.

---

[5] The fact that `String` starts with an upper-case letter helps us to remember this, since all primitive type names start with a lower-case letter.

Code 4.6   A test-rig for the Population class (`PopulationMain.java`)

```java
    // A class to act as a test-rig for the Population class.
class PopulationMain {
    public static void main(String[] args){
        // Create objects for two different towns.
        Population smallTown = new Population();
        smallTown.setCount(300);

        Population largeTown = new Population();
        largeTown.setCount(50000);

        // Print out the current states of the towns.
        System.out.println("The population of the small town is");
        System.out.println(smallTown.getCount());

        System.out.println("The population of the large town is");
        System.out.println(largeTown.getCount());
    }
}
```

Code 4.7   The Note class whose objects are attached to a display (`Note.java`)

```java
    // A class to represent a sticky note, that could
    // be stuck to a wall, door, refrigerator, etc.
    // A display object is used to show the message.
class Note {
        // Return what the message is.
    public String getMessage(){
        return message;
    }

        // Change the message.
    public void setMessage(String m){
        message = m;
        // Show the message on the display.
        NoteDisplay view = getDisplay();
        view.showMessage(message);
    }
        // Return the object used to display the message.
    private NoteDisplay getDisplay(){
        return display;
    }

    // The variable used to store the text of the message.
    // The note is blank to start with.
    private String message = "";
    // A display for the message. This represents the wall,
    // door, refrigerator, etc.
    private NoteDisplay display = new NoteDisplay();
}
```

The main changes illustrated here are concerned with a note's interaction with a `NoteDisplay` object. When something is written on a note via `setMessage`, the note sends a message to an associated NoteDisplay object. Note has the additional attribute, `display`, for this purpose. Like `message`, it is initialized as soon as a Note object is created. This involves the creation of a NoteDisplay object. When a NoteDisplay object is created, it arranges for itself to be added to the GUI, details of which are hidden from these classes. The `getDisplay` method is an accessor for this attribute. You might like to compare its structure with the `getMessage` accessor. We leave a discussion of the difference between `private` and `public` until Section 4.7.

Exercise 4.6 A short test-rig for the Note class is available in the file `NoteMain2.java`. Compile and run it to produce the output shown in Figure 4.1.

Exercise 4.7 Define a main method of your own to create some Note objects containing messages of your choice.

4.4 Review

Here are the main points we have covered in the preceding sections:

- The body of a class definition consists of member definitions: methods, fields, and nested classes.
- A class's fields are used to define attributes for its instances.
- An object's attributes are used to maintain its state.
- The more complex an object's state, the harder it is to ensure that it has been correctly implemented.
- We should consider breaking particularly complex classes down into several smaller cooperating classes.
- We recommend placing definitions of fields after the definitions of methods.
- Each instance of a class has its own copy of the instance variables defined in the class.
- Instances of a class share the same version of a class variable.
- Java has primitive types to represent commonly used data values.
- Primitive types are often used to efficiently represent part of an object's state.
- The values in the primitive types are not object references because the primitive types are not classes.
- Attributes should always be defined as `private`.
- Fields have class scope and are accessible from any methods within the class.
- A method that does not return a result is declared as `void`.
- A method that returns a result includes the type of the result in its header.
- A method that returns a result must include a return statement in its body.
- The type of the expression in a return statement must match the declared type of the method.
- A method's formal arguments are declared between parentheses in the method header.

- Java uses call-by-value for argument passing.
- The actual argument values supplied as part of a message are copied into the corresponding formal arguments of the matching method.

4.5 The SimpleSwitch Class

In order to reinforce the basics of class layout and terminology described in the previous sections, we shall create a further class definition. The example we shall use is a class that is designed to model an on/off switch. Objects of such a class might be used to control a wide range of electrical or electronic devices, such as light bulbs, heaters, or computers. Figure 4.3 shows a GUI for an application that makes use of the class we shall define. The figure shows that two switch objects are controlling independent devices, and that one switch is off and the other is on. As for the previous example, we shall start by defining a simpler version of this (SimpleSwitch) that just prints a message to the terminal when a switch is turned on or off. Later, we shall elaborate on this class to create the Switch class which is able to interact with the GUI to display its state. Code 4.8 shows a main method that creates two SimpleSwitch objects and turns one of them on.

Code 4.8 Creating and using two SimpleSwitch objects (`SwitchMain1.java`)

```
        // A test rig for the SimpleSwitch class.
class SwitchMain1 {
    public static void main(String[] args){
        // Create two Switch objects to control devices which are
        // located upstairs and downstairs.
        SimpleSwitch upstairs = new SimpleSwitch(),
                    downstairs = new SimpleSwitch();

        // Leave the upstairs switch in its default state (off) and
        // turn on the downstairs switch.
        downstairs.switchOn();
    }
}
```

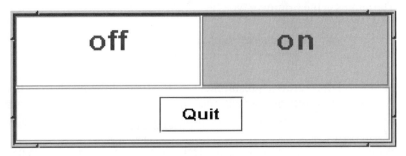

Figure 4.3 A GUI displaying the state of two on/off devices

Code 4.9   The attribute definition for the SimpleSwitch class

```
    // A simple on/off switch.
class SimpleSwitch {
    // Method definitions will go here.
    ...

    // Whether the switch is on or not.
    // true means on and false means off.
    private boolean on = false;
}
```

The result of running the program in Code 4.8 is the following single line of output printed by the `switchOn` method:

```
    Turn the switch on.
```

4.5.1   A Boolean Attribute

A SimpleSwitch object's state can take on only two possible values—on and `off`. The switch must always be in one of those two states—there is no provision for some form of intermediate "standby mode", for instance. In order to represent these two opposite state values, we need to define a single attribute within the SimpleSwitch class. Java does not have an on/off type, as such, so we must pick an appropriate type to model these values. The most appropriate Java type for this attribute is `boolean`, a *primitive type* with only two values: `true` and `false`. We can use the value `true` to indicate that a switch is in the on state, and the value `false` to indicate that the switch is in the `off` state.[6] Code 4.9 shows a beginning for the SimpleSwitch class.

The attribute is an instance variable whose name is on. The name of the variable is immediately preceded by the `boolean` reserved word to indicate its type. The attribute's declaration includes an explicit initialization of the value it should have when a SimpleSwitch object is created.[7] In fact, `boolean` fields are always automatically initialized to the value `false` without the need to do so explicitly.

The SimpleSwitch class only requires one attribute to maintain the state of its objects. More complex objects will usually require more state information to be stored than can be held in a single attribute. Just as more than one variable may be defined inside a method, so multiple fields may be defined inside a class definition. Depending upon the complexity of an object, its attributes will be some combination of primitive type values, references to other objects and references to *collections* of objects (see Chapter 10).

---

[6] If you have previously programmed in languages without a `boolean` type, you might be tempted to use a small integer type to represent on and off values. Such a type would contain many *redundant values* and is much less appropriate than the `boolean` type in this example.

[7] Notice that `false` is written without any surrounding quotation marks because it is a *boolean literal value* rather than a string.

Having defined an attribute, we now need to provide some methods that will allow other objects to interact with a switch and alter its state.

4.5.2 The Public Interface of a Class

The example in Code 4.8 shows that a switchOn message can be sent to a SimpleSwitch object, and it will presumably also have a switchOff method to perform the complementary task. In addition, we will provide a further method (isTheSwitchOn) that will enable objects to inquire whether the switch is on or off (Code 4.10).

In our design, these three methods represent the full *public interface* of the SimpleSwitch class. These are the only three messages that it is possible to send to a SimpleSwitch object in order to ask it to do something or to provide some information. Correct design of a public interface is very important. It should provide a means to interact with a class's objects that is as natural as possible—that is, the method names should reflect the way one would normally interact with such an object in the real-world. Notice that we arrange to receive a switchOff message rather than setSwitch(false), because someone is much more likely to say, "Please turn the switch off," rather than "Please set the switch to false!" A consequence of this approach is that it is sometimes necessary to create internal *bridging methods* between the public interface and the private implementation of a class.

Code 4.10 The public interface and private attribute of the SimpleSwitch class

```
    // A simple on/off switch (not attached to anything).
class SimpleSwitch {
        // Turn the switch on.
    public void switchOn(){
        ...
    }

        // Turn the switch off.
    public void switchOff(){
        ...
    }

        // Tell an enquirer whether the switch is on or not.
    public boolean isTheSwitchOn(){
        ...
    }

    // Further (bridging) methods.
    ...

    // Whether the switch is on or not.
    // true means on and false means off.
    private boolean on = false;
}
```

4.5.3 Bridging Methods

Code 4.11 shows the complete definition of the SimpleSwitch class. This includes bodies for the three public interface methods and two additional methods—getOn and setOn—that bridge between the public interface and the full implementation of the class's behavior. In fact, getOn and setOn follow the standard pattern for an attribute's accessor and mutator methods.

The body of the switchOn methods contains two statements. The first sends a println message to the System.out object to print a string on the screen. The second statement

```
setOn(true);
```

requires a little more explanation. From our earlier discussion we can see that it is a use of the class's own mutator method in which the value true is passed as an actual argument to set the attribute. However, this is the first time we have seen a method

Code 4.11   The full definition of the SimpleSwitch class (`SimpleSwitch.java`)

```
    // A simple on/off switch (not attached to anything).
class SimpleSwitch {
        // Turn the switch on.
    public void switchOn(){
        System.out.println("Turn the switch on.");
        setOn(true);
    }

        // Turn the switch off.
    public void switchOff(){
        System.out.println("Turn the switch off.");
        setOn(false);
    }

        // Tell an enquirer whether the switch is on or not.
    public boolean isTheSwitchOn(){
        return getOn();
    }

        // Return the state of the switch.
    private boolean getOn(){
        return on;
    }

        // Set the state of the switch.
    private void setOn(boolean o){
        on = o;
    }

    // Whether the switch is on or not.
    // true means on and false means off.
    private boolean on = false;
}
```

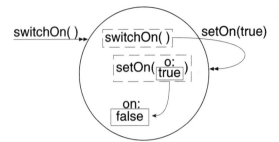

Figure 4.4   A SimpleSwitch object
sends itself a `setOn` message

used without its being attached to an object reference via a variable name and the dot symbol. The reason these are not needed, here, is that the `setOn` message is intended for the same object that received (and is currently acting on) the `switchOn` messages. We could say that a switch object sends itself the `setOn` message (Figure 4.4). This example illustrates that methods have *class scope*, and are accessible from any methods within the class, just as fields are (see Section 4.3.5).

Inside the body of a class, there is a reserved word that can be used to explicitly refer to the current object—`this`. We saw an example of its use in Section 4.3.5. We could use it to make it perfectly clear that the `setOn` message is being sent to the same object that received the `switchOn` message.

```
public void switchOn(){
    System.out.println("Turn the switch on.");
    this.setOn(true);
}
```

However, there is rarely any need to use this form in practice.

The definition of the `switchOff` method contains no new features, whereas the `isTheSwitchOn` method illustrates the way in which the expression used in a return statement does not have to be a simple variable's value. In this case, the value returned from the method is just the value returned by the object's own accessor method, `getOn`. Since `getOn` is defined to return a `boolean` value, we can see that this is suitable to be returned from `isTheSwitchOn`. Note that it is not necessary to store the result of `getOn` in a method variable before returning it from `isTheSwitchOn`, as follows:

```
public boolean isTheSwitchOn(){
    // switchState is not really necessary here.
    boolean switchState = getOn();
    return switchState;
}
```

The method variable `switchState` is really redundant here, and we prefer to use the result of `getOn` directly.

4.5.4   The Switch Class

The `Switch` class, illustrated in Code 4.12, is a more sophisticated version of the SimpleSwitch class.

Code 4.12   The Switch class that controls a DeviceDisplay (`Switch.java`)

```
    // An on/off switch with an associated display for a device.
class Switch {
        // Turn the switch on.
    public void switchOn(){
        setOn(true);
        getDisplay().showOn();
    }

        // Turn the switch off.
    public void switchOff(){
        setOn(false);
        getDisplay().showOff();
    }

        // Tell an enquirer whether the switch is on or not.
    public boolean isTheSwitchOn(){
        return getOn();
    }

        // Return the state of the switch.
    private boolean getOn(){
        return on;
    }

        // Set the state of the switch.
    private void setOn(boolean o){
        on = o;
    }

    private DeviceDisplay getDisplay(){
        return display;
    }

    // Whether the switch is on or not.
    // true means on and false means off.
    private boolean on = false;
    // A display for the status of the switch. This stands in the
    // place of a device being controlled by the switch.
    private DeviceDisplay display = new DeviceDisplay();
}
```

The main changes illustrated here are concerned with the switch's interaction with a DeviceDisplay object. Instead of printing a text message to the terminal when turned on and off, a Switch object sends a message to its associated Device-Display object to tell it to show the switch's status. This is analogous to the switch sending a message to a device to turn it on or off.

One new point worth noting is the way in which the switchOn and switchOff methods make use of the accessor for the display attribute, getDisplay.

```
public void switchOn(){
    setOn(true);
    getDisplay().showOn();
}
```

The pair of empty parentheses after `getDisplay` make it clear that this is a method call, not a variable. As we noted in Section 4.5.3, it is not always necessary to store the result of a method call in a variable before its value can be used. Here we are using the object reference returned by `getDisplay` to send a `showOn` message to the display object. This is shorthand for:

```
public void switchOn(){
    setOn(true);
    DeviceDisplay gui = getDisplay();
    gui.showOn();
}
```

In this alternative version, a method variable, `gui`, is used to hold the object reference returned by `getDisplay`, before sending the display object a `showOn` message. Either form is acceptable, and you should feel free to use whichever form you find the easier to understand. A short test-rig for the Switch class is available in the file `SwitchMain2.java`.

4.6   Review

Here are the main points we have covered in the preceding sections:

- A class should provide a public interface that matches real-world usage of its objects as closely as possible.
- It is sometimes necessary to provide bridging methods between a class's public interface and its private implementation.
- Methods have class scope and are accessible from any methods within the class.
- An object can send a message to itself without requiring an explicit object reference.

Exercise 4.8   Take a copy of the file `SwitchMain2.java` and run it to produce the window shown in Figure 4.3.

Exercise 4.9   Modify the main method so that both switches are turned on.

Exercise 4.10   The Switch class does not contain a mutator for its `display` attribute; why do you think this is?

Exercise 4.11   What happens if you replace the statement

```
downstairs.switchOn();
```

with the statement

```
downstairs.setOn(true);
```

in the main method? You will need to recompile SwitchMain2.java after making the change.

Exercise 4.12   Modify the Switch class in the file Switch.java so that the setOn method is public instead of private. Recompile this file and then try Exercise 4.11 again. What happens? What effect does this have on the GUI? Can you explain this?

Exercise 4.13   Define the class Stepper whose role is to maintain a single attribute called value of type int, whose initial value is zero. Define a public accessor (getValue) and a private mutator (setValue) for this attribute. In addition to getValue, the public interface of this class consists of two further methods: stepUp and stepDown (note that all of these method names are case-sensitive).

- stepUp should increase the value of the attribute by 1.
- stepDown should decrease the value of the attribute by 1.

None of these methods should print anything. The class StepperMain, shown in Code 4.13, contains a main method that you can use to test your implementation. It introduces the print method of System.out that can be used as an alternative to println.

Remember that you will typically be recompiling Stepper.java each time you change it

```
javac Stepper.java
```

but you test it by running the class with the main method

```
java StepperMain
```

Stepper should *not* contain a main method because the program only needs one. You should see the following output:

Code 4.13   A main method for testing the Stepper class (**StepperMain.java**)

```
       // A simple test rig for the functionality of Stepper objects.
       // Use this to test your implementation of Stepper.
class StepperMain {
    public static void main(String[] args){
        Stepper step1 = new Stepper(), step2 = new Stepper();

        System.out.print("Initial value of step1 = ");
        System.out.println(step1.getValue());
        System.out.print("Initial value of step2 = ");
        System.out.println(step2.getValue());

        step1.stepUp();
        step1.stepUp();
        step2.stepDown();

        System.out.print("Final value of step1 = ");
        System.out.println(step1.getValue());
        System.out.print("Final value of step2 = ");
        System.out.println(step2.getValue());
    }
}
```

```
Initial value of step1 = 0
Initial value of step2 = 0
Final value of step1 = 2
Final value of step2 = -1
```

Notice the different effects produced by `println` and `print`, because `print` does not add a line-terminator to what it prints.

4.7 Encapsulation

Suppose that you are an avid collector of rare books and that a collector friend of yours expresses an interest in your collection. There are at least two ways in which your friend can discover which books you have in your collection: they could ask you directly, or they could break into your house and take a look! Furthermore, if they took the latter course of action, then they might spot a book on your shelves that they are particularly keen to own, and decide to steal it. This example epitomizes the thinking behind accessor and mutator methods in class definitions.

Since an object's *state*—as represented by the values of its attributes—is crucial to the operation of that object, it is clearly very important that this state is always sensible and self-consistent; the position of a King in a chess game should always be within the coordinates of the board space; a student's course percentage should lie between 0 and 100; an ordinary bank account should not be billions of dollars overdrawn. It is in order to facilitate these requirements of validity and consistency of object state that we chose to introduce the use of the `private` *access modifier* when declaring object attributes in Section 4.3.1. The effect of including this in a field or method's declaration is to make that field or method completely inaccessible to any other part of the program outside its class scope. In contrast, defining some of the methods we have seen as `public` means that they are accessible to every part of the program.

By making attributes private, we prevent objects of all other classes both from examining their contents, and from altering those contents by direct assignment. Defining an attribute to be private is like putting an impregnable protection around your book collection; the only way to find out about your books is to ask you, and the only way to take one is also by asking, and you can refuse if you wish.[8] The same rules apply to private methods of a class; these are only accessible to objects of the class in which they are defined.

Defining attributes as `private` forces objects of other classes to request changes to another object's state only via its non-private mutator methods. In this way, an object is always in a position to check attempted changes to its state before complying with such a request. This gives the object a much better chance of ensuring that it remains in a valid and consistent state after dealing with the message. Indeed, an object is at liberty to refuse to obey a request should it decide that the request would leave it in either an invalid or inconsistent state. Safeguarding objects in this

---

[8] In fact, we have to be slightly careful about taking this analogy too far because Java permits objects of the same class to access the private methods and fields of each other directly. So, strictly speaking, one BookCollector object could freely plunder the collection of another BookCollector object with impunity. However, this is a practice we strongly condemn!

way—by keeping attributes private and channeling access to them through accessors and mutators—is known as *encapsulation*.

It is worth pointing out that Java does not enforce privacy by default, and an attribute without such a designation will be freely available to other classes. However, most authorities on object-oriented programming would require privacy of attributes as a fundamental principle of good class design. We adopt the rule that an object should even use its own accessors and mutators to examine and manipulate its own attributes, even though they can be freely within the class scope. See our stylistic conventions in Appendix F for an explanation of why we recommend this.

Consider the following concrete example of an object which is controlling the operation of a chemical process. It might need to keep the temperature and pressure of the system in a balance that ensures safe operation of the whole process. A request to raise the temperature of the process might be inconsistent with previous requests to maintain the pressure of the system within certain bounds. Such a request would be refused, therefore. Only after receiving further messages to alter the pressure bounds would the control object be willing to respond to the raise-temperature message. In a similar way, a ship object might refuse to alter its speed if the request was for a speed beyond its maximum, a bank account object might refuse to set a balance that seemed way out of line with its normal operational limits, or an airborne weapons control system might refuse to release its bombs if the aircraft was flying upside down.

4.7.1 Accessor Methods

In order to make the value of a private attribute available to an outside client, we must provide an *accessor* method. Such methods will typically be given names such as `getAttribute` where `attribute` is the name of the item of interest. This was the practice that we followed for the SimpleSwitch and Switch classes in Code 4.11 and 4.12. The bodies of accessor methods typically consist of a single return statement containing the name of the attribute whose value is required. Although some of the accessors we have seen use the `private` access modifier, `public` accessors are often the norm for attributes of primitive type, because there is usually little harm in simply revealing an attribute's value as this does not allow them to be modified.

```
// Public accessor to private attribute
public double getTemperature(){
    return temperature;
}
...
// Private attribute.
private double temperature;
```

There are occasions when public access of an accessor is inappropriate, usually when it is desirable to limit access to attributes that could result through aliasing, to not reveal their existence or to hide details of exactly how they are implemented. It was this later reason that is the explanation for the privacy of the switch classes' accessors and mutators. We preferred to hide the implementation details behind their public interface methods so as to allow a more natural interaction with their clients.

4.7.2   Mutator Methods

If an attribute of an object is kept private, then the only way for an object of another class to be able to modify its value is via a *mutator* method. Mutators will typically be given names such as `setAttribute` where `attribute` is the name of the attribute of interest. Mutator methods tend to show more variety in their implementation than accessors, since part of their purpose will often be to check that the intended modification is legitimate. Nevertheless, most contain an assignment statement to modify the current contents of the attribute with a new value. The new value replaces any previous value, which is completely lost.

```
    // Set the state of the switch.
private void setOn(boolean o){
    on = o;
}
```

None of the mutators we have seen so far has performed any checking of new attribute value. The main reason for this is that we have not yet introduced the Java statements that would allow us to check (and possibly reject) the replacement value. If a mutator does not perform any checking of its argument, then it will not need to return any form of success or failure indication. In such cases it will be defined to have a `void` return type.

One way in which a mutator could indicate acceptance or rejection of the new value would be to return a `boolean` result. Returning a value of `true` might indicate an acceptable modification, and `false` an unacceptable attempt, with no change being made to the attribute. A more advanced alternative to indicating rejection is that the mutator could *throw an exception*, a subject which is dealt with in Chapter 11.

Rather more thought should be given to which access modifier to use with a mutator than is the case with accessors. This is because they provide the potential for changing an object's state and, therefore, any behavior that depends on that state. It might well be necessary to restrict mutation only to other objects which know what they are doing—you would not let a child play with the speed controls on the bridge of an ocean liner, for instance. If in doubt, define a mutator as private until you determine a need to make it more visible. Java does, in fact, provide two levels of access midway between public and private, as we discuss in Sections 8.1.1 and 14.7.1.

4.8   Constructors—Initializing Object State

Our discussion of accessors and mutators was based upon the premise that it is essential to ensure that an object remains in a valid and consistent state throughout its life. The one issue that we have not addressed is how to ensure that an object *starts* its life in a valid state. This is the role performed by a class's *constructor*. A constructor is *never* used to receive messages from other objects, and only in special circumstances from itself. Instead, the constructor is only ever used when an object is created, and this happens automatically as part of the execution of the `new` operator that creates the object. The constructor's job is to ensure that each attribute of the instance under construction is set to an initial value that represents a valid state for objects of that class.

In order to illustrate how constructors are defined, we shall explore the example of a class whose job it is to keep track of the temperature of an industrial process. This will be displayed in the GUI shown in Figure 4.5. Code 4.14 shows the `SimpleController` class that maintains an attribute to record this temperature.

Figure 4.5   The GUI of a temperature display (`ControllerMain1.java`)

Code 4.14   A temperature controller class attached to a display

```
    // A simple class to maintain a temperature variable
    // along with an accessor and mutator.
class SimpleController {
    // A no-arg constructor for the class.
  public SimpleController(){
    // Ensure that the initial temperature is set to
    // a non-zero default value.
    setTemperature(293.0);
  }

    // Temperature accessor.
  public double getTemperature(){
    return temperature;
  }

    // Temperature mutator.
  public void setTemperature(double setting){
    temperature = setting;
    // Register the change on the display.
    getDisplay().showTemperature(setting);
  }

    // An accessor for the display object.
  private ValueDisplay getDisplay(){
    return display;
  }

  // The current temperature value (0.0 by default).
  private double temperature;
  // A display for the temperature value.
  private ValueDisplay display = new ValueDisplay();
}
```

A constructor is distinguished from all methods within a class in the following ways:

- A constructor always has the same name as the class to which it belongs.
- A constructor does not have a return type—not even `void`. This is an important difference from normal methods. If you give a constructor a return type then it ceases to be a constructor and will not be automatically called when an object is created.

A constructor that takes no arguments is called a *no-arg constructor*. The purpose of the no-arg constructor in Code 4.14 is to initialize the `temperature` attribute to a sensible value, other than the value of `0.0` which all `double` fields are given by default. You might suppose that this could be achieved without a constructor by explicitly initializing the attribute at its point of definition,

```
// The current temperature value.
private double temperature = 293.0;
```

but there would be an important difference in the effect on SimpleController objects of initializing it this way. Before reading further, try to work out what the difference would be. The following exercises might help you to work this out.

Exercise 4.14 Without making any changes to the example files, compile and run the program in `ControllerMain1.java`. You should see something like the output shown in Figure 4.5. Now modify the file `SimpleController.java` in the following ways:

- Either comment out, or remove, the statement in the constructor that sets the initial temperature value.
- Modify the declaration of the `temperature` attribute to explicitly initialize it to the value `293.0`.
- Compile `SimpleController.java` and then rerun `ControllerMain1`.

How does the output differ from that shown in Figure 4.5? Why is this?

Exercise 4.15 Is it possible to overcome this problem by initializing the attribute as follows?

```
private double temperature = setTemperature(293.0);
```

Try it.

4.8.1 Constructors with Arguments

The class shown in Code 4.14 always initializes the temperature value to `293.0`. If we wish to construct such a controller object with a different initial value, then we currently have no alternative but to do this in two stages (Code 4.15).

This is similar to the approach we used with the `SimpleNote` and `Note` classes introduced earlier in this chapter.

Code 4.15   Altering the initial setting of a SimpleController (`ControllerMain2.java`)

```
    // Illustrate changing the temperature value of a SimpleController.
class ControllerMain2 {
    public static void main(String[] args){
        // Construct a Controller, which takes on the default
        // temperature.
        SimpleController control = new SimpleController();
        // Lower the controller's default temperature.
        control.setTemperature(275);
    }
}
```

For some classes, separation of construction from initialization could represent inappropriate behavior or extremely dangerous behavior. Imagine a controller object that is designed to deliver an amount of current to an attached device and it has a particular default value for the current. If this controller is attached to a type of device whose normal operating current is much lower than the default value, then the device could be seriously damaged or destroyed as soon as the controller is created. Ideally, we need a means to pass in a required initial attribute value to a constructor when an object is constructed, rather than relying on being able to change its setting after construction. This is easily achieved in Java by defining constructors that take arguments. Code 4.16 shows the `Controller` class that is more sophisticated than the SimpleController class because it defines alternative constructors. One constructor is a no-arg constructor, allowing the default class-defined value to be used, and the other is a single-argument constructor which supplies the initial value from outside.

Defining multiple constructors in this way is an illustration of a feature of Java called *overloading*. It is applicable to any sort of method, not just constructors. It means that two or more methods have the same name within a particular class. Overloaded methods must be distinguishable in some way; either by having different numbers of arguments, or by the types of those arguments being different. The names of the formal arguments play no part in distinguishing between them. In the example in Code 4.16, the two constructors are distinguished by their different numbers of parameters.

The main method shown in Code 4.17 shows how two Controller objects can be created to make use of the different constructors. The effect on the GUI is shown in Figure 4.6. The object referred to by `control1` is constructed via the no-arg constructor, whereas that referred to by `control2` is constructed via the single-argument constructor.

4.8.2   Overloaded Constructors—`this`

One problem with defining multiple constructors is that there could potentially be a significant amount of duplication of code between them. This is particularly a problem if the initialization is complex; if an error in the coding of a constructor is identified

Code 4.16 Multiple constructors in the Controller class

```
        // A class to maintain a temperature variable.
        // Two constructors are provided to initialize an object.
class Controller {
        // A no-arg constructor for the class.
    public Controller(){
        // Ensure that the initial temperature is set to
        // a non-zero default value.
        // Make it clear what the number means by giving it a name.
        double defaultTemperature = 293.0;
        setTemperature(defaultTemperature);
    }

        // Use the initial value provided in the argument, instead
        // of the default.
    public Controller(double initialTemp){
        setTemperature(initialTemp);
    }

        // Temperature accessor.
    public double getTemperature(){
        return temperature;
    }

        // Temperature mutator.
    public void setTemperature(double setting){
        temperature = setting;
        // Register the change on the display.
        getDisplay().showTemperature(setting);
    }

        // An accessor for the display object.
    private ValueDisplay getDisplay(){
        return display;
    }

    // The current temperature value.
    private double temperature;
    // A display for the temperature value.
    private ValueDisplay display = new ValueDisplay();
}
```

during subsequent testing, the problem will need to be located in all the constructors with similar statements. Such a situation is a maintenance nightmare, and it is usually good practice to ensure that code to perform a particular task is located in one place only. In the example in Code 4.16, we see a case where both constructors call the setTemperature mutator to initialize the object's temperature attribute.

To reduce the potential effects of this problem, Java allows a constructor to invoke another constructor in the same class. It does this by using the this reserved word in a way that is quite distinct from that described in Section 4.5.3. When this is

Code 4.17 Creating objects via different constructors (`ControllerMain3.java`)

```
    // Illustrate using different constructors of a Controller.
class ControllerMain3 {
    public static void main(String[] args){
        // Construct one controller that takes on the default
        // temperature and one which takes on a lower value.
        Controller control1 = new Controller(),
                control2 = new Controller(275);
    }
}
```

Figure 4.6 The temperature settings of two newly constructed controllers

used as a method name, followed by an argument list, it is taken to mean: invoke an alternative constructor with a matching formal argument list—which could be empty. This can only be done from within a constructor, and the invocation must appear as the first statement in the original constructor. Once the alternative constructor has finished, control returns to the original constructor, and continues immediately following the use of `this`. Using `this` means that we can often locate all of the initialization statements in one constructor and have the others call it, supplying default values for one or more of the arguments. An example is shown for the Controller class in Code 4.18. However, note that the requirement that `this` be used as the first statement in a constructor means that we can no longer define a variable in the no-arg constructor to name the default initial temperature.[9]

When the no-arg constructor is used in Code 4.18, it immediately hands control over to the other constructor, passing the default value to be set in its single argument.

Code 4.19 shows a further example of a class with multiple constructors. This creates a `Point` object that might be used in a graphical application, for instance.

The Point class might be used to represent a pixel position within a graphical application, for instance. Its two constructors allow it to be initialized either from an (x,y) pair or the contents of another Point. A constructor taking a single argument of the same class is often called a *copy constructor*. Its private mutators mean that,

---

[9] In fact, we could get around this by defining the variable as a *class variable* outside the constructor, but this is beyond the scope of this chapter. See Section 7.9 for details of class variables.

Code 4.18   Using `this` to avoid duplicate constructor code

```
        // A class to maintain a temperature variable.
        // Two constructors are provided to initialize an object.
class Controller {
        // A no-arg constructor for the class.
    public Controller(){
        // Ensure that the initial temperature is set to
        // a non-zero default value.
        this(293.0);
    }

        // Use the initial value provided in argument, instead of the
        // default.
    public Controller(double initialTemp){
        setTemperature(initialTemp);
    }
    ...
}
```

Code 4.19   A basic implementation of a Point class (`Point.java`)

```
        // A class to hold details of an (x,y) coordinate.
class Point {
    public Point(int x, int y){
        setX(x);
        setY(y);
    }

    public Point(Point p){
        this(p.getX(),p.getY());
    }

    public int getX(){
        return x;
    }

    public int getY(){
        return y;
    }

    private void setX(int newX){
        x = newX;
    }

    private void setY(int newY){
        y = newY;
    }

    private int x,y;
}
```

in effect, a Point represents a fixed position once created. Note, too, that we could directly access the x and y attributes of the second constructor's argument, because private fields are accessible to objects of the same class. However, we respect the rule to use an object's accessor methods to access its attributes.

The general pattern with multiple constructors is that one constructor takes one or more arguments representing the full set of initial attribute values, and the other constructors provide subsets of these arguments. The subset constructors make use of the full-set one via `this`, although this does not preclude them from performing further initialization once the call to `this` has finished. In addition, in some classes it would be more appropriate to have more than one constructor to whom this sort of delegation is performed.

4.8.3   Object Integrity

It is worth summarizing an important point about object integrity that arises from the preceding sections on accessors, mutators, and constructors. The primary task of an object is to maintain its integrity, that is, to ensure that all of its attributes have sensible values and that their combined values represent a sensible state for that object. An object has an absolute right to refuse to obey messages requiring modifications to its state that would violate its integrity. Indeed, as we shall see in Chapter 11, an object even has the right to refuse to allow itself to be constructed if this cannot be done in keeping with these principles.

4.9   Review

Here are the main points we have covered in the preceding sections:

- The state of an object should always be valid and self-consistent.
- External objects should inquire about an object's attributes through accessor methods.
- External objects should change an object's attributes through mutator methods.
- Even methods within a class should use their own attribute accessors and mutators, rather than using the attributes directly.
- Attributes should be kept private in order to ensure validity and consistency of an object's state.
- An object can be put into a legitimate state as soon as it is created by defining a constructor for the class.
- Constructors are often overloaded to provide alternative ways to initialize objects of the class.
- Overloaded methods must be distinguishable on the basis of the number and type of their arguments.
- It is good practice to avoid duplication of initialization statements in multiple constructors, if possible.
- One constructor may invoke another by using `this` as the first statement of its body.

The following exercises will help you to test your understanding of attributes, accessors, mutators, and constructors.

Exercise 4.16 Modify the class Controller (defined in `Controller.java`) to have an additional `pressure` attribute of type `double`. Provide public accessor and mutator methods for this attribute. The initial value of this attribute should be set in the existing constructors to be four times the temperature value, but the two attributes do not need to be kept in step thereafter.

Use the `showPressure` method of the `ValueDisplay` class

```
public void showPressure(int value)
```

to display the value of `pressure` when an object is constructed and every time its value is changed via its mutator. This should use the same ValueDisplay object that currently displays the temperature.

Exercise 4.17 Define a further constructor for your answer to Exercise 4.16 that enables an initial value for both `temperature` and `pressure` to be passed in on object creation.

Why is it not possible to add a fourth constructor to the other three that receives a value for the pressure but not the temperature?

4.10   Identifiers and Name Resolution

In Section 2.2.1, we introduced a description of the role that *identifiers* play in a program. We noted that identifiers are usually names made up by the programmer, and one of their purposes is to make a program more understandable to a human reader. So far, we have encountered several different places in which identifiers are used:

- Names of classes.
- Formal argument names.
- Method names (including constructors).
- Method variable names.
- Field names.

In future chapters, we shall encounter further uses of identifiers, but it is important to be sure that you understand the difference between each of the uses given above. Code 4.20 provides an example where each occurs at least once.

Here is a list of the categories of each identifier in Code 4.20:

- Names of classes: `ExampleClassMain`, `ExampleClass`, `System`.
- Formal argument names: `args`, `updatedValue`.
- Method names (including constructors): `main`, `ExampleClass`, `getValue`, `setValue`, `println`.
- Method variable names: `obj`.
- Field names: `value`, `defaultValue`, `out`.

Notice that `ExampleClass` appears twice, as the name of a class and the name of a constructor. Note, too, that `out` appears as a field name because the `System` class defines it as a publicly visible *class variable*. Although the only method variable in the above example belongs to the main method, any method may define any number

Code 4.20 Different uses of identifiers (`ExampleClassMain.java` and `ExampleClass.java`)

```java
    // An example main method to illustrate name resolution.
class ExampleClassMain {
    public static void main(String[] args){
        ExampleClass obj = new ExampleClass();
        System.out.println(obj.getValue());
    }
}

    // An example class to illustrate name resolution.
class ExampleClass {
        // No-arg constructor for this class.
    public ExampleClass(){
        setValue(defaultValue);
    }

        // Accessor for value attribute.
    public int getValue(){
        return value;
    }

        // Mutator for value attribute.
    public void setValue(int updatedValue){
        value = updatedValue;
    }

    private int defaultValue = 10;
    private int value;
}
```

of variables for exclusive use within that method. We shall see the full utility of this in Section 7.7, when we look at *control structures*.

In a large project, there might be many thousands of names for items created by a team of programmers in a single program. So that we do not have to endlessly think up new names each time we need an identifier, Java allows us to use the same identifier to mean different things in different places within a program. There are some limitations to this, but the compiler has a set of rules that enable it to work out which particular item an identifier refers to at any one time. We shall leave a full description of these rules until Section 8.1 and give only a condensed version here that relates to the type of identifiers we have encountered so far.[10] The compiler always looks at the context in which the identifier is being used:

- Inside a method or constructor it first looks to see if there is a matching method variable or formal argument.
- It then looks to see if there is a matching method name or attribute defined in the class. This rule explains why accessor and mutator methods are able to refer to a field defined in their class.

---

[10] In particular, we largely ignore the existence of *packages*, which are dealt with in Section 8.1.

Code 4.21 Confusing (but legal) reuse of identifiers

```
class ClassName {
    // All these uses of 'name' are legal.
    public void name(int name){
        ...
    }

    ...

    private int name;
}
```

- It then looks for another class in the current context (*package* or program).
- Finally, it looks for classes in a default set of classes known as the `java.lang` package. This rule explains why the compiler accepts identifiers such as `System` and `String` without your having to define them.

If following all of these rules fails to locate a definition of an identifier, the compiler will report an error such as:

```
Undefined variable: valu
```

One of the restrictions that Java imposes on reusing identifiers is that a method variable may not have the same name as a formal argument of that method or another variable defined in the method. It is permitted, however, to use the same name for an attribute, a method and a formal argument of the method (see Code 4.21); we do not recommend this practice, however!

4.11 Case Study: A Simple Card Game (I)

We have now introduced quite a lot of the basic concepts of object-oriented programming and the associated Java syntax. Before adding yet more, we will reinforce some of what we have seen by looking at a slightly smaller problem than the port simulation.

Consider the following simple card game:

The game is played between two players using a pack of 52 cards. Only the face values of the cards are used; their suits play no role in the game. There are 4 cards of each value and the values are from 1 to 13. A dealer divides the cards from the pack equally between the two players who keep their cards in the order they receive them. Once the cards have all been distributed, the players take it in turns to pass a single card to the dealer who places it onto the top of a pile of cards. They must play their cards in the order that they received them. If a player plays a card with the same value as that currently on the top of the pile, that player receives all the cards in the pile from the dealer. The winning player adds them to the end of any cards still held. Play continues with the player who took the pile passing the first card for a new pile to the dealer. The game ends when a

Figure 4.7   A simple graphical user interface for the card game

player has no cards to play on their turn. The winner is the player with cards remaining, or the game is drawn if both have no cards.[11]

Figure 4.7 shows a simple GUI that might be used to show the most recent cards played by both players and any resulting win.

4.11.1   Identifying the Classes

What are the objects that appear in the problem description and, therefore, might appear in a program written to simulate such a game? There are five that seem obvious: the pack of cards, the cards themselves, the players, the dealer, and the pile that is won. What are the interactions that take place between these objects? Cards are distributed from the pack by the dealer. The dealer passes cards to the players. Players play cards onto the pile via the dealer. Players are given the pile by the dealer.

Such an identification of objects and interactions might serve as the basis for a full object-oriented design for a simulation of the game, and the program, implemented from the design, would contain `Card`, `Dealer`, `Pack`, `Pile`, and `Player` classes whose objects behave in the ways described.

4.11.2   Identifying the Methods

One possible design would be for the dealer to play a coordinating role; so all of the interactions we have identified will be mapped into messages that the dealer originates and sends to the player, pack, and pile objects. The player objects will have `takeCard`, `playCard`, and `takePile` methods. The `takeCard` method will have a Card object as an argument passed by the dealer during the initial deal, and the `takePile` method will have a Pile object as its argument representing the pile of won cards.

---

[11] It is probably worth noting that this is a game whose outcome is completely determined by the initial distribution of cards. The players are able to exercise no strategy in an attempt to win. This is because they are required to keep their cards in a strict order according to the deal and the way they are picked up from the pile.

Code 4.22   An outline for the `nextCard` method of Pack

```
class Pack {
    ...
    // Return the card from the top of the pack.
    public Card nextCard(){
        ...
    }
    ...
}
```

Code 4.23   An outline for the `takeCard` method of Player

```
class Player {
    ...
    // Take a card during the initial deal.
    public void takeCard(Card c){
        ...
    }
    ...
}
```

Consider the `nextCard` method belonging to Pack; it does not require any arguments because the dealer is not giving information to the pack. Rather, it is asking for something—the Card object on the top of the pack, so `nextCard` returns a Card object as its result. Code 4.22 contains an outline of this method.

For comparison, Code 4.23 shows an outline of a Player's `takeCard` method.

Exercise 4.18   What might a Player's `takePile` method header look like? Does the dealer pass an argument? Does the player return anything? Hint: It is *very* similar to the `takeCard` method.

Exercise 4.19   What might a player's `playCard` method header look like? Does the dealer pass an argument? Does the player return anything?

4.11.3   The Card Class

All cards in our game will have an attribute to hold an integer between 1 and 13. What should the constructor for Card look like? If we do not initialize the `value` attribute as a Card is being constructed, Java will give the attribute a *default value* of zero, which it gives to all integer fields not otherwise initialized; zero is not a valid card value in the game, however, which could lead to problems. We could ask the Pack object to send each Card object a `setValue` message as soon as it has been created. However, it could be easy to forget to do that, and the object would remain

---

Code 4.24 The Card class

```
class Card {
    public Card(int faceValue){
        setValue(faceValue);
    }

    public int getValue(){
        return value;
    }

    private void setValue(int replacementValue){
        value = replacementValue;
    }

    // The face value of this card.
    private int value;
}
```

---

in an inconsistent state. In addition, if the setValue method is publicly available, there would be nothing to stop an unscrupulous player from changing the values of the cards in their hand! We would like to prevent this, if possible. Code 4.24 shows the full definition for the Card class that overcomes these problems by using the setValue mutator inside the constructor. This guarantees that a card's state will be valid as soon as it is created.

By making both the value attribute *and* the setValue method private, we have prevented any other objects from being able to modify a card's value once it has been set on construction, hence we have prevented the cheating possibility described earlier. In effect, this allows us to say that all Card objects are *immutable*—they cannot be changed once they have been constructed. This can be a very useful property of objects in some applications. In this instance, it fits with real life, too—players in a card game are not usually able to modify the value of cards by scraping off some of the symbols or sticking on extra ones! We shall return to this case study in Section 10.6.

Exercise 4.20 Which of the following are *primitive types*: boolean, double, Integer, byte, int, String, char, main?

Exercise 4.21 What is the *return type* of the getBalance accessor method?

```
public long getBalance(){
    return balance;
}
```

Write a declaration for the balance attribute and its associated mutator method.

Exercise 4.22 Which of the following statements are true and which are false?

- Fields and methods are *members* of a class.
- Only attributes of primitive types may be defined.
- A method with a non-void return type must include a return statement.

- Java requires that every attribute must have both an accessor method and a mutator method.
- A method variable may have the same name as a field in the same class.
- Fields are visible from all methods in a class, regardless of order of declaration.

Exercise 4.23   What is wrong with the following method?

```
public boolean debuggingOn(){
    return "true";
}
```

Correct it.

Exercise 4.24   List all the formal argument names, method names, and field names to be found in the `Point` class shown in Code 4.19.

Exercise 4.25   Add the following two constructors to the definition of the `Note` class shown in Code 4.7.

- A *no-arg constructor* that sets the note's message to be

```
"This note is blank."
```

- A constructor with a single `String` argument that allows a message to be associated with it when a Note object is constructed.

Test your constructors by defining a main method that includes creations of objects that use both constructors; for instance,

```
Note milk = new Note("We need more milk.");
Note blank = new Note();
```

Print out the messages they contain from the main method, immediately after construction.

Exercise 4.26   If the Note class only contains the constructor with a single argument, is it still possible to create blank notes, such as this?

```
Note blank = new Note();
```

Experiment with your solution to Exercise 4.25 to find this out. (One way to remove the no-arg constructor is to surround it with a *multi-line comment*).

```
/*
   constructor here will be 'commented out'
   ...
*/
```

Exercise 4.27   Why is it important for an object to retain full control over the values of its attributes?

In this chapter, we have covered the fundamental language features that enable attributes to be defined within a class definition. We have stressed the importance of attribute privacy and the way in which attributes should be examined and modified via accessor and mutator methods. In the next chapter, we add further language features that allow us to define the behavior of objects.

Adding Sequential Behavior

CHAPTER

5

In this chapter, we start to introduce the core features of Java that enable us to add behavior to class definitions. In particular, we describe how to program statement sequences. We also describe the basics of arithmetic expressions and provide the custom-built `SimpleInput` class to ease the reading of input data.

5.1 Introduction

In previous chapters, we have shown the core syntactic features of Java that enable us to define classes with methods and attributes. So far, all of the classes we have seen in detail have been extremely primitive—little more than places where attribute values are stored, accessed, and modified by simple assignment. Our ultimate goal is to be able to create objects that perform useful tasks. In practice, objects must be able to exhibit quite sophisticated behavior that involves them in exercising choices over actions (such as whether to allow an attribute to be modified) and the need to repeat particular actions (such as running the rounds in a card game until the game is finished). We start by introducing statement sequencing and some basic features of Java's arithmetic and arithmetic operators. Choice and repetition are key features of subsequent chapters. In keeping with the practice described in Section 3.9, we illustrate many of these new features of the language via short programs implemented entirely within a main method. This will help to keep the examples relatively short and easy to try out as self-contained programs in separate source files. We shall later show how these features may be used in the context of full class definitions.

5.2 Putting Things in Order

Programs written in most *imperative programming* languages consist of doing things in sequences of steps, one after the other.[1] The following example shows what we mean by a sequence of steps (note that in this, and many of the other examples

---

[1]On the other hand, some specialist *parallel programming* languages, such as *occam*[Gal96], are designed to make it easier to program steps that are to be performed *concurrently*. Java also permits concurrent programming; see Chapter 18.

Code 5.1   A simple sequence of steps (see Code 3.4)

```
public static void main(String[] args){
    Ship argo = new Ship();

    // Ask the ship to report its initial position, course and speed.
    argo.report();
    // Ask the ship to move from its initial position.
    argo.move();
    // Ask it to change course, move and report its new settings.
    argo.setCourse(90);
    argo.move();
    argo.report();
}
```

in this chapter, we are using informal English descriptions rather than proper Java statements).

```
A sequence of steps:
    First do this. Then do that. Finally do the other.
```

We have already seen sequences in many of the main methods that we have looked at, such as those that create a ship and then ask it to do things (Code 5.1).

Each statement is performed in turn, in the order in which it is written. First, a new Ship object is created. Next, it is asked to report its initial position. It then moves, has its course changed, and so on. Each step is performed one after the other, but not until the one immediately preceding it has been completed.

One of the tasks to be performed in the design stage of solving programming problems is to determine what the necessary steps are in each aspect of a class's behavior, and then to put them in the right order so that the desired behavior is achieved. In this section, we shall look at how the order in which steps are placed makes a difference to the correct operation of a program.

Try the following exercises in order to sharpen your appreciation of statement sequencing.

Exercise 5.1   Here are a few simple sentences to accomplish the task of leaving a house and driving to the end of the road. See if you can put them into an order that makes sense.

```
Going for a drive:
    Drive to the end of the road.
    Put the key in the ignition.
    Unlock the car door.
    Start the engine.
    Walk out of the house.
    Remove the steering lock.
```

One way to find out if the order makes sense is to ask questions like, "Can I, Put the key in the ignition, before I, Unlock the car door?"—obviously not if the door is locked.

Exercise 5.2   Try putting the following sentences into an order that makes sense.

```
Leaving for work:
    Cycle to work.
    Get out of bed.
    Have breakfast.
    Get dressed.
    Wash in the bathroom.
    Wash the breakfast dishes.
```

Is there only one way to do this, or are there alternatives with the same result? Does it matter whether you, `Have breakfast` before you `Wash in the bathroom`?

Now look at the consequences of the two different orderings of these three sentences:

```
Sell your old car. Pay the money into a bank.
Write a check to buy a new car.
```

And

```
Write a check to buy a new car. Sell your old car.
Pay the money into a bank.
```

Although both orders are possible, the result of the second might well be either a bounced check or a large overdraft! From these exercises and illustrations we can see that:

- Sometimes there is only one order in which things may be done. Any other order either has no effect or just does not make sense.
- Sometimes we can achieve the same task with different orders. One order might be more natural or more efficient, but the end result is the same.
- Sometimes different orders are possible, but the outcomes are quite different.

These rules will be just as true with programs as they are in dealing with real life tasks.

One way of telling whether the order matters is to work out whether one action is *dependent upon* the outcome of an earlier action. Put another way, does an earlier action have an effect upon a later action? When an action has an effect in a program, either it *changes an object's state*, or it changes the environment in which objects within the program or system operate. Paying money into your bank account has an effect upon the state of that account, as does drawing money out. Hence the potentially different outcomes in the example of buying a new car. Burning fossil fuel has the potential to change the planet's environment and thereby the lives of the different life forms that live on it. We shall see exactly the same sorts of effects going on in the programs we write: either direct effects on individual objects, or indirect effects via an object's environment.

In Java, a common way to directly change a object's state is to send it a message via one of its mutators:

```
argo.setSpeed(5);
```

Mutators are used to make *explicit* changes to an object's attributes. Methods other than the straightforward attribute mutators may also make *implicit* changes to an object's state. A ship's move method will implicitly change its position attributes according to its current heading and speed, for instance. Understanding this can help us to work out whether alternative orderings have distinct effects or not.

Exercise 5.3   Do the following alternative statement orderings have the same effect or not?

```
Ship argo = new Ship();
argo.setSpeed(5); argo.setCourse(45); argo.move();
argo.setSpeed(3); argo.setCourse(90); argo.move();
```

And

```
Ship argo = new Ship();
argo.setSpeed(3); argo.setCourse(45); argo.move();
argo.setSpeed(5); argo.setCourse(90); argo.move();
```

Does argo end up at the same location at the end of each sequence?

To help you work out the answer, you might like to define a main method that constructs two different Ship objects and sends one of the alternative sequences of messages to each. Do they arrive at the same destination?

Exercise 5.4   Put the following sentences into a simple sequence that makes sense. You may assume that, to start with, the washing machine is turned off and is empty with its door closed.

```
Wash day:
      Open the door.
      Open the door.
      Close the door.
      Take the washing out of the machine.
      Put the washing in the machine.
      Turn the machine off.
      Turn the machine on.
      Hang the washing on the line.
      Wait for the machine to finish washing.
      Put the powder in the machine.
```

Is there more than one possible sequence that makes sense?

In the next section we shall look at some statements which commonly occur in sequences. These statements involve *arithmetic expressions*.

5.3   Arithmetic Expressions

Most of the examples that we use in this book are not particularly mathematical in nature. However, it remains the case that many computer programs are written to perform tasks involving arithmetic calculations. In this section, we shall introduce the basic *arithmetic operators* that exist in Java to manipulate the primitive numeric types.

```
class PennyBankAccount {
    ...
        // Credit the account with the given amount.
    public void credit(long amount){
        // Find out how much is currently in the account.
        long currentBalance = getBalance();
        // Add in the amount to be credited.
        currentBalance = currentBalance + amount;
        // Set the attribute from the new value.
        setBalance(currentBalance);
    }
    ...
    // How much is currently in the account, in cents.
    private long balance;
}
```

These often occur in the context of *arithmetic expressions* in assignment statements, where an arithmetic calculation is performed on the right-hand side of the assignment symbol, and the resulting value stored into the variable on the left-hand side.

5.3.1   The Addition Operator

The traditional mathematical symbol for addition (+) is used for this operator in Java. Code 5.2 shows a possible implementation of the credit method from the Penny-BankAccount that we introduced in Section 3.8.1. It uses the addition operator to calculate the account's new balance value.

   The overall purpose of credit is to change the state of the account by adding the amount passed via its formal argument into the existing balance attribute.[2] Notice that we follow the informal rule established in Chapter 4 that a class's methods use the accessor and mutator methods to manipulate an attribute, rather than directly accessing the class's fields, so the first step in the sequence involves obtaining the balance through the object's accessor, getBalance. A local copy of this value is stored in a method variable, currentBalance. The type of currentBalance must match the type of the value returned by the accessor, so it is defined as long. The balance attribute is stored as a long integer value because we wish be able to hold as large a whole number of cents as possible. The next step in the sequence is to calculate the new balance and store the result into the method variable. The right-hand side of the assignment uses the arithmetic addition operator to create a sum of the current balance value with the amount to be added. This sum is then stored back in currentBalance to complete the assignment. The final step of the sequence involves changing the state of the current PennyBankAccount object so that its balance attribute takes on the new value, using the setBalance mutator.

---

[2] For the sake of simplicity, we ignore the possible effects of using a negative amount in the actual argument at this stage.

Failure to perform this final step in the sequence will mean that the old balance remains unchanged by this method.

Method variables are ephemeral variables—they only have a limited lifespan. They come into existence when an object receives a message corresponding to the method in which they are defined and, as soon as the method ends, they disappear. Each time a method is called, method variables which are not explicitly initialized as part of their declaration have values which are undefined; otherwise, they are initialized using the expression in their declaration statement. This means that it is not possible to use a method variable to retain a value from one call of the method to the next; instance variables must be used for this purpose.

Exercise 5.5   Approximately how many dollars could we represent in a bank account if we used an `int` rather than a `long` to hold the balance in cents?

Exercise 5.6   Does the order of the statements matter in Code 5.2? For instance, could the `setBalance` statement come before the assignment statement? Can the method variable's declaration come after it is used by the assignment statement?

5.3.2   Subtraction, Multiplication, and Division

As well as an operator for arithmetic addition, there is one operator for subtraction (`-`), one for multiplication (`*`), and two for division (`/` and `%`). The addition, subtraction, and multiplication operators are used in the ways one might expect for both the primitive integer types (`byte`, `short`, `int`, and `long`) and the primitive floating point types (`double` and `float`). If the result of an integer operation is too large in the positive direction or too small in the negative direction to be represented in the number of bits of its type, then the result wraps around, and no runtime error results. In the case of floating point operations, a value of $+\infty$ or $-\infty$ results (see Section 8.2).

One of the division operators (`/`) may be used with both integer and floating point types, but it produces different effects in each case. When used between two integer types, the result is the *quotient* of the division and any remainder is discarded. For example,

```
5/3 gives a result of 1
```

When used between floating point types, the result will contain a decimal point, for example,

```
5.0/3.0 gives a result of 1.6666666666666667
```

Notice that the result is inexact because it is not possible to represent $1\frac{2}{3}$ exactly in a floating point number.

Unlike in some languages, the modulus operator (`%`) may be used with both integer and floating point operands. Between integer operands, its result is the remainder after integer division, so

```
5%3 gives a result of 2
100%9 gives a result of 1
```

Between integer operands, arithmetic expressions involving the division operators satisfy the relationship:

```
(a/b)*b + (a%b) is equal to a
```

Using the modulus operator between floating point numbers, the effect is similar but, due to the inexact representations of some numbers, can produce slightly unexpected results. For instance, 6.2 is divided twice by 3.0 and should leave a remainder of 0.2, while 9.9 is divided three times by 3.1 and should leave a remainder of 0.6, but

```
6.2%3.0 gives 0.20000000000000018
9.9%3.1 gives 0.6000000000000001
```

This serves to illustrate the general point that great care needs to be taken when using floating point arithmetic because inexact results are common due to the limitations of machine representations. Although the magnitude of any individual error may be small, a succession of calculations based upon inexact values can quickly become highly inaccurate. This is one reason why we generally prefer to use double rather than float for real numbers, because double provides greater precision.

Exercise 5.7   Write the definition of a debit method, along the lines of the credit method shown in Code 5.2, that subtracts an amount of money from the current balance. You may assume that the amount of money passed into the method will be positive.

5.3.3   Division by Zero

Programming languages are not always clear about what should happen to a program in exceptional circumstances, such as arithmetic involving an attempt to divide a number by zero. Should the program simply stop with a runtime error, or continue as if nothing wrong has occurred? The Java language defines precisely what happens in this particular circumstance because it follows a standard for computer arithmetic, known as *IEEE 754*[Ins85]. At this point in our coverage of the language, it should be sufficient to note that an attempt to divide an integer by zero will result in a runtime error which will probably cause your program to stop.[3] On the other hand, attempting to divide a floating point number by zero will result in a value of $+\infty$, $-\infty$, or NaN, but there will not be a runtime error. The Double and Float *wrapper classes*, discussed in Section 10.4, allow such results to be detected and manipulated in logical ways.

5.3.4   The Unary Negation Operator

In addition to its role as a *binary operator*, the subtraction symbol (-) may be used as a *unary operator* for negation. A unary operator is one that takes a single operand. Its operand may be a numeric value, the value stored in a numeric variable, or the

---

[3] In fact, it will result in an ArithmeticException being thrown. See Chapter 11 for more detail.

value of an arbitrary arithmetic expression. The following are all examples of its use:

```
int terminatingValue = -1;
int penalty = -bonus;
int result = -(b*c/d);
```

While the addition operator (+) may be used in a similar way for compatibility, its use has no effect on its operand.

5.3.5   Order of Precedence

When several operators are used together in an arithmetic expression, it is necessary to have rules that define which order the operators are applied in. For instance, in `5-2+1`, should the subtraction be done first, to give the answer `4`, or should the addition be done first, to give the answer `2`? The *precedence rules* in Java follow the usual rules of arithmetic: multiplication and division (including modulus) are done before addition and subtraction; otherwise, the ordering is from left to right between operators of equal precedence. Unary operators have higher precedence than binary operators. Here are some examples of how this works in practice.

```
5-2+1 is   4
5*2+1 is  11
5+2*3 is  11
8*3/6 is   4
1+9%2 is   2
-8+50 is  42
```

The order of precedence for all Java's operators is given in Table C.1.

The normal ordering imposed by the precedence rules may be changed by placing parentheses around parts of an expression. Compare the results of the following expressions with the similar-looking set above.

```
5-(2+1) is   2
5*(2+1) is  15
(5+2)*3 is  21
8*(3/6) is   0 (remember this is integer division)
(1+9)%2 is   0
```

Exercise 5.8   Test your understanding of the arithmetic operators by using the Calculator program shown in Figure 5.1. Click on the digit and operator buttons to enter an arithmetic expression and then click on the = button. The expression and the result will be displayed in the lower of the two text lines at the top of the window.

Exercise 5.9   What are the values of these expressions?

1+2+3	100−5+8	8−9
16*3	10*3−4	92−3*4
18/9	17/9	19/9
8*6/3	48/7*2	10%3
64%2	3*(17/3)+17%3	12.0+6.0
18.0/6.0	19.0/4.0	4.0*5.2+9.43

Try to work them out for yourself before checking your answers on the Calculator.

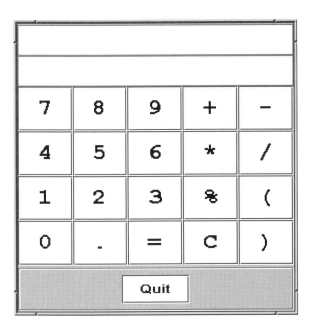

Figure 5.1 Calculator for evaluating Java arithmetic expressions (`CalculatorMain.java`)

Code 5.3   Concatenation of two strings (`StringCat.java`)

```
    // Demonstrate the string concatenation operator (+)
class StringCat {
    public static void main(String[] args){
        String s1 = "The cat ";
        String s2 = "sat on ";
        String s3 = "the mat.";
        // Create a new string from the three pieces.
        String sentence = s1+s2+s3;
        System.out.println(sentence);
    }
}
```

5.3.6 The String Concatenation Operator

We shall deal with the `String` class in detail in Section 8.3, but the addition operator (+) has a slightly unusual additional use in Java: that of *string concatenation*. If two String objects are combined with this symbol, a new String object is created that consists of a composite copy of the two operands. Code 5.3 shows a typical example. This would result in

```
The cat sat on the mat.
```

being printed. Note the presence of a space character at the end of the first two strings to ensure that the words are properly spaced when these are joined together.

String concatenation is frequently used within calls to `println` and `print` (which does not add a new line after its argument) when creating formatted output for the screen. Instead of writing two statements, as in

```
System.out.print("Unable to open the file: ");
System.out.println(filename);
```

We commonly join two strings together in a single call:

```
System.out.println("Unable to open the file: "+filename);
```

The + operator can also be used with mixed-type operands. When the item on one side of the operator is a String and that on the other side is an expression of one of the primitive arithmetic types, the arithmetic expression is evaluated and then automatically converted into a string, so

```
System.out.println("The answer is: "+(2+2));
```

would print

```
The answer is: 4
```

However, there are dangers for the unwary; what do you think the following will print?

```
System.out.println("The answer is: "+2+2);
```

It actually prints

```
The answer is: 22
```

because the normal rule of left-to-right order of evaluation for operators of equal precedence applies, even in this situation. So the first 2 is turned into a string and concatenated to `"The answer is: "`, and then the second 2 undergoes a similar conversion.

Exercise 5.10   What would be printed by the following, and why?

```
System.out.println("The answer is: "+2*2);
```

Exercise 5.11   Is the following statement allowed?

```
System.out.println("The answer is: "+2-2);
```

5.4   The Char Type

The `char` type is used to hold 16-bit representations of characters from the ISO Unicode character set (see Section 12.1.1). Literal values of type `char` are written between a pair of single quote characters (`'`), for instance `'A'`, `'q'`, `'8'`. The same quote character is used in both positions. It is important to distinguish between a single digit integer literal, such as 6, and the similar looking character literal `'6'`. The former represents a value of type `int` and the latter is a value of type `char`.

Values and variables of type `char` can be used in contexts requiring an `int` value, so the following example is permitted:

```
char c = '6';
int i = c;
System.out.println(i);
```

This will print the value `54`, which is the underlying integer value of the character `'6'`.

The concatenation operator may be used between strings and characters, so the following prints `"cats"`:

```
System.out.println("cat"+'s');
```

Further details of the `char` type may be found in Appendix A.

5.5 Type Conversion

Expressions involving operands of different types are quite common. Not all types are compatible with each other, and Java defines rules that determine which types can be mixed and which cannot. We discuss these rules in the next few sections.

5.5.1 Implicit Type Conversion

Expressions of mixed numerical types arise most frequently, particularly where one value is of an integer type (`short`, `int`, `long`) and the other is of a real type (`float`, `double`). When this occurs, an *implicit type conversion* on the operand value of the less precise type to the type of the more precise operand occurs before the operator is applied. Table 5.1 uses `int` and `double` as representatives of these types of numbers to show how they may be used with the arithmetic operators we have introduced so far. The same holds true when a `long` and an `int` are combined: the `int` is first converted to an equivalent `long` and a `long` result is produced; combining a less-precise `float` with a `double` yields a `double`, and so on.

5.5.2 Primitive Type Checking

The different sizes and value ranges of the primitive numerical types mean that it is not always possible to mix values of different types. Mixing types is most often a problem when the value of an expression of one type (the source type) is being assigned to a variable that is of a different type, or being passed as an actual argument to a formal parameter of a different type (the destination type). The following restrictions apply:

- It is not permitted to use any numerical source value where a target type of `char` is required.
- It is not permitted to use a `boolean` source value where a numerical or `char` target value is required.
- It is not permitted to use a floating point source value where an integer target value is required. This would mean the potential loss of digits after the decimal point. This is not allowed even if the digits after the decimal point are all zero,

Table 5.1 Implicit type conversions with the arithmetic operators

Operator	Left Type	Right Type	Result Type
+	int	int	int
	int	double	double
	double	int	double
	double	double	double
	String	String	String
	String	int	String
	String	double	String
	int	String	String
	double	String	String
− or *	int	int	int
	int	double	double
	double	int	double
	double	double	double
/	int	int	int (quotient)
	int	double	double
	double	int	double
	double	double	double
%	int	int	int (remainder)
	int	double	double
	double	int	double
	double	double	double

so the following is not allowed:

```
// Illegal assignment.
int i = 3.0;
```

- It is not permitted to use an integer source type where a smaller integer target type (that is, consisting of fewer bits) is required, because this would mean loss of bits. For instance an int (32-bits) source value may not be used where a short (16-bits) target type is required.
- It is not permitted to use a floating point source value where a smaller floating point target type is required. So a double (64-bits) may not be used where a float (32-bits) is required. This rules out the following

```
// Illegal assignment.
float f = 3.0;
```

because floating point literals have type double by default. This particular example can be worked around by appending the character "f" or "F" to the literal, which gives it type float, as follows:

```
// Legal assignment.
float f = 3.0f;
```

- It is not permitted to use a char source value where a short target type is required (and vice versa), even though they have the same number of bits. In effect, char values are unsigned integer values, whereas short values are signed.

After taking into account the above restrictions, the following uses are allowed:

- It is always possible to use a numeric source value where a target type of a larger numerical range is required. For instance, a `short` source value may be used where an `int` target type is required. An important (counter-intuitive) instance of this rule is that a `long` (64-bits) may be used in place of a `float` (32-bits) because the range of `float` values is larger than that of `long` values. However, the `float` type is not able to represent the complete set of `long` values, so some loss of precision is possible.
- A `char` may be used where an `int`, `long`, `double`, or `float` target type is required.

5.5.3   Primitive Type Casting

Where Java does not permit the use of a source value of one type, it is necessary to use a *cast* to force the compiler to accept the use for the target type. A cast consists of the target type written between a pair of parentheses, and placed immediately before the value to be converted from one type to another. For instance, in order to store the `int` value stored in the variable `iVariable` into the `short` variable `sVariable`, the following cast is required

```
short sVariable = (short) iVariable;
```

or to pass `double` values to `int` formal parameters:

```
public void plot(double x, double y){
    // setPixel requires integer arguments.
    setPixel((int) x, (int) y);
}
```

The only exception to the rules for converting between primitive types is that a cast cannot be used to turn a `boolean` value into a different primitive type (and vice versa) under any circumstances.

It is important to appreciate that casting from one primitive type to another usually involves a modification of the source data in order to turn it into a size and format that is suitable for the target type. Using a cast typically involves discarding some information from the source value in order to fit it into the requirements of the target type. Casting from a `double` to a `float` causes loss of precision in the resulting value. Casting from a larger integer type to a smaller involves discarding the most significant bits in favor of the least significant bits. The example in Code 5.4 demonstrates that both sign and magnitude information might be lost in the result.

This example produces the following output:

```
i = -65533
s = 3
```

By forcing you to use a cast, the compiler ensures that you acknowledge that information is likely to be lost and you are prepared to accept the consequences.

Code 5.4   Casting from an `int` to a `short` can result in a change of sign

```
    // Demonstrate the effect of casting between integer types.
public class CastExample {
    public static void main(String[] args){
        // A negative value.
        int i = -65533;
        short s;

        System.out.println("i = "+i);
        // Casting involves loss of the top 16-bits of i.
        s = (short) i;
        System.out.println("s = "+s);
    }
}
```

5.5.4   Combined Assignment Operators

The example in Code 5.2 contains the following common form of assignment

```
    currentBalance = currentBalance+amount;
```

where the intention is to add some value (`amount`) into the value held in the variable on the left-hand side of the assignment operator—a form of increment operation. This kind of update is so common that there are several variations on the assignment operator (`=`) that avoid the need to repeat the destination variable on the right-hand side. Here is how to add one value into another using the in-place assignment operator (`+=`):

```
    currentBalance += amount;
```

There must be no space between the two operator characters because they represent a single symbol. There are also combined assignment operators for the other arithmetic operators: subtraction (`-=`), multiplication (`*=`), division (`/=`), and modulus (`%=`). These can be used with any primitive arithmetic type variable on the left-hand side of the assignment.

String concatenation can also be performed with the (`+=`) operator;

```
    String greeting = "hello, ";
    greeting += "world";
```

leaves the `greeting` variable referring to the new object `"hello, world"`.

Exercise 5.12   Rewrite the following expressions using combined assignment operators.

```
    x = x + 3*y;
    x = x - 10;
    x = x * (y-10);
    x = x / (y+z);
    x = -b + x + 20;
    x = (y-3)*x;
```

Exercise 5.13   Is it possible to rewrite the following expressions using combined assignment operators in a similar way?

```
x = x * y - 10;
x = y - x;
x = (y+z)/x;
```

5.6   Reading Input Using SimpleInput

Although modern programs increasingly provide opportunities for users to supply input to them via a graphical user interface, the need to input data via a keyboard or data file still commonly arises. We discuss at length Java's many features for facilitating input-output between a wide range of input sources and output sinks in Chapter 12. Unfortunately, they make it relatively complex to perform even quite simple tasks such as reading numerical values and text. Full usage of those features requires an understanding of a considerable number of Java concepts.

In order to make it easy for you to experiment with input, therefore, we have provided a helper class, `SimpleInput`. This class is not part of the standard Java API, but has been custom-built for this book. Selected methods from this class have been listed in Table 5.2. Creating a SimpleInput object allows numbers to be read interactively from the keyboard via its `nextInt` and `nextDouble` methods. The availability of this class provides a useful means to further test your understanding of the arithmetic operators discussed above. A fuller discussion of how SimpleInput works may be found in Section 12.15.

5.6.1   Reading Numerical Values

Code 5.5 shows a program to create a SimpleInput object, read two integers, and print their sum.

We start the main method by creating a SimpleInput object whose methods will allow us to read input from the keyboard. A reference to this object is stored in the variable `keyboard`. The next step is to define two variables that will be used to hold the items read using `keyboard`. Before trying to read each item, a 'prompt' is printed

Table 5.2   Selected methods of the SimpleInput class

	Method and Arguments
	SimpleInput()
	SimpleInput(String filename)
void	discardLine()
boolean	nextBoolean()
double	nextDouble()
int	nextInt()
String	nextLine()
String	nextWord()
void	setDelimiters(String delimiters)

Code 5.5   Using SimpleInput to read two integers (`InputMain1.java`)

```
    // Demonstrate the nextInt method of the SimpleInput class.
class InputMain1 {
    public static void main(String[] args){
        // Create a SimpleInput object in order to read input from
        // the keyboard.
        SimpleInput keyboard = new SimpleInput();

        // Define variables to hold the input items.
        int firstNumber, secondNumber;

        // Prompt for the two numbers and read them.
        System.out.println("Please type an integer: ");
        firstNumber = keyboard.nextInt();
        System.out.println("Please type an integer: ");
        secondNumber = keyboard.nextInt();

        // Now print their sum.
        System.out.println("The sum is: "+(firstNumber+secondNumber));
    }
}
```

to tell the user what is expected; this is done because the methods of SimpleInput do not tell the user that they are expecting some input. (If you use the `print` method of System.out to print a prompt, you should follow this with the statement

```
System.out.flush();
```

to ensure that the prompt appears before the input is requested.) Once the first prompt has been printed, the SimpleInput object is requested to fetch an integer value from the user. When you run this program, you should type an integer—one or more digits with no spaces between—and then press the Enter or Return key. The number you type will be returned as a result from `nextInt` and stored into `firstNumber`. The main method will then print the second prompt, to which you should respond in a similar fashion. Remember to press the Enter key afterwards, as most operating systems do not send a user's keyboard input to a program until an end-of-line indication is typed. Once these two numbers have been read, the program will print out their sum for you to see. The SimpleInput class defines methods to return values of most of the primitive numeric types: `nextDouble`, `nextFloat`, `nextInt`, `nextLong`, `nextShort`.

There are two important concepts to appreciate about reading input in this way. Failure to understand these is a common source of later programming errors.

- Reading input is an essentially 'destructive' process. An item of data can typically only be read once. Once you have read an integer with a method like `nextInt` you cannot read it again. Classes like SimpleInput step past that point in the input stream and will not go back when asked for the next item of data. This means that if you want to use an item of data more than once that has been read in this way, it must be stored in a variable as soon as it has been read. Trying to read the same data item twice will simply cause a SimpleInput object to read whatever value follows the item previously read.

- Asking an object from a class like SimpleInput to read an item of data of a particular type, such as `int`, poses that object a dilemma if the next item available to it is not of the type requested. What should it do? It could either:

  - Skip over the next item and keep looking until it finds one of the right type.
  - Pretend the item it found was of the right type and return a value that is not a true representation of what it found.
  - Give up and leave the part of the program that asked it to read the item to sort out the problem.

In general, a SimpleInput object takes the first approach and will skip over inappropriate items until it finds one of the right type.[4]

5.6.2 Reading Strings

The SimpleInput class defines two methods that return a String object: `nextWord` and `nextLine`. When its `nextWord` method is called, it uses a set of delimiter characters to identify where the next word occurs on the input. By default, white space characters are used to identify word boundaries, but the set of delimiters may be changed by sending a `setDelimiters` message to the SimpleInput object. This definition means that the term word includes numbers as well as alphanumeric strings.

The `nextLine` method discards any input remaining on the current line (using the class's `discardLine` method) and returns the whole of the next as a string. The example in Code 5.6 illustrates these two methods.

If you are using the SimpleInput class to read mixed input of words and numbers, a potential problem to be aware of is that using a full stop (' . ') as a delimiter will prevent it from reading floating point numbers properly, as the same character is used as the decimal point—SimpleInput uses its delimiter set for words and numbers alike. Whenever a delimiter set includes a decimal point, you can avoid this problem by dynamically switching between delimiter sets depending upon whether you wish to read a word or number next.

5.6.3 Reading Boolean Values

The `nextBoolean` method of SimpleInput uses its `nextWord` method to find the next word on the input matching one of the four strings, `"t"`, `"true"`, `"f"`, `"false"` (the comparison is not sensitive to upper and lowercase, so `"TRUE"` will also match). When it finds one of these, it will return a `boolean` value of `true` or `false`, as appropriate (see Section 6.1.2 for more on expressions involving boolean values).

5.6.4 Reading Data from a File

The SimpleInput class is able to read its data from a file just as easily as from a user at a keyboard. This facility is particularly useful if a large amount of data must

---

[4] If it finds a floating point number when asked to read an integer, it will discard the floating point component and return the truncated integer value, however.

Code 5.6   Reading words and lines with SimpleInput (`InputMain2.java`)

```java
    // Demonstrate the nextWord method of the SimpleInput class.
class InputMain2 {
    public static void main(String[] args){
        // Create a SimpleInput object in order to read input from
        // the keyboard.
        SimpleInput keyboard = new SimpleInput();

        // Ignore spaces and punctuation when reading words.
        keyboard.setDelimiters(" ,.;:?!");
        // Read the user's name.
        System.out.println("What is your name?");
        String name = keyboard.nextWord();

        System.out.println("Please type a message for our sponsors.");
        String message = keyboard.nextLine();

        System.out.println("Hello "+name);
        System.out.println("Your message was: "+message);
    }
}
```

be supplied to a program, which is tedious to do interactively. The only difference between this use and the ones we have seen is that the name of the file containing the data is passed to the constructor, thus:

```java
    SimpleInput dataFile = new SimpleInput("data.txt");
```

Thereafter, the methods we have described are used in the normal way. If the file does not exist, or cannot be opened, a runtime error will result.

5.7 Review

Here are the main points we have covered in the preceding sections:

- The behavior of many objects involves performing a set of steps in a particular order.
- Sometimes different sequences of the same set of steps will produce different outcomes.
- Java possesses arithmetic operators for addition, subtraction, multiplication, and division.
- Division between integers discards any remainder.
- The modulus operator may be used to determine the remainder after division.
- Multiplication and division take precedence over addition and subtraction.
- Strings may be concatenated using the + operator.
- Implicit type conversions take place between operands of mixed numeric types.
- Casts can be used to create explicit type conversions, which would otherwise be rejected by the compiler.

- When a cast is required, it represents a conversion in which information will usually be lost.
- It is sometimes possible to use combined assignment operators when the destination of an assignment is used as part of the expression on the right-hand side.
- Reading a data item is typically a single-chance process; you cannot re-read something or unread it.
- The SimpleInput class (supplied with the material accompanying this book) provides a simple means to read numbers, words, and lines from the keyboard or a file.

Exercise 5.14   Modify the program shown in Code 5.5 so that it reads three integers instead of two. Add some further `println` statements to print the results of several arithmetic expressions that use the operators discussed in Section 5.3.

Exercise 5.15   Modify your solution to Exercise 5.14 so that it uses SimpleInput's `nextDouble` method to read at least one `double` value from the user and store it in an appropriate variable. Examine the effect that this has on your program's results.

Having explored some of the fundamental Java language features in the context of sequential statements, we can now begin to make use of them in extending object behavior via non-sequential control structures.

CHAPTER 6

Adding Selective Behavior

In this chapter, we discuss some of the control structures that allow objects to choose among different possible courses of action. In particular, we look at the if-statement and if-else statement. Closely associated with these statements is the usage of Boolean expressions.

6.1 Choice

A sequence of steps to accomplish a task will be the simplest form of arrangement that we can use to solve a problem—just doing one thing after another. Unfortunately, life is rarely as simple as following a course of action in which there are no decisions to be made. We will often be faced with making choices in the solutions to problems and either choosing to perform a set of actions or to skip over them (see Section 1.4.2). If we live a long way from the nearest supermarket and wish to drive there, the following simple sequence suggests itself:

```
Get in the car. Drive to the supermarket.
```

However, suppose we get in the car and find that the gas tank is nearly empty—we might not have enough gas to reach the supermarket. We ought to add a check for this between getting in the car and driving off:

```
Get in the car.
If we haven't enough gas then fill up at the gas station.
Drive to the supermarket.
```

Clearly, we would not wish to fill up with gas every time we go shopping so we only 'fill up at the gas station' *if* 'we haven't enough gas.' We choose whether or not to perform an extra action depending on the state of the car's gas tank. In programming problems, such choices are common. The following three examples provide further illustrations of the concept:

```
Get some money:
    Request money from an ATM.
    If the request is accepted then collect the amount
      requested.
```

```
Computer access:
    Request a login name from the user.
    Request a password from the user.
    If the password matches that for the user then let
    them use the computer.

Nighttime routine:
    Brush your teeth.
    Read a good book for a while.
    If it is a weekday tomorrow then set the alarm for 6:30.
    Turn out the light.
```

The common element in each case is that we only perform a dependent action (or set of actions) if we find that a particular *condition* is true.

Exercise 6.1   Can you think of any more examples of real-life situations where you either want to do something or nothing depending upon a particular condition?

6.1.1   The Simple Choice Statement

In Java, the sort of simple choices that we have seen in the previous section are programmed with *if-statements*, which have the forms shown in Code 6.1.

An if-statement is introduced by the reserved word i f, which is always followed by an opening parenthesis. Arbitrary white space is allowed around these, of course.

```
if ( condition )
{
    ...
}
```

The pair of parentheses bracket a *condition* which is used to determine whether the *dependent statements* of the if-statement are executed or not. The two different forms in Code 6.1 illustrate the fact that multiple dependent statements *must* be grouped

---

Code 6.1   The two forms of an if-statement

```
// Perform a single statement, depending upon condition.
if(condition)
    statement;
```

or

```
// Perform multiple statements, depending upon condition.
if(condition){
    statement;
    statement;
    statement;
    ...
}
```

with a pair of curly brackets, forming a *block*. In fact, we recommend that these curly brackets are always included, even when we anticipate that there will only be one dependent statement. As usual, free form layout is permitted, but we choose to be consistent in always placing the opening curly bracket immediately after the closing parenthesis of the condition, and line up the closing curly bracket with the `if` word. We also indent each dependent statement by four spaces from the `if`. Note that a terminating semicolon should never be added after the closing curly bracket of a block inside a method. An if-statement is often called an *if-then statement* because other programming languages commonly use `then` as a reserved word after the *condition*—Java does not have this.

6.1.2   Boolean Expressions

The *condition* guarding the dependent statements is a *Boolean expression*. In contrast to arithmetic expressions which produce a numerical value, a Boolean expression can have one of only two possible values: `true` or `false` (see Appendix A for more details of the `boolean` primitive type). If the value of the expression in the condition is `true`, then the dependent statements will be executed next in sequence. If the value of the condition is `false`, then the dependent statements are skipped over, and whatever immediately follows the whole if-statement is executed next. A simple if-statement provides one way of programming two possible paths through a sequence of statements—either the dependent statements are followed as a subsequence of the main sequence, or they are not. Code 6.2 illustrates this principle.

Either `A;B;C` is executed (when *condition* is `true`) or `A;C` is executed (when *condition* is `false`). The statements `A` and `C` are executed in both cases, but sometimes `B` intervenes if the condition is fulfilled.

6.1.3   Relational Operators

In order to see how Boolean expressions produce a result, we need to look at some of the operators that are typically used within them. Boolean expressions often involve the use of *relational operators*, which make it possible to compare the values resulting from expressions of similar primitive type. Table 6.1 shows the complete set of relational operators and their meanings. Notice that the test for equality (`==`) is

Code 6.2   Choosing whether to perform `B`

```
// Always perform A.
Statement-A;
if(condition){
    // Only perform B if the condition is true.
    Statement-B;
}
// Always perform C.
Statement-C;
```

Table 6.1 The relational operators

Expression	Meaning
a == b	is a equal to b?
a != b	is a not equal to b?
a > b	is a greater than b?
a < b	is a less than b?
a >= b	is a greater than or equal to b?
a <= b	is a less than or equal to b?

Code 6.3   Using an if-statement to verify mutation

```
class Ship {
    ...
    public void setSpeed(double s){
        // Only change the speed if it is not too high.
        if(s <= getMaximumSpeed()){
            speed = s;
        }
    }
    ...
}
```

not what you might have expected, but this is because a single (=) symbol is already taken up for assignment. If you mistakenly used = instead of == to compare two numbers in the Boolean expression of an if-statement, the compiler would give an error message such as:

```
Incompatible type for if. Can't convert int to boolean.
```

This is because it thinks you are trying to use the value of the variable on the left-hand side of the assignment as a Boolean expression. Java forbids the use of an arithmetic expression on its own as the condition part of an if-statement.[1]

Code 6.3 shows a common use for an if-statement in a mutator method, to prevent an attribute from being set to an inappropriate value.

Only if the new speed is below the maximum allowed is the attribute modified, otherwise it is left unchanged. Code 6.4 shows a version of the `credit` method previously seen in Code 5.2. The amount is now only added into the balance if the formal parameter holds a value that is not negative.

6.1.4   Precedence of Boolean Relational Operators

The tests for equality and inequality (!=) have a lower precedence than the other relational operators, and all have lower precedence than the arithmetic operators we have seen (see Table E.1). This means that it is possible to write many common

---

[1] This is quite different from the practice in the C and C++ programming languages.

Code 6.4   Only make a credit if the amount is not negative

```
class PennyBankAccount {
    ...
        // Credit the account with the given amount.
        // The amount must be non negative.
    public void credit(long amount){
        if(amount >= 0){
            // Find out how much is currently in the account.
            long currentBalance = getBalance();
            // Add in the amount to be credited.
            currentBalance += amount;
            // Set the attribute from the new value.
            setBalance(currentBalance);
        }
    }
    ...
}
```

conditional expressions without parentheses, such as this:

```
if(a+b > x+y){
    ...
}
```

However, it is worth including the unnecessary parentheses to make the sense absolutely clear to a human reader, thus:

```
if((a+b) > (x+y)){
    ...
}
```

A major difference between arithmetic operators and relational operators is that the former take arithmetic operands and produce an arithmetic result, whereas the latter typically take arithmetic or character operands and produce Boolean results.[2]

6.1.5   Comparing Object References

The equality operators (== and !=) may be used to compare variables containing object references, as well as values of the primitive types. However, a common mistake to make is to assume that the comparison involves comparing details of the objects themselves, whereas it simply involves comparing the references. The only thing that comparing references can tell you is whether two variables refer to the same object or not. Consider the example shown in Code 6.5.

---

[2] Section 6.1.5 shows that two of the relational operators may also be used with variables containing object references.

Code 6.5   Equality between references is not content equality (PointDemo.java)

```
    // Demonstrate the difference between reference equality
    // and content equality when using relational operators.
class PointDemo {
    public static void main(String[] args) {
        Point p1 = new Point(10,20);
        Point p2 = new Point(20,20);
        Point p3 = new Point(10,20);
        Point p4 = p1;

        if(p1 == p1){
            System.out.println("p1 == p1");
        }
        if(p1 == p2){
            System.out.println("p1 == p2");
        }
        if(p1 == p3){
            System.out.println("p1 == p3");
        }
        if(p1 == p4){
            System.out.println("p1 == p4");
        }
    }
}
```

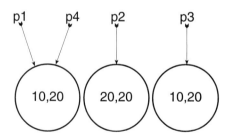

Figure 6.1   Four Point reference variables referring to three different objects (Code 6.5)

Each Point object is assumed to contain an (x, y) coordinate pair. The relationship that exists between the four variables is shown in Figure 6.1. The output from this example will be:

```
p1 == p1
p1 == p4
```

Even though p1 and p3 refer to objects with identical attribute values, the test for equality between them returns false, because they refer to different objects. We shall come back to object equality in Section 8.3, because it is often a problem that arises when comparing String objects. In Section 14.3 we discuss the correct way to test for equality of content between different objects.

Exercise 6.2 Write a main method that reads two `double` values from the user using a SimpleInput object. Write an if-statement that only prints the sum of these values if the sum is greater than zero. If the sum is less than or equal to zero, it will print nothing. Test your program with various combinations of positive and negative values to ensure that it is working correctly.

Exercise 6.3 Modify your solution to Exercise 6.2 so that it only prints the sum if it is less than or equal to zero.

6.1.6   A Bar Chart Exercise

The following exercises are designed to give you a chance to practice using simple if-statements. Figure 6.2 illustrates output from the use of a bar-charting class called `BarChart`. In this imaginary scenario, BarChart belongs to part of a poorly written library of classes to produce graphical displays of data. You would like to make use of these classes, but you do not have access to the sources in order to improve them. Rather than rewriting the classes from scratch, your task is to write some minder classes that will enable them to be used safely. One problem with the BarChart class, for instance, is that it does not check to see whether the data values it is asked to display do actually lie within the range of values of the chart. In some cases, this

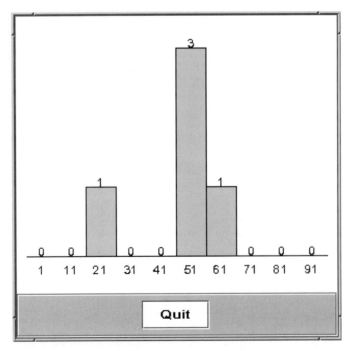

Figure 6.2 Sample output from the `BarChart` class (`BarChartMain1.java`)

```
Code 6.6    The (non-checking) BarChartMinder class (BarChartMinder.java)
```

```
    /* A minder class for the (bug-ridden) BarChart class.
     * Try to make the BarChart object, passed to the constructor,
     * more usable by protecting it from silly values.
     */
class BarChartMinder {
        // Look after the given chart.
    public BarChartMinder(BarChart c){
        setChart(c);
    }

        // Add the given value into the chart.
    public void addToChart(int value){
        BarChart display = getChart();
        display.addValue(value);
    }

    private BarChart getChart(){
        return chart;
    }

    private void setChart(BarChart c){
        chart = c;
    }

    // The chart to be looked after. This must be initialized
    // by this class's constructor.
    private BarChart chart;
}
```

leads to the chart displaying misleading data, and in others it leads to a runtime error. Code 6.6 shows the outline of a class, BarChartMinder, that maintains a BarChart attribute, passed to it via its constructor.

The public interface of BarChart contains the method, addValue, which receives an integer value to be added to the chart's display. This value is passed on to the chart via BarChartMinder's addToChart method. Code 6.7 shows the main method that creates a BarChartMinder and associated BarChart object and passes in a few (valid) values to be displayed.

This produces the output shown in Figure 6.2.

Exercise 6.4   Compile and run the program in BarChartMain1.java to check that it produces the output shown in Figure 6.2.

Exercise 6.5   The bar chart should only display bars for values in the range 1 ... 100 and each bar represents values in groups of 10: 1–10, 11–20, etc. Modify one of the argument values passed to addToChart in the main method so that it is less than 1, that is, below the minimum value of the range. Compile and run the program. What effect does this have on the program's output?

Code 6.7   Adding a few values to a BarChart via a BarChartMinder (`BarChartMain1.java`)

```
        // Illustrate the creation of a BarChart and
        // its appearance when a few values are added.
class BarChartMain1 {
    public static void main(String[] args){
        // Use a minder to check sensible use of the BarChart.
        // The chart displays values in the range [1..100]
        BarChartMinder minder = new BarChartMinder(new BarChart());

        // Add a small selection of values.
        minder.addToChart(30);
        minder.addToChart(55);
        minder.addToChart(59);
        minder.addToChart(70);
        minder.addToChart(52);
    }
}
```

Exercise 6.6   Modify one of the argument values passed to `addToChart` in the main method so that it is greater than 100, that is, above the maximum value of the range. Compile and run the program. What effect does this have on the program?

Exercise 6.7   The BarChart class defines a method whose header is

```
    public int getMax()
```

This returns the maximum integer value that should be counted in the chart's data. Modify the `addToChart` method of BarChartMinder so that it only passes on a value to its BarChart object if the value is less than or equal to the maximum. The `addToChart` method should take no further action if the value is too big. This should prevent the program from crashing with a runtime error.

Exercise 6.8   The BarChart class also defines a method whose header is

```
    public int getMin()
```

This returns the minimum integer value that should be included in the chart's data. Modify the `addToChart` method of BarChartMinder so that it does not pass on a value smaller than this minimum to its BarChart object. The method should take no further action if the value is too small. *Note:* You might find it easier, at first, to deal with only avoiding values that are too small, rather than trying to combine this with your solution to Exercise 6.7. Once you have got this part working, try to filter out all values outside the min . . . max range. In this case, make sure that you choose the data values in the main method carefully to test all possible sequences through `addToChart`, and that you know what the results on the chart should look like.

Note that the statements of the main method shown in Code 6.7 are not particularly well suited to displaying a large number of values in the bar chart. Even if the use of literal values were to be replaced by use of a SimpleInput object, displaying a chart based on several hundred values would be extremely tedious to program. What we see here is the need for a concise means to perform a small set of actions (read a value, add it to the chart) over and over again. We shall deal with how to do this in Chapter 7.

6.2   Alternative Actions

A common scenario involving conditions and dependent statements is to choose between two alternative actions:

```
Get some cash:
        Request money from an ATM.
        If there is enough money in my account then
                    collect the amount requested
        else request a smaller amount.
```

Rather than doing nothing different if the condition is false, we wish to try an alternative action instead. If the cash machine can fulfill the request from the balance held in the account, then it will do so; otherwise, the user will try again for a smaller amount. Requesting a smaller amount is only done if the condition is false. During a particular attempt to withdraw money, only one of the alternatives will ever be acted on. The user will never both take the money and ask for a smaller amount. Here is another example:

```
Decide what to eat:
        If there is any milk in the refrigerator then have
                    a bowl of cereal
        else have toast.
```

Providing an alternative action if the condition fails means that this person will not go hungry. The need to choose between alternative actions is very common in programming.

Exercise 6.9   Can you think of any more real-life situations where you either want to do one thing or an alternative if your first choice is not possible?

6.2.1   The If-Else Statement

In order to program alternative actions in Java, we use an extension of the simple if-statement: the *if-else statement*.[3] Code 6.8 shows the general form that this takes.

The reserved word `else` introduces a single statement or block of statements to be executed if the controlling condition is false. Once again, it is not necessary to use curly brackets if there is only one dependent statement in an else part, but we choose to always use them. It is important to notice the way in which semicolons are used in the two different forms. Where there is a single statement immediately following the condition, that statement must be terminated with a semicolon, as usual.

---

[3] Sometimes called an *if-then-else statement*, although Java has no `then` reserved word.

Code 6.8   The two forms of the if-else statement

```
// Select between single-statement alternatives.
if(condition)
    // Condition is true.
    statement;
else
    // Condition is false.
    statement;
```

or

```
// Select between multiple-statement alternatives.
if(condition){
    // Condition is true.
    statement;
    statement;
    statement;
}
else{
    // Condition is false.
    statement;
    statement;
    statement;
}
```

In the multiple statement case, there must be no semicolon following the block that precedes the else-part. If the following were to be written in error

```
if(condition){
    ...;
};

else{
    ...;
}
```

the compiler will report something like

```
'else' without 'if'.
    else{
    ^
```

which is confusing but correct.

Code 6.9 illustrates the different statements which are executed depending on whether the condition is true or false.

There are only two possible sequences: A;B;D or A;C;D. It is important to appreciate that, on any one pass through this sequence, either B or C will be executed,

---

Code 6.9   Choosing between either B or C

```
// Always perform A.
 Statement-A;
if(condition){
    // Only perform B if the condition is true.
    Statement-B;
}
else{
    // Only perform C if the condition is false.
    Statement-C;
}
// Always perform D.
Statement-D;
```

Code 6.10   Choosing the larger of two values (`Larger.java`)

```
    // Demonstrate the effect of an if-else statement.
class Larger {
    public static void main(String[] args){
        // Read two integers and print which is the larger.
        SimpleInput reader = new SimpleInput();

        System.out.println("Please type two integers.");
        int x = reader.nextInt(), y = reader.nextInt();

        if(x >= y){
            System.out.println(x+" is the larger.");
        }
        else{
            System.out.println(y+" is the larger.");
        }
    }
}
```

---

but never both together. If the condition is `true`, then B is executed. When the end of the B-block is reached, the C-block is skipped over. Similarly, if the condition is `false`, the B-block is skipped and the C-block executed before continuing. In both cases, execution of D follows B or C.

Code 6.10 represents a typical situation in which we wish to work out which of two variables holds the larger value.

Code 6.11 illustrates how we might enhance the `credit` method seen in Code 6.4 to report an incorrect amount rather than ignoring it silently.

Code 6.11   Report an error if a negative amount is passed to `credit`

```
class PennyBankAccount {
    ...
        // Credit the account with the given amount.
        // The amount must be non-negative.
    public void credit(long amount){
        if(amount >= 0){
            // Find out how much is currently in the account.
            long currentBalance = getBalance();
            // Add in the amount to be credited.
            currentBalance += amount;
            // Set the attribute from the new value.
            setBalance(currentBalance);
        }
        else{
            System.out.println("A negative amount: "+amount+
                               " cannot be credited to an account.");
        }
    }
    ...
}
```

Exercise 6.10   Write a main method that reads a `double` value from the user, using a SimpleInput object, and prints a message saying whether the number is positive or negative.

6.2.2   Nested If Statements

If you attempted Exercise 6.8, you will have appreciated that it is sometimes necessary to make several tests before being able to decide on the right action to take. It is common to use multiple if-else statements when trying to determine potentially complex relationships between different variables and expressions. Each condition tested helps to narrow down the relationships that apply and the easiest way to do this is to *nest* if- or if-else statements inside one another. Suppose we wished to find the largest value held in three different integer variables (x, y, z). Code 6.12 shows how we might find out the answer.

If the first condition is false, then we do not have to consider the value of x any further in the lower outer else-part. Similarly, y does not come into consideration again if the first condition is true.

Exercise 6.11   How many different triplets of values would you use to convince yourself that the program shown in Code 6.12 always produces the correct answer? Check your data by running the program once for each triplet.

Code 6.12   Finding the largest of three integers (`Largest.java`)

```
     // Demonstrate the effect of an if-else statement.
class Largest {
    public static void main(String[] args){
        // Read three integers and print which is the larger.
        SimpleInput reader = new SimpleInput();

        System.out.println("Please type three integers.");
        int x = reader.nextInt(), y = reader.nextInt(),
            z = reader.nextInt();
        // A variable to hold the answer.
        int largest;

        if(x >= y){
            // It must be either x or z.
            if(x >= z){
                largest = x;
            }
            else{
                largest = z;
            }
        }
        else{
            // It must be either y or z.
            if(y >= z){
                largest = y;
            }
            else{
                largest = z;
            }
        }
        System.out.println("The largest is: "+largest);
    }
}
```

Exercise 6.12   Write a main method that reads a `double` value from the user. Take the following actions, depending upon the value:

- If the value is positive, request a second value. Print the difference between these two numbers so that the difference is always positive. For instance, if the first value is `10.3` and the second is `4.1`, you would print the result of $10.3 - 4.1$. If the first value is `3.8` and the second is `13.4` you would print the result $13.4 - 3.8$.
- If the first value read is negative, print its positive equivalent. For instance, if its value is `-89.6` you should print `89.6`.

Nesting further if- and if-else statements inside the else-part of an outer if-else statement is so common that it is easy to produce indentation that drifts a long way across the page and requires a trail of closing curly brackets at its end (Code 6.13).

Code 6.13   Deeply nested if-else statements

```
public void m(){
    ...
    if(condition){
        ...
    }
    else{
        if(condition){
            ...
        }
        else{
            if(condition){
                ...
            }
            else{
                ...
            }
        }
    }
    ...
}
```

Code 6.14   Improved layout for cascading if-else statements

```
public void m(){
    ...
    if(condition){
        ...
    }
    else if(condition){
        ...
    }
    else if(condition){
        ...
    }
    else{
        ...
    }
    ...
}
```

In such circumstances—where there is only one statement in an else-part, and that is another if- or if-else statement—we prefer to use the layout shown in Code 6.14.

This is informally called a *cascading if-else statement*. Each else is lined up with the initial if in order to avoid the problem of drift. Notice that we have also been able to remove the curly brackets associated with all but the final else-part. This is possible because all but the final else-part consisted of a single statement, and curly brackets are optional in such circumstances.

Code 6.15   Determining which variable contains the larger value

```
if(x > y){
    System.out.println(x+" is the larger.");
}
else if(y > x){
    System.out.println(y+" is the larger.");
}
else{
    System.out.println("Both have the same value: "+x);
}
```

Code 6.16   Without else-parts, more tests are required to determine the relationship

```
if(x > y){
    System.out.println(x+" is the larger.");
}
if(y > x){
    System.out.println(y+" is the larger.");
}
if(x == y){
    System.out.println("Both have the same value: "+x);
}
```

The fact that each condition is tested in turn, until one gives a `true` value, can help to simplify the logical structure of complex methods and help us to reason about how they work. Suppose that you wish to refine the statements of Code 6.10 and print a message indicating which of the two variables (x or y) is the larger or whether they have the same value. Code 6.15 shows how this might be done with a short cascading if-else statement.

Reaching the final else-part *guarantees* that the variables contain the same value, and we do not need to explicitly test for this condition; otherwise we would have been prevented from reaching this point by one of the first two conditions giving the value `true`. Compare Code 6.15 with the version in Code 6.16 where we have no similar guarantees on reaching the third if-statement, because we have chosen not to use else-parts.

We will always reach the third test, whether the answer has already been printed or not, so an explicit test for equality must be made to cover this last case. It is a good idea to get into the habit of using if-else statements where appropriate, in order to avoid unnecessary extra testing. Indeed, not using if-else statements can lead to unexpected effects in some circumstances. Suppose we wished to both print a message about the relationship between x and y and have the larger value stored in both by the end of the tests. Would the code in Code 6.17 produce the desired effect?

What would be printed out if x is initially larger than y, for instance? Note the *dependencies* between the different statements—particularly those of the third if-statement on the previous two. Each condition is dependent upon the current

Code 6.17 Incorrect logic in determining which is larger

```
if(x > y){
    System.out.println(x+" was the larger.");
    y = x;
}
if(y > x){
    System.out.println(y+" was the larger.");
    x = y;
}
if(x == y){
    System.out.println("Both had the same value: "+x);
}
```

Code 6.18 Correct logic in determining which of two values is larger

```
if(x > y){
    System.out.println(x+" was the larger.");
    y = x;
}
else if(y > x){
    System.out.println(y+" was the larger.");
    x = y;
}
else{
    System.out.println("Both had the same value: "+x);
}
```

values of x and y, and because there are assignments to these in the first and second
if-statements, these could have a cascading effect upon the evaluation of the third
condition. Such a possibility is avoided by the correct version shown in Code 6.18.

6.2.3   Boolean Logical Operators

Sometimes it is possible to combine several tests in a single condition rather than
using multiple if-statements. Such conditions often use the *logical-and* (&& and &), the
logical-or (|| and |), and, less frequently, the *exclusive-or* ($\wedge$) operators. Tables 6.2
and 6.3 show which Boolean value is produced as a result of each, depending upon
the values of their operands.

6.2.4   The Logical-And Operators

The *logical-and* operator (&&) gives the value `true` only if both of its operands are
`true`. Code 6.19 shows a use of one of the logical-and operators to test whether three
variables contain the same value.

Table 6.2 Result values using short-circuit Boolean logical-operators

Operator	lhs	rhs	Result
&&	false	any-value	false
	true	false	false
	true	true	true
||	true	any-value	true
	false	false	false
	false	true	true

Table 6.3 Result values using fully-evaluating Boolean logical-operators

Operator	lhs	rhs	Result
&	false	false	false
	true	false	false
	false	true	false
	true	true	true
|	false	false	false
	true	false	true
	false	true	true
	true	true	true
^	false	false	false
	true	false	true
	false	true	true
	true	true	false

Code 6.19 Testing for equality of three variables

```
if((x == y) && (y == z)){
    System.out.println("x, y and z are equal.");
}
```

Only if both (x == y) and (y == z) will the message be printed. Notice that we have to write y twice in this expression; the following is not allowed:

```
// Illegal expression; && must be used.
if(x == y == z)
```

This will produce an error message from the compiler, such as:

```
Incompatible type for ==. Can't convert int to boolean.
    if(x == y == z){
           ^
```

In the example of Code 6.19, there is no need to test the value of y against z if x is not equal to y, because the whole test would give the value false—even if the values of y

---

Code 6.20   Determining whether **x** is the largest

```
if((x < y) || (x < z)){
    System.out.println(x+" is definitely not the largest.");
}
```

---

and z were the same, we already know that at least two are different. This particular and-operator (&&) takes this possibility into account and will not bother to evaluate its right operand if the left is determined to be false. For this reason, it is called a *short-circuit operator*. In contrast, the other logical-and operator (&) produces the same pattern of results from its operands, but it is a *fully-evaluating operator* because it *always* evaluates both of its operands, from left to right. There might be some circumstances where this is the desired behavior but, in all of our examples, we use the short-circuit version. The circumstances in which we must guarantee that both operands are always evaluated are relatively rare in practice.[4]

Exercise 6.13   Use a logical-and operator in your answer to Exercise 6.8 to ensure that a value to be added to the chart is both greater than or equal to the minimum value and less than or equal to the maximum value.

Exercise 6.14   Character values may be compared using the relational operators in the same way as integers. Write a method that takes a single char argument and returns true if its value is an uppercase character, in the range 'A' to 'Z'.

6.2.5   The Logical-Or Operators

The *logical-or* operator (||) gives the value false only if both of its operands are false. Code 6.20 shows an example of the double-character logical-or operator, which also exhibits short-circuit semantics.

It will only evaluate the right operand if the left operand is false. The alternative (fully-evaluating) or-operator (|) gives the same pattern of results as the short-circuit version but always evaluates both of its operands. Once again, a need for the fully-evaluating form in Boolean expressions is questionable.

Exercise 6.15   Write a method, isRoman, that takes a single char argument and returns true if its value is one of the characters: 'M', 'D', 'C', 'L', 'V', or 'I'.

6.2.6   The Logical Exclusive-Or Operator

The logical exclusive-or operator ($\wedge$)[5] gives a value of true if the left and right operands have different values, but it gives a value of false if the operands have the

---

[4] We have never found the need to use a fully-evaluating logical-and operator in a practical program.

[5] Also known as the *xor operator*.

Code 6.21   Determining whether **x** is the middle value

```
if((x < y) ∧ (x < z)){
    System.out.println(x+" is the middle value");
}
```

same value. It only comes in the fully-evaluating form because a short-circuit version would not make sense—the semantics of the operator mean that its result can only ever be determined by evaluating both operands. Code 6.21 shows an example that prints a message if the value of x is less than only one of two other values.

The effects of the exclusive-or operator can be hard to interpret, because it does not correspond closely to any natural-language phrases in common usage.

All of these logical operators have lower precedence than the arithmetic and relational operators we have seen, so, strictly speaking, it is not necessary to paren-thesize their operands as we do in Code 6.19 and Code 6.20. However, we prefer to parenthesize for the sake of clarity.

6.2.7   The Logical-Not Operator

In addition to the binary logical operators, there is a unary *logical-not* operator (!) that takes a single operand. This has the effect of negating the value of its operand so !true is false and !(x > y) means (x <= y), for instance. Care should be taken not to overuse this operator in ordinary Boolean expressions involving relational and other logical operators, because it is often clearer to find a way of rewriting the whole expression without it. A typical use is to reverse the value of a boolean result returned by a method, such as:

```
public void debit(long amount){
    if(!account.isOverdrawn()){
        // Permit the debit
        ...
    }
    ...
}
```

In addition to their use in Boolean expressions, several of the logical operators can also be used to manipulate the bit-patterns of primitive type values. These more specialized uses are discussed in Appendix C.6.

6.2.8   De Morgan's Theorem

Two rules, known as *De Morgan's Theorem*, can help to simplify Boolean expres-sions involving multiple logical-not operators in combination with other Boolean operators. These state that:

```
(!bexpr1) && (!bexpr2) can be rewritten as !(bexpr1 || bexpr2)
(!bexpr1) || (!bexpr2) can be rewritten as !(bexpr1 && bexpr2)
```

The first applies when we need to establish that both `bexpr1` and `bexpr2` are `false` (neither is `true`), and the second is `true` when at least one (but possibly both) of `bexpr1` and `bexpr2` is `false`.

As an example of the first rule, we might be searching through a collection of items looking for a particular `searchValue`, and we wish to stop if there are no more items or the value is found. This might be written as:

```
// Keep searching?
!((index > maxIndex)||(item == searchValue))
```

De Morgan's theorem allows this to be expressed slightly differently, by negating the inner expressions and switching the operator from logical-or to logical-and, giving:

```
// Keep searching?
(index <= maxIndex) && (item != searchValue)
```

In other words, we keep searching as long as we have not yet considered all items and we have not found the item we want.

As an example of the second rule, we might wish to determine whether the value in `x` is not bigger than the values in both `y` and `z`. One way this might have been written is:

```
!(x > y)||(x <= z)
```

At first glance, this does not look like it conforms to one of the rules, since only one of the two expressions contains a logical-not. However, by rewriting the right-hand side of the logical-or operator, we can put the expression into a form that is closer to what we would expect:

```
!(x > y)||!(x > z)
```

Now we can rewrite by directly using the second rule

```
!((x > y) && (x > z))
```

which corresponds more closely to the original than the description that the value in `x` should not be bigger than the values in both `y` and `z`.

6.2.9   Avoiding Boolean Literals

It is often possible to avoid using the `true` and `false` Boolean literals in conditional expressions. Consider the following method, `full`, that returns a Boolean result to indicate whether a car park is full or not. It does this by determining how many free places there are.

```java
public boolean full(){
    if(getSpaces() == 0){
        return true;
    }
    else{
        return false;
    }
}
```

It is possible to simplify this method by recognizing that the value returned in each part of the if-else statement exactly matches the value of the expression used to select it. This means that we can rewrite the method as:

```
public boolean full(){
    return getSpaces() == 0;
}
```

The same will often be the case with expressions involving Boolean variables. Consider the following example, in which a Boolean variable, `found`, is used to store the result of a search.

```
if(found == true){
    System.out.println("The value was found.");
}
```

This can be simplified to

```
if(found){
    System.out.println("The value was found.");
}
```

since the result of the comparison is exactly the same as the value of `found`; if `found` holds `true`, the expression is true, but if `found` holds `false`, the expression is false.

Exercise 6.16   Rewrite the following expression, using the logical-not operator to eliminate the use of `false`.

```
if(found == false){
    System.out.println("The value was not found.");
}
```

6.3   The Conditional Operator

The arithmetic and Boolean operators we have met so far have taken either a single operand (`-` and `!`), or a pair of operands (`*` and `&&`). In addition to these, Java has a single operator which takes three operands; as such, it is called a *ternary operator*. It consists of a pair of characters—`'?'` and `':'`—written separately between its three operands. It is called the *conditional operator*, and its general form in expressions is

```
bexpr ? expr1 : expr2
```

where `bexpr` is a Boolean expression and `expr1` and `expr2` may be of any type, although they will typically be of similar type to each other. The value of the Boolean expression is used to choose between the other two expressions as to which provides the result of the operation. Only one of these two will be evaluated. If `bexpr` is `true`, then `expr1` is evaluated and is the result of the operation; otherwise, `expr2` is evaluated as the result. In this respect, the conditional operator is regarded as a short-circuit operator.

It is often used to replace an if-else statement which is setting a variable to alternative values according to the result of its Boolean expression. Instead of

```
if(x >= y){
    larger = x;
}
else{
    larger = y;
}
```

we can write:

```
larger = (x >= y) ? x : y;
```

If bexpr is true, then x is assigned to larger, otherwise y is. Note that we can only replace an if-else statement in this way under the following circumstances:

- Each part of the if-else statement contains a single statement, which is an assignment.
- The assignment stores a value into the same variable in both parts of the if-else statement.

Use of the conditional operator is not limited to rewriting assignment statements; it can be used in any context where one of two values, decided by a Boolean expression, is required. The method in Code 6.22 uses it to return the absolute value of its actual argument—that is, it returns the positive equivalent of n.

Since the result of the conditional operator is simply a value, these operators can be nested to effect a multi-way selection. The method in Code 6.23 returns a value according to the sign of its actual argument: -1 for a negative value, 0 for a zero value and +1 for a positive value.

If the value of n is greater than or equal to zero, then the value returned by the first conditional operator will be the value returned by the second one.

Clearly, this approach could be used to nest conditional operators arbitrarily deeply, but such expressions quickly become difficult to read and understand. If care

Code 6.22   Using the conditional operator in a return statement

```
      // Return the absolute value of n.
public int abs(int n){
    return (n < 0) ? -n : n;
}
```

Code 6.23   Nested selection of a value

```
      // Return -1, 0 or 1 according to the sign of n.
public int sign(int n){
    return (n < 0) ? -1 :
           (n > 0) ?  1 : 0;
}
```

Code 6.24   Multiple nested conditional operators

```
    // Return a classification for mark.
public int classify(int mark){
    return mark >= 70 ? Distinction :
           mark >= 60 ? Merit :
           mark >= 50 ? Good :
           mark >= 35 ? Pass : Fail;
}
```

is taken with the way in which each operator is formatted, then some expressive variations on the cascading if-else statement can be written. Suppose that we wish to return an `int` value that represents a course classification from a method which takes an integer mark value as its argument. Each classification represents a band of values in which the mark might lie. By repeatedly testing the mark against each band, we can arrive at the classification. Code 6.24 shows how we might do this using multiple nested conditional operators. It also shows how these might be formatted in order to make the classification process comprehensible.

You might like to compare such a replacement for cascading if-else statements with the *switch statement* described in Section 9.20.1, in which it is difficult to express selection involving relational tests, such as that in Code 6.24.

6.4   Review

Here are the main points that we have covered in the preceding sections:

- An if-statement allows an optional sequence of statements to be executed if a Boolean condition evaluates to `true`.
- An if-else statement allows a choice of two alternative sequences of statements to be executed, depending upon whether a condition evaluates to `true` or `false`.
- Relational operators allow comparison of primitive type expressions to produce Boolean results.
- Boolean operators allow combinations of Boolean expressions to be used in an if-statement's condition.
- The and-operators and or-operators come in both short-circuit and fully-evaluating forms.
- The conditional operator is a short-circuit operator taking three operands.
- De Morgan's Theorem can sometimes be used to simplify or rewrite complex Boolean expressions.
- Boolean literal values can often be avoided in conditional expressions.

Exercise 6.17   Using if-statements, arrange the following sentences so that you can print out whether a small number is exactly divisible by 3 or by 4 or by both. You may use each sentence as many times as you wish. If a sentence is marked as a condition, this tells you that the sentence has to be written as part of the condition of an if-statement.

```
Think of a number less than 100.
Print that the number is divisible by 3 but not 4.
Print that the number is divisible by 4 but not 3.
Print that the number is divisible by both 3 and 4.
Print that the number is divisible by neither 3 nor 4.
The number is divisible by 3. (condition)
The number is divisible by 4. (condition)
```

Write a main method that prompts the user for a number and prints the answer, using statements based upon these sentences.

Exercise 6.18   What is printed when m1 is called with actual argument values of 3, 30, and 9 respectively?

```
public void m1(int i){
    if((i >= 0) && (i < 5)){
        System.out.print("P");
    }
    else if((i == 5) ||(i == 6)){
        System.out.print("Q");
    }
    else if((i > 6) && (i <= 10)){
        System.out.print("R");
    }
    else{
        System.out.print("X");
    }
}
```

Exercise 6.19   Consider the following method:

```
public int m2(int a, int b, int c){
    if((a > 1) && (b == 0)){
        c /= a;
    }
    if((a == 5) ||(c > 2)){
        c += 1;
    }
    return c;
}
```

What value is returned when m2 is called with actual argument values as follows:

```
m2(2,0,5);
m2(10,1,3);
m2(5,10,4);
m2(5,0,15);
```

Exercise 6.20   Write a method that takes two arguments of type double (x and y) and returns a result of type double. This method should return whichever is the larger of x and y, if their values differ; otherwise, it returns a value equal to 3 times their sum. Write two versions of this method, one using an if-else statement and the other using conditional operators.

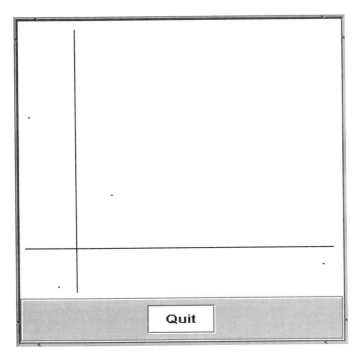

Figure 6.3 Sample output from the `Graph` class
(`GraphMain1.java`)

6.5   A Graph Exercise

In Section 6.1.6, we introduced the scenario of a poorly written library of classes to produce graphical displays of data. The exercises in this section involve another of those classes, called `Graph`. Figure 6.3 illustrates the output produced by this class when used to plot four points and two lines. The Graph class contains two methods, `drawPoint` and `drawLine`, which take one or two pairs of `double` values, respectively, representing `(x,y)` coordinates. Unfortunately, the programmer of this class has written some poor code, with the result that it will cause a runtime error if an attempt is made to plot a point that lies outside the coordinate space represented by the graphical display. Furthermore, the class will reject attempts to draw lines for which the x-value of the first pair lies to the right of the x-value of the second pair. Your task is to make the Graph class more usable by completing the `GraphMinder` class shown in Code 6.25.

The boundaries of the coordinate space are defined by the arguments of Graph-Minder's constructor. Code 6.26 shows the main method that was used to create the output shown in Figure 6.3.

Exercise 6.21   Compile and run the program in `GraphMain1.java` to check that it produces the output shown in Figure 6.3.

Code 6.25   The (non-checking) GraphMinder class (`GraphMinder.java`)

```
    /* A minder class for the (bug-ridden) Graph class.
     * Try to make the Graph object, created by the constructor,
     * more usable by protecting it from things it does not like.
     */
class GraphMinder {
        // Create a Graph and look after it.
    public GraphMinder(double minX, double maxX, double minY, double maxY){
        // Set the graph attribute.
        setGraph(new Graph(minX,maxX,minY,maxY));
    }

        // Add the given point into the graph.
    public void addPoint(double x, double y){
        Graph display = getGraph();
        display.drawPoint(x,y);
    }

        // Add the given point into the graph.
    public void addLine(double x1, double y1, double x2, double y2){
        Graph display = getGraph();
        display.drawLine(x1,y1,x2,y2);
    }

    private Graph getGraph(){
        return graph;
    }

    private void setGraph(Graph g){
        graph = g;
    }

    // The graph to be looked after. This must be initialized
    // by this class's constructor.
    private Graph graph;
}
```

Exercise 6.22   Modify `GraphMain1.java` so that an attempt is made to add a point that lies outside the coordinate space to the graph, for instance (`100.0,100.0`). What effect does this have when you recompile and run the program?

Exercise 6.23   The Graph class defines public accessor methods for the minimum and maximum x- and y-coordinate values it should allow. These are called, `getMinX`, `getMaxX`, `getMinY`, and `getMaxY`. Each returns a value of type double. Modify the `addPoint` method of the GraphMinder class so that it prevents attempts to draw points on the graph that lie outside the boundaries of the coordinate space. Note, this restriction applies to the endpoints of lines as well as individual points.

Code 6.26   Adding a few points and lines to a Graph via a GraphMinder (`GraphMain1.java`)

```
        // Illustrate the creation of a Graph and
        // its appearance when a few points are added.
class GraphMain1 {
    public static void main(String[] args){
        // Define the bounds of the coordinate space.
        double minX = -10, maxX = 50, minY = -10, maxY = 50;
        GraphMinder minder = new GraphMinder(minX,maxX,minY,maxY);

        // Draw lines through the origin.
        minder.addLine(minX,0,maxX,0);
        minder.addLine(0,minY,0,maxY);

        // Add a small selection of points, one in each quadrant.
        minder.addPoint(-3.5,-8.9);
        minder.addPoint(-9,30);
        minder.addPoint(48,-4);
        minder.addPoint(7,12);
    }
}
```

Exercise 6.24   Modify `GraphMain1.java` so that an attempt is made to draw a line in which the x-value of the first end-point is larger than the x-value of the second end-point. What effect does this have when you recompile and run the program? Modify the `addLine` method of the GraphMinder class so that such a line is drawn by the Graph class, as long as both end-points lie within the coordinate space.

Exercise 6.25   Test the operation of your version of the GraphMinder class by creating Graph objects with different coordinate spaces. Are there any circumstances in which constructing a Graph object fails? If so, can you add statements to correct the failure?

In the next chapter we add *repetition* to the behavior of objects.

Adding Repetitive Behavior

Sequence and choice provide us with two of the primary ways in which we can organize the statements in a method or piece of program to achieve particular goals. The third is through the use of repetition. Java defines three control structures to express this concept: the while loop, the do loop, and the for loop. In this chapter, we start by looking at the main concepts associated with repetition, and then move on to see how these are achieved in Java. We also deal with final variables, static variables, and static methods.

7.1 Repetition of Statements

Repetitive actions are common in everyday life.

```
Repeat every day:
    Get up, have breakfast, go off to work or classes, have lunch,
    do more work, have an evening meal, relax, go to bed.
```

with the occasional break at weekends!

Repetitions are also common within the tasks comprising part of the day's work; a postal worker's deliveries might involve:

```
Deliver a sack of letters:
    Check the address on the next letter, go to the right house,
    deliver the letter, check the address on the next letter,
    and so on, until the sack of letters is exhausted.
```

In Section 6.1.6, we noted how difficult it is to supply large amounts of test data to a program with only sequence and selection statements. This was because we lacked control structures that would allow us to repeatedly read an item of data and add it to the bar chart over and over again, without having to write the statements out possibly hundreds of times.

Repetition in a programming language always has two main elements:

- The actions to be repeated.
- A test to determine whether to stop repeating.

The termination test is a Boolean expression, just as we have seen with if-statements. In Java, the form of the test usually determines whether to keep going, in fact, rather than whether to stop. As long as the test expression gives the value `true` when evaluated, the actions are repeated at least one more time. Despite the fact that a test is fundamental to repetition, this can be the hardest part to get right, sometimes resulting in either a loop that goes on forever, or a loop that never executes at all!

Java has three sorts of loop:

- The *while loop.*
- The *do loop.*
- The *for loop.*

We shall introduce all three in this chapter.

7.2   The While Loop

The general syntax for the while loop is shown in Code 7.1.

It uses a further reserved word: `while`. As with if-statements, a single statement in the body of the loop does not require the curly brackets to create a block, although we usually include them.

To illustrate how a while loop is used, imagine that you are checking the flavor of some soup, and you need to know whether it is salty enough yet. You might express this as in Code 7.2.

When the loop is reached, the condition is tested; if it gives the value `true`, then the body of the loop is entered, and a pinch of salt is added. At the end of the loop's body, control returns back to the condition in order to test the flavor again. This is the first example we have seen where the control flow goes back to perform some action that has just been performed, rather than proceeding only down the page (see Section 1.4.2).

How many pinches of salt will be added by the while loop shown in Code 7.2? There is no definite answer to this; the body of the loop will be executed an indeterminate number of times, depending upon how salty it was to start with and how salty you like soup to be. You might add one pinch and find when you next taste it that the soup is just right. In this case, the test will give the value `false` after a

Code 7.1   Outline of the while loop

```
while(condition)
    // Repeat a single statement.
    statement;
```

or

```
while(condition){
    // Repeat multiple statements.
    statement;
    statement;
    statement;
    ...
}
```

Code 7.2   Flavoring soup with pinches of salt

```
class Cookery {
    ...
    public void saltTheSoup(){
        while(there isn't enough salt in the soup){
            Add a pinch of salt;
        }
    }
    ...
}
```

---

single *iteration*, the body will then be skipped over and whatever follows the loop executed next. On the other hand, after one pinch it might still not be salty enough and require a second, third, fourth pinch, and so on. Conversely, you might be quite concerned about the amount of salt in your food and prefer to keep it to a minimum. In this case, the first time you taste it you are quite likely to decide that it is already sufficiently salty and add no pinches at all. This is perfectly possible with a while loop; the statements in the body may be executed 0, 1, 2, ..., up to any number of times. We describe this property of an arbitrary number of iterations as *unbounded repetition*. If the body of the loop is executed at least once, then the number of further times must be determined by the dependence of the condition upon one or more statements in the loop. Here we have a condition testing saltiness and a body increasing saltiness, so the dependence is clear.

Consider what might happen if you made a mistake with the ingredients and added sugar instead of salt (Code 7.3).

In this case, no matter how many times the body of the loop is executed, the soup will never become any saltier and the loop will go on indefinitely; this is called an *infinite loop*. Infinite loops are a fairly common result of logical errors when developing programs, and they mean that a method will never finish what it is meant to do. They usually arise from exactly what we see here: the body of a loop not bringing the condition any closer to becoming `false`, which it must do if the loop is to end.

Code 7.4 shows an example of a Java method that uses a while loop properly to print some numbers up to a maximum value passed in as an argument.

Code 7.3   Flavoring soup with sugar instead of salt

```
class Cookery {
    ...
    public void saltTheSoup(){
        while(there isn't enough salt in the soup){
            Add a pinch of sugar;
        }
    }
    ...
}
```

Code 7.4   Print the numbers 1 to maximum

```java
    // Print the numbers 1 to maximum.
public void printNumbers(int maximum){
    int nextToPrint = 1;

    while(nextToPrint <= maximum){
        System.out.print(nextToPrint+" ");
        // Get ready to print the next number.
        nextToPrint += 1;
    }
    System.out.println();
}
```

The numbers are all printed on a single line before terminating the line once the loop is complete. We can confirm that the loop's condition is dependent upon the statements in the loop's body by noting that the value of nextToPrint is increased each time around the loop, and this will gradually bring it up to the value of maximum. The result of passing the value 5 as an actual argument will be as follows:

```
1 2 3 4 5
```

We shall revisit this example in later sections.

7.2.1   Reading Input with a While Loop

A while loop provides us with the means to read arbitrary amounts of input into a program, such as the numbers to be displayed in the BarChart exercises of Section 6.1.6. We shall use a SimpleInput object to help with the number reading in those examples. In order to create an appropriate loop, we need to decide what are the actions to be repeated, and how we will know when to stop the repetition. The actions to be repeated are reading a value and adding it to the chart. A common approach that is often used to indicate the end of input data is to pick an *out-of-bounds value* that is of no use to the application. When this value is input by the user, it means that the repetition should stop. For input to a BarChart application (which displays values in the range 1..100, by default) a value of -1 could serve as the terminating value. Code 7.5 illustrates what we might be tempted to write as a first attempt at programming an input-reading while loop.

This example represents a very common mistake made by many people when they start to use loops to achieve repetition. Before reading further, you should pause here and try to understand why this is not correct. If you can spot the error then it will help you a lot in devising your own loops.

Surely there is nothing wrong with the loop in Code 7.5? It contains all of the required elements: value is tested against the terminating value, and the loop's body contains the necessary statements to read each new value and add it to the chart; so what is wrong? What values would be added to the chart if the user supplied the following data?

```
3 25 -1
```

Code 7.5   Incorrect reading of data for a BarChart

```
        // Read a series of values for a BarChart.
class BarChartMain {
    public static void main(String[] args){
        // Read input from the user.
        SimpleInput keyboard = new SimpleInput();
        // Use a minder to check sensible use of the BarChart.
        // The chart displays values in the range [1..100]
        BarChartMinder minder = new BarChartMinder(new BarChart());
        // The value on which to stop.
        int terminatingValue = -1;

        System.out.println("Please input the values, -1 to finish.");
        // NB: This loop is incorrect.
        int value = 0;
        while(value != terminatingValue){
            value = keyboard.nextInt();
            minder.addToChart(value);
        }
    }
}
```

When the loop is first reached, the method variable `value` contains a value of zero. This is tested against the condition for the first time and the condition gives the value `true`, allowing the body of the loop to be entered for the first time. Read from the input, the value 3 is stored into `value` and then added to the chart. The end of the loop body having been reached, the condition is retested. Since `value` contains 3 still, the condition remains `true` and the loop body is entered once again. This process is repeated with the value 25, which is added to the chart, and then the value -1 is read. This is the terminating value, so we really want the loop to stop at this point. But the loop cannot stop until the condition is evaluated next time around. Before that point, the -1 will be added to the chart, which was not our intention. However, once it has been added, the condition evaluates to `false` and no more numbers are read.

Although adding -1 to the chart is not a huge disaster, it does represent a logical flaw in the programming of this loop, and it could represent a more serious error in other circumstances. The problem lies in the fact that we add a value to the chart before we test to see whether it is the terminating value or not. There are two common ways in which it is tempting to fix this error; Code 7.6 represents the first.

This approach is particularly tempting because it does fix the problem, but it does not address the underlying error. We avoid ever adding the terminating value to the chart by explicitly testing for it immediately before adding it. The problem with this approach is that we now test every single value twice rather than once. Having tested it once, inside the loop, we test it again almost immediately afterwards, even though its value will not have changed in between times!

Code 7.6   An inappropriate attempt to fix the logical error of Code 7.5

```
public static void main(String[] args){
    ...
    // The value on which to stop.
    int terminatingValue = -1;
    int value = 0;

    while(value != terminatingValue){
        value = keyboard.nextInt();
        // Don't add the terminating value.
        if(value != terminatingValue){
            minder.addToChart(value);
        }
    }
}
```

Code 7.7   Another incorrect attempt to fix the logical error of Code 7.5

```
public static void main(String[] args){
    ...
    // The value on which to stop.
    int terminatingValue = -1;
    int value = 0;
    while(value != terminatingValue){
        minder.addToChart(value);
        value = keyboard.nextInt();
    }
}
```

A second attempt to fix the problem is shown in Code 7.7. In this example, the order of the two statements in the body of the loop has been reversed from their original order. This approach recognizes that we should not add a value to the chart until it has been checked by the loop's condition. This is closer to what the correct version will look like, but an error remains the first time the body of the loop is executed. On the first time through, a value will be added to the chart that has not been read from the user: the zero stored in value. This, too, is a logical error. Code 7.8 shows the correct version.

We can easily overcome the error shown in Code 7.7 by ensuring that value is initialized with a legitimate data item from the user *before* the loop condition is tested for the first time. Now the only values added to the chart will be those that the user supplied and intended to have added.

The errors we have discussed in this section are particular examples of *boundary errors* or *boundary cases*—logical errors that occur at the edges of a problem. In one case, we had trouble processing the last item of data, and in the other it was the

Code 7.8 Correct reading of data values for a BarChart (`BarChartMain2.java`)

```
// Illustrate use of a while-loop to read an arbitrary
// number of values interactively from the user.
// The end of the input is indicated when the value -1 is read.
class BarChartMain2 {
    public static void main(String[] args){
        SimpleInput keyboard = new SimpleInput();
        // Use a minder to check sensible use of the BarChart.
        // The chart displays values in the range [1..100]
        BarChartMinder minder = new BarChartMinder(new BarChart());

        // The value on which to stop.
        int terminatingValue = -1;
        System.out.println("Please input the values, use "+
                        terminatingValue+" to finish.");
        int value = keyboard.nextInt();
        while(value != terminatingValue){
            minder.addToChart(value);
            value = keyboard.nextInt();
        }
    }
}
```

first item (non-item, in fact) that caused trouble. Loops are prime candidates for boundary errors because, whereas the actions to be repeated are often fairly well defined, arranging to start their execution or stop their execution is often much harder to get exactly right. It is a bit like flying an aircraft; the actual flying part is not too difficult; but getting off the ground and getting back down again are the hard parts!

Exercise 7.1 A test for whether a number is divisible by 9 is to repeatedly add up its digits, and the resulting digits, until you have a single digit. If the single digit result is 9, then the original number is divisible by 9. For instance,

```
99 -> 9+9 = 18
18 -> 1+8 = 9
```

so 99 is divisible by 9, but

```
9121 -> 9+1+2+1 (= 13) -> 1+3 = 4
```

so 9121 is not divisible by 9.

Using sequence, choice, and repetition, arrange the following sentences so that they tell whether a number greater than zero is divisible by 9. If a sentence is marked as a condition, this tells you that the sentence has to be written as part of the condition of an if-statement or a loop.

```
Divisible by 9?:
    Write a 4 digit number at the top of the page.
    Cross out the old number and replace it with the new number.
```

```
The number has more than one digit. (condition)
The number is divisible by nine. (condition)
Add up the digits to form a new number.
Print out that the number is divisible by 9.
Print out that the number is not divisible by 9.
```

Exercise 7.2   Compare the version of `printNumbers` in Code 7.4 with the following:

```
    // Print the numbers 1 to maximum.
 public void printNumbers(int maximum){
     int nextToPrint = 0;

     while(nextToPrint < maximum){
          // Get ready to print the next number.
          nextToPrint += 1;
          System.out.print(nextToPrint+" ");
     }
     System.out.println();
 }
```

There are three main differences; see if you can spot them. Do both versions print identical output for all possible actual arguments?

Exercise 7.3   Add a while loop to read user data with a SimpleInput object in the main method of one of the Graph programs of Section 6.5. It will be simplest if you stick to drawing either only points or only lines. Read either a pair of `double` values for a point, or two pairs for a line.

Exercise 7.4   In this exercise, you will write a program to decode and display an image. The file `picture.txt` contains numerical data that encodes an image. The first few lines (and the last) are as follows:

```
174 199
63 3 55 3 6 0 50 3
63 3 53 3 4 0 3 1 1 0 50 3
63 3 52 3 2 0 2 1 1 0 3 1 1 0 50 3
...
-1
```

The first line contains a pair of numbers that are the image's width and height, respectively. Each subsequent line, except the last, consists of a set of (count, color) pairs. Each distinct `color` value stands for a particular pixel color within the image. The `count` value specifies how many consecutive pixels of the associated color should be plotted. So the example above specifies that the first line of the image consists of 63 pixels of color 3, followed by a further 55 pixels of color 3, then 6 pixels of color 0, and 50 more of color 3. The sum of the count values in each line of the input file is equal to the width of the image. The first count on the final line of the file is negative (out of bounds) value, indicating the end of the image.

The `PicturePlotter` class defines the following constructor:

```
public PicturePlotter(int width,int height)
```

Creating a PicturePlotter object causes a window to appear on the screen, whose drawing area matches the given dimensions. The class also defines the following method:

```
public void plot(int x, int y, int count, int color)
```

which can be used to plot count lots of color starting at position (x,y) within the image area. The class already defines associations between the color values in the data file and the screen colors that they represent.

Write a program to read the contents of the file picture.txt and display the image it represents on a PicturePlotter object. The main method outline shown in Code 7.9 is provided to get you started.

When you have read and plotted the full image, send the PicturePlotter object a repaint message

```
public void repaint()
```

to ensure that the image is not broken up.

Exercise 7.5   (*Note: this is a harder exercise.*) The data for the picture used in Exercise 7.4 is not in its most compressed form. For instance, the first two pairs are

```
63 3 55 3
```

The same effect could be achieved with

```
118 3
```

Write a new solution to Exercise 7.4 so that multiple consecutive counts for the same color *on the same image line* only result in a single call to plot.

This is harder than it sounds, because you must not merge the pair at the end of one image line with the pair at the beginning of the next (hint: use the width of

---

Code 7.9 Outline main method for the PicturePlotter exercise (`PictureMain.java`)

```
// Exercise solution outline.
// Plot the run-length encoded text file, picture.txt
// The format of the file should be as follows
//      image-width image-height
//      count color count color count color ... (Image Line 1)
//      count color count color count color ... (Image Line 2)
//      ...
//      count color count color count color ... (Image Line N)
//      -1 (Negative count Terminator)
class PictureMain {
    public static void main(String[] args){
        // An input reader.
        SimpleInput pictureFile = new SimpleInput("picture.txt");
        // ... add the rest here ...
    }
}
```

the image to help you decide). To help you, you may assume that a pair could only be followed by a pair for the same color if the count value was 63. However, it is not safe to assume that a count of 63 means that the next pair will definitely be for the same color. Note that we have said, write a new solution, rather than suggesting that you modify your previous solution, because you might find it easier to use a completely different looping structure to solve this problem.

7.3   The Do Loop

The while loop and *do loop* differ primarily in whether the test to continue is made before the statements in the loop body are performed or afterwards. The syntax for a do loop is shown in Code 7.10.

It uses a further reserved word: do. Note the mandatory terminating semicolon following the condition part of the loop, whereas it would be an error to place one after the condition of a while loop.

In order to illustrate the main difference between the do loop and the while loop, consider a variation on the soup-flavoring example (Code 7.11).

Code 7.10   Outline of a do loop

```
do
    // Repeat a single statement.
    statement;
while(condition);
```

or

```
do{
    // Repeat multiple statements.
    statement;
    statement;
    statement;
    ...
} while(condition);
```

Code 7.11   Using a do loop to flavor soup

```
class Cookery {
    ...
    public void saltTheSoup(){
        do{
            Add a pinch of salt;
        } while(there isn't enough salt in the soup);
    }
    ...
}
```

Code 7.12   Print the numbers 1 to maximum

```
    // Start from 1 and print up to and including maximum.
public void printNumbers(int maximum){
    int nextToPrint = 1;

    do{
        System.out.print(nextToPrint+" ");
        // Get ready to print the next number.
        nextToPrint += 1;
    }
    while(nextToPrint <= maximum);
    System.out.println();
}
```

With this type of loop, the statements in the loop's body are always executed at least once, before the condition is tested for the first time. Thereafter, the behaviors of the two loops are identical: if the condition gives the value `false`, then the loop is complete, but if the condition is `true`, the body is executed once again before being retested. Thus, whereas a while loop executes its body zero or more times, a do loop executes its body one or more times. Both are *unbounded loops* because the number of iterations is determined by what happens in the loop's body. When deciding which to use, the question to ask is, "Are there any circumstances when the loop body should not be executed?" If the answer to this is yes, then you should probably use a while loop; otherwise, it might be safe to use a do loop, although our preference is to hardly ever use do loops.

Code 7.12 shows a version of `printNumbers` (previously seen in Code 7.4) that uses a do loop instead of a while loop.

Try the following exercises in order to test your understanding of how a do loop differs from a while loop.

Exercise 7.6   Does the version of `printNumbers` shown in Code 7.12 behave exactly the same as that shown in Code 7.4? If we pass in the value 5 as its actual argument, does it give the output shown previously?

     1 2 3 4 5

Exercise 7.7   Are there some values of `maximum` for which the while loop version shown in Code 7.4 does not print anything?

Exercise 7.8   Under what circumstances would it be reasonable to replace the while loop of Code 7.8 with a do loop? Can this be done safely without writing a test of `value` within the body of the loop as well as part of the terminating condition?

Make sure that you fully understand why the two versions of `printNumbers` in Code 7.4 and 7.12 behave differently in some circumstances, because this will help you to appreciate which is the right loop to use in different cases. Our experience

Code 7.13   Using a do loop to return the next negative value (see Code 7.14)

```
    // Return the next negative integer.
public int nextNegative(SimpleInput reader){
    int n;
    do{
        n = reader.nextInt();
    } while(n >= 0);
    return n;
}
```

Code 7.14   Using a while loop to return the next negative value (see Code 7.13)

```
    // Return the next negative integer.
public int nextNegative(SimpleInput reader){
    int n = 0;
    // This test will always be true first time through.
    while(n >= 0){
        n = reader.nextInt();
    }
    return n;
}
```

is that do loops offer little in the way of extra functionality over while loops, and offer more opportunities for creating logical errors or duplicate tests (such as we illustrated in Code 7.6). So there are very few practical examples of their use in this book; however, Code 7.13 illustrates one example that is appropriate.

You might like to compare the do loop version with the while loop alternative in Code 7.14.

Since the first test of the while loop in Code 7.14 is guaranteed to be `true`, and so is redundant, it is more appropriate to use a do loop, as in Code 7.13.

Exercise 7.9   What difference would it make to both Code 7.13 and Code 7.14 if the method variable n were to be initialized as follows

```
    int n = reader.nextInt();
```

before the loop is reached. Is this approach better than those shown?

7.4   Review

Here are the main points that we have covered in the preceding sections:

- Repetition of statements is commonly needed in a program.
- Repetition involves a set of statements to be repeated and a test whether to continue or not.

- Boolean expressions are used to control whether the statements of a loop are to be repeated or not.
- Java has three control structures for repetition—the while loop, do loop, and for loop (dealt with in Section 7.5).
- While loops are used to execute statements zero or more times.
- Do loops are used to execute statements one or more times.
- While loops offer more flexibility than do loops.
- Once the body of a loop has been entered, the statements within the body are responsible for ensuring that the loop will eventually terminate.
- Boundary errors are often responsible for a loop not starting or finishing.
- You should try to avoid duplicating the loop termination test inside the body of a loop; this usually suggests a logical error.

7.5   The For Loop

Some actions need to be repeated for a fixed number of times: "Knock twice and then give the password," "Add three teaspoons of sugar," etc. For these sorts of activities, a *for loop* is provided in Java. Its general form is given in Code 7.15.

The loop is introduced by the reserved word `for`, and it has two components additional to the controlling condition and the body: an initialization section that is performed once only—before the condition is evaluated for the first time—and an update expression that is performed each time around the loop *after* the body has been executed.

In some programming languages, the for loop is used to perform *bounded repetition*, in which the statements within the loop's body are performed a fixed number of times and the number of times is established when the loop is started. Although Java's for loop is often used in this way, it is, in fact, little more than a while loop with a slightly different syntax. Therefore, a for loop can be rewritten as the equivalent while loop shown in Code 7.16.

Code 7.15 Outline of the for loop

```
// Repeat a single statement
for(initialization; condition; post-body update)
    // The single statement to be repeated.
    statement;
```

or

```
// Repeat multiple statements.
for(initialization; condition; post-body update){
    // Statements to be repeated.
    statement;
    statement;
    statement;
    ...
}
```

Code 7.16   A while loop equivalent of a for loop

```
// Repeat multiple statements.
initialization;
while(condition){
    // Statements to be repeated.
    statement;
    statement;
    statement;
    ...
    post-body update;
}
```

Code 7.17   Incrementing a variable by 1

```
while(nextToPrint <= maximum){
    System.out.print(nextToPrint+" ");
    // Get ready to print the next number.
    nextToPrint++;
}
System.out.println();
```

Rewritten in this form, the relationship of the initialization and post-body update expressions to the rest of the loop is easier to see.

Within the post-body update expression, it is common to use two arithmetic operators that we have not yet discussed. These are described in the next section.

7.5.1   The Increment and Decrement Operators

The need to write assignments of the form

```
nextToPrint = nextToPrint + 1;
```

or

```
nextToPrint += 1;
```

is so common that Java has a particular operator that adds 1 to a numeric variable. The statement

```
nextToPrint++;
```

does exactly the same as the other two examples—it directly adds 1 to its operand. Code 7.17 shows this in practice in a version of the printNumbers method first seen in Code 7.4.[1]

---

[1] In fact, a counting loop such as this is more usually written with a for loop, as we shall see in Code 7.19.

An equivalent operator exists to subtract 1 from its operand (--). In both cases, the operand must be a variable of primitive numeric or `char` type (it cannot be used on a `boolean` variable).

Both ++ and -- may be written either before or after the variable to be updated. Written as statements by themselves, there is no difference between

```
--itemsLeftToProcess;
```

and

```
itemsLeftToProcess--;
```

The first form is called a *pre-decrement operator* and the second is called a *post-decrement operator*. There are some situations in which the placement of the operator before or after the variable can make a difference to the meaning or outcome of a statement. Consider the two sets of statements in Code 7.18.

This example produces the following output:

```
01
BC
```

The differences lie in whether the variable is updated *before* its value is used as part of an expression, or afterwards. With the post-increment form, the increment is only performed after the value of the variable has been retrieved, ready to be used in the current context. So, a value of 0 is passed to the first `print` call in Code 7.18. In contrast, with the pre-increment form, the increment is performed before the value of the variable is passed to its context, so the third `print` receives a value of 'B' (that is 'A'+1). It is important to understand that, in the post-increment case, the update is *not* delayed until after the call to `print` has finished, but only long enough for a copy of its value to be taken for the actual parameter. This can be illustrated with the following example:

```
int n = 0;
System.out.println(n++ + " " + n++);
```

Code 7.18   Comparing the effects of pre- and post-increment operators

```java
public void increment(){
    // Use the post-increment form.
    int n = 0;
    System.out.print(n++);
    System.out.print(n++);
    System.out.println();

    // Use the pre-increment form.
    char c = 'A';
    System.out.print(++c);
    System.out.print(++c);
    System.out.println();
}
```

which prints

```
0 1
```

as the first n++ is completed before the second n++ is performed. Incidentally, notice that we have carefully separated the increment operator (++) from the concatenation operator (+) to avoid a confusing looking string of three plus symbols, as in:

```
int n = 0;
System.out.println(n+++" "+n++);
```

Although the compiler would have no objection to the example immediately above, it would object to the similar looking

```
System.out.println(n+++" "+++n);
```

which only serves to illustrate that adding extra white space to make your meaning clear is worth doing.

In general, our advice to avoid confusion with these operators is to write an increment or decrement as a separate statement, where possible. In addition, we prefer to use the post-increment and post-decrement forms for the sake of consistency (see Section F.7).

7.5.2   Using a For Loop to Print Numbers

Code 7.19 shows a version of the printNumbers method using a for loop and the post-increment operator.

This behaves identically to that shown in Code 7.4 and it is a typical example of bounded repetition, as the number of repetitions is fixed when the loop starts. The initialization section is used to define the integer variable nextToPrint as a *loop variable*, just before the loop's condition is tested for the first time. In effect, a for loop has its own scope that extends from its header to the end of its body. A loop variable defined in the header is accessible only within this scope. The condition is used to test whether nextToPrint has a value less than or equal to maximum. If it has, then the single println statement will be executed next. Once the end of the body is reached, the post-body update expression is performed—in this case the loop variable is incremented; then the condition is tested once again to see if maximum has been exceeded. If it has, the loop has finished, otherwise the loop body's statements and the post-body update expression are executed once more. When the loop has finally finished executing, control continues with whatever statements follow the loop body. In this case, the line is terminated before ending the method.

Code 7.19   For loop version of the number printing method

```
public void printNumbers(int maximum){
    for(int nextToPrint = 1; nextToPrint <= maximum; nextToPrint++){
        System.out.print(nextToPrint+" ");
    }
    System.out.println();
}
```

An important reason why the eventual number of iterations is not actually fixed at the point the loop is started is that the condition of a for loop is always completely re-evaluated each time around the loop. This can lead to some inefficiencies if the condition involves a complex expression such as

```
for(int loopVar = 0; loopVar < (x*x+x/y+z-3); loopVar++){
    ...
}
```

but it does allow the value of the terminating expression to be altered by the loop's statements.

When the loop variable is being tested against an expression whose value does not change from one iteration to the other, it is best to evaluate the expression before reaching the loop and store its value in a variable defined for that purpose. The variable can then replace the expression in the loop's condition. If, in addition, the variable is declared as final (see Section 7.8), this makes it explicit that its value will not be modified by the loop. Code 7.20 contains an example.

Since a loop variable defined in the initialization section only exists as long as the loop is executing, an ordinary method variable must be used as the loop variable if its final value is required beyond the scope of the loop (see Code 7.21).

Repetition using for loops is bounded repetition when the number of times that the loop will be executed is controlled purely by the initialization, condition, and update of the loop variable in the for loop's header; that is, the statements in the loop body neither increase nor decrease the number of iterations. One way that they might affect the number of repetitions would be to modify the loop variable; this is not generally a good idea as it can make the loop hard to understand.

As for loops and while loops are so similar, it can sometimes be hard to decide which to use in particular circumstances. The following may be considered to be general guidelines on which to use:

Code 7.20   Removing a constant expression from the terminating condition

```
final int terminatingValue = x*x+x/y+z-3;
for(int loopVar = 0; loopVar < terminatingValue; loopVar++){
    // Loop body in which none of x, y or z is changed.
    ...
}
```

Code 7.21   Using a method variable to control a loop

```
int nextToPrint;
for(nextToPrint = 1; nextToPrint <= maximum; nextToPrint++){
    System.out.print(nextToPrint+" ");
}
System.out.println();
System.out.println("nextToPrint would be: "+nextToPrint);
```

- Use a for loop if a counter is needed, with regular increments at the end of each execution of the statements in the loop body.
- For loops are commonly used to step through an *array* (see Chapter 9 for more details).
- Use a while loop if a counter is needed, but only if it has irregular or uneven increments as part of each execution of the statements in the loop body.
- Use a while loop if it cannot be predicted in advance how many times the loop body will be executed. These situations typically occur when input is being read in a loop and used to determine when to stop the iteration.

7.5.3   Optional Header Expressions

All of the expressions in a for loop's header are optional. The most common reason for omitting the initialization section is that the variable being used to control the loop has been defined and initialized before the loop is reached. For instance, the method in Code 7.22 prints a countdown from the value of the actual argument, n, to zero.

Notice that it is necessary to retain the two semicolons when omitting one or more of the expressions. The post-body update expression is usually omitted if what happens in the body of the loop requires it to be updated irregularly (Code 7.23).

Notice that, in this case, we are violating the rule about not modifying the loop variable in the body of the loop. However, the loop is barely recognizable as a for loop, anyway!

If the terminating expression is omitted, then the loop has the potential to run indefinitely:

```
for( ; ; ){
    ...
}
```

This is equivalent to writing:

```
while(true){
    ...
}
```

Usually the body of such a loop contains a means to finish the iteration, such as a return statement or break statement (see Section 9.20.2).

Code 7.22   Omitting the initialization expression in a for loop

```
    // Print a count down from n to zero.
public void countdown(int n){
    for( ; n >= 0; n--){
        System.out.println(n);
    }
}
```

Code 7.23   Omitting the post-body update expression

```
    // Print a count down from n to zero in irregular amounts.
public void countdown(int n){
    for(; n > 0; ){
        System.out.println(n);
        if(n > 1000){
            n -= 1000;
        }
        else if(n > 100){
            n -= 100;
        }
        else if(n > 10){
            n -= 10;
        }
        else{
            n--;
        }
    }
}
```

Code 7.24   Multiple expressions in the loop initialization

```
    // Use isPrime to count the number of prime numbers from 2 to max.
public int countPrimes(int max){
    int numPrimes, possible;

    for(numPrimes = 0, possible = 2; possible <= max; possible++){
        if(isPrime(possible)){
            numPrimes++;
        }
    }
    return numPrimes;
}
```

7.5.4   The Comma Operator

The initialization and post-body update sections of a for loop may contain multiple expressions, separated by the comma operator. Sometimes it is necessary to initialize two variables at the start of the loop, one being the main loop index and the other counting occurrences of something that is detected within the loop. Code 7.24 illustrates this with an example to count the number of prime numbers in a given range.[2]

Comma-separated expressions in a for loop header are evaluated from left to right. In this example, numPrimes must be declared outside the loop because it is used in the return statement, but the syntax of comma-separated expressions means that neither of the following forms that define possible inside the loop's header is

---

[2] The isPossiblePrime method of the BigInteger class provides a prime-tester that might form the basis for the isPrime method.

allowed. The effect of the first would be to redefine `numPrimes`

```
int numPrimes;
// Not allowed.
for(int possible = 2, numPrimes = 0; possible <= max; possible++)
```

whereas the following is a syntax error:

```
int numPrimes;
// Not allowed.
for(numPrimes = 0, int possible = 2; possible <= max; possible++)
```

Exercise 7.10   Code 7.25 shows the outline of the class `ShapePrinter` with two
empty methods, `stars` and `printChar`.

Complete the body of the `stars` method so that it prints n star characters,
followed by a newline. The file `ShapePrinterMain.java` contains a main method
that will print the following shape if your implementation is correct:

```
***
*
*****
```

Exercise 7.11   Add a loop to the main method of `ShapePrinterMain` that uses
your `stars` method from Exercise 7.10 to print the following shape:

```
*
**
***
****
```

Exercise 7.12   Use your `stars` method to write a loop in the main method of
ShapePrinterMain that prints the following shape:

```
******
*****
****
***
```

Code 7.25   Outline of a class for printing lines of characters (`ShapePrinter.java`)

```
class ShapePrinter {
      // Print a line of n "*" characters.
   public void stars(int n){
      ...
   }

      // Print a line consisting of n copies of ch.
   public void printChar(int n, char ch){
      ...
   }
}
```

Exercise 7.13   Write a loop to print the following shape:

```
****
****
****
****
```

Exercise 7.14   Complete the body of the `printChar` method in the ShapePrinter class.

Exercise 7.15   Using calls to your `printChar` method from Exercise 7.14, print the following shape from within the main method of ShapePrinterMain:

```
###
-----
###
```

Exercise 7.16   How could you rewrite the body of the `stars` method so that it uses the `printChar` method to output the stars?

Exercise 7.17   Colors in graphical applications are often defined in terms of three separate red, green, and blue color component values. Normal values for these components typically lie in the range `0...255`. Figure 7.1 shows a window whose main background is colored with a particular set of RGB values that are displayed within it. The window is implemented by a `ColorDisplay` object whose public interface contains the following method:

```
public void changeColor(int red, int green, int blue)
```

Sending a `changeColor` message to a ColorDisplay object will cause it to use the given values to change its background color. Code 7.26 shows the main method that was used to create Figure 7.1.

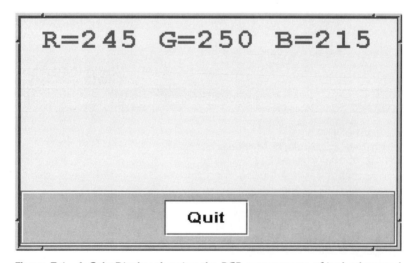

Figure 7.1   A ColorDisplay showing the RGB components of its background
(`ColorDisplayMain.java`)

Code 7.26   Creating and setting the color of a ColorDisplay (`ColorDisplayMain.java`)

```
    // A main method for iterating over RGB color component
    // values with a ColorDisplay object.
class ColorDisplayMain {
    public static void main(String[] args){
        ColorDisplay display = new ColorDisplay();

        // Set a delay of 10 milliseconds.
        display.setDelay(10);
        // Show a single color.
        display.changeColor(245,250,215);
    }
}
```

Add a for loop to the main method shown in Code 7.26 so that the value of the red component is successively changed from 0 to 255 over its full range. The ColorDisplay class pauses after each color change to make it easier to discern the changes. The length of this delay may be changed by sending it a `setDelay` message whose argument is the number of milliseconds to pause between each change.

Exercise 7.18   Add further nested for loops to your answer to Exercise 7.17 so that every combination or red, green, and blue value in the range `0..255` is used.

Exercise 7.19   Modify the headers of the for loops in your solution to Exercise 7.18 so that different step sizes are used for the red, green, and blue components. For instance, the red component might be changed by 10 units on each iteration, while the green component might be changed by 15.

7.6   Review

Here are the main points that we have covered in the preceding sections:

- For loops are often used to execute statements a fixed number of times.
- There are similarities between while loops and for loops that sometimes make it difficult to decide which to use.
- All the expressions in a for loop's header are optional, but the two semicolons are mandatory.
- The post-body update expression is evaluated after the statements in the body of the loop, but before the condition is re-tested.
- The loop's condition is re-evaluated after each iteration.
- An empty condition is equivalent to a `true` condition.
- A variable defined in the header of a for loop has a scope that is limited to the loop, and is undefined thereafter.
- The comma operator may be used to separate multiple expressions in the header of a for loop.

- The increment and decrement operators allow addition or subtraction of 1 from a primitive numeric or `char` variable.
- The pre- forms of the increment and decrement operators update the variable before its value has been used in an expression, so the updated value is used in the expression.
- The post- forms of the increment and decrement operators update the variable after its value has been used in an expression, so the original value is used in the expression.

7.7   Code Blocks and Scope

With the introduction of control structures, we have increased the level of complexity at which it is possible to write methods; methods will no longer simply contain a straight-line sequence of object creations, assignments, or message passing. Methods will contain decision making statements and looping statements, among other things. This means that it will often be necessary to define further method variables to help with the task undertaken by a method; these will contain instances of collaborating objects or intermediate results in arithmetic calculations, for instance.

A method variable may be defined within any block in the body of a method, not simply in the outermost block. Indeed, it is a good idea to define method variables in the immediate context where they are needed, rather than grouping them all at the start of the method body. We can define variables inside the bodies of if-statements and loops. For instance, suppose we wish to swap the values held in two variables x and y if x is larger than y. Swapping the values of two variables requires the introduction of a third variable to hold the value of one of them while it takes on the value of the other. Code 7.27 shows how a method variable may be defined inside a statement block purely for this purpose.

The variable `temp` has a short but useful life. It only comes into existence if x is larger than y and the body of the if-statement is entered. Its definition inside

Code 7.27 Introducing a local method variable

```
public void m(){
    int x, y;
    // Statements using x and y.
    ...
    if(x > y){
        // Swap the values held in x and y.
        // Hold onto the value of x so that it is not lost.
        int temp = x;
        // Copy y's value into x.
        x = y;
        // Copy into y the old value of x.
        y = temp;
    }
    ...
}
```

the code block means that it can only be referred to by the three statements inside that part of the method—the block is the *scope* of temp. Each code block defines a new scope, from the opening curly bracket to the closing curly bracket. The scope of a method variable lasts from its point of declaration to the end of the block in which it is defined. Note that this is different to the rule for attributes, which are accessible anywhere within the full scope of the class (see Section 4.3.5). A method variable defined inside an inner code block may not be accessed from an outer code block. Code 7.28 illustrates several nested scope levels, each with its own method variable. In practice, these code blocks would form part of control structures such as if-statements or loops, but we have omitted details of these to keep the example as straightforward as possible.

Notice, in particular, that the identifier middle has been defined in two separate code blocks in this example. This is only possible in the second use because the first use is *out of scope* by the time the second is declared. It is not possible to redeclare a method variable or formal argument that is still in scope. If we had tried to redefine outer, say, in one of the nested blocks in Code 7.28, the compiler would have given an error message such as:

```
Variable 'outer' is already defined in this method.
```

However, it is possible for a method variable or a method's formal argument to have the same name as a method or field defined at the class level. It is common practice to define a method variable with the same name as an attribute in order to hold a temporary local copy of the attribute (obtained via its accessor), for instance.

Code 7.28   Illustrating nested scope

```
public void method(int arg){
    int outer;
    {   int middle;
        {   int inner;

            // arg, outer, middle and inner are accessible.
            ...
        }
        // arg, outer and middle are accessible.
        // inner is inaccessible.
        ...
    }
    // arg and outer are accessible.
    // middle and inner are inaccessible.
    ...
    {   // This use of middle is distinct from the one above.
        int middle;

        // arg, outer and the local version of middle are accessible.
        // inner is inaccessible.
        ...
    }
}
```

Exercise 7.20   Given the following class,

```
class ExampleClass {
   public ExampleClass(){
        int value = 10;
   }

   public int getValue(){
        return value;
   }

   private int value = 0;
}
```

what will be printed by the following `println` statement?

```
ExampleClass obj = new ExampleClass();
System.out.println(obj.getValue());
```

Exercise 7.21   Is it possible to move the definition of the variable n in Code 7.13 completely inside the do loop's code block body as follows?

```
do{
    int n = reader.nextInt();
}while(n >= 0);
```

If you are unsure, write a simple main method containing a similar loop to discover the answer to this.

7.8   Final Variables and Arguments

Sometimes an arithmetic value has a particular significance in the context of a method. The number 12, for instance, could mean the month of December in a diary program, 12 noon in a clock program, or a dozen in a retail program. It is often wise to give such values of significance a name in order to make their purpose clear. In Java, this is done by declaring a *final variable* using the final modifier

```
final int DOZEN = 12;
final double NUMDEGREES = 360.0;
```

These examples show a common convention to use fully uppercase names for final variables representing constant numeric or character values.[3] This modifier may be prefixed to formal arguments, instance variables, method variables, and class variables (see Section 7.9). By labeling a variable of a primitive type in this way, we not only give it a name, but indicate that the identifier represents a *constant* value—that is, one that may not be changed.[4] Assignments to final method variables are prohibited after their declaration, as are assignments to final formal arguments. The

---

[3] This is a convention to which we choose not to adhere rigidly.

[4] Final variable is really an oxymoron, since the contents of a variable cannot be varied if it is final!

compiler will report errors if either is attempted. The final modifier is a cross between a programming tool and a compiler optimization mechanism. The compiler
can sometimes use the fact that a variable's value will not change after initialization
to make a method execute faster. Code 7.29 shows an example of a final argument
and method variable.

A little care must be taken in understanding what is meant here by the term
constant. It is fairly obvious that for a variable of a primitive type it means we cannot change that variable's value once initialized. However, what does it mean in
Code 7.30?

When the final variable contains an object reference, it does not mean that we
cannot mutate the object referred to by that variable; so the setSpeed message
sent to liner is ok. It does mean that we are not allowed to change which object
either liner or steamer refers to, so making steamer reference *"Titanic"* is not
allowed. In effect, a final variable of class type is permanently glued to the object to
which it refers. Be sure that you understand the distinction here, because it might
not be the one you expect.

Code 7.29   Defining a formal argument and local variable as final

```
class PennyBankAccount {
    ...
        // Credit the account with the given amount.
        // The amount must be non-negative.
    public void credit(final long amount){
        if(amount >= 0){
            // Find out how much is currently in the account.
            final long currentBalance = getBalance();
            // Add in the amount to be credited.
            setBalance(currentBalance+amount);
        }
        else{
            System.out.println("A negative amount: "+amount+
                               " cannot be credited to an account.");
        }
    }
    ...
}
```

Code 7.30   Final variables may not be assigned to

```
final Ship liner = new Ship("Titanic");
final Ship steamer = new Ship("Mississippi Belle");
// Mutation is valid.
liner.setSpeed(5);
// Assignment is not valid.
liner = steamer;
```

Code 7.31   Setting a final attribute from within a constructor

```
class Card {
    public Card(int faceValue){
        value = faceValue;
    }

    public int getValue(){
        return value;
    }

    // The face value of this card. This must be initialized
    // by the constructor.
    private final int value;
}
```

7.8.1   Final Fields and Constructors

There is an important exception to the rule that final variables may not be assigned to after their declaration. A final instance variable may be left uninitialized in its declaration as long as it is initialized by *all* constructors of its class or by an *instance initializer* (see Section 9.8.2). Such a variable is called a *blank final variable*. This is an important exception because it allows the advantages of final variables to be exploited for attributes that cannot be set up until an object is created. Code 7.31 illustrates this idea with the Card class introduced in Section 4.11.

It is not possible to initialize the `value` field of a Card until an actual parameter is passed to the Card's constructor. However, once the value is known, it will not be changed for the lifetime of the card, so a final variable is its most appropriate declaration. Notice that we can now entirely dispense with a mutator for this attribute—indeed, it is not possible to initialize it via a mutator, as the compiler requires that this be done directly from the constructor. At the same time, this illustrates a disadvantage with this approach. If there are restrictions on the set of values that such an attribute should take on, a mutator is the natural place to locate such checks. For a final attribute, this is not possible, so those checks must be made directly in the constructor that initializes it (and, as a consequence, duplicated in *all* constructors that initialize it).

7.9   Static Variables

Code 7.32 illustrates an obvious application for final variables in providing names for the months of the year from within a `Diary` class.

In this example, we have a case where the values of those final variables will be identical in each instance of the Diary class. However, because they are also instance variables, each instance will have its own copy. This seems a little unnecessary and a waste of space. Ideally, we would like to have one set of these variables that is available to all instances of the class. This is exactly the effect we achieve by prefixing

---

Code 7.32   A set of final variables as constants

```
class Diary {
    ...
    // Provide local meaningful names for the months.
    private final int January = 1, February = 2, March = 3;
    private final int April = 4, May = 5, June = 6;
    private final int July = 7, August = 8, September = 9;
    private final int October = 10, November = 11, December = 12;
}
```

`static` to their declaration, between `private` and `final`, as follows:

```
private static final int April = 4, May = 5, June = 6;
```

The `static` modifier may only be used on members at the class level, not on variables and arguments within methods. It has the effect of making a field into a *static variable* (also known as a *class variable*). A static variable is one that belongs to the class rather than any particular instance.

Because final variables may not be modified, it is common to see final class variables of primitive types defined with the `public` access modifier, where they may be of use to objects of other classes (Code 7.33). This is perfectly safe and does not contradict our rules on the use of accessors and mutators with attributes (partly because they are not instance attributes, of course).

It is the use of the `static` reserved word, rather than the use of `final`, that classifies a variable as a class variable. A class variable is shared between all instances of that class. If a class variable is not `final`, and its value is changed by one instance of the class, then the new value is shared by all instances. Furthermore, class variables have the distinctive property that they exist even if no instances of that particular class have been created. This means that public class variables may be accessed via either an object of the class or via the name of the class in which they are defined; for instance,

```
System.out.println("April is month number "+Diary.April);
```

is one way of accessing the `April` class variable in the Diary class. A variable defined as both `final` and `static` is sometimes known as a *class constant*.

Code 7.33   Defining public final class variables with **static**

```
class Diary {
    // These class variables may safely be made public.
    public static final int January = 1, February = 2,
                March = 3, April = 4, May = 5, June = 6,
                July = 7, August = 8, September = 9,
                October = 10, November = 11, December = 12,
    ...
}
```

The `Math` class—a standard part of the language (see Section 8.2)—defines class variables for the mathematical constants π (the ratio of a circle's circumference to its diameter) and e (the base of natural logarithms) as a means of ensuring that each program that needs them has an accurate and consistent value. These can be used directly, via the name of the Math class, as in

```
System.out.println("The value of Pi is: "+Math.PI);
System.out.println("The value of e is: "+Math.E);
```

which will produce the following output for all implementations of Java:

```
The value of Pi is: 3.141592653589793
The value of e is: 2.718281828459045
```

Closely related to static variables are *static methods*, which we discuss in Section 7.10.

7.10   Static Methods

Static methods (also known as *class methods*) have close links with *static variables*. A static method is one with the `static` reserved word in its header. So far, we have only seen the main method with this form. Static methods differ from all other methods in that they are not associated with any particular instance of the class to which they belong. They are usually accessed directly via the name of the class in which they are defined (although they may be used via an object reference). When you run a program via a Java interpreter, you pass it the name of the class containing the main method:

```
java Hello program-arguments
```

The interpreter starts the program by calling the main method using the class name you have given to it, as follows:

```
Hello.main(program-arguments);
```

It does not create an object belonging to the Hello class in order to do this.

Because static methods are not associated with an object, they are not allowed to access non-static methods or fields of the class in which they are defined. This is one reason why we try to keep the number of statements defined in a main method fairly low, and why our classes containing the main method do not define any attributes. Static methods should only be used sparingly in class definitions. The most common use for a static method is to perform a well-defined task that requires little or no state information. Code 7.34 shows that the `printNumbers` method we have discussed in this chapter could well be implemented as a static method within an arbitrary class.

Some utility classes, such as the `Math` class (see Section 8.2), consist entirely of static methods and static variables. It is never necessary to create an object of such classes, therefore, since they have no dynamic behavior. Any information the class's static methods require must usually be passed via their parameters. Since a static method has no associated object, they are usually relatively self-contained, retaining no state between calls to them. Where they must retain state, this must be stored in a static field of the class.

Code 7.34   A static method requires no access to non-static members of its class

```
    // Print the numbers 1 to maximum.
public static void printNumbers(final int maximum){
    int nextToPrint = 1;

    while(nextToPrint <= maximum){
        System.out.print(nextToPrint+" ");
        // Get ready to print the next number.
        nextToPrint += 1;
    }
    System.out.println();
}
```

A commonly used static method is `exit`, which is defined by the System class. Calling this method with a single integer argument causes the program to terminate immediately. The value of the argument can sometimes be used to indicate to the external environment why the program has finished. A non-zero value is traditionally used to indicate that a fatal error occurred. The System class also defines `currentTimeMillis`, that returns the current time as a `long` number of milliseconds since January 1, 1970, 00:00:00 GMT.

Exercise 7.22   Complete the definition of the following static method, `addDigits`:

```
    // Return the sum of the decimal digits in n. For instance,
    // addDigits(362023) would return 16.
public static int addDigits(int n)
```

The `addDigits` method should be defined in the same class as the main method. As it is a static method, it will be callable from `main`.

Exercise 7.23   Use your implementation of `addDigits` to create a program for the divisible-by-nine test, described in Exercise 7.1. Use the SimpleInput class to read numbers from a user, and print out whether they are divisible by nine or not.

7.11   Review

Here are the main points we have covered in the preceding sections:

- A method variable may be defined within any code block inside a method.
- The scope of a method variable lasts from its point of declaration to the end of the block in which it is defined.
- A method variable may not be declared if there is a method variable or formal argument with the same name in scope.
- A method variable or formal argument may have the same name as a method or field of the class in which it is defined.
- Final variables may be used to give meaningful names to significant constant values of the primitive types.

- Formal arguments may be declared as final.
- A compiler can sometimes use final declaration information to provide optimizations.
- Initialization of final fields may be left to constructors and initializer blocks.
- An object accessed via a final variable may be mutated.
- A static (class) variable is shared by all instances of that class.
- A static variable may be accessed via its class name rather than via an instance.
- A static variable exists even if no objects of its class have been created.
- A static (class) method is not associated with a particular instance of a class.
- A static method is not permitted to access any non-static members of its class.
- A static method may be accessed via its class name.
- A static method may be used even if no objects of its class have been created.

Exercise 7.24   Write a main method that generates a random integer in the range 10,000 to 99,999 and prompts the user to guess the value. Guesses that are outside the range should receive an error message reminding the user of the range. Guesses within the range that are above or below the random value should receive a message that indicates whether they are too high or too low. When the number has been guessed, print the number of within-range guesses that the user took.

You can use the following static method, defined in `GuessingMain.java`, to generate suitable random numbers.

```
    // Return a 5-digit random number.
public static int fiveDigitRandom(){
    final int min = 10000, limit = 100000;
    return min+(int)((limit-min)*Math.random());
}
```

See the discussion of the `Math` class in Chapter 8 for its usage of the static `random` method of that class.

Exercise 7.25   Write the opposite version of Exercise 7.24, in which the program tries to guess a user's choice of a 5-digit number. The program should report if it detects that the user has changed their guess or made a mistake.

Exercise 7.26   Write another version of the program described in Exercise 4.5. The `Population` class should have a constructor that takes two arguments—a name for the town and the count of its inhabitants. The name of each town should be fixed for the life of the class's objects, once constructed, but the count may be changed via a public mutator. Include in the Population class an implementation of the following method

```
public String toString()
```

which returns a descriptive string containing the name of the town and the population count the time it was called. For instance,

```
"Market Flossing. Population 3507"
```

The main method should test the Population class by creating multiple instances, ensuring that each method is called at least once. Use the `print` and `println` methods of System.out to show the states of these objects, both before and after each time the objects are altered.

Exercise 7.27   Add a further method to the Population class of Exercise 7.26 so that it is possible to change the current population count by a small positive or negative amount. Define limits for the absolute size of a change at any one time, and refuse to alter the `count` attribute if the change is too great. Implement this test in the count's mutator method. Add further statements to the main method to test this extension in the behavior implemented by the class.

By this stage of the book, we have a firm basis on which to implement general object behavior in terms of sequences of statements, choices between alternative sets of statements, and the option of repeating statements an arbitrary number of times. All object behavior is made up from these three elements. In the next chapter, we look at the way in which some pre-defined Java utility classes can help to simplify the writing of classes.

8

Packages and Utility Classes

In this chapter, we introduce Java's *package* concept—a means of grouping related classes. We follow this with a description of several utility classes, such as Math, String, and StringBuffer, that are defined in some of the standard API packages. We also introduce some standard classes that simplify the formatting of numerical values and dates.

8.1 Packages

Many modern programming languages provide facilities to allow related components to be grouped together into named *modules*. Java's module facility is known as a *package*. A package consists of a collection of classes and *interfaces* (see Chapter 13) that are related in some way. Typically, the relationship is either one in which classes perform a similar role to one another—such as classes that handle input-output—or one in which classes form a cohesive unit relating to the performance of an overall task—such as the playing of a game of chess. The Java language has associated with it a set of packages known as the *Java Platform Core Application Programming Interface (API)*.[1] A large number of packages are defined in this API and it would not be possible to describe them all in detail within the scope of this book. Nevertheless, we shall describe and make use of classes defined in quite a few of them; in particular, the packages java.applet (Chapter 20), java.awt (Chapter 16), java.io (Chapter 12), java.lang, java.util (Chapter 10), and javax.swing (Chapter 17).

The classes defined in one package are usually made available in another by importing them, via an *import statement* at the start of a .java file.[2] Here are the two forms of an import statement:

```
// Import all of the classes and interfaces from the
// javax.swing package.
import javax.swing.*;
// Import just the ArrayList class from the java.util package.
import java.util.ArrayList;
```

The first of these implicitly imports all the visible definitions from the javax.swing package, while the second explicitly imports a single class—

---

[1] At the time of writing, the API version is 1.2.

[2] Package declarations come first, however; see below.

ArrayList—from the `java.util` package. Only one package or class at a time may be imported per statement. Classes imported in this way may be used to create objects as if they were classes we had defined for ourselves, for instance,

```
// Create a ArrayList object.
ArrayList list = new ArrayList();
```

If a class has not been imported, we can still access it by using its full name, with the package as a prefix:

```
// Create a LinkedList object.
java.util.LinkedList list = new java.util.LinkedList();
```

Note that the *fully qualified class name* is required in both places.

It is important to realize that an import statement does not bring the source of imported classes into a file. Rather, roughly speaking, it is an instruction to the compiler to tell it that we shall be using classes that are defined somewhere other than the current set of source files it is compiling. As such, it brings names from another package into the current *namespace*. Bringing classes from another package into the current namespace means that we have to modify the simplified name resolution that were first introduced in Section 4.10 and extended in Section 7.7. An extended set of rules that is used by the compiler to associate an identifier with the item to which it refers is as follows:

1. Inside a method, is there a matching method variable in scope?
2. Inside a method, is there a matching formal argument?
3. Inside a method or class body, is there a matching member name defined in the class—including in interfaces implemented by this class (see Chapter 13) or super classes extended by this class (see Chapter 14)?
4. Does the identifier match a class that has been explicitly imported (e.g., `java.util.ArrayList`)?
5. Is there a matching class or interface in the current package? This could be in another file, because packages may span source files.
6. Does the identifier match a visible implicitly imported class or interface (e.g., in the `javax.swing` package imported via `import javax.swing.*`)?
7. Does the identifier match one in the `java.lang` package that is implicitly accessible without the need for an import statement?

8.1.1 Creating a Package

All classes belong to a package, whether this is stated explicitly or not (see the fifth rule, above). By default, all classes belong to the *unnamed package*—a program-wide collecting point. It is straightforward to allocate classes to a named package; this is done by including a *package declaration* at the beginning of the source file containing the classes. Code 8.1 shows a package declaration to allocate the Ship class to the `Maritime` package.

Package declarations must be placed at the start of a source file, before any import statements. It is only possible to allocate a class to one package. The same package declaration should appear at the start of all source files containing classes

---

```
package Maritime;
import java.io.*;
import java.text.NumberFormat;
import java.util.Observable;

class Ship {
    ...
}
```

---

you wish to belong to that package. Classes belonging to a package do not need to include an import statement for that package in their source file. We say that all classes in the same package share *package access*—an access level that lies midway between public and private access.

While it is straightforward to allocate classes to packages, telling the compiler and interpreter where to find classes belonging to packages is a little more tricky. We said, above, that an import statement is an instruction to the compiler to tell it that we shall be using classes that are defined somewhere other than the current set of source files it is compiling. This means that you have to tell the compiler where to look for those packages, which means that you have to set its idea of a *classpath*. A classpath is a list of places—typically folders, directories, *jar files*, or *zip files*—where the compiler and interpreter look for `.class` files. For instance, the class files for the core API are stored in the file `rt.jar`. These classes are a standard part of the Java platform installation known as the *bootstrap classes*. Their whereabouts are known to the compiler and interpreter on your system. This means that, once you have installed Java on your system, you do not usually have to take any specific action to gain access to these core classes when you import them (see Appendix G). However, as soon as you start to define your own packages and import them, you need to modify the compiler's classpath so that it can find them. In general, the `.class` files belonging to a particular package should be stored in a folder (directory) bearing the same name as the package, and the package folder should be located directly beneath a folder named in the classpath. For instance, the `Ship.class` file from Code 8.1 would be stored in a folder called `Maritime` directly beneath somewhere on the classpath. Hierarchical package names are typically reflected in nested folders. For instance, `.class` files for classes defined in the package `outer.middle.inner` would be located in a folder `outer\middle\inner`[3] on the class path. See Appendix G for further details about how to modify the classpath for the `javac` compiler of JavaSoft's Java platform.

Allocating classes to packages introduces a third level of access to the public and private access that we have seen so far, namely, *package access*. Any class, method, or class attribute that is not explicitly labeled `public`, `private`, or `protected`[4] is said to have package access and is accessible from within all other classes defined within that same package. If we choose to place our classes in the default unnamed

---

[3] Directory `outer/middle/inner` on UNIX and Linux systems.
[4] See Section 14.7.1.

package, then this is unlikely to cause any problems. If we choose to place them in named packages, however, we will need to think carefully about whether a method should be defined to have public access or package access. In Section 14.7.1, we introduce a fourth type, *protected access* which lies between public and package access in terms of accessibility.

The ability to import packages of pre-defined classes can greatly simplify the task of program creation. We gain access to a wide (and ever-increasing) range of reusable components that save us from having to reinvent things that have already been done. This brings big savings in terms of time and effort, and a generally available implementation of a commonly used class is much more likely to have been thoroughly tested and debugged than one we might create for ourselves. In the next few sections, we look at some of the classes defined in the `java.lang` package that greatly simplify the creation of programs that require math functions or involve string manipulation.

8.2   The Math Class

The `Math` class is defined in the `java.lang` package. It consists entirely of static methods and static variables, many of which are used to supply commonly used mathematical values and functions. It defines two static variables for the mathematical constants `PI` (the ratio of a circle's circumference to its diameter) and `E` (the base of natural logarithms). In addition to these, it defines the following static methods, some of which are summarized in Table 8.1.

- Trigonometric functions: `acos`, `asin`, `atan`, `cos`, `sin`, and `tan`. Each of these takes a single `double` argument and returns a `double` result. In addition, `toDegrees` and `toRadians` convert their argument from degrees to radians and vice versa.

Table 8.1   Selected methods of the Math class

	Method and Arguments
static double	abs(double value)
static int	abs(int value)
static double	cos(double radians)
static double	exp(double value)
static double	log(double value)
static double	min(double x, double y)
static double	max(double x, double y)
static int	min(int x, int y)
static int	max(int x, int y)
static double	pow(double x, double y)
static double	random()
static int	round(double x)
static double	sin(double radians)
static double	sqrt(double value)
static double	tan(double radians)
static double	toDegrees(double radians)
static double	toRadians(double degrees)

- Absolute value: abs. There are four versions for the primitive types double, float, int, and long. If the argument is negative, then its positive equivalent is returned. Care must be taken if the argument is the smallest possible int or long value, because they have no positive equivalent.
- Minimum and maximum functions: min and max. There are four versions of each of these, each taking two arguments of a different primitive numerical type and returning either the minimum or the maximum value of the pair.
- Rounding functions: ceil, floor, rint, and round. These return integer values of their floating point arguments with different characteristics.
- Random function: random. This takes no argument and returns a double value in the range 0.0 to 1.0, but not including 1.0. We use this method a lot in generating random integer values. The easiest way to generate an integer in the range

```
0 <= num < max
```

is as follows:

```
int num = (int) (max*Math.random());
```

- Common mathematical functions: exp returns the value of Math.E to the power of its argument; log returns the natural logarithm of its argument; pow raises its first argument to the power of the second; sqrt returns the square root of its argument.
- Remainder: IEEEremainder. This returns the floating point remainder of its two arguments. The name derives from the IEEE standard for floating point arithmetic[Ins85].

8.3   The String Class

The String class is defined in the java.lang package. Strings are an important part of the Java language. Unlike values of the primitive types, strings are proper objects. This class defines a large number of methods that allow strings to be examined, tested, and manipulated. Some of these have been summarized in Table 8.2. A String object is automatically created by writing a literal string between a pair of *double quote* characters ("), for instance: "This is a String object". The number of characters in a string can be determined by sending it a length message, which returns an integer:

```
String s = "hello";
System.out.println(s+" has a length of "+s.length());
```

The string "hello" has a length of 5. It is possible to represent a string with a zero length by writing just a pair of double quotes: "". If it is necessary to include a double quote character within a string, then it must be preceded by a *backslash character* to form an *escape sequence*, for example,

```
String hearsay = "She said, \"You must be mad!\"";
```

	Table 8.2 Selected methods of the String class
	Method and Arguments
	String(String s)
char	charAt(int index)
int	compareTo(String s)
String	concat(String s)
boolean	equals(Object o)
boolean	equalsIgnoreCase(String s)
int	indexOf(String s)
int	indexOf(String s, int startPos)
int	indexOf(int c)
int	indexOf(int c, int startPos)
int	length()
boolean	regionMatches(int offset,String s,int sOffset, int len)
boolean	regionMatches(boolean ignoreCase, int offset,String s,int sOffset, int len)
String	replace(char c,char replacement)
boolean	startsWith(String prefix)
String	toLowerCase()
String	toUpperCase()
String	trim()

8.3.1   String Comparisons

One of the most common tests on a string is whether it is identical to another string; that is, whether the two strings have the same length and match character-for-character. Section 6.1.5 warned us that this process cannot simply involve a use of one of the equality operators (== or !=). Code 8.2 shows a small program to read words from the user and find which is the longest word. It uses the `nextWord` method of the SimpleInput class described in Section 5.6.

This program illustrates the `equals` method of the String class, which is the correct way to test for string equality. The `equals` method of one String object takes a reference to a second String as an argument and returns a `boolean` result that indicates whether the two strings match exactly or not. As each String is read, an `equals` message is sent to it asking it to compare itself against the terminating word, "END". If there is not a match, then the body of the loop is entered and the length of the new word is determined for comparison against the longest found so far. If we had written the terminating condition of the loop as

```
word != terminatingWord
```

then this would never become `false`, because the String object returned by the `nextWord` method would never have the same object reference as that held in `terminatingWord`.

Unfortunately, the potential for confusion over comparing object references is compounded in the case of String objects because the language definition requires Java compilers to make a special case out of String literal objects. The same object reference is used for all identical literal string objects. Consider the example in Code 8.3.

Code 8.2   Find the longest word input by the user (`LongestWord.java`)

```
// Find the longest word on the input.
// Input is terminated by the word: "END", which is not
// counted.
class LongestWord {
    public static void main(String[] args){
        SimpleInput keyboard = new SimpleInput();
        String longestWord = "";
        int longestLength = 0;
        final String terminatingWord = "END";

        String word = keyboard.nextWord();
        while(!word.equals(terminatingWord)){
            final int nextLength = word.length();
            if(nextLength > longestLength){
                longestWord = word;
                longestLength = nextLength;
            }
            word = keyboard.nextWord();
        }

        if(longestLength > 0){
            System.out.println("The longest word was: "+longestWord);
        }
    }
}
```

The language rule requires that the three literal "dog" strings in Code 8.3 must be stored as a single String object. Figure 8.1 illustrates the relationship between the variables and the different String objects. What this means is that both the comparison of s1 with s3 and that of s1 with the string literal *will* succeed, contrary to the rule for other object types. After this, things appear to go wrong; creating a new String object directly always results in a new object reference, so doggy will refer to an object that is different from the one s3 refers to. Furthermore, no matter what a user types in response to the "Dog or cat?" prompt, the reference returned by nextWord will always be to a different String object, because it did not arise from a literal string in the program code. Therefore, the output from this example will always be the following:

```
s1 == s3
s1 == "dog"
Dog or cat?
You didn't type dog.
```

The only safe rule is, *never* use the equality operators in tests involving content equality; always use the equals method and you will not get it wrong.

The equalsIgnoreCase method of the String class makes a similar comparison but ignores upper and lowercase character differences between the two strings:

```
// This is true.
s1.equalsIgnoreCase("DOG")
```

Code 8.3   Literal strings share the same reference (`SameString.java`)

```java
    // Demonstrate that, Strings are treated entirely
    // differently from other objects :-(
class SameString {
    public static void main(String[] args){
        String s1 = "dog";
        String s2 = "It's a dog's life";
        String s3 = "dog";

        // Demonstrate that identical literals share the same reference.
        if(s1 == s2){
            System.out.println("s1 == s2");
        }
        if(s1 == s3){
            System.out.println("s1 == s3");
        }
        if(s1 == "dog"){
            System.out.println("s1 == \"dog\"");
        }

        // Now show where things start to go wrong.
        String doggy = new String(s1);
        if(s1 == doggy){
            System.out.println("s1 == doggy");
        }

        SimpleInput keyboard = new SimpleInput();
        System.out.println("Dog or cat?");
        String userDog = keyboard.nextWord();
        if(s1 == userDog){
            System.out.println(s1);
        }
        else{
            System.out.println("You didn't type dog.");
        }
    }
}
```

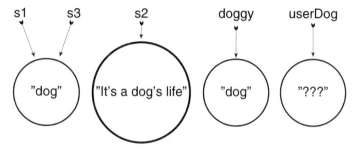

Figure 8.1 Duplicate literal strings are the same object (sometimes!)

One of the `regionMatches` methods can be used if a case-insensitive match is required on only part of a string.

8.3.2 The `compareTo` Method

In some circumstances, a simple test for equality is not what we want; rather it can be useful to know whether one string comes before or after another in *lexicographic ordering*. The `compareTo` method returns an integer indicating the Unicode distance between the two strings being compared. If the two strings are identical, then the value returned is zero. Otherwise, it is the value of the difference between the first pair of non-matching characters. This value will be negative if the string to which the message is sent comes before the actual argument string in lexicographic ordering and positive if it comes after. Here are some examples:

```
String s1 = "dog", s2 = "apple", s3 = "cat";
s1.compareTo("dog") == 0
s2.compareTo("book") == -1
s3.compareTo("apple") == 2
// There are 32 characters between the upper case and
// lower case character ranges.
s3.compareTo("Cat") == 32
```

8.3.3 The Immutability of Strings

An important characteristic of strings is that they are *immutable objects*—once defined their contents cannot be modified. A string's immutability means that it is always safe to return a reference to a private string attribute from an object's accessor—we do not need to return a copy—because any client receiving that reference will be unable to modify the attribute via the reference. Code 8.4 illustrates such an accessor for the Ship class.

Only the Ship class is able to set the name of a Ship, using its `setName` mutator, and that name cannot be altered by other objects obtaining a reference to the String object via `getName`.

A further consequence of this immutability is that building a string by concatenation—using +=, for instance (see Section 5.5.4)—might not do exactly what you would expect. In the following assignment example, we appear to append one string to another, but this is not actually what happens.

```
String noun = "dog";
// Make noun a plural.
noun += "s";
```

The result of this example is that *three* separate String objects are created—"dog", "s", and "dogs". Because the object referenced by noun is immutable, we cannot simply add an extra character onto its current contents. Instead, concatenating "s" actually requires a completely new string to be created ("dogs"), containing the combined contents of the other two strings. The variable noun is then made to refer to the newly created object.

Code 8.4   It is safe to return a reference to a String attribute

```
class Ship {
    public Ship(String name){
        setName(name);
    }

    ...

        // We don't need to copy the attribute.
    public String getName(){
        return name;
    }

        // Set the ship's name.
    private void setName(String name){
        this.name = name;
    }

    // Immutable name object.
    private String name;
}
```

Code 8.5   Illustrate mutating String methods (`StringMethods.java`)

```
    // Illustrate various 'mutating' methods of the String class.
class StringMethods {
    public static void main(String[] args){
        // Example strings to be 'mutated'
        String hello = "hello, ", world = "world.";
        String mixed = "ToWerBLocKS";
        String trailing = "I have too much space.           ";

        System.out.println(hello.concat(world));
        System.out.println(mixed.toUpperCase());
        System.out.println(mixed.toLowerCase());
        System.out.println(trailing.trim());
        System.out.println(trailing.replace(' ','*'));
    }
}
```

There are several string methods whose names appear to contradict the principle of immutability—concat, replace, toLowerCase, toUpperCase, trim; these methods simply return a new string whose contents reflect the result of the operation as it would have been on the receiver of the message, and the receiver remains unchanged. The example in Code 8.5 briefly illustrates these methods. The space characters in the strings have been shown explicitly to emphasize the effects on them.

The new strings constructed by this example would be:

```
"hello,␣world."
"TOWERBLOCKS"
"towerblocks"
"I␣have␣too␣much␣space."
"I*have*too*much*space.**********"
```

A string's immutability means that operations in which a string must be built up from pieces, or manipulated in various ways once created, are often better performed on objects of the `StringBuffer` class, which are not immutable. StringBuffer is discussed in Section 8.4.

8.3.4   Parsing Strings

A common task involving strings is that of *parsing* them, that is, examining their contents for particular characters or sequences of characters. The individual characters in a string may be referenced by their *index*—a value in the range 0 to `length()-1`. The character at a particular index may be obtained using the `charAt` method. There are several versions of the two methods for searching a string for characters and substrings—indexOf and `lastIndexOf`. Both take either a char or String argument and an optional index position from which to start the search. Code 8.6 illustrates how we might find the number of spaces in a string.

Two versions of `indexOf` are shown. The first establishes the position of the first space, starting from the beginning of the string. If there is no space, then `indexOf` returns the value -1 as strings are indexed from 0. If at least one space is found, the body of the loop is entered. In order to continue the search, the second version of `indexOf` is used. This takes a position in the string from which the search is to start; here, this will be one place beyond the position where the last space was found. If a space occurs as the last character in this example, it is not an error to pass in an index that is outside the bounds of the string.

Code 8.6   Count the number of spaces in a string

```
    // Return a count of the number of spaces in s.
public int countSpaces(String s){
    int count = 0;
    // Look for the first.
    int index = s.indexOf(' ');

    // indexOf returns -1 on failure.
    while(index >= 0){
        // We found one.
        count += 1;
        // Look for the next just after the last one.
        index = s.indexOf(' ',index+1);
    }
    return count;
}
```

Code 8.7   Count the number of times substring occurs in s

```
    // Return a count of how many times substring is found in s.
public int substringCount(String s, String substring){
    int count = 0;
    // Look for the first.
    int index = s.indexOf(substring);

    // indexOf returns -1 on failure.
    while(index >= 0){
        // We found one.
        count += 1;
        // Look for the next just after the last one.
        index = s.indexOf(substring,index+1);
    }
    return count;
}
```

Two further versions of indexOf take a string as an argument in order to detect substring matches. These work in a similar way, and Code 8.7 illustrates an example to count the number of times a particular substring occurs in a string.

In Section 12.14 we describe some other ways in which the contents of a string may be analyzed using the StringTokenizer class.

8.3.5 Converting Primitive Values to Strings

Sometimes it is necessary to obtain a string representation of a primitive type value, such as an int, double, or boolean. The following attempt to do this is not allowed in Java, however.

```
int value = 32;
...
// The following is illegal ...
// Try to make a String from an int.
String valueString = value;
```

A case where turning primitive values into strings is necessary is when they are output using one of the print or println methods of the System.out, for example,

```
System.out.print(value);
```

In order to output these values, print and println must obtain an equivalent String object. They might do this by passing the value to a valueOf method of the String class. There is one valueOf method for each primitive type in the language and they are static methods, which means that they are usually used in the form String.valueOf. The incorrect example, above, should be written as

```
int value = 32;
...
// Obtain a string representation of intValue.
String valueString = String.valueOf(value);
```

The valueOf method for boolean values returns the strings "true" and "false".

In Section 5.3.6 we saw that it is common to use + when printing mixed output consisting of strings and numbers, for instance,

```
System.out.println("The sum is: "+(x+y));
```

This suggests the following legitimate alternative to the use of valueOf if we wish to obtain a string from a primitive value:

```
int intValue = 32;
...
// Obtain a string representation of intValue.
String intString = ""+intValue;
```

You should feel free to use whichever form best communicates your intention.

Exercise 8.1 Complete the implementation of the control method shown in Code 8.8. The control method should use the nextWord method of the controller's input attribute to read words from the user until a string matching terminating-Word is read. Each word read should be interpreted as a command for the ship. If the user inputs the word "move", for instance, a move message should be sent to the ship which has been passed as a parameter to control. Commands to set a ship's speed or course should be followed by a numerical value, read with nextDouble,

---

Code 8.8 An outline of the ShipController class (`ShipController.java`)

```
        // An outline for a ShipController class.
        // The implementation of the control method is incomplete.
        // (see ShipControllerMain.java)
class ShipController {
        // Read the controlling commands from r.
    public ShipController(SimpleInput input){
        this.input = input;
    }

        // Read commands to control the ship from the SimpleInput
        // object passed to the constructor.
        // Finish this method when the specified terminating word
        // is read from the user.
    public void control(Ship s,String terminatingWord){
        final SimpleInput keyboard = getInput();
        // Add the rest here ...

    }

    private SimpleInput getInput(){
        return input;
    }

    // Read input from the user using the reference received on creation.
    private final SimpleInput input;
}
```

Code 8.9   A main method for using a ShipController (`ShipControllerMain.java`)

```
        // Set up a ShipController to allow a ship to be
        // controlled from the keyboard.
class ShipControllerMain {
    public static void main(String[] args){
        // Set up the input reader.
        SimpleInput keyboard = new SimpleInput();
        // Ask the user for a 'terminating word'.
        System.out.println("Which word will you use to end the commands?");
        String terminatingWord = keyboard.nextWord();

        // Create the controller.
        ShipController controller = new ShipController(keyboard);
        // Create the ship.
        Ship argo = new Ship();

        System.out.println("Now input your commands.");
        // Ask the controller to control the ship.
        controller.control(argo,terminatingWord);
        System.out.println("Control of the ship is over.");
    }
}
```

which is to be passed to either the `setSpeed` or `setCourse` method of the ship. Try to make your tests of user commands accept both uppercase and lowercase words. Code 8.9 contains a main method to prompt the user for what to do.

Exercise 8.2   If your skills in trigonometry are good enough, add a `moveTo` method to the ShipController class in your solution to Exercise 8.1. This should take an (x,y) position to which the ship should be moved at its current speed. Start by calculating the correct heading for the ship based upon its current (x,y) position, and then send a series of `move` messages to the ship in a loop until it arrives. Because of the limited precision of floating point numbers, it will probably not always be possible to make it arrive at the exact destination required. Instead, the termination test for the method's loop should allow for a small margin of error between the final position and the ship's current position.

Investigate whether recalculating the required heading each time around the loop, instead of just once before the loop, allows you to arrive closer to the destination point.

What happens if a ship's speed is zero when this method is called?

8.4   The StringBuffer Class

The `StringBuffer` class is defined in the `java.lang` package. In Section 8.3.3, we noted that a String object is immutable; that is, its contents cannot be changed once it has been constructed. While it is relatively easy to use the `'+'` operator and

Table 8.3 Selected methods of the StringBuffer class

	Method and Arguments
	StringBuffer()
	StringBuffer(int length)
	StringBuffer(String s)
StringBuffer	append(char c)
StringBuffer	append(double d)
StringBuffer	append(String s)
char	charAt(int index)
int	capacity()
StringBuffer	insert(int offset,char c)
StringBuffer	insert(int offset,double d)
StringBuffer	insert(int offset,String s)
int	length()
StringBuffer	replace(int start,int end,String s)
StringBuffer	reverse()
void	setCharAt(int index,char c)
void	setLength(int length)
String	subString(int start)
String	subString(int start, int end)

Code 8.10 Using a StringBuffer to created a fixed-width formatted integer

```
    // Return a string representing number right adjusted
    // in a field of the given width.
public static String formatInt(int number,int width){
    // Create space for the full width of the string.
    StringBuffer formattedInt = new StringBuffer(width);
    // Append a string version of the number.
    formattedInt.append(number);
    // How many extra spaces are required?
    int spaces = width-formattedInt.length();

    // Prefix the given number of spaces.
    for(int i = 0; i < spaces; i++){
        formattedInt.insert(0," ");
    }
    // Convert the StringBuffer to a String.
    return formattedInt.toString();
}
```

String's methods to construct new strings which are modifications of existing ones, there are many circumstances in which this is unnecessarily inefficient in terms of object construction and *garbage collection*. StringBuffer overcomes many of these inefficiencies when circumstances effectively require mutation of a string. Table 8.3 shows some of StringBuffer's methods. Code 8.10 shows a simple example of how to build a fixed-width string representation of an integer value.[5]

---

[5] The example in Code 8.10 is purely for illustrative purposes, as the java.text package provides a more comprehensive set of classes for formatting number-related data (see Section 8.6.2).

The class has three constructors taking either:

- No argument. A default initial buffer space of sixteen characters will be allocated. The buffer contains no characters to start with.
- An integer specifying an explicit amount of buffer space to create initially. The buffer contains no characters to start with.
- A String indicating the buffer's initial contents. The initial buffer space will be sixteen characters more than the length of this string.

The size of the buffer following construction is not fixed for the life of the object. New space is automatically made available to the buffer, if necessary, as further characters are added to it via its `append` and `insert` methods. It is important to understand that the buffer size is distinct from the length of the contents held in the buffer at any time—creating a buffer of a particular length does not fill the buffer with space characters, for instance. The `ensureCapacity` method makes it possible to ensure that a minimum amount of space is available in the buffer. If the final size of the buffer is known in advance of its use, it is a good idea to make sure it has this capacity, as this will reduce the need for fresh space to be allocated as its contents are built up.

As illustrated in Code 8.10, `append` methods exist to allow string representations of primitive type values to be appended, as well as Strings. The `insert` methods take an index position at which the insertion is made, pushing any existing contents from that position onwards to the right. The character at a particular position may be replaced with `setCharAt`, and `reverse` reverses the buffer's contents. Truncation of the buffer's contents is possible with the `setLength` method. If its argument is greater than the length of the current contents, then *null characters* (`'\u0000'`—see Section A.6.1) are appended up to the indicated length.

Code 8.11 shows an example of a class that uses string buffers to format strings in various ways within a fixed-width field. The `leftAdjust` method returns a String with extra spaces to the right of its argument according to its width argument. The length of the returned string should be equal to width. The `rightAdjust` method places extra spaces before its argument, and the `center` method distributes spaces on either side of its argument. The private `spaces` method does work for each of these methods by creating a buffer with the required number of space characters. The `leftAdjust` method illustrates an important feature of many of the methods of the StringBuffer class; they return the modified buffer object as their result. This makes it possible to chain together operations in a single statement, such as:

```
spaces(width-stringLength).append(s).toString()
```

The buffer returned from `spaces` has a string appended to it, and the resulting buffer is asked to return a String version of the contents of the buffer. We see a similar use in the `center` method:

```
spaces(leftSpace).append(s).append(spaces(rightSpace)).toString()
```

Code 8.11   Positioning text within a fixed-width field (`StringFormatter.java`)

```
    // Provide static methods to position or center a String within
    // a given width.
class StringFormatter {
    // Pad out s with spaces after it.
    public static String leftAdjust(String s,int width){
        final int stringLength = s.length();
        if(stringLength >= width){
            // This covers the case when width is negative, too.
            return s;
        }
        else{
            return spaces(width-stringLength).insert(0,s).toString();
        }
    }


    // Pad out s with spaces before it.
    public static String rightAdjust(String s,int width){
        final int stringLength = s.length();
        if(stringLength >= width){
            // This covers the case when width is negative, too.
            return s;
        }
        else{
            return spaces(width-stringLength).append(s).toString();
        }
    }


    public static String center(String s,int width){
        final int stringLength = s.length();
        if(stringLength >= width){
            // This covers the case when width is negative, too.
            return s;
        }
        else{
            final int numSpaces = width-stringLength;
            final int leftSpace = numSpaces/2,
                      rightSpace = numSpaces-leftSpace;
            return spaces(leftSpace).append(s).
                                append(spaces(rightSpace)).toString();
        }
    }

        // Return a StringBuffer full of spaces.
    private static StringBuffer spaces(int numSpaces){
        if(numSpaces <= 0){
            return new StringBuffer();
        }
        else{
            StringBuffer spaces = new StringBuffer();
            for(int i = 0; i < numSpaces; i++){
                spaces.append(' ');
            }
```

(Continued)

Code 8.11   (*Continued*)

```
            return spaces;
        }
    }
}
```

8.5   A Simplified Ship Class

By this point, we have covered sufficient Java to be able to present a simplified version of a complete Ship class. Code 8.12 contains a full definition for the class `SimpleShip` which, apart from its name and the way it reports its position, behaves in a way that is broadly similar to the components of the full Ship class that we have looked at in previous chapters. Mostly the class illustrates attributes, accessors, and mutators, but it also includes examples of final variables, class variables, and use of static methods from the Math class (see Section 8.2).

Code 8.12   A simplified version of the full Ship class

```
        // Simple definition of a SimpleShip class with position,
        // speed and course information.
public class SimpleShip {
    // Default position, course and speed.
    public static final double DEFAULT_X = 25.0, DEFAULT_Y = 25.0;
    public static final double DEFAULT_COURSE = 0.0, DEFAULT_SPEED = 5.0;

        // Constructors.
    public SimpleShip(double x, double y, double course, double speed){
        setPosition(x,y);
        setCourse(course);
        setSpeed(speed);
    }

    public SimpleShip(double x, double y, double course){
        this(x,y,course,DEFAULT_SPEED);
    }

    public SimpleShip(double x, double y){
        this(x,y,DEFAULT_COURSE,DEFAULT_SPEED);
    }

    public SimpleShip(){
        // Set default position, course and speed for this ship.
        this(DEFAULT_X,DEFAULT_Y,DEFAULT_COURSE,DEFAULT_SPEED);
    }

    public SimpleShip(String name){
        this();
        setName(name);
    }
```

(Continued)

Code 8.12   (*Continued*)

```
    // Public mutators.
public void setPosition(double x, double y){
    setX(x);
    setY(y);
}

public void setSpeed(double newSpeed){
    speed = newSpeed;
}

public void setCourse(double newCourse){
    // Keep degrees in the range [0..360)
    final double numDegrees = 360.0;
    if(newCourse < 0){
        newCourse = numDegrees+(newCourse%numDegrees);
    }
    course = newCourse % numDegrees;
}

    // Other public methods.
public void report(){
    String name = getName();
    if((name != null) && !name.equals("")){
        System.out.print(name+": ");
    }
    System.out.print("Position is ("+getX()+","+getY()+"), ");
    System.out.print("Course is "+getCourse()+", ");
    System.out.print("Speed is "+getSpeed());
    System.out.println();
}

public void move(){
    double radians = Math.toRadians(getCourse());
    setPosition(getX()+speed*Math.cos(radians),
                getY()+speed*Math.sin(radians));
}

    // Accessors to the basic attributes.
public double getX(){
    return x;
}

public double getY(){
    return y;
}

public double getCourse(){
    return course;
}
```

(*Continued*)

Code 8.12   (*Continued*)

```java
public double getSpeed(){
    return speed;
}

public String getName(){
    return name;
}

    // Private mutators.
private void setX(double xval){
    x   = xval;
}

private void setY(double yval){
    y   = yval;
}

private void setName(String s){
    if(s != null){
        name = s;
    }
}

/* Private data. */
// (x,y) co-ordinates in the ocean.
private double x = DEFAULT_X, y = DEFAULT_Y;
// Speed and course.
private double speed = DEFAULT_SPEED, course = DEFAULT_COURSE;
// A name for the ship.
private String name = "";
}
```

Do not worry about how the move method works to calculate a ship's new position, as this requires some understanding of trigonometry. The cos, sin, and toRadians methods are all static methods of the Math class (see Section 8.2).

The setCourse mutator illustrates usage of an if-statement to check whether the course being set is positive or negative. It also includes use of the modulus operator (%) to ensure that the new course is always a positive value less than 360 degrees (a value stored in a final variable).

The SimpleShip class may be used in similar ways to the examples shown for the Ship class in Chapter 3. Code 8.13 shows an example main method.

The main difference between this and the earlier examples is the lack of a GUI, so this example produces the following output on the terminal:

```
Position is (25.0,25.0), Course is 0.0, Speed is 5.0
Position is (30.0,25.0), Course is 0.0, Speed is 5.0
```

Code 8.13 Creating and using a SimpleShip object (`SimpleShipMain1.java`)

```
        // An illustration of object creation.
class SimpleShipMain1 {
    public static void main(String[] args){
        // Define a method variable to refer to a Ship object.
        SimpleShip argo = new SimpleShip();

        // Construct a new Ship object.
        argo.report();
        argo.move();
        argo.report();
    }
}
```

Exercise 8.3   Modify the SimpleShip class shown in Code 8.12 so that it contains a maximum speed class variable. Each time it receives a `setSpeed` message, it should use the value of this to decide how to respond. Alternative responses to a request to set a speed beyond the maximum value might be to ignore the request, or to use the maximum value instead.

Exercise 8.4   How should the SimpleShip's `setSpeed` method respond to a negative speed value? Make sure this takes into account the maximum value correctly.

Exercise 8.5   It has been decided that it is unrealistic for the `setCourse` method to permit arbitrary changes of course without its moving position. Modify the `setCourse` method so that a *change* of less than 10 degrees is the maximum permitted without automatically causing the ship's `move` method to be called. A request to change by more than 10 degrees at any one time should be implemented as a sequence of 10 degree changes, each followed by a move, followed by any remaining number of degrees less than 10. For instance, suppose that a ship's current course is 30 degrees and a request is made to set its course to 65 degrees. This would be internally implemented as three changes of 10 degrees, each accompanied by a movement, and one change of 5 degrees.

8.6   Locale-Specific Processing

Number and Date printing are two members of a group of tasks that are often referred to as *locale* specific. In other words, the results should be dependent upon the country and culture in which they are performed. A program always runs within a particular locale, and it is not usually necessary to do anything to set the runtime environment's idea of the current locale. What a programmer must bear in mind, however, is that the locales in which a program might be run could be quite different from the locale in which it was developed. The `Locale` class, defined in the `java.util` package, provides a convenient location for locale-specific information. This includes details of the correct currency symbol, which characters should be used as decimal and thousands separators when printing numbers, whether month numbers appear before

	Table 8.4 Selected methods of the Locale class
	Method and Arguments
	Locale(String language,String country)
	Locale(String language,String country,String variant)
static Locale[]	getAvailableLocales()
String	getCountry()
static Locale	getDefault()
String	getDisplayCountry()
String	getDisplayLanguage()
String	getDisplayName()
String	getVariant()

day numbers when printing dates, and so on. In Section 8.6.1, we discuss the Locale class, and in Sections 8.6.2 and 8.6.3 we discuss how numbers and dates may be formatted in locale-specific ways.

8.6.1   The Locale Class

The `Locale` class is defined in the `java.util` package. It allows locale-specific information to be conveniently located in a single object. Classes performing locale-specific tasks, such as `DateFormat` and `NumberFormat`, make use of this information in order to ensure that they format data correctly. Table 8.4 shows some of Locale's methods. A locale may be specified at three levels: country, language, and variant. Not all locales will need to differentiate at all three levels, although usage of country and language are common. The default locale for an application may be obtained via the static `getDefault` method of the Locale class. There are also several publicly available static references defined within the class, for locales such as CHINA, FRANCE, GERMANY, JAPAN, KOREA, UK, US, etc.

The country and language components of a locale are formally defined by two standards: ISO 639 for language and ISO 3166 for country. String values drawn from these standards may be passed to the constructor for Locale to create a Locale object, if a convenience reference is not already defined within the class. The static `getAvailableLocales` method returns an array of available Locale objects. Methods such as `getDisplayCountry`, `getDisplayLanguage`, and `getDisplayVariant` return strings that give user-readable descriptions of the three sub-divisions of a locale. Code 8.14 shows an example of how some of the descriptive information on the default locale may be obtained. It also shows how the default locale may be changed for the duration of the program's execution.[6]

The output from this example might be as follows:

```
United States, English, English (United States),
USA, eng
Deutschland, Deutsch, Deutsch (Deutschland),
DEU, deu
```

In neither case is there any variant information.

---

[6] Permanently setting the default locale for your environment might be a facility offered by your operating system.

Code 8.14 Printing information on the default locale (`LocaleMain1.java`)

```java
import java.util.Locale;

class LocaleMain1 {
    public static void main(String[] args){
        // Show details of the default locale.
        showLocale();
        // Set a different default.
        Locale.setDefault(Locale.GERMANY);
        showLocale();
    }

    // Print details of the default locale.
    public static void showLocale(){
        Locale loc = Locale.getDefault();
        System.out.print(loc.getDisplayCountry()+", ");
        System.out.print(loc.getDisplayLanguage()+", ");
        System.out.print(loc.getDisplayName()+", ");
        System.out.println(loc.getDisplayVariant());
        System.out.print(loc.getISO3Country()+", ");
        System.out.println(loc.getISO3Language());
    }
}
```

8.6.2 Number Formatting

The `NumberFormat` class, defined in the `java.text` package, provides methods that allow locale-specific formatting of numerical values, such as which character is used to separate thousands, and as a decimal separator. It also allows control over how many pre-decimal and post-decimal places should be included in the formatted value. Table 8.5 shows some of NumberFormat's methods. Code 8.15 shows an example that uses some of its `setMinimumFractionDigits`, `setMaximumFractionDigits`, `setMinimumIntegerDigits`, and `setMaximumIntegerDigits` methods.

A formatting object for numbers is obtained via either the `getInstance` or `getNumberInstance` method. The various `format` methods defined in the NumberFormat class take either a `double` or a `long` value. The output from this example is as follows:

```
Truncated PI = 3.14159
Truncated PI = 0,003.14159
```

In the first case, the number of decimal places is limited to five. In the second, a minimum of four digits before the decimal point is required, so the result is prefixed with leading zeros. Notice that a comma is the thousands separator in the locale used with this example.

The `getCurrencyInstance` and `getPercentInstance` methods return objects that specialize in formatting money and percentage values. The example in Code 8.16 shows a simple usage of both.

Table 8.5   Selected methods of the NumberFormat class

	Method and Arguments
static NumberFormat	getCurrencyInstance()
static NumberFormat	getInstance()
static NumberFormat	getInstance(Locale locale)
String	format(double num)
String	format(long num)
int	getMaximumFractionDigits()
int	getMaximumIntegerDigits()
int	getMinimumFractionDigits()
int	getMinimumIntegerDigits()
static NumberFormat	getNumberInstance()
static NumberFormat	getPercentInstance()
Number	parse(String s) throws ParseException
void	setMaximumFractionDigits(int max)
void	setMaximumIntegerDigits(int max)
void	setMinimumFractionDigits(int min)
void	setMinimumIntegerDigits(int min)

Code 8.15   Adjust the formatting of floating-point numbers (`NumberFormatMain1.java`)

```
import java.text.*;

class NumberFormatMain1 {
    public static void main(String[] args){
        NumberFormat formatter = NumberFormat.getNumberInstance();
        // The effect of setting minimum and maximum digits.
        formatter.setMaximumFractionDigits(5);
        System.out.println("Truncated PI = "+formatter.format(Math.PI));
        formatter.setMinimumIntegerDigits(4);
        System.out.println("Truncated PI = "+formatter.format(Math.PI));

    }
}
```

The output from this in the US locale would be:

```
$3.53
35%
```

Note the way in which the correct currency symbol has been automatically included with the monetary amount.

The `getNumberInstance` method will often return an object of the `DecimalFormat` class, which contains further methods for increased control over decimal output. Code 8.17 shows how the reference returned from `getNumber-Instance` may be cast when this is the case.

Code 8.16 Formatting monetary and percentage values (`NumberFormatMain2.java`)

```java
import java.text.*;

class NumberFormatMain2 {
    public static void main(String[] args){
        NumberFormat money = NumberFormat.getCurrencyInstance();
        System.out.println(money.format(3.53));

        NumberFormat percent = NumberFormat.getPercentInstance();
        System.out.println(percent.format(.353));
    }

}
```

Code 8.17 Using methods of DecimalFormat for format control (`NumberFormatMain3.java`)

```java
import java.text.*;

class NumberFormatMain3 {
    public static void main(String[] args){
        // The effect of including/excluding the decimal separator.
        DecimalFormat formatter =
                    (DecimalFormat) NumberFormat.getNumberInstance();
        formatter.setDecimalSeparatorAlwaysShown(true);
        System.out.println(formatter.format(3.0));
        formatter.setDecimalSeparatorAlwaysShown(false);
        System.out.println(formatter.format(3.0));
    }
}
```

In this particular example, the `setDecimalSeparatorAlwaysShown` method is used to control whether a decimal point should be shown if there is no fractional part. The output from this example is as follows:

```
3.
3
```

The `parse` methods of NumberFormat allow a String to be parsed and an object of one of the numeric wrapper classes (Section 10.4) returned. In fact, NumberFormat is a highly sophisticated class that allows general locale-specific formats for numbers to be described and data parsed and formatted according to these. Within the scope of this book, it is not possible to look further into these aspects.

Exercise 8.6 Write a program to print some monetary values in your default locale, and that of a different country.

Table 8.6	Selected methods of the DateFormat class
	Method and Arguments
Calendar	getCalendar();
static DateFormat	getDateInstance()
static DateFormat	getDateInstance(int style)
static DateFormat	getDateInstance(int style,Locale locale)
static DateFormat	getDateTimeInstance()
static DateFormat	getDateTimeInstance(int dstyle,int tstyle)
static DateFormat	getDateTimeInstance(int dstyle,int tstyle,Locale locale)
static DateFormat	getInstance()
static DateFormat	getTimeInstance()
static DateFormat	getTimeInstance(int style)
static DateFormat	getTimeInstance(int style,Locale locale)
Date	parse(String s) throws ParseException

Exercise 8.7   Select a locale with a different decimal separator character from your own and format some decimal values. Many continental European countries use a comma for the decimal separator, whereas the USA and the United Kingdom use a decimal point.

8.6.3   Date Formatting

The `DateFormat` class, defined in the `java.text` package, provides a means to format dates and times in locale-specific ways. A range of different styles—SHORT, MEDIUM, LONG, and FULL are also available. Table 8.6 shows some of NumberFormat's methods. A date formatting object is normally obtained via one of DateFormat's `getDateInstance` methods. Without an argument, this will return a DateFormat object to format dates in the default format for the current locale. Alternatively, one of the style values given above may be used to request more or less detail in the formatted date. By default, the formatter will use information from the current locale, but a version of `getDateInstance` exists that takes both a style and a Locale argument. The example in Code 8.18 illustrates each version of this method to print a particular date in the full range of formats.

Creating a `Date` object with no argument encapsulates the current date and time. The output from the example shown in Code 8.18 might be as follows:

```
Default:      May 19, 1999
Short (UK):   19/05/99
Medium:       May 19, 1999
Long:         May 19, 1999
Full:         Wednesday, May 19, 1999
```

Note the difference that using the UK locale makes to the order of the day and month number, as day numbers are traditionally written preceding the month number in the UK.[7]

---

[7] The difference between US and UK ordering has provided a fruitful source of clues in detective fiction over many years!

Code 8.18   Examples of different date formatting styles (`DateMain1.java`)

```
import java.util.Date;
import java.text.*;

class DateMain1 {
    public static void main(String[] args){
        // Obtain a Date object for now.
        Date now = new Date();
        // Use the default format for the current locale.
        DateFormat formatter = DateFormat.getDateInstance();
        System.out.println("Default:    "+formatter.format(now));
        // Select short format, for the UK.
        formatter = DateFormat.getDateInstance(DateFormat.SHORT,
                                            java.util.Locale.UK);
        System.out.println("Short (UK): "+formatter.format(now));
        // Demonstrate the MEDIUM, LONG and FULL formats for the
        // current locale.
        formatter = DateFormat.getDateInstance(DateFormat.MEDIUM);
        System.out.println("Medium:     "+formatter.format(now));
        formatter = DateFormat.getDateInstance(DateFormat.LONG);
        System.out.println("Long:       "+formatter.format(now));
        formatter = DateFormat.getDateInstance(DateFormat.FULL);
        System.out.println("Full:       "+formatter.format(now));
    }
}
```

The DateFormat class's `getTimeInstance` method fulfills a similar role for the formatting of time information. The following provides examples of the full range of time styles (`DateMain2.java`):

```
Default:    12:34:33 PM
Short:      12:34 PM
Medium:     12:34:33 PM
Long:       12:34:33 PM GMT+00:00
Full:       12:34:33 PM GMT+00:00
```

Three `getDateTimeInstance` methods provide a formatter object which will format both date and time as a single combined string. The various versions allow either the default styles to be used, or separate styles for date and time, with or without a Locale.

The `parse` method may be used to turn a string containing a date and/or time into an equivalent Date object. The example in Code 8.19 shows a literal String passed to this method.

The parsing may be either strict or lenient, set via the `setLenient` method. The output from this example might be as follows:

```
Jun 7, 2001 1:11:05 PM
```

If the DateFormat object cannot make sense of the string, then it will throw a `Parse-Exception` exception.

Code 8.19   Parse a String into an equivalent Date (`DateMain3.java`)

```java
import java.util.Date;
import java.text.*;

class DateMain3 {
    public static void main(String[] args){
        // Use the default format for the current locale.
        try{
            DateFormat formatter = DateFormat.getDateTimeInstance();
            formatter.setLenient(true);
            Date d = formatter.parse("june 7, 2001 01:11:5 pm");
            // Reformat the resulting date.
            System.out.println(formatter.format(d));
        }
        catch(ParseException e){
            System.out.println(e);
        }
    }
}
```

The object returned by the `getInstance` methods will often actually be an object of the class `SimpleDateFormat`, rather than a pure `DateFormat` object. `SimpleDateFormat` includes further methods, such as `get2DigitYearStart` and `set2DigitYearStart` for getting and setting the correct century digits.

Exercise 8.8   Write a main method that prints the current date and time. Decide whether to print this in short, medium, and long formats.

Exercise 8.9   Modify your solution to Exercise 8.8 to print the current date and time for a particular locale.

8.7   Review

Here are the main points we have covered in the preceding sections:

- Classes may be grouped into hierarchical named packages.
- A `package` declaration must be the first declaration in a file.
- All classes not assigned to a named package are part of the *unnamed package*.
- The `import` statement is used to import declarations from a package.
- An `import` statement provides access to either a single class from a package, or all classes from a package.
- Classes and members without an explicit access modifier (`public`, `private`, or `protected`) have *package access*.
- The Math class consists entirely of static variables and methods for commonly used mathematical functions.
- The String class is one of the most commonly used standard classes.
- Always use the `equals` method to test for string equality.

- String objects are immutable.
- The StringBuffer class provides mutable operations on strings.
- The Locale class, of the `java.util` package, defines locale-specific information.
- A locale may have up to three levels: country, language, and variant.
- The NumberFormat class, defined in the `java.text` package, provides a basis for locale-specific formatting of numbers.
- The DateFormat class, defined in the `java.text` package, provides a basis for locale-specific formatting of dates.

Exercise 8.10   Write a program that will encode and decode strings using a simple offset algorithm. A `Crypto` class should maintain an integer attribute which is used to add a fixed offset to each character of any message to be encrypted. A message is encrypted by passing a String argument to one of its methods, which returns the encrypted version as its result. (Use the `charAt` method of the String class to obtain the individual characters of a message.) A message is decrypted by applying the opposite operation—subtracting the offset from each character of a message. Create a class containing a main method that prompts the user for strings that are to be encrypted with a Crypto object.

Exercise 8.11   Design a class that could be used to read a file of data containing the specification of a coordinate space and the positions of points and lines within that space. For instance, the first three lines of the file might contain the following data,

```
space 0 100 0 100
point 50 50
line 10 20 8 38
```

where:

- The word `space` is followed by the minimum and maximum x- and y-values of the coordinate space.
- The word `point` is followed by the x- and y-values of a point to be plotted within the space.
- The word `line` is followed by two `(x,y)` pairs defining the endpoints of a line within the space.

Use the `GraphMinder` class from your solutions to the exercises in Section 6.5 to safely draw the data specified by the file on a `Graph` object.

Exercise 8.12   Add to your solution to Exercise 8.11 the ability to recognize and implement some further drawing commands in the data file. For instance, you might add a `square` command that takes an `(x,y)` pair, specifying the top left corner of the square, and a length value specifying the size of the square to be drawn.

In the chapters that follow, we shall use the standard classes described in this chapter over and over again in class definitions. There we shall extend the capabilities of objects by describing further control structures and some of the standard classes and objects that allow collections of data values and objects to be maintained.

CHAPTER

9

Arrays and Further Statements

I n this chapter, we look at both single and multi-dimensional arrays. Arrays allow data and objects to be grouped together in fixed size collections. We also discuss Java's remaining flow of control statements: `switch`, `break`, and `continue`. The switch statement offers an alternative to multiple if-else statements for selection, while break and continue statements are used to alter the normal flow of control through a loop.

9.1 Introduction

The need to group together related items of data or collections of objects is a common one when writing programs. The cards in a pack or a player's hand are collections of objects, as are the ships in a port and the players on a sports team's payroll. By grouping together a set of related objects or data values in a single object, it becomes possible to manipulate the group as a whole as well as in the form of individual items. In order to make such groupings possible, Java has two distinct facilities: *array* objects and the `Collection` classes. In this chapter, we shall deal only with arrays, deferring collection classes until Chapter 10. Nevertheless, we shall see that many of the techniques we demonstrate with arrays will be equally applicable to the collection classes.

9.2 Problems That Arrays Solve

Using the features of Java that we have met so far, the only way to indicate that multiple items of data are similar in type and fulfill a related purpose is to define a set of attributes with related names. For instance, suppose that you wish to define a class in which the monthly rainfall figures for a year are held; Code 9.1 shows how (without arrays) you might do this.

Not only are twelve separate attributes required, but twelve separate accessors (plus twelve mutators) would also have to be written. Furthermore, we could not write a method to return the complete set of values as a single object—something that might be useful in calculating monthly averages over a period of several years, for instance. Imagine extending this principle to a program that had to analyze yearly rainfall data for the past 300 years! The problem lies in the fact that the relationship between the values is evident from the class definition only because the attribute

Code 9.1   Storing twelve rainfall amounts, without an array

```
    // Store details of the monthly rainfall figures for a single year.
    // Amounts are in millimeters.
class YearlyRainfall {
    ...

    // Return the mean monthly rainfall for this year.
    public int meanMonthlyRainfall(){
        return (getJan()+getFeb()+getMar()+getApr()+
                getMay()+getJun()+getJul()+getAug()+
                getSep()+getOct()+getNov()+getDec()) / numMonths;
    }

    public int getJan(){
        return Jan;
    }

    public int getFeb(){
        return Feb;
    }

    ...

    private static final int numMonths = 12;
    // The twelve monthly amounts.
    private int Jan, Feb, Mar, Apr, May, Jun,
                Jul, Aug, Sep, Oct, Nov, Dec;
}
```

names have been chosen to be related. There is no direct link at the programming language level between them. This is the problem that arrays address, by allowing explicit grouping through extra features of programming language syntax.

The following list contains some further applications that might wish to group together data values or objects:

- A coursework record system, storing the individual assignment marks for a large number of students.
- Software for seat bookings in a movie theater or aircraft.
- Programs displaying popup menus with a list of menu items.

A characteristic of each of these examples is that each individual item type to be grouped is the same in each case: double, SeatDetails, MenuItem. Furthermore, the size of each collection is fixed: each student in a class takes the same number of assignments, the number of seats in a theater tends not to vary from day to day, etc. An array is a suitable object to use for grouping related items when the collection size is fixed and pre-determined, and the items to be stored in it all have the same primitive type or class. In Section 9.3, we see the syntax for defining arrays in Java.

Code 9.2   Creating a rainfall array

```
class YearlyRainfall {
    ...
    // Fixed size of the rainfall array.
    private static final int numMonths = 12;
    // Declare an attribute to hold the monthly rainfall figures.
    private int[] rainfall = new int [numMonths];
}
```

9.3   Creating Array Objects

In principle, arrays to hold primitive type values and arrays to hold object references are used in a similar way. Nevertheless, there is a subtle distinction between
them when they are created, so we shall discuss primitive type and class type arrays
separately.

9.3.1   Defining Arrays for Primitive-Type Values

Code 9.2 shows the declaration and creation of an array capable of holding twelve
related `int` values simultaneously. This array is used to store the monthly rainfall
values (in millimeters) for a single year.

An array is an object, so it has to be created like other objects, but there is
no Array class for this purpose. This leads to some differences in the syntax for the
creation of array objects when compared with that for the creation of all other objects!
In Code 9.2, an instance variable called `rainfall` is used to provide a reference
to the array object. Notice that the type of the attribute includes a pair of square
brackets '`[]`' which can be read as "array", so we say that the type of `rainfall`
is "int array" (`int[]`).[1] The type name preceding the square brackets indicates the
base type of the items that may be stored in the array. We say that an array is used
to hold a *homogeneous collection* of items, because all the items in it must be of
the same type as the base type. In the example in Code 9.1, only integers may be
stored in `rainfall`, therefore. All array elements in a newly constructed array of
primitive type are initialized to the default value for the array's base type—in this
case, 0. Figure 9.1 attempts to illustrate the contrast between the rainfall attributes
of the two classes shown in Code 9.1 and Code 9.2. In one case, we have twelve
independent and separately named locations, and in the other the twelve locations
exist as a single unified object, to which the attribute `rainfall` refers. An important
point to bear in mind is that the twelve locations within the array can be used in the
same way as the twelve independent locations. There is nothing special about using
a value retrieved from an array, and nothing special happens to a value when stored
there. See Section 9.4 for details of how items are stored and retrieved.

---

[1] In keeping with the practice of related languages, such as C and C++, it is possible to place the
square brackets after the variable name instead of after the type—`int rainfall[]`. In our opinion, it
is not so clear from this form that the brackets are really part of the variable's type.

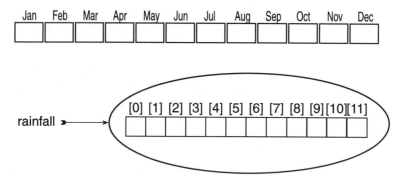

Figure 9.1 Contrasting twelve individual integer attributes with a single array object.

Code 9.3   Creating an array for String objects

```
class CardGame {
    ...
    // There are four distinct suits in this card game.
    final int numSuits = 4;
    // An array for the names of the distinct card suits.
    private String[] suitNames = new String[numSuits];
}
```

Because an array is an object, an instance of the appropriate type for an array attribute is created using `new`, just as we would in creating an instance of a class. The use of `new` must be followed immediately by the type of the items to be stored in the array. This will almost invariably be the same as the base type of the array.[2] Finally, the number of items the array is to hold is written between a second pair of square brackets. This value is the *length* of the array and it remains fixed for the life of the array object. The length may be any non-negative integer arithmetic expression, including zero. It is often useful to give the length a meaningful name using a final variable, as we have done, so that it is clear why the array has a particular length.

9.3.2 Defining Arrays for Objects

Arrays to hold objects are created in a similar way to arrays for the primitive types. Code 9.3 shows the creation of an array to hold references to four String objects.

However, the subtle distinction to recognize is that, when an array to hold objects is created, no objects are automatically stored in it. For instance, the `suitNames` array in Code 9.3 has the capacity to store references to four strings but holds none immediately following its construction. Each element of a newly constructed array for objects is automatically initialized to the `null` reference to

---

[2] Java's *polymorphism* rules do allow other compatible types to be used in some circumstances (see Section 13.3.2).

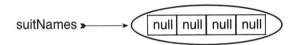

suitNames ▸━━━━━━▶ (null | null | null | null)   **Figure 9.2** The initial state of a four-
element array of object references

Code 9.4 Defining arrays with identical lengths

```
class CourseMarks {
    ...
    private final int numberOfStudents = 200;
    private double[] studentMarks = new double[numberOfStudents];
    // Ensure that this array is always the same length as studentMarks.
    private double[] deviationFromMean = new double[studentMarks.length];
}
```

indicate there is no object stored there yet (Figure 9.2). Constructing an array of object references often involves a secondary stage of content-creation, therefore. We
show some of the ways in which this can be done in Section 9.7.

9.3.3 The `length` Attribute

Once created, all array objects have an attribute called `length` that can be used
to find out their fixed size. This is not a private attribute, so it can be used directly
and Java does not provide an accessor for it. Code 9.4 illustrates how the `length`
attribute of one array could be used in the declaration of another.

Even though the `length` attribute is publicly available, the fact that it is `final`
means that you are not allowed to modify it in an effort to change the size of an
array—the compiler will reject attempts to do so; once created, an array object has
a fixed size.

9.4 Indexing an Array

Items are stored in the individual *elements* of an array. These elements are accessed
by *indexing* the array with a non-negative integer value. Index values start from `[0]`
and there are always exactly the same number of elements as the length of the array,
which is fixed when the array is created. Therein lies the root of a misunderstanding
that often occurs in the use of arrays, as this means that the index of the final element
is one less than the length of the array; the twelve elements of the `rainfall` array
are indexed from `[0]` to `[11]`, not `[1]` to `[12]`. So we would use `rainfall[0]`
for January's value, `rainfall[1]` for February's, and so on. The values `0` and
`length-1` are known as the *bounds* of the array.

Code 9.5 shows how values are stored and retrieved from various parts of the
`rainfall` array.[3] Values held in an array are used in exactly the same way as values
held in ordinary variables.

---

[3] We have omitted the use of final variables for month names in order not to obscure how index
expressions are used.

Code 9.5   Manipulating some items stored in `rainfall`

```
// Store the rainfall figure for January.
rainfall[0] = 30;
...
// Compare the December and November figures.
if(rainfall[11] > rainfall[10]){
    System.out.println("December was wetter than November.");
}
...
// Correct an error of 1 millimeter in March's rainfall total.
rainfall[2]++;
```

Code 9.6   Using final variables with `rainfall`

```
// Name the months.
final int January = 0, February = 1, ... , December = 11;
...
// Store the rainfall figure for January.
rainfall[January] = 30;
...
// Compare the December and November figures.
if(rainfall[December] > rainfall[November]){
    System.out.println("December was wetter than November.");
}
...
// Correct an error of 1 millimeter in March's rainfall total.
rainfall[March]++;
```

If, for any reason, an attempt is made to use an index outside the bounds of an array, then this will lead to a *runtime error*. The program will stop running unless steps are taken to deal with such an error. This particular kind of error is called an `ArrayIndexOutOfBoundsException`; details are covered in Chapter 11 where *exceptions* are discussed.

9.4.1   Use Final Variables for Index Names

Notice how the usual association of month names with numbers (January = 1, February = 2, etc.) does not work in the rainfall examples we have been using because array conventions force us to use index 0 for the first month. One way of overcoming this is to create final variables for each month name, corresponding to the indices that will be used (compare Code 9.6 with Code 9.5).[4]

This approach should always be used when one or more index values have a particular significance. This avoids obscuring your code with *magic numbers* and will make it both easier to read and easier to modify at a later date.

---

[4] Alternatively, there is nothing to prevent us from defining the array to have thirteen elements, numbered 0...12, and not use the first element.

Exercise 9.1   Explain what is meant by the following attribute declarations:

```
private final int numTeams = 12;
private TeamDetails[] teams = new TeamDetails[numTeams];
```

What does `teams` contain following its initialization?

Exercise 9.2   What is syntactically wrong with the following array attribute declaration?

```
private final int numStudents  = 200;
private String[] studentNames = new studentNames[numStudents];
```

Exercise 9.3   Define a class containing just a main method. Declare an array variable called `numbers` in the main method and make it refer to an array object capable of holding three integer values. Write assignment statements to store the values `10`, `20`, and `30` in the three elements of `numbers`. Write `println` statements to check that you have done this correctly.

Exercise 9.4   Add further statements to the program you wrote for Exercise 9.3 to store in the integer variable `pair` the sum of the values held in the first two elements of `numbers`. Print out the value of `pair` using `System.out.println`.

Exercise 9.5   Add the declaration of an integer variable, `error`, to your program from Exercise 9.4, and the assignment:

```
error = numbers[numbers.length];
```

What happens when you compile and run this program? Can you explain why this happens?

9.5   Accessors for Array Attributes

Classes with array attributes should provide accessors and mutators for them, just as they do for attributes containing simple primitive-type values, or references to a single object. Array mutators are dealt with in Section 9.6 and Code 9.7 shows an accessor for the `rainfall` attribute of the YearlyRainfall class.

Code 9.7   Defining an accessor for an array object

```
class YearlyRainfall {
    ...
        // Return a reference to the rainfall array.
    public int[] getRainfall(){
        return rainfall;
    }
    ...
    // Fixed size of the rainfall array.
    private static final int numMonths = 12;
    // Declare an attribute to hold the monthly rainfall figures.
    private int[] rainfall = new int [numMonths];
}
```

Notice that the return type of an accessor for an array attribute is just the type used in the attribute's declaration (int []). An important point to note is that *no copy* of the array is made when an array attribute is used like this. The attribute contains a *reference* to the array object, and it is a copy of this reference, rather than the array object, that is returned. Both references will refer to the same array object, and can be used to access (and modify) the items stored in the array in exactly the same way.

9.6   Mutators for Array Attributes

Just as array attributes have associated accessors (Section 9.5), they sometimes need mutators. These will be required if an array attribute might be used to refer to different array objects from time to time. If an array attribute will refer to the same object throughout its life, and this is initialized internally when its containing object is created, a mutator will not be necessary. Code 9.8 shows the outline of a Polyline class with a public mutator that receives an array of Point objects (see Code 4.19) representing the line's vertices.

Once again, the type information for the argument in both the mutator and the constructor is simply that corresponding to the type of the array object. An important point to appreciate is that as with array accessors, passing an array as a formal argument to a method does not cause a copy of the array to be made. The example in Code 9.8, therefore, leaves the Polyline's attribute referring to the same array object as the formal argument. If any changes are made to the contents of that array outside the class, the Polyline's private data will, in effect, be altered. This represents a potential violation of an object's encapsulation. See Section 9.11 for how to make a copy of the contents of an array object and the preferred form of this class's array mutator.

Code 9.8   A simple (potentially unsafe) mutator for an array attribute

```
    // Maintain an array of Point objects as part of a drawing package.
class Polyline {
    public Polyline(Point[] p){
        setPoints(p);
    }
    ...
        // Receive details of this polyline's points.
    public void setPoints(Point[] p){
        if(p != null){
            points = p;
        }
    }

    // The points outline a drawn shape. This attribute
    // should be initialized by the constructor.
    private Point[] points = null;
}
```

Code 9.9   An outline for the YearlyRainfall class. (`YearlyRainfall.java`)

```
        // Complete the implementation of this class.
class YearlyRainfall {
    public YearlyRainfall(){
    }

    public int getMonthAmount(int month){
        return 0;
    }

    public void setMonthAmount(int month,int amount){
    }

    public double getMean(){
        return 0.0;
    }

        // An accessor for the rainfall display.
    private RainfallDisplay getDisplay(){
        return display;
    }

    // An (optional) display for the rainfall data.
    private RainfallDisplay display = new RainfallDisplay();
}
```

Exercise 9.6   Complete the implementation of the `YearlyRainfall` class shown in Code 9.9, as outlined in earlier sections of this chapter.

YearlyRainfall should define an array attribute of twelve integers to hold the monthly rainfall values for a single year. Its accessor and mutator should both be private. Its public methods should be implemented as follows:

- `getMonthAmount`—takes a single integer argument (within the index bounds of the array attribute: 0 for January, etc.) and returns the integer rainfall amount for that month. Return -1 for an invalid month.
- `setMonthAmount`—takes an integer argument as the month and a second integer argument representing the rainfall value to be set for that particular month. The method should set the rainfall figure for the given month to the given value. Do nothing for an invalid month or amount.
- `getMean`—takes no argument and returns the mean monthly value for the whole year (the sum of the individual monthly values, divided by the number of months). The result should be returned as a `double`.

Use the `RainfallDisplay` attribute to display a chart of your data. An instance and accessor has already been defined in the outline. It has the following methods in its public interface:

```
    // Display each value in data in a separate bar.
    // The number of bars will be equal to the length of data.
    // A copy of the data is *not* made.
public void setData(int[] data)

    // Provide a set of labels for the bars.
public void setBarLabels(String[] labels)

    // Redisplay the data after it has been altered.
public void repaint()
```

You should send the display object a repaint message any time that the data stored in the YearlyRainfall's array attribute is modified, so that it can update its appearance.

Code 9.10 shows a simple main method to create a YearlyRainfall object. This main method allows a user to interactively modify the YearlyRainfall object. You should feel free to alter this for testing purposes, if you wish.

9.7 Initializing Arrays

Java contains a convenient means for initializing the contents of an array object, when it is declared, via a list of the values or objects to be stored into it. In this case, it is not necessary to use the new reserved word to create the array because its size can be calculated from the number of items listed in the *array initializer*. Code 9.11 shows the initialization of an array of integers.

The initial values for the array are listed between a pair of curly brackets. The values are separated by commas. A comma after the final item in the list is optional, but often included, as this makes it easier to add further items to the list at a later stage of program development. Notice that the closing curly bracket of the initialization

Code 9.10 A main method to test the YearlyRainfall class (`RainfallMain.java`)

```
    // Ask the user for month, amount pairs to update the
    // monthly rainfall amounts.
    // Print the mean after each change.
class RainfallMain {
    public static void main(String[] args){
        YearlyRainfall lastYear = new YearlyRainfall();

        SimpleInput keyboard = new SimpleInput();
        while(true){
            System.out.println("Month: 0-11? ");
            int month = keyboard.nextInt();
            System.out.println("Amount? ");
            int amount = keyboard.nextInt();
            int newTotal = lastYear.getMonthAmount(month)+amount;
            lastYear.setMonthAmount(month,newTotal);
            double mean = lastYear.getMean();
            System.out.println("The mean is: "+mean);
        }
    }
}
```

Code 9.11   Using an array initializer to construct an array

```
class AssignmentMonitor {
    ...
    // Differentially weight the assignments.
    private int[] assignmentWeights = {
        1, 2, 1, 5, 1,
    };
    private final int numAssignments = assignmentWeights.length;
}
```

---

must be followed by a semicolon, whereas this is not required after the closing bracket of a statement, method, or class block. Each item in the list of initializers must be compatible with the array object's base type.

An interesting feature of the example in Code 9.11 is the way in which the initialization of an attribute to record the number of elements in the array has been left until *after* the array has been created, rather than before as in previous examples. Because attributes are initialized in their order of declaration, assignmentWeights will refer to the newly created array object before numAssignments is initialized. Where array initializers are used, the approach used here is safer because it guarantees that the attribute will always have the correct value, even if later modifications to the class add or remove assignment weights from the original collection by changing the initializer.

Code 9.12 shows the initialization of an array of strings in a similar way. Notice an important difference between this example and that in Code 9.3, illustrated visually by the difference between Figure 9.2 and Figure 9.3. In Code 9.3, an array object is constructed and a reference to it stored in the attribute suitNames. Each element of that array contains a null reference. In Code 9.12, an array object is constructed in a similar way—except that its size is determined from the initializer—in addition,

---

Code 9.12   Using an array initializer with an array of object references

```
class CardGame {
    ...
    private String[] suitNames = {
        "Spades", "Hearts", "Diamonds", "Clubs"
    };
}
```

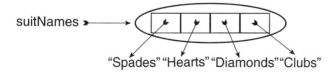

Figure 9.3   An initializer results in base type objects being created

---

Code 9.13   Explicit construction objects within an initializer

```
class UnitSquare {
    ...
    // Initialize the vertices with Point objects.
    private Point[] vertices = {
        new Point(0,0),
        new Point(0,1),
        new Point(1,1),
        new Point(1,0),
    };
}
```

---

however, four String objects are constructed, and the contents of the array initialized with references to them.

An initializer may contain more complex object constructions, such as that shown in Code 9.13, in which the contents of an array are initialized with a set of newly constructed Point objects. Notice that the Point objects are, in effect, *anonymous objects*, because they are not referred to by a variable name.

9.7.1 Anonymous Arrays

The example in Code 9.13 includes the creation of anonymous Point objects, whose attributes are initialized via their constructor. Since array objects do not belong to a particular class, they cannot be initialized in the same way when used in an anonymous context. Java, therefore, defines further syntax for the creation and initialization of *anonymous arrays*—array objects with no name in the local scope. These are used most often when creating an array that is immediately passed as an argument to a method, as follows:

```
// Create an anonymous array of integers.
YearlyRainfall y2k = new YearlyRainfall(
            new int[]{10,10,8,8,6,4,4,0,4,4,7,10,});
```

In Section 15.6.4, we discuss the related topic of *anonymous classes*.

9.7.2 Use of `final` with Array Attributes

Where an array attribute will refer to the same object throughout its life, and this is initialized directly in its declaration or in the constructor, it is appropriate to define the attribute as `final`. We would not anticipate that the names used for the suits in a game of cards would change during the course of a game, for instance (see Code 9.12). However, care must be taken in interpreting what it means for an array variable to be final. It is tempting to prefix the `suitNames` attribute with the `final` modifier and to make it `public` and `static` so as to be readily accessible to all CardGame objects and to other classes, as in Code 9.14.

Code 9.14   Defining a `final` array attribute as `public` is not safe

```
class CardGame {
    public static final  String[] suitNames = {
        "Spades","Hearts","Diamonds","Clubs"
    };
    ...
}
```

However, care must be taken in understanding what is meant by defining an array attribute as `final`. The use of `final` only guarantees that the `suitNames` variable may not be changed to refer to another array object. It does not prevent *the contents* of the array to which it refers from being modified. Hence, the following assignment is perfectly legal and likely to produce confusing results!

```
// Surreptitiously change the name of the Spades suit.
CardGame.suitNames[0] = "Shovels";
```

While it is often appropriate to define an array attribute as `final`, it is inadvisable to define it as `public`. A related issue is that returning a reference to an array from a public accessor leaves the attribute's contents vulnerable to external modification. Where this is likely to be a problem, a reference to a copy of the array, rather than the original, should be returned (see Section 9.11).

9.8 Using For Loops with Arrays

It is very common to use a for loop when something must be done to every element of an array. The for loop header in Code 9.15 is typical of this kind of use.

A loop variable, `month`, is defined and initialized to zero—the index of the first element. This variable serves to index into the array. The array's `length` attribute is used to set the limit for the loop's iterations. Note that the loop's terminating condition uses the less than operator (`<`) rather than (`<=`) because we do not wish to enter the loop with `month` equal to `12`, as the last index in the array is `11` (that is, `rainfall.length-1`). After each iteration, the loop variable is incremented ready to test against the number of months to be used to access the next element. This style of accessing all the elements of an array with a for loop is so common that you should be sure that you understand it, and could write it for yourself for an arbitrary array.

9.8.1 Iterating over an Array in Reverse

Sometimes it is necessary to traverse an array from its highest index to its lowest. We might have an array of numbers sorted into ascending order that must be printed out in descending order. Code 9.16 shows how this is done.

There are several changes to the loop's header, when compared with that in Code 9.15. The loop variable is initialized to the index of the final element of the array; the condition must include the test for equality against the initial index value, because

---

Code 9.15   Calculating a year's rainfall

```java
class YearlyRainfall {
    ...
        // Return the sum of the individual monthly values.
    public int totalRainFall(){
        // Obtain the data values.
        final int[] monthlyValues = getRainfall();
        int totalRain = 0;
        final int numMonths = monthlyValues.length;
        for(int month = 0; month < numMonths; month++){
            totalRain += monthlyValues[month];
        }
        return totalRain;
    }
    ...
    public int[] getRainfall(){
        return rainfall;
    }

    // Fixed size of the rainfall array.
    private static final int numMonths = 12;
    // Declare an attribute to hold the monthly rainfall figures.
    private int[] rainfall = new int [numMonths];
}
```

Code 9.16   Printing an array in reverse

```java
class StudentMarks {
    ...
        // Print the list of marks in reverse order.
    public void  printInReverse(){
        final double[]  numbers = getMarks();
        for(int index = numbers.length-1; index >= 0; index--){
            System.out.print(numbers[index]+" ");
        }
        System.out.println();
    }
    ...
}
```

---

we still want to enter the loop with an index of zero; and the loop variable must be decremented at the end of each iteration. It is a very common mistake to use ++ in error, simply through force of habit. The effect of that will be to cause an Array-IndexOutOfBoundsException exception to be thrown on the second execution of the loop's body (see Chapter 11).

9.8.2   Initializer Blocks

We saw in Section 9.7 that an array may be initialized as part of its declaration, thus:

```
private int[] assignmentWeights = {
    1, 2, 1, 5, 1,
};
```

This is satisfactory for most purposes as long as the initial values are relatively few, and do not involve complex calculation. If we wish to initialize an array to hold the squares of the numbers 1...100, or a `boolean` array indicating seat availability in a 150-seat theater, this is a little more tricky. Initializer blocks provide the solution, and they are often used to initialize arrays, although they are not exclusively tied to this role. The examples shown in Code 9.17 illustrate the sort of initializations we have been describing.

These initializer blocks are known as *instance initializers*, because they apply to each instance of their enclosing class. An initializer block is simply a set of statements (surrounded by a pair of curly brackets) defined at the outer level of a class definition—that is, at the same level as the attributes. An initializer block typically follows the variable it is being used to initialize, although such a block can be used for more general initialization if necessary. They are executed in the order they are defined, before the class's constructors are executed. In many ways, they are similar to no-arg constructors, but the ability to place them close to the attributes to which they apply often makes them preferable to constructors. An initializer block is permitted to initialize an uninitialized final instance variable, in the same way that a constructor is (see Section 7.8.1).

Code 9.17   Using initializer blocks to initialize arrays

```
        // An example of initializer blocks.
class SquareSeats {
    ...
    // The status of seats in a theater.
    private final  int numSeats = 150;
    private boolean[] freeSeats = new boolean[numSeats];
    {
        // All seats are free to start with.
        for(int i = 0; i < numSeats; i++){
            freeSeats[i] = true;
        }
    }

    // The first 100 squares.
    final  int numSquares = 100;
    private long[] squares = new long[numSquares];
    {
        for(int i = 0; i < numSquares; i++){
            squares[i] = i*i;
        }
    }
}
```

Code 9.18   A static initializer block

```
// Determine whether a name has been set from the environment,
// before using the default.
private static String DEFAULTNAME = "Tryphena";
private static final  String name;
static {
    String userName = System.getProperty("NAME");
    if(userName != null){
        name = userName;
    }
    else{
        name = DEFAULTNAME;
    }
}
```

An initializer prefixed with the `static` reserved word is a *static initializer*. As you might suppose, such a block may be used to initialize static variables of a class—including static final variables. Code 9.18 illustrates how a static variable might be initialized, at runtime, from information in the system properties.

Exercise 9.7   Define a class, `StudentMarks`, which has an array attribute which can hold five `double` values representing individual marks on five assignments. Define an accessor for the array and methods to retrieve and set the marks for individual assignments. (These will be similar to those described for the monthly rainfall values in Exercise 9.6.) In addition, define a method to return the mean value of the five marks. Write a class with a main method to set some sample mark values via the class's methods, and check that your class works properly.

Exercise 9.8   Add a further method to the StudentMarks class of Exercise 9.7 to return the index of the highest of the five assignment marks held in the array. This method should use a for loop to find the correct index.

Exercise 9.9   In the class you wrote for Exercise 9.8, which index is returned if there are two equal highest marks for a student; that of the first or the second occurrence? Rewrite the method so that the other occurrence is returned instead.

9.9   Array Arguments

In Section 9.6, we showed that arrays may be passed as arguments to methods. Code 9.19 shows a further example in which the values in one rainfall array are added into cumulative totals for several years stored in another array of the same size. The cumulative values are passed in as an argument to the `accumulateRainfall` method.

The principle of always determining the size of an array from its `length` attribute becomes particularly important when an array object is passed as an argument to a method, since there may well be no other means of determining this—indeed,

Code 9.19   Accumulating yearly rainfall totals

```
class YearlyRainfall {
    ...
    // Add this year's rainfall into the cumulative array.
    public void accumulateRainfall(int[] cumulative){
        final int[] monthlyValues = getRainfall();
        final int numMonths = monthlyValues.length;
        for(int month = 0; month < numMonths; month++){
            cumulative[month] += rainfall[month];
        }
    }
    ...
}
```

Code 9.20   Calculating the mean of an array of doubles

```
    // Return the mean value of the numbers in the array.
public double mean(double[] numbers){
    double sum = 0.0;
    final int howMany = numbers.length;
    // Avoid dividing by zero.
    if(howMany > 0){
        for(int i = 0; i < howMany; i++){
            sum += numbers[i];
        }
        return sum / howMany;
    }
    else{
        return 0.0;
    }
}
```

it is perfectly possible to pass arrays of different lengths to the same method at various times during the operation of a program. Code 9.20 shows a method that will calculate the mean of *any* array full of doubles, whatever its length.

9.10   The Main Method Array Argument

The main method is always passed in an array argument when a program starts. So far, we have tended to ignore this argument, but the String objects stored in it usually originate from any *command-line arguments* that were passed to the program when it was run. If we run the program in Code 9.21 with the command

```
java PrintArguments first second third
```

the values first, second, and third are turned into strings and placed in elements [0], [1], and [2], respectively, of args. Code 9.21 shows how the strings stored in this array might be printed out, one per line.

Code 9.21   Printing the command-line arguments (`PrintArguments.java`)

```
class PrintArguments {
    public static void main(String[] args) {
        final int numArgs = args.length;
        for(int n = 0; n < numArgs; n++){
            System.out.println(args[n]);
        }
    }
}
```

Code 9.22   Looking up words in a glossary (`LookupWords.java`)

```
class LookupWords {
    public static void main(String[] args) {
        GlossaryManager glossary = new GlossaryManager();

        for(int n = 0; n < args.length; n++){
            System.out.println("Looking up "+args[n]);
            System.out.println(glossary.definition(args[n]));
        }
    }
}
```

If no command-line arguments are given, then the length of the array will be zero and nothing will be printed. Command-line arguments are one way of passing information from the external environment into the program. It is then possible to have the program examine its `args` array in order to vary the way it runs each time. For instance, a program to print word definitions from a glossary might take the words to be looked up as its command-line arguments (Code 9.22).

9.11   Copying Arrays

In Section 9.6, we noted that simply copying an array reference into an array attribute leaves an object open to modification if the data held in the array object is modified externally. Wherever possible, therefore, this should be avoided by making a copy of the contents of the array referred to by the argument. The need to copy all or part of the contents of one array to another is so common, that the static `arraycopy` method is defined in the `System` class.

Code 9.23 illustrates how the `arraycopy` method of the System class may be used to create a duplicate of the data passed to the argument of a class's constructor (compare this with the previous version shown in Code 9.8).

The first argument of `arraycopy` is the array object containing the source data. The second argument specifies the index of the first value in the source data to be copied. The third argument is the array object into which the copy is to be made, and the fourth specifies the index of where the first value is to be stored in the destination. The final argument specifies how many items are to be copied from the

Code 9.23 Copying array data passed to a mutator

```
    // Maintain an array of Point objects as part of a drawing package.
class Polyline {
    public Polyline(Point[] p){
        setPoints(p);
    }
    ...
        // Make a copy of the Point data.
    public void setPoints(Point[] p){
        if(p != null){
            final int numPoints = p.length;
            points = new Point[numPoints];
            // Copy from p to points.
            System.arraycopy(p,0,points,0,numPoints);
        }
    }

    // The points outline a drawn shape. This attribute
    // should be initialized by the constructor.
    private Point[] points = null;
}
```

source array. Clearly, the destination array must have sufficient space to receive all of the copied items, and the source array must contain at least the required number of items. The source and destination array references may actually refer to the same array object, allowing data to be shifted within a single array.

9.11.1 Partially Occupied Arrays

Sometimes there is insufficient data to completely fill an array, or an array is progressively filled throughout the life of a program. Unfortunately, with an array of primitive types, there is no general way to determine whether an element of an array is "occupied". The only work around is to make use of values of the base type that are not meaningful in the context of the use of the array—*out of bounds values*. For instance, negative marks in an array of assignment marks could indicate unoccupied locations. When this approach is not possible, occupied locations must be grouped together at the start of the array and a count of how many elements are occupied must be passed with the array to any methods that need this information. The example in Code 9.24 illustrates this idea.

　　With an array of object types, on the other hand, it is possible to indicate that an element is unused by storing a null reference there. A method iterating over such an array would need to check each location for the presence of a null before attempting to send a message to the corresponding object (Code 9.25).

　　Where we do not wish to use every element of an array, it may be better to use one of the Collection classes, such as ArrayList (Section 10.2.1) or LinkedList (Section 10.2.3), for storing the objects.

Code 9.24   Passing a partially occupied array as an argument

```
    // Return the mean value of the numbers in the array.
    // Only elements 0 .. (howMany-1) contain meaningful values.
public double mean(double[] numbers, int howMany){
    double sum = 0.0;
    for(int i = 0; i < howMany; i++){
        sum += numbers[i];
    }
    if(howMany > 0){
        return sum / howMany;
    }
    else{
        return 0.0;
    }
}
```

Code 9.25   Iterating over a partially occupied array of objects

```
    // Print the occupied elements of the array.
public void printNames(String[] names){
    final int numStrings = names.length;
    for(int i = 0; i < numStrings; i++){
        // Test for occupation.
        if(names[i] != null){
            System.out.println(names[i]);
        }
    }
}
```

9.12   Searching an Unsorted Array

When iterating over an array, it is not always necessary to iterate over the whole array. Searching an array to find a particular value or object fits this kind of iteration; we do not know where in the array the item might be—it could be at the first index, the last index, somewhere near the middle, or not there at all. This means that it can sometimes be difficult to decide whether to use a while loop or a for loop for the iteration. Code 9.26 shows a method that uses a while loop to search for a particular integer value in its array argument. If we use a while loop for the iteration, many of the steps used will be similar to those in using a for loop:

- An index variable is needed.
- The loop variable must be initialized—typically to zero.
- A loop-terminating condition must be checked.
- The index variable must be incremented each time around the loop.

Code 9.26   Searching using a while loop

```
    // Return the index of value in numbers if it is there.
    // Return -1 if it is not there.
public int indexOf(int[] numbers,int value){
    // The value to return if value is not in numbers.
    final int notPresent = -1;
    int index = 0;
    // Stop if we reach the end of the array or if
    // we find the value.
    while((index < numbers.length) && (numbers[index] != value)){
        index++;
    }
    // Did we find it?
    if(index == numbers.length){
        // We didn't.
        return notPresent;
    }
    else{
        return index;
    }
}
```

Notice that, in the example in Code 9.26, the terminating condition has to take two possibilities into account:

- Has the end of the array been reached without finding the value?
- Is the value at the current index?

Notice, too, how the properties of the short-circuit version of the *and-operator* (`&&`) protect us from trying to look beyond the end of the array; if `index >= numbers.length`, then the first half of the test will be false and the second half will not be tested. Code 9.27 shows an incorrect alternative version of this method, using a for loop instead of a while loop.

This version is incorrect because an index-variable declared in a for loop's header cannot be used outside of the for loop. Technically, `index` is *out of scope* because a variable defined in the header of a for loop is only available within the header and body of that loop; that is, its scope is limited to the lifetime of the loop (see Section 7.5.2). In fact, this is easily fixed by declaring it as a normal method-variable rather than declaring it in the for loop header, just as we had to do in the while loop version. However, consider the preferred alternative search shown in Code 9.28.

This makes use of the fact that the only thing we are interested in knowing is whether the value is present or not. Once the loop has found it, the method can return straight away. This means that if the loop condition ever becomes false, it must be because the end of the array was reached and the value not found, so the statement after the loop becomes a simple return of the "not-present" value. This approach is perfectly satisfactory if we do not need to do anything within this method with the index found. However, it should be noted that some authorities consider it to be poor style to terminate a for loop prematurely in this way.

Code 9.27   (Incorrect) Searching using a for loop

```
    // Return the index of value in numbers if it is there.
    // Return -1 if it is not there.
public int indexOf(int[] numbers,int value){
    // The value to return if value is not in numbers.
    final int notPresent = -1;
    // Stop if we reach the end of the array or if
    // we find the value.
    for(int index = 0; (index < numbers.length) &&
                        (numbers[index] != value); index++){
        // There is nothing left to do here.
    }
    // Did we find it? [Error: index is out of scope.]
    if(index == numbers.length){
        // We didn't.
        return notPresent;
    }
    else{
        return index;
    }
}
```

Code 9.28   Correct search using a for loop

```
    // Return the index of value in numbers, or -1.
public int indexOf(int[] numbers,int value){
    // The value to return if value is not in numbers.
    final int notPresent = -1;
    // Stop if we reach the end of the array or find it.
    for(int index = 0; index < numbers.length; index++){
        if(numbers[index] == value){
            return index;
        }
    }
    // We didn't find it.
    return notPresent;
}
```

In Java, there is sometimes very little difference between while loops and for loops in terms of the functionality they offer. However, sometimes a little care must be exercised over the value of the variable used to index into the array. Consider Code 9.29, which is a version of the program in Code 9.26.

Here we are using a boolean variable in the loop-terminating condition to determine whether the value was found on the last iteration. If the value is found, we set found to be true and do not update the index. Compare this version with that using a similar idea in Code 9.30.

Because the loop-variable increment is performed after the body has been executed, the value of index is incremented even if the value was found. This means

Code 9.29 Searching using a while loop

```
    // Return the index of value in numbers if it is there.
    // Return -1 if it is not there.
public int indexOf(int[] numbers,int value){
    // The value to return if value is not in numbers.
    final int notPresent = -1;
    int index = 0;
    // Have we found the value, yet?
    boolean found = false;
    // Stop if we reach the end of the array or if
    // we find the value.
    while((index < numbers.length) && !found){
        if(numbers[index] == value){
            found = true;
        }
        else{
            index++;
        }
    }
    return found ? index : notPresent;
}
```

Code 9.30 (Incorrect) Searching using a for loop

```
    // Return the index of value in numbers if it is there.
    // Return -1 if it is not there.
public int indexOf(int[] numbers,int value){
    // The value to return if value is not in numbers.
    final int notPresent = -1;
    // Stop if we reach the end of the array or if
    // we find the value.
    int index;
    boolean found = false;
    for(index = 0; (index < numbers.length) && !found; index++){
        if(numbers[index] == value){
            found = true;
        }
    }
    // Error: index was incremented after the value was found.
    return found ? index : notPresent;
}
```

that it is one higher than it should be when returned outside the loop. Although this is a trivial example, it represents a common mistake that is easily made when using a for loop.

Exercise 9.10 Design a class, DayTemperatures, to record a set of hourly temperature readings over the course of a day. The class should include a method, hottestHours, that returns an array of the hottest hours. The length of this array will vary according to the number of hours in the day that have the same highest temperature. You may assume that hours are numbered according to the 24-hour clock, that is, they have values in the range 0..23. It should also include a method, meanTemperature that returns the mean temperature for the day.

Exercise 9.11   Add the class, WeeklyTemperatures, to your solution to Exercise 9.10 that stores a week's set of DayTemperatures. The class should include a method, meanDailyTemperature, that returns the mean value of the individual daily mean temperatures.

9.13   Searching a Sorted Array

The data stored in an array is often sorted in some way—increasing values of a primitive type or an attribute of an object. In Section 9.14, we show that the binary-Search methods of the Arrays class make use of this to provide an efficient search for a particular value. In this section, we look at the difference made to a search algorithm by the fact that the data being searched is sorted.

Consider the version of indexOf shown in Code 9.28; this assumes nothing about the order of the data in the array. Suppose its argument contains the values in ascending numerical order at the indicated indices shown in Figure 9.4 and we look for the value 67. After five comparisons of numbers[index] against value, the answer will be returned. Suppose we look for the value 100? Each element of the array will be considered before the loop is finished and it is ascertained that 100 is not in the array. What happens if we look for the value 2? Exactly the same as when we looked for 100, but we can clearly see that there is no point looking any further than the second element, because the array is sorted. Code 9.31 is an attempt to avoid looking any further, once it has been established that the value cannot be in the array.

How does this behave differently from the version in Code 9.28 if we search the data in Code 9.32 for the three values 67, 100, and 2? For the first two values, there is no change in the number of times the body is executed: five times for 67 before finding it, seven times for 100 before finding it is not there, but only two times for 2; so this looks like an improvement. However, a more significant difference is that *two* comparisons against the value of numbers[index] are performed each full time around the loop, rather than one. With a very large array, this could amount to a significant increase in execution time. Can we find a way to search that only looks once at each element? We are using two comparisons, rather than one, because we are trying to take into account the relative magnitudes of the target value and the next value in the array. We can observe that, most of the time, the value we are looking for is greater than the value it is being compared with. This means that both comparisons always fail except when we have found the answer. This leads us to the version in Code 9.32.

[0] [1] [2] [3] [4] [5] [6]

1	3	10	45	67	68	99

Figure 9.4   Sorted data to be searched

Code 9.31 Inefficient searching of a sorted list

```
public int indexOf(int[] numbers,int value){
    // The value to return if value is not in numbers.
    final int notPresent = -1;
    for(int index = 0; index < numbers.length; index++){
        if(numbers[index] == value){
            return index;
        }
        else if(numbers[index] > value){
            return notPresent;
        }
        else{
            // numbers[index] is still smaller.
        }
    }
    return notPresent;
}
```

Code 9.32 Searching a sorted list

```
public int indexOf(int[] numbers,int value){
    // The value to return if value is not in numbers.
    final int notPresent = -1;
    for(int index = 0; (index < numbers.length) &&
                       (numbers[index] < value); index++){
        // Nothing more to do here.
        // value > numbers[index].
    }
    if(index == numbers.length){
        return notPresent;
    }
    else if(value == numbers[index]){
        return index;
    }
    else{
        return notPresent;
    }
}
```

Here we want to keep moving along the list as long as there is another element to check *and* the next number in the array is smaller than the one we are looking for. Only if one of those two parts of the condition fails do we need to make a second comparison. For our three sample values, the numbers of comparisons against the array elements are now six for 67, eight for 100, and three for 2. For big arrays, with a random distribution of data both present and not present, this represents a significant improvement over the other versions. However, as we shall see next, we can do even better than this.

With the searching method shown in Code 9.32, each comparison we make in searching for a particular value reduces the number of future comparisons by only one, as we step element-by-element along the array. A technique known as the *binary search* method allows us to cut the number of remaining comparisons in half at each step. Let us assume that there are no duplicate values in the sorted array. With the binary search method, we recognize that, given the value at any index, all values to the left (that is, with lower indices) have values less than it, and all to the right (with higher indices) have values greater than it. Comparing the target value against an element in the middle of the array immediately allows us to eliminate one half of the array for consideration. This is similar to the technique that we might use to search a videotape containing several different programs. To find the one we want to watch, we might start looking somewhere near the middle and then either look only forward or backward of that point.

For instance, suppose we want to locate the value 67 in the array shown in Figure 9.4 and that we start by comparing it against the value at index [3]. The result of the comparison tells us that our target value is larger than the element at this index. This result eliminates not just the one at index [3] but all of the values at indices from [0] to [3] in one go, because they must all be smaller than the one we are looking for. One comparison has eliminated four elements. Now we are left having to consider only the elements shown in Figure 9.5. It looks like we just have to look at the next array element along, but this is a lucky coincidence in this case. In general, we always pick the middle element of whatever we have left to work with. So our next comparison is against the value at index [5]. This value is too large, but that doesn't mean the target value does not exist, simply that it might be in the section to the left of the comparison point. So now we have eliminated elements [5] and [6] and there is only element [4] to look at, which is our target. We have found it in three steps.

Let us look at another example, with a target value of 100 on the same data. Checking against element [3] tells us to look in the right-hand section. Checking against element [5] suggests the right-hand section again, which just consists of element [6]. Checking against that indicates looking to the right, but there are no more elements there, so the search is at an end and we know that 100 is not in the array.

Exercise 9.12 Trace out what happens when using the binary search method to look for the values 2 and 1 in the sorted data shown in Figure 9.4.

Code 9.33 gives an outline of what we have been doing in these examples.
Each time around the loop, we need three pieces of information:

- The index of the next item to check—the "middle" item.
- The index of the left-hand limit of the section we are checking. Initially this will be [0].

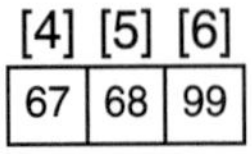

[4] [5] [6]

67	68	99

Figure 9.5   Remaining portion of data to be searched

Code 9.33   Outline of the binary search algorithm

```
Find a starting point around the middle of the array;
while(there are more elements to check){
    if(the target element is bigger than the item in the array){
        Focus on the right hand part of
        the remaining elements;
    }
    else if(the target element is smaller than
                the item in the array){
        Focus on the left hand part of
        the remaining elements;
    }
    else{
        // Found it.
        return the index;
    }
}
// Not found.
return notPresent;
```

- The index of the right-hand limit of the section we are checking. Initially this will be [length-1].

If the comparison indicates that we must look next in the right-hand section, then the left-hand limit changes to be one place to the right of where we just looked. If the comparison indicates that we must look next in the left-hand section, then the right-hand limit changes to be one place to the left of where we just looked. We must stop if the left- and right-hand limits cross—indicating failure to find the target value. Code 9.34 implements the algorithm outlined in Code 9.33.

Code 9.34   A binary search method

```
public int indexOf(int[] numbers,int value){
    // The value to return if value is not in numbers.
    final int notPresent = -1;
    int indexToSearch;
    int leftIndex = 0, rightIndex = numbers.length-1;
    // Keep going until the left and right cross.
    while(leftIndex <= rightIndex){
        // Calculate the mid-point.
        final int numItems = rightIndex-leftIndex+1;
        indexToSearch = leftIndex+(numItems/2);
        if(value > numbers[indexToSearch]){
            leftIndex = indexToSearch+1;
        }
        else if(value < numbers[indexToSearch]){
            rightIndex = indexToSearch-1;
        }
```

(*Continued*)

Code 9.34   (*Continued*)

```
    else{
        // Found it.
        return indexToSearch;
    }
  }
  return notPresent;
}
```

This method works even if there are duplicate values stored in the array—as long as the array is still sorted. In this case, however, it does not guarantee to return the index of the first occurrence of a particular value; which index it returns depends upon the length of the array and the other values stored there.

Exercise 9.13   What result is return by the version of `indexOf` in Code 9.34, when it is called with a `numbers` argument containing `10, 10, 10`, and a `value` argument of `10`?

What result is returned if the `numbers` argument holds the values `9, 10, 10, 10, 10, 11, 12, 13, 14` when `value` is `10`?

9.14   The Arrays Class

The `java.util` package defines the `Arrays` class, whose public interface consists entirely of static methods. A sample of these is shown in Table 9.1. This class provides a convenient location for commonly used operations on arrays, such as sorting their contents (`sort`), filling them with a particular value (`fill`), testing whether two arrays have the same contents (`equals`), and searching for the occurrence of a particular value (`binarySearch`). A version of most of these methods exists for arrays of each of the primitive types. Code 9.35 shows an example of how the `fill` method might be used to initialize a `boolean` array, for instance.

The `sort` method is particularly useful for sorting large amounts of data efficiently. The `binarySearch` method takes an array as its first argument and a value to be searched for. It returns the index of where in the array the value occurs. The

Table 9.1 Selected methods of the Arrays class

	Method and Arguments
static int	binarySearch(int[] arr,int key)
static int	binarySearch(double[] arr,double key)
static boolean	equals(int[] arr,int[] a2)
static void	fill(int[] arr,int val)
static void	fill(int[] arr,int from,int to,int val)
static void	sort(int[] arr)
static void	sort(int[] a,int from,int to)

Code 9.35   Filling a whole array with the same value

```
final int numSeats = 150;
boolean[] freeSeats = new boolean[numSeats];
// All seats are free to start with.
java.util.Arrays.fill(freeSeats,true);
```

contents of the array must be sorted for this method to work. See Section 9.13 for a description of the approach this method uses.

Exercise 9.14   Define a main method that contains a small unsorted array of `double` values. Use one of the static `sort` methods of the `Arrays` class to sort the values. Print the contents of the array before and after the sort.

9.15   Review

Here are the main points that we have covered in the preceding sections:

- Arrays allow a related collection of items to be grouped in a single object.
- Arrays are able to hold either primitive-type data values or references to objects.
- The type name for an array includes one or more pairs of square brackets.[5]
- When an array to hold objects is created, no containing objects are created by default. All of its locations hold a `null` reference.
- An array initializer may be used to define the initial contents of an array.
- An anonymous array may be created and initialized in a single expression.
- The `length` attribute of an array defines the number of items it can contain.
- The items in an array are indexed from `0` to `length-1`, inclusive.
- For loops are often used to iterate over the full length of an array.
- The contents of an array are not copied when an array reference is passed as an argument or copied as a result.
- The static `arrayCopy` method of the `System` class may be used to copy the whole or part of an array.
- "Empty" elements of an array of objects may be indicated with a `null` reference.
- Searching sorted data is often more efficient than searching unsorted data.
- The Arrays class provides general purpose static methods for manipulating arrays.

9.16   Case Study: A Sports League

Consider the following problem description:

> A sports league consists of a fixed number of teams. Each team has a name, a coach, and a venue where they play their matches. Initially, a team starts a season with 0 points,

---

[5] See Section 9.17 for multi-dimensional arrays.

but this will be altered as the season progresses. Design and write the classes to hold a team's details and to hold the full set of details for teams in the league.

This description leads us to two essential classes, which we shall call `League` and `TeamDetails`. It would appear that a TeamDetails object only needs to be a passive repository of information: name, coach, venue, and points.

9.16.1   The TeamDetails Class

Code 9.36 shows the class used to hold these details for a single team.

Notice that the `setPoints` mutator checks to ensure that a negative number of points is not set for any team. One decision we needed to make about the various attributes is whether they should be `final` or not. Teams regularly change their coaches, but do they ever change their venue or name? If we have confidence that neither of these values could ever be changed, then those attributes should be marked as `final`, their values set in the constructor, and the mutators removed.

9.16.2   The League Class

The problem description does not place any particular requirements on the League class, but we shall design it to contain methods to allow the following operations on either the set of teams or an individual team:

- Print out the names of the teams in the league, along with the number of points each has.
- Add some points to a team, given the team's name.
- Find a team's details, given the team's name.

Since the number of teams in the league is fixed, an array is a suitable object to hold the set of TeamDetails objects within a League object. The question arises, how should the array of TeamDetails be set up and registered with a League object? There are at least three possibilities:

- A League object could read the names, coaches, and venues from a data file or interactively from a user when it is constructed.
- A League object could be constructed with no teams, initially, and have TeamDetails objects passed to it one by one.
- A full set of TeamDetails could be set up before a League object is created, and then passed to its constructor.

In general, it is a good idea to avoid requiring an object to set itself up interactively as this tends to limit the generality of a class. Progressively initializing an object is also best avoided. The problem is that such objects can spend part of their time in a partially-initialized state. This could have a disastrous effect on the methods of the class, since they are typically written on the assumption that an object will be fully initialized. Of the three options, the third is the most acceptable and is the one we

Code 9.36   The details held on a single team (`TeamDetails.java`)

```java
       // Keep a set of details on a particular team:
       //     a name, the team's coach, and their home venue.
class TeamDetails {
    public TeamDetails(String name, String coach, String venue){
        setName(name);
        setCoach(coach);
        setVenue(venue);
    }

    public String getName(){
        return name;
    }

    private void setName(String n){
        name = n;
    }

    public String getCoach(){
        return coach;
    }

    private void setCoach(String c){
        coach = c;
    }

    public String getVenue(){
        return venue;
    }

    private void setVenue(String v){
        venue = v;
    }

    public int getPoints(){
        return points;
    }

        // Allow points to be set, but only if non-negative.
    public void setPoints(int p){
        if(p >= 0){
            points = p;
        }
    }

    // The team's basic attributes.
    private String name, coach, venue;
    // How many points this team has.
    private int points = 0;
}
```

shall choose. This means that creation of the TeamDetails object to be registered with a League object becomes the responsibility of some other part of the program. Code 9.37 shows an implementation of the League class.

Code 9.37   The class maintaining an array of TeamDetails objects (`League.java`)

```
    // Maintain an array of TeamDetails object, initialized at
    // construction. Provide methods to print the league, add points
    // to a team (given its name), and return a TeamDetails given
    // a team name.
class League {
        // Make a copy of the team list.
    public League(TeamDetails[] teamList){
        setTeams(teamList);
    }

        // Print out the name of each team in the league with the
        // number of points it has, on a single line.
    public void print(){
        final TeamDetails[] teamList = getTeams();
        final int numTeams = teamList.length;
        for(int i = 0; i < numTeams; i++){
            final TeamDetails team = teamList[i];
            System.out.println(team.getName()+" = "+team.getPoints());
        }
    }

        // Add the given number of points to the team whose name
        // matches teamName.
    public void addPoints(String teamName, int points){
        TeamDetails team = findTeam(teamName);
        if(team != null){
            team.setPoints(team.getPoints()+points);
        }
        else{
            System.err.println("Team: "+teamName+" was not found.");
        }
    }

        // Find the TeamDetails with the given name. The search
        // is case insensitive. Return null if no match is found.
    public TeamDetails findTeam(String teamName){
        final TeamDetails[] teamList = getTeams();
        final int numTeams = teamList.length;
        for(int i = 0; i < numTeams; i++){
            if(teamName.equalsIgnoreCase(teamList[i].getName())){
                return teamList[i];
            }
        }
        return null;
    }

        // Clear the points for each team in the league.
    public void clearPoints(){
```

Code 9.37   (*Continued*)

```
        final TeamDetails[] teamList = getTeams();
        final int numTeams = teamList.length;
        for(int i = 0; i < numTeams; i++){
            teamList[i].setPoints(0);
        }
    }

    public TeamDetails[] getTeams(){
        return teams;
    }

        // Take a copy of the array's data.
    private void setTeams(TeamDetails[] t){
        if(t != null){
            final int num = t.length;
            teams = new TeamDetails[num];
            System.arraycopy(t,0,teams,0,num);
        }
    }

    // The details are set from the constructor.
    private TeamDetails[] teams;
}
```

Notice that the array of TeamDetails passed in to the constructor is copied by the setTeams mutator, as described in Section 9.11. This ensures that a League's teams attribute is not affected by any subsequent changes made outside the class to the array object passed in as the constructor's argument. Code 9.38 shows a simplistic test-rig that creates a League object containing four teams and changes the points of one of them.

Code 9.38   Setting up a League object's TeamDetails (LeagueMain.java)

```
    // A minimal example program to create and manipulate a simple
    // fixed-size league of team details.
class LeagueMain {
    public static void main(String[] args){
        // Create the League object from four sample sets
        // of team details.
        League league = new League(new TeamDetails[]{
            new TeamDetails("Kestrels", "Able Amy", "Ambleside"),
            new TeamDetails("Eagles", "Brave Ben", "Big Rock"),
            new TeamDetails("Hawks", "Capable Charis", "Cheam"),
            new TeamDetails("Falcons", "Dull Dan", "Ditchfield"),
        });

        // Print the before-state of the league.
        System.out.println("======= Before =======");
```

(*Continued*)

Code 9.38 *(Continued)*

```
    league.print();

    // Give one of the teams a point.
    league.addPoints("Kestrels",1);

    // Print the after-state of the league.
    System.out.println("======== After ========");
    league.print();
  }
}
```

Notice the way in which this example uses an anonymous array, because there is no need for a named reference to the array in the remainder of the main method.

Exercise 9.15 Modify the main method of the `LeagueMain` class (shown in Code 9.38) so that it uses a `SimpleInput` object to interactively set up the teams for a League. Prompt the user for the number of teams in the league, construct a suitably-sized array to hold the TeamDetails, and then read the details for the required number of teams as strings. Add further statements to the main method to thoroughly test the League and TeamDetails classes.

Exercise 9.16 Design your own class to hold details on a sport with which you are familiar. Implement a class to hold a fixed number of teams, with methods to manipulate them in appropriate ways.

9.17 Multi-Dimensional Arrays

Some applications require multi-dimensional arrays; for example, many mathematical problems use matrices, and many games have a two-dimensional board structure. Two-dimensional array objects are created in Java using the following syntax:

```
    final int numRows = 10, numCols = 5;
    double[][] matrix = new double[numRows][numCols];
```

The effect of this is to create a ten-by-five grid for storing floating point numbers. The object referred to by `matrix` might be initialized as shown in Code 9.39.

Each dimension of the array must be indexed individually, within its own set of square brackets, that is, `matrix[row][col]`.[6] In fact, Java regards `matrix` as being an ordinary array object of length 10, in which each element of the array is

---

[6] It is **not** permitted to list the indices in a single pair of square brackets, thus `matrix[row,col]` is illegal.

Code 9.39   Initializing a matrix structure

```
// The value to store in elements other than those
// on the leading diagonal.
final double nonDiagonalValue = -1.0;
final double diagonalValue = 1.0;
// Iterate over the first dimension.
for(int row = 0; row < matrix.length; row++){
    // Iterate over the second dimension.
    for(int col = 0; col < matrix[row].length; col++){
        if(row == col){
            // The leading diagonal.
            matrix[row][col] = diagonalValue;
        }
        else{
            matrix[row][col] = nonDiagonalValue;
        }
    }
}
```

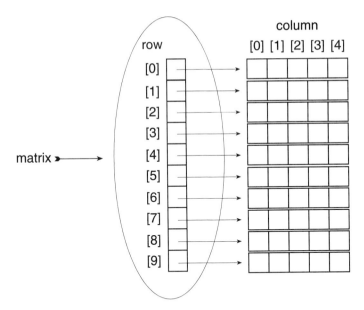

Figure 9.6   A two-dimensional array object

another array object of length 5—an array of arrays (Figure 9.6). This is reflected in the fact that the dimensions can be allocated separately, as shown in Code 9.40.

The first new-statement allocates an array whose elements will each contain a reference to one of the rows of the matrix. We delay specifying the lengths of the dimensions other than the first in the new-statement by leaving the remaining brackets empty. The loop then allocates a new array object for each of these. One implication of this is that we can change a whole row of a matrix, if we wish, simply

---

Code 9.40   Defining an array of arrays

```
final int numRows = 10, numCols = 5;
double[][] matrix = new double[numRows][];
// Allocate the rows.
for(int row = 0; row < matrix.length; row++){
    matrix[row] = new double[numCols];
}
```

Code 9.41   Initializing a two-dimensional array

```
char[][] hiddenWord = {
    { 'd', 'g', 'i', 'b' },
    { 'e', 'i', 'u', 'm' },
    { 't', 'a', 's', 'a' },
};
```

---

by assigning a different reference to the appropriate row element. Swapping rows is equally easy:

```
// Swap the rows matrix[3] and matrix[4].
double[] temp = matrix[3];
matrix[3] = matrix[4];
matrix[4] = temp;
```

No numbers are copied, only the row references are swapped. Another implication is that each row may have a different number of elements, see Section 9.17.1.

Short-hand initialization of multi-dimensional arrays is available, just as for single-dimension arrays; a pair of curly brackets is used to indicate the length of each dimension (Code 9.41). The array, hiddenWord, contains three rows and four columns.

9.17.1   Non-Rectangular Arrays

Because each row in a two-dimensional array is an array in its own right, it is perfectly possible for the rows to be different lengths. Compare the creation of a rectangular matrix in Code 9.40 with that of a triangular array in Code 9.42.

Code 9.42   Creation of a Pascal's triangle

```
final int numRows = 5;
int[][] triangle = new int[numRows][];
for(int row = 0; row < triangle.length; row++){
    triangle[row] = new int[row+1];
}
```

Code 9.43 Initialization of a triangular array

```
int[][] triangle = {
    {1},
    {1,1},
    {1,2,1},
    {1,3,3,1},
    {1,4,6,4,1},
};
```

The first row of `triangle` is of length 1, the second of length 2, and so on. There is no problem with initializing such arrays in the same way as was done with rectangular two-dimensional arrays (Code 9.43).

Exercise 9.17   In Exercise 7.17, we noted that colors in graphical applications are often defined in terms of three separate red, green, and blue color component values. For instance, black would have component values of (0,0,0) and white would be (255,255,255). The PicturePlotter described in Exercise 7.4 has the following method defined for setting a color table for the image to be displayed:

```
public void setColorTable(int[][] table)
```

Each row of the table consists of three red, green, and blue values for a single color. Modify your solution to Exercise 7.4 to set a color table on the plotter for the image before the data is read. This could just contain the values for black in row zero and white in row one, for instance, or you might like to experiment with a more complex table.

Exercise 9.18   Modify your solution to Exercise 9.17 so that the color values are read from the input file. You might modify the format of the input file so that the color table is listed after the width and height of the image. You will probably include a count of how many colors there are, for instance:

```
174 199
2
0 0 0
255 255 255
63 3 55 3 6 0 50 3
...
```

Exercise 9.19   Find two different ways of creating a two-dimensional array of integers with three elements in its first row, six in its second, and one in its third.

9.18 Review

Here are the main points that we have covered in the preceding sections:

- Arrays may have multiple dimensions.
- Each dimension of an array is treated as a separate object.

- The elements of a dimension in a multi-dimensional array may have different lengths.

9.19   Case Study: A Tic-Tac-Toe Game

The game of Tic-Tac-Toe (or Noughts and Crosses) provides a well-known example that will serve to illustrate the use of a two-dimensional grid of values. In this section, we shall look at the design of some classes to implement the game. To add some variety, we shall design these so that the game can be played within a square grid of any width greater than 2.

There are two distinct classes that should be implemented in this program; TTTGame to maintain the current state of the board—which squares are free and which are occupied, whether the game is over—and TTTManager to manage the game—whose turn it is to move, whether a player has won, displaying the state of the game. If we can keep these two aspects separate—that is, in different classes that communicate through a well-defined interface—then we should be able to make modifications to one without unduly affecting the operation of the other. Our goal is to keep the coupling between the classes relatively weak, therefore. For instance, the class managing the game might allow either two humans to play a game against each other, or one human to play against a computer player, or a random game to be played for illustrative purposes. The class maintaining the current state of the game should not have to know about any of these details. Similarly, the game manager does not need to know how the other class works out whether anyone has won, or what sort of data structure is used to store the state of the board; changes to these should not affect how a game is run.

9.19.1   The TTTGame Class

We start by identifying the attributes and methods required by the TTTGame class that maintains the current state of the game. First, it keeps track of which squares are occupied. Some form of grid, representing the board, is an obvious choice for this, and it can be held in a square two-dimensional array. An array is appropriate because the dimensions of the board are fixed for the entire length of the game and we want to be able to access its elements in a random fashion. What type should be used for the array's elements? Each square must be able to represent three possible states: empty, occupied by a Nought or occupied by a Cross, so any of the integer types, or a char type might be suitable. To make printing of the board slightly easier, we will use char and store 'X' for a Cross and 'O' for a Nought, with '.' as an arbitrary character signifying an empty square.

Methods in this class will be needed to:

- Clear the board for a new game.
- Allow a particular square on the board to be used.
- Display the board.
- Determine the current state of the game.

Code 9.44 outlines most of what we have described so far.

```java
    // This class implements the grid structure used for the board.
    // All board operations and enquiries are made via this class.
public class TTTGame {
    // The minimum grid size.
    public static final int minimumSize = 3;

    // The characters used to mark the board.
    public static final char Free = '.', Nought = 'O', Cross = 'X';

    // Game state indicators.
    public static final int NoughtWon = 0, CrossWon = 1, Drawn = 2,
                            Unfinished = 3;

    // If no grid size is specified, use the normal size of 3x3.
    public TTTGame(){
        this(minimumSize);
    }

        // Create a size-by-size grid, as long as size fits the minimum.
    public TTTGame(int size){
        if(size < minimumSize){
            System.out.println(size+" must be at least "+minimumSize);
            // Use the minimum.
            size = minimumSize;
        }
        // Create the grid.
        grid = new char[size][size];
        // Fill the grid with Free indicators.
        clearTheBoard();
    }

    public void clearTheBoard(){
        char[][] board = getGrid();
        final int size = getBoardSize();

        for(int row = 0; row < size; row++){
            for(int col = 0; col < size; col++){
                board[row][col] = Free;
            }
        }
    }

        // player wishes to play at row,col.
    public void play(int row,int col,char player){
        // Assume the move is valid.
        char[][] board = getGrid();
        board[row][col] = player;
    }

        // Print the board on standard output.
    public void showBoard(){
```

(Continued)

Code 9.44   *(Continued)*

```
        char[][] board = getGrid();
        final int size = getBoardSize();

        for(int row = 0; row < size; row++){
            for(int col = 0; col < size; col++){
                System.out.print(board[row][col]);
            }
            System.out.println();
        }
    }

    // What is the state of the game?
    // Return one of the game state indicators.
    public int gameState(){
        ...
    }

    public int getBoardSize(){
        return grid.length;
    }

    private char[][] getGrid(){
        return grid;
    }

    // The board. Initialized by the constructor according to the
    // required size.
    private final char[][] grid;
}
```

The constructor creates the rows and columns of the `grid` array to be allocated according to the requested size and then clears the board ready for a new game. Each move of the game involves a `play` message being received, with the row and column for the square and a character representing a `Nought` or a `Cross`. The `gameState` method has been left incomplete, for the time being, because this is the most complex part of the class to implement.

At this stage, we should make sure that the public interface presented in the `TTTGame` class is sufficient to play a game of Tic-Tac-Toe, whether this be between two human players or any other combination of human and computer opponents.

- A new TTTGame object is constructed.
- The first move is made by a call to `play`.
- After each move, the state of the game can be determined by a call to `game-State` in order to ascertain whether the last person to play has won, or whether the board is full and the game drawn.
- After each move, the board may be displayed, if desired, with `showBoard`.

This seems to be sufficient for a game to be played. However, note that there is no provision for the TTTGame object to respond to a `play` message with an indication that the requested square was either already occupied or the grid position was not legal. If we wished to anticipate such errors, `play` will either have to return a valid or invalid indication (via a `boolean` return type), or throw an exception indicating an error (see Chapter 11). Alternatively, we would just assume that only legal moves will be made. Related to this is the fact that there is currently no way for a player to find out which squares are occupied, or whether a particular square is free. Without such methods, players would have to rely on the game manager to tell them which squares the other player has used, and it would become the manager's responsibility to keep track of the current state of the board. This would mean, in effect, that the manager would have to maintain a grid structure that duplicates the one maintained by the TTTGame object. Such duplication of effort is rather pointless and a potential source of error. In view of this, we will add an `isSquareFree` method to the public interface of the class and an `isSquareValid` method to its private implementation.

```
// Return true if square (row,col) is free and valid, false otherwise.
public boolean isSquareFree(int row, int col)

// Return true if row,col is within the grid, false otherwise.
private boolean isSquareValid(int row,int col)
```

Now, the game manager will be able to check the legality of a player's move by asking the TTTGame object to arbitrate.

9.19.2   The TTTManager Class

Before looking further at the implementation of the TTTGame class, consider the TTTManager class shown in Code 9.45.

The controlling loop in its `play` method shows that it needs to be able to find out from the TTTGame object whether the game is over or not. An alternative to the cascading if-else statement in `reportTheResult` would be the use of a switch statement (see Section 9.20.1). Developing the TTTManager class has identified the need for some further methods in the TTTGame class, for switching players (`nextPlayer`) and determining which player has won (`hasWon`). This particular manager simply generates random moves for alternating players (`makeARandom-Move`) in order to provide a simulation. This particular manager uses a `TTTDisplay` object to show a GUI representation of the game state in `makeARandomMove` (Figure 9.7), but this could easily be replaced by use of TTTGame's `showBoard` method.

9.19.3   The gameState Method

The `gameState` method of TTTGame has been left until last because it is the hardest to write. There are four possible states that may be returned:

- The Nought player has won by forming a line across any row, down any column, or along one of the two diagonals (`NoughtWon`).
- The Cross player has done likewise (`CrossWon`).
- The board is full without either player having formed a row, and hence the game is `Drawn`.
- The game is neither won nor drawn, and so remains `Unfinished`.

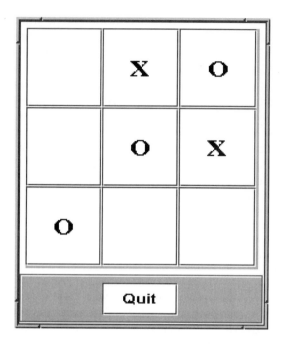

Figure 9.7 A GUI for the Tic-Tac-Toe game (`TTTMain.java`)

Code 9.45 The class that coordinates the players of a TTT game (`TTTManager.java`)

```
        // Run a game of noughts and crosses.
        // Squares are chosen randomly.
class TTTManager {
    // How big the game's board should be.
    public TTTManager(int size){
        game = new TTTGame(size);
        // Create a display for the game.
        display = new TTTDisplay(size);
    }

    // Play a single game.
    public void play(){
        final TTTGame game = getGame();
        game.clearTheBoard();
        getDisplay().clear();

        // Who plays next.
        char player = TTTGame.Nought;
        while(game.gameState() == TTTGame.Unfinished){
            makeARandomMove(player);
            if(!game.hasWon(player)){
                player = game.nextPlayer(player);
            }
        }

        reportTheResult();
    }
```

Code 9.45   (*Continued*)

```
        // Make a random move for player.
    private void makeARandomMove(char player){
        final TTTGame game = getGame();
        // We shall generate a random row and column for each move.
        int row, col;
        // Generate a valid random move.
        do{
            row = getRandomPosition();
            col = getRandomPosition();
        } while(!game.isSquareFree(row,col));
        // Play in the chosen square.
        game.play(row,col,player);
        getDisplay().showSquare(row,col,player);
    }

    private void reportTheResult(){
        final TTTGame game = getGame();
        int result = game.gameState();

        if(result == TTTGame.Drawn){
            System.out.println("The game was drawn.");
        }
        else if(result == TTTGame.NoughtWon){
            System.out.println(TTTGame.Nought+" won.");
        }
        else if(result == TTTGame.CrossWon){
            System.out.println(TTTGame.Cross+" won.");
        }
        else{
            System.out.println("Unknown result: "+result);
        }
    }

    // Return a valid random number as part of a move.
    private int getRandomPosition(){
        return (int) (Math.random() * getGame().getBoardSize());
    }

    private TTTGame getGame(){
        return game;
    }

    private TTTDisplay getDisplay(){
        return display;
    }

    // The board. Initialized in the constructor.
    private final TTTGame game;
    // A GUI for the game.
    private final TTTDisplay display;
}
```

When this method is called, how should it work out the answer? It could either work it out from scratch by examining the board, or keep a running record of it. In the latter case, each time a new square is played into, the game object must update its understanding of the state of the game so that it is ready to respond to a `gameState` request at any time. The former approach is easier to program as it is self-contained within the `gameState` method.

To determine whether a player has won, we define a `hasWon` method to examine each row, column, and diagonal in order to count the squares that this player has. Code 9.46 shows an outline of how we might approach this.

Code 9.46   Outline for determining whether a player has won

```
    // Has player won?
public boolean hasWon(char player){
    // How many of player's moves.
    int count;
    final int size = getBoardSize();
    // Look along the rows.
    for(int row = 0; row < size; row++){
        count = 0;
        for(int col = 0; col < size; col++){
            if(board[row][col] == player){
                count++;
            }
        }
        if(count == size){
            return true;
        }
    }
    // Look along the columns.
    for(int col = 0; col < size; col++){
        count = 0;
        for(int row = 0; row < size; row++){
            if(board[row][col] == player){
                count++;
            }
        }
        if(count == size){
            return true;
        }
    }
    // Look along the left-to-right diagonal.
    count = 0;
    for(int row = 0; row < numRows; row++){
        if(board[row][row] == player){
            count++;
        }
    }
    if(count == size){
        return true;
    }
```

Code 9.46   (*Continued*)

```
    // Look along the right-to-left diagonal.
    count = 0;
    for(int row = 0; row < numRows; row++){
        if(board[row][size-row-1] == player){
            count++;
        }
    }
    return count == size;
}
```

Is this a good approach? First, it checks the rows, then the columns, then each diagonal. That means two passes over the full size of the board and two passes along the rows. We can achieve the same effect with just a single pass over the board, by recognizing that the `row` and `col` loop variables can be used interchangeably for checking along the rows and down the columns. Code 9.47 shows this in action as it is implemented in the TTTGame class.

Code 9.47   Has the given player won? (`TTTGame.java`)

```
    // This class implements the grid structure used for the board.
    // All board operations and enquiries are made via this class.
public class TTTGame {
    ...
    // Game state indicators.
    public static final int NoughtWon = 0, CrossWon = 1, Drawn = 2,
                            Unfinished = 3;
    ...
    // What is the state of the game?
    // Return one of the game state indicators.
    public int gameState(){
        // Has someone won?
        if(hasWon(Nought)){
            return NoughtWon;
        }
        else if(hasWon(Cross)){
            return CrossWon;
        }
        else{
            final int size = getBoardSize();
            char[][] board = getGrid();
            // Check to see if the board is full.
            for(int row = 0; row < size; row++){
                for(int col = 0; col < size; col++){
                    if(board[row][col] == Free){
                        return Unfinished;
                    }
                }
            }
```

(*Continued*)

Code 9.47   (*Continued*)

```
                return Drawn;
        }
    }

        // Has player won?
    public boolean hasWon(char player){
        final int size = getBoardSize();
        final char[][] board = getGrid();
        // Counts for the two diagonals.
        int leftDiagonalCount = 0, rightDiagonalCount = 0;
        for(int x = 0; x < size; x++){
            // How many for player on this row.
            int rowCount = 0;
            // How many for player on this col.
            int colCount = 0;
            for(int y = 0; y < size; y++){
                // Check the row.
                if(board[x][y] == player){
                    rowCount++;
                }
                // Check the column.
                if(board[y][x] == player){
                    colCount++;
                }
            }
            if((rowCount == size) || (colCount == size)){
                return true;
            }
            // Check the two diagonals.
            if(board[x][x] == player){
                leftDiagonalCount++;
            }
            if(board[x][size-x-1] == player){
                rightDiagonalCount++;
            }
        }
        if((leftDiagonalCount == size) || (rightDiagonalCount == size)){
            return true;
        }
        else{
            return false;
        }
    }
    ...
}
```

The loop variables have been given the coordinate names x and y to show that they are not tightly tied to uniquely indexing either the rows or the columns.

Even this version shows that there are still plenty of other ways this could be done; it only tells us whether the particular player identified in the `player` argument has won—what about the other? Should we rewrite this so that it checks for both players at once? That would involve keeping two separate sets of counts. In the version shown in Code 9.46, we do not need to keep checking across that row once a square not belonging to the player is found, since a player can only win by having their piece in every square in a row (or column or diagonal). Using a *break statement* (see Section 9.20.2) would allow us to leave the inner loops if we find a mismatch, as follows:

```
if(board[row][col] != player){
    break;
}
count++;
```

What we are discussing here are trade-offs between simplicity and efficiency. The version shown in Code 9.46 is very simple but not very efficient. The version shown in Code 9.47 is more efficient, but harder to understand. Adding further refinements to either approach for the sake of efficiency would add further complexity and obscurity, and we won't pursue these ideas further here, although you might like to consider them as informal exercises. A full implementation of this class may be found in the file TTTGame.java and the main method to run the game may be found in the file TTTMain.java.

Exercise 9.20   Check that the current implementation of the Tic-Tac-Toe game is correct for grid sizes larger than three-by-three.

Exercise 9.21   The gameState method of the TTTGame class (shown in Code 9.47) iterates over the whole board looking for a Free square in order to report whether the game is Unfinished or Drawn. Add another attribute to the class that keeps a record of the number of free squares left on the board. Use the value of this attribute to simplify the gameState method.

Exercise 9.22   Design and implement a TTTPlayer class that will allow a user to input moves on the board. You may assume that the TTTManager will continue to coordinate the game, asking an object of your class for moves when required. The TTTManager class must be modified to enable it to interact with objects of this class. What must the public interface of TTTPlayer be to make this interaction possible? How should possibly incorrect moves by a human player be handled; which class should be responsible for checking this? Does the TTTPlayer need direct access to the TTTGame object? Make your implementation able to play on any valid grid size.

Exercise 9.23   Suppose you wished to write a non-interactive class that took on one side of a Tic-Tac-Toe game, and tried to win or at least draw. If this class is not to maintain its own representation of the board, would you need further methods to be added to the TTTGame class to make this possible? If so, what would they be? Design and implement such a class.

Exercise 9.24   If the TTTGame class wished to keep its idea of the current state of the game up-to-date as soon as each move has been played, what additional attributes would you add to it? What would it have to do to update these attributes after each move?

It is probably worth pointing out that, while a two-dimensional array is the obvious choice for representing the board, an imitation of the physical board is not necessarily required. The state of the game could equally well be represented by keeping a list of moves, for instance. Determining whether a square is free then becomes a check to see whether the same move already exists within the list. Does this make checking for a winning line harder?

9.20   Further Control Statements

Java defines three remaining statements that can be used to influence the flow of control through a method: the *switch statement*, the *break statement* and the *continue statement*. We discuss each of these, in turn, in the next few sections.

9.20.1   The Switch Statement

Cascading if-else statements, in which the value of an expression is compared against a succession of candidate constant values, are quite common (Code 9.48). If the values to be checked against are all compile-time constant integer expressions (including `char` expressions), we can rewrite it as a *switch statement*, as in Code 9.49.

The expression to be compared against a set of possible values is written between a pair of parentheses following the `switch` reserved word. This is followed by an opening curly bracket marking the body of the switch statement. Inside the body of the statement are listed the individual *case labels* against which the value of the expression is to be compared. Each label value is preceded by the `case` reserved word and followed by a colon symbol (`:`). One or more statements may be written for each case, and the switch statement differs from all the other control structures we have seen, thus far, in that curly brackets are not required for multiple-statements to be included within a single case. The final statement of each case is typically a *break statement*, written as the reserved word `break` followed by a semicolon. The

---

Code 9.48   A cascading if-else statement

```
if(expr == 1){
    statements1;
}
else if(expr == 6){
    statements2;
}
else if(expr == 9){
    statements3;
}
...
else{
    // None of the values matched.
    statementsN;
}
```

Code 9.49   Outline for a switch statement

```
switch(expr){
    case 1:
        statements1;
        break;
    case 6:
        statements2;
        break;
    case 9:
        statements3;
        break;
    ...
    default:
        // None of the values matched.
        statementsN;
        break;
}
```

statements following the *default label* are selected if the value of the switch expression matches none of the case labels. If there is no match and no default label, then the body of the whole statement is skipped and control continues with whatever follows it.

The type of the expression used to select a case label may be any of the integer types (`byte`, `char`, `short`, `int`, `long`). The example in Code 9.50 illustrates part of a method to select a choice from a menu based upon a user's key press.

Code 9.50   Respond to a choice from a menu

```
    // Act on the user's menu choice.
public void menuAction(char choice){
    switch(choice){
        case 'd':
            delete();
            break;
        case 'i':
            insert();
            break;
        case 'h':
            help();
            break;
        case 'q':
            quit();
            break;
        ...
        default:
            System.out.println("Unknown command: "+choice);
            break;
    }
}
```

Code 9.51   Order of labels is irrelevant to their selection

```
// Act on the user's menu choice.
public void menuAction(char choice){
    switch(choice){
        default:
            System.out.println("Unknown command: "+choice);
            break;
        case 'q':
            quit();
            break;
        case 'h':
            help();
            break;
        case 'i':
            insert();
            break;
        case 'd':
            delete();
            break;
        ...
    }
}
```

In contrast to a cascading if-else statement, the order in which the cases are listed does not necessarily imply an order in which the case labels are tested against the value of the switch expression. Where there is a large number of cases to choose from, the compiler is quite likely to find an efficient method to select the correct case directly. In addition, the default label need not be listed last; it will still only be selected if no case labels match the expression. Therefore, the example in Code 9.51 is exactly equivalent to that in Code 9.50.

The *break statement* that terminates each case is an ordinary statement that transfers control to the end of the whole switch statement. If a break statement is omitted from one of the cases, then control will *fall through* to the immediately follow-ing case, even though its case label does not match the value of the switch expression. Code 9.52 illustrates how this might be used to adjust the xpos and ypos values of a position according to a compass point direction passed into a move method.

Code 9.52   Falling through to the next case

```
class Turtle {
    // Names for the compass points.
    public static final int North = 0, South = 1,
                            East = 2, West = 3,
                            NorthEast = 4, NorthWest = 5,
                            ...;

    // Adjust (xpos,ypos) according to direction.
    public void move(int direction){
        switch(direction){
```

Code 9.52   (*Continued*)

```
            case NorthEast:
                xpos++;
                // Fall through.
            case North:
                ypos--;
                break;
            case SouthWest:
                xpos--;
                // Fall through.
            case South:
                ypos++;
                break;
            ...
        }
    }
    ...
}
```

If the value of direction is North, then the value of ypos is decremented by one. If the value of direction is NorthEast, then the value of xpos is incremented by one before falling through to the following case, where the value of ypos is decremented by one. Omitting a break statement is often the result of error, so we have been careful to include a comment to indicate that the fall through is intentional. In fact, we do not recommend that this approach be overused, as it can make program code harder to understand. Not much is saved by omitting the full set of statements from the fall through cases in many instances. Omission of break statements and use of fall through is legitimate when used in circumstances such as that shown in Code 9.53. In this example, several case labels have identical statements associated with them—it is not a case of partially completing an action under one label and completing it by using the fall through mechanism.

Code 9.53   Identical statements for different case labels

```
    // Return a classification according to the given grade.
public int classify(char grade){
    switch(grade){
        case 'A': case 'B':
            return Distinction;
        case 'C': case 'D': case 'E':
            return Merit;
        case 'P':
            return Pass;
        default:
            return Fail;
    }
}
```

In effect, case label ′A′ has no statements associated with it; if selected, control falls straight through to the statements with the ′B′ label and Distinction is returned. Similarly, there are no statements associated with label ′C′ so, when grade has that value, control falls through to the ′D′ label. Since it too has no statements, control falls through again to the ′E′ label, where the value of Merit is returned. A set of statements may be labeled by any number of cases in this way.

Note that no break statements are necessary in the example shown in Code 9.53. Writing the first two cases as

```
case 'A': case 'B':
    return Distinction;
    break;
```

for instance, would result in a Statement not reached error message from the compiler, referring to the break statement.

Although we have compared switch statements to cascading if-else statements, there are some important differences. In particular, the use of a switch is limited to those circumstances in which we have an integer expression that is to be compared against a known set of constant integer case labels. We cannot use ranges or Boolean expressions for case labels. This means that the example in Code 9.54 is illegal.

9.20.2   The Break Statement

In Section 9.20.1, we introduced the *break statement* in the context of the switch statement. We can also use a break statement to break out from a loop without waiting for the terminating condition to become false. Code 9.55 shows a modified version of Code 9.30 that avoids the error associated with that example.

The break statement in the body of the if-statement causes the loop to be terminated immediately, before the post-body update expression is executed at the end of the current iteration. Control continues with the statement immediately following the for loop.

Great care should always be exercised when including a break statement within a loop. The reason is that it introduces a means of leaving the loop that is an alternative to the normal controlling condition. Statements following the loop's body can no

Code 9.54   Illegal use of a switch statement

```
public int classify(int mark){
    // Totally illegal.
    switch(mark){
        // Relational operators are not allowed here.
        case >= 70:
            return Distinction;
        // Boolean operators are not allowed here.
        case < 70 && >= 60:
            return Merit;
        ...
    }
}
```

Code 9.55 Breaking out of a for loop

```
    // Return the index of value in numbers if it is there.
    // Return -1 if it is not there.
public int indexOf(int[] numbers,int value){
    // The value to return if value is not in numbers.
    final int notPresent = -1;
    // Stop if we reach the end of the array or if
    // we find the value.
    int index;
    boolean found = false;
    for(index = 0; index < numbers.length; index++){
        if(numbers[index] == value){
            found = true;
            // Leave now - before the index is incremented.
            break;
        }
    }
    return found ? index : notPresent;
}
```

longer assume that they have been reached solely because the terminating condition now has the value `false`. This means that it is often necessary to place a test immediately following a loop that contains a break statement, in order to determine how the loop was terminated. We see this principle in Code 9.55; the loop is left because either the value of `index` has exceeded the bounds of the array, or because the value was found and the break statement executed.

9.20.3 The Continue Statement

The *continue statement* can be used to skip immediately to the end of the loop body but without leaving the loop. Used inside a for loop, the next part of the loop to be executed will be the post-body update expression. Code 9.56 shows an example in which numbers between 1 and 100 that are not divisible by any of the three values passed to the method are to be printed.

If num is divisible by x, then the continue statement skips over all the remaining statements in the body of the loop and increments num ready for the termination test. If it is not divisible by x, then control continues with the test against the value of y and so on. Only if each test fails is the remainder of the loop executed.

Continue statements may be used in all of the loop statements we have seen—while, do, and for—however, care should be exercised in their use, as they can make it difficult to follow the logic of a loop. In general, we shall avoid their use.

9.20.4 Labeled Statements

Any statement may be preceded by a *label*, which is an identifier followed by a colon symbol:

```
    outerLoop:
    while(condition) ...
```

Code 9.56   Skip printing numbers divisible by x, y, or z

```
// Print the numbers from 1..100 that are not divisible by
// either x, y or z.
public void skipPrinting(int x, int y, int z){
    for(int num = 1; num <= 100; num++){
        if((num % x) == 0){
            continue;
        }
        if((num % y) == 0){
            continue;
        }
        if((num % z) == 0){
            continue;
        }
        // This one isn't divisible by them, so print it.
        System.out.println(num);
    }
}
```

The most common reason for using labels is to supply a target for a break or continue statement that is deeply nested within the labeled statement. If break is followed by the name of a label, control breaks out of the labeled statement:

```
outerLoop:
for(int i = 0; i < numRows; i++){
    for(int j = 0; j < numCols; j++){
        if(box[i][j] != 0){
            found = true;
            // Break out of both loops.
            break outerLoop;
        }
    }
}
```

If continue is followed by the name of a label, the label should be attached to a loop statement, and control continues to the end of the body of the labeled loop, ready for the next iteration.

In many ways, labels are an encouragement to disrupt the normal flow of control, and use of such statements tends to make the logic of a method hard to understand or reason about. We consider their use to be poor programming practice.

Care must be taken not to confuse case labels with statement labels. The example in Code 9.57 illustrates a particularly nasty error. Perhaps surprisingly, the default case will be selected in the switch statement. The problem is that case has been incorrectly omitted from in front of the South, East, and West cases. However, to the compiler, these look like statement labels, so there is no compilation error, but the statement does not do what you would expect.

Code 9.57   The default case will be (incorrectly) selected

```
final int North = 0, South = 1, East = 2, West = 3;
int dir = South;
switch(dir){
    case North: South: East: West:
        System.out.println(dir);
        break;
    default:
        System.out.println("Gotcha!");
        break;
}
```

9.21 Review

Here are the main points that we have covered in the preceding sections:

- The switch statement offers an efficient alternative to multiple if-else statements where the expression being tested is a simple integer expression.
- The expressions used for case labels must be compile-time constant expressions.
- A break statement should be used at the end of a case to prevent fall through.
- The order of cases is arbitrary.
- A default case may be used to pick up a value which matches none of the cases.
- The break statement may be used to break out of an immediately enclosing loop.
- The continue statement may be used to skip to the end of an immediately enclosing loop, ready for the next iteration.
- Statements may be labeled. A labeled statement may be used as the target of a break or continue statement.

Exercise 9.25   Rewrite the reportTheResult method of the TTTManager class (shown in Code 9.45) to use a switch statement, rather than a cascading if-else statement.

Exercise 9.26   What would be the output from method m shown in Code 9.58?

Exercise 9.27   An outline for the class CarPark is shown in Code 9.59. Complete this class according to the following requirements:

- A CarPark has a fixed capacity, set on construction.
- The getSpaces method returns the number of empty locations in the car park.
- The full method returns true if there are no free locations in the car park, otherwise it returns false.
- A Car is added to the car park via its park method, which returns an integer indicating the location of the car. This location will be used later as an argument to the collect method.

- A Car is removed via the `collect` method, which takes a location number as its argument. The location becomes free. The value `null` should be returned if the location number is outside the bounds of the array, or if there is no Car at the location.

A dummy `Car` class (Code 9.60) can be used to test your implementation.

Code 9.58   A loop containing break and continue statements

```
public void m(){
    System.out.println("Start of loop.");
    for(int i = 0; i < 5; i++){
        if(i == 2){
            continue;
        }
        else if(i == 3){
            break;
        }
        else{
            System.out.println(i);
        }
        System.out.println("End of iteration.");
    }
    System.out.println("End of loop.");
}
```

Code 9.59   An outline of the CarPark class (`CarPark.java`)

```
    // Exercise outline.
class CarPark {
        // Create parking spaces for capacity cars.
    public CarPark(int capacity){
    }

        // How many free spaces?
    public int getSpaces(){
    }

        // Is the car park full?
    public boolean full(){
    }

        // Park the given car, and return its location number.
    public int park(Car c){
    }

        // Collect the car from the given location.
    public Car collect(int location){
    }
}
```

Code 9.60   The Car class, for testing CarPark (`Car.java`)

```
    // A dummy class for the CarPark class to use.
public class Car {
    public Car(String license){
        this.license = license;
    }

    public String getLicense(){
        return license;
    }

    private final String license;
}
```

In this chapter, we have introduced the ability to create arrays—fixed-sized collections of values or objects. In the next chapter, we shall see how to create flexible- and arbitrary-sized collections of objects, using classes from the `java.util` package.

10

Collection Classes

In this chapter, we look at classes which allow data and objects to be grouped together in flexible-size collections. The main classes considered from the `java.util` package are `ArrayList`, `LinkedList`, and `HashMap`. We conclude the chapter with a brief introduction to recursion.

10.1 Introduction

As we saw in Chapter 9, the need to group together related items of data or collections of objects is a common one when writing programs. By grouping together a set of related objects or data values in a single object, it becomes possible to manipulate the group as a whole as well as the individual items. Arrays are a little more specialized than general collections, but they are easier to understand and use. They are also preferred for storing values of the primitive types. However, the collection classes provide an important flexibility and generality over arrays which means that we shall often use them in preference to arrays. In particular, arrays are fixed in the number of items that they can hold, whereas collections are designed to hold dynamically varying numbers of objects.

10.2 The Need for Flexible-Size Collections

In order to illustrate a situation in which a collection class might be preferred over an array, consider the case of a radio show that offers a prize at random to one of many callers that phone in. The names of the callers over a limited period must be collected before the prize is awarded (see Code 10.1).

The exact number of callers to the show cannot be anticipated in advance because it could depend on many factors—the time of day, the nature of the prize, and so on. If we choose to use an array to hold the names, then there are two approaches we could use:

- Define a very large array that should be more than big enough to hold the names of all the callers.
- Define a smaller array and place a limit on the number of callers to match the size of the array.

Code 10.1   Collect the names of callers to a radio show (`RadioShowMain.java`)

```
    // Collect an arbitrary number of callers to a radio show phone-in
    // competition. Then randomly select one as the prize winner.
class RadioShowMain {
    public static void main(String[] args){
        // Read the names of users.
        SimpleInput keyboard = new SimpleInput();
        // Read names until 'end' is typed.
        final String endMarker = "end";

        // Collect callers to a particular program.
        RadioShow show = new RadioShow("Win with Walter");

        System.out.println("Give the callers' names. Finish with "+
                            endMarker);
        // Read the first name.
        String name = keyboard.nextWord();
        while(!name.equalsIgnoreCase(endMarker)){
            show.addCaller(name);
            name = keyboard.nextWord();
        }

        // Report how many there are.
        int howMany = show.numCallers();
        System.out.println("There are: "+howMany+" callers to "+
                            show.getProgram());
        // Randomly select a winner.
        int which = (int) (Math.random()*howMany);
        System.out.println(show.selectCaller(which)+" is the winner.");
    }
}
```

Neither approach is entirely satisfactory; we have no guarantees that the first option really will provide enough space—a really good prize offered during one show could easily overflow the available space. Furthermore, a lot of unwanted space could be wasted on most occasions. The second option is also unsatisfactory because it could exclude a number of legitimate callers and undermine the attractiveness of the competition.

In situations where we can neither accurately predict the amount of space we require, or where the amount could vary significantly under different circumstances, it makes much more sense to use a flexible collection object.

The `ArrayList` class is one of several classes, defined in the `java.util` package, that provide an alternative to the use of arrays when objects need to be grouped in flexible-sized collections. While these classes have many similarities to arrays, they also have two main important differences, one of which is a pro and the other a con:

- They are not fixed in size—they grow and shrink according to the number of objects they are currently holding.
- They cannot ordinarily hold values of the primitive types.

On the positive side, their variable size is particularly useful when it is not known how many objects will have to be stored in the collection before it is created, or when the number of items might increase and decrease arbitrarily, from time to time. On the negative side, their inability to hold values of the primitive types is a little frustrating at times, but a work-around is possible through the use of *wrapper classes* (see Section 10.4). In the next section, we look at how to create and use an ArrayList object.

10.2.1   The ArrayList Class

The `ArrayList` class is defined in the `java.util` package, which means that it must be imported explicitly, by including the statement

```
import java.util.ArrayList;
```

or implicitly, by including the statement

```
import java.util.*;
```

at the head of any file containing classes that make use of it. As its name suggests, the class is implemented using an underlying array attribute, which means that we can efficiently access the items it holds using an integer index. A sample of its methods is shown in Table 10.1. An ArrayList object starts with a particular *capacity* but the varying size property is implemented quite simply by creating a new array with a larger capacity if the original becomes full and more space is required. The details

Table 10.1 Selected methods of the ArrayList class

	Method and Arguments
	ArrayList()
	ArrayList(Collection c)
	ArrayList(int capacity)
boolean	add(Object o)
void	add(int index,Object o)
boolean	addAll(Collection c)
boolean	addAll(int index,Collection c)
void	clear()
boolean	contains(Object o)
void	ensureCapacity(int capacity)
Object	get(int index)
int	indexOf(Object o)
boolean	isEmpty()
Iterator	iterator()
int	lastIndexOf(Object o)
ListIterator	listIterator()
Object	remove(int index)
boolean	remove(Object o)
Object	set(int index,Object o)
int	size()
Object[]	toArray()
Object[]	toArray(Object[] arr)
void	trimToSize()

Code 10.2   A class with an ArrayList attribute (`RadioShow.java`)

```java
import java.util.ArrayList;

    // Record a collection of callers to a radio phone-in program.
class RadioShow {
    public RadioShow(String prog){
        program = prog;
    }

        // Add the given caller to the current list.
    public void addCaller(String c){
        ArrayList callers = getCallers();
        callers.add(c);
    }

        // Replace one caller with another.
    public void replaceCaller(int which,String newCaller){
        ArrayList callers = getCallers();
        callers.set(which,newCaller);
    }

        // How many callers in the collection?
    public int numCallers(){
        return getCallers().size();
    }

    ...

    public String getProgram(){
        return program;
    }

    private ArrayList getCallers(){
        return callers;
    }

    // Which program they are calling into.
    private final String program;
    // The collection of caller names.
    private ArrayList callers = new ArrayList();
}
```

of this are entirely hidden from the user of the class by virtue of encapsulation. It is possible to go on adding items, *ad infinitum*, without taking any special action, because that is handled by the ArrayList itself. The class contains an `ensureCapacity` method that can be used to set a minimum capacity at any time, or an ArrayList can be created with an explicit initial capacity passed to one of the class's constructors. The radio show example in Code 10.1 implies that a `RadioShow` object will be used to collect the callers' names as a collection of String objects. Code 10.2 shows the outline of this class, including the declaration of an ArrayList attribute to hold the names.

If we had been defining an ordinary array to hold the names, we might have defined the `callers` attribute as

```
private String[] callers = new String[maxCallers];
```

whereas the ArrayList for the strings has been defined in Code 10.2 as

```
private ArrayList callers = new ArrayList();
```

The differences between the two are important to appreciate. You will notice that a major distinction between an array and an ArrayList is that the type of item to be held in an array (String, in this case) is part of the array's declaration, but it is not part of an ArrayList's; we simply create an object of type ArrayList, with no mention of the String class. This feature is common to all of the collection classes defined in the `java.util` package and it has important implications for the way in which we use collection objects. In effect, an object partially *loses its identity* when it is placed in a collection. We shall discuss the implications of this in Section 10.2.2.

Each item stored in an ArrayList has a unique index but, instead of using square-bracket syntax, a collection has methods to add, access, and remove elements from it. The `addCaller` method of the RadioShow class illustrates the ArrayList's `add` method. The first item added to the collection is given index 0 and the subsequent items are automatically given index values of 1, 2, etc. As we shall see, these indices may be used to retrieve an item from the collection via its `get` method. The number of items in a collection can be determined from its `size` method, as used by `numCallers` in Code 10.2. The occupant of a particular index may be replaced by using the `set` method, as shown in `replaceCaller`. A reference to the previous occupant is returned by `set` but a runtime error[1] will result if the index had not previously been used (that is if the index is greater than or equal to `size()`). A new item may be inserted at a particular index with the `add` method, which takes two arguments: the index for insertion and the object to be inserted. Existing items from this index position onwards are moved along by one place to make room.

All items may be removed from a collection by using its `clear` method, or a single item may be removed from a particular index by using the `remove` method. In this latter case, all items after the removed item are moved down by one to fill the gap, and the size of the collection is reduced by one. The current capacity of the array list is not reduced when one or more items are removed, which makes adding further items less likely to require the capacity to be increased (and the existing contents copied to a new array). If necessary, the current capacity of an array list can be reduced to exactly match the number of items it holds by using its `trimToSize` method. This ensures that extra (unused) space is not wasted, but it should probably only be done if the collection is unlikely to expand again in the near future.

The location of a particular object may be found using either the `indexOf` or `lastIndexOf` method. Both take a reference to the object to be located and return its integer index. If the object is not in the collection, both methods return -1. Clearly, the existence of both methods shows that the same object may occur more than once in the collection but, for some reason, there is no method to locate

---

[1] An `IndexOutOfBoundsException` exception.

other occurrences between the first and last. For a class that does not permit multiple occurrences of an object, see one of the `Set` classes, such as `HashSet`.

As can be seen, there are many similarities between arrays and ArrayList objects—particularly in terms of the relationship between elements and indices. Care must be taken to recognize that an element's index in a collection might change over time as other elements in the collection are added and removed. This will happen automatically if elements with lower indices are removed or extra items are inserted before it.

In the next section, we look at some of the complications that arise from the fact that an object partially loses its identity when placed in a collection, because the collection's declaration does not contain any information about the type of objects it will contain.

10.2.2   Collections and Object Identity

We sometimes need to make a distinction between the type of a variable and the type of the object to which the variable refers. We do this by using the terms *static type* and *dynamic type*. The dynamic type of an object is the name of the class used to construct it, whereas the static type of an object is the declared type of the variable we are using to refer to it. In all of the examples we have seen in the first few chapters, the static and dynamic types of the objects have been identical to each other. An object always remains aware of its own dynamic type, but we can sometimes lose track of an object's original static type. This is what happens when we place an object in a collection such as an ArrayList. The collection classes are merely passive repositories of objects; they have little interest in sending messages to the objects they store, so they do not need to keep any record of their original static types. One of the consequences of this fact is that a collection is not limited to holding objects of only a single class. Although we will not need to make use of this facility in this chapter, a collection may hold a mixture of different object types all at the same time. We say that it can hold a *heterogeneous collection* of objects. This is in contrast to an array which holds a *homogeneous collection* of objects or values of the type it was declared to hold. Inevitably, this flexibility provided by collections brings a penalty with it. We cannot simply `get` an object from a collection and store it straight into a variable of the type we know it to be, as follows:

```
ArrayList callers = getCallers();
// Get the first caller - compilation error.
String caller = callers.get(0);
```

If we were to try this, the compiler would say something like:

```
Explicit cast needed to convert java.lang.Object to java.lang.String.
```

The error message refers to a cast which was first described in Section 5.5.3. A cast is needed whenever an attempt is made to assign a value of one type to a variable of an incompatible type; when assigning a floating point value to an integer variable, for instance. The compiler would complain in the example above for a similar reason— an attempt being made to assign what is retrieved from the collection into a variable of type String. It is not easy to see what the problem is, at first, because we know that the only things stored in the `callers` array list are String objects. However, that fact is unknown to the compiler at the point we access an item of the collection. Because the collection could contain items of absolutely any object type, it is not prepared to assume that we know what we are doing. We have to make it clear that we know what type of object is stored at that particular index, and that it is compatible with the variable we are assigning the reference to. As with the primitive types, this is done with a cast as follows:

```
ArrayList callers = getCallers();
// Get the first caller.
String caller = (String) callers.get(0);
```

The full version of the `selectCaller` method of the RadioShow class is shown in Code 10.3. Such a cast is called a *downcast* (see Section 14.3.3). It is a very common error to forget to include the required cast when retrieving objects from a collection, so you should familiarize yourself with the "Explicit cast needed" error message shown above. Even though we have included the correct cast, the interpreter will still check at runtime that we have used the right one. If, for any reason, the object returned from the collection is not actually of the right type for the cast, a *runtime error* will result in the form of a `ClassCastException` exception and the program will stop running. See Section 13.4 for details of the `instanceof` operator, which allows us to determine whether an object is of the right type for the cast we wish to use.

Clearly, the ArrayList class must use some static type to refer to objects it stores in the collection because its `add` method needs a type for its formal parameter. As shown in Table 10.1, the headers of the `add` and `get` methods actually look like this:

```
public boolean add(Object o)
public Object get(int index)
```

The static type that `add` uses for the formal argument and `get` uses for its return type is `Object`, which is a class that is defined in the `java.lang` package. This helps to explain what the compiler means when it reports:

```
Explicit cast needed to convert java.lang.Object to java.lang.String.
```

The collection both receives and returns items for the collection as values belonging to the Object class. This is an important class because all objects that are created

---

Code 10.3 Using a cast when retrieving an object from a collection (`RadioShow.java`)

```
import java.util.ArrayList;

    // Record a collection of callers to a radio phone-in program.
class RadioShow {
    ...
    public String selectCaller(int which){
        ArrayList callers = getCallers();
        return (String) callers.get(which);
    }
    ...
}
```

belong to it, as well as to their full dynamic type. We describe this class in detail in Section 14.9. For the time being, it should be sufficient to understand that the collection classes only handle what they think of as Objects.

Although we suggested above that arrays are different from array lists, in this respect, there *is*, in fact, some flexibility about the types of objects that may be held in an array. We can, for instance, define an array of Objects, and store within it any type of object we like:

```
Object[] oddArray = {
    "hello, world",
    new Ship(),
    new ArrayList(),
};
```

As long as we know what type of object is stored at each location (or can find out) we can access these objects with an appropriate downcast:

```
String greeting = (String) oddArray[0];
Ship argo = (Ship) oddArray[1];
ArrayList data = (ArrayList) oddArray[2];
```

Exercise 10.1   You are a collector of sporting souvenirs and plan to keep track of the free coins you have collected from a local store. There are 20 coins to collect, each with the name of a player. You need to know how many of each coin you have so that you can organize swaps of your duplicates for those you do not have. Design a class, `Coin`, that holds as attributes the name of a player and a count of the number of times you have that particular coin. It should have a `toString` method

```
public String toString()
```

that returns a string containing a concatenation of these attributes, separated by a space. Include the following `addToCount` method

```
public void addToCount(int more)
```

to increment the `count` attribute by the value of its single integer argument. Write a main method to create a few Coin objects and print their attributes via the toString method. Test the `addToCount` method.

Exercise 10.2   Design a class, `CoinCollection`, that holds references to Coin objects that you created in your solution to Exercise 10.1. It should hold the references in an ArrayList. CoinCollection should have the following methods in its public interface.

```
public void addToCollection(String player)
public void printDuplicates()
public void swap(String give, String get)
```

The `addToCollection` method will create a new Coin object for the player and add it to the collection, if not already present; otherwise, it will add one to the count of the existing Coin for the player. The `printDuplicates` method will use the `toString` method of Coin to print a list of the Coins for which the count is greater than one.

The `swap` method will reduce the count attribute by one of the Coin whose name attribute matches the `give` argument, and increase the count by one for the Coin whose name matches the `get` attribute. If a Coin does not already exist for the player matching the `get` attribute, then a new Coin is created and added to the collection.

In the next section, we look at the `LinkedList` class, which is closely related to the `ArrayList` class. When gathering together multiple objects in a collection, the choice of class to use will often be primarily between the ArrayList class and the LinkedList class.

10.2.3 The LinkedList Class

The `LinkedList` class is defined in the `java.util` package. In terms of the methods it defines, it bears a strong resemblance to the ArrayList class discussed in Section 10.2.1. This can be seen from a selection of its methods shown in Table 10.2. Both classes have `add`, `clear`, `indexOf`, `remove`, and `set` methods in common. However, there are also significant differences and it is important to appreciate these

Table 10.2 Selected methods of the LinkedList class

	Method and Arguments
	LinkedList()
	LinkedList(Collection c)
boolean	add(Object o)
void	add(int index,Object o)
boolean	addAll(Collection c)
boolean	addAll(int index,Collection c)
void	addFirst(Object o)
void	addLast(Object o)
void	clear()
boolean	contains(Object o)
Object	get(int index)
Object	getFirst()
Object	getLast()
int	indexOf(Object o)
boolean	isEmpty()
Iterator	iterator()
int	lastIndexOf(Object o)
ListIterator	listIterator()
Object	remove(int index)
boolean	remove(Object o)
Object	removeFirst()
Object	removeLast()
Object	set(int index,Object o)
int	size()
Object[]	toArray()
Object[]	toArray(Object[] arr)

in order to come to the correct decision when choosing between using an ArrayList or LinkedList as the most appropriate class for managing a flexible-size collection of objects. In order to illustrate the differences, we shall take a closer look at the simple card game introduced in Section 4.11.

In the course of a game of cards, the number of cards in a player's hand will vary as they are played and won; this makes a flexible collection class the obvious choice to hold them. However, the simple nature of this game places particular constraints on the way in which cards are added and removed from the collection. A player is required to play cards in the order they are received, and cards won from the pile must be added to the back of the hand, so that they are the last to be played. This means that a player never needs to access the cards from random locations within their hand, only taking them from the front and adding them to the back. Furthermore, because a player always removes cards from the front of the collection, using an ArrayList would mean that the remaining cards are continually being moved along by one position each time a card is removed. The implementation of the LinkedList class means that it offers features that are much better suited to this particular situation than those of the ArrayList class. In particular, it defines methods to directly access the first and last items in a collection, and removing or inserting items does not cause a wholesale shift of all the existing items. Figure 10.1 illustrates a possible structure for the LinkedList class, in which references are only kept to nodes at the start and end of the list. The nodes contain links to each other, and it is the nodes that refer to the individual objects stored in the collection. (Section 15.6.7 describes how a similar class

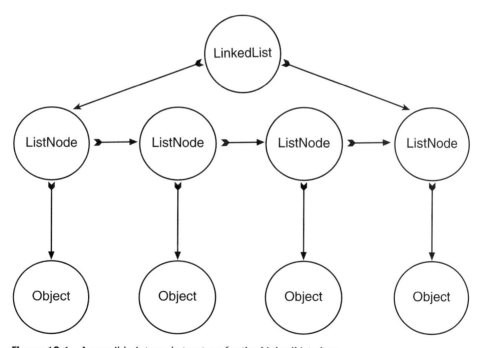

Figure 10.1   A possible internal structure for the LinkedList class

---

Code 10.4 Using a LinkedList to hold a collection of Card objects (`Hand.java`)

```
import java.util.LinkedList;

    // Maintain a collection of Card objects for a player.
    // Mostly a case of delegating to an underlying collection
    // and casting the result where required.
class Hand {
    public void add(Card c){
        if(c != null){
            getCards().add(c);
        }
    }

    public Card getNextCard(){
        return (Card) getCards().removeFirst();
    }

        // Add the given pile to the end of this one.
    public void addPile(Pile pile){
        getCards().addAll(pile.getCards());
    }

    public int numCards(){
        return getCards().size();
    }

    private LinkedList getCards(){
        return cards;
    }

    // Store the cards in a linked list, because we only need
    // access at either end.
    private final LinkedList cards = new LinkedList();
}
```

---

might be implemented.) On the deficit side, access to an item at an arbitrary location is slower than it would be with an equivalent ArrayList. In LinkedList, its position can only be found by starting at the head of the list and working along, node by node.

Code 10.4 shows the Hand class designed to store an arbitrary number of Card objects in a LinkedList for a player's hand. The LinkedList class defines distinctive methods to access the first and last items in the collection (getFirst, getLast), remove them (removeFirst, removeLast), and add new items to those positions (addFirst, addLast). The getNextCard method of the Hand class illustrates usage of the removeFirst method, which both returns a reference to the first item in the collection, and removes it. The addPile method of Hand shows the way in which the entire contents of another collection (e.g., another LinkedList, or an ArrayList) may be added to the end of a LinkedList using addAll. Another version of the same method exists to insert another collection at a particular index position.

Exercise 10.3 You are a keen collector of small animal figures, manufactured by FurryFigure pottery and you wish to keep track of your collection. Define a class, `FurryFigure`, that has attributes to record the type of animal (`"Cat"`, `"Dog"`, `"Weasel"`, etc.), a description (`"Green, with tail curled around it"`, etc.), the price you paid for it in cents, and an integer year when it was bought. The constructor should take values for all of these attributes and any mutators required should be private. Provide a public accessor for each attribute. Define a `toString` method

```
public String toString()
```

that returns a single string containing all of the attribute values.

Define a main method that creates a few FurryFigure objects and prints their details using the `toString` method.

Exercise 10.4 Add to your solution to Exercise 10.3 a class, `FurryFigure-Collection`, that uses a LinkedList to keep track of your FurryFigure objects. Its public interface should include the following methods:

```
public void addToCollection(FurryFigure figure)
public void printDescriptions(String animalType)
public int investment()
public LinkedList findAll(String searchString)
```

The `addToCollection` method adds `figure` to the collection. The `print-Descriptions` method should print the descriptions of all animals of the given type, for instance,

```
printDescriptions("Weasel")
```

prints the descriptions of all Weasels. The `animalType` attribute should not be case-sensitive. The `investment` method should return the amount of money used to purchase the entire collection as a number of cents. The `findAll` method should return a new LinkedList object containing references to all FurryFigure objects in the collection whose descriptions include the given word, which is case-insensitive. For instance,

```
find("tail")
```

will find all objects with the word `"tail"` somewhere in their descriptions. (You might like to use the `indexOf` method of the String class to help with this.)

Define a main method that creates a FurryFigureCollection object, adds a few FurryFigure objects to it, and tests its methods.

10.2.4 The HashMap Class

All of the examples using arrays, ArrayLists, and LinkedLists have used integer indices to access the data within a collection. This is not always the most convenient way in which to index data. There is often a need to look for an item in a collection based upon one of the item's attributes—a database search based on a person's name,

Table 10.3 Selected methods of the HashMap class

	Method and Arguments
	HashMap()
	HashMap(int capacity)
	HashMap(int capacity,float factor)
	HashMap(Map m)
void	clear()
boolean	containsKey(Object key)
boolean	containsValue(Object value)
Set	entrySet()
Object	get(Object key)
boolean	isEmpty()
Set	keySet()
Object	put(Object key,Object value)
void	putAll(Map m)
Object	remove(Object key)
int	size()
Collection	values()

for instance, or a dictionary search for the definition of a word. The HashMap class, defined in the java.util package, permits just such an association between an item and its *key value*. A sample of its methods is shown in Table 10.3. The key may, in fact, be any Object and it is used internally by the HashMap to generate an index position into the collection. The details of how this index generation is done are not important to understand at this stage.[2] Code 10.5 shows a GlossaryManager class that manages a glossary of words and their definitions, and allows a user to lookup words in it.

Code 10.5 Using a HashMap for a glossary (GlossaryManager.java)

```
import java.util.HashMap;

    // Illustrate the HashMap class by using one to create a glossary.
    // The contents of the glossary are read from a file as pairs of lines.
class GlossaryManager {
    public static final String defaultFile = "glossary.txt";

    public GlossaryManager(){
        this(defaultFile);
    }
    // Set up the glossary from the given file.
    public GlossaryManager(String glossaryFile){
        SimpleInput file = new SimpleInput(glossaryFile);
        HashMap gloss = getGlossary();
```

---

[2] Section 14.9 describes how a key's hashCode method may be used to create an integer index position.

Code 10.5   (*Continued*)

```
        String word = file.nextLine();
        while(!word.equalsIgnoreCase(endMarker)){
            String definition = file.nextLine();
            if(gloss.put(word,definition) != null){
                System.out.println(word+" is defined more than once.");
            }
            word = file.nextLine();
        }
    }

    // Interact with the user to look up words.
    public void interact(){
        System.out.println("There are: "+getGlossary().size()+
                            " words in the glossary.");

        SimpleInput keyboard = new SimpleInput();
        System.out.println("Input words to be looked up. Use "+
                            endMarker+" to finish.");
        String word = keyboard.nextLine();
        while(!word.equalsIgnoreCase(endMarker)){
            System.out.println(word+": "+definition(word));
            word = keyboard.nextLine();
        }
    }

    // Always return a non-null string, even if it is an error message.
    public String definition(String word){
        HashMap gloss = getGlossary();
        String definition = (String) gloss.get(word);
        if(definition != null){
            return definition;
        }
        else{
            return "I have no definition for "+word;
        }
    }

    private HashMap getGlossary(){
        return glossary;
    }

    private HashMap glossary = new HashMap();
    private final String endMarker = "end";
}
```

When a GlossaryManager is created, it reads pairs of lines from the file passed to its constructor. The first line of each pair consists of one or more words to be defined, such as "attribute" or "popup menu". The second line of each pair is a definition for the previous line. The first line is used as the key for the definition on the second line, which is added to the HashMap via its put method. This method returns null if the key has not previously been used, so a test has been included to guard against a word having multiple definitions.

The `interact` method allows the user to query the glossary by reading lines which should be in a similar form to the first of the glossary file's pairs. The `get` method of the HashMap takes this string as the key, and returns a reference of type Object if a definition with matching key is found in the glossary. This reference is cast to String before it is used, just as we saw with items retrieved from the other collection classes. Code 10.6 defines a main method that creates a GlossaryManager. The file that contains the glossary should be a simple text file.

The HashMap class also defines the methods `isEmpty`, `containsKey`, and `containsValue`, all of which return `boolean` results. The `size` method returns the number of items in the collection. The `remove` method takes a single key argument and removes the item with that key, if any; it also returns a reference to the item as its result. The `clear` method may be used to discard the full contents of the collection. As you can see, it offers a public interface which is similar to that of the ArrayList and LinkedList classes in many ways.

Exercise 10.5   The SimpleShip class contains the following constructor

```
public SimpleShip(String name)
```

which constructs a SimpleShip with a given name. Its `getName` accessor returns a reference to this name. Define a class that uses a HashMap attribute to store

---

Code 10.6 A main method for the GlossaryManager class (`GlossaryMain.java`)

```
/* Read a file of word and definition pairs and then allow
 * interactive querying of the glossary.
 * The file should contain each word on a separate line, followed
 * by its definition on the next line.
 * The end of the file should be marked by the word: end
 */
class GlossaryMain {
    public static void main(String[] args){
        GlossaryManager gloss;
        // Check for the name of a glossary file.
        if(args.length == 1){
            // Set up the glossary from the file.
            gloss = new GlossaryManager(args[0]);
        }
        else{
            // Use the default (GlossaryManager.defaultFile).
            gloss = new GlossaryManager();
        }
        // Allow the user to look up words in the glossary.
        gloss.interact();
    }
}
```

SimpleShip objects, using their name as the key. The public interface of the class should include methods to add and remove ships from the collection.

Exercise 10.6   Extend your solution to Exercise 10.5 so that there is a limit to the number of SimpleShips that can be stored. An attempt to add further ships beyond its capacity will be rejected, either with a printed error message, or the `addShip` method returning a `boolean` result.

10.2.5   The Legacy Collection Classes

Prior to version 1.2 of the Java API, the main collection classes in the `java.util` package were `Vector` and `Hashtable`, with `Enumeration` (see Section 13.7.3) fulfilling a similar role to `Iterator` (see Section 13.7.1). Vector is similar in underlying implementation to the ArrayList class, but offers a rather different public interface. For instance, it defines the methods `addElement` and `removeElementAt` for basic insertion and removal. From version 1.2, extra methods have been added to make its interface consistent with that of ArrayList. However, apart from any need to understand and interact with legacy software, there should be little need to use the Vector class.

The legacy Hashtable class is also similar to the newer HashMap class, and has been retrofitted from version 1.2 to make it compatible.

An Enumeration defines only two methods, `hasMoreElements` and `nextElement`. Therefore, it cannot be used to modify the associated collection. An Enumeration object is returned by the `elements` method of both Vector and Hashtable, but is not used by any of the newer classes. Either Iterator or ListIterator should be used in preference.

10.3   Review

Here are the main points that we have covered in the preceding sections:

- Classes in the `java.util` package support arbitrary-sized collections of objects.
- ArrayList, LinkedList, and HashMap are probably the most important general-purpose collection classes.
- Objects partially lose their identity when placed in a general-purpose collection.
- The collection classes hold and return their data using the `Object` type.
- When an object is retrieved from a collection, it will usually be necessary to use a downcast to the required type.
- The ArrayList class provides efficient random-access to its collection.
- The LinkedList class provides efficient access to the items at either end of its collection, and relatively low-cost insertion and deletion of items.
- The HashMap class allows items to be accessed via an object *key value* rather than a numerical index.
- The `java.util` package contains several legacy classes.

10.4   The Primitive Value Wrapper Classes

An advantage that both ArrayList and LinkedList have over arrays is that their size is not predetermined at the time of their construction. This means that they are to be preferred to arrays when the amount of data to be held is not known in advance. However, when the items to be collected are of a primitive type, this presents a potential problem, since both classes are only able to hold object types. The solution to this is to enclose a primitive value in an object of its corresponding *wrapper class*, which can be stored in a collection.

Wrapper classes exist for all of the numeric primitive types, with their class names differing only from the corresponding primitive type names by an initial capital letter: `Boolean`, `Byte`, `Double`, `Float`, `Integer`, `Long`, and `Short`. In addition, the `Character` class is available to wrap `char` values and provide character-related methods. All of these classes are defined in the `java.lang` package. In the next few sections, we briefly look at the Integer, Double, and Character classes.

10.4.1   The Integer and Double Classes

A primitive `int` value may be enclosed in an `Integer` wrapper by passing it to the class's constructor. Table 10.4 shows a sample of the methods of this class. A `double` value may be enclosed in a `Double` wrapper in a similar way. For example,

```
SimpleInput keyboard = new SimpleInput();
// Read two primitive values.
int inum = keyboard.nextInt();
double dnum = keyboard.nextDouble();
// Wrap the primitive value in an object wrapper.
Integer wrappedInt = new Integer(inum);
Double wrappedDouble = new Double(dnum);
...
```

Code 10.7 illustrates how this approach might be used to store an arbitrary number of integers in an ArrayList and then print them out in reverse order. Each of the integers read is added to the ArrayList in an Integer wrapper. When the contents of list is printed, each object returned by it must be cast to the Integer type. The value is then retrieved from its wrapper by using the `intValue` method of this object. Each of the wrapper classes for the numeric types contains the following set of methods—`byteValue`, `doubleValue`, `intValue`, `longValue`, and `shortValue`—so that the enclosed value may be returned as a value of any of the other numeric types if required.

The numeric wrapper classes contain various static methods that take a string containing a number and extract from it into either a primitive or wrapper type that represents the value of the number. The most general of these is `valueOf` which is available in all of them. The integer types have a version which takes a `radix` argument which can be used to indicate that the string is encoded in a base other than decimal, such as hexadecimal (radix 16) or octal (radix 8). With the Integer class, there are four distinct ways that can be used to extract an `int` value from a String (Code 10.8). The `parseInt` methods return an `int` value, whereas the `valueOf`

Table 10.4 Selected methods of the Integer class	
	Method and Arguments
	Integer(int value)
	Integer(String s)
byte	byteValue()
static Integer	decode(String s)
double	doubleValue()
float	floatValue()
static Integer	getInteger(String property)
int	intValue()
long	longValue()
static int	parseInt(String s)
static int	parseInt(String s,int radix)
short	shortValue()
static String	toBinaryString(int value)
static String	toHexString(int value)
static String	toOctalString(int value)
String	toString()
static String	toString(int value)
static String	toString(int value,int radix)
static Integer	valueOf(String s)
static Integer	valueOf(String s,int radix)

and `decode` methods return an Integer object. All will result in a runtime error[3] if their string arguments do not contain only an integer in string form. The Double class defines an equivalent static `parseDouble` method.

The Integer and Long classes also have the static methods `toBinaryString`, `toOctalString`, and `toHexString`, which take an integer argument and return a string representation of the value in either binary, octal, or hexadecimal notation (see Section B.2.3). All of the numeric wrapper classes contain definitions of `MIN_VALUE` and `MAX_VALUE`, which specify the positive minimum and maximum values of the corresponding primitive type (the positive values in the case of the floating point types). The example in Code 10.9 produces the following output:

```
-2147483648 2147483647
4.9E-324 1.7976931348623157E308
```

In Section 5.3.3, it was pointed out that division by zero between floating point numbers does not result in a runtime exception but a value of $+\infty$, $-\infty$, or `NaN`. The static `isInfinite` method of Double takes a `double` argument and returns `true` if the answer is infinite. Similarly, the static `isNaN` method returns `true` if its argument is Not a Number (such as `0.0/0.0`). The Double class also defines class constants `NEGATIVE_INFINITY` and `POSITIVE_INFINITY` to make it possible to distinguish between different infinities (for example, `-1.0/0.0` and `1.0/0.0`).

---

[3] A `NumberFormatException` exception.

Code 10.7   Storing primitive values in a collection (`WrapperMain.java`)

```java
import java.util.ArrayList;

    // Demonstrate the way in which primitive int values may
    // be wrapped in Integer objects for storage in a collection.
class WrapperMain {
        // Read an arbitrary number of integers and print
        // them in reverse.
    public static void main(String[] args){
        SimpleInput keyboard = new SimpleInput();
        ArrayList numbers = new ArrayList();
        // The terminating value.
        final int endValue = -1;

        System.out.println("Input the numbers, "+endValue+
                            " to finish.");
        // Read the first number.
        int num = keyboard.nextInt();
        // Keep reading until the end of input is indicated.
        while(num != endValue){
            numbers.add(new Integer(num));
            num = keyboard.nextInt();
        }
        // Print the numbers in reverse.
        final int howMany = numbers.size();
        for(int i = howMany-1; i >= 0; i--){
            Integer val = (Integer) numbers.get(i);
            System.out.print(val.intValue()+" ");
        }
        System.out.println();
    }
}
```

The `Byte`, `Long`, and `Short` classes contain similar methods to the Integer class, and the `Float` class is similar to Double.

10.4.2   The Boolean Class

The `Boolean` class can be used to provide an object that wraps a primitive `boolean` value. A selection of its methods is shown in Table 10.5. Its two constructors take either a primitive `boolean` argument or a String. In the latter case, if the argument matches "`true`" (regardless of case), the wrapped value will be `true`, otherwise it will be `false`. The `booleanValue` method returns the wrapped value. The static `valueOf` method takes a String argument and returns a Boolean object whose value follows the same rule as for the constructor.

10.4.3   The Character Class

The `Character` class provides an object wrapper for a primitive-type `char` value. Of more importance, however, is the large number of static methods that it defines

---

Code 10.8 Distinct ways to extract an **int** value from a String (`StrToIntMain.java`)

```
        // Demonstrate the different ways of parsing a string
        // containing an integer.
public class StrToIntMain {
    public static void main(String[] args) throws Exception {
        for(int i = 0; i < args.length; i++){
            int i1 =  Integer.parseInt(args[0]);
            // Specify radix 10.
            int i1a = Integer.parseInt(args[0],10);
            // Extract the int value from the resulting Integer.
            int i2 =  Integer.valueOf(args[0]).intValue();
            int i3 =  Integer.decode(args[0]).intValue();
            int i4 =  new Integer(args[0]).intValue();

            // All these should contain the same answer.
            System.out.println(i1+" "+i1a+" "+i2+" "+i3+" "+i4);
        }
    }
}
```

Code 10.9 The minimum and maximum values of the Integer and Double classes

```
    // Print the min/max values of the Integer and Double ranges.
class NumberRangeMain {
    public static void main(String[] args){
        System.out.println(Integer.MIN_VALUE+" "+Integer.MAX_VALUE);
        System.out.println(Double.MIN_VALUE+" "+Double.MAX_VALUE);
    }
}
```

---

to manipulate a character value or classify one; for instance, as to whether it is a digit, letter, and so forth. A selection of its methods is shown in Table 10.6. These methods are particularly important, given Java's association with the Unicode character set, which supports a much richer character set than most other programming languages. The class defines a single constructor, taking the `char` value to be wrapped and its `charValue` method returns the wrapped character. The static `toLowerCase` and

Table 10.5 Selected methods of the Boolean class

	Method and Arguments
	Boolean(boolean value)
	Boolean(String s)
boolean	booleanValue()
static boolean	getBoolean(String property)
String	toString()
static Boolean	valueOf(String s)

Table 10.6 Selected methods of the Character class

	Method and Arguments
	Character(char value)
static int	digit(char c,int radix)
static int	getNumericValue(char c)
static int	getType(char c)
static boolean	isDigit(char c)
static boolean	isLetter(char c)
static boolean	isLetterOrDigit(char c)
static boolean	isLowerCase(char c)
static boolean	isSpaceChar(char c)
static boolean	isTitleCase(char c)
static boolean	isUpperCase(char c)
static boolean	isWhitespace(char c)
static char	toLowerCase(char c)
static char	toTitleCase(char c)
static char	toUpperCase(char c)

toUpperCase methods convert their single char arguments to the appropriate case, while isLowerCase and isUpperCase return boolean results for their single arguments. The static isDigit, isLetter, and isWhitespace methods also return boolean results, and there are several other methods of this form for different classifications. It is important to note that these are static methods, so they operate on the argument value passed into them, rather than on a wrapped char attribute. They are general purpose methods, therefore, usable from any part of a program.

10.5 Iterating over a Collection

In Section 9.8, we described how to iterate through an entire array using a for loop. Since the items in an ArrayList or LinkedList have indices, we could use a similar technique to iterate through both using their get methods with successive index values. However, in Section 10.2.3, we noted that indexed access to the items of a LinkedList is not very efficient. Furthermore, when iterating through a collection, it is sometimes necessary to add or remove items from it. Making sure that we keep the indices synchronized when doing this can become very messy.

Fortunately, both classes provide a way to iterate through their elements which overcomes these problems. This is identical in both classes and the same approach is also commonly used by other collection classes. What this means is that we can write code to iterate through a collection that is largely independent of the particular underlying collection—be it an ArrayList, LinkedList, or something else. As a result, it becomes much easier to change which particular collection class we are using should the need arise.

In order to iterate over the items in a collection, it is simply necessary to ask the collection to return an Iterator object (Table 10.7), via its iterator method.[4]

---

[4] Iterator is actually an *interface* defined in the java.util package; see Chapter 13.

Table 10.7 Methods of the Iterator interface	
	Method and Arguments
boolean	hasNext()
Object	next()
void	remove()

Code 10.10   Iterating over a LinkedList (`IteratorMain1.java`)

```java
import java.util.*;

    // Demonstrate non-modifying iteration over a collection.
class IteratorMain1 {
    public static void main(String[] args){
        // Create a small list of cards.
        LinkedList list = new LinkedList();
        list.add(new Card(3));
        list.add(new Card(7));
        list.add(new Card(5));

        // Iterate over the list.
        Iterator cards = list.iterator();
        while(cards.hasNext()){
            Card c = (Card) cards.next();
            System.out.print(c.getValue()+" ");
        }
        System.out.println();
    }
}
```

Code 10.10 shows how this might work in practice. An iterator object has only three methods in its public interface: `hasNext`, `next`, and `remove`. This example shows the normal pattern for use of such an object which does not involve removing items from the collection. Once an Iterator object has been obtained from the collection object, the `hasNext` method is used to indicate whether there are any more items in the collection. If it returns the value `true`, then the next item is obtained via the `next` method. As you might expect, the item is returned as an Object, and so it must be cast to an appropriate type before it can be used. The output from the example in Code 10.10 is as follows:

    3 7 5

The example in Code 10.11 shows the way in which items could be removed from a collection as an iteration proceeds. This particular example uses an ArrayList, rather than a LinkedList, to show that this makes no difference to the way in which an Iterator object is obtained or used. A small list of numbers is created, and this is then iterated over to remove the negative values. Note that no special action is required to take into account whether we remove a number from the list or not in

Code 10.11   Removing items from a collection during iteration

```
import java.util.*;

    // Demonstrate modifying iteration over a collection.
class IteratorMain2 {
    public static void main(String[] args){
        // Create a small list of numbers.
        ArrayList list = new ArrayList();
        list.add(new Integer(3));
        list.add(new Integer(-7));
        list.add(new Integer(5));
        list.add(new Integer(9));

        // Iterate over the list, removing negative values.
        Iterator numbers = list.iterator();
        while(numbers.hasNext()){
            Integer num = (Integer) numbers.next();
            if(num.intValue() < 0){
                numbers.remove();
            }
        }

        // Now show what remains.
        numbers = list.iterator();
        while(numbers.hasNext()){
            Integer num = (Integer) numbers.next();
            System.out.print(num.intValue()+" ");
        }
        System.out.println();
    }
}
```

the first loop. The second loop simply iterates over the (modified) list to confirm that
only the negative values have been removed, giving the output:

```
    3 5 9
```

In addition to the `iterator` method, both ArrayList and LinkedList provide the
`listIterator` method, which returns a `ListIterator` object. This is more sophisticated than an Iterator in that it allows movement both backwards and forwards
over the items in a collection. In addition to the standard Iterator methods, it provides
`hasPrevious`, `previous`, `nextIndex`, `previousIndex`, `add`, and `set`, the last
of which allows an item in the collection to be replaced by a different object.

Exercise 10.7   An organization maintains details of the PCs on its network. The
details of each PC are stored in an object of class `PCDetails`, which contains a
name for the PC, its owner, and two integers indicating which part of the network
it is on (its `netid`) and which host number it is for that part of the network (its
`hostid`). PCs are added to (and removed from) the network on a regular basis and

Code 10.12   An outline for the PCDatabase class (`PCDatabase.java`)

```
        // Exercise outline.
        // Complete the following class.
class PCDatabase {
        // Add pc to the network with netid net and hostid host.
    public void addToNetwork(PCDetails pc,int net,int host){
    }

        // Move the pc with the given name to the given part of
        // the network (net) with the hostid host.
    public void movePC(String name,int net,int host){
    }

        // Change the hostid of the pc with the given name to be host.
        // It retains its current netid.
    public void movePC(String name,int host){
    }

        // Print the name, netid, hostid and owner of the given pc.
    public void printDetails(String name){
    }

        // Print details of all the pcs in the database, one per line.
    public void printAll(){
    }
}
```

moved around between parts of the network, which may require a change to the values of their `netid` and `hostid`.

Design and write the class PCDatabase, which holds a single PCDetails object for each PC. Code 10.12 shows an outline for its public interface. The PCDetails class is defined in the file `PCDetails.java`.

10.6 Case Study: A Simple Card Game (II)

In this section, we return to a fuller exploration of the simple card game that was introduced in Section 4.11. Now that we have introduced most of the fundamental control structures of Java, and how to create collections of objects, we can outline how these might be used to write full versions of the classes that go to make up a program to play the game.

10.6.1 The Player Class

In Code 10.4, we showed the Hand class that could be used to hold the cards belonging to a player. Its methods allowed a single card to be added to the player's hand, the first card to be removed and played onto the accumulating pile of cards, and a pile won by the player to be added to their current set of cards. Code 10.13 shows the Player

Code 10.13   The card game's Player class (`Player.java`)

```
class Player {
       // Receive a card from the dealer.
    public void takeCard(Card c){
        getHand().add(c);
    }


       // Play the next card from the hand. Return null if
       // we have no more cards.
    public Card playCard(){
        if(numCards() > 0){
            // We have at least one card.
            return getHand().getNextCard();
        }
        else{
            return null;
        }
    }


       // Add the cards from the pile to the hand.
    public void takePile(Pile p){
        getHand().addPile(p);
    }

    private int numCards(){
        return getHand().numCards();
    }

    private Hand getHand(){
        return hand;
    }

    // A collection to hold the player's cards.
    private Hand hand = new Hand();
}
```

class that implements the methods identified in Section 4.11 that are required by a
player. Most of the functionality is delegated to the player's Hand attribute. The only
method of significance is the `playCard` method which must only attempt to remove
a card from the collection if there is at least one there. Otherwise, `null` is returned
to indicate that the player has no more cards. This value will have to be detected
by the part of the program coordinating the players' actions, as it indicates that this
player has lost the game.

10.6.2   The Pile Class

The `Pile` class needs to receive the individual cards played in each round. We will
need to know if the top two cards match because this means that the pile is won by
the player who has laid the most recent card. The Pile class is the most obvious place

Code 10.14 The card game's Pile class (`Pile.java`)

```java
import java.util.LinkedList;

    // Maintain a pile of cards for a single round in the game.
    // At the end of the round, the pile is given to the winner
    // of the round.
class Pile {
    // Do the top two cards match?
    public boolean snap(){
        int howMany = numCards();
        if(howMany < 2){
            return false;
        }
        else{
            LinkedList pile = getCards();
            Card top = (Card) pile.getLast();
            Card previous = (Card) pile.get(howMany-2);

            // See if the values are the same.
            return top.getValue() == previous.getValue();
        }
    }

    // Add a card to the end of the pile.
    public void addCard(Card c){
        getCards().add(c);
    }

    public int numCards(){
        return getCards().size();
    }


    // A Player needs access to the cards when they are won.
    public LinkedList getCards(){
        return cards;
    }

    private LinkedList cards = new LinkedList();
}
```

to locate this functionality, which we define as its snap method (see Code 10.14). The Pile class uses a LinkedList since we are only ever interested in the cards at one end of the pile and not in the middle. We can see that the takePile method of the Player class and the getCards method of Pile introduce a degree of coupling among the Player, Pile, and Hand classes. Transfer of the cards in a won pile to a player's hand means that the hand must know, to some extent, how the pile is implemented.[5]

_____

[5] In fact, the coupling could be reduced to a great extent by making the transfer in terms of the Collection interface, but details of interfaces have been left until Chapter 13.

10.6.3 The Pack Class

The `Pack` class only plays a small role at the beginning of the game. It is responsible for creating the basic Card objects that will be passed around between the different objects for the remainder of the game. Once those cards have been dealt, a Pack has no further useful life. Code 10.15 shows the Pack class, which has only two methods in its public interface: `shuffle` and `nextCard`.

Code 10.15 The card game's Pack class (`Pack.java`)

```
import java.util.ArrayList;

class Pack {
    // Shuffle the cards in the pack.
    public void shuffle(){
        // Repeatedly swap pairs of cards around in the pack.
        final ArrayList pack = getPack();
        final int cardsInDeck = pack.size();
        final int shuffleTimes = 10*cardsInDeck;
        for(int i = 0; i < shuffleTimes; i++){
            // Generate the indices of two cards to move.
            int first = (int) (Math.random()*cardsInDeck),
                second = (int) (Math.random()*cardsInDeck);
            Object card = pack.get(first);
            // Replace the second with the first ...
            card = pack.set(second,card);
            // ... and vice versa.
            pack.set(first,card);
        }
    }


    // Return the card on the top of the pack, or null
    // if there are no more.
    public Card nextCard(){
        ArrayList pack = getPack();
        final int numCards = pack.size();
        if(numCards > 0){
            // Remove the last.
            return (Card) pack.remove(numCards-1);
        }
        else{
            return null;
        }
    }

    private ArrayList getPack(){
        return pack;
    }

    // The cards in the pack.
    private final ArrayList pack = new ArrayList();
    {
        // Construct a pack of 52 cards, 4 copies of values 1..13.
        final int numDuplicates = 4;
```

Code 10.15   (*Continued*)

```
        final int low = 1, high = 13;
        for(int i = 0; i < numDuplicates; i++){
            for(int value = low; value <= high; value++){
                pack.add(new Card(value));
            }
        }
    }
}
```

Notice the way in which an *instance initializer* has been used to construct the required number of Card objects when a Pack is created. The technique used to shuffle the pack is fairly arbitrary but is one reason for choosing an ArrayList rather than a LinkedList as the basis of the implementation. The `shuffle` method repeatedly generates two random indices within the collection, and swaps the two cards at those positions. Notice the way in which the return value from the `set` method is used to retain a reference to the card at the second index when it is replaced by the card from the first index:

```
        // Replace the second with the first ...
        card = pack.set(second,card);
```

The fact that we wish to index arbitrarily into the collection makes an ArrayList a better choice than a LinkedList in this case. In the `nextCard` method, we are careful to remove a card from the high-index end of the collection, rather than the low-end, because then no shifting down of the remaining cards is necessary following removal. Notice, also, that we do not need to cast the reference returned from the uses `get` and `set` in `shuffle`, because we do not need to use the returned object as a Card; this makes it possible to use Object as the type of the `card` variable.

There are quite a lot of important concepts illustrated by this class, so you should make sure that you fully understand it before moving on further with the material in this chapter.

10.6.4   The Dealer Class

In terms of logical structure and control flow, the `Dealer` class is the most complex class in the card game program. The way we have implemented it means that this class represents much more than simply a dealer of cards; it is really the object that coordinates all the other objects that participate in the game: the Pack, the Players, and the Pile. Therefore, it contains the highest degree of coupling with these other classes, since it must be familiar with the public interfaces of all of them. A change to the public interface of any of them will probably require a change in the Dealer class. Classes which play a coordinating role are quite common in object-oriented programs. The Dealer class defines only two methods, `dealTheCards` and `superviseAGame`. It is also responsible for maintaining an array containing the two Player objects that are participating in the game (Code 10.16).

```
class Dealer {
        // Create a new pack and distribute cards to the players.
    public void dealTheCards(){
        final Player[] players = getPlayers();
        int nextPlayer = 0;
        // Select the first player to receive a card.
        Player player = players[nextPlayer];

        // Distribute the cards until they run out.
        final Pack pack = new Pack();
        pack.shuffle();
        Card card = pack.nextCard();
        while(card != null){
            player.takeCard(card);
            // Calculate the index of the next player.
            nextPlayer = (nextPlayer+1) % numPlayers;
            player = players[nextPlayer];
            // Get the next card, if any.
            card = pack.nextCard();
        }
    }

        // The cards have been distributed; play a game.
    public void superviseAGame(){
        // Where to show the game.
        CardDisplay display = new CardDisplay(numPlayers);
        display.clear();

        final Player[] players = getPlayers();
        // Select the first player to play a card.
        int nextPlayer = 0;
        Player player = players[nextPlayer];

        // Create a pile for the first round.
        Pile pile = new Pile();
        // Request the first card of the round.
        Card cardPlayed = player.playCard();

        while(cardPlayed != null){
            display.showCard(cardPlayed,nextPlayer);
            // Add it to the pile.
            pile.addCard(cardPlayed);
            if(pile.snap()){
                display.report("Snap!"+
                            "Player: "+nextPlayer+" wins "+
                            pile.numCards()+" card(s).");
                display.clear();
                // player wins the cards in the pile.
                player.takePile(pile);
                // Create a new pile for the next round.
                pile = new Pile();
            }
```

Code 10.16   (*Continued*)

```
                else{
                    // Select the next player for this round.
                    nextPlayer = (nextPlayer+1) % numPlayers;
                    player = players[nextPlayer];
                }
                // Ask the player for the next card (if any).
                cardPlayed = player.playCard();
            }
            // Determine who has won.
            if(nextPlayer == 0){
                display.report("Player 1 has won.");
            }
            else{
                display.report("Player 0 has won.");
            }
        }

        private Player[] getPlayers(){
            return players;
        }

        // Setup the players.
        private static int numPlayers = 2;
        private final Player[] players = new Player[numPlayers];
        {
            for(int i = 0; i < numPlayers; i++){
                players[i] = new Player();
            }
        }
    }
```

The `dealTheCards` method creates a Pack object, asks it to shuffle the cards, and then distributes the cards one-by-one until the pack is exhausted. The technique used to select each Player object in turn from the array of Players is worth noting because it illustrates a common pattern. We need to repeatedly iterate over the array, and then start again when we have reached the end. For an array of two elements, we need to generate index values that go:

```
    0 1 0 1 0 1 etc.
```

For an array of 4 elements, the index values would need to go:

```
    0 1 2 3 0 1 2 3 0 1 2 3 etc.
```

In other words, the index values must run from 0 to `length-1` and then restart at 0. The easiest way to achieve this is to increment the index variable *modulus the length of the array*, in this case the number of players in the game. Hence, the index of the next player is generated by writing:

```
    nextPlayer = (nextPlayer+1) % numPlayers;
```

Code 10.17   The main method for the card game (`CardGameMain.java`)

```
    // The main method for the simple Card Game case study.
class CardGameMain {
    public static void main(String[] args){
        Dealer d = new Dealer();
        d.dealTheCards();
        d.superviseAGame();
    }
}
```

A similar technique is used in the `superviseAGame` method to select who is to play the next card. Note that this will work, without modification, if the number of players is increased from two to any larger value.[6]

The `superviseAGame` method coordinates the two players for the whole game, and is responsible for deciding and reporting the winner of the game. It starts by creating a Pile object to contain the first batch of cards to be won. A card is requested from the first player and then iteration continues in the while loop until the next player has no more cards. Each card is added to the current pile, and the pile is asked to compare the top two cards via its `snap` method. If there is a match, then the winning player is handed the pile and a fresh Pile object is created for the next round. If there is no match, the next player is selected and the process repeats.

The `CardDisplay` object created by the dealer in `superviseAGame` provides a GUI for the game (see Figure 4.7). The details of its implementation are beyond this stage of the book.

The game is run from the main method shown in Code 10.17.

Exercise 10.8   Make any necessary modifications to the card game program described in this section, so that it can be played by more than two players. If the number of cards in the Pack cannot be distributed equally between the players, what should be done with the excess? For instance, in a 3-player game, each may receive 17 cards from a 52-card pack with one left over. The logic for determining the end of the game will need to be modified significantly. A player is out of the game when they have no more cards to play, but more than one player might still have cards to play.

Exercise 10.9   Develop a program to play a more sophisticated card game, whose rules are as follows:

> The card game is played with a pack of N different cards (for instance, $N == 52$). Each card has a value between one and $N/4$. Each card belongs to one of four numerical *suits*, which may have associated names. A game consists of a number of rounds between P players. At the start of each round, every player receives C ($C == N/P$) cards. The remaining $N\%P$ cards are turned face up so that everyone can see them. A single game

---

[6] However, with more than two players, the logic for determining the end of the game and who has won is more complicated (see Exercise 10.8).

consists of C rounds in which each player plays a single card in turn. The player of the first card in the first round of a game is decided randomly. Thereafter, the winner of each round plays the first card of the next round of that game, if there is one. After the first card of a round has been played, the remaining players play one card each in turn. These players must follow the suit of the first player if possible. A round is won by the player who plays the highest card of the lead suit. A game is won by the player or players who have won the most rounds in that game.

You may reuse or modify any of the classes developed in this section in your solution.

10.7   Queue and Stack Collections

Two sorts of collections that we regularly meet in programming problems are *queues* and *stacks*. Queues are familiar from many everyday life contexts: checkout lines in a cafeteria, traffic jams, bus queues, and other first-come first-served situations. Queues are often referred to as *first in, first out* (*FIFO*) data structures (Figure 10.2). The first item to arrive in the queue is the first one to leave. It is replaced at the head of the queue by the second item, which is then the next to leave. In the meantime, other items might arrive, and these must join the back of the queue. Stacks are slightly less common in everyday life—papers arriving in an in-tray, shopping trolleys in a supermarket, a pile of trays in a restaurant, the discard pile in a game of cards—but they are important in many computing applications, such as the implementation of programming languages. Stacks are often referred to as *last in, first out* (*LIFO*) data structures (Figure 10.3). The most recent item to arrive in the stack is the first one to leave. A newly arrived item pushes down or covers the existing contents of the stack. Many card games illustrate the practical use of both a queue and a stack. In the game introduced in Section 4.11, the cards in each player's hand are held in a queue since they must be played in the order they are received. In more sophisticated card games, such as the Rummy family, there are usually two piles of cards from which players may draw cards to replace those in their hands—a pile of unseen cards (the *stock*) and a discard pile. A player plays a card face up onto the top of the discard pile and the next

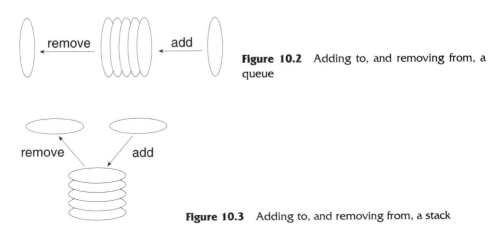

Figure 10.2 Adding to, and removing from, a queue

Figure 10.3 Adding to, and removing from, a stack

player may choose to take either that card from the discard pile or an unseen card from the top of the stock. The discard pile acts like a stack as new cards are added. When the stock is exhausted, the discard pile is inverted to act as a replacement stock. This replacement stock then behaves like a queue—the first card entered into it (when it was a discard pile) will be the first to be removed, and so on.

From the descriptions above, we can see that implementations of both queues and stacks would probably have methods similar to the following. In this particular case, we have designed the methods around a card game:

```
// Add an item to the queue/stack.
public void add(Card c);
// Remove (and return) the next item from the queue/stack.
public Card next();
```

In addition, it is often useful to be able to find out how long a queue or stack is, and to take a look at the next item in line without removing it, so we will add the following methods to the other two:

```
// How many items in the queue/stack?
public int size();
// Return a reference to the next in line, without removing it.
Card peek();
```

Queues and stacks are ideal candidates for implementation with the aid of a Linked-List, because it provides methods which give us direct access to the first and last item in the list, which tend to be the only positions of interest when using a queue or a stack.

10.7.1 A Queue for Cards

Code 10.18 shows the definition of a CardQueue class along these lines. The CardQueue class has a LinkedList attribute and associated accessor. The queue's add method uses the list's add method to place the latest arrival at the end of the queue. The next method returns the card that has been longest in the queue, via the list's removeFirst method. Notice that very little new functionality is provided in this class that is distinct from that provided by the LinkedList class and a CardQueue object asks its LinkedList attribute to do most of its work! This principle of handing over responsibility to another object to implement part of the service offered by a class is called *delegation*. It is a commonly used technique in object-oriented programming, and we shall meet it again in Chapter 12 when we discuss some of the many classes that perform input and output. In effect, a CardQueue object forms a kind of *wrapper* around the linked list object, providing access to its functionality via a more limited public interface than the full linked list provides. A Queue object imposes *FIFO semantics* upon an otherwise random-access object. It also frees users of the class from needing specific knowledge of how the queue is implemented. If, at some later time, we preferred to use something other than a LinkedList to hold the items in the queue, only the internals of the Queue class would need to be changed and not its public interface to the objects within the program that make use of it. This fits in with our goals of *encapsulation* and

Code 10.18   A FIFO queue class for Cards (`CardQueue.java`)

```java
import java.util.LinkedList;

        // An implementation of a FIFO queue of cards.
class CardQueue {
    // Add a card to the queue.
    public void add(Card c){
        // Add it to the end.
        getQueue().add(c);
    }

    // Remove (and return) the next card from the queue.
    public Card next(){
        if(size() > 0){
            return (Card) getQueue().removeFirst();
        }
        else{
            return null;
        }
    }

    // Return (but don't remove) the next card from the queue.
    public Card peek(){
        if(size() > 0){
            return (Card) getQueue().getFirst();
        }
        else{
            return null;
        }
    }

    // How many cards in the queue?
    public int size(){
        return getQueue().size();
    }

    // Return a reference to the collection.
    private LinkedList getQueue(){
        return queue;
    }

    // The collection of objects.
    private LinkedList queue = new LinkedList();
}
```

information hiding. Code 10.19 shows a main method that illustrates the order in which cards are added and removed from a CardQueue. The output from this example will be:

```
Queue length = 3 Removed: 3
Queue length = 2 Removed: 5
Queue length = 1 Removed: 7
```

Code 10.19   Demonstrating the CardQueue class (`QueueDemoMain.java`)

```
class QueueDemoMain {
    public static void main(String[] args){
        CardQueue queue = new CardQueue();
        // Add a few cards to the queue.
        queue.add(new Card(3));
        queue.add(new Card(5));
        queue.add(new Card(7));

        // Empty the queue.
        for( ; queue.size() > 0; ){
            System.out.print("Queue length = "+queue.size());
            Card c = queue.next();
            System.out.println(" Removed: "+c.getValue());
        }
    }
}
```

Code 10.20   Outline for a queue of Ship objects

```
class ShipQueue {
    // Add a ship to the queue.
    public void add(Ship s){
        // Add it to the end.
        getQueue().add(s);
    }

    // Remove (and return) the next ship from the queue.
    public Ship next(){
        if(size() > 0){
            return (Ship) getQueue().removeFirst();
        }
        else{
            return null;
        }
    }

    ...
}
```

Although the CardQueue class has been specifically designed to store Card objects, creating a class to hold a queue of objects of any other type would simply be a case of changing every reference to Card in Code 10.18 into the desired type. The add and next methods for a queue of Ship objects waiting to enter a port would look like that shown in Code 10.20, for instance.

10.7.2   A Stack for Cards

The java.util package does, in fact, already contain a Stack class for maintaining a stack of Objects. We prefer not to use it, however, because its public interface is little different from that of the other collection classes; in particular, it does not actually impose LIFO semantics on objects it maintains. We give further reasons for our dislike of the class in Section 14.3.1.

Code 10.21 shows the definition of a `CardStack` class along similar lines to the CardQueue class in Code 10.18. The CardStack class differs from the equivalent CardQueue class only in its `next` and `peek` methods. The different effects of LIFO and FIFO semantics may be seen by comparing the output from the example shown

Code 10.21   A LIFO stack class for cards (`CardStack.java`)

```java
import java.util.LinkedList;

        // An implementation of a LIFO stack of Cards.
class CardStack {
    // Add a card to the stack.
    public void add(Card c){
        // Add it to the end.
        getStack().add(c);
    }

    // Remove (and return) the last card from the stack.
    public Card next(){
        if(size() > 0){
            return (Card) getStack().removeLast();
        }
        else{
            return null;
        }
    }

    // Return (but don't remove) the last card from the stack.
    public Card peek(){
        if(size() > 0){
            return (Card) getStack().getLast();
        }
        else{
            return null;
        }
    }

    // How many items in the stack?
    public int size(){
        LinkedList stack = getStack();
        return stack.size();
    }

    // Return a reference to the collection.
    private LinkedList getStack(){
        return stack;
    }

    // The collection of objects.
    private LinkedList stack = new LinkedList();
}
```

in Code 10.19 with that produced from a similar program that uses a CardStack instead of a CardQueue:

```
Stack length = 3 Removed: 7
Stack length = 2 Removed: 5
Stack length = 1 Removed: 3
```

As you can see, the three cards are removed in the opposite order, as you might expect. As with the CardQueue class, it is trivial to modify the CardStack class to maintain a stack of any type of object, simply by replacing the use of Card for an alternative class in the arguments and return types of its methods.

The similarity between the public interfaces of the CardQueue and CardStack classes is something that we shall be able to exploit when we discuss *interfaces* in Chapter 13. In essence, the two different classes present a similar public interface to their clients—the ability to add, remove, and examine objects from an infinite collection; furthermore, there will be some circumstances in which clients will only be interested in that interface and not specific details of whether that interface is implemented by a queue, a stack, or some other data structure. As we have seen with the ArrayList and LinkedList classes, several classes within the `java.util` package offer similar interfaces, although the underlying implementations are slightly different.

10.8 Review

Here are the main points that we have covered in the preceding sections:

- Primitive-type values must be enclosed in an object wrapper before being added to an object collection.
- Wrapper classes exist for all of the primitive types.
- Iterator and ListIterator objects provide easy iteration operations on object collections.
- Collections are often manipulated with LIFO (stack) or FIFO (queue) semantics.
- The LinkedList is well suited to providing an underlying collection for a stack or queue.

10.9 Passing `this` to Another Object

There are some circumstances in which an instance of a class needs to be able to refer to itself via a reference. This arises most often when an object needs to tell another object about itself—i.e., to pass a reference to itself in a message to an object. We can use the `this` reference to do this. The method `sayHelloTo` in Code 10.22 shows an example of its use. The `Talker` class has two methods concerned with sending a message to another Talker object (`sayHelloTo` and `talkTo`). It also defines a `listen` method to print out any message it receives. The main method, shown in Code 10.23, creates two Talker objects and asks one to say hello to the other. When Aristotle receives the `sayHelloTo` message, he sends a "Hello" greeting to Plato. Aristotle then sends a `talkTo` message to the Plato object. It is here that `this` is

Code 10.22   Passing this to another object (`Talker.java`)

```java
        // A simple illustration of 'this' as a reference to
        // the current object.
class Talker {
    // I have a name.
    public Talker(String myName){
        name = myName;
    }

    // Say hello to friend and then ask them to talk to me.
    public void sayHelloTo(Talker friend){
        friend.listen("Hello",getName());
        friend.talkTo(this);
    }

    // Talk to friend.
    public void talkTo(Talker friend){
        System.out.println(getName()+" was asked to talk to "+
                        friend.getName());
        // Reply.
        friend.listen("Goodbye",getName());
    }

    // Message received.
    public void listen(String greeting,String whoFrom){
        System.out.println(getName()+" received the message: "+
                        greeting+" from "+whoFrom);
    }

    public String getName(){
        return name;
    }

    // My name.
    private final String name;
}
```

Code 10.23   Ask two philosophers to talk to each other (`TalkerMain.java`)

```java
class TalkerMain {
    public static void main(String[] args){
        Talker talker1 = new Talker("Aristotle"),
                talker2 = new Talker("Plato");

        // Ask Aristotle to say hello to Plato.
        talker1.sayHelloTo(talker2);
    }
}
```

used; its effect is that Plato receives a reference to the Aristotle object, in order to enable him to communicate back to Aristotle. This raises the interesting observation that, in general, objects do not know from whom they receive messages, unless the sending object chooses to tell them. The main method in Code 10.23 results in the following output:

```
Plato received the message: Hello from Aristotle
Plato was asked to talk to Aristotle
Aristotle received the message: Goodbye from Plato
```

Exercise 10.10   Suppose the second statement in the `sayHelloTo` method in Code 10.22 is

```
friend.sayHelloTo(this);
```

rather than

```
friend.talkTo(this);
```

What would be printed by the program? Can you work out why? Later sections will explain this effect.

10.10   Introduction to Recursion

"Which came first, the chicken or the egg?" is a familiar conundrum. Did the first chicken hatch from the first egg? If so, what produced the first egg—surely the first chicken—and so on *ad infinitum*. This example illustrates a principle called *infinite recursion*: the answer to the question lies in finding the answer to another question, which involves finding the answer to the first question, and so on. We can produce a similar effect in a program by allowing a method to call itself. The `chickenOrEgg` method in Code 10.24 illustrates such a method (the fact that it is a static method is immaterial). The first call to `chickenOrEgg` prints its argument and calls the method again with the name of the thing from which it must have originated. The first call cannot finish until this second call has finished. However, the second call will print its argument and make a third call, and so on for a fourth call, fifth call, ... We might represent the hierarchy of calls as follows:

```
1: chickenOrEgg("Chicken") prints Chicken and calls
2:  chickenOrEgg("Egg"), which prints Egg and calls
3:    chickenOrEgg("Chicken"), which prints Chicken and calls
4:      chickenOrEgg("Egg"), which prints Egg and calls
5:        chickenOrEgg("Chicken"), which prints Chicken and calls
   ...
```

Each call is nested within the previous one and the output just goes on and on. Indeed, it would go on forever except for the fact that the virtual machine will probably eventually run out of memory at some point. The reason is that the virtual machine has to keep track of all the outstanding calls to `chickenOrEgg` which are never completed because they have made another call to the same method before

Code 10.24   An infinitely recursive method (`ChickenOrEgg.java`)

```
       // An illustration of infinite recursion.
class ChickenOrEgg {
    public static void main(String[] args){
        // Start the recursion.
        chickenOrEgg("Chicken");
        // This point is never reached ...
        // ... so the program never ends naturally.
    }

    // Which came first?
    public static void chickenOrEgg(String which){
        System.out.println(which);
        if(which.equals("Chicken")){
            chickenOrEgg("Egg");
        }
        else{
            chickenOrEgg("Chicken");
        }
    }
}
```

Code 10.25   Infinite recursion printing consecutive numbers (`InfinitePrint.java`)

```
       // An illustration of infinite recursion.
class InfinitePrint {
    public static void main(String[] args){
        // Start the (infinite) recursion.
        sequencePrint(0);
    }
        // A recursive method. Print n, n+1, etc.
    public static void sequencePrint(long n){
        System.out.print(n+" ");
        sequencePrint(n+1);
        System.out.println("End of sequencePrint: "+n);
    }
}
```

reaching the end.[7] Code 10.25 provides a further example of infinite recursion. You might like to run this program to see how big a number it is able to print before your virtual machine runs out of memory. Note that the statement at the end of sequencePrint can *never* be executed. Normally, a compiler will give a message

---

[7] In fact, it is possible that some compilers will translate the chickenOrEgg method in such a way that the virtual machine will not run out of memory, but this is a topic for courses on compiler writing rather than introductory object-oriented programming!

such as

```
Classify.java:107: Statement not reached.
        x = 9;
        ^
```

for an unreachable statement, but it is unlikely to do so in this particular case.

In practice, we do not usually want to write methods that call themselves infinitely and result in the virtual machine running out of memory, and we shall see how to avoid this shortly. What we have illustrated with these two examples is that recursion can offer an alternative to using iteration when we want some actions to be performed repeatedly. Both the chickenOrEgg and sequencePrint methods caused the statements in their bodies to be performed over and over again, but neither used any form of looping control structure, such as a while, do or for loop. The repetition was achieved by calling a method that had already been called *but had not yet finished*—that is, the method was still active, or its completion was pending. For a normal method belonging to an object, we might say that a method is recursive if an object receives a message via that method before the object has finished dealing with a previous message sent via the same method. In both of the examples we have seen, the object receiving the original message sent the recursive message to itself, and this is often the way that recursion is used. It is called *direct recursion*. However, there is nothing to stop the subsequent (recursive) call originating from a different method, either from within the same object or another. In this case, the recursion is called *indirect recursion*. If two or more methods are involved in simultaneous indirect recursion, then this is called *mutual recursion*. An example of mutual recursion is provided by the solution to Exercise 10.10 in Section 10.9. The exercise asked what would happen in the sayHelloTo method if one Talker object sent a sayHelloTo message to another Talker object. The result would be an example of infinite mutual recursion.

10.10.1 Avoiding Infinite Recursion

All of the examples used in Section 10.10 involved infinite recursion. How can we avoid problems associated with *stack overflow* if recursion always involves a method calling itself, either directly or indirectly? For comparison with the recursive version shown in Code 10.25, Code 10.26 shows an iterative version of the sequencePrint

---

Code 10.26 Infinite iteration

```
    // An iterative method. Print n, n+1, etc.
public void sequencePrint(long n){
    while(true){
        System.out.print(n+" ");
        n++;
    }
    // This point is never reached.
}
```

method, which serves to illustrate that infinite execution is not a result of the use of recursion *per se*. In Section 7.2, we pointed out that a loop will continue indefinitely unless the actions in the body of the loop do something that will eventually lead to the loop's Boolean expression becoming `false`. We could do this in the example in Code 10.26 by checking the value of n to see whether it has reached a particular limit (Code 10.27). In a similar way, we can control the *depth of recursion* in the example in Code 10.25 by providing a terminating condition in the recursive method (Code 10.28). The important distinctive feature of the example in Code 10.28 over the similar example in Code 10.25 is that there is now an *escape route* from the recursion—a path through the method that does not result in yet another recursive call being made. The recursion only continues if the value of n passed in is less than the value of the local variable `limit`. Once it reaches the terminating value, the recursion *unwinds*. This means that all of the pending `println` statements at the end of the `sequencePrint` methods are finally executed. As a result, we obtain

---

Code 10.27   Placing a limit on the number of iterations

```
public void sequencePrint(long n){
    final long limit = 10;
    while(n < limit){
        System.out.print(n+" ");
        n++;
    }
    System.out.println("End of sequencePrint.");
}
```

Code 10.28   Placing a limit on the depth of the recursion (`LimitedRecursivePrint.java`)

```
        // An illustration of depth-limited recursion.
class LimitedRecursivePrint {
    public static void main(String[] args){
        sequencePrint(0);

    }

        // A recursive method. Print n, n+1, etc.
    public static void sequencePrint(long n){
        final long limit = 10;
        if(n < limit){
            System.out.print(n+" ");
            sequencePrint(n+1);
            System.out.println("End of sequencePrint: "+n);
        }
    }
}
```

the following output from this program:

```
0 1 2 3 4 5 6 7 8 9 End of sequencePrint: 9
End of sequencePrint: 8
End of sequencePrint: 7
End of sequencePrint: 6
End of sequencePrint: 5
End of sequencePrint: 4
End of sequencePrint: 3
End of sequencePrint: 2
End of sequencePrint: 1
End of sequencePrint: 0
```

Take the time to be sure that you understand why the output appears in this order, and with this particular formatting.

In the case of direct recursion, the key to employing recursion as a useful programming tool is to ensure that there is at least one non-recursive path through the recursive method.

10.10.2   The Factorial Function

A particular example that is often used to illustrate recursion is the definition of the *factorial function* and, simply for the sake of completeness, we include a discussion of it here. The factorial function plays an important role in many mathematical applications. It is represented by the symbol ' ! ' (which is unrelated to Java's use of the same symbol for Boolean negation). For positive integers it is defined as follows:

$$0! = 1$$
$$n! = n \times (n - 1)! \text{ for } n > 0$$

Notice that the factorial function is defined recursively; the value of $n!$ is defined in terms of the value of $(n - 1)!$. An example would be that $3! = 3 \times 2!$. If we expand this fully, we get:

$$3! = 3 \times 2!$$
$$= 3 \times (2 \times 1!)$$
$$= 3 \times (2 \times (1 \times 0!))$$
$$= 3 \times (2 \times (1 \times 1))$$
$$= 3 \times 2 \times 1 \times 1$$
$$= 6$$

In other words, $n!$ is equal to $n \times (n-1) \times (n-2) \times \ldots 1$, for $n > 0$. Infinite recursion is avoided in the definition of the factorial function by the provision of a non-recursive case corresponding to 0!. This is known as the *base case* and provides the necessary escape route. We can write a recursive `factorial` method that implements the factorial function. This is shown in Code 10.29 and it can be seen that it mirrors the recursive definition quite closely. The recursive sequence of calls required to evaluate `factorial(3)` would be as follows:

```
factorial(3)
   return 3 * factorial(2)
      return 3 * (return 2 * factorial(1))
         return 3 * (return 2 * (return 1 * factorial(0)))
            return 3 * (return 2 * (return 1 * (return 1)))
```

Code 10.29 A recursive method to calculate n!

```
public static long factorial(long n){
    if(n == 0){
        // The (non-recursive) base case.
        return 1;
    }
    else{
        return n * factorial(n-1);
    }
}
```

Code 10.30 An iterative method to calculate n!

```
public static long factorial(long n){
    // The base case.
    long product = 1;
    for(long i = 1; i <= n; i++){
        product *= i;
    }
    return product;
}
```

Once the call to `factorial(0)` is reached, the recursion is able to unwind and the pending multiplications take place from right to left.

While the factorial function is commonly used to introduce recursion, it is not a particularly compelling example of the use of recursion as an alternative to straightforward iteration. Since the value of n! is simply the product of the numbers $n \ldots 1$, it makes more sense to implement this function using a for loop, as shown in Code 10.30. Where recursion really comes into its own is in solving problems for which a *divide and conquer* approach is the most appropriate. We shall describe this type of problem in more detail in Section 10.10.3.

10.10.3   Divide and Conquer Problems

In Section 10.10, recursion was introduced as a technique that has close similarities to iteration for achieving repetition, but that does not involve the use of loops. The examples in that section were quite simple and merely served to illustrate the fact that a second call may be made to a method before the first call has been completed. An area of problem solving that lends itself particularly well to the use of recursion is that of *divide and conquer* problems; searching is one such problem area. A divide and conquer approach to problem solving often works well when a large set of data must be processed in some way. We might have a relatively efficient technique for processing small amounts of the data, but that does not work well with large amounts. If the original data can be divided into many smaller parts, then there is a chance that the whole can be processed relatively efficiently. Another requirement that

---

Code 10.31   Binary search outline

```
Find the mid-point;
if(the target element is too big){
    Try again to the right;
}
else if(the target element is too small){
    Try again to the left;
}
else{
    We have found it.
}
```

---

sometimes lends itself well to divide and conquer is the need to identify and process a single item, or small number of items, from the large data set. If the data can be partitioned efficiently to identify the required item, or items, then the time taken for the overall task might be significantly reduced over operating on the data as a whole. Consider the case of a detective faced with the prospect of having to take statements from 100 different crime suspects. If a reliable eye-witness states that the criminal had a beard, the number of suspects may be significantly reduced by quickly visiting each suspect and eliminating from consideration all those not having a beard. If a subsequent witness asserts that the criminal had very short hair, a further division of the remaining pool of suspects might be possible following a second visit, leaving a much small number of full interviews to be conducted than the original number required. This technique is also found in the game *Animal, Vegetable, or Mineral* where someone secretly chooses an object whose identity is to be guessed and the other participants must ascertain what the object is simply by asking questions which elicit a Yes or No answer. To increase the likelihood of guessing the object, each question should be designed to reduce the number of potential objects as quickly as possible, until only one possible answer is left.[8]

What we have described is something very similar to what we were doing with the binary search search on sorted data described in Section 9.13. In looking for a particular value, we checked for it in the middle of the sorted array and, if not found, repeated the task to either the left or the right of the mid-point, depending upon whether the value we were seeking was smaller than the mid-point value or larger than it. An informal outline of the binary search is shown in Code 10.31. In Code 9.34, we implemented the "Try again" statements by building an iterative wrapper around the mid-point selection and the if-statement. Many algorithms that involve trying again can often be expressed succinctly using recursion as an alternative to iteration. The important point to remember is to provide a non-recursive escape route from the method as a terminating condition, in order to avoid it recursing infinitely. When the problem involves reducing the original data at each recursive step, the terminating condition usually involves either finding the item you want or running out of data to

---

[8] There is usually a limit on the number of questions that may be asked before the chooser is considered to have won.

Code 10.32   Recursive outline for a binary search

```
    // Recursively look for value in part of numbers.
    // Return its index if found, or -1 if not.
public int indexOf(int[] numbers, int value,which-part-to-examine){
    // The return value indicating that value is not present.
    final int notPresent = -1;

    if(no-more-items-left){
        // The search is complete and value is not present.
        return notPresent;
    }
    else{
        int index = find-the-mid-point;
        if(value > numbers[index]){
            // Look to the right of index.
            return indexOf(numbers,value,right-hand-side);
        }
        else if(value < numbers[index]){
            // Look to the left of index.
            return indexOf(numbers,value,left-hand-side);
        }
        else{
            // Found it.
            return index;
        }
    }
}
```

process because it has all been eliminated from consideration. Code 10.32 extends the binary search outline of Code 10.31 by showing outline statements for the recursion. The first test in the method provides the escape route for the recursion to unwind. If there is still data left to examine, then we find the middle item in the remaining part of the array to be considered and compare it against the value sought. If we do not find a match, then one of two possible recursive calls is made, with a narrower band of the array to be searched. If we do find a match, then this provides a second escape route, by returning the index of the located item and causing the process to unwind. How is the narrowing achieved? The iterative version in Code 9.34 maintained local variables for the index of the left-most item still to be considered (`leftIndex`) and the index of the right-most (`rightIndex`). In the recursive version, these indices must be passed in as arguments to the method. Code 10.33 shows the full recursive version of the binary search. Notice that we have changed the method header so that it takes values for `leftIndex` and `rightIndex` directly as arguments. This means that the outer-most call to the recursive version of `indexOf` must pass actual argument values for these, so instead of calling `indexOf` as something like

```
        indexOf(numbers,55);
```

it would now be called as

```
        indexOf(numbers,55,0,numbers.length-1);
```

Code 10.33   Recursive version of binary search

```
    // Recursively look for value in
    // numbers[leftIndex]..numbers[rightIndex].
    // Return its index if found, or -1 if not.
public int indexOf(int[] numbers, int value,
                        int leftIndex, int rightIndex){
    // The return value indicating that value is not present.
    final int notPresent = -1;
    // How many items to search?
    final int numItems = rightIndex-leftIndex+1;

    if(numItems <= 0){
        // The search is complete and value is not present.
        return notPresent;
    }
    else{
        // Calculate the mid-point.
        int index = leftIndex+(numItems/2);
        if(value > numbers[index]){
            // Look to the right.
            return indexOf(numbers,value,index+1,rightIndex);
        }
        else if(value < numbers[index]){
            // Look to the left.
            return indexOf(numbers,value,leftIndex,index-1);
        }
        else{
            // Found it.
            return index;
        }
    }
}
```

```
[0] [1] [2] [3] [4] [5] [6] [7] [8]
 1 | 3 |10 |20 |37 |55 |71 |92 |99
```

Figure 10.4   Sorted data for a recursive search

with the third and fourth arguments supplying the initial left and right limits of the
search. A search for the value 3 in the array shown in Figure 10.4 would result in the
following set of recursive calls

```
indexOf(numbers,55,0,8);      // Look right
    indexOf(numbers,55,5,8);      // Look left
        indexOf(numbers,55,5,6);   // Look left
            indexOf(numbers,55,5,5); // Found
```

with the index value 5 being returned from the final call.

10.11   Review

Here are the main points that we have covered in the preceding sections:

- An object may pass its this reference to another object.
- A method may be recursive; that is, it may call itself.
- Care must be taken to avoid infinite recursion with a recursive method.

- Several methods may be mutually recursive.
- Recursion can be considered as an alternative to iteration in some circumstances.
- Recursion is particularly important in solving *divide and conquer* problems.

Exercise 10.11   The program shown in Code 10.34 prints the number of times a set of positive values can be split in half (integer divided by 2). Rewrite the `halve` method so that it uses recursion rather than iteration.

Exercise 10.12   Extend your solution to Exercise 10.11 so that it handles negative numbers correctly. For instance, the result returned for a negative value, x, should be the same as that returned for its positive equivalent, -x.

Exercise 10.13   Create a class called `LineFill` which is able to format a sequence of words into lines of a fixed length. In general, joining words together, each separated from the preceding word by a single space, will not completely fill a line of a given width. The job of this class is to distribute the spare spaces, as evenly as possible,

---

Code 10.34   Repeatedly halve a set of values (`SplitInTwo.java`)

```
        // Count how many a sample of positive values
        // can be split in two.
public class SplitInTwo {
    public static void main(String[] args){
        final int[] values = {
            // Powers of 2.
            0, 1, 2, 4, 1024,
            // Other even numbers.
            6, 22, 100,
            // Odd numbers (powers of 2 plus 1).
            9, 257, 2049,
            // Other odd numbers.
            7, 37, 101, 1149,
        };
        final int numValues = values.length;
        for(int i = 0; i < numValues; i++){
            System.out.println(values[i]+" halves "+
                               halve(values[i])+" times.");
        }
    }

        // Return how many times num can be (integer) divided by 2.
    public static int halve(int num){
        int times = 0;
        while(num > 1){
            num /= 2;
            times++;
        }
        return times;
    }
}
```

Code 10.35   The public interface of the LineFill class (`LineFill.java`)

```
    /* Outline of a class to format lines.
     * Words are added one-by-one to a line of a particular length.
     * Consecutive words should be separated by a single space.
     * If adding a word would cause a line to exceed its given
     * length then the current line must be printed and a new one
     * started. The (possibly incomplete) contents of a line may be
     * 'flushed'.
     */
class LineFill {
    public LineFill(int width){
    }

        // Add the word to the current line if there is room.
        // Otherwise print the line and use word to start a new one.
    public void addWord(String word){
    }

        // Print the current line and clear it ready for the next.
    public void flush(){
    }
}
```

between the words. The constructor of the class should take an integer argument specifying the length of the lines it is to create. Thereafter, words are added one-by-one to the line via its `addWord` method, which takes a single String argument. Consecutive words should initially be separated by a single space. If adding a word would cause a line to exceed its given length, then the line's current contents must be filled with the extra spaces, and then printed (using the `println` method of System.out). The word which caused overflow will then be the first on the next line.

The (possibly incomplete) contents of a line may be printed at any time via the class's `flush` method, which takes no parameters. In this case, the line should not be padded to its full length.

Code 10.35 shows an outline for the class containing the headers for its public interface. Code 10.36 shows a main method that could be used to test your LineFill class. As an example, consider a line length of 40 characters and the following words to be formatted (punctuation is considered to be attached to any immediately preceding letters).

Once upon a time, there were three chickens who wanted to cross a very wide road. At first, they looked for a safe place to cross, but could not find one.

The first seven words will fit on the first line as follows (an index line has been added showing the length of the line):

```
12345678901234567890123456789012345678 90
Once upon a time, there were three
```

but the eighth (chickens) would cause the line to overflow, leaving six spaces to be redistributed. Starting from the left of the line, an extra space may be inserted between each word pair to give

```
Code 10.36   Test-rig for the LineFill class (LineFillMain.java)
```

```
        // A test-rig for the LineFill class.
        // Read words until STOP is read. Output lines
        // with a maximum length of lineWidth characters.
class LineFillMain {
    public static void main(String[] args){
        final int lineWidth = 60;
        final String terminator = "STOP";
        LineFill formatter = new LineFill(lineWidth);
        SimpleInput keyboard = new SimpleInput();

        System.out.println("Type words to be formatted. "+lineWidth+
                        " characters per line. Type "+terminator+
                        " to stop input.");
        String word = keyboard.nextWord();
        while(!word.equals(terminator)){
            formatter.addWord(word);
            word = keyboard.nextWord();
        }
        formatter.flush();
    }
}
```

```
123456789012345678901234567890123456789 0
Once   upon   a   time,   there   were   three
```

which is then printed, with chickens starting the next line. The second line is already completely filled without any room for extra space when an attempt to add road is made. This results in

```
123456789012345678901234567890123456789 0
chickens who wanted to cross a very wide
```

being printed. When place is added, the third line is as follows

```
123456789012345678901234567890123456789 0
road. At first, they looked for a safe
```

requiring an extra space before At and one before first. The remaining words fit on the fourth line which, when flushed, looks like this

```
123456789012345678901234567890123456789 0
place to cross, but could not find one.
```

because a flushed line may have trailing spaces.

Exercise 10.14 The effect of always adding spaces from left to right in a line can create an unbalanced effect. Modify your LineFill class from Exercise 10.13 so that it fills from the left or right on alternate lines.

In the next chapter, we consider how to anticipate and handle circumstances that could give rise to runtime errors, via Java's *exception handling* mechanism.

PART

II

Further Language Features

CHAPTER 11

Exceptions

In this chapter, we look at the exception handling mechanism of Java. We see the way in which exceptions make it possible for any part of a program to indicate that an unexpected circumstance has arisen. Of equal importance is the ability for error-recovery mechanisms to be included to deal with these problems.

11.1 The Need for Exceptions

When a class presents a public interface to the outside world, it immediately leaves objects of that class open to things going wrong. While the internal definition of a class might be entirely self-consistent, the public interface methods potentially permit other parts of the program to make unreasonable requests on these objects. In Section 4.7, we discussed the essential reasons why it is important to keep an object's attributes under the control of its accessor and mutator methods. However, that is not enough to prevent other objects from trying to alter the state inappropriately, either maliciously or inadvertently. For instance, the fact that we might have a mutator for a ship's speed will not, of itself, prevent attempts to move the ship forward when it is still tied up to the dock side, or the fact that seat booking for a theater is controlled by an object will not prevent someone from trying to book a seat when there are none available.

As a general principle, therefore, the designer of a class must anticipate that messages might be sent which are impossible for its objects to fulfill; either because they are inappropriate for the class as a whole, or because the current state of an object makes it impossible for it to respond at that particular time. For instance, objects of a Ship class with a maximum speed should never obey a request to go beyond that speed, but a ship operating in a speed-restricted area should not respond to a request to break the speed limit, even if it is within its maximum allowed speed.

Faced with a request it cannot (or should not) fulfill, how should an object react? The following are some possibilities:

- Print an error message and do nothing.
- Terminate the program—with or without an error message.
- Silently ignore the request and do nothing.
- Perform the request anyway.

- Fake an appropriate or modified action.
- Request a correction interactively.
- Return the wrong answer.
- Return an error indication.

You might like to think of the relative merits of these approaches in different situations—particularly life-threatening or safety-critical situations! Is it always better to do something rather than nothing, on the grounds that the client must have a reason for asking you to do something? Is a wrong answer better than no answer? Will it always be possible to interact with a user in order to resolve the dilemma?

In the next few sections, we discuss how Java's exception-handling facilities may be used for dealing with such problematic situations.

11.2   Throwing Exceptions

Java's exception-handling mechanism is an attempt to resolve the dilemma faced by an object when it is asked to perform a task that it is either unwilling or unable to perform. When such a situation arises, an object may *throw an exception*. Such a course of action is, in effect, a failure indication. Some examples of exceptions that we have seen in previous chapters are:

- `ArithmeticException`; thrown when an attempt is made to perform integer division by zero.
- `ArrayIndexOutOfBoundsException`; thrown by an array when an out-of-bounds index is used.
- `IndexOutOfBoundsException`; thrown by a collection object when an out-of-bounds index is used.
- `ClassCastException`; thrown by the runtime interpreter when an inappropriate cast is used on an object reference.
- `NumberFormatException`; thrown by methods of the numerical wrapper classes when a String does not contain a valid number.

11.2.1   The Throw Statement

An exception is an object, which means that throwing an exception involves creating an object of an appropriate class. The easiest exception class to use is `Runtime-Exception`, defined in the `java.lang` package. This is a class concerned with representing non-specific exceptions. The example in Code 11.1 shows how an exception may be thrown by creating a RuntimeException object, and using it in a *throw statement*. The result of running this program will be something like the following output:

```
Exception in thread "main" java.lang.RuntimeException
    at java.lang.Throwable.<init>(Throwable.java:68)
    at java.lang.Exception.<init>(Exception.java:33)
    at java.lang.RuntimeException.<init>(RuntimeException.java:37)
    at UncheckedMain1.main(UncheckedMain1.java:5)
```

Code 11.1   Throwing an exception (`UncheckedMain1.java`)

```
    // Illustrate the effect of throwing an unchecked exception.
class UncheckedMain1 {
    public static void main(String[] args){
        // Terminate the whole program with a runtime exception.
        throw new RuntimeException();
    }
}
```

What we see here is a *stack trace*, which is an attempt by the runtime system to give us a picture of which part of a program the interpreter was executing when the exception was thrown. The most useful information comes at the end where we see both the name of the file and the line number on which the exception was thrown (`UncheckedMain1.java:5`). The RuntimeException class has both a no-arg constructor and one that takes a string argument. The string is often used to convey a diagnostic message describing the nature of the problem. Modifying the example shown in Code 11.1 so that the exception is thrown as follows

```
        throw new RuntimeException("I just can't cope!");
```

produces the following output

```
    Exception in thread "main" java.lang.RuntimeException: I just can't cope!
        at java.lang.Throwable.<init>(Throwable.java:78)
        at java.lang.Exception.<init>(Exception.java:42)
        at java.lang.RuntimeException.<init>(RuntimeException.java:47)
        at UncheckedMain2.main(UncheckedMain2.java:5)
```

where we see the diagnostic message included in the output with the stack trace.

11.2.2   Exception Objects

Because an exception is an object, it can be treated in a similar way to all other objects. The exception classes define several methods, which make it possible to send messages to their objects. Code 11.2 illustrates several of these methods as well as the important fact that it is not the *creation* of an exception object that causes a program to stop, but the *throwing* of the exception. The main methods of interest associated with exceptions are:

- `getMessage`: an accessor for the string passed to its constructor.
- `printStackTrace`: prints the stack trace as it existed when the object was created.
- `toString`: returns a String representation of the object's class and its diagnostic message.

Use of these methods is common when thrown exceptions are caught by another part of the program; we discuss *catching exceptions* in Section 11.3. The final statement in Code 11.2 actually throws the exception, and the program fails at that point. The

s to an exception object (`UncheckedMain3.java`)

```
          .ianipulation of an exception object.
          in3 {
        .c void main(String[] args){
      .ninate the whole program with a runtime exception.
    .meException e = new RuntimeException("I just can't cope!");
   .em.out.println("Message is: "+e.getMessage());
  printStackTrace(System.out);
 system.out.println("String version is: "+e.toString());

  // Now throw the exception.
  throw e;
}
```

output from this example, that precedes the final stack trace, is as follows:

```
Message is: I just can't cope!
java.lang.RuntimeException: I just can't cope!
    at java.lang.Throwable.<init>(Throwable.java:78)
    at java.lang.Exception.<init>(Exception.java:42)
    at java.lang.RuntimeException.<init>(RuntimeException.java:47)
    at UncheckedMain3.main(UncheckedMain3.java:6)
String version is: java.lang.RuntimeException: I just can't cope!
```

The final stack trace, resulting from the throw statement, will be identical to what is printed by `printStackTrace`.

11.2.3 The Throws Clause

The examples we have seen so far have not illustrated the way in which exceptions would normally be used in practice, simply their effect. In Section 11.1, we suggested that a ship might refuse to obey a request to exceed the maximum speed for its class. Code 11.3 illustrates how such a refusal might be implemented by throwing a runtime exception. The version of the `setSpeed` method in Code 11.3 indicates that it might throw an exception by including a *throws clause* as part of its header. The clause names the type of exception that it might throw. If the absolute value of the new speed is beyond the maximum, then the method creates and throws a RuntimeException object. A meaningful diagnostic string is created from the actual parameter value and the maximum in order to help anyone trying to fix the problem. As soon as the exception is thrown, control proceeds no further within the `setSpeed` method—it is terminated automatically without reaching the end. If an exception is thrown in a method with a return type, no return statement will be executed and so no result will be returned.

A method wishing to throw several different types of exception lists them all separated by commas in the throws clause

```
public void method() throws RuntimeException, NumberFormatException
```

Code 11.3   Throwing an exception on receiving an invalid request

```
class Ship {
    // Objects of this class must not exceed this limit.
    public static final double maximumSpeed = 10.0;
    ...
    public void setSpeed(double s) throws RuntimeException {
        // Check the validity of the request.
        if(Math.abs(s) > maximumSpeed){
            // Too fast. Don't proceed.
            throw new RuntimeException("Speed "+s+
                        " is beyond the maximum of "+maximumSpeed);
        }
        else{
            speed = s;
        }
    }
    ...
}
```

The exceptions form part of the *method signature*, along with its return type and argument types.

11.2.4   Object Construction Failure

It is common to use exceptions from within a constructor to prevent an object from being created if the actual argument values passed to it are inappropriate. Code 11.4 illustrates an example of such a use. `Circle` objects must have a positive radius and a runtime exception will be thrown if this is not the case. Throwing an exception in a constructor (or indirectly via one of the methods it invokes) is the accepted way to indicate failure to create a valid instance of a class, for whatever reason. You should make it a policy to refuse to complete the construction of an object that cannot be placed in a valid initial state.

11.2.5   Checked and Unchecked Exceptions

Java divides exceptions into two categories: *checked exceptions* and *unchecked exceptions*. `RuntimeException` is classified as an *unchecked exception* (as are all the other exceptions we have described so far). One major difference between these categories is that a method does not need to declare that it might throw an unchecked exception in a throws clause, whereas a checked exception must be listed there. Even though it is not necessary to indicate that a method might throw an unchecked exception, it is clearly an aid to good program documentation if a method declares this as part of its signature, and this is the practice we shall typically follow.

A full description of how exceptions are created and used cannot be undertaken until after the discussion of *inheritance* in Chapter 14. It will then be possible to define our own exceptions, but for the time being it will be necessary to use those that are

Code 11.4   Constructing a circle with a negative radius will fail (`Circle.java`)

```
      // Attempts to create a circle with a non-positive radius
      // will fail.
class Circle {
     public Circle(double r) throws RuntimeException {
          if(r <= 0){
             throw new RuntimeException("The radius must be positive: "+r);
          }
          radius = r;
     }

     public double circumference(){
          return 2*Math.PI*getRadius();
     }

     public double area(){
          final double r = getRadius();
          return Math.PI*r*r;
     }

     public double getRadius(){
          return radius;
     }

     private final double radius;
}
```

provided for us, such as RuntimeException. In the next section, we look at how thrown exceptions may be caught, rather than causing a program to stop.

Exercise 11.1   The Exception class (defined in java.lang) is a checked exception. Modify the main method shown in Code 11.2 so that an Exception object rather than a RuntimeException object is created. Recompile the program and note the error message given by the compiler.

Exercise 11.2   Modify the header of the main method in your solution to Exercise 11.1 as follows:

```
     public static void main(String[] args) throws Exception
```

Will the compiler now allow you to compile and run this version?

Exercise 11.3   Define the class ClosedShape, which takes an array of Point objects as a single argument to its constructor. The constructor should throw a RuntimeException if the number of points in the array is less than four or if the last point in the array does not contain the same (x,y) as the first point. Create main methods to test that the constructor fails under the correct conditions.

Code 11.5   Outline of the try statement

```
try{
    statement;
    ...
}
catch(Exception e){
    statement;
    ...
}
finally{
    statement;
    ...
}
```

11.3   Catching Exceptions

So far, we have been using the terms *runtime error* and *exception* as if they were synonymous; that an exception will necessarily result in a runtime error and program termination. Although in some programming languages this would be the case, Java permits an exception to be a non-fatal error. It does this by allowing us to anticipate when an exception might be thrown and arrange to *catch* it. An exception will only lead to a fatal runtime error if it is not caught or handled by some part of the program. Catching an exception means that there is a chance to deal with whatever caused the problem and to attempt a recovery. This might then mean that the program is able to continue as normal, but this will not always be possible. Nevertheless, good programming practice dictates that the possibility of exceptions occurring should be anticipated and catered for. In the next section, we look at the way in which exceptions may be caught.

11.3.1   The Try Statement

We have seen that an exception is thrown either when an illegal operation occurs (such as integer division by zero) or when the part of the program that is currently being executed chooses to create an exception object and throw it. When an exception is thrown, rather than terminating immediately, the runtime system will look for an *exception handler* that knows how to deal with that particular exception. The exception handler could be in any part of the program that is in the current *runtime stack*.[1] An exception handler has the general form shown in Code 11.5.

In its most general form, a try statement has three sections: the *try clause*, the *catch clause*, and the *finally clause*. Unlike the other Java statements we have seen, there is no alternative single-statement version of the try statement that omits the curly brackets in the blocks of any of these clauses. Either the catch clause or the finally clause may be omitted, and we shall defer discussion of the finally clause until Section 11.4.

---

[1] It is the runtime stack that is printed by the printStack method of the exception classes.

Code 11.6 Catching a RuntimeException exception when a Circle is created (`CircleMain2.java`)

```
// Illustrate construction failure. A negative radius will
// cause creation of a Circle object to fail.
// Catch the exception.
class CircleMain2 {
    public static void main(String[] args){
        SimpleInput keyboard = new SimpleInput();
        // Allow up to 5 circles to be created.
        final int max = 5;
        System.out.println("Please input "+max+" radius values.");
        for(int i = 0; i < max; i++){
            try{
                double radius = keyboard.nextDouble();
                Circle c = new Circle(radius);
                System.out.println("Area = "+c.area());
            }
            catch(RuntimeException e){
                System.out.println(e.getMessage());
            }
        }
    }
}
```

An exception handler is introduced with the reserved word `try`, and the normal sequence of statements we want to be executed are enclosed between the pair of curly brackets immediately after it. These are the statements we hope will be performed without an exception being thrown. Placing them inside a try clause, however, signifies to the compiler and runtime system that they are *protected statements*. The catch clause supplies an alternative set of statements that will endeavor to take over control if an exception is thrown during execution of any of the protected statements. Code 11.6 illustrates a try statement written to anticipate problems with attempting to create a number of Circle objects, based upon radius values read from the user.

Inside the body of the for loop, the normal execution path involves reading a number from the user, creating a Circle object based upon this value, and printing the area of that circle. As we saw in Code 11.4, the constructor of Circle will reject attempts to create a circle with a negative radius, by throwing a RuntimeException. If this occurs, the second of the three protected statements would be abandoned part way through, and control would pass immediately to the catch clause that is designed to handle such an eventuality. Because exceptions are objects, the header of the catch clause includes a pair of parentheses giving the class of the exception being caught (`RuntimeException`) and a user-defined variable name (e) to hold a reference to the exception object. As was illustrated in Code 11.2, exception objects contain methods that can be used in handling the error; in this case, we use its `get-Message` method to print the message it contains for the benefit of the user. Once the statements in the catch clause have been executed, control continues normally with whatever follows the whole try statement, rather than returning to the protected statements. Clearly, it is important to ensure that it makes sense to execute whatever

Code 11.7 Anticipating more than one exception

```
try{
    // The protected statements.
    ...
}
catch(IndexOutOfBoundsException e){
    // Statements to deal with an out of bounds error.
    ...
}
catch(ArithmeticException e){
    // Statements to deal with an arithmetic error.
    ...
}
catch(RuntimeException e){
    // Statements to deal with a general runtime error.
    ...
}
```

follows the whole try statement under the alternative circumstances that the protected statements either succeeded or failed. The effect of catching the exception in Code 11.6, therefore, is that a negative value read from the user does not cause the whole program to fail, but `max` attempts to create Circle objects will always be made, even though they might not all succeed.

Exercise 11.4 Modify the ClosedShape class that you wrote for Exercise 11.3 so that it throws a checked `Exception` rather than an unchecked `RuntimeException` on construction failure. Without adding an exception handler, recompile and run one of the main methods to see the effect.

Exercise 11.5 Add an exception handler to the main method in Exercise 11.4 to catch and report the exception thrown by the ClosedShape class.

11.3.2 Anticipating Multiple Exceptions

If several different exceptions might be thrown by the protected statements, these are listed with separate catch clauses as in Code 11.7. The type of exception thrown by the protected statements will be checked against the type of the exception named in each catch clause in turn, until a match is found. Where there are multiple catch clauses, at most one will be executed for an exception thrown in the protected statements. Furthermore, if the selected catch clause were to throw an exception for any reason, this would not be handled by the current set of catch clauses, but *propagated* (see Section 11.3.3). Notice that it is not necessary to give distinct identifiers to the exception objects named in the different catch clauses because the scope of the variable used to name a caught exception is limited to the catch clause in which it is defined.[2]

---
[2] It is common practice to use the identifier e for this.

The fact that the catch clauses are checked in order for a match against the type of the thrown exception object means that the order can make a difference in how a particular exception is handled. Exception types tend to differ in how specific they are to a particular type of error. For instance, an ArrayIndexOutOfBounds-Exception is a more specific type than an IndexOutOfBoundsException, and both are more specific types than RuntimeException. The rule is that clauses for the more specific types should come before those for the more general types,[3] so a catch clause for an ArrayIndexOutOfBoundsException exception must precede any for an IndexOutOfBoundsException exception, and both must precede one for a Runtime-Exception exception. If this rule is not followed, the compiler will give an error such as:

```
ExampleMain.java:25: catch not reached.
    catch(ArrayIndexOutOfBoundsException e)
    ^
```

Exercise 11.6 Code 11.8 shows a main method that includes array indexing and integer division. Both of these tasks could result in unchecked exceptions being thrown. Enclose all of the statements in the body of the for loop within a try-catch statement. This should catch the two exceptions that could result from its statements. Print an appropriate error message, and continue with the next iteration of the loop.

11.3.3 Exception Propagation

What happens if there is no exception handler immediately enclosing the statements where the exception is first thrown? The program does not necessarily stop straight away, but the answer partly depends upon whether the exception is a checked exception or an unchecked exception. The try statement in which the exception occurred might, itself, be nested within another try statement in the same method. In this case, the catch clauses of the enclosing try statement are checked for a match, and so on until either a match is found or all containing try statements within the current method have failed to provide one. Thereafter, if the exception is an unchecked exception, or if the exception type is listed in the throws clause of the method, it will be propagated out to the calling method, where a similar process will be followed. Code 11.9 shows an example in which the exception thrown by the Circle constructor is not caught straight away, but propagated to the immediately calling method.

In this example, the createCircles method is required to return an array that contains exactly max Circle objects. A failure to create one of these should result in a failure for the whole method. Notice that it does not directly throw an exception, itself, nor does it define an exception handler. A RuntimeException thrown by the

---

[3] Specifically, it is not possible to list a catch clause for a *sub class* after a catch clause for its *super class*. See Chapter 14 for further details of super classes and sub classes.

Code 11.8   Ask the user to nominate operands and a destination for a result
(`ArrayExceptionMain.java`)

```
// Exercise outline.
// Interactively prompt the user for 3 indices into an
// array of integers. Divide the two operands, and store
// the result at the destination.
class ArrayExceptionMain {
    public static void main(String[] args){
        // Some random values.
        final int[] values = { 10, 0, 30, 40, 100, 5, 2 };
        final int numValues = values.length;
        final SimpleInput keyboard = new SimpleInput();

        // Allow 5 changes.
        final int numChanges = 5;
        for(int change = 0; change < numChanges; change++){
            // Show the values.
            for(int i = 0; i < numValues; i++){
                System.out.print(values[i]+" ");
            }
            System.out.println();
            // Ask for the indices of the operand values.
            int operand1, operand2;
            System.out.println("Operands: ");
            operand1 = keyboard.nextInt();
            operand2 = keyboard.nextInt();

            int result = values[operand1]/values[operand2];
            System.out.println("The result is: "+result);
            // Ask for where it should be stored.
            System.out.println("Destination: ");
            int destination = keyboard.nextInt();
            values[destination] = result;
        }
    }
}
```

Circle constructor will be propagated out to the method that called `createCircles`
to see if it has a handler. In this example, it does have one, so the exception will be
reported there, and a fresh attempt made to create a complete set of circles. However,
if no exception handler were to be found enclosing the call to `createCircles`, then
this process of looking for an exception handler would have been repeated once again
one level further up the runtime stack. Only if the main method is reached, and it
does not handle the exception, is a runtime failure finally reported, with the program
terminating.

   If the original exception is a checked exception, the rules are slightly different
from those given above. A checked exception *must* either be handled immediately
within a catch clause, or its type must be included in the throws clause of any method
where it might arise or be propagated. Only unchecked exceptions may be omitted

Code 11.9 Propagation of an uncaught exception (`CircleMain3.java`)

```java
     // Illustrate exception propagation.
class CircleMain3 {
    public static void main(String[] args){
        // Require 5 circles to be created.
        Circle[] circles = null;
        do{
            try{
                final int max = 5;
                circles = createCircles(max);
            }
            catch(RuntimeException e){
                System.out.println(e.getMessage());
            }
        }
        while(circles == null);
        // Got them all.
        for(int i = 0; i< circles.length; i++){
            System.out.print(circles[i].getRadius()+" ");
        }
        System.out.println();
    }

        // Return an array containing max Circle objects.
        // The array must be returned full, or not at all.
    public static Circle[] createCircles(int max) throws RuntimeException {
        SimpleInput keyboard = new SimpleInput();
        Circle[] circles = new Circle[max];
        System.out.println("Please input "+max+" radius values.");
        for(int i = 0; i < max; i++){
            double radius = keyboard.nextDouble();
            circles[i] = new Circle(radius);
        }
        return circles;
    }
}
```

from a throws clause and still propagated to a calling method. The compiler will ensure that these rules are followed for checked exceptions and will not allow you to ignore the possibility that a checked exception might arise. A common checked exception that we shall encounter later in this chapter is IOException (defined in the java.io package). Even though unchecked exceptions will be automatically propagated, and do not have to be explicitly programmed for, it is good practice either to write handlers for them or to include their possible occurrence in the throws clause of a method.

In Section 11.3.2, we noted that an exception thrown in a catch clause will not be handled by the current exception handler. This can sometimes be useful when a method wishes to partially handle the exception, but leave further recovery to its caller. A catch clause can propagate an exception by rethrowing it once it has done the work it needs to do. This simply involves using an ordinary throw statement as the final statement of the clause, as follows:

```
try{
    // Protected statements
    ...
}
catch(Exception e){
    // Partial recovery.
    ...
    // Rethrow the exception.
    throw e;
}
```

The catch clause does not need to create a new exception object to do this.

We can see that a great deal of thought needs to be put into whether a class fully handles exceptions locally or propagates them to the callers of its methods. In general, recovery will often be easier, and the recovery action more specific, if it is performed close to where the problem was discovered. There are some situations where it is impossible to avoid an exception being thrown, simply because we do not have access to enough information before it happens, or enough control over the objects we are using to help us with a task. We shall see this, in particular, in the sections dealing with input-output. In such cases, the exception must be propagated further from the point at which it was thrown in order to provide a more complete context for the recovery.

11.3.4   The Error Exception

For those exceptions from which it is impossible to provide a reasonable recovery strategy, it is preferable to throw an unchecked `Error` exception, which is also defined in the `java.lang` package. A typical situation that cannot usually be recovered from is insufficient memory available to the program, for which recovery probably also requires memory—a *Catch 22* situation. An Error exception should really only be used as a last resort, since it is the ultimate admission of program failure.

11.4   The Finally Clause

The full form of the try statement includes a *finally clause*. This has a fairly specialized role, and is often omitted. The statements of a finally clause are *always* performed, whether control reached the natural end of the try clause, or was interrupted by an exception. Code 11.10 provides an outline of the full form that we can use to discuss the possible flows of control when a finally clause is included. In the example in Code 11.10, suppose that `T2` might throw an exception that is caught by the catch clause. If an exception is not thrown, then the sequence of statements will be: `T1; T2; T3; F`. If `T2` does throw an exception, then the sequence will be: `T1; T2; C; F`. The primary purpose of a finally clause is to enable a method to perform any essential housekeeping operations, whichever route is taken. The most common example is the closing of files associated with the method's task. Clearly, care must be taken in the finally clause that only statements appropriate to both the try and catch clauses are performed; this is another reason why they are often omitted.

```
public void method(){
    try{
        // T2 might throw an exception.
        Statement-T1;
        Statement-T2;
        Statement-T3;
    }
    catch(Exception e){
        Statement-C;
    }
    finally{
        Statement-F;
    }
}
```

It might appear that the finally clause behaves no differently from simply writing normal statements immediately after the try and catch clauses. Where the finally clause differs, however, is that its statements are executed even if one of the other clauses causes the method to terminate—via a return statement or a propagated exception. In the case of a return statement, the return is delayed until the finally clause has completed. The only deviation from this rule is when the finally clause, itself, causes an exception to be thrown, or contains a return statement; both take precedence over a prior return.

Code 11.11 illustrates the case where a thrown exception is propagated. This is an example similar to those that we shall meet in subsequent sections on input-output.

```
import java.io.*;

class FileCombiner {
    ...
        // Append the contents of the source file to the
        // destination file. Propagate any exception.
    public void append(String source, String destination)
                                        throws IOException {
        // Read from source.
        FileReader inFile = null;
        // Append to the destination.
        FileWriter outFile = null;
        try{
            inFile = new FileReader(source);
            outFile = new FileWriter(destination,true);
            ...
        }
        finally{
            // Only close the reader and writer if they were
            // opened successfully.
```

Code 11.11   (*Continued*)

```
                if(inFile != null){
                    inFile.close();
                }
                if(outFile != null){
                    outFile.close();
                }
            }
        }
        ...
    }
```

The append method attempts to open two files and then append the contents of the source file to the destination file. If this is successful, then the two files should be closed at the end of the method. However, either of the attempts to create a File-Reader or FileWriter object could fail, in which case a checked IOException exception will be thrown. If the first open succeeds but the second fails, we should still close the first file. The semantics of the finally clause mean that its statements will be executed whether the method is completed successfully, or an exception is thrown. In the latter case, the absence of a catch clause means that the IOException will be propagated, as it is declared in the method's throws clause. Notice that the two variables, inFile and outFile, must be defined outside the try clause; otherwise, they will not be in scope within the finally clause.

11.5 Review

Here are the main points that we have covered in the preceding sections:

- Classes should be designed to anticipate potential failure of their operations.
- Java provides for a method to throw an exception when it is unable or unwilling to complete an action.
- An exception is an object which is constructed in the normal way.
- Most exception objects are created by passing a diagnostic string to their constructor. This string is available via their getMessage method in the appropriate handler.
- An exception is thrown via a throw statement.
- A thrown exception may be caught by an exception handler in any part of the current runtime stack.
- An exception not caught by an exception handler will result in a program terminating.
- Exceptions may be checked or unchecked.
- Checked exceptions must be declared in the throws clause of any method that throws or propagates them. Declaration is optional (but recommended) for unchecked exceptions.
- A checked exception must be either caught or explicitly propagated.
- An exception is caught in a catch clause of a try statement.

- Different exceptions may be handled by multiple catch clauses in a single try statement.
- An exception will be handled by only one catch clause in a single try statement.
- Catch clauses for sub class exceptions must be listed before catch clauses for exceptions of their super class (see Chapter 14).
- The finally clause of a try statement is always executed.
- One or other of the catch and finally clauses may be omitted in a try statement.
- An exception thrown in a catch or finally clause of an exception handler is not recaught by that handler.
- The Error exception class should be used for exceptions that should not be caught. This class should be used as a last resort.

Exercise 11.7   Modify your solution to Exercise 9.27 so that the array manipulation statements are inside the try-part of a try-catch-finally statement, rather than the try statement being inside the loop. An exception will cause the iteration to end, with the catch sections printing appropriate error messages, as before. The finally section should print the contents of the array before the program finishes.

Exercise 11.8   Modify your solution to the `CarPark` Exercise 9.27, so that both the `collect` and `park` methods could throw a checked exception.

- The `collect` method should throw an exception if its argument is outside the bounds of the array, or if the given location is empty. Pass different message strings to the constructor in these two cases.
- The `park` method should throw an exception if an attempt is made to park a car when the car park is full.

You will need to include exception handlers in all classes that use these methods.

In this chapter, we have discussed the way in which exceptions may be used to indicate that something unexpected has occurred to interrupt a program's normal flow of control. Class designers must pay attention to anticipating the possible occurrence of exceptions, and to take appropriate corrective action. In the next chapter, we look at some of the standard input-output classes that are available in Java. Interacting with an external file system is an area where exceptions are common.

Input-Output

CHAPTER

12

In this chapter, we look at how file-system input and output can be performed using the Reader, Writer, and Stream classes of the `java.io` package. We also present an implementation of the `SimpleInput` class.

12.1 Input-Output

Input-output is often one of the more complex topics to describe in a programming language. The reason for this is that input-output occurs at a program's interface to the outside world, where things are often far from consistent or standardized across different systems. The input-output facilities must accommodate a potentially wide variety of operating system and hardware characteristics that make up the platform on which programs will run. Here are just a few examples of some of these differences:

- Operating systems have different conventions for how an end-of-line is to be indicated in a file.
- The same operating system might use completely different *character set encodings* to represent information in different countries.
- Some character sets use 8 bits to represent a character, whereas others use 16.
- Computers store binary representations of numbers internally in different ways (for example, *little-endian*, *big-endian*).
- Filename and path name conventions vary from system to system.

One of the ways in which the designers of Java have sought to isolate programmers from many of these differences is through the provision of the package of input-output classes, `java.io`. In addition, a particularly significant design decision was the use of the *Unicode character set*[Con96] for the representation of strings and the primitive type `char` (see Section 12.1.1 for more information on Unicode). Objects of the Reader classes of the `java.io` package take data read from files that are stored according to the conventions of the host operating system and automatically convert it into Unicode for use internally within the program. When it is written out, objects from the Writer classes convert it back from Unicode into the host's representation. In addition, Stream classes exist that will retain the original byte nature of input-output, where this is required.

In the next few sections, we introduce the basics of file-based input-output in Java: opening and closing files, and reading and writing both text and data.

12.1.1   The Unicode Character Set

The Unicode character set[Con96] has been designed to make it easier to exchange and display information that makes use of a wide range of different symbols. For instance, as well as being able to represent the familiar Latin based alphabet of the English language, it also allows scripts such as Arabic, Hebrew, Cyrillic, Thai, and so on, to be used. One consequence of this is that Java identifiers may be composed of letters and digits drawn from non-English alphabets (see Section 2.2.1). An *escape sequence* starting with \u indicates a Unicode character value. The value of the character is given using exactly four *hexadecimal* digits so '\u0035' represents the character '5' and '\u007a' represents the character 'z'. Several classes of the java.io package have been designed to convert from whatever character encoding is used in the external file system into Unicode, and vice-versa, (see Section 12.3 and Section 12.9). If conversion is not possible, a CharConversionException will be thrown. The Character wrapper class for primitive char variables defines several static methods that are concerned with testing Unicode characteristics of an individual character. For instance, its isLetter and isDigit methods can be used to test whether a particular character is a Unicode letter or digit. This means not simply the Latin symbols—'A'–'Z', 'a'–'z', and '0'–'9'—but also letters and digits in other supported languages and scripts. The isJavaIdentifierStart and isJavaIdentifierPart methods return true if a particular character may start an identifier or be part of an identifier after the initial character.

12.2   The File Class

Operating systems vary in the way in which their file systems are organized, the length of file names, the characters permitted in file names, the characters used to separate components of a file name, and so on. The File class of the java.io package attempts to free the programmer from worrying about many of these differences by providing objects which attempt to iron them out. Table 12.1 shows a selection of some of its methods. A File object represents an *abstract path name* for a file system item. It maintains information on both files and folders—or directories as the class's terminology prefers. A single File object holds information such as the name of the file, where it resides in the file system, the name of its parent directory, how big the file is, and so on. In programs that read from and write to parts of the file system, a File object offers the opportunity to ensure that a file exists and is readable or writable before attempting to open it. This is useful because attempting to open a file that does not exist is likely to result in a FileNotFoundException exception being thrown (see Section 12.4).

In its simplest form, the constructor of File takes the name of a file as a String:

```
File fileInfo = new File("Letter.txt");
```

In this case, we have specified a *relative filename* rather than an *absolute filename*. A relative filename is taken to refer to a file relative to the current directory in which

Table 12.1 Selected methods of the File class

	Method and Arguments
	File(String path)
	File(String parentPath,String child)
	File(File parentPath,String child)
boolean	canRead()
boolean	canWrite()
boolean	createNewFile()
static boolean	createTempFile(String prefix,String suffix)
static boolean	createTempFile(String prefix,String suffix,File folder)
boolean	delete()
void	deleteOnExit()
boolean	exists()
File	getAbsoluteFile()
String	getAbsolutePath()
File	getCanonicalFile()
String	getCanonicalPath()
String	getName()
String	getParent()
File	getParentFile()
String	getPath()
boolean	isAbsolute()
boolean	isDirectory()
boolean	isFile()
boolean	isHidden()
long	lastModified()
long	length()
String[]	list()
File[]	listFiles()
static File[]	listRoots()
boolean	mkdir()
boolean	renameTo(File newName)
boolean	setLastModified(long time)
boolean	setReadOnly()

the program is running, whereas an absolute filename indicates a path from the root (or top level) of the file system. No exception is thrown if the filename refers to a file that does not exist, but the contents of the created object will be of less use than when the file does exist. Information about the file is gathered from the file system and becomes available to the program via the File object's methods. A test for a file's existence can be made with its `exists` method, which returns a `boolean` result:

```
File fileInfo = new File("Letter.txt");
if(fileInfo.exists()){
    System.out.println(fileInfo.getName()+" exists.");
}
```

A file might exist, but we might not have permission to read or overwrite its contents; these permissions can be ascertained with the `canRead` and `canWrite` methods. Code 12.1 illustrates these principles using the `checkReadability` method of the `CombineFile` class, which is part of a program to create a single combined output file out of multiple input files.

Code 12.1   Check a file before opening it for reading (`CombineFiles.java`)

```java
import java.io.*;

    // Combine the files whose names are given to combineFiles to
    // the file named in the constructor.
class CombineFiles {
    public CombineFiles(String whereTo){
        // Keep a copy of the name of the combined file.
        destination = whereTo;
    }

        // Write these files to the 'destination' file.
    public void combineFiles(String[] filesToCombine){
        // Where the files will be appended to.
        FileWriter outputFile = null;
        try{
            checkReadability(filesToCombine);
            // Append to the destination file.
            outputFile = new FileWriter(getDestination(),true);
            for(int n = 0; n < filesToCombine.length; n++){
                // Copy the next file into the destination.
                try{
                    FileReader inputFile = new FileReader(filesToCombine[n]);
                    copyFile(inputFile,outputFile);
                    inputFile.close();
                }
                catch(FileNotFoundException e){
                    System.out.println("Unable to open "+filesToCombine[n]);
                }
                catch(IOException e){
                    System.out.println(e.toString());
                }
            }
        }
        catch(IOException e){
            System.out.println(e.toString());
        }
        finally{
            if(outputFile != null){
                try{
                    outputFile.close();
                }
                catch(IOException e){
                    System.out.println("Unable to close "+getDestination());
                }
            }
        }
    }

        // Throw a FileNotFoundException if any of the files
        // is readable or does not exist.
    public void checkReadability(String[] filesToRead)
                                    throws FileNotFoundException {
        // Build up an error message for bad files.
        StringBuffer notFound = new StringBuffer();
        final int numFiles = filesToRead.length;
        for(int i = 0; i < numFiles; i++){
```

Code 12.1   (*Continued*)

```
        File details = new File(filesToRead[i]);
        if(!details.exists()){
            notFound.append(filesToRead[i]);
            notFound.append(" does not exist. ");
        }
        else if(!details.canRead()){
            notFound.append(filesToRead[i]);
            notFound.append(" is not readable. ");
        }
        // else - ok.
    }
    if(notFound.length() != 0){
        throw new FileNotFoundException(notFound.toString());
    }
}

...

    // Return a copy of the destination filename.
    public String getDestination(){
        return destination;
    }

    // The name of the combined file.
    private final String destination;
}
```

The `checkReadability` method takes an array of filenames and establishes whether all of the files exist and are readable. It does this by creating a File object for each and querying its `exists` and `canRead` methods. If any of the files is not valid, then it creates an error message and throws an exception at the end of the method. Other methods defined in the File class are as follows:

- String path methods: these return an absolute file system path name (`getAbsolutePath`), a system-dependent unique (canonical) path name (`getCanonicalPath`), the last part of the path name (`getName`), the name of the containing directory (`getParent`), and a file system path name (`getPath`). Because operating systems use different conventions for separating the components of a path name, the class defines class constants for the different separators: `separatorChar` (a char) and `separator` (a String).
- File path methods: these return File objects similar to the String accessor methods described above: `getAbsoluteFile`, `getCanonicalFile`, and `getParentFile`.
- Boolean checking methods: return `true` if the abstract path is an absolute path name (`isAbsolute`), a directory/folder (`isDirectory`), an ordinary file (`isFile`), or is hidden (`isHidden`).
- Manipulation methods: to remove it (`delete` and `deleteOnExit`), rename it (`renameTo`), change its modification time (`setLastModified`), and set its read-status (`setReadOnly`).

- Listing methods: obtain an array of Strings for its contents if it is a directory (list) and an array of File objects (listFiles). The static listRoots method returns an array of File objects for the file system roots, or top-level directories.
- File creation methods: create a new file (createNewFile), create a temporary file (createTempFile — such a file will be deleted automatically on exit), and create a new directory (mkdir).

The lastModified method returns a long value which encodes the date and time at which the file was last modified. This value can be passed to a Date object in order to obtain a representation that is easier to manipulate, if required.

Exercise 12.1   Use the static listRoots method of the File class to find out the file-system root directories in your environment. Use the toString method of the File objects returned to print the name. Alternatively, use the getCanonicalPath method. This might throw an IOException, which will need to be caught. If your environment has a disk drive without a disk in it, an exception will probably be thrown in such a case.

Exercise 12.2   Use the getAbsolutePath method of the File class to print the absolute path name of your current working directory. The name of the current directory is referred to by the name "." on many operating systems.

Exercise 12.3   Write a main method that tests each of the command line arguments to see if they are the names of files which exist. For each file which exists, print out whether it is readable, its absolute path name, and whether it is a directory or not.

12.2.1   A Directory Lister

Code 12.2 uses several of the methods of the File class in an example that maintains a File attribute for a file-system directory. The purpose of the class is to provide different listings of the contents of the directory. The DirectoryLister class uses the File object to print either a simple list of names of the contents of the directory (printContents) or a more detailed listing that includes file types and read/write permissions (printFullDetails). Note that the constructors and setDirectory mutator of this class prevent a DirectoryLister object from being constructed if either the directory does not exist, or the parameters refer to something that is not a directory. In this way, they ensure that a DirectoryLister cannot be sent messages to which it would be meaningless to respond. A short example of the output from printFullDetails might be as follows:

```
drw May 11, 1999 SCCS
frw May 9, 1999 UncheckedMain2.class
fr- May 9, 1999 UncheckedMain2.java
```

This example uses the DateFormat class of the java.text package to format the last modified dates of each file (see Section 8.6.3).

Code 12.2   Providing short and long directory listings (`DirectoryLister.java`)

```java
import java.io.*;
import java.util.Date;
import java.text.DateFormat;

    /* Maintain a File object relating to a particular directory (folder).
     * Construction of a DirectoryLister will fail if either the given
     * directory name does not exist or the name does not relate to a
     * directory. Methods are provided to print a simple list of the
     * directory's contents, or a more detailed list including the type
     * and permissions for each file, the date on which it was last
     * modified and its name.
     */

class DirectoryLister {
    // Construct from the name of a directory.
    public DirectoryLister(String dirname)
                    throws FileNotFoundException, Exception {
        this(new File(dirname));
    }

    // Construct from a File object that should refer to a directory.
    public DirectoryLister(File dir)
                    throws FileNotFoundException, Exception {
        setDirectory(dir);
    }

        // Print the contents of this directory. Only print
        // the names, one per line, without further details.
    public void printContents(){
        // Include the directory's full path as a heading.
        System.out.println(getPath());
        File details = getDirectory();

        String[] list = details.list();
        final int numFiles = list.length;
        for(int i = 0; i < numFiles; i++){
            System.out.println(list[i]);
        }
    }

        // Print details of the contents of this directory.
        // Include file type, read/write permission and date
        // of last modification.
        // This appears in the form
        //        frw Dec 25, 1999 filename

    public void printFullDetails(){
        // Format the file modification time.
        DateFormat formatter = DateFormat.getDateInstance();
        // Obtain the path of this directory.
        String path = getPath();
        File details = getDirectory();
        // Obtain the list of file objects for the contents.
        File[] list = details.listFiles();
        final int numFiles = list.length;

        System.out.println(path);
        // A buffer used to form the descriptions.
        StringBuffer info = new StringBuffer();
```

(Continued)

Code 12.2   *(Continued)*

```java
        for(int i = 0; i < numFiles; i++){
            final File f = list[i];
            // Don't include hidden files
            if(!f.isHidden()){
                info.setLength(0);
                info.append(f.isDirectory() ? "d" : f.isFile() ? "f" : "-");
                info.append(f.canRead() ? "r" : "-");
                info.append(f.canWrite() ? "w" : "-");

                // Include the date on which the file was last modified.
                Date modified = new Date(f.lastModified());
                info.append(" "+formatter.format(modified));
                info.append(" "+f.getName());
                System.out.println(info);
            }
        }
    }

    // Try to return the canonical path, but use the absolute
    // path if that fails.
    public String getPath(){
        File details = getDirectory();
        String path = "";
        try{
            path = details.getCanonicalPath();
        }
        catch(IOException e){
            // Cannot obtain the canonical path, for some reason.
            // Use the absolute path.
            path = details.getAbsolutePath();
        }
        return path;
    }

    // Check that the file exists and is a directory.
    public void checkForDirectory(File f) throws FileNotFoundException, Exception {
        if(!f.exists()){
            throw new FileNotFoundException(f.getName());
        }
        else if(!f.isDirectory()){
            throw new Exception(f.getName()+" is not a directory.");
        }
        // else - ok.
    }

    public File getDirectory(){
        return directory;
    }

    // Set the Directory to be used. This must be a directory.
    public void setDirectory(File d) throws FileNotFoundException,
                                            Exception {
        checkForDirectory(d);
        directory = d;
    }

    // Assert: directory.exists() && directory.isDirectory().
    private File directory;
}
```

Exercise 12.4   Compile and run the program in the file `DirectoryLister-Main.java` to see the type of output it produces on your file system. Give the program some command line arguments that test its error handling, such as directory names that do not exist and names that are ordinary files, rather than directories.

12.2.2   A Recursive Directory Lister

A file system is usually hierarchical in nature; that is, a directory may contain both files and directories (sub-directories). The sub-directories themselves may contain files and directories, and so on. The definition of such a hierarchical file system is *recursive*: a directory consists of a named collection of zero or more files and directories. The recursion is terminated by a directory containing no sub-directories. In addition to the functionality currently provided by the DirectoryLister class, it would be useful to be able to list both the contents of a directory and all of its sub-directories (and all of their sub-directories, and so on). This process is called *navigating a file system*, and it is a problem with a recursive solution. Having printed the contents of the top-level directory, we need to identify the sub-directories it contains, create DirectoryLister objects for each and ask each of those to recursively print their contents. Code 12.3 shows part of a new class, `RecursiveLister`. This is identical to the existing DirectoryLister with the addition of two further methods, `printNestedContents` and `getSubDirectories`. The `printNested-Contents` method first prints the contents of the top-level directory. It then uses the `getSubDirectories` method to obtain a list of File objects for all of the sub-directories contained within it. For each of these sub-directories, it creates a new RecursiveLister object and asks it to print its contents recursively. Note the use of a variable-sized `ArrayList` object to collect together a list of the directories, and the use of its `toArray` method to convert this into a fixed-size array once the list is complete.

Exercise 12.5   Run the program in the file `RecursiveListerMain.java` to assure yourself that the `printNestedContents` method does what it should.

Exercise 12.6   In what order will the files in the directory structure shown below be printed by a RecursiveLister?

```
root
    subdir1
        a1
        b1
    subdir2
        a2
        subdir21
          b2
        c2
    subdir3
        a3
        b3
```

Code 12.3   Recursively print the contents of a directory (`RecursiveLister.java`)

```java
class RecursiveLister {
    // Construct from the name of a directory.
    public RecursiveLister(String dirname)
                        throws FileNotFoundException, Exception {
        this(new File(dirname));
    }

    // Construct from a File object that should refer to a directory.
    public RecursiveLister(File dir)
                        throws FileNotFoundException, Exception {
        setDirectory(dir);
    }

    /* Print the contents of this directory and all nested
     * directories. This is not handled by recursion of this method
     * but by recursively creating further RecursiveLister
     * objects for each sub directory.
     */
    public void printNestedContents(){
        // Print the contents of this directory.
        printContents();
        // Find each directory in the current directory.
        File[] directories = getSubDirectories();
        final int numDirectories = directories.length;
        for(int i = 0; i < numDirectories; i++){
            try{
                RecursiveLister subdir = new RecursiveLister(directories[i]);
                subdir.printNestedContents();
            }
            catch(Exception e){
                System.err.println(e);
            }
        }
    }

    // Return an array of File objects representing the
    // sub-directories within this directory.
    // Return an array of all the subdirectories within
    // this directory.
    public File[] getSubDirectories(){
        ArrayList directories = new ArrayList();
        File details = getDirectory();
        final String path = getPath();
        String[] list = details.list();
        final int numFiles = list.length;
        for(int i = 0; i < numFiles; i++){
            File f = new File(path+File.separator+list[i]);
            if(f.isDirectory()){
                directories.add(f);
            }
        }
        // Return the directories collection as an array.
        File[] fileArray = new File[directories.size()];
        directories.toArray(fileArray);
        return fileArray;
    }
    ...
}
```

Exercise 12.7   Add a method to RecursiveLister that uses the `printFull-`
`Details` method to recursively print the full details of a directory's contents. You
should not modify `printFullDetails` in order to do this.

In fact, slight care needs to be taken with any attempt to recursively traverse a hierarchical file system. Many file systems are not strictly tree-like in structure, allowing
lower level directories to contain links to items at higher levels. This could lead to a
RecursiveLister performing infinite recursion.

   The close similarity of the DirectoryLister class to that of RecursiveLister suggests that it ought to be possible to re-use the functionality of the former in the latter.
As we shall see in Chapter 14, this is where class *inheritance* provides big benefits
for code re-use. We shall return to the RecursiveLister class in Exercise 14.17 of that
chapter.

12.3   Readers, Writers, and Streams

In Section 12.1, we noted that the data stored in a file system in one environment might be quite different from the format used in a different environment,
while the internal character format expected by Java programs is Unicode. It is
important to recognize the existence of such differences, and the need that often
arises to convert an external format into a different internal format. Java's input-
output classes are designed around two different views of the way in which external data must be handled. The *stream classes* are designed to deliver an ordered
stream of `byte` values that capture the external representation of data. The *reader
and writer classes*, on the other hand, are designed to convert a wide range of
external representations of character-based data to and from the internally used
Unicode representation. When the requirement is to process text files, therefore,
the primary classes to select are the reader and writer classes. The waters appear
to be somewhat muddied in that combined classes also exist, such as `Input-`
`StreamReader` and `OutputStreamWriter`; such classes share the general characteristics of the reader and writer classes when interacting with the internal (program) level, and the stream classes when interacting with the external (file
system) level.

   Input-output of text files is the easiest place to start, so the next few sections
describe some of the available reader and writer classes.

12.4   The FileReader and FileWriter Classes

The most basic operation to be performed on a file is to open it—so that we can
read its contents, or write new contents to it. Because the exact nature of the outside
world is usually out of the programmer's control, even such a simple task as opening
a file can go wrong: a file we wish to read might have restricted access permission for
security reasons, for instance. For this reason, we will need to make a lot of use of
the exception-handling features of Java that we met in Chapter 11.

Code 12.4   Open and close a file for reading

```
void processInputFile(String filename){
    try{
        // Try to open the file.
        FileReader inputFile = new FileReader(filename);
        // Process the file's contents.
        ...
        // Close the file now that it is finished with.
        inputFile.close();
    }
    catch(FileNotFoundException e){
        // The file could not be opened.
        System.out.println("Unable to open "+filename);
    }
    catch(IOException e){
        // The file could not be read or closed.
        System.out.println("Unable to close "+filename);
    }
}
```

12.4.1   Opening and Closing a File

Code 12.4 shows the outline of a method that might be used to open, process, and then close a file whose name has been passed to it as an argument. A text file is opened by creating a new object of the class `FileReader` which is imported from the `java.io` package. A selection of its methods is shown in Table 12.2. The name of the file to be opened is passed to the object's constructor (alternative constructors take a File object or a `FileDescriptor` object). If the required file cannot be found (or, indeed, cannot be opened for any other reason), a `FileNotFoundException` exception is thrown by the constructor and the new object is not created; otherwise, the new FileReader object contains attributes that enable data to be read from the opened file. An important point to note is that, even though we might have used the `exists` and `canRead` methods of a File object first of all to establish that a file does indeed exist and is readable, we must still cater for a FileNotFoundException

Table 12.2   Selected methods of the FileReader class

	Method and Arguments
	FileReader(String filename)
	FileReader(File file)
	FileReader(FileDescriptor file)
void	close()
int	read()
int	read(char[] buffer)
int	read(char[] buffer,int bufferOffset,int numChars)
long	skip(long numChars)

exception when creating the FileReader object. The compiler is not able to appreciate that use of a File object's `exists` and `canRead` methods are for the express purpose of eliminating the possibility of the open failing.

When the data from a file has been processed, the file should be closed in order to indicate to the operating system that we have finished with it. For this we use the `close` method of the FileReader object. Although unlikely, this could result in an `IOException` exception being thrown, and so we must provide a catch section to deal with it. In the example in Code 12.4, the more specific test for a FileNotFoundException must be made before the test for an IOException, as described in Section 11.3.2. Closing a file also frees resources in the *virtual machine* (VM), and so remembering to close it is doubly important because the VM might have a limit on the number of files that may be open simultaneously.

In order to write text to a file, we can use a `FileWriter` object. A selection of its methods is shown in Table 12.3. A FileWriter is created and used in an analogous way to a FileReader (see Code 12.5). A FileWriter has four constructors, three of

---

Code 12.5   Opening a file for writing.

```
void processOutputFile(String filename){
    try{
        FileWriter outputFile = new FileWriter(filename);
        // Process the file's contents.
        ...
        outputFile.close();
    }
    catch(FileNotFoundException e){
        System.out.println("Unable to open "+filename);
    }
    catch(IOException e){
        System.out.println("Unable to close "+filename);
    }
}
```

Table 12.3   Selected methods of the FileWriter class

	Method and Arguments
	FileWriter(String filename)
	FileWriter(String filename,boolean append)
	FileWriter(File file)
	FileWriter(FileDescriptor file)
void	close()
void	flush()
String	getEncoding()
void	write(int c)
void	write(char[] buffer)
void	write(char[] buffer,int bufferOffset,int numChars)
void	write(String s)
void	write(String s,int sOffset,int numChars)

Code 12.6 Copying text from one file to another (`CombineFiles.java`)

```
class CombineFiles {
    ...
    void copyFile(FileReader inputFile,FileWriter outputFile)
                    throws IOException {
        // Provide space for a small number of characters to be read.
        final int bufferSize = 1024;
        char[] buffer = new char[bufferSize];
        // Read the first chunk of characters.
        int numberRead = inputFile.read(buffer);
        // Keep going as long as something was read.
        while(numberRead > 0){
            // Write out what was read.
            outputFile.write(buffer,0,numberRead);
            // Read the next chunk, if any.
            numberRead = inputFile.read(buffer);
        }
        outputFile.flush();
    }
    ...
}
```

which correspond to those of the FileReader class. A fourth is added because the one taking a single file name String argument will open a file for writing destructively. This means that, if a file of that name already existed, its contents will be lost and overwritten by opening it. The additional constructor takes two arguments: a filename String and a `boolean mode` argument. The second argument indicates whether an existing file should be opened in *append mode* or not. If the actual argument has the value `true`, then any existing contents will not be lost. Rather, new data written to the file will be appended after its existing contents. This approach would be used by a program writing continuous log files, for instance.

Closing an output file explicitly is particularly important because it causes any internal buffers to be flushed. The `flush` method can be used for this purpose, too. Failure to ensure that internal buffers are flushed can result in some data not being written. You should not assume that the end of a program automatically closes files and flushes buffers, because this is not the case.

12.4.2 Reading and Writing Text Files

A FileReader object has several different `read` methods that allow us to read a single character from the text file into a variable, or one or more characters from the file into a character array. A FileWriter object has a complementary set of `write` methods. Code 12.6 shows an example to copy the text from one file to another between the reader and writer objects passed as its arguments. It uses one version of `read` and one version of `write` to do this. The corresponding input and output files have already been opened successfully when this method is called. The `read` method takes a `char` array of any length as its actual argument and the Reader object tries to fill that array with Unicode versions of the characters read from the input file. As a result, it indicates how many characters it was able to read, which might be fewer than the array can hold. This value is stored in `numberRead` so that it can be checked and so that it can be used when writing out the characters. When the end of the file is reached, the value returned will be `-1`. The data that is read will have been held in the file in the character set that is used by the operating system storing it. This will not usually be the form in which we wish to process it; rather, we want to read it as a stream of Unicode characters. This conversion process is automatically done for us by the FileReader object.

The FileWriter's `write` method takes an array containing the characters to be written as its first argument, the index in that array of the first character to be written, and how many characters to write (because the array might not be full). Just as a FileReader automatically converts from the file system's external representation to internal Unicode form, a FileWriter performs the opposite conversion. Both reading and writing might throw an `IOException` exception, so the method includes a throws clause.

One of the `read` methods of the Reader class is analogous to the three-argument `write` method we used above:

```
numberRead = inputFile.read(buffer,0,buffer.length);
```

Here, the second argument is the first index of the array into which to read the characters, and the third determines how many to read if possible. Similarly, there is a single-argument `write` method

```
outputFile.write(buffer)
```

which is equivalent to

```
outputFile.write(buffer,0,buffer.length);
```

It wasn't possible to use the single argument `write` in `copyFile` because we have no guarantee that the whole of the array was filled with characters by `read`. In particular, the final read from the file is unlikely to fill the buffer, unless the file length is an exact multiple of the number of bytes we try to read each time.

12.4.3   Reading a Whole File

The example in Code 12.6 iteratively copies a file by repeatedly reading and writing relatively small pieces. It is possible to attempt to read the complete contents of a file with a single `read`, provided sufficient buffer space is available. Code 12.7 illustrates this approach in a simple example that copies the contents of a file named on the command line to the file named `output.txt`. This example uses the FileReader constructor that takes a File argument to open the file. It also uses the `length` method of File to determine the number of bytes in the file to be read, and then

---

Code 12.7 Copying a file with a single read and write (`Copy.java`)

```java
import java.io.*;

        // Illustrate the way to read a file in a single read.
class Copy {
    public static void main(String[] args) throws IOException {
        if(args.length == 1){
            FileReader reader = null;
            FileWriter writer = null;
            try{
                final String outputFile = "output.txt";
                // Use a File in order to find out the file's length.
                final File f = new File(args[0]);
                // Open the input and output files.
                reader = new FileReader(f);
                writer = new FileWriter(outputFile);
                // Attempt to read the whole file in a single read.
                final int fileSize = (int) f.length();
                // Allocate sufficient space.
                char[] buffer = new char [fileSize];

                if(fileSize != f.length()){
                    throw new IOException("File size mismatch.");
                }
                else if(reader.read(buffer,0,fileSize) != fileSize){
                    throw new IOException("Read failure.");
                }
                else{
                    writer.write(buffer);
                    writer.flush();
                    System.out.println(outputFile+" written.");
                }
            }
            finally{
                if(reader != null){
                    reader.close();
                }
                if(writer != null){
                    writer.close();
                }
            }
        }
    }
}
```

---

allocates a char array that exactly matches this value. There are several potential problems with this:

- If the number of bytes does not match the number of characters, the program will report a read failure.

Code 12.8 Copying a file one character at a time

```
    // Illustrate copying character-by-character.
void copyFile(FileReader inputFile,FileWriter outputFile){
    try{
        // Read the first character.
        int nextChar = inputFile.read();
        // Have we reached the end of file?
        while(nextChar != -1){
            outputFile.write(nextChar);
            // Read the next character.
            nextChar = inputFile.read();
        }
        outputFile.flush();
    }
    catch(IOException e){
        System.out.println("Unable to copy a file.");
    }
}
```

- The program assumes that it will be possible to input the file in a single read operation. This assumption might be invalid for a very large file or on some operating systems.
- The length method of File returns a value of type long, but a value of this type cannot be used to specify the size of an array. If the size of the file is too large to fit into the size of an int, this approach will fail.
- A very big file will require a single very large array to contain it. Memory limitations in a particular environment might prohibit this approach.

12.4.4 Reading Single Characters

The FileReader and FileWriter classes each include a method to either read or write a single char. Code 12.8 shows examples of these because the read method is slightly unusual. The character read on each call to read is returned as the method's result. This causes a slight problem, because the return value has also been chosen to indicate when the end of file has been reached. However, there is no *out-of-bounds value* within the range of the char type that could be used to signal the end of file; all values are valid within the Unicode character set. As a consequence, the return type of read has been defined as int, rather than char; when the end of the file is reached, the non-char out of bounds value -1 is returned.

This causes a complication because Unicode characters should really be stored in variables of the primitive type char, but nextChar must be defined as an int in Code 12.8. If we had tried to define it as a char, the compiler would have given the error message:

```
    Incompatible type for declaration.
    Explicit cast needed to convert int to char.
        char nextChar = inputFile.read();
                ^
```

In other words, we are trying to store the integer returned from `read` into a character variable. This is all rather messy and confusing—we say that the meaning of the return value of `read` is *overloaded*; it is being used for two different purposes which are incompatible. If it has a Unicode character to return, this version of `read` is casting it into an integer before returning it. For the sake of compatibility, the complementary version of `write` takes a single integer argument which it assumes is a Unicode character cast to an integer, and it casts it back to type `char` before arranging for it to be written out.

The file `CombineFiles.java` contains versions of the pieces we have looked at in these sections to implement a complete file copying program. A main method may be found in `CombineFilesMain.java`.

Exercise 12.8   Use a FileReader to read the contents of a text file and report the percentage of letter characters in the file. Use the static `isLetter` method of the Character class for the classification.

Exercise 12.9   Use the FileReader and FileWriter classes to write a program that makes a copy of a file with all multiple consecutive space characters replaced by a single space. For instance, the following two lines in the input file

```
multiple␣spaces␣␣␣should␣be␣␣compressed,
even␣trailing␣spaces␣␣␣
```

should appear as follows

```
multiple␣spaces␣should␣be␣compressed,
even␣trailing␣spaces␣
```

in the resulting file. Use the static `isSpaceChar` method of the Character class for testing.

Exercise 12.10   Use a FileReader to read the contents of a text file character-by-character and report the percentage of digit characters in the file. Use the static `isDigit` method of the Character class for the classification.

12.5   The Buffered Reader and Writer Classes

In most of the examples above, we used an array, `buffer`, in order to make the copying slightly more efficient than it would have been had we copied the files one character at a time—it reduces the number of times the body of the main copying loop is executed, for instance. The `java.io` package contains classes that also provide buffering mechanisms that are slightly different in implementation, but similar in intent. Reading and writing files involves interacting with *peripheral devices* that are part of the system's environment. Such interactions are relatively slow compared with the speed at which the computer's CPU can operate when executing a program's instructions. For this reason, the `BufferedReader` and `BufferedWriter` classes try to overcome some of these overheads. Tables 12.4 and 12.5 show a sample of their methods. When a `read` message is sent to a BufferedReader object, it might actually read more data from the file than was specifically asked for. It will hold on to that

	Table 12.4 Selected methods of the Buffered-Reader class
	Method and Arguments
	BufferedReader(Reader r)
	BufferedReader(Reader r,int bufferSize)
void	close()
int	read()
int	read(char[] buffer)
int	read(char[] buffer,int bufferOffset,int numChars)
String	readLine()
long	skip(long numChars)

	Table 12.5 Selected methods of the Buffered-Writer class
	Method and Arguments
	BufferedWriter(Writer w)
	BufferedWriter(Writer w,int bufferSize)
void	close();
void	flush();
void	newLine();
void	write(int c)
void	write(char[] buffer)
void	write(char[] buffer,int bufferOffset,int numChars)
void	write(String s)
void	write(String s,int sOffset,int numChars)

which is left over so that it can respond to the next read-request promptly, without having to make an external request. Similarly, a BufferedWriter object might bundle up several small write requests in its own internal buffer and only make a single external write-to-file operation when it considers that it has enough data to make the write worthwhile, when its internal buffer is full, or a specific request is made via a call to its `flush` method. These classes have the further advantage that we can use them to read and write text in terms of a whole line of a file, which is often the sort of granularity we will require. Furthermore, each line is handled as a String object rather than an array of characters.

It is not possible to open a file directly simply by constructing a Buffered Reader or Writer object. Instead we construct one from an existing FileReader or FileWriter object. This is the result of a design decision on the part of the class designers. It has the advantage of not duplicating file-opening functionality in many different classes. Code 12.9 shows how FileReader and FileWriter objects are wrapped in BufferedReader and BufferedWriter objects, respectively. Notice that we only close the outermost `reader` and `writer`, and not the `inputFile` and `outputFile` objects. To close both would be an error. This is because the buffered classes simply act as wrappers around the objects they were constructed with, which they retain as an attribute. These buffered objects have the same set of `read` and `write` methods as the unbuffered objects but they delegate all their input-output operations to those

---

Code 12.9   Creating a Buffered Reader and Writer

```
try{
    // Open the file and create the buffered reader.
    FileReader inputFile = new FileReader(inputFilename);
    BufferedReader reader = new BufferedReader(inputFile);
    // Open the file and create the buffered writer.
    FileWriter outputFile = new FileWriter(outputFilename);
    BufferedWriter writer = new BufferedWriter(outputFile);
    // Use reader and writer.
    ...
    // Close the files.
    reader.close();
    writer.close();
}
catch(FileNotFoundException e){
    System.out.println(e.getMessage());
}
catch(IOException e){
    System.out.println(e.getMessage());
}
```

Code 12.10   Creating a Buffered Reader and Writer

```
try{
    // Open the file and create the buffered reader.
    BufferedReader reader =
        new BufferedReader(new FileReader(inputFilename));
    // Open the file and create the buffered writer.
    BufferedWriter writer =
        new BufferedWriter(new FileWriter(outputFilename));
    ...
}
```

---

attributes. Closing a BufferedReader causes it to close the underlying FileReader automatically.

Because the Buffered Reader and Writer objects take over the full roles of the File Reader and Writer objects, we do not really need the `inputFile` and `output-File` variable names, and will commonly write these as anonymous object creations, as shown in Code 12.10. The BufferedReader class adds a `readLine` method that returns a String, and BufferedWriter adds both a `write` method that takes a String argument, and a `newLine` method that outputs a line terminator. Code 12.11 shows how these buffered objects might be used to copy a file line-by-line in the form of strings. Each line is returned as a String object from the Reader's `readLine` method. A `null` reference is returned at the end of the file. When a line of text is read, the line termination is removed so when the line is written to the file associated with the Writer, a line termination must be added with its `newLine` method.

Code 12.11   Reading and writing a file line-by-line

```
// Copy everything from inputFile to outputFile.
void copyFile(BufferedReader reader,BufferedWriter writer)
            throws IOException {
    // Read the first line.
    String line = reader.readLine();
    while(line != null){
        // Write the whole line.
        writer.write(line);
        // Add the newline character.
        writer.newLine();
        // Read the next line.
        line = reader.readLine();
    }
}
```

Code 12.12   Selecting particular lines from a file (`SelectLines.java`)

```
public void selectLines(String filename, int n)
                    throws FileNotFoundException, IOException {
    LineNumberReader reader =
                    new LineNumberReader(new FileReader(filename));
    // Read the first line.
    String line = reader.readLine();
    while(line != null){
        if((reader.getLineNumber() % n) == 0){
            // This line is to be printed.
            System.out.println(line);
        }
        line = reader.readLine();
    }
    reader.close();
}
```

12.5.1   The LineNumberReader Class

A class related to BufferedReader is `LineNumberReader`. Objects of this class keep track of the number of the line just read from the associated file. There is no complementary LineNumberWriter class. Code 12.12 shows a method to read from a file and print only every n^{th} line; all exceptions are left for the caller to handle. The `getLineNumber` method of a LineNumberReader returns the number of the current line.

12.5.2   The CharArray Reader and Writer Classes

Reader and Writer functionality is not exclusively tied to external files. The `CharArrayReader` class makes it possible to create a reader that takes its source from the array of characters passed to one of its constructors. The class defines read methods just like the FileReader class. Similarly, the `CharArrayWriter` class makes it possible to write to a dynamically expanding array of characters. An initial size for the array may be passed as the argument to one of its two constructors. Its `toArray` method returns a reference to the data that has been written to it.

Exercise 12.11 Write a program to print the lines of a text file with each line preceded by its line number and a space. Display the line number within a fixed width of 5 characters so that text of each line is aligned. For instance, if the first three lines of the file are

```
first
second
third
```

these will be printed as:

```
ᵾᵾᵾᵾ1ᵾfirst
ᵾᵾᵾᵾ2ᵾsecond
ᵾᵾᵾᵾ3ᵾthird
```

Exercise 12.12 Define and implement a class that is able to read a file and detect duplicate consecutive lines within it. The class should contain methods that are able to do the following:

- Write a new file containing only the non-duplicate lines.
- Write a new file containing one copy of each of only the duplicate lines.
- Write a new file containing the non-duplicate lines and a single copy of the duplicate lines.

You do not need to detect duplicate lines that do not immediately follow one another.

12.6   Review

Here are the main points that we have covered in the preceding sections:

- Input-output involves communication with a program's external environment.
- Host operating systems have different characteristics that make up part of a program's external environment.
- Environments differ in the character sets they use, and the binary format they use for storing data, for instance.
- Java uses the Unicode character set internal representation of `char` data.
- A File object provides an internal abstract path name for an external file or directory.
- A File object allows operating system characteristics of an external file or directory to be accessed and manipulated.
- The Reader and Writer classes free a program from needing to be aware of the external encoding of character data.
- The Reader classes transform external host-dependent character data into internal Unicode format.

- The Writer classes transform internal Unicode character data into an appropriate external host dependent format.
- Text files may be read and written with the FileReader and FileWriter classes.
- Reader classes define `read` methods to read both single characters and arrays of characters.
- Writer classes define `write` methods to write both single characters and arrays of characters.
- The BufferedReader and BufferedWriter classes provide internal buffering to improve the efficiency of input-output operations.
- Readers and writers should always be closed when a program has no further need for the data to which they refer.
- Buffered data will not be automatically flushed when a program terminates.

12.7 The Stream Classes

The alternative to using reader and writer classes for input and output is to use one of the stream classes. Unlike readers and writers, which deal with `char` data, stream classes manipulate a sequenced stream of `byte` data, typically associated with binary format files. For instance, a binary image file is not intended to be processed as text, and so no conversion would be appropriate when such a file is read for display in a program. An important feature of the stream classes is that they are not entirely tied to data held in external files. Specialist classes exist to deliver a stream of bytes to and from other sources and sinks, such as an internal array of bytes. `InputStream` defines the core of the input functionality. A selection of its methods is shown in Table 12.6. Other major input stream classes which build on the core functionality provided by the `InputStream` class are as follows:

- `BufferedInputStream`: deliver a buffered stream of bytes. Read operations may be fulfilled from an internal buffer, and, in some cases, this offers the opportunity to mark and re-read positions within the stream.
- `ByteArrayInputStream`: deliver a stream of bytes from the array (or part of it) passed to its constructor.

Table 12.6 Selected methods of the InputStream class

	Method and Arguments
	InputStream()
int	available()
void	close()
void	mark(int limit)
boolean	markSupported()
int	read()
int	read(byte[] buffer)
int	read(byte[] buffer,int bufferOffset,int numBytes)
void	reset()
long	skip(long numBytes)

- `DataInputStream`: deliver a stream of bytes in such a way that primitive type values may be read in a machine-independent way (see Section 12.8).
- `FileInputStream`: deliver a stream of bytes from a file, details of which are passed to the constructor as a File, FileDescriptor, or String.
- `ObjectInputStream`: deliver an object as a stream of bytes. An introduction to this class is given in Section 12.12.
- `PipedInputStream`: deliver a stream of bytes from a *pipe*. Connected to the other end of the pipe is usually another object writing a stream of bytes via a `PipedOutputStream` object.
- `PushbackInputStream`: deliver a stream of bytes, but allow a limited number of bytes that have already been read to be pushed back into the stream and re-read subsequently. Such functionality is useful when it is necessary to look ahead at the input data in order to be able to decide what to do next, but not lose the data in the process.
- `SequenceInputStream`: deliver a single stream of bytes from a sequence of multiple input streams. As soon as the end of the first stream is reached, delivery continues seamlessly with the next in sequence, and so on.

For most of these input stream classes, there is an equivalent output stream class: `BufferedOutputStream`, `ByteArrayOutputStream`, `DataOutputStream`, `FileOutputStream`, `ObjectOutputStream`, and `PipedOutputStream` (there are no PushbackOutputStream and SequenceOutputStream classes). Each of these is based upon the core functionality provided by the `OutputStream` class, a selection of whose methods are shown in Table 12.7.

Code 12.13 illustrates how the FileInputStream and FileOutputStream classes may be used to make a byte-identical copy of a file. The only significant difference between the approach taken in this example and the `copyFiles` method shown in Code 12.6 is the use of a `byte` array to hold the data rather than a `char` array. However, you should not confuse the similarities at the program level from the major differences taking place within the different stream and reader and writer classes. The FileInputStream object does not transform the byte-level data being read from the file *in any way*, whereas the corresponding FileInputReader object in Code 12.6 is continuously mapping raw byte data into Unicode character data before delivering it to the program.

Table 12.7 Selected methods of the Output-Stream class	
	Method and Arguments
	OutputStream()
void	close()
void	flush()
void	write(int b)
void	write(byte[] buffer)
void	write(byte[] buffer,int bufferOffset,int numBytes)

Code 12.13 Make a byte-identical copy of the file named in the program's argument
(`StreamExampleMain.java`)

```
import java.io.*;

    // Illustrate the FileInputStream and FileOutputStream classes
    // by making a binary copy of the command line argument in the
    // file output.bin.
class StreamExampleMain {
        // Any Exceptions caused program termination.
    public static void main(String[] args)
                        throws FileNotFoundException, IOException {
        if(args.length == 1){
            final String outputFile = "output.bin";
            FileInputStream inFile = new FileInputStream(args[0]);
            FileOutputStream outFile = new FileOutputStream(outputFile);
            // Provide space for a small number of bytes to be read.
            final int bufferSize = 1024;
            byte[] buffer = new byte[bufferSize];
            // Read the first chunk of bytes.
            int numberRead = inFile.read(buffer);
            // Keep going as long as something was read.
            while(numberRead > 0){
                // Write out what was read.
                outFile.write(buffer,0,numberRead);
                // Read the next chunk, if any.
                numberRead = inFile.read(buffer);
            }
            inFile.close();
            outFile.close();
        }
        else{
            System.err.println("Usage: java StreamExampleMain binary-file");
        }
    }
}
```

All of the input stream classes define the method `available` which returns an integer number of bytes that an object could deliver without blocking. They also define a `mark` method which can be used to remember the current position in the stream, with a view to returning to it subsequently. However, implementation of marking is optional and is only likely to be implemented by a particular class if its `markSupported` method returns the value `true`.

12.8   The Data Stream Classes

The `DataInputStream` and `DataOutputStream` classes are particular examples of *filter stream* classes; other filter input streams are provided by BufferedInput-Stream and PushbackInputStream. Such input classes are constructed using an existing InputStream object, to which they delegate the basic task of reading a stream of bytes. Their role is to filter or manipulate the raw bytes in some way. In the case of DataInputStream, its main task is to interpret the byte data as values of the primitive data types. It is important not to confuse this role with the interpretation of the contents of a text file as consisting of words and numbers—a task for which we have regularly been using the SimpleInput class. Because these are stream classes, the underlying data is assumed to be in a binary format rather than human-readable text format. DataInputStream defines one method for each primitive type, such as `readInt` and `readDouble`. Although Java includes no concept of unsigned integer types, this class defines two methods to interpret one or two bytes of data as unsigned values: `readUnsignedByte` and `readUnsignedShort`. Its two `read-Fully` methods take an array of bytes to be filled, and its `skip` method attempts to discard the number of bytes indicated in its argument. Although not a primitive type, a String may be read using one of the class's two `readUTF` methods. *UTF* is a multi-byte transformation format that provides efficient storage of Unicode strings. In particular, although each Unicode character occupies two bytes, UTF allows the space requirement to be reduced when only a single byte of most values is significant. However, the payoff is that some characters will require three bytes in this format.

The DataOutputStream class provides compatible methods to write primitive-type-values (`writeInt`, `writeDouble`, etc.) and String objects (`writeUTF`). Code 12.14 illustrates use of these two classes. In order to associate the stream reader

Code 12.14   Read and write a sample of binary data (`DataStreamMain.java`)

```
import java.io.*;

    // Illustrate the DataInputStream and DataOutputStream
    // classes by writing some sample data, and then reading
    // it back in.
class DataStreamMain {
    public static void main(String[] args){
        try{
            // The name of the binary file to be written/read.
            final String datafile = "data.bin";
            writeData(datafile);
            readData(datafile);
        }
        catch(IOException e){
            System.err.println(e.toString());
        }
    }

        // Write a string, and an array of doubles to the given file.
    public static void writeData(String file) throws IOException {
        DataOutputStream out = null;
        try{
            final String message = "Einstein I'm not.";
            final double[] vals = { Math.PI, Math.E };
            final int numValues = vals.length;

            out = new DataOutputStream(new FileOutputStream(file));
            out.writeUTF(message);
```

Code 12.14   (*Continued*)

```
            // Indicate how many values there are.
            out.writeInt(numValues);
            for(int i = 0; i < numValues; i++){
                out.writeDouble(vals[i]);
            }
        }
        finally{
            if(out != null){
                out.close();
            }
        }
    }

    // Read a string, and an array of doubles from the given file.
    public static void readData(String file) throws IOException {
        DataInputStream in = null;
        try{
            in = new DataInputStream(new FileInputStream(file));
            System.out.println(in.readUTF());
            // Read how many values there are.
            final int numValues = in.readInt();
            for(int i = 0; i < numValues; i++){
                System.out.print(in.readDouble()+" ");
            }
            System.out.println();
        }
        finally{
            if(in != null){
                in.close();
            }
        }
    }
}
```

---

and writer with external files, the files are opened with file input and output stream objects.

Exercise 12.13   Write a program that uses a DataOutputStream to write out the command line arguments passed to its main method to a binary file. Write a method that reads these strings back in using a DataInputStream.

Exercise 12.14   Devise an encoding scheme for binary data that will enable you to read and write binary files containing arbitrary primitive data and strings. Precede each item to be written by a single byte whose value indicates the type of the binary data that follows. For instance, a byte value of zero might mean that an int follows next, whereas a byte value of one might mean that a String is next, and so on. Write an encoder and a decoder that use this scheme.

12.9   The Stream Reader and Writer Classes

The `InputStreamReader` and `OutputStreamWriter` classes are important for two reasons:

- They provide a bridge between the byte-level functionality of the stream classes and the character-level reader and writer classes.
- They make explicit provision for indicating the character set encoding of a file in the external file system.

They should be regarded as reader and writer classes, concerned with supplying and delivering character data, rather than as stream classes delivering byte data. Their `read` and `write` methods take `char` arguments, therefore. Both classes take an object of any of the appropriate input or output stream classes as an argument to their constructors, to which they delegate the byte-level task of reading or writing. A selection of the methods of InputStreamReader is shown in Table 12.8. One constructor of the InputStreamReader class takes an additional String argument denoting the *character set encoding* which was used to create the text data held in the input file. A selection of the methods of the OutputStreamWriter class is shown in Table 12.9. One of the OutputStreamWriter constructors takes an encoding string which will be used to dictate the external format in which the textual data should be stored. Both classes have a `getEncoding` method that can be used to query the encoding being used, which is returned as a String. The documentation for the `native2ascii` tool, supplied with the Java platform, lists the encoding names that may be used for a wide range of common character sets: `"8859_1"` is ISO Latin-1, `"8859_6"` is ISO

Table 12.8	Selected methods of the InputStreamReader class
	Method and Arguments
	InputStreamReader(InputStream stream)
	InputStreamReader(InputStream stream,String encoding)
void	close()
String	getEncoding()
int	read()
int	read(char[] buffer)
int	read(char[] buffer,int bufferOffset,int numChars)

Table 12.9	Selected methods of the OutputStreamWriter class
	Method and Arguments
	OutputStreamWriter(OutputStream stream)
	OutputStreamWriter(OutputStream stream,String encoding)
void	close()
void	flush()
String	getEncoding()
void	write(int c)
void	write(char[] buffer)
void	write(char[] buffer,int bufferOffset,int numChars)
void	write(String s)
void	write(String s,int sOffset,int numChars)

Code 12.15   Converting a file from one external encoding to another (`EncodingMain.java`)

```
import java.io.*;

    /* Illustrate the InputStreamReader and OutputStreamWriter classes
     * by making a copy of the command line argument in the
     * file output.txt. The input file will be assumed to be stored
     * in the system-default character encoding. The output file
     * will be written using an arbitrary Japanese encoding, simply for
     * illustrative purposes.
     */
class EncodingMain {
        // Any Exceptions caused program termination.
    public static void main(String[] args)
                        throws FileNotFoundException, IOException {
        if(args.length == 1){
            // Which output encoding to use - arbitrary in this example.
            final String outputEncoding = "JIS";
            // Get the system default encoding for the input file.
            String inputEncoding = System.getProperty("file.encoding");
            if(inputEncoding == null){
                // Use the output encoding for lack of anything else.
                inputEncoding = outputEncoding;
            }

            // Set up the file names.
            final String inputFile = args[0], outputFile = "output.txt";
            InputStreamReader inFile = new InputStreamReader(
                        new FileInputStream(inputFile),inputEncoding);
            OutputStreamWriter outFile = new OutputStreamWriter(
                        new FileOutputStream(outputFile),outputEncoding);
            System.out.println("Reading "+inputFile+
                        " in encoding "+inFile.getEncoding()+
                        " and writing to "+outputFile+
                        " in "+outFile.getEncoding());
            // Provide space for a small number of characters to be read.
            final int bufferSize = 1024;
            char[] buffer = new char[bufferSize];
            int numberRead = inFile.read(buffer);
            while(numberRead > 0){
                outFile.write(buffer,0,numberRead);
                numberRead = inFile.read(buffer);
            }
            inFile.close();
            outFile.close();
        }
        else{
            System.err.println("Usage java EncodingMain text-file");
        }
    }
}
```

Latin/Arabic, `"8859_8"` is ISO Latin/Hebrew, and `"JIS"` is one of the Japanese character sets, for instance. The example in Code 12.15 illustrates conversion of a file from the system default encoding to an alternative encoding. In order to associate the stream reader and writers with external files, the files must be opened with file input and output stream objects, which are passed to the appropriate constructors. We attempt to determine the default file encoding from the system's properties, via the static getProperty method of the System class. The property to obtain is "file.encoding".

12.10   The RandomAccessFile Class

The RandomAccessFile class provides a set of methods that is a combination of those provided by both the DataInputStream and DataOutputStream class, discussed in Section 12.8. An object of this class should be created when access to binary data is required, but in a non-sequential form. Although some of the input stream classes provide a limited ability to mark and return to previous positions in the stream, their primary purpose is to deliver a sequential stream of data. In contrast, a RandomAccessFile object supports arbitrary navigation around the binary data stored in a file. The same object may be used to both read and write the file.

The class defines two constructors, taking either a String or File object to specify the file to be manipulated. Both constructors take a second mode argument which is a string containing either "r", for read-only access, or "rw", for both read and write access—an IllegalArgumentException will be thrown if this argument contains anything else. The contents of the file are navigated over using an index value of type long. The getFilePointer method returns the index of the current read-write position within the file. The seek method takes a long argument and moves the current index position to that value (provided it is within the current length of the file). The setLength method may be used to either truncate or extend the length of the file. In the case of extension, the contents of the extended portion are undefined.

Exercise 12.15   The file hiddenword.bin contains a single-word String hidden within a binary file. The file offset of the String within the file is stored in a long value at the start of the file. Write a program that uses a RandomAccessFile object to read the long offset at the start of this file, and then seeks to that position in order to read the hidden word with the readUTF method. Print out the message to show you have found it.

Exercise 12.16   The file message.bin contains a multi-word String hidden within a binary file. The length of the string is written as an int value at the start of the file. This is immediately followed by a long value denoting the offset of the first char of the message within the file. Each character is immediately followed by a long offset for the next character. Write a program that uses a RandomAccessFile object to decode the message.

Exercise 12.17   Write a program that uses a RandomAccessFile object to encode an arbitrary string within a binary file, as described in Exercise 12.16. Use a Random object (defined in java.util) to generate random locations for the characters of

Code 12.16   Creating a Reader and Writer for System.in and System.out

```
BufferedReader stdinReader =
                new BufferedReader(new InputStreamReader(System.in));
PrintWriter stdoutWriter = new PrintWriter(System.out,true);
```

the message. How might you build in safeguards to ensure that the message does not become corrupted by the encoding process?

12.11   Readers and Writers for System Input-Output

Access to standard input, standard output, and standard error streams is provided via the public static `System.in`, `System.out`, and `System.err` variables. These are usually automatically associated with a user's keyboard and screen. `System.in` is an input stream object, while `System.err` and `System.out` are both `Print-Stream` objects. We can associate a reader or writer with these source and sink objects by wrapping them in reader and writer objects, as shown in Code 12.16. For `System.in`, an InputStreamReader is appropriate. This can be further wrapped in a BufferedReader if line-based input is required. For standard output and standard error, an `OutputStreamWriter` could be used, but we often want to retain the functionality of the familiar `print` and `println` methods. If this is the case, then the appropriate Writer to create is a `PrintWriter`. The second argument to the Print-Writer constructor requests that the output will be *flushed* whenever the `println` method is used. This avoids the need to write explicit calls to the `flush` method in order to cause pending output to appear on the screen. PrintWriter is different from most of the other input-output classes in that it does not throw an IOException on error; it is necessary to send it a `checkError` message, which returns `true` if an error has occurred. As a side-effect, this method also flushes the stream. It is worth noting that the `close` method is typically not used with objects created from the standard input and output streams.

The current streams to which the `err`, `out`, and `in` streams of the System class refer may be altered via its static `setErr`, `setOut`, and `setIn` mutators. The first two take a PrintStream argument and the third takes an input stream object.

12.12   Reading and Writing Objects

It is a common requirement for programs that maintain collections of objects to be able to store object data in a file, so that it is available on a future run of the same program. One possible approach to storing persistent object data would be for a class to implement methods that allow the attributes of an object to be both written to and read from a file. The format in which the data is to be written would be decided on by the designer of the class and might be a binary format, encoded text, or some other arbitrary format. There are several problems with this approach:

- Having to create new read/write methods for each class whose objects can be stored is a repetitious and tedious process. One of the benefits of using an object-oriented language is that it can often free programmers from having to reinvent things, through facilities such as *inheritance* (see Chapter 14).
- The most compact storage technique is likely to be a binary format of some sort. However, the problem with binary formats is that they are often not portable between different operating systems. Since Java is a portable language, it would be nice to have an equally portable format for transferring associated object data between machines.
- Where a class implementation is likely to exist in different versions, it may be hard to be sure that the version used to retrieve data is compatible with the version used to store it.

Given the unsatisfactory aspects of requiring class designers to come up with their own solution to storing and retrieving object data, Java provides facilities that almost entirely free the programmer from having to work out how to achieve it. The `ObjectInputStream` and `ObjectOutputStream` classes of the `java.io` package make this relatively simple to do via their `readObject` and `writeObject` methods, respectively. This is a process called *object serialization*. However, in order to use this process, we need to understand how to use the associated `Serializable` *interface* from the same package. Therefore, we defer further discussion of reading and writing objects until Section 13.10.

12.13   The StreamTokenizer Class

Reading data from files often involves extracting information that is not simply textual. Files may contain a mixture of text and numerical data that is necessary to read as complete words or numbers. Objects of the `StreamTokenizer` class are able to extract the different types of data that are present in an input file, and to make them available as either a String or a `double` numerical value. A sample of its methods is shown in Table 12.10. A StreamTokenizer object is constructed from a reader object that controls from where the stream of tokens is to be read. When StreamTokenizer's `nextToken` method is called, it examines the next section of input character-by-character and pieces together a contiguous sequence of related characters into a single token to be returned. Tokens may be separated by arbitrary

	Table 12.10 Selected methods of the StreamTokenizer class
	Method and Arguments
	StreamTokenizer(Reader r)
int	lineno()
void	lowerCaseMode(boolean mode)
int	nextToken()
void	parseNumbers()
void	wordChars(int lower,int upper)

Code 12.17 Using a StreamTokenizer to parse data

```
class Parser {
    ...
        // Use a StreamTokenizer to return the next double.
    public double nextNumber() throws IOException {
        // Create a StreamTokenizer object to parse the numbers.
        StreamTokenizer stream = new StreamTokenizer(getReader());
        // Read the next token.
        while(stream.nextToken() != StreamTokenizer.TT_NUMBER){
            // Check to make sure we have not reached EOF.
            if(stream.ttype == StreamTokenizer.TT_EOF){
                throw new IOException("End of file.");
            }
        }
        // Return the number.
        return stream.nval;
    }
    ...
    private BufferedReader getReader(){
        return reader;
    }

    private BufferedReader reader;
}
```

numbers of white space characters, which are not included in the values returned. There are two main types of token that it will identify: words and numbers. When it finds a word, it returns the identification TT_WORD and when it finds a number it returns TT_NUMBER. When it reaches the end of the input, it will return the value TT_EOF. Code 12.17 shows an example method that takes a BufferedReader object for an open file and returns the next number token found in that file. It keeps on executing the body of the while loop until a TT_NUMBER value is returned. The public attribute ttype of the stream contains the type of the token most recently identified, so this is used inside the loop to make sure that it did not reach the end of the file before finding the next number. If the latest token is a number, its value is stored in the public double attribute, nval; if the latest token is a word, its value is stored in the public String attribute, sval (neither has an accessor method). The files Parse-Main.java and NumberParser.java use a method similar to nextNumber in order to print out the numbers in the files passed to the full program as command-line arguments.

If it is necessary to tokenize the standard input stream, then this can be done quite simply by wrapping System.in in an associated reader, as was done in Section 12.11. Code 12.18 shows a method to count how many words and numbers there are on the standard input. The StreamTokenizer class is a little less useful than might be supposed at first. It is primarily intended for tokenizing text files that are program source files, This is clear from its methods to set its idea of what should be regarded as comment characters.

Code 12.18   Counting tokens on the standard input

```java
import java.io.*;

    // Print a count of the number of words and numbers on the
    // standard input.
class StdinCount {
    public static void main(String[] args){
        // Create a stream tokenizer from a standard input reader.
        StreamTokenizer stream =
                new StreamTokenizer(new InputStreamReader(System.in));
        // Count words and numbers.
        int wordCount = 0, numberCount = 0;

        try{
            while(stream.nextToken() != StreamTokenizer.TT_EOF){
                if(stream.ttype == StreamTokenizer.TT_WORD){
                    wordCount++;
                }
                else if(stream.ttype == StreamTokenizer.TT_NUMBER){
                    numberCount++;
                }
                else{
                    // Don't count this.
                }
            }
            System.out.println("Word(s) = "+wordCount);
            System.out.println("Number(s) = "+numberCount);
        }
        catch(IOException e){
            System.out.println(e.getMessage());
        }
    }
}
```

12.14   The StringTokenizer Class

The StringTokenizer class is defined in the java.util package, rather than java.io. A selection of its methods is shown in Table 12.11. Its purpose is to allow String objects to be tokenized on the basis of a set of *delimiters*. By default the delimiters are the *white space* characters: space (' '), tab ('\t'), newline ('\n'), and carriage return ('\r'). Code 12.19 shows how we might print all of the words found in a string. The string to be tokenized is passed to the constructor of StringTokenizer. The tokenizer's hasMoreTokens method returns true if there is at least one more token to return, and the next token is obtained with the nextToken method. Its countTokens method returns the number of tokens left. If this example is tried on the following string

```java
"A sentence. However, this one contains a comma.";
```

	Table 12.11 Selected methods of the StringTokenizer class
	Method and Arguments
	StringTokenizer(String s)
	StringTokenizer(String s,String delim)
	StringTokenizer(String s,String delim,boolean returnDelims)
int	countTokens()
boolean	hasMoreElements()
boolean	hasMoreTokens()
Object	nextElement()
String	nextToken()
String	nextToken(String delim)

Code 12.19 Tokenize a string on white space characters

```
    // Print the tokens in s, delimited on white space characters.
public void printTokens(String s){
    StringTokenizer tokenizer = new StringTokenizer(s);

    while(tokenizer.hasMoreTokens()){
        System.out.println(tokenizer.nextToken());
    }
}
```

then eight tokens will be returned:

```
"A" "sentence." "However," "this" "one" "contains" "a" "comma."
```

Notice that the punctuation characters form part of the words to which they are attached because only white space characters delimit the tokens. If we wish to exclude punctuation, these characters could be registered as delimiters in the constructor. Code 12.20 shows an example that makes it possible to read a file, line by line, and identify the words delimited by punctuation and space characters. The set of delimiters passed into the constructor of a StringTokenizer is remembered and used in each call to nextToken. A different set of delimiters may be set by passing a String parameter to nextToken. These delimiters are used for the remainder of the tokenizing, unless a further set is supplied to replace them. This makes it possible to parse strings which are partitioned in different ways along their length.

In the examples above, the delimiters form no part of the tokens returned. Sometimes it is necessary to have the delimiters returned in addition to the tokens. The third of StringTokenizer's constructors takes a boolean argument which, when it has the value true, will cause delimiters to be returned as tokens. For instance, suppose we wished to tokenize a simple Java expression using white space and the arithmetic operators as delimiters and extract the operands as tokens, but we also wish the operators to be available as tokens. The example in Code 12.21 performs this task using the constructor that takes three arguments to ensure that the delimiters are also returned. Notice that we allow space characters to delimit the operands, in addition to the operators. It is not possible to request the tokenizer to return

Code 12.20 Print the words found in a file (`WordFinder.java`)

```java
import java.io.*;
import java.util.*;

        // This class finds words delimited by punctuation characters
        // in the file passed to its constructor.
        // The delimiters may be changed via setDelimiters.
class WordFinder {
    public void findWords(String filename){
        try{
            // Open the file (FileReader) and construct a
            // BufferedReader object using it.
            BufferedReader in = new BufferedReader(
                                        new FileReader(filename));
            findWords(in);
            in.close();
        }
        catch(IOException e){
            System.err.println(e);
        }
    }

        // Read the file, line by line, and break it up.
    public void findWords(BufferedReader in) throws IOException {
      String line = in.readLine();
      while(line != null){
        // Break up the line based upon the current delimiters.
        StringTokenizer tokenizer =
                    new StringTokenizer(line,getDelimiters());
        while(tokenizer.hasMoreTokens()){
            String s = tokenizer.nextToken();
            // Print the next word.
            System.out.println(s);
        }
        line = in.readLine();
      }
    }

    public String getDelimiters(){
        return delimiters;
    }

    public void setDelimiters(String d){
        delimiters = d;
    }

    // What to use to break up words: punctuation, white space and quotes.
    private String delimiters = ",;:.`' ";
}
```

Code 12.21   Tokenize an arithmetic expression

```
class Parser {
    ...
        // Tokenize expr, which consists of operators and operands.
    public void tokenizeExpr(String expr){
        // Allow for spaces.
        final String space = " ";
        // The operators expected.
        final String operator = "+-*/%";
        // Return delimiters as tokens.
        StringTokenizer tokenizer =
                new StringTokenizer(expr,space+operator,true);

        while(tokenizer.hasMoreTokens()){
            String token = tokenizer.nextToken();
            // Work out whether we have white space, operator or operand.
            if(space.indexOf(token) >= 0){
                // White space - ignore it.
            }
            else if(operator.indexOf(token) >= 0){
                System.out.println("Operator: "+token);
            }
            else{
                System.out.println("Operand: "+token);
            }
        }
    }
    ...
}
```

only the operator delimiters and not the space ones, however. This means that we
need to examine the returned token in order to determine whether it is an operator
character, an operand, or a space character. If the token is a delimiter, then it will be a
string containing the single delimiter character matched.[1] The String class's `indexOf`
method makes it simple to check whether a single character delimiter token occurs
in either the `space` string or the `operator` string. Passing the string "a␣*␣␣␣␣b"
to `tokenizeExpr` produces the output

```
Operand: a
Operator: *
Operand: b
```

and passing "a+++b" produces:

```
Operand: a
Operator: +
Operator: +
```

---

[1] This will be the case even if multiple delimiters occur together — each is returned as an individual
token.

```
Operator: +
Operand: b
```

StringTokenizer is probably of more general utility than the StreamTokenizer class. In Section 12.15, we show how it forms the basis of the SimpleInput class.

12.15   Case Study: The SimpleInput Class

In all of the input-output classes we have discussed in this chapter, none provides general purpose facilities for reading arbitrary words and numbers of different types from a user at the keyboard or from a text file. The StreamTokenizer class comes close (see Section 12.13), but is rather too closely tied to programming language input. The approach we have taken in this book is to create the `SimpleInput` class, which is actually based upon the StringTokenizer class (see Section 12.14). In this section, we provide a description of how the SimpleInput class works. Usage of this class was introduced in Section 5.6.

Code 12.22 contains the full definition. The comments have been written in a form suitable for the `javadoc` tool, which we will not explain here (see Appendix H).

Code 12.22   The SimpleInput class (`SimpleInput.java`)

```java
import java.io.*;
import java.util.StringTokenizer;

    /** A helper class that allows words, numbers, and booleans
     *  to be read from an input stream. This can be either System.in
     *  or a named file.
     *  All methods throw a RuntimeException object if EOF is reached
     *  when a value is requested.
     *  @author David J. Barnes (d.j.barnes@ukc.ac.uk)
     *  @version Version 1.3 (1st Jan 1999)<br>
     *  Version 1.2 did not include the discardLine method.<br>
     *  Version 1.1 did not correctly discard the current line when
     *  nextLine() was used.<br>
     *  Version 1.0 used a StreamTokenizer as the basis for its input.
     *  This has been replaced by a StringTokenizer to make parsing
     *  of floating point numbers more flexible.<br>
     */

public class SimpleInput {
    /** Take input from System.in.
     */
    public SimpleInput(){
        // Use standard input.
    }

    /** Take input from the named file.
     *  @param file Read input from the named file.
     *  @throws java.lang.RuntimeException if file cannot be opened.
     */
    public SimpleInput(String file) throws RuntimeException {
```

Code 12.22   (*Continued*)

```java
        // Try to make sure it exists.
        File details = new File(file);
        if(!details.exists()){
            throw new RuntimeException(file+" does not exist.");
        }
        else if(!details.canRead()){
            throw new RuntimeException(file+" exists but is unreadable.");
        }
        else if(!details.isFile()){
            throw new RuntimeException(file+" is not a regular file.");
        }
        else{
            // We should be ok.
            try{
                setReader(new BufferedReader(new FileReader(details)));
            }
            catch(FileNotFoundException e){
                throw new RuntimeException("Failed to open "+file+
                        " for an unknown reason.");
            }
        }
    }

    /** @return The next number from the input stream as a short.
     *  Non-numerical input is skipped. A floating point number on the
     *  input is truncated.
     *  @throws java.lang.RuntimeException if end-of-file
     *  has been reached.
     */
    public short nextShort() throws RuntimeException {
        return (short) nextNumber();
    }

    /** @return The next number from the input stream as a short.
     *  Non-numerical input is skipped. A floating point number on the
     *  input is truncated.
     *  @throws java.lang.RuntimeException if end-of-file
     *  has been reached.
     */
    public int nextInt() throws RuntimeException {
        return (int) nextNumber();
    }

    /** @return The next number from the input stream as a long.
     *  Non-numerical input is skipped. A floating point number on the
     *  input is truncated.
     *  @throws java.lang.RuntimeException if end-of-file
     *  has been reached.
     */
    public long nextLong() throws RuntimeException {
        return (long) nextNumber();
    }
```

(*Continued*)

Code 12.22   *(Continued)*

```
/** @return The next floating point number from the input stream
 *  as a float.
 *  Non-numerical input is skipped. A floating point number on the
 *  input is truncated.
 *  @throws java.lang.RuntimeException if end-of-file
 *  has been reached.
 */
public float nextFloat() throws RuntimeException {
    return (float) nextNumber();
}

/** @return The next floating point number from the input stream
 *  as a double.
 *  Non-numerical input is skipped.
 *  @throws java.lang.RuntimeException if end-of-file
 *  has been reached.
 */
public double nextDouble() throws RuntimeException {
    return nextNumber();
}

/** @return The next floating point number from the input stream
 *  as a double.
 *  Non-numerical input is skipped.
 *  @throws java.lang.RuntimeException if end-of-file
 *  has been reached.
 */
private double nextNumber() throws RuntimeException {
    // Number will refer to an appropriate Double when one is found.
    // Return number.doubleValue();
    Double number = null;
    do{
        String numString = null;
        try{
            numString = nextToken();
            // See if it is a proper number.
            number = new Double(numString);
        }
        catch(NumberFormatException e){
            // That wasn't a recognized number.
            // Try replacing 'd/D' with 'e'.
            numString = numString.toLowerCase();
            numString = numString.replace('d','e');
            try{
                number = new Double(numString);
            }
            catch(NumberFormatException ex){
                // Failed again.
            }
        }
    } while(number == null);
    return number.doubleValue();
}
```

Code 12.22   (*Continued*)

```
/** @return The next token from the input stream as a String.
 *  This does not distinguish numbers from words.
 *  @throws java.lang.RuntimeException if end-of-file
 *  has been reached.
 *  @see java.util.StringTokenizer
 */
public String nextWord() throws RuntimeException {
    return nextToken();
}

/** @return A boolean value corresponding to the next boolean
 *  word on the input stream.
 *  This will be either true, false, t, or f, ignoring case.
 *  Numerical input and non-boolean words are skipped.
 *  @throws java.lang.RuntimeException if end-of-file
 *  has been reached.
 */
public boolean nextBoolean() throws RuntimeException {
    for(; ;){
        String s = nextWord();
        if(s.equalsIgnoreCase("t") || s.equalsIgnoreCase("true")){
            return true;
        }
        else if(s.equalsIgnoreCase("f") || s.equalsIgnoreCase("false")){
            return false;
        }
    }
}

/** @return The next line on the input stream as a string.
 *  This will discard the remainder of the current line, if any.
 *  @throws java.lang.RuntimeException if end-of-file
 *  has been reached.
 */
public String nextLine() throws RuntimeException {
    try{
        discardLine();
        BufferedReader reader = getReader();
        String line = reader.readLine();
        // Check for EOF.
        if(line == null){
            throw new RuntimeException("End of input.");
        }
        return line;
    }
    catch(IOException e){
        // Pass it on as an unchecked exception.
        throw new RuntimeException(e.getMessage());
    }
}
```

(*Continued*)

Code 12.22 *(Continued)*

```
/** This will discard the remainder of the current line, if any.
 *  @since Version 1.3
 */
public void discardLine(){
    setTokenizer(new StringTokenizer(""));
}

/** @return The delimiters currently in use by the string
 *  tokenizer.
 *  By default these are " ".
 */
public String getDelimiters(){
    return delimiters;
}

/** Mutator for the delimiters to be used in tokenizing the input.
 *  @param The new string of delimiters.
 *  By default these are " ".
 */
public void setDelimiters(String d){
    if((d != null) && (d.length() > 0)){
        delimiters = d;
    }
}

/** @return The next token from the input. Tokens are
 *  delimited by the current set of delimiters.
 *  @throws java.lang.RuntimeException if end-of-file
 *  has been reached.
 */
private String nextToken() throws RuntimeException {
    StringTokenizer t = getTokenizer();
    final String delimiters = getDelimiters();
    if(!t.hasMoreTokens()){
        do{
            String line = nextLine();
            t = new StringTokenizer(line,delimiters);
            setTokenizer(t);
        } while(!t.hasMoreTokens());
    }
    return t.nextToken(delimiters);
}

/** Accessor for the buffered reader associated with the input stream.
 *  @see java.io.BufferedReader
 */
private BufferedReader getReader(){
    return reader;
}

/** Mutator for the buffered reader associated with the input stream.
 *  @param The reader.
 *  @see java.io.BufferedReader
```

Code 12.22   (*Continued*)

```
   */
   private void setReader(BufferedReader r){
      reader = r;
   }

   /** @return The internal string tokenizer.
    *  @see java.util.StringTokenizer
    */
   private StringTokenizer getTokenizer(){
      return tokenizer;
   }

   /** Mutator to set the internal string tokenizer.
    *  @param The new string tokenizer.
    *  @see java.util.StringTokenizer
    */
   private void setTokenizer(StringTokenizer t){
      tokenizer = t;
   }

   // A reader for System.in that is shared by all objects
   // that are created with the no-arg constructor
   private static final BufferedReader stdinReader =
                  new BufferedReader(new InputStreamReader(System.in));
   // By default use standard input.
   private BufferedReader reader = stdinReader;
   // The delimiters used in tokenizing.
   private String delimiters = " ";
   // The tokenizer.
   private StringTokenizer tokenizer = new StringTokenizer("");
}
```

12.15.1 The Attributes

The SimpleInput class reads input from the source object referred to by its `reader` attribute. By default, this is an alias for `stdinReader`, which refers to a reader object wrapping standard input (`System.in`). This is a static reference in order to ensure that all SimpleInput objects being used to read from standard input share the same reference — there is only one System.in object, after all. If the user wishes to read from a file, the single-arg constructor can be used to open a file and set the `reader` attribute appropriately. In both cases, input is channeled through a BufferedReader object, which means that input is line based.

The `tokenizer` attribute is used to refer to a succession of StringTokenizer objects. A new StringTokenizer is created for each line of input. The `tokenizer` refers to the object that holds whatever was left of the line after the previous token was returned. The first line is not read until the first request for an item of input is received, so a tokenizer with an empty line is created by default.

12.15.2 The nextToken Method

All requests for input, except nextLine, are ultimately channeled through the nextToken method. This uses the current tokenizer to look for the next token, which will be delimited by a character in the set defined by the delimiters attribute. If the current tokenizer has no more tokens, then a request is made to nextLine for the next input line and a new StringTokenizer is constructed to manage it. In order to handle blank lines properly, this process is enclosed within a loop. Once it knows that there is another token, nextToken finally returns the next one extracted by the tokenizer.

12.15.3 The nextNumber Method

All requests for primitive type numerical values are delegated to the nextNumber method. This requests a token from nextToken and then tries to parse this as a recognizable floating point number by constructing a Double object from it. This is able to parse numbers in a form such as 3.5e-2. It makes a second attempt if the first failed by checking to see if a number has been written in a non-Java alternative form, such as 3.5d-2. If the second attempt fails, the loop repeats by checking the next token. When a number is found, a double value is returned from the Double object wrapping it. Methods of SimpleInput that return non-double values, such as next-Float and nextInt, simply cast the value returned by nextNumber, with a possible loss of precision.

The remaining methods of the class are reasonably straightforward.

12.16 Review

Here are the main points that we have covered in the preceding sections:

- The Stream classes provide access to the byte-based format of external data.
- Classes based upon the InputStream class allow byte-based data to be input.
- Classes based upon the OutputStream class allow byte-based data to be output.
- The DataInputStream and DataOutputStream classes define methods to read and write primitive data, type values and Strings as binary data in a host-independent format.
- The InputStreamReader and OutputStreamWriter classes provide Reader and Writer functionality with streams.
- The RandomAccessFile class allows a file to be both read and written via a single object reference.
- Reader functionality for System.in can be provided by using an InputStream-Reader.
- Writer functionality for System.out can be provided by using a PrintWriter.
- Complete objects may be read and written using the ObjectInputStream and ObjectOutputStream classes. Details may be found in Section 13.10.
- The StreamTokenizer class simplifies the parsing of input files which consist of programming-language-like tokens.

- The StringTokenizer class may be used to tokenize Strings, based upon variable delimiter sets.
- Programs must often take into account details of the external environment that are locale-specific.

Exercise 12.18   Write a program that uses a BufferedReader and BufferedWriter to read a text file line-by-line and write a new copy with the lines sorted. The `Collections` class of the `java.util` package defines a `sort` method with the following header

```
public void sort(List list)
```

that will take either an ArrayList or LinkedList of Strings as an argument and sort them. The names of the input and output files should be passed as command-line arguments to the program.

Exercise 12.19   Exercise 7.4 simplified the task of reading textual image data by using the SimpleInput class. Modify your solution to that exercise to read the input data line-by-line with a `BufferedReader`. Split up each line with a StringTokenizer and use one of the static methods of the `Integer` class to extract the individual numerical values.

Exercise 12.20   Modify your solution to Exercise 12.19 so that comment lines may be included in the data file. A comment line should contain a hash symbol (`'#'`) as its first character. Comment lines contain no image data and should be discarded by the decoder. They allow human readable text to be added to the file, for instance,

```
# The image width and height.
174 199
# Start of the image data.
63 3 55 3 6 0 50 3
```

In this chapter, we have looked at the ways in which the classes of the `java.io` package help to isolate a program from the different characteristics that make up the underlying file system environment. In the next chapter, we begin to explore the topics of *interfaces* and *polymorphism*, which are fundamental building blocks in exploiting the power of an object-oriented language.

CHAPTER 13

Interfaces

In this chapter, we describe the `interface` facility of Java and introduce the concept of polymorphism. We look at several common interfaces that we have used informally in previous chapters, such as `Collection`, `Iterator`, and `List`. We also introduce further standard interfaces, such as `Comparable` and `Comparator`, that allow objects to be sorted, and `Serializable` that allows whole objects to be read and written externally.

13.1   What is an Interface?

So far, we have used the term public interface informally, to mean the set of public methods belonging to an object that enable objects of other classes to interact with it. More formally, `interface` is a reserved word in Java that plays a similar role to the `class` reserved word. An interface provides a way of describing a set of public methods and fields that *a range of classes* might all provide. This is sometimes known as *interface inheritance*, to distinguish it from *class inheritance*, which we discuss in Chapter 14. Classes implementing the same interface are distinct from each other, but related by the fact that they implement a common set of methods. The most important distinction between an interface and a class is that the former describes only the *method signatures*, without defining how these are implemented. This separation of *what* from *how* is an important part of the *information hiding* concept of software engineering. Among other things, such a separation allows us to develop a range of different implementations that all meet the specification of the interface, yet potentially differ in various ways. The requirement to be able to vary implementations might be on grounds of varying speed, memory size, or cost, in different circumstances, for instance.

Everyday life is full of the concept of interfaces, although we typically do not think about life in those terms. Manufacturers of competing items of technology conform to the idea that the interface of their product must be familiar to potential users, although their underlying implementation is necessarily different from that of their competitors—cheaper, faster, more efficient, better looking, etc. Video Cassette Recorders (VCRs) have a basic interface that differs little from manufacturer to manufacturer: tapes may be loaded, ejected, played, paused, stopped, rewound, and advanced. Here, the interface is a set of facilities. Users of VCRs take these facilities for granted and have little trouble working out how to use them across a wide range of different machines. Different manufacturers might choose to add further features to enhance their product, such as variable speed playing and recording, index marking, and so on, but these things are not the essence of what makes a VCR a VCR.

Consider another example—non-technological this time; movie theaters (cinemas) have an interface that differs little from town to town, and even country to country: they show movies, they charge money to customers who wish to see those movies, customers sit down to view them, certification systems place age limits on the audiences, refreshments are usually available. Beneath the common interface, details may differ widely from cinema to cinema: entrance price, number of screens, size of the auditorium, comfort of the seats, quality of the sound system. However, someone wishing to see a movie in an unfamiliar town should have little difficulty interacting with the local cinema, providing they are old enough and can afford the price of a ticket!

Some further examples of common interfaces with different underlying implementations are banks, supermarkets, telephone networks, and computer operating systems. In some cases, it is precisely the areas where differences lie in essentially similar operations that cause people problems. An example might be the different ways that VCRs have for allowing their clocks to be set.

Exercise 13.1   Can you think of any more everyday examples of objects and organizations that provide a common interface with different underlying implementations?

Exercise 13.2   Can you think of any everyday examples where the interfaces are consistent within one country but differ between countries?

13.2   Interface Definitions

A Java interface definition describes the names of the methods and the values of the fields that a class implementing that interface will provide. As we pointed out above, an important feature of an interface is that it describes the methods without constraining their implementation in any ways other than their name, their return type, and their argument types—no details of the method bodies are given in an interface definition. Code 13.1 shows an interface definition that might fit our model of the basic facilities provided by a VCR.[1]

An interface is introduced by the reserved word `interface` followed by an identifier giving it a name, `VCR` in this case. Its body consists of only *method signatures* (method headers) and fields. None of the method headers has an associated body. This is fundamental to the idea that interfaces describe *what* will be provided by an implementing class, rather than *how* it will be implemented. The various classes that implement this interface in their own particular way will provide their own versions of the method bodies. A method without a body is called an *abstract method* and an

---

[1] For the sake of simplicity, we have omitted any recording functionality from the VCR, making it more like a video cassette player.

Code 13.1   Basic interface for a VCR (VCR.java)

```
    // An interface for a simple (play-only) Video Cassette Recorder (VCR).
interface VCR {
    // All methods return true if successful,
    // or false otherwise - typically if there is no tape loaded.

        // Return false if a tape is already loaded.
    public boolean loadTape(String tapeName);
        // Return false if no tape is loaded.
    public boolean eject();
        // Main functions.
    public boolean play();
    public boolean pause();
    public boolean stop();
        // Fast-forward and rewind.
    public boolean ff();
    public boolean rew();
        // A method to enquire about the video's current status.
    public int getStatus();
        // Status enquiry values, returned by status().
    public static final int PLAYING = 0, PAUSED = 1, STOPPED = 2,
                            FORWARD = 3, BACKWARD = 4, NOTAPE = 5;
}
```

interface as a whole is said to be abstract.[2] An interface also differs from an ordinary class in that it never has any constructors.

Fields defined within an interface are always public *class constants*—this is true even if the reserved words `public static final` are omitted. The compiler will not allow you to define a field in an interface as `private`, therefore. An interface method is not permitted to be static. Even though all interface fields are automatically `public static final`, we recommend that these reserved words are specifically included in order to avoid any misconception. What this feature of interfaces guarantees is that all classes that implement a particular interface will have a set of names with common underlying values. This is quite important for the sake of consistency across implementations. In the example in Code 13.1, for instance, all classes implementing this interface should return the value `PLAYING` in reply to the `getStatus` message if they are currently playing a tape. Unfortunately, Java provides no way of *enforcing* this behavior from implementations. This means that, in order to ensure consistent implementations, an interface definition should always be clearly documented, so that there is no room for doubt in the mind of the implementor as to what is required of a conforming implementation.

---

[2] There is an `abstract` reserved word which you will sometimes see prefixing an interface header or a method signature in the interface. As a matter of style, we prefer not to use it in the context of an interface.

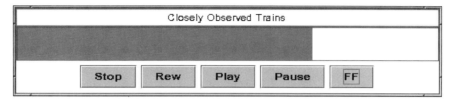

Figure 13.1   A GUI for demonstrating VCR functionality (`VideoStoreMain.java`)

Code 13.2   A class implementing the VCR interface (`NoFrillsVCR.java`)

```
class NoFrillsVCR implements VCR {
    ...
}
```

13.3   Implementing an Interface

A class indicates that it is an implementation of an interface by including an *implements clause* in its header. This consists of the reserved word `implements`, followed by the name of the interface being implemented (Code 13.2).

By so doing, it promises to provide implementations of the methods listed in the interface.[3] In this sense, an interface is like a *contract* that implementing classes agree to abide by. Code 13.3 shows a full implementation for the `NoFrillsVCR` class. This particular example has a dummy GUI to demonstrate the way in which it might be used to control a VCR machine. This is illustrated in Figure 13.1.

Apart from the `implements VCR` addition to the class header, an implementing class definition is just like any other class definition that we have seen so far. There is a full definition of each of the method's bodies. An implementing class is also perfectly free to define further methods and variables that are not part of the interface, for its own purposes—`NoFrillsVCR` has the private mutator `setStatus`, for instance.

Definitions of the class constants defined within the interface are not repeated in the implementing class. They are freely available within the class body without qualification with the interface name,[4] and they can be used as if they are defined directly within the class (see the `play` method in Code 13.3, for instance). Because these fields are static variables, this means that there are always three different ways of referring to them from outside a defining class:

- Via the interface name, e.g., `VCR.STOPPED`.
- Via an implementing class name, e.g., `NoFrillsVCR.STOPPED`.
- Via an object reference of an implementing class, e.g., `cheap.STOPPED`.

Of these three, the first is to be preferred since it is the most general and least likely to require change as the result of later program modifications.

---

[3] See Section 15.1 for the implication if not all of the method bodies are defined.

[4] See Section 13.9.1 for the only exception to this rule.

Code 13.3   An outline implementation of the VCR interface

```
        // A no-frills implementation of the VCR interface.
        // Basic operations and single speed FF and REW.
class NoFrillsVCR implements VCR {
    public boolean play(){
        if(getStatus() != NOTAPE){
            setStatus(PLAYING);
            getGui().start(PLAYING_SPEED);
            return true;
        }
        else{
            return false;
        }
    }

    public boolean pause(){
        if(getStatus() != NOTAPE){
            setStatus(PAUSED);
            // The GUI does not visually distinguish between stop and pause.
            getGui().stop();
            return true;
        }
        else{
            return false;
        }
    }

    public boolean stop(){
        if(getStatus() != NOTAPE){
            setStatus(STOPPED);
            getGui().stop();
            return true;
        }
        else{
            return false;
        }
    }

        // Only wind forward if the tape is stopped.
    public boolean ff(){
        if(getStatus() == STOPPED){
            setStatus(FORWARD);
            getGui().start(FAST_SPEED);
            return true;
        }
        else{
            return false;
        }
    }

        // Only wind backward if the tape is stopped.
    public boolean rew(){
        if(getStatus() == STOPPED){
            setStatus(BACKWARD);
            // Negative speed for reverse.
```

Code 13.3   (*Continued*)

```
                getGui().start(-FAST_SPEED);
                return true;
            }
            else{
                return false;
            }
        }

        // Load the requested tape.
        // Return false if a tape is already loaded.
        public boolean loadTape(String tapeName){
            if(getStatus() == NOTAPE){
                setStatus(STOPPED);
                getGui().changeTape(tapeName);
                return true;
            }
            else{
                return false;
            }
        }

        public boolean eject(){
            if(getStatus() != NOTAPE){
                setStatus(NOTAPE);
                getGui().changeTape("");
                return true;
            }
            else{
                return false;
            }
        }

        public int getStatus(){
            return status;
        }

        private void setStatus(int s){
            status = s;
        }

        private TapeDemo getGui(){
            return gui;
        }

        // This object's current status attribute.
        private int status = NOTAPE;
        // The two speeds for normal and ff/rew.
        private static final int PLAYING_SPEED = 1, FAST_SPEED = 5;
        // A GUI to demonstrate this implementation.
        private TapeDemo gui = new TapeDemo("No Frills VCR",this);
        { gui.setLocation(20,20);
        }
}
```

13.3.1 Multiple Implementations of a Single Interface

One of the main reasons for defining an interface is the anticipation that it will be
implemented by more than one class. Any number of different classes may implement a single interface. An interface simply defines a minimum set of methods that
an implementing class must provide. There is nothing to prevent an implementing
class from adding further features to its class definition to enhance that set, or from
providing more sophisticated versions of the basic methods. The `UpMarketVCR` class
of Code 13.4 includes a `setSpeed` method to allow fine grain control over the fast
forward and rewind speed, for instance.

Code 13.4   An alternative implementation of the VCR interface (`UpMarketVCR.java`)

```
        // An up-market implementation of the VCR interface.
        // Basic operations plus variable speed FF and REW.
        // FF and REW operate even if the tape is not STOPPED.
class UpMarketVCR implements VCR {
    ...
        // Increase the forward speed.
    public boolean ff(){
        if(getStatus() != NOTAPE){
            // If we are already moving forward, simply increase speed,
            // otherwise set the basic FAST_SPEED.
            if(getStatus() == FORWARD){
                setSpeed(getSpeed()+1);
            }
            else{
                setStatus(FORWARD);
                setSpeed(FAST_SPEED);
            }
            getGui().start(getSpeed());
            return true;
        }
        else{
            return false;
        }
    }

        // Increase the rewind speed.
    public boolean rew(){
        if(getStatus() != NOTAPE){
            // If we are already moving backward, simply increase speed,
            // otherwise set the basic FAST_SPEED.
            if(getStatus() == BACKWARD){
                setSpeed(getSpeed()-1);
            }
            else{
                setStatus(BACKWARD);
                setSpeed(-FAST_SPEED);
            }
            getGui().start(getSpeed());
            return true;
        }
```

Code 13.4   (*Continued*)

```
            else{
                return false;
            }
        }
    ...
    private int getSpeed(){
        return speed;
    }

        // Allow the speed to be set externally.
    public void setSpeed(int s){
        if(Math.abs(s) <= MAX_SPEED){
            speed = s;
        }
    }
    ...
    private TapeDemo getGui(){
        return gui;
    }

    // This object's current status attribute.
    private int status = NOTAPE;
    // The normal playing speed, initial fast speed and maximum speed
    // for ff/rew.
    private static final int PLAYING_SPEED = 1, FAST_SPEED = 5,
                             MAX_SPEED = 15;
    private int speed = PLAYING_SPEED;
    // A GUI to demonstrate this implementation.
    private TapeDemo gui = new TapeDemo("Up Market VCR",this);
    { gui.setLocation(40,40);
    }
}
```

In this example, the same set of interface methods has been implemented, but additional sophistication has been added to the functionality. Additional methods do not become part of the interface; rather, they are ordinary methods that belong to a class that happens to implement a particular interface. Methods such as setSpeed, therefore, would only be available via a reference to an object of the UpMarketVCR class and not through one to an object of a different implementing class, such as NoFrillsVCR.

13.3.2   Using Implementations of Interfaces

The real value of implementing the same interface by different classes can only be appreciated when considering how objects of implementing classes are passed to other objects. These receiving objects will typically only be interested in details of the interface, rather than the underlying implementation or further methods additional to those in the interface. Suppose we have a class that has been designed to

---

Code 13.5   Testing distinct implementations (`VideoTester1.java`)

```
    // Test different implementations of the VCR interface.
class VideoTester1 {
    public void cheapVideoTest(){
        System.out.println("Testing the cheap video player.");
        NoFrillsVCR cheap = new NoFrillsVCR();
        if(cheap.loadTape("Gone With The Wind")){
            if(cheap.play()){
                System.out.println("Playing cheap video.");
            }
            // Test other functions, too ...
        }
        else{
            System.out.println("Failed to load the tape.");
        }
    }

    public void expensiveVideoTest(){
        System.out.println("Testing the expensive video player.");
        UpMarketVCR expensive = new UpMarketVCR();
        if(expensive.loadTape("Closely Observed Trains")){
            if(expensive.play()){
                System.out.println("Playing expensive video.");
            }
            // Test other functions, too ...
        }
        else{
            System.out.println("Failed to load the tape.");
        }
    }
}
```

---

test for conformance to the VCR interface design—it might ensure that the correct values are returned in all cases from the `getStatus` method, for instance. It might be imagined that this class will need a test method for each particular implementing class so that the type of the actual argument, representing an object to be tested, matches the type of the formal argument for the respective test function (Code 13.5).

A separate method to test each different implementation results in a large amount of duplicated code. However, the consistency of the interface defined by both classes means that all the testing methods really need to know is that the object they are dealing with belongs to a class that implements the VCR interface, since they are only interested in using the methods and fields defined in that interface. This means that our VCR tester class really only needs one `videoTest` method that will accept any VCR-implementing object as an argument. So Code 13.5 can be rewritten more concisely, as in Code 13.6.

The type of the first argument to `videoTest` is the interface name, rather than an implementing class name. The compiler will check that the actual argument to `testVCR` is an object of a legitimate implementing class. Why does this work?

Code 13.6   Accepting any VCR-implementing argument

```
    // Test different implementations of the VCR interface.
class VideoTester2 {
    public void cheapVideoTest(){
        System.out.println("Testing the cheap video player.");
        videoTest(new NoFrillsVCR(),"Gone with the Wind");
    }

    public void expensiveVideoTest(){
        System.out.println("Testing the expensive video player.");
        videoTest(new UpMarketVCR(),"Closely Observed Trains");
    }

        // Test any implementation of the VCR interface.
    private void videoTest(VCR video,String tape){
        if(video.loadTape(tape)){
            if(video.play()){
                System.out.println("Playing ...");
            }
            // Test other functions, too ...
        }
        else{
            System.out.println("Failed to load: "+tape);
        }
    }
}
```

Because `videoTest` is only going to use the methods and fields defined within the interface, it only needs to know that the object passed to it is capable of receiving those messages. The point being made here is an important one, and is vital when we come to the subject of *class inheritance* in Chapter 14:

> An object of any class implementing a particular interface type may be used as an actual argument where a formal argument of that interface type is required.

We call the interface type a *super type* of any implementing class, and the class is correspondingly called a *sub type* of the interface it implements. This principle of substitutability goes further than we have suggested above. In fact, an object of a sub type may be used *anywhere* that an object of one of its super types is required. This is a principle known as *polymorphism*. We saw earlier examples of this idea in Section 10.2.2, where we noted that objects of any type could be stored in a collection expecting references of type `Object`, because all classes have Object as one of their super types.

Exercise 13.3   Identify the methods that the `CardQueue` (Section 10.7.1) and `CardStack` (Section 10.7.2) classes have in common. Define an interface to reflect these common methods.

Exercise 13.4   Modify the class headers of the CardQueue and CardStack classes so that they now implement the interface you defined in your solution to Exercise 13.3.

Write a method that takes an argument of your interface type and demonstrates each of the interface methods. Test it by passing various CardQueue and CardStack objects to it.

Exercise 13.5   Given the following interface

```
interface Logger {
    public void report(String message);
}
```

defined in the file Logger.java, define two classes, ScreenLogger and File-Logger, that implement the Logger interface. ScreenLogger's implementation should print the parameter to the screen. FileLogger's implementation should write the message to a file. Both should end the message with a newline. Define a main method to test your implementations.

13.4 The instanceof Operator

Sometimes it is necessary to know whether an object, whose *static type* is an interface type, has a *dynamic type* of a particular implementing sub type—that is, if it is an instance of a particular class. To this end, Java provides the instanceof operator. It takes an object reference as its left operand and a class or interface type as its right operand. Code 13.7 shows how this might be used within the videoTest method of Code 13.6 to determine whether the actual argument is an instance of a class that implements additional features.

Having determined that a particular actual argument is an instance of the Up-MarketVCR class, we want to invoke one of the extra methods of that class. However, we cannot do this directly via the video variable, because its type is declared to be the basic VCR interface type in the formal argument definition. Instead, we must provide an object reference of the correct class and copy the video reference into this variable with an appropriate *cast* (see Section 10.2.2). The cast is guaranteed to succeed, in this case, because we have made sure that the instance is of the right class.

Where there might be several tests of an object to determine its type, it is important that the most detailed sub types are tested for first, rather than the least

Code 13.7 Using the instanceof operator

```
class VideoTester {
    private boolean testVCR(VCR video,String tape){
        ...
        if(video instanceof UpMarketVCR){
            // Test its extra features.
            UpMarketVCR betterVCR = (UpMarketVCR) video;
            // Play at twice the normal speed.
            betterVCR.setSpeed(2);
        }
        ...
    }
}
```

Code 13.8 An interface for collecting constants

```
interface PieceNames {
    public static int Pawn = 0, Rook = 1, Knight = 2, Bishop = 3,
                        Queen = 4, King = 5;
}
```

detailed super types. If the order is reversed, the later tests are unlikely to be reached. For instance, the following test will always succeed in the first condition, and is therefore incorrect because *all* classes have Object as a super type.

```
// Super types should be tested for after sub types.
if(video instanceof Object){
    // Condition is always true.
    ...
}
else if(video instanceof VCR){
}
else if (video instanceof UpMarketVCR)
    ...
```

The first condition can never be false. Similarly, the second test is equally incorrect because an UpMarketVCR will always have VCR as a super type, and so the third condition could never be `true` if the second is `false`.

   If the left operand of `instanceof` has the value `null`, then the result will always be `false`.

13.5 Interfaces without Methods

It is common practice to define an interface without any methods. Such an interface is not intended to be implemented by any classes, but serves as a collection point for names of related significant values, such as global program constants or status values. For instance, someone designing a program to play a game of chess would prefer to create variable names for the game's pieces rather than littering the code with a lot of *magic numbers*. These names do not belong to any one class, but would be used by many classes throughout the whole program. The interface in Code 13.8 serves as one such collection point.

   Some programming languages provide an *enumerated type* feature that fulfills a similar naming role;[5] Java does not possess such a feature,[6] so an interface with no methods is about as close as you can get without resorting to a *singleton class*. What it cannot provide, however, is any runtime checking that a variable which should only hold a value defined in the interface really does. The following example is perfectly legal, for instance:

```
int piece = PieceNames.King;
int badPiece = piece+1; // Nonsense, but not an error.
```

---

[5] Pascal, for instance, and enum in C and C++.

[6] This should not be confused with Java's `Enumeration` interface, which is quite different—see Section 13.7.3.

As can be seen, the problem lies in the fact that the interface simply provides names for int values and the variables defined to hold those values are ordinary integer variables—they are not of type PieceName—so all normal integer operations are valid on them. Nevertheless, despite their shortcomings, interfaces without methods do provide a useful naming feature that should be used where appropriate.

Exercise 13.6   The interface NumberGenerator has the following definition:

```
interface NumberGenerator {
    // Return the next integer in sequence.
    public int nextNumber();
}
```

Implementing classes should return an increasing sequence of integers in response to repeated calls to nextNumber. For instance, the implementing class, EvenNumbers, would return the values 0, 2, 4, etc., while the implementing class OddNumbers, would return the values 1, 3, 5, etc.

Define the classes EvenNumbers and OddNumbers that separately implement the NumberGenerator interface. Both classes will need a variable that keeps track of either the last value returned, or the next value to be returned. Be careful to ensure that the first value returned from each class is the correct one. Code 13.9 contains a main method to test your implementations.

Exercise 13.7   Add the further following method to the NumberGenerator interface, and define implementations of it within both of the EvenNumbers and

---

Code 13.9   Test-rig for the EvenNumbers and OddNumbers classes
(NumberGeneratorMain.java)

```
        // Test-rig for the EvenNumbers and OddNumbers implementations
        // of the NumberGenerator interface.
class NumberGeneratorMain {
    public static void main(String[] args){
        EvenNumbers even = new EvenNumbers();
        // Generate a short sequence of even numbers.
        sequence(even);
        OddNumbers odd = new OddNumbers();
        // Generate a short sequence of odd numbers.
        sequence(odd);
    }

        // Generate a few numbers using the NumberGenerator interface.
    public static void sequence(NumberGenerator numbers){
        int n = numbers.nextNumber();
        while(n < 20){
            System.out.print(n+" ");
            n = numbers.nextNumber();
        }
        System.out.println();
    }
}
```

OddNumbers classes.

```
// Return the next number in the sequence that is divisible
// by divisor.
public int nextDivisibleBy(int divisor);
```

The nextDivisibleBy method should return the next integer in the sequence that is exactly divisible by its divisor argument. For instance, if an EvenNumbers object has just returned the number 12 and a call is made to nextDivisibleBy with an argument of 5, the result would be the value 20. You might like to think about what should happen if an even number is passed as an argument to the implementation of this method in the OddNumbers class.

Exercise 13.8 Define a class, RandomNumbers, that also implements the Number-Generator interface with its nextNumber and nextDivisibleBy methods. The java.util package defines the class Random. This class defines a nextInt method that returns a random positive or negative integer. Use an object of the Random class in your implementation of RandomNumbers. The nextNumber method should always return a value that is bigger than the last one returned. For instance, this class might return the numbers 0, 3, 16, 100, etc.

Add some statements to the main method shown in Code 13.9 to test your implementation.

Exercise 13.9 Design and implement a class, PriorityList, with an attribute that is one of the standard collection classes. All objects that are to be stored in the collection will implement the Priority interface shown in Code 13.10. PriorityList should have an add method with the following header:

```
// Add item to the list if it implements the
// Priority interface.
public void add(Object item) throws RuntimeException
```

It should only add item to its collection if it implements the Priority interface; otherwise, it should throw a RuntimeException exception. When an item is added to the collection, its position is determined by the value returned by its getPriority method, in relation to the priority of the items already in the collection. Those items with higher priority values should be stored at lower indices than those with lower values. Include in your implementation a method, listPriorities, that iterates over the collection, printing out the priority value of each item in it.

Create one or more classes that implement the Priority interface in order to test PriorityList.

Code 13.10 An interface for implementing a priority mechanism (`Priority.java`)

```
// Classes implementing this interface indicate that they
// should be ordered by their priority.
interface Priority {
    public int getPriority();
    public void setPriority(int p);
}
```

13.6   Review

Here are the main points that we have covered in the preceding sections:

- An interface contains only method signatures (headers) and/or fields.
- An interface never contains a method body.
- Fields defined in an interface are always `public static final`.
- A method in an interface may not be `static`.
- A class `implements` an interface.
- An implementing class defines a body for each method signature in the interface definition.
- An interface is often implemented by more than one class.
- An interface provides a means of ensuring consistency of interaction with objects of implementing classes—a contract.
- Implementing classes may define further methods and variables, but these do not form part of the interface.
- For the sake of generality, interface fields should be accessed externally via the interface name, rather than an implementing class name.
- Polymorphism allows an object of any implementing class (a sub type) to be used where an object of the interface type (its super type) is required.
- The `instanceof` operator makes it possible to determine whether an object implements a particular interface.
- When using `instanceof`, sub types should be checked before super types.
- An interface without method signatures is a convenient collecting point for program- or package-wide constants.

13.7   Common Interfaces

In this section, we investigate some of the more commonly used interfaces drawn from a number of packages, such as `java.io`, `java.lang`, and `java.util`.

13.7.1   The Iterator Interface

In Chapter 10, we introduced the concept of collections of objects. Collections based around implementations using arrays (`ArrayList`) or linked lists (`LinkedList`) are common in programs, as are collections that use other mechanisms to group their data, such as `HashMap`. Not all collections use a simple indexing strategy to access their elements, and yet it is a common requirement to be able to iterate through the complete set of elements they contain. It might be necessary to increase the salary of all employees by a fixed percentage, for instance, or register a collection of students for a particular course. In such instances, we are often not particularly interested in the order in which we access the items—indeed, the notion of order is irrelevant in some contexts—rather, we simply want to access them all. For this purpose, the `java.util` package defines the `Iterator` interface shown in Code 13.11.

We saw examples of the use of Iterator in Section 10.5, although we did not point out that Iterator is, in fact, an interface rather than a class. Classes which maintain collections will usually include an `iterator` method which returns an

Code 13.11   The Iterator interface from the java.util package

```
public interface Iterator {
    // Are there any more items?
    public boolean hasNext();
    // Return the next item. The exception is unchecked.
    public Object next() throws NoSuchElementException;
    // Remove the last item returned. The exceptions are unchecked.
    public void remove() throws IllegalStateException,
                                UnsupportedOperationException;
}
```

object of a class implementing the Iterator interface. The rules of polymorphism mean that it is not necessary to know the name of the class that implements the Iterator interface on behalf of a particular collection class. A further advantage of this approach is that clients do not need to know anything about how the collection is organized—an important requirement for *information hiding*. In fact, one reason for the similarity of many of the collection classes we have seen so far, is the fact that they are implementations of the Collection interface (defined in the java.util package). In addition to iterator, this contains methods such as add, clear, remove, removeAll, and toArray, which we have seen as being an integral part of the ArrayList and LinkedList collection classes. Both of these classes also share the List interface (from java.util) as a common super type. This adds methods such as indexOf, lastIndexOf, and listIterator, to those defined in the simpler Collection interface.

13.7.2   Implementing an Iterator

Where you wish to provide access to the elements stored within a collection, it is a good idea to provide it in this standard way. If you are using one of the standard collection classes, such as ArrayList or LinkedList, to hold your data, then this is easy since they already have the iterator method expressly for this purpose. Where your collection is custom-built, you will need to define a specific class that implements the Iterator interface and has details of how you are holding the data. This is often best done using an *inner class*, and we shall see how to do this in Section 15.6. However, it is fairly simple to illustrate how it can be done if the data is held in an array. We can build an implementation of the Iterator interface that is general enough to work with a filled array of any object type. Code 13.12 shows this.[7]

The remove method is optional, in the sense that an iterator may be defined to provide read-only access to the underlying collection. If remove is not implemented, then it should simply throw the UnsupportedOperationException exception as the single statement in its body. We have chosen to implement removal simply by setting the appropriate index in the array to contain the null value. Careful

---

[7] A ready-made alternative to this example is provided by the asList method of the Arrays class.

Code 13.12   Iterator implementation for an array of objects (`ArrayIterator.java`)

```java
import java.util.*;

        // Iterate over an array of objects.
class ArrayIterator implements Iterator {
        // Retain a reference to the data to be iterated over.
    public ArrayIterator(Object[] data){
        array  = data;
    }

        // Definitions of the interface methods.
    public boolean hasNext(){
        return getLastIndex()+1 < getArray().length;
    }

    public Object next() throws NoSuchElementException {
        if(hasNext()){
            int index = getLastIndex()+1;
            // Update the value for next time.
            setLastIndex(index);
            return getArray()[index];
        }
        else{
            throw new NoSuchElementException();
        }
    }

        // Remove an element by setting it to null.
    public void remove() throws IllegalStateException,
                            UnsupportedOperationException{
        int index = getLastIndex();
        if(index < 0){
            throw new IllegalStateException();
        }
        else{
            getArray()[index] = null;
        }
    }

        // Accessors and mutators for the LastIndex and array attributes.
    private int getLastIndex(){
        return lastIndex;
    }

    private void setlastIndex(int n){
        lastIndex = n;
    }

    private Object[] getArray(){
        return array;
    }

    // The array of objects to be iterated over.
    private final Object[] array;
    // The index of the last element returned.
    private int lastIndex = -1;
}
```

management of the index value into the collection is needed. An important design decision is whether the index maintained by the iterator should refer to the last item returned, or the next item to be returned. Either is possible, but careful consideration must be given to the operation of each of the methods to avoid *boundary errors*. For instance, what happens if the `next` method is called when the full collection has already been iterated over? What should happen if `remove` is called before the first item has been returned?

Exercise 13.10   Test the implementation of the `ArrayIterator` class using the main method shown in Code 13.13. The main method passes its String array argument to an ArrayIterator object in order to create an Iterator. Running the program as follows

```
java ArrayIteratorMain first second third
```

should produce the following output:

```
first
second
third
```

Exercise 13.11   What should be the effect on the contents of the `args` array if the following statement is added just after the end of the loop?

```
strings.remove();
```

Test the effect by printing out the contents of the array immediately afterwards— either using a fresh Iterator, or using the array directly.

Code 13.13   A main method to test the ArrayIterator class (`ArrayIteratorMain.java`)

```java
import java.util.Iterator;

    // A test rig that shows an implementation of the
    // java.util.Iterator interface for an array of objects.
class ArrayIteratorMain {
    public static void main(String[] args) {
        if(args.length > 0){
            // Iterate over the arguments passed in.
            Iterator strings = new ArrayIterator(args);
            while(strings.hasNext()){
                System.out.println((String) strings.next());
            }
        }
        else{
            System.out.println("Usage: java ArrayIteratorMain str ...");
        }
    }
}
```

Code 13.14 The Enumeration interface from the java.util package

```
public interface Enumeration {
        // Will nextElement return another object?
    public boolean hasMoreElements();
        // The exception is unchecked.
    public Object nextElement() throws NoSuchElementException;
}
```

Exercise 13.12   What should be the effect on the program if the following statement is added just before the start of the loop?

```
    strings.remove();
```

Try it out to test your understanding.

Exercise 13.13   Modify the `ArrayIterator` implementation of Code 13.12 so that the `next` method does not return `null` references from the array of objects. You will need to think carefully about the interaction between the `lastIndex` attribute and the implementation of the `hasNext` method.

Exercise 13.14   The `ListIterator` interface (defined in the `java.util` package) provides for both forward and backward movement over the items in a collection. Modify the original version of ArrayIterator, so that it implements the following methods of ListIterator, in addition to those already implemented: `hasPrevious`, `previous`. The remaining methods should throw the `UnsupportedOperation-Exception` exception. Write a main method to test your implementation.

Exercise 13.15   Complete the implementation of the ListIterator interface that you started in Exercise 13.14. Since the `add` operation implies that the underlying collection is not fixed in size, you should feel free to omit the implementation of this method.

13.7.3   The Enumeration Interface

A legacy interface, closely related to the Iterator interface, is `Enumeration`,[8] shown in Code 13.14. An example we can use to illustrate this idea is the `Properties` class which is defined in `java.util`. An object of this class keeps a table of String key/value pairs, rather like a specialized HashMap.[9] The String value associated with a particular key may be retrieved with its `getProperty` method. In order to find out its complete set of keys, the class provides the `propertyNames` method which returns an object of a class that implements the Enumeration interface. The `System`

---

[8] This should not be confused with enumerated types—a feature of languages, such as Pascal and C—that Java does not possess.

[9] In fact, the Properties class is built from the legacy `Hashtable` class, which fulfills a similar role to HashMap.

Code 13.15   Printing the system properties

```
import java.util.*;

        // Print out the complete set of System properties.
class ShowProperties {
    public static void main(String[] args){
        Properties props = System.getProperties();
        Enumeration propNames = props.propertyNames();
        while(propNames.hasMoreElements()){
            // Get the property name, which is the key.
            String name = (String) propNames.nextElement();
            // Look up its value in the properties.
            String value = props.getProperty(name);
            System.out.println(name+" = "+value);
        }
    }
}
```

class maintains a collection of system properties—things that relate to the program and its running environment, such as the current user, details of the operating system and working directory, and so on. For this, it uses an object of the Properties class. Code 13.15 shows how we might print a complete list of the system properties. Here is a fragment of the output it might produce:

```
user.timezone = Europe/London
user.name = djb
os.arch = x86
os.name = Windows NT
java.vm.vendor = Sun Microsystems Inc.
java.vendor.url = http://java.sun.com/
```

Exercise 13.16   Write a program that creates a `Properties` object containing only those properties from the system properties with the prefix "`user.`". (*Hint:* use the `startsWith` method of the String class to look for matches.)

Exercise 13.17   Write a program similar to that for Exercise 13.16 that selects the set of system properties that start with the prefixes passed to the program as its command-line arguments. If no arguments are given, then all properties should be selected. The selected properties should be stored in a HashMap object. From the HashMap, print the keys and values as follows:

- Use the `values` method of the HashMap to obtain a `Collection` object. Use the Collection's `iterator` method to iterate over, and print, the full set of values.
- Use the `keySet` method of the HashMap to obtain an object from a class implementing the `Set` interface (defined in `java.util`). A Set is a special collection in which there are no duplicate values. Use the Set's `iterator` method to iterate over, and print, the full set of keys.

Code 13.16   The Comparable interface defined in the `java.lang` package

```
public interface Comparable {
    public int compareTo(Object o) throws ClassCastException;
}
```

13.7.4 The Comparable Interface

The `Comparable` interface is defined in the `java.lang` package. It is similar to the `Comparator`, discussed in Section 13.7.5. The Comparable interface is shown in Code 13.16. The Comparable interface defines a single method, `compareTo`, whose task is to return an integer value describing the comparative relationship between the object receiving the message, and the method's argument. The value returned should be negative if the receiving object should precede the argument in some ordering, positive if the receiving object comes after the object, and zero if the two objects are equal. Code 13.17 illustrates a simple class that implements this interface.

Code 13.17   A class implementing the Comparable interface (`Student.java`)

```
    /* A simple implementation of the Comparable interface.
     * Students with higher marks come before those with lower marks.
     * Otherwise, the ordering for identical marks is alphabetical
     * on names.
     */
class Student implements Comparable {
    public Student(String name, int mark){
        this.name = name;
        this.mark  = mark;
    }

        // In comparing this Student to the given Object, it is necessary
        // to ensure that o is, indeed, a Student.
    public int compareTo(Object o) throws ClassCastException {
        if(o == null){
            // Student should come before null objects.
            // Return a token negative value.
            return -1;
        }
        else{
            // This could result in a ClassCastException, if o is
            // not a Student.
            Student s = (Student) o;
            // Compare marks first. Higher marks come first.
            // So we want a negative result if our mark is higher.
            int markDifference = s.getMark() - getMark();
            if(markDifference != 0){
                return markDifference;
            }
            else{
                // Marks are the same. Compare names.
                return getName().compareTo(s.getName());
            }
        }
    }
```

Code 13.17   (*Continued*)

```
    // Return a String representation of the student name mark.
    public String toString(){
        return getName()+" "+getMark();
    }

    public int getMark(){
        return mark;
    }

    public String getName(){
        return name;
    }

    private final String name;
    private final int mark;
}
```

The Student class maintains two attributes, the student's mark and their name. In implementing the Comparable interface, the idea is that students with higher marks should be placed before those with lower marks in any comparison. If the marks of two students are equal, then their names are used to order them alphabetically (this role is performed by the existing compareTo method of the String class which, itself, implements the Comparable interface). Now that we have a way of ordering two Student objects, it becomes easy to sort a complete array of Student objects. The Arrays class, briefly introduced in Section 9.14, contains methods to sort efficiently not only arrays of primitive values, but also to sort arrays of objects. The requirement is that the objects in the array implement the Comparable interface. When the sort method wishes to check the relative ordering of two elements, it uses the fact that they define a compareTo method to check the relationship. Code 13.18 shows a main method that shows this approach using a small array of Student objects. The output from this example will be as follows:

```
Upminster 100
Battlement 50
Hobart 50
Barking 0
```

The Collections class contains similar sort methods designed to work on collections that implement the List interface.

Exercise 13.18   Modify the TeamDetails class, shown in Section 9.16.1, so that it implements the Comparable interface. A team with more points should come before a team with fewer points. Teams with equal points should be ordered alphabetically by name. Add a public sort method to the League class, shown in Section 9.16.2, that delegates to the appropriate sort method of the Arrays class defined in java.util. The sort method should be called whenever one of the points-changing methods of League is used.

Code 13.18   Sorting an array of Comparable objects (`ComparableMain.java`)

```java
import java.util.Arrays;

    // Illustrate use of Arrays.sort on an array of objects
    // that implement the Comparable interface.
class ComparableMain {
    public static void main(String[] args){
        final Student[] students = {
            new Student("Hobart",50),
            new Student("Battlement",50),
            new Student("Barking",0),
            new Student("Upminster",100),
        };
        // Sort the data.
        Arrays.sort(students);
        // Demonstrate that it has been sorted.
        final int numStudents = students.length;
        for(int i = 0; i < numStudents; i++){
            System.out.println(students[i].toString());
        }
    }
}
```

13.7.5   The Comparator Interface

The Comparator interface (defined in `java.util`) contains two methods, shown in Code 13.19. The `compare` method fulfills a similar role to the `compareTo` method of the Comparable interface, discussed in Section 13.7.4. It returns a negative, positive, or zero value depending upon whether the first argument should precede, follow, or is equal to the second. If the two arguments belong to classes that already implement the Comparable interface, then this method could be trivially implemented as

```java
public int compare(Object o1,Object o2) throws ClassCastException {
    return o1.compareTo(o2);
}
```

However, the Comparator interface is normally used in two distinct circumstances:

- When objects to be sorted belong to a class that does not implement the Comparable interface, and you do not have access to the source of the class in order to amend it. The Comparator interface makes it possible to sort such items based upon their accessible attributes.

Code 13.19   The Comparator interface defined in the java.util package

```java
public interface Comparator {
    public int compare(Object o1,Object o2) throws ClassCastException;
    public boolean equals(Object o);
}
```

- When a sort order of some objects is required that is different from that provided by their class's normal implementation of the Comparable interface.

Implementation of the equals method is slightly less obvious than that of compare. Its purpose is to return true if its argument represents an implementation of Comparator that would return the same results for all arguments. That is, it allows two Comparator implementations to be compared. This is potentially complex to implement for all arguments, and so it is often sufficient to omit it from the implementing class. The reason that this is possible is that all objects have a default version of the equals method; see Section 14.9 for more details. Code 13.20 defines an implementation of the Comparator class for illustrative purposes.

The implementation of compare goes to considerable lengths to ensure that null references are handled correctly. The approach is to define these as being placed after any valid data. The comparison between two Student objects is a simplified version of that defined in the compareTo method of Code 13.17. In this case, we only order the students on their marks and not their names. A further version of the sort methods defined in the Arrays class takes an array of objects to be sorted, and an object implementing the Comparator interface. Code 13.21 shows a simple main method that uses this version. The output from this example is as follows:

```
Upminster 100
Hobart 50
Battlement 50
Barking 0
```

Code 13.20   An implementation of Comparator (`ComparatorExample.java`)

```java
import java.util.Comparator;

class ComparatorExample implements Comparator {
    public int compare(Object o1,Object o2) throws ClassCastException {
        if(o1 == o2){
            return 0;
        }
        else if(o1 == null){
            // Always place null objects towards the end.
            return 1;
        }
        else if(o2 == null){
            return -1;
        }
        else{
            // Either of these casts might fail.
            Student s1 = (Student) o1, s2 = (Student) o2;
            // Only distinguish on mark, not name.
            return s2.getMark()-s1.getMark();
        }
    }
}
```

Code 13.21   An implementation of the Comparator interface (`ComparatorMain.java`)

```
import java.util.Arrays;

    // Illustrate use of Arrays.sort on an array of objects
    // that implement the Comparator interface.
class ComparatorMain {
    public static void main(String[] args){
        final Student[] students = {
            new Student("Hobart",50),
            new Student("Battlement",50),
            new Student("Barking",0),
            new Student("Upminster",100),
        };
        // Sort the data using a Comparator.
        Arrays.sort(students,new ComparatorExample());
        // Demonstrate that it has been sorted.
        final int numStudents = students.length;
        for(int i = 0; i < numStudents; i++){
            System.out.println(students[i].toString());
        }
    }
}
```

Notice that the ordering is different from the similar data used in the example of Code 13.18 because no account has been taken of the name ordering.

Exercise 13.19   Define the class, `PointComparator`, that implements the Comparator interface in order to produce an ordering of `Point` objects (see Code 4.19). Points should be ordered in increasing value of their x-attribute. Points with identical x-attribute should be ordered by increasing y-attribute. So the following points, $(0,0), (0,5), (1,3)$, are in order.

13.7.6   The FileFilter and FilenameFilter Interfaces

The `FileFilter` and `FilenameFilter` interfaces are both defined in the `java.io` package. Both define a single method, `accept`, which returns a `boolean` result. The purpose of these interfaces is to allow classes to be defined that indicate whether a given file or filename is to be accepted for some purpose. For instance, when a user wishes to select a file from the file system, the list of possibilities might be filtered in some way, such as only files with a given suffix are offered. Code 13.22 shows the FileFilter interface. Code 13.23 shows the FilenameFilter interface.

Exercise 13.20   Define an implementation of the `FileFilter` interface that only accepts its argument if the path name ends in the suffix `".java"`. The test should not be sensitive to case.

Code 13.22   The FileFilter interface defined in the `java.io` package

```
public interface FileFilter {
    // Should the given path name be accepted?
    public boolean accept(File pathname);
}
```

Code 13.23   The FilenameFilter interface defined in the `java.io` package

```
public interface FilenameFilter {
    // Should name in the given directory be accepted?
    public boolean accept(File directory,String name);
}
```

Exercise 13.21   Define an implementation of the `FilenameFilter` interface that only returns `true` if the directory is writable and the name does not yet exist within it.

13.8   Implementing Empty Interfaces

Occasionally, an interface is defined containing neither method signatures nor fields. It might appear that such an interface could have no useful purpose. In fact, an empty interface fulfills an important role as a *marking interface*. A class implementing such an interface needs to add nothing to its existing functionality, but by doing so it marks itself out in some way. Three of the more important empty interfaces are `Event-Listener` (see Section 13.9), `Serializable` (see Section 13.10), and `Cloneable`. Cloning is concerned with making a duplicate copy of an object. If a programmer wishes this to be possible, then a class must implement the Cloneable interface; additional code will not necessarily be required. When an attempt is made to clone an object, a check will be made to ensure that it belongs to a class that implements the Cloneable interface; otherwise, a `CloneNotSupportedException` exception will be thrown. We discuss cloning in detail in Section 15.3.

13.9   Implementing Multiple Interfaces

The use of interfaces becomes very important when we look at programs with *Graphical User Interfaces* (*GUIs*) in later chapters. Various devices, such as the keyboard and mouse, which supply input *events* to such programs, will expect parts of the programs to be *listening* for those events to occur on the devices—events such as button presses, mouse movements, and keyboard strokes. In order to further facilitate this interaction, the `java.awt.event` package contains a number of interface definitions, such as `ActionListener`, `KeyListener`, and `MouseListener`. A program wishing to respond to events must define classes that implement the

Code 13.24   Implementing multiple interfaces

```java
import java.awt.event.*;

class MultiEventHandler implements ActionListener, KeyListener {
    // Implementation of the ActionListener interface
    public void actionPerformed(ActionEvent e){
        ...
    }

    // Implementation of the KeyListener interface
    public void keyPressed(KeyEvent e){
        ...
    }

    public void keyReleased(KeyEvent e){
        ...
    }

    public void keyTyped(KeyEvent e){
        ...
    }
    ...
}
```

appropriate interfaces.[10] Of particular significance is that an object within the program might need to be able to respond to events of different types, such as both mouse and keyboard events. This means that it must be possible for its class to implement more than one interface. This is permitted in Java; each interface to be implemented is listed as part of a comma-separated list in the class header (Code 13.24).

Components within a GUI notify listener objects when an event of interest to them has occurred. In order for them to know whom to notify, listeners must register an interest in their events. For instance, a JButton object (from the javax.swing package) will tell listeners when it has been pressed. Its class defines the addActionListener method so that objects implementing the ActionListener interface can register with a button. This method has a single argument of type ActionListener for which the MultiEventHandler class defined in Code 13.24 is suitable (Code 13.25).

At this stage, we shall not go further into detail about how events are generated or handled; this is covered in Chapter 16. A point to note, however, is that the basic rule of polymorphism applies to classes implementing multiple interfaces as well as single interfaces; an object implementing multiple interfaces may be used anywhere that an object of any one of those interface types is required. JButton's addActionListener method only requires an object implementing the ActionListener interface, but this does not prevent us from using a MultiEventHandler object for this purpose.

---

[10] Classes which act as event listeners also implicitly implement the empty EventListener interface.

Code 13.25 Registering an interest in events

```
// Define an object to handle all the events of interest.
MultiEventHandler handler = new MultiEventHandler();
// Define a button to be pressed in order to start
// something happening.
JButton startButton = new JButton("Start");
// Register an interest in knowing when the
// startButton is pressed.
startButton.addActionListener(handler);
...
```

13.9.1   Conflict Resolution with Multiple Interfaces

A question we shall return to in Section 14.3.2 is, what happens if two interfaces implemented by a single class have a method or field with the same name? The following rules define what happens in each possible case:

- A method defined with different numbers of arguments in the multiple interfaces simply becomes a normal *overloaded method* in the implementing class. Such a method will have multiple method bodies—one to go with each signature.
- A method defined with identical headers in the multiple interfaces will have a single method body, which stands as the implementation of each. Clearly, this only makes sense if the intent of the methods in the different interfaces is the same or very similar.
- If the only difference is in the exceptions the method signatures define as being thrown, then this presents more of a problem, because it is not possible to define overloaded methods that only differ in the exceptions they throw. One possibility is to define the combined method to throw no exceptions, since an implementation may throw fewer checked exceptions than are defined in the interface. Alternatively, if the two signatures have some exceptions in common, the implementation could be defined to throw just the common subset.
- Where there are field names in common between the multiple interfaces, those names cannot be used unqualified in the implementation. Each usage of an overloaded field name must be fully qualified with the name of the interface in which it was defined.

Exercise 13.22   Consider the interfaces shown in Code 13.26. How many methods must a class implementing both `Int1` and `Int2` define?

Exercise 13.23   How many methods must a class implementing both `Int1` and `Int3` define?

Exercise 13.24   How many methods must a class implementing both `Int1` and `Int4` define?

Code 13.26   Four similar interfaces

```
interface Int1 {
    public void method();
}

interface Int2 {
    public void method(int arg);
}

interface Int3 {
    public void method();
}

interface Int4 {
    public void method() throws Exception;
}
```

Exercise 13.25   How many methods must a class implementing both `Int2` and `Int4` define?

13.10   The Serializable Interface

In Section 12.12, we noted that the `ObjectInputStream` and `ObjectOutput-Stream` classes of the `java.io` package free a class designer from having to do much of the work involved in saving and retrieving whole objects from files. This involves a process called *object serialization*. In order to fully describe how whole objects may be read and written, it is necessary to introduce the `Serializable` interface, defined in the `java.io` package. Code 13.27 shows its definition.

Serializable is a *marking interface*, with no fields or methods. Any class which implements the Serializable interface can be stored in and retrieved from files without any further intervention on the part of the programmer. The example in Code 13.28 shows two classes which implement this interface as part of a program that maintains a persistent collection of objects representing World Wide Web *bookmarks*.

Both classes are straightforward. The `Bookmark` class contains String attributes representing the *Uniform Resource Locator (URL)* of a Web page (for instance, `"http://www.javasoft.com/"`) and a title for the page (`"JavaSoft Home Page"`). The `BookmarkCollection` class holds a LinkedList of Bookmarks and provides methods to add a new bookmark and obtain an array of references to the complete collection. As a LinkedList is an arbitrary choice for the collection (an

---

Code 13.27   The Serializable interface defined in the `java.io` package

```
public interface Serializable {
}
```

Code 13.28   Maintain a collection of WWW bookmarks

```java
import java.io.Serializable;
import java.util.*;

        // Keep a record of a Web page's URL and a title for it.
        // The title is not necessarily the page's HTML title but
        // could be user defined. However, a URL string may not
        // be altered once set.
class Bookmark implements Serializable {
    public Bookmark(String url,String title){
        this.url = url;
        setTitle(title);
    }

    public String getUrl(){
        return url;
    }

    public String getTitle(){
        return title;
    }

        // Allow external changes to the title.
    public void setTitle(String t){
        if(t != null){
            title = t;
        }
    }

    private String title;
    private final String url;
}

class BookmarkCollection implements Serializable {
        // Add a new bookmark to the collection.
    public void add(Bookmark mark){
        getCollection().add(mark);
    }

        // Make the collection available as an array.
    public Bookmark[] getBookmarks(){
        Collection collection = getCollection();
        Bookmark[] bookmarks = new Bookmark[collection.size()];

        collection.toArray(bookmarks);
        return bookmarks;
    }

    private Collection getCollection(){
        return collection;
    }

    // The type of Collection is arbitrary.
    private Collection collection = new LinkedList();
}
```

Code 13.29   Writing a Serializable Bookmark

```
try{
    // An illustrative Serializable object.
    Bookmark mark = new Bookmark(
                "http://www.javasoft.com/","JavaSoft Home Page");
    // Open the file where the bookmark is to be stored.
    FileOutputStream fstream = new FileOutputStream("bookmarkfile");
    // Open an object stream associated with the bookmark file.
    ObjectOutputStream ostream = new ObjectOutputStream(fstream);
    ostream.writeObject(mark);
    ostream.close();
}
catch(NotSerializableException e){
    System.err.println("Saving failed: "+e.toString());
}
catch(IOException e){
    System.err.println("Saving failed: "+e.toString());
}
```

ArrayList could equally well have been used, for instance), most of its usage is handled through the Collection interface that both implement. This makes it relatively easy to use an alternative Collection implementation, should this be required.

In order to allow objects of the Bookmark and BookmarkCollection classes to be stored in files, nothing needs to be added to these classes, aside from their implementation of the Serializable interface. This means that it is possible to use them in a program that allows a user to add new references to a bookmark collection over a period of time. Code 13.29 shows the steps involved in constructing a single Bookmark object and writing it to a file.

The process of reading and writing objects is performed by objects of the ObjectInputStream and ObjectOutputStream classes. It is these classes that define how to read and write the individual components of any class in an appropriate portable byte-based format. In order to construct an ObjectOutputStream object, it is necessary to have available an object representing the stream on which to write the objects. Such a stream is provided by the FileOutputStream class (see Section 12.7). An object is then written to the stream by passing it as a parameter to the writeObject method of ObjectOutputStream. It is important to close the ObjectOutputStream once all of the objects have been written to ensure that the data is flushed to the file system. If the object passed to writeObject belongs to a class that does not implement the Serializable interface, a NotSerializable-Exception exception will be thrown.

Reading objects from an object input file follows a complementary process, shown in Code 13.30. Notice that the readObject method of ObjectInputStream constructs an object of the appropriate class, but this is returned as a reference of type Object, which must be downcast before assignment.

The example in Code 13.31 shows a demonstration class that is able to read and write a BookmarkCollection and allows a user to add new bookmarks to it. A main method to demonstrate this may be found in the file BookmarkMain.java.

Code 13.30   Reading a Bookmark from a file

```
try{
    // Open the file where the bookmark is stored.
    FileInputStream fstream = new FileInputStream("bookmarkfile");
    // Open an object stream associated with the bookmark file.
    ObjectInputStream istream = new ObjectInputStream(fstream);
    // Obtain the object.
    Bookmark mark = (Bookmark) istream.readObject();
    istream.close();
}
catch(Exception e){
    System.err.println("Reading failed: "+e);
}
```

Code 13.31   Reading and writing a BookmarkCollection

```
import java.io.*;
import java.util.StringTokenizer;

    // Demonstrate use of Object Serialization by reading and
    // writing a BookmarkCollection object.
    // Read and write to the file passed to the constructor.
    // Fail with a runtime exception if the file is inaccessible.
class BookmarkDemo {
    public BookmarkDemo(String filename) throws RuntimeException {
        this.filename = filename;
        File bookmarkFile = new File(filename);
        if(bookmarkFile.exists()){
            if(!bookmarkFile.canRead()){
                throw new RuntimeException(filename+" is unreadable.");
            }
            else if(!bookmarkFile.canWrite()){
                throw new RuntimeException(filename+" is unwritable.");
            }
            else{
                // Ok. Read the saved collection.
                collection = readCollection();
            }
        }
        else{
            // There is no existing collection.
            collection = new BookmarkCollection();
        }
    }

    // Interactively read new bookmarks from the user.
    // The URL "quit" terminates the input.
    // Save the new state of the collection on completion.
    public void updateCollection(){
        final BookmarkCollection collection = getCollection();
```

(*Continued*)

```
        final SimpleInput reader = new SimpleInput();
        System.out.println("Supply each URL and title on a single line.");
        System.out.println(
            "Separate the URL from the title with an @ character, e.g.");
        System.out.println("http://www.javasoft.com@JavaSoft Home Page");
        System.out.println("Finish with a blank line.");
        String line = reader.nextLine();
        while(line.length() > 0){
            StringTokenizer tokenizer = new StringTokenizer(line,"@");
            final String url = tokenizer.nextToken();
            // Take the remainder of the line as the title.
            final String title = tokenizer.nextToken();
            collection.add(new Bookmark(url,title));
            line = reader.nextLine();
        }
        saveCollection();
    }

    // Print them out.
    public void printCollection(){
        Bookmark[] marks = getCollection().getBookmarks();
        for(int i = 0; i < marks.length; i++){
            final Bookmark mark = marks[i];
            System.out.println(mark.getUrl()+" "+mark.getTitle());
        }
    }

    // Try to read a Bookmark collection. Throw a RuntimeException
    // on failure.
    private BookmarkCollection readCollection() throws RuntimeException {
        try{
            final String filename = getFilename();
            // Open the input stream for the associated file.
            ObjectInputStream istream = new ObjectInputStream(
                    new FileInputStream(filename));
            BookmarkCollection collection =
                        (BookmarkCollection) istream.readObject();
            istream.close();
            return collection;
        }
        catch(Exception e){
            throw new RuntimeException("Reading failed: "+e);
        }
    }

    private void saveCollection(){
        try{
            final String filename = getFilename();
            // Open the output stream for the associated file.
            ObjectOutputStream ostream = new ObjectOutputStream(
                    new FileOutputStream(filename));
            ostream.writeObject(getCollection());
            ostream.close();
```

Code 13.31   (*Continued*)

```
        }
        catch(IOException e){
            System.err.println("Saving failed: "+e);
        }
    }

    private BookmarkCollection getCollection(){
        return collection;
    }

    public String getFilename(){
        return filename;
    }

    // Where the bookmarks are to be stored persistently.
    private final String filename;
    private final BookmarkCollection collection;
}
```

Notice that, in this example, it is a BookmarkCollection object that is passed to `writeObject`. The process of writing out that object's LinkedList attribute causes further (recursive) invocations of `writeObject` on the individual Bookmark objects contained within it—a process known as *swizzling*. This illustrates how powerful the technique of object serialization is, and how little effort is required on the part of the programmer to make use of its benefits.

Exercise 13.26   Create a serialized version of the `League` and `TeamDetails` classes described in Section 9.16. Define a main method that adds some points to the teams and then serializes the state of the league. Add statements to the main method that will cause it to de-serialize this version if the filename in which it is stored is passed as a command-line argument to the program.

13.10.1   Controlling Serialization

Fields defined as `static` within a class are not written out as part of object serialization. When a serialized object with static fields is de-serialized, the static fields are left unmodified. In addition, sometimes it is inappropriate to have particular fields written out as part of the serialization process, because their values will not necessarily make sense when the object is de-serialized. A typical example of this would be fields that refer to open file streams, readers, or writers. A field may be prevented from being serialized by using the `transient` reserved word as part of its declaration. There seems to be no fixed position for this word within a declaration, but we recommend that it be placed immediately after any access modifier, in a similar position to where a `static` reserved word would be placed, as follows:

```
            // Don't serialize this field.
      private transient FileWriter outfile;
```

Transient fields will be given the default initial value for their type when an object is de-serialized.

By default, all non-static and non-transient fields of an object will be written automatically as part of the serialization process. If more control is required, two methods may be defined in a serializable class to allow finer control over which fields are written and in which order. These are:

```
      void readObject(ObjectInputStream in);
      void writeObject(ObjectOutputStream out);
```

These methods may use their arguments to control their own input and output. Clearly, the readObject method should de-serialize the fields in the same order as they are written by the writeObject method that wrote them. Usage of these methods is more specialized than we wish to explore further.

Each serializable class is given its own version identification in a serial-VersionUID field. The value of this is written out as part of an object's serialization. This prevents possible problems if a class undergoes changes between some of its objects being serialized and then de-serialized. It also helps to ensure that objects de-serialized from a remote location across a network are compatible with the class definitions available in the receiving host's environment. The version number of a particular class can be determined from the serialver tool that is part of the Java platform. For instance, running this command on one version of the Bookmark class shown in Code 13.28 produced the following output:

```
   Bookmark: static final long serialVersionUID = 3493142387118876503L;
```

If the class were to be changed in the future, perhaps through the addition of further fields, then an attempt to de-serialize old versions would result in an Invalid-ClassException exception being thrown. Where it is necessary for a new version of a class to retain the old version number, the declaration of serialVersionUID may be explicitly included within the class definition, with its old value.

A means of determining the version number of a Serializable class, from within a program, is via the static lookup method of the ObjectStreamClass (defined in the java.io package).

Exercise 13.27   Use the serialver tool of the Java platform to find out the serial version UID of the serializable classes in your solution to Exercise 13.26.

Exercise 13.28   Add a field to one of the serializable classes in your solution to Exercise 13.26 and see what happens when you try to de-serialize a saved old version.

13.10.2   The Externalizable Interface

The Externalizable interface is provided for programmers who need finer control over the serialization of their classes. It defines two method signatures, shown in Code 13.32. The implementations of readExternal and writeExternal would

Code 13.32   The Externalizable interface, defined in the `java.io` package

```
public interface Externalizable {
    public void readExternal(ObjectInput in)
                        throws IOException, ClassNotFoundException;
    public void writeExternal(ObjectOutput out) throws IOException;
}
```

use their arguments to read or write the primitive and object attributes of the class. This process is similar to the use of `readObject` and `writeObject` mentioned in Section 13.10.1.

13.11 Review

Here are the main points that we have covered in the preceding sections:

- An `Iterator` implementation is returned by the `iterator` method of classes implementing the `Collection` interface.
- The `Enumeration` interface is a legacy interface used by some classes to permit read-only enumeration over a collection of objects.
- The `Arrays` class defines static methods to allow arrays of objects to be sorted.
- The `Comparable` interface allows a class to define an ordering for its objects, for sorting purposes.
- The `Comparator` interface allows sorts to be performed on objects not implementing the Comparable interface.
- The `FileFilter` and `FilenameFilter` classes allow file selection on arbitrary criteria.
- An empty interface, such as `Cloneable`, may be used as a marker interface.
- A single class may implement multiple interfaces.
- Methods with the same name in multiply-implemented interfaces will have separate implementations if their arguments differ.
- Identical method signatures in multiply-implemented interfaces only need to be implemented once.
- Identically-named methods that differ only in the exceptions they throw must be implemented by a single method throwing a subset of the declared exceptions.
- Identically-named fields in multiply-implemented interfaces must be distinguished by qualifying them with their defining interface name.
- Implementing the `Serializable` interface permits an object to be read and/or written externally.
- Fields which are `static` or `transient` are not written as part of a serialized object.
- When an object is de-serialized, its version identification is checked to ensure that it matches the latest class definition.
- The `Externalizable` interface allows complete control over the serialization process.

13.12   Case Study: A Stopwatch Interface

In this section, we shall look at some of the considerations that might be taken into account when defining an interface that might have alternative implementations. In discussing the design, it is important to remember that the interface defines *what* implementing classes will do, rather than *how* they will do it.

> Design an interface that could be used as the basis for classes implementing a stop watch or digital timer.

While the emphasis on design at the first stage does not absolve us from a responsibility to ensure that implementations are possible, it does mean that we are not having to give primary consideration to the loops and if-statements that are going to be used. Instead, we are mostly concerned with the messages that will be sent to implementing objects to achieve the behavior characteristic of objects implementing that particular interface. So, for a stopwatch, we need some basic operational methods that will enable us to start, stop, and reset it. We also need to be able to find out how much time has elapsed since it was started. It might also be useful to be able to suspend and resume its timing.

13.12.1   Argument and Result Types

Before we can create an outline of the interface, we need to consider what arguments and results, if any, each of these methods might have. Java has at least two classes that deal with quantities of time, `GregorianCalendar` and `Date`, both of which are defined in the `java.util` package. Looking at these might help us to ensure that our interface is reasonable and implementable. For instance, both classes represent time to the nearest millisecond, so we can avoid major problems by ensuring that we do not try to represent time with a greater precision than is possible. Given the availability of these classes, the method to return how much time has elapsed could return a Date or GregorianCalendar object, or a simpler `long` value representing a number of milliseconds.

Do any of the basic operational methods need to return a status or error indication? What should happen if a `suspend` message is sent before the timer has been started? They could return a `boolean` result to indicate success or failure, or throw an exception on invalid use; alternatively, the message could just be ignored with no ill effects.

Code 13.33 contains an outline of a design for the `StopWatch` interface that provides answers to these questions. We have decided that inappropriate messages will be ignored and the elapsed time is returned as a number of milliseconds since the timer was started. In a sense, these decisions are arbitrary, but they are reasonable.

At this stage, we should move to thinking about whether this interface is adequate and complete, and how implementations of the interface might work. This does not have to involve full detail, but should be enough to satisfy ourselves that what we have defined is sufficient for the task we have in mind. The example of a VCR interface (Code 13.1) contained a method to inquire about the status of an object. If the operational methods of StopWatch are not going to return a success or failure indication, then it might be useful if objects interacting with an implementation could

Code 13.33   Outline StopWatch interface

```
        // A simple millisecond Stop Watch interface.
interface StopWatch {
    public void reset();
    public void start();
    public void stop();
    public void suspend();
    public void resume();

        // How many milliseconds have elapsed.
    public long getElapsedTime();
}
```

inquire about its current state, in order to avoid sending inappropriate messages at any stage. This means we must think about what *set of states* a timer object may be in and how it moves from one state to another when an operational message is sent. There are four possible states that we might identify:

- RESET—the timer is set at zero, and has not yet been started. It should be in this state on creation or following receipt of a `reset` message.
- RUNNING—the timer is running and measuring elapsed time. It will be in this state immediately following a `start` message.
- STOPPED—the timer is not currently measuring elapsed time, although it has been at some point in the past. It will be in this state immediately following a `stop` message.
- SUSPENDED—the timer is not currently measuring elapsed time, although it has been at some point in the past and it might be again in the future. It will be in this state immediately following a `suspend` message.

This list describes some of the ways in which a timer will get into those states, but it is incomplete. We need to consider what happens for each state when each of the possible messages is sent. When a sensible message is sent: for instance, if the `start` message is sent to a timer in the RESET state, it will make a *transition* to the next appropriate state, in this case, RUNNING. What should happen when an inappropriate message is sent, for instance, if the `suspend` message is sent to a timer in the STOPPED state? The message could be ignored, with no resulting transition. Alternatively, we could choose to add a further ERROR state, to which a transition is made if the timer is ever sent an inappropriate message. The only way out of the ERROR state would be to send a `reset` message. We have already made the decision to ignore inappropriate messages, but programs controlling sensitive data or critical applications might need to respond in some way to inappropriate messages, which could be indications of access violations or system failures elsewhere. An ERROR state, and accompanying exception, might be appropriate in these circumstances.

Table 13.1 shows the list of valid transitions from a From State on each particular state-changing message defined in the interface. Blank entries in the table indicate that a particular message has no effect upon the current state. In other applications, these might be filled with transitions to an error state.

Table 13.1 Destination states on each valid message

		Message			
From State	Reset	Start	Stop	Suspend	Resume
RESET		RUNNING			
RUNNING	RESET		STOPPED	SUSPENDED	
STOPPED	RESET				
SUSPENDED	RESET		STOPPED		RUNNING

As a further guide to implementors, we must document additional information about the expected behavior of conforming implementations of the interface:

- In the RESET state, getElapsedTime will return 0.
- Except in the RESET state, getElapsedTime returns the sum of all time periods the timer has been in the RUNNING state since the last time it was in the START state.
- Time spent in the RESET, STOPPED, or SUSPENDED states does not count towards the elapsed time.

Describing the interface in this level of detail may seem tedious, but it is vital if implementors are to be sure they have a valid implementation, and users of implementing objects are to be confident of consistent behavior.

Code 13.34 shows a full version of the interface, including a getState inquiry function.

Code 13.34   Full version of the StopWatch interface

```
    // A simple millisecond Stop Watch interface.
interface StopWatch {
    public void reset();
    public void start();
    public void stop();
    public void suspend();
    public void resume();

    // The cumulative time while in the RUNNING state.
    public long getElapsedTime();

    // Enquiry function for the current state, returns
    // one of RESET, RUNNING, SUSPENDED and STOPPED.
    public int getState();

    // The states the watch may be in.
    public static final int RESET = 0, RUNNING = 1, SUSPENDED = 2,
                    STOPPED = 3;
}
```

13.12.2   Implementing the StopWatch Interface

The design of the StopWatch interface, described in the previous section, gave us quite a lot of insight into how an implementation must behave, without going into any detail as to how the elapsed time would be calculated. We can use that discussion to begin our implementation by using as a skeleton that part of the implementation concerned with managing the state changes listed in Table 13.1. Code 13.35 shows such a skeleton for the `TimingDevice` class.

Code 13.35 State changes within a StopWatch implementation

```java
    // Implement just the state transitions of the
    // StopWatch interface, for testing purposes.
class TimingDevice implements StopWatch {
    public TimingDevice(){
        // Make sure everything is reset initially.
        reset();
    }

    public void reset(){
        setState(RESET);
    }

    public void start(){
        if(getState() == RESET){
            setState(RUNNING);
        }
    }

    public void stop(){
        int state = getState();
        if((state == RUNNING) || (state == SUSPENDED)){
            setState(STOPPED);
        }
    }

    public void suspend(){
        if(getState() == RUNNING){
            setState(SUSPENDED);
        }
    }

    public void resume(){
        if(getState() == SUSPENDED){
            setState(RUNNING);
        }
    }

        // A dummy version of getElapsedTime to complete the implementation.
        // For testing purposes only.
    public long getElapsedTime(){
        return 0L;
    }
}
```

Code 13.36 Testing the state changes in a prototype StopWatch implementation
`(TimerStateTest.java)`

```
        // A driver program to test some of the state transitions of
        // an implementation of the StopWatch interface.
class TimerStateTest {
    public static void main(String[] args){
        boolean ok = true;
        final StopWatch timer = new TimingDevice();
        if(timer.getState() != StopWatch.RESET){
            System.err.println("State should be RESET after construction.");
            ok = false;
        }
        timer.start();
        if(timer.getState() != StopWatch.RUNNING){
            System.err.println("State should be RUNNING after start.");
            ok = false;
        }
        timer.suspend();
        if(timer.getState() != StopWatch.SUSPENDED){
            System.err.println("State should be SUSPENDED after suspend.");
            ok = false;
        }
        timer.resume();
        if(timer.getState() != StopWatch.RUNNING){
            System.err.println("State should be RUNNING after resume.");
            ok = false;
        }
        timer.stop();
        if(timer.getState() != StopWatch.STOPPED){
            System.err.println("State should be STOPPED after stop.");
            ok = false;
        }
        if(ok){
            System.out.println("Tests passed ok.");
        }
    }
}
```

With the dummy method for `getElapsedTime`, we could already test the state-change behavior of our putative implementation against the specification by creating a TimingDevice object and sending appropriate sequences of messages to it, as in Code 13.36.

Clearly this is not a thorough set of tests, but any failure will help us to correct the most basic elements of the behavior before we start work on the timing details. Where we are programming a complex class, it is often a good idea to build it in stages, making as certain as possible that each stage is working before moving on to the next.

As we discussed earlier, the `GregorianCalendar` and `Date` classes both contain functionality that we might consider using in the implementation of the timing parts of TimingDevice. However, much of the original definition of Date has been *deprecated* as of version 1.1. This means that the deprecated aspects of its definition should not be relied upon to be available in future implementations of the class. Nevertheless, the GregorianCalendar class, itself, is defined in terms of the Date class, and there is still enough non-deprecated functionality in Date for the purposes of maintaining the sort of timer we require. In particular, creating a Date object initializes it to the current time, and its `getTime` method returns this value as a `long` number of milliseconds since January 1, 1970, 00:00:00 GMT.

It might be thought that a StopWatch object will have to run continuously in parallel with the other parts of the program that are using it, so that it always has the elapsed time available when requested. This, after all, is the way that a stopwatch works in real life. However, we shall see that a StopWatch can operate as a purely passive object, only calculating the elapsed time when requested via its `getElapsedTime` method. Simplistically, as long as it knows when it was started (i.e., when it entered the RUNNING state for the first time) it can always calculate the elapsed time from then until the point of the request. Code 13.37 shows versions of the `start` and `getElapsedTime` methods that implement this idea.

Code 13.37   A Simplified version of TimingDevice

```
class TimingDevice implements StopWatch {
    ...
    public void start(){
        if(getState() == RESET){
            // Record the current time.
            setStartTime(new Date());
            setState(RUNNING);
        }
    }

    public long getElapsedTime(){
        // Find out the current time.
        Date now = new Date();
        // Return the difference between now and the start time.
        return now.getTime() - getStartTimeInMillis();
    }

    private long getStartTimeInMillis(){
        if(startTime != null){
            return startTime.getTime();
        }
        else{
            // The timer hasn't been started.
            Date dummy = new Date();
            return dummy.getTime();
        }
    }

    private void setStartTime(Date when){
        startTime = when;
    }

    // When we started.
    private Date startTime;
}
```

The problem with this implementation is that it assumes that the timer is continuously in the RUNNING state, from the time it was started. This will not be true if the timer is in the RESET, STOPPED, or SUSPENDED states when `getElapsed-Time` is called. We could, therefore, have `getElapsedTime` check the current state; if the state is RUNNING we perform this calculation, otherwise ... what? If the state is RESET then the elapsed time is zero, by definition, but in the other two states we would have needed to have calculated the elapsed time when the clock was stopped, or suspended, and use that value instead. However, there is a further hitch with the RUNNING state. Just because the timer is running at present does not mean that it has been running continuously since it was started. There might have been one or more suspensions in the meantime.

How can we cater for all of these possibilities without making a real mess of what should be a relatively simple task? We clearly need a record of how much time had cumulatively elapsed at the point the timer is suspended or stopped; so can we use this information to simplify the RUNNING case? If we modify the use of the `startTime` attribute so that it records when the timer most recently entered the RUNNING state—not just when the `start` message was sent—then we can. We will change its name to `latestStartTime` to reflect this fact. Each time the timer is reset, stopped, or suspended, the current elapsed time is calculated and stored in a another field, `elapsed`. Whenever the timer enters the RUNNING state, the current time is stored in `latestStartTime`. It is then a combination of the values in these two variables that is used when the elapsed time is requested. Code 13.38 shows the full definition of the TimingDevice class that illustrates how this functionality is achieved.

Code 13.38 Control of the elapsed time calculation

```java
        // Implementation of the StopWatch interface.
import java.util.*;

class TimingDevice implements StopWatch {
    public TimingDevice(){
        // Make sure everything is reset to start with.
        reset();
    }

    public void reset(){
        setState(RESET);
        setElapsed(0);
    }

    public void start(){
        if(getState() == RESET){
            setLatestStartTime(new Date());
            setState(RUNNING);
        }
    }

    public void stop(){
        if(getState() == RUNNING){
```

Code 13.38   (*Continued*)

```
            // Calculate the elapsed time at this point.
            recordElapsedTime();
            setState(STOPPED);
        }
        else if(getState() == SUSPENDED){
            setState(STOPPED);
        }
        else{
            // Inappropriate action.
        }
    }

    public void suspend(){
        if(getState() == RUNNING){
            recordElapsedTime();
            setState(SUSPENDED);
        }
    }

    public void resume(){
        if(getState() == SUSPENDED){
            // Set the resumption time.
            setLatestStartTime(new Date());
            setState(RUNNING);
        }
    }

    public long getElapsedTime(){
        // We must calculate how much time has passed since the
        // elapsed time was last calculated.
        long increment = 0;
        if(getState() == RUNNING){
            Date now = new Date();
            increment = now.getTime()-getStartTimeInMillis();
        }
        // Set the new value.
        setElapsed(getElapsed() + increment);
        return getElapsed();
    }

    public int getState(){
        return state;
    }

    private void setState(int s){
        state = s;
    }

        // Calculate how much has elapsed to this point.
    private void recordElapsedTime(){
        Date now = new Date();
        // Find out how much time has passed since
```

(*Continued*)

Code 13.38   *(Continued)*

```
         // latestStartTime.
         long increment = now.getTime()-getStartTimeInMillis();
         // Add it in to what has elapsed so far.
         setElapsed(getElapsed()+increment);
      }

      private long getElapsed(){
         return elapsed;
      }

      private void setElapsed(long time){
         elapsed = time;
      }

      private long getStartTimeInMillis(){
         return getLatestStartTime().getTime();
      }

      private Date getLatestStartTime(){
         return latestStartTime;
      }

      private void setLatestStartTime(Date now){
         latestStartTime = now;
      }

      // Current state: RESET, RUNNING, SUSPENDED, STOPPED.
      private int state = RESET;
      // Keep track of the most recent start time and
      // how much time has elapsed in the preceding periods.
      private Date latestStartTime;
      private long elapsed = 0;
   }
```

13.12.3   Testing the StopWatch Implementation

Having implemented the elapsed time calculation, this needs testing. The `sleep` method of the `Thread` class is defined as follows:

```
         // Suspend the current thread for the given number
         // of milliseconds.
      public static void sleep(long milliseconds)
                              throws InterruptedException;
```

This provides a convenient general way of allowing time to pass in a program by putting the program to sleep for the given period. We shall utilize this to allow known periods of time to elapse. Its argument is the number of milliseconds to sleep for, so a value of 5000 means 5 seconds. The sleep method can throw an `InterruptedException` exception, so calls to it should be enclosed within a try statement. Code 13.39 shows some statements to test a timer's basic operations with

Code 13.39   Testing some of TimingDevice functionality (`TimingDeviceMain.java`)

```
            // Simple timing tests of a TimingDevice implementation.
class TimingDeviceMain {
    public static void main(String[] args){
        try {
            final StopWatch timer = new TimingDevice();
            final long timeToSleep = 5000L;

            // A basic timing test.
            timer.start();
            Thread.sleep(timeToSleep);
            timer.stop();
            System.out.println("Elapsed time = "+timer.getElapsedTime()+
                    " which should be about "+timeToSleep+" milliseconds.");

            // Reset for the second test.
            timer.reset();
            // Include a suspend-resume pair in the timing period.
            timer.start();
            Thread.sleep(timeToSleep);
            timer.suspend();
            Thread.sleep(timeToSleep);
            timer.resume();
            Thread.sleep(timeToSleep);
            System.out.println("Elapsed time = "+timer.getElapsedTime()+
                    " which should be about "+2*timeToSleep+
                    " milliseconds.");
        }
        catch(InterruptedException e){
            System.err.println(e);
        }
    }
}
```

a couple of simple start-stop and start-suspend-resume sequences. An example of the output from running this program might be as follows:

```
Elapsed time = 5007 which should be about 5000 milliseconds.
Elapsed time = 9994 which should be about 10000 milliseconds.
```

The results given by these test programs will not exactly match the sleep times because there are small time overheads associated with what is going on in the program. Nevertheless, the answers should be within a few milliseconds of what we would expect.

Exercise 13.29   Use the `TimingDevice` class to time how long it takes to sort a large array of `Student` objects.

Exercise 13.30   For increased accuracy, sort the same set of data repeatedly, varying numbers of times. Use the `suspend` and `resume` methods between iterations while the unsorted data is recreated each time.

Exercise 13.31   Compare the time it takes to sort randomly ordered data with data that is already sorted.

Exercise 13.32   Add a further field to the StopWatch interface, ERROR. Create a new implementation of the interface so that inappropriate transitions always cause a timer to enter the ERROR state, rather than ignoring them. Only a `reset` will cause the timer to leave the ERROR state. Calls to `getElapsedTime` while in the ERROR state should result in a RuntimeException exception being thrown. You may reuse as much of the TimingDevice class as you wish in creating your new implementation.

Exercise 13.33   Does the addition of an ERROR field to the interface make Timing-Device an invalid implementation?

Exercise 13.34   The more sophisticated card game described in Exercise 10.9 means that players are potentially faced with several decisions to be made in each round:

- A player might randomly play a card that follows suit.
- A player might always play their highest card of the required suit, in an attempt to win.
- A player starting a round might be able to determine that they have a definite winning card, from those that have been played in previous rounds.
- A player unable to follow suit in a round must make a decision about the best card to discard.
- A player who is able to follow suit, but is unable to win the round, might discard the lowest card of the required suit.
- . . . and so on.

These decisions allow for a range of possible player strategies to be developed, all of which are defined by classes that implement the same interface. Design a `CardPlayer` interface that contains the required methods for any player to participate in the game. Develop a range of strategic implementations that implement this interface, and play the different versions off against each other.

In this chapter, we have described *interface inheritance*—the way in which interfaces may be used to describe *what* implementing classes must do, rather than *how* they must do it. This allows objects to interact with objects of other classes implementing a particular interface, purely in terms of the interface definition. This is permitted by Java's rules of *polymorphism*, which state that an object of a sub type (implementing class) may be used anywhere that an object of its super type (interface) is required. Issues of polymorphism are particularly important in the next chapter, when we look at *class inheritance*.

CHAPTER 14

Class Inheritance

In this chapter, we introduce the concept of class inheritance in Java. Inheritance is one of the distinguishing features of object-oriented languages and it is a powerful and expressive capability. Inheritance provides the ability to derive new classes that inherit much of their code and functionality from the classes on which they are based. Among other things, this permits software re-use and further exploitation of polymorphism.

14.1 The Need for Re-use

Many programming projects involve different classes that bear quite a strong similarity to each other. We have seen several pairs of similar classes in previous chapters, such as `ArrayList` and `LinkedList`, `NoFrillsVCR` and `UpMarketVCR`, and `SimpleShip` and `Ship`. While each class of a pair has functionality which is distinctive of its particular role, much of their functionality is identical. A mechanism that allowed the common aspects to be shared would clearly be advantageous, from the viewpoint of smaller programs, and code maintenance. As we shall see, these are some of the benefits that inheritance brings. However, before we look at how inheritance does this, we consider alternative approaches to sharing common functionality.

14.1.1 Alternatives to Inheritance

As an illustration of what inheritance provides that other programming styles do not, consider the characteristics of the general Ship class that we have used in earlier chapters. All ships have attributes, such as their current position, course and name. We have also suggested that some ships might carry passengers and/or cargo. In effect, we have identified typical characteristics possessed by different sorts of ships and lumped them all together in a single class definition. Clearly, not all ships will necessarily be able to carry bulky cargo—a passenger ferry operating in the English Lake District, for instance; not all ships will carry ordinary fare-paying passengers—an ocean-going oil tanker, for instance.

With our current model of ships, and the Java facilities we have met so far, there are three possible ways of modeling vessels in such a way that common characteristics are shared, but differences can also be represented:

1. Define a different class for each category of ship. These new classes would re-implement most of the functionality and attributes of a common Ship class, but lack those things which do not apply to ships of the new class, and add new parts for distinctive features.
2. Define a single Ship class containing functionality for every different type of ship. This would be an all singing, all dancing class.
3. Add a ship-type attribute to the Ship class that denotes the category of each particular ship object. Methods would then disallow inappropriate usage according to the value of this attribute.

None of these solutions is particularly satisfactory.

1. The first approach means we have to write a lot of duplicate code in each class for the common elements that do not change from one ship to another (such as movement and position calculation).
2. The second approach means we have no guarantees that no one will inappropriately try to use the cargo-manipulating methods on a passenger ferry, for instance. In effect, the only means of identifying what sort of vessel it is comes from its programmer-defined name, which might be entirely arbitrary. No compile-time or runtime checks will be possible as safeguards against inappropriate method use.
3. The third approach looks to be the best of the three. However, it still has the disadvantage that every specialist method has to be cluttered up with tests to ensure that it has only been called on the correct sort of ship.

Code 14.1 illustrates the third approach.

As an illustration of the problems we get if we try to build such tagged classes, suppose we decide to introduce a new type of boat called `Dinghy`. As well as adding dinghy-specific methods to the class to handle behavior involving oars, we need to examine every type-dependent method and ensure that it is programmed correctly for the new type. Some changes that are required will not be immediately obvious. In Code 14.1, it is no longer sufficient to simply reject the `loadCargo` message on the basis of whether the type is PassengerShip or not; the test must either be amended to be an exclusive test that rejects Dinghys, too, or completely changed to be an inclusive test that checks for the type being CargoShip or Ferry. There will be many such situations to be thought about carefully and the process of making such changes to a working class contains many opportunities for getting things wrong. Not only is the Dinghy behavior unlikely to work properly, but we risk introducing errors into previously working code.

14.1.2 Delegation

A fourth alternative to inheritance is provided by *delegation*. This is probably the most viable alternative if inheritance is not available in a language. Using delegation, a single class would be created that implements the attributes and behavior common to all types of ship. Specialist classes would then be created to define the distinctive characteristics of the more detailed types. Each specialist class would contain an

Code 14.1   Tagging an object with its type (unattractive)

```
class Boat {
    // Possible types of boat.
    public static int CargoShip = 0, PassengerShip = 1, Ferry = 2;

    public Boat(String name, int type){
        this.name = name;
        this.type = type;
        ...
    }

    public void loadCargo(Cargo c){
        if(getType() != PassengerShip){
          // Ok
          ...
        }
        else{
          // Inappropriate use.
          ...
        }
    }
    ...
    // Which type of Boat. Used to detect appropriate use of methods.
    private final int type;
    private final String name;
}
```

attribute referring to an object of the common-behavior class. In addition to their specialist methods, they would also define simplified methods for the common behavior. Messages received by these common-behavior methods would be delegated directly to the common-class attribute. Code 14.2 illustrates this approach.

When a CargoShip object receives a setCourse message, it passes it straight on to its ship attribute. This means that a cargo ship maintains none of the common attributes for itself; all of these are maintained solely by its delegate. An advantage of delegation is that any changes or enhancements to the common functionality only affect the definition of the delegate class, and modifications to the delegating classes will only be required if the changes involve result-type or argument alterations, or additional methods.

14.1.3   Inheritance as a Solution

It is rare for a single solution to meet the objections of all competing alternatives, but inheritance does so in the case of those listed in Section 14.1.1. The main reason is that it tackles the underlying problem in a completely different fashion from the ideas we suggested there. Central to inheritance is the task of isolating the common elements of the classes which have related behavior and attributes, as we did with delegation in Section 14.1.2. These common elements are located in what is known as a *super class*. The various distinctive features of the different classes—and only the

Code 14.2   Delegation as an alternative to inheritance

```
class CargoShip {
    public CargoShip(String name){
        // Create the delegated object.
        ship = new Ship(name);
        ...
    }
    ...
    public void setCourse(double c){
        // Delegate.
        getShip().setCourse(c);
    }

    public void loadCargo(Cargo c){
        // Specialist behavior, don't delegate.
        addCargo(c);
    }
    ...
        // Return a reference to the object implementing the common
        // functionality.
    private Ship getShip(){
        return ship;
    }

    private final Ship ship;
}
```

distinctive features—are then placed in new *sub classes* which inherit the common features from their super class.

We say that sub classes *derive* their behavior from the super class on which they are based. The process of deriving sub classes from super classes addresses the three problem areas of Section 14.1.1 in the following ways:

- The derivation process allows the code of the super class to be accessed directly via the sub classes, so no duplicate code needs to be written. A benefit of this is that, if an error is found in the common code, it only needs to be fixed in one class (the super class) rather than many.
- Specialization methods, such as `loadCargo`, are only written in the sub classes of vessels that are able to carry cargo, so it is not possible to send such messages to ships unable to respond to them.
- There is no cluttering of code with tests of the object's type.
- All objects are aware of their dynamic type without needing an explicit field to denote this. This is also much more secure than relying on programmers to exercise discipline in their choice of identifiers.

On first hearing, inheritance sounds rather like delegation; however, unlike delegation, the sub classes do not also have to include definitions of the methods defined in the super class.[1]

---

[1] As we shall see, however, there are some occasions when they do for the purposes of *overriding*.

It will be easier to illustrate the principles of inheritance if we look initially at a smaller example than the Ship class, which we do in the next section.

14.2   An Example of Inheritance

As an introduction to the way in which inheritance is achieved in Java, consider the following scenario:

> A company manufactures a range of different controllers which are attached to heaters. A heater's temperature setting is able to be varied over a small range, but a controller's sophistication in manipulating a heater varies according to its price. All heater controllers have basic on/off switches, but the simplest controller is unable to vary the temperature setting of its attached device. At the next level of sophistication, limited temperature level control is possible within the device's allowed range. The most sophisticated controllers allow varying numbers of on/off time periods, in addition to temperature level setting.

What is described here is a range of different controllers with some attributes and behavior in common, in addition to their own distinctive features. This makes them prime candidates for describing in an *inheritance hierarchy*, so that common functionality is shared in a super class and distinctive functionality introduced in different sub classes. In reality, heater controller objects would be connected to a physical heating device, but such real-world device manipulation is beyond the scope of this book. Instead, we have chosen to simulate such operation by attaching a controller to an object of class `Heater` that provides a GUI displaying the temperature setting of a heating device, and whether it is on (green) or off (red). Figure 14.1 illustrates a sample display consisting of five Heater objects, two of which are off (the fourth and fifth) and the remainder of which are on. The numerical values represent the (fixed) temperature at which the heating devices are set.

14.2.1   The HeaterController Class

In designing a suitable inheritance hierarchy for the family of controllers, we start by isolating those elements that are common to all types of controllers—the state of being either on or off, and the ability to externally alter this state. We describe these elements in the `HeaterController` class, shown in Code 14.3. This will be the super class for all controller classes to be created, because all controllers will share this functionality. Such a class is little different from any other class we have defined—it has public interface methods (`switchOn`, `switchOff`, and `isOn`), attributes (`heater`

Figure 14.1 Visualization of the state of five Heater objects (`HeaterControllerMain. java`)

Code 14.3   Basic functionality of all controllers (`HeaterController.java`)

```java
        // A heater controller with only on/off capability.
class HeaterController {
        // Public status mutators.
    public void switchOn(){
        setOn(true);
    }

    public void switchOff(){
        setOn(false);
    }

        // Public enquiry method.
    public boolean isOn(){
        return getOn();
    }

        // Protected (non-public) internal methods.
    protected boolean getOn(){
        return on;
    }

    protected void setOn(boolean state){
        if(on != state){
            // A change of state.
            on = state;
        }
        // Make sure that the heater always matches this state.
        getHeater().setOn(on);
    }

    protected Heater getHeater(){
        return heater;
    }

    // The (GUI) device to which we are attached.
    private final Heater heater = new Heater();

    // The current state of the heater.
    private boolean isOn;
    {    // Make sure the heater is initially off.
        switchOff();
    }
}
```

and on), accessors (`getOn` and `getHeater`), and a mutator (`setOn`). The only special provision made for the fact that we are going to derive other classes from it is the use of the `protected` reserved word, rather than `private`, for three of its non-public methods. We shall explain the meaning of `protected` in Section 14.7.1. HeaterController objects are used just like any others; Code 14.4 shows a simple example.

Code 14.4   Using the basic functionality of a HeaterController

```
HeaterController c = new HeaterController();

// Warm up the room.
c.switchOn();
...
// The room is warm enough - switch the heater off.
c.switchOff();
```

Switching the controller on or off results in the `setOn` method relaying an appropriate message to the Heater device it is controlling. This is similar to the idea of pressing a switch on a wall-mounted device causing an electrical signal to be transmitted to a heating element.

Figure 14.1 results from running the program shown in Code 14.5. This example creates a `HeaterControllerDemo` object to randomly turn Heater objects on and off via an array of Heater-Controllers.

Code 14.5   Randomly switch HeaterController objects (`HeaterControllerDemo.java`)

```
    /* Demonstration rig for the HeaterController class.
     * Create an arbitrary number of HeaterControllers and
     * randomly turn them on and off.
     * A GUI provides a visualization via the Heater class.
     */
class HeaterControllerDemo {
    // Repeatedly select a random controller.
    // Change its state at random intervals.
    public void run(){
        while(true){
            // Select a random controller.
            final HeaterController c = randomController();
            // Change its state if possible.
            if(turnItOff()){
                if(c.isOn()){
                    c.switchOff();
                }
            }
            else{
                c.switchOn();
            }
            // Pause a little.
            delay();
        }
    }

    // Randomly decide whether to turn a controller off.
    private boolean turnItOff(){
        return Math.random() < 0.5;
    }
```

(Continued)

Code 14.5   (*Continued*)

```
        // Randomly select a controller to adjust
    private HeaterController randomController(){
        final HeaterController[] controllers = getControllers();
        // Which controller to select.
        int which = (int) (Math.random()*controllers.length);
        return controllers[which];
    }

    private void delay(){
        try{
            // Sleep for 1 second.
            Thread.sleep(1000);
        }
        catch(InterruptedException e){
        }
    }

    private HeaterController[] getControllers(){
        return controllers;
    }

    // Create an arbitrary number of HeaterController objects
    // to be manipulated.
    // Initialize the individual controller objects.
    private final HeaterController[] controllers;
    {
        // How many controllers to create.
        final int numControllers = 5;
        controllers = new HeaterController[numControllers];
        for(int i = 0; i < numControllers; i++){
            controllers[i] = new HeaterController();
        }
    }
}
```

14.2.2   Extending the HeaterController Class

When we come to define a class to represent the next degree of controller sophistication, we wish to provide control of Heater objects that allows them both to be switched on and off and to have their temperature level setting adjusted. Inheritance allows us to *extend* our existing HeaterController class in order both to re-use the functionality it provides and to add further methods particular to a new level-varying class, which we shall call `VariableController`. How this is achieved is shown in Code 14.6.

The class header of VariableController differs from those we have seen so far in its use of the reserved word `extends`. This indicates that VariableController is not a complete class in its own right, but a *sub class* of the super class whose name immediately follows `extends`. As we would expect, a VariableController object can

Code 14.6   VariableController as a sub class of HeaterController (`VariableController.java`)

```java
        // A class that extends the facilities of its super class,
        // HeaterController, to add temperature-level setting.
class VariableController extends HeaterController {
    // Class constants for basic temperatures.
    public static final int DefaultLevel = 16,
                            MinLevel = 5, MaxLevel = 30;

    // Additional attributes and methods peculiar to
    // VariableController functionality.

        // An accessor for the attached heater's current
        // temperature level.
    public int getLevel(){
        // The device keeps track of its current temperature setting.
        return getHeater().getTemperature();
    }

        // Set the heater's level within an allowed range.
    public void setLevel(int level) throws RuntimeException {
        if((MinLevel <= level) && (level <= MaxLevel)){
            // Adjust the heater.
            getHeater().setTemperature(level);
        }
        else{
            // The value is out of the allowed range.
            throw new RuntimeException("Illegal level setting: "+level);
        }
    }
}
```

Code 14.7   Sub classes typically have their own functionality

```java
VariableController v = new VariableController();
...
if(v.getLevel() == v.MinLevel){
    v.setLevel(v.DefaultLevel);
}
...
```

respond to messages relating to the functionality it defines for itself, as illustrated in
Code 14.7.

The temperature level to be set is checked by its setLevel method against
a valid range, before being relayed to the Heater. An inappropriate level results
in an exception being thrown. Note that there is no need for a VariableController
to maintain its own level attribute because the Heater does this. Although it is
sometimes necessary to duplicate such information, having a value defined in two
different places is a recipe for the two values becoming inconsistent, and we will
often try to avoid it.

Code 14.8   Sub classes inherit their super class's public interface

```
VariableController v = new VariableController();

// Warm up the room.
v.switchOn();
...
// The room is warm enough - switch the heater off.
v.switchOff();
```

In addition to providing its own distinctive functionality, the rules of inheritance state that a sub class inherits all of the attributes and methods of its super class. This means, in effect, that the VariableController class automatically contains the switchOn, switchOff, isOn, getOn, setOn, and getHeater methods, and the on and heater attributes, even though they are not listed directly in the VariableController class body. It is important to distinguish this feature of inheritance from the related idea of delegation, discussed in Section 14.1.2. One thing that inheritance provides, therefore, is *code re-use* without duplication. As well as responding to messages distinctive of a VariableController (getLevel and setLevel), such objects respond equally to the public interface messages (isOn, switchOn, and switchOff), in exactly the same way that simpler Heater-Controller objects do. Compare Code 14.8 with Code 14.4, which illustrates this.

A demonstration of the VariableController class is available in the file VariableControllerMain.java. This turns Heater objects on and off via their attached controller, and randomly alters their temperature setting. Its appearance is shown in Figure 14.2. The fact that a VariableController object has all of the functionality of a more basic HeaterController object leads us to the important statement that:

A VariableController object *is also a* HeaterController object.

By this we mean that we can always use a VariableController object wherever a plain HeaterController object is required, because it contains all of the same methods and attributes. In fact, we can generalize this to say that:

An instance of a sub class may be used anywhere that an instance of its super class is required. In other words, a sub class instance *is an* instance of the super class.

Figure 14.2   Visualization of Heaters controlled with VariableControllers (Visual-ControllerMain.java)

Code 14.9   Polymorphism allows a sub class reference to be stored in a super class variable

```
HeaterController c = new VariableController();

// Warm up the room.
c.switchOn();
...
// The room is warm enough - switch the heater off.
c.switchOff();
```

A consequence of this is that we could write Code 14.8 as in Code 14.9. However, the opposite relationship is not allowed, so the following assignment is illegal.

```
// Illegal: the sub class/super class relationship
VariableController vc = new HeaterController();
```

The compiler will reject it with a message such as:

```
Incompatible type for declaration. Explicit cast needed to convert
HeaterController to VariableController.
```

Attempting to correct this by including a cast will keep the compiler happy.

```
VariableController vc = (VariableController) new HeaterController();
```

However, this simply defers the inevitable until runtime, when a ClassCast-Exception exception will occur. Since the object referred to by vc is only an instance of the more basic HeaterController class, it would be unable to respond to messages such as setLevel. Hence, an assignment of a super-type reference to a sub-type variable is always treated as unsafe.

This principle is a further example of *polymorphism* in Java, which was introduced in the context of interfaces in Section 13.3.2. This leads us to note that the sub classing relationship with extends bears a strong resemblance to the sub-typing relationship with implements. The most significant difference, however, is that when a class is extended, we do not have to redefine the bodies of the methods in the super class—their definitions are inherited by the sub class. This has important implications when we consider the issue of *multiple inheritance*, which is permitted with interfaces but not permitted with class inheritance (see Section 14.3.2). In Section 14.4, we shall take a look at some further examples of inheritance to supplement the discussion in this section. Before that, however, we shall explore the nature of the is-a relationship, that is crucial in helping us to understand polymorphism and inheritance.

14.3   The Is-A and Has-A Relationships

When analyzing a problem and looking for the components that will serve as the basis for the essential classes of the solution, it is important to bear in mind the possibility of using inheritance relationships as part of the design. This is what we did with the heating controller example of the previous section. It is quite likely that such relationships will not always be as immediately obvious from the problem description as they were in that case. Instead, they will have to be *synthesized* from the objects and classes that have been identified as part of the description analysis.

Consider the problem of writing a program to play a game of chess against a human opponent. The obvious objects in the problem are the human player, the computer player, the board, the various pieces of the game—king, queen, rook, knight, bishop, and pawn—and possibly the squares, on the board. In such a complex problem, it is well worth spending time at the design stage looking for relationships between classes, because it could save us a good deal of effort at the implementation stage. We might start by looking for relationships between these objects that indicate common attributes and/or common behavior that will allow us to capture those common features in one or more super classes, from which more specialized sub classes are then derived. As a first attempt, the human player and computer player are likely to share common features. Looking further, we might think that the players, the squares, and the piece types all have the concept of color in common, so that might be one possibility for a super class containing just color information. However, a class consisting of a single attribute (even plus its accessor and mutator) is a little tenuous, and further thought might also lead us to recognize that the color of the board's squares is completely unrelated to the color of the pieces. So we have one appropriate example, and one inappropriate. How can we make sure that we identify appropriate inheritance relationships?

A particularly helpful guide to identifying the inheritance relationship is to characterize it as an *is-a relationship*, as we did in the previous section. What this means is that if we can say that one object *is a sort of* or *is a type of* some class or category, then we may be able to represent this as an inheritance relationship between the object's class and the category. For instance, a cargo ship is a type of vessel, a German Shepherd is a sort of dog, a flute is a sort of wind instrument, and so on. In the chess program, a rook is a type of piece, as are the king, queen, knight, bishop, and pawn. These different piece types have attributes and behavior in common—color, position on the board, and the fact that they are not allowed to move to a square containing a piece of their own color—as well as their own distinctive characteristics—movement geometry, being in check, etc. Similarly, the human and computer objects are both players or opponents with aspects in common (a human player is-a player and a computer player is-a player). From this we can clearly see why an inheritance relationship involving color is inappropriate: a rook is not a color, neither is a player. Instead we would say that a piece *has-a* color, a player *has-a* color, a vessel *has-a* name. The *has-a* relationship represents an attribute of a class or object, and it is sometimes referred to as *aggregation*. It is very common for programmers new to inheritance to confuse the is-a and has-a relationships, so it is important that you are clear in your mind about the difference.

The is-a relationship corresponds to the sub type/super type relationship of polymorphism. This means that we can use a VariableController wherever an ordinary HeaterController is needed, or a `Rook` wherever a basic `ChessPiece` is needed; a VariableController *is a* HeaterController by inheritance, and a Rook *is a* ChessPiece. Any message that may be sent to a HeaterController may be sent to a VariableController, and any message that may be sent to a ChessPiece may be sent to a Rook (or `Knight`, `Bishop`, `King`, `Queen`, `Pawn`).

In Section 14.4, we provide some further examples of inheritance that reinforce the is-a relationship. We do this in the context of using inheritance for the purpose of specialization.

14.3.1   Inappropriate Inheritance

The characterization of inheritance as representing an is-a relationship is an important one. The fact that polymorphism allows a sub class object to be used wherever a super class reference is required, reinforces the strength of this relationship. It follows that it is important to be able to recognize where inheritance is not the correct relationship to be used between classes, and it is so easy to get this wrong that it is worth providing some examples to illustrate the problem.

An inheritance relationship is often mistakenly used to create a new class simply because an existing class supplies most of the functionality that is required by the new class, and the additional functionality can be supplied via a few extra methods. An example of this can be seen in the relationship between the Stack and Vector classes defined in the java.util package. The Stack class defines the basic push and pop methods, as well as empty, peek (examine the top item without removing it), and search (look for an item in the stack). It has been built on a Vector because a Vector already provides a convenient class to manage an arbitrary-sized collection of data. In Section 10.7, we outlined the semantics of a stack as being a last in, first out (LIFO) data structure: access to the items stored in the stack should be entirely via the top-most item. The problem with Stack extending Vector is that, as a consequence, it inherits all of the Vector's methods that have nothing to do with stack-like behavior. It is perfectly possible to send messages such as set and get to access arbitrary items within the underlying collection. This should not be possible with a Stack; a proper LIFO stack is not a Vector. A much better approach would be to design a class that utilized a Vector's data collection abilities via a Vector attribute, to which push and pop operations delegate their requirements. This is the approach we took with the CardQueue and CardStack classes in Section 10.7.

As a further example, consider a class required to return random numbers over a fixed integer range: 1 . . . 6, say, in order to simulate the rolls of a die. The Random class, defined in java.util, contains a nextInt method that takes an argument, n, and returns a random number in the range 0 . . . (n-1). It is tempting to define a Die class as in Code 14.10.

While this class works perfectly adequately, it is inappropriate because a Die is not a general purpose random number generator, although its definition suggests that it is. What does it mean to send a nextDouble message to a Die, for instance, or a nextInt message without an argument; yet both are perfectly possible because of the way it has been implemented? A more appropriate implementation is shown in Code 14.11.

Once again, the preferred solution is to use an attribute of the existing functional class, and delegate to it. We prefer to say that a Die has a Random attribute, rather than that it is a Random number generator. Similarly, a Stack has a Vector attribute, but it is not a general purpose collection.

Code 14.10   Inappropriate inheritance to implement a die

```java
import java.util.Random;

    // Inappropriate inheritance
class Die extends Random {
        // Return an integer in the range 1..6
    public int roll(){
        final int range = 6;
        // Use the inherited nextInt method.
        return 1+nextInt(range);
    }
}
```

Code 14.11   A die implemented with a Random attribute (`Die.java`)

```java
import java.util.Random;

    // Simulate the roll of a die.
class Die {
        // Return an integer in the range 1..6
    public int roll(){
        final int range = 6;
        return 1+getRand().nextInt(range);
    }

    protected Random getRand(){
        return rand;
    }

    private static final Random rand = new Random();
}
```

Exercise 14.1   Which of the following pairs are appropriate is-a relationships and which are has-a relationships?

```
Dog, Animal
Aircraft, Wing
Ferry, Boat
Person, Parent
Niece, Uncle
Window Manager, GUI
Computer, Chip
Computer, Hardware
Card, Deck
Fruit, Tomato
Apple, Pip
Polygon, Point
Car, Fuel Tank
```

For those that are is-a relationships, indicate which is the super class and which is the sub class.

Exercise 14.2   Consider the pair of classes, `Teacher` and `Principal`. Is there a single obvious is-a or has-a relationship between these?

14.3.2   Multiple Inheritance

An important decision in the design of object-oriented programming languages is whether to permit *multiple inheritance* or not. Multiple inheritance means that a class directly extends more than one class, or implements more than one interface.[2] There are some situations in which extending multiple classes might seem reasonable. Consider a database maintained by a school, in which items of data are held on the teaching staff (`Teacher`) and the parents of pupils in the school (`Parent`). A teacher who is also a parent in the school might be represented by a class `ParentTeacher`, that extends both Teacher and Parent for its functionality. A problem arises if the ParentTeacher class inherits distinct versions of the same method from its two super classes; which should receive a matching message?

We saw in Section 13.9.1 that implementing multiple interfaces is permitted in Java, and there are rules to resolve conflicts when similar definitions appear in the multiple interfaces. There is not a problem with implementing multiple interfaces because there will only be a single implementation of the matching signatures. It is the problem of such conflict resolution that is one of the reasons for the decision to rule that multiple inheritance of classes is *not* permitted. For classes, Java is a *single inheritance* language. However, there is nothing to prevent a class from extending a class in addition to implementing one or more interfaces. (In effect, this happens whenever a class implements an interface, since all classes extend the Object class by default.) The `extends` clause always precedes the `implements` clause in the class header, for instance,

```
class SubClass extends SuperClass implements Interf1, Interf2
```

Furthermore, an interface is permitted to extend one or more interfaces, as shown in Code 14.12. Clearly, because these are all interfaces, the `ParentTeacher` interface inherits no implementation from its super-type interfaces.

14.3.3   Downcasts and Upcasts

In Section 10.2.2, we noted that a cast from the Object super type to a more detailed type is called a *downcast*; for example,

```
// Downcast from Object to VariableController.
VariableController controller = (VariableController) list.getFirst();
```

Conversely, when an object reference of a sub type is stored in a variable of one of

---

[2] Note that multiple inheritance does not refer to a class extending a super class, where that super class extends its own super class. That is always permitted.

Code 14.12   An interface may extend one or more interfaces

```
interface Teacher {
    // ...
}

interface Parent {
    // ...
}

interface ParentTeacher extends Parent, Teacher {
    // ...
}
```

its super types, this is referred to as an *upcast*; for example,

```
// Upcast from VariableController to Object.
list.add(controller);
```

Java's rules of *polymorphism* mean that an explicit upcast is not usually required. The terms refer to the direction in which the inheritance hierarchy is traversed as a result of the cast. Super classes are always considered to be above sub classes in the hierarchy, so the Object class is always the uppermost class in any object's type hierarchy, and the object's dynamic type is always the lowest. The fact that multiple inheritance for classes is disallowed in Java means that the class hierarchy is always linear. That for interfaces, however, may be more branching. An upcast, therefore, means a cast in the direction of the Object super class, whereas a downcast means a cast in the direction of the dynamic type of the object.

14.4   Inheritance for Specialization

In Section 14.2, we used an example involving heating controllers to introduce inheritance at the simplest level. In that example, the VariableController class extended the capabilities of its super class by adding the ability to manipulate the temperature level of a heating device to which it was attached. We noted that, by virtue of polymorphism, it is possible to use a VariableController wherever an object of its super class might be required, because it possessed all of the HeaterController's functionality as well as its own. It is important to note that the methods of VariableController did not modify the behavior of its super class in any way; in this respect it provides an example of inheritance purely for the purpose of extending behavior. In later sections, we shall see some ways in which a sub class extends but also modifies the super class behavior in various ways. In this section, we provide a few more examples of super class and sub class pairings to reinforce the issues involved. As a result, this will throw up some other issues that need addressing in relation to the way in which the super class and sub class elements of an extending class relate to one another.

A nice example of simple sub class extension is provided by the LineNumber-Reader class of the java.io package (Code 14.13). This extends the Buffered-Reader class by keeping track of the line number of the input file to which the

Code 14.13   An outline of LineNumberReader defined in the `java.io` package

```
public class LineNumberReader extends BufferedReader {
    ...
    public int getLineNumber(){
        ...
    }

    public void setLineNumber(int lineNumber){
        ...
    }
    ...
}
```

object refers. It provides an accessor (`getLineNumber`) and a mutator (`setLine-Number`) for the attribute, that are additional to the methods defined in Buffered-Reader. Otherwise, LineNumberReader provides the same public interface as its super class via inheritance. A principle to bear in mind when considering the relationship between a sub class and its super class is that *inheritance represents specialization*. By this we mean that a sub class usually provides a more specialized service to clients than its super class—in this case, the specialization is line numbering. If you like, the sub class adds value to the super class, as we saw with the VariableController class adding further capabilities to the basic HeaterController class.

As a further example of specialization, consider a supermarket wishing to maintain a database of details of the items it sells. We might create a class, `Sellable-Item`, that maintains a common set of attributes for all items on sale: item description, manufacturer, item price, and so on. Some, but not all, items will be perishable and require an associated Sell-by (or Best-before) date. It would not be appropriate to include such an attribute in the general SellableItem class, so we would create a sub class, `PerishableItem`, that extends SellableItem in order to encapsulate this additional information (Code 14.14). Once again, Perishable-Item represents a specialization of the more general class of which it is an extension.

Code 14.14   A class for perishable supermarket items

```
class PerishableItem extends SellableItem {
    ...
    public Date getSellbyDate(){
        return sellBy;
    }
    ...
    private final Date sellBy;
}
```

Code 14.15   A balance-holding account class (`BalanceAccount.java`)

```java
class BalanceAccount {
    public void credit(long amount) throws RuntimeException {
        if(amount < 0){
            throw new RuntimeException("Negative credit: "+amount+
                                       " is not allowed.");
        }
        setBalance(getBalance()+amount);
    }

    public void debit(long amount) throws RuntimeException {
        if(amount < 0){
            throw new RuntimeException("Negative debit: "+amount+
                                       " is not allowed.");
        }
        setBalance(getBalance()-amount);
    }

    public long getBalance(){
        return balance;
    }

    private void setBalance(long b) {
        balance = b;
    }

    private long balance = 0L;
}
```

Exercise 14.3   The class `BalanceAccount` (Code 14.15) has an attribute, `balance`, of type `long`, with a public accessor and private mutator.

It has public `credit` and `debit` methods which take a single argument of type `long`, representing an amount to be added to or subtracted from the balance. Both throw a RuntimeException if their argument value is less than zero.

Define the class `PayInterestAccount`, which is a sub class of Balance-Account. It has an attribute, `rate`, of type `double` with public accessor and mutator methods. This represents a percentage interest rate, so a value of `1.0` means that one percent interest is paid on the balance in the account. Its public method, `creditInterest`, adds an amount of interest to the current balance in the account. The amount of interest to add is 1/12 of the rate as a percentage, multiplied by the current balance. For instance, given a balance of 1000 and a rate of 1.0, the amount credited would be $(1000 \times 1.0 \div 100) \div 12$.

What will happen if the account balance is negative when a `creditInterest` message is received? What *should* happen in your opinion? Define a main method to test the implementations of BalanceAccount and PayInterestAccount.

Exercise 14.4   The Radio class (Code 14.16) has a single attribute, `frequency`, of type double, with a public accessor and mutator.

Code 14.16   A class maintaining a radio frequency attribute (`Radio.java`)

```java
class Radio {
    // Radios cannot be set below this frequency.
    public static final double MIN_FREQUENCY = 80000000.0;
    // Step up or down by the following amount.
    public static final double INCREMENT = 0.1;

    public void up(){
        try{
            setFrequency(getFrequency()+INCREMENT);
        }
        catch(RuntimeException e){
            // This should never happen. Restore it to a legitimate
            // value.
            setFrequency(MIN_FREQUENCY);
        }
    }

    public void down(){
        try{
            setFrequency(getFrequency()-INCREMENT);
        }
        catch(RuntimeException e){
            // We have hit the minimum. Take no further action.
        }
    }

    public double getFrequency(){
        return frequency;
    }

    // f must be at least MIN_FREQUENCY.
    public void setFrequency(double f) throws RuntimeException {
        if(f < MIN_FREQUENCY){
            throw new RuntimeException("Frequency: "+f+
                                " is below the minimum of "+
                                MIN_FREQUENCY);
        }
        frequency = f;
    }

    private double frequency = MIN_FREQUENCY;
}
```

It has two further public methods, up and down, which increase or decrease the value of frequency by 0.1 (with the restriction that it must never be set below 80000000.0). The mutator throws a RuntimeException if this is ever attempted.

Define the class PresetsRadio as a sub class of Radio. Its constructor should take an array of double values representing frequency values of different radio stations. The accessor and mutator for this array are both public. It has two further public methods, stationUp and stationDown, which select the next station from the array of frequencies and set the frequency value appropriately. Both methods should wrap around when the start or end of the array is reached. Define a main method to test the implementations of Radio and PresetsRadio.

How should `stationUp` and `stationDown` deal with a frequency that is below the minimum? Do you think it is a good idea for the minimum frequency and increment values to be defined as class constants? Give reasons for your answers.

14.4.1   Structural Similarity between Classes

Another example of inheritance might be provided by a lending library that keeps loan records on both books and music Compact Discs (CDs). All items available to be lent are likely to have a common set of attributes. These might include things such as a title and an accession or identification number. In addition, particular types of items will have their own characteristic attributes; a book will have the name of its authors and perhaps the number of pages, whereas a CD will have the name of the recording artist and might have the number of tracks. Code 14.17 shows a possible bare outline for this particular class hierarchy.

Code 14.17   A lending library inheritance hierarchy

```
    // Store common attributes for a library's lendable items.
class LoanItem {
    ...
    public String getTitle(){
        return title;
    }

    public String getAccessionNumber(){
        return accessionNumber;
    }

    private final String title, accessionNumber;
}

    // Maintain additional attributes for books.
class Book extends LoanItem {
    ...
    public int getNumPages(){
        return numPages;
    }

    // Allow for multiple authors.
    private final String[] authors;
    private final int numPages;
}

    // Maintain additional attributes for music CDs.
class MusicCD extends LoanItem {
    ...
    public int getNumTracks(){
```

Code 14.17   (*Continued*)

```
        return numTracks;
    }

    // Allow for multiple artists.
    private final String[] artists;
    private final int numTracks;
}
```

The LoanItem example differs from most of those we have seen previously in that it envisages distinct sub classes with the same super class—in effect, the `Book` and `MusicCD` classes are *sibling sub classes* sharing the same parent class. This form of hierarchy is common in practice and there are many examples in the core packages of the Java API. For instance, the `Reader` class in the `java.io` package has several immediate sub classes: `BufferedReader`, `CharArrayReader`, `InputStream-Reader`, etc. A point to note is that, in Java, two classes do not possess any special privileges with respect to each other simply by virtue of their being sibling sub classes.

The example classes in Code 14.17 illustrate a further important point about class design and inheritance. You might have noticed that the two sub classes, Book and MusicCD, have the same attribute types in each case. At first sight, it is tempting to dispense with the duplication present in defining two sub classes, and encapsulate the similar attributes in a single general class that looks after an array of strings and an integer. Such an approach would regard the structural similarity of the two classes as being more important than their semantic differences: a book and a music CD really have nothing in common at the level these separate classes are describing.

Using a single class definition for structurally similar types is quite likely to be based upon the mistaken belief that a single common class is more efficient than separate similar-looking classes,[3] but this thinking is erroneous. It is often possible to identify such inappropriate merging of classes from the name given to the combined class, or the names given to the shared attributes; it would be difficult to find a shared name for the book and CD `int` attributes that would accurately describe its use for both a number of pages and a number of music tracks, for instance (`numItems?`). A particular problem with merging classes is that it creates a much stronger coupling between the types than is naturally present in the problem area, and one of the principles of object-oriented design is that the classes in the design should fit as closely as possible with the naturally occurring classes in the problem area. Furthermore, it makes it harder to develop the single class in the future in ways which continue to reflect the real-life objects it is seeking to model. In this example, at some point in the future it might be necessary to include the total playing time as an attribute of a CD, for instance. There is no comparable attribute for books (reading time?!) and the structural similarity that originally gave rise to their merging would no longer apply. This would, in effect, finally force the separation of the combined class into separate classes, similar to those we have now. Such a task is likely to have

---

[3] This belief often applies not just within an inheritance hierarchy, in fact.

far-reaching consequences on those parts of the program that access and manipulate its objects; each reference to the combined class will have to be tracked down and replaced with one or other of the separate class names.

As a general rule, therefore, structural similarity between classes should not be taken as an indication that they may be combined into a single class. Far more important is behavioral and functional similarity, which can often be exploited via inheritance. It is far better to keep semantically distinct classes separate at the outset rather than be forced to try to separate them retrospectively.

14.5   Sub Class Initialization (I)

The examples we have used so far demonstrate that an object of a sub class inherits all of the methods and attributes of its super class. Because of this, it is clear that when a sub class object is created, the super class components of that object must also be initialized properly. For instance, when a VariableController (Code 14.6) object is created, there will be a requirement to ensure that the on and `heater` attributes of its HeaterController super class (Code 14.3) are set up properly. Furthermore, the order in which the component parts are initialized could be important because correct initialization of the sub class parts might require information from the super class parts, whereas the opposite is much less likely since the super class will generally be self-contained with respect to any sub classes.

Since object initialization often involves constructors, a related issue is what to do if the super class's constructor takes arguments? A way must be found for these to be passed via the sub class's constructors. The approach that Java takes is to stipulate that a super class's components *must* be initialized before the sub class's constructor and methods take full control. This means that an arrangement must be made in a sub class constructor for an appropriate super class constructor to be invoked. We can illustrate this using the `Bookmark` class, described in Section 13.10 (Code 13.28). This stores a World Wide Web URL and associated title. A possible sub class of Bookmark, `AnnotatedBookmark`, allows a descriptive string to be associated with the URL and its title (Code 14.18). An AnnotatedBookmark object might be created as follows:

```
new AnnotatedBookmark("http://www.javasoft.com/","JavaSoft Home Page",
                "A starting point for information on Java.");
```

The values for the `url` and `title` attributes of the Bookmark class are passed into the sub class's constructor when an AnnotatedBookmark object is created. Because the super class part of the object must be initialized first, these attribute values must be handed straight on to the super class's constructor for initialization of the full object. This is done by using the `super` reserved word, followed by any actual argument values required by the appropriate super class constructor being invoked.

```
public AnnotatedBookmark(String url,String title,String description){
    // Pass on two of the arguments to the super class.
    super(url,title);
    ...
}
```

```
Code 14.18    Outline of an annotated WWW bookmark (AnnotatedBookmark.java)

    // Add a description string to a Bookmark.
class AnnotatedBookmark extends Bookmark {
    public AnnotatedBookmark(String url,String title,String description){
        // Pass on two of the arguments to the super class.
        super(url,title);
        setDescription(description);
    }

    public String getDescription(){
        return description;
    }

    public void setDescription(String d){
        description = d;
    }

    private String description;
}
```

Once the Bookmark super class constructor has finished, the AnnotatedBookmark constructor continues its initialization of the remaining elements of the object.

When a sub class constructor explicitly invokes a super class constructor, this must be the sub class constructor's first statement. If it fails to include an explicit call, then a hidden implicit call to its super class's *no-arg constructor* is automatically inserted before any statements in the body of the sub class's constructor:

```
super();
```

This implicit call would clearly cause a problem if its super class does not have a no-arg constructor. In order to ease this problem, all classes *that have no constructor defined explicitly* have a simple default no-arg constructor defined implicitly. This constructor has public access, takes no arguments, and has no statements in its body. Such a constructor might seem pointless, but we shall see in Section 14.5.1 that it is not.

A default no-arg constructor does not solve the initialization problem completely, because a class with at least one explicit argument-taking constructor is *not* supplied with a default no-arg constructor. This will lead to a compile-time error if an explicit super class constructor invocation has not been used in an immediate sub class.

14.5.1   The Default No-Arg Constructor

In order to understand how a default no-arg constructor helps to solve the super class initialization problem, consider a variation on the VariableController class, shown in Code 14.19.

In this version, we have added a constructor to the class originally shown in Code 14.6. The rules of object initialization tell us that the no-arg constructor of HeaterController will be called automatically before any statements of the

Code 14.19   Default invocation of a no-arg constructor

```
class VariableController extends HeaterController {
    ...
        // Set the heater to an explicit initial level on construction.
    public VariableController(int initialLevel) throws RuntimeException {
        setLevel(initialLevel);
    }
    ...
}
```

VariableController constructor are executed. The effect would be as if the sub class constructor had been written as:

```
    // Set the heater to an explicit initial level on construction.
    public VariableController(int initialLevel) throws RuntimeException {
        // Implicit call to super class's no-arg constructor inserted.
        super();
        setLevel(initialLevel);
    }
```

The fact that the HeaterController class has no explicit constructor means it will be supplied with a default one, having no statements in its body (Code 14.20).

In fact, the default no-arg constructor shown in Code 14.20 is not strictly accurate. Since we have stated that all constructors not including an explicit call to their super class constructor have an implicit call inserted, a default no-arg constructor is no exception. You might think that this is unnecessary in the case of HeaterController, because it does not extend any class. However, *all classes* that do not explicitly extend a class implicitly extend the Object class defined in the java.lang package. This is what lies behind the fact, pointed out in Section 10.2.2, that an object belongs to both its full dynamic type and the Object type. An object is both an instance of its created type and an instance of the Object type. The Object type is discussed in more detail in Section 14.9. In the light of this, a full outline for the header of the HeaterController class and its implicit no-arg constructor is shown in Code 14.21.

It is important to remember that a class only has a default no-arg constructor if it has no other constructors. This means that the introduction of a single-argument constructor for VariableController in Code 14.19 means that we can no longer

Code 14.20   The default no-arg constructor for the HeaterController class

```
class HeaterController {
        // Default (implicit) no-arg constructor.
    public HeaterController(){
        // Empty body.
    }
    ...
}
```

Code 14.21   The implicit super class and no-arg constructor of HeaterController

```
    // This class (implicitly) extends Object.
class HeaterController extends Object {
    // Default (implicit) no-arg constructor.
    public HeaterController(){
        // (Implicit) invocation of the Object class's no-arg constructor.
        super();
    }
    ...
}
```

construct such objects as follows

```
        // Illegal because VariableController does not have a
        // no-arg constructor.
        VariableController v = new VariableController();
```

for which the compiler would give the error message

```
    No constructor matching VariableController() found in
                                class VariableController.
```

Even though its HeaterController super class does have an implicit no-arg constructor, the compiler requires that either VariableController is also given an explicit no-arg constructor or that an appropriate integer argument is supplied to match its only constructor. If we wish to construct a VariableController without specifying an initial temperature level, then a second explicit no-arg constructor must be defined (Code 14.22). It is not necessary to place any statements in the body of the no-arg constructor. By default, the HeaterController's no-arg constructor will be called to initialize the super class elements of the object. No further initialization of the sub class elements is required.

Code 14.22   Providing an explicit no-arg constructor.

```
class VariableController extends HeaterController {
    ...
        // Set the heater to an explicit initial level on construction.
    public VariableController(int initialLevel) throws RuntimeException {
        setLevel(initialLevel);
    }

        // Explicit no-arg constructor, to allow construction without
        // a specific initial level.
    public VariableController() {
    }
    ...
}
```

14.5.2 Constructor Arguments and Order of Initialization

The requirement to initialize the super class components of an object before the sub class components places limits on the values that may be used for the actual arguments passed via `super`. A sub class constructor may only pass expressions based upon its own formal arguments and static variables. In particular, it may not pass values of non-static attributes to the super class constructor, even if these are final variables (constants). Any sub class attributes (even final fields) are only initialized to their defined values once the super class constructor has finished, until that time they are regarded as containing the default value for their type. This is only really significant if the super class somehow manages to access attributes of its sub class from within the super class constructor. An example of such a special case is discussed in Section 15.2.

Exercise 14.5 The Shape class has a single constructor that takes an array of Point objects as its only argument.

```
class Shape {
    public Shape(Point[] points){
        this.points = points;
    }
    ...
}
```

The `ColoredShape` class is a sub class of Shape. It has a final integer attribute, `color`, passed to its constructor along with the array of points required to initialize the super class components. Define the constructor of ColoredShape.

14.6 Creating Exception Sub Classes

A very common example of inheritance is the creation of new checked and unchecked exception classes to distinguish between the different error situations that might arise within a program (see Section 11.2.5). If we indicate all errors by throwing a basic checked `Exception` or unchecked `RuntimeException` object, it can be difficult for exception handlers to distinguish between the many potential reasons for the error. This, in turn, might make choosing an appropriate recovery strategy difficult. It is preferable to define a new class for each category of exception that can arise and distinguish between these in the catch sections of exception handlers.

We can illustrate this by reference to the original VariableController class defined in Code 14.6. In that example, the `setLevel` method throws a RuntimeException if an attempt is made to set the controller to an inappropriate temperature. Instead, we would like to define a `HeaterLevelException` that reports details of the invalid argument, so that the handler dealing with the problem is able to both identify the type of problem and the value that caused it. Code 14.23 shows the modified `setLevel` method.

New exception classes are created in exactly the same way as any other sub class. New checked exceptions will be sub classes of Exception, and new unchecked

Code 14.23   Throwing a HeaterLevelException exception

```java
class VariableController {
    ...
    public void setLevel(int level) throws HeaterLevelException {
        if((MinLevel <= level) && (level <= MaxLevel)){
            // Adjust the heater.
            getHeater().setTemperature(level);
        }
        else{
            // The value is out of the allowed range.
            throw new HeaterLevelException("Illegal level setting: "+level);
        }
    }
    ...
}
```

Code 14.24   A sub class of RuntimeException (`HeaterLevelException.java`)

```java
    // An illegal temperature level has been set on a heater.
class HeaterLevelException extends RuntimeException {
    public HeaterLevelException(String message){
        // Pass on the error message to the super class.
        super(message);
    }
}
```

exceptions will be sub classes of RuntimeException. Code 14.24 shows the definition of the new unchecked exception class, HeaterLevelException, used by the `setLevel` method in Code 14.23.

The argument string is passed on from the sub class constructor to the super class constructor in the usual way, via `super`. Notice that the new class adds no additional attributes or behavior to its super class. Its sole purpose is to provide a more discriminating object type than Exception or RuntimeException to an exception handler. In this respect, such sub classes fulfill a role which is a little different from the specialization role we have mostly associated with inheritance up to this point. Despite the fact that they add no new functionality to their super class, their role of adding type discrimination is an important one, and an aid to improving program correctness. Code 14.25 shows how the new exception might be handled in a version of the VariableController class that incorporates the various changes we have made in earlier sections: `VariableLevelController`. An object of a new exception class is thrown and handled in exactly the same way as any other objects of its Exception super class.

The close association of an exception with a particular class whose objects throw it makes exception sub classes ideal candidates for implementing as *top-level classes*. These are discussed in Section 15.5.

Code 14.25   Catching a HeaterLevelException exception

```
try{
    // Use the default initial temperature setting.
    VariableLevelController v = new VariableLevelController();
    ...
    v.setLevel(100);
    ...
} catch(HeaterLevelException e){
    System.err.println(e.getMessage());
}
```

Exercise 14.6   Suppose that the class TimerFailure is a sub class of the checked Exception class. Given the following method header

```
    public void setStartTime(Time t) throws TimerFailure
```

would the following throw statement be legal within the body of setStartTime if it is not enclosed within a try statement?

```
    throw new Exception("Unable to set the start time.");
```

Give your reasons.

Exercise 14.7   If the TimerFailure class described in Exercise 14.6 were a sub class of the unchecked RuntimeException, rather than the checked Exception class, would the following throw statement be legal within the body of setStartTime if it is not enclosed within a try statement?

```
    throw new RuntimeException("Unable to set the start time.");
```

Give your reasons.

Exercise 14.8   Is the following throw statement legal according to the definition shown in Code 14.24?

```
    throw new HeaterLevelException();
```

If not, why?

Exercise 14.9   Modify your solution to Exercise 11.5, so that the constructor of ClosedShape throws two different exceptions according to whether the problem was too few points, or the last point not matching the first point. The exceptions thrown should be sub classes of Exception that you have defined.

14.7   Access Control

In the next few sections, we investigate some of the implications of inheritance for the access control (visibility) rules that apply to classes and their members. We need to consider what access rights a sub class has to its super class's members, and to appreciate that classes defined in one package are regularly extended by classes defined in different packages. .

14.7.1 Protected Access

Until the introduction of `protected` in Section 14.2, we had used two other reserved words to indicate differing levels of access control (or visibility) of attributes and methods defined in classes and interfaces—`public` and `private`. In addition to these two levels, there is *package access*, which requires no reserved word (see Section 8.1.1). Declaring an attribute or method as `public` allows objects of any class to access it. In Section 4.7, we gave reasons why this is not a good approach for ordinary object attributes—it makes it impossible for an object to restrict access to its attributes, and hence ensure that it is always in a valid and consistent state. Declaring an attribute or method as `private` restricts access so that it is only accessible to objects which are of the same class as that in which it is defined. The rule on privacy even applies to a class which extends another class—the methods of the sub class do not have access to the private elements of the super class, and vice-versa. Given the close relationship between the components of the sub class and the components of the super class within an object of the sub class, such a rule is often too restrictive to be convenient. Although package access offers an alternative to public and private access, it is inadequate if a sub class belongs to a different package from that of its super class, which is a commonly occurring situation. For this reason, Java adds *protected access* as a level between public access and package access. Attributes and methods declared as `protected` are available, without restriction, both to all classes defined in the same package and to all classes which extend that class (either directly or indirectly) whether they are defined in the same package or not. This means that protected access can be viewed as a slightly less restrictive form of package access for the benefit of sub classes. It could be characterized as giving your house keys to trusted members of your family or friends.

A couple of examples should help to illustrate these rules. Code 14.26 contains an artificial three-level inheritance hierarchy. All of the classes are defined in the same named package, `generations`.

At the top of the inheritance hierarchy is the `Grandparent` class. It has a private attribute, `top`, to which access is gained via its public accessor and package access mutator. This mutator will only be accessible to classes defined in the `generations` package. A similar pattern is repeated in the `Parent` class, which extends Grandparent, but its mutator has protected access, allowing sub classes defined in packages other than `generations` to access it. The `Child` class directly extends the Parent class and, hence, indirectly extends the Grandparent class; this means it is a sub class of both Parent and Grandparent. Child's `setBottom` mutator has been declared as public to complete the illustration. It will be available to all classes in all packages throughout the program. Grandparent's private attribute, `top`, is accessible to neither Parent nor Child; it can only be set or examined via the public `getTop` and package access `setTop` methods. Similarly, Parent's private attribute, `middle`, is inaccessible to Child other than through its public accessor and protected mutator.

Code 14.26   Access Control via `protected` (`ProtectedMain.java`)

```
package generations;

class Grandparent {
    public int getTop(){
        return top;
    }

    void setTop(int t){
        top = t;
    }

    private int top;
}

class Parent extends Grandparent {
    public int getMiddle(){
        return middle;
    }

    protected void setMiddle(int m){
        middle = m;
    }

    private int middle;
}

class Child extends Parent {
    public int getBottom(){
        return bottom;
    }

    public void setBottom(int b){
        bottom = b;
        setMiddle(bottom/2);
        setTop(bottom/3);
    }

    private int bottom;
}
```

14.7.2 Class Visibility

All three classes in Code 14.26 have no explicit access control reserved word for the classes themselves, which means that they have the default package access and so may only be instantiated from within the `generations` package. A class or interface may have one of only two forms of visibility: package or public. If we anticipate that classes defined in other packages will want to import, instantiate, or extend classes we create, it will be necessary to give them an explicit public access. Code 14.27 illustrates a two-class parent-child hierarchy in which the `Parent` and `Child` classes are defined in different packages.

Code 14.27   Class and constructor access between packages

```
package generation1;

    // This class must be public in order to allow
    // classes in other packages to extend or instantiate it.
public class Parent {
    public int getMiddle(){
        return middle;
    }

    // Protected access.
    protected void setMiddle(int m){
        middle = m;
    }

    private int middle;
}

package generation2;

import generation1.Parent;

class Child extends Parent {
    public int getBottom(){
        return bottom;
    }

    // Public access.
    public void setBottom(int b){
        bottom = b;
        setMiddle(bottom/2);
    }

    private int bottom;
}
```

In order to enable the Child class in package `generation2` to extend the Parent class in package `generation1`, Parent must be declared as a public access class. The fact that Parent's `setMiddle` mutator has been given protected access means that the Child class is able to use it, which would not be the case if it had only been given package access.

14.7.3 Constructor Accessibility

Importing and extending classes from other packages means that we have to give careful thought to constructor accessibility, as well as class accessibility. In the example in Code 14.27, neither class has an explicit constructor, so both will be supplied with an implicit default no-arg constructor. In Section 14.5, we pointed out that default no-arg constructors are always public. This means that Child's default constructor will have access to that of Parent. However, if Parent had an explicit constructor, then it would be necessary to give it either public or protected access in order to allow Child to extend the class. If an explicit no-arg constructor in Parent had been given either package or private access, for instance, the compiler would give a potentially confusing message such as

```
Child.java:5: No constructor matching Parent() found in
              class generation1.Parent.
```

when compiling the Child class, because the constructor that does exist is effectively invisible at that point.

14.7.4 Guidelines on Access Control

With the introduction of protected access, we recommend a modification to the advice given in Section 4.7 on access control. These are our guidelines on what form of access control to use in different circumstances:

- An object's attributes should always be declared as private, rather than public, package or protected, even if the class is to be extended.
- Access to private attributes of primitive type may safely be granted via accessors with public access. Greater care should be taken when returning references to private attributes of object types since this could potentially allow circumvention of validating mutators via an alias. Use either public or protected access as appropriate.
- Use protected access mutators as a general rule, unless public access is required. Public access mutators should take particular care over validation of their arguments to ensure that an object is not left in an inconsistent state.
- Methods intended purely for internal use by a class should be protected, to make possible future extension by classes in other packages easier than with package access.
- General methods intended for the receipt of messages from other classes should be public.
- Constructors should normally provide either package or public access. If the class has package access, then no harm is done in providing public constructors.
- Classes and interfaces should have either package or public access, depending upon a program's requirement.

These rules make it slightly easier to extend classes than it would be if the choice of access was simply between public and private, even when it has not been envisaged that a class might be extended in the future. Using at least protected access for its methods means that a package access class can be made extensible by classes in other packages relatively easily, by amending its constructors to at least protected level and giving public access to the class.

There is one further issue of protected accessibility that should be noted here. Since protected access lies between public and package access, the protected methods and attributes of a class are accessible to all classes defined in the same package, even if those other classes do not extend it. This renders the difference between public, protected, and package access almost indistinguishable within a package. This might present a problem if the *unnamed package* is used through-out a program (see Section 8.1.1). To prevent this effect, it is a good idea to make use of packages, where appropriate, to reflect the overall structure of a program.

Exercise 14.10   Consider the case of a public class whose only constructor has pro-tected access. What would be the effect of this on where instances of that class could be constructed? Would it prevent sub classes being defined and used in another package?

Exercise 14.11   Could it ever make sense to give a constructor private access? Give your reasons.

14.8   Review

Here are the main points that we have covered in the preceding sections:

- Objects from different classes often exhibit broadly similar behaviors.
- Inheritance provides a mechanism to capture similarities between classes.
- Delegation provides the most viable alternative to inheritance.
- The common functionality is placed in a super class.
- A sub class extends a super class to add distinctive behavior.
- Inheritance allows a sub class to re-use the functionality of its super class largely without the need for re-implementation.
- Inheritance is characterized by the *is-a* relationship between classes.
- Polymorphism formalizes the is-a relationship by allowing a sub class object to be used wherever a super class object is required.
- Care must be taken not to confuse the is-a relationship with a *has-a* relationship. The has-a relationship suggests use of an attribute, rather than inheritance.
- Java implements a single-inheritance model for class inheritance; a class may directly extend only a single super class.
- Inheritance often represents a specialization relationship between sub class and super class.
- New exception classes are often created as a means of providing greater type discrimination, even though they add no additional behavior to their super classes.
- The super class elements of a class are always initialized before the non-static sub class fields.
- Each sub class constructor must invoke an appropriate super class constructor as its first statement.
- Without an explicit use of `super` in a sub class constructor, the super class's no arg constructor will be invoked automatically.
- The `protected` reserved word extends package access by allowing sub classes access to protected members of their super class.

Code 14.28   A simplified version of some of class Object's methods

```
public class Object {
    public boolean equals(Object o);
    public int hashCode();
    public String toString();
    public Class getClass();
    protected Object clone() throws CloneNotSupportedException;
    ...
}
```

14.9   The Object Class

We have seen that if a class Child extends a class Parent, which itself extends a class Grandparent (Code 14.26), then objects of class Child inherit the non-private methods and attributes of both the Parent and Grandparent super classes. Access control rules permitting, polymorphism makes it possible to send a Grandparent message to an object of class Child and such an object may be used anywhere that an object of either class Parent or class Grandparent is required. As we pointed out in Section 14.5.1, *all classes* in a Java program are sub classes, even if they do not explicitly extend another class, because they are all sub classes of class `Object` (defined in the `java.lang` package). Therefore, all classes in a program automatically inherit Object's methods. Knowing that all classes share Object as a super class helps us to understand how polymorphism allows utility classes, such as ArrayList, LinkedList, and HashMap, to handle general collections of Objects as opposed to collections of a specific type (see Chapter 10).

Code 14.28 shows a simplified version of the main public and protected methods of interest that are defined in the Object class.[4] The purposes of the methods shown in Code 14.28 may be summarized briefly as follows:

- `equals` returns `true` if this object is equal to the object referenced by the method's argument, and `false` otherwise. By default, the method only regards two objects as being equal if they have the same object reference value. This behavior is identical to use of the equality operator (`==`) with two objects. So, by default

    ```
    p1.equals(p2)
    ```

    will give the same result as

    ```
    p1 == p2
    ```

    In practice, as we saw in Section 6.1.5, this default behavior is too restrictive and not particularly useful, so we often need to alter it. What we usually want equality to mean is something we shall explore in Section 14.10.

---

[4] The `clone`, `getClass`, and `hashCode` methods are actually *native methods*, and `getClass` is a *final method*.

- hashCode returns an integer *hash code* value that is used by collection classes such as HashMap in the java.util package. Hash codes are often associated with *(key,object)* pairs that must be efficiently stored and accessed. The key is passed to a *hash function* to produce an integer hash code. This value can be used as an index into a linear data structure, indicating where the object should be located. The hash function will always return the same code for the same key, and so the key can be used to retrieve the data when required. Such mechanisms are used by many database applications and for symbol table storage in a compiler, for instance.
- The toString method is an important one, but it is often not invoked directly on an object variable. Whenever an object is used in a context that requires a String, an implicit toString message is sent to it. Object's definition of this method returns a String consisting of the object's class name, followed by an at character (@) and then the object's hash code value as returned by hash-Code. While such default behavior does not provide a particularly meaningful description of a complex object—it contains no information on the object's attribute values, for instance—the fact that all objects inherit this method from their Object super class is very important. We shall see how to overcome its limitations in Section 14.10.
- The getClass method returns an object of class Class, which is defined in the java.lang package. A Class object for a given class contains detailed information on the members of that class. We describe the Class class in more detail in Section 15.7. Of interest at this point is the fact that Class defines the method getName, which returns a String object containing the name of the class to which an object belongs. This is used by the toString method of Object as described above.

```
public Object {
    ...
    public String toString(){
        return getClass().getName()+"@"+
                    Integer.toHexString(hashCode());
    }
    ...
}
```

- clone allows an object to create an identical copy of itself. This provides a means by which accessor methods can return a reference to an attribute of an object type without allowing the receiver to gain write access to the real attribute via an *alias* (see Section 14.7.4). Instead, the accessor sends a clone message to the object attribute and returns the cloned copy as its result. Cloning used recursively will create a *deep copy* of an object rather than a *shallow copy*. We shall see how to use the clone method in Section 15.3.

In order to illustrate the way in which classes inherit the default behavior of the Object class's equals, hashCode, and toString methods, we shall use the OldPoint class shown in Code 14.29. (This is the same as the earlier definition of the Point class shown in Code 4.19.)

An OldPoint object maintains an (x,y) coordinate pair and might be used in a program for plotting graphs or drawing geometrical lines and shapes.

Code 14.29 A class inheriting default behavior from the Object class (`OldPoint.java`)

```java
                // A class to hold details of an (x,y) coordinate.
                // This class uses the default definitions of equals
                // and toString from its Object super class.
class OldPoint {
    public OldPoint(int x, int y){
        setX(x);
        setY(y);
    }

    public OldPoint(Point p){
        this(p.getX(),p.getY());
    }

    public int getX(){
        return x;
    }

    public int getY(){
        return y;
    }

    private void setX(int newX){
        x = newX;
    }

    private void setY(int newY){
        y = newY;
    }

    private int x,y;
}
```

Code 14.30 shows an `ObjectMain1` class that creates three points and uses the default behavior of the `toString` and `equals` method. The default behavior of `hashCode` will also be seen in the output from `toString`.

The output from ObjectMain1 might be:

```
p1 is OldPoint@1ef5785
p2 is OldPoint@5af559
p3 is OldPoint@1a1ab5e
p1 equals p1
p1 == p1
```

Notice how the use of the three OldPoint variables in the String context of `println` causes their `toString` method to be called implicitly. The resultant hash codes that are printed serve to show that they contain distinct object references. Note, too, that the `equals` method allows us to compare any two objects for equality, even if they are not of the same class

```java
        if(p1.equals(s)) ...
```

Code 14.30   Illustrating the default behavior of `toString` and `equals` (`ObjectMain1.java`)

```java
        // Demonstrate the default behavior of the toString, equals,
        // and hashCode methods a class inherits from its Object
        // super class.
class ObjectMain1 {
    public static void main(String[] args) {
        OldPoint p1 = new OldPoint(10,20);
        OldPoint p2 = new OldPoint(20,20);
        OldPoint p3 = new OldPoint(10,20);
        String s = "I am not a point.";

        // Illustrate toString.
        System.out.println("p1 is "+p1);
        System.out.println("p2 is "+p2);
        System.out.println("p3 is "+p3);

        // Illustrate the default equals test.
        if(p1.equals(p1)){
            System.out.println("p1 equals p1");
        }
        if(p1.equals(p2)){
            System.out.println("p1 equals p2");
        }
        if(p1.equals(p3)){
            System.out.println("p1 equals p3");
        }
        if(p1.equals(s)){
            System.out.println("p1 equals s");
        }

        // Illustrate reference equality, for comparison.
        if(p1 == p1){
            System.out.println("p1 == p1");
        }
        if(p1 == p2){
            System.out.println("p1 == p2");
        }
        if(p1 == p3){
            System.out.println("p1 == p3");
        }
    }
}
```

whereas it is not possible to use the equality operator (`==`) between references of different types. The default behavior of the `equals` method is seen to be equivalent to using the equality operator, even though p1 and p3 contain the same x and y attribute values.

In order to see how we can usefully use the fact that all classes inherit these methods from their Object super class, we need to deal with the topic of *overriding*. This is covered in Section 14.10.

14.10   Overriding Methods

We saw in Section 14.9 that, since all classes implicitly inherit from the Object class, they have methods available to them such as `toString` and `equals`. Code 14.29 in that section defined an OldPoint class that we used to illustrate the default behavior of those methods. While inheritance has distinct advantages in promoting code reuse and avoiding duplication of code, we would often prefer the inherited methods to exhibit behavior that is more in keeping with the attributes and characteristics of the sub class rather than that of the super class. For instance, we would like an `equals` message sent to a point object to return `true` for the more general condition that the attribute values of the two point objects are identical. Fortunately, Java's inheritance rules allow us to *redefine* a super class method in one or more of its sub classes; such redefinition is called *method overriding*.

A method is overridden by defining the alternative version in the sub class, using the same method header as that in the super class. Code 14.31 shows a new definition of a Point class with methods overriding Object's versions of `toString` and `equals`.

Code 14.31   Overriding the default `equals` and `toString` methods (`Point.java`)

```java
        // A class to hold details of an immutable (x,y) coordinate.
class Point {
    public Point(int x, int y){
        this.x = x;
        this.y = y;
    }

    public Point(Point p){
        this(p.getX(),p.getY());
    }

        // Return a string representation of the (x,y) pair.
    public String toString(){
        return "("+getX()+","+getY()+")";
    }

        // Return true if o is a Point with the same (x,y)
        // pair as this Point.
    public boolean equals(Object o){
        if(o == this){
            // The same object.
            return true;
        }
        else if(o == null){
            return false;
        }
        else if(o instanceof Point){
            Point p = (Point) o;
            return getX() == p.getX() && getY() == p.getY();
        }
        else{
            return false;
```

Code 14.31   (*Continued*)

```
        }
    }

    public int getX(){
        return x;
    }

    public int getY(){
        return y;
    }

    private final int x,y;
}
```

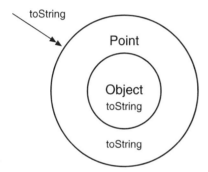

Figure 14.3   Messages are normally received by the outermost class layer of an object

A Point object receiving a toString message is now able to handle it itself, via the overriding version of the method. Figure 14.3 illustrates the structure of a Point as two concentric layers. Both the outer (Point) layer and the inner (Object) layer define a version of the toString method, but messages sent to an object are normally received by the outermost layer (even messages an object sends to itself[5].) It is the dynamic-type of an object that is used in selecting the appropriate version of a method, rather than the static-type. Effectively, the super class version of the method is prevented from receiving it because the overriding version gets it first. The new version of toString returns a String representation of the object that includes the values of its x and y attributes. This is much more informative than the default representation.

The overriding equals method is more complicated. Notice that its formal argument is of type Object rather than Point, because it must match the corresponding argument's type in the signature of the super class version. It is a common error to forget this. Potentially, an object of any class could be passed as the actual argument of this method, as was illustrated with a String object in Code 14.30. In testing for equality, this must be taken into account, rather than assuming that the argument will

---

[5] See Section 14.10.1 for an exception to this rule.

always be another Point object. Furthermore, the object reference passed in could have the `null` value, and this must also be tested for. Once established that the argument is a non-null Point reference, the test for equality simply involves ensuring that the two pairs of x and y attributes have the same values. Notice that this involves using a cast from Object to Point in order to be able to use Point methods on the argument.

Using the new version of Point, the output from a main method similar to that shown in Code 14.30 (`ObjectMain2.java`) would be:

```
p1 is (10,20)
p2 is (20,20)
p3 is (10,20)
p1 equals p1
p1 equals p3
p1 == p1
```

We can see that the overriding `toString` method prints the point details in a much more suitable format than before, and that the point referred to by p1 is considered equal to that referred to by p3.

Overriding the `toString` and `equals` methods of a class is very common, and you should always consider whether to include them in definitions of any classes you create. Code 14.32 shows a simple Polygon class, both of whose `toString` and `equals` methods make use of the corresponding methods in the Point objects which it has as an attribute.

Code 14.32 A Polygon with `toString` and `equals` methods (`Polygon.java`)

```
    // Maintain a set of Point objects representing a polygon.
    // Throw an exception if insufficient points are supplied.
class Polygon {
    // A polygon must have at least three points.
    public static int minPoints = 3;

    public Polygon(Point[] points) throws InvalidPolygonException {
        if(points.length < minPoints){
            throw new InvalidPolygonException(
                "A polygon must have at least "+minPoints+" points.");
        }
        this.points = points;
    }

        // Return a string containing the list of point details
        // held in the attribute Point[] points;
    public String toString(){
        Point[] points = getPoints();
        // Start with the first point.
        String result = "["+points[0];
        for(int i = 1; i < points.length; i++){
            // Add a separating space.
            result += " ";
```

Code 14.32   (*Continued*)

```
            // points[i].toString() is implicitly called here:
            result += points[i];
        }
        result += "]";
        return result;
    }

    // Return true if o is a Polygon with equal Points
    // in the same order. Otherwise return false.
    public boolean equals(Object o){
        if(o == this){
            // The same object.
            return true;
        }
        else if(o == null){
            return false;
        }
        else if(o instanceof Polygon){
            Polygon p = (Polygon) o;
            // Make sure they have the same number of points.
            final int length = getNumPoints();
            if(length == p.getNumPoints()){
                final Point[] myPoints = getPoints(),
                              otherPoints = p.getPoints();
                for(int i = 0; i < length; i++){
                    if(!myPoints[i].equals(otherPoints[i])){
                        // Mismatch.
                        return false;
                    }
                }
                // No failure, so a complete match.
                return true;
            }
            else{
                return false;
            }
        }
        else{
            return false;
        }
    }

    public int getNumPoints(){
        return points.length;
    }

    public Point[] getPoints(){
        return points;
    }

    private final Point[] points;
}
```

A typical output from the `toString` method of this might be:

```
[(0,0) (1,0) (1,1)]
```

An example program to demonstrate the `toString` and `equals` methods may be found in the file `PolygonMain.java`.

Exercise 14.12 The `equals` method of Polygon in Code 14.32 only returns `true` if the two polygons have identical points *in the same order*. For instance, a polygon with the points in the order `[(0,0) (1,0) (1,1)]` would be regarded as different from one with the same points in the order `[(1,1) (0,0) (1,0)]`. Modify the Polygon class so that different rotational orderings of the same points all return `true`.

14.10.1 Restrictions on Overriding

A method can only override a method in its super class if the super class method is not a private method. In addition, the method signatures in the super and sub class must be identical in terms of name, return type, and argument types. This latter rule is the reason why the argument to an overriding `equals` method must always be Object rather than that of the class in which it is being overridden. There is some flexibility in the visibility of an overriding method, whether the arguments are `final` or not, and the exceptions thrown by it. This flexibility may be summarized as follows:

- An overriding method may be more visible than that in the super class.
- Arguments that are `final` in the super class version do not have to be marked as such in the sub class version.
- Any checked exception thrown by the sub class version must match the type of one thrown by the super class version, or be a sub class of such an exception. However, the sub class version does not have to throw any exceptions that are thrown by the super class version. We shall see an example of this restriction and some of its implications in Section 14.11.1.

One reason for the final rule is that the overriding version of a method is actually able to invoke the super class version of the same method. We shall see how the sub class version of a method can invoke the super class version in Section 14.11. In doing so, it might choose to catch and handle the exceptions for itself, rather than propagating them.

Unlike the rule for non-static methods, a static method is selected by the static-type of an object reference, rather than the dynamic-type. This means that a static method defined in a super class is not overridden by a method with an identical header in a sub class. This is illustrated by the example in Code 14.33. The result of running it will be:

```
super class version
super class version
sub class version
```

Code 14.33   A static method cannot be overridden (`StaticOverrideMain.java`)

```
        // Demonstrate the static methods are not overridden in
        // sub classes.
class StaticOverrideMain {
    public static void main(String[] args){
        // The parent class.
        StaticSuper parent = new StaticSuper();
        parent.method();
        // Use a parent type variable with an object of the child class.
        parent = new StaticSub();
        parent.method();
        // Use a child type variable with an object of the child class.
        StaticSub child = new StaticSub();
        child.method();
    }
}

class StaticSuper {
    public static void method(){
        System.out.println("super class version");
    }
}

class StaticSub extends StaticSuper {
        // This does not override the super class version.
    public static void method(){
        System.out.println("sub class version");
    }
}
```

14.11   Styles of Method Overriding

Section 14.10 demonstrated that a message sent to a non-static method of an object
is handled by the sub class's version of an overridden method, rather than that in
the super class. Since the class of an object might be multi-layered, involving several
levels of an inheritance hierarchy (Figure 14.3), the rule is that a message is handled
by the outermost layer defining an appropriate method. We can think of this as if
all messages arrive at the outermost layer of the object's dynamic type (that is, the
lowest level of the inheritance hierarchy) and, in effect, trickle through the layers
until a matching method is found.[6]
    Sometimes simply selecting the outermost version of a method is too restrictive.
We often want the sub class version of a method to supplement the behavior of the
super class's method, rather than replacing it completely. What this means in practice
is that we need a mechanism to enable a method defined in a sub class to invoke the
method in a super class that it overrides. Java permits a sub class method to call a

---

[6] In practice, compilers are able to create more efficient mechanisms for locating the appropriate
method.

method of its super class by using the `super` reserved word.

```
public void method(int arg){
    ...
    // Invoke the super class version of this method.
    super.method(arg);
    ...
}
```

This is a use of `super` that is additional to its use for object construction (Section 14.5). There is no similar restriction as to where this is invoked within the sub class method—it does not have to be the first statement of the method. Note that the name of the super class is *not* used to invoke the overridden method, as that would imply that the method is static.

When a sub class method is invoked, we can characterize at least three different ways in which it might relate to the method that it overrides:

- The sub class version implements its own behavior within the context of the attributes and behavior of the sub class and then calls the super class version so that it can perform a similar task within the super class context (*overriding for breadth*).
- The sub class version checks to see whether it can respond to the message on its own and only calls the super class version of the method if it cannot (*overriding for chaining*).
- The sub class version calls the super class version first of all and then uses or manipulates the result or effects of that call in some way (*overriding for restriction*).

We shall look at each of these approaches in turn.

14.11.1   Overriding for Breadth

As an illustration of overriding for breadth, consider the VariableController class introduced in Code 14.6. Suppose that we would like to override the `switchOn` method of its super class so that it sets the initial temperature level to `defaultLevel` whenever the heater is switched from off to on. The HeaterController super class takes care of switching the heater on, but some additional behavior is also needed. We could completely override the existing `switchOn` method of the HeaterController class (Code 14.3), but it makes more sense to re-use the existing functionality that is there. Using the existing functionality avoids duplicating code unnecessarily and allows the sub class to benefit from any future changes to its super class's version of the extended method.

Code 14.34 shows how a `switchOn` method of VariableController would set the default temperature level and then call its super class's method. If the switch is off, then the overriding method sets the level before invoking the super class's version of the method.

Notice that the sub class version of `switchOn` has to deal with the added complication of the fact that `setLevel` might throw a HeaterLevelException exception. This illustrates an important point about the signatures of super class and sub class

Code 14.34   Extending the `switchOn` method of HeaterController

```
class VariableController extends HeaterController {
    // Class constants for basic temperatures.
    public static int DefaultLevel = 16, MinLevel = 5, MaxLevel = 30;
    ...
        // Extend the behavior in the super class.
    public void switchOn() throws RuntimeException {
        if(!isOn()){
            try{
                setLevel(DefaultLevel);
            }
            catch(HeaterLevelException e){
                // This should never happen.
                throw new RuntimeException(e.getMessage());
            }
        }
        super.switchOn();
    }
}
```

methods. The signature of `switchOn` in the HeaterController class is:

```
public void switchOn();
```

Section 14.10.1 pointed out that the signature of an overriding method must not throw *checked* exceptions that are not sub classes of exceptions thrown by the super class method. This means that it would not have been possible to pass on the Heater-LevelException exception by defining the overriding method signature as:

```
public void switchOn() throws HeaterLevelException
```

Instead, if we wish to indicate an exception to the caller, then we have to compromise by throwing an equivalent *unchecked* exception from the overriding method.

The reason for this rule lies in the implications of polymorphism, which mean that an object of a sub class may be used wherever an object of the super class is required. Consider the implications for the following example if VariableController's version of `switchOn` is allowed to throw a checked exception:

```
public void processController(HeaterController c){
    c.switchOn();
    ...
}
```

The formal type for the argument `c` is HeaterController, but polymorphism allows the dynamic type of the actual argument to be either HeaterController or Variable-Controller. If it is the latter, then the `switchOn` call would have to be embedded in an exception handler (or `processController` would have to have a throws-clause in its signature) because it could throw a checked exception. If, instead, it is a basic HeaterController, then no exception handler is required. The compiler cannot know which of these will be the case when the program runs—indeed, different invocations of `processController` might well have different actual argument types during the run of a program. The only solution to this is to mandate the restriction on signatures described above. If, however, VariableController's version of `switchOn` throws an unchecked exception, then the compiler does not require an exception handler to be present.

14.11.2 Overriding for Chaining

With overriding for chaining, the sub class version of a method checks to see whether it can respond to the message on its own and only calls the super class version of the method if it cannot. This is common in event handling classes, such as those that are used in building user interfaces. Code 14.35 illustrates this approach. We shall see further examples of this in Chapter 16 when we look at graphical programming using the *Abstract Windowing Toolkit (AWT)*.

14.11.3 Overriding for Restriction

In Section 14.3, we noted that all of the pieces in a game of chess share piece-like characteristics and behavior, such as color and the ability to move. We can encapsulate the essentials of a piece in a super class, `ChessPiece` (Code 14.36). The ChessPiece class manages the `color` attribute of pieces and implements the basic move validity checks that are relevant to all of its sub classes—the destination square must be distinct from the source square, and the destination square must not be occupied by a piece of the same color. Sub classes for the particular specializations of Bishop, King, Knight, Pawn, Queen, and Rook would extend ChessPiece in their own ways. As part of that extension, each sub class must implement its own move-validity

---

Code 14.35   Chaining behavior to filter command handling

```
class MyCommandProcessor extends CommandProcessor {
    ...
        // Try to process command. If this is done return true,
        // otherwise ask the super class to respond.
    public boolean process(String command){
        if(command.equals(myCommand)){
            takeAction();
            // We were able to respond.
            return true;
        }
        else{
            // Let the super class version have a go.
            return super.process(command);
        }
    }
    ...
    // The command I know how to respond to.
    private final String myCommand = "...";
}
```

Code 14.36   A super class for the common behavior of chess pieces

```
        // A super class for the different piece types.
public class ChessPiece {
    public ChessPiece(int color){
        this.color = color;
    }

        /* Check basic move validity:
         *    + The destination square must be distinct from the
         *      source square.
         *    + The destination square must not contain a piece of our
         *      own color.
         */
    public boolean validMove(Move m, Board board){
        // Make sure from and to are distinct.
        if(m.getFrom().equals(m.getTo())){
            return false;
        }
        else{
            // Check the destination square.
            ChessPiece capturedPiece = board.getPieceAt(m.getTo());
            if(capturedPiece == null){
                // The square is empty.
                return true;
            }
            else if(capturedPiece.getColor() == getColor()){
                // Cannot capture our own piece.
                return false;
            }
            else{
                return true;
            }
        }
    }

    public int getColor(){
        return color;
    }

    // The color of this piece. Fixed for its life.
    private final int color;
}
```

---

checking in a method that overrides `validMove`, but still uses the basic checking of the super class. Such further checking will place additional limitations or restrictions on the moves accepted as valid by the super class version of the method. For instance, a Rook needs to check that it is moving along a row or column and that the path between the source and destination square is clear; a Bishop needs to check that it is moving along a diagonal and that its path is clear; a Knight needs to check that it is moving two squares in one direction and one in another. Code 14.37 illustrates how the Rook class might extend ChessPiece.

Code 14.37   A Rook's more restricted valid move-checking

```
public class Rook extends ChessPiece {
    public Rook(int color){
        super(color);
    }

    // Is this a valid move for a rook?
    public boolean validMove(Move m,Board board){
        // Check the basic validity.
        if(!super.validMove(m,board)){
            return false;
        }
        else{
            // The move must be wholly along a row or column and
            // all intervening squares must be empty.
            if(m.colDistance() == 0){
                // A move along a row.
                return board.clearPath(m);
            }
            else if(m.rowDistance() == 0){
                // A move along a column. Check the path is clear.
                return board.clearPath(m);
            }
            else{
                // A non-linear move.
                return false;
            }
        }
    }
}
```

This is a typical example of overriding for restriction. A further example is provided by cloning in Section 15.3.1.

14.12   Super Class Behavior and Overriding

It is important to realize that the overridden methods of an extended object apply even within the context of the super class. That is, if an overridden method is called from within the super class part of an object, it will be the sub class version that is called and not that in the super class. The only exceptions to this rule are calls to private or static methods, since these are not overridden by equivalent sub class versions. In other words, *all* messages, sent to an object via non-private and non-static methods, always arrive at its outermost layer, no matter from where they originated; even if they originated from within an inner layer of the object itself. This can make it difficult to understand how an object will behave under certain circumstances. To illustrate this, consider the Transaction class shown in Code 14.38.

```java
import java.io.*;

        /* Hold an amount of money representing a credit or debit
         * transaction. The amount is a long integer.
         * The toString() method formats the amount in a width
         * determined by getFormatWidth().
         * The printAmount() prints the formatted amount to the
         * specified Writer.
         */

public class Transaction {
    public Transaction(long amount) {
        this.amount = amount;
    }

        // Return the formatted amount as a string.
        // The amount should be right adjusted in a field of
        // the length returned by getFormatWidth().
    public String toString(){
        // Get the formatted version of the amount.
        String amount = formattedAmount();

        // Create a prefix of spaces to fill the remaining format width.
        int prefixLength = getFormatWidth()-amount.length();

        StringBuffer prefix = new StringBuffer();
        for(int i = 0; i < prefixLength; i++){
            prefix.append(" ");
        }
        prefix.append(amount);
        return prefix.toString();
    }

        // Print the amount formatted as a string.
    public void printAmount(Writer writer) throws IOException{
        writer.write(toString());
    }

    public long getAmount(){
        return amount;
    }

    // Return amount in the form: "dollars.cents"
    protected String formattedAmount(){
        long amount = getAmount();
        long dollars = amount/centsPerDollar;
        long cents = amount % centsPerDollar;

        // Make up the result from its components.
        String result = dollars+".";
```

(*Continued*)

Code 14.38   (*Continued*)

```
        // Make sure that the number of cents is always two digits.
        if(cents < 10){
            result += "0"+cents;
        }
        else{
            result += cents;
        }
        return result;
    }

    // Return the width in which to format the amount.
    protected int getFormatWidth(){
        return defaultFormatWidth;
    }

    private static final int centsPerDollar = 100;

    // The default width of the formatted amount.
    private final int defaultFormatWidth = 10;

    // The amount of the credit, debit or transfer.
    private final long amount;
}
```

Transaction maintains the transaction amount as an attribute and enables it to be printed in a formatted form via a Writer object passed to its printAmount method. It would appear from the definition of Transaction that the toString method will always format amounts in a width of ten characters (the value of its default-FormatWidth field). However, this class is part of a set of classes concerned with recording monetary transactions in a financial application. Credit and debit operations on an account are recorded by constructing Credit and Debit objects to hold and format the amount of each individual transaction.[7] These two classes are shown in Code 14.39.

Both Credit and Debit extend Transaction. Credit and Debit objects are required to format themselves with different field widths, so that they may be printed in distinct columns on a statement of the account. For this purpose, they define their own getFormatWidth methods. However, the formatting itself is performed in the toString method of the Transaction class. The important point to note is that, even though Transaction has its own definition of getFormatWidth, *it is the overridden version that is used* according to the dynamic type of the object receiving the toString message. From this discussion it can be seen that the following output

```
                        ⎵⎵⎵⎵⎵⎵⎵⎵⎵⎵⎵⎵⎵⎵⎵⎵⎵⎵10.00
                ⎵⎵⎵⎵⎵⎵⎵⎵⎵⎵⎵⎵⎵⎵⎵⎵⎵⎵⎵⎵⎵⎵⎵⎵⎵⎵⎵⎵⎵⎵⎵⎵⎵⎵⎵⎵⎵-20.00
```

---

[7] Details of the other accounts involved in these transactions have been omitted for the sake of simplicity.

Code 14.39   Maintain credit and debit transaction details (`Credit.java` and `Debit.java`)

```java
        // Maintain a positive Transaction amount.
        // Format the amount in a width of 25 characters.
public class Credit extends Transaction {
    public Credit(long amount) throws InvalidTransactionException {
        super(amount);
        if(amount <= 0){
            throw new InvalidTransactionException(
                        "Credits must be greater than zero: "+amount);
        }
    }

    protected int getFormatWidth(){
        return creditFormatWidth;
    }

    // The width of the print field.
    private final int creditFormatWidth = 25;
}

        // Maintain a negative Transaction amount.
        // Format the amount in a width of 50 characters.
public class Debit extends Transaction {
    public Debit(long amount) throws InvalidTransactionException {
        super(amount);
        if(amount >= 0){
            throw new InvalidTransactionException(
                        "Debits must be less than zero: "+amount);
        }
    }

    protected int getFormatWidth(){
        return debitFormatWidth;
    }

    // The width of the print field.
    private final int debitFormatWidth = 50;
}
```

would result from the example shown in Code 14.40. The implication of this is that it will not always be possible to understand the dynamic behavior of a super class purely from the context of its own definition. The apparent behavior of its methods might be significantly altered when responding to messages through a sub class object with overriding methods. There are clearly dangers inherent in the fact that a super class's behavior may be fundamentally changed by overriding methods in a sub class. If a class makes assumptions on the basis of its own defined behavior, those assumptions could easily prove to be ill-grounded in some circumstances. It behooves designers of classes to take great care not to make too many assumptions about the context in which each particular method might operate. See Section 14.12.2 for details of how to prevent a class from being sub-classed or a method from being overridden.

Code 14.40   Sub-type methods are used even via super-type references (`BankTest.java`)

```java
import java.io.*;

class BankTest {
    public static void main(String[] args){
        try{
            // Create a Writer out of System.out for the print
            // method of Transaction.
            PrintWriter writer = new PrintWriter(System.out,true);
            Transaction t1 = new Credit(1000);
            Transaction t2 = new Debit(-2000);

            t1.printAmount(writer);
            writer.println();
            t2.printAmount(writer);
            writer.println();
        }
        catch(Exception e){
            System.err.println(e.getMessage());
        }
    }
}
```

14.12.1   Sub Classes and Attributes

A sub class may define its own version of attributes defined in its super classes. In effect, the super class versions of an overridden attribute will be hidden from within sub classes that redefine them.[8] In contrast to the effect that we saw with methods in Section 14.12, a reference to an attribute is resolved from the class context in which it is used, or the static type of the object through which it is accessed. If the `toString` method of `Transaction` in Code 14.38 were to use the value of the attribute `formatWidth` directly, therefore, all transactions would be formatted in a field width of ten characters, regardless of the fact that both Credit and Debit define their own versions of that attribute. In practice, this would force sub classes of Transaction to define their own versions of `toString` to achieve the effect they desire.

14.12.2   Final Classes and Methods

In Section 14.12, we discussed the possible danger to a super class if one or more of the methods that it uses are overridden in sub classes. Overriding methods could easily damage the integrity of the super class elements if care is not taken. It is possible to prevent a whole class from being sub-classed by defining it as a *final class*—using the `final` reserved word in its class header immediately before the `class` reserved

---

[8] Note that our approach to defining attributes as `private` effectively hides them from sub classes anyway.

Code 14.41   Final and non-final methods in Calendar

```
public abstract class Calendar implements Serializable, Cloneable {
    ...
    // Final methods.
    public final int get(int field);
    public final void set(int field,int value);
    public final void setTime(Date date);
    ...
    // Non-final methods.
    public TimeZone getTimeZone();
    public int getFirstDayOfWeek();
}
```

word. An example is the String class in the java.lang package:

```
public final class String implements Serializable, Comparable
```

As well as safeguarding super class integrity, final classes provide the compiler opportunities to create code that is more efficient than usual. The compiler knows that the dynamic type of an object whose static type is final must be identical to that static type. Hence, it knows the identity at compile time of any references to methods defined in the final class, since they cannot have been overridden.

Defining a whole class as final is rather drastic, since it completely prevents any further sub class from being created from it. Rather, it is preferable to permit sub classes to extend a class in the usual way, but designate specific methods as final, preventing only them from being overridden in a sub class. An example is provided by the Calendar class[9] in the java.util package (Code 14.41).

The methods concerned with manipulating the internal representation of Calendar objects—such as get, set, and setTime—are declared as final, whereas others—such as getTimeZone and getFirstDayOfWeek—are not. This makes it possible to extend the class, as is done by GregorianCalendar, without risking compromising the integrity of the underlying representation.

14.13   Review

Here are the main points that we have covered in the preceding sections:

- All classes implicitly extend the Object class.
- All classes inherit a set of common methods from their Object super class.
- The equals method should be overridden to provide a class-specific test for content equality of its objects.
- The toString method should be overridden to provide a class-specific string visualization of its objects.

---

[9] Calendar is also an *abstract class* and abstract classes cannot be final since they must be extended to be of use—see Section 15.1 on abstract classes.

- An overriding method must match the name, return type, and formal argument types of its super class method.
- An overriding method may throw fewer exceptions than its super class version, but all checked exceptions must be instanceof-equivalent to those thrown by the overridden version.
- An overriding method may be more visible than the super class version.
- Private methods are not overridden.
- Static methods are not overridden.
- An overriding method may invoke the overridden version via the `super` prefix.
- Overriding is usually for breadth, chaining, or restriction.
- A reference to an overridden (non-private) method from within a super class is always handled by the outermost implementation of the method—that is, the lowest method in the class hierarchy.
- A direct reference to a field from within a super class never refers to a field with that name in an extending class.
- A method may be marked as `final` to prevent its being overridden.
- A class may be marked as `final` to prevent its being extended.

Exercise 14.13   The `Counter` class is defined in Code 14.42. Define the class `HourCounter` to extend Counter so that its `value` attribute only takes on the values in the range `[0...23]`. After reaching `23`, it wraps around to zero again. Implement this constraint by overriding the `setValue` method. Write a main method that constructs an HourCounter and demonstrates that it works as required.

Exercise 14.14   Define the class `MinuteCounter` to extend the Counter class shown in Code 14.42. The `value` attribute of MinuteCounter should only take on values in the range `[0...59]`, after which it wraps around to zero. Demonstrate that this works.

Code 14.42   A simple incrementing counter (`Counter.java`)

```
class Counter {
    public int getValue(){
        return value;
    }

    public void step(){
        setValue(getValue()+1);
    }

    protected void setValue(int v){
        value = v;
    }

    private int value = 0;
}
```

Exercise 14.15 How might you use your experience of writing HourCounter in Exercise 14.13 and MinuteCounter in Exercise 14.14 to define the general class `WraparoundCounter` that maintains an arbitrary positive limit on the counter's value? How would HourCounter and MinuteCounter classes be rewritten in terms of WraparoundCounter?

Exercise 14.16 Prevent a WraparoundCounter from being constructed with a negative limit.

Exercise 14.17 In Section 12.2.2, we pointed out that the `RecursiveLister` class shares most of its functionality with the non-recursive `DirectoryLister` class. Rewrite RecursiveLister so that it extends DirectoryLister, and hence remove the duplicated functionality from RecursiveLister.

Exercise 14.18 The `Die` class, shown in Code 14.11, is really a specialization of a more general requirement for a random number generator that returns integers within a particular range of values. Create a new class, `RandomRange`, which has a constructor taking two integer arguments. These specify a lower and an upper value for the range of random integers to be returned. Include a single argument constructor whose argument specifies the upper bound, with a default lower bound of zero. The class should include a public method to return a random integer that lies within the bounds $[lower...upper]$. Throw a `RandomRangeException` exception if inappropriate arguments are passed to the constructor.

Create a class `Die` as a sub class of RandomRange. This should return values in the range $[1...6]$.

In this chapter, we have covered the final major language feature of object-oriented languages: class inheritance. Inheritance is a powerful facility that enables common behavior exhibited by related classes in the problem domain to be captured in common super classes. Sub classes extend a super class to provide additional or specialized behavior. In the next chapter, we discuss abstract classes and nested classes.

CHAPTER

15

Abstract and Nested Classes

In this chapter, we look at abstract classes, nested classes, and nested interfaces. Abstract classes are always incomplete in some sense. Often, this is because one or more of their methods has no body. There is some resemblance between abstract classes and interfaces. Abstract classes are completed by creating sub classes. Java's nested class feature allows a class to be defined inside the body of an enclosing class or method.

15.1   Abstract Classes

Abstract classes are distinguished by the fact that you may not *directly* construct objects from them using the `new` operator. There are usually two main reasons for defining such a class that cannot be instantiated. These reasons are not mutually exclusive:

- A class is abstract if one or more methods of the class has not been implemented.
- A class can be made abstract if objects of the class would have no meaningful independent existence.

Abstract classes exist solely as a basis for creating sub classes with fleshed-out functionality, therefore.

15.1.1   Incomplete Abstract Classes

A class will be abstract if one or more of its methods is abstract. An abstract method consists of only a method header prefixed by the `abstract` reserved word. This must appear before the return type, but may either precede or follow an access specifier. A class with one or more abstract methods must also include `abstract` before the word `class` in its header. A class will also be abstract if it implements an interface, but fails to define a body for one of the methods of the interface—interface methods are always abstract, by default.

Since an abstract class is often incomplete, in effect, it must be extended to be of any use. Code 15.1 gives an outline of the `Number` class from the `java.lang` package illustrating how an abstract class is defined. Number is extended by classes

Code 15.1   Outline of the Number class, defined in the `java.lang` package

```
public abstract class Number implements Serializable {
    public abstract int intValue();
    public abstract long longValue();
    public abstract double doubleValue();
    public abstract float floatValue();

        // Return the number as a byte value.
    public byte byteValue(){
        ...
    }

        // Return the number as a short value.
    public short shortValue(){
        ...
    }

    // Private attributes and methods.
    ...
}
```

such as `Double` and `Integer` in `java.lang`, and `BigDecimal` and `BigInteger` in `java.math`. Because Number is abstract, it is not possible to construct a Number object directly using `new`.

```
// This is not allowed.
Number n = new Number();
```

An attempt to do so will result in a compiler error message such as:

```
class java.lang.Number is an abstract class. It can't be instantiated.
```

If an abstract class cannot be instantiated, what use does it have? Abstract classes are useful in that they can define a common set of methods that must be implemented by their sub classes, but which do not necessarily have a common implementation independent of those sub classes. In other words, all sub classes of Number will provide a `floatValue` method, but each will define it in a way that is specific to the type of number it represents—`int`, `float`, `double`, etc. In some ways, abstract classes are similar to interfaces, but there are significant differences; see Section 15.1.3 for more details.

Code 15.2 shows part of how the Double class might flesh out two of the abstract methods of its super class. The `AbstractList` class, defined in `java.util`, is another example of an incomplete abstract class. Sub classes must implement its abstract `get` and `size` methods. `ArrayList` and `LinkedList` are two of its sub classes.

If a class extends a class with abstract methods, but does not provide implementations of all of the abstract methods, then the sub class itself becomes abstract and must be declared as such.

Code 15.2   Possible implementation of `java.lang.Double`

```
    // Provide an object wrapper for a value of primitive type double.
public class Double extends Number {
    public Double(double value){
        this.value = value;
    }

    // Use this as the accessor to the wrapped value.
    public double doubleValue(){
        return value;
    }

    // This probably involves loss of information.
    public float floatValue(){
        return (float) doubleValue();
    }

    // This probably involves loss of information.
    public int intValue(){
        return (int) doubleValue();
    }

    // This probably involves loss of information.
    public long longValue(){
        return (long) doubleValue();
    }

    // The value being wrapped.
    private final double value;
}
```

15.1.2   Complete Abstract Classes

A class may also be designated as abstract, even if it has no abstract methods. This use of the abstract designation is for classes that are complete in the sense that none of their methods is abstract, but incomplete in the sense that they lack attributes or methods that would make instantiations meaningful as separate objects. This can be illustrated quite well by considering further the classes that might exist in a program to implement a game of chess, previously discussed in Section 14.11.3. While it makes sense to create objects of Bishop, King, Knight, Pawn, Queen, and Rook classes, an object of their ChessPiece super class has no valid separate existence within the context of a game. In which case, while none of its methods might be abstract, we would include the `abstract` designation in the class header of ChessPiece to indicate that no such objects should be created directly (Code 15.3).

15.1.3   Abstract Class or Interface?

There are obvious similarities between abstract classes and interfaces because the abstract methods of a class have no bodies. There is often a fine dividing line between

---

Code 15.3   ChessPiece is a complete, but abstract, super class

```
    // All the methods in this class are complete and functional.
public abstract class ChessPiece {
    ...
}
```

---

deciding whether to implement a class as an abstract class or as an interface, particularly where most of a class's methods are abstract. Take the case of the Number class from the `java.lang` package; only two of its public methods, `byteValue` and `shortValue`, are not abstract. Defining Number as an interface would require all implementing classes to implement this identical functionality for themselves. If a super class requires a constructor—particularly a constructor with arguments—then there is little choice but to use an abstract class rather than an interface, as interfaces do not have constructors. On the other side of the coin, if sub classes of an abstract class must extend another class as well, then this would be prohibited by the lack of multiple inheritance in Java, and one of the multiple super classes would have to be an interface.

15.2   Sub Class Initialization (II)

In Section 14.5.2, we noted that an invocation of `super` from a sub class constructor may only pass actual arguments based upon the class's static fields and the sub class constructor's own formal arguments, because the sub class's non-static fields only become available to it once the super class elements have been initialized. We can use an abstract class example to illustrate this important feature about the order in which the super class and sub class elements of an object are initialized. Code 15.4 shows a simple abstract super class, `Parent`, and a sub class, `Child`.

The initialization of `attribute` in Child to contain a reference to the String object "`Child`" only takes place *after* the super class constructor of Child is complete. So the output from running this program will be:

```
Setting attribute to Parent
Child
```

15.3   Object Cloning

In Section 14.9, we noted that all classes inherit a `clone` method from their Object super class, but we did not describe the method in detail there. In essence, a clone is a copy of an object that is identical to the original. One of the main areas in which the need for clones arises is in accessor methods. Our guidelines on access control (Section F.10) require that modification of an object's attributes should only be performed via its mutators, as this allows the mutators to ensure that an object remains internally consistent. However, an accessor that returns an attribute which is an object reference potentially allows modifications to be made to that attribute

Code 15.4 Illustrating super class and sub class order of initialization
(`InitializationOrderMain.java`)

```java
    // Demonstrate that a sub class's attribute is not initialized
    // until after its super class's constructor has completed.
class InitializationOrderMain {
    public static void main(String[] args){
        Child child = new Child();
        System.out.println(child.getAttribute());
    }
}

abstract class Parent {
    public Parent(){
        setAttribute("Parent");
    }

    abstract public void setAttribute(String value);
}

class Child extends Parent {
    public String getAttribute(){
        return attribute;
    }

    public void setAttribute(String value){
        System.out.println("Setting attribute to "+value);
        attribute = value;
    }

    // Not initialized until after the Parent constructor.
    private String attribute = "Child";
}
```

without the ability of the owning object to intervene. For instance, the Polygon class shown in Code 14.32 returns a reference to its array of Point objects from its public `getPoints` accessor. There is nothing to stop any object which obtains such a reference from modifying the contents of the array, without the Polygon being aware that this is going on. Preferable, therefore, would be for `getPoints` to return a copy of the array so that any changes made to the copy could not affect the original.

15.3.1   Deep and Shallow Copying

Whenever we copy an object, we need to decide how far to go. In copying an array of Points, for instance, is it sufficient simply to create a new array object containing references to the existing Point objects—a *shallow copy* (Figure 15.1)—or must new Point objects be created as well, to go in the array copy—a *deep copy* (Figure 15.2)?

Code 15.5 illustrates a way of creating a deep copy of a Polygon's array attribute in the absence of cloning. A new array for the points is constructed, followed by a new

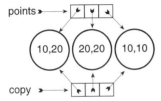

Figure 15.1 A shallow copy of a polygon's point array

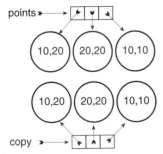

Figure 15.2 A deep copy of a polygon's point array

Code 15.5 An (unattractive) deep copy alternative to cloning

```
     // Not a general solution to cloning.
class Polygon {
     ...
          // Return a duplicate of the points attribute.
     public Point[] getPointsCopy(){
          final int numPoints = getNumPoints();
          // Create a copy of the array.
          final Point[] copy = new Point[numPoints];
          for(int i = 0; i < numPoints; i++){
               // Make a copy of the Point.
               final Point p = points[i];
               copy[i] = new Point(p.getX(),p.getY);
          }
          return copy;
     }
     ...
}
```

set of Point objects constructed from the (x,y) values of the original set. The original is left completely independent of this deep copy, hence preserving the integrity and privacy of the polygon's real attribute.

While this approach works in this case, its weakness lies in its reliance on being able to create a complete and identical copy of an object via its constructor. This assumes that it will be possible to obtain a complete set of the attributes of the object to be copied, in order to pass them to the constructor. In the case of Point, this is possible—it has only two simple attributes, both of whose values are directly obtainable via its public accessors. What about copying more complex objects whose

---

Code 15.6   Use array cloning to return a shallow copy of the Polygon's Point data

```
class Polygon {
    ...
        // Return a shallow copy of the Point data.
    public Point[] getPointsCopy(){
        return (Point[]) points.clone();
    }
    ...
}
```

---

current state might have been reached by a series of interactions with other objects over quite a long period? For instance, an object might have been constructed by reading data from a file passed to its constructor, or by interacting with a user. An object of one class might have attributes which it is not prepared to reveal to an object of another class wishing to clone it. In practice, therefore, the only practical approach is to make object copying *the responsibility of the object being copied*; that is, an object must be asked to return a copy of itself. This is the purpose of the `clone` method inherited from the Object class.

Array objects are able to clone themselves already, so a (shallow copy) version of `getPointsCopy` using this approach is shown in Code 15.6. Note that it is necessary to cast the result of `clone` as this is always returned as a reference of type Object.

The default version of `clone` defined in the Object class works by creating a new object corresponding to the dynamic type of the object to which the original `clone` message was sent (`Point[]` in the example in Code 15.6). A shallow copy of each of the attribute values in the original is transferred to the copy. Attributes are copied at all levels of the inheritance hierarchy between the Object class and the class of the dynamic type. What is returned from `getPointsCopy`, therefore, is a shallow copy of the array object whose elements refer to *the same* Point objects as the original (Figure 15.1). While we have prevented another object from modifying the contents of a Polygon's `points` attribute, we would not have prevented it from altering the Point objects referred to by that array if the points were mutable objects. If we wish the clone to be completely independent of the original, then it will be necessary to implement a version of `getPointsCopy` that creates a deep copy of the array (Figure 15.2). This means that the Point objects must also be requested to clone themselves. Code 15.7 shows what is required of the `getPointsCopy` method of Polygon to achieve this. Each element of the array clone is filled with a reference to a cloned Point from the original array. Once again, notice the requirement to cast the Object reference returned from Point's `clone` method.

This example is not quite complete, however, since we have assumed that it is possible to create a clone of a Point object. Although all classes inherit a `clone` method from their Object super class, a class must explicitly indicate that it may be cloned by implementing the `Cloneable` interface defined in the `java.lang` package. Cloneable is an empty interface which simply acts as a marker (Section 13.8),

Code 15.7   Deep copy of an array attribute (`Cloning/Polygon.java`)

```
class Polygon {
    ...
        // Return a deep copy of the Point data.
    public Point[] getPointsCopy(){
        // Clone the array.
        Point[] copy = (Point[]) points.clone();
        // Clone the points.
        final int numPoints = getNumPoints();
        for(int i = 0; i < numPoints; i++){
            copy[i] = (Point) points[i].clone();
        }
        return copy;
    }
    ...
}
```

indicating that a class might be willing to allow its objects to be cloned.[1]

If an attempt is made to clone an object of a class that does not implement Cloneable, then a checked `CloneNotSupportedException` exception is thrown by the class. Code 15.8 shows a Cloneable version of the Point class that is suitable for use with the deep copy version of `getPointsCopy` shown in Code 15.7.

Code 15.8   A Cloneable Point (`Cloning/Point.java`)

```
        // A cloneable point class.
        // A class to hold details of an (x,y) coordinate.
public class Point implements Cloneable {
    public Point(int x, int y){
        this.x = x;
        this.y = y;
    }

    public Point(Point p){
        this(p.getX(),p.getY());
    }

        // Return a string representation of the (x,y) pair.
    public String toString(){
        return "("+getX()+","+getY()+")";
    }
        // Return true if o is a Point with the same (x,y)
```

(*Continued*)

---
[1] As we shall see in Section 15.3.2, implementation of Cloneable is no guarantee that an object of that class may be cloned, as this might be prohibited elsewhere within the object's inheritance hierarchy.

Code 15.8   *(Continued)*

```
        // pair as this Point.
    public boolean equals(Object o){
        if(o == this){
            // The same object.
            return true;
        }
        else if(o == null){
            return false;
        }
        else if(o instanceof Point){
            Point p = (Point) o;
            return getX() == p.getX() && getY() == p.getY();
        }
        else{
            return false;
        }
    }

    public Object clone() {
        try{
            return super.clone();
        }
        catch(CloneNotSupportedException e){
            // This should never happen!
            throw new Error("Cloning error in Point: "+e);
        }
    }

    public int getX(){
        return x;
    }

    public int getY(){
        return y;
    }

    private final int x,y;
}
```

The clone method of Object only has protected access, so it must be overridden with public access in a Cloneable class if that class wishes to permit general cloning. This is allowed under the rules described in Section 14.10.1. Notice that there is no need to supplement the default cloning process in this particular case, because a Point's attributes are both of primitive type, so there is no difference between a deep copy and a shallow copy. What it must do, however, is either hand on any failure of the cloning process, as follows

```
        public Object clone() throws CloneNotSupportedException {
            return super.clone();
        }
```

Code 15.9 A deep copy clone of Polygon (`Cloning/Polygon.java`)

```java
class Polygon implements Cloneable {
    ...
        // Create a deep copy clone.
    public Object clone(){
        try{
            // Create a basic shallow copy.
            Polygon p = (Polygon) super.clone();
            // Replace p's shallow copy of points with a deep copy
            // that is returned by getPoints.
            p.setPoints(getPointsCopy());
            return p;
        }
        catch(CloneNotSupportedException e){
            // This should never happen!
            throw new Error("Cloning error in Polygon: "+e);
        }
    }
    ...
}
```

or provide an exception handler. For a class such as this, an exception probably represents an unrecoverable failure of some form and so we have chosen to catch it and throw a terminating Error exception.[2]

An important point to note is that we have not yet demonstrated how to clone a Polygon object, just how to clone an array attribute belonging to the Polygon. It is only when a class contains an attribute that is an object reference that a deep copy version of the cloning process for the class needs to be considered. For the sake of completeness, we illustrate how to create a deep copy clone of a Polygon (Code 15.9).

Polygon's `clone` method firstly creates a shallow copy clone via its super class version. It is then only necessary to replace the array attribute in the clone with a deep copy of the original's array, which is available from the deep copy version of `getPointsCopy` illustrated previously. Note that, in effect, this prevents the `points` attribute for the class being declared as final. The file `CloningMain.java` in the `Cloning` directory contains a test-rig for these cloning examples.

There is a good case for implementing different accessors for the object attributes of a class; a public cloning version for granting access to other objects, and a more restricted access non-cloning version for granting access from within the object.

Although it is specifically concerned with cloning a Polygon, the `clone` method in Code 15.9 serves to illustrate the general principles associated with deep copy cloning. The deep copy cloning process typically involves a process of overriding for restriction (Section 14.11.3); firstly, invoking the immediate super class's `clone` method, and then amending the resulting object in whatever way is required to create

---

[2] Note that the `clone` method in Code 15.8 illustrates the point that an overriding method may throw fewer exceptions than the super class version (see Section 14.10.1).

Code 15.10 The NotCloneable class may be cloned through a Cloneable sub class

```
    // This class should not be cloned for some reason.
class NotCloneable {
    ...
}

    // Implement Cloneable, even though the super class does not.
class Cloner extends NotCloneable implements Cloneable {
    ...
    public Object clone() throws CloneNotSupportedException {
        return super.clone();
    }
}
```

Code 15.11 Prevent cloning by overriding `clone`

```
class NotCloneable {
    ...
        // Prevent sub class cloning by throwing an exception.
    public Object clone() throws CloneNotSupportedException {
        throw new CloneNotSupportedException("Don't clone me!");
    }
    ...
}
```

deep copy versions of this sub class's object attributes, before returning the cloned object. In a class hierarchy several levels deep, this process will typically have to be repeated recursively at each level of the hierarchy in order to produce a true deep copy.

15.3.2   Preventing Cloning

There are some circumstances in which a class might wish to prevent its objects from being cloned. For instance, objects that use a resource that it is not possible to share, such as a writable record of a database. To prevent cloning, it is insufficient to simply not implement the Cloneable interface, because this can be thwarted by a sub class that does implement the interface. Code 15.10 shows a `NotCloneable` class that should not be cloned for some reason. However, because the `Cloner` sub class implements Cloneable, this wish will be thwarted.

In order to prevent cloning, it is necessary to take a more active step by overriding the `clone` method and throwing a CloneNotSupportedException exception from it. Code 15.11 shows how NotCloneable should properly fulfill its goal.

When the sub class's version of the `clone` method invokes its super class's version, this will prevent the message from reaching the version defined in the Object class. This also illustrates that, simply because an object belongs to a class that implements Cloneable, this is no guarantee that it may be cloned.

Conversely, in overriding the `clone` but not implementing the Cloneable interface, this example illustrates that a class could anticipate normal future cloning by a sub class, without requiring it for its own objects. Designers should give serious consideration as to whether there could be a future need for a full `clone` method in their classes, even if they do not directly require it.

15.4   Review

Here are the main points that we have covered in the preceding sections:

- An `abstract` method has no body.
- Methods defined in an interface are always abstract.
- A class is abstract if any of its methods are abstract.
- An abstract class must include `abstract` in its header.
- A class may be designated as abstract even if it has no abstract methods.
- An abstract class may not be directly instantiated.
- The `clone` method should be overridden to allow an object to be cloned.
- By default, cloning produces a shallow copy of an object.
- A deep copy of an object should be created if it is necessary to prevent modifications to an object.

Exercise 15.1   Determine whether the `Random` and `LinkedList` classes, defined in `java.util`, implement the Cloneable interface, or define public `clone` methods.

Exercise 15.2   Determine whether the `ArrayList` and `LinkedList` classes, defined in `java.util`, implement the Cloneable interface. If so, do they clone a deep or shallow copy?

Exercise 15.3   If class `Die` extends `RandomRange`, and Die implements the Cloneable interface but RandomRange does not, will it be possible to clone Die objects? Modify your solution to Exercise 14.18 in order to see whether you are right.

Exercise 15.4   Modify your solution to Exercise 14.15 so that the Wraparound-Counter class actively prevents its sub classes from cloning it.

15.5   Top-Level Classes and Interfaces

We commonly use statements nested inside one another in the body of a method. We can think of a method body as being the outermost level of the nesting and statements within it as being at further levels of nesting—typically surrounded by a pair of curly brackets. Code 15.12 illustrates three such levels of statement nesting: the outer level of the method body, a middle level of the loop body, and the innermost level of the if-statement's true-part. Just as statements may be nested, Java allows us to define classes and interfaces inside one another. A class that is not nested inside another is called a top-level class. This means that all of the classes we have written up to this point are top-level classes. There are two different sorts of classes that may be defined inside an outer level class: *nested top-level classes* and *inner classes*. This is rather confusing from a naming point of view, because we now have two sorts of top-level

Code 15.12 Three levels of nested statements

```
    // Return the sum of the values > 0 from the input.
    // A value of 0 terminates the numbers.
public static int sumPositives(SimpleInput reader){
    // Outer-level statement - method body.
    int sum = 0;
    int num = reader.nextInt();
    while(num != 0){
        // Middle level - loop body.
        if(num > 0){
            // Innermost level - true-part.
            sum += num;
        }
        num = reader.nextInt();
    }
    return sum;
}
```

classes: nested and non-nested. In the remainder of this section, we concentrate on nested top-level classes and interfaces and we prefer to use the term *static nested class* rather than nested top-level class. We discuss inner classes in more detail in Section 15.6.

15.5.1 Static Nested Classes

We have seen that packages provide one way to group related classes. Parts of a program wishing to use classes from a package can do so individually

```
// Use the LinkedList class.
import java.util.LinkedList;
```

or as a whole:

```
// Use the LinkedList, Random, Calendar and Date classes.
import java.util.*;
```

If two classes are members of the same package, it does not necessarily mean that they are tightly *coupled*—that is, dependent upon one another. For instance, the Random and LinkedList classes both belong to the `java.util` package but there is no coupling between them at all. On the other hand, Calendar and Date belong to the same package, and these are coupled because Calendar uses the Date class to provide some of its functionality.

Sometimes it is useful to be able to suggest a stronger degree of coupling between classes, indicating, for instance, that one class only has a significance in the context of another. Static nested classes provide a way to show this. Consider the VariableController and HeaterLevelException classes discussed in Section 14.6. The HeaterLevelException class is very closely tied to the existence of the Variable-Controller class, and it would be hard to justify its existence otherwise. The clearest

---

Code 15.13   A static top-level class

```
        // A class that extends the facilities of its super class,
        // HeaterController, to add temperature-level setting.
class VariableController extends HeaterController {
    // Class constants for basic temperatures.
    public static final int DefaultLevel = 16,
                            MinLevel = 5, MaxLevel = 30;

            // An illegal temperature level has been set.
    public static class HeaterLevelException extends RuntimeException {
        public HeaterLevelException(String message){
            super(message);
        }
    }

        // An accessor for the attached heater's current
        // temperature level.
    public int getLevel(){
        // The device keeps track of its current temperature setting.
        return getHeater().getTemperature();
    }

        // Set the heater's level within an allowed range.
    public void setLevel(int level) throws HeaterLevelException {
        if((MinLevel <= level) && (level <= MaxLevel)){
            // Adjust the heater.
            getHeater().setTemperature(level);
        }
        else{
            // The value is out of the allowed range.
            throw new HeaterLevelException(
                            "Illegal level setting: "+level);
        }
    }
}
```

---

way to indicate such a dependence is to define HeaterLevelException as a static
nested class within VariableController (Code 15.13). A static nested class is defined
inside its *enclosing class* at the same level as the enclosing class's methods. Interfaces
defined inside another class or interface are always static.

The static reserved word immediately precedes the class or interface
reserved word. The nested class or interface may be given an access modifier in the
same way as the other methods and attributes of the enclosing class or interface. If
it is intended that the nested class should be accessible to other classes, then public,
protected, or package access is appropriate, otherwise private access could be used
if it is intended purely for the enclosing class's use. From within the enclosing class,
the nested class is used in exactly the same way as if it were another top-level class. A
static nested class only has access to static members of its enclosing class—including
private ones. It has no access to any instance variables or non-static methods of its

Code 15.14 Catching a static nested exception class object

```
try{
    VariableController v = new VariableController();
    ...
    v.setLevel(100);
    ...
} catch(VariableController.HeaterLevelException e){
    System.err.println(e);
}
```

enclosing class. The fact of its being nested only makes a difference to other classes. The full name of the nested class has the enclosing class's name as a prefix, so the fully qualified name of the nested class in Code 15.13 is

```
VariableController.HeaterLevelException
```

and this is what will be used by other classes. Code 15.14 shows the way in which it would be used in a typical exception handler. When a Java compiler translates a class containing a static nested class, it will create a separate `.class` file for each separate class. The name of the `.class` file for the nested class will contain a `$` character in place of the dot separating the two components of its name. This is reflected in the name of the class returned by the `getName` method of the `Class` class (see Section 15.7). Therefore, the output from the example in Code 15.14 will be:

```
VariableController$HeaterLevelException: Illegal level setting: 100
```

The close association of exception sub classes with the classes that throw them makes exception classes ideal candidates for implementing as static nested classes.

Although placing a static nested class within a class suggests that the enclosing class will typically be responsible for instantiating it, an instance of a static nested class can exist entirely independently of instances of its enclosing class. If the nested class is visible to other classes, they may create instances of it using its fully qualified name.

Exercise 15.5 Modify your solution to Exercise 14.18 so that RandomRange-Exception is defined as a static nested class within the RandomRange class. What consequent changes must be made to any classes that create and use RandomRange objects?

15.6 Inner Classes

In Section 15.5, we introduced the idea of nesting the definition of one class inside another, as a way of indicating a particularly close association between the nested class and its enclosing class. In addition to static nested classes, Java also permits *non-static nested classes* which are also known as *inner classes*. In contrast to the static variety, an instance of a non-static nested class can only exist within the context of an instance of its enclosing class. In other words, an instance of an inner class always has an associated *enclosing object*. One difference between a top-level class and an inner class is that a non-static inner class is not allowed to have static methods or variables. An inner class object has unqualified access to all of the methods and fields of its enclosing object—even the `private` ones. There is a danger in this in that it is all too easy to put too much functionality into an inner class's methods. One result is to couple the inner class too closely to its enclosing class. It is better to have an inner class object simply call an enclosing class method to perform the major part of its task, if possible.

Non-static inner classes are used in several different ways, which we discuss in the next few sections.

15.6.1   Subordinate Inner Classes

Inner classes are often used as a way to break up potentially large classes into two or more related but smaller classes. The enclosing class provides the major functionality of the class and one or more inner classes provide associated but subordinate functionality. We informally describe inner classes used in this way as *subordinate inner classes*. One purpose that they fulfill is to free their enclosing object from having to deal with subordinate activities and, hence, help to keep the enclosing classes simpler than they might otherwise have to be. The enclosing class typically has an attribute of the inner class, to which it delegates responsibility for particular tasks.

Consider the `LoggingShip` example in Code 15.15, which keeps a running record of its position after every move.[3]

Code 15.15   Log a ship's position after every move (`LoggingShip.java`)

```
import java.util.*;

        // Simple definition of the Ship class with position,
        // speed and course information.
        // The Ship maintains a log of its position after each
        // move using an inner class ShipLog object.
public class LoggingShip extends SimpleShip {
    public LoggingShip(){
        // Log the ship's initial position.
        getLogger().log();
    }

        // Extend move so that it records the new position.
    public void move(){
        super.move();
        getLogger().log();
    }
```

(Continued)

---

[3] For the sake of simplicity, we have defined LoggingShip as a sub class of SimpleShip. However, the case for using an inner class in this example is even more compelling if we choose to make logging part of the core functionality of all ships.

Code 15.15 (*Continued*)

```
    // Return whatever information the logger has collected.
public Iterator getLog(){
    return getLogger().getLog().iterator();
}

    // Delegate the role of logging information to
    // a ShipLog object.
protected class ShipLog {
    protected void log(){
        // Get the enclosing ship's position.
        Position p = new Position(getX(),getY());
        // Add it to the log.
        getLog().add(p);
    }

    protected LinkedList getLog(){
        return positionLog;
    }

    private LinkedList positionLog = new LinkedList();
}

protected ShipLog getLogger(){
    return logger;
}

private final ShipLog logger = new ShipLog();
}
```

Defined inside LoggingShip is an inner class, ShipLog, and an instance is created as an attribute called logger. When a ship is created, and each time it moves, it sends a log message to the logger. In this example, the logger maintains a collection to which it adds a new Position object each time it receives a log message. An inner class's direct access to the enclosing class's methods can be seen in ShipLog's use of getX and getY within its log method. These are references to methods of its enclosing object, which a LoggingShip inherits from its SimpleShip super class. It is important to note that it is not ShipLog that inherits the method but LoggingShip. However, ShipLog has free access to its enclosing class's members. Furthermore, the getLog method of ShipLog is not accessible via a reference to a LoggingShip object; if an external object wishes to obtain a copy of the ship's log, then it sends a getLog message to the ship object, which the ship then delegates to its logger attribute.

Code 15.16 shows a simple main method that illustrates how a ship's log might be obtained and printed after a few moves. The code of the main method is completely unaware that the logging function is performed by an inner class object. This is part of the ship's encapsulation of its implementation.

In view of the fact that inner class objects have access to the private data of their enclosing object, care should always be taken not to allow them to be used to provide

Code 15.16 A simple example of using a LoggingShip (`LoggingShipMain.java`)

```
import java.util.Iterator;

    // A demonstration of the logging features of a LoggingShip.
class LoggingShipMain {
    public static void main(String[] args){
        LoggingShip ship = new LoggingShip();
        ship.setSpeed(5);
        ship.move();
        ship.move();
        ship.move();

        // Find out where the ship has been.
        Iterator log = ship.getLog();
        System.out.print("The positions moved through are: ");
        while(log.hasNext()){
            Position p = (Position) log.next();
            System.out.print(p+" ");
        }
        System.out.println();
    }
}
```

back door access to that data. Unless there is very good reason to do otherwise, an enclosing object's attributes should continue to be manipulated in the inner class via their accessors and mutators, in the usual way.

It can sometimes be difficult to decide whether to create an inner class or not. In the LoggingShip example, there would have been nothing to stop us from defining all of the ShipLog functionality directly inside its enclosing class, rather than resorting to an inner class. As the main method in Code 15.16 is unaware of the existence of an inner class object, it would not be affected by a modification that moved the logging functionality from the inner class to the enclosing class. This possibility for diversity of implementation is typical of the subordinate usage of inner classes, in contrast to the interpretational use described in Section 15.6.2. However, as described above, inner classes do provide us with the opportunity to encapsulate a small set of specialized behavior in a separate subordinate class, each of whose instances is closely tied to a single instance of the enclosing class. The case for using an inner class becomes more compelling if we were to add additional sophistication to the logging features in this particular example. We might wish to keep the current course and speed, as well as the position, or only keep a log of the most recent 100 positions, say. Instead of having the logger return an Iterator over the positions, we could even have it send a pretty printed report to an output file. All of these additional features have nothing to do with the essential behavior of a ship object, and so they demand to be placed in a separate class. Yet, the close association of the data with the ship to which it belongs suggests an inner class is the most appropriate solution.

15.6.2   Interpretational Inner Classes

In Section 15.6.1, we described the subordinate role that inner classes often provide to their enclosing class; objects external to the class are typically not aware of the separation between the inner and enclosing functionality. There is also a further use for inner classes which is almost always to provide explicit external access to some or all of an enclosing object's data. We refer to these as *interpretational inner classes*, since their role is often to provide a view or interpretation of that data in a form which will be familiar to the external object, but independent of the actual representation in the enclosing object. This view is often via one of the common collection interfaces, such as `Iterator` or `Enumeration`.

Code 15.17 illustrates a class, `DataValues`, which has been designed to store an arbitrary number of `double` values, placing them in `Double` wrappers.

Code 15.17   A collection of data for which we wish to provide interpretations or selections

```
import java.util.*;
import java.io.PrintWriter;

        /* An example of creating an inner class Iterator.
         * Collect an arbitrary number of double values.
         * Provide access to individual items and the mean value,
         * for instance.
         * Allow selection of all positive values in the collection.
         */
public class DataValues {
        // Add a value to the collection.
    public void add(double d){
        getNumbers().add(new Double(d));
    }

        // Get a value from the collection.
    public double get(int index) throws IndexOutOfBoundsException {
        Double d = (Double) getNumbers().get(index);
        return d.doubleValue();
    }

        // Calculate the mean of the values in the collection.
    public double mean(){
        final int howMany = numItems();
        if(howMany > 0){
            double sum = 0.0;
            for(int i = 0; i < howMany; i++){
                sum += get(i);
            }
            return sum / howMany;
        }
        else{
            return 0.0;
        }
    }
```

Code 15.17   (*Continued*)

```
        // Print the collection.
    public void print(PrintWriter writer){
        final int howMany = numItems();
        for(int i = 0; i < howMany; i++){
            writer.print(get(i)+" ");
        }
        writer.println();
        writer.flush();
    }

        // Return how many items in the collection.
    public int numItems(){
        return getNumbers().size();
    }

    // Possibly other methods relating to the data.
    ...

    protected LinkedList getNumbers(){
        return numbers;
    }

    // A collection of Double objects.
    private final LinkedList numbers = new LinkedList();
}
```

DataValues provides methods to add a value, determine how many are stored, retrieve an individual value, calculate the mean value, and it could have other methods relating to ways in which the data is to be manipulated. It is not envisaged that items will be deleted from the collection. We shall use the `DataValues` class to illustrate different ways in which inner classes might be used to provide interpretations or selections of the data managed by its instances. For instance, we might want to be able to select all the positive values from the collection and be able to use an Iterator over them. Code 15.18 illustrates one way to achieve this using an Iterator associated with a LinkedList. Note that this particular example does not yet use an inner class. The `getPositives` method works by creating a new linked list and copying into it the set of positive values from the full set of values. It then returns an iterator object from the new linked list. An object receiving this iterator is able to iterate through the collection of positive data which is independent of the full collection held by the DataValues object. This has both a positive and a negative effect:

- On the positive side, the object receiving the iterator is not able to modify the actual data held in the full collection. The iterator's `remove` method will only operate on the copy.
- On the negative side, the iterator will not be aware of any additions to the actual collection that might be made following the creation of the copy. Furthermore, each request to `getPositives` results in a distinct copy of the collection being created. If the actual collection is constantly being added to over time,

Code 15.18   Selecting the positive values from the collection

```
public class DataValues {
    ...
        // Return an iterator over the positive values in the collection.
    public Iterator getPositives(){
        final int howMany = numItems();
        LinkedList positives = new LinkedList();
        for(int i = 0; i < howMany; i++){
            double d = get(i);
            if(d > 0){
                positives.add(new Double(d));
            }
        }
        return positives.iterator();
    }
    ...
}
```

and several external objects are viewing it through different iterators returned by separate calls to `getPositives`, then these different external objects will potentially have conflicting views of the positive data values contained in the full collection.

The only way to solve these problems is to ensure that any iterator over the positive values is always operating over the full set of values, rather than a copy. This is where an inner class facilitates an acceptable solution. Code 15.19 illustrates an inner class, `PositiveSelector`, inside the DataValues class. PositiveSelector implements the Iterator interface and a new instance is created whenever a `getPositives` message is received by a DataValues object.

PositiveSelector implements the three methods of the Iterator interface—`has-Next`, `next`, and `remove`—however, because we do not want it to be used to modify the actual collection, the `remove` method simply throws an `Unsupported-OperationException` exception. This retains the benefit of the previous solution. The inner class uses an attribute, `index`, to keep track of the next element of the collection to examine to see whether it is positive or not. Both `hasNext` and `next` use the class's `nextPosition` method to look ahead in the collection to see if there is another positive number present. Because a PositiveSelector always accesses the real collection, we have overcome the problem discussed above of further items being added to it after the selector has been created. Furthermore, all PositiveSelectors of a particular DataValues object will be representing the same collection of data; hence, clients will have consistent views of that data. The file `DataValuesMain.java` contains a main method to illustrate the DataValues class.

We shall return to use this example in Section 15.6.3 and Section 15.6.4, in order to illustrate further aspects of Java's inner classes.

Code 15.19   Using an inner class to select the positive data values (`DataValues.java`)

```java
import java.util.*;
import java.io.PrintWriter;

    /* An example of creating an inner class Iterator.
     * Collect an arbitrary number of double values.
     * Provide access to individual items and the mean value,
     * for instance.
     * Allow selection of all positive values in the collection.
     */
public class DataValues {
    ...
        // Obtain an iterator over the positive values in the collection.
    public Iterator getPositives(){
        return new PositiveSelector();
    }

        // An inner class to allow identification of the positive
        // values (> 0) in the collection.
    protected class PositiveSelector implements Iterator {
        public boolean hasNext(){
            return nextPosition() >= 0;
        }

            // Return the next positive data item, if there is one.
        public Object next() throws NoSuchElementException {
            // Find out where the next (if any) occurs.
            int i = nextPosition();
            if(i >= 0){
                Object o = getNumbers().get(i);
                // Next time, start looking from the following position.
                setIndex(i+1);
                return o;
            }
            else{
                throw new NoSuchElementException();
            }
        }

            // Disallow removal.
        public void remove() throws UnsupportedOperationException {
            throw new UnsupportedOperationException();
        }

            // Return the index of the next positive number in the
            // collection.  If there is none, return NOITEM.
        protected int nextPosition(){
            int i = getIndex();
            final int howMany = numItems();
            while(i < howMany){
                if(get(i) > 0){
                    return i;
                }
```

(Continued)

Code 15.19   (*Continued*)

```
            i++;
        }
        return NOITEM;
    }

    protected int getIndex(){
        return index;
    }

    protected void setIndex(int i){
        index = i;
    }

    // The index of the next item to be examined.
    private int index = 0;
    // An illegal index to indicate no item is available.
    private final int NOITEM = -1;
    }

    protected LinkedList getNumbers(){
        return numbers;
    }

    // A collection of Double objects.
    private final LinkedList numbers = new LinkedList();
}
```

Exercise 15.6   Define the class `Plotter`, which implements the outline shown in Code 15.20.[4] A Plotter object must keep a record of the argument values passed to each call of its `plot` method. When its `dumpData` method is called, it must list these values, one set per line. Implement the Plotter class so that it uses an inner class object to hold each set of `plot` argument values it receives. Objects of this inner class should be stored in a collection attribute belonging to Plotter. The `dumpData` method should iterate over the collection to write the values out. The output from the first few calls with the image data shown in Exercise 7.4 would be:

```
0 0 63 3
63 0 55 3
118 0 6 0
124 0 50 3
0 1 63 3
63 1 53 3
...
```

---

[4] This is similar in functionality to the `PicturePlotter` class described in Exercise 7.4.

Code 15.20   Outline of a data plotting class

```
class Plotter {
        // Plot count pixels of color, starting at x,y and
        // moving right horizontally.
    public void plot(int x, int y, int count, int color){
        ...
    }

        // Output the arguments to each previous call to plot.
    public void dumpData(){
        ...
    }
}
```

15.6.3   Local Inner Classes

The PositiveSelector class of the example in Code 15.19 was used in only one method of the DataValues class, getPositives. Unlike the examples of subordinate inner class used in Section 15.6.1, we see that the enclosing DataValues object retains no reference to the inner class object; its purpose, after all, is to provide a view of the enclosing object's data to an external object. Such localized use of an inner class—from within a single method—can be made explicit by defining it as a *local inner class*. A local inner class is defined *inside a method* rather than at the same level as the enclosing class's methods and variables. Local inner classes may be defined within any block inside a method, just like method variables. They are not prefixed with an access reserved word since, necessarily, their access is local to the block in which they are defined. Furthermore, they cannot be defined as static or final. In addition to the methods and attributes of the enclosing class, they have access to any final local variables or final arguments defined within the enclosing blocks of their enclosing method. In all other ways they are the same as non-local inner classes.

Code 15.21 defines a variation on the getPositives method and Positive-Selector class we have seen previously. It defines a method, selectAbove, which takes a parameter used to set a lower limit on the values of the data collection which are to be selected. For instance, selectAbove(0.0) would be equivalent to selectPositives(). The methods of the AboveSelector class are identical to PositiveSelector, with the single exception of the if-statement in the body of next-Position. Instead of testing against 0, we test against the value of limit, which is the argument of selectAbove. This must be declared as final in order to be accessible to the local class.

15.6.4   Anonymous Classes

The example of Code 15.21 adapted that of Code 15.19 to localize class definition and instance creation within a single method selectAbove. In this section, we describe an alternative adaptation of the PositiveSelector class of Code 15.19. This involves the creation of a more general inner class, called Selector, whose basic

Code 15.21 A local inner class which uses an enclosing method's `final` argument

```
import java.util.*;
import java.io.PrintWriter;

    /* An example of creating a local inner class Iterator.
     * Collect an arbitrary number of double values.
     * Provide access to individual items and the mean value,
     * for instance.
     * Allow selection of all values above a limit in the collection.
     */
public class DataValues {
    ...
        // Obtain an iterator over the values above limit in
        // the collection.
        // The argument must be final to be accessible to the
        // local class.
    public Iterator selectAbove(final double limit){
            // A local inner class to allow identification of
            // values > limit in the collection.
        class AboveSelector implements Iterator {
            ...
                // Return the index of the next positive number in
                // the collection.  If there is none, return noItem.
            protected int nextPosition(){
                int i = getIndex();
                final int howMany = numItems();
                while(i < howMany){
                    // Test against the argument limit specified.
                    if(get(i) > limit){
                        return i;
                    }
                    i++;
                }
                return NOITEM;
            }
            ...
        }

        return new AboveSelector();
    }
    ...
}
```

implementation is identical to that of PositiveSelector but which is designed to permit the simple creation of sub classes that iterate over arbitrary sets of values from the data collection. In order to do this, we shall introduce the ability to create *anonymous classes*.

We have already illustrated generalization of the PositiveSelector class (Code 15.19) in the AboveSelector class of Code 15.21. AboveSelector selected all values from the collection above a particular limit, rather than just values above zero. We could easily modify the AboveSelector class in a similar fashion to create a new class that selects the values below a limit, or to create a class that selects those values within a pair of limits. Both of these changes would require only a modification of the test condition in the `nextPosition` method, leaving the other methods unaltered. This discussion suggests that what we really need is a super class that provides the general functionality, with sub classes providing particular specialisms, such as selecting positive values, negative values, values within a range, and so on. Code 15.22 shows the class `DataSelection`. This contains an inner class, `Selector`, which embodies the general functionality that we are describing. The modifications to AboveSelector are the introduction of the Boolean method `select` and its use in `nextPosition` in place of the test involving a relational operator.

Code 15.22   An inner super class for general data selection (`DataSelection.java`)

```
import java.util.*;
import java.io.PrintWriter;

    // Collect an arbitrary number of double values.
    // Provide access to individual items and the mean value,
    // for instance.
    // Allow selection of values from the collection on different criteria.
public class DataSelection {
    // Methods applying to the whole collection.
    ...
    // Methods for various criteria.

        // Obtain an iterator over the values above limit in the collection.
    public Iterator selectAbove(final double limit){
        ...
    }

        // Obtain an iterator over the values below limit in the collection.
    public Iterator selectBelow(final double limit){
        ...
    }

        // Obtain an iterator over the values in the range
        // [lower .. upper] in the collection.
    public Iterator selectRange(final double lower, final double upper){
        ...
    }

        // A local inner super class to allow selection of
        // values in the collection.
    protected class Selector implements Iterator {
        public boolean hasNext(){
            return nextPosition() >= 0;
        }

            // Return the next positive data item, if there is one.
        public Object next() throws NoSuchElementException {
```

(Continued)

Code 15.22   (*Continued*)

```
        // Find out where the next (if any) occurs.
        int i = nextPosition();
        if(i >= 0){
            Object o = getNumbers().get(i);
            // Next time, start looking from the following position.
            setIndex(i+1);
            return o;
        }
        else{
            throw new NoSuchElementException();
        }
    }

    // Disallow removal.
    public void remove() throws UnsupportedOperationException {
        throw new UnsupportedOperationException();
    }

    // Decide whether to select this particular value.
    // This method would normally be overridden in
    // an inner sub class.
    public boolean select(double d){
        return true;
    }

    // Return the index of the next positive number in the
    // collection.  If there is none, return NOITEM.
    protected int nextPosition(){
        int i = getIndex();
        final int howMany = numItems();
        while(i < howMany){
            // Test against the selection criteria.
            if(select(get(i))){
                return i;
            }
            i++;
        }
        return NOITEM;
    }

    protected int getIndex(){
        return index;
    }

    protected void setIndex(int i){
        index = i;
    }

    // The index of the next item to be examined.
    private int index = 0;
    // An illegal index to indicate no item is available.
    private final int NOITEM = -1;
}
```

Code 15.22   (*Continued*)

```
    protected LinkedList getNumbers(){
        return numbers;
    }

    // A collection of Double objects.
    private final LinkedList numbers = new LinkedList();
}
```

The DataSelection class is essentially the same in purpose and behavior as the
DataValues class shown in Code 15.17. The signatures of three methods (select-
Above, selectBelow, and selectRange) have been included to illustrate the
sort of selections that might be required. The selectAbove method could be implemented using a local inner class to extend Selector, as shown in Code 15.23. This
illustrates no new features of Java.

  This two-stage purpose of defining a local inner class simply for the purpose
of constructing an object immediately afterwards is so common that Java allows
us to define the class anonymously, effectively combining its definition with object
creation. This is similar to the way in which anonymous arrays may be created, for
instance (see Section 9.7.1); Code 15.24 shows full definitions of the three select
methods of DataSelection, each of which creates an *anonymous class* for the sub
classes of Selector.

  An anonymous class is created as part of an expression involving the new
operator. This is followed by the name of a super class for the anonymous class
and arguments for the super class's constructor. The body of the anonymous class
then follows, containing any methods and variables it requires. Note that the return
statements in which these examples are defined require their normal terminating
semicolon, which looks slightly unusual following a closing curly bracket. As with
local classes, anonymous classes are able to access any final variables and arguments

Code 15.23   Selecting values above `limit` using a local inner sub class

```
class DataSelection {
    ...
        // Obtain an iterator over the values above limit in the collection.
    public Iterator selectAbove(final double limit){
        class PositiveSelector extends Selector {
            public boolean select(double d){
                return d > limit;
            }
        }
        return new PositiveSelector();
    }
    ...
}
```

Code 15.24   Returning anonymous sub class objects (`DataSelection.java`)

```
public class DataSelection {
    ...
        // Obtain an iterator over the values above limit
        // in the collection.
    public Iterator selectAbove(final double limit){
        return new Selector(){
            // Provide the selection criteria.
            public boolean select(double d){
                return d > limit;
            }
        };
    }

        // Obtain an iterator over the values below limit
        // in the collection.
    public Iterator selectBelow(final double limit){
        return new Selector(){
            // Provide the selection criteria.
            public boolean select(double d){
                return d < limit;
            }
        };
    }

        // Obtain an iterator over the values in the range
        // [lower .. upper] in the collection.
    public Iterator withinRange(final double lower, final double upper){
        return new Selector(){
            // Provide the selection criteria.
            public boolean select(double d){
                return (d >= lower) && (d <= upper);
            }
        };
    }
    ...
}
```

of their enclosing method. Anonymous classes may also be used to implement interfaces, as shown in Code 15.25. As we shall see in Chapter 16, anonymous classes are particularly common for implementing *listener* interface implementations for handling user interface events.

Anonymous classes may not have a constructor, since this would mean they would require a name. However, where their super class's constructor requires arguments, these are placed in the parentheses immediately after the class name, in the usual way. The lack of a constructor is not a significant problem, since the same purpose can often be achieved in an instance initializer block. Each anonymous class is compiled to a separate .class file, the name of which is that of its enclosing class followed by a $ character and a number, 1, 2, ..., depending upon the number of anonymous classes defined within an enclosing class.

Code 15.25   Returning an anonymous class implementation of an interface

```
        // Return an Iterator over the data values.
    public Iterator iterator(){
        // Provide implementations of each method of Iterator.
        return new Iterator(){
            public boolean hasNext(){
                ...
            }
            ...
        }
        ...
    }
```

Exercise 15.7   Complete the body of the following method:

```
    public static Iterator steps(final int stepSize)
```

The method should return an anonymous object that implements the Iterator interface. The hasNext method always returns true and the remove method throws an UnsupportedOperationException exception. The next method returns Integer objects containing successive integer values, starting at zero and increasing each time by stepSize. So a call to steps with an actual argument value of 3 will return an infinite sequence starting:

```
    0  3  6  9  12 ...
```

Test your implementation from the main method shown in Code 15.26.

15.6.5   Inner Classes and `this`

Because an inner class object has access to the members of its enclosing class, there is room for confusion over the meaning of this in the context of an inner class. Within an inner class, this always refers to an instance of that inner class. The enclosing object of an inner class instance must be referred to as Enclosing.this, where Enclosing is the name of the immediately enclosing class. Code 15.27 illustrates one inner class nested inside another inner class. In Code 15.27, three different this objects will be accessible from the innermost object: this, Middle.this, and Outer.this.

15.6.6   External Creation of Inner Class Objects

While inner classes performing a subordinate role are often not directly visible to external objects, and interpretational inner classes are often accessed via an interface, it is sometimes necessary for inner classes to be directly accessible from outside their enclosing class. A distinguishing feature of an inner class object is its tie to a particular instance of its enclosing class (Enclosing.this). This association

Code 15.26   A test-rig for the `steps` method (`AnonymousMain.java`)

```
import java.util.Iterator;

        // Exercise outline.
        // Complete the body of steps.
class AnonymousMain {
    public static void main(String[] args){
        Iterator i = steps(3);
        while(i.hasNext()){
            System.out.println(i.next()+" ");
        }
    }

        // Return an anonymous implementation of Iterator.
        // That returns an infinite sequence
        //      0, 0+stepSize, 0+2*stepSize, ...
    public static Iterator steps(final int stepSize){
        // ...
    }
}
```

Code 15.27   Accessing enclosing instances (`this`) from an inner class

```
class Outer {
    // 'this' accessible from here.
    ...
    class Middle {
        // 'this' and 'Outer.this' accessible from here.
        ...
        class Innermost {
            // 'this', 'Middle.this' and 'Outer.this' accessible from here.
            ...
        }
        ...
        private Innermost i = new Innermost();
    }
    ...
    private Middle m = new Middle();
}
```

is created automatically and implicitly as part of the instantiation of the inner class
object. This is in contrast to any association between objects of top-level classes, which
is created by explicitly passing a reference to one object as an argument to a method
of another object. As a consequence of the implicit association of an inner class
object with its enclosing instance, it is not possible to instantiate an inner class object
directly from outside its enclosing class; such an object would have no associated

enclosing object. As with static nested classes, an inner class may be referred to by prefixing its name with the names of all of its enclosing classes. For instance, the full class name of the Innermost class of Code 15.27 is `Outer.Middle.Innermost`. However, although it is possible to use this type name to define a variable to hold an object reference obtained from an enclosing object, it is not possible to use it directly to create an instance of an inner class, such as:

```
// This is illegal ...
new Outer.Middle();
```

The reason for this lies in the fact that any object of the Middle class must have an instance of the Outer class as its enclosing object, and here it has none. However, it is still possible to create an object of an inner class from outside its enclosing class. In order to do so, we must provide an enclosing object as part of its creation. The syntax to do this is as follows:

```
// We need a reference to an appropriate enclosing-class object.
Outer outerObj = new Outer();
...
// Create an object of class Outer.Middle
Outer.Middle middleObj = outerObj.new Middle();
```

There are two points to note about this example:

- The `new` used to create the inner class object must be prefixed by a reference to an object of the appropriate enclosing class.
- The name of the constructor used for the inner class object is the unqualified class name, i.e. `Middle` rather than `Outer.Middle`.

We can extend this particular example further by creating an instance of the innermost class of Code 15.27 as follows:

```
Outer.Middle.Inner innerObj = middleObj.new Inner();
```

Remember that these qualified forms are only required if the objects are being created from outside the immediately enclosing class of the object being created.

15.6.7 Linked Data Structures

In Chapter 10, we introduced the `LinkedList` collection class, which supported the maintenance of arbitrary-sized collections of objects. Figure 10.1 illustrated a possible internal implementation of that class. Inner classes are an ideal means of implementing such classes. Code 15.28 shows a class, `Queue`, that maintains a *first in, first out (FIFO) queue* of objects, using a subordinate inner class, `Node`. Each Node object is only responsible for maintaining a reference to a single item in the queue, and to the next in line. References to the nodes at the beginning and end of the queue are stored in the `head` and `tail` attributes of Queue. Note that these attributes refer to nodes, and not the queue items, themselves.

Code 15.28   An object queue (`Queue.java`)

```java
// Maintain a queue of objects. This class provides a more limited
// set of capabilities than java.util.LinkedList, for instance.
// Use an inner class, Node, to provide the internal structure
// of the queue.
public class Queue {
    // Add an object to the tail of the queue.
    public void add(Object o){
        Node n = new Node(o);
        Node tail = getTail();
        if(tail != null){
            tail.setNext(n);
        }
        else{
            // Whole queue is empty.
            setHead(n);
        }
        setTail(n);
    }

    // Return (and remove) the object at the head of the queue.
    // Return null if the queue is empty.
    public Object next(){
        Object item = null;
        Node head = getHead();
        if(head != null){
            item = head.getItem();
            // Drop the node from the head.
            Node nextNode = head.getNext();
            setHead(nextNode);
            if(nextNode == null){
                // Empty queue.
                setTail(nextNode);
            }
        }
        return item;
    }

    // Return a reference to the object at the head of the queue,
    // without removing it.
    // Return null if the queue is empty.
    public Object peek(){
        Object item = null;
        Node head = getHead();
        if(head != null){
            item = head.getItem();
        }
        return item;
    }

    // Return the length of the queue.
    public int size(){
        int length = 0;
```

Code 15.28   (*Continued*)

```
        Node node = getHead();
        while(node != null){
            length++;
            node = node.getNext();
        }
        return length;
    }

    // Maintain a reference to a single item in the queue, and
    // a reference to the next in line.
    protected class Node {
        public Node(Object item){
            this.item = item;
        }

        public Object getItem(){
            return item;
        }

        public Node getNext(){
            return next;
        }

        public void setNext(Node n){
            next = n;
        }

        private final Object item;
        private Node next = null;
    }

    protected Node getHead(){
        return head;
    }

    protected void setHead(Node n){
        head = n;
    }

    protected Node getTail(){
        return tail;
    }

    protected void setTail(Node n){
        tail = n;
    }

    // References to the node at the head and tail of the queue.
    // Both references are null when the queue is empty.
    private Node head = null, tail = null;
}
```

Exercise 15.8   Modify the implementation of the `size` method of the `Queue` class, shown in Code 15.28, so that it does not have to be calculated dynamically.

Exercise 15.9   Implement a *last in, first out (LIFO)* stack using an inner class.

Exercise 15.10   Implement a more general linked queue data structure whose `add` method has the following signature:

```
public void add(Object o,int priority)
```

Objects are placed in the queue such that those with the highest priority are placed nearer the head of the queue. No change will be required to the `remove` method.

15.7   The Class Class

In Section 14.9, we saw that the Object class defines the method `getClass`. This returns an object of type `Class`, which is defined in the `java.lang` package. The `Class` for an object contains useful information about the object's type and `Class` objects exist for all object types, array types, and the primitive types, even though the latter are not object types. Each class used by a program has been loaded by a `ClassLoader` object. A reference to the loader for a Class is available via the `getClassLoader` method of a Class object.

A particularly important role played by `Class` is to enable *reflection*—the ability to find out what methods, fields, constructors, and so on, are defined for a class and to create what are, in effect, dynamic programs. For instance, a string typed by a user could be turned directly into the name of a message to be sent to an object, enabling a more sophisticated version of Exercise 8.1 to be created.

Code 15.29 shows an example that uses some of the methods defined in the `Class` class to print information about a variety of types.

Code 15.29 An illustration of some of the methods of the Class class (`ClassExampleMain.java`)

```
    // Illustrate methods of the java.lang.Class class.
class ClassExampleMain {
    public static void main(String[] args){
        // Create some objects whose classes will be examined.
        final String obj = new String();
        final int[] arr = new int[10];

        // Obtain class objects for the String, the array
        // and the primitive int type.
        final Class[] classes = {
            obj.getClass(),
            arr.getClass(),
            int.class,
        };
        // Show details of the example classes.
        final int numClasses = classes.length;
```

Code 15.29   (*Continued*)

```
        for(int i = 0; i < numClasses; i++){
            showClassDetails(classes[i]);
        }
    }

    // Show a few details on the given class.
    public static void showClassDetails(Class c){
        // The class's name.
        System.out.println(c.getName());
        if(c.isPrimitive()){
            System.out.println(" Is a primitive type.");
        }
        else if(c.isArray()){
            Class baseType = c.getComponentType();
            System.out.println(" Is an array of: "+baseType.getName());
        }
        else{
            // A class.
            final Class superClass = c.getSuperclass();
            if(superClass != null){
                System.out.println(" Extends: "+superClass.getName());
            }
            if(c.isInterface()){
                System.out.println(" Is an interface.");
            }
            // See if this class implements one or more interfaces.
            final Class[] interfaces = c.getInterfaces();
            for(int i = 0; i < interfaces.length; i++){
                System.out.println(" Implements: "+
                                    interfaces[i].getName());
            }
        }
    }
}
```

The main method illustrates that a Class object can be obtained via the getClass method of any class or array object. In addition, a primitive type name (including void) followed by .class provides a reference to a Class object for the primitive types. The showClassDetails method of Code 15.29 illustrates the get-ComponentType, getInterfaces, getName, getSuperclass, isArray, is-Interface, and isPrimitive methods in order to print a simple diagnostic output for each of the three Class objects. The output is as follows:

```
    java.lang.String
     Extends: java.lang.Object
     Implements: java.io.Serializable
     Implements: java.lang.Comparable
    [I
     Is an array of: int
```

```
int
   Is a primitive type.
```

The output [I is the name used for the int[] type.

The Class class defines several additional methods whose return types are defined in the `java.lang.reflect` package, such as `Constructor`, `Field`, and `Method`, which contain Class information about constructors, fields, and methods, respectively. A detailed examination of these is beyond the scope of this book, but the example in Code 15.30 illustrates several of them in an application to create an object of an arbitrary class, and control it via interactive commands from a user.

Code 15.30   Dynamically send messages to an object from user commands
(`DynamicProgram.java`)

```java
import java.lang.reflect.*;

    // Interactively control an object of objectClass.
    // The assumption is that this Class has a no-arg constructor.
class DynamicProgram {
    public DynamicProgram(Class objectClass) throws RuntimeException {
        // Make sure objectClass has a no-arg constructor.
        try{
            Constructor noArgConstructor =
                        objectClass.getConstructor(new Class[0]);
            subject = noArgConstructor.newInstance(new Object[0]);
        }
        catch(NoSuchMethodException e){
            throw new RuntimeException(objectClass.getName()+
                                    " must have a no-arg constructor.");
        }
        catch(IllegalAccessException e){
            throw new RuntimeException(e.toString());
        }
        catch(InstantiationException e){
            throw new RuntimeException(e.toString());
        }
        catch(InvocationTargetException e){
            throw new RuntimeException(e.toString());
        }
    }

        // Interactively read commands from the user and send
        // them as messages to the subject object.
    public void run(){
        // The Object to be controlled.
        final Object subject = getSubject();
        final Class subjectClass = subject.getClass();
        final Method[] methods = subjectClass.getMethods();
        final SimpleInput reader = getReader();
        final String terminatingCommand = "quit!";
        System.out.println("Type "+terminatingCommand+" to finish.");
        String command = getCommand();
```

Code 15.30   (*Continued*)

```java
        while(!command.equalsIgnoreCase(terminatingCommand)){
            // Make sure the command maps to a method.
            Method method = matchMethod(methods,command);
            if(method != null){
                invokeMethod(method,subject);
            }
            else{
                System.err.println("No match found for: "+command);
            }
            command = getCommand();
        }
    }

    // Invoke the given method, with appropriate arguments,
    // on subject.
    // This method only copes with arguments of primitive type
    // int and double.
    protected void invokeMethod(Method method,Object subject){
        try{
            final Class[] argumentClasses = method.getParameterTypes();
            final int numArgs = argumentClasses.length;
            final Object[] args = new Object[numArgs];
            final SimpleInput reader = getReader();
            for(int i = 0; i < numArgs; i++){
                if(argumentClasses[i] == int.class){
                    args[i] = new Integer(reader.nextInt());
                }
                else if(argumentClasses[i] == double.class){
                    args[i] = new Double(reader.nextDouble());
                }
                else{
                    System.err.println(
                        "Only numerical arguments are possible.");
                    return;
                }
            }
            method.invoke(subject,args);
        }
        catch(IllegalAccessException e){
            System.err.println(e);
        }
        catch(InvocationTargetException e){
            System.err.println(e);
        }
    }

    protected Method matchMethod(Method[] methods, String command){
        final int numMethods = methods.length;
        for(int i = 0; i < numMethods; i++){
            if(methods[i].getName().equalsIgnoreCase(command)){
                return methods[i];
            }
```

(*Continued*)

Code 15.30   *(Continued)*

```
        }
        return null;
    }

    protected String getCommand(){
        System.out.print("Command: ");
        System.out.flush();
        return getReader().nextWord();
    }

    protected Object getSubject(){
        return subject;
    }

    protected SimpleInput getReader(){
        return reader;
    }

    // The instance to be controlled.
    private final Object subject;
    // Where commands are read from.
    private final SimpleInput reader = new SimpleInput();
}
```

The constructor of DynamicProgram takes a Class argument, representing the class of object it is to create. It checks that this has a no-arg constructor, by using the class's getConstructor method. This takes an array of Classes as its argument, which should have a length of zero for a no-arg constructor. It then uses the Constructor object's newInstance method (again taking a zero-length array for its argument) to create an instance of the class. This is saved in the subject attribute for later use. As can be seen, several exceptions might arise as a result of these efforts. All should cause the constructor to fail.

The class's run method is responsible for reading command strings from the user and matching these against the methods of the subject's class. An array of Method objects is obtained via the getMethods method of Class. The matchMethods method of DynamicProgram is used to search this array for a method name matching the user's command. If one is found, it must be established whether it takes any arguments or not. In this limited example, the invokeMethod of DynamicProgram only checks for arguments of the primitive types int and double. The appropriate method is called via its invoke method. This takes the object to receive the message as its first argument, and an array of arguments as it second. The arguments must all be of Object types, so it is necessary to wrap primitive argument values in an appropriate wrapper class.

The example in Code 15.30 may be driven from the main method shown in Code 15.31. This takes a single command line argument naming the class to use in order to create the subject to be controlled. The main method uses the forName method of the Class class in order to ensure that the class name is fully resolved within

```
    // A test-rig for the DynamicProgram class. The name of a class
    // with a no-arg constructor should be passed as a single
    // command line argument. An object of this class will then
    // be dynamically controlled interactively.
class DynamicProgramMain {
    public static void main(String[] args){
        if(args.length != 1){
            System.err.println("Usage: DynamicProgramMain class-name");
        }
        else{
            try{
                // Resolve the class name into a Class
                final Class objectClass = Class.forName(args[0]);
                // Create an object to run the class dynamically.
                final DynamicProgram program =
                                new DynamicProgram(objectClass);
                program.run();
            }
            catch(ClassNotFoundException e){
                System.err.println("Unable to find class: "+args[0]);
            }
        }
    }
}
```

the interpreter's current context. An appropriate class to use might be `SimpleShip`. Interactive commands, such as

```
move
setCourse 90
report
```

could then be used to control it.

15.8   Review

Here are the main points that we have covered in the preceding sections:

- Class and interface definitions may be nested.
- The fully qualified name of a nested class contains the name of its enclosing class as a prefix.
- The compiler includes a $ character in the `.class` file name for nested classes.
- An unnested class is a top-level class.
- A static nested class is a static top-level class.
- A static nested class only has access to the static members of its enclosing class.
- A non-static nested class is an inner class.
- An inner class may not have static members.
- An object of an inner class has unqualified access to the members of its enclosing class, even private members.

- Inner classes often provide functionality that is subordinate to the main behavior of their enclosing class.
- Inner classes often provide access to data of their enclosing class via a well-known interface.
- An inner class defined inside a method is a local inner class.
- Local inner classes may access the final arguments and final method variables of their enclosing method.
- An anonymous class is a local inner class without a name.
- An anonymous class implicitly extends an existing class or implements an interface.
- Inner classes must prefix `this` with the name of their enclosing class in order to obtain an explicit reference to their enclosing object.
- Objects of the `Class` class contain detailed information on the implementation of a program's classes.
- A class object exists for all of the primitive types, including `void`.
- Reflection, using the `java.lang.reflect` package, allows dynamic programs to be created.

In introducing abstract classes and nested classes, we have now described most of the major features of the Java programming language. In future chapters, we shall build on all of the fundamental language features we have covered up to this point, when we explore programs that involve graphical user interfaces, networking, concurrency, and simulation.

PART

III

GUI Packages

CHAPTER

16

AWT Applications

In this chapter, we introduce some of the graphical capabilities of Java through the development of `Frame`-based Applications. The Abstract Windowing Toolkit (AWT) provides a powerful collection of classes that simplify the creation of applications with graphical user interfaces. This chapter builds heavily on the concepts of interfaces and inheritance that were introduced in previous chapters.

16.1 The Abstract Windowing Toolkit

One of the major attractions of Java is that it is relatively easy to create programs that make use of the graphical facilities of modern personal computers and workstations. This is made possible by the large library of class definitions to be found in the `java.awt` package. These are known as the *Abstract Windowing Toolkit (AWT)*, and they provide ready-made definitions of classes to handle windows, menus, buttons, dialogs, fonts, events, sound, and so on. Furthermore, they do so in a way that makes *Graphical User Interfaces (GUIs)* appear broadly similar across the whole range of different platforms. Many of the classes we describe are part of a large collection of classes known as the *Java Foundation Classes (JFC)*. Within the scope of this book, there is not room to describe the full set of classes defined within this and its associated packages. Nevertheless, we shall describe enough to create reasonably sophisticated GUIs. In Chapter 17, we shall cover a further set of JFC classes, known as *Swing*. The Swing classes build heavily on the AWT classes.

There are two main styles of Java programs that use the AWT: *Applications* and *Applets*. Applications have a slightly smaller set of AWT facilities available to them than Applets, but they are closer to the style of programs that we have seen so far in this book. Applets are the programs that are often run within Web browsers to provide sophisticated Web pages. The security restrictions associated with applets mean that, outside of Web browsers, they have little to offer over standard applications. In this chapter, we shall deal only with Applications, but most of the principles will apply equally well to Applets, which are dealt with in Chapter 20. In using the AWT, we shall see many examples of the power of Object-Oriented programming, particularly through the use of inheritance and interfaces.

16.2   The Frame Class

All programs that make use of the AWT import the `java.awt` package. Defined within this package are many of the fundamental classes that are used to build applications with graphical user interfaces. Of these classes, `Component` and `Container` provide the major building block super classes for applications. The starting point for all AWT applications is the `Frame` class. Frame represents what we traditionally think of as a rectangular window. In the AWT inheritance hierarchy, Frame exists several levels below the Object class; Frame extends `Window`, which extends `Container`, which extends `Component`, which extends `Object`. Code 16.1 shows a simple program to create an instance of the `Frame` class, which is defined in the `java.awt` package. This results in a small empty rectangular window appearing on the screen, with dimensions approximately 100×100 *pixels*, illustrated in Figure 16.1.

From the fundamental abstract Component class, Frame inherits its basic methods that allow us, among other things, to set the size of the frame (`setSize`), whether it is visible or not (`setVisible`), and perform basic drawing within the window (`paint`). Many of the methods defined in Component are overridden and extended in its sub classes and, as we discuss in Section 16.2.1, overriding `paint` will be a primary means of controlling what appears in a window.

Code 16.1 already illustrates the power of the AWT. In order to display a window on the screen, we do not need to know anything about the way in which graphics are implemented by the window manager running in the current working environment. All of those details are taken care of in the implementations of the sub classes of Component.

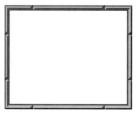

Figure 16.1   A basic Frame with no contents
(`BasicFrame.java`)

Code 16.1   Creating a Frame object (`BasicFrame.java`)

```
        // Create a simple frame.
import java.awt.*;

public class BasicFrame {
    public static void main(String[] args){
        Frame frame = new Frame();
        final int width = 100, height = 100;
        frame.setSize(width,height);
        frame.setVisible(true);
    }
}
```

Figure 16.2   Drawing text in a Frame
(`AWTWorld.java`)

Exercise 16.1   Compile and run the program illustrated in Code 16.1. Does the window manager automatically place the frame at a particular position on the screen or does it prompt you to place it? Can you perform all of the normal window management operations on the frame? Will the window manager allow you to close the window in the normal way?

If you tried Exercise 16.1, then you might have been surprised to find that the window did not disappear almost as soon as it was created, when control reached the end of the main method. The reason it remains on the screen is that an instance of the Frame class runs in a separate *thread of control* from the part of the application that created it (see Chapter 18 for a detailed explanation of threads). This means that this program does not end as soon as the end of the main method is reached; in fact, the program will continue displaying the frame until interrupted by an external event—such as the user pressing an interrupt key in the window from which the application was run.[1] Attempting to close the window using the window manager's normal commands for this does not usually work unless further code is added to the application; we say that the window must be listening for a message from the window manager telling it to close. In Section 16.3, we introduce a means of achieving this, although a detailed discussion of how it works is left until Section 16.20.

16.2.1   The `paint` Method

Code 16.1 illustrated the creation of a Frame object directly. Most of the time, however, we will want to define sub classes of Frame in order to have greater control over a window's contents. In particular, because Frame is a sub class of the Container class, this will allow us to add further components to it, such as menus, buttons, labels, text areas, and so on. In addition, we will sometimes override a frame's `paint` method in order to draw graphics or text within the window. We can illustrate this with the program in Code 16.2 which is an AWT-equivalent of a hello-world program, whose output is illustrated in Figure 16.2.

Here we see the power of inheritance; everything to do with window creation is performed for us in the constructors of the super classes of the `HelloWorld` class, and all we need to add is what we want to appear on the frame's surface. Passing a string to the frame's constructor provides the window manager with a title for the frame.

---

[1] On UNIX and Windows systems this is usually the *Control C* key.

Code 16.2   Creating a sub class of Frame (`AWTWorld.java`)

```java
import java.awt.*;

        // Paint a string in the graphics context of a Frame.
public class AWTWorld {
    public static void main(String[] args){
        HelloWorld world = new HelloWorld();
        world.setVisible(true);
    }
}

        // Extend Frame to provide control over the frame's contents.
class HelloWorld extends Frame {
    public HelloWorld(){
        // Give this frame a title.
        super("Hello World");
        // Set the frame's size.
        final int width = 150, height = 100;
        setSize(width,height);
    }

        // Override Frame's paint method.
    public void paint(Graphics g){
        // Define the drawing position.
        final int xpos = 10, ypos = 50;
        g.drawString("Welcome to Earth!",xpos,ypos);
    }
}
```

Exercise 16.2   Compile and run the program illustrated in Code 16.2. What does your window manager do with the title passed to the constructor of Frame by the constructor of HelloWorld? Some window managers include a title bar and others do not. Some use the title when the window is displayed as an *icon*.

An interesting feature of the program in Code 16.2 is that there is no explicit call to `paint` written into the program. If you tried Exercise 16.2, then you will know that the string is displayed, nevertheless. The reason is that `paint` is called automatically whenever an object belonging to a sub class of Component needs to be displayed.

Exercise 16.3   Demonstrate that `paint` is automatically called when a window is resized by running the example in Code 16.2, which you can find in the file `AWT-World.java`. Adjust the size of the frame using the window manager. Each time it is grown or shrunk, the text will be redrawn.

In order for a Component to paint itself, it needs a *graphics context* in which to draw. This is supplied as a `Graphics` object argument to `paint`. We shall describe this object in more detail in Section 16.5. The `drawString` method of Graphics takes a string to be drawn and an (x, y) coordinate position for the text to appear. The coordinates are integer offsets measured from the top-left corner of the frame. The position is taken by `drawString` to indicate the bottom-left corner of the first character, so the base of our string appears 10 pixels in from the left edge of the frame and 50 pixels from the top edge.

Exercise 16.4   What happens to the position of the text if the value of `xpos` in Code 16.2 is set to 0? Why do you think this is?

16.2.2   The `repaint` Method

Closely related to the `paint` method is `repaint`, whose simplest version is:

```
public class Component {
    ...
        // Simplified version of repaint.
    public void repaint(){
        Graphics g = getGraphics();
        update(g);
        paint(g);
    }
    ...
}
```

Unlike `paint`, `repaint` does not take an argument. In fact, one of its tasks is to obtain a graphics context for `paint` to draw on. Having obtained the appropriate graphics context, `repaint` passes this to the `update` method of Component

```
public void update(Graphics g);
```

whose task is to clear the graphics context before it is passed on to `paint`. While it is not usually necessary to override `repaint`, there are some specialized circumstances in which it is necessary to override `update`—specifically in order to prevent its clearing of the graphics context (see Section 16.24 for details of this). In fact, `repaint` causes the `update` and `paint` to be performed in a separate thread and, itself, returns to its caller almost immediately.

It is important to understand the relationship between the `paint` and `repaint` methods and when each is called automatically on a frame. The `repaint` method is always called when a frame needs to be completely redrawn, such as when the window is resized. Only `paint` is called when the frame's contents simply need restoring, such as when its window has been partially hidden and is then exposed, or when a minimized window is restored. The fact that `repaint` obtains the appropriate graphics context for a frame or component, and arranges for `update` to clear it, provides a convenient means for getting a component to completely redraw itself. In contrast to `paint`, therefore, you will often see explicit calls to `repaint` that have been written by the programmer.

16.3   A Mechanism for Closing Windows

In Section 16.2, we pointed out that the window manager cannot be used to close a Frame unless the frame is specifically listening for such messages. In this section, we briefly introduce a simple outline for the main method that can be used with most AWT applications. As well as constructing an object of the appropriate Frame sub class and making the frame visible, the main method will attach a *window listener* to the frame that will respond to messages from the host system's window manager. Specifically, this listener will close the frame and exit the program, without reference to the application. This is rather a brute force approach, but it is simple to implement and convenient for the example programs in this chapter. In practice, a program might need to close files or free other resources before it exits.

In Code 16.2, the main method used to construct an object of the `HelloWorld` class was as follows:

```
public class AWTWorld {
    public static void main(String[] args){
        HelloWorld world = new HelloWorld();
        world.setVisible(true);
    }
}
```

The two stages are construction of an instance of the new sub class of Frame, and making the frame visible. The frame object executes in a separate thread from the main method and so continues to run even though the main method has been completed at that point. In order to make the frame responsive to window-closing messages from the window manager, we can attach a window listener object to the frame using the `addWindowListener` method that it inherits from its Window super class. We have defined the class `WindowCloser` to listen for window-closing messages and exit the program. An explanation of how WindowCloser works is left until Section 16.20, but this should not stop us from using it as a black-box object that provides us with some necessary functionality. Code 16.3 shows how we can attach such an object to an application between constructing it and making it visible.

Notice that we do not need a variable name for the WindowCloser object; we can construct it and pass it straight to the application's `addWindowListener` method.

Code 16.3 Attaching an object to listen for window-closing messages

```
public class AWTWorld {
    public static void main(String[] args){
        HelloWorld world = new HelloWorld();
        world.addWindowListener(new WindowCloser());
        world.setVisible(true);
    }
}
```

Code 16.4 A standard template for the main method of AWT applications

```
public class AWTWorld {
    public static void main(String[] args){
        Frame frame = new HelloWorld();
        frame.addWindowListener(new WindowCloser());
        frame.setVisible(true);
    }
}
```

Exercise 16.5 Amend the source of the file AWTWorld.java so that a Window-Closer object is attached to the HelloWorld object, as shown in Code 16.3. Use the host window manager's method for closing a window to check that it works.

Exercise 16.6 Amend the definition of the HelloWorld class which is in the file AWTWorld.java so that it adds the window listener to itself, rather than this being done by the main method. Will this produce the same effect?

We find that the three steps illustrated in Code 16.3 are common to the main method of most of the AWT applications that we shall write:

- Construct an object from a sub class of Frame.
- Attach a WindowCloser object to respond to window-closing messages.
- Make the frame visible.

We can reuse this pattern for the main method over and over again, therefore. In fact, we can make a further refinement to it that illustrates its generality. Because the main method needs to know nothing about the specific methods of the application object it is creating, there is no need for the static type of the variable it defines to be anything other than Frame. Polymorphism allows us to use the general template of Code 16.4 for future examples.

Notice that the only parts of this template that need to be changed for each application are the name of the class containing the main method—which will match the name of the file containing it—and the dynamic type of the frame object being constructed.

16.4 The Canvas Class

As long as we have the whole of the frame's area available to draw on, and that is all we want to do in terms of user interface, adding further functionality to a Frame's paint method will be sufficient for our needs. However, Frame is a sub class of Container and, in general, we will use it to hold different sorts of user-interface components—menus, buttons, and so on—all at the same time. In this case, any part of the frame used for drawing becomes just one such component, sharing the available space with the others. For tasks involving drawing, there is a specialized drawing area component called Canvas. When we wish to include a drawing in a container, we

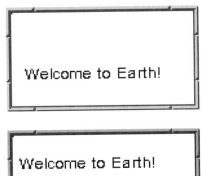

Figure 16.3 Drawing a string at `(10,50)` on a Canvas within a Frame

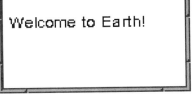

Figure 16.4 Drawing directly on a Frame at `(10,50)`

first create a sub class of the `Canvas` class and override its `paint` method to do the required drawing. An object of this sub class is then added to a Frame. Code 16.5 shows the first step in building up a frame with multiple components. Its appearance is shown in Figure 16.3 with the Frame version shown for comparison alongside it in Figure 16.4. The reason for the difference between the two images will be explained shortly.

A new component is added to a Frame with the `add` method inherited from Container. Components are usually added in the Frame sub class's constructor because their positioning and appearance is an essential part of its creation. An object of any class derived from the Component class may be added to a container in this way, and we shall later see the addition of buttons, labels, and text components, for instance. In addition, any number of components may be added to a container, although this will raise issues of how the limited space is shared among the multiple components. We begin to address these issues in Section 16.6.

`Canvas` has a `paint` method, just as Frame does, and we have overridden it in `WelcomeCanvas` to draw the required string. Notice that this means that there is no longer any need for an overridden `paint` method in the Frame class. You will notice from a comparison of Figure 16.3 with Figure 16.4, that the position of the string drawn on the Canvas is slightly different from that drawn on the Frame. The main reason for this is that the width and height of a Frame, as determined by `getSize`, include any space used for its border and title, whereas the dimensions returned from the canvas's `getSize` method refer entirely to the internal space granted to it when added to its Container. In addition, the `(0,0)` position of the Canvas's Graphics argument is the top left position of the canvas, and not the top left of the frame. This will be true for any component within a container. If you tried Exercise 16.4, you will have discovered that the left edge of the text was slightly obscured by the frame's border. The reason for this is that the frame's `(0,0)` position is the outer edge of its window.

A component's position within its parent container can be determined with the `getBounds` method inherited from Component. This returns a `Rectangle` object whose `width` and `height` attributes will be identical to those returned by `getSize`.

Code 16.5   Drawing a string on a Canvas added to a Frame (`AWTWelcome.java`)

```
    // Paint a string in the graphics context of a Canvas within a Frame.
import java.awt.*;

public class AWTWelcome {
    public static void main(String[] args){
        Frame frame = new WelcomeFrame();
        frame.addWindowListener(new WindowCloser());
        frame.setVisible(true);
    }
}


        // Extend Frame to provide control over the frame's contents.
class WelcomeFrame extends Frame {
    public WelcomeFrame(){
        // Give this frame a title.
        super("Welcome");
        // Set the frame's size.
        final int width = 150, height = 100;
        setSize(width,height);
        add(new WelcomeCanvas());
    }
}

class WelcomeCanvas extends Canvas {
        // Override Canvas's paint method.
    public void paint(Graphics g){
        // Define the drawing position.
        final int xpos = 10, ypos = 50;
        g.drawString("Welcome to Earth!",xpos,ypos);
    }
}
```

Its x and y attributes give the offset from the top-left corner of the parent container. It is important to make use of one of the `getSize` or `getBounds` methods, rather than assuming that the component still has the size it had when it was created, since the user usually has complete control over resizing the containing window.

16.5   The Graphics Class

The exact details of how to draw on different platforms under a range of possible window managers are determined by sub classes that extend the abstract `Graphics` class and an application does not need to know any of these details. Instead, a platform-dependent instance of a sub class of Graphics is passed as an actual argument to the `paint` method of any component within a Frame when it needs to be drawn. Each sub class of Graphics provides appropriate implementations of the many `draw` methods.

In Code 16.2, the Graphics object passed to the `paint` method represented the complete area of the frame, including any title, border, and the central drawing area, while, in Code 16.5, it represented the drawing area allotted to the canvas

Code 16.6   Drawing a resizable oval

```java
import java.awt.*;

        // Draw an oval on a Canvas added to a Frame.
class OvalFrame extends Frame {
    public OvalFrame(){
        final int width = 200, height = 100;
        setSize(width,height);
        // Create a canvas in which to draw and
        // add it to this Frame (Container).
        add(new OvalCanvas());
    }
}

    // Draw an oval within the canvas.
public class OvalCanvas extends Canvas {
    // Adjust the size of the oval according to the size of the canvas.
    public void paint(Graphics g){
        // Find out the size of this component.
        Dimension size = getSize();
        final int width = size.width, height = size.height;
        // Allow a small gap inside the drawing area.
        final int gap = 5;

        // Make sure there is enough space
        final int spaceRequired = 2*gap+2;
        if((width >= spaceRequired) && (height >= spaceRequired)){
            g.drawOval(gap,gap,width-2*gap,height-2*gap);
        }
    }
}
```

within its containing frame. In Sections 16.2.1 and 16.4, we illustrated drawing using the drawString method of the Graphics class. This takes an (x,y) position for the bottom-left corner of the String to be drawn. Implementations of the Graphics class contain methods for drawing lines, arcs, ovals, polygons, images, rectangles, and strings. These methods all use a coordinate system in which the top left of the drawing area is (0,0). It should be noted that there is only scope to describe the simplest techniques using the AWT's basic Graphics class. More sophisticated classes, such as the Graphics2D sub class of Graphics, take these concepts even further by making it possible to draw virtually any geometric shape.

16.5.1   The drawOval Method

Code 16.6 shows an example that uses the drawOval method of the Graphics object to draw an oval within a canvas contained within a frame.[2] This is illustrated in Figure 16.5. The drawOval method takes an (x,y) position for the top-left corner

---

[2] In future examples, we shall omit details of the class containing the main method, where this simply constructs a Frame object, attaches a window listener, and makes the frame visible.

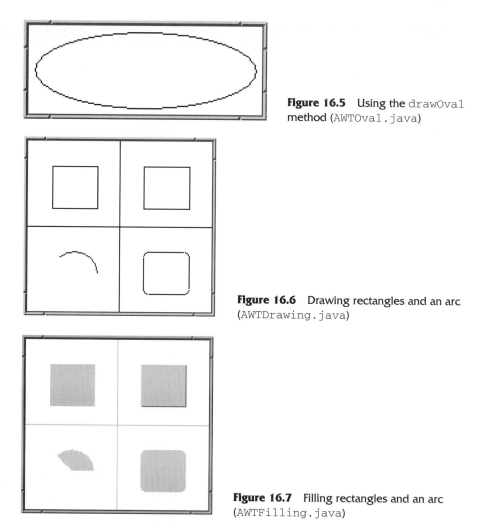

Figure 16.5 Using the `drawOval` method (`AWTOval.java`)

Figure 16.6 Drawing rectangles and an arc (`AWTDrawing.java`)

Figure 16.7 Filling rectangles and an arc (`AWTFilling.java`)

of a rectangle enclosing the oval, along with the width and height of this bounding box. The value of `gap` in Code 16.6 is simply used to offset the oval from the sides of the drawing area slightly, for the sake of giving it a better appearance. The `paint` method of `OvalCanvas` has been designed to ensure that the oval will completely fit within the drawing area of the frame, even if the window is resized by the user. This has been done by calculating the oval's diameter from the size of the canvas in which it is being drawn, rather than hard-wiring fixed coordinate positions into the code with *magic numbers*.

16.5.2 Drawing and Filling Shapes

In addition to drawing strings (Section 16.2.1) and ovals, the Graphics class provides methods for drawing and filling lines, rectangles, and arcs. Figures 16.6 and 16.7 illustrate the effect of these. Code 16.7 shows the class used to draw Figure 16.6.

Code 16.7 Drawing rectangles and an arc (`DrawCanvas.java`)

```java
import java.awt.*;

class DrawCanvas extends Canvas {
    public void paint(Graphics g){
        Dimension size = getSize();

        final int offset = 25;
        final int shapeWidth = size.width/4;
        final int shapeHeight = size.height/4;

        // Provide extra color contrast for the 3DRectangle.
        g.setColor(Color.black);

        // Divide the frame into four.
        int y = size.height/2;
        g.drawLine(0,y,size.width,y);
        int x = size.width/2;
        g.drawLine(x,0,x,size.height);

        // Draw a rectangle in the top-left quadrant.
        g.drawRect(offset,offset,shapeWidth,shapeHeight);
        // Draw a 3d rectangle in the top-right quadrant.
        g.draw3DRect(size.width/2+offset,offset,
                    shapeWidth,shapeHeight,true);
        // Draw a 135 degree arc, counter-clockwise, in the third quadrant.
        final int startAngle = 0, angle = 135;
        g.drawArc(offset,size.height/2+offset,
                shapeWidth,shapeHeight,startAngle,angle);
        // Draw a round-cornered rectangle in the fourth quadrant.
        // The roundness of the corners.
        final int roundDiameter = 10;
        // Draw a 3d rectangle in the top-right quadrant.
        g.drawRoundRect(size.width/2+offset,size.height/2+offset,
                    shapeWidth,shapeHeight,roundDiameter,roundDiameter);
    }

}
```

Illustrated in this example are the drawLine, drawRect, draw3DRect, draw-RoundRect, and drawArc methods of the Graphics class. Figure 16.7 was created by replacing the draw methods of Code 16.7 with the corresponding fill versions (see FillCanvas.java). All take an (x,y) pair for the top-left corner of their bounding rectangle (including drawArc) and a width and height for the same. The area of the 3DRect is actually 1 pixel wider and 1 pixel higher than specified. The effect of this shape is meant to be as if a source of light were present at its top-left corner. The fifth argument indicates whether the rectangle should appear raised (true) or depressed (false). It can be difficult to see any difference between a normal rectangle and a 3D-effect rectangle, so the effect has been enhanced by using

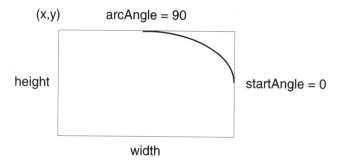

Figure 16.8 How the arguments to drawArc are used

the setColor method to draw the shapes in a contrasting color in these examples (see Section 16.11.4 for more information on using color).

The drawArc method takes two further arguments indicating the start angle and the number of degrees swept by the arc. Starting angles are measured from the 3 o'clock position and positive sweeps move anti-clockwise (Figure 16.8). The arc illustrated in Figure 16.6 could have been drawn alternatively with a negative arc angle as follows:

```
g.drawArc(offset,size.height/2+offset,shapeWidth,shapeHeight,135,-135);
```

The drawRoundRect method makes it possible to draw rectangles with rounded corners. Its fifth and sixth arguments represent the width and height of the oval whose curves are used to produce the rounding. The larger the values for these, the more of the rectangle's sides will be occupied by the curve of the oval rather than straight lines.

16.5.3 Drawing Polygons

The drawPolygon, drawPolyline, and fillPolygon methods of the Graphics class provide the ability to draw general shapes with arbitrary orientations. The distinction between a polygon and a polyline is simply that the former is automatically closed by ensuring that the final point is always joined by a line to the first point. Figure 16.9 illustrates the use of all three methods, produced by the example in Code 16.8.

Code 16.8 Using the polygon and polyline methods of Graphics (PolyCanvas.java)

```
import java.awt.*;

class PolyCanvas extends Canvas {
        // Draw three diamond shapes, side by side.
    public void paint(Graphics g){
        Dimension size = getSize();

        // Define the width and height of the shapes.
        final int width = size.width/4, height = size.height/2;
        // Shift right between drawing the shapes.
```

Code 16.8   (*Continued*)

```
        final int shapeGap = 5;

        // Offset from the edges.
        int gap = (size.width-(3*width+2*shapeGap))/2;
        if(gap < 0){
            gap = 5;
        }

        // The (x,y) coordinate pairs of the first shape.
        final int[] xvals = {
                gap, gap+width/2, gap+width, gap+width/2,
        };
        final int[] yvals = {
                height, height/2, height, 3*height/2,
        };

        // Draw a polygon shape.
        g.drawPolygon(xvals,yvals,xvals.length);

        // Shift the coordinate space to the right.
        g.translate(width+shapeGap,0);

        // Fill a Polygon object.
        Polygon poly = new Polygon(xvals,yvals,xvals.length);
        g.fillPolygon(poly);

        // Shift again.
        g.translate(width+shapeGap,0);

        // Draw a polyline.
        g.drawPolyline(xvals,yvals,xvals.length);
    }
}
```

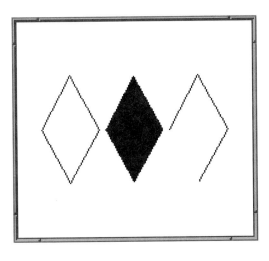

Figure 16.9 Polygon and Polyline examples (`AWTPolygon.java`)

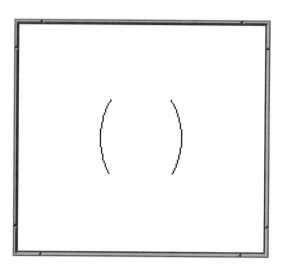

Figure 16.10 Parts of an oval outside the central clip region do not appear (`AWTClipping.java`)

The `drawPolygon` and `fillPolygon` methods come in two forms, either taking three arguments of integer coordinate positions and a number of points, or taking a single object of the `Polygon` class, which itself is constructed from the raw point data. The example in Code 16.8 uses two four-element arrays to draw the first polygon. Notice that the last point is joined up to the first. The `translate` method of the graphics context is used to shift the coordinate space to the right by the width of the polygon plus a small offset to produce a gap between the first and second shape. The points are then used to construct a Polygon object, which is filled with the current drawing color. Finally, the drawing origin is shifted again, via `translate`, to position the third shape, which is a polyline, and so the last point is not joined to the first.

16.5.4   Clipping

The `setClip` method allows a clipping region to be defined within the graphics context. Anything drawn outside the clipping region will not appear. One version of the method takes a position for the top left of the rectangular clipping area, along with its width and height. Code 16.9 shows how the result of using `drawOval` is affected by an overlapping clipping area in the center of the canvas. From Figure 16.10, it can be seen that the upper and lower parts of the oval do not appear because they lie outside the clipping region. The clipping bounds for a graphics context may be found by using its `getClipBounds` method, which returns a Rectangle. The `clipRect` method defines the position and dimensions of a rectangular area that can be used to limit the current clipping bounds. The new clipping bounds correspond to the area which is defined by its intersection of the current bounds and the rectangular area defined by `clipRect`.

The `clearRect` method takes the same arguments as `drawRect` and `fill-Rect`. It clears the defined rectangular area. The `copyArea` method copies an area of the specified dimensions offset from its original position. If the offset values are positive, the area is copied down and to the right of its origin. Negative offsets indicate a copy left and up. The example in Code 16.10 illustrates how to simulate

Code 16.9   Clipping an oval (`ClipCanvas.java`)

```java
import java.awt.*;

class ClipCanvas extends Canvas {
        // Draw an oval within a clipping area.
    public void paint(Graphics g){
        Dimension size = getSize();

        // Define the oval's position.
        final int x = size.width/3, y = size.height/4;
        // Define the width and height of the oval.
        final int width = size.width/3, height = size.height/2;

        // Define a clipping rectangle in the central area.
        g.setClip(size.width/4,size.height/3,size.width/2,size.height/3);

        // Draw the oval.
        g.drawOval(x,y,width,height);
    }
}
```

Code 16.10   Use of `copyArea` and `clearRect` (`CopyCanvas.java`)

```java
import java.awt.*;

class CopyCanvas extends Canvas {
    CopyCanvas{
        setBackground(Color.white);
    }

        // Draw a rectangle and then move a quadrant west.
    public void paint(Graphics g){
        Dimension size = getSize();
        // The dimensions of the main rectangle.
        final int width = size.width/3, height = size.height/3;
        // Where to place the main rectangle.
        final int x = size.width/3, y = size.height/3;

        g.fillRect(x,y,width,height);
        // Copy a chunk.
        final int chunkWidth = width/2, chunkHeight = height/2;
        // Where from.
        final int chunkX = x+width/4, chunkY = y+height/4;
        // Copy it to just inside the left edge of the canvas.
        final int xoffset = -(chunkX-5), yoffset = 0;
        g.copyArea(chunkX,chunkY,chunkWidth,chunkHeight,xoffset,yoffset);
        // Clear the removed area.
        g.clearRect(chunkX,chunkY,chunkWidth,chunkHeight);
    }
}
```

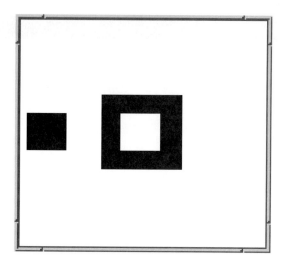

Figure 16.11 Moving a rectangle with `copyArea` and `clearRect` (`AWTCopying.java`)

the effect of cutting out a rectangular area of a shape by combining `clearRect` and `copyArea`. The effect may be seen in Figure 16.11.

This example firstly fills a rectangular area in the center of the canvas. A smaller area from inside the rectangle is copied to the left of the canvas with `copyArea`. The appearance of having moved this piece out of the original is effected by clearing the removed area, with `clearRect`.

Further methods of the Graphics class will be covered in later sections; `getColor`, `setColor`, `setPaintMode`, and `setXORMode` use the `Color` class (Section 16.11.4); `getFont`, `getFontMetrics`, `setFont`, and `setFontMetrics` use the `Font` class (Section 16.11.3).

16.6 Container Layout

A common component required in user interfaces is provided by the `Button` class. A user indicates an action to the application, through the user interface, by pressing a button. In contrast to Frame and Canvas components, we usually use Button objects directly, without creating sub classes. A Button has an associated label which is passed to its constructor and indicates its purpose: `"Save"`, `"Cancel"`, `"Quit"`, and so on. As it is a sub class of Component, a Button object is added to a Container in the same way as we saw a Canvas added to a Frame in Code 16.5. However, as we shall demonstrate, adding multiple components to a container requires a little care. Code 16.11 shows an attempt to add both a canvas and a button to a Frame.

Unfortunately, this example is flawed for reasons which will not be immediately obvious. Try the following exercises before reading further in this section in order to see the problem in practice.

Exercise 16.7 Modify the constructor of `OvalFrame` in the file `OvalFrame.java` so that a Quit button is added to the frame, as shown in Code 16.11. Compile and run the program using the main method in `AWTOval.java`. Notice the effect—it probably will not be what you expect.

Code 16.11   Adding a button to a Frame (incorrectly)

```
class OvalFrame extends Frame {
    public OvalFrame(){
        final int width = 100, height = 200;
        setSize(width,height);

        // Create a canvas in which to draw.
        OvalCanvas canvas = new OvalCanvas();
        // Add it to the containing frame.
        add(canvas);

        // Create a button with the label "Quit".
        Button quitButton = new Button("Quit");
        // Add it to the containing frame.
        add(quitButton);
    }
}
```

Exercise 16.8   Reverse the order in which the canvas and button are added to the frame in your solution to Exercise 16.7, rerun the program, and observe the difference. Why do you think this effect occurs?

The problem with the example in Code 16.11 is that it does not specify how the two components are to share the available space. By default, multiple components added to a frame are placed directly on top of one other, as if the others did not exist; this produces an effect which is not what we usually want.

In order to control the way in which multiple components are displayed within a container, each sub class of Container uses a *layout manager*. It is the responsibility of the layout manager to arrange the order of the components and share out the available space among them according to their needs. A component indicates the space it requires through its getMinimumSize and getPreferredSize accessors, both of which return a Dimension object containing public integer height and width attributes. There are several layout manager classes defined in the java.awt package, and we shall look at each in turn—BorderLayout, CardLayout, FlowLayout, GridLayout, and GridBagLayout. If none of these meets the set of requirements we have for a particular application, then it is always possible to write our own by implementing the LayoutManager interface. Each sub class of Container has a default layout manager, but this may be changed by passing a suitable object to its setLayout method. It is frequently necessary to do this in order to achieve the desired results.

16.6.1   The BorderLayout Class

A Frame's layout is managed by an object of the BorderLayout class. This style of layout is designed around the idea of dividing the full area of the container into a large central area and four smaller areas arranged around its borders. The five areas are called North, South, East, West, and Center. Unless you indicate otherwise,

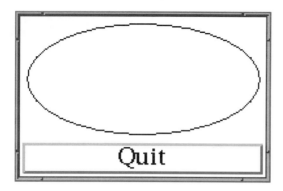

Figure 16.12 Positioning multiple components within a Frame using constraints (`AWTOvalLayout.java`)

Code 16.12 Multiple components with a BorderLayout (`OvalLayoutFrame.java`)

```
    // Draw an oval on a Canvas added to a Frame.
    // Include a (non-functional) quit button.
class OvalLayoutFrame extends Frame {
    public OvalLayoutFrame(){
        final int width = 200, height = 150;
        setSize(width,height);

        // Create a canvas in which to draw.
        OvalCanvas canvas = new OvalCanvas();
        // Add it to this Frame (Container).
        add(canvas,"Center");

        // Add a (non-functional) button for quitting the application.
        Button quitButton = new Button("Quit");
        add(quitButton,"South");
    }
}
```

---

all components added to a Frame are placed in the center of the layout, one on top of the other—hence the problem illustrated by Exercise 16.7. This problem is cured by the example shown Code 16.12 where the canvas is added to the Center and the button is added to the South in order to keep them apart. The effect is illustrated in Figure 16.12.

The argument passed to add to indicate a component's position is known as a *constraint*. If a constraint is given which the layout manager does not understand, an exception will be thrown giving an error message, such as:

```
java.lang.IllegalArgumentException: cannot add to layout:
        unknown constraint: Esst
```

Figure 16.13 shows the positioning and typical space allocation of all five areas in a border layout. In general, the Center area receives the lion's share, with the other four areas arranged around it. Because the central area of a border layout takes the

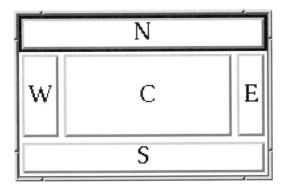

Figure 16.13 The five positions in a BorderLayout (`AWTBorder.java`)

majority of the available space, it is usually not practical to add a drawing canvas to any position other than the center, since not enough space would be allocated to it for anything to appear.

Exercise 16.9   Write an application to produce the effect shown in Figure 16.13. Each area contains a single button. Experiment with resizing the window to see how the proportion of available space is reallocated between the different areas.

16.7   Activating Buttons

Adding a button to a frame does not give us any extra functionality; it simply makes a labeled button appear within the frame. Pressing on the button with the mouse has no apparent effect. The reason is that, although the press is detected by the button, it is not the responsibility of the button to implement the action associated with the press—such as quitting the application. Clearly, a general purpose button cannot know what the action associated with its label means. One approach we could take is to create sub classes of the Button class, each with the desired functionality. However, it is more common to take a quite different approach to that one. This means that there will be a distinction between a component such as Canvas, which we usually sub class in order to implement desired functionality, and Button which we almost never sub class.

Responsibility for responding to a button press is always delegated to another part of the application. The part that responds could be the overall Frame sub class object, a sub component of the application, or an object of a custom-defined class, for instance. As a result, it will be necessary to establish a linkage between a button and the part of the application that must respond to its being pressed. We call the part of an application that responds a *listener*, and we say that a listener must register an interest in events occurring on the button. When the button is pressed, the button notifies all registered listeners. These objects are called listeners because they implement an interface which extends the empty `EventListener` interface, defined in the `java.awt.event` package.

Code 16.13   The ActionListener interface

```
public interface ActionListener extends EventListener {
    public abstract void actionPerformed(ActionEvent e);
}
```

16.7.1   The ActionListener Interface

Pressing a button results in the button sending an `ActionEvent` object to its listeners. ActionEvent is defined in the `java.awt.event` package and is a sub class of the more general AWT event class, `AWTEvent`, defined in the `java.awt` package. AWTEvent is a sub class of the more general `EventObject`, defined in the `java.util` package.

An object registers an interest in button events by sending an `addAction-Listener` message to the button:

```
Button quitButton = new Button("Quit");
// Listener registers an interest in events on the button.
quitButton.addActionListener(listener);
```

As an argument, a reference to the listener object is passed so that the button will be able to contact it when an event has occurred. The `addActionListener` message is usually sent just after the button has been created. An object can de-register as a listener by sending a `removeActionListener` message to a button, with a reference to itself as the argument.

In order to be eligible to listen for ActionEvents on a button, a class must implement the `ActionListener` interface, which has a single method shown in Code 16.13.

The `EventListener` interface is empty (see Section 13.8), and so `action-Performed` is the only method to be implemented. When pressed, a Button object sends an `actionPerformed` message, along with the appropriate ActionEvent object, to all its listeners. Code 16.14 shows a class implementing each of these concepts: button creation, registering as a listener to events coming from that button, and a simple implementation of the method receiving notification of an event. You will use the pattern that it illustrates over and over again in programs that use buttons.

Code 16.14   Listening for a button press (`QuitOvalFrame.java`)

```
import java.awt.*;
import java.awt.event.*;

       // Example showing a Canvas and a Button.
class QuitOvalFrame extends Frame implements ActionListener {
    static final String quitString = "Quit";

    public QuitOvalFrame(){
        final int width = 200, height = 200;
        setSize(width,height);
```

Code 16.14   (*Continued*)

```
    add(new OvalCanvas(),"Center");

    // Arrange to quit the application.
    Button quitButton = new Button("Quit");
    // We wish to know about button presses.
    quitButton.addActionListener(this);
    add(quitButton,"South");
  }

    // Implement the ActionListener interface.
    // Receive events from the quit button.
 public void actionPerformed(ActionEvent e){
    // The quit button has been pressed.
    System.exit(0);
  }
}
```

Notice the need to import from the `java.awt.event` package.

The simple nature of the action performed when the button is pressed suggests that we might prefer to implement the action listener as an *anonymous class* (see Section 15.6.4). This alternative is illustrated in Code 16.15. In this case, the Frame sub class does not need to declare the ActionListener interface in its header.

16.7.2   Listening to Multiple Buttons

If the only required response is to an event sent from the quit button, then the definitions of `actionPerformed` in Code 16.14 and Code 16.15 are sufficient. In general, however, an object might need to register itself as a listener to events occurring on a number of different buttons. In this case, we need some way of determining from which button a particular event has come. This can be done by setting a distinguishing *action command* on a button, using its `setActionCommand` method:

```
    Button quitButton = new Button("Quit");
    quitButton.addActionListener(this);
    quitButton.setActionCommand("Quit");
```

The action command is a string that the button object will include in an `action-Command` attribute of the ActionEvent objects it sends to listeners. It follows that the action commands used for different buttons should be distinct. It is common practice to use the same string for the action command as for the button's label.[3] When an event is received in `actionPerformed`, the associated action command can be retrieved by sending the `getActionCommand` message to the ActionEvent argument. A string comparison can then be made against the expected command values. Code 16.16 illustrates this approach.

---

[3] This approach can be a problem if a program is to be used in different countries, where the labels will need to be translated but the essential functionality of the application is unchanged.

Code 16.15 Implementing a simple listener as an anonymous class

```java
import java.awt.*;
import java.awt.event.*;

        // Example showing a Canvas and a Button.
class QuitOvalFrame extends Frame {
    static final String quitString = "Quit";

    public QuitOvalFrame(){
        final int width = 200, height = 200;
        setSize(width,height);

        add(new OvalCanvas(),"Center");

        // Arrange to quit the application.
        Button quitButton = new Button("Quit");
        // We wish to know about button presses.
        quitButton.addActionListener(new ActionListener(){
            public void actionPerformed(ActionEvent e){
                // The quit button has been pressed.
                System.exit(0);
            }
        });
        add(quitButton,"South");
    }
}
```

Code 16.16 Retrieving an event's action command attribute (`MultiButtonFrame1.java`)

```java
import java.awt.*;
import java.awt.event.*;

    // Example showing a listener to multiple buttons.
class MultiButtonFrame1 extends Frame implements ActionListener {
    // Labels (and action commands) for two buttons.
    static final String BOTTOM = "Bottom", TOP = "Top";

    public MultiButtonFrame1(){
        final int width = 200, height = 200;
        setSize(width,height);

        // Place a dummy button at the top of the frame.
        Button top = new Button(TOP);
        top.setActionCommand(TOP);
        // We wish to know about button presses.
        top.addActionListener(this);
        add(top,"North");

        Button bottom = new Button(BOTTOM);
        bottom.setActionCommand(BOTTOM);
```

Code 16.16   (*Continued*)

```
        // We wish to know about button presses.
        bottom.addActionListener(this);
        add(bottom,"South");
    }

        // Implement the ActionListener interface.
        // Receive events from the buttons.
    public void actionPerformed(ActionEvent e){
        final String command = e.getActionCommand();
        if(command.equals(TOP)){
            System.out.println(TOP+" received.");
        }
        else if(command.equals(BOTTOM)){
            System.out.println(BOTTOM+" received.");
        }
        else{
            System.out.println("Unexpected command "+command+
                               " received.");
        }
    }
}
```

Notice that the strings set on the buttons must be accessible to both the constructor and the `actionPerformed` method. Alternatively, an anonymous class object could be created to handle each individual button. This would require no action command, since the action listener is directly associated with the button to which it is attached. Code 16.17 illustrates this approach.

Code 16.17   Listening to multiple buttons with dedicated anonymous class instances (`MultiButtonFrame2.java`)

```
import java.awt.*;
import java.awt.event.*;

    // Example showing a listener to multiple buttons.
class MultiButtonFrame2 extends Frame {
    public MultiButtonFrame2(){
        // Labels (and action commands) for two buttons.
        final String BOTTOM = "Bottom", TOP = "Top";
        final int width = 200, height = 200;
        setSize(width,height);

        // Place a dummy button at the top of the frame.
        final Button top = new Button(TOP);
        top.addActionListener(new ActionListener(){
            public void actionPerformed(ActionEvent e){
                System.out.println(top.getLabel()+" pressed.");
            }
        });
```

(*Continued*)

Code 16.17   *(Continued)*

```
        add(top,"North");

        final Button bottom = new Button(BOTTOM);
        bottom.addActionListener(new ActionListener(){
            public void actionPerformed(ActionEvent e){
                System.out.println(bottom.getLabel()+" pressed.");
            }
        });
        add(bottom,"South");
    }
}
```

Notice that it is common to define the variable holding the button as final, so that the anonymous class object is able to use it. This example also illustrates use of the getLabel accessor for a button's label text; there is a corresponding setLabel mutator.

In the remainder of our coverage of the AWT, we will tend to use the set-ActionCommand approach to button identification. In Chapter 17, however, we commonly use the anonymous class approach.

16.7.3   Determining the Event Source

Requesting the associated action command from an ActionEvent assumes that one has been set on the component dispatching the event. An alternative means of determining the source of the event is to use the getSource method that ActionEvent inherits from its EventObject super class. This returns an Object reference to the issuing object, which might be used as shown in Code 16.18. This approach has the advantage it that is applicable to all event types—not just ActionEvents. This approach has the disadvantages that references to the event-generators must be available to actionPerformed, and different components generating what are essentially the same events must be checked for separately.

Code 16.18   Determining the source of an event (`MultiButtonFrame3.java`)

```
import java.awt.*;
import java.awt.event.*;

    // Example showing a listener to multiple buttons.
    // Use the event's source to detect which was pressed.
class MultiButtonFrame3 extends Frame implements ActionListener {
    public MultiButtonFrame3(){
        final int width = 200, height = 200;
        setSize(width,height);

        // Add the two buttons to the frame.
        Button top = getTop();
```

Code 16.18   (*Continued*)

```
        top.addActionListener(this);
        add(top,"North");

        Button button = getBottom();
        bottom.addActionListener(this);
        add(bottom,"South");
    }

        // Work out which button was pressed.
    public void actionPerformed(ActionEvent e){
        Object source = e.getSource();

        if(source == getTop()){
            Button b = (Button) source;
            System.out.println(b.getLabel()+" pressed.");
        }
        else if(source == getBottom()){
            Button b = (Button) source;
            System.out.println(b.getLabel()+" pressed.");
        }
        else{
            System.out.println("Unexpected event from: "+source);
        }
    }

    protected Button getTop(){
        return top;
    }

    protected Button getBottom(){
        return bottom;
    }

    // Two buttons within the frame.
    private final Button top = new Button("Top"),
                        bottom = new Button("Bottom");
}
```

16.8   Using Different Layouts

The BorderLayout class described in Section 16.6 provides one way of arranging multiple components within a frame. A disadvantage is that it offers a rather limited layout in that only five fixed-position areas are available and most of the space is given over to the central one.

16.8.1   The FlowLayout Class

The FlowLayout class provides an alternative type of layout manager. The principle on which a FlowLayout object works is to arrange components from left to right in the order in which they are added to the container. When the horizontal space in one row is used up, it starts a new row from left to right, and so on (Figure 16.14).

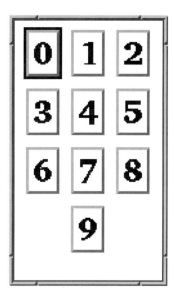

Figure 16.14   FlowLayout within a Frame
(`AWTFlowLayout.java`)

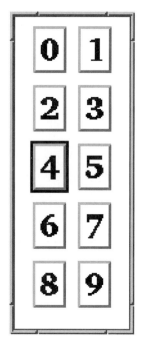

Figure 16.15   FlowLayout within a resized Frame

Components are centered within each row. If the window holding a panel is resized, then the order will remain the same, but their arrangement in rows might change to fit the new width (Figure 16.15). The default BorderLayout layout manager for a Frame may be changed by using its `setLayout` method inherited from its Container super class. Code 16.19 illustrates changing a Frame's layout manager to an instance of FlowLayout.

Code 16.19   Changing to a FlowLayout layout manager in a Frame (`FlowFrame.java`)

```
    // Contain multiple buttons within a Frame using a FlowLayout.
class FlowFrame extends Frame {
    public FlowFrame(){
        final int width = 125, height = 175;
        setSize(width,height);
        setBackground(Color.white);

        // Use a FlowLayout layout manager instead of BorderLayout.
        setLayout(new FlowLayout());

        // Add an arbitrary number of (non-operational) buttons,
        // in this case ten.
        final int numButtons = 10;
        for(int b = 0; b < numButtons; b++){
            add(new Button(""+b));
        }
    }
}
```

Exercise 16.10   Compile and run the main method for the class shown in Code 16.19, which may be found in the file `AWTFlowLayout.java`. Its initial appearance should be as shown in Figure 16.14. Experiment with resizing the window to see how the arrangement of the buttons changes with increasing and decreasing window width.

16.8.2   The GridLayout Class

When components are added to a container managed by an object of the FlowLayout class (Section 16.8.1), they are added from left to right until the width of the container is full, and then a new row is started. If such a window is resized, the arrangement of these components may change if the width is increased or reduced. The GridLayout class provides an alternative layout manager that maintains the same grid layout structure, in terms of numbers of rows and columns, even when its container is resized. This is achieved by resizing the individual components to fit within the new container's dimensions. Code 16.20 contains a program similar to that in Code 16.19, but this time using a GridLayout layout manager in the frame containing a number of buttons. Its appearance is shown in Figure 16.16.

When a GridLayout object is created, the number of rows and columns it is to have are passed as actual arguments to the constructor. Each cell of the grid has the same dimensions. Components added to a container are then laid out accordingly. If there are not enough items to completely fill the last row, then a blank space is left at the right-hand end of the row. If there are not enough items to fill all of the rows, then *blank rows are not included*. If there are too few components, then the number of columns may be reduced. Figure 16.17 illustrates a 4 × 4 grid with 10 buttons, where the number of columns has been reduced to avoid a blank row.

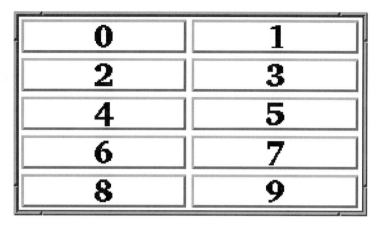

Figure 16.16   5×2 GridLayout with 10 Buttons (`AWTGridLayout.java`)

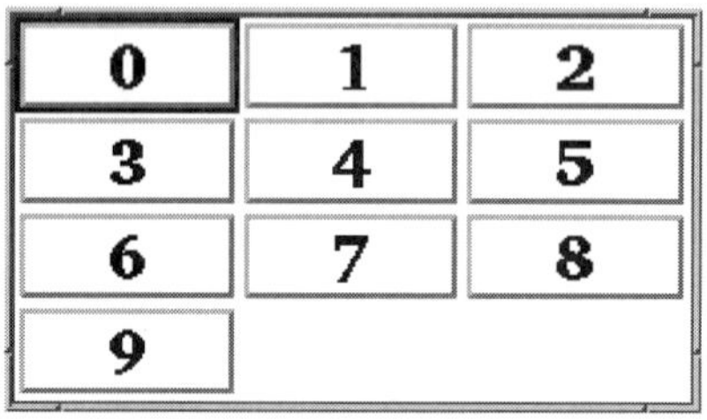

Figure 16.17   A 4 × 4 grid with reduced columns

Code 16.20   A GridLayout example (`GridFrame.java`)

```
    // Contain multiple buttons within a Frame using a GridLayout.
class GridFrame extends Frame {
    public GridFrame(){
        final int width = 275, height = 175;
        setSize(width,height);
        setBackground(Color.white);

        // Use a GridLayout layout manager instead of BorderLayout.
        final int rows = 5, cols = 2;
        setLayout(new GridLayout(rows,cols));

        // Add an arbitrary number of (non-operational) buttons,
        // in this case ten.
        final int numButtons = 10;
        for(int b = 0; b < numButtons; b++){
            add(new Button(String.valueOf(b)));
        }
    }
}
```

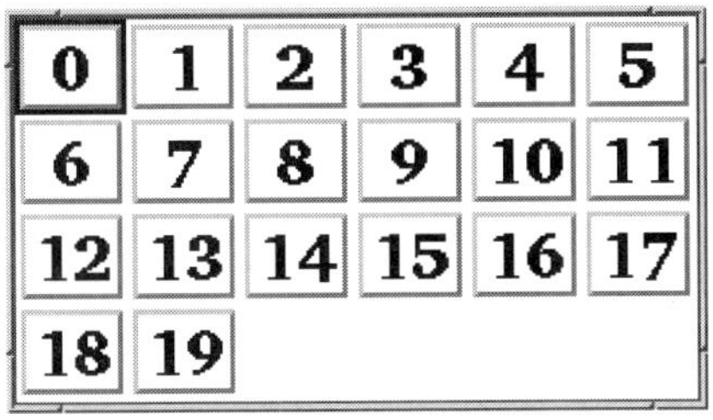

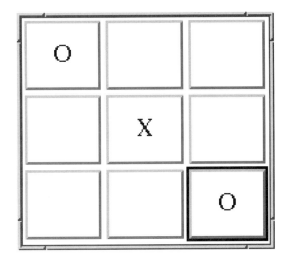

Figure 16.18 A 0×6 grid's row calculation with 20 components

Figure 16.19 The GUI of a Tic-Tac-Toe game (`AWTOXO.java`)

The number of rows and columns may be changed with the layout object's `setRows` and `setColumns` methods. There are also `getRows` and `getColumns` methods. If either row or column value is set to zero, then it is calculated from the number of components and the value of the non-zero dimension. For instance, if there were 20 components and 4 rows, 20 divides exactly by 4 to give 5 columns. If there were 20 components and 6 columns, this does not divide exactly so the next largest multiple of 6 would result in 4 rows (Figure 16.18). If there are too many components for the dimensions of the grid, then the number of columns is expanded to accommodate them.

Exercise 16.11   Compile and run the program in Code 16.20 whose main method may be found in the file `AWTGridLayout.java`. Notice the effect when the window is made smaller or larger.

The example in Code 16.21 illustrates the use of a GridLayout to form the basic interface of a Noughts and Crosses (Tic-Tac-Toe) game, such as we looked at in Section 9.19. Its appearance is shown in Figure 16.19.

Code 16.21 A user interface for Noughts and Crosses (`TicTacToeFrame.java`)

```java
import java.awt.*;
import java.awt.event.*;

        /* The basis for a Noughts and Crosses (TicTacToe) game
         * using a GridLayout of Buttons.
         * This class simply creates a 3x3 grid of buttons
         * as a View of a TicTacToe game.
         */
class TicTacToeFrame extends Frame implements ActionListener {
    public TicTacToeFrame(){
        final int width = 200, height = 200;
        setSize(width,height);
        setBackground(Color.white);

        // Use a Grid Layout
        setLayout(new GridLayout(rows,cols));

        // Add each button to the frame and the board.
        Button[][] board = getBoard();
        for(int r = 0; r < rows; r++){
            for(int c = 0; c < cols; c++){
                Button square = new Button("");
                // Give it a unique action command corresponding to
                // its index.
                square.setActionCommand(String.valueOf(r*cols+c));
                // Tell us about button presses.
                square.addActionListener(this);
                board[r][c] = square;
                add(square);
            }
        }

    }

        // Work out which square was selected from the value
        // stored in its action command.
    public void actionPerformed(ActionEvent event){
        String command = event.getActionCommand();

        // See if it was a number
        try{
            int value = Integer.parseInt(command);
            if((0 <= value) && (value < (rows*cols))){
                // O.K.
                if(selectSquare(value)){
                    // Swap symbol for next time.
                    toggleSymbol();
                }
                else{
                    System.out.println("Square already taken.");
                }
            }
        }
```

Code 16.21   (*Continued*)

```
        catch(NumberFormatException e){
            // It wasn't.
            System.out.println("Unknown command: "+command);
        }
    }

    // Select the given squares and set the appropriate symbol.
    // Return true if the square was free.
    protected boolean selectSquare(int value){
        int row = value/cols;
        int col = value%cols;
        Button[][] board = getBoard();
        Button square = board[row][col];

        if(square.getLabel().equals("")){
            square.setLabel(nextSymbol);
            // Redisplay the board.
            repaint();
            return true;
        }
        else{
            return false;
        }
    }

    protected String getSymbol(){
        return nextSymbol;
    }

    // Change the symbol to be use for the next square.
    protected void toggleSymbol(){
        if(nextSymbol == Nought){
            nextSymbol = Cross;
        }
        else{
            nextSymbol = Nought;
        }
    }

    protected Button[][] getBoard(){
        return board;
    }

    // The board's dimensions.
    private static final int rows = 3, cols = 3;
    // The strings used for the two choices.
    private static String Nought = "O", Cross = "X";
    // Which symbol to use next.
    private String nextSymbol = Nought;
    // The board of buttons.
    private Button[][] board = new Button[rows][cols];
}
```

Each square in the example is implemented as a Button stored in a GridLayout. Associated with each square is an identification number that is passed as a String to the button's `setActionCommand` message. On receipt of an event indicating selection of a particular square, the identifying number is retrieved with the event's `getActionCommand` method and used to set the square's label to either a Nought or a Cross. The example in Code 16.21 is a simplified version of that used in Section 9.19; for instance, it includes no detection of the end of the game.

16.9   The Panel Class

Like Frame, Panel is a sub class of Container, so it can hold multiple components. By default, a Panel uses a `FlowLayout` layout manager to arrange those components. In Section 16.8.1, we pointed out that one of the disadvantages of the default BorderLayout layout management of a frame is that only five areas are available for the placement of components. If we want to have more than five components in a frame we would appear to be stuck. However, the Panel class provides a solution to this problem. As a sub class of Container, we can add multiple components to a Panel, but since Container is also a sub class of Component, we can add a multi-component Panel to a frame as a single component. This effect is illustrated in Figure 16.20, where a Panel containing three buttons has been placed in the `North` border area of a Frame. Code 16.22 illustrates the principal mechanisms for doing this, omitting details of how the buttons interact with their listener and how the color of the drawing is set.

Instead of adding the color buttons directly to the frame, they are added to a Panel. The panel is then added to the frame, along with the canvas and quit button. No constraint argument to `add` is required by the Panel's FlowLayout layout manager. As far as the frame is concerned, there is only a single object occupying the `North` position in its border layout—the panel. It has no particular interest in the buttons contained within the panel. Any messages the frame has to pass on to its components (such as `repaint`) are sent to the canvas and panel objects, and the panel is left to relay those messages on to its components in turn.

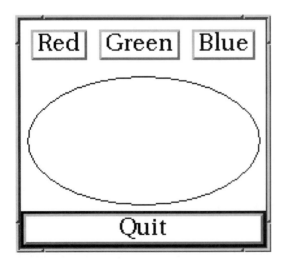

Figure 16.20   Using a multi-component Panel in a Frame (`AWTPanel.java`)

Code 16.22   Adding buttons to a panel (`PanelFrame.java`)

```java
class PanelFrame extends Frame implements ActionListener {
    public PanelFrame(){
        final int width = 200, height = 200;
        setSize(width,height);
        setBackground(Color.white);

        // Create a panel for the three buttons.
        Panel buttonPanel = setupButtonPanel();
        // Add the panel to the Frame
        add(buttonPanel,"North");
        ...
    }

        // Create a panel for the three buttons.
    protected Panel setupButtonPanel(){
        Panel buttonPanel = new Panel();
        // Add the three color buttons to the panel.
        addButton(redString,buttonPanel);
        addButton(greenString,buttonPanel);
        addButton(blueString,buttonPanel);
        return buttonPanel;
    }

    // Add a new button with label and command s.
    // Use the label as the associated command.
    protected void addButton(String label, Panel buttonPanel){
        Button b = new Button(label);
        b.addActionListener(this);
        b.setActionCommand(label);
        buttonPanel.add(b);
    }

    ...

    // Where to draw the oval.
    private OvalCanvas canvas = new OvalCanvas();
    // The labels for the buttons.
    private static final String
        redString = "Red", greenString = "Green", blueString = "Blue";
}
```

16.10   The Label Class

Label is a sub class of Component that allows a passive piece of text to be placed in a container. Unlike a Button, a label has no visible boundary to show its limits. This makes it ideal for use in titles or as a label for other components in a container. The text a label contains may be passed to its constructor or set via its setText method. The length of the text determines the amount of space the label occupies. Section 16.11.3 shows how the font used for the text of a label may be changed from the default, and this will affect the dimensions of the label. The alignment of the text

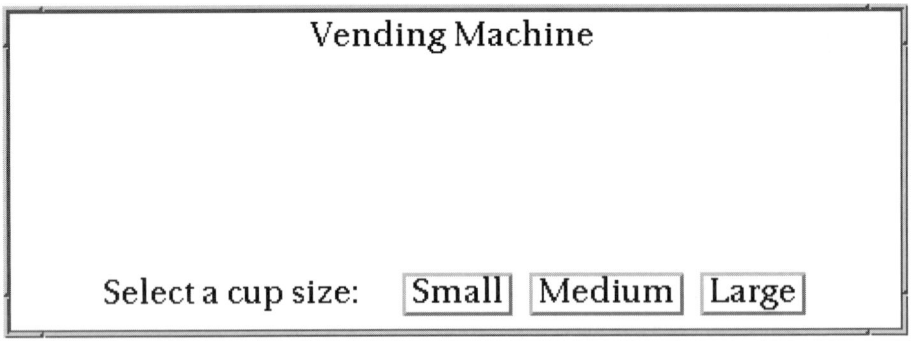

Figure 16.21 Using Labels for a title and prompt (`AWTLabel.java`)

Code 16.23 Using Label components (`VendingMachine.java`)

```java
import java.awt.*;

        // Display a centered title Label at the top of the frame
        // and label three Buttons at the bottom.
class VendingMachine extends Frame {
    public VendingMachine(){
        final int width = 400, height = 200;
        setSize(width,height);
        setBackground(Color.white);

        Label title = new Label("Vending Machine",Label.CENTER);
        add(title,"North");

        Panel buttonPanel = new Panel();
        buttonPanel.add(new Label("Select a cup size: "));
        buttonPanel.add(new Button("Small"));
        buttonPanel.add(new Button("Medium"));
        buttonPanel.add(new Button("Large"));

        add(buttonPanel,"South");
    }
}
```

within a label may be set with one of the values CENTER, LEFT, or RIGHT defined in the class. Figure 16.21 shows the use of two Labels as a title and a label for buttons in a frame. One of the labels uses a CENTER alignment, and the other uses the default LEFT alignment. Code 16.23 shows how this example was created.

16.11 System-Dependent Details

The AWT does quite a good job of isolating programmers from the need to know much about the low level details of the different potential systems that their programs might be run on. However, there are some system-dependent details that will affect the general *look-and-feel* of an AWT-based application. For instance, objects of the basic AWT component classes are provided by host-dependent *peer objects*. This means that the same program running under different window managers might have subtle differences in its visual appearance. In the next few sections, we describe some of the AWT classes that are affected by these differences. It is worth noting that the more advanced Swing classes, described in Chapter 17, go to some considerable lengths to remove even these few differences.

16.11.1   The Toolkit Class

The `Toolkit` class has the general role of supporting the creation of host-dependent *peer objects* for the AWT component types. These are what ultimately give applications a particular look-and-feel in each host windowing environment. Most of its methods are `protected` and not of general interest to most programmers. The toolkit's main methods of interest are a disparate collection concerned with providing information on the host system's properties (`getProperty`), colors (`getColorModel`), and screen (`getScreenResolution`, `getScreenSize`) as well as supporting image manipulation (`createImage`, `getImage`), printing (`getPrintJob`), and access to the system's clipboard (`getSystemClipboard`). Examples of how some of these methods are used are provided in subsequent sections. Toolkit is an abstract class, and an instance of an appropriate sub class can be obtained through its static `getDefaultToolkit` method.

16.11.2   The GraphicsEnvironment Class

The `GraphicsEnvironment` class provides information on the fonts and graphics devices available to a program. We describe fonts in more detail in Section 16.11.3. A `GraphicsDevice` might be a screen, a printer, or an image buffer, for instance. An instance of an implementation of GraphicsEnvironment may be obtained via its static `getLocalGraphicsEnvironment` method.

16.11.3   The Font Class

All sub classes of Component inherit a `setFont` method, which means that we can vary the size, style, and typeface of the text that appears on Labels, Buttons, Text and Menu components, and so on. Thoughtful use of font styles and sizes can significantly enhance the visual appearance of a user interface. There are three different ways of describing fonts, which can be confusing. A font can be described by its *logical name* (such as `"SansSerif"`), by its *family name* (such as `"Helvetica"`), or by its *face name* (such as `"Helvetica Bold"`). The `getName` method of the Font class returns a font's logical name, while `getFamilyName` returns its family name. The `getFontName` method returns the host name of the installed font.

One constructor of the `Font` class takes three arguments. The first names the font required, using either a logical name (`"Dialog"`, `"DialogInput"`, `"Monospaced"`, `"SansSerif"`, `"Serif"`, `"Symbol"`), or a face name. The second gives the style (PLAIN, BOLD, or ITALIC—values defined in the Font class). The third

Figure 16.22 An example of the SansSerif font in different sizes (`AWTFontSizes.java`)

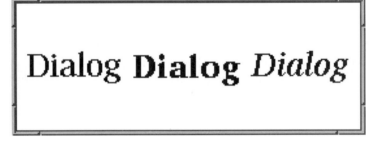

Figure 16.23 Plain, Bold, and Italic styles (`AWTFontStyles.java`)

gives the point size (smaller point sizes mean smaller characters). The style values may be bitwise-or'd together to give bold-italic, for instance (see Appendix C.6 for details of the bit manipulation logical operators). Figure 16.22 shows a range of font sizes displayed in the `SansSerif` style. This was produced by the example in Code 16.24 .

A font will not necessarily be available in all requested sizes. Figure 16.23 illustrates the standard styles. The names of the fonts that are available to a program, additional to the standard ones, will vary from system to system. You should not rely on a potentially specialized font being available without checking and providing an alternative, if necessary. A `GraphicsEnvironment` object will tell you which fonts are provided via its `getAvailableFontFamilyNames` method. Code 16.25 shows how this list may be printed.

Code 16.24   Displaying labels in a range of font sizes (`FontSizes.java`)

```java
import java.awt.*;

    // Display a range of labels in order to illustrate different
    // font sizes.
class FontSizes extends Frame {
    public FontSizes(){
        final int width = 250, height = 250;
        setSize(width,height);
        setBackground(Color.white);

        // The font sizes to display.
        final int[] sizes = { 8, 12, 16, };
        // Display one font size per row.
        setLayout(new GridLayout(sizes.length,1));

        // Which font to use.
        final String fontName = "SansSerif";
        // Create a centered label for each size.
        for(int i = 0; i < sizes.length; i++){
            // Use the font name as the label's text.
            Label label = new Label(fontName,Label.CENTER);
            // Set the required font.
            label.setFont(new Font(fontName,Font.PLAIN,sizes[i]));
            add(label);
        }
    }
}
```

Code 16.25   Finding the available fonts (`AWTFontNames.java`)

```java
import java.awt.*;

        // Find out the names of the fonts available in this environment.
class AWTFontNames {
    public static void main(String[] args){
        // Get the default graphics environment.
        GraphicsEnvironment env =
                GraphicsEnvironment.getLocalGraphicsEnvironment();
        // Get the font names.
        final String[] fontNames = env.getAvailableFontFamilyNames();
        final int numNames = fontNames.length;

        System.out.println("The following font families are available.");
        for(int i = 0; i < numNames; i++){
            System.out.println(fontNames[i]);
        }
    }
}
```

ascent → 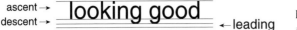 ← leading

descent →

Figure 16.24   Relationship of ascent, descent and leading

A sample of the its output might be:

```
The following font families are available.
Courier
Default
Dialog
dialog.bold
dialog.bolditalic
dialog.italic
...
```

The `getAllFonts` method of GraphicsEnvironment returns an array containing a reference to an instance of all the available Font classes.

A font has associated with it a set of *font metrics* which provide details of the height and widths of individual characters within that font. The Component and Graphics classes both have a `getFontMetrics` method which takes a Font as an actual argument and returns a `FontMetrics` object associated with that font. The Graphics class also has a no-arg version of the method that returns the metrics object for the current drawing font. The characters in a font all have the same height space available to them but they make use of this in differing ways. The full height is divided into three areas—*leading*, *ascent*, and *descent*—from top to bottom, with the ascent region occupying the major proportion of the height (Figure 16.24). The leading represents the amount of space between this character and the characters in the line below. The ascent is the space between the character and its *baseline*—the line upon which it sits. Beneath the baseline is the descent area, used for characters such as 'g', 'j', and 'y' whose tails fall below the baseline. A plain serif font of size twelve might have a height of sixteen pixels with values for the leading, ascent, and descent of one, twelve, and three pixels, respectively. Fonts typically allocate variable widths to their characters. The width of a single character or string of characters may be determined via the `charWidth` and `stringWidth` methods of FontMetrics. In the serif font, mentioned above, the width of 'i' might be three pixels, while that of 'T' might be seven pixels.

Exercise 16.12   Create several labels and add them to a Frame using different font characteristics to see the effects on the text that is displayed.

Exercise 16.13   Create an application that displays a label using the font name "Dialog Bold". The program should check to make sure that this font family is available before constructing a Font object that uses it. Use GraphicsEnvironment's `getAvailableFontFamilyNames` method to check this.

In Chapter 13, we developed an implementation for a stopwatch interface. If we wanted to create a graphical view of the digits of the watch, then a label to represent each digit would be the ideal component to do this. Setting a large font for each label would enhance the display's readability. Figure 16.25 shows how this might look.

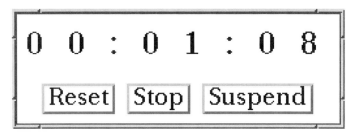

Figure 16.25   A stopwatch display (`AWTWatch.java`)

Figure 16.26   A two-digit counter display
(`AWTCountdown.java`)

Figure 16.26 shows a simpler example than the stopwatch display that we can use to illustrate how the elements of the more complex display are achieved. The class that produces this two-digit display is shown in Code 16.26. A particular point to note is that components use the font of their parent container, so setting a new font for the frame causes the labels it contains to use that font.

Code 16.26   Part of a two-digit counter class (`Countdown.java`)

```java
import java.awt.*;

    // Displays two Labels in a Frame.
    // These are used as a two-digit countdown.
public class Countdown extends Frame {
    public Countdown(){
        final int width = 100, height = 75;
        setSize(width,height);
        setBackground(Color.white);

        // Use a FlowLayout to keep the digits together in the
        // center of the frame.
        setLayout(new FlowLayout());
        // Set the font for the Frame.
        final int fontSize = 20;
        setFont(new Font("SansSerif",Font.BOLD,fontSize));

        // Add the digit labels to the frame.
        add(getHighDigit());
        add(getLowDigit());
    }

        // Give a countdown of the required number of seconds.
    public void countdown(int seconds){
        updateDisplay(seconds);
```

(*Continued*)

Code 16.26   *(Continued)*

```
    // Tick away the seconds.
    try{
        // One second in milliseconds.
        final int oneSecond = 1000;
        while(seconds > 0){
            Thread.sleep(oneSecond);
            seconds--;
            updateDisplay(seconds);
        }
    }
    catch(InterruptedException e){
    }
}

    // Show the number of seconds as two separate digits.
protected void updateDisplay(int seconds){
    // Make sure seconds fits within two digits.
    seconds %= 100;
    // Extract the two components.
    int highDigit = seconds / 10;
    int lowDigit = seconds % 10;
    // Set the text of the two components.
    getHighDigit().setText(Integer.toString(highDigit));
    getLowDigit().setText(Integer.toString(lowDigit));
    // Make sure the display is updated.
    repaint();
}

protected Label getHighDigit(){
    return highDigitDisplay;
}

protected Label getLowDigit(){
    return lowDigitDisplay;
}

// The two labels used for the two digits.
private Label highDigitDisplay = new Label("0",Label.CENTER);
private Label lowDigitDisplay = new Label("0",Label.CENTER);
}
```

The counter is started when a countdown message is received, indicating the number of seconds to tick away. The updateDisplay method breaks up the seconds into single-digit values. These values are stored in the text of the two labels. Once the labels have been changed, repaint is called to update the display. In order to animate the display, we need to know when each second has passed. The easiest way to do this is to use the static sleep method of the Thread class to wait one second and then change the text in the labels to reflect the new time.

Exercise 16.14   Design an application, similar to that shown in Code 16.26, and illustrated in Figure 16.26, that is able to adapt the number of labels it needs to the number of digits to be displayed. For instance, three labels will be needed if the counter has a value in the range 100–999. Consider whether the number of labels should be reduced when the counter reaches a value that requires fewer labels. What effect might reducing the number of labels have on the visual organization of the display?

Exercise 16.15   Design an application, similar to that shown in Code 16.26, but whose display is closer to that shown in Figure 16.25. That is, the argument passed to `countdown` represents a number of seconds that should be displayed as hour, minute, and second pairs, with a separator between the pairs.

16.11.4   The Color Class

The `Color` class allows a range of colors to be described. As with Fonts, thoughtful and restrained use of color can significantly enhance the impact of a user interface. However, it is all too easy to overdo the use of color and produce lurid and distracting combinations that only serve to distract from the otherwise positive aspects of a user interface.

For convenience, thirteen Color names are provided as public static Color objects in the class. These have the names: `black`, `blue`, `cyan`, `darkGray`, `gray`, `green`, `lightGray`, `magenta`, `orange`, `pink`, `red`, `white`, and `yellow`. The exact appearance of these to the user will be dependent upon several things, such as the window manager's settings, the monitor hardware, and the way in which a user's eyes process what they see. The `setBackground` mutator of a Component takes a Color object as its argument. Whenever the `update` method clears a component, this is the color it will use. There is a corresponding `setForeground` mutator that determines the color in which all graphical drawing operations are performed. Alternatively, the `setColor` method of a Graphics object may be used to change the color in which drawing is done. The `getBackground` and `getForeground` accessors return an appropriate Color object if one has been set. The example in Code 16.27 shows how the color values for the standard names might be displayed, each in a Label with a background of a particular color. This is illustrated in Figure 16.27 (in shades of gray, of course!).

Code 16.27   Representing the standard Color names

```
import java.awt.*;

        // Provide a Frame for a set of colored Labels.
class ColoredFrame extends Frame {
    public ColoredFrame() {
        final int width = 300, height = 200;
```

(Continued)

Code 16.27   *(Continued)*

```
            setSize(width,height);
            setBackground(Color.white);
            setLayout(new FlowLayout());
            setupColoredLabels();
        }

    protected void setupColoredLabels() {
        // The name of each Color. This will be the label's string.
        String[] standardColorNames = {
            "black", "blue", "cyan", "darkGray",
            "gray", "green", "lightGray", "magenta",
            "orange", "pink", "red", "white", "yellow",
        };

        // References to the standard Color objects.
        Color[] standardColors = {
            Color.black, Color.blue, Color.cyan, Color.darkGray,
            Color.gray, Color.green, Color.lightGray, Color.magenta,
            Color.orange, Color.pink, Color.red, Color.white, Color.yellow,
        };

        // Add a label of each color to the frame.
        for(int i = 0; i < standardColors.length; i++){
            Label label = new Label(standardColorNames[i]);
            label.setBackground(standardColors[i]);
            add(label);
        }
    }
}
```

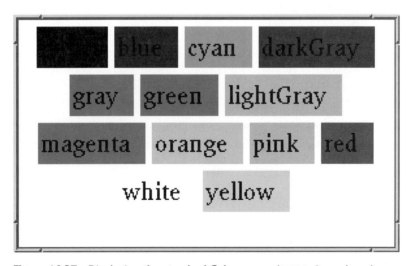

Figure 16.27   Displaying the standard Color names (AWTColor.java)

The `setBackground` method has been used to set the background of the frame and of each label. A color name is displayed in the label's foreground color, which is black by default. This means that the text of the label with a black background will not be visible, and the outline of the label with a white background merges with the background of its container.

16.12   The RGB Color Model

A particular color is often described according to the *RGB Color Model*[FVFH90], that is in terms of the amount of each of the three primary color components it contains: red, green, and blue. Integer values for each of these color components, in the range [0 ... 255], are passed to the constructor to create a `Color` object. This allows for over 16 million different color values, which is far more than is required for most applications. Alternatively, a single integer argument may be used in which the blue value occupies bits 0–7, the green value occupies bits 8–15, and the red value occupies bits 16–23. A third constructor takes three `float` arguments for the red, green, and blue values in the range [0.0...1.0]. In all cases, the larger the value of a component, the greater its contribution to the final color. The same saturated red color might be created in each of the following three ways:

```
new Color(255,0,0);
new Color(255 << 16);
new Color(1.0,0.0,0.0);
```

The second of these three examples uses the *left shift operator* (see Appendix C.6.2). Black is produced from values of 0 for each component and white is produced from the maximum value of each (255 or 1.0). Grays are created by using equal amounts of each component. The value of each color component can be determined with the accessors `getRed`, `getGreen`, and `getBlue`. Once created, a Color object is immutable and variations in its values can only be produced by creating new Color objects. The `brighter` and `darker` methods both return new objects in which the components of the object are scaled: `brighter` increases the amount of the non-zero components and `darker` reduces them. The example in Code 16.28 illustrates the use of several of these methods in an application that displays a random color in the background of a Canvas within a Frame. The appearance of this application is shown in Figure 16.28.

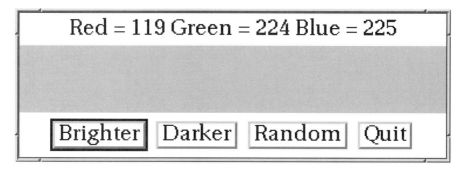

Figure 16.28 Generating and manipulating random Colors (Code 16.28) (`AWTRGB.java`)

Code 16.28 Display and manipulate a random color in a Canvas (`AWTRGB.java`)

```java
import java.awt.*;
import java.awt.event.*;

        // Display a Canvas with a background Color that
        // can be manipulated. Allow the user to use the
        // deeper and brighter methods, as well as generating
        // random colors.
class RGBFrame extends Frame implements ActionListener {
    public RGBFrame(){
        final int width = 375, height = 150;
        setSize(width,height);
        setBackground(Color.white);

        // Add the canvas that will display the color examples.
        Canvas canvas = getCanvas();
        canvas.setSize(width,2*height/3);
        // Start with a black background.
        canvas.setBackground(Color.black);
        add(canvas,"Center");

        // Add a label for a description of the current background color
        // at the top of the frame.
        add(getLabel(),"North");
        describeColor();

        // Add a panel of buttons for user actions at the bottom
        // of the frame.
        Panel buttonPanel = new Panel();
        for(int i = 0; i < buttonLabels.length; i++){
            Button b = new Button(buttonLabels[i]);
            b.addActionListener(this);
            buttonPanel.add(b);
        }
        add(buttonPanel,"South");
    }

        // Act on a button press.
    public void actionPerformed(ActionEvent e){
        String command = e.getActionCommand();
        if((command == null) || command.equals("")){
            return;
        }
        else if(command.equals("")){
            return;
        }

        Canvas canvas = getCanvas();
        // Obtain the current background to manipulate.
        Color c = canvas.getBackground();

        if(command.equals(brighterString)){
            c = c.brighter();
        }
```

Code 16.28   (*Continued*)

```
        else if(command.equals(darkerString)){
            c = c.darker();
        }
        else if(command.equals(randomString)){
            // Random number for RGB value.
            final int numColorValues = 256*256*256;
            c = new Color((int) (Math.random()*numColorValues));
        }
        else if(command.equals(quitString)){
            System.exit(0);
        }
        canvas.setBackground(c);
        describeColor();
        repaint();
    }

    // Extract the component color values from the canvas's
    // background color to create the text for the label.
    protected void describeColor(){
        Label label = getLabel();
        Color c = getCanvas().getBackground();
        if(c != null){
            label.setText("Red = "+c.getRed()+" Green = "+c.getGreen()+
                        " Blue = "+c.getBlue());
        }
        else{
            label.setText("");
        }
    }

    protected Canvas getCanvas(){
        return canvas;
    }

    protected Label getLabel(){
        return label;
    }

    private Canvas canvas = new Canvas();
    // Center the text of the label
    private Label label = new Label("",Label.CENTER);
    // Strings for the button labels.
    private String brighterString = "Brighter",
                darkerString = "Darker",
                randomString = "Random",
                quitString = "Quit";
    private String[] buttonLabels = {
        brighterString, darkerString, randomString, quitString,
    };
}
```

The integer values of the red, green, and blue components of the canvas's color are displayed in the text of a Label at the top of the frame. This text is set in the describeColor method. Buttons at the bottom of the frame allow the current color to be brightened or darkened, or a new random color to be generated. When the Random button is pressed, a random integer is generated, which is then passed as an argument to the constructor of a new Color object.

16.12.1   The HSB Color Model

In addition to the RGB color model, the Color class supports the *HSB Color Model*, whose three component values denote hue, saturation, and brightness.[4] The contribution of each of these to a color is represented by a value in the range [0.0 ... 1.0]. While there is no constructor for this model, the static getHSBColor method fulfills a similar role. The hue value is used to select from the spectrum: red $\left(\frac{0.0}{6.0}\right)$, yellow $\left(\frac{1.0}{6.0}\right)$, green $\left(\frac{2.0}{6.0}\right)$, cyan $\left(\frac{3.0}{6.0}\right)$, blue $\left(\frac{4.0}{6.0}\right)$, magenta $\left(\frac{5.0}{6.0}\right)$. The brightest colors have larger brightness values. The saturation value corresponds to the intensity of a color, for instance a pure red might have a saturation value of 1.0 while the saturation value in a pink might be only 0.3. The class defines static methods to convert from the RGB model to HSB (RGBtoHSB) and vice versa (HSBtoRGB).

Exercise 16.16   Modify the example shown in Code 16.28 so that the HSB values of the canvas's background color are displayed in the Label, instead of the RGB values. You will probably need to increase the width of the frame to accommodate the floating point values. You might like to use the NumberFormat class of the java.text package to restrict the number of decimal places printed (see Section 8.6.2).

16.12.2   The Exclusive-Or Color Mode

The setColor method of the Graphics class takes a Color object to set the color in which subsequent draw and fill operations will be performed, and Section 16.5 discussed the basic draw and fill methods of the Graphics class. When multiple shapes are drawn on a graphics context, care must be taken that the desired effect is achieved. For instance, Figure 16.29 shows two different ways in which a pair of overlapping rectangles might appear. In the second image, it is impossible to distinguish that there are two rectangles and not a single large rectangle. One possible approach is to draw them in different colors, but Figure 16.30 shows that this gives the appearance of a narrow rectangle to the left of the wider rectangle. A third approach is to try represent the overlapping region in a distinctive color, as in Figure 16.31. Fortunately, this does not require trying to work out the area of overlap and drawing it separately from the other parts of the rectangles. The setXORMode method of the Graphics class instructs the Graphics object that drawing is to be conducted in *exclusive-or mode* until further notice. The normal mode is *paint mode*, in which drawing always overwrites what is already on the graphics context. It is possible

---

[4] This is sometimes known as the HSV color model—hue, saturation, and value.

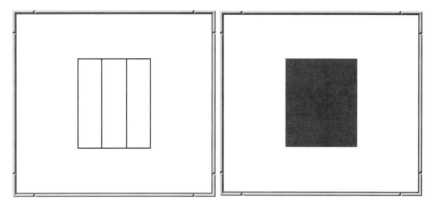

Figure 16.29 Overlapping rectangles using `drawRect` and `fillRect`

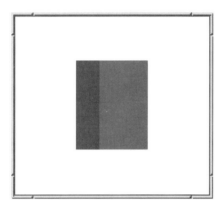

Figure 16.30 Overlapping rectangles in PaintMode

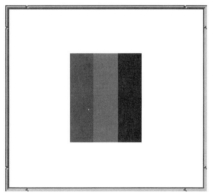

Figure 16.31 Overlapping rectangles in XORMode (`AWTXOR.java`)

to switch back to paint mode with the `setPaintMode` method of the Graphics class, which takes no arguments. The `setXORMode` method takes a Color argument representing the exclusive-or color. The effect of the Boolean and bit manipulation exclusive-or operations is described in Section 6.2.6 and Appendix C.6, respectively. The effect with colors is a little different, but related to those concepts. In general, when drawing is performed in exclusive-or mode, and drawing in the current color

Code 16.29   Using XORmode for draw and fill operations (`XORCanvas.java`)

```java
import java.awt.*;

class XORCanvas extends Canvas {
        // Draw two overlapping rectangles.
    public void paint(Graphics g){
        Dimension size = getSize();

        // Define the width and height of the shapes.
        final int shapeWidth = size.width/4, shapeHeight = size.height/2;

        // The x and y shift for the second shape.
        final int xShift = shapeWidth/2, yShift = 0;
        // Evenly space between the sides and top.
        final int xPos = (size.width-(shapeWidth+xShift))/2,
                yPos = (size.height-(shapeHeight+yShift))/2;

        // Fill the first rectangle.
        g.setColor(Color.red);
        g.fillRect(xPos,yPos,shapeWidth,shapeHeight);
        g.setXORMode(Color.green);
        // Fill the second rectangle.
        g.fillRect(xPos+xShift,yPos+yShift,shapeWidth,shapeHeight);
    }
}
```

overlaps with earlier drawing in a different color, the exclusive-or color is used to create a different color in the overlapping area—hence the effect in Figure 16.31.

The exclusive-or color, itself, will appear in the overlapping region of two parts of the image drawn in the same color. However, it can be quite difficult to obtain the exact effect that you want. Code 16.29, for instance, illustrates a canvas in which an attempt is made to draw two overlapping rectangles filled in red, with the overlapping portion displayed in green.

However, the effect is similar to that in Figure 16.31, with the left third displayed in red, the middle third in green, and the right third in blue (or other non-red color). Why does the right section not appear in red? The problem is that, once exclusive-or mode is set, any drawing will combine the existing colors on the canvas, so the color of the second rectangle combines with the background color of the canvas to produce a non-red result. We can retain the red color in both rectangles by setting the exclusive-or color to be the background color:

```java
g.setXORMode(getBackground());
```

This produces the appearance of Figure 16.32 . Clearly, it is possible to produce a wide variety of effects with exclusive-or mode. The problem with it is the unpredictability of the color combinations the exclusive-or color will produce.

A further feature of this mode, from which it derives its name, is that drawing an image a second time causes it to be removed and the area it covered restored to

Figure 16.32   Using the background color for the exclusive-or color

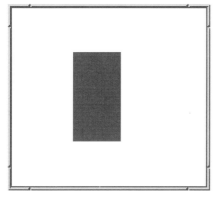

Figure 16.33   Drawing the second rectangle twice erases it

its former state. This is illustrated in Figure 16.33, where the second rectangle has been erased to leave the first in its original state.

16.13   The TextComponent Class

The `TextComponent` class extends Component to provide methods which allow display and user-editing of arbitrary text. It is extended by both `TextField` and `TextArea` (Section 16.13.2) for single-line and multi-line input, respectively. Figure 16.34 illustrates a common combination of Label and TextField as a prompt-and-response pair for user input. TextComponent implements a cursor marking the position where user input will appear. All input to the field, along with any associated editing, cursor movement, and highlighting, is handled by it. The full text it contains is available to the program via its `getText` method. A portion of the text which has been highlighted by the user may be accessed via the `getSelectedText` method, and the end points of this area are returned by `getSelectionStart` and

Figure 16.34   Combining a Label and TextField (`AWTForm1.java`)

`getSelectionEnd`. The ability to edit the displayed text may be turned on or off via the `setEditable` method, which takes a `boolean` argument.

16.13.1 The TextField Class

`TextField` adds the ability to turn input echoing off via its `setEchoChar` method. This takes a `char` argument which is displayed instead of normal input in order to give the user feedback as to the number of characters they have entered. The most obvious use for this is password entry, as shown in Figure 16.34.

When the Return key is typed in a TextField, an ActionEvent is sent by the field to any action listeners that have registered with it via its `addActionListener` method. This is similar to what we saw with buttons in Section 16.7. However, we cannot use the normal approach of requesting the action command from an Action-Event originating from a TextField in order to determine the source of the event. This is because requesting the action command simply retrieves the String the field holds—i.e., it is the equivalent of using `getText` on the TextField object. This is useful, but it does not help us to identify which object sent the event. Instead we need to use the approach of identifying the source of the event, using `getSource`. This will return a reference to the object that sent the event, which we can use to compare with a reference to the text field object. Code 16.30 shows this approach in action, and is illustrated in Figure 16.34. A Panel is used to contain two Label and TextField pairs for name and password entry. Echoing has been turned off in the password text field.

Code 16.30 Responding to ActionEvents in TextField components (`LoginFrame.java`)

```
import java.awt.*;
import java.awt.event.*;

    // Display a pair of labeled text fields.
    // Detect when the Return key is typed in either field.
public class LoginFrame extends Frame implements ActionListener {
    public LoginFrame(){
        final int width = 600, height = 75;
        setSize(width,height);
        setBackground(Color.white);

        // How many characters may be entered in either field.
        final int fieldWidth = 10;

        // A panel for the label and field pairs
        Panel panel = new Panel();

        Label nameLabel = new Label("Name: ");
        TextField nameField = new TextField("",fieldWidth);
        Label passwordLabel = new Label("Password: ");
        TextField passwordField = new TextField("",fieldWidth);
        // Hide passwords.
        passwordField.setEchoChar('?');
```

Code 16.30   (*Continued*)

```
        // Let us know about action events.
        nameField.addActionListener(this);
        passwordField.addActionListener(this);
        // Group the labels and the fields as a unit.
        panel.add(nameLabel);
        panel.add(nameField);
        panel.add(passwordLabel);
        panel.add(passwordField);
        // Add to the Frame.
        add(panel,"North");
    }

    public void actionPerformed(ActionEvent e){
        Object source = e.getSource();
        if(source instanceof TextField){
            TextField field = (TextField) source;

            if(field.echoCharIsSet()){
                System.out.println("The password is secret!");
            }
            else{
                System.out.println("Name = "+field.getText());
            }
        }
    }
}
```

The `actionPerformed` method in Code 16.30 receives an ActionEvent whenever a Return key is typed in either of its text fields. Once we have determined that a text field object sent the event, we can cast the Object reference to its proper type. We then distinguish between the name field and password field by checking whether an echo character has been set. If it has, then we know that the source was the password field and so we do not print its text. Otherwise, we use the `getText` method to find out what is in it.

Two of TextField's constructors take a `columns` argument, used as `field-Width` in Code 16.30. The effect of this on the size of the field is both dependent upon the type of font associated with field and platform dependent. It specifies the field width in terms of the width of an average character, such as `'n'`, in the current font. Such a width would accommodate fewer `'m'` characters but more `'.'` characters, for instance.

16.13.2   The TextArea Class

The `TextArea` class extends `TextComponent` to provide a class that handles multi-line text input to a program, complete with both horizontal and vertical scrollbars, if desired. The most general form of the constructor allows us to specify the initial

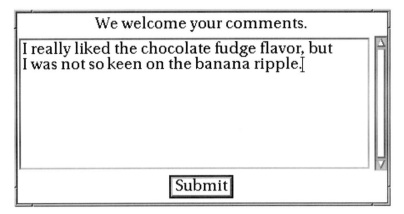

Figure 16.35   Combining a TextArea and Button (`AWTTextArea.java`)

contents of the area, the numbers of rows and columns, and whether it has scrollbars:

```
final int numRows = 10, numCols = 60;
String initialString = "";
TextArea comments = new TextArea(initialString,numRows,numCols,
                              TextArea.SCROLLBARS_NONE);
```

If the scrollbars argument is missing, it defaults to SCROLLBARS_BOTH, meaning that there will be both horizontal and vertical scrollbars. To request just one scrollbar, use SCROLLBARS_HORIZONTAL_ONLY or SCROLLBARS_VERTICAL_ONLY. It is not possible to register as an ActionListener with a TextArea, so you must either associate a button with it, or attach a TextListener (Section 16.13.4), which will notify you of any change to the text. Code 16.31 shows an example of a TextArea used for submitting comments. Its appearance is illustrated in Figure 16.35. The Submit button sends the usual ActionEvent message when pressed.

Code 16.31   Using a TextArea for a comments form (`CommentsForm.java`)

```
import java.awt.*;
import java.awt.event.*;

    // Display a labeled text area and a submit button.
public class CommentsForm extends Frame
                                implements ActionListener {
    public CommentsForm(){
        final int width = 450, height = 250;
        setSize(width,height);
        setBackground(Color.white);

        // Place a centered label at the top.
        Label welcome = new Label("We welcome your comments.",
                                Label.CENTER);
        add(welcome,"North");
```

Code 16.31   (*Continued*)

```
        // A central TextArea for comments.
        // How many characters are allowed to be entered.
        final int numRows = 10, numCols = 40;
        Label nameLabel = new Label("Comments: ");
        TextArea comments = new TextArea("",numRows,numCols,
                            TextArea.SCROLLBARS_VERTICAL_ONLY);
        comments.setBackground(Color.white);
        setComments(comments);
        // Add to the Frame.
        add(comments,"Center");

        // Add a Submit button.
        Button submit = new Button(submitString);
        submit.setActionCommand(submitString);
        submit.addActionListener(this);
        // Place the button in a Panel to limit its size.
        Panel p = new Panel();
        p.add(submit);
        add(p,"South");
    }

        // The Submit button has been pressed.
    public void actionPerformed(ActionEvent e){
        final String command = e.getActionCommand();
        if(command.equals(submitString)){
            System.out.println("Comments = "+comments.getText());
        }
        else{
            System.err.println("Unknown command: "+command);
        }
    }

    protected TextArea getComments(){
        return comments;
    }

    protected void setComments(TextArea commentArea){
        comments = commentArea;
    }

    // The label and action command of the submit button.
    private final String submitString = "Submit";
    // The text area.
    private TextArea comments;
}
```

The TextArea class also has the methods `insert`, `append`, **and** `replace-`
`Range` to modify the areas contents from within the program. The `insert` method
takes a string and a character position after which to insert the string. The `ap-`
`pend` method takes a string to be appended to the end of the text in the area. The

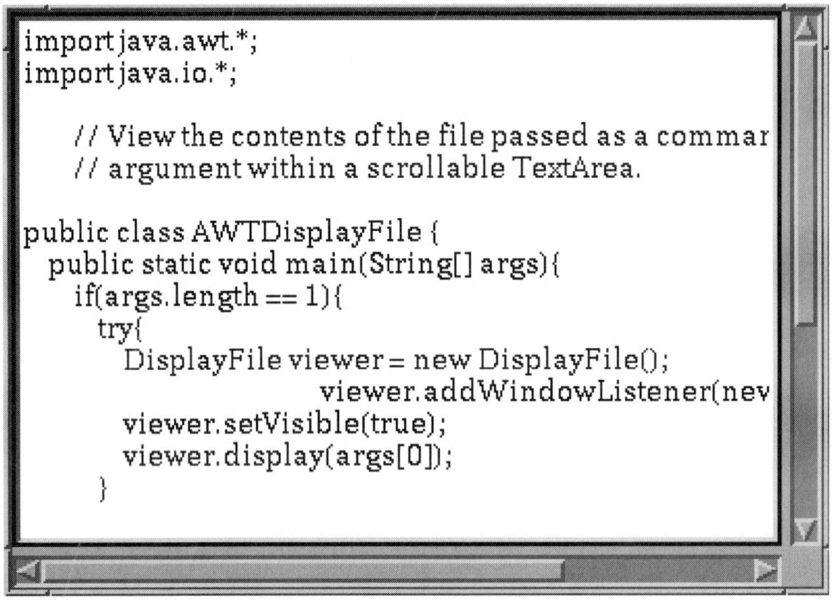

```
import java.awt.*;
import java.io.*;

    // View the contents of the file passed as a commar
    // argument within a scrollable TextArea.

public class AWTDisplayFile {
  public static void main(String[] args){
    if(args.length == 1){
      try{
        DisplayFile viewer = new DisplayFile();
                     viewer.addWindowListener(nev
        viewer.setVisible(true);
        viewer.display(args[0]);
      }
```

Figure 16.36 A TextArea for file viewing (`AWTDisplayFile.java`)

replaceRange method takes a string along with a starting and ending index and
replaces the subrange of the indexed text with the string.

16.13.3   A File Viewer using TextArea

A TextArea is commonly used to view the contents of a file in a scrollable area
(Figure 16.36). The example in Code 16.32 defines the DisplayFile class, whose
constructor adds a single TextArea to a Frame. The contents of a file whose name is
passed to its display method is loaded into the TextArea.

Code 16.32   A simple file viewer (`DisplayFile.java`)

```
import java.awt.*;
import java.io.*;

        // Allow the contents of a file to be viewed within
        // a TextArea. The area has both vertical and horizontal
        // scrollbars, and is made non-editable.
public class DisplayFile extends Frame {
    public DisplayFile(){
        final int width = 400, height = 300;
        setSize(width,height);
        // Create the viewing area for the file's contents.
        final int numRows = 10, numCols = 80;
        TextArea area = new TextArea("",numRows,numCols,
                        TextArea.SCROLLBARS_BOTH);
```

Code 16.32   (*Continued*)

```
        area.setFont(new Font("Helvetica",Font.PLAIN,10));
        // Don't allow changes.
        area.setEditable(false);
        add(area);
        setContents(area);
    }

        // Display the contents of the given file in the viewing area.
    public void display(String filename) throws Exception {
        // Make sure the file exists.
        File details = new File(filename);
        if(!details.exists()){
            throw new Exception(filename+" does not exist.");
        }
        else if(!details.canRead()){
            throw new Exception("You don't have permission to view: "+
                                filename);
        }
        else if(details.length() > Integer.MAX_VALUE){
            // We can't cope with the file's size.
            throw new Exception("The file is too big to display.");
        }
        else{
            loadFile(details);
        }
    }

        // Load the contents of the given file into the TextArea.
        // The existence and readability of the file should have
        // already been ascertained, but failure must still be
        // anticipated.
    protected void loadFile(File details) throws Exception {
        final String filename = details.getName();
        BufferedReader reader = null;
        try{
            // Read the file into a single array.
            int fileSize = (int) details.length();
            char[] buffer = new char [fileSize];
            // Keep track of how much has been read.
            int totalCharsRead = 0;

            // Open the file and read it.
            reader = new BufferedReader(new FileReader(filename));
            while(totalCharsRead < fileSize){
                // Try to read the remainder in one go.
                int charsRead = reader.read(buffer,totalCharsRead,
                                            fileSize-totalCharsRead);
                totalCharsRead += charsRead;
            }

            // Place the text into the TextArea.
            TextArea area = getContents();
```

(*Continued*)

Code 16.32   *(Continued)*

```
            area.setText(String.valueOf(buffer));
        }
        catch(IOException e){
            throw new Exception("Read failure: "+e.getMessage());
        }
        finally{
            if(reader != null){
                reader.close();
            }
        }
    }

    protected TextArea getContents(){
        return contents;
    }

    protected void setContents(TextArea c){
        contents = c;
    }

    private TextArea contents;
}
```

The TextArea is prevented from allowing changes to the text it displays by sending it a setEditable message with a `false` argument value. In the `loadFile` method, we recognize that the length of a file may be too big to store in an integer, so we restrict the size of files that can be displayed to `Integer.MAX_VALUE` characters. The contents of the file are read into a single array of `char`. Once read, the array of characters is converted into a String object and placed in the TextArea with its setText method. We shall use this example in Section 16.25, and those that follow, as we build a more fully-fledged file viewer as an introduction to the menu classes.

16.13.4   The TextListener Interface

If an object wishes to be informed of every change to a TextComponent, it must implement the TextListener interface (Code 16.33) and register itself as a listener via the component's addTextListener method.

Code 16.33 The TextListener interface

```
public interface TextListener extends EventListener {
    public abstract void textValueChanged(TextEvent e);
}
```

Code 16.34   Responding to a TextEvent

```
class FileEditor implements TextListener {
    ...
        // Respond to TextEvents
    public void textValueChanged(TextEvent e){
        Object source = e.getSource();
        if(source instanceof TextArea){
            setChanged(true);
        }
    }
    ...
    // Has the current file been edited?
    private boolean changed = false;
}
```

The implementation of textValueChanged is very similar to the implementation of actionPerformed illustrated in Code 16.30. Since TextComponents already handle the basic editing requirements of TextFields and TextAreas, it is not often necessary for an application to take detailed action when notified of a TextEvent. The most common need is that of a text editor which needs to know whether the text of a file has been changed or not. This will enable it to warn the user if they tried to leave the editor without having saved any changes. Code 16.34 shows such an implementation of textValueChanged that sets a boolean status attribute if notified of a TextEvent.

16.14   The GridBagLayout Class

The GridBagLayout class represents the most sophisticated of the layout managers defined in the java.awt package. Consequently, it is also the most complex to explain and understand. Its major advantages over the simpler GridLayout layout manager are the ability to define grids in which components occupy multiple cells (Figure 16.37) and the juxtaposition of components is less regular (Figure 16.38). The programmable interface of the GridBagLayout class is relatively simple as most

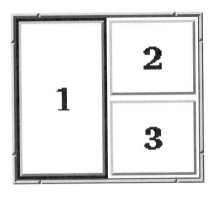

Figure 16.37   Spanning multiple cells with a GridBagLayout

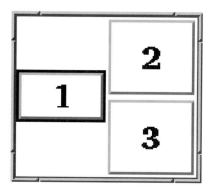

Figure 16.38   Irregular arrangements with a
GridBagLayout

of the methods are not called directly by the programmer, but by the Container whose components are being managed. The main power of this class comes from its interaction with objects of the GridBagConstraints class.

When a component is added to a container managed by a GridBagLayout object, the component is normally associated with a GridBagConstraints object;[5] alternatively, constraints may be associated with a component by sending the layout manager a setConstraints message with a reference to the component and its constraints. The layout manager uses the constraints of all components, in combination, to determine the placement of individual components and how to divide up the available area of the container among them. Within the space allocated to a component, the constraints further determine how it should be positioned and sized. A component's constraints consist of values for the following attributes: gridx, gridy, gridwidth, gridheight, anchor, fill, weightx, weighty, insets, ipadx, and ipady. All of these attributes have type int, apart from the weight attributes, which are of type double, and insets, which is an object of the Insets class. We shall explain each of these attributes in turn, making incrementally small changes to examples. Where possible, we have illustrated some of these changes with paired figures. In these examples, we have chosen to use Button components because they have a visual representation whose boundaries are easy to see. Nevertheless, the principles apply equally well to all the sub classes of Component.

We start by illustrating the grid attributes, which are relatively straightforward. Each component is placed at a cell position within the grid managed by the layout manager. This position is indicated by the values of the gridx and gridy attributes of its associated constraint object, with position (0,0) located at the top left of the grid. A component may straddle more than one cell horizontally and/or vertically by specifying a value for the gridwidth and/or gridheight attributes, respectively. Figure 16.39 illustrates the layout of six buttons in a grid of two rows and four columns. Button "1" has a grid height of two, and thus spans two rows, and button "4" has a grid width of two, and thus spans two columns. The example in Code 16.35 shows how this is done.

---

[5] For conciseness, we shall refer to these GridBag objects simply as layout and constraints objects in the remainder of this discussion.

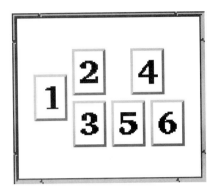

Figure 16.39 Spanning multiple rows and columns (`GridBagLayoutExample.java`)

Code 16.35 Setting grid positions, widths and heights

```
import java.awt.*;

        // Layout a number of buttons to illustrate positioning
        // and row and column spanning with a GridBagLayout.
class GridBagLayoutFrame extends Frame {
    public GridBagLayoutFrame(){
        final int width = 150, height = 150;
        setSize(width,height);
        setBackground(Color.white);

        // Use a slightly larger than normal font.
        setFont(new Font("SansSerif",Font.BOLD,20));

        // Create the layout manager.
        GridBagLayout layout = new GridBagLayout();
        setLayout(layout);
        setupComponents();
    }

        // Setup the required set of components in this container.
    protected void setupComponents(){
        // Create the constraints. Reuse this object with each button.
        GridBagConstraints constraints = new GridBagConstraints();

        // Create each button, set up its constraints and
        // add it to the frame.
        final int singleCell = 1, wider = 2, higher = 2;
        initBasicConstraints(constraints,0,0,singleCell,higher);
        addButton("1",constraints);

        initBasicConstraints(constraints,1,0,singleCell,singleCell);
        addButton("2",constraints);

        initBasicConstraints(constraints,1,1,singleCell,singleCell);
        addButton("3",constraints);
```

(Continued)

```
        initBasicConstraints(constraints,2,0,wider,singleCell);
        addButton("4",constraints);

        initBasicConstraints(constraints,2,1,singleCell,singleCell);
        addButton("5",constraints);

        initBasicConstraints(constraints,3,1,singleCell,singleCell);
        addButton("6",constraints);
    }

        // Initialize the x,y width,height values for the constraints.
    protected void initBasicConstraints(GridBagConstraints constraints,
                              int x, int y, int width, int height){
        constraints.gridx = x;
        constraints.gridy = y;
        constraints.gridwidth = width;
        constraints.gridheight = height;
    }

        // Add a button to the Frame with the given label and constraints.
    protected void addButton(String label, GridBagConstraints constraints){
        Button b = new Button(label);
        add(b,constraints);
    }
}
}
```

Applications in which a large number of components are added to a container managed by a GridBagLayout are often messy to look at because of the large number of constraints that must be set for each. They typically contain many *magic numbers* for positions and widths. Where possible, much of the constraint setting should be placed in short utility methods, such as initBasicConstraints in Code 16.35, and final variables used to give names to values of particular significance, as we have done with singleCell, wider, and higher for the width and height attributes. In addition, the GridBagConstraints class defines the static final variable RELATIVE to assist with positioning. When this is used for the value of gridx, a component is placed in the column to the right of the most recently added component, or in the row below for the value of gridy. Somewhat confusingly, this name is overloaded for use with gridwidth and gridheight attributes where it means the last-but-one row, in the case of gridwidth, and column in the case of gridheight. The static final variable REMAINDER is defined for the width and height attributes to indicate that a component is to occupy the remaining columns or rows, respectively.

When a GridBagConstraints object is passed to the add method of a container, a copy of the constraints is made[6] so that it is safe to modify that particular object for use with future components.

---

[6] Using its clone method (see Section 15.3).

Exercise 16.17   Modify the example in Code 16.35 so that button "6" is not added to the Frame. What effect does this have on button "5"?

The example in Figure 16.39 illustrates that, although two of the buttons have been designated as occupying multiple cells, by default they do not occupy the full width or height of the space that has been allocated to them. Each component in the Figure occupies the minimum space required to display it in full. If it is required to have a component make fuller use of its allotted space, then the `fill` attribute of its constraints must be set. This may take on one of four values: BOTH, NONE, HORIZONTAL, and VERTICAL, to indicate in which direction it should expand beyond its minimum requirement. Setting the `fill` attribute of `constraints` for button "4" as follows

```
constraints.fill = GridBagConstraints.BOTH;
addButton("4",constraints);
```

produces the result shown in Figure 16.40. In this case, there is only spare room for it to expand horizontally.

Where a component has more space allocated to it than it occupies, the `anchor` attribute of its constraints may be used to position it within that space. By default, this has the value CENTER, but there are values for the eight points of the compass—NORTH, NORTHEAST, EAST, etc. Figure 16.41 illustrates the effect of setting the `anchor` attribute for button "1" to be SOUTH, as follows:

```
constraints.anchor = GridBagConstraints.SOUTH;
addButton("1",constraints);
```

In all of the examples we have seen so far in this section, the components have been grouped together in the central area of the container, surrounded by additional space. Even when the `fill` attribute of the constraints was made use of, a large amount of unused space existed outside the block of components. The reason that the components do not make more use of the available space is that the `weightx` and `weighty` attributes of their constraints have the value 0.0 by default. When this is the case, components are allotted the minimum space they require to be displayed within their cells, and space left over appears around the edge of the group. Although

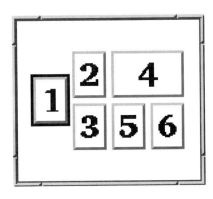

Figure 16.40   Filling the available space for button "4"

Code 16.36   Setting default grid bag constraint values

```
// Initialize the x,y width,height values for the constraints.
// Each component has an equal non-zero weight.
protected void initBasicConstraints(GridBagConstraints constraints,
                        int x, int y, int width, int height){
    constraints.gridx = x;
    constraints.gridy = y;
    constraints.gridwidth = width;
    constraints.gridheight = height;
    constraints.weightx = 1.0;
    constraints.weighty = 1.0;
}
```

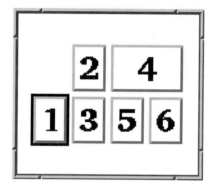

Figure 16.41   Anchoring button "1" to the SOUTH of its available space

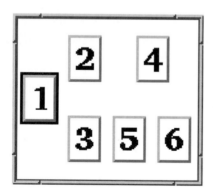

Figure 16.42   Using equal, non-zero, weights for each component

any `double` values may be used for the weights, it is typical that only values in the range `0.0` to `1.0` are used. We start by modifying `initBasicConstraints` from Code 16.35 so that the weights of all components are set to `1.0` (Code 16.36).

The effect of this can be seen in Figure 16.42, which should be contrasted with the effect of all zero weights in Figure 16.39. Each component now has a larger allotment of the available space and so each is more distant from the others. In Figure 16.42, the `fill` and `anchor` constraints of each component still have the

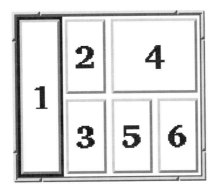

Figure 16.43 Filling all available space within the container

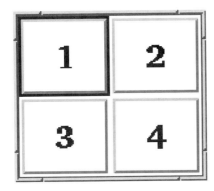

Figure 16.44 Equally weighted components

default values of NONE and CENTER, respectively. In contrast, Figure 16.43 illustrates the effect of setting the fill attribute to BOTH and gives a clearer idea of how much space is available in each cell.

It is easy to misunderstand the effect of the weight attributes because, unlike the other constraint attributes, they apply to all the components in a particular row or column and not simply to an individual component. For instance, reducing the weighty attribute of button "3" in Figure 16.43 to 0.5 will not make it appear half the size of buttons "5" and "6"; indeed, it will have no effect. When determining how much space to allocate to components, above their minimum requirement, the container determines the relative weight of each row from the *maximum* constraint value of weighty for each component in that row. Similarly, it determines the relative weight of each column from the maximum constraint value of weightx for each component in that column. In order to illustrate these effects of this, Figure 16.44 shows a rectangular arrangement of four buttons, each filling its allotted space and with equal non-zero weight attributes. In contrast, Figure 16.45 illustrates the same set of components but with those in the upper row having one half of the weighty of those in the lower row, and those in the right column having one quarter of the weightx of those in the left column. Code 16.37 shows the class used to create this effect.

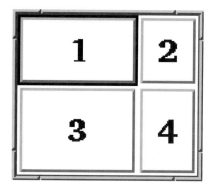

Figure 16.45 Differentially weighted components
(`GridBagWeightExample.java`)

Code 16.37 Allocating differential weights to components (`GridBagWeightFrame.java`)

```java
import java.awt.*;

    // Layout a number of buttons to illustrate the weight
    // attributes of a component's constraints.
class GridBagWeightFrame extends Frame {
    public GridBagWeightFrame(){
        final int width = 150, height = 150;
        setSize(width,height);
        // Use a slightly larger than normal font.
        setFont(new Font("SansSerif",Font.BOLD,20));

        // Create the layout manager.
        GridBagLayout layout = new GridBagLayout();
        setLayout(layout);
        setupComponents();
    }

    // Setup the required set of components in this container.
    protected void setupComponents(){
        // Create the constraints. Reuse this object with each button.
        GridBagConstraints constraints = new GridBagConstraints();

        // Create each button, set up its constraints and
        // add it to the frame. Reduce the weight attributes
        // of some of the buttons.
        final int singleCell = 1;
        final double shorter = 0.5, narrower = 0.25;

        initBasicConstraints(constraints,0,0,singleCell,singleCell);
        constraints.weighty = shorter;
        addButton("1",constraints);

        initBasicConstraints(constraints,1,0,singleCell,singleCell);
        constraints.weighty = shorter;
        constraints.weightx = narrower;
        addButton("2",constraints);

        initBasicConstraints(constraints,0,1,singleCell,singleCell);
        addButton("3",constraints);
```

Code 16.37   *(Continued)*

```
    initBasicConstraints(constraints,1,1,singleCell,singleCell);
    constraints.weightx = narrower;
    addButton("4",constraints);
    }

    // Initialize the x,y width,height values for the constraints.
    // Each component has an equal non-zero weight.
protected void initBasicConstraints(GridBagConstraints constraints,
                          int x, int y, int width, int height){
    constraints.gridx = x;
    constraints.gridy = y;
    constraints.gridwidth = width;
    constraints.gridheight = height;
    constraints.weightx = 1.0;
    constraints.weighty = 1.0;
    constraints.fill = GridBagConstraints.BOTH;
    }

    // Add a button to the Frame with the given label and constraints.
protected void addButton(String label, GridBagConstraints constraints){
    Button b = new Button(label);
    add(b,constraints);
    }
}
```

The differential space allocation is achieved by setting the `weighty` constraints attributes for buttons "1" and "2" to the value of `shorter` (one half) for the upper row and the `weightx` attributes for buttons "2" and "4" to the value of `narrower` (one quarter) for the right-hand column.

The `insets` attribute of a component's constraints is used to specify the size of a marginal area to be placed around that component. This is also known as *external padding*. A `Insets` object has attributes `top`, `left`, `bottom`, and `right` (measured in pixels) to allow irregular borders to be described. By default, the values of these are all zero. The effect of adding padding can be seen in Figure 16.46, in which a small

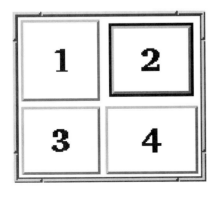

Figure 16.46 The effect of external padding around a component
(`GridBagInsetsExample.java`)

Code 16.38 Providing external padding with the `insets` constraint
(`GridBagInsetsFrame.java`)

```java
        // Layout a number of buttons to illustrate the insets
        // attributes of a component's constraints.
class GridBagInsetsFrame extends Frame {
    ...
        // Setup the required set of components in this container.
    protected void setupComponents(){
        // Create the constraints. Reuse this object with each button.
        GridBagConstraints constraints = new GridBagConstraints();

        // Create each button, set up its constraints and
        // add it to the frame.
        final int singleCell = 1;
        // Keep track of the default insets constraint.
        Insets defaultInsets = constraints.insets;

        initBasicConstraints(constraints,0,0,singleCell,singleCell);
        addButton("1",constraints);

        initBasicConstraints(constraints,1,0,singleCell,singleCell);
        // Define a small marginal inset for this button.
        final int margin = 5;
        Insets border = new Insets(margin,margin,margin,margin);
        constraints.insets = border;
        addButton("2",constraints);
        // Restore the default insets.
        constraints.insets = defaultInsets;

        initBasicConstraints(constraints,0,1,singleCell,singleCell);
        addButton("3",constraints);

        initBasicConstraints(constraints,1,1,singleCell,singleCell);
        addButton("4",constraints);
    }
}
```

border has been added around button "2" in an otherwise regular arrangement of four buttons. Code 16.38 contains a version of the `setupComponents` method, previously seen in Code 16.37, in order to achieve this.

Notice that the default `insets` attribute has been restored after adding the second button in order to give the remaining buttons the same margin.

The `ipadx` and `ipady` constraints attributes specify an amount of *internal padding* to be added to the minimum size of a component. This will only be noticeable if a component is not already filling space in addition to its minimum requirement, made available from spare space in the container. Figure 16.47 shows a frame in which the `fill` constraint of each button is set to NONE but button "2" has `ipadx` and `ipady` constraints set to a value of 20. As a result, it appears significantly larger than the other three buttons.

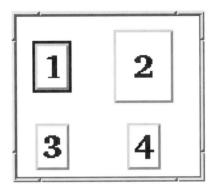

Figure 16.47   Internal padding added to a component (`GridBagIpadExample.java`)

We have now given examples of the use of all of the attributes defined in the GridBagConstraints class. For many applications, simply being able to place components so that they span multiple rows and columns will be a sufficient advance over the more basic GridLayout layout manager. Where more control is required, however, the GridBagLayout and GridBagConstraints classes give considerable flexibility over the organization, placement, and the allocation of space to components within a container. However, it is important to remember that constraints will often interact in unexpected ways and it can take a lot of effort to produce the desired effect. It is particularly important to be sure that you understand:

- The difference between external padding (`insets`) and internal padding (`ipadx`, `ipady`).
- The weight values for a component must be seen in the context of the weight values of all other components in the same row or column.

16.15   The CardLayout Class

The `CardLayout` class provides yet another layout manager for containers. It is so named because it displays the components in a container as if they were stored in a deck of cards: only the topmost is visible at any one time. Components in the deck are usually cycled through by moving the topmost to the bottom of the deck, revealing the one below it.

We can illustrate how a CardLayout layout manager is used with the example application whose main Frame sub class is shown in Code 16.39.

The CityFrame class has the central area of its frame occupied by a `CityDeck` panel, which will contain a number of city names to be displayed one at a time. At the South of the frame is a control panel that contains buttons which are used to select the city to be displayed: `First`, `Next`, `Last`, and `Random`. Figures 16.48 and 16.49 illustrate the initial appearance of the application and its appearance immediately after the Next button has been pressed.

The central area of the frame is implemented by the CityDeck class, which extends the Panel class and uses a CardLayout layout manager to manipulate the multiple label items it contains. Code 16.40 illustrates this class.

Code 16.39 Controlling frame containing a panel using a CardLayout (`CityFrame.java`)

```java
import java.awt.*;
import java.awt.event.*;

    // Place a panel with several labels in the center of the
    // frame, and a control panel in the South.
    // Use the control panel to cycle through the cities.
class CityFrame extends Frame {
    public CityFrame(){
        final int width = 250, height = 150;
        setSize(width,height);

        // The panel where the city names are to be shown.
        CityDeck deck = new CityDeck();
        add(deck,"Center");
        // Create the control panel. The deck will respond to
        // button presses.
        createControls(deck);
    }

        // Create a set of buttons in a panel.
    protected void createControls(ActionListener deck){
        Panel controlPanel = new Panel();
        // Strings associated with the control buttons.
        String controlStrings[] = {
            "First", "Next", "Last", "Random", "Quit",
        };
        for(int b = 0; b < controlStrings.length; b++){
            Button control = new Button(controlStrings[b]);
            control.setActionCommand(controlStrings[b]);
            control.addActionListener(deck);
            controlPanel.add(control);
        }
        add(controlPanel,"South");
    }
}
```

Berlin

First Next Last Random Quit

Figure 16.48 The initial view of the CityDeck (`AWTCities.java`)

Brussels

First Next Last Random Quit

Figure 16.49 The CityDeck after pressing the Next button

Code 16.40   Inserting items into the deck

```java
import java.awt.*;
import java.awt.event.*;

public class CityDeck extends Panel implements ActionListener {
    public CityDeck(){
        // Set the layout manager.
        setLayout(new CardLayout());

        // Give the labels an appropriately sized font.
        final int fontSize = 20;
        setFont(new Font("SansSerif",Font.BOLD,fontSize));

        // Add the city names to the deck.
        for(int city = 0; city < cityNames.length; city++){
            // Center the label's text.
            Label label = new Label(cityNames[city],Label.CENTER);
            // Use the label's text as a constraint, which is
            // needed by the layout manager.
            add(label,label.getText());
        }
    }

    public void actionPerformed(ActionEvent e){
        String command = e.getActionCommand();
        CardLayout layout = (CardLayout) getLayout();

        if(command.equals("First")){
            layout.first(this);
        }
        else if(command.equals("Next")){
            layout.next(this);
        }
        else if(command.equals("Last")){
            layout.last(this);
        }
        else if(command.equals("Random")){
            int randomIndex =
                    (int) (Math.random() * cityNames.length);
            String constraint = cityNames[randomIndex];
            layout.show(this,constraint);
        }
        else if(command.equals("Quit")){
            System.exit(0);
        }
        else{
            // Catch the error if extra buttons have been added.
            System.err.println("Unknown command "+command);
        }
        repaint();
    }

    // The names of the cities.
    private static final String cityNames[] = {
        "Berlin", "Brussels", "London", "Paris", "Rome", "Vienna",
    };
}
```

Each component that is added to the panel being managed by a CardLayout layout manager must be accompanied by a *constraint*. This is simply an arbitrary string that is uniquely associated with that component and can be used to randomly look it up with the manager's show method. For this purpose, we have used the text stored in the label, as it is different for each item to be displayed, and so serves to identify the label uniquely. The CityFrame class registers the CityDeck panel as the object listening to the button presses. The actionPerformed method identifies which of the buttons has been pressed and sends the layout manager the appropriate first, last, or next message to select an item to be displayed at the top of the deck. Repeatedly selecting the Next button eventually causes the deck to cycle and display the first city name. If the Random button is selected, then the layout manager is sent a show message with a random constraint value selected from the array of city names.

16.16   Adding and Removing Components

Sometimes it is necessary to vary the components on display in a user interface. With a frame containing buttons controlling an object within a program, we can vary the buttons displayed according to the current state of the object being controlled. Consider an implementation of the StopWatch interface, discussed in Section 13.12.1. When the implementation has not yet been started, there is no point providing a button to suspend it—that only needs adding once the timer is running. Similarly, when running, the start button may be removed, and only restored once the timer has been reset. Figures 16.50 and 16.51 illustrate these variations in displayed buttons.

An object may be removed from a Container object in several different ways (Code 16.41).

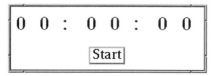

Figure 16.50   Only the Start button is available initially (AWTWatch.java)

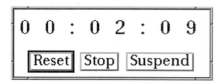

Figure 16.51   Available buttons once the timer is running.

Code 16.41   Remove methods of Container

```
public abstract class Container extends Component {
    public void remove(int indexOfComponent);
    public void remove(Component component);
    public void removeAll();
    ...
}
```

When a component is added to a container, it is allocated to the next available index (as with objects added to an `ArrayList` or `LinkedList`) so it can be removed by quoting its index. However, as an earlier component is removed, the indices of the components that follow it are reduced to avoid leaving a gap, so care must be taken with assuming that a component retains the index it had when first added to a container. More reliable is to pass to the `remove` method a specific reference to the object to be removed. The third method, `removeAll`, causes all components to be removed in one go.

Think through the following exercise before reading any further in this section.

Exercise 16.18   Suppose that three buttons—Reset, `Suspend`, and `Stop`—were added to an empty Panel. If pressing the `Suspend` button causes it to be removed and a `Resume` button added (in that order), what would be the order of the buttons in the control panel?

Suppose that the the `Resume` button is now pressed, causing it to be removed and the `Suspend` button restored. Would the Reset, `Suspend`, and `Stop` buttons be in the same order as they were before? If not, why?

Exercise 16.18 illustrates that the order of the buttons appearing in the interface could vary from time to time if care is not taken with a sequence of `add` and `remove` messages. Such variation is confusing to users and should be avoided wherever possible. One way to prevent it is to `add` a component to a container at a specific index position using the following method of the Container class:

```
add(Component component,Object constraints,int index);
```

The `constraints` argument may be `null`, but the `index` must not be larger than the number of components currently in the container. This method, and the `remove` methods we have discussed, are illustrated in Code 16.42. This example shows how the displayed buttons on the user interface of a timer controller might be added and removed when the timer's state is altered by one of the buttons being pressed.

Code 16.42   Modifying the buttons on a stopwatch controller (`Watch.java`)

```
        // Digital display of a Timer running object.
        // A control panel at the bottom of the frame
        // allows the timer functions to be operated.
import java.awt.*;
import java.awt.event.*;

class Watch extends Frame implements ActionListener {
    ...

    public void actionPerformed(ActionEvent e) throws RuntimeException {
        String command = e.getActionCommand();
        // Make sure that suspend and resume always appear in the
        // same position.
```

(Continued)

Code 16.42 *(Continued)*

```
        final int suspendResumeIndex = 2;
        // Obtain the panel containing the buttons.
        Panel controlPanel = getControlPanel();

        if(command.equals(controlStrings[Reset])){
            // We could have come from any state, so remove everything.
            controlPanel.removeAll();
            controlPanel.add(controlButtons[Start]);
            timer.reset();
        }
        else if(command.equals(controlStrings[Start])){
            controlPanel.remove(controlButtons[Start]);
            controlPanel.add(controlButtons[Reset]);
            controlPanel.add(controlButtons[Stop]);
            controlPanel.add(controlButtons[Suspend],
                                        null,suspendResumeIndex);
            timer.start();
        }
        else if(command.equals(controlStrings[Suspend])){
            controlPanel.remove(controlButtons[Suspend]);
            controlPanel.add(controlButtons[Resume],
                                        null,suspendResumeIndex);
            timer.suspend();
        }
        else if(command.equals(controlStrings[Resume])){
            controlPanel.remove(controlButtons[Resume]);
            controlPanel.add(controlButtons[Suspend],
                                        null,suspendResumeIndex);
            timer.resume();
        }
        else if(command.equals(controlStrings[Stop])){
            controlPanel.removeAll();
            controlPanel.add(controlButtons[Reset]);
            timer.stop();
        }
        else{
            throw new RuntimeException("Unknown command "+command);
        }
        // Make everything fit in the new arrangement.
        pack();
        repaint();
    }
    ...
}
```

When the size and number of the components within a container are varying dynamically, it is not sufficient simply to `repaint` the container's contents after making the changes. The reason for this is that the space originally allocated to a component or group of components may be inadequate to display the new set. This is the case when we remove the single `Start` button from the timer and replace it with three others. In such cases, it is necessary to invoke the `pack` method within the Frame (inherited from the Window class) so that the relative proportions of the various areas within the frame may be adjusted to cater for the needs of the current arrangement of components. This is best done at the end of the method where the changes have been made (in our example, in `actionPerformed`), just before `repaint` is called. The file, `Watch.java`, implements a full user interface for the stopwatch timer along these lines. Compile the file `AWTWatch.java` in order to run it.

16.17   Listening for MouseEvents

When a mouse is clicked over a Button, the button responds to the mouse event directly without the application needing to become involved. The button is able to distinguish between a valid press, in which a press-release pair happens entirely within the area of the button, from an invalid one, in which either the press or the release event occurs outside the button. In the former case, it informs any listeners of an action event and in the latter case it informs no one of what has occurred. We see similar mouse monitoring in the TextField and TextArea classes, for instance. This encapsulation of behavior within components considerably simplifies the design of applications that use them. Nevertheless, there are some applications that do require us to detect and respond to mouse events directly. For such applications, there are two interfaces related to mouse events: `MouseListener` and `MouseMotion-Listener`, shown in Code 16.43. Any object that needs to respond to mouse events will need to implement one or both of these interfaces.

When a mouse event occurs within a component, an object of class `MouseEvent` is sent to any objects that have registered themselves as a listener of the appropriate type. A mouse event object contains methods to reveal the integer x and y positions within the component at which the event occurred (`getX`, `getY`) or an object of the `Point` class with the same information (`getPoint`), as well as the type of event that occurred: `MOUSE_CLICKED`, `MOUSE_DRAGGED`, `MOUSE_ENTERED`, `MOUSE_EXITED`, `MOUSE_MOVED`, `MOUSE_PRESSED`, or `MOUSE_RELEASED`.

The simplest way to illustrate how these work, in practice, is to develop an application to use them.

Code 16.43   The MouseListener and MouseMotionListener interfaces

```
public interface MouseListener extends EventListener {
    public void mouseClicked(MouseEvent e);
    public void mouseEntered(MouseEvent e);
    public void mouseExited(MouseEvent e);
    public void mousePressed(MouseEvent e);
    public void mouseReleased(MouseEvent e);
}

public interface MouseMotionListener extends EventListener {
    public void mouseDragged(MouseEvent e);
    public void mouseMoved(MouseEvent e);
}
```

Design a class, `DrawingCanvas` (as a sub class of Canvas) that will allow the mouse to be used for free-hand drawing on its surface. Drawing of a free-hand line takes place when a button is pressed and the mouse is dragged with the button held down. As soon as the button is released drawing stops. Single mouse clicks will draw dots on the canvas.

We shall assume that drawing on the canvas is not meant to be continuous; that is, drawing will be initiated when a mouse button is pressed and terminated when it is released. This means that the application will be in one of two possible states: *drawing* or *not drawing*. This allows us to make a distinction between the interfaces shown in Code 16.43. The MouseMotionListener interface is only relevant when the application is in the drawing state, and mouse movements can be ignored otherwise. Initially, the application should listen for the mouse events notified to a MouseListener. Only when a MOUSE_PRESSED event is received does it need to behave as a MouseMotionListener. Similarly, when a MOUSE_RELEASED event is received, it can cease to be a registered MouseMotionListener. Code 16.44 shows a class that illustrates these principles. The full program may be found in the file `AWTMouseDrawing1.java`.

Code 16.44   Using MouseEvents to draw on a Canvas

```java
import java.awt.*;
import java.awt.event.*;

        // Allows free-hand drawing with the mouse.
public class DrawingCanvas extends Canvas
              implements MouseListener, MouseMotionListener {
    public DrawingCanvas(){
        addMouseListener(this);
    }

    public void clear(){
        Graphics g = getGraphics();
        update(g);
    }

    // The MouseListener methods.
    public void mousePressed(MouseEvent e){
        // Pick up the point and remember it.
        setLastPoint(e.getPoint());
        setDrawing(true);
    }

    public void mouseReleased(MouseEvent e){
        if(getDrawing()){
            drawToPoint(e.getPoint());
            setDrawing(false);
        }
    }

    public void mouseClicked(MouseEvent e){
        // Draw a dot.
        Graphics g = getGraphics();
```

Code 16.44   (*Continued*)

```
        int x = e.getX();
        int y = e.getY();
        g.drawLine(x,y,x,y);
    }

    public void mouseEntered(MouseEvent e){
        // Not interested in this event.
    }

    public void mouseExited(MouseEvent e){
        // Cancel any drawing.
        setDrawing(false);
    }

    // The MouseMotionListener methods
    public void mouseDragged(MouseEvent e){
        drawToPoint(e.getPoint());
    }

    public void mouseMoved(MouseEvent e){
        drawToPoint(e.getPoint());
    }

        // Draw from lastPoint to p2 and make p2 the new lastPoint.
    protected void drawToPoint(Point p2){
        Graphics g = getGraphics();
        Point p1 = getLastPoint();
        g.drawLine(p1.x,p1.y,p2.x,p2.y);
        setLastPoint(p2);
    }

    protected boolean getDrawing(){
        return drawing;
    }

    protected void setDrawing(boolean d){
        // Make sure this represents a change of state.
        if(d != drawing){
            if(d){
                addMouseMotionListener(this);
            }
            else{
                removeMouseMotionListener(this);
            }
            drawing = d;
        }
    }

    protected Point getLastPoint(){
        return lastPoint;
    }
```

(*Continued*)

Code 16.44   (*Continued*)

```
protected void setLastPoint(Point p){
    lastPoint = p;
}

// Are we drawing at the moment?
private boolean drawing = false;
// Where we last drew to.
Point lastPoint;
}
```

On construction, the canvas registers itself as a listener to the basic set of discrete mouse events. The two major methods of importance are `mousePressed` and `mouseReleased`. When the mouse is pressed, the application must move from the non-drawing state to the drawing state. It does this in `setDrawing`, but first it remembers the point at which the mouse was pressed with `setLastPoint`. It will use this point to join up to as soon as the next mouse event is received. The `setDrawing` method determines whether the application is moving into the drawing state, in which case it must listen for mouse motion events, or into the non-drawing state, in which case it is no longer interested in these. When the mouse is released, the point of release is joined up to the previous point, with `drawToPoint`, and the drawing state changed. If the mouse moves out of the application area while in the drawing state, then this is taken to indicate cancellation of the drawing. If the mouse is clicked at any time, then this does not affect the current state but results in a single point being plotted. For the mouse motion events, it is simply necessary to obtain the current mouse position and join up to the previous position. The current position is remembered for the next time. A simple example of a drawing produced with this program can be seen in Figure 16.52.

Exercise 16.19   Experiment with the program that is held in the file `AWTMouse-Drawing1.java` to satisfy yourself that it works as described.

Exercise 16.20   How might the program behave differently if drawing is not cancelled when the mouse exits the application area? Modify the program to test your ideas.

Exercise 16.21   What happens to the drawing if the application window is resized? Why is this? How could the DrawingCanvas class be modified to prevent this happening?

The class illustrated in Code 16.44 implements the MouseListener and MouseMotionListener interfaces in the class where the drawing appears—a sub class of Canvas. There is, however, an alternative. We could implement these methods in a

Figure 16.52   A free-hand drawing using Mouse Listeners

completely separate specialist class. This class would need access to a graphics context on which it would draw, but this approach has the advantage that the drawing
would not need to be specifically tied to drawing on a Canvas; it could draw on
any appropriate sub class of Component which has a suitable graphics context and
will allow it to listen to mouse events. This approach is possible because it is the
Component class which defines the `addMouseListener` and `addMouseMotion-
Listener` methods inherited by Canvas. Just as we saw with the Button class, above,
this means that we can keep the specialist event-handling functionality in a separate
class. Code 16.45 illustrates such a specialist class, `MouseResponder`. Most of its
listener methods are identical to those we have seen in Code 16.44, so we have only
included `mousePressed` and `mouseReleased` as samples.

   The role of a MouseResponder is purely to act as a listener to mouse events and
implement their actions on the graphics context of an associated component. For this
to be possible, it is necessary to give the MouseResponder a reference to the component on which the drawing is to be done—this is done by passing it to its constructor. This enables it to register as a listener, and to obtain the component's graphics

Code 16.45 A specialist drawing class for Mouse Events (`MouseResponder.java`)

```java
import java.awt.*;
import java.awt.event.*;

        // Implement free-hand drawing on the component passed
        // on construction.
class MouseResponder implements MouseListener, MouseMotionListener {
    public MouseResponder(Component component){
        setDrawingComponent(component);
        // Listen for mouse events on the component.
        component.addMouseListener(this);
    }

    // The MouseListener methods.
    public void mousePressed(MouseEvent e){
        // Pick up the point and remember it.
        setLastPoint(e.getPoint());
        setDrawing(true);
    }

    public void mouseReleased(MouseEvent e){
        if(getDrawing()){
            drawToPoint(e.getPoint());
            setDrawing(false);
        }
    }

    ...

    // Return the Graphics object belonging to the component.
    private Graphics getGraphics(){
        return getDrawingComponent().getGraphics();
    }

    private Component getDrawingComponent(){
        return drawingComponent;
    }

    private void setDrawingComponent(Component component){
        drawingComponent = component;
    }

    ...

    // The component to be drawn on.
    private Component drawingComponent;
}
```

context, in `getGraphics`. The full version of this example may be found in the file `AWTMouseDrawing2.java`. From the user's point of view, there is no difference between this and the equivalent program in the file `AWTMouseDrawing1.java`.

In Section 16.18, we shall see a further example of this form of separation of responsibility when we consider the AWT's Adapter classes, which simplify

```
public abstract class MouseAdapter implements MouseListener {
    public void mouseClicked(MouseEvent e){}
    public void mouseEntered(MouseEvent e){}
    public void mouseExited(MouseEvent e){}
    public void mousePressed(MouseEvent e){}
    public void mouseReleased(MouseEvent e){}
}

public abstract class MouseMotionAdapter implements MouseMotionListener {
    public void mouseDragged(MouseEvent e){}
    public void mouseMoved(MouseEvent e){}
}
```

implementation of interfaces such as MouseListener and MouseMotionListener. Use of adapters makes such separation even more compelling in the absence of multiple inheritance in Java.

16.18   MouseAdapter and MouseMotionAdapter

The `java.awt.event` package defines additional classes, `MouseAdapter` and `MouseMotionAdapter`, that are closely related to the mouse listener interface we discussed in Section 16.17. These provide trivial implementations of the MouseListener and MouseMotionListener interfaces, respectively, in which each method body is empty (Code 16.46).

The situation quite often arises where a class is only interested in one or two of the events handled by a listener interface. In such situations, it can be a nuisance to have to implement all of the methods. The Adapter classes offer the alternative of creating a sub class of the Adapter class and overriding only the methods of interest. Clearly, this approach will only work if the class that would have implemented the interface is not already extending another class, since Java forbids multiple inheritance. This will be the case if you are defining specialist listener classes for events, rather than adding the functionality to a Component sub class, as we illustrated with the MouseResponder class in Section 16.17. Code 16.47 illustrates this principle with a class that responds to double-clicks on the mouse by plotting a point on the graphics context of an associated component.

Since double-clicks are of interest, the `ClickPlotter` class overrides the `mouseClicked` method of MouseAdapter. It uses the `getClickCount` method of the MouseEvent to check whether it represents a double-click or not.

16.19   KeyListener and KeyAdapter

In Section 16.17, we saw that specialist components, such as Buttons, often handle raw mouse events and make them available in some other form to an application. Similarly, keystrokes are often handled by specialist components in a graphical user interface, such as TextFields and TextAreas. However, just as sometimes parts of

Code 16.47   Creating a sub class of MouseAdapter (`ClickPlotter.java`)

```
    // Illustrate the use of MouseAdapter to select a particular event
    // without having to implement the whole MouseListener interface.

import java.awt.*;
import java.awt.event.*;

        // Plot a point where the mouse is double-clicked.
class ClickPlotter extends MouseAdapter {
    public ClickPlotter(Component comp){
        setComponent(comp);
    }

        // Plot double-click points.
    public void mouseClicked(MouseEvent e){
        if(e.getClickCount() == 2){
            final int x = e.getX(), y = e.getY();
            getGraphics().drawLine(x,y,x,y);
        }
    }

    protected Graphics getGraphics(){
        return getComponent().getGraphics();
    }

    protected Component getComponent(){
        return component;
    }

    protected void setComponent(Component c){
        component = c;
    }

    private Component component;
}
```

an application need to handle mouse events for themselves, the same is sometimes true of keyboard events. When this is the case, the `KeyListener` interface may be implemented (Code 16.48) and the Component class defines an `addKeyListener` method to enable an implementing class to register for KeyEvents.

As can be seen, KeyEvents are sent to registered listeners on `KEY_PRESSED`, `KEY_RELEASED`, and `KEY_TYPED` events. In general, it is usually `KEY_TYPED` events that are of most interest. An alternative to implementing the KeyListener interface is to extend the `KeyAdapter` class and override its `keyTyped` method, just as we saw with the MouseAdapter class in Section 16.18.

An illustration of when it is necessary to listen for key events is provided by the fact that many user interfaces allow the same operation to be performed by either pressing a button or typing a particular key. The reason for this is that it can help to reduce the amount of device-switching that a user is forced to do. They are provided

Code 16.48   The KeyListener interface

```
public interface KeyListener {
    public void keyPressed(KeyEvent e);
    public void keyReleased(KeyEvent e);
    public void keyTyped(KeyEvent e);
}
```

Code 16.49   A class responding to keystrokes (`KeyResponder.java`)

```
import java.awt.*;
import java.awt.event.*;

    // Respond to clear and quit commands from the keyboard.
    // This is used by the DrawingCanvas class in AWTMouseDrawing3.java
class KeyResponder extends KeyAdapter {
    public KeyResponder(ClearableCanvas canvas){
        drawingCanvas = canvas;
    }

    // Override KeyAdapter's implementation of keyTyped.
    public void keyTyped(KeyEvent e){
        char charTyped = e.getKeyChar();

        if((charTyped == 'c') || (charTyped == 'C')){
            ClearableCanvas canvas = getDrawingCanvas();
            canvas.clear();
        }
        else if((charTyped == 'q') || (charTyped == 'Q')){
            System.exit(0);
        }
    }

    protected ClearableCanvas getDrawingCanvas(){
        return drawingCanvas;
    }

    // The application.
    private ClearableCanvas drawingCanvas;
}
```

with the choice of using either the mouse or the keyboard, according to what is most convenient for the current position of their hands. The free-hand drawing program, described in Section 16.17, provides buttons to allow the user to clear the drawing area and quit the application. The program in the file AWTMouseDrawing3.java is a modification to that example that allows these same operations to be performed through the keyboard, by pressing the 'C' and 'Q' keys as an alternative to using the Clear and Quit buttons. This is implemented by registering a KeyResponder object, illustrated in Code 16.49, as a key listener on the canvas.

When a key is typed over the canvas's area, the KeyResponder's `keyTyped` method receives a KeyEvent. This method examines which key has been pressed via the event's `getKeyChar` method. If it is an upper or lowercase `'C'` or `'Q'`, then it sends the appropriate `clear` or `quit` message to the drawing canvas object that was passed to its constructor. KeyEvents are described further when discussing menu shortcuts in Section 16.25.1.

16.20   WindowListener and WindowAdapter

Classes implementing the `WindowListener` interface (Code 16.50) are able to handle `WindowEvent` objects which are sent to sub classes of the `Window` class. An `addWindowListener` method is defined in Window, therefore, rather than Component.

The `WindowAdapter` class offers a trivial implementation of each of the WindowListener methods. Of interest to the Frame sub class of most applications is the `windowClosing` method which usually signifies that the application should terminate. An application responding to this event is able to free any resources it might be using, such as open files, and save any data before causing the application to exit. Code 16.51 illustrates the class that we introduced in Section 16.3 and have been using to listen for window closing events on frames. It frees the resources of the window with which it is associated and then hides the window. Whether the program is exited at the same time is determined by its `exitOnClose` attribute, which is `true` by default.

Code 16.50   The WindowListener interface

```
public interface WindowListener {
    public void windowActivated(WindowEvent e);
    public void windowClosed(WindowEvent e);
    public void windowClosing(WindowEvent e);
    public void windowDeactivated(WindowEvent e);
    public void windowDeiconified(WindowEvent e);
    public void windowIconified(WindowEvent e);
    public void windowOpened(WindowEvent e);
}
```

Code 16.51   A class responding to window closing events (`WindowCloser.java`)

```
import java.awt.*;
import java.awt.event.*;

        // Just handle WINDOW_CLOSING events.
        // The constructor's argument determines whether to exit
        // the program when the window is closed.
```

Code 16.51   (*Continued*)

```
public class WindowCloser extends WindowAdapter {
    public WindowCloser(){
        // Exit by default.
        this(true);
    }

    public WindowCloser(boolean exitOnClose){
        setExitOnClose(exitOnClose);
    }

    public void windowClosing(WindowEvent e){
        // Find out which window has been closed.
        Window w = e.getWindow();
        // Hide it.
        w.setVisible(false);
        // Free its resources.
        w.dispose();
        if(exitOnClose()){
            System.exit(0);
        }
    }

    protected boolean exitOnClose(){
        return this.exitOnClose;
    }

    protected void setExitOnClose(boolean b){
        exitOnClose = b;
    }

    private boolean exitOnClose = false;
}
```

Section 16.3 shows how the WindowCloser object is used and attached to a Frame.

16.21   The Image Class

A common requirement in GUIs is to display graphical images loaded from local files. The Image class is an abstract class that makes it possible to display images in different formats, such as GIF and JPEG. Images are loaded into an application (but not displayed) by sending a getImage message to a Toolkit object. Code 16.52 shows a main method to load local images in this way.

This example uses the ImageViewer class shown in Code 16.53. ImageViewer extends the Frame class and its sole responsibility is to display the image in its paint method via the drawImage method of the Graphics argument. Its appearance is illustrated in Figure 16.53.

Code 16.52   Obtaining images with the `getImage` method of Toolkit (`ImageExample.java`)

```java
import java.awt.*;
import java.io.File;

        // Load and display the image files passed as command-line
        // arguments.
class ImageExample {
    public static void main(String[] args){
        // Get the default toolkit for this environment.
        Toolkit tk = Toolkit.getDefaultToolkit();

        for(int i = 0; i < args.length; i++){
            File f = new File(args[i]);
            if(f.exists() && f.isFile() && f.canRead()){
                System.out.println("Loading: "+args[i]);
                Image graphic = tk.getImage(args[i]);
                // Display it.
                new ImageViewer(graphic);
            }
            else{
                System.err.println("Unable to load: "+args[i]);
            }
        }
    }
}
```

Figure 16.53   An image displayed with the ImageViewer

Code 16.53   A class to display an Image within a frame of matching size (`ImageViewer.java`)

```java
        // View an image in a frame that exactly surrounds it.
import java.awt.*;
import java.awt.event.*;
import java.awt.image.*;

class ImageViewer extends Frame {
    public ImageViewer(Image image){
        setImage(image);
        setup();
    }

        // Obtain the image from the producer.
    public ImageViewer(ImageProducer producer){
        setImage(createImage(producer));
        setup();
    }

        // Perform common frame setup for the two constructors.
    protected void setup(){
        // Dimensions are adjusted once the dimensions of
        // the image are known.
        final int initialWidth = 200, initialHeight = 200;
        setSize(initialWidth,initialHeight);
    }

    public void paint(Graphics g){
        // Make sure it appears just within the frame's insets.
        Insets insets = getInsets();
        g.drawImage(getImage(),insets.left,insets.top,this);
    }

    // Override Frame.imageUpdate - the implementation of ImageObserver.
    public boolean imageUpdate(Image img,int infoflags,int x, int y,
                               int width, int height){
        // Find out what has changed.
        boolean result = super.imageUpdate(img,infoflags,x,y,width,height);
        // See if the image is complete.
        if((infoflags & ImageObserver.ALLBITS) != 0){
            // Set the frame's size according to the image size.
            Insets insets = getInsets();
            // Include in the width and height the insets space required
            // for the frame's decoration.
            int newWidth = insets.left+width+insets.right;
            int newHeight = insets.top+height+insets.bottom;
            setSize(newWidth,newHeight);
        }
        else if((infoflags &
                  (ImageObserver.ABORT | ImageObserver.ERROR)) != 0){
            System.err.println("Image error.");
        }
        else{
```

(Continued)

Code 16.53   *(Continued)*

```
            // Ignore.
        }
        return result;
    }

    protected Image getImage(){
        return image;
    }

    protected void setImage(Image i){
        image = i;
    }

    private Image image;
}
```

An important point to bear in mind when trying to understand ImageViewer is that the call to the Toolkit's `getImage` method returns before the image has been fully loaded from its file. You are probably familiar with the concept of images appearing in pieces from the way that many Web browsers behave. In effect, the retrieval of the image is taking place as a separate *thread* to the one in which the ImageViewer object is running. The ImageViewer's Frame super class is kept informed of the progress of the image's arrival via its implementation of the `ImageObserver` interface, which is defined in the `java.awt.image` package. We have chosen to override this method so that we can detect when the image has been completely loaded—as indicated by the `ALLBITS` flag being set in its `infoflags` argument—or when there is an error in image retrieval, perhaps because the resource is of an unknown image type. Once the image is complete, its width and height are used to resize the Frame so that the frame fits exactly around the image. The `paint` method of ImageViewer uses the `drawImage` method of its Graphics argument. Its second and third argument specify an `(x,y)` offset for the image. The fourth argument must be an ImageObserver implementation. Component is such an implementation and, hence, so is the Frame.

Exercise 16.22   Using the following `drawImage` method of Graphics

```
    public void drawImage(Image i,int x, int y, int width, int height,
                          ImageObserver observer);
```

modify the ImageViewer class shown in Code 16.53 so that the original image is scaled to twice its original width and height (the scaling is performed in `drawImage` by specifying the increased `width` and `height` arguments). Make sure that the frame still exactly fits around the scaled image.

Exercise 16.23   Modify the ImageViewer class shown in Code 16.53 so that it extends Canvas rather than Frame. Write a new class that extends Frame and takes an Image argument to its constructor. Add an instance of your new ImageViewer class to the frame in order to display the image. Modify the ImageExample class shown in Code 16.52 to pass each image to a new instance of your new Frame class.

Exercise 16.24   Further modify the ImageExample class so that all the image file-names passed to the program from the command line are displayed in a single Frame containing multiple instances of your Canvas classes. You might like to do this by passing an array of Images to the constructor of the Frame sub class that you defined in your answer to Exercise 16.23 or by adding a `showImage` method in the sub class of Frame.

In addition to loading Image data from local files, the `getImage` method of the Toolkit class will load image files from remote locations. Given a *Uniform Resource Locator (URL)*, in the form of a URL object, this method will retrieve the designated image across a network. The URL class is defined in the `java.net` package. URLs are familiar to anyone who has used a Web browser. The following creates a URL object referring to a remote image file:

```
new URL("http://www.cs.ukc.ac.uk/people/staff/djb/Book/redBall.gif")
```

We discuss URL objects in more detail in Section 19.3.

16.21.1   The MediaTracker Class

If one or more images must be retrieved from a remote location across a network, this could take a considerable amount of time. This is one of the reasons that Toolkit's `getImage` returns immediately, rather than waiting until the image finishes loading. The `MediaTracker` class provides a way for an application to wait for an image to load, and to assign loading priorities to multiple images. A MediaTracker is created by passing a reference to a component (usually the object creating the tracker) to its constructor. Code 16.54 shows an example to load a set of images based on an array of file names. Passing one or more images to its `addImage` method provides a means to keep track of their loading. In addition to the image, an integer `id` is passed. This serves a dual purpose; related images may be given the same value, and the ID serves as a priority level. Lower values indicate higher priorities for retrieval. In this example, we use the ID to check that all the images have finished loading via `checkID`. Note that this does not guarantee that all the images could be found. The `isErrorAny` method returns `true` if one or more images could not be loaded. The `getErrorsAny` method returns an array of the images for which there were errors. The media tracker has four methods for waiting for the images to load, two versions of `waitForAll`, and two of `waitForID`. The pairs differ in whether they take a `long` argument indicating how long we are prepared to wait.

16.21.2   The Cursor Class

It is possible to change the cursor associated with the mouse according to an application's current state. For instance, a waiting cursor could be set to give the user feedback while waiting for images to load or a server to respond. Cursors are set on a per-component basis, and a component's current cursor may be determined via its `getCursor` method. For temporary changes of cursor, a reference to the current

Code 16.54   Monitor image loading with a MediaTracker (`ImageLoader.java`)

```java
import java.awt.*;

    // A non-visual component that uses a MediaTracker to monitor
    // image loading.
class ImageLoader extends Component {
    // Get the images.
    public Image[] retrieveImages(String[] files) {
        final int numImages = files.length;
        Image[] images = new Image[numImages];
        if(numImages > 0){
            // Use a Toolkit to load the images.
            Toolkit tk = Toolkit.getDefaultToolkit();
            // Use a MediaTracker to monitor the loading.
            MediaTracker tracker = new MediaTracker(this);
            for(int i = 0; i < numImages; i++){
                System.out.println("Loading: "+files[i]);
                images[i] = tk.getImage(files[i]);
                // Give each a separate ID for checking.
                tracker.addImage(images[i],i);
            }
            // Loading initiated, wait a limited time for them to arrive.
            try{
                final long waitingTime = 5*1000;
                tracker.waitForAll(waitingTime);
            }
            catch(InterruptedException e){
                System.out.println("Interrupted.");
            }
            System.out.println("Checking.");
            // Check each.
            for(int i = 0; i < numImages; i++){
                if(tracker.checkID(i)){
                    System.out.println("Loaded: "+files[i]);
                }
                else{
                    System.out.println("Failed to load: "+files[i]);
                    images[i] = null;
                }
            }
            if(tracker.isErrorAny()){
                System.out.println("There were errors.");
            }
        }
        return images;
    }
}
```

cursor should be obtained before setting a new one. This makes it possible to restore the previous one accurately. Code 16.55 illustrates this approach with one of the predefined cursors available in the `Cursor` class.

Code 16.55   Temporary cursor change while waiting (`CursorImageLoader.java`)

```java
import java.awt.*;

    // A visual component that uses a MediaTracker to monitor
    // image loading. Set a 'waiting' cursor while waiting for
    // the images to load.
class CursorImageLoader extends Frame {
    public CursorImageLoader(){
        final int width = 200, height = 200;
        setSize(width,height);
    }

        // Get the images.
    public Image[] retrieveImages(String[] files) {
        final int numImages = files.length;
        Image[] images = new Image[numImages];
        if(numImages > 0){
            // Replace the current cursor to indicate that a wait might be
            // required.
            final Cursor oldCursor = getCursor();
            setCursor(Cursor.getPredefinedCursor(Cursor.WAIT_CURSOR));
            ...
            // Loading initiated, wait a limited time for them to arrive.
            try{
                final long waitingTime = 5*1000;
                tracker.waitForAll(waitingTime);
            }
            catch(InterruptedException e){
                System.out.println("Interrupted.");
            }
            // Restore the previous cursor.
            setCursor(oldCursor);
            ...
        }
        return images;
    }
}
```

This example is a modified version of that shown in Code 16.54. While waiting for
the images to load, a different cursor is shown.

16.22   The Scrollbar Class

Scrollbars are commonly used to control which part of a large text area or image is
displayed within a limited field of viewport. We saw the ability to include scrollbars in
a TextArea object in Section 16.13.2, for instance, and the ScrollPane class fulfills
a similar role for images. It is also possible to create stand alone scrollbars that can be
used either to scroll custom-built viewports or, more commonly, to act as sliding scales
controllers of integer-based attributes within an application. Figure 16.54 shows the
form of a Scrollbar component. The visual representation of a Scrollbar consists

Figure 16.54   A horizontal scrollbar

Figure 16.55   Scrollbar dimensions

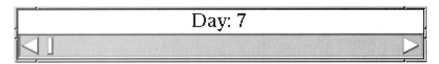

Figure 16.56   Day-monitoring scrollbar (Code 16.58)

of a rectangular bar containing a slider. At either end of the bar are triangular-shaped unit-adjustment controls. The slider moves from left to right in a horizontal slider and up and down in a vertical slider. A Scrollbar object maintains a simple integer attribute within a configurable range. The current value of the attribute is represented by the position of the left-hand edge of the slider within the area in which it moves. The attribute's value may be changed via the visual control in one of three main ways:

- Moving the slider—*tracking*.
- Clicking the mouse on either slide of the slider—*block adjustment*.
- Clicking the mouse on a unit-adjustment control—*unit adjustment*.

Each of these actions causes the attribute to take on the value corresponding to the updated position of the slider.

   When a Scrollbar is created, the five arguments to its constructor specify its orientation (`HORIZONTAL` or `VERTICAL`), the initial value of the attribute, the width of the slider (in attribute units rather than pixels), the minimum value of the attribute's range, and the maximum value of the attribute's range. In fact, the name of the final argument is misleading because it should be equal to the maximum value of the range plus the width of the slider (Figure 16.55). Code 16.56 shows how a Scrollbar might be constructed to control the page in a diary or calendar. The appearance of this example is shown in Figure 16.56.

   A scrollbar's `setBlockIncrement` and `setUnitIncrement` methods allow the size of the block and unit increments to be defined; in this case, clicking in the bar increments the day value up or down by a week, and the unit adjustments change its value by a single day. Care needs to be taken in allocating sufficient space to a scrollbar. If it must be possible to identify each value within the range, it will be

Code 16.56   Creating a Scrollbar to select a day in the year

```
        // Display a 1..daysInYear calendar with a Scrollbar slider.
class DayOfYear extends Frame implements AdjustmentListener {
    public DayOfYear(){
        final int width = 400, height = 75;
        setSize(width,height);

        // The maximum and minimum values on the scale,
        // allowing for leap years.
        final int firstDay = 1, daysInYear = 366;
        // The slider represents a week.
        final int daysInWeek = 7;
        final int sliderWidth = daysInWeek;

        Scrollbar bar = new Scrollbar(Scrollbar.HORIZONTAL,
                          firstDay,
                          sliderWidth,
                          // The range - allow for the slider's width.
                          firstDay,daysInYear+sliderWidth);

        // Set increments for clicking in the scrollbar and
        // using the end adjusters.
        bar.setBlockIncrement(daysInWeek);
        bar.setUnitIncrement(1);
        ...
    }
    ...
}
```

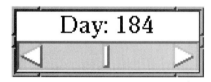

Figure 16.57   Allowing insufficient width for the size of the range

necessary to make the width (or height) of the scrollbar larger than the number of values in the range. If there is insufficient space to allocate at least one pixel per value (plus the space needed for the unit adjusters at either end) the slider might look disproportionately large, and be hard to use for fine adjustment. Figure 16.57 illustrates this problem with the DayOfYear class. Note how large the 7-day wide slider is in proportion to the year's width of the scrollbar.

When a scrollbar is adjusted, it generates an AdjustmentEvent object to any registered listeners that implement the AdjustmentListener interface (Code 16.57). The Scrollbar class is a sub class of the Adjustable class, and an AdjustmentEvent provides access to the object that generated it via its get-Adjustable method. Code 16.58 shows a program to create a scrollbar and listen for adjustments to it. The associated Adjustable is identified in the implementation of adjustmentValueChanged.

Code 16.57   The AdjustmentListener interface from `java.awt.event`

```
public interface AdjustmentListener extends EventListener {
    public void adjustmentValueChanged(AdjustmentEvent e);
}
```

Code 16.58   Listing for adjustments to a scrollbar (`DayOfYear.java`)

```
          // Illustrate the Scrollbar Component with
          // a horizontal scrollbar representing day numbers
          // values in the range 1 .. 366. A label displays
          // the current setting of the scrollbar.
import java.awt.*;
import java.awt.event.*;

          // Display a 1..daysInYear calendar with a Scrollbar slider.
class DayOfYear extends Frame implements AdjustmentListener {
    public DayOfYear(){
        final int width = 400, height = 75;
        setSize(width,height);

        // The maximum and minimum values on the scale,
        // allowing for leap years.
        final int firstDay = 1, daysInYear = 366;
        // The slider represents a week.
        final int daysInWeek = 7;
        final int sliderWidth = daysInWeek;

        Scrollbar bar =
                new Scrollbar(Scrollbar.HORIZONTAL,
                              firstDay,
                              sliderWidth,
                              // The range - allow for the slider's width.
                              firstDay,daysInYear+sliderWidth);

        // Set increments for clicking in the scrollbar and
        // using the end adjusters.
        bar.setBlockIncrement(daysInWeek);
        bar.setUnitIncrement(1);

        // Let me know when the bar is moved.
        bar.addAdjustmentListener(this);

        // Create a label for the day display.
        // Allow enough space for the maximum day.
        Label display = new Label(labelPrefix+daysInYear,Label.CENTER);
        setDayDisplay(display);

        // Display the label and scrollbar one above the other.
        Panel panel = new Panel();
```

(Continued)

Code 16.58   (*Continued*)

```
        final int rows = 2, cols = 1;
        panel.setLayout(new GridLayout(rows,cols));
        panel.add(display);
        panel.add(bar);

        add(panel);

        // Set the label to the initial value.
        display.setText(labelPrefix+bar.getValue());
    }

    // Implement AdjustmentListener
    public void adjustmentValueChanged(AdjustmentEvent e){
        // Get the bar on which the adjustment happened.
        Adjustable bar = e.getAdjustable();

        // Get the new value.
        int value = bar.getValue();

        // Change the display label.
        Label display = getDayDisplay();
        display.setText(labelPrefix+value);
    }

    protected Label getDayDisplay(){
        return dayDisplay;
    }

    protected void setDayDisplay(Label label){
        dayDisplay = label;
    }

    // Prefix for the day number display.
    private static final String labelPrefix = "Day: ";
    // A display for the current day.
    private Label dayDisplay;
}
```

The current value of the scrollbar's attribute is displayed in a Label next to it. This is kept up-to-date by retrieving the current position using the Adjustable's `getValue` method in `adjustmentValueChanged`.

16.23 The ScrollPane Class

The `ImageViewer` class described in Section 16.21 was designed to display small images in an adjustable frame exactly fitting the image's dimensions. Sometimes a graphical area to be viewed is too large to be conveniently displayed in its entirety and it is more convenient to provide a viewport into part of its area, along with horizontal and/or vertical scrollbars. This need is catered for by the `ScrollPane` class which

Figure 16.58   An image displayed within a ScrollPane

provides complementary functionality to that of the `TextArea` class with scrollable text. ScrollPane is a sub class of the `Container` class but it only manages a single component, which is typically a graphic of some sort. In the following discussion, we shall assume that it is an image. It is a sub class of Container simply in order to be able to implement a particularly restrictive layout policy. For instance, although the class has a `setLayout` method, you are not permitted to set a new layout. In addition, this method is `final` in order to prevent this restriction from being overridden in any sub classes. Figure 16.58 shows an example of an image displayed within a ScrollPane. When a ScrollPane is constructed, a scrollbar policy may be specified. This is one of the values `SCROLLBARS_AS_NEEDED`, `SCROLLBARS_ALWAYS`, or `SCROLLBARS_-NEVER`, of which the first is probably the most economical of space since it removes the horizontal and/or vertical scrollbar if the full width and/or height of the item being viewed is visible. Code 16.59 shows a simple class that adds an `ImageCanvas`[7] object to a ScrollPane contained within a Frame.

Control over the actions of the scrollbars is possible by obtaining the `Adjustable` objects responsible for horizontal and vertical scrolling. These are obtained via the `getHAdjustable` and `getVAdjustable` methods of the ScrollPane. The example in Code 16.59 sets arbitrary unit increment values as an illustration of use of these. An application can determine which part of the image is visible through the viewport via the `getScrollPosition` method, which returns a `Point` object describing the coordinates of the image displayed at the top left-hand corner of the scroll pane. The two `setScrollPosition` methods may be used to manipulate the visible portion of the image by specifying the position of the image to appear at the top left as either a Point or an `(x,y)` pair of integers. How much of the image is displayed can be determined from the `getViewportSize` method, which returns a `Dimension` object. If it is necessary for the application to be informed when the image is scrolled, it can implement the `AdjustmentListener` interface and register with the horizontal and vertical Adjustables. This technique was demonstrated in the context of the `Scrollbar` class in Section 16.22.

---

[7] `ImageCanvas` is a variation on the `ImageViewer` class (see Section 16.21) which displays an image in a Canvas whose size exactly matches that of the image.

Code 16.59   Viewing an ImageCanvas through a ScrollPane

```java
import java.awt.*;

        // Provide a Frame for a ScrollPane which contains
        // an ImageCanvas displaying Image.
public class ScrollPaneFrame extends Frame {
    ScrollPaneFrame(Image i){
        final int initialWidth = 200, initialHeight = 200;
        setSize(initialWidth,initialHeight);

        // Only include scrollbars if necessary.
        ScrollPane pane = new ScrollPane(ScrollPane.SCROLLBARS_AS_NEEDED);
        // Get the horizontal adjustment controls and set the
        // scrolling increments.
        final int hIncrement = 5, vIncrement = 2;
        Adjustable horizontal = pane.getHAdjustable(),
                   vertical = pane.getVAdjustable();
        horizontal.setUnitIncrement(hIncrement);
        vertical.setUnitIncrement(vIncrement);

        // Add the component to be scrolled to the scroll pane.
        Canvas canvas = new ImageCanvas(i);
        pane.add(canvas);
        // Add the scroll pane to the frame.
        add(pane);
    }
}
```

16.24   Animation

Graphics and animation are a popular combination, and it is relatively simple to create a basic animation framework with the classes of the AWT. The basic steps in animation involve drawing an image, updating the data on which the image is based, and then redrawing it. Typically, repetition of these steps is performed over and over again in a loop of some sort. Often the redrawing step involves erasing the previous image before drawing it in its new state. In Section 16.2.1, we discussed the relationship among the paint, update, and repaint methods of the Graphics class. These are the methods that we shall typically use to create animations when using the AWT. We noted there that the repaint method obtains a Graphics object associated with its Component object. This graphics context is then passed to update which clears it by filling it with the component's background color. The Graphics object is then passed to paint to be drawn on.

```java
public void repaint(){
    Graphics g = getGraphics();
    update(g);
    paint(g);
}
```

This existing hierarchy of methods already provides the basics of the standard erase-draw combination that is typical of animation.

Code 16.60 The main method and containing frame for a simple animation
(`AWTAnimate1.java`)

```java
import java.awt.*;

public class AWTAnimate1 {
    public static void main(String[] args){
        AnimationFrame frame = new AnimationFrame();
        frame.addWindowListener(new WindowCloser());
        frame.setVisible(true);
        // Hand over to the frame to run forever.
        frame.run();
    }
}

    // Repeatedly request a canvas to paint itself.
class AnimationFrame extends Frame {
    public AnimationFrame(){
        // Set the frame's size.
        final int width = 200, height = 200;
        setSize(width,height);

        add(getCanvas());
    }

    public void run(){
        // Animate the drawing 50 times per second.
        final int sleepTime = 1000/50;
        AnimatedArcCanvas canvas = getCanvas();
        while(true){
            try{
                Thread.sleep(sleepTime);
                // Perform the next animation step.
                canvas.step();
            }
            catch(InterruptedException e){
            }
        }
    }

    protected AnimatedArcCanvas getCanvas(){
        return animationCanvas;
    }

    private AnimatedArcCanvas animationCanvas = new AnimatedArcCanvas();
}
```

An animation usually requires a controlling object that determines the length
of the delay between the animation steps and which causes the next erase-draw pair
to take place. In Java, this can be done most conveniently using *threads*, which are
described in Chapter 18. In this chapter, we shall create a similar effect by defining
a `run` method in the parent frame that repeatedly sends `step` messages to the
animation component it contains. This `run` method is called from the application's
main method. Code 16.60 illustrates the main method and parent frame for a simple

Figure 16.59   Progressive steps in an animation

animation. The frame contains a single canvas, called `AnimatedArcCanvas`, which implements the animation. The `AWTAnimate1` class contains the usual main method, with an addition statement that sends a `run` message to the frame it has created. The constructor of `AnimationFrame` constructs an `AnimatedArcCanvas`, which is the only component it contains. The `run` method of AnimationFrame repeatedly sleeps for an appropriate length of time and then asks the AnimatedArcCanvas to draw the next step in its animation. Other than this, it does not concern itself at all with how the animation is performed.

Code 16.61 contains AnimatedArcCanvas to show how a simple animation can be achieved. This object progressively draws a filled arc through 360 degrees before starting again. A snapshot from three steps within this animation is shown in Figure 16.59.

Code 16.61   A simple animation of an arc

```
    // Illustrate a basic animation of a filled arc drawn full circle.
import java.awt.*;

    // Animate an arc through a full circle before starting again.
class AnimatedArcCanvas extends Canvas {
    public void paint(Graphics g){
        Dimension size = getSize();

        final int x = size.width/4, y = size.height/4;
        final int width = size.width/2, height = size.height/2;

        final int sweep = getAngle();
        g.fillArc(x,y,width,height,startAngle,sweep);
    }

        // Perform the next animation step.
    public void step(){
        // Update the angle.
        setAngle(getAngle()+angleIncrement);

        // Clear last step and draw the current arc
        repaint();
    }
```

(Continued)

Code 16.61   *(Continued)*

```
protected int getAngle(){
    return angle;
}

protected void setAngle(int a){
    if(Math.abs(a) <= circleDegrees){
        angle = a;
    }
    else{
        // Time to restart.
        angle = 0;
    }
}

// Always start at the 3 o'clock position.
private final int startAngle = 0;
// The number of degrees in a circle.
private final int circleDegrees = 360;
// Update the angle by a fixed amount.
private final int angleIncrement = 12;
// How many degrees of sweep for the arc.
private int angle = 0;
}
```

AnimatedArcCanvas maintains an `angle` attribute which it uses to determine how much of the arc to draw each time the `paint` method is called. Each time its `step` method is called, it updates the amount of the arc to be drawn and then uses its `repaint` method to clear the previous image and draw a new one.

Exercise 16.25   Compile and run the program in AWTAnimate1.java. What do you think of the quality of the animation; is it smooth? Does the quality vary with the size of the window? Experiment with different values of the `sleepTime` variable in the `run` method to see how this affects the visual impression.

Exercise 16.26   Modify the program in AWTAnimate1.java so that the filled arc it draws always sweeps the same small angle (2 degrees, say) but continues to move counterclockwise. This should give it the appearance of an inverted clock hand moving backwards (Figure 16.60). Remember that positive sweep values move counterclockwise and negative values move clockwise. It should only be necessary to modify the AnimatedArcCanvas class in order to achieve this. Experiment with different sleep times, as described in Exercise 16.25, and form an impression of the visual impact of the animation.

16.24.1   Avoiding Flicker in Animation

If you have run the program AWTAnimate1.java, shown in Code 16.61, you probably will have noticed that the animation is not particularly smooth, and there is often *flicker* within the image. This does not create a particularly pleasing impression. The

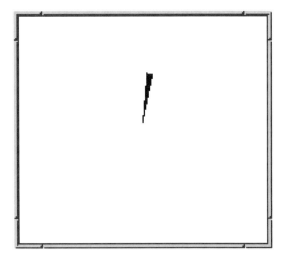

Figure 16.60   A fixed-sweep moving arc

Code 16.62   A possible default implementation of `update`

```
public void update(Graphics g){
    // Determine the size of this component.
    Dimension size = getSize();
    // Fill it with the current background color.
    g.setColor(getBackground());
    g.fillRect(0,0,size.width,size.height);
    // Set the drawing color.
    g.setColor(getForeground());
    // Do the drawing.
    paint(g);
}
```

---

main reason for this lies at the heart of the erase-draw pair and its implementation by the `repaint`, `update`, and `paint` methods. Before each new version of the arc is drawn, the complete graphics context of the canvas is cleared in the `update` method whose default definition might be as shown in Code 16.62.

It is the clearing process that is one of the causes of the image's flicker. A second cause is the time that it takes for the image to be created—i.e., the geometry of the arc to be calculated and drawn. Both of these causes can be tackled in separate ways. We shall first address ways of avoiding those elements of flicker which are due to the canvas being repeatedly cleared at each step. In fact, in this particular animation example, there is no need to clear the previous version of the arc in most cases, since the next step will simply be extending the area drawn in the previous step. It is only once the sweep completes the full 360 degrees that the old arc needs to be cleared. There are two approaches we could take, therefore:

- Override the `update` method in AnimatedArcCanvas so that it does not clear the canvas before calling `paint`.
- Avoid using `repaint` (and hence `update`) in `step` and simply call `paint` directly.

In both cases, the old version of the circle must be cleared when the angle returns to the starting angle. Code 16.63 shows an improved version of AnimatedArcCanvas that uses the second approach to limit the amount of flicker.

Code 16.63   Avoiding unnecessary clearing by avoiding `repaint`

```
        // Illustrate animation of a filled arc drawn full circle.
        // This approach tries to limit flicker by taking advantage
        // of the fact that the arc only needs to be cleared when it
        // returns to its starting position.
import java.awt.*;

    // Animate an arc through a full circle before starting again.
class AnimatedArcCanvas extends Canvas {
    public void paint(Graphics g){
        Dimension size = getSize();

        final int x = size.width/4, y = size.height/4;
        final int width = size.width/2, height = size.height/2;

        int sweep = getAngle();
        if(sweep == 0){
            // Clear the area or the arc.
            g.clearRect(x,y,width,height);
        }
        g.fillArc(x,y,width,height,startAngle,sweep);
    }

        // Perform the next animation step.
    public void step(){
        // Update the angle.
        setAngle(getAngle()+angleIncrement);

        // Draw the current arc with this component's graphics context.
        paint(getGraphics());
    }

    protected int getAngle(){
        return angle;
    }

    protected void setAngle(int a){
        if(Math.abs(a) <= circleDegrees){
            angle = a;
        }
        else{
            // Time to restart.
            angle = 0;
        }
    }

    // Always start at the 3 o'clock position.
    private final int startAngle = 0;
```

Code 16.63   (*Continued*)

```
    // The number of degrees in a circle.
    private final int circleDegrees = 360;
    // Update the angle by a fixed amount.
    private final int angleIncrement = 12;
    // How many degrees of sweep for the arc.
    private int angle = 0;
}
```

In this new version, `paint`, rather than `repaint`, is called from within `step`. The component's graphics context is obtained via its `getGraphics` method to pass as an argument to `paint`. The clearing of the canvas when the arc has completed 360 degrees is checked for and performed within `paint`. This involves a test to see whether the value of the sweep angle has returned to zero. If it has, then the rectangular area enclosing the arc is cleared. This approach significantly reduces the amount of flicker as the arc moves around. Test this for yourself by running this version of the program, which may be found in the file `AWTAnimate2.java`.

Exercise 16.27   Try the alternative approach to flicker reduction by implementing an overriding version of the `update` method for the AnimatedArcCanvas in the original version of `AWTAnimate1.java`. Remember that you will still need to arrange for the arc to be cleared once the sweep angle has returned to zero.

Exercise 16.28   The `paint` method of `AWTAnimate1.java` fills the complete arc each time it is called. Modify it so that it only fills the additional `angleIncrement` of the arc each time. Are there any circumstances in which this approach will not work?

With the example of the sweeping arc, it was possible to eliminate the flicker by taking advantage of the fact that it was not necessary to clear the previous image at each step—each step redrew an extended version of what was drawn by the previous step. Clearly, not all animations are of this nature. Exercise 16.26, for instance, required that an arc with the same small sweep be animated so that it looked like an inverted clock hand. In that case, it was necessary to erase the arc drawn in the previous step before drawing the next. Rather than clearing the whole canvas, an alternative approach is to erase the previous image by painting it again using the background color instead of the foreground color. This means that the only part of the canvas that is erased is the part that needs erasing. This approach might be important if there are other features on the canvas that should remain undisturbed. The example in Code 16.64 illustrates this approach with a clockwise sweeping arc, whose appearance was shown in Figure 16.60.

The arc's attributes are maintained by the `MovingArc` class, which takes an incremental value for the arc's angle. Its `step` method calculates the new angle for the arc at each animation step by adding this increment to its previous angle. Notice that the `paint` method of `MovingArcCanvas` simply draws the arc at its

Code 16.64   Animation of a clockwise moving small arc

```java
    // Illustrate clearing of the previous step in an animation by
    // re-painting with the background color.
import java.awt.*;

    // Continuously animate a moving arc.
class MovingArcCanvas extends Canvas {
    public void paint(Graphics g){
        Dimension size = getSize();

        final int x = size.width/4, y = size.height/4;
        final int width = size.width/2, height = size.height/2;

        MovingArc arc = getArc();
        final int startAngle = arc.getAngle();
        final int arcWidth = arc.getWidth();
        g.fillArc(x,y,width,height,startAngle,arcWidth);
    }

        // Perform the next animation step.
    public void step(){
        Graphics g = getGraphics();

        // Clear last arc.
        g.setColor(getBackground());
        paint(g);

        getArc().step();

        // Draw the current arc
        g.setColor(getForeground());
        paint(g);
    }

    protected MovingArc getArc(){
        return arc;
    }

    // Move clockwise.
    private final int increment = -1;
    private final MovingArc arc = new MovingArc(increment);
}

    // Maintain the attributes of a moving arc.
    // The increment per step (and hence its direction)
    // is set at construction.
class MovingArc {
    public MovingArc(int inc){
        increment = inc;
    }

        // Move to the next position.
    public void step(){
```

Code 16.64   (*Continued*)

```
        setAngle(getAngle()+getIncrement());
    }

    public int getWidth(){
        return arcWidth;
    }

    public int getAngle(){
        return angle;
    }

    protected void setAngle(int a){
        if(a <= fullCircle){
            angle = a;
        }
        else{
            // Time to restart.
            angle = startAngle;
        }
    }

    protected int getIncrement(){
        return increment;
    }

    private final int increment;
    // Always start at the 3 o'clock position.
    private final int startAngle = 0;
    private final int fullCircle = startAngle+360;
    private int angle = startAngle;
    private final int arcWidth = 6;
}
```

---

current angle—it is not aware of whether it is drawing or erasing the arc on any particular call. The process of erasing the previous arc and painting the new one is performed entirely in the `step` method of MovingArcCanvas. The current graphics context for the component is obtained and its drawing color set to the component's background color. The previous arc is then re-painted, causing it to be erased. Now the MovingArc object can be asked to calculate its new position, the drawing color is set to the component's foreground color and the arc painted in its new position. Note that the first time MovingArcCanvas's `step` method is called there will be no previous arc to erase, but this is of no consequence in this particular case.

Exercise 16.29   Modify the program in the file `AWTMovingArc.java` so that the MovingArcCanvas class has an array of MovingArc objects, rather than just one. Each MovingArc should be given a distinct increment argument to its constructor to create arcs that move in different directions by differing amounts—you could even have a stationary arc if the increment value is zero. You will need to modify both the

Figure 16.61 Multiple MovingArc objects

paint and step methods of MovingArcCanvas to iterate over the elements of the array. The result might look something like that shown in Figure 16.61.

16.24.2 Double-Buffering in Animation

In some of the examples in Section 16.24.1, we were not able to fully eliminate the erasing of the image at each step, and hence ended up reintroducing a degree of flicker to those animations. At the start of that section, we noted that a second contributing factor to flicker is the time it takes to calculate and draw the image. The example animations we have looked at so far have been particularly simple in this respect; the problem is more noticeable in images of greater complexity. A technique that can be used to overcome this aspect of the flicker problem is *double buffering*. The principal idea behind this technique is that the next version of the image can be drawn behind the scenes, in a separate graphics context, and then copied to the canvas's graphics context when the drawing is complete. The assumption is that it will be relatively quick to copy the contents of one graphics context to another, compared to the time it takes to compute and draw the image. The example in Code 16.65 implements this idea in a modification of the moving arc example. It uses the same MovingArc class shown in Code 16.64 to maintain details of the animated arc, so we have only shown the DoubleBufferCanvas class, which replaces the MovingArcCanvas shown there.

The DoubleBufferCanvas class makes use of the fact that an Image object has a graphics context that can be drawn on (see Section 16.21). This newly drawn image can then be transferred to the canvas's graphics context via the drawImage method of the Graphics class. The step method arranges first of all for the MovingArc object to advance itself, it then causes the new image of the arc to be drawn offscreen, in the Image's graphics context, and finally paints it onto the screen. This means that the paint method has been reduced to simply copying the offscreen image; all of the rendering of the image has already been performed by drawOffscreenImage. The first task of drawOffscreenImage is to ensure that it has a valid Image object

Code 16.65   Using double buffering to eliminate flicker (`DoubleBufferCanvas.java`)

```
    // Illustrate double buffering to eliminate flicker.
import java.awt.*;

    // Continuously animate a MovingArc.
    // Use double buffering to avoid flicker.
class DoubleBufferCanvas extends Canvas {
        // Perform the next animation step.
        // Render the image of the arc in the offscreen graphics context.
    public void step(){
        // Move the arc on.
        getArc().step();
        // Draw the current arc in the offscreen image.
        drawOffscreenImage();
        // Paint it to the onscreen one.
        paint(getGraphics());
    }

    public void paint(Graphics g){
        // Copy the offscreen image to this component's context.
        g.drawImage(getImage(),0,0,this);
    }

        // Draw the arc in its current position in the offscreen image.
    protected void drawOffscreenImage(){
        Dimension size = getSize();
        // Make sure we have a suitable offscreen image.
        Image offscreenImage = getImage();
        if((offscreenImage == null) ||
                (offscreenImage.getWidth(this) != size.width) ||
                (offscreenImage.getHeight(this) != size.height)){
            // Create a new one.
            offscreenImage = createImage(size.width,size.height);
            setImage(offscreenImage);
        }

        // Perform the drawing.
        final int x = size.width/4, y = size.height/4;
        final int width = size.width/2, height = size.height/2;
        MovingArc arc = getArc();
        final int startAngle = arc.getAngle();
        final int arcWidth = arc.getWidth();

        // Obtain the offscreen graphics context.
        Graphics g = getImage().getGraphics();

        // Clear the previous image.
        g.clearRect(0,0,size.width,size.height);

        // Draw this one.
        g.fillArc(x,y,width,height,startAngle,arcWidth);
    }
```

(Continued)

Code 16.65 *(Continued)*

```
protected MovingArc getArc(){
    return arc;
}

protected Image getImage(){
    return image;
}

protected void setImage(Image i){
    image = i;
}

// Move clockwise.
private final int increment = -1;
// The arc to be animated.
private final MovingArc arc = new MovingArc(increment);
// An image to provide an off-screen graphics context.
private Image image = null;
}
```

---

on which to draw. If it is the first time it has been called, then it will need to create an image whose size matches the size of the canvas. The other circumstance in which it will need to create one is if the size of the frame has been changed since the image was created—the size of the image must match that of the component so that a proper pixel-by-pixel copy of its graphics context can be achieved. The arc is then drawn on the offscreen image's graphics context in exactly the same way as was done in the paint method of MovingArcCanvas in Code 16.64. Notice that, before this is done, any previous image is removed by using clearRect. Unlike in previous versions, this will not contribute to any flicker because it is done on the offscreen image, not the onscreen one, so the user will not be aware that it has taken place.

The visual impression created by the double buffering version of the moving arc program is considerably better than that of the previous version. Double-buffering is a powerful standard technique that goes a long way towards producing pleasing animation, particularly when the images are quite complex and quite time-consuming to draw. In Section 20.9, we discuss using animation with *applets*.

16.25 The Menu Classes

In Section 16.13.2, we introduced a DisplayFile class that displayed the contents of a file in a TextArea, which could be scrolled both horizontally and vertically. In this and the next few sections, we shall use parts of the DisplayFile class to build a more complete file browser application that will allow files to be loaded dynamically and their text searched. This will be used as a vehicle to introduce the various classes of the AWT that allow menus to be included in an application. We shall also demonstrate the FileDialog class for selecting a file to be displayed. The appearance of the final result is shown in Figure 16.62, and we shall refer to this in the discussion that follows.

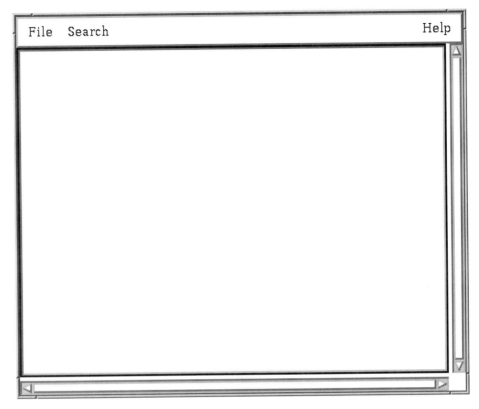

Figure 16.62   A file browser

       The main classes in the `java.awt` package for creating menus are `Menu`, `MenuItem`, and `PopupMenu`. `MenuItem` is a sub class of the abstract `MenuComponent` class. In addition, we shall cover the `MenuBar` and `MenuShortcut` classes. Menus are usually contained within a `MenuBar` that has been associated with a Frame via its `setMenuBar` method (Frame implements the `MenuContainer` interface). The menu bar for the file browser can be seen along the top of the frame in Figure 16.62 containing three Menus whose names are `"File"`, `"Search"`, and `"Help"`. The name for a Menu is set via its constructor, and a Menu is added to a MenuBar by sending the menu bar object an `add` message. Since help menus often occupy a distinctive position in applications, this can be indicated by adding such a menu to the bar with its `setHelpMenu` method. Code 16.66 shows how we might simplistically create the basic appearance of the browser shown in Figure 16.62, but without any functionality in place.

       In order to be useful, a Menu must have one or more MenuItems added to it. The File menu of the browser will have two items—`"Open"` and `"Quit"`. We will also place a horizontal-line separator between these two items, using Menu's `addSeparator` method. Furthermore, we would like the Quit item to offer the chance to `"Cancel"` or `"Really quit"`. This means that the Quit item will really be a further Menu nested within the File menu. This is possible because Menu is

Code 16.66   Adding a MenuBar to a Frame

```
        // Illustrate setting up the appearance of the FileBrowser
        // application. No functionality is present in the menus, yet.
public class FileBrowser extends Frame {
    public FileBrowser(){
        // Create the viewing area for the file's contents.
        final int numRows = 10, numCols = 80;
        TextArea area = new TextArea("",numRows,numCols,
                            TextArea.SCROLLBARS_BOTH);
        add(area);
        // Save the text area as an attribute.
        setContents(area);

        // Setup the appearance of the menu bar.
        MenuBar bar = new MenuBar();
        bar.add(new Menu("File"));
        bar.add(new Menu("Search"));
        bar.setHelpMenu(new Menu("Help"));
        setMenuBar(bar);
    }
    ...
}
```

Code 16.67   Creating the File menu with a nested Quit menu

```
public class FileBrowser extends Frame {
    ...
        // Create the File menu with items Open and Quit.
    protected Menu createFileMenu(){
        Menu fileMenu = new Menu("File");

        // Open is a simple item.
        MenuItem openItem = new MenuItem("Open");

        // Quit is a sub-menu.
        Menu quitMenu = new Menu("Quit");
        // Add the sub-menu items to Quit.
        quitMenu.add(new MenuItem("Cancel"));
        quitMenu.add(new MenuItem("Really quit"));

        // Add the items to this menu.
        fileMenu.add(openItem);
        // Add a separator between Open and Quit.
        fileMenu.addSeparator();
        fileMenu.add(quitMenu);
        return fileMenu;
    }
    ...
}
```

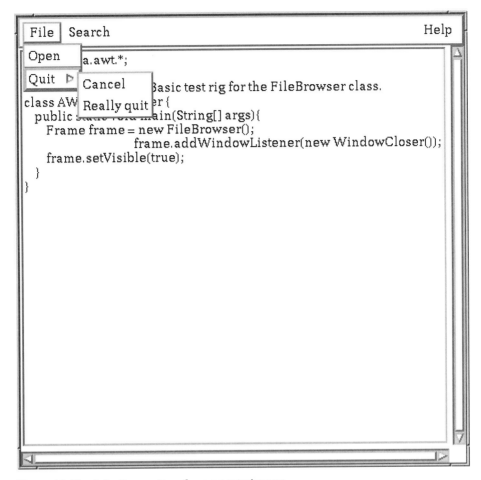

Figure 16.63 Selecting an item from a nested menu

a sub class of MenuItem. Figure 16.63 shows the appearance of the frame when the Quit item is selected. Code 16.67 shows how to create the File menu in this way; note that we have moved creation of the menus to separate methods because of their complexity. For the time being, we shall leave further discussion of the setup of the Search and Help menus until later.

When a menu item is selected, it results in an ActionEvent being sent to any action listeners that have registered with it. The FileBrowser implements the ActionListener interface and adds itself as an action listener when creating the menus, therefore. Each menu item needs an associated action command to identify it when the action event is received.

```
protected Menu createFileMenu(){
    ...
    MenuItem openItem = new MenuItem("Open");
    openItem.setActionCommand("Open");
    // Add the browser as an action listener.
```

```
        openItem.addActionListener(this);
        ...
    }
```

16.25.1   The MenuShortcut Class

As an alternative to selection via the mouse, a *shortcut key* may be attached to a menu item. A shortcut is defined by the `MenuShortcut` class, an object of which may be passed to the constructor of a `MenuItem`, or it may be set after construction by sending it a `setShortcut` message. The particular key used to select an item should be specified via one of the class constants defined in the `KeyEvent` class of the `java.awt.event` package. These constants have the prefix `VK_` followed by a name for each key available. For instance, `VK_F1` refers to the F1 function key, `VK_X` refers to the X key, and `VK_NUM_LOCK` to the Num Lock key. In order to distinguish these shortcuts from ordinary key events destined for text components, you will usually have to hold down the Ctrl key when activating them. When a shortcut key is attached to a menu item, it is displayed alongside the item's name in the menu. The following example shows both how to create a menu item with a shortcut and how

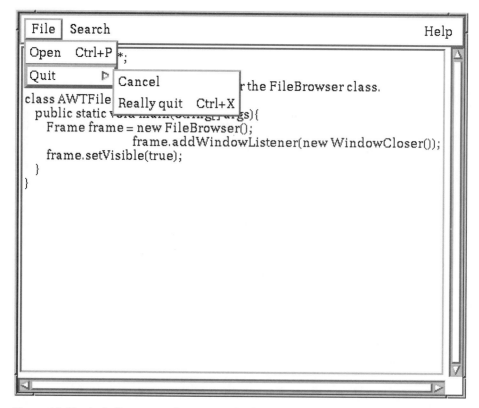

Figure 16.64   Including menu shortcuts in the file browser

to set one on an existing item:

```
// Activate with the F1 key
MenuItem openItem = new MenuItem("Open",
                               new MenuShortcut(KeyEvent.VK_F1));
...
MenuItem exitItem = new MenuItem("Really quit");
// Activate with X key
exitItem.setShortcut(new MenuShortcut(KeyEvent.VK_X));
```

The appearance of the menus in the file browser is illustrated in Figure 16.64.

16.26   The FileDialog Class

When the Open menu item is selected in the file browser, we wish to present the user with the opportunity to select a file to be opened. The `FileDialog` class, which extends the `Dialog` class discussed in Section 16.29, makes this very easy because it takes care of determining which files are available in the selected folder or directory and presenting them in an easily selectable way. Figure 16.65 shows the appearance of the FileDialog created in Code 16.68 in a UNIX environment. Code 16.68 shows the `selectFile` method of the FileBrowser that displays the FileDialog.

The constructor of FileDialog requires a reference to the Frame object in which it will be displayed. The constructors optionally take a title and a mode which has a value of either LOAD or SAVE. The title and mode are merely advisory to the host window manager, and their effect is platform dependent. When an application uses both LOAD and SAVE dialogs, the title string appearing in the title bar of the dialog could be used as a prompt to the user to distinguish between them. In

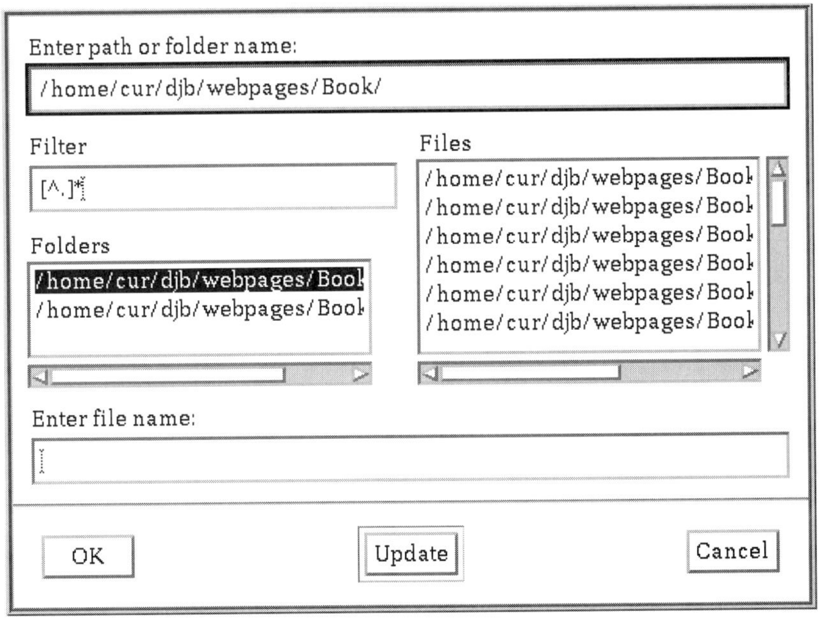

Figure 16.65   A FileDialog in a UNIX environment

Code 16.68   Creating a FileDialog for file selection

```
public class FileBrowser extends Frame {
    ...
        // The user has requested to open a file.
        // Show a FileDialog in LOAD mode.
    protected void selectFile(){
        FileDialog dialog =
                new FileDialog(this,"Open File",FileDialog.LOAD);
        dialog.setDirectory("/home/pkg/ftp/pub/djb/Book");
        dialog.setFile("");
        dialog.show();

        // Get the filename selected.
        String filename = dialog.getFile();
        if((filename != null) && (filename.length() != 0)){
            // Prefix the directory name, if any.
            String directory = dialog.getDirectory();
            if((directory != null) && (directory.length() != 0)){
                filename = directory+filename;
            }
            try{
                // Load the file.
                loadFile(filename);
            }
            catch(Exception e){
                System.err.println(e);
            }
        }
    }
    ...
}
```

addition, the SAVE mode could be used by the window manager to ensure that an existing file is not overwritten unintentionally, although this is not a standard part of the FileDialog's semantics. The `setDirectory` method of FileDialog allows its initialization from the contents of the given folder or directory, and the `setFile` method allows a default file name to be provided.

16.27   The PopupMenu Class

Popup menus are a common feature of many user interfaces. They have the advantage of keeping the main area of an interface less cluttered since they only appear when their functionality is specifically requested by the user. Furthermore, they are often used to save the user from having to move the mouse to a particular location to trigger them, or to provide a context-sensitive menu according to the position of the mouse when they are triggered. The `PopupMenu` class extends the Menu class, and so they are constructed from MenuItems in exactly the same way as we saw in Section 16.25. The main additional method of the class is `show`, which is used to display them within a particular Component at the specified `(x,y)` position.

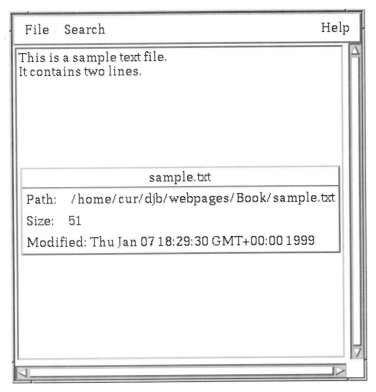

Figure 16.66   A PopupMenu showing details of the current file

The slightly tricky aspect of using popup menus is that of detecting when they should be displayed, and this is made more complicated by the incompatible conventions of different window managers. Some window managers regard the *press* of a mouse button as the popup trigger, whereas others regard the *release* as the trigger. In addition, the particular mouse button acting as the trigger may be platform dependent. An application wishing to show a popup menu must firstly provide an implementation of the `MouseListener` interface. To overcome some of the platform dependent aspects, MouseEvents have an `isPopupTrigger` method that returns `true` if the event is to be regarded as the platform's trigger. For platform independence, this should be checked for in the implementations of both the `mousePressed` and `mouseReleased` methods of the MouseListener interface, although it will return `true` in only one of those on any particular platform. Once detected, the `(x,y)` position associated with the event can be used to position the popup menu via its `show` method.

In order to demonstrate the use of a popup menu, the file browser will display details of the current file in one when a popup trigger is received. The appearance of this menu may be seen in Figure 16.66. This particular application introduces some complications into this process, however. Because the whole of the body of the Frame is covered by the TextArea used to display the file's contents, the popup trigger mouse events will be sent to the TextArea, rather than the Frame. In addition, the TextArea

object will already be listening for mouse events independent of the popup menu
action, and so it will be necessary to take some measures to prevent these two actions
from interfering with each other. Instead of directly using an object of class TextArea
to display the file, therefore, we shall create a sub class, `FileViewArea`, so that we
have more control over events received at the user interface. Code 16.69 shows the
FileViewArea class that displays the popup menu.

Code 16.69   Displaying a PopupMenu over the TextArea

```
import java.awt.*;
import java.awt.event.*;
import java.io.*;
import java.util.Date;

        // Display the contents of a file in a TextArea with
        // two scrollbars. Maintain details of the current file
        // so that these can be displayed with a popup menu.
public class FileViewArea extends TextArea implements MouseListener {
    FileViewArea(int rows, int cols){
        super("",rows,cols,SCROLLBARS_BOTH);

        // Create a popup menu for displaying the file's details.
        PopupMenu popup = new PopupMenu();
        setPopup(popup);
        add(popup);
        // Trigger the popup on mouse events.
        addMouseListener(this);
    }

    public void display(File details,String text){
        setDetails(details);
        setText(text);
    }

        // Methods of MouseListener.
    public void mousePressed(MouseEvent e){
        if(e.isPopupTrigger()){
            showPopup(e.getX(),e.getY());
            e.consume();
        }
    }
    public void mouseReleased(MouseEvent e){
        if(e.isPopupTrigger()){
            showPopup(e.getX(),e.getY());
            e.consume();
        }
    }

        // Display details of the current file.
    protected void showPopup(int x, int y){
        File details = getDetails();
        if(details != null){
            PopupMenu popup = getPopup();
```

Code 16.69   (*Continued*)

```
            // Clean it out from the last time it was used.
            popup.removeAll();
            popup.setLabel(details.getName());
            popup.add(new MenuItem("Path:     "+details.getPath()));
            popup.add(new MenuItem("Size:     "+details.length()));
            popup.add(new MenuItem("Modified: "+
                            new Date(details.lastModified())));
            popup.show(this,x,y);
        }
    }

        // The remaining methods are of no interest.
    public void mouseClicked(MouseEvent e) {}
    public void mouseEntered(MouseEvent e) {}
    public void mouseExited(MouseEvent e) {}

    protected File getDetails(){
        return details;
    }

    protected void setDetails(File d){
        details = d;
    }

    protected PopupMenu getPopup(){
        return popup;
    }

    protected void setPopup(PopupMenu p){
        popup = p;
    }

    // Details of the currently displayed file.
    File details = null;
    // The popup menu used to display the file's details.
    PopupMenu popup;
}
```

In FileViewArea's constructor, the popup menu is added via Component's add method which takes a PopupMenu argument, but it does not appear at this stage. Both the mousePressed and mouseReleased methods of MouseListener try to ascertain whether a popup trigger has been received, as described above. Notice that, when the trigger is detected, a consume message is sent to the mouse event so that no other listener to the same event will try to respond to it. This is important in this case because the TextArea super class might also try to act on it and should be prevented from doing so. In showPopup, the name of the file is used as the label of the popup (setLabel) and then various details are added as items. None of the items requires an action command or listener since they are only displayed to provide information. The showPopup method reuses the same popup menu each time it is called—the one that was added to this component in the constructor. This means that it must remove any menu items created the last time it was displayed, via `removeAll`, before the current details are added.

Exercise 16.30   Make the following changes to the popup menu managed by the `FileViewArea` class:

- Instantiate the PopupMenu with the label `"File Details"` in the constructor of FileViewArea.
- In the `showPopup` method, add the name of the file as a MenuItem, rather than setting the name as the label of the menu.
- If the path of the file is not an absolute path (as determined by the `isAbsolute` method of the `File` class), display an additional MenuItem in the popup menu that contains the string returned from the `getAbsolutePath` method of the File class.

16.28   The CheckboxMenuItem Class

The `CheckboxMenuItem` class is a further sub class of MenuItem. It includes a `boolean` state indicator attribute that is displayed next to the menu item's label. Such components are commonly used in menus that indicate whether a particular program option is turned on or off, for example, whether the sound is on in a game, whether a toolbar is to be included in the display, whether hints are to be shown on program start up, and so on (Figure 16.67). A CheckboxMenuItem can be created by passing its label and initial state to its constructor:

```
CheckboxMenuItem openItem = new CheckboxMenuItem("Sound?",true);
```

Associated with the state attribute are the `getState` and `setState` accessor and mutator. The window manager under which the example in Figure 16.67 was gen-

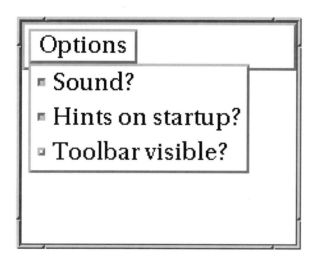

Figure 16.67   Options displayed with CheckboxMenuItem components

erated indicates the state of the item with either a raised or a depressed rectangle. Other window managers use either a tick to indicate a `true` state or no symbol for a `false` state. This latter case can make a CheckboxMenuItem hard to distinguish from a normal MenuItem. We recommend, therefore, that the label of a Checkbox-MenuItem should always include a question mark, or equivalent, to make it clear to the user that it indicates a `boolean` state.

Selecting a CheckboxMenuItem causes its state to *toggle* to the opposite value. CheckboxMenuItem implements the `ItemSelectable` interface so that listeners may register an interest in being notified when its state changes. They do this by sending an `addItemListener` message to it. The `getSelectedObjects` method of ItemSelectable is really designed for components that might have multiple selectable items, and so returns an array as its result. For a CheckboxMenuItem, this method will return an array containing a single object. If the menu item's state is `true`, then the array will contain the label of the item; if its state is `false`, then the array contains a `null` object. A related class that implements ItemSelectable is `Checkbox`, which is described in Section 16.30.

16.29   The Dialog Class

Continuing our discussion of a simple file browser, we shall further develop it in this and the next few sections through the design of a search dialog window. An image of the final version of this is shown in Figure 16.68. Within the `Dialog` window are five main elements:

- A TextField containing the string to be searched for.
- A list of strings previously searched for—a `Choice`.
- Selection of case sensitivity, if required—a `Checkbox`.
- Selection of the search direction—a `CheckboxGroup`.
- Buttons to undertake or cancel a search.

In order to take the new elements of the AWT step-by-step, we start by introducing a simplified version of the dialog containing just the text field and the `"Find"` and `"Cancel"` buttons. This will enable us to concentrate on the basics of how to set up and use a Dialog without allowing the class definition to become too cluttered with the detail of the various new components contained within it.

Up to this point, multiple components of a user interface have been grouped in a sub class of `Container`; either a Frame or a Panel. When the search dialog is displayed, we do not wish to add a new Panel to the current display of the browser since there is no room for it. Rather, we wish to create a new window somewhere in the vicinity of the browser window, containing the components we need to allow the search details to be specified. The `Dialog` class is designed for this purpose; it is a sub class of `Window` and so it is also a sub class of `Container`.

In order to create the search dialog window, we shall define a sub class of Dialog, called `SearchDialog`, and add the required components within its constructor. When a Dialog is constructed, it is associated with a parent Frame, a reference to which must be passed to its constructor. A dialog is displayed by sending it a `show` message. Dialogs come in two forms, *modal* and *non-modal*. A modal dialog blocks input to the parent frame until the dialog is closed, whereas a non-modal dialog

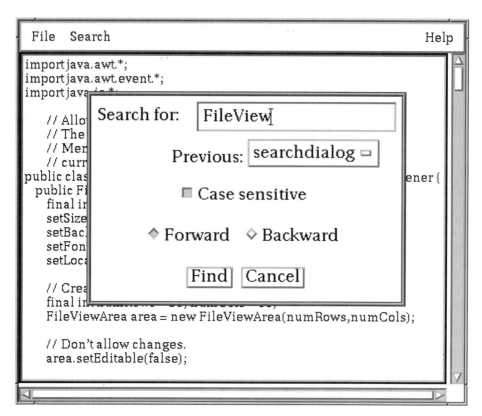

Figure 16.68   A search dialog window in the file browser

co-exists with the parent. Modal dialogs are probably the more common variety because they make it simpler to program the interaction between the dialog and the parent frame. However, you should consider carefully whether the user will ever need to gain access to the parent before the dialog is complete. We can compare the difference between the two approaches with the following two search scenarios:

- Modal search dialog: the search is initiated, causing the parent frame to display the dialog by sending it a `show` message. The parent frame then waits for the dialog to close itself, which is indicated by the `show` method returning. The frame then requests the search string from the dialog and undertakes the search.
- Non-modal search dialog: the search is initiated in a similar way to the modal case, but the `show` message returns immediately. This means that a way must be found to let the parent know when the search string is available.

Typically, there is a higher degree of *coupling* between the dialog and parent in the non-modal case than the modal case. Furthermore, it is important that the user does not interact with the parent frame in such a way as to invalidate the dialog or create an inconsistent state between the two objects. It is the greater complexity of interaction between elements of the user interface in the non-modal case that often makes modal dialogs the preferred choice. We shall use the modal model for our search dialog.

Code 16.70   Displaying the search dialog

```
public class FileBrowser extends Frame implements ActionListener {
    ...
        // Take whatever action is required by the menu.
    public void actionPerformed(ActionEvent e){
        String command = e.getActionCommand();
        if((command == null) || (command.length() == 0)){
            // No valid command.
        }
        else if(command.equalsIgnoreCase("Find")){
            SearchDialog search = getSearch();
            // Offset the search dialog slightly from the main frame.
            Point location = getLocation();
            final int offset = 75;
            location.x += offset;
            location.y += offset;
            search.setLocation(location);

            search.show();
            // Determine what to look for.
            String searchString = search.getSearchString();
            if(searchString.equals("")){
                // No search.
            }
            else if(!findString(searchString)){
                System.err.println("No match.");
            }
        }
        ...
    }
    ...

    // Construct the search dialog.
    private SearchDialog search = new SearchDialog(this);
}
```

Code 16.70 shows the `actionPerformed` method of the FileBrowser class that causes the search dialog to be displayed.

Because a Dialog is an independent Window, the host operating system's window manager will have some discretion over where it is placed, unless we indicate a preference. With some window managers, this could result in the dialog being placed at the top left corner of the screen, regardless of the position of the parent frame. We can set its position by sending it a `setLocation` message. In Code 16.70, we request the position of the top left corner of the parent frame (`getLocation`) and create a position for the dialog that is slightly below and to the right of this. The `show` message then causes the dialog to appear, and the parent is blocked until the dialog is closed, since the dialog is modal. Once the dialog is closed, we request the search string from it and attempt to find the given string in the browser's text area. Notice that hiding the dialog does not cause its components to be destroyed, so the search string remains available. Code 16.71 shows an outline for the `SearchDialog` class that just includes a field for the search string and buttons for confirming or cancelling the search.

Code 16.71   A simplified SearchDialog class

```
import java.awt.*;
import java.awt.event.*;

        // Implement a Search Dialog to enable strings to be searched
        // for in the current file. A text field contains the string
        // to be searched for.

class SearchDialog extends Dialog implements ActionListener {
    public SearchDialog(Frame frame){
        // A modal dialog is required.
        super(frame,"Search",true);
        final int width = 310, height = 200;
        setSize(width,height);
        final int rows = 2, cols = 1;
        setLayout(new GridLayout(rows,cols));

        // Setup the two panels.
        setupSearchPanel();
        setupButtonPanel();
    }

        // Return the string to be searched for.
    public String getSearchString(){
        String s = "";
        TextField field = getSearchField();

        if(field != null){
            s = field.getText();
        }
        return s;
    }

        // Implementation of ActionListener.
        // Respond to either the Return key being typed in
        // the TextArea or one of the Find/Cancel buttons
        // being pressed.
    public void actionPerformed(ActionEvent e){
        // The command to be acted on.
        String command;

        // Separate an event generated by typing Return in a
        // text component from one generated by a button.
        if(e.getSource() instanceof TextComponent){
            command = startFindString;
        }
```

Code 16.71   (*Continued*)

```
        else{
            command = e.getActionCommand();
        }

        // Obey the command.
        if(command == null){
        }
        else if(command.equals("")){
        }
        else if(command.equals(startFindString)){
            // Hide the dialog.
            setVisible(false);
        }
        else if(command.equals(cancelFindString)){
            // Clear the search string.
            setSearchString("");
            // Hide the dialog.
            setVisible(false);
        }
        else{
            System.err.println("Unknown action command: "+command);
        }
    }

    // Set up the Search text field.
    protected void setupSearchPanel(){
        // The string and previous strings.
        Panel searchTextPanel = new Panel();
        final int searchLength = 20;
        TextField searchField = new TextField("",searchLength);
        // Let the dialog know when the Return key is pressed.
        searchField.addActionListener(this);
        searchTextPanel.add(new Label("Search for:"));
        searchTextPanel.add(searchField);
        setSearchField(searchField);
        add(searchTextPanel);
    }

    // Set up the buttons for Find and Cancel.
    protected void setupButtonPanel(){
        ...
    }

    ...

    // The field containing the search string.
    private TextField searchField;
    // Action commands for the button actions.
    private final String startFindString = "StartFind",
                         cancelFindString = "CancelFind";
}
```

The constructor of SearchDialog uses the constructor of its super class that takes three arguments: the parent Frame, a title for the Dialog, and a Boolean value of `true` to indicate that the dialog is modal. Both the title and modal arguments are optional.

As a replacement for the default BorderLayout layout manager, a GridLayout layout manager has been used to organize the panels containing the components of the dialog. As we introduce more elements of the dialog, more panels will be added. Greater control over the layout would have been possible by using a GridBagLayout layout manager, but we have chosen GridLayout for the sake of keeping the class simple. A Panel is used to contain the components in each row of the grid. The `setupSearchPanel` method is responsible for creating the search TextField and the `setupButtonPanel` sets up the `Find` and `Cancel` buttons. The class implements the ActionListener interface so that it can respond to two sorts of events; button presses and the Return key being pressed in the text field. Both types of event are used to indicate that the dialog is complete and an appropriate action should be taken. The action, when either the find button is pressed or the Return key is pressed, is the same, and simply requires that the dialog window is closed. It will be the responsibility of the parent frame to request the current search string. When the cancel button is pressed, the search string is cleared before the dialog is closed—an empty search string is used to indicate to the parent that no search is to be performed. Note that the `actionPerformed` method cannot simply send a `getActionCommand` message to the ActionEvent object it receives in order to work out what to do (see Section 16.13). It must first determine whether the event was originated by the TextComponent or one of the buttons. In the case of the TextComponent, this will have resulted from the Return key having been pressed and `command` is set to be the equivalent of pressing the `Find` button.

The example in Code 16.71 gives us the basis of a dialog class to which we can add further components, both to illustrate further classes of the AWT and to enhance the search facilities of the dialog.

Exercise 16.31   Suppose the `actionPerformed` method in Code 16.71 simply sent a `getActionCommand` message to its ActionEvent argument without first establishing the source of the event. Why would this be wrong? *Hint:* What would be the consequence if the string to be searched for is `"Cancel"`?

Exercise 16.32   Modify the browser so that selecting the `About` menu item in the `Help` menu produces a modal Dialog box containing some text about the program. The dialog should include an `Ok` button that is used to close it.

16.30   The Checkbox Class

The search dialog, introduced in Section 16.29 and illustrated in Figure 16.68, allows a user to specify whether the search is to be *case sensitive* or not. The component used to allow this choice is a `Checkbox`. A Checkbox normally consists of a label and a Boolean state. When the box is selected, it represents a state of `true`. In the example in Figure 16.68, the box is not selected, indicating a search that is not case sensitive. The state of a check box is switched by clicking in the box. Window managers represent the state of a box differently from one another; some indicate selection by displaying a tick in the box, while others indicate this by a depression in the box. The case sensitive check box is constructed as follows:

```
// By default, the search is not case sensitive.
Checkbox caseSensitive = new Checkbox("Case sensitive",false);
```

This could be added directly to the dialog, but a better layout results if it is first added to a Panel of its own. Both the label and the initial state are optional arguments to the constructor, but both may be set using the `setLabel` and `setState` mutators. The `getState` accessor may be used to determine the state of a check box.

Sometimes it is necessary to be informed of a change of state of a check box when it happens. Classes interested in this information can implement the `Item-Listener` interface, from the `java.awt.event` package, and register themselves as listeners with a check box via its `addItemListener` method. Whenever the state of the box is changed, an `ItemEvent` is sent to such listeners. Checkbox implements the `ItemSelectable` interface which includes a `getSelectedObjects` method. This method is defined to return an array of Objects, and a Checkbox returns an array with a single Object, which is the String of its label. An ItemListener registered with several Checkboxes can determine which one's state has changed by examining this label. Other classes implementing ItemSelectable, such as `List` (Section 16.32), return multiple objects in their array.

16.30.1   The CheckboxGroup Class

In addition to the case sensitive check box, described in Section 16.30, the search dialog contains two further check boxes, labeled `"Forward"` and `"Backward"`. In Figure 16.68, these have a slightly different appearance from the former in that the square shape has been turned on its end to appear as a diamond. The reason for this is that they have been allocated to a `CheckboxGroup`. Some window managers display grouped checkboxes as circles rather than diamonds. A CheckboxGroup is not another AWT Component sub class; rather, it is a way of associating closely related check boxes such that selection of one excludes the others from being selected. That is, at any time, only one of the boxes may be selected. Such grouped check boxes are commonly known as *radio buttons*, because they behave like the mechanical wave-band selection buttons on radios in the days before digital displays. In this case, we either want the search direction to be forwards from the current cursor position or backwards—these options are mutually exclusive. A Checkbox may be assigned to a Checkbox group either at construction or by passing the appropriate group object to its `setCheckboxGroup` method. The selected check box may be determined by sending a `getSelectedCheckbox` message to the group object. Code 16.72 shows the `setupCheckBoxes` method of SearchDialog that creates all of the check boxes for the dialog.

Note that a Panel is necessary to visually group the `forward` and `backward` check boxes because the CheckboxGroup object is only used to enforce the mutual exclusion property—it is not a Component. It is the individual box objects that are added to the panel, therefore, rather than the group object.

Code 16.72 Allocating Checkboxes to a CheckboxGroup

```
class SearchDialog extends Dialog implements ActionListener {
    ...
    protected void setupCheckBoxes(){
        // The case-sensitive check box in its own panel.
        // Placing it in a panel improves the layout.
        Checkbox caseSensitive = new Checkbox("Case sensitive",false);
        setCaseSensitive(caseSensitive);
        Panel caseSensitivePanel = new Panel();
        caseSensitivePanel.add(caseSensitive);
        add(caseSensitivePanel);

        // Group the direction boxes in a panel.
        Panel checkPanel = new Panel();
        CheckboxGroup direction = new CheckboxGroup();
        Checkbox forward = new Checkbox(forwardLabel,direction,true);
        Checkbox backward = new Checkbox(backwardLabel,direction,false);
        checkPanel.add(forward);
        checkPanel.add(backward);
        setDirection(direction);
        add(checkPanel);
    }
    ...
}
```

16.31 The Choice Class

The final component of the search dialog is an instance of the Choice class. This is illustrated in Figure 16.68 with the label "Previous". A Choice component maintains a collection of zero or more item strings and allows selection of a single one of these. The selected item is displayed within the visible portion of the component, to the right of its label. The remainder of the collection of items is hidden and is only displayed as a popup list or *drop down list* when the component is selected with the mouse. In common with the Checkbox and CheckboxMenuItem classes, Choice implements the ItemSelectable interface and so provides the getSelected-Objects method. For convenience, it also has a getSelectedItem method that returns the currently selected string.

In the search dialog, we use a Choice to retain previous search strings. This means that further items are continuously being added throughout a run of the application. To prevent unlimited expansion of the collection, we do not include duplicate strings. There are two stages at which we manipulate the Choice component:

- Each time an item is selected from it, that item is copied into the search text field.
- Each time a search is initiated, the current contents of the text field are added to the Choice, unless already present.

Note that, when storing the contents of the text field into the Choice, we do not attempt to distinguish between a string that has just been typed by the user and one that

Code 16.73   Listening for events on a Choice component

```
class SearchDialog extends Dialog implements ItemListener,
                                             ActionListener {
    ...
        // Implementation of ItemListener.
        // A selection has been made from the Choice.
    public void itemStateChanged(ItemEvent e){
        if((e.getStateChange() & ItemEvent.SELECTED) ==
                                        ItemEvent.SELECTED){
            // Get the selected string.
            Object o = e.getItem();
            if(o instanceof String){
                String s = (String) o;
                // Copy the selected string to the search field.
                TextField field = getSearchField();
                field.setText(s);
            }
            else{
                System.err.println("Item isn't a string.");
            }
        }
        else{
            System.err.println("Choice wasn't selected.");
        }
    }
    ...
}
```

originated from the Choice in the first place. Such a check is unnecessary because it is already covered by the decision not to retain duplicate search strings in the Choice.

In order to copy a selected item into the text area, the dialog must register itself as a listener with the Choice. This means that it must implement the Item-Listener interface from the java.awt.event package. This interface contains a single method, itemStateChanged, which receives an ItemEvent. The particular event of interest is SELECTED. The event's getItemSelectable method will return a reference to the object in which the event occurred, and the getItem method will return the selected string. Code 16.73 shows the itemStateChanged method of SearchDialog. The test of the change of state examines the value returned by getStateChange by masking it with the bit-pattern for the SELECTED event. If what remains is the SELECTED pattern, then it has established that this event has occurred. Once it has been established that a valid string from the Choice has been selected, the text of the search field is set with the selected text. Since the SearchDialog is presumed to be only listening for ItemEvents on the Choice, any event other than item selection would represent a programming error.

When a search is initiated, the current string must be added to the Choice for future reference. This is handled in the actionPerformed method of SearchDialog, shown in Code 16.74. This is an expanded version of that previously shown in Code 16.71.

Code 16.74 Adding the current search string to the Choice

```
class SearchDialog extends Dialog implements ItemListener,
                                             ActionListener {
    ...
    // Implementation of ActionListener.
    public void actionPerformed(ActionEvent e){
        ...
        else if(command.equals(startFindString)){
            // Get things ready for Find.
            String s = getSearchString();
            if((s != null) && !s.equals("")){
                // Copy the latest string to the list of previous strings.
                // Don't add if it is already there.
                Choice choiceList = getPreviousStrings();
                int numItems = choiceList.getItemCount();
                int index;
                for(index = 0; index < numItems; index++){
                    String previous = choiceList.getItem(index);
                    if(s.equals(previous)){
                        // Found it.
                        break;
                    }
                }
                if(index == numItems){
                    // It wasn't found.
                    choiceList.add(s);
                }
            }
            // Hide the dialog.
            setVisible(false);
        }
        ...
    }
}
```

Having retrieved the search string from the text field (getSearchString), the first stage is to check that this string is not already present in the Choice. The number of items stored in a Choice is returned by its getItemCount method and an individual item string is returned by getItem. If the current string is not found, then it is added to the choice.

Exercise 16.33 Modify the file browser to include a menu that contains the names of all files browsed during the current session. Each time a new file is loaded, the name of the previous file should be added as a new MenuItem. An alternative to reloading a previous file from the File menu is to select its name from this list. Try to avoid duplicate names appearing in the list. There is no need to retain the contents of the FileViewArea for files other than the current one.

Exercise 16.34 Further extend your solution to Exercise 16.33 so that the File-ViewArea of previously loaded files is retained. This should make switching between different files quicker. You might like to consider using a `CardLayout` layout manager (Section 16.15) in the main Frame to effect the switching of views.

16.32   The List Class

The `List` class is a sub class of Component that is similar to the Choice class in that it implements the `ItemSelectable` interface. In contrast, List implements the interface in the most general way since it allows multiple items to be selected, whereas Choice only permits a single selection. The example in Figure 16.69 shows the class `QuestionAsker` which extends the Container class and uses a List component to provide possible answers to a question. The question is posed in a Label at the top of the frame, and a Button has been provided to signal that selection of the set of answers is complete. In this particular example, two items in the list have been selected by the user. A scrollbar appears at the right of the list to indicate that there are further items in the non-visible portion of the list. The implementation of QuestionAsker is shown in Code 16.75. For illustrative purposes, the class implements the ItemListener interface in order to demonstrate the way in which an ItemListener can monitor the activity taking place on a component that implements the ItemSelectable interface, as List does.

The List component is created in the `setupAnswerList` method. The constructor is passed an integer representing the number of items that should appear in the visible area by default, space permitting. The second argument indicates whether multiple selections should be allowed—by default they are not. The `setMultiple-Mode` method of List allows the mode to be changed once a List has been constructed. The containing object registers itself as a listener to events occurring on it. The effect of this is that the QuestionAsker is notified, via `itemStateChanged`, each time

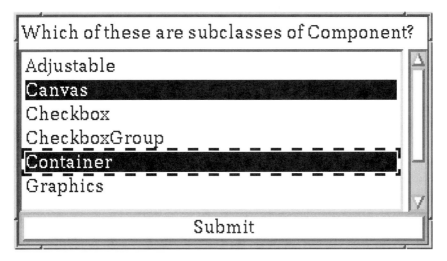

Figure 16.69   Selecting multiple items from a List

```
import java.awt.*;
import java.awt.event.*;

        // Define a Container holding a Question label, a List
        // of possible answers and a Submit button.
public class QuestionAsker extends Container
                    implements ActionListener, ItemListener {
    QuestionAsker(String question,String[] possibleAnswers){
        // For simplicity, use a BorderLayout.
        setLayout(new BorderLayout());

        // Display the question.
        add(new Label(question),"North");

        // Store the answers in a list.
        List answers = setupAnswerList(possibleAnswers);
        setAnswerList(answers);
        add(answers,"Center");

        // The button to be pressed when the answer is complete.
        Button b = new Button("Submit");
        b.addActionListener(this);
        add(b,"South");
    }

        // Implementation of ActionListener.
        // Respond when the submit button is pressed.
    public void actionPerformed(ActionEvent e){
        // Get the final list of selections.
        List list = getAnswerList();
        String[] answers = list.getSelectedItems();
        if((answers == null) || (answers.length == 0)){
            System.out.println("There were no answers selected.");
        }
        else{
            System.out.print("The answers selected were: ");
            for(int i = 0; i < answers.length; i++){
                System.out.print(answers[i]+" ");
            }
            System.out.println();
        }
        System.exit(0);
    }

        // Implementation of ItemListener.
        // Monitor when an item is selected or de-selected.
    public void itemStateChanged(ItemEvent e){
        // Obtain information about which item has been (de)selected.
        Object o = e.getItem();
        if((o != null) && (o instanceof Integer)){
            // The index of the item.
            int index = ((Integer) o).intValue();
            int stateChange = e.getStateChange();
```

Code 16.75   (*Continued*)

```
            if((stateChange & ItemEvent.SELECTED) ==
                                         ItemEvent.SELECTED){
                System.out.println("Item "+index+" selected.");
            }
            else if((stateChange & ItemEvent.DESELECTED) ==
                                         ItemEvent.DESELECTED){
                System.out.println("Item "+index+" de-selected.");
            }
            else{
                System.err.println(
                        "Unidentified state change to item: "+index);
            }
        }
        else{
            System.err.println("Unknown item event: "+e+" on "+o);
        }
    }

    // Setup the List from an array of possible answer strings.
    protected List setupAnswerList(String[] possibleAnswers){
        // Create the List to contain the possible answers.
        // Allow one row per answer.
        // Allow multiple selected items.
        List answers = new List(possibleAnswers.length,true);
        // Add the possibleAnswers to the list.
        for(int i = 0; i < possibleAnswers.length; i++){
            answers.add(possibleAnswers[i]);
        }
        // Notify this object of changes to the list.
        answers.addItemListener(this);
        return answers;
    }

    protected List getAnswerList(){
        return answerList;
    }

    protected void setAnswerList(List list){
        answerList = list;
    }

    private List answerList;
}
```

---

an item is either selected or deselected in the list. The resulting ItemEvent has an Integer attribute representing the index of the item in the list which has undergone a state change. The nature of the state change is determined from the result of the getStateChange method of the ItemEvent. In addition to DESELECTED and SELECTED, the other possible state indications are ITEM_FIRST, ITEM_LAST, and ITEM_STATE_CHANGE. In practice, monitoring of individual changes to a List is not normally required and only the final list of selections will be of interest. The `Submit` button of the application generates an `ActionEvent` which is handled in the container's `actionPerformed` method. It uses this notification to determine the final set of selected items by sending the List a `getSelectedItems` message, which returns an array of the selected strings.

An item may be selected or deselected under program control by passing its index to either the `select` or `deselect` method of the List. A particular item may be brought into view by passing its index to the `makeVisible` method. The two `remove` methods take either an integer or a string argument and remove the indicated item; `removeAll` clears the list.

16.33   Review

In this chapter, we have covered some of the major classes of the Abstract Windowing Toolkit. These classes remove many of the platform-dependent elements usually required to create Graphical User Interfaces. As such, they considerably simplify the amount of effort required to create applications with GUIs. The AWT is based around the concept of an application Frame acting as a Container for multiple Components. Layout managers handle the division of space between the competing components within a container. Classes exist that support the inclusion of fundamental GUI components, such as buttons, labels, text area, drawing canvases, and hierarchical menus.

In the next chapter, we consider the Swing classes—a set of more sophisticated classes that build upon the foundation provided by the AWT.

CHAPTER

17

Swing

In this chapter, we look at a selection of classes from the Swing packages. These provide a further set of components that extend the capabilities of the Abstract Windowing Toolkit. In many ways, the Swing classes are more sophisticated than their AWT counterparts. Of particular significance is the greater control they provide over an application's look-and-feel.

17.1   Introduction

The Swing classes are part of a wider collection known as the *Java Foundation Classes (JFC)*. They build on many of the classes and concepts of the AWT, such as layout managers, Color, Font, Graphics, and the event-handling interfaces. Within the scope of this book, however, it is only possible to provide an overview of many of them. For more detailed coverage, you should consult a specialist book which is dedicated to the Swing classes, such at that by Topley[Top98].

   The design of the Swing classes involves a completely different approach to that taken with the AWT classes. The Swing classes are written entirely in Java, in contrast to the AWT classes which are built on top of platform-specific *peer* components. One effect is that a Swing application can take the same *look-and-feel* to different platforms, rather than relying on the look-and-feel that is provided by peer classes on a particular platform (see Section 17.19).

   Swing component classes have names with a J prefix that indicate their similarity to equivalent AWT classes, for instance, JButton, JFrame, JLabel, and JPanel. In this chapter, we shall take much of their AWT-like functionality for granted, because it can be inferred from the descriptions of the related super classes in Chapter 16. Several Swing classes enhance the functionality of the AWT classes, and we shall concentrate on these aspects. For instance,

- There is more consistent support for combining text and graphics within components (in the form of the Icon interface).
- The JScrollPane class brings scrolling capabilities to all components.
- Menu bars and text components take on characteristics that are more consistent with other components.

17.2   The JFrame Class

Swing applications are built from user-created classes that extend the JFrame class at the top level. JFrame, itself, extends the AWT Frame class and shares many similarities with it, but it also defines a more sophisticated model of an application's visual representation. A JFrame contains a single JRootFrame object which contains a JLayeredPane. The JLayeredPane is a container for multiple overlapping components occupying different layers or levels within the overall frame. We describe JLayeredPane in Section 17.11.4. The default components housed by the JLayered-Pane are a *content pane* container, an optional JMenuBar, and a transparent *glass pane* component that is positioned above all the other components in the frame. One of the differences between a JFrame and a Frame is that the full area of the content pane is available to draw on—there is no need to take the edges and title bar into account when drawing onto it or when specifying the coordinate positions for components to be placed on it. Other classes which have a root frame and similar structure are JDialog, JWindow, JApplet, and JInternalFrame.

17.2.1   A JFrame Oval Application

We shall discuss the basic features of how to create an application with a JFrame by presenting a version of the oval drawing program first introduced in Section 16.5. This serves to illustrate some of the immediate similarities and differences between the Swing classes and those of the underlying AWT.

Code 17.1 shows a class containing a main method that creates an object belong to a sub class of JFrame.

Many of the Swing classes, such as JFrame, are defined in the javax.swing package. By default, a JFrame object is invisible, so it must be made visible before it can be seen by the user. Code 17.2 shows the SwingOvalFrame class that we have defined for this example.

The first significant difference between this example and those based on an AWT Frame is that components are not added directly to the Frame, but to the frame's content pane—obtained via its getContentPane method. The content pane is an object that is a sub class of the AWT Container class, allowing multiple components to be added to it. Notice that usage of the AWT classes means that it is necessary to include an import of java.awt in addition to javax.swing.

Code 17.1   Creating a JFrame object (`SwingOvalMain.java`)

```
import javax.swing.*;
import java.awt.*;

public class SwingOvalMain {
    public static void main(String[] args) throws Exception {
        JFrame frame = new SwingOvalFrame();
        frame.setVisible(true);
    }
}
```

Code 17.2   A sub class of JFrame (`SwingOvalFrame.java`)

```
import javax.swing.*;
import java.awt.*;
import java.awt.event.*;

        // Draw an oval within a JFrame.
class SwingOvalFrame extends JFrame {
    public SwingOvalFrame(){
        super("Swing Oval Frame Demo");
        final int width = 200, height = 175;
        setSize(width,height);

        // Get the frame's content pane, to which the components
        // will be added.
        Container pane = getContentPane();

        // Create a component in which to draw and
        // add it to this Frame's content pane.
        JComponent oval = new SwingOvalDrawing();
        pane.add(oval,"Center");

        // Add a quit button.
        JButton quitButton = new JButton("Quit");
        quitButton.addActionListener(new ActionListener(){
            public void actionPerformed(ActionEvent e){
                System.exit(0);
            }
        });
        pane.add(quitButton,"South");
    }
}
```

The default layout manager for the content pane is BorderLayout, as it is for a Frame. The drawing of the oval will be performed on a sub class of `JPanel` that we have called `SwingOvalDrawing`. A `JButton` (see Section 17.7.1) has been added to the content pane in much the same way as Buttons are added to AWT containers. A standard action listener has been attached, in order to close the application.[1]

17.2.2 The JPanel Class

The `JPanel` class provides a fundamental sub class of JComponent that can be used either as a container or as a drawing surface. There is no JCanvas class in the Swing libraries; instead, it is usual to create a sub class of either JPanel or JComponent to provide a drawing surface. Code 17.3 shows the definition of SwingOvalDrawing used in Code 17.2.

Instead of overriding the `paint` method, `paintComponent` is the equivalent

---

[1] We have encapsulated this common functionality in `QuitJButton.java` for subsequent use (see Code 17.6).

Code 17.3   Drawing on a JPanel (`SwingOvalDrawing.java`)

```
import javax.swing.*;
import java.awt.*;

        // Draw an oval within the panel.
public class SwingOvalDrawing extends JPanel {
    // Adjust the size of the oval according to the size
    // of the component.
    public void paintComponent(Graphics g){
        super.paintComponent(g);
        // Find out the size of this component.
        Dimension size = getSize();
        // Allow a small gap inside the drawing area.
        final int gap = 1;
        final int width = size.width-2*gap, height = size.height-2*gap;

        // Make sure there is enough space
        if((width > 0) && (height > 0)){
            g.drawOval(gap,gap,width,height);
        }
    }
}
```

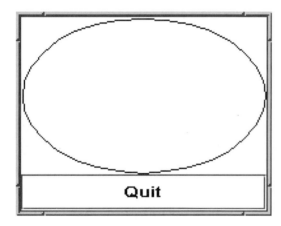

Figure 17.1 A Swing version of an Oval drawing program (`SwingOvalMain.java`)

for Swing components. As the super class's version of this method will sometimes perform useful work, we invoke it from within the sub class version. Figure 17.1 shows the visual appearance of this application, which is not significantly different from the equivalent AWT version illustrated in Figure 16.12.

17.3   The JComponent Class

Most of the component classes that we discuss in this chapter are immediate sub classes of the `JComponent` class. An important distinction between a JComponent and an AWT Component is that JComponent extends `Container`, so there is not the same distinction between a container and a component in Swing as there is in the AWT. JComponents have a layout manager, therefore, and it is possible to add multiple components to them; a feature that is regularly used. Swing adds further layout managers to those in the AWT, and these are described in Section 17.11. In the following sections, we describe some of the more important component sub classes of JComponent and interfaces closely associated with them.

17.4   The JLabel Class

The JLabel class is the most basic of the sub classes of JComponent, yet it performs a particularly useful role. As you might expect, it defines similar functionality to the AWT Label class, providing a convenient means to place a passive String object within a user interface. In addition to hosting a String, a JLabel is able to display an object of a class that implements the Icon interface, such as ImageIcon (see Section 17.5). This makes a JLabel the easiest way to arrange for an image to be displayed within a GUI. Code 17.4 shows how this can be done (Figure 17.2).

The QuitJPanel object used here is simply a panel that contains a Quit button that causes the application to exit when pressed (Code 17.5). See Section 17.6 for details of the border it uses to outline the panel. The QuitJButton class, used by QuitJPanel, is another utility class, shown in Code 17.6. See Section 17.5 for details of the Icon interface it is able to use. Details of applets (referred to in one of the comments) may be found in Chapter 20.

A further advance over its AWT equivalent is the ability to associate a JLabel with another component, via JLabel's setLabelFor method. The main purpose of this is to allow a char or int keycode mnemonic to be set on the label (set-DisplayedMnemonic) as a proxy for its associated component. See Section 17.7.1 for a description of the related setMnemonic methods associated with buttons.

Code 17.4   Using a JLabel to display an image (`SwingImageFrame.java`)

```
import javax.swing.*;
import java.awt.*;

    // Show the way in which a JLabel may be used to display an image.
class SwingImageFrame extends JFrame {
    public SwingImageFrame(){
        final int width = 195, height = 275;
        setSize(width,height);
        Container contents = getContentPane();

        // The label to hold the image.
        final JLabel image = new JLabel(new ImageIcon("apple.gif"));

        contents.add(image,"Center");
        contents.add(new QuitJPanel(),"South");
        pack();
    }
}
```

Figure 17.2 Using a JLabel to display an image (SwingImageFrame.java)

Code 17.5 A utility class for containing a Quit button (QuitJPanel.java)

```
import java.awt.Color;
import javax.swing.*;
import javax.swing.border.EtchedBorder;

    // A convenience class that contains an active Quit button
    // for terminating a program.
public class QuitJPanel extends JPanel {
    public QuitJPanel(){
        super();
        setBackground(Color.white);
        setBorder(new EtchedBorder(EtchedBorder.LOWERED));
        add(new QuitJButton());
    }
}
```

Code 17.6 A Quit button utility class (QuitJButton.java)

```
import java.awt.Color;
import javax.swing.*;
import java.awt.event.*;

    // Always quit an application when pressed.
class QuitJButton extends JButton implements ActionListener {
    public QuitJButton(String s,Icon i){
        super(s,i);
```

Code 17.6   (*Continued*)

```
            addActionListener(this);
    }

    public QuitJButton(String s){
        this(s,null);
    }

    public QuitJButton(Icon i){
        this("",i);
    }

    public QuitJButton(){
        this(label,null);
    }

    public void actionPerformed(ActionEvent e){
        // Exit is prohibited from an applet.
        try{
            System.exit(0);
        }
        catch(RuntimeException ex){
        }
    }

    private static final String label = "Quit";
    {
        setBackground(Color.white);
    }
}
```

When the mnemonic is activated, the label will send a `requestFocus` message to the component it is labeling. This overcomes the problem of components on which it is not possible to display mnemonics directly, such as text components.

17.5   The Icon Interface

Many basic Swing components, such as JLabel and AbstractButton, define a `set-Icon` method which enables an image to be displayed within them. Such images are often provided by classes implementing the `Icon` interface, shown in Code 17.7.

Code 17.7   The Icon interface

```
public interface Icon {
    public int getIconHeight();
    public int getIconWidth();
    public void paintIcon(Component c, Graphics g, int x, int y);
}
```

Implementations of the interface simply draw on the graphics context passed to their paintIcon method at the specified (x,y) position. It is quite easy to create implementations; Code 17.8 shows one that creates colored circle icons.

Code 17.8   An implementation of the Icon interface (`CircleIcon.java`)

```java
import javax.swing.Icon;
import java.awt.*;

        // A circular icon.
class CircleIcon implements Icon {
    public static final int defaultWidth = 10;
    public static final Color defaultColor = Color.blue;

    public CircleIcon(){
        this(defaultWidth,defaultColor);
    }

    public CircleIcon(int w){
        this(w,defaultColor);
    }

    public CircleIcon(Color c){
        this(defaultWidth,c);
    }

    public CircleIcon(int w,Color c){
        width = w;
        color = c;
    }

        // The Icon interface.
    public int getIconWidth(){
        return width;
    }

    public int getIconHeight(){
        // The height is the same as the width.
        return width;
    }

    public void paintIcon(Component c, Graphics g, int x, int y){
        g.setColor(color);
        g.fillArc(x,y,width,width,0,360);
    }

    public Color getColor(){
        return color;
    }

    private final int width;
    private final Color color;
}
```

If you do not wish to create your own implementation, the Swing ImageIcon class provides several constructors that allow an icon to be created from either a byte array or another Image, to be loaded either from a local filename, or loaded from a remote location via a URL object (see Section 19.3). A string description for such icons may be supplied.

17.6 The Border Interface

The JComponent class defines a setBorder method that allows a decorative border to be added to any Swing component. Such borders might be used to give the effect of a raised or depressed button, for instance. The Border interface is defined in the javax.swing.border package, and several convenient implementations are provided there. Figure 17.3 illustrates a selection of these attached to several JPanel objects, each of which contains a descriptive string.

The standard classes implementing this interface are BevelBorder, CompoundBorder, EmptyBorder, EtchedBorder, LineBorder, Matte-Border, SoftBevelBorder, and TitledBorder. Code 17.9 illustrates several of these in practice. The samples in the main area of the frame are created in the setupBorders method, although an etched border is also attached to the panel containing the quit button (QuitJPanel.java). The BevelBorder and SoftBevel classes give a 3D effect by using distinct highlight and shadow colors for their sides,

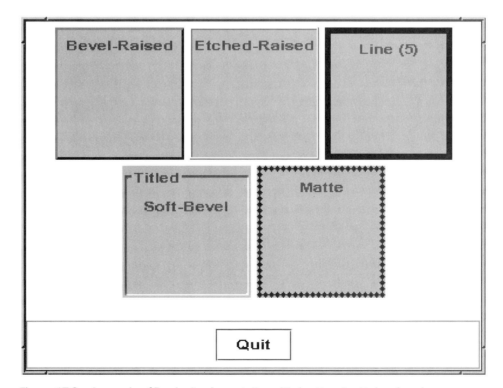

Figure 17.3   A sample of Border implementations (SwingBorderMain.java)

Code 17.9   A sample of the classes implementing the Border interface
(`SwingBorderFrame.java`)

```java
import javax.swing.*;
import javax.swing.border.*;
import java.awt.*;

        // Show a range of different Borders around JPanels.
class SwingBorderFrame extends JFrame {
    public SwingBorderFrame() {
        final int width = 400, height = 320;
        setSize(width,height);
        Container contents = getContentPane();

        JPanel labelPanel = new JPanel();
        setupBorders(labelPanel);
        contents.add(labelPanel,"Center");
        contents.add(new QuitJPanel(),"South");
    }

        // Add panels to the display with various borders.
        // Each panel contains a descriptive label.
    protected void setupBorders(Container display){
        // Shared font and size.
        final Font f = new Font("SansSerif",Font.BOLD,12);
        final int width = 110;
        final Dimension size = new Dimension(width,width);
        // A thickness for the LineBorder.
        final int lineThickness = 5;

        // Label and Border pairs for each panel.
        Object[][] borders = {
            {"Bevel-Raised",
             new BevelBorder(BevelBorder.RAISED,Color.cyan,Color.blue)
            },
            {"Etched-Raised", new EtchedBorder(EtchedBorder.RAISED)
            },
            {"Line ("+lineThickness+")",
             new LineBorder(Color.black,lineThickness)
            },
            {"Soft-Bevel",
             new TitledBorder(
                    new SoftBevelBorder(SoftBevelBorder.LOWERED),"Titled")
            },
            {"Matte", new MatteBorder(new CircleIcon(5))
            },
        };

        // Create a bordered panel containing a descriptive label.
        final int numBorders = borders.length;
        for(int i = 0; i < numBorders; i++){
            JPanel panel = new JPanel();
            JLabel label = new JLabel((String) borders[i][0]);
            panel.setBorder((Border) borders[i][1]);
            label.setFont(f);
```

Code 17.9   (*Continued*)

```
            panel.setPreferredSize(size);
            panel.add(label);
            display.add(panel);
        }
    }
}
```

---

as if there is a light source to the top left of the component. The line thickness of a LineBorder is specified on construction. The MatteBorder class tiles an icon or draws a line of a specified color. The TitledBorder class allows a title string to be justified within the border (CENTER, LEFT, or RIGHT) or positioned relative to the border (ABOVE_BOTTOM, ABOVE_TOP, BELOW_BOTTOM, BELOW_TOP, BOTTOM, or TOP).

17.7   The AbstractButton Class

The AbstractButton class provides the abstract super class of several button-like classes: JButton, JToggleButton, and JMenuItem. These have in common the display of a String and Icon, notification of events to ActionListener, Change-Listener and ItemListener objects, and association with a keycode mnemonic (Section 17.7.1).

17.7.1   The JButton Class

Code 17.10 illustrates the way in which a JButton may be created with an associated Icon.

Code 17.10   The "Go" and "Stop" buttons display both a String and an Icon
(`SwingButtonFrame.java`)

```
import javax.swing.*;
import java.awt.*;
import java.awt.event.*;

    // Two JButtons (Go and Stop) control a horizontal JProgressBar.
    // Used mainly as an example of the former.
class SwingButtonFrame extends JFrame {
    public SwingButtonFrame(){
        final int width = 300, height = 100;
        setSize(width,height);
        Container contents = getContentPane();

        // The reaction timer, which is a progress bar.
        final ReactionTimer reaction =
                    new ReactionTimer(JProgressBar.HORIZONTAL);
```

(*Continued*)

Code 17.10   (*Continued*)

```java
    // The two buttons that will manipulate the timer.
    final AbstractButton go =
            new JButton("Go",new ImageIcon("Go.gif"));
    final AbstractButton stop =
            new JButton("Stop",new ImageIcon("Stop.gif"));
    // Enable the go button, and attach key mnemonics to both.
    go.setEnabled(true);
    go.setMnemonic('g');
    stop.setEnabled(false);
    stop.setMnemonic('s');

    // When the go button is pressed, it must start the timer
    // and enable the stop button.
    go.addActionListener(new ActionListener(){
        public void actionPerformed(ActionEvent e){
            go.setEnabled(false);
            reaction.start();
            stop.setEnabled(true);
        }
    });

    // When the stop button is pressed, it must stop the timer
    // and enable the go button.
    stop.addActionListener(new ActionListener(){
        public void actionPerformed(ActionEvent e){
            reaction.stop();
            stop.setEnabled(false);
            go.setEnabled(true);
        }
    });

    // Group the two buttons.
    JPanel buttonPanel = new JPanel();
    buttonPanel.add(go);
    buttonPanel.add(stop);

    contents.add(reaction,"Center");
    contents.add(buttonPanel,"South");
    }
}
```

The SwingButtonFrame class is part of an application that simulates a reaction timer. Initially, the "Go" button is enabled and the "Stop" button is disabled (Figure 17.4). When the "Go" button is pressed, a ReactionTimer (based upon the JProgressBar class, described in Section 17.24) is started. The buttons swap states and the progress bar moves from left to right (Figure 17.5). When the "Stop" button is pressed, the progress bar stops and the buttons swap states again.

The way in which JButtons respond to mouse clicks is familiar from examples with Button objects in Chapter 16. The only significant difference we see here is the second argument to the constructor of a JButton which is an ImageIcon (see

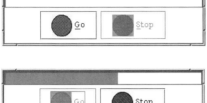

Figure 17.4 The go button enabled and no progress

Figure 17.5 The stop button enabled and some progress

Section 17.4). Both the String and Icon arguments are optional. The JButton class inherits several methods for manipulating icons from its AbstractButton super class. By default, the icon will be displayed centrally to the left of the string, if both are present, but four methods allow the horizontal and vertical alignment and positioning to be adjusted (for instance, setHorizontalAlignment and setHorizontalText-Position). A disabled button will have its icon and text grayed out automatically, but an alternative icon may be set for this purpose via the setDisabledIcon method.

The example in Code 17.10 also illustrates use of one of the two setMnemonic methods that JButtons inherit from AbstractButton. The version used here takes a char argument. When this character is pressed in combination with the ALT key, it is equivalent to pressing the associated button. As can be seen from the figures, the mnemonic key is indicated within the label's button for ease of reference. The second version of the method takes an int keycode value. Names for keycode values are defined in the KeyEvent class of the java.awt.event package. The JComponent class offers a general approach to the association of keyboard shortcuts with components via its registerKeyboardAction methods. These are described in Section 17.9.

17.7.2 The JToggleButton Class

The JToggleButton class extends the AbstractButton class to provide a button with two states, selected and not-selected. Its state is reflected in its visual appearance. Code 17.11 shows a frame that contains two toggle buttons in a central panel. The visual appearance after one of these has been pressed is shown in Figure 17.6.

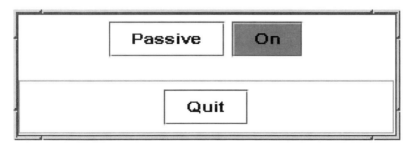

Figure 17.6 Two JToggleButtons, one of which is selected (SwingToggleMain.java)

```java
import javax.swing.*;
import java.awt.*;
import java.awt.event.*;

        // Display two JToggleButtons.
class SwingToggleFrame extends JFrame {
    public SwingToggleFrame() {
        final int width = 300, height = 120;
        setSize(width,height);
        Container contents = getContentPane();

        // Create two JToggleButtons. One listens for
        // changes, the other is passive.
        final JToggleButton passiveButton = new JToggleButton("Passive");
        // Initially the second button is selected.
        final JToggleButton activeButton = new JToggleButton("On");
        activeButton.setSelected(true);
        // Make the text on the button respond to its state.
        activeButton.addItemListener(new ItemListener(){
            public void itemStateChanged(ItemEvent e){
                int change = e.getStateChange();
                if(change == ItemEvent.SELECTED){
                    activeButton.setText("On");
                }
                else{
                    activeButton.setText("Off");
                }
            }
        });

        // Add the buttons to a central panel.
        final JPanel togglePanel = new JPanel();
        togglePanel.add(passiveButton);
        togglePanel.add(activeButton);
        contents.add(togglePanel,"Center");
        contents.add(new QuitJPanel(),"South");
    }
}
```

Selection and de-selection of a JToggleButton can be detected by attaching an `Item-Listener`. The `getStateChange` of the resulting `ItemEvent` can be used to determine whether the button has been `SELECTED` or `DESELECTED`. Although `passiveButton` in Code 17.11 has no attached listener, it still responds to selection and de-selection by altering its visual appearance. Different look-and-feels will represent selection in their own way. JToggleButton is the immediate super class of `JCheckBox` (Section 17.7.3) and `JRadioButton` (Section 17.7.4).

Figure 17.7   A selected JCheckBox (`SwingCheckBoxMain.java`)

17.7.3   The JCheckBox Class

The `JCheckBox` class is a sub class of JToggleButton and inherits its two-state be-havior. It is similar to the AWT `Checkbox` class.[2] Code 17.12 shows an example that creates a JCheckBox and listens for changes to its status. Figure 17.7 shows its appearance when the check box has been selected.

Code 17.12   A JCheckBox component that responds to changes of status

```
import javax.swing.*;
import java.awt.*;
import java.awt.event.*;

    // Display a JCheckBox component and respond to events on it.
    // The text of a status label is changed when the state of the
    // check box is changed.
class SwingCheckBoxFrame extends JFrame {
    public SwingCheckBoxFrame() {
        final int width = 300, height = 125;
        setSize(width,height);
        Container contents = getContentPane();

        // The status label and strings for it.
        final String willHear = "You will be hearing from us.",
                wontHear = "You won't be hearing from us.";
        final JLabel status = new JLabel(wontHear,JLabel.CENTER);

        // Create a JCheckBox component. It listens for
        // changes and modifies the status label's string.
        final JCheckBox checkbox =
                new JCheckBox("Check the box to receive email from us.");
        // Initially the check box is not selected.
        checkbox.setSelected(false);

        // Make the text in the label respond to changes of state.
        checkbox.addItemListener(new ItemListener(){
```
(Continued)

---

[2] Note, however, the confusing difference in the case of the B in box.

Code 17.12 *(Continued)*

```
        public void itemStateChanged(ItemEvent e){
            int change = e.getStateChange();
            if(change == ItemEvent.SELECTED){
                status.setText(willHear);
            }
            else{
                status.setText(wontHear);
            }
        }
    });

    // Add the components to a central panel.
    final JPanel togglePanel = new JPanel();
    // Place the check box immediately above the status label.
    togglePanel.add(checkbox);
    togglePanel.add(status);
    contents.add(togglePanel,"Center");
    contents.add(new QuitJPanel(),"South");
    }
}
```

Because JCheckBox is a sub class of JToggleButton, it can respond to status changes in a similar way to that shown in Code 17.11.

17.7.4   The JRadioButton Class

Like JCheckBox, the JRadioButton class is a sub class of JToggleButton, and inherits its two-state behavior. This component represents a formal class to fulfill the role described in Section 16.30.1 for mutually exclusive groups of AWT check boxes. In the AWT, multiple Checkbox components can be added to a CheckboxGroup object that manages them in such a way that only one of the check boxes may be selected at any one time. In fact, although the Swing library defines JRadioButton as a separate class, it still needs a ButtonGroup object to supply the mutual exclusion, which does not arise simply from creating multiple radio buttons. Code 17.13 shows

Code 17.13   A pair of grouped JRadioButtons (`SwingRadioButtonFrame.java`)

```
import javax.swing.*;
import java.awt.*;
import java.awt.event.*;

    // Display two grouped JRadioButton components.
    // Respond to events on one of them.
    // The text of a status label is changed when the state of the
    // Yes button is changed.
class SwingRadioButtonFrame extends JFrame {
    public SwingRadioButtonFrame() {
```

Code 17.13   (*Continued*)

```
        final int width = 300, height = 150;
        setSize(width,height);
        Container contents = getContentPane();

        // The status label and strings for it.
        final String willHear = "You will be hearing from us.",
                     wontHear = "You won't be hearing from us.";
        final JLabel status = new JLabel(wontHear,JLabel.CENTER);

        // A question to prompt a Yes/No answer.
        final JLabel question =
                new JLabel("Would you like to receive email from us?",
                           JLabel.CENTER);
        // Create the radio buttons. One listens for
        // changes and modifies the status label's string.
        // Initially the no button is selected.
        final JRadioButton yesButton = new JRadioButton("Yes",false),
                           noButton  = new JRadioButton("No",true);

        // Make the text in the status label respond to changes of state.
        yesButton.addItemListener(new ItemListener(){
            public void itemStateChanged(ItemEvent e){
                int change = e.getStateChange();
                if(change == ItemEvent.SELECTED){
                    status.setText(willHear);
                }
                else{
                    status.setText(wontHear);
                }
            }
        });

        // Group the buttons to achieve mutual exclusivity.
        ButtonGroup answerGroup = new ButtonGroup();
        answerGroup.add(yesButton);
        answerGroup.add(noButton);

        // Group the radio buttons in their own panel.
        JPanel answerPanel = new JPanel();
        answerPanel.add(yesButton);
        answerPanel.add(noButton);

        // Add the components to a central panel in a single column.
        final JPanel radioPanel = new JPanel();
        final int rows = 3, cols = 1;
        radioPanel.setLayout(new GridLayout(rows,cols));
        radioPanel.add(question);
        radioPanel.add(answerPanel);
        radioPanel.add(status);

        contents.add(radioPanel,"Center");
        contents.add(new QuitJPanel(),"South");
    }
}
```

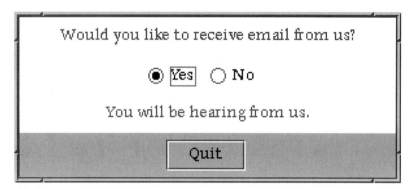

Figure 17.8   Two JRadioButtons grouped associated via a ButtonGroup (`SwingRadioButtonMain.java`)

Code 17.14   The ChangeListener interface defined in the `javax.swing.event` package

```
public interface ChangeListener extends EventListener {
    public void stateChanged(ChangeEvent e);
}
```

an example consisting of a pair of Yes/No radio buttons with an associated question and status label. Its appearance is shown in Figure 17.8.

The way in which status changes to a JRadioButton are monitored is similar to that for toggle buttons and check boxes, via attached ItemListeners.

17.7.5   The ChangeListener Interface

Many of the component classes include an `addChangeListener` method to support event notification to classes that implement the `ChangeListener` interface (defined in the `javax.swing.event` package). This interface is shown in Code 17.14.

The `ChangeEvent` class is a trivial sub class of the standard `EventObject` class. It adds no additional functionality.

17.8   Tool Tips

The JComponent class defines the `setToolTipText` method that makes it possible to associate a small popup text label with any Swing component. Such tips serve as a guide to the user as to the functionality of components—particularly where a component contains no other text. Figure 17.9 shows a tool tip attached to a Quit button. A tip appears if the mouse remains stationary over its associated component for a delay time that is configurable. It disappears if the mouse is moved away. Code 17.15 shows how this tool tip was created.

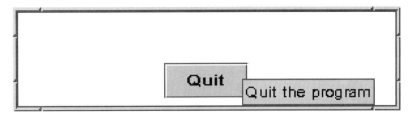

Figure 17.9   A tool tip attached to a button (`SwingToolTipMain.java`)

Code 17.15   Setting a tool tip on a component and configuring the manager
(`SwingToolTipFrame.java`)

```
import javax.swing.*;
import java.awt.*;
import java.awt.event.*;

        // Set a tool tip for a Quit button.
        // Make the delay relatively short before tips are shown.
class SwingToolTipFrame extends JFrame {
    public SwingToolTipFrame() {
        final int width = 300, height = 100;
        setSize(width,height);
        Container contents = getContentPane();

        JButton quit = new JButton("Quit");
        quit.addActionListener(new ActionListener(){
            public void actionPerformed(ActionEvent e){
                System.exit(0);
            }
        });

        // Set a small delay (in milliseconds) before tips are shown.
        ToolTipManager manager = ToolTipManager.sharedInstance();
        manager.setInitialDelay(250);
        // Set the tool tip for the quit button.
        quit.setToolTipText("Quit the program");

        JPanel buttonPanel = new JPanel();
        buttonPanel.add(quit);
        contents.add(buttonPanel,"South");
    }
}
```

The behavior of all tool tips is controlled by a *singleton* ToolTipManager, which is available via the static sharedInstance method of its class. The manager registers itself as a listener to mouse events for components with tool tips, and it controls how long to delay before showing the tip (setInitialDelay), how long to leave the tip displayed after the mouse has moved (setDismissDelay), and how long before redisplaying it again (setReshowDelay). The argument to each of these methods is a number of milliseconds. Tool tips may be globally enabled or disabled via the manager's setEnabled method.

17.9   The KeyStroke Class

In Section 17.7.1, we discussed the way in which a keyboard mnemonic may be associated with a button. The JComponent class offers a general mechanism for associating a keyboard shortcut with a component, via its registerKeyboard-Action methods. The example in Code 17.16 illustrates both of these methods, and the several ways of obtaining a KeyStroke object. Its appearance is shown in Figure 17.10.

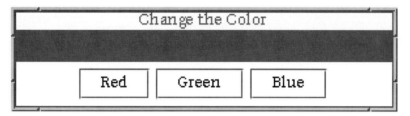

Figure 17.10   The panel's color is changed via keystrokes associated with the buttons (SwingKeyStrokeMain.java)

Code 17.16   Setting keyboard shortcuts on components (SwingKeyStrokeFrame.java)

```java
import javax.swing.*;
import java.awt.*;
import java.awt.event.*;

    // Illustrate the registerKeyboardAction methods of
    // The JComponent classes.
    // The color of a central panel may be changed via different
    // key stroke combinations attached to three buttons.
class SwingKeyStrokeFrame extends JFrame {
    public SwingKeyStrokeFrame() {
        final int width = 300, height = 100;
        setSize(width,height);

        Container contents = getContentPane();
        final JLabel promptLabel = new JLabel("Change the Color",JLabel.CENTER);
        final JPanel colorPanel = new JPanel();
        // Set up the buttons to change the color of the panel.
        final JPanel buttonPanel = setupButtons(colorPanel);

        // Cause the program to exit if the Q key is typed
        // over the application.
        colorPanel.registerKeyboardAction(
            new ActionListener(){
                public void actionPerformed(ActionEvent e){
                    // Print the associated command message.
                    System.out.println(e.getActionCommand());
                    System.exit(0);
                }
            },
            "Goodbye",
            KeyStroke.getKeyStroke('Q'),
            JComponent.WHEN_IN_FOCUSED_WINDOW
        );
        contents.add(promptLabel,"North");
```

Code 17.16   (*Continued*)

```
        contents.add(colorPanel,"Center");
        contents.add(buttonPanel,"South");
    }

        // Setup three buttons to be activated on different
        // keystroke combinations. Each should set the panel
        // to a different background color.
    protected JPanel setupButtons(final JPanel colorPanel){
        final JButton red = new JButton("Red"),
                    green = new JButton("Green"),
                    blue = new JButton("Blue");
        final JPanel panel = new JPanel();

        // Define the common background setting action in a named
        // local class.
        class BackgroundSetter implements ActionListener {
            BackgroundSetter(Color color){
                this.color = color;
            }

            public void actionPerformed(ActionEvent e){
                colorPanel.setBackground(color);
                colorPanel.repaint();
            }

            private final Color color;
        }

        // Red when SHIFT-R is released.
        red.registerKeyboardAction(
            new BackgroundSetter(Color.red),
            KeyStroke.getKeyStroke(KeyEvent.VK_R,
                            InputEvent.SHIFT_MASK,true),
            JComponent.WHEN_IN_FOCUSED_WINDOW
        );
        red.setEnabled(true);

        // Green when CTRL-G is pressed and the button has the focus.
        green.registerKeyboardAction(
            new BackgroundSetter(Color.green),
            KeyStroke.getKeyStroke(KeyEvent.VK_G,InputEvent.CTRL_MASK),
            JComponent.WHEN_FOCUSED
        );

        // Blue when 'b' is pressed.
        blue.registerKeyboardAction(
            new BackgroundSetter(Color.blue),
            KeyStroke.getKeyStroke('b'),
            JComponent.WHEN_ANCESTOR_OF_FOCUSED_COMPONENT
        );

        panel.add(red);
        panel.add(green);
        panel.add(blue);

        return panel;
    }
}
```

The example shown in Code 17.16 registers a KeyStroke object with each button. Triggering any one of these keyboard shortcuts will cause the color of the central panel to be changed to either red, green, or blue. In addition, a KeyStroke has been registered with the central panel, causing the application to exit when an uppercase 'Q' key is released. Registering a keystroke requires at least three arguments: an ActionListener to be activated, a KeyStroke to activate the listener, and a focus condition that must be met for the listener to be notified. The three condition values are defined in the JComponent class: WHEN_FOCUSED (when this component has the focus), WHEN_IN_FOCUSED_WINDOW (when this component's window has the focus), and WHEN_ANCESTOR_OF_FOCUSED_COMPONENT (when this component, or one of its ancestor components, has the focus). One of the register methods includes an additional String argument, which will be set as the actionCommand of the Action-Event if the event is triggered. This version is illustrated in the keyboard action associated with the colorPanel variable in Code 17.16.

The easiest way to obtain an appropriate KeyStroke object is via one of the KeyStroke class's static getKeyStroke methods. The first version takes a single char argument. This has been used with both the colorPanel and blue objects. The second version takes a keycode argument (as defined in the KeyEvent class of the java.awt.event package) and a modifier (as defined in the InputEvent class of the java.awt.event package). The green button illustrates this version. Its event will be sent to the associated listener when CTRL+G is typed, but only when this button has the focus. The third version takes a keycode, a modifier and a boolean value indicating whether the event should be triggered on key release rather than press. This is illustrated by the red button, which is triggered when SHIFT+R is released. The getKeyStrokeForEvent method of KeyStroke allows the key stroke that triggered a particular KeyEvent to be obtained.

17.10   The JOptionPane Class

The JOptionPane class provides static convenience methods that enable dialogs with a common set of user-interaction styles to be constructed easily. The three standard styles are message dialogs, confirmation dialogs, and input dialogs, which are provided by the methods showMessageDialog, showConfirmDialog, and showInputDialog, respectively. In addition, the showOptionDialog method allows more user control over the options available with a confirmation dialog.

17.10.1   The showMessageDialog method

Message dialogs are entirely informational. They offer the user the opportunity to read a message and then dismiss the dialog by clicking on an "OK" button, but no other choice of actions. Figure 17.11 shows the message dialog that is produced by the example in Code 17.17.

The arguments to showMessageDialog are common to most of the other dialog methods, so we shall describe them in some detail here. The first argument is a Component that is used to provide a relative position for the dialog. In addition, the Frame to which the component belongs will be used as the dialog's parent frame. The second argument is the message to be displayed in the dialog. While this will usually

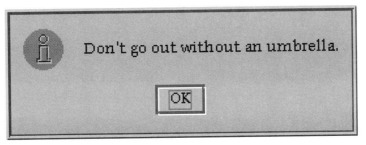

Figure 17.11 An informational message dialog using
`showMessageDialog(SwingOptionMain1.java)`

Code 17.17   Displaying a message dialog when a button is pressed
(`SwingOptionFrame1.java`)

```java
import javax.swing.*;
import java.awt.*;
import java.awt.event.*;

        // Display a Message Dialog when a button is pressed.
class SwingOptionFrame1 extends JFrame {
    public SwingOptionFrame1() {
        final int width = 300, height = 100;
        setSize(width,height);
        final Container contents = getContentPane();

        // A button to trigger the message.
        JButton advice = new JButton("Advice");
        advice.addActionListener(new ActionListener(){
            public void actionPerformed(ActionEvent e){
                JOptionPane.showMessageDialog(
                        contents,
                        "Don't go out without an umbrella.",
                        "Helpful Advice",
                        JOptionPane.INFORMATION_MESSAGE);
            }
        });

        // A panel to hold the buttons in the frame.
        JPanel panel = new QuitJPanel();
        panel.add(advice);
        contents.add(panel,"South");
    }
}
```

be a string, the formal argument type is Object, and we discuss the effect of this
below. The remaining three arguments—a string that is used as a title for the dialog,
an integer option type, and an Icon—are all optional, and we have omitted the Icon
in this particular case. The message type may be one of five standard values defined
in the JOptionPane class: ERROR_MESSAGE, INFORMATION_MESSAGE, WARNING_-
MESSAGE, QUESTION_MESSAGE, and PLAIN_MESSAGE. If the title, message type,

and icon arguments are all omitted, an INFORMATION_MESSAGE is assumed. The look, and, feel manager should be able to provide a representative icon to include in the dialog based upon the message type. Only if you wish to supply your own image is it necessary to use the Icon argument, therefore. It is up to you to choose which message type best suits the information you are giving the user.

A rather interesting effect results from using something other than a simple string for the second (message) argument:

- A Component object is displayed in its normal representation.
- An Icon is displayed within a label.
- The contents of an array are displayed vertically.
- Any other object is displayed via the string it returns from its toString method.

These rules are applied recursively in the case of an array. Figure 17.12 shows the result of passing an array of strings as the message argument.

17.10.2   The showConfirmDialog method

Unlike a message dialog, a confirmation dialog allows the user to choose from two or more courses of action as a result of pressing a button in the dialog. The show-ConfirmDialog method of JOptionPane is very similar to the showMessage-Dialog method, but with the addition of an integer "option type" argument immediately after the title argument. This argument determines how many option buttons will appear in the dialog, their labels, and their meanings. Figure 17.13 shows a confirmation dialog containing a WARNING_MESSAGE. This dialog was produced by the statements shown in Code 17.18.

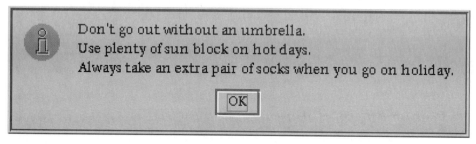

Figure 17.12   Displaying an array of strings in a message dialog (SwingOptionMain2.java)

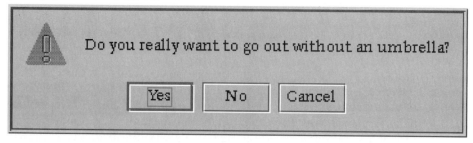

Figure 17.13   A YES_NO_CANCEL confirmation dialog (SwingOptionMain3.java)

Code 17.18   Displaying a YES_NO_CANCEL confirmation dialog (`SwingOptionFrame3.java`)

```
         // Display a Confirm Dialog when a button is pressed.
class SwingOptionFrame3 extends JFrame {
    public SwingOptionFrame3() {
        ...
        JButton advice = new JButton("Advice");
        advice.addActionListener(new ActionListener(){
            public void actionPerformed(ActionEvent e){
                int choice = JOptionPane.showConfirmDialog(
                        contents,
                        "Do you really want to go out without an umbrella?",
                        "Sanity Check",
                        JOptionPane.YES_NO_CANCEL_OPTION,
                        JOptionPane.WARNING_MESSAGE);
                switch(choice){
                    case JOptionPane.CANCEL_OPTION:
                        System.out.println("Ok, think again.");
                        break;
                    case JOptionPane.CLOSED_OPTION:
                        System.out.println("You'll regret it.");
                        break;
                    case JOptionPane.NO_OPTION:
                        System.out.println("A wise decision.");
                        break;
                    case JOptionPane.YES_OPTION:
                        System.out.println("You'll regret it.");
                        break;
                }
            }
        });
        ...
    }
}
```

The available option types for the fourth argument are `DEFAULT_OPTION`, `YES_NO_OPTION`, `YES_NO_CANCEL_OPTION`, and `OK_CANCEL_OPTION`. This method returns an integer that indicates which option the user chose, or whether the dialog window was closed (`CLOSED_OPTION`). The value returned for the "Yes" button (`YES_OPTION`) is identical to that returned for the "OK" button (`OK_OPTION`) so it is not possible to use both in a switch statement.

Using an option type of `DEFAULT_OPTION` produces a dialog equivalent to a message dialog, and omitting all but the parent and message arguments produces a `YES_NO_CANCEL_OPTION` dialog.

17.10.3   The `showInputDialog` method

The `showInputDialog` method creates a dialog that allows user input. The set of arguments is closest in form to those of a message dialog, with two important (optional) additions. In its simplest form, the user is invited to enter input into a text field, which is returned from the method in a reference of type Object. Figure 17.14

Figure 17.14   An ERROR_MESSAGE input dialog (SwingOptionMain4.java)

Code 17.19   Displaying an ERROR_MESSAGE input dialog (SwingOptionFrame4.java)

```
        // Display an Input Dialog when a button is pressed.
class SwingOptionFrame4 extends JFrame {
    public SwingOptionFrame4() {
        ...
        // A button to trigger the dialog.
        JButton locate = new JButton("Locate");
        locate.addActionListener(new ActionListener(){
            public void actionPerformed(ActionEvent e){
                Object response = JOptionPane.showInputDialog(
                        contents,
                        "www.jawasoft.com not found",
                        "Please supply a new URL",
                        JOptionPane.ERROR_MESSAGE);
                if(response == null){
                    System.out.println(
                        "The dialog was closed or cancelled.");
                }
                else if(response instanceof String){
                    String s = (String) response;
                    System.out.println("You typed: "+s);
                }
                else{
                    System.out.println("You selected: "+
                                        response.toString());
                }
            }
        });
        ...
    }
}
```

shows a confirmation dialog containing a ERROR_MESSAGE. This dialog was produced by the statements shown in Code 17.19. If the dialog is closed or cancelled, then a null reference is returned.

Two further arguments allow an array of selection values and an initial selection value to be offered to the user by the dialog. Code 17.20 shows the relevant statements to use this form of the method.

Code 17.20   Supplying an array of possible values in an input dialog
(`SwingOptionFrame5.java`)

```
        // Display an Input Dialog when a button is pressed.
        // The dialog offers the user a choice of input values.
class SwingOptionFrame5 extends JFrame {
    public SwingOptionFrame5() {
        ...
        // Some possible responses to offer the user.
        final String[] locations = {
            "www.javasoft.com",
            "www.netscape.com",
            "www.infoseek.com",
        };

        // A button to trigger the dialog.
        JButton locate = new JButton("Locate");
        locate.addActionListener(new ActionListener(){
            public void actionPerformed(ActionEvent e){
                Object response = JOptionPane.showInputDialog(
                        contents,
                        "www.jawasoft.com not found",
                        "Please supply a new URL",
                        JOptionPane.ERROR_MESSAGE,
                        (Icon) null,
                        locations,
                        locations[0]);
                if(response == null){
                    System.out.println(
                                "The dialog was closed or cancelled.");
                }
                else if(response instanceof String){
                    String s = (String) response;
                    System.out.println("You selected: "+s);
                }
                else{
                    System.out.println("You selected: "+
                                        response.toString());
                }
            }
        });
        ...
    }
}
```

Notice that it is necessary to supply an Icon using this form, because of the position that the selection values take in the argument list. However, a `null` reference is perfectly acceptable. The array of possible values will be offered to the user in an appropriate component. Figure 17.15 shows these particular options in a `JComboBox` (Section 17.23). The final argument of this form of the method specifies which of the list of values will be shown by default.

Figure 17.15   An input dialog with selection values
(SwingOptionMain5.java)

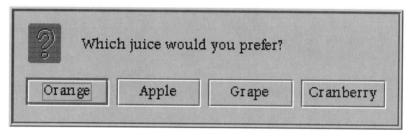

Figure 17.16   An option dialog with arbitrary button labels
(SwingOptionMain6.java)

17.10.4   The showOptionDialog method

There is only one version of the showOptionDialog method, and this takes eight
arguments. The first six match those of a confirmation dialog—parent component,
message, title, option type, message type, and icon. These are followed by an array
of Object references—the options—and a single Object reference—the initial value.
The array of objects is used to create a set of buttons. If the objects are strings then
these will provide the labels for the buttons. Figure 17.16 shows an option dialog
created by the example in Code 17.21.

Code 17.21   Creating an option dialog with arbitrary labels (SwingOptionFrame6.java)

```
import javax.swing.*;
import java.awt.*;
import java.awt.event.*;

        // Display an Option Dialog when a button is pressed.
        // The dialog offers the user a choice of different options.
class SwingOptionFrame6 extends JFrame {
    public SwingOptionFrame6() {
        final int width = 300, height = 100;
        setSize(width,height);
        final Container contents = getContentPane();

        // The button labels.
        final Object[] options = {
```

Code 17.21   (*Continued*)

```
            "Orange",
            "Apple",
            "Grape",
            "Cranberry",
    };

    // A button to trigger the dialog.
    JButton activity = new JButton("Drink");
    activity.addActionListener(new ActionListener(){
        public void actionPerformed(ActionEvent e){
            int choice = JOptionPane.showOptionDialog(
                    contents,
                    "Which juice would you prefer?",
                    "Drink Choice",
                    JOptionPane.DEFAULT_OPTION,
                    JOptionPane.QUESTION_MESSAGE,
                    (Icon) null,
                    options,
                    options[0]);
            if(choice >= 0){
                System.out.println("You selected: "+options[choice]);
            }
            else{
                System.out.println("You selected: "+choice);
            }
        }
    });
    ...
  }
}
```

If an array argument is supplied, the option type argument is ignored, so we have chosen DEFAULT_OPTION as an arbitrary value. When one of the buttons is selected, an integer index into the array of options is returned. If the dialog is closed without a selection, then −1 is returned, the value of CLOSED_OPTION. Clearly, this value should be excluded before indexing directly into the array. The initial value argument is used to indicate which of the options should have the input focus by default.

It is not necessary for the options array to contain strings; any Object will do, so Icons are possible, as well as any other Component type.

17.11   Swing Layout Managers

Swing adds further layout managers to those available with the AWT: BoxLayout and OverlayLayout. In addition, the Box and JLayeredPane classes are components used to achieve particular layouts.

17.11.1   The BoxLayout Class

The BoxLayout layout manager can be used as a convenient alternative to a Grid-Layout which has a single row or column. A BoxLayout layout manager is created

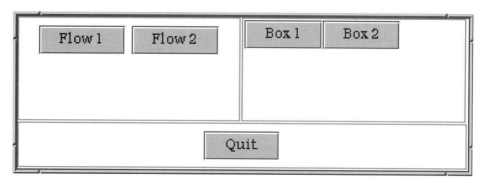

Figure 17.17 Contrasting BoxLayout with FlowLayout (`SwingBoxMain1.java`)

slightly differently from other layout managers in that the component to be managed is passed to its constructor. This is required in addition to the usual setting of a container's layout manager with its `setLayout` method. Code 17.22 shows an example which serves to illustrate the contrast between a BoxLayout and FlowLayout. The initial appearance of this application is shown in Figure 17.17.

Code 17.22   Side-by-side panels with BoxLayout and FlowLayout layout managers (`SwingBoxFrame1.java`)

```
import javax.swing.*;
import javax.swing.border.*;
import java.awt.*;

    // Illustrate the effect of BoxLayout compared with FlowLayout.
    // Place two pairs of buttons in panels managed by different
    // layout managers.
class SwingBoxFrame1 extends JFrame {
    public SwingBoxFrame1() {
        final int width = 375, height = 150;
        setSize(width,height);

        Container contents = getContentPane();

        // This panel will use the default FlowLayout.
        JPanel flowPanel = new JPanel();
        flowPanel.setBorder(new EtchedBorder(EtchedBorder.LOWERED));

        // This panel will use a horizontal BoxLayout.
        JPanel boxPanel = new JPanel();
        boxPanel.setLayout(new BoxLayout(boxPanel,BoxLayout.X_AXIS));
        boxPanel.setBorder(new EtchedBorder(EtchedBorder.LOWERED));

        // Add two buttons to each panel.
        flowPanel.add(new JButton("Flow 1"));
        flowPanel.add(new JButton("Flow 2"));
        boxPanel.add(new JButton("Box 1"));
        boxPanel.add(new JButton("Box 2"));
```

Code 17.22   (*Continued*)

```
    // Place the two panels side-by-side within a central panel.

    JPanel centerPanel = new JPanel();
    final int rows = 1, cols = 2;
    centerPanel.setLayout(new GridLayout(rows,cols));
    centerPanel.add(flowPanel);
    centerPanel.add(boxPanel);

    contents.add(centerPanel,"Center");
    contents.add(new QuitJPanel(),"South");
  }
}
```

The BoxLayout used to managed the contents of boxPanel will lay out its components horizontally (X_AXIS), as opposed to vertically (Y_AXIS). Initially, there is sufficient width in the frame for both panels to lay out their contents horizontally. If the width is reduced, however, the available horizontal space may be insufficient (Figure 17.18). In this case, the flow layout manager is able to reorganize its components vertically, whereas the box layout manager does not have that freedom. In Section 17.11.2, we discuss some of the ways in some degree of variation may be exercised in laying out components within a box layout.

17.11.2   The Box Class

The Box class is a sub class of Container, managed by a BoxLayout layout manager. Its constructor takes a single X_AXIS or Y_AXIS argument (defined in BoxLayout). Its static createHorizontalBox and createVerticalBox methods provide an alternative means of creating a Box object. It provides further methods that add additional flexibility to the way in which components are arranged by the layout manager. These are based on the idea of creating invisible components that take up part of

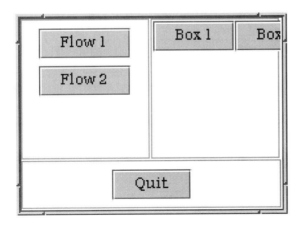

Figure 17.18   Insufficient width for a horizontal box layout (SwingBoxMain1.java)

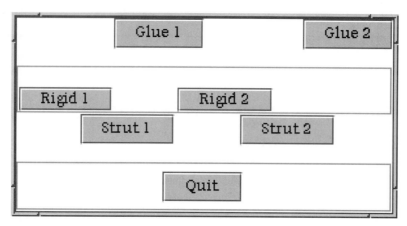

Figure 17.19 Diverse spacing of components within horizontal boxes
(SwingBoxMain2.java)

the available space within the container, and hence force the visible components
into particular arrangements. The example in Code 17.23 illustrates each of the three
types of invisible components: *glue*, *rigid areas*, and *struts*. Its appearance is shown
in Figure 17.19.

Code 17.23   Varieties of spacer within containers managed by horizontal BoxLayouts
(SwingBoxFrame2.java)

```java
import javax.swing.*;
import javax.swing.border.*;
import java.awt.*;

    // Compare the effects of glue, rigid areas and struts
    // within two Boxes and a JPanel.
class SwingBoxFrame2 extends JFrame {
    public SwingBoxFrame2() {
        final int width = 300, height = 175;
        setSize(width, height);

        Container contents = getContentPane();

        // This box will contain horizontal glue.
        Box glueBox = Box.createHorizontalBox();
        glueBox.add(Box.createHorizontalGlue());
        glueBox.add(new JButton("Glue 1"));
        glueBox.add(Box.createHorizontalGlue());
        glueBox.add(new JButton("Glue 2"));

        // This panel will contain rigid areas. Use a bordered panel in
        // order to show the relative size of each area, and the positioning
        // of the buttons within them.
        JPanel rigidPanel = new JPanel();
        rigidPanel.setBorder(new EtchedBorder(EtchedBorder.LOWERED));
        rigidPanel.setLayout(new BoxLayout(rigidPanel, BoxLayout.X_AXIS));
```

Code 17.23   *(Continued)*

```
        rigidPanel.add(new JButton("Rigid 1"));
        // Separate the two buttons.
        final int areaWidth = 50, areaHeight = 40;
        rigidPanel.add(Box.createRigidArea(
                        new Dimension(areaWidth,areaHeight)));
        rigidPanel.add(new JButton("Rigid 2"));

        // This box will contain horizontal struts.
        Box strutBox = Box.createHorizontalBox();
        final int strutWidth = 50;
        // Fix the first button from the left side.
        strutBox.add(Box.createHorizontalStrut(strutWidth));
        strutBox.add(new JButton("Strut 1"));
        // Fix the second button from the first.
        strutBox.add(Box.createHorizontalStrut(strutWidth));
        strutBox.add(new JButton("Strut 2"));

        // Place the three containers vertically within a panel.
        JPanel centerPanel = new JPanel();
        final int rows = 3, cols = 1;
        centerPanel.setLayout(new GridLayout(rows,cols));
        centerPanel.add(glueBox);
        centerPanel.add(rigidPanel);
        centerPanel.add(strutBox);

        contents.add(centerPanel,"Center");
        JPanel quitPanel = new QuitJPanel();
        contents.add(quitPanel,"South");
    }
}
```

The three types of invisible components are available in the following ways via methods of the Box class:

- *glue*—createGlue, createHorizontalGlue, and createVertical-Glue. Glue expands to take up any leftover space around components. Horizontal glue inserted into a horizontal box has differing effects, depending upon where it is placed. As the first component, it will tend to push the remaining components to the right. Inserted as the last component, it will push them to the left. Inserted between components, it will act as a spacer. An analogous effect is obtained with vertical glue in a vertical box.
- *rigid areas*—createRigidArea. This method takes a single Dimension argument. A rigid area has a fixed width and height. It both provides spacing between components in one direction and enforces a minimum spacing in the other direction. Using a value of zero for the height in a horizontal box, or the width in a vertical box, will give a similar effect as using a strut, but without further constraining the other overall dimension of the container. Figure 17.19 illustrates the effect on the visible components if there is insufficient space to

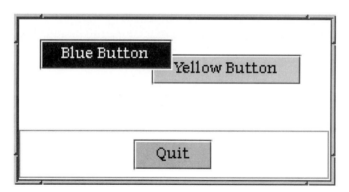

Figure 17.20   Overlapping buttons using an OverlayLayout
layout manager (`SwingOverlayMain.java`)

accommodate the height of a rigid area within a horizontal box layout; notice
that the two buttons in the second layer are slightly squashed.

- *struts*—`createHorizontalStrut` and `createVerticalStrut`. These
  provide a fixed-size spacer between adjacent components, or from the edge
  of the container. Resizing the container has no effect on the size of the strut.

Each method returns a Component reference that is added directly to a Box or other
container.

17.11.3   The OverlayLayout Class

Layout managers usually arrange components within a container so that they do not
overlap. The `JLayeredPane` class provides a class that allows overlapping components, but it does this by not having a layout manager. In contrast, the `Overlay-
Layout` class provides a regular layout manager that allows components to over-
lap. All JComponents have an *alignment point* that can be determined using their
`getAlignmentX` and `getAlignmentY` accessors inherited from their `Container`
super class.[3] These are values of type `float`. The Component class defines names
for standard alignments: `BOTTOM_ALIGNMENT` (1.0), `CENTER_ALIGNMENT` (0.5),
`LEFT_ALIGNMENT` (0.0), `RIGHT_ALIGNMENT` (1.0), and `TOP_ALIGNMENT` (0.0).

When an OverlayLayout object is constructed, a reference to the container
it is to manage must be passed as an argument. When components are added to
the container, the layout manager will overlap them about their alignment points.
Code 17.24 shows an example that uses an overlay layout manager. Figure 17.20
shows the effect this produces.

The alignment point for the `blueButton` is halfway from its top, and in the
final quarter of its width. The alignment point for `yellowButton` is its top left
corner. (Note that floating point literals—`0.85F` and `0.50F`—have been used in
order to match the formal argument types of the alignment methods.)

---

[3] At the time of writing, the corresponding mutators are only implemented by the JComponent
class, rather than its super class.

Code 17.24   Using an OverlayLayout layout manager to overlap components
(`SwingOverlayFrame.java`)

```
import javax.swing.*;
import java.awt.*;

        // Illustrate an OverlayLayout layout manager to
        // overlap components.
        // Two buttons are overlapped within a panel.
class SwingOverlayFrame extends JFrame {
    public SwingOverlayFrame() {
        final int width = 250, height = 150;
        setSize(width,height);

        Container contents = getContentPane();

        // Create two buttons to be overlapped.
        JComponent blueButton = new JButton("Blue Button");
        blueButton.setBackground(Color.blue);
        blueButton.setForeground(Color.white);

        JComponent yellowButton = new JButton("Yellow Button");
        yellowButton.setBackground(Color.yellow);

        // Set the alignment points.
        blueButton.setAlignmentX(0.85F);
        blueButton.setAlignmentY(0.50F);
        yellowButton.setAlignmentX(Component.LEFT_ALIGNMENT);
        yellowButton.setAlignmentY(Component.TOP_ALIGNMENT);

        // Add them to a panel with an OverlayLayout
        // layout manager.
        JPanel centerPanel = new JPanel();
        centerPanel.setLayout(new OverlayLayout(centerPanel));
        centerPanel.add(blueButton);
        centerPanel.add(yellowButton);

        contents.add(centerPanel,"Center");
        contents.add(new QuitJPanel(),"South");
    }
}
```

An overlay layout manager uses the minimum size of each component in calculating how to lay out the contents of a container. In the example in Code 17.24, the minimum size of the buttons can be calculated from their labels. For some other components (panels, for instance), it will be necessary to set an explicit minimum size, using their `setPreferredSize` method, before adding them to their container.

17.11.4   The JLayeredPane Class

The `JLayeredPane` class is not a layout manager, but it provides layout functionality; in particular, the ability to place components in layers and manipulate the layers to change the nested ordering of those components. In addition, a single layer may

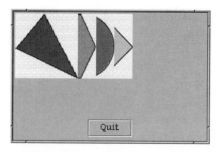

Figure 17.21   Four images within a single layer

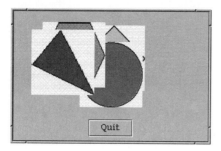

Figure 17.22   The images' positions within their layer have been altered

contain multiple components, and the position of a component within a layer may be altered. We shall start by illustrating positioning within a single layer, before discussing the role of multiple layers. Figure 17.21 illustrates an application in which four images have been placed in a JLayeredPane so that they overlap. The images occupy the same layer, which is known as the DEFAULT_LAYER. Figure 17.22 shows the state of the application after the positions of these images within their layer have been altered several times. Code 17.25 shows a class that places a JLayeredPane in the center of its content pane and displays each image within a JLabel.

Code 17.25   A Frame containing a JLayeredPane to show overlapping images (`SwingLayerFrame1.java`)

```
import javax.swing.*;
import java.awt.*;
import java.awt.event.*;

    // Display a layer of images in a JLayeredPane.
    // The names of the image files should be passed to
    // the constructor.
class SwingLayerFrame1 extends JFrame {
    public SwingLayerFrame1(String[] images) {
        final int width = 275, height = 200;
        setSize(width,height);
        final Container contents = getContentPane();

        // Place a JLayeredPane within the frame to manage the
        // layering.
        contents.add(getPane(),"Center");
```

Code 17.25   (*Continued*)

```
    setupImages(images);

    contents.add(new QuitJPanel(),"South");
}

    // Place a component holding each image into the layered pane.
protected void setupImages(String[] images){
    final Container contents = getContentPane();
    final JLayeredPane pane = getPane();
    // Where to place the first image.
    final int initialX = 2, initialY = 2;
    // By how much to offset each image from the previous one.
    final int initialXOffset = 25;
    // Where to locate each image.
    Point initialLocation = new Point(initialX,initialY);

    final int numImages = images.length;
    for(int i = 0; i < numImages; i++){
        final JComponent image = createImage(images[i]);
        // Without a layout manager, we set the required size
        // explicitly.
        image.setSize(image.getPreferredSize());
        image.setLocation(initialLocation);
        pane.add(image);

        // Place the next in a different initial location.
        initialLocation.x += initialXOffset;
    }
}

    // Locate the image in a JLabel.
    // The component should listen for mouse clicks and move
    // itself as a result.
    // This is used to illustrate some of the within-layer
    // methods of JLayeredPane.
protected JComponent createImage(String imageFile){
    final JLabel label = new JLabel(new ImageIcon(imageFile));
    label.addMouseListener(new MouseAdapter(){
        public void mousePressed(MouseEvent e){
            final JLayeredPane pane = getPane();
            // Where is this component within its layer?
            int position = pane.getPosition(label);
            // Where is this position within the container.
            Point where = label.getLocation();
            if(position == 0){
                // Shift it right and down slightly.
                final int shiftOffset = 2;
                where.x += shiftOffset;
                where.y += shiftOffset;
            }
            else{
                // Move it up one layer.
```

(*Continued*)

Code 17.25   (*Continued*)

```
                    pane.setPosition(label,position-1);
                }
                label.setLocation(where);
            }
        });
        return label;
    }


    protected JLayeredPane getPane(){
        return pane;
    }

    // The (layered) pane in which the labels will be stored.
    private final JLayeredPane pane = new JLayeredPane();
}
```

By default, a JLayeredPane has no layout manager, so we have explicitly set the size and position of each component before adding it to the pane. The location of each component has been offset slightly from the others in order to show that components can overlap each other arbitrarily. We have illustrated movement within layers by attaching a MouseListener to each label. The listener responds to mouse clicks.

When a component is added to a layer, it is given a position at the back of the current set of components within the same layer. Position 0 is the uppermost. Code 17.25 illustrates both the getPosition and the setPosition methods of the layered pane. Both methods take a reference to the component as an argument. In this example, when the mouse is clicked over an image that is not at the top of its layer, it is raised by one position. In the case of the image at the top of the layer, its position is shifted down and right when clicked over. The method moveToFront is equivalent to using setPosition with a position value of 0. The method moveToBack is equivalent to setting a position value of −1.

The example in Code 17.25 places all components within a single layer and does not make full use of the layering capabilities of a JLayeredPane. The class is able to manage a set of numbered layers, with components in higher numbered layers always appearing above those in lower numbered layers. It is important not to be confused by a component's layer and its position within a layer. A component's place in a hierarchy of components is determined firstly by its layer number, and then its position within that layer. While the actual numbers used for layers can be arbitrary, the class defines a set of named Integer objects for layers common to many applications. These are DEFAULT_LAYER (0), DRAG_LAYER (400), FRAME_CONTENT_-LAYER (−30000), MODAL_LAYER (200), PALETTE_LAYER, (100), and POPUP_LAYER (300). The names reflect the purposes for which the layers are used for components within standard applications, with dragged components appearing on the top of an application, popup components above modal components, and so on. Layer numbers between 0 and 99 are a reasonable set for user layers. Care must be taken in distinguishing between the occasions when a layer number is represented as a primitive int value or as an Integer object. We shall see both uses in the following example.

Code 17.26 shows part of an application that is similar to the one shown in Code 17.25.

Code 17.26   Placing a component within a particular layer of a JLayeredPane (`SwingLayerFrame2.java`)

```java
import javax.swing.*;
import java.awt.*;
import java.awt.event.*;

    // Display layers of images in a JLayeredPane.
    // The names of the image files should be passed to
    // the constructor.
class SwingLayerFrame2 extends JFrame {
    ...
        // Place a component holding each image into the layered pane.
    protected void setupImages(String[] images){
        final Container contents = getContentPane();
        final JLayeredPane pane = getPane();
        // Where to place the first image.
        final int initialX = 2, initialY = 2;
        // By how much to offset each image from the previous one.
        final int initialXOffset = 25;
        // Where to locate each image.
        Point initialLocation = new Point(initialX,initialY);
        // Which layer to place the next image in.
        int nextLayer = JLayeredPane.DEFAULT_LAYER.intValue();

        final int numImages = images.length;
        for(int i = 0; i < numImages; i++){
            final JComponent image = new JLabel(new ImageIcon(images[i]));
            // Without a layout manager, we set the require size
            // explicitly.
            image.setSize(image.getPreferredSize());
            image.setLocation(initialLocation);

            // Add it to its own layer.
            pane.add(image,new Integer(nextLayer));

            // Attach a mouse listener to it that will enable the
            // image to be moved around.
            new SwingMouseResponder(image);

            // Place the next in a different initial location and layer.
            initialLocation.x += initialXOffset;
            nextLayer++;
        }
    }
    ...
}
```

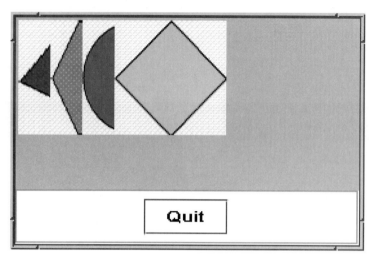

Figure 17.23   A series of images, each in its own layer (SwingLayerMain2.java)

This time, each JLabel has been added to the pane with a second Integer argument, which contains the number of the layer it is to occupy. This corresponds to the add method the JLayeredPane class inherits from its Container super class, which takes a second Object constraints argument. The result of the for loop in setupImages will be to place each image in its own layer, with the later images above the lower ones. Figure 17.23 illustrates the initial appearance of this application. Notice that the appearance is not dissimilar to that of the previous application shown in Figure 17.21, illustrating that (visually) there is no difference between components occupying the same layer or different layers. The practical differences have been illustrated in this example by attaching a SwingMouseResponder object to each image as it is added to the layered frame (see Code 17.27). This class is based on the MouseResponder example, which was used to draw on AWT components in Chapter 16.

Code 17.27   Allow a component in a JLayeredPane to be manipulated
(SwingMouseResponder.java)

```
import javax.swing.*;
import java.awt.Point;
import java.awt.event.*;

    // Implement free-hand movement of the given component.
    // This is assumed to be contained within a JLayeredPane.

class SwingMouseResponder implements MouseListener, MouseMotionListener {
    SwingMouseResponder(JComponent component){
        setComponent(component);
        // Listen for mouse events on the component.
        component.addMouseListener(this);
    }

        // The MouseListener methods.
    public void mousePressed(MouseEvent e){
        // Pick up the point and remember it.
```

Code 17.27   (*Continued*)

```
        setLastMousePoint(e.getPoint());
        setMoving(true);

        // Bring it to the top of its layer.
        final JComponent c = getComponent();
        final JLayeredPane pane = (JLayeredPane) c.getParent();
        pane.setPosition(c,0);
    }

        // Complete the final movement and finish moving.
    public void mouseReleased(MouseEvent e){
        if(getMoving()){
            moveToPoint(e.getPoint());
            setMoving(false);
        }
    }

        // Respond to a double click.
        // If the component is in the highest layer, move it to the bottom,
        // otherwise move it up one layer.
    public void mouseClicked(MouseEvent e){
        if(e.getClickCount() > 1){
            final JComponent c = getComponent();
            final JLayeredPane pane = (JLayeredPane) c.getParent();
            final int layer = pane.getLayer(c);
            if(layer == pane.highestLayer()){
                // Place it at the bottom of the lowest layer.
                pane.setLayer(c,pane.lowestLayer());
            }
            else{
                // Place it topmost within the next layer up.
                pane.setLayer(c,layer+1,0);
            }
        }
    }

    public void mouseEntered(MouseEvent e){
        // Not interested in this event.
    }

    public void mouseExited(MouseEvent e){
        // Cancel any movement.
        setMoving(false);
    }

        // The MouseMotionListener methods
        // These will only be active if we are moving.
    public void mouseDragged(MouseEvent e){
        moveToPoint(e.getPoint());
    }

    public void mouseMoved(MouseEvent e){
        moveToPoint(e.getPoint());
    }

        // Move from the current point by the relative distance
        // from lastMousePoint to p2.
        // Make p2 the new lastMousePoint.
```

(Continued)

```java
    protected void moveToPoint(Point p2){
        final Point p1 = getLastMousePoint();
        // Calculate the offset.
        final int xdiff = p2.x-p1.x, ydiff = p2.y-p1.y;
        // Apply it to the component's current position.
        final JComponent c = getComponent();
        final Point loc = c.getLocation();
        loc.x += xdiff;
        loc.y += ydiff;
        c.setLocation(loc);
    }

    protected JComponent getComponent(){
        return component;
    }

    protected void setComponent(JComponent c){
        component = c;
    }

    protected boolean getMoving(){
        return moving;
    }

        // Make sure this represents a change of state.
        // Changing the state requires that we either listen
        // for mouse motion events, or stop doing so.
    protected void setMoving(boolean m){
        if(m != moving){
            final JComponent c = getComponent();
            if(m){
                c.addMouseMotionListener(this);
            }
            else{
                c.removeMouseMotionListener(this);
            }
            moving = m;
        }
    }

    protected Point getLastMousePoint(){
        return lastMousePoint;
    }

    protected void setLastMousePoint(Point p){
        lastMousePoint = p;
    }

    // Are we moving at the moment?
    private boolean moving = false;
    // Where the mouse last moved to.
    Point lastMousePoint;
    // The component to be moved.
    private JComponent component;
}
```

SwingMouseResponder listens for mouse events on its attached component. When a mouse button is pressed, it allows the component to be dragged within its container. When a mouse button is pressed over an image (`mousePressed`), it is raised to the top of its layer, but its layer is not changed. As a consequence, it remains behind any components in layers with higher numbers. The `mouseClicked` method shows how a component's layer may be manipulated. If the mouse is double-clicked over an image, its current layer is obtained via the layered pane's `getLayer` method. This is compared with the number of the highest layer containing any components (`highestLayer`). If it is already in the highest layer, then it is pushed down to the bottom of the lowest layer with `setLayer`. Otherwise, it is raised to the top of a layer with the next numeric value—which could currently have no components in it. Notice that all of these methods for manipulating layers, apart from the original `add`, use primitive `int` values, rather than Integer objects.

17.11.5   The JDesktopPane and JInternalFrame Classes

The `JDesktopPane` class is a specialized sub class of JLayeredPane whose purpose is to provide virtual desktop management within its containing frame. It is common for objects of this class to contain `JInternalFrame` objects. JInternalFrame defines a lightweight frame with very similar structure and functionality to the JFrame class. Code 17.28 shows a class that is similar to that shown in Code 17.26, but with each image added to a JInternalFrame within a JDesktopPane. The effect is shown in Figure 17.24.

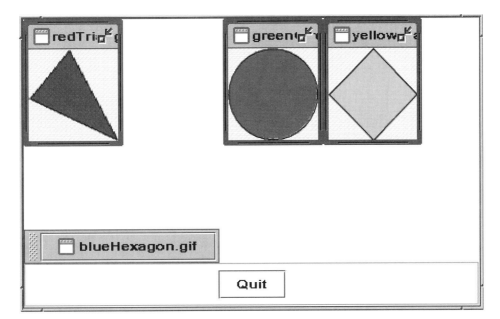

Figure 17.24   JInternalFrame objects in a JDesktopPane (`SwingLayerMain3.java`)

```java
import javax.swing.*;
import java.awt.*;

    // Display the images within their own JInternalFrame
    // in a JDesktopPane.
class SwingLayerFrame3 extends JFrame {
    public SwingLayerFrame3(String[] images) {
        final int width = 475, height = 250;
        setSize(width,height);
        final Container contents = getContentPane();

        // Place a JDesktopPane within the frame to manage the
        // layering.
        contents.add(getPane(),"Center");

        setupImages(images);

        contents.add(new QuitJPanel(),"South");
    }

        // Place a component holding each image into a separate
        // JInternalFrame in the desktop pane.
    protected void setupImages(String[] images){
        final Container contents = getContentPane();
        final JDesktopPane desktop = getPane();
        // Where to place the first internal frame.
        final int initialX = 0, initialY = 0;
        // Where to locate each internal frame.
        Point initialLocation = new Point(initialX,initialY);

        final int numImages = images.length;
        for(int i = 0; i < numImages; i++){
            final JComponent image = new JLabel(new ImageIcon(images[i]));
            // Set the image's preferred size.
            image.setSize(image.getPreferredSize());

            // Create an internal frame to hold the image.
            JInternalFrame imageFrame = new JInternalFrame();

            // Add the image to the frame's content pane.
            imageFrame.getContentPane().add(image);
            imageFrame.setLocation(initialLocation);
            imageFrame.setResizable(true);
            imageFrame.setIconifiable(true);
            imageFrame.setTitle(images[i]);

            imageFrame.pack();

            // Add all frames to the same layer.
            desktop.add(imageFrame);

            // Place the next directly alongside.
            initialLocation.x += imageFrame.getSize().width;
```

Code 17.28   (*Continued*)

```
        }
    }

    protected JDesktopPane getPane(){
        return desktop;
    }

    // The desktop in which the labels will be stored.
    private final JDesktopPane desktop = new JDesktopPane();
}
```

A JInternalFrame has a similar internal structure to a JFrame, and components are added to its content pane, rather than directly to the frame itself. A JInternalFrame may have a range of properties set on it. The example in Code 17.28 turns on the ability to resize and minimize the internal frames, and sets a title for each based upon the name of the image it is displaying. The effect of minimizing one of these frames can be seen in Figure 17.24.

17.11.6   The JApplet Class

Applets, in general, are discussed in Chapter 20. Those built with the Swing classes should extend JApplet, which is a sub class of the Applet class. As with the JFrame class, components are added to the JApplet's content pane, rather than to the JApplet itself. Code 20.4 contains an example.

17.11.7   The JRootPane Class

It is the JRootPane class that is responsible for managing the overall contents of the four heavyweight Swing containers— JApplet, JDialog, JFrame, and JWindow—in addition to the single lightweight container—JInternalFrame. A root pane contains a glass pane and a layered pane. The glass pane is an invisible pane placed directly above the remaining contents of the container, and always covering its full area. It is the glass pane that is responsible for intercepting mouse events, for instance. The layered pane hosts the content pane—to which the container's child components are always added—and an optional menu bar (see Section 17.12). A root pane has its own specialized layout manager that, for instance, resizes the content pane if a menu bar is added to, or removed from, the container.

17.12   The Swing Menu Classes

As you might expect, there are strong similarities between the Swing menu classes and the AWT menu classes, simply because the fundamental roles they play are very similar. However, as we see with other classes, there is an increased generality available with the Swing classes that makes them both easier to use and more flexible.

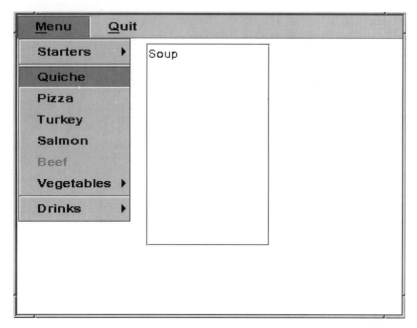

Figure 17.25   A JMenuBar with two JMenus (`SwingMenuMain1.java`)

17.12.1   The JMenuBar Class

The `JMenuBar` class is a sub class of JComponent, so menu bars may be added to any component of a Swing application. This contrasts with the `MenuBar` class of the AWT, which may only be attached to a Frame. Nevertheless, JMenuBars are most commonly attached to JFrame objects, which have a `setJMenuBar` method.[4] The `add` method of JMenuBar receives a `JMenu` object to be added to the bar. The `setHelpMenu` method is provided to receive a Help menu, which look-and-feel managers might choose to treat in a specialized manner. The `getMenu` method may be used to access an individual menu in the menu bar via an integer index.

17.12.2   The JMenu and JMenuItem Classes

The `JMenu` class provides the ability to create sophisticated hierarchical menu structures. Although the obvious components to add to a JMenu are `JMenuItem` objects, several `add` methods are defined to allow menu items to be created from three other types: `Action`, `Component`, and `String`. Since JMenu is a sub class of JMenu-Item, nested menus are easily created. Furthermore, since JMenuItem is a sub class of `AbstractButton`, there are strong similarities between menu items and buttons, particularly in terms of their appearance and response to events. In this section, we provide a brief introduction to some of the capabilities of Swing menus via an application to allow a meal to be chosen from a restaurant menu.

The basic appearance of the application is shown in Figure 17.25. This illustrates a JMenuBar attached to the application's JFrame, and two JMenus attached to the

---

[4] In fact, this method delegates the operation to the equivalent method of JRootPane.

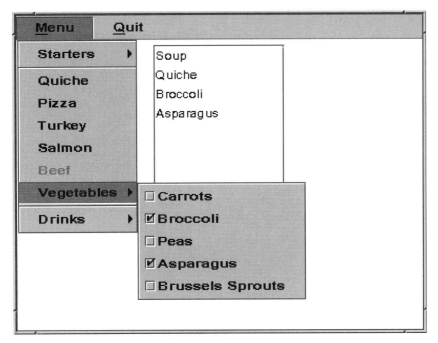

Figure 17.26   An example of JCheckBoxMenuItems in a menu

menu bar. In the center of the frame is a JList to which items are added from the menu as they are selected. The first menu is divided into three areas; the upper and lower areas consist of submenus (indicated by the arrow symbols to the right of "Starters" and "Drinks"). The central area consists of five JMenuItems and a further submenu. The "Beef" menu item is grayed-out to show that it cannot be selected.

The "Vegetables" submenu is shown in Figure 17.26. This illustrates that one or more JCheckBoxMenuItem objects may be added to a menu, as may JRadio-ButtonMenuItem objects. Both behave in a similar way to the JCheckBox and JRadioButton classes, described in Section 17.7.3 and 17.7.4.

The "Drinks" submenu (Figure 17.27) illustrates that Icons may be associated with menu items, as you might expect from their AbstractButton super class. Code 17.29 contains the frame class that creates the application shown in Figure 17.25 through Figure 17.27.

Code 17.29   An illustration of various JMenu capabilities (`SwingMenuFrame1.java`)

```
import javax.swing.*;
import java.awt.*;
import java.awt.event.*;

        // An illustration of JMenuBar, JMenu and associated
        // menu components.
class SwingMenuFrame1 extends JFrame {
    public SwingMenuFrame1() {
```

(Continued)

Code 17.29   *(Continued)*

```
        final int width = 350, height = 275;
        setSize(width,height);

        JMenuBar bar = new JMenuBar();
        // Place the menu bar.
        setJMenuBar(bar);
        // Add the first menu.
        JMenu foodMenu = createRestaurantMenu();
        foodMenu.setMnemonic('M');
        bar.add(foodMenu);

        // Add a second menu to quit the application.
        JMenu quit = new JMenu("Quit");
        quit.setMnemonic('Q');
        // Allow a second chance.
        quit.add(new JMenuItem("Cancel"));
        // Confirm quitting.
        Action reallyQuit = new AbstractAction("Really quit"){
            public void actionPerformed(ActionEvent e){
                System.exit(0);
            }
        };
        quit.add(reallyQuit);
        bar.add(quit);

        // List the chosen menu items in a central area.
        final int listWidth = 125, listHeight = 200;
        JScrollPane pane = new JScrollPane(getItemList());
        pane.setPreferredSize(new Dimension(listWidth,listHeight));
        JPanel panel = new JPanel();
        panel.add(pane,"Center");
        Container contents = getContentPane();
        contents.add(panel);
    }

    /* Create a JMenu with a set of restaurant menu items.
     * There are three separate areas for Starters, Main Course
     * and Drinks. The first two are nested JMenus.
     */
    protected JMenu createRestaurantMenu(){
        // The menu, to which all items are ultimately added.
        final JMenu menu = new JMenu("Menu");

        // A sub-menu for the starters.
        final JMenu starters = new JMenu("Starters");
        starters.add(new SelectableMenuItem("Soup"));
        starters.add(new SelectableMenuItem("Melon"));
        starters.add(new SelectableMenuItem("Avocado"));
        menu.add(starters);

        menu.addSeparator();

        // The main course choices.  The beef is off.
        menu.add(new SelectableMenuItem("Quiche"));
        menu.add(new SelectableMenuItem("Pizza"));
```

Code 17.29   (*Continued*)

```java
        menu.add(new SelectableMenuItem("Turkey"));
         menu.add(new SelectableMenuItem("Salmon"));
         JMenuItem beef = new SelectableMenuItem("Beef");
         beef.setEnabled(false);
         menu.add(beef);
         // The vegetables are in a sub menu.
         menu.add(setupVegetables());

         menu.addSeparator();

         // The drinks are in a sub menu.
         menu.add(setupDrinks());

         return menu;
    }

         // Allow a selection of vegetables. Any number of
         // these may be chosen.
    protected JMenuItem setupVegetables(){
         final String[] choices = {
              "Carrots", "Broccoli", "Peas", "Asparagus", "Brussels Sprouts",
         };
         final int numVegetables = choices.length;

         // Add each item as a check box.
         final JMenu vegetables = new JMenu("Vegetables");
         for(int i = 0; i < numVegetables; i++){
            final JCheckBoxMenuItem item = new JCheckBoxMenuItem(choices[i]);
              // Listen for selection or deselection and add or remove
              // the item from the application's list.
              item.addItemListener(new ItemListener(){
                   public void itemStateChanged(ItemEvent e){
                        int change = e.getStateChange();
                        // Get the data items for the list.
                        final DefaultListModel model =
                                (DefaultListModel) getItemList().getModel();
                        if(change == ItemEvent.SELECTED){
                            model.addElement(item.getText());
                        }
                        else{
                            model.removeElement(item.getText());
                        }
                   }
              });
              vegetables.add(item);
         }
         return vegetables;
    }

         // Return a menu item for the drinks.
         // Provide a colored icon for each.
    protected JMenuItem setupDrinks(){
         Object[][] choices = {
              {"Apple", Color.green},
```

(*Continued*)

```
            {"Red Grape", Color.red},
            {"White Grape", Color.white},
        };
        final int numDrinks = choices.length;

        final JMenu drinks = new JMenu("Drinks");
        for(int i = 0; i < numDrinks; i++){
            final JMenuItem item = new SelectableMenuItem(
                                (String) choices[i][0],
                                new CircleIcon((Color) choices[i][1]));
            drinks.add(item);
        }
        return drinks;
    }

    /* A JMenuItem that adds its associated text to the
     * central JList when it is selected.
     * By implementing ActionListener, the item can respond
     * to its selection by adding its text to the list.
     */
    protected class SelectableMenuItem extends JMenuItem
                                    implements ActionListener {
        public SelectableMenuItem(String item,Icon icon){
            super(item,icon);
            addActionListener(this);
            // Position the text to the right of the icon.
            setHorizontalTextPosition(JMenuItem.RIGHT);
        }

        public SelectableMenuItem(String item){
            super(item);
            addActionListener(this);
        }

        // Add the text of this item to the list when selected.
        public void actionPerformed(ActionEvent e){
            JMenuItem item = (JMenuItem) e.getSource();
            // Get the data items for the list.
            final DefaultListModel model =
                    (DefaultListModel) getItemList().getModel();
            model.addElement(item.getText());
        }
    }

    protected JList getItemList(){
        return itemList;
    }

    // Which items have been selected from the menu.
    private JList itemList = new JList(new DefaultListModel());
}
```

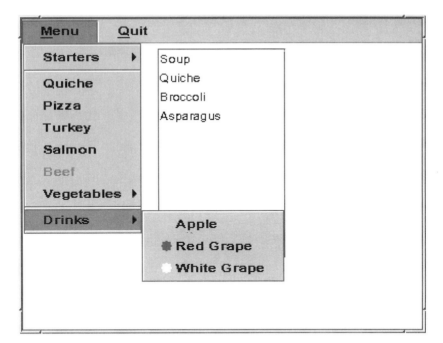

Figure 17.27   Icons may be attached to menu items

The constructor of `SwingMenuFrame1` creates a JMenuBar and adds two menus to it. The first menu is put together in `createRestaurantMenu`. The second menu "`Quit`" contains a "`Cancel`" and "`Really quit`" option. The latter is interesting because it illustrates the way in which `Action` objects may be added to a menu. When a menu receives an object implementing the Action interface, it creates a JMenuItem to associate with it and the argument is registered as an action listener on the item. The effect, here, is that selecting the "`Really quit`" menu item causes the application to exit. A shortcut mnemonic has been associated with both menus via the `setMnemonic` method inherited from Abstract-Button.

Most of the items added to the restaurant menu are JMenuItem objects, but these have been created via the inner class, `SelectableMenuItem`. This has been done because we wish there to be a common action for all menu selections: they should add themselves to the JList that is accumulating selections in the center of the frame. The SelectableMenuItem implements the ActionListener interface for this purpose. If an Icon is associated with a menu item, the appropriate constructor arranges for the icon to be placed to the left of the menu's label. The effect of this can be seen in Figure 17.27.

The `setupVegetables` method creates a number of JCheckBoxMenuItem objects. Associated with each of these is an ItemListener that either adds or removes the menu item from the JList.

The "`Beef`" menu item illustrates that an item may be disabled via the `setEnabled` method. Separators are placed between menu items with the `add-Separator` method of JMenu.

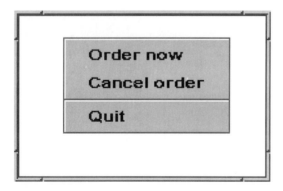

Figure 17.28 A JPopupMenu
(SwingMenuMain2.java)

17.12.3 The JPopupMenu Class

Rather curiously, the JPopupMenu class is not a sub class of either JMenu or JMenuItem, but JComponent. Yet it has a similar set of methods to JMenu. Code 17.30 illustrates how a simple popup menu may be created and popped up when the appropriate trigger is received. The appearance of this menu is shown in Figure 17.28.

Code 17.30 A JPopupMenu, popped up when the appropriate trigger is received (SwingMenuFrame2.java)

```
import javax.swing.*;
import java.awt.*;
import java.awt.event.*;

    // Illustrate a JPopupMenu.
class SwingMenuFrame2 extends JFrame {
    public SwingMenuFrame2() {
        final int width = 200, height = 150;
        setSize(width,height);
        Container contents = getContentPane();

        setupPopupMenu();
        setupPopupListener();
    }

    // Create the popup menu's contents.
    protected void setupPopupMenu(){
        JPopupMenu menu = getPopup();
        JMenuItem order = new JMenuItem("Order now");
        JMenuItem cancelOrder = new JMenuItem("Cancel order");
        // Listeners may be attached to the popup menu items
        // in the normal way.
        // ...
        // Quit option.
        Action quit = new AbstractAction("Quit"){
            public void actionPerformed(ActionEvent e){
                System.exit(0);
            }
        };
```

Code 17.30   (*Continued*)

```
        menu.add(order);
        menu.add(cancelOrder);
        menu.addSeparator();
        menu.add(quit);
    }

        // Listen for mouse events that could be the menu trigger.
    protected void setupPopupListener(){
        // Listen for a popup trigger.
        addMouseListener(new MouseAdapter(){
            public void mousePressed(MouseEvent e){
                checkForPopup(e);
            }

            public void mouseReleased(MouseEvent e){
                checkForPopup(e);
            }

            public void mouseClicked(MouseEvent e){
                checkForPopup(e);
            }

            protected void checkForPopup(MouseEvent e){
                if(e.isPopupTrigger()){
                    final Point p = e.getPoint();
                    // Show the popup within the frame.
                    getPopup().show(SwingMenuFrame2.this,p.x,p.y);
                }
            }
        });
    }

    protected JPopupMenu getPopup(){
        return popup;
    }

    // The menu to be fleshed out.
    private final JPopupMenu popup = new JPopupMenu();
}
```

As with a JMenu, JPopupMenus may have arbitrary JMenuItems added to them, and separators may be used to provide visual grouping of related items. The show method of the menu is used to display it within the containing frame when a mouse event trigger is received.

17.13   The JToolBar Class

The JToolBar class provides a convenient grouping for a set of controls, which are often placed towards the top of an application's frame—in the North of a BorderLayout, for instance. The controls are often buttons containing icons. Code 17.31 shows

Code 17.31   Configuring a JToolBar with navigational buttons (`SwingToolBarFrame.java`)

```java
import javax.swing.*;
import java.awt.*;
import java.awt.event.*;

        // Display a floatable JToolBar.
class SwingToolBarFrame extends JFrame {
    public SwingToolBarFrame() {
        final int width = 300, height = 300;
        setSize(width,height);
        Container contents = getContentPane();

        // Create a toolbar.
        JToolBar toolBar = setupToolBar();
        toolBar.setFloatable(true);

        contents.setBackground(Color.white);
        contents.add(toolBar,"North");
        contents.add(new QuitJPanel(),"South");
    }

        // Setup a toolbar to contain four arrow buttons.
    protected JToolBar setupToolBar(){
        // Four buttons for the bar.
        JButton left = new JButton(new ArrowIcon(ArrowIcon.LEFT));
        JButton right = new JButton(new ArrowIcon(ArrowIcon.RIGHT));
        JButton up = new JButton(new ArrowIcon(ArrowIcon.UP));
        JButton down = new JButton(new ArrowIcon(ArrowIcon.DOWN));

        // Add dummy listeners to the buttons.
        left.addActionListener(dummyActionListener("Back"));
        left.setToolTipText("Back");
        right.addActionListener(dummyActionListener("Forward"));
        left.setToolTipText("Forward");
        up.addActionListener(dummyActionListener("Up"));
        left.setToolTipText("Up");
        down.addActionListener(dummyActionListener("Down"));
        left.setToolTipText("Down");

        // Add the buttons to the bar.
        JToolBar bar = new JToolBar(JToolBar.HORIZONTAL);
        bar.add(left);
        bar.add(right);
        bar.addSeparator();
        bar.add(up);
        bar.add(down);
        return bar;
    }

        // Create a dummy ActionListener that just prints the
        // report string when it receives an event.
    protected ActionListener dummyActionListener(final String report){
        return new ActionListener(){
```

Code 17.31   (*Continued*)

```
        public void actionPerformed(ActionEvent e){
            System.out.println(report);
        }
    };
  }
}
```

---

an application that displays four navigational buttons in a toolbar. The appearance of this is shown in Figure 17.29 . A JToolBar has an orientation of either HORIZONTAL or VERTICAL. As a sub class of JComponent, it acts as a container and components may be added directly to it via its add method. Four arrow icons (see ArrowIcon.java) have been associated with buttons in this example. The addSeparator method provides additional spacing between logical groupings of components.

It is not necessary for a toolbar to remain fixed in the position that it was assigned to in its parent. If a toolbar's floatable attribute is set to true, then it may be dragged to a new position with the mouse. Figure 17.30 illustrates a detached toolbar. If the parent component of the toolbar uses a BorderLayout layout manager, then a toolbar will sometimes attach itself to a free border area in preference to floating free.

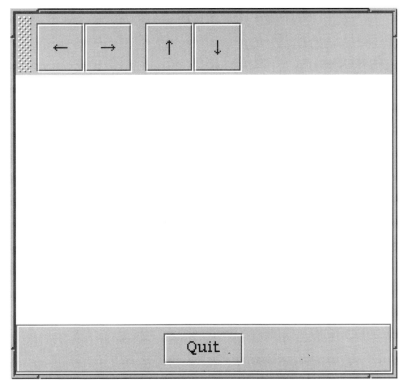

Figure 17.29   A JToolBar containing navigational controls (SwingToolBarMain.java)

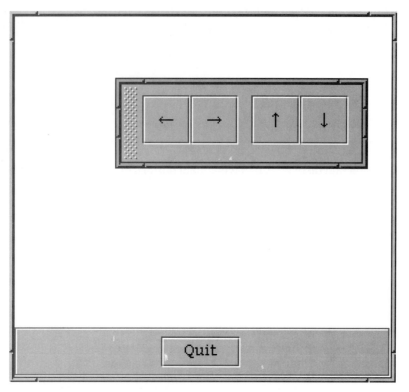

Figure 17.30   A floating JToolBar

17.14   The JScrollPane Class

The JScrollPane class provides a general component that can be used to scroll any component contained within it. Code 17.32 shows the way in which a JLabel displaying an image can be provided with scrollbars (Figure 17.31).

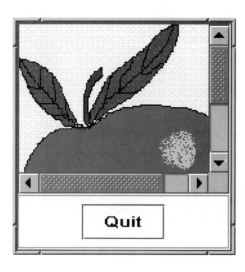

Figure 17.31   Using a JScrollPane to view an image (SwingScrollMain1.java)

Code 17.32   Displaying an image within a JScrollPane (`SwingScrollFrame1.java`)

```
import javax.swing.*;
import java.awt.*;

    // Display an image in a scroll pane.
class SwingScrollFrame1 extends JFrame {
    public SwingScrollFrame1() {
        final int width = 175, height = 200;
        setSize(width,height);
        Container contents = getContentPane();

        // Create a scroller for the image.
        final JScrollPane scroller = new JScrollPane(getLabel());

        contents.add(scroller,"Center");
        contents.add(new QuitJPanel(),"South");
    }

        // Show the image in the scroll area.
    public void setImage(String file){
        try{
            getLabel().setIcon(new ImageIcon(file));
        }
        catch(Exception e){
            JOptionPane.showMessageDialog(
                    getContentPane(),
                    e.toString(),
                    "Image Failure",
                    JOptionPane.ERROR_MESSAGE);
        }
    }

    protected JLabel getLabel(){
        return label;
    }

    // Label for the image.
    private final JLabel label = new JLabel();
}
```

A JScrollPane has policies for both its horizontal and vertical scroll bars. These may be set on construction, or via its `setHorizontalScrollBarPolicy` and `setVerticalScrollBarPolicy` methods. Values for these are defined in the `ScrollPaneConstants` interface, which JScrollPane implements. It contains values such as VERTICAL_SCROLLBAR_AS_NEEDED, VERTICAL_SCROLLBAR_-ALWAYS, VERTICAL_SCROLLBAR_NEVER, and similarly for the horizontal scroll bar. By default, scrollbars will be created as they are needed, that is, when the pane is too small to fully display the component it contains. The two `JScrollBar` objects may be obtained via the scroll pane's `getHorizontalScrollBar` and `get-VerticalScrollBar` methods. The example in Code 17.37 shows how an

`AdjustmentListener` can be attached to these scroll bars in order to receive notification of when they are moved.

17.14.1   The JViewport Class

A JScrollPane is really a composite object, consisting of a `JViewport`, two scroll bars, four corner components, and two header components. It is the JViewport that provides the viewing area into the client component, and so it is the viewport that moves over the component when the scroll bars are adjusted. So, when a component is added to a scroll pane via its `add` method, the component is passed on to the associated viewport to manage. This model of general scrolling makes it much easier to wrap a wide variety of components in scroll panes, without having to provide scrolling functionality directly in the wrapped components. Sections 17.15.3 and 17.17 provide illustrations of typical uses with JTextArea objects, for instance.

The JViewport object associated with a scroll pane may be obtained via the pane's `getViewport` method. An object implementing the `ChangeListener` may register itself with the viewport, via its `setChangeListener` method. It will then receive notification of events which cause the viewport to move.

17.14.2   The Corner Components

Four separate arbitrary components may be placed at the corners of a JScrollPane via its `setCorner` method. The first argument of this method is a String having one of the values `LOWER_LEFT_CORNER`, `UPPER_LEFT_CORNER`, `LOWER_RIGHT_CORNER`, or `UPPER_RIGHT_CORNER`. The second argument is the component to be placed at that position.

17.14.3   The Header Components

Components may be placed at the top and left of the viewport via the scroll pane's `setColumnHeaderView` and `setRowHeaderView` methods, respectively. These might be `JLabel` components containing text or images to label the scrollable component. A column header will scroll horizontally and a row header will scroll vertically as the scrollbar directly opposite is adjusted. A particular use is made of the column header component by the scroll panes associated with the `JTable` class; the column header is filled with the individual header descriptions of the table's columns that are managed by the table's `JTableHeader` object.

17.15   The JTextComponent Class

The `JTextComponent` class is the super class of several text manipulation classes. It is defined in the `javax.swing.text` package although its sub classes are in the usual `javax.swing` package. The functionality of this class and some of its sub classes is closely related to that of the `TextField` and `TextArea` classes of the AWT, but in several areas the functionality is much more sophisticated. There is much better provision for text involving multiple fonts, styles, and colors, for instance, as

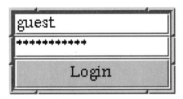

Figure 17.32   Display a JTextField and a JPasswordField (`SwingTextMain1.java`)

well as mixed text and images, and documents containing *markup*, such as *HyperText Markup Language (HTML)*[Worb]. Most of these changes result from text components being responsible for the management of an underlying document model—an object that is from a class that implements the `Document` interface (also defined in the `javax.swing.text` package). The `getDocument` method of JTextComponent returns a reference to this object.

    Three of the methods inherited by its sub classes permit material to be copied between the document and the system clipboard:

```
public void cut();
public void copy();
public void paste();
```

All three operate on the currently selected area in the text component, or at the caret position (in the case of `paste`) if there is no selected text.

    Two further methods allow the contents of a file to be read easily into the component, or the contents of the component written to a file:

```
public void read(Reader r,Object description) throws IOException;
public void write(Writer w) throws IOException;
```

The second argument to `read` may be `null`, but, if not, it will typically be either a descriptive `String`, a `File`, or a `URL` object (see Section 19.3). Clearly, it is not necessary for the Reader and Writer arguments to be associated only with an external file. An example of use of the `read` method can be seen in Section 17.15.3.

17.15.1   The JTextField Class

The `JTextField` class is used to manage a document consisting of a single line of text. By default, the underlying document is an instance of the `PlainDocument` class, which represents text in a single font and color. A number of columns for the field may be specified on construction or via its `setColumns` method. The value is interpreted as the number of m-width characters in the current font. Code 17.33 illustrates the creation of a JTextField and a `JPasswordField` object (see Section 17.15.2) within a vertical box. Its appearance may be seen in Figure 17.32.

    When the "Login" button is pressed, the contents of the two fields are retrieved and printed. This example includes the use of the `setHorizontalAlignment` method, whose argument may be either CENTER, LEFT, or RIGHT.[5] When there is sufficient space to display the full text, this value is used to justify the contents within

---

[5] The alignment will be LEFT by default, so the setting in this case is not strictly necessary.

Code 17.33   Using a JTextField and a JPasswordField for logging in (`SwingTextFrame1.java`)

```
import javax.swing.*;
import java.awt.*;
import java.awt.event.*;

        // Display a JTextField and JPasswordField.
        // When the Login button is pressed, retrieve the
        // text they both contain.
class SwingTextFrame1 extends JFrame {
    public SwingTextFrame1() {
        final int width = 300, height = 100;
        setSize(width,height);
        Container contents = getContentPane();

        // Place both fields in a vertical box.
        Box box = Box.createVerticalBox();
        final JTextField name = new JTextField("guest",10);
        name.setHorizontalAlignment(JTextField.LEFT);
        final JPasswordField password = new JPasswordField(10);
        box.add(name);
        box.add(password);
        contents.add(box,"Center");

        // Display the contents of the fields when a button is pressed.
        JButton login = new JButton("Login");
        login.addActionListener(new ActionListener(){
            public void actionPerformed(ActionEvent e){
                System.out.println("Name = "+name.getText());
                String pwd = new String(password.getPassword());
                System.out.println("Password = "+pwd);
                System.exit(0);
            }
        });
        contents.add(login,"South");
        pack();
    }
}
```

the field. When the text is too long for the available space, the alignment value is used to determine whether the central, left, or right portion should be in the visible area. Further characters may be added, but these will only be seen if they are added within the visible area.

17.15.2   The JPasswordField Class

The JPasswordField class is a sub class of JTextField, designed for receiving input of text that should not be echoed. Section 17.15.1 includes an illustration of its use. Rather than using the getText method of JTextComponent, the getPassword method should be used. This returns a char array containing the characters typed.

17.15.3 The JTextArea Class

The JTextArea class is designed for a document containing multi-line text. The biggest observable difference between this class and the related AWT class, Text-Area, is the absence of direct scrollbar support in the Swing class. In fact, this is an improvement, since it simplifies the JTextArea class and is an acknowledgement that scrollbar support is a general requirement of a different sort of component, and not something that should be tied to particular components. This means that it is common to add a JTextArea component to a JScrollPane object as soon as it is created. Code 17.34 illustrates an application that contains a central text area within a scroll pane, that is used to display the contents of a file. The appearance of this is shown in Figure 17.33.

The appearance of the GUI is created in the constructor. A file is loaded into the text area via the showFile method. This makes use of the text area's read method inherited from its JTextComponent super class. A JTextArea manages scrolling by implementing the Scrollable interface, through which it responds to events from its enclosing JScrollPane.

Where there is no associated scroll pane, line wrapping may be enabled on the text area via the setLineWrap method. The argument of the associated setWrap-StyleWord determines whether lines are wrapped at word boundaries (true) or character boundaries (false).

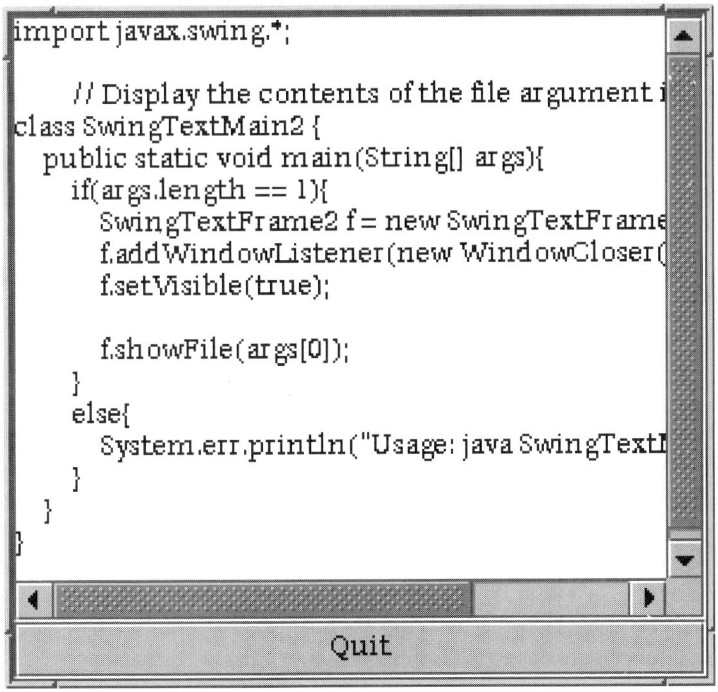

```
import javax.swing.*;

    // Display the contents of the file argument i
class SwingTextMain2 {
  public static void main(String[] args){
    if(args.length == 1){
      SwingTextFrame2 f = new SwingTextFrame
      f.addWindowListener(new WindowCloser(
      f.setVisible(true);

      f.showFile(args[0]);
    }
    else{
      System.err.println("Usage: java SwingTextI
    }
  }
}
```

                                 Quit

Figure 17.33 Display of a file within a scrollable text area
(SwingTextMain2.java)

Code 17.34   A JTextArea within a JScrollPane (`SwingTextFrame2.java`)

```java
import javax.swing.*;
import java.awt.*;
import java.awt.event.*;
import java.io.*;

    // Display the contents of a file in a scrolling text area.
class SwingTextFrame2 extends JFrame {
    public SwingTextFrame2() {
        final int width = 300, height = 300;
        setSize(width,height);
        Container contents = getContentPane();

        // Add a text area wrapped in a scroll pane.
        JScrollPane scroller = new JScrollPane(getText());
        contents.add(scroller,"Center");
        contents.add(new QuitJPanel(),"South");
    }

        // Show the given file in the text area.
    public void showFile(String filename){
        try{
            FileReader infile = new FileReader(filename);
            getText().read(infile,null);
            infile.close();
        }
        catch(IOException e){
            JOptionPane.showMessageDialog(
                    getContentPane(),
                    e.toString(),
                    "File Failure",
                    JOptionPane.ERROR_MESSAGE);
        }
    }

    protected JTextArea getText(){
        return text;
    }

    // The text area used to display the file.
    private final JTextArea text = new JTextArea();
}
```

17.16   The JEditorPane Class

The JEditorPane class provides capabilities to display and edit text that is markedup
in formats such as HTML and *Rich Text Format (RTF)*. This is possible because it
delegates the editing process to an object of a sub class of the abstract EditorKit
class, which is able to format marked-up text in an appropriate way. An object of
the DefaultEditorKit class is able to display and support editing of plain text.
More sophisticated editing is provided by sub classes of StyledEditorKit, such

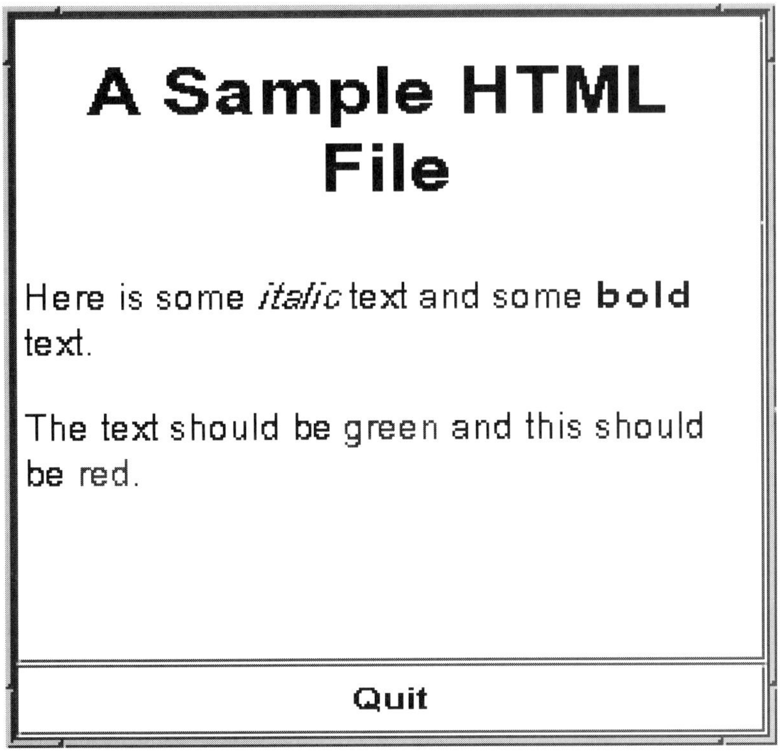

Figure 17.34   HTML text displayed within a JEditorPane (`SwingTextMain3.java`)

Code 17.35   A sample HTML file (`sample.html`); see Figure 17.34

```
<html>
<head><title>A Sample HTML File</title></head>
<body>
<center><h1>A Sample HTML File</h1></center>
Here is some <i>italic</i> text and some
<b>bold</b> text.
<p>
The text should be <font color="green">green</font> and this
should be <font color="red">red</font>.
</body>
</html>
```

as `HTMLEditorKit` and `RTFEditorKit`. Code 17.36 shows an example in which a document is displayed in an editor pane placed within a scroll pane. Figure 17.34 shows the effect of this using the HTML sample shown in Code 17.35.

The constructor of JEditorPane takes either a `URL` object or a string containing a URL. If the URL can be resolved, the document will be displayed according to its type (assuming that a suitable EditorKit is available). If the URL cannot be resolved, an IOException will be thrown. The example in Code 17.36 also illustrates that

Code 17.36   Displaying a document in a JEditorPane (`SwingTextFrame3.java`)

```java
import javax.swing.*;
import java.awt.*;
import java.awt.event.*;
import java.io.*;

    // Display the contents of a URL document in an editor pane.
class SwingTextFrame3 extends JFrame {
    public SwingTextFrame3() {
        final int width = 300, height = 300;
        setSize(width,height);
        Container contents = getContentPane();
        contents.add(new QuitJPanel(),"South");
    }

        // Show the given file in the text area.
    public void showDocument(String url){
        try{
            JEditorPane ed = getEditor();
            if(ed == null){
                ed = new JEditorPane(url);
                ed.setEditable(false);
                getContentPane().add(new JScrollPane(ed),"Center");
            }
            else{
                ed.setPage(url);
            }
            validate();
        }
        catch(IOException e){
            JOptionPane.showMessageDialog(
                    getContentPane(),
                    e.toString(),
                    "URL Failure",
                    JOptionPane.ERROR_MESSAGE);
        }
    }

    protected JEditorPane getEditor(){
        return editor;
    }

    protected void setEditor(JEditorPane e){
        editor = e;
    }

    private JEditorPane editor;
}
```

the editor's document may be changed via its `setPage` method. Unfortunately, a full discussion of the facilities available via this complex class is beyond the scope of this book. For more detailed coverage, you should consult a specialist book which is dedicated to the Swing classes, such as that by Topley[Top98].

17.16.1   The JTextPane Class

The `JTextPane` class is a sub class of JEditorPane, and hence offers further sophistication. It is concerned with the display and editing of documents which are implementations of the `StyledDocument` interface. Style characteristics may be set at several levels within a document: the document as a whole, the level of a paragraph, and the level of characters within a paragraph. The attributes at a particular level consist of things such as such as font family, font style, font size, text background, and foreground colors. The meaning of the term paragraph is simply a run of consecutive characters of arbitrary length. Objects of this class are appropriate for use via the GUI controls of text manipulation tools such as word processors and document markup programs. For instance, when a user highlights a portion of text in the text display area and then selects a font change button, appropriate messages would be sent to the underlying document to set modified attributes on the selected text. Further discussion of the facilities available via this complex class is beyond the scope of this book.

17.17   The JSplitPane Class

The `JSplitPane` class allows a single viewing area to be split into two parts with a movable divider between them. Figure 17.35 shows the appearance of one in which the contents of two files are viewed side by side. The two areas may be arranged either horizontally (`HORIZONTAL_SPLIT`) or vertically (`VERTICAL_SPLIT`), and they are referred to as either the left and right panes, or the top and bottom panes, respectively. Code 17.37 shows the example used to produce Figure 17.35.

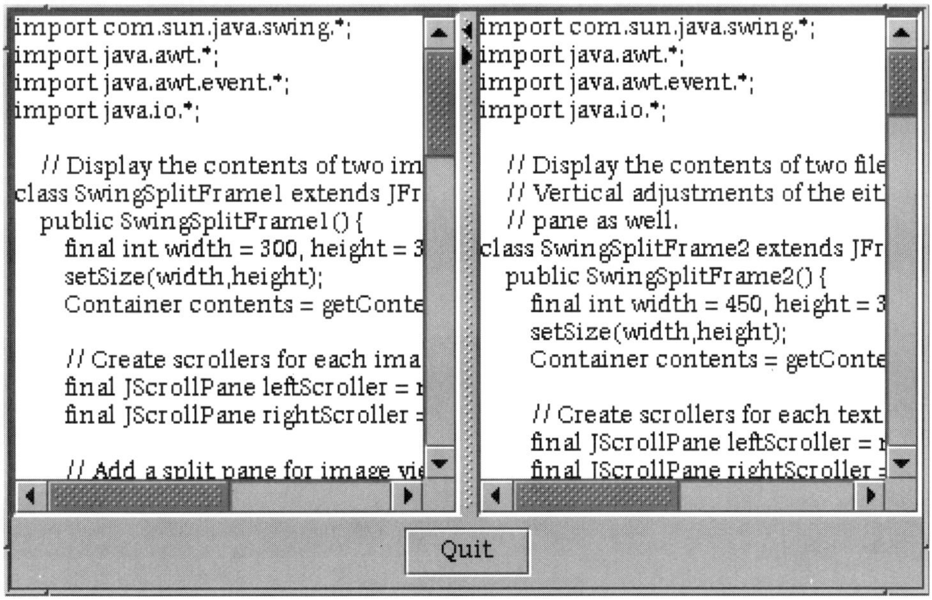

Figure 17.35   Viewing two similar files side by side (`SwingSplitMain2.java`)

Code 17.37   Two files displayed in a JSplitPane (`SwingSplitFrame2.java`)

```java
import javax.swing.*;
import java.awt.*;
import java.awt.event.*;
import java.io.*;

    // Display the contents of two files in a vertically split pane.
    // Vertical adjustments of the either pane should move the other
    // pane as well.
class SwingSplitFrame2 extends JFrame {
    public SwingSplitFrame2() {
        final int width = 450, height = 300;
        setSize(width,height);
        Container contents = getContentPane();

        // Create scrollers for each text area.
        final JScrollPane leftScroller = new JScrollPane(getLeft());
        final JScrollPane rightScroller = new JScrollPane(getRight());

        // Listen for adjustments on one vertical scroll bar and
        // relay them to the other.
        final JScrollBar leftV = leftScroller.getVerticalScrollBar(),
                         rightV = rightScroller.getVerticalScrollBar();

        linkVerticalScrollBars(leftV,rightV);

        // Add a split pane for document viewing.
        JSplitPane pane = new JSplitPane(JSplitPane.VERTICAL_SPLIT);
        // Add both scrollers to the split pane.
        pane.setLeftComponent(leftScroller);
        pane.setRightComponent(rightScroller);
        // Set the divider at the mid-point.
        pane.setDividerLocation(0.5);

        contents.add(pane,"Center");
        contents.add(new QuitJPanel(),"South");
    }

        // Show the given file in the text area.
    public void showFiles(String file1,String file2){
        try{
            FileReader infile = new FileReader(file1);
            JTextArea left = getLeft();
            left.read(infile,null);
            infile.close();

            infile = new FileReader(file2);
            JTextArea right = getRight();
            right.read(infile,null);
            infile.close();
        }
        catch(IOException e){
            JOptionPane.showMessageDialog(
```

Code 17.37   (*Continued*)

```
                              getContentPane(),
                              e.toString(),
                              "File Failure",
                              JOptionPane.ERROR_MESSAGE);
        }
    }

    // Listen for adjustments on one vertical scroll bar and
    // relay them to the other.
    protected void linkVerticalScrollBars(final JScrollBar left,
                                          final JScrollBar right){
        left.addAdjustmentListener(new AdjustmentListener(){
            public void adjustmentValueChanged(AdjustmentEvent e){
                right.setValue(e.getValue());
            }
        });

        right.addAdjustmentListener(new AdjustmentListener(){
            public void adjustmentValueChanged(AdjustmentEvent e){
                left.setValue(e.getValue());
            }
        });
    }

    protected JTextArea getLeft(){
        return left;
    }

    protected JTextArea getRight(){
        return right;
    }

    // Default sizes for the text areas.
    private final int textWidth = 50, textHeight = 25;
    private final JTextArea left = new JTextArea(textWidth,textHeight),
                           right = new JTextArea(textWidth,textHeight);
}
```

An AdjustmentListener has been attached to the vertical scroll bars of each pane so that their movements are relayed to each other. This has the effect of keeping the two files more or less in step, an effect which could be used by a file comparison program, for instance.

The mouse may be used to drag the divider and, hence, adjust the relative proportion of space allocated to the two components. Using the setContinuous-Layout method makes it possible to set whether the two components are continuously redisplayed during this process (true) or only redisplayed when the adjustment has finished (false). This attribute should be set to true when the user needs feedback from the visual effect of repositioning on the components, in order to decide on its correct position.

The divider's location may be set in one of two ways via the `setDivider-Location` methods. A positive integer value specifies either the offset from the left edge (in the case of a horizontal split) or the top edge (in the case of a vertical split). A floating point value in the range `0.0` to `1.0` is used as a proportion of the overall width or height, so `0.5` sets the divider in the middle of the pane.

The `setOneTouchExpandable` method takes a `boolean` argument and adds extra functionality to the divider if the value is `true`. Figure 17.35 illustrates two small triangular symbols on the divider because the one-touch-expandable feature has been turned on. Clicking on one of these symbols will cause the divider to move fully to either the left or the right of this particular pane. The pane remembers the last location of the divider (`getLastDividerLocation`) and this will be the position it moves to when the other triangle is selected.

17.18   The JTabbedPane Class

The `JTabbedPane` class fulfills a similar role to the `CardLayout` layout manager, but does so with a more sophisticated and familiar look-and-feel. Each JComponent is added to the pane with an associated Tab, which is a string. The tab strings are grouped to the `TOP`, `BOTTOM`, `LEFT`, or `RIGHT` of the component viewing area. At any time, only one of the components added to the pane is selected and visible. A different component may be viewed by selecting its tab. The JColorChooser class uses a JTabbedPane to provide alternative means for choosing a color (see Section 17.20.1). Figure 17.36 illustrates an application designed to provide alternative views of a data set. Code 17.38 shows the class used to create this tabbed pane.

The `SwingBarChart` and `SwingCumulativeChart` objects added to the tabbed pane are custom-created JComponents based upon the BarChart class introduced in Chapter 6. Each has been added to the pane via one of its several `add` methods. The first string argument will be used as the Tab string in each case, and the components are added sequentially. Other `add` methods allow a component to be inserted at a particular index within the collection of components.

When a new component is selected within the tabbed pane, a `ChangeEvent` will be sent to any listeners that have registered via its `addChangeListener` method. A reference to the tabbed pane that has issued the ChangeEvent is available via the `getSource` method of the event in `stateChanged`. The tabbed pane's

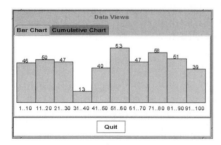
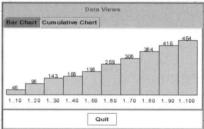

Figure 17.36   A JTabbedPane permits alternative views of a data set
(`JTabbedMain.java`)

Code 17.38   Adding components to a JTabbedPane (`SwingTabbedFrame.java`)

```
import javax.swing.*;
import javax.swing.event.*;
import java.awt.*;

    // Display a JTabbedPane with alternative data views.
    // Illustrate receipt of a ChangeEvent when a tab
    // is selected.
class SwingTabbedFrame extends JFrame {
        // Receive the data to be displayed.
    public SwingTabbedFrame(RangeCounts data) {
        final int width = 450, height = 300;
        setSize(width,height);
        Container contents = getContentPane();

        // A tabbed pane to hold the alternative views of the data.
        JTabbedPane pane = new JTabbedPane();
        pane.add("Bar Chart",new SwingBarChart(data));
        pane.add("Cumulative Chart",new SwingCumulativeChart(data));
        // Be notified of changes to the selected pane.
        pane.addChangeListener(new ChangeListener(){
            public void stateChanged(ChangeEvent e){
                // Get a reference to the pane.
                JTabbedPane p = (JTabbedPane) e.getSource();
                // Report the selected component.
                System.out.println("Tab: "+p.getSelectedIndex()+
                                " selected.");
            }
        });

        contents.add(new JLabel("Data Views",JLabel.CENTER),"North");
        contents.add(pane,"Center");
        contents.add(new QuitJPanel(),"South");
    }
}
```

`getSelectedIndex` and `getSelectedComponent` methods may be used to identify which component is now visible. This information could be used to notify the component of its new visibility; a component's initialization might be delayed until it is absolutely necessary, for instance, or it might need to check for changes to its context in order to determine whether it needs to recompute its appearance.

17.19 Pluggable Look-and-Feel

One of the most significant differences between the Swing classes and their counterparts in the AWT is that the Swing classes are written entirely in Java. One effect is that a Swing application can take control over its *look-and-feel*—it is not dependent upon that provided by host-dependent peers. This makes it much more possible for an application to have an identical look-and-feel on different platforms.

17.19.1 The UIDefaults Class

One of the ways in which this is achieved is by separating the way a component is visualized from the functionality it provides. Details of the colors, fonts, borders, margins, and so on, are kept completely separate. This means that it becomes relatively easy to change these settings without affecting the basic component functionality at all. The `UIDefaults` class is responsible for maintaining associations between component properties and their implementations. The UIDefaults class is a sub class of the legacy `Hashtable` class (see Section 10.2.5). Code 17.39 shows how a complete set of the properties it maintains may be determined.

A (sorted) sample of its output might be as follows:

```
Button.background
Button.border
Button.disabledText
Button.focus
Button.font
Button.foreground
Button.margin
Button.select
Button.textIconGap
Button.textShiftOffset
ButtonUI
CheckBox.background
CheckBox.border
```

A particular look-and-feel will have its own set of defaults associated with it. In the next section, we show how the look-and-feel of an application may be set.

17.19.2 The UIManager Class

The `UIManager` class consists entirely of static methods used to access, enquire about, and manipulate the set of look-and-feel classes that are available to an

---

Code 17.39   Printing all the UIDefaults properties (`ShowUIDefaults.java`)

```java
import javax.swing.*;
import java.util.*;

        // Show the complete list of UIDefaults properties.
class ShowUIDefaults {
    public static void main(String[] args){
        UIDefaults defaults = UIManager.getDefaults();
        Enumeration keys = defaults.keys();
        while(keys.hasMoreElements()){
            System.out.println(keys.nextElement());
        }
        // Exit because of the separate thread.
        System.exit(0);
    }
}
```

Code 17.40   Finding out the installed look-and-feels (`LookAndFeelMain1.java`)

```java
import javax.swing.*;

        // Print details of the installed look and feel names.
class LookAndFeelMain1 {
    public static void main(String[] args){
        // Obtain an array of all the installed look and feel types.
        UIManager.LookAndFeelInfo[] info =
                            UIManager.getInstalledLookAndFeels();

        if(info != null){
            System.out.println("Installed Look and Feels.");
            // Print the name and class for each one.
            for(int i = 0; i < info.length; i++){
                final UIManager.LookAndFeelInfo look = info[i];
                System.out.println(look.getName()+
                                " Class: "+look.getClassName());
            }
        }

        // Exit, because use of the UIManager has created a separate thread.
        System.out.flush();
        System.exit(0);
    }
}
```

---

application. Code 17.40 shows how names for the set of installed look-and-feels can be determined.

The `getInstalledLookAndFeels` method returns an array of objects belonging to a static nested class of UIManager. The `LookAndFeelInfo` class provides the methods `getName` and `getClassName` to reveal names for the installed look-and-feels. It is these names that can be used when selecting a particular look-and-feel for an application. Typical output from running the example in Code 17.40 is as follows:

```
Installed Look and Feels.
Metal Class: javax.swing.plaf.metal.MetalLookAndFeel
CDE/Motif Class: com.sun.java.swing.plaf.motif.MotifLookAndFeel
Windows Class: com.sun.java.swing.plaf.windows.WindowsLookAndFeel
```

showing the three commonly available styles known as `Metal`, `Motif`, and `Windows`. It is important to realize that, although a look-and-feel might be installed on a particular platform, it might not be available to applications for proprietary reasons, for instance.

Code 17.41 shows the way in which a particular look-and-feel may be selected for an application via one of the UIManager's two `setLookAndFeel` methods. One takes a class name, in the form of a string, and the other a `LookAndFeel` object. Figure 17.37 shows the effect of setting the *Motif*™ look-and-feel on the example previously shown with the *Metal* look-and-feel in Figure 17.24.

```java
import javax.swing.*;
import javax.swing.*;

    // Display the arguments as images in a JDesktopPane.
    // Explicitly set the Motif look-and-feel for this.
class SwingLayerMain4 {
    public static void main(String[] args) {
        if(args.length > 0){
            // Explicitly set the look and feel.
            try{
                UIManager.setLookAndFeel(
                    "com.sun.java.swing.plaf.motif.MotifLookAndFeel");
            }
            catch(Exception e){
                System.err.println(e);
            }
            // Pass in the image names.
            SwingLayerFrame3 f = new SwingLayerFrame3(args);
            f.addWindowListener(new WindowCloser());
            f.setVisible(true);
        }
        else{
            System.err.println("Usage: java SwingLayerMain4 file.gif ...");
        }
    }
}
```

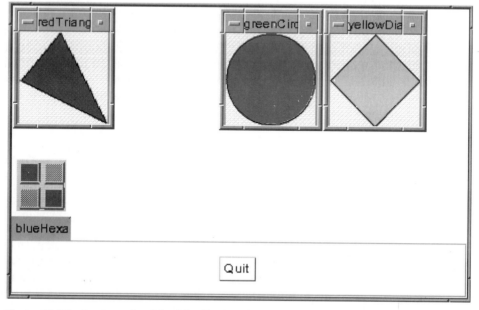

Figure 17.37   An example of the *Motif* look-and-feel (`SwingLayerMain4.java`)

An alternative to setting the look-and-feel from a program is to place a setting in a `swing.properties` file. The UIManager will check for such a file in the `lib` directory directly beneath the installation directory of the Java platform, for instance `jdk1.2/lib/swing.properties` (see Appendix G). The following line might be used to set the default look-and-feel for Swing applications to be Metal:

```
swing.defaultlaf=javax.swing.plaf.metal.MetalLookAndFeel
```

17.20   The JDialog Class

The `JDialog` class provides a wrapper for components that need to appear in a dialog context, such as those that allow a user to exercise a choice. Section 17.10 described the `JOptionPane` that provides commonly used dialog functionality for simple warning, error, and alert dialogs, for instance. JDialog is a sub class of the AWT `Dialog` class, so dialogs can be either modal or non-modal. The class is similar to JFrame in that it has a content pane to which its child components should be added. Two classes that are commonly wrapped in a JDialog are `JColorChooser` (Section 17.20.1) and `JFileChooser` (Section 17.21).

17.20.1   The JColorChooser Class

The `JColorChooser` class makes it simple to interactively select a color value from a palette. While it is possible to create a JColorChooser object via one of its three constructors, it is often more convenient to have one created via the class's static `showDialog` method. This takes care of providing functional "OK", "Cancel", and "Reset" buttons, for instance. Figure 17.38 shows the appearance of this dialog. The

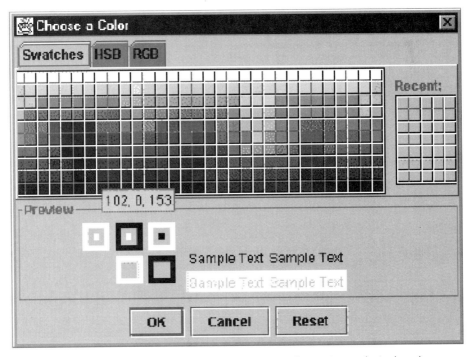

Figure 17.38   A JDialog containing a JColorChooser (`SwingColorMain1.java`)

upper portion of the color chooser contains an area for choosing a color with the mouse. The effect of the choice is shown in different contexts in the lower preview portion. The most recent choices are maintained for reference in a color block to the right. Code 17.42 shows part of an application that uses a JColorChooser to select the background of a central panel via its "Change" button.

Code 17.42   Setting the background color of a panel via a JColorChooser
(`SwingColorFrame1.java`)

```java
import javax.swing.*;
import java.awt.*;
import java.awt.event.*;

    // Illustrate a JColorChooser by allowing one to change the
    // background of a central panel.
class SwingColorFrame1 extends JFrame {
    public SwingColorFrame1(){
        final int width = 400, height = 200;
        setSize(width,height);

        final Container contents = getContentPane();

        JLabel label = new JLabel("Change the Background.",JLabel.CENTER);
        contents.add(label,"North");
        // Add a panel, whose background color will be changed.
        contents.add(getPanel(),"Center");

        // Set up Change + Quit buttons.
        final JPanel buttonPanel = new JPanel();
        setupButtons(buttonPanel);
        contents.add(buttonPanel,"South");
    }

        // Allow a JColorChooser to change the background color of
        // the central panel.
    protected void setupButtons(JPanel buttonPanel){
        final JButton quit = new QuitJButton("Quit"),
                      change = new JButton("Change");

        // The action to take when the Change button is pressed.
        // Show a color chooser and use the selected color.
        change.addActionListener(new ActionListener(){
            public void actionPerformed(ActionEvent e){
                final JPanel p = getPanel();
                Color c = JColorChooser.showDialog(
                        SwingColorFrame1.this,"Choose a Color",
                        p.getBackground());
                if(c != null){
                    p.setBackground(c);
                }
            }
        });
        buttonPanel.add(change);
        buttonPanel.add(quit);
    }
```

Code 17.42   (*Continued*)

```
protected JPanel getPanel(){
    return panel;
}

// The panel whose background color is to be changed.
private final JPanel panel = new JPanel();
}
```

The `showDialog` method takes a Component object as a parent for where the dialog is to be shown. A string provides a title for the dialog, and the third Color argument indicates the initial color for the chooser. When the "OK" button on the dialog is pressed, the currently selected color is returned from `showDialog`. If the "Cancel" button is selected, then `null` is returned. Both buttons cause the dialog to disappear. The "Reset" button restores the initial color but the dialog remains in place. Figure 17.38 shows that there are, in fact, two different ways of selecting colors. A JTabbedPane offers selection via a palette of swatches, HSB ranges (Figure 17.39), or RGB JSlider controls (Figure 17.40).

Each call to `showDialog` creates a new JColorChooser. If you wish to reuse a chooser, then the static `createDialog` alternative is available. This offers more flexibility than using `showDialog` because it allows you to attach your own ActionListener objects to the "OK" and "Cancel" buttons. The file

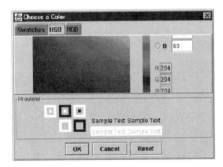

Figure 17.39   HSB color selection

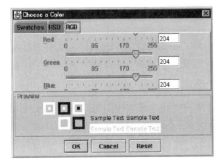

Figure 17.40   RGB color selection

Code 17.43 Employ a re-usable JColorChooser (`SwingColorFrame2.java`)

```
class SwingColorFrame2 extends JFrame {
    ...
    // Allow a re-usable JColorChooser to change the background color of
    // the central panel.
    protected void setupButtons(JPanel buttonPanel){
        final JButton quit = new QuitJButton("Quit"),
            change = new JButton("Change");

        // The action to take when the Change button is pressed.
        // Show a color chooser and use the selected color.
        change.addActionListener(new ActionListener(){
            public void actionPerformed(ActionEvent e){
                final JPanel p = getPanel();
                final JColorChooser chooser = getChooser();
                JDialog dialog = JColorChooser.createDialog(getPanel(),
                    "Choose a Color",true,chooser,
                    // Set the background if Ok is pressed.
                    new ActionListener(){
                        public void actionPerformed(ActionEvent e){
                            getPanel().setBackground(chooser.getColor());
                        }
                    },
                    // Do nothing if Cancel is pressed.
                    null);
                dialog.show();
            }
        });
        buttonPanel.add(change);
        buttonPanel.add(quit);
    }
    ...
}
```

`SwingColorFrame2.java` is a slight variant on the class shown in Code 17.42 that uses this approach. The only changes are the creation of a JColorChooser attribute and modifications to the `actionPerformed` method associated with the change button to display it (Code 17.43).

The first argument of `createDialog` is the dialog's panel, the second is a title for the dialog, the third is whether the dialog should be modal or not. The fourth argument is the JColorChooser object to display (here it is an attribute of the containing object). The fifth and sixth arguments must be objects that implement the ActionListener interface. The fifth will receive an ActionEvent if the "OK" button is pressed and the sixth will if the "Cancel" button is pressed. In both cases, the dialog will be removed. The `ColorSetter` class in the above example is the following simple inner class that retrieves the color chooser's color and uses it to set the panel's background (Code 17.44).

Code 17.44 An inner class used to act on the color chooser's "OK" button
(`SwingColorFrame2.java`)

```
class SwingColorFrame2 {
    ...
        // Set the central panel's color from the color chooser.
    protected class ColorSetter implements ActionListener {
        public void actionPerformed(ActionEvent e){
            getPanel().setBackground(getChooser().getColor());
        }
    }
    ...
    // The (reusable) color chooser.
    private final JColorChooser chooser = new JColorChooser();
}
```

17.21   The JFileChooser Class

The `JFileChooser` class provides a dialog to allow a user to interactively select files
and folders (directories) from the host file system. Figure 17.41 shows the appearance
of such a dialog. The central area contains a display of files and folders which may
be selected or used to navigate part of the underlying file system. The upper area
provides navigational and display controls via a combo box and several buttons. The
lower area contains a text field for entering a file name or for storing the result of a

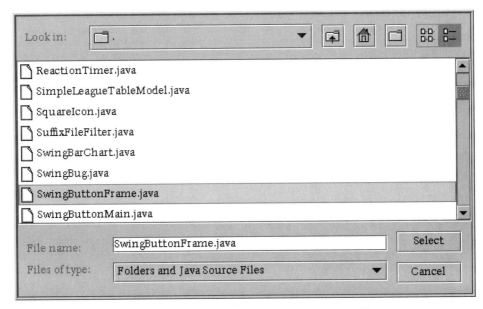

Figure 17.41 A JFileChooser, showing only folders and Java source files
(`SwingFileChooserMain.java`)

selection. A second combo box allows different file filters to be applied in order to restrict the type of files displayed in the central area. Two buttons allow a selection to be confirmed or cancelled; both result in the dialog being closed. The example in Code 17.45 shows one of the ways in which a JFileChooser may be created, and several of the ways in which its behavior may be customized.

Code 17.45   Using a JFileChooser to select a Java source file
(`SwingFileChooserFrame.java`)

```java
import javax.swing.*;
import javax.swing.filechooser.FileFilter;
import java.awt.*;
import java.awt.event.*;
import java.io.*;

        // Display a JFileDialog and allow .java files to be
        // selected. The selected files are displayed in a JList
        // within the frame.
class SwingFileChooserFrame extends JFrame {
    public SwingFileChooserFrame() {
        final int width = 300, height = 300;
        final Container contents = getContentPane();

        setSize(width,height);

        // Place a JList in the center to display the selected files.
        contents.add(getFileList(),"Center");
        JPanel buttonPanel = new QuitJPanel();
        JButton select = new JButton("Choose a File");
        select.addActionListener(new ActionListener(){
            public void actionPerformed(ActionEvent e){
                chooseFrom(".");
            }
        });
        buttonPanel.add(select);
        contents.add(buttonPanel,"South");
    }

        // Choose one or more files from the given folder.
    public void chooseFrom(String folder){
        final Container contents = getContentPane();
        final JLabel where = new JLabel(folder,JLabel.CENTER);
        contents.add(where,"North");

        // Make sure that folder is a directory.
        File source = new File(folder);
        while((folder != null) && !source.isDirectory()){
            folder = JOptionPane.showInputDialog(this,
                        folder+" is not a folder. Try again",
                        "Type a Folder Name",
                        JOptionPane.ERROR_MESSAGE);
            if(folder != null){
                source = new File(folder);
```

Code 17.45   *(Continued)*

```
                }
            }
        if(folder != null){
            displayChooser(source);
        }
    }

    // Display only .java files and folders within the source folder.
    // Only allow .java files to be selected.
    protected void displayChooser(File source){
        // Set up the dialog.
        final JFileChooser chooser = new JFileChooser();
        chooser.setCurrentDirectory(source);
        // Only files may be selected.
        chooser.setFileSelectionMode(JFileChooser.FILES_ONLY);
        // Only allow single selections.
        chooser.setMultiSelectionEnabled(false);
        // Only .java files may be chosen.
        final FileFilter choosableFiles =
                    new SuffixFileFilter("java","Java Source Files");
        // Only display folders and .java files.
        chooser.setFileFilter(new FileFilter(){
            public boolean accept(File f){
                return (f != null) &&
                    (f.isDirectory() || choosableFiles.accept(f));
            }

            public String getDescription(){
                return "Folders and Java Source Files";
            }
        });
        chooser.addChoosableFileFilter(choosableFiles);

        // Show the file chooser..
        if(chooser.showDialog(this,"Select") ==
                        JFileChooser.APPROVE_OPTION){
            // Transfer the selected file to the file list.
            final DefaultListModel model =
                    (DefaultListModel) getFileList().getModel();
            File selection = chooser.getSelectedFile();
            model.addElement(selection);
        }
    }

    protected JList getFileList(){
        return fileList;
    }

    // The list of selected files.
    private final JList fileList = new JList(new DefaultListModel());
}
```

Most of the work related to creating and using the JFileChooser is to be found in the `displayChooser` method. The JFileChooser class has six constructors that allow a chooser to be created with either an explicit starting directory or the user's home directory, by default. An optional `FileSystemView` argument may be included to provide the object with file system specific information. FileSystemView is defined in the associated `javax.swing.filechooser` package. A starting directory for the chooser may be set after construction with `setCurrentDirectory`. By default, a file chooser will display all non-hidden files and folders within the designated folder. The user has a considerable degree of control over what is displayed via the `setFileHidingEnabled` and `setFileFilter` methods. The former turns file hiding on or off; the exact details of which files would normally be hidden is usually a characteristic of the host operating system. We discuss file filters in Section 17.21.1.

File selection refers to what may be returned as an end result of the dialog. If the dialog is being used to select a name in order to save the contents of a file, selecting a folder would probably be inappropriate. By default, all files and folders will be displayed, but only files are selectable. It is also possible to control selection of files or folders via the argument to `setFileSelectionMode`: `FILES_AND_DIRECTORIES`, `FILES_ONLY`, or `DIRECTORIES_ONLY`. In addition, more specific characteristics of naming or content type may be specified via one or more calls to `addChoosableFileFilter`, which takes a FileFilter argument.

Once created and configured, a dialog may be displayed via one of three static methods of the JFileChooser class: `showDialog`, `showOpenDialog`, or `showSaveDialog`. All three take a Component argument representing the parent to which the dialog should belong; this is often the containing JFrame. The names of both `showOpenDialog` and `showSaveDialog` reflect the fact that file dialogs are typically used to select either the name of a file to be opened or to be saved to. The result produced by each is a dialog whose approve button has either an "Open" or "Save" label. The `showDialog` method is the most general; its second argument is the text to be used to label the approve button. When the dialog is closed, all three methods return either `APPROVE_OPTION` or `CANCEL_OPTION` to indicate the result. If the result is `APPROVE_OPTION`, then the selected file or folder may be retrieved with `getSelectedFile`, which returns a `File` object.[6] In the example shown in Code 17.45, we added details of the selected file to the application's JList.

17.21.1   The FileFilter Class

The `FileFilter` abstract class is defined in the `javax.swing.filechooser` package. It is used by several methods of the JFileChooser class to filter out files and folders that should not be displayed in a dialog, or that are not selectable. This simple class is shown in Code 17.46.

Writing a file filter simply involves examining the details recorded in the File argument of `accept` and returning `true` if the file should be accepted. The description string is used in the file chooser's combo box, as shown in Figure 17.41. Code 17.47

---

[6] The API of the class supports multiple file selection via `setMultipleSelection` and `getSelectedFiles`. At the time of writing, however, these methods are not implemented.

Code 17.46   The FileFilter class defined in the `javax.swing.filechooser` package

```java
public abstract class FileFilter {
    public abstract boolean accept(File f);
    public abstract String getDescription();
}
```

Code 17.47   A sub class of FileFilter to select suffixed files (`SuffixFileFilter.java`)

```java
import javax.swing.filechooser.FileFilter;
import java.io.*;

    // Filter files on the given suffix.
    // The suffix may include the preceding dot.
public class SuffixFileFilter extends FileFilter {
    public SuffixFileFilter(String suffix){
        this(suffix,suffix+" files");
    }

    public SuffixFileFilter(String suffix,String description){
        // Include a leading dot.
        if(suffix.charAt(0) != '.'){
            this.suffix = "."+suffix;
        }
        else{
            this.suffix = suffix;
        }
        this.description = description;
    }

    public boolean accept(File f){
        boolean ok = false;
        if(f != null){
            final String name = f.getName();
            if(name != null){
                final int nameLength = name.length();
                int dotIndex = name.lastIndexOf(".");
                ok = (dotIndex >= 1) &&
                    getSuffix().equalsIgnoreCase(name.substring(dotIndex));
            }
        }
        return ok;
    }

    public String getDescription(){
        return description;
    }

    public String getSuffix(){
        return suffix;
    }

    private final String description, suffix;
}
```

shows the `SuffixFileFilter` filter class, which has been written to accept files whose names match a given suffix. The SuffixFileFilter class is used in the example in Code 17.45 to select files with a `.java` suffix. The `getAcceptAllFileFilter` method of JFileChooser returns an implementation of FileFilter that accepts all files.

17.22   The JList Class

The `JList` class is similar in concept to the AWT `List` class. Arbitrary objects may be stored in a JList and selected, either singly or multiply. The list items are managed by an associated object of a class that implements the `ListModel` interface, such as `DefaultListModel`. Selection and de-selection of items is managed by an object belonging to a class that implements the `ListSelectionModel` interface, such as `DefaultListSelectionModel`. The selection model associated with a particular list is able to enforce exclusive selection of a single item, selection of a contiguous range of items, or arbitrary selection of a range of items.

17.22.1   List Selections

Code 17.48 shows an example of a JList allowing arbitrary multiple selection of its items. The effect is shown in Figure 17.42.

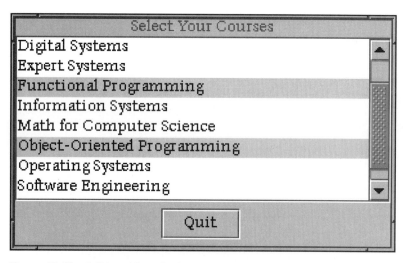

Figure 17.42   A JList with multiple selections (`SwingListMain1.java`)

Code 17.48   Listening for selection events on a JList (`SwingListFrame1.java`)

```
import javax.swing.*;
import javax.swing.event.*;
import java.awt.*;

        // Display listContents in a JList. Monitor selection
        // and de-selection of items in the list.
```

Code 17.48   *(Continued)*

```
class SwingListFrame1 extends JFrame {
    public SwingListFrame1(Object[] listContents) {
        final int width = 300, height = 200;
        setSize(width,height);
        Container contents = getContentPane();

        // Display a title.
        contents.add(new JLabel("Select Your Courses",JLabel.CENTER),
                    "North");

        // Manage the listContents in a JList.
        final JList list = new JList(listContents);
        // Request a minimum of 6 visible items.
        final int minVisible = 6;
        list.setVisibleRowCount(minVisible);
        // Allow multiple selections.
        list.setSelectionMode(
                ListSelectionModel.MULTIPLE_INTERVAL_SELECTION);
        // Detect when items are selected.
        list.addListSelectionListener(new ListEventMonitor());

        // Place the list in a scroll pane.
        contents.add(new JScrollPane(list),"Center");
        contents.add(new QuitJPanel(),"South");
    }

    // A ListSelectionListener that reports changes in a list's
    // selections.
    protected class ListEventMonitor implements ListSelectionListener {
        public void valueChanged(ListSelectionEvent e){
            // The list that has been changed.
            JList listSource = (JList) e.getSource();
            // Gain access to the list data.
            ListModel data = listSource.getModel();
            // Get the boundaries of the change.
            final int first = e.getFirstIndex(), last = e.getLastIndex();
            if(first < 0){
                // Initial 'de-selection'.
            }
            else if(first == last){
                String item = data.getElementAt(first).toString();
                if(listSource.isSelectedIndex(first)){
                    System.out.println(item+" selected.");
                }
                else{
                    System.out.println(item+" de-selected.");
                }
            }
            else{
                String top = data.getElementAt(first).toString(),
                        bottom = data.getElementAt(last).toString();
                if(listSource.isSelectedIndex(first)){
```

(Continued)

Code 17.48   (*Continued*)

```
                    System.out.println("Selection between: "+top+
                                    " and "+bottom);
            }
            else{
                System.out.println("De-selection between: "+top+
                                " and "+bottom);
            }
        }
      }
    }
  }
}
```

A list with more than only a few items should be placed in a JScrollPane (see Section 17.14) to provide a vertical scroll bar if space for the list is insufficient. The `setVisibleRowCount` requests a minimum number of items to appear in the visible portion of the list. The required list selection mode may be set via `set-SelectionMode` which can take a value of `MULTIPLE_INTERVAL_SELECTION`, `SINGLE_INTERVAL_SELECTION`, or `SINGLE_SELECTION`, whose values are defined in the ListSelectionModel interface in the `javax.swing.event` package. A single item is usually selected by clicking over it with a mouse. An interval is selected by clicking the mouse while holding down the *Shift* key. A single additional item is added to those already selected by holding down the *Ctrl* key while clicking the mouse.

In the example in Code 17.48, a `ListSelectionListener` has been defined by the `ListEventMonitor` inner class. Whenever an item in the list is selected or de-selected, a `ListSelectionEvent` event will be received by registered listeners. The source of the event is the JList object, and access to the items in it is obtained via its associated data model (`getModel`). A little care needs to be exercised in interpreting the meaning of a ListSelectionEvent because it could represent either selection or de-selection of either a single item or a range of items. Furthermore, the range cannot necessarily be interpreted as meaning that all items within that range are now in the same state. The selection state of individual items can be established via the JList's `isSelectedIndex` method, which returns `true` if the item at the given index is selected, and `false` otherwise. Because a single selection can trigger a series of events, the `getValueIsAdjusting` method is provided by ListSelectionEvent. This should return `true` if the current event is one of a series and `false` if it is the last.

17.22.2   List Changes

Code 17.49 shows how new items may be added to the data model of a list. Its appearance is shown in Figure 17.43. In order to be able to add and remove items from the list, the ListModel functionality has been provided by a `DefaultListModel` object. Whenever the contents of the data model is altered, the list model notifies any registered `ListDataListener` objects by issuing a `ListDataEvent` object.

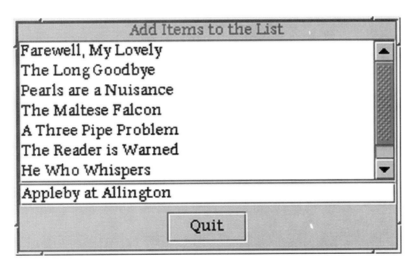

Figure 17.43   Adding new items to a JList (`SwingListMain2.java`)

Code 17.49   Listening for additions to a JList (`SwingListFrame2.java`)

```
import javax.swing.*;
import javax.swing.event.*;
import java.awt.*;
import java.awt.event.*;

        // Display a JList and allow additions through a JTextField.
        // Monitor additions to the list.
class SwingListFrame2 extends JFrame {
    public SwingListFrame2(){
        final int width = 300, height = 200;
        setSize(width,height);
        Container contents = getContentPane();

        // Display a title.
        contents.add(new JLabel("Add Items to the List",JLabel.CENTER),
                "North");

        // Use a DefaultListModel object to manage the list.
        final JList list = new JList(new DefaultListModel());
        // Detect when items are selected.
        list.getModel().addListDataListener(new ListDataMonitor());

        // Provide a text field. Text entered here is added to the list
        // as a new item.
        final JTextField inputLine = new JTextField("");
        // Pressing Enter causes the text to be added to the list.
        inputLine.addActionListener(new ActionListener(){
            public void actionPerformed(ActionEvent e){
                // Add the text as a new item in the list.
                final JTextField line = (JTextField) e.getSource();
```

(Continued)

Code 17.49   *(Continued)*

```
                final DefaultListModel model =
                                (DefaultListModel) list.getModel();
            model.addElement(line.getText());
            line.setText("");
        }
    });

    // Place the list and input line in a panel.
    JPanel panel = new JPanel();
    panel.setLayout(new BorderLayout());
    panel.add(new JScrollPane(list));
    panel.add(inputLine,"South");

    contents.add(panel,"Center");
    contents.add(new QuitJPanel(),"South");
}

    // A ListDataListener that reports changes in the
    // contents of a list's data model.
protected class ListDataMonitor implements ListDataListener {
    public void intervalAdded(ListDataEvent e){
        final ListModel model = (ListModel) e.getSource();
        final int first = e.getIndex0(), last = e.getIndex1();

        if(first == last){
            Object item = model.getElementAt(first);
            System.out.println("Added: "+item.toString());
        }
        else{
            System.out.println("Interval added: "+first+" to "+last);
        }
    }

    public void intervalRemoved(ListDataEvent e){
        System.out.println("Interval removed.");
    }

    public void contentsChanged(ListDataEvent e){
        System.out.println("Contents changed.");
    }
}
}
```

An inner `ListDataMonitor` class has been used to implement the listener functionality. It implements three methods, `intervalAdded`, `intervalRemoved`, and
`contentsChanged`, only the first of which will be called in this example. The indices of the elements affected in the model are available via the `getIndex0` and
`getIndex1` methods of the ListDataEvent object.

   In the application in Code 17.49, items are added to the list by entering a line
of text in a JTextField. An ActionListener object attached to the text field extracts

the text of the line and adds it as an item to the list. The field is then cleared ready for another line. Adding an item will cause the `intervalAdded` method of the ListDataMonitor object to be called.

17.23   The JComboBox Class

The `JComboBox` class is similar to the JList class. The major differences are that it is only possible to make a single selection with a JComboBox and, in its passive state, it displays only a single item from its associated ListModel. The contents of a JComboBox are typically String or Icon objects. Figure 17.44 shows a JComboBox in its passive state at the top of a frame. The arrow to the right of the box indicates that a drop down list is hidden beneath the most recently selected item. Clicking on the box causes the remainder of the list to appear (Figure 17.45). The example in Code 17.50 shows how to create a combo box containing a list of colored icons. We use an implementation of the Icon interface, `SquareIcon`, that is similar to `CircleIcon`, shown in Code 17.8.

A JComboBox may either be constructed from an array of Objects, the contents of a `Vector`, or with an empty list model. The `DefaultComboBoxModel` provides a convenient implementation of the `MutableComboBoxModel`, to which items may be added as required, either via the model's `addElement` method or the box's `addItem` method which delegates to the model. The example in Code 17.50 uses the former approach in its `setupComboBox` method. A selection from the box can be detected by attaching an ItemListener to it. The source of the ItemEvent is the box, and its `getSelectedItem` method returns a reference to the selected item. This item becomes the one shown on the box in its passive state. If the combo box is editable (`setEditable`) then new Strings may be added to the list.

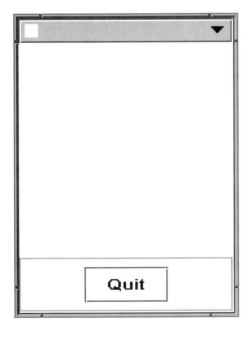

Figure 17.44   An unselected JComboBox

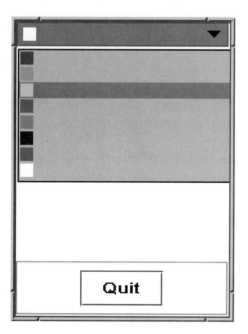

Figure 17.45   A selected JComboBox

Code 17.50   Using a JComboBox to set the background color of a central panel
(SwingComboFrame.java)

```
import javax.swing.*;
import java.awt.*;
import java.awt.event.*;

        // Display a JComboBox that allows the background color
        // of the central panel to be selected.
class SwingComboFrame extends JFrame {
    public SwingComboFrame() {
        final int width = 175, height = 250;
        setSize(width,height);
        Container contents = getContentPane();

        setupComboBox();
        contents.add(getBox(),"North");
        contents.add(getPanel(),"Center");
        JPanel buttonPanel = new JPanel();
        buttonPanel.add(new QuitJButton());
        contents.add(buttonPanel,"South");
    }

        // Add colored labels to the combo box.
    protected void setupComboBox(){
        // Color/Name pairs.
        final Color[] colors = {
            Color.red, Color.orange, Color.yellow, Color.green,
            Color.cyan, Color.blue, Color.magenta, Color.white,
        };
```

Code 17.50   (*Continued*)

```
        // Add SquareIcon elements to the box's model.
        final JComboBox box = getBox();
        final DefaultComboBoxModel model =
                        (DefaultComboBoxModel) box.getModel();
        final int numColors = colors.length;
        for(int i = 0; i < numColors; i++){
            model.addElement(new SquareIcon(colors[i]));
        }

        // Act on selections.
        box.addItemListener(new ItemListener(){
            public void itemStateChanged(ItemEvent e){
                if(e.getStateChange() == ItemEvent.SELECTED){
                    SquareIcon icon = (SquareIcon) box.getSelectedItem();
                    // Change the central panel's background color.
                    getPanel().setBackground(icon.getColor());
                }
            }
        });

        // The user should not be able to enter a new item.
        box.setEditable(false);
    }

    protected JComboBox getBox(){
        return box;
    }

    protected JPanel getPanel(){
        return panel;
    }

    // A color choosing combo box.
    private final JComboBox box = new JComboBox(new DefaultComboBoxModel());
    // A central panel to be colored.
    private final JPanel panel = new JPanel();
}
```

17.24   The JProgressBar Class

The JProgressBar class provides a visualization for progress made over an integer range. The example in Code 17.10 used a class based on the JProgressBar to implement a reaction timer, for instance. (The implementation of this is shown in Code 17.52.) The constructors of JProgressBar allow the limits of the range to be specified and an orientation for the bar (HORIZONTAL or VERTICAL). By default, the range is [0...100] and the orientation is horizontal. A progress bar does not drive itself; the value on which it bases its indication of progress is set via its setValue mutator. Code 17.51 show an example of a thread that sleeps periodically and updates the bar with the amount of time it has slept. Its appearance is shown in Figure 17.46.

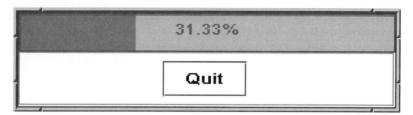

Figure 17.46   A JProgressBar with painted string (`SwingProgressMain.java`)

Code 17.51   Periodically updating a JProgressBar (`SwingProgressFrame.java`)

```java
import javax.swing.*;
import java.awt.*;
import java.awt.event.*;
import java.text.*;

    // Show a JProgressBar and periodically update it.
class SwingProgressFrame extends JFrame implements Runnable {
    public SwingProgressFrame() {
        final int width = 300, height = 100;
        setSize(width,height);

        Container contents = getContentPane();
        contents.add(getBar(),"Center");
        contents.add(new QuitJPanel(),"South");
    }

    // Sleep for short periods and add the sleep time to the
    // value of the bar.
    public void run(){
        final int sleepTime = 100;
        // A formatter for the percentage progress
        NumberFormat formatter = NumberFormat.getNumberInstance();
        formatter.setMinimumFractionDigits(2);
        formatter.setMaximumFractionDigits(2);

        final JProgressBar bar = getBar();
        bar.setValue(0);
        // Don't assume some one else isn't changing the bar's data.
        while(bar.getValue() < bar.getMaximum()){
            try{
                Thread.sleep(sleepTime);
                bar.setValue(bar.getValue()+sleepTime);
                // Show what percentage has been done.
                double percentDone = 100*bar.getPercentComplete();
                bar.setString(formatter.format(percentDone)+"%");
            }
            catch(InterruptedException e){
            }
        }
    }
}
```

Code 17.51   (*Continued*)

```
    protected JProgressBar getBar(){
        return bar;
    }

    // Let it run for the equivalent of 30 seconds.
    private final int min = 0, max = 30*1000;
    private final JProgressBar bar =
        new JProgressBar(JProgressBar.HORIZONTAL,min,max);
    {
        bar.setStringPainted(true);
    }
}
```

The getPercentComplete method returns the percentage progress as a double
value in the range 0.0 to 1.0. Notice that the class allows an additional string to be
included on the bar, set via its setString method. This string will only be painted
if requested via the setStringPainted method. An object wishing to be notified
of changes to the bar's value may register as a ChangeListener in the normal way,
via addChangeListener.

17.24.1   The Timer Class

The Timer class can be used to fire ActionEvents periodically at registered listeners.
The example in Code 17.52 shows one being used by the ReactionTimer class,
previously seen in the example in Code 17.10. The period between events has been
specified as an argument to the Timer's constructor.

Code 17.52   Using a Timer to advance a JProgressBar (`ReactionTimer.java`)

```
import javax.swing.*;
import java.awt.*;
import java.awt.event.*;

    // Maintain a Timer linked to this JProgressBar.
    // At every timer increment, adjust the bar by increment.
    // Used by the SwingButtonFrame class.
class ReactionTimer extends JProgressBar implements ActionListener {
    // How many milliseconds to update.
    public static final int increment = 50;
    public static final int min = 0, max = 100*increment;

    public ReactionTimer(int orientation){
        super(orientation,min,max);
    }

    public void start(){
        setValue(0);
```

                                                                    (*Continued*)

Code 17.52   *(Continued)*

```
        getTimer().start();
    }

    public void stop(){
        getTimer().stop();
    }

    public void actionPerformed(ActionEvent e){
        // The timer has ping'ed.
        setValue(getValue()+increment);
    }

    protected Timer getTimer(){
        return timer;
    }

    // At every increment, the Timer notified this object to
    // update the progress bar.
    private final Timer timer = new Timer(increment,this);
}
```

The ReactionTimer registers as an action listener via the constructor's second argument. The Timer does not send events until it receives a `start` message. Thereafter, it will continue to send events until it receives a `stop` message. A distinct initial delay may be set via its `setInitialDelay` method. A timer may be restarted via its `restart` message, and it will reuse the initial delay, if one has been set.

17.25   The JSlider Class

The `JSlider` class provides a visual representation for, and manipulation of, an index position within a discrete bounded range of integers. The slider may be annotated with major and minor tick marks, and optional labels at the major tick positions. Figure 17.47 shows an application whose user interface contains two JSliders. The sliders are used to control the values to be displayed in the two labels at the top of the frame, which are arbitrarily described as temperature and pressure in this example. The upper slider is used to control the absolute value of the temperature and the lower slider provides a multiplier for the temperature in order to calculate the pressure value. Moving either slider results in the values in both labels being changed. Code 17.53 shows the frame class used to create this application.

Code 17.53   Using two JSlider components to control temperature and pressure levels
(`SwingSliderFrame.java`)

```
import javax.swing.*;
import javax.swing.event.*;
import javax.swing.border.*;
import java.awt.*;
```

Code 17.53   (*Continued*)

```
import java.awt.event.*;

        /* Use two JSlider objects to control a related pair of
         * temperature and pressure values.
         * One slider controls the temperature and the other provides
         * a scaling factor with which to derive the pressure from
         * the temperature.
         * The units are arbitrary.
         */
class SwingSliderFrame extends JFrame {
    public SwingSliderFrame() {
        final int width = 360, height = 200;

        setSize(width,height);

        // Set up listeners for the two sliders.
        setupTemperatureSlider();
        setupPressureSlider();
        // Show the initial values.
        showTemperatureAndPressure();

        // A panel for the temperature and pressure displays.
        JPanel displayPanel = new JPanel();
        displayPanel.add(getTemperatureDisplay());
        displayPanel.add(getPressureDisplay());

        // Place the display and two JSliders vertically above
        // each other.
        JPanel groupedPanel = new JPanel();
        final int rows = 3, cols = 1;
        groupedPanel.setLayout(new GridLayout(rows,cols));
        groupedPanel.add(displayPanel);
        groupedPanel.add(getTemperatureSlider());
        groupedPanel.add(getScalingSlider());

        final Container contents = getContentPane();
        contents.add(groupedPanel,"Center");
        contents.add(new QuitJPanel(),"South");
    }

        // Attach a listener to the slider controlling the range of
        // possible temperatures.
    protected void setupTemperatureSlider(){
        getTemperatureSlider().addChangeListener(new ChangeListener(){
            public void stateChanged(ChangeEvent e){
                JSlider slider = (JSlider) e.getSource();
                // Only update when movement has settled down.
                if(!slider.getValueIsAdjusting()){
                    showTemperatureAndPressure();
                }
            }
        });
```

(*Continued*)

Code 17.53   *(Continued)*

```
    }

        // Attach a listener to the slider controlling the scaling of
        // the temperature to produce a pressure.
    protected void setupPressureSlider(){
        // Add a listener to change the displays.
        getScalingSlider().addChangeListener(new ChangeListener(){
            public void stateChanged(ChangeEvent e){
                // Update continuously.
                showTemperatureAndPressure();
            }
        });
    }

        // Determine the new values from the two sliders and
        // display them.
    protected void showTemperatureAndPressure(){
        final JSlider tempSlider = getTemperatureSlider();
        final int temperature = tempSlider.getValue();
        final int pressure = temperature*getScalingSlider().getValue();

        getTemperatureDisplay().setText("T = "+temperature);
        getPressureDisplay().setText("P = "+pressure);
    }

    protected JLabel getTemperatureDisplay(){
        return temperatureDisplay;
    }

    protected JLabel getPressureDisplay(){
        return pressureDisplay;
    }

    protected JSlider getTemperatureSlider(){
        return temperatureSlider;
    }

    protected JSlider getScalingSlider(){
        return scalingSlider;
    }

    // Two labels to hold the dependent values.
    private final JLabel temperatureDisplay = new JLabel("T = 12345"),
                         pressureDisplay = new JLabel("P = 12345");
    {
        final Font f = new Font("SansSerif",Font.BOLD,16);
        temperatureDisplay.setFont(f);
        temperatureDisplay.setBorder(
                BorderFactory.createBevelBorder(BevelBorder.RAISED));
        pressureDisplay.setFont(f);
        pressureDisplay.setBorder(
                BorderFactory.createBevelBorder(BevelBorder.RAISED));
    }
```

Code 17.53   (*Continued*)

```
        // A slider for controlling the temperature value.
    private final int minTemperature = 200, maxTemperature = 300,
                    initialTemperature = 273;
    private final JSlider temperatureSlider =
            new JSlider(JSlider.HORIZONTAL,
                minTemperature,maxTemperature,initialTemperature);
    {
        // Display major and minor ticks on the scale.
        temperatureSlider.setPaintTicks(true);
        temperatureSlider.setMajorTickSpacing(25);
        temperatureSlider.setMinorTickSpacing(5);
        temperatureSlider.setPaintLabels(true);
    }

        // A slider for the scaling the pressure. The current pressure
        // will be the current temperature scaled by this value.
        // Use the JSlider defaults for the scaling range.
    private final JSlider scalingSlider = new JSlider();
    {
        scalingSlider.setPaintTicks(true);
        scalingSlider.setMajorTickSpacing(10);
        scalingSlider.setPaintLabels(true);
    }
}
```

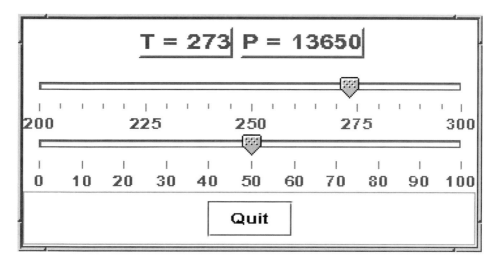

Figure 17.47   The appearance of two JSliders, with tick marks and labels
(SwingSliderMain.java)

JSliders may be positioned either vertically or horizontally, and the end points of their range may be specified via the constructor or the class's mutator methods. The `scalingSlider` object in Code 17.53 uses the *no-arg constructor*, which means it will be placed horizontally and have a minimum value of 0, a maximum value of 100 and an initial value of 50. The `setMajorTickSpacing` method sets large tick marks at every multiple of its argument. In addition, the `setPaintLabels` method may be used to annotate the major tick marks with numeric labels (an alternative set of labels may be set with the `setLabelTable` method). The `temperature-Slider` object in Code 17.53 has its range set via the constructor. It has minor tick marks sets via its `setMinorTickSpacing` method. The minor tick spacing should normally exactly divide the major tick spacing, otherwise mismatches arise in the slider's appearance.

Movements of the slider give rise to ChangeEvents being passed to any registered ChangeListeners. Responding to these events usually involves inquiring of the slider object what its current value is. The slider's `getValueIsAdjusting` method can be used to differentiate between an event that is one of a series—as the slider is being moved—or because it has reached a resting place. Its use can be seen in `setupTemperatureSlider` in Code 17.53 where we choose to only update the temperature and pressure display once movement has ceased. Adjustments of the scaling slider, on the other hand, cause continuous adjustment of the values.

17.26   The JTable Class

The `JTable` class provides an extremely sophisticated component for the display and editing of data. The data is presented in a rectangular grid of cells, much like a spreadsheet in appearance, but where each cell may be occupied by an arbitrary object—not just a GUI component. In general, each column is devoted to a homogeneous display of a particular class type, while each row is made up from a heterogeneous collection of class types. However, since all classes share Object as a common super class, there is nothing to prevent a column from containing heterogeneous data. The JTable class is another of the Swing classes in which the presentation and manipulation of the data view is kept as separate as possible from the underlying data model. What this means, in practice, is that a single JTable object consists of multiple objects of different classes collaborating together. The different classes involved are `JTableHeader` and `TableColumn`, along with implementations of the `TableColumnModel` and `TableModel` interfaces. Each of these classes and interfaces, except JTable, are defined in the `javax.swing.table` package.

In the remainder of this section, we shall give a flavor of what is possible with the JTable class by creating a table to represent and edit the data in a fixed-size sports league, such as that described in Section 9.16. Figure 17.48 shows the final appearance of this application. Code 17.54 shows the main method that was used to create the `League` object containing the data, and pass it on to the application to be displayed.

Before showing how the finished editable version of the table is created, we shall describe how to define a simpler read-only version. This version is created by the main method in `SwingTableMain1.java`, which is almost identical to that shown in Code 17.54.

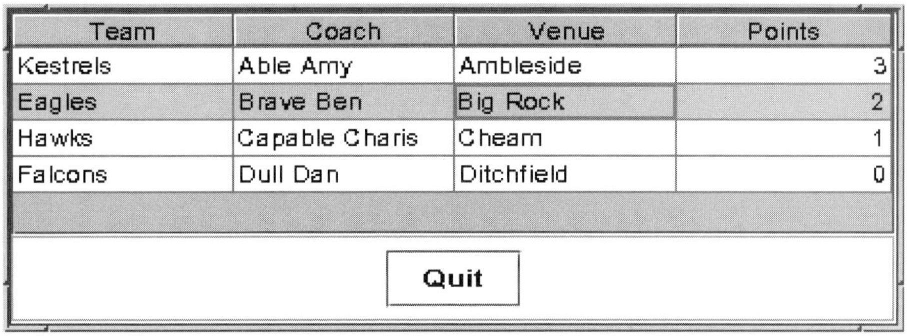

Figure 17.48   A JTable containing details from a `League` object
(SwingTableMain2.java)

Code 17.54   Creating the data to be displayed in the table (`SwingTableMain2.java`)

```
import javax.swing.*;

class SwingTableMain2 {
    public static void main(String[] args){
        SwingTableFrame2 f = new SwingTableFrame2();
        // Create the League object from four sample sets of team
        // details.
        League league = new League(new TeamDetails[]{
            new TeamDetails("Kestrels", "Able Amy", "Ambleside"),
            new TeamDetails("Eagles", "Brave Ben", "Big Rock"),
            new TeamDetails("Hawks", "Capable Charis", "Cheam"),
            new TeamDetails("Falcons", "Dull Dan", "Ditchfield"),
        });

        f.setLeague(league);

        f.addWindowListener(new WindowCloser());
        f.setVisible(true);
    }
}
```

17.26.1   The AbstractTableModel Class

The way in which the data view is kept separate from the data in the underlying model, is by having the JTable interact with the model via an object that belongs to a class implementing the `TableModel` interface. The JTable class defines a `setModel` method which can be used to associate the GUI classes with the underlying model. Code 17.55 shows a sub class of JFrame that creates a JTable object, sets up its data model, and displays the table within a JScrollPane.

In the frame's constructor, we associate a preferred size for the table via its `setPreferredScrollableViewportSize` method. The dimensions, in this case, are

---

Code 17.55   Creation of a JTable and placement within a scroll pane
(`SwingTableFrame2.java`)

```
import javax.swing.*;
import java.awt.*;

class SwingTableFrame2 extends JFrame {
    public SwingTableFrame2() {
        // setSize(width,height);
        Container contents = getContentPane();

        // Define the table's preferred size, to avoid a lot of
        // blank space within the scroll pane.
        final int tableWidth = 400, tableHeight = 100;
        getTable().setPreferredScrollableViewportSize(
                    new Dimension(tableWidth,tableHeight));

        // Add the table to the frame within a scroll pane.
        contents.add(new JScrollPane(getTable()),"Center");
        contents.add(new QuitJPanel(),"South");

        pack();
    }

        // Receive the League to be displayed.
    public void setLeague(League teams){
        // An appropriate table model is needed.
        getTable().setModel(new LeagueTableModel(teams));
    }

    protected JTable getTable(){
        return table;
    }

    private final JTable table = new JTable();
}
```

---

based upon a knowledge of how the data will need to be displayed. The data that
belongs to the model is passed to the frame via its `setLeague` method. We have
wrapped this in an object of class `LeagueTableModel` which implements the Table-
Model interface, and so it may be passed to the table's `setModel` method. From
this point on, whenever the table needs access to the data, it will obtain it via the
LeagueTableModel object.

   The easiest way to create a class such as LeagueTableModel is to extend
the `AbstractTableModel` class. This implements most of the methods of the
TableModel interface except for three: `getRowCount`, `getColumnCount`, and
`getValueAt`. Code 17.56 shows a simplified version of LeagueTableModel that
completes this implementation in order to supply data from a League object to a
JTable.

```java
import javax.swing.*;
import javax.swing.table.*;
import java.awt.*;

    // Implement only the required methods of AbstractTableModel.
class SimpleLeagueTableModel extends AbstractTableModel {
    public SimpleLeagueTableModel(League l){
        league = l;
    }

        // Implementations of the abstract methods.

    public int getRowCount(){
        return getTeams().length;
    }

    public int getColumnCount(){
        return numColumns;
    }

    public Object getValueAt(int row, int col){
        final TeamDetails[] teams = getTeams();
        final int numTeams = teams.length;
        if((row >= 0) && (row < numTeams) &&
           (col >= 0) && (col < numColumns)){
            final TeamDetails team = teams[row];
            switch(col){
                case TEAM:
                    return team.getName();
                case COACH:
                    return team.getCoach();
                case VENUE:
                    return team.getVenue();
                case POINTS:
                    return new Integer(team.getPoints());
                default:
                    return null;
            }
        }
        else{
            return null;
        }
    }

    protected TeamDetails[] getTeams(){
        return getLeague().getTeams();
    }

    protected League getLeague(){
        return league;
    }

    // This information is closely tied to the implementation of
    // TeamDetails.
    private static final int numColumns = 4;
    private static final int TEAM = 0, COACH = 1, VENUE = 2, POINTS = 3;

    // The team details.
    private final League league;
}
```

Both TableModel and AbstractTableModel are defined in the `javax.swing.-table` package. Each row of the table will display the information contained in a single `TeamDetails` object. The number of rows in the table is simply the number of teams in the league. The number of columns is slightly harder to calculate since it is tied closely to the definition of the TeamDetails class (`getColumnCount`). The `getValueAt` method must interpret a column index as a particular field within TeamDetails. We can see that there is a very high degree of *coupling* between the class representing the data in the model to the table (SimpleLeagueTableModel), and the class containing the data of the model (TeamDetails). The SimpleLeagueModel class needs to know the name of each accessor method of the TeamDetails class and, in the case of the `points` attribute, it needs to know that it must wrap an int value in an Integer object. If the TeamDetails class were to add further attributes that must be displayed in the table, then the TableModel class would also need changes to keep up with it.

There are three alternatives that could be taken in this case:

- We could have the TeamDetails class, itself, either extend AbstractTableModel or implement TableModel.
- We could add a method to TeamDetails that maps a column index into an Object representation of one of its fields.
- We could use reflection to determine the names and arguments of the appropriate methods.

In this particular case, we have preferred to leave TeamDetails unmodified, and therefore unaware that it might be being used in this context. Different projects will have different requirements for the solution to similar problems.

17.26.2   The TableModel Interface

The implementation of SimpleLeagueTableModel in Code 17.56 leads to the creation of a read-only table of the league's details shown in Figure 17.49. Not only is it not possible to modify the data, but the headers are rather uninformative default headers, because the table model has supplied no alternatives. Code 17.57 shows the complete set of methods defined in the TableModel interface.

A	B	C	D
Kestrels	Able Amy	Ambleside	0
Eagles	Brave Ben	Big Rock	0
Hawks	Capable Charis	Cheam	0
Falcons	Dull Dan	Ditchfield	0

Quit

Figure 17.49 · A read-only presentation of the League's data (`SwingTableMain1.java`)

Code 17.57   The TableModel interface

```
public interface TableModel {
        // Methods left abstract in AbstractTableModel.
    public int getColumnCount();
    public int getRowCount();
    public Object getValueAt(int row, int col);

        // Methods to enable editing.
    public boolean isCellEditable(int row, int col);
    public void setValueAt(Object value, int row, int col);

        // Column information.
    public String getColumnName(int columnIndex);
    public Class getColumnClass(int columnIndex);

        // Attach and remove change-listeners.
    public void addTableModelListener(TableModelListener listener);
    public void removeTableModelListener(TableModelListener listener);
}
```

The getColumnName method allows a header to be associated with each column. If a table is wrapped in a JScrollPane, the scroll pane is able to keep the headers associated with the data as a table is scrolled either horizontally or vertically (see Section 17.14.3). The getColumnClass is used by the view to determine how the cells in a column should be displayed. In order to permit editing of a table's cells, the isCellEditable method must return true for each editable cell. This is often simply a case of checking the column index. If editing of one or more cells is possible, the setValueAt method must arrange for the value argument to be written into the data model. It should not be necessary to alter the addTableModelListener or removeTableModelListener methods.

Code 17.58 shows the LeagueTableModel class that overrides several of these methods to provide more informative headers and the ability to edit the Points column of the table.

Code 17.58   Overriding methods of AbstractTableModel to enhance the table
(LeagueTableModel.java)

```
import javax.swing.*;
import javax.swing.table.*;
import java.awt.*;

    // Implement the methods of AbstractTableModel that make it
    // possible to edit some of the data, and have headers displayed.
class LeagueTableModel extends AbstractTableModel {
    public LeagueTableModel(League l){
        league = l;
    }
```

(Continued)

Code 17.58 *(Continued)*

```
    // Implementations of the abstract methods.

public int getRowCount(){
    return getTeams().length;
}

public int getColumnCount(){
    return numColumns;
}

public Object getValueAt(int row, int col){
    final TeamDetails[] teams = getTeams();
    final int numTeams = teams.length;
    if((row >= 0) && (row < numTeams) &&
       (col >= 0) && (col < numColumns)){
        final TeamDetails team = teams[row];
        switch(col){
            case TEAM:
                return team.getName();
            case COACH:
                return team.getCoach();
            case VENUE:
                return team.getVenue();
            case POINTS:
                return new Integer(team.getPoints());
            default:
                return null;
        }
    }
    else{
        return null;
    }
}

    // Only a team's points may be changed.
public boolean isCellEditable(int row, int col){
    return col == POINTS;
}

    // Implement the required change, if the cell is editable.
public void setValueAt(Object value,int row, int col){
    if(isCellEditable(row,col)){
        try{
            final TeamDetails[] teams = getTeams();
            final TeamDetails team = teams[row];
            switch(col){
                case POINTS:
                    int points = Integer.parseInt((String) value);
                    team.setPoints(points);
                    fireTableCellUpdated(row,col);
                    break;
            }
        }
        catch(Exception e){
            JOptionPane.showMessageDialog(null,e,
```

Code 17.58   (*Continued*)

```java
                                            "Value Setting Error",
                                            JOptionPane.ERROR_MESSAGE);
            }
        }
    }

    public String getColumnName(int col){
        final String[] headers = getHeaders();
        if(col < headers.length){
            return headers[col];
        }
        else{
            return "???";
        }
    }

    public Class getColumnClass(int col){
        if(col < numColumns){
            // Pick up the class from an arbitrary cell
            // in this column.
            return getValueAt(0,col).getClass();
        }
        else{
            Object o = new Object();
            return o.getClass();
        }
    }

    protected TeamDetails[] getTeams(){
        return getLeague().getTeams();
    }

    protected League getLeague(){
        return league;
    }

    protected String[] getHeaders(){
        return headers;
    }

    // This information is closely tied to the implementation of
    // TeamDetails.
    private static final int numColumns = 4;
    private static final int TEAM = 0, COACH = 1, VENUE = 2, POINTS = 3;
    private static final String[] headers = new String[numColumns];
    static {
        headers[TEAM] = "Team";
        headers[COACH] = "Coach";
        headers[VENUE] = "Venue";
        headers[POINTS] = "Points";
    };

    // The team details.
    private final League league;
}
```

Notice that the `setValueAt` method must notify any listeners of a change to the data model by calling `fireTableCellUpdated`.

17.27   The JTree Class

The `JTree` class is one of Swing's more sophisticated components, so we can only provide a flavor of its capabilities in this section. One of its most common uses is to display the contents of a hierarchical file system, with folders (directories) representing the internal nodes of the tree and files as the leaf nodes. However, as the example we shall present shows, it can present any data structure that is tree-like, such as the contents of a document or the managerial structure of a business. Figure 17.50 shows the appearance of a typical JTree within an application. In addition to the JTree in the central area of this application, a JTextField allows names for new nodes to be entered. The visual representation of a JTree is kept separate from the underlying data model and node storage by interfaces such as `TreeModel` and `TreeNode` that are defined in the `javax.swing.tree` package. Convenient implementations of these are provided by the `DefaultTreeModel` and `DefaultMutableTreeNode` classes, both of which are defined in the same package. These are the fundamental building blocks of a JTree.

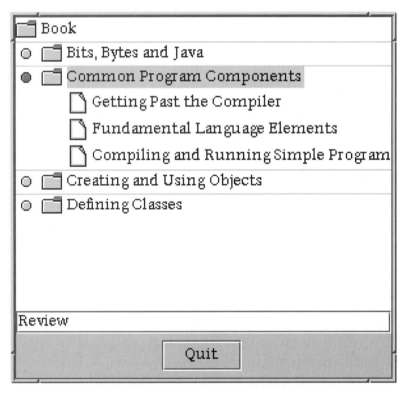

Figure 17.50   A JTree displaying the chapter and section structure of a book (`SwingTreeMain.java`)

Code 17.59 shows a class that creates the example shown in Figure 17.50. Most of the relevant functionality is defined in the `setupBookTree` and `addNode` methods. The several constructors of JTree allow a new tree to be created using an array of Objects, a `Hashtable`, a `Vector`, an existing TreeModel, or TreeNode. Alternatively, we have chosen to use the no-arg constructor and later pass the model to be used via the `setModel` method, once it has been created in `setupBookTree`.

Code 17.59   Creating and adding nodes to a JTree (`SwingTreeFrame.java`)

```java
import javax.swing.*;
import javax.swing.tree.*;
import java.awt.*;
import java.awt.event.*;

class SwingTreeFrame extends JFrame {
    public SwingTreeFrame() {
        final int width = 300, height = 300;
        setSize(width,height);
        Container contents = getContentPane();

        setupBookTree();
        setupInputLine();
        JPanel treePanel = new JPanel();
        treePanel.setLayout(new BorderLayout());
        treePanel.add(getBook(),"Center");
        treePanel.add(getInputLine(),"South");
        contents.add(treePanel,"Center");
        contents.add(new QuitJPanel(),"South");
    }

    protected void setupBookTree(){
        final DefaultMutableTreeNode root =
                        new DefaultMutableTreeNode("Book");
        // The first string in each row is the chapter title; the remaining
        // strings are some of the section headings.
        final String[][] contents = {
            {"Bits, Bytes and Java",
              "The Challenge","A Simple Model of a Computer",
              "Bits and Bytes","The Central Processing Unit",
            },
            {"Common Program Components",
              "Getting Past the Compiler","Fundamental Language Elements",
              "Compiling and Running Simple Programs",
            },
            {"Creating and Using Objects",
              "Why So Much for So Little?",
              "What are Object-Oriented Languages?",
              "Modeling the Operation of a Port", "...",
            },
            {"Defining Classes",
              "Usage of the Main Method's Class",
              "Object State and Complexity",
              "The Outline of a Class Definition",
```

(Continued)

Code 17.59   (*Continued*)

```
            "The SimpleSwitch Class",
            "Encapsulation", "...",
        },
    };
    final int numChapters = contents.length;
    for(int i = 0; i < numChapters; i++){
        DefaultMutableTreeNode chapterNode =
                        new DefaultMutableTreeNode(contents[i][0]);
        final int numSections = contents[i].length;
        for(int j = 1; j < numSections; j++){
            chapterNode.add(new DefaultMutableTreeNode(contents[i][j]));
        }
        root.add(chapterNode);
    }
    DefaultTreeModel model = new DefaultTreeModel(root);
    getBook().setModel(model);
}

// Add a listener to the input line.
// This will add its text to the tree when Enter is pressed.
protected void setupInputLine(){
    final JTextField line = getInputLine();
    line.addActionListener(new ActionListener(){
        public void actionPerformed(ActionEvent e){
            String text = line.getText();
            if(!text.equals("")){
                addNode(text);
                // Clear the line.
                line.setText("");
            }
        }
    });
}

// Find the currently selected node and add text as a child.
protected void addNode(String text){
    // Add the text as a new node.
    TreePath path = getBook().getSelectionPath();
    if(path != null){
        Object o = path.getLastPathComponent();
        if(o instanceof DefaultMutableTreeNode){
            DefaultMutableTreeNode node = (DefaultMutableTreeNode) o;
            node.add(new DefaultMutableTreeNode(text));
            DefaultTreeModel model =
                    (DefaultTreeModel)getBook().getModel();
            // Tell the tree to redisplay the modified node.
            model.reload(node);
        }
    }
}

protected JTree getBook(){
    return book;
```

Code 17.59   (*Continued*)

```
    }

    protected JTextField getInputLine(){
        return inputLine;
    }

    // Maintain the book structure in a tree.
    private final JTree book = new JTree();
    // Allow nodes to be added to the book-tree.
    private final JTextField inputLine = new JTextField();
}
```

The nodes of a tree are created from a hierarchy of objects whose class implements the TreeNode interface. It is important to distinguish between a node and the Object it holds. Objects of any class may be stored within a node. Internal nodes have a single parent and the root of the tree is distinguished by having no parent. A node may have zero or more children and is called a leaf node if it has no children. The `DefaultMutableTreeNode` class allows a node to be created with a given Object as its contents. When the node is created, it is possible to indicate that it is not allowed to have child nodes attached to it. This sort of node would be appropriate for holding a reference to an ordinary file object (i.e., one that is not a folder or directory). The `add` method of `DefaultMutableTreeNode` takes another node object as its argument and adds it to its list of children, if these are allowed. This is the approach taken in `setupBookTree` in Code 17.59. A parent node is set up containing the name of a chapter, and multiple child nodes are added to it representing sections within the chapter. This example could be extended to allow subsection children of the section nodes, for instance. The chapter nodes are added as children of the root node that is created at the start of the method. Once all of the nodes have been created, a DefaultTreeModel object is created to manage them. This takes the root to its constructor, and this model is then set for the JTree.

The application in Code 17.59 contains a JTextField that allows a user to create new chapters and sections. A listener attached to the field adds a new node containing the text of the line by calling the frame's `addNode` method. The `addNode` method uses the `getSelectionPath` method of JTree to find out the currently selected node; this could be the root node, an internal node, or a leaf node. This returns a `TreePath` object which identifies a unique path from the root of the tree to the selected node. Individual elements of the path may be extracted from this via its `getPathComponent` method, and the number of components is available via its `getPathCount` method. In this example, we are only interested in identifying the node at the end of the path, which is available via `getLastPathComponent`. Having retrieved this, we add a new child node to it. It is then necessary to inform the tree model managing the nodes that the contents of the tree have been changed. In order to do this, we have used the `reload` method of DefaultTreeModel, passing a reference to the node that has changed. The version of `reload` with no arguments will cause the whole tree to be reloaded. Notifying the model of changes will cause any listeners that have registered with it to be informed. We have not shown details of any listener interfaces associated with trees, such as `TreeExpansionListener`, `TreeModelListener`, and `TreeSelectionListener`.

17.28   Review

Within the scope of this book, it has only been possible to provide an overview of the Swing classes. The Swing classes build on many of the classes and concepts of the AWT, such as layout managers, Color, Font, Graphics, and the event-handling interfaces. A significant difference is the fact that the JComponent super class is, in fact, a Container; this makes it possible to readily combine multiple components within such basic items as labels and buttons, for instance. Also of note is the potential for an application to take its look-and-feel from one host platform to another, providing consistency to its users.

PART

IV

Advanced Features

18

Threads

In this chapter, we look at the ways in which Java makes it possible to separate a program into concurrently running threads. Threads are a standard part of the Java language and provide capabilities to design a single program to run in independent parts. These parts of the program may be given different priorities and the activities of collaborating threads may be synchronized. However, the power of threads brings with it a number of new problems of which the designer of multithreaded programs needs to be aware; problems such as race hazards, starvation, livelock, and deadlock.

18.1 Multiprocessing

In everyday life, we often perform multiple tasks at the same time: listening to the radio while doing the washing up, making a sandwich while waiting for the coffee to brew, and so on. In modern programming environments, we also take for granted the ability to run multiple programs concurrently and independently. Users expect to be able to edit their files, read their email, catch up on their favorite newsgroups, print documents, and download remote Web pages, while possibly sharing their computer and network with tens or hundreds of other users. The state of the art has been reached as part of a long progression from the early days of computing when a whole machine would be given over to a single user for hours at a time, through the *multiprogramming systems* that enabled a machine's resources to be shared among multiple programs run in batch mode, to the *timesharing systems* that allowed multiple users interactive access with the illusion of having the whole machine to themselves, and now networked and distributed systems made up of large collections of many different types of computer, seemingly integrated into a seamless whole.

Central to these changes has been the development of *operating systems*[TW97] with their ability to control multiple *processes*. One of the key roles of an operating system is to share a finite set of resources between these processes, ensuring that each process receives its fair share of the CPU cycles available and equitable access to the machine's memory and peripheral devices. Each process runs in its own *address space* that keeps it from interfering with other processes running on the same machine. On the other hand, sometimes processes need to communicate with one another in order to work collaboratively on a task, and an operating system must provide *interprocess communication* mechanisms to make this possible. Most of the key operating systems concepts we use today were developed in the 1960s and 1970s, which means that a great deal of experience has been built up with them and they are well understood. The designers of Java have taken many of these concepts and integrated them directly into the language in the form of *threads*. By doing so, Java joins the distinctive ranks of other languages, such as Ada[Cul96] and occam[Gal96], in having concurrent processing features existing as first class citizens alongside the more common features found in most other mainstream non-concurrent programming languages, such as C[KR78], FORTRAN[NL98], Pascal[JW78], and C++[Str97].

A single Java application may consist of multiple threads of control, each apparently running concurrently with every other. As a consequence, threads are sometimes know as *lightweight processes* by analogy with full-scale processes managed by the operating system. In contrast to full-scale processes, threads are not the responsibility of the operating system, as such, but the runtime system created by the Java Virtual Machine, which runs as a single process within the host operating system. This distinction between operating system processes and Java threads is important because it means that Java's multithread capabilities are not inhibited by a failure of the host operating system to provide a true multiprocessing environment. Just as processes run in their own address space, each thread maintains its own copy of the *runtime stack* and the *program counter*, although the object population of a program is shared between all of its threads.

In this chapter, we look at the fundamental features of the Java language that allow multiple threads to be created within a single application program, and how those threads may be organized either to work independently or to collaborate on a combined task.

18.2   A Single Thread of Control

All Java applications have at least one thread of control, named `main`, in which the main method runs. We see this in the runtime errors that programs sometimes report:

```
Exception in thread "main" java.lang.ArithmeticException: / by zero
        at ComplexArithmetic.main(ComplexArithmetic.java:26)
```

An individual thread executes its statements in sequence, one after the other, just as we saw in Chapter 5. Each step completes before the next starts. This makes it possible to reason about a program in order to try to ensure that a program does what we intend it to. For instance, if we write the statements

```
setX(10);
System.out.print(getX()+" ");
setX(getX()+1);
System.out.println(getX());
```

we can have confidence that this part of the program will print

```
10 11
```

because the first `setX` will be completed before we try to print it the first time, and the second `setX` will complete before we print it the second time. As long as there is a single thread of execution, nothing can interfere with the clear logic and predictable outcome of these statements.

In introducing the concept of multiple threads of control, it will be important to distinguish between multiple objects and multiple threads; a program can have multiple objects without necessarily having multiple threads. Indeed, most of the programs you will write will probably consist of multiple objects executing within the same thread of control. These objects communicate by sending messages to each other and receiving replies back, but, at any one time, only one object is in control. When an actor sends a message to an agent, the actor must wait passively for the agent to respond. That agent might, itself, become an actor in respect of another agent and each actor must wait in turn for the recipient of its message to respond before it can continue. This is because there is only a single thread of control—only one object at a time can be in charge. Within a single thread of control we might simulate multiple objects operating independently, but the fact remains that they really are only active one after another. In order to illustrate this, consider the example in Code 18.1.

Code 18.1 Scheduling multiple ships in a single thread of control (`PseudoRandomShip.java`)

```java
import java.util.Random;

    // Create a number of ships and repeatedly ask them
    // to move and report.
class PseudoRandomShip {
    public static void main(String[] args){
        final int defaultShips = 5;
        int numShips = defaultShips;
        Ship[] ships;

        if(args.length == 1){
            try{
                numShips = Integer.parseInt(args[0]);
                if(numShips <= 0){
                    numShips = defaultShips;
                }
            }
            catch(Exception e){
            }
        }

        ships = new Ship[numShips];

        // Create the ships with a random course.
        final int numDegrees = 360;
        final Random randomCourse = new Random();
        final int fast = 5;
        for(int i = 0; i < ships.length; i++){
            ships[i] = new Ship();
            ships[i].setCourse(randomCourse.nextInt(numDegrees));
            ships[i].setSpeed(fast);
        }
```

Code 18.1   (*Continued*)

```
        // Interleave their movements.
        while(true){
            for(int i = 0; i < ships.length; i++){
                final Ship s = ships[i];
                s.move();
                s.report();
            }
        }
    }
}
```

This example creates five ships with random courses and then repeatedly asks each to move and report its position. When the program runs, the appearance on the display is of each ship moving independently along its own course. However, as we can see from the code, each ship must take its turn to move in line with the others; the first ship is asked to move and report its course, then the second ship, then the third ship, and so on. Within the single thread of control occupied by the main method, each ship is scheduled in turn via the inner for loop and the repetition is accomplished by the outer while loop. The second ship cannot start to move until the first has moved and reported its new position. Similarly for all five ships. However, what we shall describe in this chapter are the features of the Java language that permit each ship to be given its own thread of control so that it can take charge of its own sequencing, and not be made to wait in line for the other ships to move first. We shall revisit this example in Section 18.4.1.

18.3   Thread Basics

In Chapter 16, we saw that creation of a frame-based application automatically results in a second thread of control coming into existence; after the main method has constructed a GUI, it continues independently of that user interface. When the main method finishes, the runtime system waits for the GUI component of the program to terminate before the program as a whole is ended. In the examples in that chapter, the two threads of control remained largely independent of each other and there was no need to explain the details of how multithreaded programs work in general.

In order to create your own thread, an object of the Thread class (defined in java.lang) or one of its sub classes must be created and started running. A selection of its methods is shown in Table 18.1. Code 18.2 illustrates a simple program in which class ThreadCounter extends the Thread class. This allows a ThreadCounter object to be created which will run in a different thread of control from that of the main method.

In this example, we create one ThreadCounter object, secondThread. Throughout its lifetime, a thread object is in one of several possible states. Immediately following construction it is in the *new thread state*, but it is not yet running. This can be seen from the first result of sending a Thread object the isAlive message,

Table 18.1 Selected methods of the Thread class

	Method and Arguments
	Thread()
	Thread(Runnable r)
	Thread(Runnable r,String threadName)
	Thread(String threadName)
	Thread(ThreadGroup group,Runnable r)
	Thread(ThreadGroup group,Runnable r,String threadName)
	Thread(ThreadGroup group,String threadName)
static int	activeCount()
void	checkAccess()
static Thread	currentThread()
static void	dumpStack()
String	getName()
int	getPriority()
ThreadGroup	getThreadGroup()
void	interrupt()
static boolean	interrupted()
void	join()
void	join(long milliseconds)
void	join(long milliseconds,long nanoseconds)
void	run()
void	setDaemon(boolean on)
void	setName(String threadName)
void	setPriority(int priority)
static void	sleep(long milliseconds)
static void	sleep(long milliseconds,long nanoseconds)
void	start()
String	toString()
static void	yield()

Code 18.2 Creating a second thread of control

```java
        // Illustrate the creation and running of a simple thread.
public class ThreadExample {
    public static void main(String[] args){
        // Create a new Thread object.
        ThreadCounter secondThread = new ThreadCounter();

        if(!secondThread.isAlive()){
            System.out.println("Second thread is not yet alive.");
        }
        // Start the second thread running.
        secondThread.start();
        if(secondThread.isAlive()){
            System.out.println("Second thread is now alive.");
        }
        // Let secondThread have a go.
        Thread.yield();
        if(!secondThread.isAlive()){
            System.out.println("Second thread is no longer alive.");
        }
```

Code 18.2   (*Continued*)

```
        System.out.println("First thread has finished.");
    }
}

    // Objects of this class run in a separate thread.
class ThreadCounter extends Thread {
    // Print the numbers [1..max]
    public void run(){
        final int max = 10;
        System.out.println("Started running.");
        for(int i = 1; i <= max; i++){
            System.out.print(i+" ");
        }
        System.out.println();
        System.out.println("End of run reached.");
    }
}
```

---

which returns `false` while it is in the new thread state. Once constructed, a thread may be started by sending it the `start` message, which takes no arguments. It is within the `start` method that the division between the original thread of control and the new thread of control begins. The thread now enters the *runnable state* and the `start` method automatically calls the thread's `run` method, which sub classes of Thread should always override, because Thread's version does nothing useful.[1] Meanwhile, the original call to `start` has returned because it is in a separate thread. At this stage, there are two independent threads of control available to be run. We can determine that the second thread is runnable because the `isAlive` message now returns `true`. However, in the example in Code 18.2, the newly created thread is not able to start executing its `run` method because the original thread is still running, and only a single thread at a time can actually have control of the CPU. In order for the second thread to run, it must gain control of the CPU in some way. The way we illustrate this in this simple example is for the first thread to explicitly yield control to it, which it does with the static `yield` method of the Thread class. Now the second thread can start executing its `run` method, which it does to completion. Once its `run` method has finished, the second thread enters the *dead state* and the `main` thread's `yield` call finishes causing the thread containing the main method to run again. The state of the second thread can be checked by sending it an `isAlive` message, which now returns `false`. Although it is impossible to restart a thread that is in the dead state, the Thread object retains all of its attributes and will respond to messages in the normal way.

    Because the second thread has finished, the first thread's call to `yield` terminates, and it can run to completion. When the end of the main method is reached, the

---

[1] Note that it is a mistake to call a Thread's `run` method directly; this is only ever done indirectly via `start`.

program only finishes when all other threads have finished.[2] In this case, since `sec-ondThread` had died, the program ends immediately. The output from Code 18.2 will be as follows:

```
Second thread is not yet alive.
Second thread is now alive.
Started running.
1 2 3 4 5 6 7 8 9 10
End of run reached.
Second thread is no longer alive.
First thread has finished.
```

As we shall see, this example is crude both in the first thread's use of `yield` and in the second thread's greedy use of the available processor, but it serves to illustrate the basic concepts of thread creation and the main states of its lifecycle. In the next section, we shall look at some of the other ways in which multiple threads can share the processor time.

18.3.1 Threads and Anonymous Classes

Sometimes the overridden `run` method of a Thread sub class is relatively short, and only a single instance is required. Such sub classes are ideal for implementing as an anonymous class. Code 18.3 shows an example that uses this approach. This is equivalent to the example shown in Code 18.2.

Exercise 18.1   Write a program that creates two new threads. One should print a finite sequence of positive numbers and the other a finite sequence of negative numbers. Both sequences should be relatively long—1000 numbers, say. Neither thread should yield once it has control. (You should use the `flush` method with `System.out` if you are using only its `print` method to print each number.) Run your program to see whether or not the output is interleaved. If the output is not interleaved, increase how many are printed by each thread to 100,000, say. Does this make any difference?

Exercise 18.2   Modify your solution to Exercise 18.1 so that each thread yields to the other after printing a few numbers. Does this produce the expected interleaving?

18.3.2 The Runnable Interface

In Section 18.3, we illustrated the basic concepts of thread creation by extending the Thread class. Apart from implementing the essentials of the basic thread mechanism, a raw Thread object has little useful functionality, so sub classes that override its `run` method are sometimes created. However, Java's lack of multiple class inheritance means that sub-classing Thread is often impossible; that is, when the class to be threaded is already extending another class. An important alternative to extending Thread is to have a class implement the `Runnable` interface which has a single

---

[2] With the exception of *daemon threads*, such as the *garbage collector* (Section 18.11).

Code 18.3 Implementing a simple thread as an anonymous class
(AnonymousThreadExample.java)

```java
    // Illustrate the creation and running of a simple thread.
    // Use an anonymous class for the thread.
public class AnonymousThreadExample {
    public static void main(String[] args){
        Thread secondThread = new Thread(){
            public void run(){
                final int max = 10;
                System.out.println("Started running.");
                for(int i = 1; i <= max; i++){
                    System.out.print(i+" ");
                }
                System.out.println();
                System.out.println("End of run reached.");
            }
        };

        if(!secondThread.isAlive()){
            System.out.println("Second thread is not yet alive.");
        }
        secondThread.start();
        if(secondThread.isAlive()){
            System.out.println("Second thread is now alive.");
        }
        // Let secondThread have a go.
        Thread.yield();
        if(!secondThread.isAlive()){
            System.out.println("Second thread is no longer alive.");
        }
        System.out.println("First thread has finished.");
    }
}
```

Code 18.4 The Runnable interface from java.lang

```java
public interface Runnable {
    public abstract void run();
}
```

method, run (Code 18.4). Since there is often no need to override any of Thread's methods apart from run, implementing Runnable will be our preferred approach to creating threads. Code 18.5 illustrates its use in implementing a program that is similar to that shown in Code 18.2.

The run method in Runnable has the same signature as that in the Thread class[3] so there is little change to the GreedyCounter class which replaces

---

[3] In fact, Thread implements Runnable.

Code 18.5 Implementing Runnable for use in a Thread (`RunnableExample.java`)

```
            // Illustrate the creation and running of a simple thread
            // using the Runnable interface.
public class RunnableExample {
    public static void main(String[] args){
            // Create the runnable object.
            Runnable counter = new GreedyCounter();
            // Pass the runnable object to a new thread.
            // Give the thread a name.
            Thread secondThread = new Thread(counter,"counter");

            if(!secondThread.isAlive()){
                System.out.println("Second thread is not yet alive.");
            }
            secondThread.start();
            if(secondThread.isAlive()){
                System.out.println("Second thread is now alive.");
            }
            // Let secondThread have a go.
            Thread.yield();
            if(!secondThread.isAlive()){
                System.out.println("Second thread is no longer alive.");
            }
            System.out.println("First thread has finished.");
    }
}


    // Objects of this class may be run in a separate thread.
    // Implementation provided for Runnable.run().
class GreedyCounter implements Runnable {
    // Print the numbers [1..max]
    public void run(){
            final int max = 10;
            System.out.println("Started running.");
            for(int i = 1; i <= max; i++){
                System.out.print(i+" ");
            }
            System.out.println();
            System.out.println("End of run reached.");
    }
}
```

`ThreadCounter` of Code 18.2. The major change is in the creation of the `sec-ondThread` object in the main method. Implementing Runnable does not automatically make an object runnable as a separate thread, so we cannot send a `start` message to `counter` in Code 18.5. In order to have it run in a separate thread of execution, it is necessary to create an associated Thread object and pass the Runnable to its constructor. The effect of this is that, when `secondThread` is started, the minimal `run` method of Thread calls the implementing `run` method of the Runnable it was constructed with. As a result, the example in Code 18.5 runs in exactly the same way as that in Code 18.2, and the same output results. We have also passed to the Thread constructor a name for the thread. If a Runnable needs a reference to the Thread object responsible for it, it can obtain this by calling the static `currentThread` method of the Thread class.

```
public void run(){
    // Which thread am I running in?
    Thread myThread = Thread.currentThread();
    // What is my name?
    String myName = myThread.getName();
    ...
}
```

Exercise 18.3   Modify the example shown in Code 18.5 so that the greedy counter is implemented as an anonymous implementation of Runnable.

Exercise 18.4   Modify your solution to Exercise 18.2 so that it uses implementations of Runnable, rather than sub classes of Thread.

18.3.3 Scheduling and Thread Priorities

As soon as a second thread of execution is started and made runnable, the Java run-time system is faced with the need to make a decision about which thread should be allocated the resources of the CPU and made to become the currently running thread. Of course, there may be tens or hundreds of threads all competing for this resource, so how does the runtime system resolve this competition, in general? Responsibility for making this decision lies with a part of the runtime system called the *scheduler*. When considering a thread for allocation as the currently running thread, the first consideration of the scheduler is the state of each thread. We have seen that a thread may be in one of at least three possible states during its lifecycle: *new thread*, *runnable*, and *dead* are the states we have seen so far. Only threads in the runnable state are eligible to become the current thread and so the scheduler maintains a separate queue of such threads to make the decision easier. Its second consideration is the *priority level* of a runnable thread. A thread's priority level lies in the range MIN_PRIORITY (1) to MAX_PRIORITY (10), as defined in the Thread class, and a newly created thread inherits the priority of the thread that created it. The thread in which the main method runs has a priority referred to as NORM_PRIORITY (5), so the priority of secondThread in Code 18.5 will also have a priority level of 5. The scheduler's queue of runnable threads will be ordered by priority level, with those threads of higher priority nearer the head of the queue than those of lower priority. An alternative approach would be to maintain separate queues for each priority level. When there is more than one thread with equally highest priority, the scheduler allocates the CPU to the one at the head of the queue—typically the one that has been waiting the longest.

Once a thread has been made the current thread, how do other runnable threads ever get the chance to run? The answer to this depends upon the implementation of the scheduler in a particular JVM:

- Some schedulers allow the current thread to retain control of the CPU as long as it remains in the runnable state.
- Some schedulers allocate a limited *timeslice* to the current thread. The amount of time allocated is known as a *quantum*. Once its quantum has expired, the current thread is moved to the end of the queue for its priority level and the next runnable thread is made the current thread. Of course, the thread whose quantum has expired may be the only runnable thread at its priority level and, assuming it remains the highest priority runnable thread, it will be reassigned to being the current thread.

With both approaches, a thread may be *preempted*—forced to yield control before it has finished—if another thread with a higher priority becomes runnable. Preemption is no respecter of where a thread has currently got to in its task—it might even occur when it is halfway through loading or storing a variable's value. This unpredictability of how much work a thread may accomplish during the period that it is running is one of the things that makes programming threads safely particularly difficult and can lead to situations such as *race hazards*, which we describe in Section 18.6.

Other ways in which a thread may cease to be the current thread are that it might voluntarily yield control (as the main method's thread does in Code 18.5) or move out of the runnable state for any of several possible reasons, such as we discuss in Section 18.4 and Section 18.8.

A thread's priority may be set independently of the level inherited from its creator by sending it a setPriority message. Code 18.6 illustrates the effect of setting the priority of secondThread to be higher than the priority of the thread that starts it running. The main method determines the priority of the main thread using getPriority and sets the priority of secondThread to be slightly higher just before starting it. This example uses the same implementation of the Greedy-Counter class as shown in Code 18.5 and an identical logic is used for the printing of progress messages in the main method. However, compare the output that results from this version from that shown in Section 18.3:

```
Second thread is not yet alive.
Started running.
1 2 3 4 5 6 7 8 9 10
End of run reached.
Second thread is no longer alive.
First thread has finished.
```

The second output is identical except for the absence of "Second thread is now alive". The reason for this is that, as soon as the counter thread is started, the scheduler places it before the main thread in the run queue in view of its higher priority. As a result, the first thread is preempted and cannot continue until the counter thread has finished and died. Once it is allowed to continue, the main thread makes its second check to see whether counter is alive, which it isn't, and so no message is printed this time. It then yields control to any other runnable thread, but there is no other runnable thread so main is made current again and completes its statements.

This example is important because it illustrates that a thread might lose control without having yielded it voluntarily. While it is true that, in this case, we can easily anticipate that this is going to happen because we deliberately set the new thread's

Code 18.6   Setting a priority on a Thread (`PriorityExample.java`)

```
        // Illustrate the setting of a priority on a newly
        // created thread.
public class PriorityExample {
    public static void main(String[] args){
        // Create the runnable object.
        Runnable counter = new GreedyCounter();
        // Pass the runnable object to a new thread.
        // Give the thread a name.
        Thread secondThread = new Thread(counter,"counter");

        if(!secondThread.isAlive()){
            System.out.println("Second thread is not yet alive.");
        }
        // Modify the new thread's priority to be greater than
        // this threads.
        Thread myThread = Thread.currentThread();
        secondThread.setPriority(myThread.getPriority()+1);

        secondThread.start();
        if(secondThread.isAlive()){
            System.out.println("Second thread is now alive.");
        }
        // Let secondThread have a go.
        Thread.yield();
        if(!secondThread.isAlive()){
            System.out.println("Second thread is no longer alive.");
        }
        System.out.println("First thread has finished.");
    }
}
```

priority, in general a thread may be preempted *at any time* if the scheduler decides that another thread should take over, and a thread can do nothing to guarantee that this does not happen. This has important consequences for the design of concurrent programs because it is essential to ensure that objects do not leave themselves or other parts of the system in an inconsistent state in the event of the thread in which they are running being preempted by another thread. We shall look at mechanisms in Java that limit the opportunity for inconsistency in Section 18.7.

Exercise 18.5   Write a program that creates two implementations of the Runnable interface. One should print a finite sequence of positive numbers and the other a finite sequence of negative numbers. After printing a few numbers, each should reduce its priority level by one before printing any more. What effect does this have on the output? Is the effect predictable?

Exercise 18.6   Modify your solution to Exercise 18.5 so that each periodically sets its priority to a random value between MAX_PRIORITY and MIN_PRIORITY. What effect does this have on the output? Is the effect predictable?

18.4   Fair Threads

In all of the examples we have seen so far, the run methods have been allowed to run to completion once they are part of the current thread of control. This is a particularly greedy approach to the use of resources that are meant to be shared among multiple threads. If the scheduler does not operate a timeslicing policy, then there is nothing to stop a greedy thread from running to completion and excluding all other threads from having a chance to do some work. You should make it a policy in designing a class that is to be run in a thread to ensure that it will give other threads a chance to run, in case your program should run on a non-timeslicing JVM. We have seen that one possibility is for a thread to voluntarily invoke the yield method of the Thread class. The thread remains in the runnable state but it is moved to the back of the queue for threads of the same priority. The problem with this approach is that it never gives threads of lower priority a chance to run, which is known as *thread starvation*. The only way to be sure of giving other threads a fair chance of taking over as the current thread is for a thread to move out of the runnable state and into a *not runnable state*. At some later point it can move back into the runnable state, when other threads have had a chance to run.

18.4.1   Yielding by Sleeping

The simplest way for a thread to take itself out of the runnable state voluntarily for a limited period is for it to enter the *sleeping state* by calling the sleep method of Thread with the number of milliseconds for which it is to remain not runnable (Code 18.7).

Code 18.7   Using sleep to achieve fairness (FairCounter.java)

```
class FairCounter implements Runnable {
    public FairCounter(int min,int max){
        this.min = min;
        this.max = max;
    }

    // Print the numbers [min..max]
    public void run(){
        final int max = getMax();
        for(int i = getMin(); i <= max; i++){
            System.out.print(i+" ");
            try{
                // Let someone else have a go.
                Thread.sleep(100);
            }
            catch(InterruptedException e){
                // Someone woke us up.
            }
        }
        System.out.println();
    }
    ...
}
```

   After printing each number, a `FairCounter` object sleeps for 100 milliseconds
before trying to print the next. Note that it is possible for a thread to have its sleep
deliberately interrupted by another thread sending an `interrupt` message, so it
is necessary to include the sleep in a try-catch statement anticipating receipt of an
`InterruptedException` exception. By sleeping, a thread removes itself from the
queue of runnable threads until the sleep period has expired, at which point it is
returned to the back of the runnable queue for threads of that priority. The example
in Code 18.8 illustrates how three FairCounter objects might be created and run in
separate threads.

Code 18.8   Running multiple FairCounters in separate threads (`FairCoordinator.java`)

```
        // Illustrate the creation and running of multiple threads
        // that let other threads have a go from time to time.
class FairCoordinator implements Runnable {
    public FairCoordinator() {
        initCounters();
    }

        // Set up an array of threads to run multiple Counters.
    protected void initCounters(){
        // Where the threads are to be stored.
        Thread[] counters = getCounters();

        // Create the counters and threads.
        for(int i = 0; i < counters.length; i++){
            // Specify the range over which the counter operates.
            final int min = 10*i+1, max = min+9;
            counters[i] = new Thread(new FairCounter(min,max));
        }
        System.out.println("All counters created.");
    }

    public void run(){
        // Find out my priority.
        Thread myThread = Thread.currentThread();
        int myPriority = myThread.getPriority();
        Thread[] counters = getCounters();

        for(int i = 0; i < counters.length; i++){
            // Ensure that the threads don't start until I
            // am ready for them to run.
            counters[i].setPriority(myPriority-1);
            counters[i].start();
        }

        System.out.println("All counters ready to run.");
        waitForCountersToFinish(myPriority);
        System.out.println("All the threads have finished.");
    }
```

(Continued)

Code 18.8   (*Continued*)

```
    protected void waitForCountersToFinish(int myPriority){
        // Crank down my priority below the other threads in order to
        // let them battle it out with the minimum of interference.
        Thread myThread = Thread.currentThread();
        myThread.setPriority(myPriority-1);
        do{
            try{
                Thread.sleep(500);
            }
            catch(InterruptedException e){
            }
        } while(stillRunning());
    }

        // Return true if at least one counter is still alive.
    protected boolean stillRunning(){
        Thread[] counters = getCounters();
        for(int i = 0; i < counters.length; i++){
            if(counters[i].isAlive()){
                return true;
            }
        }
        return false;
    }

    protected Thread[] getCounters(){
        return counters;
    }

    // Create the array to hold the threads.
    private final int numCounters = 3;
    private final Thread[] counters = new Thread[numCounters];
}
```

Because each thread periodically puts itself to sleep, the other threads receive an opportunity to accomplish part of their task from time to time. As a result, each succeeds in completing its task at roughly the same time as the others and the output should appear as follows:

```
All counters created.
All counters ready to run.
1 11 21 2 12 22 3 13 23 4 14 24 5 15 25 6 16 26 7 17 27 8 18 28 9 19 29 10 20 30

All the threads have finished.
```

You can see from this that the periods of activity are interleaved in an orderly fashion. One reason for this is that each thread sleeps for the same period of time and the effect is of a *round robin allocation* as the current thread. If we assume that the time taken to print a number is considerably less than the time for which a thread sleeps,

Table 18.2 Sample of the Fair-Counter states and output		
Runnable	*Sleeping*	*Output*
c0 c1 c2		
c1 c2	c0	1
c2	c0 c1	1 11
	c0 c1 c2	1 11 21
c0	c1 c2	
	c1 c2 c0	1 11 21 2
c1	c2 c0	1 11 21 2
etc.		

and also ignore the presence of the threads for the `main` and `coordinator` threads, Table 18.2 shows the states of the three FairCounter threads and the numbers that have been printed as time progresses down the table.

Exercise 18.7   In Table 18.2, we ignored the `coordinator` thread, which periodically checks to see whether all of the FairCounter threads have finished. Add a `println` statement to the `run` method of Controller to show when it is active, and hence amend the table of thread activity.

The orderly arrangement of FairCounter activity is unusual and arises from the fact that they use their available time to do a similar task and then sleep for the same amount of time. We can get a more accurate picture of the way in which thread activity is interleaved by making the FairCounters sleep for different amounts of time. For instance, if we change the argument of `sleep` in the FairCounter's `run` method to take the value of `max`, we might see something similar to the following interleaving of output:

```
All counters created.
All counters ready to run.
1 11 21 2 12 3 22 4 13 5 23 6 14 7 24 15 8 16 9 25 10 17
26 18 27 19 28 20
29 30
All the threads have finished.
```

Because the thread counting from 1 to 10 only sleeps for 10 milliseconds at a time, it might move from the sleeping state to the runnable state before an earlier sleeping thread wakes from its 20 or 30 millisecond sleep. Hence it finishes its overall task before the other two, with the thread counting from 21 to 30 being the slowest to finish. This example illustrates that it can be difficult to coordinate the activities of independent threads. One thread cannot make assumptions about the amount of progress that has been made by another because that progress may be dependent upon many things—whether the scheduler operates a timeslicing policy, whether other threads of higher priority are blocking lower priority threads from running, how long a thread chooses to sleep, and so on.

Exercise 18.8   Write a program that runs two new threads. One thread should sleep for 100 milliseconds before printing the current time, while the other should sleep for 1000 seconds before printing the current time. Give each thread a name and include its name with the time. How closely do the sleeping periods match against the reported times?

Exercise 18.9   Modify your solution to Exercise 18.8 so that the two threads have different priorities. Does this make a significant difference to the correspondence between the sleeping times and the reported times? Reverse the priorities to see if this makes a difference.

We conclude this section by revisiting the example presented in Code 18.1. That example was used to show the way in which a program with a single thread of control might schedule multiple objects in order to give the appearance of concurrency. Responsibility for asking the ships to move lay with a loop running forever in the main method. Each ship was asked, in turn, to move and report its position. With the availability of threads, we can now make each ship responsible for its own propulsion and reduce the role of the main method to being one of simply starting the ship threads running. Code 18.9 shows the revised main method. The run method of Ship might look like that in Code 18.10.

Code 18.9   Creating multiple ships, each in its own thread of control (`RandomShip.java`)

```
import java.util.Random;

        // Create a ship, ask it to report its position and then move.
class RandomShip {
    public static void main(String[] args){
        final int defaultShips = 5;
        int numShips = defaultShips;
        Ship[] ships;

        if(args.length == 1){
            try{
                numShips = Integer.parseInt(args[0]);
                if(numShips <= 0){
                    numShips = defaultShips;
                }
            }
            catch(Exception e){
            }
        }

        ships = new Ship[numShips];

        // Create the ships with a random course.
```

Code 18.9   (*Continued*)

```
        final int numDegrees = 360;
        final Random randomCourse = new Random();
        final int fast = 5;
        for(int i = 0; i < ships.length; i++){
            ships[i] = new Ship();
            ships[i].setCourse(randomCourse.nextInt(numDegrees));
            ships[i].setSpeed(fast);
        }

        // Start them moving under their own control.
        for(int i = 0; i < ships.length; i++){
            new Thread(ships[i]).start();
        }
    }
}
```

Code 18.10   The run method of Ship

```
class Ship extends Observable implements Runnable {
    ...
        // Implementation of the Runnable interface.
    public void run(){
        while(true){
            move();
            report();
            // Be prepared to yield, in case we are not sleeping for
            // some reason.
            Thread.yield();
        }
    }
    ...
}
```

After each move, a ship reports its position. Each ship is fair in that it sleeps for a random period related to its speed whenever it moves, and hence allows other threads to run. However, it also deliberately yields in case its sleep time is zero. Responsibility for the scheduling of these threads is now down to the runtime system, and the varying sleep times of the individual ships allow their activities to be interleaved in a way that would have been too complex to try to program in the version without threads. This example helps to illustrate some of the additional expressive power that threads bring to a programming language.

18.4.2   The Join Method

In the example in Code 18.8, the FairCoordinator's waitForCountersToFinish method uses the approach of periodically checking to see whether any of the counters is still alive. Since it has nothing more useful to get on with while it is waiting, an

Code 18.11   Using `join` to await a thread's death (`JoinCoordinator.java`)

```
class JoinCoordinator {
    ...
    protected void waitForCountersToFinish(int myPriority){
        // Crank down my priority below the other threads in order to
        // let them battle it out with the minimum of interference.
        Thread myThread = Thread.currentThread();
        myThread.setPriority(myPriority-1);

        // Wait for all the counters to finish.
        Thread[] counters = getCounters();
        for(int i = 0; i < counters.length; i++){
            // Anticipate being interrupted before the
            // join is complete.
            boolean interrupted;
            do{
                try{
                    interrupted = false;
                    counters[i].join();
                }
                catch(InterruptedException e){
                    interrupted = true;
                }
            }
            while(interrupted);
        }
    }
    ...
}
```

alternative to this active approach might be to wait passively to be informed when
a counter thread dies. It can do this by using one of the `join` methods of Thread.
Code 18.11 is an alternative version of `waitForCountersToFinish`. Sending the
`join` message to a thread causes the client to be suspended pending the death of
the thread on which it is waiting. If the thread has already died, then `join` returns
immediately. The for loop in this example waits for each thread to die in turn, and the
order in which they die is not significant. As with `sleep`, a thread waiting with `join`
could be interrupted by another thread, and so it is necessary to use an exception
handler to deal with this. In this example, interruptions are ignored by trying the
`join` again. Two further forms of `join` exist, both of which take a length of time to
allow to elapse before giving up the wait. These might be used in situations where the
thread being waited for is not guaranteed to die, perhaps through thread starvation or
an inability to obtain the resources it requires. In this respect, using a time argument
to `join` is safer than waiting indefinitely.

18.4.3   Deprecated Thread States

Versions of the Java API prior to version 1.2 included a `suspend` method in the
Thread class. Sending this message to a thread causes it to enter the *suspended*

state. A suspended thread may be returned to the running state by sending it a `resume` message. However, both of these methods are now deprecated and will ultimately be removed from the Thread class. One of the reasons for their discontinuation is that they take no account of what a thread is currently doing; telling a thread to suspend itself could easily lead to other parts of the system being left in an inconsistent state, or to resources being tied up in the suspended thread that are needed elsewhere. We shall look at how these sorts of things can happen in later sections. A further Thread method that is now deprecated, for similar reasons, is `stop`, which abruptly kills a thread by throwing a `ThreadDeath` exception at it. This is usually too brute force an approach for comfort, and alternative means of letting a thread know that it should terminate should usually be found.

18.4.4   Yielding by Blocking

One way in which a thread may become not runnable involuntarily is for it to attempt to perform input-output that is blocked. For instance, a thread requesting user input via the keyboard will become not runnable and enter the *blocked state* while it waits for the user to respond. We shall see an example of this in Section 18.6.

In the next section, we shall see some of the problems that threads can also bring!

18.5   Review

Here are the main points that we have covered in the preceding sections:

- Concurrency in everyday life is common.
- Operating systems make it possible for concurrent tasks to be conducted on a single computer, often by multiple users.
- Non-concurrent programs execute within a single thread of control.
- Within a single thread of control, statements are executed sequentially.
- The thread of control in which the main method operates is called `main`.
- Graphical Java applications typically have at least two threads of control.
- The Thread class supports multiple threads of control.
- Concurrent objects may be constructed from a sub class of Thread that includes an overridden `run` method.
- A class that implements the Runnable interface may be used to create objects that run concurrently.
- A Runnable object must be passed to a Thread object before it can be run.
- A thread is started via its `start` method.
- When a thread is started, it enters the runnable state.
- A thread may `yield` control to another runnable thread.
- A thread enters the dead state when its run method finishes. It cannot be resurrected.
- Multiple threads are managed by a scheduler.
- The scheduler will only run one thread at a time.

- A thread may only be run by the scheduler if the thread is in the runnable state.
- Some schedulers allocate a limited timeslice to a thread before giving other threads a chance to run.
- A thread may be blocked when it performs input or output.
- Threads have a priority level; threads with a lower priority cannot run if there is one more eligible thread at a higher priority level.
- A running thread may be preempted by another eligible thread.
- A greedy thread might starve other threads from running.
- A threaded class should be designed to give other threads a chance to run, for instance, by having its object periodically go to sleep.
- A thread may wait for another to finish via `join`.

18.6   Resource Sharing Between Threads

All of the examples we have seen in this chapter have involved threads that were largely independent of one another; that is, aside from ensuring that a thread behaved fairly in giving other threads an opportunity to run, no coordination was required between them. By its very nature, an object-oriented program consists of multiple objects collaborating together to achieve a result. Where some of these objects run in separate threads, it is almost inevitable that some of them will need to synchronize their activities at some point in their lifetimes. In a simple way we have seen this with the `join` method, where one thread waits for another to finish its task. More common, however, is the need to cooperate over the use of one or more *resources*. A resource can be anything within the environment of a program; a single byte of memory, an object, an array of objects, an input-output device, and so on.

Bank accounts have been used several times in this book to illustrate various aspects of class design and object interaction, and they serve as a useful exemplar of real-life situations in which concurrent activities must be coordinated in order to accurately accomplish a complex task. A bank maintaining an account must permit various competing operations to access details of the account and make changes to it. For instance, it is common for customers to set up direct debit mandates between themselves and companies, allowing those companies to directly debit an account without the intervention of the account holder; banks pay out regular standing orders; checks must be cleared and the corresponding amounts transferred between accounts; account holders deposit cash at bank branches and withdraw money through cash-points (ATM's) all over the world.

Consider a simplified version of real life in which separate threads are used to represent regular direct debit operations, regular deposits of money, and interactive cash withdrawal through an ATM. Code 18.12 shows a main method which sets up these threads which share access to a simple `UnsafeAccount` object representing the bank account.

The UnsafeAccount's `credit` and `debit` methods ensure that only valid amounts are credited to and debited from the account, and that no attempt is made to set a negative balance.

Code 18.12   Creating threads that share access to an UnsafeAccount object

```
        // Basic operations on a bank account.
interface Account {
    public boolean credit(long amount);
    public boolean debit(long amount);
    public long getBalance();
}

        // An illustration of how a Race Hazard can occur.
        // This program is unsafe.
class RaceHazard {
    public static void main(String[] args){
        // Access to this account is shared by three threads.
        Account acc = new UnsafeAccount();

        // Make regular debits of a given amount.
        new Thread(new DirectDebit(acc)).start();
        // Make regular deposits into the account.
        new Thread(new Saver(acc)).start();
        // Allow the user to withdraw money interactively.
        new Thread(new ATM(acc)).start();
    }
}

        // Maintain details of the account's balance and
        // implement credit and debit operations on it.
        // This implementation is unsafe.
class UnsafeAccount {
    public UnsafeAccount(){
        final int initialBalance = 600;
        setBalance(initialBalance);
    }

        // Return whether the debit was successful or not.
    public boolean debit(long amount){
        System.out.println();
        System.out.println("Debit: "+amount);
        if(amount >= 0){
            return setBalance(getBalance()-amount);
        }
        else{
            return false;
        }
    }

        // Return whether the debit was successful or not.
    public boolean credit(long amount){
        System.out.println();
        System.out.println("Credit: "+amount);
```

(Continued)

Code 18.12   *(Continued)*

```
if(amount >= 0){
        return setBalance(getBalance()+amount);
    }
    else{
        return false;
    }
}

public long getBalance(){
    return balance;
}

// The balance may not go negative. Return true
// on success, false on failure.
protected boolean setBalance(long amount){
    if(amount >= 0){
        balance = amount;
        return true;
    }
    else{
        return false;
    }
}

// How much is in the account.
private long balance;
}
```

Now consider the implementation of the DirectDebit, Saver, and ATM classes in Code 18.13 which share access to an implementation of Account. Each class extends AccountUser which simply provides them with an accessor and mutator for the Account object they manipulate. The DirectDebit thread withdraws 100 dollars approximately every 100 milliseconds, as long as the account would remain in balance. The Saver thread deposits 500 dollars approximately every 10 seconds. The ATM thread's run method firstly determines how much money is available in the customer's account and then asks the customer how much they wish to withdraw. The amount requested by the customer is checked to ensure that it is within balance before being debited from the account. Taken individually, each class seems to be well behaved—none tries to manipulate the account in such a way as to take the balance below zero. However, when all three threads run together, circumstances can sometimes conspire to make a customer's withdrawal via the ATM object fail.

Exercise 18.10   Before reading further, see if you can work out under what circumstances a withdrawal via the ATM might fail.

The key to understanding the main problem with this example is to remember that a thread may move out of the runnable state if it is blocked by an attempt to

Code 18.13   Classes sharing access to a single Account object

```
    // Regular debits are made from the account if there are
    // sufficient funds.
class DirectDebit extends AccountUser implements Runnable {
    public DirectDebit(Account account){
        super(account);
    }

    public void run(){
        Account account = getAccount();
        final long debitAmount = 100;
        final long sleepTime = 100;

        while(true){
            try{
                if(account.getBalance() >= debitAmount){
                    if(!account.debit(debitAmount)){
                        System.out.println("Direct debit failed!");
                    }
                }
                Thread.sleep(sleepTime);
            }
            catch(InterruptedException e){
            }
        }
    }
}

    // Allow the user to specify how much they wish to withdraw
    // within the balance of the account.
class ATM extends AccountUser implements Runnable {
    public ATM(Account account){
        super(account);
    }

    public void run(){
        Account account = getAccount();
        SimpleInput keyboard = new SimpleInput();
        final long sleepTime = 100;

        while(true){
            try{
                // Find out the maximum amount that may be withdrawn.
                long available = account.getBalance();
                if(available > 0){
                    System.out.print("You have "+available+
                        " available, how much do you want? ");
                    System.out.flush();
                    // Request the amount from the user.
                    long amount = keyboard.nextLong();
                    // Check its validity.
```

(Continued)

Code 18.13   (*Continued*)

```
                    if(amount <= 0){
                        System.out.println("The amount must be positive.");
                    }
                    else if(amount > available){
                        System.out.println("That is too much.");
                    }
                    else{
                        // This should be ok, but ...
                        if(!account.debit(amount)){
                            System.out.println("The ATM debit failed!");
                        }
                    }
                }
                Thread.sleep(sleepTime);
            }
            catch(InterruptedException e){
            }
        }
    }
}


        // Top up the account with a regular amount.
class Saver extends AccountUser implements Runnable {
    public Saver(Account account){
        super(account);
    }

    public void run(){
        Account account = getAccount();
        final long creditAmount = 500;
        // We don't get paid very often!
        final long sleepTime = 10000;

        while(true){
            try{
                account.credit(creditAmount);
                Thread.sleep(sleepTime);
            }
            catch(InterruptedException e){
            }
        }
    }
}
```

perform input or output. Having determined the available balance in the account, the
ATM's run method asks the user how much they wish to withdraw. If the user does
not reply immediately, then this thread will become blocked waiting for a response.
In the meantime, the DirectDebit thread could wake from its sleep and debit the
account, in which case the amount available is no longer what the customer has been
told it is. If the customer attempts to withdraw the full amount that they believe to

be in the account, this debit will fail because there are no longer sufficient funds available. This situation is known as a *race hazard* or *race condition*. A race hazard between two threads describes the situation where they take actions based upon their own understanding of the current state of part of the system but one of these actions is invalidated or corrupted by the other. This happens most commonly when there is a separation between an inquiry about the system and a modifying action based upon the result of that inquiry—that is, the two steps are *non-atomic*. Between those two steps, another thread might have intervened to change the state before the first had the chance to complete its action. Such race hazards will always be a potential problem in an environment which implements timesliced scheduling and/or preemptive scheduling because a thread might take over at any point during another thread's activity. In the particular example of the bank accounts, the UnsafeAccount object prohibits the cash withdrawal if it would take the balance below zero. In situations where a lesser amount is withdrawn, however, there will be no such warning and the customer may be left with a false impression of how much money really remains in the account. Indeed, this particular situation is not the only place in which a race hazard may occur in Code 18.13; there is a similar separation of inquiry from action in the `debit` method of DirectDebit.

Rather more subtle, but even more dangerous, is the example of UnsafeAccount's mutator, `setAmount`, reproduced in Code 18.14.

Exercise 18.11   Before reading further, try to use your understanding of how a timeslicing scheduler works to spot the race hazard in Code 18.14. Remember that a thread may be interrupted *at any point* in its activity if its quantum expires—even in mid-statement.

We can explain the race hazard of Code 18.14 as follows. Suppose that the shared UnsafeAccount object holds a balance of 500 dollars and the DirectDebit thread has just sent a `debit` message of 100 dollars to it. This method calculates the new balance to be 400 dollars and calls the `setBalance` mutator. The condition of the if-statement is evaluated and the value of `amount` is found to be positive. At this point, before the assignment is made, the DirectDebit thread's quantum expires and it is sent to the back of the runnable queue to await its next turn. Suppose that

Code 18.14   A potential race hazard in the UnsafeAccount class

```
    // Danger: this method contains a potential race hazard.
protected boolean setBalance(long amount){
    if(amount >= 0){
        balance = amount;
        return true;
    }
    else{
        return false;
    }
}
```

the ATM thread is at the head of the runnable queue and is about to send its own
`debit` message for 150 dollars, and that this transaction is completed, leaving a
balance of 350 dollars. At this point, the ATM thread goes back to sleep, allowing
the DirectDebit thread to resume where it left off—in the body of the if-statement
of `setBalance`. The problem is that this thread has no idea that the balance has
been modified since it last had control at this point, and it sets the balance to the
value it calculated last time, namely 400 dollars. The balance in the account should
be 250 dollars and has been corrupted; in effect, the ATM transaction has been lost.

The race hazard that can arise when a customer attempts to withdraw the
full amount from their account was easy both to explain and to demonstrate in
practice; it simply required that the customer delay in responding long enough for
the DirectDebit thread to wake and reduce the real available balance. While it is
relatively easy to explain the problem with `setBalance`, demonstrating it is a lot
harder because it requires a particular set of time-dependent circumstances to arise.
Such a set of circumstances might arise only very rarely and the result is a bug that
is very hard to track down because it is almost impossible to reliably reproduce. It
might be argued that such a problem is so unlikely to arise in practice that it is not
worth worrying about, but these are the sort of problems that could cause millions
of dollars to disappear without a trace from a bank and aircraft to fall out of the
sky inexplicably, so they should be taken seriously. Fortunately, the problem of race
hazards has been well understood for a long time and mechanisms exist within Java
to avoid their arising if used properly. We discuss these in the next section.

Exercise 18.12   Write a program that creates two threads that share access to a
single instance of the `Resource` class, shown in Code 18.15. Each thread should
repeatedly attempt to get the value of the `value` attribute and then change it. One

---

Code 18.15   A class to be used as a shared resource (`Resource.java`)

```
    // Exercise outline.
    // A shared resource. Its value attribute should only
    // be adjusted by +1 or -1 via setValue.
    // Used to illustrate race hazards.
class Resource {
    public int getValue(){
        return value;
    }

        // Value should only be changed by 1 at most.
    public void setValue(int v){
        if(Math.abs(value-v) != 1){
            System.out.println("Mismatch: "+value+" "+v);
        }
        value = v;
    }

    private int value;
}
```

thread should increment it by one and the other decrement it by one. In order to simulate the way in which race hazards can arise, one thread should yield to the other between getting and setting the value, while the other thread should only yield after it has set the value. The Resource object will report a mismatch that results from a race condition occurring.

Exercise 18.13   The explicit yielding in Exercise 18.12 is only required if the scheduler does not operate a timeslicing policy. Try removing the calls to `yield` to see whether a mismatch occurs with your JVM.

18.7   Avoiding Race Hazards

In Section 18.6, we looked at some of the problems that can arise when potential race hazards are ignored. At the heart of such problems is the fact that a resource is shared between threads and the actions of those threads on the resource are non-atomic, leading to competing actions overlapping or interleaving. A further race hazard that we did not mention in those particular examples is the fact that access to the 64-bit primitive types, `long` and `double`, is not guaranteed to be atomic but might be separated into two separate 32-bit accesses. This means that a thread might be preempted partway through a write operation into such a variable, and, if the preempting thread writes to the same location, the final value of the variable will be corrupt.

   While we cannot, in general, eliminate the non-atomic nature of all sequences of actions, we can identify *critical sections* of an object's behavior which should not be interfered with until completed. Such situations typically involve the getting or setting of a shared `long` or `double` attribute or any *access-process-mutate* sequence of operations on an object shared between threads. Java provides a mechanism to limit the potential for this problem to occur by allowing an object to be *locked* by a thread, so that no other thread may access that object until the lock is released.[4] An object may be locked in one of two ways, by sending a message to one of its `synchronized` methods, or by making it the subject of a *synchronized statement*. We will look, first of all, at synchronized methods and discuss synchronized statements in Section 18.7.3.

18.7.1   Synchronized Methods

An object with one or more synchronized methods is defined to be a *monitor*[Hoa74, BH75]. Only one thread at a time is allowed to actively use a synchronized method of a monitor, and, when it does so, the monitor is locked by that thread. When a client thread sends a message via a synchronized method, it is said to be trying to acquire the object's lock. The runtime system first checks to see whether the monitor is already locked; if it is, then the client thread is placed at the back of a queue of other threads which are also waiting to acquire that particular lock. If the monitor

---

[4] In fact, this is a slight simplification as it is not possible to obtain completely exclusive access to an object by locking it, as we discuss below.

Code 18.16   Avoiding a race hazard with a synchronized method

```
    // Prevent a potential race hazard by locking this object.
protected synchronized boolean setBalance(long amount){
    if(amount >= 0){
        balance = amount;
        return true;
    }
    else{
        return false;
    }
}
```

is not already locked, the client thread acquires the lock and is able to proceed. We can apply this idea to the `setBalance` mutator shown in Code 18.14. We saw in Section 18.6 that a problem could arise if a thread was preempted partway through its setting of the balance and another thread made a change before the first got a chance to complete the mutation. We can avoid this situation arising by designating `setBalance` as `synchronized` (Code 18.16).

Once a thread has acquired the object lock, no other thread may acquire the same lock until the first has completed its use of `setBalance`, even if the first thread is preempted before the method has completed. As soon as the synchronized method from which the lock was obtained has been completed, the lock is released and another thread waiting to acquire it is allowed to proceed, relocking it in the process, of course. Which other methods of the UnsafeAccount class should be synchronized to reduce the potential for race hazards? The rules about the non-atomic nature of `long` and `double` suggest that the `getBalance` accessor should also be a synchronized method. In addition, both `credit` and `debit` exhibit the tell-tale access-process-mutate behavior which leaves them open to race hazards. Code 18.17 shows `SaferAccount` as an alternative version of the original UnsafeAccount class.

Code 18.17   Bank account class with synchronized methods (`SaferAccount.java`)

```
        // Maintain details of the account's balance and
        // implement credit and debit operations on it.
        // Use synchronized methods, where appropriate,
        // to reduce the potential for race hazards.
class SaferAccount implements Account {
    SaferAccount(){
        final int initialBalance = 600;
        setBalance(initialBalance);
    }

        // Return whether the debit was successful or not.
    public synchronized boolean debit(long amount){
        System.out.println();
        System.out.println("Debit: "+amount);
        if(amount >= 0){
```

Code 18.17   (*Continued*)

```
            return setBalance(getBalance()-amount);
        }
        else{
            return false;
        }
    }

        // Return whether the debit was successful or not.
    public synchronized boolean credit(long amount){
        System.out.println();
        System.out.println("Credit: "+amount);
        if(amount >= 0){
            return setBalance(getBalance()+amount);
        }
        else{
            return false;
        }
    }

    public synchronized long getBalance(){
        return balance;
    }

    // The balance may not go negative. Return true
    // on success, false on failure.
    protected synchronized boolean setBalance(long amount){
        if(amount >= 0){
            balance = amount;
            return true;
        }
        else{
            return false;
        }
    }

    // How much is in the account.
    private long balance;
}
```

There are a couple of points to note about SaferAccount that will explain some of
the features and limitations of Java's implementation of monitors. Race hazards only
arise when a resource or object is shared between threads. There is never a need to
designate a constructor as synchronized because a particular instance will only ever
be created by a single thread, even if it is shared thereafter. Note that, in the case of
the SaferAccount class, the newly created account is temporarily locked during its
creation by the constructor's use of its synchronized mutator, anyway.

Both credit and debit are synchronized methods which call other synchronized methods within the same instance—getBalance and setBalance. This does
not present a problem because Java's monitors are *reentrant*, by which is meant that

a thread possessing the lock on an object reacquires it when it enters another synchronized method in the same object, and is not made to wait with other threads trying to acquire the lock.

It should be carefully noted that an object is only locked from other threads which are trying to gain access via synchronized methods in the class, or via a synchronized statement on the object (Section 18.7.3). Where a class has both synchronized and unsynchronized methods, there is nothing to prevent a thread sending messages to a locked object via its unsynchronized methods. The assumption is that the unsynchronized methods do not provide the potential for race hazards to arise.

When a synchronized method is overridden in a sub class, the overriding method does not also have to be synchronized. If it is not synchronized, then the object will not be locked when its statements are executed. However, the object will become locked if the overriding version uses its synchronized super class version, but only for the duration of the super class method.

18.7.2   Volatile Attributes

It is not possible to designate an attribute as synchronized. This presents a potential problem; even if an object is locked by a thread's use of one of its synchronized methods, there is nothing to stop another thread directly accessing the locked object's attributes, because an object is only locked to access via its synchronized methods. This fact serves to strengthen the case made in Section 4.7 that attributes should be kept private and only examined and manipulated through a class's designated accessors and mutators—even by the class's own methods.

When an attribute *is* used directly by multiple threads, but access to it is not channeled through synchronized accessor and mutator methods for some reason, the attribute should be designated as `volatile`:

```
protected volatile long sharedAttribute;
```

Use of `volatile` signals to the compiler that it should not make optimizations that are based upon assumptions that the attribute's value remains unchanged for the duration of a particular sequence of statements in a method. This is necessary because a compiler will often load the value of a variable into one of the runtime system's registers when that variable is used several times within a statement sequence, for the sake of efficiency. The value in the register will be invalidated if another thread modifies the attribute's variable unseen to the statements of that particular method. Use of `volatile` warns the compiler to reload the attribute's value directly from its memory location on each use. This only applies to instance and class variables, of course, because each thread possesses its own copy of any method variables on its runtime stack, and these are free from interference by other threads. Since we eschew direct access to attributes and recommend that synchronized accessor and mutator methods are used where multiple threads are involved, the use of `volatile` does not feature any further in our examples.

Exercise 18.14   Would making the `getValue` and `setValue` methods of the Resource class in Exercise 18.12 synchronized cure the race hazard that arises? If not, why?

Exercise 18.15   Modify the Resource class from Exercise 18.12 so that it has a single synchronized method that can be used by the two threads to alter its `value` attribute atomically.

18.7.3   The Synchronized Statement

In Section 18.7, we demonstrated that the SaferAccount class of Code 18.17 removes some of the potential for race hazards that we identified with the use of the UnsafeAccount class in Section 18.6; however, it is not a complete solution. Recall the problem with the `run` method of the ATM class in Code 18.13, where the user is informed of the account's balance and invited to withdraw some money within the bounds of that balance. Assuming that this class is now manipulating a SaferAccount object and is using synchronized versions of `getBalance` and `debit`, the original race hazard *still exists*. Why is this? The problem is that the account object it manipulates is only locked by the ATM's thread while it responds, individually, to the `getBalance` and `debit` messages. In between those two points, the account object is not locked by the ATM's thread and the DirectDebit thread is free to acquire the lock and reduce the account's balance. What this illustrates is that the *critical section* of the ATM's access-process-mutate behavior does not lie within a single method of the account object, but straddles several of its methods, each used separately. What the ATM thread needs is a means to lock the account object for the full duration of this critical section so as to exclude other threads from acquiring the lock. Java's solution to this is the *synchronized statement*, which has the general form shown in Code 18.18.

The `expression` denotes the object for which a lock is to be acquired. It could be a variable containing an object reference, or a general expression that produces an object reference. For the ATM thread, the expression will be a reference to the account object it wishes to manipulate during its critical section (Code 18.19).

If another thread already has the lock on the account, then the ATM thread will have to wait to enter the body of the synchronized statement until it acquires it. Once it has done so, all other threads are prevented from using the account's synchronized methods until the lock is released when the end of the synchronized statement is reached. Note the importance of reentrant locks in this example; the lock on the account object is not acquired by using one of the account's synchronized methods, but the thread possessing the lock is still permitted to use the `getBalance` and `debit` methods on the locked object within its critical section.

Code 18.18   Outline of the synchronized statement

```
synchronized(expression){
    // Object of expression is locked.
    statements of the critical section ...
}
```

Code 18.19 Locking the account for the duration of the critical section

```
                // Lock the account each time a debit is required.
public void run(){
    Account account = getAccount();
    SimpleInput keyboard = new SimpleInput();
    final long sleepTime = 100;

    while(true){
        try{
            // Critical section: acquire the lock on the account.
            synchronized(account){
                // Find out the maximum amount that may be withdrawn.
                long available = account.getBalance();
                if(available > 0){
                    System.out.print("You have "+available+
                        " available, how much do you want? ");
                    System.out.flush();
                    // Request the amount from the user.
                    long amount = keyboard.nextLong();
                    // Check its validity.
                    if(amount <= 0){
                        System.out.println("The amount must be positive.");
                    }
                    else if(amount > available){
                        System.out.println("That is too much.");
                    }
                    else{
                        // This should be ok, but ...
                        if(!account.debit(amount)){
                            System.out.println("The debit failed!");
                        }
                    }
                }
            }
            // The lock has been released.
            Thread.sleep(sleepTime);
        }
        catch(InterruptedException e){
        }
    }
}
```

Although we have now solved the race hazard posed by use of the ATM thread, the solution is not entirely satisfactory because we have no guarantee over how quickly the user will respond to the request for the amount to be debited. The account object remains locked until a response is received and the ATM releases it. Locking out other threads could lead to their starvation and the system as a whole eventually grinding to a halt. Rather than allowing the ATM thread to lock the account indefinitely, it might be better to impose a timeout on account locking and force the ATM to release the thread if it receives no response from the user within a set period. However, this approach is also not ideal as, in some circumstances, it can lead to the need to back out of partially completed transactions. Although we shall not explore this particular example any further, it is important to be aware of some of the problems that can arise when a thread acquires exclusive use of a resource but is unable to proceed for some reason. Such a situation can easily lead the whole system to a state of *deadlock*, which is a topic that we shall address in Section 18.9.

A synchronized statement can sometimes be used within a method as an alternative to making the whole method synchronized. Instead of writing

```
public synchronized void method(){
    non-critical parts;
    critical section;
    more non-critical parts;
}
```

an object can lock itself for just the critical section within the method by using `this` in the statement's lock expression, and writing the method as:

```
public void method(){
    non-critical parts;
    synchronized(this){
        critical section;
    }
    more non-critical parts;
}
```

Although excluding other threads from interfering with a critical section of an object's behavior is an important solution to the problem of race hazards, the additional problems that can arise from locking out other threads for a long time mean that the use of a synchronized statement in this way to limit the period of the lockout should be seriously considered. However, synchronized statements used outside the object being locked do have their limitations in comparison with synchronized methods. They assume that other competing threads will be well behaved attempting to acquire the lock for themselves in a similar way, but this is something that cannot be enforced. If another thread simply goes ahead and uses the locked object without guarding this access with a synchronized statement, the lock cannot prevent this if the locked object's methods are not synchronized.

Exercise 18.16   Modify your solution to Exercise 18.13 to use a synchronized statement in order to avoid the race condition.

18.7.4   Synchronized Collection Objects

You might consider using a synchronized statement to enforce shared access to a collection object, such as an `ArrayList` or `LinkedList`. However, a safer way is to use one of the static methods of the `Collections` class (defined in `java.util`) to obtain a properly synchronized version of one of the collection classes. Two of the methods designed for this purpose are `synchronizedCollection` and `synchronizedList` (there are others for `Map` and `Set` objects). Each takes an object implementing a particular collection interface type and creates a synchronized collection that is backed by the argument to maintain the data within it. However, even though all the methods of the returned object are synchronized, care must be taken not to thwart the synchronization via an unsynchronized Iterator over it, for instance. If the data in the collection is accessed via any reference other than that returned by Collections' method, it should be enclosed within a synchronized statement for safety. For instance,

```
List data = Collections.synchronizedList(new LinkedList());
...
// Safely iterate over the data.
synchronized(data){
    ListIterator iterator = data.listIterator();
    while(iterator.hasNext()){
        // Move back and forth over the data, via iterator.
        ...
    }
}
```

18.7.5   Static Synchronized Methods

Static methods of a class may also be synchronized and entry to one of these by a thread prevents entry by another thread to other static synchronized methods of that class, but it does not prevent threads using non-static synchronized methods. In effect, a class with static synchronized methods has a class monitor associated with it that is distinct from any monitors associated with instances of that class. A thread entering a static synchronized method acquires the lock for the class, therefore. A typical use for such synchronized class methods would be to act as accessors and mutators to static (class) variables shared between threads.

18.8   Producer-Consumer Threads

Most of the thread examples we have looked at so far have involved either independent threads, which ignore each other, or competing threads which must be prevented from interfering with each other's activities. A common set of problems involves the need to enable threads to share a resource in order to collaborate over a common task. These problems are typically characterized as *Producer-Consumer* problems, where one thread acts as a producer of data and a second consumes the data the first has produced. Such threads typically share a resource which acts as a buffer for the produced items. This buffer might have enough space to hold either a single item of data or multiple items in the form of a queue. In the former case, it will be necessary to ensure that the producer does not overwrite the last item it produced before the consumer has had a chance to consume it. In the latter case, it will be necessary to ensure that a producer does not try to add further items to a full queue and it must be made to wait until the consumer has freed some space in the queue. Conversely, in both cases a reader must not try to take data from an empty buffer. Such co-ordination of activities requires more subtle synchronization mechanisms than are provided by the basic monitor tools we have seen so far, and Java provides these in the fundamental `wait` and `notify` methods that are inherited by all objects from their `Object` ancestry, rather than the Thread class.

We shall begin our consideration of Producer-Consumer problems by looking at an approach that does not work, as an understanding of this will help us to see why synchronization features in addition to those we have already seen are needed. Consider the implementation of a `Buffer` class as shown in Code 18.20.

Code 18.20   Unsuitable implementation of a shared buffer

```
    // Provide a buffer between a Producer and a Consumer.
    // This implementation is unsuitable.
class Buffer {
    // Wait until an item is available and return it.
    public synchronized int retrieve(){
        while(!itemAvailable()){
            try{
                // Give the producer time to produce something.
                Thread.sleep(100);
            }
            catch(InterruptedException e){
            }
        }
        // Consume it.
        setAvailable(false);
        return getItem();
    }

    // Wait until the buffer is free, then fill it.
    public synchronized void store(int item){
        while(itemAvailable()){
            try{
                // Give the consumer time to consume the last item.
                Thread.sleep(100);
            }
            catch(InterruptedException e){
            }
        }
        // Fill it.
        setItem(item);
        setAvailable(true);
    }

    // Is there an item in the buffer?
    public synchronized boolean itemAvailable(){
        return available;
    }

    // Public access and mutation is only available
    // through retrieve() and store().
    protected synchronized void setAvailable(boolean a){
        available = a;
    }
```

(*Continued*)

Code 18.20   (*Continued*)

```
protected synchronized int getItem(){
    return item;
}

protected synchronized void setItem(int i){
    item = i;
}

// Whether there is an item in the buffer or not.
private boolean available = false;
// The buffered item.
private int item;
}
```

The Buffer acts as the shared resource between a producer and a consumer. The producer stores an item into the buffer for retrieval by the consumer. We have done our best to limit the opportunities for race hazards to occur over shared access to the Buffer by making all of its methods synchronized,[5] but this implementation will not work in general.

Exercise 18.17   Before reading further, try to use your understanding of how monitor locking works to spot the problem with the example in Code 18.20. What happens if the consumer's thread ever gets to the buffer before the producer's?

The implementation of Buffer in Code 18.20 works fine as long as the producer and consumer remain in *lock-step* with the producer always writing to the buffer before the consumer attempts to read from it. In that case, the producer acquires the lock on the buffer via `store`, finds the buffer is empty, stores the value it has produced, releases the lock, and then does something else, giving the consumer a chance to run. The consumer then acquires the lock via `retrieve`, finds an item available, retrieves the item, releases the lock, and does something with the item it has retrieved. When the producer returns, it finds the buffer empty and the two threads follow the same pattern, *ad infinitum*. However, suppose the consumer arrives first, acquires the lock via `retrieve` and then finds the buffer to be empty. There is nothing else for it to do except wait until the producer produces something. So it waits by sleeping *inside the monitor*. The problem with this is that the producer cannot enter the monitor in order to store the next item, because the monitor is permanently locked by the waiting consumer, and there is no resolution for this. Similarly, if the producer happens to be much faster than the consumer and it attempts to store the next item before the previous one has been retrieved, it will prevent the consumer from consuming the previous item by its holding on to the monitor. From this we

---

[5] However, this does not mean that we recommend that a class's methods should all be made synchronized. It is too crude a mechanism and as likely to result in deadlock and thread starvation as to prevent race hazards.

can see that a thread must not hold on to a monitor and block other threads from
gaining access, when those other threads are its only means of escape.

One possible solution from this dilemma is to remove the waiting code to the
producer and consumer and leave the `retrieve` and `store` methods in the Buffer
as ordinary accessor and mutator methods (Code 18.21).

Code 18.21   Making the producer and consumer responsible for synchronized behavior

```
        // Provide a buffer between a Producer and a Consumer.
        // This implementation relies on the good behavior
        // of the collaborators.
class Buffer {
    public synchronized int retrieve(){
        // Consume the item.
        setAvailable(false);
        return getItem();
    }

    public synchronized void store(int item){
        // Fill the buffer.
        setItem(item);
        setAvailable(true);
    }
    ...
}

class Producer extends BufferUser implements Runnable {
    public Producer(Buffer b){
        super(b);
    }

        // Run forever storing consecutive integers into the buffer.
    public void run(){
        int i = 0;
        Buffer buffer = getBuffer();

        while(true){
            if(!buffer.itemAvailable()){
                // Store the next item into the empty buffer.
                buffer.store(i);
                i++;
            }
            // Sleep briefly.
            delay(100);
        }
    }
}

        // Implement a consumer reading integers from a shared buffer.
class Consumer extends BufferUser implements Runnable {
    public Consumer(Buffer b){
        super(b);
    }
```

(Continued)

Code 18.21   (*Continued*)

```
        // Run forever retrieving integers from the buffer.
    public void run(){
        int i = 0;
        Buffer buffer = getBuffer();

        while(true){
            if(buffer.itemAvailable()){
                i = buffer.retrieve();
                System.out.print(i+" ");
                System.out.flush();
            }
            // Sleep briefly.
            delay(100);
        }
    }
}
```

The producer and consumer use the approach of *polling* the buffer to see whether
it is available. In fact, this version works fine, but it is unsatisfactory for two reasons. Firstly, it relies on the producer and consumer being well behaved; that is,
that they guard their respective attempts to store and retrieve by an appropriate
querying of the buffer via itemAvailable. The buffer makes no attempt to ensure that the same value is not retrieved more than once, or that a previous value
is not overwritten before it has been retrieved. Although this particular producer
and consumer are well coordinated in this respect, there is no guarantee that others using the same buffer will be so. Secondly, it is inadequate because the times
chosen for the producer and consumer to sleep before trying again are completely
arbitrary. If a consumer finds that the buffer is empty and sleeps for 100 milliseconds, it could be that the producer is on the point of writing to the buffer and
the consumer would spend a considerable amount of time doing nothing when it
could be engaged in useful activity. This problem is exacerbated by the fact that
the producer will not be able to write its next data value into the buffer until the
consumer has woken. Both threads could spend much of their time doing nothing.
Conversely, if one of the threads is much slower than the other, polling the buffer
is likely to be inefficient in its use of processor resources because the faster thread
will repeatedly wake and check the buffer with little chance of its finding anything
there yet.

There is yet a third problem with the approach taken in Code 18.21; if there
happens to be more than one consumer sharing the same buffer with the producer,
we are back to the familiar race hazard situation, again! A consumer waking to find
that there is something in the buffer (getAvailable) could find that it has gone by
the time it gets to retrieve it, because another consumer might have got there first,
through separation of its access and process steps. To solve this third problem we
would have to lock the buffer for these two steps.

```
synchronized(buffer){
    if(buffer.itemAvailable()){
        i = buffer.retrieve();
        System.out.print(i+" ");
    }
}
```

However, solving this minor problem still leaves us with the other two and the need for a proper solution.

18.8.1   The Wait and Notify Methods

Recall that the reason we rewrote the example in Code 18.20 was that a thread, having acquired the lock, was unable to make use of the locked object until another thread performed some operation on that object, but that it was impossible for another thread to release it because the original thread retained the lock. In order to solve this specific sort of problem, Java provides a mechanism for a thread to release control of a lock without leaving the synchronized method or statement in which it finds it cannot make progress. If a thread has acquired a lock, it can release control of it by performing a wait inside the synchronized section. This method is defined in the Object class. The effect of this is to allow another thread which is waiting to acquire the lock to do so. When there is more than one thread waiting to acquire the lock, the one that has been waiting the longest should obtain it. The assumption is that this second thread will do something that will ultimately lead to the release of the first thread. Code 18.22 illustrates how wait is used in the retrieve method of Buffer.

As with the sleep method, it is possible for a thread's wait to be interrupted and an exception handler must be provided, but this is not the normal method by which a thread is informed that its wait is over.

Code 18.22   The consumer releases the lock if an item is unavailable

```
class Buffer {
    // Wait until an item is available and return it.
    public synchronized int retrieve(){
        while(!itemAvailable()){
            try{
                // Wait to be notified of an item becoming available.
                wait();
            }
            catch(InterruptedException e){
            }
            // There should be something for me, now.
        }
        // Consume it.
        setAvailable(false);
        return getItem();
    }
    ...
}
```

A thread that waits moves from the runnable state to the *waiting state*. There are two further forms of `wait`, both of which take a length of time that the thread is willing to wait, after which time it is moved back to the runnable state and must wait to reacquire the monitor, along with any other threads that wish to do so. When there is no timeout associated with the wait, the thread remains in the waiting state until another thread with the lock issues a `notify` for that particular monitor—`notify` is also defined in the Object class. A thread waiting with a timeout will be woken before the timeout expires if it receives a notification. Where there are several threads waiting to be notified, only the thread that has been waiting the longest for the monitor is moved back to the runnable state and added to the queue of threads waiting to acquire the monitor. The fact that a thread has previously held the monitor and voluntarily relinquished it gives it no particular privilege in reacquiring it. As we shall see, this can lead to problems.

In our example of a single producer and a single consumer, the `wait` and `notify` mechanisms work well in solving the problems associated with previous efforts to program the producer-consumer relationship, and Code 18.23 shows the

Code 18.23   Using **wait** and **notify** to coordinate a producer and consumer

```
        // Provide a buffer between a Producer and a Consumer.
class Buffer {
        // Wait until an item is available and return it.
    public synchronized int retrieve(){
        while(!itemAvailable()){
            try{
                // Wait to be notified of an item becoming available.
                wait();
            }
            catch(InterruptedException e){
            }
        }
        // Retrieve the item before we notify waiting threads.
        int item = getItem();
        // Consume it.
        setAvailable(false);
        return item;
    }

        // Wait until the buffer is free, then fill it.
    public synchronized void store(int item){
        while(itemAvailable()){
            try{
                // Wait to be notified of the buffer being empty.
                wait();
            }
            catch(InterruptedException e){
            }
        }
        // Fill it.
        setItem(item);
        // Notify waiting threads there is something there.
        setAvailable(true);
    }
```

Code 18.23   (*Continued*)

```
        // Public access and mutation is only available
        // through retrieve() and store().
    protected synchronized void setAvailable(boolean a){
        // Determine whether the status is being changed.
        boolean statusChange = a != available;

        available = a;
        if(statusChange){
            // A change in status. Notify a waiting thread.
            notify();
        }
    }
    ...
}

class Producer extends BufferUser implements Runnable {
    Producer(Buffer b){
        super(b);
    }

        // Run forever storing consecutive integers into the buffer.
    public void run(){
        int i = 0;
        Buffer buffer = getBuffer();

        while(true){
            // Store the next item into the empty buffer.
            buffer.store(i);
            i++;
            // Sleep briefly.
            delay(100);
        }
    }
}

        // Implement a consumer reading integers from a shared buffer.
class Consumer extends BufferUser implements Runnable {
    Consumer(Buffer b){
        super(b);
    }

        // Run forever retrieving integers from the buffer.
    public void run(){
        int i = 0;
        Buffer buffer = getBuffer();

        while(true){
            i = buffer.retrieve();
            System.out.print(i+" ");
            // Sleep briefly.
            delay(100);
        }
    }
}
```

---

relevant methods of Buffer and the way in which these are used by the `Producer` and `Consumer` threads.

Whenever either of these threads changes the state of the buffer from empty to full or vice-versa, a `notify` is issued from `setAvailable` to wake up the other party if it happens to be waiting.

The `notifyAll` method can be used to wake all threads waiting on a particular monitor, if this is desired. Note that a thread does not lose control of the lock by issuing a notify, but only when it leaves the synchronized method or statement it entered to acquire the lock.

Exercise 18.18   Modify the producer-consumer example described in this section so that the buffer is able to hold more than one item. A consumer always removes the item that has been longest in the buffer, so the buffer acts like a FIFO queue. Experiment with varying production and consumption rates in the Producer and Consumer classes.

18.8.2   Wait and Notify in a Synchronized Statement

Because `wait` and `notify` are methods of the Object class, when they are used within a synchronized statement, the object associated with the particular monitor must be indicated if it is not `this`. For instance, suppose an `Author` object has obtained locks on the objects `paper` and `pen` in nested synchronized statements, and that `paper` is an object shared with an `Origami` object. If the author wishes to release the paper from time to time, in order to let the origami object use it, then it must specifically send the `wait` message to the paper. Similarly, the origami object must send the `notify` message to the paper object when it releases it. Code 18.24 illustrates this.

If a `wait` or `notify` message is sent to an object on which the thread does not hold the lock, then an `IllegalMonitorStateException` exception will be thrown. In the example in Code 18.24, it is not sufficient for the Author to release the lock by leaving the synchronized statement because, with a non-timeslicing scheduler, there is no guarantee that the Origami thread will ever get a chance to run.

The Producer-Consumer version of Code 18.23 solves the problems we identified earlier in the following ways. Firstly, we no longer rely on the producer and consumer being well behaved. If the buffer is already full when the producer wishes to store the next item, it is made to wait until it becomes empty. Similarly, the consumer is made to wait until notified by the producer that there is an item in the buffer. Secondly, the amount of time a waiting thread is delayed is only the length of time it takes the other thread to perform the complementary activity and release it with `notify`. Both producer and consumer can work at full tilt with the minimum of delay between their two activities.

Code 18.24   Using `wait` and `notify` in synchronized statements

```
class Author implements Runnable {
    public Author(Object paper, Object pen){
        this.paper = paper;
        this.pen = pen;
    }

        // Use the pen and paper for writing.
    public void run(){
        while(true){
            Object pen = getPen();
            synchronized(pen){
                Object paper = getPaper();
                synchronized(paper){
                    System.out.println("Writing.");
                    try{
                        // Release the paper.
                        paper.wait();
                    }
                    catch(InterruptedException e){
                    }
                }
            }
        }
    }
    ...
}

class Origami implements Runnable {
    public Origami(Object paper){
        this.paper = paper;
    }

    public void run(){
        while(true){
            Object paper = getPaper();
            synchronized(paper){
                System.out.println("Origami.");
                // Release the paper.
                paper.notify();
            }
        }
    }
    ...
}
```

So, it begins to look like everything in the garden is rosy. However ...

Exercise 18.19   Before reading further, you might like to consider why we have written the bodies of the `store` and `retrieve` methods in Code 18.23 in a loop.

18.8.3 Livelock

When a thread wakes from a call to `wait`, it will be for one of three possible reasons:

- The timeout associated with the `wait` has expired.
- It was sent an `interrupt` message.
- Another thread has issued a `notify` or `notifyAll` on the monitor it is waiting for.

In all three cases, there is no guarantee that the condition it has been waiting for to come `true` is indeed `true`. This is easy to appreciate in the first and second cases, but less so in the third case.

- If the timeout has expired, this must be because another thread has not yet issued a notification to this one. The woken thread might wish to take some action other than returning to the waiting state in this case, as it could be an indication of there being something wrong with the behavior of the other threads if the timeout was a long one. A thread can give potentially useful debugging information to a programmer by using the static `dumpStack` method of Thread when something appears to be wrong.
- If the thread has been interrupted, then it will need some means of determining why this was, probably by retrieving data from the InterruptedException object.
- If the thread was woken because another thread sent it a notification, doesn't this mean that the condition it was waiting on must now be true? In the case of a single producer and a single consumer this will be so, but, in general, if multiple threads are competing for a monitor there is no guarantee that a notification means that the required resource is available because someone else might get there first.

In order to illustrate how a resource might remain unavailable following a notification, consider the case of a single producer and two consumers. Suppose that one of the consumers acquires the lock, closely followed by the producer and the second consumer attempting to do so and being made to queue for the lock. Table 18.3 illustrates a possible scenario for the states of these three threads as time progresses from top to bottom. The first consumer, after acquiring the lock at step 1, has to wait because there is nothing in the buffer. Its wait releases the lock to the producer at

Table 18.3 Livelock with a single producer and two consumers

Step	Consumer 1	Producer	Consumer 2
1	has lock	queuing for lock	queuing for lock
2	waiting state	has lock	queuing for lock
3	waiting state	produces and notifies	queuing for lock
4	queuing for lock	sleeping	has lock
5	queuing for lock	sleeping	consumes and notifies
6	has lock	sleeping	sleeping
7	waiting state	has lock	sleeping
8	waiting state	produces and notifies	queuing for lock
9	queuing for lock	sleeping	has lock
etc.			

step 2, while the second consumer is left on the queue for the lock. At step 3, the producer is able to store its item in the buffer and issue a notification to waiting threads. This releases the first consumer at step 4, who joins the second consumer in the queue for the lock. Because the second consumer has been waiting the longest (the first consumer's time within its wait does not count for this purpose), it acquires the lock next. The second consumer takes the item in the buffer at step 5 without having to wait, and issues a notify for which there are no waiting threads. The first customer now reacquires the lock and returns to the beginning of the while loop in which it had been waiting in `retrieve`. However, the test for `itemAvailable` fails, because the second consumer has already retrieved the only item produced so far. This means that the first consumer is forced to reenter the waiting state in the body of the loop at step 7. Meanwhile, the producer has woken from its sleep and acquires the lock. At step 8, it produces and notifies the waiting first consumer, but by this time the second consumer has also woken and beaten it to the head of the queue for the monitor. So the second consumer will be able to consume the item, as before. The result is that the first consumer will be forever waking only to find that it is never able to consume anything. This situation is known as *livelock* and there is no straightforward solution within the basic thread primitives of the Java language.[6]

Exercise 18.20   Modify your solution to Exercise 18.18 so that the producer produces items for different consumers. Each item should be tagged with the identity of the consumer to which it belongs. A consumer only removes an item from the buffer if it is tagged with its identity.

Exercise 18.21   Modify your solution to Exercise 18.20 so that a consumer removes any single item from the buffer that is tagged with the consumer's identity. Note that this means the buffer will no longer operate as a FIFO data structure, and its behavior will need considerable modification.

18.9   Deadlock

The example in Code 18.24 illustrated that a thread may attempt to hold the lock on more than one monitor at the same time. We have seen that two threads competing for a single resource can be problematic, and a further set of problems can arise when multiple threads are competing for access to multiple resources. The main problem happens if two threads each possess a resource that is required by the other. Consider two impoverished authors sharing an office in which there is a single pen and a single piece of paper. Theoretically, at least one of them should be able to get some work done, but suppose one gets the pen first and the other gets the piece of paper. Neither can get any work done because each has the resource the other needs. Exactly the same thing can happen with two threads where each acquires the lock to one of a pair of resources that they both need. Such a situation is known as *deadlock* because

---

[6] The interested reader might like to look at suggestions as to how this might be addressed in the context of Java in [Wel98].

neither thread can proceed. The first indication you often get that it has happened is that your program completely locks up and becomes totally unresponsive. Deadlocks often arise from complex interactions between multiple threads and the resources they are competing over but a common theme will be a circularity in the resource dependencies. For instance, thread T1 has locked resource R1 and requires resource R2, which has been locked by thread T2. T2 requires resource R3, which is locked by thread T3, and T3 requires resource R1. Unless one thread is prepared to give up its resource and break the chain, deadlock results.

Designers of concurrent systems have been aware of the potential for deadlock for a considerable time and the conditions likely to lead to deadlock have been identified[CES71]. In terms of Java's threads, these might be described as follows:

- A monitor can be either free (not locked) or locked by a single thread.
- A thread holding a lock is allowed to obtain further locks.
- A thread cannot be forced to release a lock—release is at the thread's discretion.
- A chain of two or more threads exists, each of which is waiting to acquire a lock held by the next thread in the chain (as we saw above).

If all four of these conditions can apply, as they can in Java, there is the potential for deadlock to arise. These conditions suggest that one way to avoid deadlock might be for a thread to check before attempting to acquire a lock that it will succeed in doing so. Unfortunately, this is thwarted by the fact that Java's rules on monitor locking specify that the test and acquisition steps are atomic — in order to avoid race hazards. A more readily accessible avoidance method is to define an ordering for resources being competed over, and to insist that threads try to acquire them strictly according to this ordering. For instance, the authors sharing an office might agree that the paper should always be acquired before the pen; an author who fails to acquire the paper is forbidden from attempting to acquire the pen. This allows the author with the paper to acquire the pen also, and hence to get some work done. The idle author must wait patiently for the active author to release the resources and so acquire them in due course (Code 18.25).

Code 18.25   Ordered acquisition of resources

```
class PoorAuthors {
    public static void main(String[] args){
        // The only pen and paper available.
        Paper paper = new Paper();
        Pen pen = new Pen();
        // Let the authors share the pen and paper.
        Thread WarAndPeace = new Thread(
                        new PoorAuthor(paper,pen),"Tolstoy");
        Thread Karamazov = new Thread(
                        new PoorAuthor(paper,pen),"Dostoyevsky");

        // Let writing commence ...
```

Code 18.25   (*Continued*)

```
            WarAndPeace.start();
            Karamazov.start();
            // Will they every stop?!
    }
}

class PoorAuthor implements Runnable {
    public PoorAuthor(Object paper, Object pen){
        this.paper = paper;
        this.pen = pen;
    }

        // Use the pen and paper for writing.
    public void run(){
        Object paper = getPaper();
        Object pen = getPen();
        // Find out my name.
        String myName = Thread.currentThread().getName();

        while(true){
            // Lock both the pen and paper.
            synchronized(paper){
                synchronized(pen){
                    System.out.println(myName+" gets some writing done.");
                    // Release the pen and paper.
                }
            }
            // Take a break.
            try{
                Thread.sleep(100);
            }
            catch(InterruptedException e){
            }
        }
    }

    protected Object getPen(){
        return pen;
    }

    protected Object getPaper(){
        return paper;
    }

    private final Object paper, pen;
}
```

You might like to compare Code 18.25 with the origami example in Code 18.24 and note the different way in which the respective PoorAuthor objects release control of the shared resources. In Code 18.25, it would not be sufficient for a PoorAuthor to release the paper and pen with consecutive `wait` messages on these objects

```
paper.wait();
pen.wait();
```

as the second author would be able to gain control of the paper, but the pen would not be released by the first author until the second sent a `notify` for the paper, and the two threads are deadlocked. The first author must release both resources, and then give the second author a chance to be scheduled in case they are running on a non-timeslicing scheduler.

In a situation where a thread only discovers partway through its task that it needs to obtain a resource earlier in the order than those it already has, that thread would have to voluntarily release its existing resources and reacquire them in the correct order. There are some circumstances where this backing off is neither practicable nor necessary—because acquisition of the earlier resource would not form a circular chain, anyway—and it is up to the designer of the program to decide how these situations should be dealt with. In any case, it is important to be aware that deadlocks can arise, and the circumstances that make them more likely to do so.

Exercise 18.22   Write a program in which several threads require a pair of arbitrary resources, which they obtain and then use for a period before releasing them. The resources should be stored in an array, and the threads should randomly decide on which pair to use each time they wish to use them. Determine whether this program is likely to deadlock or not.

Exercise 18.23   Experiment with ways to avoid deadlock in your solution to Exercise 18.22.

18.10   Thread Groups

Each thread belongs to a single named group of threads, to which it is assigned on creation, and remains for the duration of its life. The `ThreadGroup` class is defined in the `java.lang` package. A selection of its methods is shown in Table 18.4. The `main` thread, in which the main method is executed, belongs to the group whose name is also `main`. By default, a Thread is allocated to the group of the thread which created it, but a reference to an alternative group may be passed to its constructor instead. A ThreadGroup object is constructed by passing a name for the group to its constructor:

```
ThreadGroup folders = new ThreadGroup("database");
```

Each ThreadGroup object has a parent ThreadGroup and a new group is made a child of the group to which its creating thread group belongs, by default. So, a user's thread groups form a tree-structured hierarchy rooted in the `main` group. A new group may be made a child of a group other than the default by passing a reference to the alternative group object as an argument to its constructor, in addition to the new group's name:

```
ThreadGroup programs = new ThreadGroup(folders,"programs");
```

Table 18.4   Selected methods of the ThreadGroup class

	Method and Arguments
	ThreadGroup(String groupName)
	ThreadGroup(ThreadGroup parentGroup,String groupName)
int	activeCount()
int	activeGroupCount()
void	checkAccess()
int	enumerate(Thread[] threads)
int	enumerate(Thread[] threads,boolean recurse)
int	enumerate(ThreadGroup[] groups)
int	enumerate(ThreadGroup[] groups,boolean recurse)
int	getMaxPriority()
String	getName()
ThreadGroup	getParent()
void	interrupt()
static boolean	interrupted()
void	list()
boolean	parentOf(ThreadGroup group)
void	setDaemon(boolean daemon)
void	setMaxPriority(int priority)
String	toString()

Code 18.26 is another version of the example shown in Code 18.8 and Code 18.11. It uses a ThreadGroup to provide an alternative to `join` in order to determine when all of the counters have finished.

Code 18.26   Using `activeCount` to determine when all threads have died (`GroupCoordinator.java`)

```
        // Illustrate the creation and running of multiple threads
        // assigned to their own ThreadGroup.
        // Use ThreadGroup.activeCount to determine when all the threads
        // have finished.
public class ThreadGroupExample {
    public static void main(String[] args){
        Thread coordinator = new Thread(
                        new GroupCoordinator(),"coordinator");
        coordinator.start();
    }
}

class GroupCoordinator implements Runnable {
    public GroupCoordinator() {
        initCounters();
    }

        // Set up an array of threads to run multiple Counters.
    protected void initCounters(){
        // Where the threads are to be stored.
        Thread[] counters = getCounters();
```

(Continued)

Code 18.26   (*Continued*)

```java
        // The group for the counter threads.
        ThreadGroup group = getGroup();

        // Create the counters and threads.
        for(int i = 0; i < counters.length; i++){
            // Specify the range over which the counter operates.
            final int min = 10*i+1, max = min+9;
            // Place this thread in a ThreadGroup.
            counters[i] = new Thread(group,new FairCounter(min,max));
        }
        System.out.println("All counters created.");
    }

    public void run(){
        Thread[] counters = getCounters();

        for(int i = 0; i < counters.length; i++){
            counters[i].start();
        }

        System.out.println("All counters ready to run.");
        waitForCountersToFinish();
        System.out.println("All the threads have finished.");
    }

    protected void waitForCountersToFinish(){
        // The group to which the counters belong.
        ThreadGroup group = getGroup();
        do{
            try{
                Thread.sleep(500);
            }
            catch(InterruptedException e){
            }
        } while(group.activeCount() > 0);
    }

    protected Thread[] getCounters(){
        return counters;
    }

    protected ThreadGroup getGroup(){
        return counterGroup;
    }

    // Create the array to hold the threads.
    private final int numCounters = 3;
    private final Thread[] counters = new Thread[numCounters];
    // Create the group to hold the counter threads.
    private final ThreadGroup counterGroup = new ThreadGroup("counters");
}
```

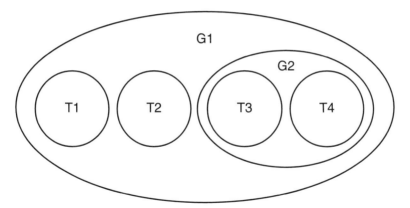

Figure 18.1   A hierarchy of thread groups

The GroupCoordinator assigns the threads controlling the FairCounter objects to a group named `counters` in `initCounters`. The GroupCoordinator then periodically sleeps in `waitForCountersToFinish` and tests the `activeCount` of the thread group, sleeping again if there is still at least one counter still active.

18.10.1   Thread Group Security

A major reason for grouping threads is for security purposes, and the `Security-Manager` class of `java.lang` manages the security rules for groups of threads. ThreadGroups provide a measure of security because a thread is not allowed to modify another thread unless both belong to the same group, or the modifying thread belongs to a group which contains the group of the thread to be modified. In the diagram in Figure 18.1, thread `T1` may modify any of the threads `T2`–`T4`, but `T3` may only modify `T4`. Thread grouping and thread security are particularly important issues in Applet environments, where potentially hostile threads loaded from remote sites can be allocated to their own groups in order to prevent them from interfering with the host system's threads. The `checkAccess` method of both the Thread and ThreadGroup classes may be used by a thread to determine whether it has the right to modify another thread or group; a `SecurityException` exception is thrown if it does not have this right. Another way in which threads in a group may be limited by a controlling group is via ThreadGroup's `setMaxPriority` method which takes a priority level as its actual argument. The method sets a ceiling for the priority level of any newly created threads within the group, but does not affect any existing threads. This provides a means to prevent a rogue thread from running itself at too high a priority and hence deny system resources to other threads with a more legitimate right to them.

18.11   Daemon Threads

Daemon threads are an alternative to the more normal user threads. Daemon threads are typically used to carry out low-priority tasks that should not take priority over the main task of the program. They can be used to do useful work when all other user threads are blocked, for instance, by input-output operations. A particular example of a daemon thread is the *garbage collector* which attempts to recycle portions of memory into the available pool (see Section 18.12). If all user threads have finished, and only daemon threads are left, a program will terminate. This helps to illustrate the subservient nature of such threads; if there are no user threads left to serve, the daemon threads have no further use. Threads have a `boolean` attribute—with associated `getDaemon` accessor and `setDaemon` mutator—to determine whether they are a daemon thread or not. Normally a thread inherits its daemon status from that of the thread that created it. If `setDaemon` is used on a thread to circumvent this pattern, this must be before the thread is started.

A ThreadGroup may also be designated as a daemon. This does not alter the status of the threads within it, however. It simply indicates that if the group ever becomes empty—through its threads all being stopped, and its contained thread groups are destroyed—then it too should be destroyed.

Exercise 18.24   Write a program that creates two new user threads. One should print a finite sequence of positive numbers and the other a finite sequence of negative numbers. Each should periodically sleep after printing some numbers. Include a demon thread in your program that prints the current time whenever it gets a chance to run.

18.12   Garbage Collection

Every object created in a program occupies some of the memory available to the virtual machine at runtime. The amount of space it occupies depends primarily upon the number and type of attributes defined by its class; a class with a single integer attribute will occupy less memory than one with multiple primitive-type attributes and collection attributes, for instance. Objects of variable-sized collection classes, such as ArrayList, require more or less memory depending upon how many object references are stored in the collection. The amount of memory available to the whole program might initially be tens or hundreds of megabytes, but this could be quickly used up if a program creates hundreds or thousands of large objects. The total amount of memory available to a program can be determined by sending a `totalMemory` message to an object of the `Runtime` class. The amount of memory that is still free at any particular time can be found out by sending it a `freeMemory` message. Objects that are no longer required, but still occupy memory, are responsible for *memory leaks*. The existence of memory leaks means that there will be less free memory available than there could potentially be.

Code 18.27 contains a program to show the total memory and the amount of free memory in a trivial program.

Exercise 18.25   Run the program in the file `Memory.java` to find out how much memory is available to programs on your system, and how much is occupied by the simplest of programs.

Code 18.27   Finding total and free amounts of memory

```
        // How much memory is available on this system?
class Memory {
    public static void main(String[] args){
        Runtime details = Runtime.getRuntime();
        final long totalMemory = details.totalMemory();
        long freeMemory = details.freeMemory();

        System.out.println("Free: "+freeMemory+" bytes out of "+
                                totalMemory);
    }
}
```

Exercise 18.26   Add some statements to create some objects in the main method of `Memory.java` (e.g., some strings) and see what effect this has on the amount of free memory.

In order to try and prevent them from running out of memory, all Java programs have a *garbage collector* that recycles objects that have been used but are no longer required. By recycling them, the memory they occupy becomes available again for the creation of new objects. Programs often create objects that are ephemeral, that is, they have a very short lifetime. Objects are often created inside a method in order to help an object carry out a particular task. Once the method is finished, there is no further use for those objects. Consider the `printWords` method in Code 18.28, for instance. Its purpose is to split the string passed as its argument into separate words and print each word out.

The method uses a `StringTokenizer` to identify the individual words, which are separated by either spaces or punctuation characters. Each word identified by the tokenizer is returned as a separate String object from `nextToken`. Once this has been printed, that particular String is no longer required and becomes eligible to be garbage collected. Finally, at the end of the method, the tokenizer object has no further use and can be recycled. How does the garbage collector know for sure that an object is no longer needed? We can only send a message to an object if we have a reference to it, so an object only has a use in a program if there is a reference

---

Code 18.28   Creating ephemeral objects that will be garbage collected

```
public void printWords(String sentence){
    StringTokenizer tokenizer = new StringTokenizer(sentence," ,;.:?!");

    while(tokenizer.hasMoreTokens()){
        String s = tokenizer.nextToken();
        System.out.println(s);
    }
}
```

Code 18.29 Only `tokenizer` can be garbage collected

```
public String[] getWords(String sentence){
    StringTokenizer tokenizer = new StringTokenizer(sentence," ,;.:");
    // Allocate space for each word.
    final int numWords = tokenizer.countTokens();
    String[] words = new String[numWords];

    for(int i = 0; i < numWords; i++){
        words[i] = tokenizer.nextToken();
    }
    return words;
}
```

to it available somewhere in the program. As long as a usable reference exists, an object will not be garbage collected, and it does not matter whether the reference is stored in an attribute, a method variable, an argument, a collection object, and so on. Only objects with no references to them become eligible for garbage collection. The only references which do not count are those which are in objects which themselves are unreferenced. Contrast the objects which can be garbage collected in Code 18.28 with those that can at the end of the `getWords` method in Code 18.29.

This method constructs an array to hold a reference to each word identified in the argument and returns the array of references at the end of the method. Assuming that the result of this method is stored in a variable in the method that called `get-Words`, then there will still be an available reference to both the array object and each of the individual word-string objects created by this method. Only the tokenizer object is eligible for garbage collection at the end of the method, therefore. However, once there is no longer a reference to the returned array, all of the string objects are likely to become eligible for garbage collection, too, unless further references to them have been made in another part of the program.

It is sometimes possible to help out the garbage collector when it is known that a referenced object is no longer required. For instance, a method might open, use, and close a FileReader at the start of the method, and then go on to perform other tasks before the method finishes. It is quite likely that the FileReader object is of no further use within the method, but it cannot be garbage collected because a reference to it still exists. This problem can be avoided by assigning a `null` value to the variable once the object is no longer required. This removes the only remaining reference to the object, and frees it for garbage collection.

```
FileReader reader = new FileReader(filename);
// Use the reader.
...
reader.close();
// Detach reader from its associated object.
reader = null;
// The FileReader can now be garbage collected.
...
```

The fact that it is possible to garbage collect a particular object does not necessarily mean that its memory will be recycled straight away. The garbage collector only performs its recycling from time to time, because it runs as a daemon thread; it tries not to take away processor resources from the task that your program is trying to achieve, but only runs when nothing else is happening. One way to force the garbage collector to be run is to send a Runtime object a gc message, or to use the static gc method of the System class.

18.12.1   Finalization

Sometimes it is necessary for an object to be aware that it is about to be garbage collected, so that it can perform some housekeeping operations: typically freeing resources, such as locks or open files, that it still has control over. Before being garbage collected, an object goes through a process known as *finalization*. In version 1.2 of the Java API, finalization is performed periodically by a low-priority thread that is separate from the garbage collector thread, whereas in previous versions it was performed by the garbage collector itself. Finalization is also performed on all objects when a program exits. It involves a finalize message being sent to an object. All classes inherit an empty finalize method from their Object super class and this may be overridden if it is necessary to add finalization actions. Code 18.30 shows an outline for such a method. Such methods should always explicitly invoke their super class's version which they are overriding, to ensure that finalization on the object is complete.

Code 18.31 shows a finalize method for a class that implements file locking of some sort. If an object of the class still has a lock on a file when it is garbage collected, then it is important that the lock is released, otherwise no other objects will be able to obtain the lock. If the finalization actions performed in the method could result in exceptions being thrown, then these can be handled with a normal exception handler. However, any unhandled exceptions will be ignored and not result in a runtime failure. While finalization does happen automatically, it can be explicitly invoked by sending a Runtime object a runFinalization message, or using the static runFinalization method of the System class.

Finalization of an object only takes place if there are no references to that object remaining within the program. However, it would theoretically be possible for a finalization method to cause new references to the object to come into being. This sort of behavior is strictly frowned upon and the preferred alternative is to create

Code 18.30   An outline finalize method

```
protected void finalize() throws Throwable {
    // Ensure that finalization of the super class is performed.
    super.finalize();
    ...
}
```

Code 18.31   Releasing a lock as part of finalization

```
class Locker {
    ...
    protected void finalize() throws Throwable {
        // Ensure that finalization of the super class is performed.
        super.finalize();
        // See if we still have the lock.
        if(haveLock()){
            releaseLock();
        }
    }
    ...
}
```

Code 18.32   Create several short-lived objects (`ShortLifeMain.java`)

```
    // A test-rig for the ShortLife class that should implement a
    // finalize method.
class ShortLifeMain {
    public static void main(String[] args){
        final int numObjects = 5;
        ShortLife b;
        for(int i = 0; i < numObjects; i++){
            b = new ShortLife();
        }
    }
}
```

---

a clone of the object (Section 15.3). An important reason why it should not be done is that finalization of an object is only ever done once. If an object is put back into circulation by its `finalize` method, it will not undergo further finalization when it next has no outstanding references.

Exercise 18.27   Define a class `ShortLife` that has a `finalize` method that reports that an object has been finalized. Test your class with the main method shown in Code 18.32. Does running this program with your class produce any output? If not, why?

Exercise 18.28   Add an explicit invocation of the garbage collector to main method shown in Code 18.32, and rerun your solution to Exercise 18.27. Does it produce any output this time?

Exercise 18.29   Check the memory availability immediately before and immediately after the call to the garbage collector in your solution to Exercise 18.28.

18.13   **Review**

Here are the main points that we have covered in the preceding sections:

- When multiple threads share a resource, there are many opportunities for things to go wrong.
- A race hazard arises when one thread's assumptions about the state of a resource are invalidated by the actions of another thread.
- A race hazard is likely to arise when there is a separation between access and mutation operations on a shared resource.
- A section of code in which there is potential for a race hazard is called a critical section.
- Race hazards can be avoided by locking a shared resource object against access by all competing threads.
- An object is locked when one of its synchronized methods is called.
- An object with one or more synchronized methods is called a monitor.
- An object is locked when it is made the target of a synchronized statement.
- When an object is locked by a thread, other threads may not enter one of the object's synchronized methods, or the body of a synchronized statement of which it is the target.
- A monitor is reentrant by the thread which has the associated lock.
- An object lock is released when a synchronized method or statement is finished.
- A locked object may be accessed via its non-synchronized methods.
- An attribute cannot be declared as synchronized. Locking must be achieved via synchronized methods or a synchronized statement.
- Static methods may be synchronized.
- Classes with static synchronized methods have a class lock which is distinct from any locks associated with its objects.
- A shared resource may be declared as `volatile` to avoid inappropriate compiler optimization.
- The `Collections` class defines static methods to create synchronized shared Collection objects.
- A thread with an object lock that is unable to proceed may `wait` in order to release the lock.
- Actions involving a thread entering the waiting state should always be included within a loop.
- A thread that has performed some action that might allow a thread to proceed should `notify` waiting threads.
- A waiting thread that has been notified is not guaranteed to be able to continue with its desired action; another thread might have got there first.
- Deadlock arises when threads compete for multiple resources.
- The most common deadlock situation arises when two threads have each locked a resource required by the other.
- Acquisition of multiple resources should be ordered in an effort to prevent deadlock.
- A thread belongs to a named thread group.
- Thread groups may be nested.

- Thread groups provide a degree of security control.
- Daemon threads run when no user thread is eligible to run.
- The existence of daemon threads does not prevent a program from terminating when there are no more user threads.
- The garbage collector is an example of a daemon thread.
- The garbage collector is able to recycle objects to which there are no remaining references.
- An object's `finalize` method is called when it is garbage collected.
- Objects should not resurrect themselves within their finalize methods.

Networking

I n this chapter, we look at some of the standard Java classes that allow programs to interact with non-Java programs across a network. These include the ability to retrieve resources from the Internet via the `URL` class, and the essential components needed to conduct reliable client-server communication over a TCP/IP network, using the `Socket` and `ServerSocket` classes. We also show how efficient but potentially unreliable networked communication may be achieved using the `DatagramSocket` and `DatagramPacket` classes.

19.1 The Internet and the World Wide Web

The invention of the *World Wide Web (WWW)* by Tim Berners-Lee in 1989 revolutionized the way in which ordinary individuals looked at the world of networked computers. Within a few years, networking concepts, hitherto largely the province of academics using the global *Internet*, were commonplace in many homes around the world. Electronic mail, bulletin-boards (news groups), file transfer, chat rooms and, in particular, Web browsing became a regular part of everyone's vocabulary. At the heart of the design of Java is a concern to allow programs to communicate across networks. Many non-programmers experience this in the form of *applets* providing active content within a Web page, but the language includes classes to allow you to create and use networked programs in a much wider context. In this chapter, we look at the main classes in the `java.net` package that include, among other things, the ability to retrieve files from remote locations, connect to different networked services and write programs that provide networked services to client programs.

19.1.1 Firewalls

Some organizations protect their networks by requiring that all access to and from the external networking world is directed through a firewall or proxy machine. Most of the examples in this chapter assume that you have direct access to the Internet. If this is not the case, and your organization does operate a proxy, you will need to make the Java runtime environment know this. There are two ways to do this. You can either provide details via the system properties from within a program

```
        Properties properties = System.getProperties();
        // Indicate that a proxy should be used.
        properties.put("proxySet","true");
        // Indicate the name of my proxy, and its port number.
        properties.put("proxyHost","proxy.thisOrg.org");
        properties.put("proxyPort","3000");
```

or you can supply values for these when you run the interpreter

```
java -DproxySet=true -DproxyHost=proxy.thisOrg.org -DproxyPort=3000 ...
```

where `"proxy.thisOrg.org"` and `"3000"` should be replaced by the values for your environment.

19.2   Uniform Resource Locators

One of the attractive aspects of the World Wide Web is that it makes global resources available to an individual almost as readily as those on their own machine. To appreciate this, it helps to understand something about where a resource is located—its absolute or relative context. When a user reads the contents of a local file into a program using the classes of the `java.io` package, the file is retrieved from the context of that user's working environment. For instance, when a `FileReader` object is constructed with a file name argument such as

```
        FileReader reader = new FileReader("file.txt");
```

the location of the file has been (implicitly) specified as a *relative filename*—i.e., relative to the folder or directory from which the program is being run. Alternatively, a file name may be referred to via an *absolute filename*, using either of something such as

```
        "C:/myprogs/file.txt"
        or
        "C:\myprogs\file.txt"
```

on Windows-based systems, or

```
        "/usr/me/myprogs/file.txt"
```

on UNIX-based systems. Even such absolute path names have an implicit context which makes them, in reality, relative; that is, they refer to the file space on the user's machine, rather than a machine on another continent. Some operating systems allow file spaces to be shared between multiple machines, in which case the machine context will be organizational rather than individual, but the same notion of local contextual interpretation of a name applies.

A *Uniform Resource Locator (URL)* extends the concept of file access from a purely local context to one in which resources are named uniformly, irrespective of where they might be physically located. It does so by encoding both a *location* for the *resource* (often a file) and a *scheme*—or *protocol*—for its retrieval.[1] The most

---

[1] While *scheme* is the approved terminology in WWW documentation, we shall often use *protocol* in keeping with Java's API documentation.

familiar URLs have the following typical form:

```
http://www.javasoft.com/index.html
```

This consists of the scheme—http (*HyperText Transfer Protocol*)—a *hostname* where the resource is located—www.javasoft.com—and a *path* to the resource (file) on that host—/index.html. Sometimes the hostname has an additional *port* number associated with it, such as:

```
http://www.javasoft.com:80/index.html
```

We discuss the use of ports in Section 19.11. The scheme refers to how the resource will be retrieved from the host that looks after it—in effect, it specifies the way in which a client program will communicate with the server program running on the resource's host machine. It is important to appreciate that the protocol says nothing at all about the type of data (if any) contained in the resource. For instance, HTTP may be used to retrieve image data, such as GIF and JPEG files, just as readily as textual information, such as *HyperText Markup Language (HTML)* files. In the next section, we describe how the URL class may be used to retrieve both remote and local resources from within a Java program.

19.3   The URL Class

The URL class, defined in the java.net package, provides a simple means to access a Web resource. A URL object is first constructed by passing a URL-format String to its constructor. Code 19.1 shows how to construct a URL object and determine its component parts.

Code 19.1   Constructing a URL (`URLConstructionExample.java`)

```java
        // An example of how to construct a URL object and print
        // out its constituent elements. Note that this example
        // does not retrieve the associated resource.

import java.net.*;

class URLConstructionExample {
    public static void main(String[] args){
        try{
            URL resource = new URL("http://www.javasoft.com:80/index.html");
            System.out.println("Protocol: "+resource.getProtocol());
            System.out.println("Port: "+resource.getPort());
            System.out.println("Host: "+resource.getHost());
            System.out.println("File: "+resource.getFile());
        }
        catch(MalformedURLException e){
            System.err.println(e);
        }
    }
}
```

This example prints the following output:

```
Protocol: http
Port: 80
Host: www.javasoft.com
File: /index.html
```

Note that the result of `getFile` includes the slash character (/) as a prefix of the filename, to indicate that the path of the resource is an absolute path as far as the host's HTTP server is concerned. It is not usually necessary to include an explicit port in the text of the URL; if this is omitted, then a value of -1 is returned by `getPort` and a default port number appropriate to the specified protocol will be used.[2]

The constructor of URL checks to make sure that the format of its argument is valid and, if not, it will throw a `MalformedURLException` exception. Passing the check does not guarantee anything about the availability of the resource, simply that the URL object is satisfied that all of the appropriate components have been included in the constructor's argument. An example of a malformed URL might be:

```
www.javasoft.com/index.html
```

You might find this surprising, since it is common to omit the protocol part when entering URLs into Web browsers. This is simply because browsers will typically assume the HTTP protocol is required if not specified by the user. The URL class makes no such assumptions and will reject URLs that do not include a proper protocol. Furthermore, the constructor will reject protocols that it does not recognize.

Two further constructors allow the protocol, host, filename, and, optionally, the port to be specified separately. The following two constructions are identical to the one we have seen so far:

```
new URL("http","www.javasoft.com",80,"/index.html");
new URL("http","www.javasoft.com","/index.html");
```

Note that, in the first of these, the port is specified as an integer rather than as a string. In both cases, the "://" elements are omitted.

Exercise 19.1 Run the example shown in Code 19.1 to be sure that you have access to sites outside your own. If it does not work, you might need to set proxy settings, as described in Section 19.1.1.

Exercise 19.2 Modify the example shown in Code 19.1 so that it prints details of the URLs given in its command line arguments. Run this example with the names of some local and external URLs with which you are familiar.

19.4   Retrieving a Resource

Having constructed a URL object, the next step is usually to retrieve the associated resource from the host server. The simplest way to retrieve it is with the `openStream` method of URL. If the URL is recognized by the host, then the resource is

---
[2] The default port for HTTP is 80.

transferred to the client program via an implementation of `InputStream` returned from `openStream`. Code 19.2 shows a program to fetch the resources named as the program arguments.

Code 19.2   Fetch copies of the given URLs

```
import java.net.*;
import java.io.*;

        // Fetch the URLs passed as program arguments.
class URLFetch {
    public static void main(String[] args) {
        for(int i = 0; i < args.length; i++){
            // For illustrative purposes, handle all exceptions here.
            try{
                URLHandler handler = new URLHandler(args[i]);
                handler.fetch();
            }
            catch(Exception e){
                // There was a problem with this one.
                System.err.println("Exception: "+e+" with "+args[i]);
            }
        }
    }
}

        // Create a URL from the given String.
        // Fetch its contents on request.
class URLHandler {
    public URLHandler(String url) throws Exception {
        resource = new URL(url);
    }

        // Fetch the resource. Save it in a local file that matches
        // the suffix of the resource. Use index.html if no suffix
        // is found.
    public void fetch() throws Exception {
        URL resource = getResource();
        // Use the resource file name as the basis of a local
        // name in which to save it.
        String filename = resource.getFile();
        // Provide a default name.
        String localName = "index.html";

        // Find the last part of the resource name.
        int lastPart = filename.lastIndexOf('/');
        if(lastPart >= 0){
            // Skip the final slash.
            lastPart++;
            // Make sure there is something there.
            if(lastPart < filename.length()){
                localName = filename.substring(lastPart);
            }
```

(Continued)

```
    }

    System.out.println("Saving "+filename+" as "+localName);

    copyFile(resource.openStream(),localName);
}

    // Copy the input sam to the file named in localName.
protected void copyFile(InputStream inputStream, String localName)
                                              throws IOException {
    OutputStream outputStream = new FileOutputStream(localName);
    // Create the buffer for the transfer.
    final int buffLen = 1024;
    byte[] buffer = new byte[buffLen];
    int bytesRead = inputStream.read(buffer);
    while(bytesRead > 0){
        outputStream.write(buffer,0,bytesRead);
        bytesRead = inputStream.read(buffer);
    }
    inputStream.close();
    outputStream.close();
}

protected URL getResource(){
    return resource;
}

private final URL resource;
}
```

The main method creates a URLHandler object to look after each URL that is passed as an argument to the program. All handling of exceptions has been left to the main method in order to simplify the methods of URLHandler. The remote resource is obtained from the host server by calling the fetch method. Its first task is to devise a name for the local copy of the resource. It looks for the final '/' character in the filename component of the URL and uses what follows as the local name. For instance, the URL http://www.footpad.cv/welcome.html would be saved as welcome.html. By convention, if there is no trailing filename component, then index.html is used as the default.

URLs referring to HTML pages via the HTTP protocol are probably those that are the most familiar, but URLs are not exclusive to this pairing. Retrieving HTML pages can be of fairly limited use unless a sub class of the abstract ContentHandler is available for HTML, and these are usually only to be found as part of Web browsers or HTML editing tools. Nevertheless, URL objects can be used to retrieve resources of other types, such as text files or images, and the example in Code 19.2 could be used to retrieve local copies of the following URLs, for instance.

```
http://www.cs.ukc.ac.uk/people/staff/djb/Book/sample.txt
http://www.cs.ukc.ac.uk/people/staff/djb/Book/redBall.gif
```

A particular form of the URL notation exists to treat local resources in a similar way to remote resources; this uses the `file` scheme. It might be used to refer to two local files in the following ways on Windows-based systems or UNIX-based systems, respectively.

```
file:/C:/myprogs/file.txt
file:/usr/me/myprogs/file.txt
```

Notice that, in both cases, a single '`/`' character follows the scheme component and that there is no host component. The example we saw in Code 19.2 would copy such resources without needing any modification. This sort of consistency of access between local and remote resources is used by Web browsers in their bookmarks record, for instance. It might also be used in pre-caching programs that periodically look to see whether any of a collection of resources of interest has changed since they were last retrieved, and automatically fetch new versions as local files if they have. In Section 19.6, we describe how to obtain such last modified information.

A further protocol with which the `openStream` method may be used is the *File Transfer Protocol (FTP)*. A host server using HTTP behaves differently from one using FTP—because they are quite distinct protocols; the more modern HTTP is designed to provide information on a resource—such as its content type and size—that FTP was never designed to provide. Furthermore, although the format of URLs using these two schemes is the same, the host and path components of an FTP-retrieved resource are often different from those of a corresponding HTTP resource, even though they might be located at the same physical organization. We shall see some of the consequences of the differences between HTTP and FTP in Section 19.6. Once again, the example in Code 19.2 would work using the FTP protocol to create local copies of the following resources, because it simply requests the contents of the resource to be transferred, using `openStream`. The following two URL strings could be passed as arguments to that program, therefore.

```
ftp://ftp.cs.ukc.ac.uk/pub/djb/Book/sample.txt
ftp://ftp.cs.ukc.ac.uk/pub/djb/Book/redBall.gif
```

Exercise 19.3   Create a modified version of the `URLHandler` class, shown in Code 19.2, that checks to see whether the string passed to its constructor is a properly formed URL. If it is not, then it should imitate the behavior of some Web browsers by attempting to prefix a suitable protocol onto it. It could use the first few characters of the string to help with this. For instance, a string starting "www" should have "`http://`" prefixed onto it, while one starting "`ftp.`" might have "`ftp://`" prefixed onto it.

19.5   Displaying Images with URLs

We can use URLs not simply to copy a local or remote image resource, but to load and display it as part of a Graphical User interface. The `Toolkit` class in the `java.awt` package has the capability to retrieve image data specified by a URL object passed to one of its `getImage` methods. Code 19.3 shows a class to retrieve and display an image via the URLs passed to its constructor. It displays the image in an `Image-Viewer` created for the purpose (see Code 16.53).

Code 19.3   Retrieve and display Image URLs (`ImageURLHandler.java`)

```
import java.net.*;
import java.awt.*;

        // Check that the files have a valid suffix and that
        // the protocol is either http:// or file:/
class ImageURLHandler {
    public ImageURLHandler(String url) throws Exception {
        resource = new URL(url);
    }

        // Show the image associated with this URL.
        // Check that the file has a valid suffix and that
        // the protocol is either http:// or file:/
    protected void show() throws Exception {
        URL resource = getResource();
        // Check the suffix.
        if(!imageSuffix(resource.getFile())){
            throw new Exception(
                    "Unknown image suffix: "+resource.getFile());
        }

        // Check the protocol.
        String protocol = resource.getProtocol();
        if(protocol.equalsIgnoreCase("http") ||
                    (protocol.equalsIgnoreCase("file") &&
                    resource.getHost().equals(""))){
            // Load the image via the Toolkit.
            Toolkit tk = Toolkit.getDefaultToolkit();
            Image image = tk.getImage(resource);
            // Display the image.
            new ImageViewer(image);
        }
        else{
            throw new Exception(
                    "Only http or local file requests accepted: "+
                    resource.toExternalForm());
        }
    }

    // This version is prepared to accept common GIF and JPEG suffixes.
    protected boolean imageSuffix(String filename){
        int dot = filename.lastIndexOf('.');
        if(dot < 0){
            return false;
        }
        else{
            filename = filename.substring(dot).toLowerCase();
```

Code 19.3   (*Continued*)

```
            return filename.equals(".gif") ||
                    filename.equals(".jpg") ||
                    filename.equals(".jpeg");
        }
    }

    protected URL getResource(){
        return resource;
    }

    private final URL resource;
}
```

The show method of ImageURLHandler checks that the URL appears to refer to a resource likely to hold a displayable image, and that the scheme is either http or specifies a local file. If these conditions are satisfied, then a reference to the default Toolkit object is obtained so that the image may be retrieved with its getImage method. The resulting Image object is then passed to one of the constructors of ImageViewer.

19.6   The URLConnection Class

One way in which HTTP differs from FTP is that it provides a client with the ability to retrieve information from the server about a resource, such as its size, when it was last modified, what type of data it consists of, and so on. Code 19.4 shows a program to print out HTTP-relevant information on the URLs passed as command line arguments. Access to this information is provided by the URLConnection class, an instance of which may be obtained from the openConnection method of a URL object. When the scheme is http, the object returned from openConnection is a sub class of HttpURLConnection.

The getDate, getExpiration, and getLastModified methods return dates in the form of the number of milliseconds since January 1, 1970, so the implicit toString method of the Date class has been used to format these values. Running this program on URLs such as

```
http://www.javasoft.com/index.html
http://www.cs.ukc.ac.uk/people/staff/djb/Book/sample.txt
http://www.cs.ukc.ac.uk/people/staff/djb/Book/redBall.gif
```

might produce the following output:

```
Filename: /index.html
Content type: text/html
Content length: -1
Content date: Sat Jun 12 15:54:25 GMT+01:00 1999
Content expiration date: Sat Jun 12 22:22:30 GMT+01:00 1999
Content last modified: Thu Jan 01 01:00:00 GMT+01:00 1970
```

Code 19.4　Print HTTP header information for a resource (`URLDetails.java`)

```
        // Obtain details on the resources whose URLs are
        // passed as command line arguments.
import java.net.*;
import java.util.Date;

class URLDetails {
    public static void main(String[] args) {
        for(int i = 0; i < args.length; i++){
            try{
                URL url = new URL(args[i]);
                URLConnection connection = url.openConnection();

                // Strictly speaking, most of these are only relevant
                // for the HTTP protocol.
                System.out.println("Filename: "+url.getFile());
                System.out.println("Content type: "+
                                connection.getContentType());
                System.out.println("Content length: "+
                                connection.getContentLength());
                System.out.println("Content date: "+
                                new Date(connection.getDate()));
                System.out.println("Content expiration date: "+
                                new Date(connection.getExpiration()));
                System.out.println("Content last modified: "+
                                new Date(connection.getLastModified()));
                System.out.println();
            }
            catch(Exception e){
                System.err.println("Exception: "+e);
            }
        }
    }
}
```

```
Filename: /people/staff/djb/Book/sample.txt
Content type: text/plain
Content length: 51
Content date: Sat Jun 12 16:00:21 GMT+01:00 1999
Content expiration date: Thu Jan 01 01:00:00 GMT+01:00 1970
Content last modified: Thu Jan 07 19:29:30 GMT+01:00 1999

Filename: /people/staff/djb/Book/redBall.gif
Content type: image/gif
Content length: 132
Content date: Sat Jun 12 16:00:22 GMT+01:00 1999
Content expiration date: Thu Jan 01 01:00:00 GMT+01:00 1970
Content last modified: Thu Jan 07 19:29:30 GMT+01:00 1999
```

The `getContentType` method returns the content type of the resource as a *Multipurpose Internet Mail Extensions (MIME)* media type name, such as text/html, image/gif and text/plain. Notice that the first example shows that `getContentLength` is not always able to determine the size of the resource in bytes. The reason for this is often that the resource is actually generated by the server in response to a request, rather than existing as a static file. This is particularly the case when interacting with *Common Gateway Interface (CGI)* scripts on a server (see Section 19.7).

In Section 19.4, we saw how to retrieve the raw data associated with a resource via the `openStream` method of URL. Because an HTTP server maintains information about the content type of a resource, the alternative to `openStream` is to use the `getContent` method of either URL or URLConnection if the scheme is `http`. The MIME content type of the resource, as indicated by the server, is used to assign an appropriate sub class of `ContentHandler` to handle the resource. This means that an appropriate object for the content type will be returned from `getContent`. For `text` MIME types the returned object is likely to be a sub class of `InputStream`, and this would be used in the same way as we saw with `openStream` in Code 19.2. For `image` MIME types the returned object is likely to be an implementation of the `ImageProducer` interface defined in the `java.awt.image` package. The simplest way to obtain the image from such a producer is to pass the producer to the `createImage` method of the Component class. Code 19.5 shows a main method to detect an ImageProducer and pass it to the appropriate constructor of ImageViewer (Code 16.53).

Code 19.5   Detecting an ImageProducer returned by `getContent` (`URLImageProducer.java`)

```java
import java.net.*;
import java.awt.image.ImageProducer;

    // Detect an ImageProducer returned from URLConnection.getContent
    // and pass it to an ImageViewer for display.
class URLImageProducer {
    public static void main(String[] args) {
        for(int i = 0; i < args.length; i++){
            try{
                URL url = new URL(args[i]);
                URLConnection connection = url.openConnection();
                Object o = connection.getContent();
                // Show an image, if we have one.
                if(o instanceof ImageProducer){
                    new ImageViewer((ImageProducer) o);
                }
                else{
                    System.err.println(
                            "The URL does not appear to refer to an image.");
                }
            }
            catch(Exception e){
                System.err.println("Exception: "+e);
            }
        }
    }
}
```

Exercise 19.4 Write a program that will only fetch a requested resource if the content type is `"text"` of some form, such as `"text/plain"` or `"text/html"`.

19.7   The Common Gateway Interface (CGI)

Web servers provide access to a repository of static resources, such as Web pages. In addition, many allow clients to interact with programs that produce *dynamic* resources. The most common standard to enable this is the *Common Gateway Interface (CGI)*[Wora] which allows programs to be written in any language and interact with clients. Some people refer to these programs as *CGI scripts* or *cgi-bin scripts*. A CGI script is simply another resource on the server and so it has a normal URL associated with it. An example of a CGI resource is

```
http://www.cs.ukc.ac.uk/people/staff/djb/cgi-bin/echo.pl
```

What makes it different from most other resources, however, is that a client is typically not interested in the script *per se* but what it will do for the client. The resource returned from a CGI URL is not the script, therefore, but a resource that the script creates and returns dynamically. To enable it to do its work of generating the resource, a client usually sends the script some information to process. Within the scope of this book it is not possible to go into much detail about the operation of CGI scripts, but we shall give enough detail to show how a Java program can send data via its GET and POST methods and retrieve a dynamic resource.

19.7.1   The CGI GET Method

The purpose of the resource associated with the CGI URL shown above is to echo back whatever text is sent to it. The text to be echoed is sent as a key-value pair in the form

```
Echo=string
```

where `Echo` is the key and `string` is the value. Before it can be sent to a CGI script, the value must be encoded so that all spaces are replaced by `'+'` characters and non-alphanumeric characters as three-character strings in the form `"%xx"`, where each x is a hexadecimal digit. The static `encode` method of the `URLEncoder` class is provided for this express purpose.

The simplest way to send information to a CGI script is to include the encoded key-value pair as part of the URL, separated from the file component with a `'?'` character. The following URL sends the string `"hello world\n"` to the echo script described above:

```
http://www.cs.ukc.ac.uk/people/staff/djb/cgi-bin/echo.pl?Echo=hello+world%0A
```

The script will arrange to have this echoed back as:

```
hello world
```

When sent in this way as part of a URL, the key-value pair is made available to the script via its `QUERY_STRING` environment variable. The resource the script sends back has to contain a little bit more than the echoed string, in fact, because it must indicate to the client the MIME content type of the resource it is returning, so that an appropriate content handler may be created. For this particular example, what the script actually sends back is:

```
Content-type: text/plain

hello world
```

A CGI script is not limited to returning textual resources. It could send text, images, audio files, binary data, and so on. As long as the content type is indicated, and the client program has an appropriate content handler available, it should be able to deal with it.

The example in Code 19.6 shows a program that turns its command line arguments into an encoded key-value pair and sends it to a CGI URL using an object of

---

Code 19.6   Sending a string to a CGI echo script

```java
// Examples of using the CGI GET method to send a
// string to a server and have it echoed back.
// The string to send is the concatenation of the program
// arguments, separated by newlines, and the key name it is sent with
// is "Echo". The URL expecting this is
// http://www.cs.ukc.ac.uk/people/staff/djb/cgi-bin/echo.pl

import java.io.*;
import java.net.*;

public class CGIGetExample {
    public static void main(String[] args) {
        if(args.length < 1){
            System.err.println("Usage: java CGIGetExample string ... ");
            System.exit(1);
        }

        // Form the string to send from the command line arguments.
        // Each argument is separated from the others by a newline.
        String request = args[0];
        // Append the rest.
        for(int i = 1; i < args.length; i++){
            request += "\n"+args[i];
        }
        // The key expected by the script.
        final String key = "Echo";
        // Encode the request for sending and prefix the key.
        request = key+"="+URLEncoder.encode(request);

        try{
            System.out.println("Sending: "+request);
            // Encode the request as part of the URL.
```

(Continued)

Code 19.6   (*Continued*)

```java
        CGIClient client = new CGIClient(
            "http://www.cs.ukc.ac.uk/people/staff/djb/cgi-bin/echo.pl"+
            "?"+request);
        System.out.println(client.getResponse());
    }
    catch(Exception e){
        System.err.println(e);
    }
    }
}


    // Maintain the URLConnection attribute for a CGI URL.
public class CGIClient {
    // Set up the URL connection.
    public CGIClient(String resourceURL) throws MalformedURLException,
                                    IOException {
        URL resource = new URL(resourceURL);
        connection = url.openConnection();
        // Indicate that we shall wish to read the script's response.
        connection.setDoInput(true);
    }

    // Get the response from the connection.
    public String getResponse() throws IOException {
        // Read back the response;
        BufferedReader reader = new BufferedReader(
                new InputStreamReader(getConnection().getInputStream()));

        String response = "";
        String line = reader.readLine();
        while(line != null){
            response += line+"\n";
            line = reader.readLine();
        }
        reader.close();
        return response;
    }

    protected URLConnection getConnection(){
        return connection;
    }

    private final URLConnection connection;
}
```

the CGIClient class. The response is read back from the server using the object's getResponse method, which assumes the returned resource will be of type text.

The constructor of CGIClient obtains a URLConnection from the openConnection method of the URL object. It then indicates that it will read from the connection by sending it a setDoInput message with the argument value true. In the `getResponse` method, the connection's input stream is used as the basis for constructing a `BufferedReader` which is then used to read the echoed response, line by line.

Exercise 19.5   Write a program to use the CGI GET method to retrieve the following resource:

```
http://www.cs.ukc.ac.uk/people/staff/djb/cgi-bin/whoAmI.pl
```

This will return to you some of the information that a Web server is able to find out about you whenever you request a resource.

Exercise 19.6   Modify your solution to Exercise 19.5 so that its query string contains the key `"Env"` with a value taken from the list of environment details. For instance,

```
Env=SERVER_PORT
```

19.7.2   Setting Request Properties

If the key-value pair is not known at the time that the URL is constructed, then it cannot be included as a query string in the normal way. An alternative means of passing the query string to the script is to set one of the *request properties* that are sent to the server when a resource is retrieved. When a client connects to an HTTP server, it sends the request for a resource in the following form:

```
GET /index.html HTTP/1.0
propertyX: valueX
propertyY: valueY
propertyZ: valueZ
```

The string `HTTP/1.0` following the filename specifies the version of the HTTP protocol it is using. It then sends zero or more property-value pairs, terminated by a blank line. Setting properties and their values for a URLConnection object is done via its `setRequestProperty` method. This takes two arguments: the property name and its value. In the case of sending a query to the echo CGI script, these might be `QUERY_STRING`[3] as the property, and the key-value pair as the property's value.

```
connection.setRequestProperty("QUERY_STRING",request);
```

An example may be found in the file `CGIGetClient.java`, with a main method that demonstrates this class and the `CGIClient` class in `CGIGetExamples.java`.

19.7.3   The CGI POST Method

The examples above use the CGI GET method to send data to a script. It is becoming increasingly common to use the more flexible POST method, instead. A script's

---

[3] In fact, the server will prefix `HTTP_` onto any properties it sends to the CGI script in this way, so the script will pick up the key-value pair from its `HTTP_QUERY_STRING` environment variable.

Code 19.7 Using the CGI POST method

```
        // Use the POST method to send a string to a CGI script.
        // This involves writing to the URL connection.
class CGIPostClient extends CGIClient {
    public CGIPostClient(String resource) throws Exception {
        super(resource);
    }

        // Write whatToPost to the URL connection and read
        // back the response.
    public String post(String whatToPost) throws IOException {
        URLConnection connection = getConnection();

        // Indicate that we wish to send output to the script.
        connection.setDoOutput(true);
        // Send whatToPost.
        Writer writer = new OutputStreamWriter(
                                        connection.getOutputStream());
        writer.write(whatToPost);
        writer.close();

        return getResponse();
    }
}
```

REQUEST_METHOD environment variable tells it whether data is being sent with GET or POST. In the case of POST, its CONTENT_LENGTH and CONTENT_TYPE variables tell it how much and what type of data to expect.[4] The data is received by the script on its standard input. In order to support the POST method, a URLConnection object allows you to write on an OutputStream to the server. In order to do this, it is necessary to send a `setDoOutput` message to the connection object with an argument value of `true`. What you write to a CGI script using post can be anything; it does not have to be a key-value pair. It is up to the script how it interprets what you send.

Code 19.7 illustrates the `CGIPostClient` class to post an encoded string passed to its `post` method and return the server's response. It extends the CGI-Client class shown in Code 19.6 for its `connection` attribute and `getResponse` method.

The stream for writing to the server is obtained from the `getOutputStream` method of URLConnection. This has been wrapped in an `OutputStreamWriter` in order to write the String `whatToPost`. Once the stream has been closed, the response is fetched from the server. This class may be tested via a similar test-rig to that shown for the CGIClient in Code 19.1.

---

[4] The content type is likely to be `application/x-www-form-urlencoded`.

Exercise 19.7   Write a program that uses the CGI POST method to send an arbitrary message to the URL.

    http://www.cs.ukc.ac.uk/people/staff/djb/cgi-bin/talkToMe.pl.

Print out what you receive back. Try including either "hello" or "goodbye" somewhere within the text of what you send.

19.8 Review

Here are the main points that we have covered in the preceding sections:

- A Uniform Resource Locator (URL) is used to refer to a resource on the World Wide Web.
- A URL encodes a location for a resource, and a scheme for its retrieval.
- The *HyperText Transfer Protocol (HTTP)* corresponds to the *http* scheme most commonly used by Web browsers.
- A URL location consists of a host, where the resource is located, and a path to the resource on that host.
- The *file* scheme can be used to retrieve a local resource.
- The URL class encapsulates the components of a Uniform Resource Locator.
- The openStream method of the URL class returns an InputStream that can be used to retrieve a resource.
- The getImage method of a Toolkit object can be used to read a resource that corresponds to image data from the open stream.
- The URLConnection class makes information about a resource available to a client from the resource's server.
- A resource may be either a static item or a dynamically created item.
- Common Gateway Interface (CGI) scripts are often used on a server to create dynamic resources.
- The CGI GET method may be used to supply input to a CGI script as part of the resource string.
- The CGI POST method may be used to send more complex information to the standard input of a CGI script.
- The setRequestProperty method of a URLConnection object may be used to send resource-related properties to the server.

19.9 Internetworking with TCP/IP

When we transfer a file from the file store of one computer to that of another across a network, we expect that this will produce an identical copy of the file's data, free from corruption. Similarly, when we enter a Web site we expect to see the pages as they were designed to look and we are dissatisfied if parts are missing. We do not expect to see portions of text rearranged or images and sentences corrupted. In both cases, our expectation is of *reliable* transfer of data from one machine to another across the network. In some respects, this is an unreasonable expectation; the networks over which the data is transferred are inherently unreliable—individual bits are easily corrupted by electromagnetic interference, machines acting as intermediaries in the transfer may be prone to crash, parts of the route used by the transfer become congested resulting in data becoming lost. So how can reliable transfer take place in the face of such inherent unreliability?

Much of the work on providing reliable transfer, over what we now refer to as the *Internet*, was conducted in the 1960s and 1970s in the development of the *Arpanet*. The developers of the Arpanet were concerned to design internetworking systems over which reliable communications could be conducted in the face of hostile military action. Out of this research came an understanding of how to accomplish this through the use of particular *protocols*. The most familiar set of protocols used by the Internet community is known as the *TCP/IP protocol suite*. In the sections that follow, we shall give a simplified explanation of the infrastructure that TCP/IP provides for reliable networking, in order to help to explain further classes of the `java.net` package. For further details of the TCP/IP protocol suite, independent of the Java language, you might like to read a book such as that by Douglas Comer[Com95], and for details of networking in general one such as that by Andrew Tanenbaum[Tan96]. For further use of Java for writing network applications, Todd Courtois' book[Cou98] provides a good introduction.

When a large piece of data is to be transferred across a network, it is broken into pieces, called *datagrams* in TCP/IP terminology. Each datagram might consist of something like 1500 bytes and is transferred independently of the others from the sender to the receiver. This means that datagrams could potentially take different routes to their destination. Furthermore, some might be lost as a result of congested parts of the network needing to discard datagrams that they are unable to cope with. The way in which datagrams are created and processed is defined by the *Internet Protocol (IP)*.

When datagrams arrive randomly at their destination, it is the responsibility of a *transport entity* at the receiving end to put them back together again in the right order and without duplication. It communicates with a peer transport entity at the sending end using a *transport protocol* that both understand. The two transport protocols most relevant to our Java context are the *Transmission Control Protocol (TCP)* and the *User Datagram Protocol (UDP)*. If reliable communication is required, TCP is used because this allows the receiving entity to detect when data has been lost, been corrupted, arrived out of order, or been duplicated for some reason. We say that the combination of TCP over IP provides a *reliable two-way stream of data* between the sender and receiver. What this means, in practice, is that applications built using TCP/IP do not, themselves, have to worry about whether the data they send will be received correctly at the other end of the communication; that is handled by the TCP and IP layers of the system. An application writer using TCP over IP can have confidence that their data will arrive in the right order and uncorrupted.

Of course, there is a cost associated with such reliability, both in terms of extra processing time and extra data to allow errors to be detected and corrected. Furthermore, a communication using TCP requires that a *connection handshake* take place between the sender and receiver before any data can be transferred. Writers of some applications choose to build on the alternative UDP transport protocol, therefore, either for reasons of speed or because their applications will be run over highly reliable networks. Classes defined in the `java.net` package allow program writers to choose to use either reliable TCP communication (`Socket` and `ServerSocket`) or (potentially) unreliable UDP communication (`DatagramSocket` and `Datagram-Packet`). We describe TCP-based applications in Section 19.11 and UDP-based applications in Section 19.13.

19.10   The InetAddress Class

In order to engage in communication across a network, a machine needs an *Internet address*—also often known as an *IP address*. These are usually statically allocated by the network manager of your local organization, or dynamically allocated by an *Internet Service Provider (ISP)*. A statically allocated address means that your machine always has the same address, whereas a dynamically allocated address is given to your machine for only a limited time (such as the duration of the connection to your ISP) and you might receive a different one the next time you connect. The current generation of Internet addresses consist of four bytes, often written in *dotted decimal notation* such as `127.35.5.9`, with the higher-order bytes written first. At any one time, a numeric address can only refer to a single machine—addresses may not be shared, although a single machine may have more than one address. Numeric addresses can be difficult to remember, so most machines have symbolic alphanumeric names associated with them, such as `elm.ukc.ac.uk` or `socks.co.cv`. The `InetAddress` class in the `java.net` package is used to represent Internet addresses. It has no constructor and an InetAddress object is usually obtained through either its `getLocalHost` or `getByName` methods, both of which are static. The example in Code 19.8 illustrates how these may be used to obtain details about the local machine or details passed in on the command line.

Running this without arguments might produce output such as the following:

```
The local host is called: elm.ukc.ac.uk and its address is: 129.12.3.255
```

The argument to `getByName` may be either a symbolic name or an address in dotted decimal form, so running it with arguments such as

```
www.javasoft.com socks.co.cv 204.160.241.83
```

might produce the output:

```
The host is called: www.javasoft.com and its address is: 204.160.241.83
Unknown host: socks.co.cv
The host is called: web2.javasoft.com and its address is: 204.160.241.83
```

This output illustrates that a single IP address (in this case `204.160.241.83`) may have more than one symbolic name. Similarly, but in contrast to numeric addresses, the same symbolic name may be shared by different machines. One reason for this is that it enables the burden borne by a popular name to be shared between machines. An array of all InetAddress objects for a single symbolic name may be obtained with the static `getAllByName` method. Finally, sending a `getAddress` message to an InetAddress object will result in an array of the raw `byte` values of the address being returned. The most significant byte of the address is stored in element 0.

Code 19.8   Obtaining an InetAddress object for the local machine (`PrintInetDetails.java`)

```
    // Print out Internet address information about the local machine.
import java.net.*;

public class PrintInetDetails {
    public static void main(String[] args){
        if(args.length == 0){
            try{
                InetAddress myDetails = InetAddress.getLocalHost();
                System.out.println("The local host is called: "+
                            myDetails.getHostName()+
                            " and its address is: "+
                            myDetails.getHostAddress());
            }
            catch(UnknownHostException e){
                System.err.println("Unknown host: "+e.getMessage());
            }
        }
        else{
            for(int i = 0; i < args.length; i++){
                try{
                    InetAddress details = InetAddress.getByName(args[i]);
                    System.out.println("The host is called: "+
                                details.getHostName()+
                                " and its address is: "+
                                details.getHostAddress());
                }
                catch(UnknownHostException e){
                    System.err.println("Unknown host: "+e.getMessage());
                }
            }
        }
    }
}
```

Exercise 19.8   Modify the example in Code 19.8 so that it uses `getAllByName` rather than `getByName` on its command line arguments. You might like to see what this produces with popular Web search site names, such as `www.yahoo.com` and `www.infoseek.com`.

19.11   The Socket Class

Applications built using TCP/IP often use the *client-server* model of communication; two examples are Web page delivery, using HTTP, and file transfer, using FTP. In the client-server model, a server offers a particular service by *passively waiting* for a client to request that service. In this model, servers are more like shops that wait for customers to arrive, rather than door-to-door sales-people who actively seek out customers to buy what they are offering. The question arises, how do clients know

Code 19.9   Connecting to a daytime service

```
try{
    // The well-known port of the TCP daytime service.
    final int DaytimePort = 13;
    // Try to establish a connection with the given host.
    Socket daytime = new Socket(hostname,DaytimePort);
    ...
}
catch(UnknownHostException e){
    throw new Exception("Unknown host: "+e.getMessage());
}
catch(IOException e){
    throw new Exception("IOException on socket creation: "+
                        e.getMessage());
}
```

where a service is being offered? HTTP and FTP are services that are typically offered at what are referred to as *well-known ports*. A *port* is simply an integer value that an operating system uses to associate incoming and outgoing data with a particular client or server. The well-known port numbers for HTTP and FTP servers are 80 and 21, respectively. On a UNIX system, you can find the port numbers assigned to particular services in the file /etc/services. Services are not limited to being offered at well-known ports; a service may be offered at any port number assigned by the server's host operating system. In general, we say that a server *listens* at a port for clients to connect to that service. When a client application wishes to contact a server, it must be allocated its own port number by the client's host operating system in order to take part in the two-way TCP communication. Typically, the port number used by a client is arbitrary and will vary from one run of the client to another. The combination of an Internet address and TCP port number is known as a *TCP endpoint*.

A two-way reliable TCP stream connection is established between two end-points in Java by creating an object of the Socket class in the client. The constructor's arguments specify the endpoint of the server—either as a hostname String or an InetAddress—and the port number on which it is listening. The example in Code 19.9 illustrates the construction of a Socket by a client intending to contact a TCP *daytime server*—a service that returns the current date and time,[5] which is listening on the well-known port number 13.

If the name of the host you are trying to contact is not recognized for some reason, then the constructor will throw an UnknownHostException exception. If the socket cannot be established for some other reason, then an IOException exception will be thrown. A possible reason for failure is that the server is too busy to accept further connections, or it refuses to accept connections on that port from outside the local organization.

Once a connection has been established, two-way communication is available

---

[5] The daytime service is defined in the Internet RFC 867.

between the client and server. The sending and receiving paths are represented by an
InputStream and OutputStream in the Socket. Accessors to these are provided
by its getInputStream and getOutputStream methods. The TCP protocol, itself, provides buffering of data between a client and server. The sizes of the send and
receive buffers may be inspected and altered via Socket's getReceiveBuffer-
Size, getSendBufferSize, setReceiveBufferSize, and setSendBuffer-
Size methods.

Communication between a client and server is often performed in terms of lines
of text, so it is common to wrap these streams in the associated BufferedReader
and BufferedWriter classes that were introduced in Section 12.5. These are useful
because they provide readLine and newLine methods, respectively, for line-based
communication. Where byte-based transfer of data is required, the raw Stream objects are to be preferred, however.

The daytime service, contacted in Code 19.9, does not expect any input from
the client but simply sends a single line of output indicating the current date and time.
Code 19.10 illustrates the full version of DaytimeClient that uses this service. Its
run method illustrates the way in which the InputStream object is wrapped in a
BufferedReader for line-based communication.

Code 19.10   Contacting and using a daytime server (DaytimeClient.java

```
import java.net.*;
import java.io.*;

        // Contact the daytime server running on hostname.
class DaytimeClient {
        // Contact the server at the appropriate port and set
        // the socket attribute for the run() method to use.
    public DaytimeClient(String hostname) throws Exception {
        // The well-known port of the TCP daytime service.
        final int DaytimePort = 13;
        try{
            socket = new Socket(hostname,DaytimePort);
        }
        catch(UnknownHostException e){
            throw new Exception("Unknown host: "+e.getMessage());
        }
        catch(IOException e){
            throw new Exception("IOException on socket creation: "+
                              e.getMessage());
        }
    }

        // Obtain the time of day from the daytime server.
    public void run() {
        Socket daytime = getSocket();
        try{
            // Get the stream used by the server to send data.
            InputStream inStream = daytime.getInputStream();
            // Wrap the stream in a BufferedReader.
            BufferedReader reader = new BufferedReader(
                    new InputStreamReader(inStream));
```

Code 19.10   (*Continued*)

```
            // The server will only send a single line.
            String response = reader.readLine();
            System.out.println(response);
            // Close the connection now it is finished with.
            daytime.close();
        }
        catch(IOException e){
            System.err.println(e.getMessage());
        }
    }

    protected Socket getSocket(){
        return socket;
    }

    private final Socket socket;
}
```

The program expects the name of the host running a daytime service to be supplied as a command line argument. Output from this program, run with a suitable host name, might be something like:

```
Sat Jun 12 16:00:35 1999
```

A simple example of two-way communication can be seen with use of the *echo service*[6] which is provided as a debugging tool for network applications. An echo server accepts connections on well-known port 7 and simply sends back any data it receives from the client. The example in Code 19.11 shows the run method of an echo client, which is similar in all other respects to the daytime client of Code 19.10. Notice the use of the flush method of BufferedWriter to ensure that the data to be sent is flushed out of its buffers and passed on to the TCP layer for sending. If this is not used appropriately, then your client could hang indefinitely, waiting for a response from the server to a message that it has not received. The output from this example might be something like:

```
Sending: Hello, echo server.
The response is: Hello, echo server.
Sending: Goodbye.
The response is: Goodbye.
```

Exercise 19.9   Write a TCP client that reads lines of text interactively from a user and sends them to an echo server. It is sometimes worth knowing that the Internet Address 127.0.0.1 can be used as an address for your local machine.

---

[6] Defined in RFC 862.

```java
import java.net.*;
import java.io.*;


        // Contact the echo server running on hostname.
class TCPEchoClient {
        // Contact the server at the appropriate port and set
        // the socket attribute for the run() method to use.
    public TCPEchoClient(String hostname) throws Exception {
        try{
            // The well-known port of the TCP echo service.
            final int EchoPort = 7;
            socket = new Socket(hostname,EchoPort);
        }
        catch(UnknownHostException e){
            throw new Exception("Unknown host: "+e.getMessage());
        }
        catch(IOException e){
            throw new Exception("IOException on socket creation: "+
                                e.getMessage());
        }
    }

        // Send the sample strings to the echo server and read
        // back the responses.
    public void run(String[] sampleStrings) {
        Socket echo = getSocket();

        try{
            // Wrap the input stream in a BufferedReader.
            BufferedReader reader = new BufferedReader(
                    new InputStreamReader(echo.getInputStream()));
            // Wrap the output stream in a BufferedWriter.
            BufferedWriter writer = new BufferedWriter(
                    new OutputStreamWriter(echo.getOutputStream()));

            // Send each string and read the response.
            for(int i = 0; i < sampleStrings.length; i++){
                String sample = sampleStrings[i];
                System.out.println("Sending: "+sample);

                writer.write(sample);
                writer.newLine();
                // Make sure the data is flushed to the stream.
                writer.flush();

                // Read the response.
                String response = reader.readLine();
                System.out.println("The response is: "+response);
            }
            // Close the connection now it is finished with.
            echo.close();
```

Code 19.11   (*Continued*)

```
        }
        catch(IOException e){
            System.err.println(e.getMessage());
        }
    }

    protected Socket getSocket(){
        return socket;
    }

    private final Socket socket;
}
```

19.11.1   A TCP Client Super Class

The examples in Code 19.10 and Code 19.11 exhibit a similar pattern of Socket
creation and input-output stream wrappers that will be present in many of the TCP
clients you write. It makes sense, therefore, to create a super class which classes may
extend to add their own particular functionality. Code 19.12 illustrates a possible
super class, TCPEndpoint, one of whose constructors is responsible for establishing
the connection and setting the socket attribute.

Code 19.12   A super class for TCP clients (and servers) (`TCPEndpoint.java`)

```
        // A class that maintains the attributes of a TCP endpoint.
        // This class looks after the socket attribute and
        // buffered reader and writer associated with the
        // two streams of a TCP communication.
        // Typical clients and servers extend this class to provide
        // the functionality applicable to their application.
import java.net.*;
import java.io.*;

class TCPEndpoint  {
        // Contact the server at the appropriate port and set
        // the socket attribute for the run() method to use.
    public TCPEndpoint(String hostname,int port) throws Exception {
        try{
            Socket socket = new Socket(hostname,port);
            // Setup the socket attribute and associated streams.
            setSocket(socket);
        }
        catch(UnknownHostException e){
            throw new Exception("Unknown host: "+e.getMessage());
        }
        catch(IOException e){
```

(*Continued*)

Code 19.12   (*Continued*)

```
            throw new Exception("IOException on socket creation: "+
                                    e.getMessage());
        }
    }

    // A connection has already been established.
    // Setup the socket attribute and associated streams.
    public TCPEndpoint(Socket socket) throws Exception {
        setSocket(socket);
    }

    // Get the next line from the server.
    protected String getLine() throws IOException {
        return getReader().readLine();
    }

    // Flush the given line to the server.
    protected void sendLine(String line) throws IOException {
        bufferLine(line);
        getWriter().flush();
    }

    // Send the given line to the server without flushing.
    protected void bufferLine(String line) throws IOException {
        BufferedWriter writer = getWriter();
        writer.write(line);
        writer.newLine();
    }

// Close the socket.
    protected void close() {
        Socket sock = getSocket();
        try{
            sock.close();
        }
        catch(IOException e){
            // Not much we can do about this.
        }
    }

    protected Socket getSocket(){
        return socket;
    }

    // Setup the socket attribute and create an
    // associated Reader and Writer for the associated
    // streams.
    protected void setSocket(Socket s) throws Exception {
        if(s != null){
            socket = s;
            // Wrap the input stream in a BufferedReader.
```

(*Continued*)

Code 19.12   (*Continued*)

```
        setReader(new BufferedReader(
                new InputStreamReader(socket.getInputStream())));
        // Wrap the output stream in a BufferedWriter.
        setWriter(new BufferedWriter(
                new OutputStreamWriter(socket.getOutputStream())));
    }
    else{
        throw new Exception("Null socket passed to setSocket.");
    }
}

protected BufferedReader getReader(){
    return reader;
}

protected void setReader(BufferedReader r){
    reader = r;
}

protected BufferedWriter getWriter(){
    return writer;
}

protected void setWriter(BufferedWriter w){
    writer = w;
}

private Socket socket;
// Buffered reader and writer for the socket's streams.
private BufferedReader reader;
private BufferedWriter writer;
}
```

In addition to the `socket` attribute, a `reader` and `writer` attribute are made available as buffered wrappers around the raw socket streams. The `sendLine` method simplifies the sending of a String plus newline and the `getLine` method returns a String from the server. The `sendLine` method always flushes the buffered writer; when this is not required, the `bufferLine` method can be used to add a line to the output buffer without necessarily causing it to be flushed. In Section 19.12, we shall see that some aspects of TCP servers also have a similar use for such a class, so the TCPEndpoint class includes a second constructor, taking a Socket argument, for this purpose.

Code 19.13 shows an example program that uses TCPClient to create the class `HTTPClient` that retrieves a single file from an HTTP server listening on well-known port `80`. An HTTP server expects to receive a request for a resource. When it receives a request, it sends the resource back to the client, assuming that the resource is available. The HTTPClient's `retrieve` methods sends a simple `GET` request and reads back the server's response. Once the resource has been sent, the server closes

Code 19.13   A simple HTTP client as a sub class of TCPClient (`HTTPClient.java`)

```
import java.net.*;
import java.io.*;

        // Use the HTTP server running on hostname.
class HTTPClient extends TCPEndpoint {
        // Contact the server at the appropriate port and set
        // the socket attribute for the run() method to use.
    public HTTPClient(String hostname) throws Exception {
        // The well-known port of the HTTP service.
        super(hostname,HTTPPort);
    }

        // Retrieve the given filename from the HTTP server.
    public String retrieve(String filename) throws IOException {
        try{
            // Send the retrieval command.
            // Use the HTTP/0.9 Simple-Request.
            sendLine("GET "+filename);
            // The line to be returned will be built up in this.
            StringBuffer line = new StringBuffer();
            // Read and print the responses.
            String response = getLine();
            while(response != null){
                line.append(response+"\n");
                response = getLine();
            }
            return line.toString();
        }
        finally{
            // Close the connection now it is finished with.
            close();
        }
    }

    // The well-known port of the HTTP server.
    private static final int HTTPPort = 80;
}
```

its end of the socket connection, and this is indicated by the end of the file being detected on the client's input stream. As a consequence, the `getLine` method inherited from TCPClient will return `null`. If the server does not recognize the request, or does not have the resource, it will send back a diagnostic message to the client.

19.12   The ServerSocket Class

In Section 19.11, we looked at how to use the Socket class to write client applications. In this section, we examine how to write servers, as provided for by the `ServerSocket` class of the `java.net` package. In the simplest case, there are two stages in the life of a server; first it constructs a `ServerSocket` object through which it listens for connections, and then it interacts with a client that has contacted it. Later we shall see that this pattern is often modified to make servers more flexible and able to interact with multiple clients concurrently, but the simple model will suffice to introduce the basics of writing servers. Code 19.14 illustrates a program that behaves a little like an echo server. A `LineLengthServer` listens for a connection from a single client and then reads lines sent to it from the client. For each line received it responds with the length of that line (excluding the newline character).

Code 19.14 A simple line-length server for a single client (`LineLengthServer.java`)

```java
import java.net.*;
import java.io.*;

    // A simple server that accepts a client connection
    // and sends back the length of the strings it
    // receives from the client.
class LineLengthServer {
    public LineLengthServer(int port) throws Exception {
        try{
            // Listen on the given port.
            serverSocket = new ServerSocket(port);
        }
        catch(BindException e){
            throw new Exception("Failed to create a server socket: "+
                    e.getMessage());
        }
    }

    // Read strings and return their length (as a String)
    // to the client.
    public void run() throws Exception {
        ServerSocket serverSocket = getServerSocket();
        Socket clientSocket = null;
        try{
            System.out.println("Listening for a client on port: "+
                        serverSocket.getLocalPort());
            // Wait for a client to make contact.
            clientSocket = serverSocket.accept();
            // Contact ...
            System.out.println("A client has arrived.");

            // Wrap the input stream in a BufferedReader.
            BufferedReader reader = new BufferedReader(
                    new InputStreamReader(clientSocket.getInputStream()));
            // Wrap the output stream in a BufferedWriter.
            BufferedWriter writer = new BufferedWriter(
                    new OutputStreamWriter(clientSocket.getOutputStream()));

            // Read lines until the client terminates.
            String request = reader.readLine();
            while(request != null){
```

(Continued)

Code 19.14   *(Continued)*

```
                    // Write the length of the line as a String.
                    writer.write(String.valueOf(request.length()));
                    writer.newLine();
                    writer.flush();
                    request = reader.readLine();
                }
            }
            catch(IOException e){
                throw new Exception("IOException talking to the client: "+
                                    e.getMessage());
            }
            finally{
                if(clientSocket != null){
                    System.out.println("The client has gone.");
                    // Close the socket to the client.
                    clientSocket.close();
                }
            }
            serverSocket.close();
        }

        protected ServerSocket getServerSocket(){
            return serverSocket;
        }

        // The socket on which the listening is done.
        private final ServerSocket serverSocket;
    }
```

The first stage in the life of a server is enacted by constructing a `ServerSocket` object. This requires the number of the port on which the server will listen. The number chosen by an ordinary user-written server, as opposed to a system server, should be larger than `1023`, since lower-valued port numbers are reserved for system services such as those we have seen using well-known port numbers. Indeed, it is probably safer to choose a five-digit port number in order to reduce the chances of trying to listen on a port that is already assigned to another server running on your machine. If the requested port is unavailable, then a `BindException` exception will be thrown, otherwise the ServerSocket object will be ready for the server to listen on. A server listens by sending an `accept` message to the ServerSocket. The Server-Socket will now block indefinitely until a client tries to connect. When a connection is established, `accept` returns a Socket object representing the server's endpoint for the communication. This can now be used in exactly the same way as we saw clients using it in Section 19.11. In the example in Code 19.14, a LineLengthServer communicates with a single client. It continues reading lines until the client closes the connection, at which point the server finishes. Before finishing, the server closes both the Socket it received from `accept` and the ServerSocket it created in its constructor. These two sockets are completely independent and we shall see the importance of this shortly.

Notice that, once a server has been contacted by a client, its basic usage of the resulting endpoint Socket will often be very similar to that of a client. In fact, there is such a similarity between clients and servers in this respect that we can use the TCPEndpoint class shown in Code 19.12 to perform a similar socket and stream management role for both clients and servers. It is for this reason that the class contains a second constructor that takes a Socket argument for the benefit of sub classes used by a server.

Exercise 19.10   Write a server-client pair that will help you to estimate the time it takes for a message to be sent from the client to the server and back. The client should repeatedly send messages to the server which sends back a single byte reply. Calculate the time as a mean for all messages sent and received. Run the client over a significant period of time to see whether the time varies much.

Exercise 19.11   Modify your solution to Exercise 19.10 so that the client periodically resets its accumulated time. Is there much variation in the calculated time at the end of each period?

Exercise 19.12   Modify your solution to Exercise 19.11 so that the server echoes back the message it receives. Experiment with varying message sizes to see whether this affects the journey time.

19.12.1   Server Timeout

The example in Code 19.14 was simplified in a number of respects from the style of servers we would normally write. In the first respect, the server only dealt with a single client; once the client had finished, the server closed its ServerSocket. This is not necessary; indeed it would be more usual for a server to stick around waiting for further clients to make contact. This is achieved quite simply by sending a further accept message to the ServerSocket once the first client has terminated its end of the connection.

The server of Code 19.14 is simplified in a second respect in that it is prepared to block indefinitely waiting for clients. Sometimes it is preferable to give clients a limited time to make contact and for the server then to give up waiting, which will free resources in the operating system. To complement this approach, if a server is not already running when a potential client makes contact, some operating systems have the ability to start the service automatically. The setSoTimeout method of ServerSocket makes it possible to set a timeout on the waiting time of accept. If the timeout expires, accept throws an InterruptedIOException exception. Code 19.15 shows an alternative line-length server, MultiLineLengthServer. Its run method removes both of the simplifications present in the earlier version. In addition, MultiLineLengthServer devolves responsibility for client interaction to an inner class, LineLengthResponder, which is a sub class of TCPEndpoint (Code 19.12). In Section 19.12.3, we shall look at further improvements to the design of servers that allow them to process multiple clients concurrently rather than sequentially.

Code 19.15   Serving multiple clients in succession (`MultiLineLengthServer.java`)

```java
import java.net.*;
import java.io.*;

        // A simple server that accepts a client connection
        // and sends back the length of the strings it
        // receives from the client.

        // Multiple clients are handled consecutively.
        // This version differs from LineLengthServer in that
        // the service functionality is devolved from the listener
        // to the separate class LineLengthResponder, which is
        // a sub class of TCPEndpoint.
class MultiLineLengthServer {
    public MultiLineLengthServer(int port) throws Exception {
        try{
            // Listen on port.
            serverSocket = new ServerSocket(port);
        }
        catch(BindException e){
            throw new Exception("Failed to create a server socket: "+
                            e.getMessage());
        }
    }

        // Read strings and return their length (as a String)
        // to the client.
    public void run() throws Exception {
        ServerSocket serverSocket = getServerSocket();
        // Wait up to 30 seconds for clients.
        final int timeToWait = 30000;
        boolean keepWaiting = true;

        while(keepWaiting){
            Socket clientSocket = null;
            try{
                // Wait for a client to make contact.
                System.out.println("Listening for a client on port: "+
                        serverSocket.getLocalPort());
                // Set how long we are prepared to wait.
                serverSocket.setSoTimeout(timeToWait);
                clientSocket = serverSocket.accept();

                // Contact ...
                System.out.println("A client has arrived.");
                // Devolve action to a separate object.
                LineLengthResponder responder =
                            new LineLengthResponder(clientSocket);
                responder.run();
                // Client has finished.
            }
            catch(InterruptedIOException e){
                // We timed out waiting for a client.
```

Code 19.15   (*Continued*)

```
            keepWaiting = false;
            System.out.println("No more clients after: "+
                                    timeToWait/1000+" seconds.");
        }
        finally{
            if(clientSocket != null){
                System.out.println("The client has gone.");
            }
        }
    }
    // No more clients, so close the socket.
    serverSocket.close();
}

    // Read lines and return their length until the
    // client terminates.
    protected class LineLengthResponder extends TCPEndpoint {
        public LineLengthResponder(Socket socket) throws Exception {
            super(socket);
        }

        public void run(){
            try{
                String request = getLine();
                while(request != null){
                    // Write the length of the line as a String.
                    sendLine(String.valueOf(request.length()));
                    request = getLine();
                }
            }
            catch(IOException e){
                System.err.println("IOException talking to the client: "+
                            e.getMessage());
            }
            // Close the socket to the client.
            close();
        }
    }
    protected ServerSocket getServerSocket(){
        return serverSocket;
    }

    // The socket on which the listening is done.
    private final ServerSocket serverSocket;
}
```

19.12.2   Rejecting Prospective Clients

Some servers are designed to only offer services to local clients and should therefore reject connection attempts by non-local clients. A straightforward way to do this is to check the InetAddress details of the client against the local details of the server.

Code 19.16   Rejecting access by non-local clients

```
public void run(){
    ...
    clientSocket = serverSocket.accept();

    // Contact ... Check for local-only clients.
    byte[] myAddress = clientSocket.getLocalAddress().getAddress();
    byte[] clientAddress = clientSocket.getInetAddress().getAddress();

    // Make sure we are compatible.
    // This assumes matching higher-order bytes.
    if((clientAddress[0] != myAddress[0]) ||
                   (clientAddress[1] != myAddress[1])){
        throw new Exception("Connection from non-local client: "+
                   clientSocket.getInetAddress().getHostName());
    }
    // Access permitted.
    ...
}
```

If, for instance, all legitimate clients share the same two higher-order bytes of their IP address with those of the server, the server might include the check shown in Code 19.16 immediately following the return of the `accept` call.

19.12.3   Handling Concurrent Clients

In Section 19.12.1, we illustrated the ways in which the ServerSocket class may be used to create a server handling multiple clients sequentially. In practice, many servers need to be able to serve multiple clients *concurrently*. A busy HTTP server might receive many connection requests per second. If users of browser clients are required to queue for attention for long periods, then they will soon desert such a site and look elsewhere. For this reason, it has long been the practice in server design to separate the listening functionality of a server from the service it is providing. Using this approach, a listener's role is almost entirely to accept client connections and play no part in the client-server interaction. Each time the listener's `accept` message to the ServerSocket returns, it immediately hands the socket over to a *slave thread* and returns to listen for the next client.[7] The slave thread implements the server's functionality and is only concerned to deal with a single client, rather than listening for other clients. Such a separation of roles, made possible by the use of threads, considerably simplifies the design of the listener and slave classes. It is made possible because, even though the separate threads use the same address-port endpoint, they do so in two different ways: the listener waits for new incoming connection attempts with `accept` on the ServerSocket, and the slave deals with client communications

---

[7] In addition, where non-local clients must be rejected, this can be performed by the listening object before handing over to the slave thread in the case of legitimate access.

via `receive` on the Socket.[8] As long as neither attempts to do the other's job, they are able to share use of the same endpoint.

We can illustrate these concepts with an example of a server that returns random integers to its clients on request. The listening functionality is implemented by the `RandomServiceListener` class shown in Code 19.17.

Code 19.17 Handle multiple client by creating separate slave threads
(`RandomServiceListener.java`)

```java
import java.net.*;
import java.io.*;

    // A server that accepts multiple client connections.
    // The service, implemented by the RandomService class,
    // sends random integers when requested.
class RandomServiceListener {
    public RandomServiceListener(int port) throws Exception {
        try{
            // Listen on port.
            serverSocket = new ServerSocket(port);
        }
        catch(BindException e){
            throw new Exception("Failed to create a server socket: "+
                        e.getMessage());
        }
    }

    // Listen for clients. When each arrives, hand the socket
    // over to a RandomService slave.
    public void listen() throws Exception {
        ServerSocket serverSocket = getServerSocket();
        // Wait up to 30 minutes for new clients.
        final int timeToWait = 1*60*1000;
        boolean keepWaiting = true;

        while(keepWaiting){
            try{
                // Wait for a client to make contact.
                serverSocket.setSoTimeout(timeToWait);
                Socket clientSocket = serverSocket.accept();
                // Let a separate Thread handle it.
                new Thread(new RandomService(clientSocket)).start();
            }
            catch(InterruptedIOException e){
                // We timed out waiting for a client.
                keepWaiting = false;
            }
            catch(IOException e){
```

(Continued)

---

[8] It is important to appreciate that client interactions with the two threads are not kept separate by virtue of the threads using different socket objects, but by the way they use the address-port endpoint pair.

Code 19.17   *(Continued)*

```
              throw new Exception("IOException: "+ e.getMessage());
          }
      }
      // No more clients, so close the socket.
      serverSocket.close();
  }

  protected ServerSocket getServerSocket(){
      return serverSocket;
  }


  // The socket on which the listening is done.
  private final ServerSocket serverSocket;
}
```

As can be seen when compared with the example in Code 19.14, all of the server functionality has been removed from the main loop in the `listen` method. Responding
to requests is now the responsibility of the RandomService class. RandomService
implements the `Runnable` interface so that it can be run in a separate thread. Separation of listening from service means that the RandomService class is an ideal sub
class of the `TCPEndpoint` described in Section 19.12; it is shown in Code 19.18.
The `run` method of RandomService simply waits for the client to request a random
integer and returns one as a String. It does not examine the text of the request.

Exercise 19.13   Write a client for the random number service. You might like to
base it on your solution to Exercise 19.9 since both involve sending a line to the
server and reading back the response.

Exercise 19.14   Modify the random number server of Code 19.18 so that it examines
the `request` sent by the client and acts on it. The client should be allowed to send
any of the following commands:

- NEXT—send a random integer.
- RANGE min max—min and max are the lower and upper bounds on the inte-
  gers that should be returned.
- LIMIT n—The effect is the equivalent to

      RANGE -n n

  and n should be a positive integer.

Responses from the server should be a single line with two parts: a 3-digit *status code*
and a *value*. For valid requests, the status code should be `200` followed by a value
for each command as follows:

- NEXT—the value is the random integer.
- RANGE—the value is min max.
- LIMIT—the value is -n n.

Code 19.18 Service functionality of the Random Number server (`RandomService.java`)

```
import java.net.*;
import java.io.*;
import java.util.Random;

        // Provide random integers to the client on request.
        // The text of any request is ignored but used
        // as a prompt for when to send each number.
class RandomService extends TCPEndpoint implements Runnable {
    public RandomService(Socket s) throws Exception {
        super(s);
    }

        // Supply random integers on request to the client.
    public void run(){
        // The random number generator for this client.
        Random random = new Random();
        try{
            String request = getLine();
            while(request != null){
                // We are not interested in the text of the request.
                sendLine(""+random.nextInt());
                request = getLine();
            }
        }
        catch(IOException e){
            System.err.println("IOException: "+e.getMessage());
        }
        finally{
            close();
            System.out.println("Thread terminating.");
        }
    }
}
```

For invalid requests, the status code should be `400` and the value should be an explanatory string. For instance, a request such as `RANGE 20 10` might produce the response:

```
400 Upper value of range must be >= lower value in RANGE 20 10.
```

Modify your client so that it thoroughly tests the server with valid and invalid requests.

Exercise 19.15 Design a server that users can log in to, as might be implemented by a game-server or chat-server. The listener should simply accept a connection and hand over to a slave thread to process the login procedure. A client's first action must be to identify itself by the message:

```
LOGIN name
```

Failure to do so will cause the connection to be closed without a reply. A client that sends the login message will be eligible to join the group of existing clients, but the slave should not confirm this. The slave thread should hand over the socket to a manager thread that has details of all the current client's sockets. It should pass the user's name with the socket to the manager. If the name is unique, the manager will confirm the connection to the client with the message:

```
WELCOME name
```

If the name is not unique, that is, there is another client already logged on with the same name, the manager should reply to the client with the message

```
REJECTED name
```

and immediately close the socket.

Implement the following client commands:

- WHO—the manager should respond with a list of who is logged in.
- LOGOUT—the client wishes to log out. The manager closes their socket.

Clients should not need to identify themselves in any messages they send, but the manager should prefix any client-client message with the login name of the client who sent it.

Exercise 19.16   Extend your solution to Exercise 19.15 by adding the following command:

- SHOUT message—send message to everyone logged in. The manager would relay it to all the other clients.

Note that this is distinct from the other commands in that clients will receive messages from the manager that they have not initiated.

Exercise 19.17   Enhance your solution to Exercise 19.15 by devising further commands that clients and the manager might use to interact with each other. For instance, a client might like to be told when someone leaves. In this case, the reply might be delayed considerably from the time the request was made.

19.12.4   Generic Listeners

As we pointed out above, the RandomServiceListener class in Code 19.17 actually has no functionality that ties it to specifically acting as a multi-client listener for the RandomService class, apart from its instantiation of a RandomService slave. It could equally well instantiate an echo service slave, for instance, and there is no reason why a similar looking class should not act as a *generic listener* for all slaves which can be instantiated with a single Socket argument to their constructor. Java does have the facilities that would allow us to pass the Class of the slave service to such a generic listener (see Section 15.7). Such a generic listener is illustrated in Code 19.19. What this means is that the listening class can be written once and used by all future server slave classes to accept client connections for them, without having to be reimplemented for each new service.

Code 19.19   A class to implement listening for a class of Runnable slave
(`GenericListener.java`)

```java
    // A generic server that accepts multiple client connections.
    // The service is implemented by the Class passed to the
    // constructor. The nature of this service is of no interest
    // to the listener.

import java.net.*;
import java.io.*;
import java.lang.reflect.Constructor;

class GenericListener {
    GenericListener(Class serviceType,int port) throws Exception {
        try{
            // The class of the slave service.
            this.serviceType = serviceType;
            // Listen on the given port.
            serverSocket = new ServerSocket(port);
        }
        catch(BindException e){
            throw new Exception("Failed to create a server socket: "+
                        e.getMessage());
        }
    }

        // Listen for clients. When each arrives, hand the socket
        // over to a slave.
    public void listen() throws Exception {
        ServerSocket serverSocket = getServerSocket();
        boolean keepWaiting = true;

        // Obtain a Constructor for the slave service so that
        // it can be instantiated.
        Class serviceType = getServiceType();
        // In order to be found, the constructor must be public.
        Constructor serviceConstructor =
                    serviceType.getConstructor(constructorArgs);
        // An array is needed for the constructor's actual parameter.
        // This is filled in with the socket reference once the accept
        // call returns.
        Object[] args = new Object[constructorArgs.length];

        while(keepWaiting){
            try{
                // Wait for a client to make contact.
                serverSocket.setSoTimeout(getTimeToWait());
                Socket clientSocket = serverSocket.accept();
                // Fill in the constructor's Socket parameter.
                args[0] = clientSocket;
                // Create an instance of the service class.
                Runnable slave =
                        (Runnable) serviceConstructor.newInstance(args);
                // Let a separate Thread handle it.
```

(Continued)

Code 19.19   (*Continued*)

```
                new Thread(slave).start();
            }
            catch(InterruptedIOException e){
                // We timed out waiting for a client.
                keepWaiting = false;
            }
            catch(IOException e){
                throw new Exception("IOException: "+ e.getMessage());
            }
        }
        // No more clients, so close the socket.
        serverSocket.close();
    }

    protected ServerSocket getServerSocket(){
        return serverSocket;
    }

    protected Class getServiceType(){
        return serviceType;
    }

    protected int getTimeToWait(){
        return timeToWait;
    }

    protected void setTimeToWait(int time){
        timeToWait = time;
    }

    // The class of the service offered by the slave.
    private final Class serviceType;
    // The constructor of the slave service is expected to
    // take a single parameter of class Socket.
    protected static final Class[] constructorArgs = {
        Socket.class,
    };
    // The socket on which the listening is done.
    private final ServerSocket serverSocket;
    // By default, wait up to 30 minutes for new clients.
    // After that, quit.
    private int timeToWait = 1*60*1000;
}
```

19.13   The User Datagram Protocol

The *User Datagram Protocol* (UDP) differs significantly from the Transmission Control Protocol (TCP) in at least two respects:

- No automatic error correction is provided between the two applications using it to communicate.
- No persistent connection exists between the two applications.

It might be thought that UDP offers no advantages over TCP, therefore, but the major advantage that it does have lies in the very reasons for the difference between the two protocols—speed of communication. There are several situations where the overheads of TCP connection establishment and error correction are a disadvantage to applications using it:

- Where the amount of data to be transferred is relatively small, such as in credit card verification transactions.
- Where the communication path between the applications is relatively error free, such as in a local area network.
- Where the presence of occasional errors is not particularly important, such as in low-quality audio transmission.

In such circumstances, use of UDP offers an attractive alternative to use of TCP.

19.13.1   The Datagram Classes

The two main classes in the `java.net` package associated with UDP communication are `DatagramSocket` and `DatagramPacket`. Unlike a Socket, a DatagramSocket is not associated with a particular receiving endpoint, but is simply used as a means of obtaining a UDP port from the local operating system in order to send UDP packets. Its no-arg constructor leaves the operating system to allocate a port to the application, whereas the application may request to use a particular port with the other constructors—a server would use one of these to offer its service on a particular port, for instance. The four constructors of the DatagramPacket class are as follows:

```
public DatagramPacket(byte[] buffer,int numBytes,InetAddress receiver,
                      int receiverPort);
public DatagramPacket(byte[] buffer,int numBytes);
public DatagramPacket(byte[] buffer,int offset,int numBytes,
                      InetAddress receiver, int receiverPort);
public DatagramPacket(byte[] buffer,int offset,int numBytes);
```

The first is used to construct a packet to be sent to a particular destination and the second is used to receive a packet. The remaining two are identical, except that their `offset` argument indicates from where in the buffer the data should be stored. The example in Code 19.20 illustrates a UDP daytime client. You might like to compare it with the equivalent TCP example shown in Code 19.10.

Code 19.20   A UDP daytime client (`UDPDaytimeClient.java`)

```
import java.net.*;
import java.io.*;

        // Contact the daytime server running on hostname.
class UDPDaytimeClient {
    public UDPDaytimeClient(String hostname) throws UnknownHostException,
                                                SocketException {
        // Obtain an InetAddress for the host.
```
(Continued)

Code 19.20   (*Continued*)

```
        server = InetAddress.getByName(hostname);
        // Create a datagram socket for sending and receiving.
        socket = new DatagramSocket();
    }

    // Send a dummy packet to a UDP daytime service
    // and read the reply.
    public void run(){
        // The well-known port of the UDP daytime service.
        final int DaytimePort = 13;

        try{
            // Get the socket we are using.
            DatagramSocket socket = getSocket();
            // Get the address of the server.
            InetAddress server = getServer();

            // Create a datagram packet to send as a prompt.
            // Its contents are irrelevant.
            DatagramPacket prompt =
                new DatagramPacket(new byte[1],1,server,DaytimePort);
            // Create a buffer and packet for receiving the reply.
            final int bufferSpace = 80;
            byte[] replySpace = new byte[bufferSpace];
            DatagramPacket reply =
                new DatagramPacket(replySpace,replySpace.length);

            // Send the prompt.
            socket.send(prompt);
            // Receive the reply.
            socket.receive(reply);

            // Print out the reply and where it came from.
            System.out.println("Reply received from "+
                reply.getAddress().getHostAddress()+" port "+
                reply.getPort());

            System.out.write(replySpace,0,reply.getLength());
            socket.close();
        }
        catch(IOException e){
            System.err.println("IOException: "+e.getMessage());
        }
    }

    protected InetAddress getServer(){
        return server;
    }

    protected DatagramSocket getSocket(){
        return socket;
    }

    // Whom we are contacting.
    private final InetAddress server;
    // The socket we are using.
    private final DatagramSocket socket;
}
```

The constructor of `UDPDaytimeClient` uses the static `getByName` method of InetAddress to obtain the address of the server to which it is to be connected, and it stores a reference to this in its `server` attribute. It then creates a DatagramSocket attribute so that it can send and receive packets. In order to obtain the time of day from the server, the `run` method of the client must first send a packet to the server via the `send` method of its socket. The contents of this packet are irrelevant, and they will be ignored by the server. However, notice that this sending of a dummy packet by the client is not something that the corresponding TCP client had to do. The reason for the difference is that constructing a TCP Socket established a connection with the server—the server became aware of the client at that point—but constructing a UDP DatagramSocket makes no contact with the server, so it is not aware of the client's existence at this stage. Sending a dummy packet acts as a prompt to the server to send the time of day in reply and, in addition, the packet it receives contains the address and port of the client. These may be extracted via the `getAddress` and `getPort` methods of DatagramPacket. It uses these to create and send its reply to the correct destination.

In the `run` method in Code 19.20, the client prepares a DatagramPacket in which to receive the server's reply. It must guess how long the reply will be when it creates the `byte` array to pass to the DatagramPacket's constructor. If there is insufficient space, then the extra data will be lost. The number of bytes in the buffer can be determined from the `getLength` method of DatagramPacket. The `receive` method of DatagramSocket blocks until a reply arrives. Alternatively, a timeout may be set on the socket via its `setSoTimeout` method. If the timeout expires before the reply is received, then an `InterruptedIOException` exception is thrown.

For comparison with the TCP echo client shown in Code 19.11, an outline for the corresponding UDP echo client is shown in Code 19.21. `UDPEchoClient` differs from the basic daytime client shown in Code 19.20 by extending a `UDPUser` super class that maintains the common attributes of UDP clients, such as the socket they use and the server's InetAddress (their `correspondent`).

Code 19.21   Outline of a UDP echo client (`UDPEchoClient.java`)

```
      // Contact the UDP echo server running on hostname.
class UDPEchoClient extends UDPUser {
   public UDPEchoClient(String hostname) throws UnknownHostException,
                                                SocketException {
      super(hostname);
   }

      // Send the given strings to the UDP echo service.
   public void run(String[] sampleStrings){
      try{
         // The well-known port of the UDP echo service.
         final int EchoPort = 7;

         // Get the socket we are using.
         DatagramSocket socket = getSocket();
         // Get the address of the server.
```

(Continued)

```
            InetAddress server = getServer();

            // Create an array of byte[] equivalents of the strings
            // to be sent.
            final int numStrings = sampleStrings.length;
            byte[][] byteStrings = new byte[numStrings][];

            // Keep track of the longest. We need to know this
            // in order to create the packet for the replies.
            int maxBytes = -1;
            for(int i = 0; i < numStrings; i++){
                // Turn the String into an array of bytes.
                byteStrings[i] = sampleStrings[i].getBytes();
                // See if this is the longest so far.
                final int length = byteStrings[i].length;
                if(length > maxBytes){
                    maxBytes = length;
                }
            }

            // Create a datagram packet to send.
            // We use the same packet for each byte string.
            DatagramPacket packet =
                    new DatagramPacket(byteStrings[0],0,server,EchoPort);
            // Create a buffer and packet for receiving the reply.
            byte[] replySpace = new byte[maxBytes];
            DatagramPacket reply =
                new DatagramPacket(replySpace,replySpace.length);

            // Send each byte[] string in turn.
            for(int i = 0; i < byteStrings.length; i++){
                // Setup up the packet for this string.
                packet.setData(byteStrings[i]);
                packet.setLength(byteStrings[i].length);

                System.out.println("Sending: "+sampleStrings[i]);
                // Send the packet (repeatedly if necessary)
                // and receive the reply.
                sendAndReceive(packet,reply);

                // Print out the reply.
                System.out.print("Received: ");
                System.out.write(replySpace,0,reply.getLength());
                System.out.println();
            }
            socket.close();
        }
        catch(IOException e){
            System.err.println("IOException: "+e.getMessage());
        }
    }
}
```

In order to send a String, a client must turn it into an array of equivalent `byte` values, using one of String's `getBytes` method.[9] Notice that we have used the same DatagramPacket for sending each of the separate byte-versions of the strings by using the packet's `setData` and `setLength` methods inside the for loop. We have also used the same packet for receiving the replies. This means that the space it contains must be large enough for receiving back the longest string we send. Hence the calculation of `maxBytes` as the Strings are turned into `byte` arrays. UDPEchoClient uses the `sendAndReceive` method that it inherits from its UDP-Client super class, which we discuss in the next section.

19.13.2   A UDP Client Super Class

Remember that UDP is an inherently unreliable protocol. If a string sent by the client is lost on its way, or the reply is lost for some reason, no attempt will be made by the network to recover from this, or even notify a client that there is a problem. It is entirely up to the client and server to sort this out for themselves. In view of this, the `sendAndReceive` method of the UDPClient class shown in Code 19.22 repeatedly tries to send the packet until a reply is received.

Code 19.22   Cope with lost packets by resending (`UDPUser.java`)

```
    // A class that maintains the common attributes of a UDP user.
    // This class looks after the socket attribute and
    // the InetAddress of the other end of the 'connection'.
    // Typical clients extend this class to provide
    // the functionality applicable to their application.
    // It can also be used by server slave threads.
import java.net.*;
import java.io.*;

class UDPUser {
    // Typically used by a client to keep track
    // of the server.
    public UDPUser(String hostname) throws UnknownHostException,
                                           SocketException {
        // Obtain an InetAddress for the host.
        correspondent = InetAddress.getByName(hostname);
        // Create a datagram socket for sending.
        socket = new DatagramSocket();
    }

    // Typically used by a server slave to keep track
    // of the client.
    public UDPUser(InetAddress correspondent) throws SocketException {
        this.correspondent = correspondent;
```
                                                        (*Continued*)

---

[9] One version returns the byte version in the host platform's default representation, and the other in a specific encoding.

Code 19.22 *(Continued)*

```
        // Create a datagram socket for sending.
        socket = new DatagramSocket();
    }

        // Send packet and make sure that a reply is received.
        // Retry if necessary, but with a longer timeout.
        // Give up after too long, with an IOException.
    protected void sendAndReceive(DatagramPacket packet,
                                  DatagramPacket reply)
                                         throws IOException {
        boolean keepTrying = true;
        // How long to wait for a reply. This is variable.
        int timeToWait = getRetryTime();
        // How many tries before giving up.
        int retriesLeft = 10;
        DatagramSocket socket = getSocket();
        while(keepTrying){
            socket.setSoTimeout(timeToWait);
            socket.send(packet);
            try{
                // Receive the reply.
                receive(reply);
                // Got it.
                keepTrying = false;
            }
            catch(InterruptedIOException e){
                if(retriesLeft > 0){
                    // Wait for longer next time.
                    timeToWait += timeToWait*2+1;
                    retriesLeft--;
                    System.out.println("Timeout: try to resend.");
                }
                else{
                    throw new IOException("Giving up:"+
                        "no reply received after multiple attempts.");
                }
            }
        }
        setRetryTime(timeToWait);
    }

        // Send a packet, but don't wait.
    protected void send(DatagramPacket packet) throws IOException {
        DatagramSocket socket = getSocket();
        socket.send(packet);
    }

        // Receive a packet.
    protected void receive(DatagramPacket packet)
                        throws IOException, InterruptedIOException {
        DatagramSocket socket = getSocket();
        socket.receive(packet);
    }
```

Code 19.22   (*Continued*)

```
    protected void close(){
        getSocket().close();
    }

    protected InetAddress getCorrespondent(){
        return correspondent;
    }

    protected DatagramSocket getSocket(){
        return socket;
    }

    protected int getRetryTime(){
        return retryTime;
    }

    protected void setRetryTime(int t){
        retryTime = t;
    }

    // How long to wait before retrying a failed send.
    private int retryTime = 500;
    // With whom we are corresponding.
    private final InetAddress correspondent;
    // The socket we are using.
    private final DatagramSocket socket;
}
```

Error detection is attempted by setting a timeout on the socket. If an InterruptedIOException exception is received, it means that no reply has been received within that time, so it tries again. Each time it tries again with an increased timeout value. It does this in an attempt to avoid increasing possible congestion, which could be the reason it did not receive a reply in the first place. Of course, there is no guarantee that the data it expects has not simply been delayed. If it has, then repeating the request will result in it receiving duplicate replies from the same data.

Another point that should be noted when comparing use of TCP and UDP is that a DatagramSocket simply associates its user with a port on the local host; there is no association between the socket and a particular server. This means that the client could potentially receive packets via the socket from a quite different sender than the one it thinks it is receiving them from; another process only needs to know the port and InetAddress it is using. Strictly speaking, therefore, a UDP client should always check who has sent a packet it has received before it acts on it, by using the packet's getAddress and getPort methods.

Exercise 19.18   Experiment with the retry time used by the UDP client shown in Code 19.22 so that clients end up resending before the server has had time to reply to a datagram.

Exercise 19.19   Is it possible to modify the UDPUser class so that it is able to detect duplicate responses?

19.13.3   UDP Servers

In Section 19.12.3, we looked at the way in which the listening aspect of a TCP server can be separated from the service aspect by passing the server's Socket endpoint to a slave thread to handle an individual client, allowing the listener to return to waiting for further connections. This is made possible because the separate threads use the server's endpoint in two different ways: the listener waits for incoming connection attempts with accept and the slave deals with client communications via receive. With DatagramSockets the division between listening and responding is not clear cut because there is not a clear distinction between establishing a connection and transferring data. If we are to implement a similar separation of listening and responding with UDP servers, a different way must be found to hand over the client to the slave thread, once initial contact has been made.

The usual way in which listener-slave separation is accomplished with UDP is to have the slave request a new port number from the operating system, which is then communicated to the client in some way — often as part of the acknowledgement of the connection request. Initially, a server will listen on a specific port number. The client then requests the service at that particular port number. When a client request is received by the server, the request is passed to a slave which takes responsibility for providing the service, allowing the original server to go back to listening, exactly as we saw with TCP sockets. However, the client must now switch the destination port of its datagrams because further datagrams to the original port would be interpreted as fresh connection requests. The client can determine the alternative port when it receives the connection response by using the getPort method on the arriving DatagramPacket.

We can illustrate this procedure with a practical example based upon the *Trivial File Transfer Protocol (TFTP)*[10] which is built on UDP. The idea of TFTP is to provide an unsophisticated file transfer capability that lacks the frills of FTP. This makes it relatively easy to use from within *bootstrapping* programs for diskless machines. With the full version of TFTP, a client can request to transfer files either to or from a server in text or binary mode. Files are transferred in fixed-sized data packets of 512 bytes each, plus a small amount of header information. Each packet sent must be acknowledged before the next is sent. The final packet is indicated by a size of less than 512 bytes.

In our example, we shall restrict clients to reading files in binary mode using simple filenames. A client encodes a read-request (RRQ) in the initial packet sent to the server. The name of the file is encoded as a sequence of non-zero bytes with the end marked by a zero byte. The listening component of the server in our implementation is responsible for checking that an incoming packet contains an RRQ value. Thereafter, it hands over to the slave process. Code 19.23 shows an outline of

---

[10] Defined in RFC 1350.

the listener part of the server, UDPFileServer, and definitions shared between the
client and the server in the interface UDPFileTransfer.

The slave part of the service is implemented by UDPFileTransferSlave.
Its constructor receives the original packet from the client. From this it extracts the
client's port number and the name of the file to be transferred. It also creates its own
DatagramSocket to use in replying to the client so that it has a port number that is

---

Code 19.23   Outline of the listener part of a simple UDP file server

```
      // Definitions for a simple UDP file transfer server.
      // The protocol is modeled on the Trivial File Transfer
      // Protocol (TFTP) described in RFC 1350.
      // Only sending of a file is implemented, and the
      // transfer mode is binary (i.e. octet).

import java.net.*;
import java.io.*;

public interface UDPFileTransfer {
    // The (arbitrary) port of the file transfer service.
    public static final int ServerPort = 20069;
    // Opcode numbers.
    public static final int RRQ = 1, DATA = 3, ACK = 4, ERROR = 5;
    // Error values.
    public static final int FileNotFound = 1, AccessViolation = 2,
                    IllegalOperation = 4, UnknownPort = 5;
    // The size (in bytes) of the Opcode and block number.
    public static int opcodeSize = 2, blockNumberSize = 2;
    // The maximum size of any data that may be transferred.
    public static int MaxDataPacket = 512;
    // Define the length of a DATA header.
    public static int dataHeaderLength = opcodeSize+blockNumberSize;
    // Define the length of a full data packet.
    public static int fullDataPacket = dataHeaderLength+MaxDataPacket;
}

        // Listener for a simple UDP file transfer server.
      // The part of the server that listens for connections.
      // As soon as a valid read request (RRQ) is received,
      // responsibility is handed over to a UDPFileTransferSlave run
      // as a separate thread.
class UDPFileServer {
      // Request a socket on the desired port.
    public UDPFileServer() throws SocketException {
        // Request to use a particular port.
        socket = new DatagramSocket(UDPFileTransfer.ServerPort);
    }

      // Listen for RRQ packets.
    public void run(){
        // Allocate space and a packet for receiving RRQ requests.
        byte[] data = new byte[UDPFileTransfer.fullDataPacket];
        DatagramPacket request = new DatagramPacket(data,data.length);
```
                                                                (Continued)

Code 19.23   (*Continued*)

```
        DatagramSocket socket = getSocket();

        // Timeout after a period of inactivity.
        boolean keepGoing = true;
        while(keepGoing){
            try{
                // Wait for transfer requests to come in.
                socket.receive(request);

                System.out.println("Request received.");
                // Make sure the request is valid by checking some
                // basic packet format conditions.
                int length = request.getLength();

                if(!lengthOk(length)){
                    System.err.println("Illegal request length: "+length);
                }
                else if(!isReadRequest(data)){
                    System.err.println("Non RRQ packet received.");
                }
                else{
                    // Hand over to a slave.
                    new Thread(new UDPFileTransferSlave(request)).run();
                }
            }
            catch(SocketException e){
                System.err.println("Failed to create a slave thread.");
            }
            catch(IOException e){
                keepGoing = false;
            }
        }
        socket.close();
    }

    // Is the length of the request ok?
    protected boolean lengthOk(int length){
        // Allow at least one byte for a filename and a 0 terminator.
        return length >= (UDPFileTransfer.opcodeSize+1+1);
    }

    protected boolean isReadRequest(byte[] data){
        return (data[0] == 0) && (data[1] == UDPFileTransfer.RRQ);
    }

    ...
}
```

distinct from the listener's. Code 19.24 has an outline of this class to illustrate these points, but we have omitted most of the detail.

Of course, the client is responsible for switching to use the slave's port and there is nothing the server can do to enforce this. Full implementations of both

Code 19.24   Constructor for a slave component of a UDP file server

```
             // Slave for a simple UDP file transfer server.
import java.net.*;
import java.io.*;

        // Handle simple file transfer to a single client.
class UDPFileTransferSlave implements Runnable {
        // The requested filename is encoded in the packet.
    public UDPFileTransferSlave(DatagramPacket request)
                             throws SocketException {
        // Create a datagram socket for sending.
        socket = new DatagramSocket();
        // Keep track of the client's port.
        clientPort = request.getPort();
        // Extract the name of the file to be transferred.
        setFilename(request.getData(),request.getLength());
    }
    ...
}
```

the server and client for this application may be found in the files, `UDPFile-Client.java`, `UDPFileServer.java`, `UDPFileTransfer.java`, and `UDP-FileTransferSlave.java`. Test-rig programs containing trivial main methods for the client and server may be found in `UDPFileClientTest.java` and `UDP-FileServerTest.java`, respectively.

Exercise 19.20   Write a UDP echo server so that the listener hands off connections to a slave thread. How must the client shown in Code 19.21 (defined in `UDPE-choClient.java`) be modified to work with this server?

Exercise 19.21   Modify the UDP echo server that you wrote in Exercise 19.20 so that the slave fails to respond to packets occasionally. How does this affect clients? How are clients affected if the listener drops occasional packets?

Exercise 19.22   There are several common methods between the UDPFileClient and UDPFileTransferSlave classes, such as `twoByteEncode`. This arises because of the way in which both examine and manipulate the similarly formatted packets they send to each other. In addition, both currently extend the UDPUser class whose components manage their DatagramSocket attribute and the InetAddress attribute that refers to their correspondent. Define a new intermediate class to contain the common methods of UDPFileClient and UDPFileTransferSlave. The new class should extend UDPUser and be extended by the client and server slave classes of this application.

Exercise 19.23   In the Trivial File Transfer Protocol (TFTP—RFC 1350), upon which the examples in this section are based, the next DATA packet is not sent until the ACK for the previous one has been received. If no ACK is received within a timeout period, the most recently sent DATA packet is retransmitted before the ACK arrives. In the original description of TFTP, the last DATA packet was to be resent if a duplicate ACK was received. Suppose a particular ACK is delayed, but not

lost, and the last DATA packet is resent before it arrives. What situation could arise
if both copies of the last packet arrive at the client? (This is known as the *Sorcerer's
Apprentice Syndrome*). How might this problem be fixed?

Exercise 19.24 The `transfer` method of the simple file transfer server implemented in `UDPFileTransferSlave.java` can exhibit the Sorcerer's Apprentice
Syndrome; modify it to prevent this happening.

Exercise 19.25 The TFTP protocol defined in RFC 1350 assumes that the client
knows the names of the files stored on the server. Design an extension to the protocol
that allows clients to request which files the server has.

Exercise 19.26 Implement the extensions to the TFTP protocol you designed in
your answer to Exercise 19.25 by modifying the UDPFileTransfer client and server
described above.

19.14 Review

- The Transmission Control Protocol (TCP) offers reliable transmission of a
  sequential stream of bytes.
- The `InetAddress` class encapsulates a 4-byte Internet Address.
- A numeric Internet Address uniquely identifies a single machine.
- A machine may have more than one Internet Address and more than one
  symbolic name.
- A symbolic name may be shared by multiple machines.
- The `Socket` class allows a client to establish a TCP connection with a server.
- A TCP connection is established between two (address,port) pairs.
- It is usually necessary for a client to know the port number on which a server
  is listening for connections.
- The `ServerSocket` class allows a server to listen for client connections on a
  particular port.
- The `accept` method of ServerSocket blocks until a client establishes contact.
- The `accept` method returns a Socket object, which the server uses to commu-
  nicate with the client.
- Concurrent clients are usually managed by the server handing over client com-
  munication to a slave thread.
- The User Datagram Protocol (UDP) is an alternative to TCP.
- UDP offers unreliable transmission of datagrams, with no guarantee of data-
  gram delivery.
- UDP is appropriate where network reliability is high, or speed is more impor-
  tant than reliability.
- The `DatagramSocket` class is used to create a UDP endpoint.
- Creating a DatagramSocket does not establish a connection between a client
  and a server.
- The `DatagramPacket` class is used to send a packet of byte data between two
  UDP processes.
- A UDP process must manage its own error-recovery strategy.

PART

V

Applets

20

Applets

I n this chapter, we describe the creation of specialist programs known as applets. Applets are most closely associated with the ability to provide active content within Web pages. They have several distinguishing features, such as their lack of a user-defined main method, and the security restrictions that limit their abilities to perform some normal tasks. This chapter draws heavily on the material covered In Chapter 16 and Chapter 17.

20.1   Introduction

In Chapter 1, we noted the Java language was being developed around the same time that the World Wide Web was undergoing a revolution in terms of its power and availability. Java's provision of a secure environment in which to run programs that have been downloaded from another site make it an ideal companion for providing active content on web sites. Such programs are called *applets* in Java. Indeed, it was primarily the existence of applets that attracted many people to the language in the first place. In this chapter, we look at applets in the context of the *Abstract Windowing Toolkit (AWT)* that was introduced in Chapter 16. Applets bear many similarities to the graphical applications introduced there and use the classes of the AWT to provide most of their functionality. We start by looking at some simple applets which are broadly similar in functionality to the early AWT applications we described. We then assume that you have a reasonable familiarity with the AWT and develop some slightly more sophisticated programs.

20.2   The Applet Class

All applets are written by defining a sub class of the `Applet` class, defined in the `java.applet` package. Code 20.1 shows a simple hello-world applet. The Applet sub class must be defined with `public` access and its constructor, if it has one, must also be `public`. By default, it only has a public no-arg constructor. The Applet class shares many similarities with the Frame class in terms of the way in which it is used as a starting point for the creation of a graphical user interface. For instance, both extend the Container class: Frame does so via its immediate super class, Window, and

---

Code 20.1   A simple hello-world applet (`HelloApplet.java`)

```
import java.applet.*;
import java.awt.*;

        // Paint a string in the graphics context of an Applet.
public class HelloApplet extends Applet {
        // Override Applet's paint method.
    public void paint(Graphics g){
        // Define the drawing position.
        final int xpos = 10, ypos = 50;
        g.drawString("Welcome to Earth!",xpos,ypos);
    }
}
```

Applet does so through its immediate super class, Panel. In addition, basic drawing may be performed within an Applet by overriding its `paint` method, as shown in Code 20.1. However, as well as the similarities, there are several important differences between applets and applications that need to be appreciated. When starting to write applets, the most significant difference to understand is that you do not write a main method as the program's starting point. Applets typically run within the context of a Web browser or applet viewer, and it is the responsibility of these controlling programs to initialize and start an applet via its `init` and `start` methods inherited from the Applet class. How this is done is hidden from the applet's programmer.

20.3 Running an Applet

An applet is run by including a reference to its `.class` file in a file written using the *HyperText Markup Language (HTML)*. Such a file will usually have a ".html" or ".htm" suffix. Code 20.2 shows a simple example of an HTML file whose sole purpose is to allow an applet to be run.

Code 20.2   A sample HTML file suitable for running an applet (`hello.html`)

```
<html>
<head>
</head>
<body>
    <applet code="HelloApplet.class" width=200 height=200>
    An applet to display a greeting string.
    </applet>
</body>
</html>
```

Figure 20.1 Running HelloApplet
with the appletviewer

The HTML file is loaded into a Web browser just like a normal Web page, or passed to a viewer such as `appletviewer`.[1] Figure 20.1 shows the result of passing the example shown in Code 20.2 to `appletviewer` with the command

```
appletviewer hello.html
```

The first four and the last two lines of the example in Code 20.2 are standard pieces of HTML notation, known as *HTML tags*, which should be included in all HTML files, whether they contain applets or not. The part which is distinctive of running applets starts with an opening *applet tag* (`<applet>`) and ends with a closing tag (`</applet>`).[2] Embedded within the opening tag are a number of *tag attributes*, such as `code`, `width`, and `height`. Further attributes are available but these three are the minimum requirement (see Section 20.5.1 for others). The `code` attribute names the class file containing the sub class of Applet you wish to run, and the `width` and `height` attributes define the dimensions of the applet within the viewer or browser—they do not define the size of the browser. Any text between the opening and closing applet tags, as in the example, is optional and will not normally appear

---

[1] `appletviewer` is distributed by JavaSoft with the Java platform. It provides a convenient means for developing and debugging applets without invoking the full power of a Web browser. However, applets which run within `appletviewer` might still fail to run within some browsers, due to incompatibilities.

[2] You might have spotted that HTML tags usually appear in nested pairs like brackets, with the characters `</` indicating the terminating half of a pair.

with the applet. It is provided as a form of documentation and as something to be displayed by browsers that do not know about applets. The class file is often located in the same place as its referring HTML file. Once a viewer or browser has loaded the HTML file, it then makes a further retrieval of the associated class file.

In the remainder of this chapter, we shall normally simply use the term viewer or applet viewer as a general term to mean a program able to run an applet, regardless of whether it is a Web browser, `appletviewer`, or some other applet-aware program. We shall also refer to the system on which an applet is run as the *client system* or *host system*, and the system from which the applet originates as the *server system*.

20.3.1   The `codebase` Attribute

Most applets will typically consist of objects created from many classes. Standard classes that exist in packages on the client system will be retrieved by the viewer via its `CLASSPATH` environment variable in the normal way. However, as was indicated above, an applet's specialized class files will normally be retrieved from the directory on the server referred to in the URL of the applet's HTML file. For instance, suppose the HTML file of Code 20.2 was retrieved from the following URL, therefore

```
http://www.cs.ukc.ac.uk/people/staff/djb/Book/hello.html
```

the viewer would expect to retrieve the HelloApplet.class file with the URL:

```
http://www.cs.ukc.ac.uk/people/staff/djb/Book/HelloApplet.class
```

Including a `codebase` parameter in the applet tag directs the viewer to load the class files from another URL, which could be either relative to the URL of the HTML file or an absolute URL. Assuming that the hello applet was retrieved via

```
http://www.cs.ukc.ac.uk/people/staff/djb/Book/hello.html
```

the following alternatives would be equivalent in directing the viewer to retrieve the class files from the `Applets` sub-directory relative to the original URL:

```
codebase="Applets"
codebase="http://www.cs.ukc.ac.uk/people/staff/djb/Book/Applets"
```

20.4   Applet Initialization

Figure 20.2 displays an applet based on the `OvalCanvas` class introduced in Code 16.6. Code 20.3 shows the Applet sub class, `OvalApplet`, that does this. As a matter of style, we generally choose not to define constructors for sub classes of Applet. Instead, we leave initialization actions to its `init` method, which is always called shortly after instantiation. The main reason for this is that only a limited amount of the applet's context is available at its point of creation, for instance its size will not have been set. This limits the amount of setup it is possible to perform in the constructor, so it might as well all be left to `init`. Following construction, an applet's `setStub` method is called to register an `AppletStub` with it. This provides an applet with contextual information such as details of the document from which

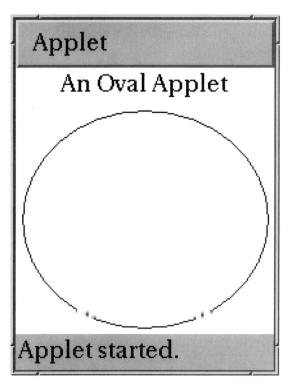

Figure 20.2   An Applet displaying a TextLabel and OvalCanvas (`OvalApplet.java`)

Code 20.3   A Label and OvalCanvas in an Applet Panel

```java
import java.awt.*;
import java.applet.*;

        // Display a central OvalCanvas and a descriptive Label.
public class OvalApplet extends Applet {
    public void init(){
        // Use a BorderLayout rather than the default FlowLayout.
        setLayout(new BorderLayout());
        // Add a label at the top.
        add(new Label("An Oval Applet",Label.CENTER),"North");
        Canvas c = new OvalCanvas();
        // Give the canvas half the extent of this applet.
        Dimension size = getSize();
        c.setSize(size.width/2,size.height/2);
        add(c,"Center");
    }
}
```

it was loaded. After registration of the stub, an applet's `init` method is called. The `init` method is called only once, when the applet has been loaded by the viewer. This is typically overridden to initialize any components that will be required by the applet for the full period of its existence.

Code 20.4   A Swing JApplet adds components to its content pane (`SwingOvalApplet.java`)

```
import java.awt.*;
import javax.swing.*;

        // Display a central OvalCanvas and a descriptive Label.
public class SwingOvalApplet extends JApplet {
    public void init(){
        final Container contents = getContentPane();
        // Use a BorderLayout rather than the default FlowLayout.
        contents.setLayout(new BorderLayout());
        // Add a label at the top.
        contents.add(new JLabel("A Swing Oval JApplet",JLabel.CENTER),
                     "North");

        // An an oval-drawing canvas.
        Component c = new OvalCanvas();
        // Give the canvas half the extent of this applet.
        Dimension size = getSize();
        c.setSize(size.width/2,size.height/2);
        contents.add(c,"Center");
    }
}
```

OvalApplet's `init` method firstly replaces its default FlowLayout layout manager (inherited from its Panel super class) with a BorderLayout object, so as to be able to arrange the separate components of its interface. This is followed by creation of a Label and OvalCanvas placed at its North and Center, respectively.

20.4.1   Swing Applets

There is very little difference between applets built with the AWT Applet class and those built with the Swing `JApplet` class. JApplet, in fact, is a sub class of the Applet class. As with the `JFrame` class (described in Chapter 17), components are added to the JApplet's *content pane*, rather than to the JApplet itself. Code 20.4 contains a JApplet equivalent to the Applet shown in Code 20.3.

20.5   Java Archive Files

Each class file required by an applet, and that is not already on the host system's class path, requires a separate retrieval from the server. Programs consisting of many class files might, therefore, take a long time to start running as a large number of file transfers are made from the server to the viewer's host machine. Multiple small transfers are typically less efficient than a single large transfer, so the Java platform provides a tool that makes it possible to bundle all the files required to run an applet into a single *Java Archive (JAR) file*; this tool is called `jar`. Files created with it should be given a `.jar` suffix, by convention.

A JAR file is created with a `jar` command in the following form:

```
jar cf file.jar files-to-be-stored
```

The `c` argument to `jar` indicates that a `.jar` file is to be created. The `f` argument indicates that the name of the file to be created comes next. If the `f` argument is omitted, then so must the file name, and the contents of the archive will be written to standard output. The names of all the files to be stored in the archive are then listed at the end of the command. The following command creates the file `oval.jar` containing the class files for the example in Code 20.3:

```
jar cf oval.jar OvalApplet.class OvalCanvas.class
```

Several further arguments may be passed to `jar` for inspection and management of an archive file:

- The `t` argument to `jar` lists the contents of an archive, for instance,

  ```
  jar tf oval.jar
  ```

- The `v` argument requests *verbose* information, so

  ```
  jar tvf oval.jar
  ```

  might produce:

  ```
    0 Tue Jun 29 10:18:46 GMT+01:00 1999 META-INF/
   66 Tue Jun 29 10:18:46 GMT+01:00 1999 META-INF/MANIFEST.MF
  911 Tue Jun 29 09:20:44 GMT+01:00 1999 OvalApplet.class
  552 Tue Jun 29 09:18:56 GMT+01:00 1999 OvalCanvas.class
  ```

  Notice that the archive contains a *manifest file* (`MANIFEST.MF`) that was placed there automatically when the archive was created (see details of the `m` argument).

- The `x` argument extracts a copy of the named files from the archive. It is possible to examine the contents of this file by extracting it from the archive using

  ```
  jar xf oval.jar OvalCanvas.class
  ```

- The `u` argument allows a file in an archive to be updated—replaced by a later version, for instance,

  ```
  jar uf oval.jar OvalApplet.class
  ```

- The `C` argument indicates that a directory name follows for where the source files are located, for instance,

  ```
  jar cf oval.jar -C ovals OvalApplet.class OvalCanvas.class
  ```

  tells the archiver to look for the class files in the `ovals` directory.

- The `m` argument allows a user-created *manifest file* to be added to an archive, rather than the default created by `jar`. All JAR files contain a manifest file. The contents of that in `oval.jar` might be as follows:

  ```
  Manifest-Version: 1.0
  Created-By: 1.2 (Sun Microsystems Inc.)
  ```

Code 20.5   The HTML file for running the OvalApplet

```
<html>
<head>
<title>An Oval Applet</title>
</head>
<body>
    <applet code="OvalApplet.class"
            archive="oval.jar"
            width=200 height=200>
    An applet to display an Oval.
    </applet>
</body>
</html>
```

This is a very simple manifest file, because the archive has not been signed—provided with authentication information. Signed archive files contain more detailed information that is beyond the scope of this book.

Instead of allowing `jar` to define its own manifest file when an archive is created, the `c` argument may include `m` as a further argument, indicating that a manifest file name is included on the command line. The order of `f` and `m` arguments should be replicated in the order of the respective file names that follow. For instance, the following command creates an archive called `arch.jar` using the file `manifest.ex` as the basis for its manifest file:

```
jar cfm arch.jar manifest.ex files-to-be-stored
```

In order to run the example shown in Code 20.3 using a JAR file, a slightly more sophisticated HTML file is required. This is shown in Code 20.5. In addition to the `code` attribute of the applet tag, an `archive` tag attribute names the `.jar` file containing the required class files (including `OvalApplet.class`).

Using this approach, only two file transfers will be required from the server: the HTML file and the JAR file. Multiple archive files may be listed in a single attribute by separating their names with commas in the attribute's value string. Notice that, in this example, an additional HTML tag pair has been added at the head of the HTML file. This pair allows a title for the containing page to be displayed by a Web browser; it is worth getting into the habit of using this for identification purposes.

20.5.1   Further `<applet>` Attributes

In addition to `archive`, `code`, `codebase`, `height`, and `width`, there are several other attributes that may be included in an applet tag to communicate information to the presenting applet viewer.

- `align`—specifies an alignment for the applet, such as *left*, *right*, *top*, *bottom*, and *middle*.
- `alt`— specifies some alternative text to be displayed if the viewer is unable to support the applet.

- hspace and vspace—these specify an amount of space that should be placed on either side, or above and below, an applet within the viewer.
- name—specifies a name for this applet. Naming an applet allows other applets to locate it, if necessary.
- object—an alternative to the code attribute. This attribute names a file containing a serialized version of an applet; that is, an applet that has already been initialized. If this attribute is present, the browser will load the named file and de-serialize the applet. An important difference is that the applet's init method is not called once it has been de-serialized; only its start method.

20.6 Retrieving Remote Images

Applets are commonly used to display images—often animated images. Images can be supplied to an applet in both of the ways we have seen with class files: separately retrieved or bundled in a JAR file. Loading an image from a JAR file is slightly more complicated than retrieving it separately, so we shall discuss the non-bundled case first of all. This has the advantage of being applicable when the images to be displayed are to be retrieved from a location that is different from the applet writer's site. Applet's getImage methods take a URL object, and an optional filename, specifying the location of the image to be retrieved. URL objects corresponding to the locations of the originating HTML file and the applet's originating class file are obtainable via its getDocumentBase and getCodeBase methods, respectively. Code 20.6 shows an applet that retrieves the file apple.gif from the directory from which its launching HTML file was retrieved, by using getDocumentBase.[3]

Code 20.6 Retrieving an image file (`AppleApplet.java`)

```
import java.applet.*;
import java.awt.*;

        // Retrieve an image file from the same location as the
        // originating HTML file (the Document Base).
public class AppleApplet extends Applet {
    public void init() throws RuntimeException {
        // Get the apple image.
        setImage(retrieveImage("apple.gif"));
    }

        // Scale the image to the full size of the applet.
    public void paint(Graphics g){
        final Dimension size = getSize();
        Image image = getImage();
        if(image != null){
            g.drawImage(image,0,0,size.width,size.height,this);
        }
    }
}
```

---

[3] In this case, using getCodeBase would have the same effect.

Code 20.6   (*Continued*)

```
    // Get the image, which is located in fileName relative
    // to the document which loaded this applet.
protected Image retrieveImage(String fileName) throws RuntimeException {
    Image appleImage = getImage(getDocumentBase(),fileName);
    // Wait for it to load.
    MediaTracker tracker = new MediaTracker(this);
    tracker.addImage(appleImage,0);
    try{
        tracker.waitForAll();
    }
    catch(InterruptedException e){
    }
    // Make sure loading was successful.
    if(tracker.isErrorAny()){
        throw new RuntimeException("Image loading problem: "+fileName);
    }
    else{
        return appleImage;
    }
}

protected Image getImage(){
    return image;
}

protected void setImage(Image i){
    image = i;
}

    // The image to be displayed in the full size of the applet.
    private Image image;
}
```

Because retrieval of the image could take a significant time, the applet uses a Media-Tracker to wait for the image to arrive fully (see Section 16.21.1). If there is a problem with retrieving the file, a RuntimeException exception is thrown to terminate the applet from within retrieveImage. If it is desired to retrieve an image that is not located at the same place as the originating document, then the single argument version of getImage might be used with a full URL object, for instance,

```
getImage(
    new URL("http://www.cs.ukc.ac.uk/people/staff/djb/Book/redBall.gif"));
```

20.7   Parameterizing an Applet

The example in Code 20.6 is tied to the filename apple.gif as its image. It would make the applet more general if the name of the file to be displayed could be supplied externally. This is possible using <param> tags between the opening and closing

Code 20.7   Specifying a name and value pair with a `<param>` tag (`image.html`)

```
<html>
<head>
<title>A Parameterized Image - Separate Retrieval</title>
</head>
<body>
    <applet code="ImageApplet.class"
            archive="image.jar"
            width=200 height=200>
    An applet to display an image named below.
    <param name="image" value="apple.gif">
    </applet>
</body>
</html>
```

applet tags in the HTML file. Code 20.7 illustrates how a typical `name` and `value` pair may be specified.

Any number of parameters may be specified in this way. Their values are retrieved via an applet's `getParameter` method. This takes a String indicating the `name` part and the corresponding `value` part is returned as its result. Code 20.8 shows the small modification needed to AppleApplet's `init` method to parameterize it in this way.

Code 20.8   Retrieve an image named in an applet's parameter (`ImageApplet.java`)

```
import java.applet.*;
import java.awt.*;

        // Retrieve an image file from the same location as the
        // originating HTML file (the Document Base).
public class ImageApplet extends Applet {
    public void init() throws RuntimeException {
        // Get the image named in the parameters.
        String imageName = checkParameter(
                            parameterInfo[imageParameter][0]);
        setImage(retrieveImage(imageName));
    }

    ...

        // Supply information on the applet's purpose.
    public String getAppletInfo(){
        return "Display an image named in the "+
                parameterInfo[imageParameter][0]+" parameter.";
    }

        // Supply information on the parameters used.
    public String[][] getParameterInfo(){
        return parameterInfo;
    }
```

Code 20.8   (*Continued*)

```
        // Retrieve the given parameter from the applet's properties.
    protected String checkParameter(String parameter)
                                throws RuntimeException {
        String value = getParameter(parameter);
        if(value == null){
            throw new RuntimeException("Parameter: "+
                                    parameter+" is missing.");
        }
        return value;
    }

    ...

    // Information on the parameters of this applet.
    private final int imageParameter = 0;
    private final String[][] parameterInfo = {
        {"image", "string",
         "Name of the image, relative to the document base."
        },
    };
}
```

Applets which expect parameters to be set in their HTML file should override their super class's `getParameterInfo` method to provide information on the details of those parameters. This technique has been illustrated in Code 20.8. The overriding version of the method returns a reference to a two-dimensional array. Each row of the array should contain exactly three strings describing the name, type, and usage, respectively, of a single parameter. Notice how the `init` method uses the information held in this array to pass the name of a required parameter to `getParameter`.

Because of security restrictions on applets (see Section 20.12), an applet has only limited access to the host's System properties, so use of <param> tags is the best way to customize an applet's environment and behavior from an external source.

In addition to overriding `getParameterInfo`, the applet in Code 20.8 also overrides its super class's `getAppletInfo` method. This returns a single string containing a short description of the purpose of the applet. The information from these two methods is displayed by `appletviewer` on selection of the *"Info..."* menu item beneath its *"Applet"* menu.

20.8   Bundling Images

In Section 20.5, we discussed the advantages of bundling all the files required by an applet into a single Java archive file. Since image files are often quite large, those advantages can be extended by including images in the same archive as the required class files. They are added in exactly the same way as class files. The disadvantage is that a slightly more complex approach is required to unbundle them from within the applet. An image stored in an archive file is not extracted simply via a call to `getImage`. Instead, the file must be identified as a *resource* via the applet's `Class-Loader` object. The `getResource` and the `getResourceAsStream` methods of

---

Code 20.9   Creating an Image from a file in the applet's archive (`JarImageApplet.java`)

```
import java.applet.*;
import java.awt.*;
import java.io.*;

        // Retrieve an image file from a Jar archive associated
        // with the applet.
public class JarImageApplet extends Applet {
    public void init() throws RuntimeException {
        // Get the image name.
        String imageName = checkParameter(parameterInfo[imageParameter][0]);
        setImage(extractImage(imageName));
    }
    ...
        // Retrieve fileName from this applet's archive file.
    protected Image extractImage(String fileName)
                                    throws RuntimeException {
        try {
            // Identify the resource via the applet's ClassLoader.
            InputStream imageStream =
                        getClass().getResourceAsStream(fileName);
            // Read the whole Image as a single byte array.
            byte imageBytes[] = new byte[imageStream.available()];
            imageStream.read(imageBytes);
            // Turn the data into an Image.
            Toolkit tk = Toolkit.getDefaultToolkit();
            return tk.createImage(imageBytes);
        }
        catch(Exception e){
            throw new RuntimeException(e.toString());
        }
    }
    ...
}
```

---

the `Class` class, delegate the location of a resource to the class loader. Code 20.9 illustrates an applet that uses the `getResourceAsStream` method to obtain an image file as a resource from the applet's associated archive file.

Only the `extractImage` method of `JarImageApplet` is distinctive from the image displaying applets we have seen so far. It obtains a Class object for the applet, via `getClass`, and then obtains an `InputStream` for the image file via `getResourceAsStream`. It creates an Image object by reading the full contents of the stream into a `byte` array and then passing this data to the `createImage` method of a `Toolkit` object. In Section 20.9.1, we show how this approach can be used to load multiple images from an archive in order to create image animations.

20.9   Applet Animation

In the context of a Web browser, an applet's code will be downloaded from a remote site onto the host system, and this will typically happen only once during a browser session. Once an applet has been loaded and initialized (via `init`) it is marked as *active* and will respond to an `isActive` message by returning the value `true`. Immediately following this, it will be sent a `start` message. If the applet code involves animation, then this is the signal for it to start the animation. If the containing page is left within the browser, then the applet will be sent a `stop` message. Following a call to `stop`, `isActive` will return `false`. An applet may be repeatedly started and stopped in this way if the user returns to and leaves the containing page. It is important that an applet respect the implication of a `stop` message and release computational resources of the host that it might be using, otherwise a user visiting several applet-containing pages in succession could find their machine slowly grinding to a halt as still-running applets compete for its limited resources. Parts of an applet responsible for animation and computation can use their `isActive` method to determine whether they should be performing work or not. One implication of this is that it is important to distinguish between the tasks performed in `init`, which is only ever called once, and those performed in `start`, which may be called multiple times. It is probably best to think of `start` as a form of restart in order to avoid placing inappropriate once-only code there.

Code 20.10 shows an applet that controls an analogue `Clock` object, which is setup to run in a separate thread via the applet's `init` method. The visual appearance of the Clock object is shown in Figure 20.3.

Notice that the `init` method performs the once-only task of starting the clock's thread. The `start` method has been written to assume that the clock's thread is in a suspended state whenever it is called, so the `init` method must ensure that this is true the first time `start` is called. Whenever a `stop` message is received, the clock's thread is suspended so that it does not consume resources unnecessarily.

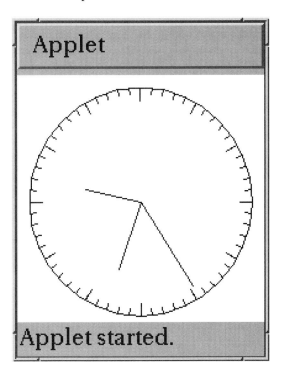

Figure 20.3 An analogue clock applet (Code 20.10)

Code 20.10   Starting and stopping a Clock object running in its own thread
(`ClockApplet.java`)

```java
        // Run a simple clock.
import java.applet.*;
import java.awt.*;

public class ClockApplet extends Applet {
    public void init(){
        Clock clock = getClock();
        // Give the clock a size.
        final Dimension size = getSize();
        clock.setSize(size.width,size.height);
        // Add it the drawing area.
        add(clock);
        // Start and suspend the clock's thread.
        // It will be (re)started properly by the start method.
        clock.setAnimationRunning(false);
        new Thread(clock).start();
    }

        // (Re)start the clock ticking.
    public void start(){
        getClock().setAnimationRunning(true);
    }

        // Suspend the clock from ticking so that it does not
        // consume any resources.
    public void stop(){
        getClock().setAnimationRunning(false);
    }

    protected Clock getClock(){
        return clock;
    }

    // The analogue clock to be run in its own thread.
    private final Clock clock = new Clock();
}
```

Applet's destroy method indicates the end of its life, enabling it to completely release any resources it might be maintaining in anticipation of being restarted. In the case of the clock applet, the separate clock thread could be permanently stopped and the applet's resources released for garbage collection by setting its clock and thread attribute to null.[4]

---

[4] This is currently prevented by their being final variables, to which an assignment of null would not be allowed.

Code 20.11   An HTML file for a multi-image animation applet (`multiimage.html`)

```
<html>
<head>
<title>Animated Images</title>
</head>
<body>
    <applet code="MultiImageApplet.class"
            archive="bites.jar"
            width=250 height=250>
    An applet to display an image animation named below.
    The separate images are .gif files with the prefix named via imagebase,
    i.e. bite0.gif, bite1.gif, etc.
    <param name="imagebase" value="bite">
    The frametime parameter is used to set the time (in milliseconds)
    between frames in the animation.
    <param name="frametime" value="500">
    </applet>
</body>
</html>
```

20.9.1   Multiple Image Animation

In Section 20.8, we described how a single image file can be bundled in a JAR file and extracted from within an applet. Java supports the GIF89 animated image format, so image animation within applets requires no special effort if the image being displayed is in a format such as that. However, more programmer control can be exercised over an animation if it is created out of multiple image files. Archive files are ideal for holding such images and requiring only a single transfer from the server. If the individual image files are given names with a consistent prefix and consecutive numerical suffixes, a simple loop can be written to extract them from the archive. The example in Code 20.11 shows an HTML file used to supply the components of an applet to perform animation of a series of images. In this particular example, successive images will be called `bite0.gif`, `bite1.gif`, and so on.

The setup of the applet's visual appearance is performed by the class `Multi-ImageApplet`, shown in Code 20.12.[5] The MultiImageApplet class's `init` method is responsible for extracting the separate image files (`extractImages`) and setting up the visual appearance of the applet (`setupButtons` and `setupImageAnima-tor`). The applet runs an `ImageAnimator` object in a separate thread to implement the animation, with its `start` and `stop` methods defined in a similar way to that illustrated with the ClockApplet in Code 20.10. The animation can be controlled by the user via `"Start"` and `"Stop"` buttons, which are interfaces to the applet's `start` and `stop` methods. As well as using a `<param>` tag to indicate the base name of the

---

[5] At the time of writing, many browsers do not support classes introduced in version 1.2 of the API, so we have used Vector instead of ArrayList in this example.

Code 20.12 Setup an applet's contents for a multi-image animation
(`MultiImageApplet.java`)

```java
import java.applet.*;
import java.awt.*;
import java.awt.event.*;
    // Use a non-1.2 class in deference to browsers.
import java.util.Vector;
import java.io.InputStream;

        /* Maintain a thread which cycles through an array of
         * Image objects. The files for the Images are bundled with
         * the associated .jar file.
         *
         * The animation is parameterized via
         *     imagebase - the base name for the image files
         *     frametime - the (long) time (in milliseconds) between images.
         */
public class MultiImageApplet extends Applet {
    public void init() throws RuntimeException {
        // Setup the layout and extract the images.
        setLayout(new BorderLayout());
        setupButtons();
        setupImageAnimator();
        // Start and suspend the thread ready for Applet.start().
        ImageAnimator animator = getAnimator();
        animator.setAnimationRunning(false);
        new Thread(animator).start();
    }

    public void start(){
        getAnimator().setAnimationRunning(true);
    }

    public void stop(){
        getAnimator().setAnimationRunning(false);
    }

        // Supply information on the parameters used.
    public String[][] getParameterInfo(){
        return parameterInfo;
    }

        // Provide a Start and Stop button for the animation.
        // In effect these are Suspend and Resume.
    protected void setupButtons(){
        Panel p = new Panel();
        Button start = new Button("Start");
        Button stop = new Button("Stop");
        p.add(start);
        p.add(stop);
        add(p,"South");

        // Attach appropriate listeners to the buttons.
        start.addActionListener(new ActionListener(){
```

Code 20.12   (*Continued*)

```
        public void actionPerformed(ActionEvent e){
            MultiImageApplet.this.start();
        }
    });

    stop.addActionListener(new ActionListener(){
        public void actionPerformed(ActionEvent e){
            MultiImageApplet.this.stop();
        }
    });
}

    // Extract the images from the associate archive file.
    // The base name for the GIF images is specified by the
    // applet parameter "imagebase".
    // Construct an ImageAnimator as a
protected void setupImageAnimator() throws RuntimeException {
    // Get the image.
    String baseName = checkParameter(
                    parameterInfo[imagebaseParameter][0]);
    Image[] images = extractImages(baseName);
    ImageAnimator animator = new ImageAnimator(images);
    // See if the animation's frame time has been set.
    String frameTime = getParameter(
                    parameterInfo[frametimeParameter][0]);
    if(frameTime != null){
        try{
            long time = Long.parseLong(frameTime);
            animator.setFrameTime(time);
        }
        catch(Exception e){
        }
    }
    // The animator is based upon a Canvas and so needs a size.
    Dimension size = getSize();
    animator.setSize(size.width,size.height);
    add(animator,"Center");
    setAnimator(animator);
}

    // Get the images, which are located in the archive
    // loaded with this applet. The image names are of the form
    //          baseName+number+.gif
    // where number starts at 0.
protected Image[] extractImages(String baseName)
                                throws RuntimeException {
    // Build a vector until we know how many there are, then
    // set the Image[] attribute.
    Vector images = new Vector();
    try{
        // Compose the individual file names, from the base name
        // a number and the image type suffix.
```

(*Continued*)

Code 20.12   (*Continued*)

```java
            for(int i = 0; ; i++){
                images.addElement(extractImage(baseName+i+".gif"));
            }
        }
        catch(Exception e){
            if(images.size() == 0){
                throw new RuntimeException(
                               "Failed to load any images "+
                               e.getMessage());
            }
        }
        // Copy them into an array.
        final int numImages = images.size();
        Image[] imageArray = new Image[numImages];
        for(int i = 0; i < numImages; i++){
            imageArray[i] = (Image) images.elementAt(i);
        }
        return imageArray;
    }

    // Retrieve fileName from this applet's archive file.
    protected Image extractImage(String fileName) throws RuntimeException {
        try {
            InputStream imageStream =
                       getClass().getResourceAsStream(fileName);
            Toolkit tk = Toolkit.getDefaultToolkit();
            byte imageBytes[] = new byte[imageStream.available()];
            imageStream.read(imageBytes);
            return tk.createImage(imageBytes);
        }
        catch(Exception e){
            throw new RuntimeException(e.toString());
        }
    }

    // Retrieve the given parameter from the applet's properties.
    protected String checkParameter(String parameter)
                               throws RuntimeException {
        String value = getParameter(parameter);
        if(value == null){
            throw new RuntimeException("Parameter: "+parameter+
                                       " is missing.");
        }
        return value;
    }

    protected ImageAnimator getAnimator(){
        return animator;
    }

    protected void setAnimator(ImageAnimator a){
        animator = a;
    }
```

Code 20.12   *(Continued)*

```
    // The image animator.
    private ImageAnimator animator;
    // Information on the parameters of this applet.
    private final int imagebaseParameter = 0, frametimeParameter = 1;
    private final String[][] parameterInfo = {
        {"imagebase", "string",
         "Base name of the image files in the JAR file."
        },
        {"frametime", "long", "Time in milliseconds between frames."},
    };
}
```

---

image files, the delay time between the images can be specified via the frametime parameter in the HTML file.

Code 20.13 shows the class responsible for the animation process. It uses a *double buffering* technique (described in Section 16.24.2) to reduce image flicker.

Code 20.13   Cycle through an array of images (`ImageAnimator.java`)

```
import java.awt.*;

    /* The constructor receives the array of images to be
     * cycled through. The time between frames may be varied
     * externally during the animator's life via its
     * setFrameTime method.
     *
     * Provide for 'suspend' and 'resume' operations by
     * polling the animationRunning attribute. Objects may suspend
     * and resume the thread in which the animator runs by
     * using its setAnimationRunning mutator.
     */
class ImageAnimator extends Canvas implements Runnable {
    public ImageAnimator(Image[] images){
        setImages(images);
    }

        // Repeatedly select a single image from the images array.
        // Draw this in an offscreen image before painting it on
        // the canvas.
    public void run(){
        // Create a full-size image for double buffering.
        final Dimension size = getSize();
        final Image offscreenImage = createImage(size.width,size.height);
        setOffscreenImage(offscreenImage);
        final Graphics offscreenGraphics = offscreenImage.getGraphics();

        // Obtain details of the list of images.
        final Image[] images = getImages();
```

(Continued)

Code 20.13   (*Continued*)

```
    final int numImages = images.length;
    // Which of the multiple images to show next.
    int nextImage = 0;

    while(true){
        try{
            // Clear the previous image and draw the new one off screen.
            offscreenGraphics.clearRect(0,0,size.width,size.height);
            offscreenGraphics.drawImage(images[nextImage],0,0,this);
            // Render it on the canvas.
            paint(getGraphics());

            // Sleep before selecting the next image.
            // This time may be externally varied.
            Thread.sleep(getFrameTime());
            // Make sure it is ok to continue.
            checkStatus();
            // Select the next image.
            nextImage++;
            if(nextImage >= numImages){
                // Wrap around.
                nextImage = 0;
            }
        }
        catch(Exception e){
        }
    }
}

    // Render the offscreen image on the canvas.
public void paint(Graphics g){
    Image image = getOffscreenImage();
    if(image != null){
        g.drawImage(image,0,0,this);
    }
}

public long getFrameTime(){
    return frameTime;
}

    // Allow the frame time to be set externally.
public void setFrameTime(long milliseconds){
    if(milliseconds >= 0L){
        frameTime = milliseconds;
    }
}

protected Image[] getImages(){
    return images;
}

protected void setImages(Image[] i){
```

Code 20.13 (*Continued*)

```
        images = i;
    }

    protected Image getOffscreenImage(){
        return offscreenImage;
    }

    protected void setOffscreenImage(Image i){
        offscreenImage = i;
    }

    // Check to see whether we are running or not.
    protected void checkStatus(){
        while(!getAnimationRunning()){
            try{
                wait();
            }
            catch(InterruptedException e){
            }
        }
    }

    public synchronized boolean getAnimationRunning(){
        return animationRunning;
    }

    public void setAnimationRunning(boolean r){
        synchronized(this){
            animationRunning = r;
            if(animationRunning){
                notify();
            }
            else{
                // This will suspend itself by polling via checkStatus.
            }
        }
    }

    // The full set of images to be animated.
    private Image[] images;
    // The offscreen image to be displayed by paint.
    private Image offscreenImage;
    // The time between image changes (milliseconds).
    private long frameTime = 100;
    // Whether the animation is suspended or not.
    private boolean animationRunning = true;
}
```

The ImageAnimator uses each iteration of its run method to render the next image on the graphics context of an offscreen Image object. It then passes this to its overridden paint method to render on the screen. The bites.jar file contains a

Figure 20.4   Successive images from a multi-image animation (`bites.jar`)

sequence of images representing a series of bites removed from the familiar apple image (Figure 20.4). On each iteration it sleeps for its current frame time, allowing this period to be varied externally, although the current implementation of the applet does not take advantage of this possibility.

20.10   The AppletContext Class

An Applet will have a limited means of interacting with the viewer in which it is run via an object which implements the `AppletContext` interface. The accessor for this object is `getAppletContext`. It is possible to associate a name with an applet via the `name` parameter of the applet tag. This makes it possible for one applet to make contact with another running in the viewer via AppletContext's `getApplet` method. This method takes a String parameter containing the name of another applet and returns an Applet reference. An `Enumeration` of all the applets known by the viewer is obtainable via the context's `getApplets` method.

The `showStatus` method of Applet is delegated to the same method in the applet's context, by default. This allows the applet to display a String in the browser's status area. This is commonly used when an applet is monitoring the mouse and needs to display position-sensitive information to the user. This approach can be used to implement an *image map*. An image map is an image in which particular areas are known as *hot spots*, that is, they will react in particular ways as the mouse is moved over them or a mouse button clicked over one of them. Reacting to mouse actions is the responsibility of the applet, rather than any special attribute of the image it displays. An applet might change color, play different sounds, or animate itself in different ways according to mouse interactions with the image map. This idea is illustrated in a very simple way by the applet in Code 20.14, which also uses one of the `showDocument` methods of AppletContext.

The `ImageMapApplet` class is based upon the JarImageApplet class illustrated in Code 20.9. In addition to reading an `image` parameter from the applet tag, it allows a `destination` parameter to indicate the URL of a document to be transferred to. The `setupMapper` method attaches a `MouseListener` and a `MouseMotionListener` to the applet. The applet regards the central area of the image as sensitive. If a mouse button is clicked within the central area, then the applet will ask the browser to transfer to the destination document. As the mouse is moved,

Code 20.14   An applet implementing a simple image map to transfer to a different URL
(`imagemap.html`)

```
import java.applet.*;
import java.awt.*;
import java.awt.event.*;
import java.net.*;
import java.io.*;

        // Illustrate the principles of image maps by drawing
        // an image and monitoring mouse movements over it.
        // The mouse's position is displayed in the applet's
        // status line within the browser.
        // Clicking in the central portion of the image causes a
        // transfer to the URL indicated by the 'destination' parameter.
public class ImageMapApplet extends Applet {
    public void init() throws RuntimeException {
        // Get the image name.
        String imageName = checkParameter(
                            parameterInfo[imageParameter][0]);
        setImage(extractImage(imageName));

        // Destination parameter is optional as there is a default.
        String whereTo = getParameter(
                            parameterInfo[destinationParameter][0]);
        if(whereTo != null){
            setDestination(whereTo);
        }
    }

    public void start(){
        // Setup the mouse listener objects.
        setupMapper();
    }

        // Scale the image to the full size of the applet.
    public void paint(Graphics g){
        final Dimension size = getSize();
        Image image = getImage();
        if(image != null){
            g.drawImage(image,0,0,size.width,size.height,this);
        }
    }

        // Supply information on the parameters used.
    public String[][] getParameterInfo(){
        return parameterInfo;
    }

        // Retrieve fileName from this applet's archive file.
    protected Image extractImage(String fileName)
                            throws RuntimeException {
        try {
            // Identify the resource via the applet's ClassLoader.
            InputStream imageStream =
                            getClass().getResourceAsStream(fileName);
```
(Continued)

Code 20.14   (*Continued*)

```
        // Read the whole Image as a single byte array.
        byte imageBytes[] = new byte[imageStream.available()];
        imageStream.read(imageBytes);
        // Turn the data into an Image.
        Toolkit tk = Toolkit.getDefaultToolkit();
        return tk.createImage(imageBytes);
    }
    catch(Exception e){
        throw new RuntimeException(e.toString());
    }
}

protected void setupMapper(){
    // Monitor mouse movements and display the (x,y) position
    // in the status line.
    addMouseMotionListener(new MouseMotionAdapter(){
        public void mouseMoved(MouseEvent e){
            if(inTransferArea(e)){
                showStatus("Goto: "+getDestination());
            }
            else{
                showStatus("");
            }
        }
    });

    // Detect button presses and transfer to a new URL if
    // the button is pressed in the central area of the image.
    addMouseListener(new MouseAdapter(){
        public void mousePressed(MouseEvent e){
            // Decide whether to transfer to the destination.
            if(inTransferArea(e)){
                try{
                    showStatus("Transferring.");
                    AppletContext context = getAppletContext();
                    context.showDocument(new URL(getDestination()));
                }
                catch(Exception except){
                    showStatus("Transfer failed.");
                }
            }
            else{
                showStatus("Outside the area.");
            }
        }
    });
}

    // Return true if the mouse is currently in the transfer area.
protected boolean inTransferArea(MouseEvent e){
    Dimension size = getSize();
    final int xBorder = size.width/4, yBorder = size.height/4;
    final int x = e.getX(), y = e.getY();
    if((x < xBorder) || (x > (size.width-xBorder))){
```

```
            return false;
        }
        else if((y < yBorder) || (y > (size.height-yBorder))){
            return false;
        }
        else{
            return true;
        }
    }

    // Retrieve the given parameter from the applet's properties.
    protected String checkParameter(String parameter)
                            throws RuntimeException {
        String value = getParameter(parameter);
        if(value == null){
            throw new RuntimeException("Parameter: "+
                                    parameter+" is missing.");
        }
        return value;
    }

    protected Image getImage(){
        return image;
    }

    protected void setImage(Image i){
        image = i;
    }

    protected String getDestination(){
        return destination;
    }

    protected void setDestination(String d){
        destination = d;
    }

    // The image to be displayed in the full size of the applet.
    private Image image;
    // Where to transfer to.
    private String destination = "http://www.javasoft.com/";
    // Provide information on the parameters expected by this applet.
    private final int imageParameter = 0, destinationParameter = 1;
    private final String[][] parameterInfo = {
        {"image", "string",
         "Name of the image, relative to the document base."
        },

        { "destination", "URL", "Where to transfer to.",
        },
    };
}
```

the `mouseMove` method constantly checks to see whether a button click would cause a transfer at that point. If it would, then it uses the `showStatus` method to display the destination, otherwise the status area is cleared. When a button is clicked, the `mouse-Pressed` method displays a message if the click is outside the area; otherwise it creates a URL object from the destination string and passes this to the applet context's `showDocument` method. A successful transfer will mean that the applet is stopped.

An image map can be as complex as you wish it to be. The difficult part is to work out where the current mouse position is in relationship to the displayed area. For instance, if the image displays a geographical area and you wish to display position-sensitive information on buildings or towns, the applet will need access to a lot of accurate coordinate information about the image. Particular care must be taken if the image could be scaled as a result of browser resizing, for instance.

20.11   Playing Audio Clips

The `java.applet` package provides some limited facilities for playing audio files in Applets, mainly via implementations of the `AudioClip` interface. The audio file formats supported are *aiff*, *au*, and *wav*, as well as MIDI-based formats *MIDI type 0*, *MIDI type 1*, and *RMF*. The Applet class has two `getAudioClip` methods which take URL objects and return an AudioClip. Version 1.2 of the API also added `newAudioClip` as a class method. In addition, the `play` methods of Applet and AppletContext take a URL and play the audio file associated with it. Implementations of AudioClip define three methods: `play`, `stop`, and `loop`. The `play` method always plays the clip from its beginning. Code 20.15 shows part of an applet that plays an audio clip each time the mouse enters the applet's area. The core of the class is based upon the AppleApplet class (shown in Code 20.6), so only the distinctive additions have been included here.

Code 20.15   Playing an AudioClip whenever the mouse enters the applet's area (`audio.html`)

```
import java.applet.*;
import java.awt.*;
import java.awt.event.*;
import java.net.*;

    // Display an image and play a sound clip whenever the
    // mouse enters the applet's area.
    // The image and sound are indicated by the parameters
    // "image" and "sound", respectively.
    // Both are retrieved relative to the document base.
public class AudioApplet extends Applet {
    // Set up the image and a MouseListener.
    public void init() throws RuntimeException {
        // Check that the parameters have been provided.
        for(int i = 0; i < parameterInfo.length; i++){
            checkParameter(parameterInfo[i][0]);
        }
        // Get the image.
        showStatus("Loading the image.");
```

Code 20.15   (*Continued*)

```
        setImage(retrieveImage(getParameter(
                          parameterInfo[imageParameter][0])));
        showStatus("");
        // Get the sound clip.
        showStatus("Loading the audio clip.");
        final AudioClip clip = getAudioClip(getDocumentBase(),
                      getParameter(parameterInfo[soundParameter][0]));
        addMouseListener(new MouseAdapter(){
            public void mouseEntered(MouseEvent e){
                // Play the audio clip.
                clip.play();
            }
        });
        showStatus("");
    }

    ...

    // Information on the parameters of this applet.
    private final int imageParameter = 0, soundParameter = 1;
    private final String[][] parameterInfo = {
        {"image", "image file",
         "Name of the image, relative to the document base."
        },
        {"sound", "audio file",
         "Name of the audio file to be played, relative to the document base."
        },
    };
}
```

The AudioClip object is created by retrieving the audio file named in the applet's sound parameter. Playing of the clip is delegated to the MouseListener which responds to MouseEntered events.

20.12   Applet Security Restrictions

Applet programs bear a strong similarity to the application programs described in Chapters 16 and 17. Aside from the absence of an explicit main method, applets use a similar set of classes for their visual appearance and programming. However, despite the similarities, there are some important differences between applets and non-applet Java programs. One of the most important differences—one that gives rise to the most frequently asked question about applets—is that an applet running in a browser is not allowed to access the file system of its host. This represents one particular element of a set of security restrictions that are applied to applets. The reasons behind these restrictions lie in the fundamental distinction between applets and non-applet programs: an applet is automatically run on a host without a specific request to do so from a user, and that host is almost always different from the server from which the applet was downloaded. Without security restrictions, users of applets would be open to a wide range of potentially damaging invasions of their system simply from browsing the Web. The main security restrictions fall into the following categories:

- Restricted access to the host file system.
- Restricted access to properties of the host system.
- Inability to create new processes on the host system.
- Restricted ability to create network connections.
- Inability to load libraries or define native method calls.
- Inability to create and manipulate different ThreadGroups.

We address some of these restrictions in the following sections.

Applet security is maintained by a `SecurityManager` object, whose role is to implement a particular *security policy*. Attempted violations of that policy result in a `SecurityException` exception being thrown. By default, an applet is regarded as *untrusted*, but security restrictions may be lifted for *trusted applets*.[6] A restriction applied to all applets is that, once set, a security manager cannot be removed or replaced. This prevents applets from circumventing a strict security policy by installing a more benign manager!

20.12.1   Access to the File System

Maintaining the privacy and integrity of a host's file system is considered to be an essential requirement of applet security. This restriction extends not merely to preventing untrusted applets from reading, writing, renaming, and deleting of files and directories but also determining whether a particular file or directory exists, its size, type, or date of last modification, for instance.

20.12.2   Access to System Properties

Access to the client system is limited in various ways. For instance, it is only possible to determine the values of a limited set of system properties from an applet via the static `getProperty` method of the `System` class. These are:

- `file.separator`
- `java.class.version, java.vendor, java.vendor.url, java.version`
- `line.separator`
- `os.arch, os.name, os.version`
- `path.separator`

As you might expect from the lack of access to the file system, input and output to and from the system console using `System.in`, `System.out`, and `System.err` is also prohibited.

20.12.3   Process Execution

An applet may not start a new process running on its host system. This prevents both malicious consumption of the host's resources and circumventing system access

---

[6] The details of how to create trusted applets are beyond the scope of this book.

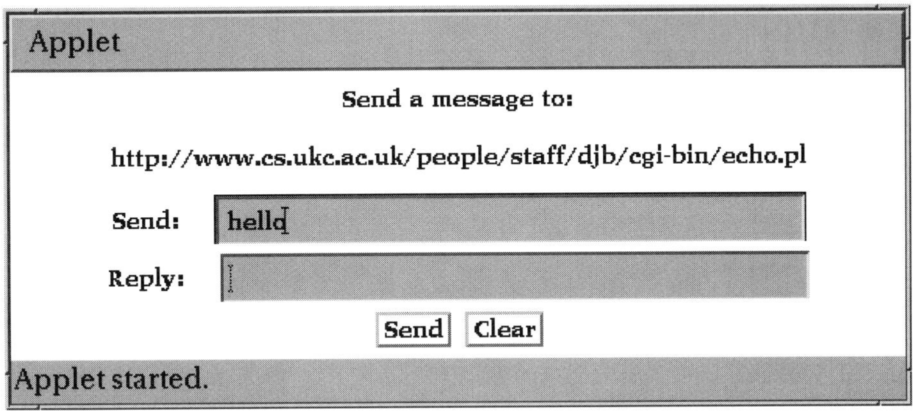

Figure 20.5   Sending a line to a CGI echo script (`cgiapplet.html`)

restrictions by running other programs that are not restricted in the same way as the applet. An applet may also not invoke the static `exit` method of the System class, since this would cause its containing viewer to terminate.

20.12.4   Network Connections

An applet is only allowed to open a network connection to the host named in the applet tag's `codebase` parameter, or the host that supplied its associated HTML file. This means that an applet cannot even open a network connection to the host on which it is running, unless it originated from there. Furthermore, the host name used when opening a connection must be in the same form as it appeared in the URL used to load the HTML file.

   An applet is also limited in which ports it is allowed to listen to and accept network connections on (see Chapter 19). Port numbers less than 1024 are usually regarded as privileged, and these are out of bounds to an applet. In addition, an applet may only accept a connection from its originating server, as with the limits on its opening connections.

   Applets are commonly used to interact with *CGI scripts* (see Section 19.7) on their originating server. Figure 20.5 shows a simple interface allowing a single line of text to be sent to a CGI script when the Send button is pressed and the reply is then displayed. The applet used to create this is shown in Code 20.16.

Code 20.16   An applet to interact with a CGI script (`CGIApplet.html`)

```
import java.applet.*;
import java.awt.*;
import java.awt.event.*;
import java.net.*;

        // This applet connects to a CGI script, sends a
        // QUERY_STRING to it and reads the response.
        // The URL of the script is specified by the "server" parameter.
```
(Continued)

Code 20.16   (*Continued*)

```
            // The key of the query string to send is specified by the "key"
            // parameter.
            // The value of the query to be sent is input to a TextLine
            // and the response is displayed in a second TextLine when
            // the applet's Send button is pressed.
            // The applet uses a CGIClient object to conduct the interaction
            // with the CGI server.
public class CGIApplet extends Applet {
        // Setup the visual appearance of the applet.
    public void init() throws RuntimeException {
            // Provide rows for a header Label, two TextFields and a pair
            // of buttons.
            final int rows = 5, cols = 1;
            setLayout(new GridLayout(rows,cols));
            setupHeader();
            setupTextFields();
            setupButtons();
            // Check that all of the parameters are present.
            for(int i = 0; i < parameterInfo.length; i++){
                checkParameter(parameterInfo[i][0]);
            }
    }

        // Supply information on the parameters used.
    public String[][] getParameterInfo(){
        return parameterInfo;
    }

        // Create a CGIClient to send line as a query string to
        // a server. Both the server and they key for the query string
        // are supplied as parameters (server and key) to the applet.
        // Normal network restrictions apply to the applet's ability
        // to connect to the server.
    protected void sendLineToServer(String line){
        try{
            // Obtain the server URL and CGI key to use from the
            // parameters of this applet.
            String server = getParameter(
                            parameterInfo[serverParameter][0]);
            if(server == null){
                throw new RuntimeException("Missing 'server' parameter.");
            }
            String serverKey = getParameter(
                            parameterInfo[keyParameter][0]);
            // Encode the line to be sent as the key's value.
            String keyValue = URLEncoder.encode(line);
            if(keyValue == null){
                throw new RuntimeException("Missing 'key' parameter.");
            }

            // Create a client of the server and send the query.
            CGIClient client = new CGIClient(
                            server+"?"+serverKey+"="+keyValue);
```

Code 20.16   (*Continued*)

```
            // Obtain and store the server's response in the reply line.
            String reply = client.getResponse();
            // Replace newline characters with spaces.
            reply = reply.replace('\n',' ');
            getReplyLine().setText(reply);
        }
        catch(Exception e){
            // Something went wrong. Show the exception as the reply.
            getReplyLine().setText(e.toString());
        }
    }

    protected void setupHeader(){
        String server = getParameter(
                            parameterInfo[serverParameter][0]);
        if(server != null){
            Label header = new Label("Send a message to:",Label.CENTER);
            add(header);
            header = new Label(server,Label.CENTER);
            add(header);
        }
    }

        // Provide Send and Reply lines of text.
    protected void setupTextFields(){
        Panel sendPanel = new Panel();
        sendPanel.add(new Label("Send: "));
        TextField sendLine = getSendLine();
        sendPanel.add(sendLine);
        // Pressing Enter in the field should cause the line to be sent.
        sendLine.addActionListener(new ActionListener(){
            public void actionPerformed(ActionEvent e){
                TextField send = getSendLine();
                sendLineToServer(send.getText());
            }
        });
        add(sendPanel);

        Panel replyPanel = new Panel();
        replyPanel.add(new Label("Reply: "));
        replyPanel.add(getReplyLine());
        add(replyPanel);
    }

        // Provide Send and Clear buttons. The Send action attempts
        // to send its contents to a server.
    protected void setupButtons(){
        Panel buttonPanel = new Panel();

        Button sendButton = new Button("Send");
        // Pressing this button should cause the line to be sent.
        sendButton.addActionListener(new ActionListener(){
```

                                                                        (*Continued*)

Code 20.16   (*Continued*)

```
        public void actionPerformed(ActionEvent e){
            TextField send = getSendLine();
            sendLineToServer(send.getText());
        }
    });
    buttonPanel.add(sendButton);

    Button clearButton = new Button("Clear");
    clearButton.addActionListener(new ActionListener(){
        public void actionPerformed(ActionEvent e){
            getSendLine().setText("");
            getReplyLine().setText("");
        }
    });
    buttonPanel.add(clearButton);

    add(buttonPanel);
}

    // Retrieve the given parameter from the applet's properties.
protected String checkParameter(String parameter)
                            throws RuntimeException {
    String value = getParameter(parameter);
    if(value == null){
        throw new RuntimeException("Parameter: "+
                                parameter+" is missing.");
    }
    return value;
}

protected TextField getSendLine(){
    return sendLine;
}

protected TextField getReplyLine(){
    return replyLine;
}

final int lineWidth = 40;
private TextField sendLine = new TextField("",lineWidth),
                replyLine = new TextField("",lineWidth);

// Provide information on the parameters expected by this applet.
private final int serverParameter = 0, keyParameter = 1;
private final String[][] parameterInfo = {
    { "server", "URL", "The server URL of the CGI script to contact.",
    },
    { "key",     "String",
      "The query string key name expected by the CGI script for input.",
    },
};
}
```

Code 20.17   An HTML file to deliver CGIApplet

```
<html>
<head>
<title>A Cgi Applet</title>
</head>
<body>
    <applet code="CGIApplet.class"
            archive="cgiapplet.jar"
            width=475 height=180
    >
    An applet to send a message to a CGI script located on
    its originating server.
    <param name="server"
            value="http://www.cs.ukc.ac.uk/people/staff/djb/cgi-bin/echo.pl"
    >
    The key expected by the script in its QUERYSTRING
    <param name="key" value="Echo">
    </applet>
</body>
</html>
```

It uses an object of the `CGIClient` class to perform its interaction with the server, and this class was described in Section 19.7.1. The URL of the server on which the CGI script is held is supplied to the applet via a parameter in the HTML file. Similarly, the key of the query string is parameterized in this way. Code 20.17 shows such a file.

Pressing the Send button in the example illustrated in Figure 20.5 would cause the following query to be sent:

```
http://www.cs.ukc.ac.uk/people/staff/djb/cgi-bin/echo.pl?Echo=hello%0A
```

Of course, the `server` parameter in this particular example will only work if the applet was served from a URL involving `www.cs.ukc.ac.uk`, otherwise the applet will cause a security exception to be thrown.

20.13   Review

Here are the main points that we have covered in the preceding sections:

- Applets make it possible to use Java to provide active content within a Web page.
- Applets are typically built from classes defined in the AWT and Swing packages.
- An applet program has no user-defined main method.
- An applet is run in an applet viewer via an HTML file.
- An applet's class and constructor must both have public access.

- Applet initialization is normally carried out in its overriding `init` method rather than a constructor.
- A Java archive (JAR) file may be used to bundle an applet and its resources in a single file.
- An applet may be externally parameterized via `<param>` tags within its associated HTML file.
- An applet is able to load and play audio files.
- A number of security restrictions apply to applets, such as lack of access to the host system.

PART

VI

Java for Simulation

Simulation

S imulations represent an important set of object-oriented programs. Object-oriented concepts, such as inheritance, lend themselves well to event-driven simulations and the creation of software components that may be reused in many different simulation applications. In this final chapter, therefore, we deal with the basic elements of event-driven (discrete) simulation. We do this mainly through the presentation of two case studies. Through the presentation of the case studies, we also endeavor to show some of the decision-making processes that must be gone through in turning an open-ended problem statement into an implementation.

21.1 Using Simulation as a Modeling Tool

Simulation is important because it provides us with the opportunity to efficiently model aspects of the real world. We can often gain valuable insights into the way things behave, or will behave, if we can create a model and build a simulation based upon that model. This can have significant benefits—particularly financial benefits. For instance, it is typically much cheaper to build a simulation of a new aircraft or racing car design than it is to build the real thing. Furthermore, it is much safer to experiment with a simulation of a safety-critical system, such as a nuclear power station, than it is to experiment with the real thing. The simulation can be used to test the effects of pushing the system to its limits (and beyond) without endangering life. However, it is important to understand that a simulation is only as good as the underlying model upon which it is based. A simulation of traffic movement for a proposed traffic management scheme that assumes constant hourly rates of traffic flow into and out of a city might give satisfying results, but they will not be accurate results. Instead, the model of traffic flow must be based upon realistic information that is related to typical patterns of vehicle use during working and leisure hours, with appropriate variations for weekdays and weekends.

21.2 Continuous and Discrete Simulation

At the heart of most simulations is the passage of time. Simulations may be classified in two ways according to the way in which they view the passage of time: *continuous simulations* and *discrete simulations*. In a continuous simulation, time ticks past at a regular rate that is applicable to the particular simulation scenario. If we are modeling the growth of an insect population in a field, time might pass at the regular rate of one day per tick. If we are modeling the growth of a bacterial infection, it might pass at the rate of one minute per tick. At each tick, all the objects in the simulation are informed of the passage of time and updated accordingly. The tick length must be carefully chosen so that the step-like illusion of time that it creates does not have a significant impact on the validity of the simulation. It must also be computationally efficient. There is little point choosing a tick rate of one day to simulate the growth of a peat bog, for instance; a tick rate in years would be more reasonable!

In a discrete simulation, time passes at an irregular rate that is determined by the primary events of interest in the simulation—the arrival of a car at a junction, the change of a traffic light, a pedestrian pressing a button at a street crossing, and so on. In a discrete simulation we are only interested in the times at which particular events occur, and not the time between events. This might mean that the clock in a discrete simulation makes a five-second leap between two events at one point, but a one-second leap between two similar events at a later point.

We can compare the difference between these two approaches by considering how they might both simulate the movement of gas molecules in a container. In a continuous simulation, at each clock tick the molecule objects would update their positions according to their current speed and direction. Molecules which collide with each other or hit the walls of the container would calculate their new energy level, speed, and direction ready for the next clock tick. In a discrete simulation, the only events of interest might be the collisions. The set of predictable collisions for the molecules would be calculated and scheduled as a series of events. As each collision event occurs, a new set of collisions is calculated and added to the scheduled list of events. The events are ordered by their time of occurrence and, as each event occurs, the simulation clock is advanced to reflect this.

In the remainder of this chapter, we shall concern ourselves only with discrete simulations. We look at the way in which events are scheduled and ordered and the simulation driven by the occurrence of events. We shall do this by examining a case study based upon the behavior of an ice cream vendor.

21.3   Events and the Simulation Scheduler

In all event-driven simulations, we shall need at least two classes: `Event` and `Scheduler`. We shall call these the *simulation classes* of the problem. The Event class is the super class of all events of significance in the simulation. From it we shall derive sub classes that signify the events that drive the simulation from step to step. The major role of the Event class is to record the time at which a particular event is to be performed, and to provide an abstract `perform` method for when the event occurs. Code 21.1 defines this class.

A common theme of Event objects is that they cause further events to be scheduled when performed. For this reason, the `perform` method is passed a reference to a scheduler.

Code 21.1   The super class of all events in a simulation (`Event.java`)

```java
    // The super class of all events in a simulation.
    // Maintain the time of the event and provide an abstract
    // perform method for the scheduler to use.
abstract public class Event {
    public Event(long eventTime){
        setWhen(eventTime);
    }

        // Each type of event defines its own behavior when triggered.
    abstract public void perform(Scheduler s);

    public long getWhen(){
        return when;
    }

    protected void setWhen(long w){
        when = w;
    }

    // When this event is due to happen.
    private long when;
}
```

The Scheduler class maintains a record of the current simulation time and a queue of events that have not yet occurred, ordered by the time at which they are to take place. Its `run` method repeatedly sends a `perform` message to the Event at the head of the queue. Code 21.2 defines this class.

From the definition of Scheduler's `run` method we can see the way in which the simulation clock changes at an irregular rate, according to the time at which each next event is set to occur, using `setTime`. Note that the time of the next event might be the same as the current time on the clock, signifying coincident events, but we do not attempt to distinguish this case.

Code 21.2   The scheduler for an event-driven simulation (`Scheduler.java`)

```java
import java.util.*;

        // The Scheduler for an event-driven simulation.
public class Scheduler {
        // Continuously process the events in the queue,
        // until stopTime.
    public void run(long stopTime){
        ArrayList events = getEvents();
        long now = getTime();

        // Terminate if there are no more events or if time
        // has expired.
        while((events.size() > 0) && (now <= stopTime)){
```

Code 21.2   (*Continued*)

```
        // Obtain the next event
        Event e = (Event) events.remove(0);

        setTime(e.getWhen());
        now = getTime();
        if(now <= stopTime){
            if(getTraceEvents()){
                // Print a trace.
                System.out.println("=> "+e);
            }
            // Give the event a reference to the scheduler.
            e.perform(this);
        }
    }
}


    // Add the given event to the appropriate place in
    // the event queue. The queue is ordered by event time.
public void schedule(Event newEvent) throws RuntimeException {
    long eventTime = newEvent.getWhen();
    if(eventTime >= getTime()){
        ArrayList events = getEvents();
        final int numEvents = events.size();
        for(int index = 0; index < numEvents; index++){
            Event e = (Event) events.get(index);
            if(eventTime < e.getWhen()){
                // Insert the new one here.
                events.add(index,newEvent);
                return;
            }
        }
        // Place it at the end.
        events.add(newEvent);
    }
    else{
        throw new RuntimeException(
                    "Attempt to schedule an event too late.");
    }
}

public boolean getTraceEvents(){
    return traceEvents;
}

public void setTraceEvents(boolean trace){
    traceEvents = trace;
}

public long getTime(){
    return time;
}
    // Make sure time only moves forward.
```

(*Continued*)

Code 21.2   (*Continued*)

```
    protected void setTime(long t) throws RuntimeException {
        if(t >= getTime()){
            time = t;
        }
        else{
            throw new RuntimeException(
                "Attempt to set the clock back to "+t+" from "+getTime());
        }
    }

    protected ArrayList getEvents(){
        return events;
    }

    // Whether to trace events or not.
    private boolean traceEvents = true;
    // The event queue ordered by event time.
    private ArrayList events = new ArrayList();
    // The current time.
    private long time = 0L;
}
```

An important part of the design of the run method is that an event is always removed from the queue before it is performed. The reason for this is that its performance is likely to result in further events being scheduled and it is conceivable that these new events might occur at the same time as the current event. Depending upon the implementation of the schedule method, this could mean that they are added to the queue in front of the current event, which would result in the wrong event being removed if removal is left until after the current event has been completed. In fact, this cannot arise in the example in Code 21.2 because new events are always added after existing events scheduled for the same time.

The implementation of the schedule method in Code 21.2 ensures that a new event is never scheduled for a time that has already passed. If this occurs, then it indicates an incorrectly created Event object, and results in an exception being thrown. For valid events, the correct insertion position in the queue is identified to ensure that the events remain strictly ordered according to the time at which they should occur.

The Event and Scheduler classes provide the fundamental framework upon which particular event-driven simulations may be built to model specific scenarios, such as traffic simulations, molecule movements, buying ice creams, and so on. In the next sections, we shall look at the particular classes of events of interest in a case study concerning an ice cream vendor.

21.4   Case Study—An Ice Cream Vendor

In this and the next few sections, we shall consider the following problem and design a discrete event-driven simulation based upon it.

> An ice cream vendor serves customers. Customers arrive at irregular intervals, wishing to buy a random number of ice creams. The vendor is only able to serve one customer at a time. Customers who arrive when the vendor is busy must join a queue which has no limit to its length. The length of time it takes to serve a customer is directly proportional to the number of ices they wish to buy.

As with other programs, our first task is to identify the major classes and objects inherent in the problem, and the interactions between them. The two obvious classes are Vendor and Customer. You might like to argue that IceCream should also be a class, with an attribute such as flavor but no behavior.[1] Whether it should be or not depends upon the level at which you wish to study this particular problem. We shall call Vendor and Customer the *primary classes* of the problem. In a program that is not a simulation, the interaction between the vendor and customer objects is probably limited to the customers requesting some number of ices from the vendor. A simulation enriches such an application by allowing us to model the time-dependent aspects of the scenario, in particular the fact that the vendor's processing of a customer's request involves the passage of time, during which other customers might arrive and be forced to queue. We shall explore these issues shortly.

For any simulation, it is important to define the information we wish to determine from the simulation, because this will influence the design of the participating classes, the interactions between them, and the attributes they must maintain. For this case study, we might wish to calculate the mean time a customer must wait in the queue before being served. In a particular context, this information might be used by a theme park to determine whether a single vendor is able to satisfactorily serve a particular flow of customers, or whether there is sufficient capacity in the system to warrant allowing multiple ice cream vendors to sell their wares.

In the following sections, we shall continue to explore this case study by introducing classes common to discrete simulations and specific sub classes that relate to this particular scenario.

21.4.1   Events in the Ice Cream Case Study

In a non-simulation application, interaction between objects of the primary classes would typically involve a Customer object simply sending a serveMe message to a Vendor object, with an actual argument value corresponding to the number of ice creams required. Completion of the serveMe method would typically indicate that the ice creams had been delivered. Such a model of interaction allows for no concept of the passage of time, during which intervening events might occur. When writing simulations, therefore, it is often necessary to rethink the normal form of *message-response* interaction and replace it with a pair of events representing *initiation* of an action and *completion* of that same action. What this means for the ice cream scenario is that we replace the serveMe message from the customer to the vendor with a Serve initiation event and a FinishServing completion event. Separation of these two events in time allows events for new customers arriving to occur in between. This suggests that we will need to define an Arrival event for customers.

---

[1] Apart from melting!

Arrival, Serve, and FinishServing represent the complete set of Event sub classes that we need to drive the simulation.

How will these events work together in practice? Here are the main actions associated with each event:

- Arrival—A new Customer object is created and passed to the vendor. If the vendor is free, then a Serve event will be scheduled to indicate that the customer is to be served immediately. If the vendor is occupied with another customer, then the newly arriving customer will not be served immediately. This suggests that a queue of waiting customers will need to be maintained by the vendor.
- Serve—Its primary purpose is to schedule a FinishServing event at an appropriately distant time in the future—the problem description states that the length of time it takes to serve a customer is proportional to the number of ice creams they wish to buy.
- FinishServing—Indicates that the vendor has finished serving the customer at the head of the queue and is now free to serve the next. The vendor removes the current customer from the head of the queue and must schedule a Serve event for the next in line. If there is no waiting customer, then the vendor will remain idle until the next customer arrives.

It is important to distinguish between the queue of Arrival events in the Scheduler—signifying customers that have not yet arrived but will at a future time—and the queue of customers in the vendor—the result of Arrival events having occurred in the past. Furthermore, it is important to distinguish between the *construction* of an event—which represents the scheduling of a particular action that is to occur at some time in the future—and the *performance* of that event. An event's construction causes it to be added to the scheduler's queue of events. An event's performance happens when it reaches the head of the queue and it is sent a `perform` message.

We have now identified the primary classes of the problem—Vendor and Customer—and the simulation classes—Arrival, Serve, and FinishServing (in addition to Event and Scheduler). We have also looked at the basic tasks to be undertaken as each event occurs. One of the hardest things to get right in the design of the simulation classes is to ensure that each has access to all the other objects that it needs to fulfill its role. For instance, a Serve event will need to ensure that the associated customer is able to interact with the vendor in order to buy the required number of ice creams. In the following sections, we shall examine the different possibilities for achieving this, and the implementation of each of the event classes that we have identified for this case study.

21.4.2 The Arrival Class

Arrival events will be of particular importance in the ice cream simulation because they are the ultimate cause of all other events. If no customers arrive, then there will be no Serve events and no FinishServing events generated.[2] One of the factors

---

[2] The only event will be the ice cream vendor going out of business!

affecting the accuracy of this particular model will be how we determine the arrival rate of customers and the distribution of arrival times. It is common to describe the distribution of arrival times in a simulation such as this using a *Poisson distribution*. This is an exponential distribution in which the random time difference between successive arrivals may be calculated with a formula such as $gap = -mean \times \log_e r$, where *mean* is the mean time difference that we want between arrivals and r is a random number in the range $[0\ldots1]$. For a properly accurate simulation, the mean arrival rate would vary according to the time of day and the weather conditions, but we will not attempt to include this level of accuracy in our simulation.

There are two ways in which the arrival events could be scheduled:

- Either, before the start of the simulation, we could generate the full set of customer arrival events for the duration of the simulation.
- Or, at the point that each arrival event is performed, calculate the time of the next and schedule it.

Both approaches are possible in our particular simulation. In general, however, it will not always be possible to precalculate all the arrival times in advance, since other factors inherent in the simulation could easily affect the scheduling of these future events. We have adopted the latter approach of scheduling the next arrival each time an arrival event is performed.

The performance of an arrival event means that a new customer has arrived at the vendor. A new Customer object must be created, therefore, and passed to the vendor to deal with. This means that the Arrival event object must be able to refer to the Vendor object at the time it is performed. How does it obtain a reference to the vendor in order to enable it to interact with the newly created customer? There are at least three possibilities:

- The vendor could be globally available to arrival events, perhaps as a `public static` reference in the Vendor class, or via a static `getVendor` method in the same. The problem with this approach is that it might limit the inclusion of multiple Vendor objects in the simulation. It also ties the reference to be made available via a particular class name—Vendor—which limits the potential for creating sub classes of a basic Vendor class.
- The vendor could be made available via some other object in the program that is already known to Arrival objects, such as the Scheduler object which is passed as an argument to the `perform` method. The problem with this is that is makes the scheduler more specific to a particular simulation than we would like it to be. At the moment, the Scheduler class is scenario-independent, and so re-usable in other simulations.
- The vendor could be made available via the constructor of the Arrival class. This frees the class from too much detailed knowledge about other classes in the system and has the advantage that it does not preclude multiple vendors from being present in the simulation.

We shall use the third approach, of passing the vendor to the constructor of the Arrival object. Code 21.3 shows our implementation of Arrival, which extends the Event super class. When an arrival event is performed, it schedules the next arrival (according to a Poisson distribution), creates the arriving customer, and informs the

```java
        // A customer arrives to buy ice creams.
public class Arrival extends Event {
    public Arrival(long eventTime,Vendor v){
        super(eventTime);
        vendor = v;
    }

        // On arrival, schedule the next arrival and add the customer
        // to the vendor's queue.
    public void perform(Scheduler scheduler){
        long now = scheduler.getTime();

        Vendor vendor = getVendor();
        // Schedule the next arrival.
        scheduler.schedule(new Arrival(nextArrivalTime(now),vendor));

        // Inform the vendor.
        vendor.arrival(new Customer());
    }

    public String toString(){
        return getWhen()+" Arrival";
    }

        // Calculate when the next customer should arrive.
    protected long nextArrivalTime(long now){
        // Simulate a Poisson distribution of arrivals.
        return now + (long)(-meanArrivalTime*Math.log(Math.random()));
    }

    protected Vendor getVendor(){
        return vendor;
    }

    // From whom the ice creams are bought.
    private final Vendor vendor;
    // The mean time between customer arrivals.
    private final double meanArrivalTime = 60.0;
}
```

vendor that a new customer has arrived. Notice how this event is simply a means to schedule further events and to bring the main participants of the primary classes together. It plays no role in the actual purchase of ice creams or queuing of customers. These tasks are left to the customer and vendor to organize between them. This separation of roles between the primary classes and the simulation classes is an important one to bear in mind when designing the different categories of class in a simulation.

21.4.3　The Serve Event

The Serve event class is much simpler than the Arrival class since it is not required to schedule any future events or construct any new objects. Its performance represents

Code 21.4 Enable the customer to be served by the vendor (`Serve.java`)

```
        // A customer reaches the head of the queue to be served.
public class Serve extends Event {
    public Serve(long eventTime,Customer c, Vendor v){
        super(eventTime);
        vendor = v;
        customer = c;
    }

        // Ask the vendor to serve the customer.
    public void perform(Scheduler scheduler){
        getVendor().serve(getCustomer());
    }

    public String toString(){
        return getWhen()+" Serve";
    }

    protected Customer getCustomer(){
        return customer;
    }

    protected Vendor getVendor(){
        return vendor;
    }

    private final Customer customer;
    private final Vendor vendor;
}
```

the point at which a customer arrives at the head of the vendor's queue and is able to request their desired number of ice creams. As we saw with the Arrival class, its purpose is to enable objects of the primary classes, Vendor and Customer, to interact with each other. It receives a reference to both the Vendor and Customer objects in its constructor, therefore, and brings these together when performed. Code 21.4 shows its implementation.

21.4.4   The FinishServing Event

A FinishServing event is scheduled to be performed at some time after its paired Serve event; the gap between them represents the time taken by the vendor to serve the associated customer. In our simulation, this is simply proportional to the number of ice creams bought. This Serve-FinishServing event pairing is the characteristic simulation replacement of the message-response interaction between two objects that we find in non-simulation applications. As with the Serve event, a FinishServing event schedules no further events and creates no new objects. Its role is simply to inform the vendor that the current customer is leaving so that the vendor can serve the next in line. Code 21.5 shows its implementation.

Code 21.5 Notify the vendor that a customer has left (`FinishServing.java`)

```
        // A customer leaves after buying ice creams.
public class FinishServing extends Event {
    public FinishServing(long eventTime,Vendor v){
        super(eventTime);
        vendor = v;
    }

        // Let the vendor know that they have left.
    public void perform(Scheduler scheduler){
        getVendor().departure();
    }

    public String toString(){
        return getWhen()+" FinishServing";
    }

    protected Vendor getVendor(){
        return vendor;
    }

    private final Vendor vendor;
}
```

21.4.5   The Vendor and Customer Classes

We complete our description of the ice cream simulation with a discussion of the Vendor and Customer classes. Customers play an entirely passive role in this simulation and it is the Vendor class that contains the active elements. A Customer object simply maintains details of how many ice creams it wishes to buy. This is calculated when a customer is created. Code 21.6 shows its definition.

A simple random number is used for the ice cream calculation. A more accurate simulation would use a more realistic and complex formula.

Code 21.6 Record the number of ice creams to be bought

```
    // Calculate how many ice creams are required, and return
    // this value when required.
public class Customer {
    public int getNumIces(){
        return numIceCreams;
    }

    // Limit their gluttony.
    final int maxIceCreams = 10;
    // They must buy at least one.
    private final int numIceCreams = 1+(int)(Math.random()*maxIceCreams);
}
```

The Vendor class is at the heart of the simulation. It is responsible for maintaining a queue of customers, in arrival order, and for scheduling the Serve and FinishServing events each time a new customer reaches the head of the queue. Each of the event classes described in Section 21.4.2 send a message to the vendor notifying it of the need to take a particular action in response to the event's occurrence. These messages inform the vendor of a new customer's arrival, that it is time to start serving a particular customer, and that it is time to stop serving the customer at the head of the queue. Code 21.7 contains a full implementation for the Vendor class.

Code 21.7   The Ice Cream Vendor (`Vendor.java`)

```java
    // An Ice Cream Vendor which maintains a queue of waiting
    // customers. The time to serve a customer depends upon the
    // number of ices they require.
class Vendor {
    public Vendor(Scheduler s){
        scheduler = s;
    }

    // Add this customer to the tail of the queue.
    public void arrival(Customer customer){
        Queue q = getQueue();
        q.add(customer);
        if(q.size() == 1){
            // Serve this customer now.
            takeNextInLine();
        }
    }

    // Serve this customer.
    public void serve(Customer customer){
        Scheduler s = getScheduler();
        // How long before this customer leaves?
        long saleTime = timeToSell(customer.getNumIces());
        s.schedule(new FinishServing(s.getTime()+saleTime,this));
    }

    // We have just finished serving the customer at the head
    // of the queue.
    public void departure() throws RuntimeException {
        Queue q = getQueue();
        if(q.size() > 0){
            // Discard head of queue.
            q.next();
            takeNextInLine();
        }
        else{
            throw new RuntimeException(
                    "Last customer is missing from the vendor's queue.");
        }
    }
```

(Continued)

Code 21.7   (*Continued*)

```
      // Serve the person at the head of the queue, if any.
   protected void takeNextInLine(){
      System.out.println(queue.size()+" customer(s) waiting.");
      Queue q = getQueue();
      if(q.size() > 0){
         Customer customer = (Customer) queue.peek();
         Scheduler s = getScheduler();
         // Serve the customer now.
         s.schedule(new Serve(s.getTime(),customer,this));
      }
   }

      // How long it will take to sell the given number
      // of ice creams.
   protected long timeToSell(int numIceCreams){
      return numIceCreams*timePerIceCream;
   }

   protected Queue getQueue(){
      return queue;
   }

   protected Scheduler getScheduler(){
      return scheduler;
   }

      // How long to serve a single ice cream, in seconds?
   private final long timePerIceCream = 15;
      // The queue of customers.
   private final Queue queue = new Queue();
   private final Scheduler scheduler;
}
```

When the vendor receives notification of a new customer, via its `arrival` method, its response is to add the customer to the queue it maintains. It then needs to determine whether it should serve the new customer straight away or not. If, after adding the customer the queue contains a single item, then the vendor assumes that it was not already occupied serving another and it calls its own `takeNextInLine` method. This schedules a Serve event for the current time, which it obtains from the scheduler.

Exercise 21.1   Before reading further, consider why we might have chosen to schedule a Serve event at this point, rather than scheduling a FinishServing event straight away. What information are we interested in learning from the simulation?

Code 21.8 Creation of the ice cream simulation (`IceCreamMain.java`)

```
public class IceCreamMain {
    public static void main(String[] args){
        // The single scheduler for all events.
        final Scheduler scheduler = new Scheduler();
        final Vendor vendor = new Vendor(scheduler);

        // Schedule the first arrival to kick things off.
        scheduler.schedule(new Arrival(0L,vendor));

        // When to stop - in seconds.
        final long stopTime = 3600L;
        scheduler.run(stopTime);
    }
}
```

When the vendor receives a `serve` message, this indicates that a Serve event has been performed. This requires it to schedule a future FinishServing event, based upon the length of time it will take to serve the given customer. We have made a simplistic assumption that all ice creams take the same length of time to serve.[3]

Exercise 21.2   Why do we not remove the customer being served from the head of the queue at this point?

The performance of a FinishServing event causes a `departure` message to be sent to the vendor. The customer being served is still at the head of the queue since we deliberately did not remove them when the Serve event was performed. They are now removed and the queue checked to see whether another customer is waiting. If there is one, then a further Serve event is scheduled, otherwise the vendor will remain inactive until it receives its next `arrival` message.

21.4.6   Running the Simulation

To complete the simulation, Code 21.8 shows the main method that is used to create and initiate it. Notice that the whole simulation is initiated by seeding it with a single arrival event. When performed, this event will schedule the next arrival and indirectly cause a Serve event to be scheduled for the first customer, and so on until the stop time is reached. Below is part of a sample run for a short portion of the simulation. The output includes the time of the event, its type, and the length of the

---

[3] One argument in favor of the inclusion of an `IceCream` class as a primary class might be that it would allow us to program more complex behavior, such as different amounts of time to serve different types of ice cream, and varying popularity of different ices.

vendor's queue each time it is examined to see if there is another customer to be
served.

```
=> 0 Arrival
1 customer(s) waiting.
=> 0 Serve
=> 12 Arrival
=> 15 FinishServing
1 customer(s) waiting.
=> 15 Serve
=> 90 FinishServing
0 customer(s) waiting.
=> 104 Arrival
1 customer(s) waiting.
=> 104 Serve
=> 155 Arrival
=> 174 Arrival
=> 212 Arrival
=> 239 FinishServing
3 customer(s) waiting.
...
11 customer(s) waiting.
=> 3482 Serve
=> 3536 Arrival
=> 3555 Arrival
=> 3587 FinishServing
12 customer(s) waiting.
=> 3587 Serve
=> 3600 Arrival
```

Notice the way in which further customers often arrive between the Serve and Finish-
Serving event pairing. This explains the importance of retaining the current customer
at the head of the queue while they are being served. The length of the customer
queue is used to determine whether the vendor is free or not when a new customer arrives. If the customer currently being served had been removed when the
Serve event was performed, then the vendor would appear to be free on the arrival
of a new customer and a second Serve event would be incorrectly scheduled before
the first's FinishServing event had been performed. Retaining the current customer
in the queue means that we do not need a separate `occupied` attribute in the
vendor.

Exercise 21.3 Create an event-driven simulation in which customers arrive at a
bank. The bank should have multiple cashiers who are able to serve any customer.
If a cashier is not free when a customer arrives, then the customers must wait in a
first-in, first-out queue. Customers arrive according to a Poisson distribution with a
mean arrival time of 120 seconds. Customers spend a random amount of time with
a cashier, between 60 and 600 seconds (this does not follow a Poisson distribution).
You may reuse the `Event` and `Scheduler` classes of the Ice Cream simulation to
help with this exercise.

At the end of the simulation, report the mean time customers spent waiting in
the queue.

21.5   Review

Here are the main points that we have covered in the preceding sections:

- Simulation is an important tool to use in understanding dynamic systems.
- Object-oriented languages are well suited to creating simulations.
- In a continuous simulation, time passes at a constant rate.
- In an event-driven simulation, time passes at an irregular rate determined by the time when each event of interest occurs.
- In an event-driven simulation, a scheduler maintains a queue of events ordered by time of occurrence.
- An event object keeps a record of when it should occur.
- Events in a simulation often occur according to a Poisson distribution.
- The Scheduler class and Event super class are typically independent of a particular simulation scenario.
- Distinct sub classes of Event should be created for each type of event that can occur within a particular scenario.
- The passage of time required by an action is often marked by separate Start-Action and Stop-Action events.
- Care should be taken not to couple the event sub classes too closely to the primary classes of the problem.

21.5.1   Extended Case Study—A Gas Station

In order to reinforce the ideas introduced in previous sections, we shall tackle a larger simulation that illustrates the way in which common themes often occur in such programs. In doing so, we shall see how to re-use the Event and Scheduler classes, as we claimed it would be possible to do. This simulation revolves around the day-to-day activities of a gas station.

> A new gas station is due to open shortly. The owners wish to simulate its operation in order to determine whether certain operating parameters they have in mind for it are correct. In particular, they are interested in discovering what typical waiting times for drivers are likely to be, depending on the number of cashiers employed. They also plan to schedule a tanker delivery to refill the tanks every eight hours, and wish to discover if they are likely to run out of fuel before it arrives.

Once we have a basic understanding of the purpose of the simulation, we can begin to investigate the ways in which the gas station might operate. Here is a typical scenario, from driver arrival to departure.

> A driver arrives at the gas station requiring a random amount of fuel of a particular type. The driver selects a suitable pump and requests delivery of the fuel. Once the delivery is complete, the driver pays an available cashier. Payment will be by either cash, credit card, or check. Once payment is complete, the driver leaves the gas station.

From this we can begin to identify the primary classes of the problem domain: Driver, Pump, Cashier. These will interact in various ways: a Driver requests fuel from a Pump and a Pump delivers the fuel; the Driver pays the Cashier in some way. What other classes might be needed?

- Will it be necessary to have a Fuel class—is it necessary to model different types of fuel?
- Do the different payment methods require their own classes?
- Do we need a class for the gas station itself? This might contain collection objects for the pumps and cashiers, for instance.
- Are there any further classes implicit in the statement; what about the tanks from which the pumps draw their fuel? It has been stated that one of the goals of the simulation is to test whether the proposed fuel supply strategy is adequate, so we shall certainly need to model fuel levels in some way. To this end, we should keep a Tank class distinct from Pump.

What about the simulation classes required; what are the markers of the passage of time in the simulation?

- Drivers will arrive and spend time in the gas station before leaving.
- Delivery of fuel from the pumps will take time, and we are required to monitor the amount of time drivers spend waiting for cashiers to become available.
- In order to determine whether a particular fuel supply strategy is acceptable or not, we shall need to schedule events to model the arrival of tankers to refill the tanks.

From looking at these issues, it is clear that we need some more information about the parameters of the simulation to gain a clearer picture of how it might be programmed. In real life, we would need to investigate the whole problem area in detail in order to gain a proper understanding of it. We would also need to obtain further information from the customer. In order to provide some answers to some of these questions, here are some imaginary timings and other parameters that the simulation will be based upon.

- Drivers arrive according to a Poisson distribution with a mean arrival spacing of 60 seconds.
- The payment methods used are 40% by cash, 40% by credit card, and 20% by check.
- Transactions take 20 seconds for cash, 40 seconds for credit card, and 90 seconds for check.
- A cashier is only able to serve one driver at a time.
- Unleaded fuel is required by 50% of drivers, leaded fuel by 30%, and diesel by 20%.
- On average, a driver requiring unleaded or leaded fuel requires 80 liters, whereas an average diesel driver requires 200 liters.
- The gas station has one tank for each type of fuel.
- Each fuel tank has a capacity of 90,000 liters and is full at the start of the simulation.
- There are six pumps connected to the unleaded tank, two to the leaded tank, and two to the diesel tank. Two of the unleaded pumps are paired with the leaded pump and one is paired with a diesel pump. There are three unpaired

unleaded pumps and one unpaired diesel pump. A paired pump is only able to dispense one type of fuel at a time.

- A tanker will always be able to fill all the tanks to capacity.

You might be able to think of other issues that we have not addressed in this list. For instance, how long does it take to refill the tanks from the tanker, and is the gas station able to continue normal deliveries while this is going on? A proper analysis of the system would need to consider these and other questions, and you should feel free to amend and correct the description as you think fit.

From the possible primary classes we have identified, we shall build the simulation around interactions between the two main classes: `GasStation` and `Driver`. Most of the events in this simulation represent things that happen to a driver and they occur within the context of the gas station—the two classes will have many interactions. When a new Driver object is created as a result of a DriverArrival event, that driver will receive a reference to the gas station object, and progress through the simulation via interactions with it. During this progression, the driver will also receive a reference to an assigned pump and then to an assigned cashier as other events are triggered for it.

In order to develop this case study further, we shall separate the development of the classes into the natural division of event classes and primary classes. This will help us to develop a prototype that should help to show whether we are heading in the right direction or not.

21.6   The Gas Station's Event Classes

In order to keep coupling between the primary classes and the event classes to a minimum, most of the Event sub classes will be designed to have a reference simply to the driver with which they are associated. When performed, they will notify the gas station (obtained via the driver) of the need to take some action, but they will not otherwise involve themselves in details of pumps, tanks, and so on. In order to gather the required statistics on the time a driver spends on various activities within the gas station, we will require a driver object to keep a record of all of the events associated with it, from arrival to departure. On departure it will be possible to access these and analyze the time intervals between them.

The following event classes will be used to mark the progression of a driver from arrival to departure:

- `DriverArrival`: A new driver is constructed, representing their arrival. This event will be responsible for scheduling the next arrival, according to a Poisson distribution. The first arrival is scheduled before the start of the simulation.
- `StartPumping`: A pump supplying the correct fuel type has become available for a particular driver.
- `StopPumping`: A pump has completed its delivery after a time based upon the amount of fuel delivered. The driver must now try to pay for the delivered fuel.
- `StartPaying`: A cashier is available for a particular driver to pay.
- `StopPaying`: The payment transaction has been completed after a time based upon the driver's payment method. Note that the length of time for this

transaction is not dependent upon the amount of fuel delivered. A `Driver-Departure` event is scheduled.

- `DriverDeparture`: A driver leaves the gas station.
- `Refill`: A tanker arrives to refill all of the gas station's tanks. The first Refill event is scheduled to occur eight hours from the start of the simulation. Each occurrence schedules the next refill in a further eight hours time.

Each of these event classes can be sub classes of the same Event class that was defined for the Ice Cream simulation and shown in Code 21.1. They all have the basic requirement to maintain an attribute describing the time at which they will occur, and a `perform` method that describes their behavior. In addition, we can use the same `Scheduler` class as was illustrated in Code 21.2.

21.6.1   The StartPumping and StopPumping Events

Code 21.9 shows how we might think of implementing two of these event classes, `StartPumping` and `StopPumping`.

Code 21.9   Possible implementations for two of the event classes

```
class StartPumping extends Event {
    public StartPumping(long eventTime,Driver d){
        super(eventTime);
        driver = d;
        d.addEvent(this);
    }

    public void perform(Scheduler scheduler){
        Driver d = getDriver();
        GasStation station = d.getStation();
        station.startPumping(d);
    }

    public String toString(){
        return getWhen()+" StartPumping";
    }

    protected Driver getDriver(){
        return driver;
    }

    private final Driver driver;
}

class StopPumping extends Event {
    public StopPumping(long eventTime,Driver d){
        super(eventTime);
        driver = d;
        d.addEvent(this);
    }
    public void perform(Scheduler scheduler){
        Driver d = getDriver();
```

Code 21.9   (*Continued*)

```
        // Now pass the driver to the gas station for payment.
        GasStation station = d.getStation();
        station.stopPumping(d);
    }

    public String toString(){
        return getWhen()+" StopPumping";
    }

    protected Driver getDriver(){
        return driver;
    }

    private final Driver driver;
}
```

Notice how an attempt has been made to keep knowledge of the methods of the Driver and GasStation classes to a minimum in both classes. Each receives a reference to their associated Driver object via its constructor and their primary roles are simply to make sure that the event is recorded in the driver's list of events (`addEvent`) and that the gas station is notified of their occurrence. This latter task is accomplished using method names that closely match the event class's name (`startPumping`, `stopPumping`). Even though these events are associated with pump activities, they do not get involved with a Pump class. Furthermore, a StartPumping event is not required to schedule the corresponding StopPumping event; this would require a knowledge of how long the delivery is to take, which requires the amount of delivered fuel to be known. Such knowledge would introduce the sort of further coupling between event classes and primary classes that we are keen to avoid.

As a result of keeping these two event classes relatively simple with respect to the primary classes, we notice that there are strong similarities between them. This suggests that they are ideal candidates for extending from a common super class which implements their common elements. Code 21.10 shows the `DriverEvent` super class that reflects this. This is used as the super class of StartPumping and StopPumping.

The DriverEvent class ensures that the event is added to the driver's event record, and maintains the driver as an attribute with associated accessor (`getDriver`). It does not implement the abstract `perform` method, inherited from its Event super class, and so it remains as an abstract class. In addition, DriverEvent can act as a super class for the StartPaying, StopPaying, and DriverDeparture classes.

21.6.2   The DriverArrival and Refill Classes

The two remaining event classes, DriverArrival and Refill, do not conform to the pattern of the other events, and so they are not sub classes of DriverEvent. Nevertheless, their `perform` methods follow a similar pattern, and the amount of detailed knowledge of the primary classes that they need to have is kept very limited. Code 21.11 illustrates both of them.

Code 21.10   The super class for driver events (`DriverEvent.java`)

```java
abstract class DriverEvent extends Event {
    public DriverEvent(long eventTime,Driver d){
        super(eventTime);
        driver = d;
        d.addEvent(this);
    }

    public String toString(){
        return getWhen()+" UnknownDriverEvent";
    }

    protected Driver getDriver(){
        return driver;
    }

    private final Driver driver;
}
```

Code 21.11   The DriverArrival and Refill events

```java
        // An event denoting the arrival (creation) of a new Driver
        // at the gas station.

class DriverArrival extends Event {
    public DriverArrival(long eventTime,GasStation f){
        super(eventTime);
        station = f;
    }

    public void perform(Scheduler scheduler){
        GasStation station = getStation();
        // Schedule the next arrival.
        long now = scheduler.getTime();
        scheduler.schedule(new DriverArrival(nextArrivalTime(now),station));

        Driver d = new Driver(station);
        // Register this event with the driver for the record.
        d.addEvent(this);

        // Let the gas station know a new driver has arrived.
        station.arrival(d);
    }

    public String toString(){
        return getWhen()+" DriverArrival";
    }
```

Code 21.11   (*Continued*)

```
        // Calculate when the next driver should arrive.
    protected long nextArrivalTime(long now){
        // Simulate a Poisson distribution of arrivals.
        return now + (long)(-meanArrivalTime*Math.log(Math.random()));
    }

    protected GasStation getStation(){
        return station;
    }

    // Mean arrival time of drivers, in seconds.
    private final double meanArrivalTime = 60.0;
    private final GasStation station;
}

        // Refill all tanks in the gas station.
class Refill extends Event {
    // Time between refills.
    public static final long refillPeriod = 8L*60*60;

    public Refill(long eventTime,GasStation f){
        super(eventTime);
        station = f;
    }

    public void perform(Scheduler scheduler){
        GasStation station = getStation();
        // Schedule the next refill.
        long now = scheduler.getTime();
        scheduler.schedule(new Refill(nextRefillTime(now),station));

        station.refill();
    }

    public String toString(){
        return getWhen()+" Refill";
    }

        // Calculate when the next refill should occur.
    protected long nextRefillTime(long now){
        // Simulate a Poisson distribution of arrivals.
        return now + refillPeriod;
    }

    protected GasStation getStation(){
        return station;
    }

    private final GasStation station;
}
```

Both events receive a reference to the gas station to their constructor. The `perform` method of DriverArrival schedules the next arrival and then constructs a new Driver object, which it passes to the gas station. Note that it also adds itself as the first event of the driver's collection of events. The `perform` method of Refill simply schedules the next refill event and informs the gas station that it has occurred.

Exercise 21.4   Would it be possible to redesign the DriverArrival class so that it conformed to the pattern of the DriverEvent class? What other classes would need to be changed? What might be the advantages and disadvantages of taking this approach?

21.6.3   Prototyping the Simulation

One advantage of the light coupling between the simulation classes and the primary classes of the problem is that we can put together a prototype of the program quite easily, even at this relatively early stage. Putting together a prototype will often give us insights into the design we are creating and help us to test its adequacy. It can often give a sense of achievement to have got something working, even if there is still a considerable way to go before the solution is complete. We simply need to provide an outline of the Driver and GasStation classes, since these are the only two primary classes with which the event classes interact. The Driver class will need to maintain a reference to the gas station and provide an `addEvent` method, while the GasStation class will need to provide a dummy method corresponding to the messages sent by the `perform` methods of each of the event classes. However, note that even with this degree of coupling, the event classes make no assumptions about what tasks will be performed within those methods. At this stage, we will not need to worry about any of the other primary classes, such as Tank, Pump, Cashier, etc.

Code 21.12 shows a non-functional prototype for the Driver class. Notice that it is not necessary for the prototype version of `addEvent` to do anything with the

---

Code 21.12   A prototype Driver class

```
class Driver {
    public Driver(GasStation s){
        station = s;
    }

    public GasStation getStation(){
        return station;
    }

    public void addEvent(Event e){
    }

    private final GasStation station;
}
```

event it receives. A driver object is largely acting as a container for a reference to the gas station, so that the event classes can gain access to it via the driver reference they have as an attribute. Code 21.13 shows a possible prototype for the GasStation class. Each method associated with an event as the driver passes through the gas station schedules the next event at an arbitrary point in the future. It is not necessary for the departure and refill to schedule future events.

Code 21.13 A prototype GasStation class

```
class GasStation {
    public GasStation(Scheduler s){
        scheduler = s;
    }

    public void arrival(Driver d){
        Scheduler scheduler = getScheduler();
        scheduler.schedule(new StartPumping(scheduler.getTime()+1,d));
    }

    public void startPumping(Driver d){
        Scheduler scheduler = getScheduler();
        scheduler.schedule(new StopPumping(scheduler.getTime()+1,d));
    }

    public void stopPumping(Driver d){
        Scheduler scheduler = getScheduler();
        scheduler.schedule(new StartPaying(scheduler.getTime(),d));
    }

    public void startPaying(Driver d){
        Scheduler scheduler = getScheduler();
        scheduler.schedule(new StopPaying(scheduler.getTime()+1,d));
    }

    public void stopPaying(Driver d) {
        Scheduler s = getScheduler();
        s.schedule(new DriverDeparture(s.getTime(),d));
    }

    public void departure(Driver d){
    }

        // Refill all of the tanks.
    public void refill(){
    }

    protected Scheduler getScheduler(){
        return scheduler;
    }

    // The simulation scheduler.
    private final Scheduler scheduler;
}
```

Code 21.14 The main method for the gas station simulation (`GasMain.java`)

```java
class GasMain {
    public static void main(String[] args){
        Scheduler scheduler = new Scheduler();
        GasStation station = new GasStation(scheduler);

        // Schedule the first arrival, to kick things off.
        scheduler.schedule(new DriverArrival(0L,station));
        // Schedule a tank refill event at the appropriate time.
        scheduler.schedule(new Refill(scheduler.getTime()+
                                    Refill.refillPeriod,station));

        final long stopTime = 24L*60*60;
        scheduler.run(stopTime);
    }
}
```

With these two prototype classes, we can run a prototype simulation to check that we have the basic scheduling logic correct, and that a driver progresses smoothly through the system. Code 21.14 shows the main method that creates the GasStation, Scheduler, and schedules the first Driver and Refill events before starting the simulation running for a period of twenty-four hours.

The following output illustrates a few events from such a prototype run:

```
=> 0 DriverArrival
=> 1 StartPumping
=> 2 StopPumping
=> 2 StartPaying
=> 3 StopPaying
=> 3 DriverDeparture
=> 85 DriverArrival
=> 86 StartPumping
=> 87 StopPumping
=> 87 StartPaying
=> 88 StopPaying
=> 88 DriverDeparture
=> 101 DriverArrival
=> 102 StartPumping
etc.
```

As can be seen, we appear to be getting the sort of output we would expect, with events occurring in the correct order, and drivers arriving at the right sort of intervals. Such a prototyping approach, that helps to build a reasonable degree of confidence in one part of the system, will enable us to concentrate on the other parts of the system as we flesh out the primary classes of the problem; in particular the GasStation class.

21.6.4   Discussion of the Primary Classes

In the previous few sections, we identified the events that represent the progress of a driver through the gas station, and we built a prototype of the simulation based upon these. As we start to develop the primary classes of the simulation, we might find it necessary to rework the event classes in the light of experience. It is rarely possible to get things right the first time, and the illumination provided by hindsight is often considerable. In Section 21.5.1, we identified some obvious primary classes—Cashier, Driver, and Pump—and tentatively explored the need for others—Tank, FuelType, and PaymentMethod. The simulation framework gives us the basis from which to explore whether we have all the classes we require, and the ways in which they might interact with one another. In looking at how the primary classes interact, we will also need to keep in mind how much interaction they should have with the event classes. Our goal in designing the event classes was to keep coupling between the two categories as separate as possible. It will only be as we flesh out the primary classes that we shall discover whether we can stick to this goal or not.

Rather than plunging straight into the design of the primary classes, we shall use the dummy methods of Code 21.13 to seek resolutions of some of these questions.

- `arrival`: A newly created Driver object has arrived at the gas station. On arrival the driver will either be assigned a suitable free pump or be required to join a queue until one becomes free. Assignment of a suitable pump implies that the driver has an associated fuel type requirement. It must also be possible to tell whether a pump is free or not.
- `startPumping`: A pump is free and has been assigned to the driver. A Stop-Pumping event must be scheduled corresponding to the time it will take to deliver the fuel. This means that there must be a required amount of fuel associated with the driver. At what stage should the fuel be removed from the associated tank? What happens to the delivery if there is insufficient fuel available or if the tank is empty?
- `stopPumping`: The time for delivery of the fuel has passed and the driver leaves the pump and must find a cashier. Can we schedule the StartPaying event straight away? Should the pump be released at this point? If there is no free cashier, then the driver will have to wait in a queue.
- `startPaying`: A cashier is free and has been assigned to the driver. It must be possible to tell whether a cashier is free or not. Should the pump be released at this point or was it released by the StopPumping event? A StopPaying event must be scheduled corresponding to the payment method used by the driver. So the driver must have an associated payment method.
- `stopPaying`: The transaction is complete and a Departure event must be scheduled. The cashier is freed and can serve another waiting driver, if there is one.
- `departure`: The collection of events associated with a departing driver can be analyzed to update the required list of statistics. Alternatively, should analysis be left until the end of the simulation, and what differences could this make?
- `refill`: A tanker arrives to refill all of the tanks. How long should this take? If it takes a finite amount of time, should there be a StartRefill and StopRefill pair of events? Should the gas station stop serving drivers until the delivery is complete?

Notice that trying to find answers has raised a whole new set of questions! This is typical of problem solving and you might think it is a bad sign. On the contrary, it is an important indicator that we are actually understanding a lot about the overall complexity of the problem. It is the fact that we have insights into what will be going on that causes us to ask further questions. Each question needs to be resolved in some way, otherwise we might find it necessary to undo a lot of work at a later stage, which could be time consuming and costly. Some of these questions will have right and wrong answers. To some there will be answers that are stylistically better than other answers. To other questions there will be no absolute answer and we shall need to make reasoned decisions about the way to resolve them. The basis of our decision might be what we feel most competent to do, relative implementation cost, internal consistency, and so on. The important point is to have asked the question in the first place, rather than be surprised by it when we have already committed to going in the wrong direction.

We can illustrate this process with a couple of the questions raised above. Firstly, at what point should the fuel be removed from the tank: when delivery starts or finishes? Does it really matter—can we find a situation in which the results might be different if we do one or the other? In Section 21.4.1, we pointed out that simulations often replace *message-response* interaction between objects with an *initiation-completion* pair of events. This latter model of interaction allows for intervening events to occur between the initiation and completion. Appreciating this helps us to answer this particular question. Consider a possible effect with the solution in which we do not remove the fuel from the tank until delivery is complete. Suppose that the level in a particular fuel tank is low (100 liters), when a StartPumping event occurs. If that driver requests 80 liters, there should be no problem delivering this amount and a corresponding StopPumping event is scheduled. Suppose that a further Start-Pumping event for a second driver occurs at or just after the first driver's. Associated with this is a request for 40 liters of the same fuel type from a different pump. It looks like this request can also be granted (because the tank still has 100 liters in it) and a second StopPumping event is scheduled. Because the second amount is less than the first, the second StopPumping event will be triggered next and the level in the tank reduced to 60 liters. When the time for the first StopPumping event occurs, the level in the tank will be reduced to -20 liters, which is an error! What we see here is an example of a *race hazard*, covered in detail in Chapter 18 in the context of *threads*.

The simplest way to resolve this problem is to remove the fuel from the tank when the StartPumping event occurs, that is, as soon as it has been established that there is enough fuel. This will prevent performance of the second StartPumping event from trying to deliver more fuel than is now available. This small example illustrates one way in which the simulation will not be able to model real life accurately. In real life (depending upon the time difference between the commencement of the two deliveries), either the second driver would obtain the full amount or both would run out simultaneously. The only way to get close to this sort of interaction would be to subdivide the delivery process into a sequence of partial-delivery events that were interleaved for the two drivers.

This situation illustrates one of the limitations of a discrete simulation when compared with a continuous simulation. The two deliveries are really two continuous, mutually dependent processes. With a discrete simulation, although two events might have the same time of occurrence, one will necessarily be performed before the other. If one has the potential for a side effect on the performance of the other, inaccuracy might result.

In this particular simulation, there is nothing in the specification that suggests this degree of realism is required and so we shall not attempt to properly resolve such conflicts.

The second question we shall consider is when should a pump be freed for another user: when the StopPumping event occurs, or when the StartPaying event occurs? Is there any difference in effect between the two? If a driver moves straight from their pump to a free cashier, then there will be no difference, because both events will be scheduled for the same time. There is only a distinction when a driver must queue before a cashier becomes free. In the case where we do not release the pump until the StartPaying event occurs, the pump remains occupied all the time that the driver is queuing. This models the real-life situation in which a cashier must query a pump to find out how much to charge the customer, and only then releases the pump. One reason for this is that the systems used by many gas stations are not able to buffer multiple deliveries and to make previously delivered amounts available to the cashier once a pump has been re-used. This situation is made more complex by the fact that customers do not always present themselves in delivery order to a cashier, particularly where a gas station has a shop that an earlier customer is browsing before paying.

The alternative release points could also make a difference to the statistics resulting from the simulation. In the case where a pump is not freed until a driver starts paying, other drivers will be held in the queue for a pump. If a pump is freed as soon as the delivery is finished, subsequent drivers will complete their deliveries but be made to wait in the queue for a cashier rather than the queue for a pump. Since a particular purpose of the simulation is to be able to analyze driver waiting times, where a driver waits could have an impact on the interpretation of the results. As this simulation does not require any accounting information to be generated, there will be no need for a cashier to obtain the amount delivered from a pump (which, in turn, means that a pump does not need to retain this information), so we could eliminate the cashier-release scenario from consideration if we wished, and release a pump as soon as fuel delivery has been completed. However, since we plan to extend this example later to include charging, we will choose the approach of having the cashier release the pump when a StartPaying event occurs.

Having considered possible solutions to two of the questions in some detail, we shall deal with the others more briefly.

- What should happen if the tank for a particular fuel type is empty and at what point will this be detected? Having taken the decision to remove fuel from a tank at the start of delivery, it should be possible to tell whether a driver's request can be satisfied at the point a pump is assigned to them. It is here that we shall check whether there is fuel available or not. In the case that there is no fuel of that type, a DriverDeparture event will be scheduled instead of a StartPumping event. This means that the set of events collected by departing drivers will either be *DriverArrival-StartPumping-StopPumping-StartPaying-StopPaying-DriverDeparture*, or *DriverArrival-DriverDeparture*. This will have to be borne in mind when analyzing the results of the simulation.
- The only statistics required for the Refill event are whether fuel is likely to run out or not before this occurs. A possible impact of the refilling is that drivers

could be made to queue longer if the refilling of the tanks causes delivery to stop. In this case, we decide not to create a StartFilling-StopFilling pair, in the interests of simplicity—what happens to drivers who are partway through their delivery when the tanker arrives, for instance? If this were to be a real-life programming problem, such a question should be resolved by reference to the commissioning customer.

21.6.5   Lockable Resources

The discussion above has helped to confirm that the Cashier and Pump classes both represent resources with which drivers must interact. They are similar in that both can be either free or occupied and can handle only a single driver at a time. Drivers must, therefore, join a queue if there is no cashier or pump available at the time they are required. In this respect, they appear to have similarities with the Vendor class of the Ice Cream simulation, described in Section 21.4.5. However, there are some significant differences between the two simulations. In the ice cream simulation, there was a single vendor who served all customers. In this simulation, there will be multiple pumps and the number of cashiers will be varied in order to determine the effect on waiting times of providing multiple cashiers. This means that we need to decide how a driver is allocated to a particular cashier or pump. Should each such resource have its own queue, so that a driver is assigned to a particular pump queue on arrival and a queue for a particular cashier following fuel delivery? Alternatively, should drivers join general queues so that they are passed to a pump or cashier when one becomes free? The best way to maximize throughput is to maintain general queues and, since making sure that customers are not kept waiting is an underlying goal of the gas station, that is the approach we shall take.

There is a difference between pumps and cashiers, however, in that a driver may be served by any cashier, but a driver is only able to obtain fuel from a pump attached to a tank containing the right type of fuel. When a cashier becomes free, the driver who has been queuing for the longest time will be served (first-in, first-out), but when a pump becomes free there might be no driver who is able to use it, even though there are drivers queuing for a pump. When a driver arrives at the gas station, the station will need to find out if there is a suitable pump free; as we have seen, the existence of drivers in a queue does not mean that there is not. This means that the pump queue will not exhibit first-in, first-out semantics. Similarly, when a driver goes to pay, it must be possible to find out which cashiers are occupied. This suggests that we can define the Cashier and Pump classes to share a common super class which we call `Lockable` (Code 21.15). The Lockable class provides us with the ability to release and lock an object and to find out whether the object is free or not.

We shall look at how the Cashier and Pump classes extend Lockable when we have determined what further behavior, if any, they require.

21.6.6   Interactions Among the Primary Classes

Up to this point we have seen that we can prototype the simulation without needing to know too much about how objects of the primary classes interact with one another. Code 21.13 suggested that the GasStation class would provide the main *locus of*

Code 21.15   The super class of Cashier and Pump (`Lockable.java`)

```
        // An object that may be free or occupied.
abstract class Lockable {
    public void lock(){
        setFree(false);
    }

    public void release(){
        setFree(true);
    }

    public boolean isFree(){
        return free;
    }

    protected void setFree(boolean f) throws RuntimeException {
        if(free != f){
            // This is a change of state.
            free = f;
        }
        else{
            throw new RuntimeException("Lock was already set to: "+free);
        }
    }

    // Whether this is free or not.
    private boolean free = true;
}
```

control, shepherding a driver through the simulation from event to event and causing it to interact with a pump and cashier. Following a driver's progress has highlighted that there are three attributes associated with each Driver object: a fuel type, an amount of fuel required, and a payment method. These could be set up either as part of the object's construction, or when required by the appropriate stages of the simulation: pump selection, delivery, and paying (we would not be interested in the payment method of a driver who leaves because there is no fuel in the tanks, for instance). For the sake of simplicity, we shall set these up when a driver is constructed. Now we turn to discussing how drivers interact with pumps and cashiers, how pumps interact with tanks, how different payment methods and fuel types are to be implemented, and so on.

When a suitable pump becomes free, a driver is assigned to it and delivery must take place as a consequence of a StartPumping event. Because the StartPumping event results in the GasStation's `startPumping` method being called, there are three ways in which the delivery could be managed:

- The gas station could instruct the driver to request the fuel it requires:

    ```
    driver.fillUp();
    ```

- The gas station could instruct the pump to request the required fuel from the driver:

```
pump.deliver(driver);
```

- The gas station could instruct the pump to deliver an amount of fuel of the required type, both obtained from the driver:

```
pump.deliver(driver.getFuelType(),driver.getAmount());
```

Each approach represents a different amount of *coupling* between the three classes. From the gas station's point of view, the first is the simplest since it leaves everything to the driver. The driver is assumed to know how to request fuel from a pump. The second approach places responsibility on the pump to request the fuel type and amount from the driver. The third approach exhibits the strongest coupling between the gas station and the other two classes, and is the least attractive, therefore. Since it is easier for a driver to supply fuel type and amount to the pump than it is for the pump to request those two items, the first approach is the one we have implemented. The driver's `fillUp` method sends a `deliver` method to its assigned pump and returns the supplied amount:

```
class Driver {
    ...
    public long deliver(){
        Pump p = getPump();
        return p.deliver(getFuelType(),getAmount());
    }
    ...
}
```

For a pump to deliver an amount of fuel to a driver, the pump must request that amount of fuel from one of the tanks. The pump must first identify which of the tanks to which it is attached can deliver the right fuel type, and then send it a `deliver` message. The tank will calculate how much it can deliver and, as we discussed in Section 21.6.4, reduce its level by that amount immediately. The pump is then able to return the delivered amount to the driver who, in turn, returns it to the gas station. The gas station uses this value to work out the time for the associated StopPumping event. If charging for fuel were to be introduced into the simulation, either the driver or the pump would have to remember how much fuel was delivered, so that a cashier could later access it. Code 21.16 shows the Pump and Tank classes.

Code 21.16 The Pump and Tank classes

```
    // A Pump is connected to one or more tanks and can deliver
    // fuel to a single customer from one of the tanks.
    // It is assumed that a Pump will not be connected to more than
    // one tank of the same fuel type.

class Pump extends Lockable {
    public Pump(Tank[] connectedTanks){
        tanks = connectedTanks;
    }
```

Code 21.16   (*Continued*)

```
    // An indication that the request fuel type is not available.
public static class FuelTypeNotAvailable extends Exception {
}

    // Can we deliver the required amount of the given fuel?
public long deliver(FuelType type,long amount)
                            throws FuelTypeNotAvailable {
    // Make sure we can supply the right type of fuel.
    Tank tank = getTankWithType(type);
    if(tank == null){
        throw new FuelTypeNotAvailable();
    }
    else{
        // Remove the fuel from the tank.
        return tank.deliver(amount);
    }
}

    // Can we deliver some of the required fuel type?
public boolean canSupply(FuelType type){
    Tank tank = getTankWithType(type);
    return tank.canDeliver();
}

    // Has this pump the required fuel type?
public boolean hasFuelType(FuelType type){
    return getTankWithType(type) != null;
}

    // Return the tank with the correct fuel type, or null
    // if there isn't one..
protected Tank getTankWithType(FuelType type){
    Tank[] pumpTanks = getTanks();
    for(int i = 0; i < pumpTanks.length; i++){
        if(pumpTanks[i].getFuelType().equals(type)){
            return pumpTanks[i];
        }
    }
    return null;
}

protected Tank[] getTanks(){
    return tanks;
}

// The tanks to which this pump is connected.
private final Tank[] tanks;
}

    // A Tank holds fuel of a particular type.
class Tank {
```

(*Continued*)

Code 21.16 (*Continued*)

```java
        // Set how much this tank can hold. This is fixed for life.
    public Tank(long max,FuelType type){
        capacity = max;
        fuelType = type;
        // The tank is full to start with.
        refill();
    }

    public long getCapacity(){
        return capacity;
    }

    public FuelType getFuelType(){
        return fuelType;
    }

        // Can this tank deliver some of the amount required?
    public boolean canDeliver(){
        return getLevel() > 0;
    }

        // Deliver the required amount, if possible.
        // Return the actual amount delivered.
    public long deliver(long amount){
        long delivered = 0L;
        if(amount > 0L){
            long currentLevel = getLevel();
            if(amount <= currentLevel){
                setLevel(currentLevel-amount);
                delivered = amount;
            }
            else{
                // Deliver what we have.
                setLevel(0L);
                delivered = currentLevel;
            }
        }
        return delivered;
    }

        // Refill the tank to its full capacity.
    public void refill(){
        setLevel(getCapacity());
    }

    public long getLevel(){
        return level;
    }

    protected void setLevel(long newLevel){
        level = newLevel;
    }
```

Code 21.16   (*Continued*)

```
    // How much the tank can hold.
    private final long capacity;
    // What sort of fuel it holds.
    private final FuelType fuelType;
    // How much is in the tank.
    private long level;
}
```

The final interaction is between a driver and a cashier as a result of a StartPaying event. In fact, in the current version of the simulation, no messages need to be sent between them. This is just a time-passing interaction. If proper charging were to be added, then the cashier would have to obtain the amount of fuel delivered so that the day's takings could be calculated. In this version, however, the cashier simply acts as a lockable resource. Code 21.17 shows that the Cashier class currently adds no further functionality to its Lockable super class.

The Driver class is shown in Code 21.18. Its only significant functional method is fillUp, which we described above.

Code 21.17 The current Cashier class just provides a type name (`Cashier.java`)

```
      // A Cashier may be free or occupied.
class Cashier extends Lockable {
}
```

Code 21.18 A driver collects its associated events (`Driver.java`)

```
      // A customer of the gas station.
class Driver {
    public Driver(GasStation s){
        station = s;
    }

      // Try to fill up. Return how much can be delivered.
    public long fillUp() throws Pump.FuelTypeNotAvailable {
        Pump p = getPump();
        return p.deliver(getFuelType(),getAmount());
    }

    public GasStation getStation(){
        return station;
    }

    public void addEvent(Event e){
```

(*Continued*)

Code 21.18   (*Continued*)

```
        getEventList().add(e);
    }

        // A free pump has been found. Delivery is about to start.
    public void setPump(Pump p){
        pump = p;
    }

        // A free cashier has been found. Payment is about to start.
    public void setCashier(Cashier c){
        cashier = c;
    }

    public FuelType getFuelType(){
        return fuelType;
    }

    public PaymentMethod getPaymentMethod(){
        return payment;
    }

    public Event[] getEvents(){
        // Return the queue of events into an array for calculation
        // of statistics.
        Queue eventQueue = getEventList();
        Event[] events = new Event[eventQueue.size()];
        eventQueue.toArray(events);
        return events;
    }

    public long getAmount(){
        return amount;
    }

    public Pump getPump(){
        return pump;
    }

    public Cashier getCashier(){
        return cashier;
    }

    protected Queue getEventList(){
        return eventList;
    }

    // Have access to a FuelFactory, for generating random
    // instances of a FuelType. This is a singleton so may be
    // shared by all Drivers.
    private static final FuelFactory fuelFactory =
                            FuelFactory.getInstance();
    // Request a random fuel type.
    private final FuelType fuelType = fuelFactory.randomFuelType();
```

Code 21.18   (*Continued*)

```
    // Request a random amount of fuel.
    private final long amount = fuelType.randomAmount();
    // Obtain a random payment method from the singleton
    // payment factory method.
    private final PaymentMethod payment =
            PaymentFactory.getInstance().randomPaymentMethod();

    private final GasStation station;
    // The pump and cashier will be allocated when free.
    private Pump pump = null;
    private Cashier cashier = null;
    // Keep track of the events that occurred for this driver.
    private Queue eventList = new Queue();
}
```

A driver collects its associated events (`addEvent`) and keeps track of the cashier and pump objects allocated to it. However, its `fuelType` and `payment` attributes illustrate features of two other classes, `FuelFactory` and `PaymentFactory` which are discussed in the following sections.

21.6.7 The Fuel and Payment Classes

The `FuelType` class is particularly important in this simulation. Drivers arrive requiring a particular type of fuel; a check must be made to ensure that this type can be supplied; a pump must identify from which of its attached tanks to draw the fuel; if proper payment were to be implemented, each fuel type would have an associated cost. The description of the scenario in Section 21.5.1 indicates that each fuel type has a probability of being required and a mean amount required per driver. We can capture these differences in sub classes of a basic FuelType super class, such as `Diesel`, `Leaded`, and `Unleaded`. If we regard the amount of fuel required by a particular driver as completely separate from the type of fuel, we can see that a fuel type class does not need to maintain any per-instance state. That is, an Unleaded instance for one driver need be no different from an Unleaded instance for any other. This makes the fuel type classes ideal candidates for being implemented as *singleton* classes (see Appendix E.2). Each sub class of FuelType needs to provide little more than a `getInstance` method and the mean amount of fuel associated with that particular fuel type. Code 21.19 shows the FuelType super class and Diesel sub class implementing these ideas. The Unleaded and Leaded classes closely follow Diesel.

Notice that the Diesel class contains no information about the probability of its being allocated to a particular driver. We shall discuss the reason for this in due course. The `meanAmount` method of the fuel type sub classes is used by the `randomAmount` method of FuelType to allocate a random amount of fuel required by a particular driver. This method represents the only public interface required by the other classes of the simulation.

Code 21.19   The Diesel singleton class and its FuelType super class

```java
import java.util.Random;

        // The super class of all fuel types.
abstract class FuelType {
        // particular fuel type.
    public long randomAmount(){
        final Random r = getRandom();
        return Math.abs(r.nextLong()) % (2*meanAmount());
    }

        // Return the mean amount of fuel to be delivered for this
        // particular fuel type.
    abstract protected long meanAmount();

        // Generate a random amount of fuel to be delivered for this
    protected static Random getRandom(){
        return random;
    }

    private static final Random random = new Random();
}

class Diesel extends FuelType {
    public static FuelType getInstance(){
        return instance;
    }

    public String toString(){
        return "Diesel";
    }

        // Return the mean amount of fuel to be delivered for this
        // particular fuel type.
    protected long meanAmount(){
        return 200L;
    }

        // Prevent arbitrary construction.
    protected Diesel(){
    }

    private static final FuelType instance = new Diesel();
}
```

21.6.8   The FuelFactory Class

The next issue to address is how a particular fuel type is assigned to each new driver. One solution would be to make the driver class aware of the percentage likelihood of each fuel type being allocated and have a newly constructed Driver object make its own choice of fuel type. If a new sub class of FuelType were to be added, then the Driver class would also need modification with this approach, which represents a strong coupling between these classes. A preferable, weaker coupling solution is to allocate a random fuel type via a *factory class* (see Appendix E.4). Such a class would be the single place in the simulation where detailed knowledge of the range of individual fuel types available is located. This decouples the Driver class from interacting directly with the sub classes of FuelType and means that changing the range of fuels available has no direct impact on the Driver class. The `FuelFactory` class maintains a collection of references to all of the singleton instances of the different fuel types, and returns them as required. Code 21.20 illustrates this class. Notice that it, too, is a singleton class.

Code 21.20 Supply different fuel types according to their probabilities (`FuelFactory.java`)

```java
import java.util.HashMap;

    /* Keep a reference to a singleton instance of each FuelType
     * class. To add a new FuelType sub class:
     *       (i)   Define the sub class, e.g GreenGas.
     *       (ii)  Add an instance to the fuels array
     *             GreenGas.getInstance().
     *   (iii) Calculate the percentage likelihood of it being
     *         requested and redistribute the percentages between
     *         all of the fuel types as recorded in the
     *         typePercentages array.
     */

class FuelFactory {
        // Provide access to the singleton instance of this class.
    public static FuelFactory getInstance(){
        return factory;
    }

        // Return a random instance of the FuelType class.
    public FuelType randomFuelType() throws RuntimeException {
        // Generate a random fuel type.
        final int num = (int) (Math.random() * 100.0);
        for(int i = 0; i < typePercentages.length; i++){
            if(num < typePercentages[i]){
                return fuels[i];
            }
        }
        throw new RuntimeException(
                    "Failure in FuelFactory.randomFuelType()");
    }

        // type should be "Diesel", etc.
    public FuelType getFuel(String type) throws RuntimeException {
        Object fuel = fuelRegistry.get(type.toLowerCase());
        if((fuel != null) && (fuel instanceof FuelType)){
            return (FuelType) fuel;
        }
```

(Continued)

Code 21.20   (*Continued*)

```
        else{
            throw new RuntimeException("Unknown fuel type: "+type+
                                        " passed to: "+
                                        "FuelFactory.getFuel()");
        }
    }

        // Prevent arbitrary creation.
    protected FuelFactory(){
    }

        // The unique set of FuelType objects.
    private final FuelType[] fuels = {
        Diesel.getInstance(),
        Leaded.getInstance(),
        Unleaded.getInstance(),
    };

    // Provide a registry of fuel types. Each fuel type may be
    // looked up by the name returned by its toString method.
    private final HashMap fuelRegistry = new HashMap();
    {
        // Initialize the registry of fuel types. This allows
        // lookup by fuel name.
        for(int i = 0; i < fuels.length; i++){
            fuelRegistry.put(fuels[i].toString().toLowerCase(),fuels[i]);
        }
    }

    // Cumulative percentage for each fuel type.
    //     Assert: typePercentages[typePercentages.length-1] == 100
    //     Assert: typePercentages.length == fuels.length
    private static final int[] typePercentages = { 20, 50, 100 };

    // The singleton instance of this class - returned by instance().
    private static FuelFactory factory = new FuelFactory();
}
```

A randomFuelType message is sent to the factory when a new Driver is created. The FuelFactory maintains details of the cumulative probabilities of the different fuel types in its typePercentages attribute. It checks a random number against these values to determine which fuel type to return. The probability that a particular fuel will be allocated to a customer is better placed in the fuel factory rather than the individual fuel classes. This is because the probability for an individual fuel type is dependent upon the collective values for all other fuel types. Adding a new fuel type is likely to reduce the probabilities of all the previous types. It is easier to ensure that all are modified when a fuel type is added/removed if the values are located in one place.

Access to the fuel type singletons is also required by the gas station's tanks. At the start of the simulation, each tank must be associated with a particular fuel

---

Code 21.21   PaymentMethod and its sub class Credit

```java
abstract class PaymentMethod {
    // How long it takes to pay with this method.
    abstract public int paymentTime();
}

class Credit extends PaymentMethod {
    public static PaymentMethod getInstance(){
        return instance;
    }

    // How long to pay with this method, in seconds.
    public int paymentTime(){
        return 40;
    }

    public String toString(){
        return "Credit";
    }

    // Prevent unwanted instantiation.
    protected Credit(){
    }

    private static final PaymentMethod instance = new Credit();
}
```

---

type. The fuel factory provides a `getFuel` method for this purpose. Its parameter is a string for the name of the fuel, and this is used as a key to a HashMap of fuel types.

The various payment methods can be handled in a similar way to the different fuel types. Code 21.21 illustrates the abstract super class, `PaymentMethod`, and one of its sub classes, `Credit`.

The `PaymentFactory` class provides the associated mechanism for allocating a random payment method to a newly constructed Driver object.

21.6.9   The GasStation Class

Code 21.22 shows the completed GasStation class, whose prototype was originally shown in Code 21.13. This pulls together all of the issues that we have discussed in the last few sections, as a driver progresses from arrival to departure. Note that we have omitted details of how the statistical analysis is performed, for the sake of clarity. The main method for the complete simulation may be found in the file `Gas-Main.java`. The following exercises should help you to test your understanding of how the program works, and the effect of some of the design decisions we have addressed in this case study.

Code 21.22   The final version of the class representing the gas station (`GasStation.java`)

```java
import java.util.*;

class GasStation {
    public GasStation(Scheduler s){
        scheduler = s;
    }

    // *** Methods corresponding to each of the events.

        // Find a pump for the driver, if there is one, otherwise
        // add them to the queue.
    public void arrival(Driver d){
        // See if there is a pump free.
        Pump pumpToUse = findPump(d.getFuelType());

        if(pumpToUse != null){
            assignPump(pumpToUse,d);
        }
        else{
            addToPumpQueue(d);
        }
    }

    public void startPumping(Driver d){
        try{
            long amountDelivered = d.fillUp();
            // Schedule the StopPumping event.
            Scheduler scheduler = getScheduler();
            scheduler.schedule(new StopPumping(scheduler.getTime()+
                                amountDelivered*timePerLiter,d));
        }
        catch(Pump.FuelTypeNotAvailable e){
            System.out.println(
                "Assigned pump doesn't have the right fuel type.");
        }
    }

        // The driver has finished delivery of fuel. Go
        // to pay for it.
    public void stopPumping(Driver d){
        Cashier[] cashiers = getCashiers();
        for(int i = 0; i < cashiers.length; i++){
            final Cashier c = cashiers[i];
            if(c.isFree()){
                assignCashier(c,d);
                return;
            }
        }
        // No free cashier.
        addToCashierQueue(d);
    }

    public void startPaying(Driver d){
```

Code 21.22   (*Continued*)

```
    // Free the pump.
    releasePump(d.getPump());
    // Schedule the StopPaying event.
    PaymentMethod payment = d.getPaymentMethod();
    Scheduler scheduler = getScheduler();
    scheduler.schedule(new StopPaying(scheduler.getTime()+
                                      payment.paymentTime(),d));
}

    // The driver has finished paying and is about to leave.
public void stopPaying(Driver d) throws RuntimeException {
    // Schedule a DriverDeparture event, for statistical purposes.
    Scheduler s = getScheduler();
    s.schedule(new DriverDeparture(s.getTime(),d));

    // Free the cashier for the next in line.
    Cashier c = d.getCashier();
    if(c != null){
        c.release();
        Queue q = getCashierQueue();
        if(q.size() > 0){
            Driver nextDriver = (Driver) q.next();
            assignCashier(c,nextDriver);
        }
    }
    else{
        throw new RuntimeException("Driver without a Cashier.");
    }
}

    // The driver is about to leave, either through completing
    // purchase of fuel, or because no fuel was available.
public void departure(Driver d){
    // Collect the driver's events for statistical analysis.
    // ... Omitted for clarity ...
}

    // Refill all of the tanks.
public void refill(){
    Tank[] tanks = getTanks();
    for(int i = 0; i < tanks.length; i++){
        System.out.println(tanks[i].getFuelType()+
                           " down to: "+tanks[i].getLevel());
        tanks[i].refill();
    }
}

// *** Methods concerned with manipulation of the pumps and cashiers.

    // Allocate the free pump to the given driver.
protected void assignPump(Pump p,Driver d){
    Scheduler s = getScheduler();
```

(*Continued*)

Code 21.22   (*Continued*)

```
        if(p.canSupply(d.getFuelType())){
            // Claim the pump.
            p.lock();
            // Inform the driver.
            d.setPump(p);
            s.schedule(new StartPumping(s.getTime(),d));
        }
        else{
            // We have no fuel of this type. The driver will leave.
            s.schedule(new DriverDeparture(s.getTime(),d));
            System.out.println("*** No fuel ***");
        }
    }


    // Find a free pump supplying the given type of fuel.
    protected Pump findPump(FuelType type){
        Pump[] pumps = getPumps();
        for(int i = 0; i < pumps.length; i++){
            if(pumps[i].isFree() && pumps[i].hasFuelType(type)){
                return pumps[i];
            }
        }
        return null;
    }


    // The pump has been released by the driver it was
    // assigned to paying the cashier.
    protected void releasePump(Pump p) throws RuntimeException {
        if(p != null){
            p.release();
            ArrayList list = getPumpQueue();
            final int numWaiting = list.size();
            for(int i = 0; i < numWaiting; i++){
                Driver d = (Driver) list.get(i);
                Pump pumpToUse = findPump(d.getFuelType());
                if(pumpToUse != null){
                    // Found one who can use it.
                    list.remove(i);
                    assignPump(pumpToUse,d);
                    return;
                }
            }
            // No one can use the pump that has been freed.
        }
        else{
            throw new RuntimeException("No pump assigned to Driver.");
        }
    }


    // Assign the free cashier to the given driver.
    protected void assignCashier(Cashier c,Driver d){
        c.lock();
        d.setCashier(c);
```

Code 21.22   (*Continued*)

```
    Scheduler s = getScheduler();
    s.schedule(new StartPaying(s.getTime(),d));
}

    // Add the driver to the queue.
protected void addToPumpQueue(Driver d){
    ArrayList list = getPumpQueue();
    list.add(d);
    System.out.println("Pump queue length = "+list.size());
}

    // Add the driver to the queue.
protected void addToCashierQueue(Driver d){
    Queue q = getCashierQueue();
    q.add(d);
    System.out.println("Cashier queue length = "+q.size());
}

protected ArrayList getPumpQueue(){
    return waitingForPump;
}

protected Queue getCashierQueue(){
    return waitingForCashier;
}

protected Tank[] getTanks(){
    return tanks;
}

protected Pump[] getPumps(){
    return pumps;
}

protected Cashier[] getCashiers(){
    return cashiers;
}

protected Scheduler getScheduler(){
    return scheduler;
}

// Queue of drivers waiting for a free pump.
// Removal could be from arbitrary locations.
private final ArrayList waitingForPump = new ArrayList();

// Queue of drivers waiting for a free Cashier.
// Removal will be queue-like.
private final Queue waitingForCashier = new Queue();

private final long tankCapacity = 90000L;
private final int numTanks = 3;
```

                                                                         (*Continued*)

Code 21.22   *(Continued)*

```
    // Attributes relating to fuel and pumps.
// Have access to a FuelFactory.
private static final FuelFactory fuelFactory =
                                FuelFactory.getInstance();

// Indices for the FuelType objects stored in tanks[].
private final int DIESEL = 0, LEADED = 1, UNLEADED = 2;

// One Tank for each fuel type.
private final Tank[] tanks = new Tank[numTanks];
{
    tanks[DIESEL] =
            new Tank(tankCapacity,fuelFactory.getFuel("Diesel"));
    tanks[LEADED] =
            new Tank(tankCapacity,fuelFactory.getFuel("Leaded"));
    tanks[UNLEADED] =
            new Tank(tankCapacity,fuelFactory.getFuel("Unleaded"));
}

// How long to deliver a liter of fuel, in seconds.
private final long timePerLiter = 1L;

private final int numPumps = 7;
// Connect the pumps to the tanks.
private final Pump[] pumps = new Pump[numPumps];
{
    pumps[0] = new Pump(new Tank[] {tanks[UNLEADED],tanks[LEADED]});
    pumps[1] = new Pump(new Tank[] {tanks[UNLEADED],tanks[LEADED]});
    pumps[2] = new Pump(new Tank[] {tanks[UNLEADED],tanks[DIESEL]});
    pumps[3] = new Pump(new Tank[] {tanks[UNLEADED]});
    pumps[4] = new Pump(new Tank[] {tanks[UNLEADED]});
    pumps[5] = new Pump(new Tank[] {tanks[UNLEADED]});
    pumps[6] = new Pump(new Tank[] {tanks[DIESEL]});
}

    // Create the required number of cashiers.
private final Cashier[] cashiers = {
    new Cashier(),
};

// The simulation scheduler.
private final Scheduler scheduler;
}
```

Exercise 21.5 Modify the simulation so that an impatient driver does not wait in the queue if the queue's length is greater than some value.

Exercise 21.6 Determine the difference it makes in waiting times if the pump is freed at the end of a StopPumping event rather than a StartPaying event.

Exercise 21.7   Add a new sub class of FuelType, `CleanDiesel`. This is required by 5% of drivers, and the alternative Diesel is now required by only 15% rather than 20%. On average, a driver requires 100 liters of this new fuel type.

Exercise 21.8   Add cost-per-liter to the fuel types and calculate the day's takings at the end of the simulation.

Exercise 21.9   Rather than scheduling a regular Refill event, have the GasStation periodically check the levels in the tanks and schedule fuel-type associated refills when required.

Exercise 21.10   Modify the behavior of Refill events so that a tanker only delivers one type of fuel.

Exercise 21.11   Implement buffering of delivery amounts so that both pump release by StopPumping and customer charging are possible. Assume that drivers present themselves to the cashiers in delivery order.

Exercise 21.12   Modify the simulation so that a driver does not wait in the queue if the queue's length is greater than some number, but only if the tank in their car is more than 10 percent full. This requires a class to be designed and implemented to model the driver's tank. Are there any similarities between this and the gas station's tank that could be exploited through inheritance?

Exercise 21.13   You might like to consider creating a dynamic visualization of the state of the simulation. This could include details of queue lengths and tank contents, for instance.

Exercise 21.14   Create your own complex simulation from scratch. There are many real-life scenarios with dynamic behavior that you might like to consider modeling, such as traffic flow within a city, aircraft movements into and out of an airport, and animal populations within an environment.

21.7 Review

In the extended case study, the main points we have made have largely been concerned with the need to fully explore the problem area before becoming too committed to a final implementation. Questions will arise at the design stage that can only be addressed by further study of the problem area or reference to a customer. A prototyping or staged implementation approach often gives important insights into the viability of a chosen design, and can highlight the need for changes much earlier than would otherwise have been apparent.

APPENDIX A

The Primitive Data Types

A.1 Introduction

There are eight primitive data types in Java; five of these represent numerical types of varying range and precision—double, float, int, long, and short. Unlike some languages, Java is completely prescriptive about the sizes and value ranges of its primitive types. This is crucial for the portability of programs—the property that they will run identically on different types of computers. Values of these types occupy between 2 and 8 bytes of memory. The remaining three primitive types are used to representing single-bit values (boolean), single byte values (byte), and 2-byte characters from the ISO Unicode character set (char). These data types allow the efficient representation and implementation of simple valued data. However, none of these is an object type. In the next few sections, we illustrate some of the characteristics of each of these types. Section 5.5.3 outlines Java's rules for converting between values of different primitive types. Section 10.4 describes a set of classes providing wrapper objects that enable primitive values to be stored in object collections.

A.2 The Boolean Type

The boolean type is used to represent a state that can only be either true or false. As such, its value requires only a single binary digit of memory. An uninitialized Boolean attribute is given an initial value of false by default. Expressions that yield a Boolean value are commonly used to control the flow of execution through a sequence of statements. They are used as conditions for if-statements and looping statements.

A.3 The Integer Types

The short, int, and long types are integer (whole number) types, able to store both positive and negative values—there is no unsigned type in Java. Uninitialized attributes of integer types have an initial value of 0 by default.

A.3.1   Integer Ranges

Their size and ranges are as follows:

- `short`—occupies 2 bytes and can store values in the range `-32768` to `32767`.
- `int`—occupies 4 bytes and can store values in the range `-2147483648` to `2147483647`.
- `long`—occupies 8 bytes and can store values in the range `-9223372036854775808` to `9223372036854775807`.

Notice that all of these types have a negative limit that is one more than their positive limit. The different types could be used as follows:

- For objects needing to represent relatively small values—the numbers of cards in a player's hand, channels on a TV set, people in an organization, ships in a harbor, and so on—the `short` type would be more than adequate.
- Numbers likely to be in the tens of thousands and small billions should be stored in items of type `int`—populations of European countries, number of aphids in a field of barley, number of positions analyzed per second by a PC-based chess program.
- For larger whole-number quantities, the `long` type should be used—elapsed time in milliseconds, total world population, the total number of positions analyzed in a game of chess by a world champion level chess program.

Despite the large range of the `short` type, the `int` type is more commonly used, except where the wider range of `long` is required.

A.3.2   Integer Literals

A literal integer value written as a string of digits will be assumed to be of type `int`, by default. A `long` literal is indicated by adding an `L` or `l` suffix to the digits, such as `20000000000L`. The upper case suffix is to be preferred, to avoid confusion of `l` with the digit 1. There is no distinct notation for `byte` or `short` literals, so an `int` literal value within the appropriate range may be assigned to a `short` or `byte` variable without a *cast*. An integer literal with `0` as its first digit is taken as an *octal* value (see Section B.2.3) and one with `0x` or `0X` as its first two characters is taken as a *hexadecimal* value (see Section B.2.3).

A.4   The Floating Point Types

The *floating point* types are used to represent values from the set of real numbers—numbers with an integer and a fractional part. Java uses the IEEE 754-1985[Ins85] standard for representing floating point numbers and performing calculations using these types. Uninitialized attributes of these types are given an initial value of `0.0` by default.

A.4.1   Floating Point Ranges

The size and ranges of these types are as follows:

- `float`—occupies 4 bytes and can store positive and negative values in the range `1.4E-45` to `3.4028235E38`.
- `double`—occupies 8 bytes and can store positive and negative values in the range `4.9E-324` to `1.7976931348623157E308`.

Either should be used where a fractional part may be needed—to represent a value that is not a whole number. For instance, the 100 meter athletics world record time in seconds, the mean mark obtained by all students taking an assignment (the individual marks might be whole numbers but the mean is probably a real number), the number of light years to the nearest galaxy. They should also be used for whole numbers that are too large to store in an item of type `long`, although neither is able to exactly represent the full set of `long` values, even though the number ranges of both are larger.

A.4.2   Floating Point Literals

A literal floating point value will be assumed to be of type `double` by default. A literal value within the range for the `float` type may *not* be assigned to a `float` variable without a *cast*. A `float` literal is indicated by adding an F or f suffix to the literal, such as `100.45F`. An explicit D or d suffix may be used to type a literal as a double, but this is rarely done. Floating point literals may be written using exponent notation, which includes an upper or lowercase e character, such as `1.0045e3`.

Because the `double` type can store values which are both bigger and more precisely represented than the `float` type, applications should probably always use `double` in preference to `float`, where the extra space requirements do not prohibit this, although better precision is generally more important than conserving space. The `double` type is also the default real type used by other parts of the language, as with type `int`. We will almost always use `double` for real numbers.

It is worth noting that some numbers cannot be exactly represented in either the `double` or the `float` types—numbers such as π, $\frac{1}{3}$, and $\sqrt{2}$. Their values can only be *approximated* using the primitive real data types, either because they have an infinite number of decimal places or simply because the primitive data types have only a limited precision.

A.5   The Byte Type

The `byte` type occupies a single byte, and is able to hold values in the range -128 to $+127$. Uninitialized attributes of the `byte` type have an initial value of 0 by default. A `byte` variable could be used to represent ordinary small whole numbers—the numbers of letters in the alphabet, tracks on a CD, marks deducted from an assignment for being late. More frequently, `byte` is used to represent the raw binary value of an item of data being processed by a program from an external source, such as an encrypted message passed across a network, or the compressed version of a data file.

A.6   The Char Type

The `char` type occupies two bytes and is used to hold 16-bit representations of characters from the ISO Unicode character set (see Section 12.1.1). Uninitialized attributes of the `char` type have an initial value of `'\u0000'` by default (see Section A.6.1). For those used to writing programs assuming 7-bit ASCII character values, this can make life more complicated than they anticipate it might be. For instance, as well as being able to represent the familiar Latin-based alphabet of the English language, Unicode also allows scripts such as Arabic, Hebrew, Cyrillic, Thai, and so on, to be used.

A.6.1   Character Literals

Literal values of type `char` are written between a pair of single quote characters (`'`), for instance, `'A'`, `'q'`, `'8'`. The same character is used in both positions. It is important to distinguish between a single digit integer literal, such as 5, and the similar looking character literal `'5'`. The former represents a 32-bit integer value of type `int` and the latter is a 16-bit value of type `char`, with an underlying value drawn from the Unicode character set (it has an equivalent integer value of 53).

A.6.2   Escape Sequences

Some characters are difficult to represent as a single character written between quotes and *escape sequences* exist to make them easier to identify. An escape sequence consists of a *backslash character* (\) followed by a single character. For instance, a *newline* is represented as `'\n'`, a *tab character* as `'\t'` and a *carriage return* as `'\r'`. It is important to have symbolic values for some characters as their external representation might differ from one operating system to another—this is particularly true of line termination. Escape sequences are also available for representing a single quote character (`'\''`) and backslash itself (`'\\'`).

A.6.3   Octal Character Literals

A character with a Unicode value in the range 0–255 may be represented by an *octal character constant* of the form `'\ddd'`, where up to three octal digits specify the character's value. Unlike the numeric literals (Section B.2.4), the number will be interpreted as an octal value without an initial zero digit, so the character constant `'\7'` represents a *bell character* on some systems and `'\65'` is another way of writing the more straightforward `'5'`.

Octal character constants are insufficient for representing the full range of the 16-bit Unicode character set, so an escape sequence starting with \u indicates a Unicode character value. The value of the character is given using exactly four hexadecimal digits, so `'\u0035'` represents the character `'5'` ($3 \times 16 + 5$) and `'\u007a'` represents the character `'z'` (decimal 122).[1]

---

[1] For reasons of source-to-source translation, more than one u may occur between the backslash and the digits, so `'\uuu007a'` is a perfectly acceptable representation of the character `'z'`, although there would be little need to use this form in normal code.

B
Number Representations

B.1 Introduction

In Section 1, we discussed the way in which varying numbers of binary digits can be used to represent different numbers of binary patterns. We noted that 8 bits (a byte) allow 256 (2^8) distinct binary patterns to be represented, whereas 16 bits allow for 65536 (2^{16}) patterns. In this appendix, we look at the way in which these patterns are used to represent ranges of integer values. We also discuss the way in which integers can be written in different *number bases*, such as *octal* (base 8) and *hexadecimal* (base 16). We include some exercises to assist those readers new to this notation.

B.2 Number Bases

When a value is written in a program as a sequence of decimal digits (0–9), it is usually interpreted as a decimal value—this is certainly what a human reader would normally expect. However, sometimes it is more convenient to represent values in bases other than base 10, *decimal*. The most frequently occurring alternatives in programming contexts are base 2 (*binary*), base 8 (*octal*), and base 16 (*hexadecimal*). We shall look at each of these in the next few sections.

B.2.1 Base 2 and Base 10 Notations

In everyday life, we commonly write numbers in *decimal notation*. It is also called base 10 notation because each digit position in a number represents a power of 10, such as 10^2, 10^1, 10^0; indeed it is common to refer to the digits of a number as hundreds, tens, and units. For instance, the number 347 can be described as composed of three hundreds, four tens, and seven units; or as $3 \times 10^2 + 4 \times 10^1 + 7 \times 10^0$. Following a similar pattern, the digits of an unsigned number written in binary (base 2) notation each correspond to a power of 2: 2^2, 2^1, 2^0. So we can readily convert a binary number to equivalent decimal notation using a similar technique. For instance, the 4-digit binary number 1101 is equivalent to $1 \times 2^3 + 1 \times 2^2 + 0 \times 2^1 + 1 \times 2^0$, or 13 (base 10). It is sometimes necessary to make clear which base is being used to represent a number. It could be easy to mistake 1101 for one thousand, one hundred and one unless the base is clear from the context, so we sometimes write the base as a subscript on a number for clarification, for instance 1101_2 is 13_{10}. The base also determines the range of digits that can appear within a number; the maximum will be one less than the base. For instance, base 10 numbers have digits in the range $[0...9]$, base 8 numbers have digits in the range $[0...7]$, and so on. As we shall see later with hexadecimal numbers, bases above 10 require that we supplement the usual $[0...9]$ digit set with letters. The `toBinaryString` methods of the `Integer` and `Long` classes return a String binary representation of their integer argument values (see Section 10.4.1).

Exercise B.1   What is the decimal representation of 010110_2?

Exercise B.2   How can you tell that the number `10120` is not written in base 2 notation?

B.2.2   Twos-Complement Notation

In Section B.2.1, we saw how to convert from binary notation to a positive decimal number by multiplying each `1` digit by an appropriate power of two and summing the results. We shall commonly want to represent both positive and negative integers in binary form, and so a convention is needed to allow a positive number to be distinguished from a negative number. In decimal notation, the convention is to indicate a negative number by prefixing the decimal digits with a minus sign (`'-'`). This is not an option with numbers stored as a sequence of bits in the memory of a computer because each bit can only take on a value of `0` or `1`. Instead, the convention commonly adopted is to regard the bits of an integer as being in *twos-complement notation*. In twos-complement notation, the most significant bit (i.e., the left-most bit in a string of binary digits) is treated as a *sign bit*: a value of `0` in this position indicates that the integer has a positive sign and a value of `1` means that it has a negative sign. Using this convention, it is straightforward to work out the value of a positive number in the way we saw in Section B.2.1, but slightly harder to work out the value of a negative one. We shall illustrate the process using only 8 bits, although the same principles also apply for larger numbers of bits (such as 16 and 32).

   Take the number 01001001_2; if this has been written in twos-complement notation, then the most significant bit tells us that the number is positive. From the remaining digits (`1001001`), we can determine that the decimal value is `64+8+1`, which is `73`. Similarly, the number 01111111_2 is the maximum positive number that we can represent in eight bits, and has the value `64+32+16+8+4+2+1`, which is `127`. Decoding negative numbers is a little more complex, so, before showing how to decode the binary pattern for a negative number, we will demonstrate how to negate a positive decimal using twos-complement notation, as that is slightly easier to understand. The negative equivalent for a positive number is found by firstly *complementing* the bits in its binary representation and then adding `1` to the result. Complementing means to turn each `0` bit into a `1` and every `1` bit into a `0`. For instance, the complement of `01101` is `10010`. Java's complement operator ($\sim$) is used to produce the complement of a binary number. To find the 8-bit twos-complement representation for -1_{10}, we take the 8-bit twos-complement representation of $+1_{10}$, which is 00000001_2, complement it to produce `11111110` and then add `1` to give

11111111. Similarly, we can find the 8-bit twos-complement representation of -43_{10} by taking that for $+43_{10}$ (00101011), complementing it (11010100), and adding 1 to give 11010101. This same process can be performed for any of the positive numbers in the 8-bit twos-complement range, [0...127].

Exercise B.3   Find the 8-bit twos-complement binary representation for -2, -3, -4, -71, and -127.

Exercise B.4   What happens if you apply the twos-complement process to the 8-bit pattern for 0_{10}? Is this what you would expect?

A useful feature of twos-complement notation is that the process works in reverse; negating the binary representation of a negative number gives the positive representation of the result, so to negate a number such as -43 (11010101_2) we complement it (00101010) and add 1 to give 00101011. This gives a simple method for working out the equivalent decimal value of a twos-complement bit-pattern whose most significant bit is 1, indicating that it represents a negative number; simply turn it into the equivalent positive bit pattern, using the complement-plus-one process, convert this pattern to its decimal form, and add a minus sign. For instance, given the 8-bit twos-complement pattern 10001100, we recognize that this is a negative number from the sign bit. Complementing this gives 01110011 and adding 1 gives 01110100, whose decimal equivalent is 116 $(64 + 32 + 16 + 4)$, so 10001100_2 is -116_{10}. However, there is one exception to this rule; consider the 8-bit pattern 10000000. What happens if we try to use this method to find its value? Complementing gives the pattern 01111111 and adding 1 gets us back where we started: 10000000, a value which is negative. The value of this pattern is, in fact, -128_{10} and this illustrates an interesting feature of twos-complement notation: we can represent one more negative value than the set of positive values. That is, for 8 bits of data, the range of values is [-128...127]; for 16 bits the range is [-32768...32767], and so on.[1] The problem only arises when the binary representation of a negative number consists entirely of zero bits apart from the sign bit. When converting on paper from negative to positive, you can always treat this as a special case, or you might like to consider the following alternative approach. Instead of complementing and adding 1 to the resulting bit pattern, take the negative bit pattern and sum the powers of two where the *zeros* occur. Then add one to decimal sum and negate the answer. For the example of 10001100, above this means we form the sum $64 + 32 + 16 + 2 + 1$, which is 115, then add 1 and negate to give -116. This works for the special case of 10000000 by giving $64 + 32 + 16 + 8 + 4 + 2 + 1$, which is 127, then add 1 and negate to give -128.

B.2.3   Octal and Hexadecimal Representation

In addition to base 2 and base 10, base 8 (octal) and base 16 (hexadecimal) representations for numbers are also common in computer applications. Both seek to provide a compact alternative representation to binary form, and hexadecimal is

---

[1] This feature affects the behavior of the `Math.abs` method which returns -32768 when passed an argument of -32768, for instance.

more compact than decimal. Neither, typically, is concerned with representing a sign to distinguish between positive and negative integers. In octal notation, the digits [0...7] are used to represent 3-bit groups of binary digits. Where the number of bits does not divide equally into groups of three (8 bits and 16 bits, for instance), the group containing the most significant bits will represent fewer bits ($2+3+3$ for 8 bits and $1+3+3+3+3+3$ for 16 bits). Just as with binary and decimal notation, each octal digit represents a multiple of a power of the base of the notation: 8^2, 8^1, and 8^0. Therefore, the octal number 162 represents the value $1 \times 64 + 6 \times 8 + 2 \times 1$, which is 114_{10}. The first digit represent the left-most 2 bits of an 8-bit binary number, the second digit represents the next 3 bits, and the final digit represents the right-most 3 bits. It is easy to reconstruct a binary number from its octal representation by translating each octal digit into its binary equivalent and concatenating the parts. So, 162_8 is converted to binary notation by concatenating 01, 110, and 010 to give 01110010_2.

Exercise B.5   What are the octal representations of 00101010_2 and 11100011_2?

Exercise B.6   What are the 8-bit binary representations of 031_8 and 277_8?

Exercise B.7   What are the 8-bit octal representations of 68_{10} and -10_{10}?

Hexadecimal notation (base 16) is made slightly more interesting by the fact that its digits have to represent values in the range [0...15], but there are no natural decimal digits in the range [10...15]. In order to solve this problem, the letters [A...F] are used for these (in either upper or lowercase form). Each hexadecimal digit represents a group of 4 binary digits, and conversion between binary and hexadecimal format is similar to that shown for octal. The value 10011110_2 is represented as $9E_{16}$, therefore, and $1F7A_{16}$ converts to 0001111101111010_2. Converting from hexadecimal to decimal consists of multiplying the hex digits by the appropriate powers of 16 (1, 16, 256, 4096, etc.); $1F7A_{16}$ converts to $1 \times 4096 + 15 \times 256 + 7 \times 16 + 10$, which is 8058. The toOctalString and toHexString methods of the Integer and Long classes return a String octal and hexadecimal representation of their integer argument values (see Section 10.4.1).

Exercise B.8   What are the hexadecimal representations of the binary values 10110100_2 and 00011110_2?

Exercise B.9   What are the 16-bit binary representations of $F0C6_{16}$, $ABCD_{16}$, and $FFFF_{16}$?

Exercise B.10   What are the 16-bit hexadecimal representations of 135_8, 4096_{10}, and -1_{10}?

B.2.4   Octal and Hexadecimal Literals

As described in Section B.2.3, octal notation only uses the digits 0–7, and each digit position is interpreted as being multiplied by successive powers of 8. For the compiler to interpret an integer literal as an octal value in Java, the initial digit must be 0. So the value 027 is understood to mean $2 \times 8^1 + 7 \times 8^0$ which is 23_{10}. In hexadecimal notation, the digits 0–9 are supplemented with the letters A–F (either upper or lowercase) to stand for the values 10–15. An integer literal must be preceded by the characters $0x$ or $0X$ for it to be interpreted by the compiler as a hexadecimal value. Each digit position is interpreted as being multiplied by successive powers of 16. So the value $0x27f$ is interpreted as $2 \times 16^2 + 7 \times 16^1 + 15$ which is 639_{10}.

An integer type numeric literal will usually be assumed to be of type int by the compiler. Where the value is too large to be held in an int (i.e., it requires more than 32 bits), then the compiler will give an error message, for instance,

```
Program.java: Numeric overflow.
        int i = 0x1ffffffffff;
                ^
```

The value $0x1ffffffffff$ requires at least 33 bits. We cannot even get around this by declaring the receiving variable as long,

```
long l = 0x1ffffffffff;
```

produces the same error message. Instead, we have to indicate to the compiler that the value itself is of type long. This is done by appending either L or l to the end of the value (an uppercase L is preferred). So the following are both valid:

```
long l1 = 0x1ffffffffffL;
long l2 = 2199023255551L;
```

APPENDIX

C

Java Operators

C.1 Introduction

In this appendix, we supplement and summarize some of the material on operators covered in Chapter 5. We also discuss the specialist *bit manipulation operators* which were not covered there, and we give a full table of *operator precedences*.

C.2 Operator Precedences

Table C.1 shows the precedence of all the Java operators. Those operators with the highest precedence appear towards the top of the table. In addition to traditional operators, such as + and &&, the table includes array indexing, argument lists, and type casts, as these are commonly used as components of expressions. The table illustrates that array indexing, argument lists, and type casts take precedence over all arithmetic operators. This results in an expression such as

```
x+arr[i]
```

Table C.1 Operator precedences

Style	Operators
postfix	`[ ] . (arguments) ++ --`
unary (prefix)	`++ -- + - ! ~`
unary	`new (cast)`
binary	`* / %`
binary	`+ -`
binary	`<< >> >>>`
binary	`< > >= <= instanceof`
binary	`== !=`
binary	`&`
binary	`^`
binary	`|`
binary	`&&`
binary	`||`
ternary	`? :`
binary	`= += -= *= /= %= >>= <<= >>>= &= |= ^=`

being given the natural interpretation of adding the value of x to the value stored at arr[i], rather than trying to add x to arr.

The high precedence of the cast operator means that it is often necessary to parenthesize the expression to which it applies. For instance,

```
return (int) Math.random()*100;
```

means

```
return ((int) Math.random())*100;
```

because the cast takes precedence over the multiplication. What is probably meant is

```
return (int) (Math.random()*100);
```

which requires the explicit parentheses.

C.3   Arithmetic Operators

The binary arithmetic operators, +, -, *, /, and % are available for all the numeric types (see Section 5.3). Versions of these operators combined with the assignment operator provide useful short-hands for in-place modification of a variable (see Section 5.5.4). Both + and - are available as unary operators. The remaining unary arithmetic operators ++ and -- exist in both prefix and postfix forms (see Section 7.5.1).

C.4   Relational Operators

Table C.2 shows the complete set of relational operators and their meanings.

Table C.2   The relational operators

a == b	is a equal to b?
a != b	is a not equal to b?
a > b	is a greater than b?
a < b	is a less than b?
a >= b	is a greater than or equal to b?
a <= b	is a less than or equal to b?

C.5   Boolean Logical Operators

Two of the binary Boolean logical operators have short-circuit versions—&& (*logical-and*) and || (*logical-or*). If the overall result can be determined from the value of the left operand, then the right operand is not evaluated. There are three fully-evaluating binary Boolean operators—& (*logical-and*), | (*logical-or*), and ^ (*exclusive-or*). Versions of these fully-evaluating operators are also used for bit manipulation of binary data (see Appendix C.6). Table C.3 shows the truth tables for all of the short-circuit binary Boolean logical operators. Table C.4 shows the truth tables for all of the fully-evaluating binary Boolean logical operators. Java has a single binary Boolean logical

Table C.3 Result value using short-circuit boolean logical-operators

	Lhs	Rhs	Result
&&	false	any-value	false
	true	false	false
	true	true	true
||	true	any-value	true
	false	false	false
	false	true	true

Table C.4 Result value using fully-evaluating Boolean logical operators

&	false	false	false
	true	false	false
	false	true	false
	true	true	true
|	false	false	false
	true	false	true
	false	true	true
	true	true	true
^	false	false	false
	true	false	true
	false	true	true
	true	true	false

operator—! (*logical-not*)—which inverts the value of its operand. See Section 6.2.3 for more details of all these operators.

C.6 Bit Manipulation Operators

Three of the *bit manipulation operators* look similar to their Boolean versions—&, | , and ^. These are interpreted as bit manipulation operators when they have operands of the following types—byte, char, int, long, and short. The bit manipulation operators may not be used between primitive floating point operands. They operate as follows:

- The bit manipulation and-operator will produce a 1 bit in the result at every position where the corresponding bits in its operands are both 1, otherwise it produces a 0 bit.
- The bit manipulation or-operator produces a 1 bit wherever at least one of the operands has a 1 bit.
- The bit manipulation exclusive-or operator produces a 1 bit only if the corresponding bits in the operands are different.

Table C.5 shows these results in tabular form for a single bit in each operand and the result. As can be seen, the rows of this table are identical to those for the

Table C.5 Result bit using bit manipulation operators

	Left	Right	Result
&	0	0	0
	1	0	0
	0	1	0
	1	1	1
|	0	0	0
	1	0	1
	0	1	1
	1	1	1
^	0	0	0
	1	0	1
	0	1	1
	1	1	0

corresponding operators in Table C.4, with each `false` value replaced by `0` and each `true` value replaced by `1`.

As an example of each operator, consider the following examples.[1] The 32-bit integer `14` has the bit pattern

    00000000000000000000000000001110

and `9` has the bit pattern

    00000000000000000000000000001001

If these two numbers are and-ed together, the result is `8`

    00000000000000000000000000001000

as the only two bits that are set in the same position in both operands are at the fourth position from the right. In other words (omitting leading zeros),

```
// 00001110 & 00001001 == 00001000
(14 & 9) == 8
```

Examples of the or- and exclusive-or operators are as follows:

```
// 00010001 | 00000011 == 00010011
(17 | 3) == 19
// 00001011 ^ 00001001 == 00000010
(11 ^ 9) == 2
```

In addition to these three operators, the *complement operator* (∼) takes a single operand and produces a result in which the operand's bits have been inverted, that is, each `1` bit in the operand produces a `0` bit in the result, and each `0` bit produces a `1` bit (analogous to the not-operator (`!`) on Boolean types). Integer values represented in *twos-complement notation* will have their sign changed by the complement operator, since the most significant bit (the left-most bit) determines the sign of the value—a

---

[1] We omit the leading zeros in many of these examples to conserve space.

0 in the most significant bit indicates a positive number and a 1 indicates a negative one. Some examples are as follows (note, we use 16-bit examples, rather than 32 bits for the sake of space):

```
// ~0000000000000000 == 1111111111111111
~0 == -1
// ~1111111111010101 == 0000000000101010
~-43 == 42
```

C.6.1   Bit Masks

Combinations of the bit manipulation operators are often used to identify and manipulate selected bits within a number. Many of the Event classes defined in the java.awt.event package (described in Chapter 16) encode items of information as a set of bit values within a single integer. For instance, the InputEvent class defines a getModifiers method that returns an int. The integer encodes information about whether particular keys—Alt, Ctrl, Shift, etc.—were pressed when the event was generated. We might test whether the Shift key was down as follows

```
// Was the Shift key down?
((e.getModifiers() & InputEvent.SHIFT_MASK) == InputEvent.SHIFT_MASK)
```

or whether either the Alt or Ctrl keys were down:

```
// Was either the Alt or Ctrl key down?
((e.getModifiers() & (InputEvent.ALT_MASK|InputEvent.CTRL_MASK)) != 0)
```

C.6.2   Bit Manipulation Operators

Three operators allow the bits in an integer value to be *shifted*, either left (bits move from less significant to more significant positions) or right (bits move to less significant positions). The issue of what to do at either end of the shifted number arises; with a left shift ($<<$) it is usual to lose the most significant bit and replace the least significant bit with a 0. Java provides two different operators for a right shift ($>>$ and $>>>$). The left operand of both is the number to be shifted and the right operand is the number of bit positions to shift to the right. With the $>>$ operator, the most significant bit from before the shift is replicated in the left-most position—this is called *sign extension*— the sign of the result matches the sign of the operand. With the $>>>$ operator, the most significant bit in the result is always 0. Here are some examples to illustrate these operators. Each Java expression is preceded by the bit-patterns it manipulates.

```
// 00000000000000000000000000000100 << 1 == 00000000000000000000000000001000
(4 << 1) == 8

// 00000000000000000000000000000100 >> 1 == 00000000000000000000000000000010
(4 >> 1) == 2

// 11111111111111111111111111111011 >> 1 == 11111111111111111111111111111101
(-5 >> 1) == -3

// 11111111111111111111111111111011 >>> 1 == 01111111111111111111111111111101
(-5 >>> 1) == 2147483645
```

Notice how filling the most significant bit in the last example (-5 >>> 1) turns a small negative operand into a large positive value.

The value of the right operand in a shift operation is sometimes modified so that it is compatible with the type of the left operand. In particular, you cannot shift an operand by more bits than exist in its length. A 32-bit int may only be shifted by a maximum of 31 bits and an 8-bit byte may only be shifted by up to 7 bits, that is, they may be shifted by a maximum of one less bit than they contain. In order to achieve this, the right operand is always *masked* by a bit pattern equal to the size of the type in bits, less one. For an 8-bit byte this will be the value 0111 (i.e., the bit-pattern for 7) and for a 32-bit int this will be the value 011111 (the bit pattern for 31), for instance.

A left-shift of one or more bits is sometimes used as an efficient alternative to integer multiplication by a power of two. Left-shifting by 1-bit multiplies an integer by 2, left-shifting by 2-bits multiplies by 4, and so on. Sign extending right-shifting almost works for division, too, unless the number being shifted is -1!

The example in Code C.1 uses a bit manipulation operator to count the number of 1-bits in an integer.

Code C.1   Report on the number of bits in a list of integers (`CountBitsMain.java`)

```java
// Use bit-wise operators to count the number of 1-bits in
// a list of integers.
class CountBitsMain {
    public static void main(String[] args){
        final int numValues = args.length;
        if(numValues > 0){
            // Turn each argument into an integer.
            for(int i = 0; i < numValues; i++){
                try{
                    int num = Integer.parseInt(args[i]);
                    String bits = Integer.toBinaryString(num);
                    int numBits = countOneBits(num);
                    System.out.println(bits+" has "+numBits+" ones.");
                }
                catch(NumberFormatException e){
                    System.out.println(args[i]+" is not an integer.");
                }
            }
        }
        else{
            System.out.println("java CountBitsMain num ...");
        }
    }

    // Return the number of 1-bits in num.
    public static int countOneBits(int num){
        int numBits = 0;
        while(num != 0){
            if((num & 0x01) == 1){
                numBits++;
```

Code C.1   *(Continued)*

```
        }
        // Shift in zeros at the left.
        num >>>= 1;
      }
      return numBits;
   }
}
```

The 1-bits are calculated in the `countOneBits` method. The right-most bit is tested each time around the loop. The main method uses the `toBinaryString` method of the `Integer` class to print a binary representation of the argument values (see Section 10.4.1).

APPENDIX D
Java Reserved Words

Table D.1 lists the reserved words (keywords) of Java that have a particular significance and so may not be used as identifiers. In addition to these, the Boolean literal values `false` and `true` and the reference value `null` have a similar status, although they are not strictly reserved words.

Table D.1 Reserved words in Java

Word	Purpose	Word	Purpose
abstract	Abstract class	interface	Interface definition
boolean	Primitive type	long	Primitive type
break	Block break	native	Native method
byte	Primitive type	new	Object creation
case	Switch statement	package	Package naming
catch	Exception handler	private	Access modifier
char	Primitive type	protected	Access modifier
class	Class definition	public	Access modifier
const	Unused	return	Method return
continue	Iteration	short	Primitive type
default	Switch statement	static	Class association
do	Iteration statement	strictfp	Class modifier
double	Primitive type	super	Super class reference
else	If-statement	switch	Switch statement
extends	Sub type definition	synchronized	Synchronized access
final	Final designation	this	This object
finally	Exception handler	throw	Throw an exception
float	Primitive type	throws	Exception thrown
for	Iteration statement	transient	Do not serialize
goto	Unused	try	Exception handler
if	If-statement	void	No return type
implements	Interface implementation	volatile	Unpredictable change
import	Package import	while	Iteration statement
instanceof	Type test		
int	Primitive type		

APPENDIX

E

Common Design Patterns

E.1   Introduction

In 1995, an influential book[GHJV95]describing a number of object-oriented design patterns was published. This was based on an earlier work[AIS+77] concerned with architectural design patterns. Both recognized that patterns, or themes, tend to recur in various disciplines. For instance, we have seen the *iterator pattern* used repeatedly to access the elements of an arbitrary collection of items. This frees the user of an `Iterator` object from having to know how the underlying collection is organized. Being aware of these patterns, and where it is appropriate to use them, can save a lot of work in both the design and implementation stages of a programming problem, and the existence of patterns is an aid to software re-use. Work has continued on identifying and cataloging new object-oriented design and implementation patterns. In this appendix, we explore just a few of the more common patterns: *Singleton*, *Model-View*, and *Factory*.

E.2   The Singleton Pattern

The principle behind the *singleton pattern* is that it is sometimes necessary to ensure that only a single instance of a particular class exists at any one time. Such an instance is called a singleton. An object with a reference to an instance of the singleton class will have an alias to the same object referred to by all others. Singletons are mostly used when either multiple instances must be prevented, or instances would have no unique state and would behave identically. There are several situations in which it does not make sense to have multiple instances of a class. It is usual to run only a single window manager during a login session, for instance; multiple instances of a CD player competing to play the same disk could produce unpleasant results; and so on.

   The first step in creating a singleton class is to prevent ordinary creation of instances. The easiest way to do this is to give the class a private constructor. The effect of this will be that an instance can only be created internally by the class's own methods. The second step is to provide a `getInstance` method that returns a reference to the singleton instance. The instance can be stored in a private class variable since it will be the only one in existence, and it can be returned by a class method. Code E.1 illustrates these principles. An example of a singleton class is the

---

Code E.1 Providing a singleton instance

```
    // An implementation of the Singleton pattern.
class Singleton {
    public static Singleton getInstance(){
        return instance;
    }

    // Other functionality ...
    ...

        // Prevent external construction.
    private Singleton(){
    }

    // The solo instance.
    private static Singleton instance = new Singleton();
}
```

Swing `ToolTipManager`, whose `sharedInstance` method returns the shared object (see Section 17.8).

Rather than automatically creating the singleton instance when the class is loaded, it is quite common to create it on demand, as shown in Code E.2. If an instance is never required, one will not be created unnecessarily.

If the instance could be shared by different threads, the example in Code E.2 provides the potential for a *race hazard* to occur; notice the tell-tale separation of

---

Code E.2 Creating a singleton on demand

```
class Singleton {
        // Create the instance on demand.
    public static Singleton getInstance(){
        if(instance == null){
            // The first request; create it.
            instance = new Singleton();
        }
        return instance;
    }

    // Other functionality ...
    ...

        // Prevent external construction.
    private Singleton(){
    }

    // The solo instance.
    private static Singleton instance;
}
```

Code E.3   Avoiding a race hazard on instance creation

```
class Singleton {
    public static Singleton getInstance(){
        if(instance == null){
            // Avoid a possible race-hazard.
            synchronized(Singleton.class){
                // Double-check in case someone else got there.
                if(instance == null){
                    instance = new Singleton();
                }
            }
        }
        return instance;
    }

    // Prevent external construction.
    private Singleton(){
    }

    // The solo instance.
    private static Singleton instance;
}
```

test-and-set operations in `getInstance` (see Section 18.6). If it is necessary to avoid this possibility, the example in Code E.3 provides a solution. The synchronized statement obtains a *monitor* on the class object before setting the instance. Notice that we only incur the penalty of locking the class if the instance needs to be set. The (minor) disadvantage of this is that a double-check of `instance` is necessary to make sure that it is still unset inside the critical section. This is because another thread could have set it between the test and obtaining the lock.

E.2.1   Enumerated Types

We can use the idea of defining a private constructor in a related context—simulating the *enumerated type* facility that is present in some languages. Code E.4 defines a class, `TeamColor`, whose instances can be used to represent color names assigned to teams in a competition, say. A variable of the enumerated type would be defined with the `TeamColor` type and its value would have to be the same as one of the four immutable static variables (or `null`), since further construction is not permitted by virtue of the constructor's visibility.

```
TeamColor whichTeam = TeamColor.Red;
```

One benefit of this approach over that described in Section 13.5, is that it provides slightly better type checking—it is not possible to store an invalid value in a variable of the enumerated type. In addition, *reference equality* is valid between variables of this type—two teams of the same color must be referring to the same instance of `TeamColor`.

Code E.4   Simulating an enumerated type

```
    // Simulate an 'enumerated type'.
public class TeamColor {
        // Immutable instances.
    public static TeamColor Red = new TeamColor("Red");
    public static TeamColor Green = new TeamColor("Green");
    public static TeamColor Blue = new TeamColor("Blue");
    public static TeamColor Yellow = new TeamColor("Yellow");

        // Prevent external construction.
    private TeamColor(String name){
        this.name = name;
    }

    public String toString(){
        return getName();
    }

    private String getName(){
        return name;
    }

    private final String name;
}
```

```
            if(playerA.getTeam() == playerB.getTeam()){
                // They are on the same team.
                ...
            }
```

E.3   The Model-View Pattern

Many applications involve the need to present a graphical representation of some data. An important early design decision is how closely coupled the representation should be to the underlying data. Where the data might change, the representation will need to be updated in order to maintain an accurate picture. For instance, a Graphical User Interface (GUI) monitoring stock market prices must be as accurate as possible second-by-second in order to keep dealers up-to-date, and the lives of many people could depend on the accurate plotting of aircraft positions on the radar screens of air-traffic controllers.

The first important point to note is that the data and its representation really are separate entities. While the data received by a share-dealing system might have a rigidly defined format, the way in which that data is presented to a dealer could be many and varied. For instance, the way in which data on rapidly changing commodity prices is presented could be quite different from that in which more stable stocks is shown. The separation of data from its representation is referred to as the *Model-View pattern*. Quite often a third element is added to create the *Model-View-Controller (MVC) pattern*. In the MVC pattern, those elements of the system which are able to

---

Code E.5   The Observable interface defined in the `java.util` package

```
public interface Observer {
        // The observerable wishes to notify us of a change.
    public void update(Observable o, Object arg);
}
```

---

control or modify the data (the model) are also defined separately. In the remainder of this section, we shall concentrate just on the model-view pattern.

There are at least two ways in which the model and the view might interact:

- The view could repeatedly, or periodically, *poll* the model to see whether it has changed or not.
- The view could wait passively to be informed by the model of any change that has occurred to it.

It is the latter mode of working that is usually referred to as model-view. The `java.util` package defines the `Observer` interface and `Observable` class that support the model-view pattern. Code E.5 shows the Observer interface.

The Observable class already defines a fully functioning set of methods to support objects that need to keep an Observer up-to-date. An Observer registers with an Observable by sending it an `addObserver` message. When an Observable object wishes to inform its observers of something, it marks itself as having changed via its `setChanged` method, and then calls one of its two `notifyObservers` methods. Both versions result in all registered observers receiving an `update` message, as defined in the Observer interface. The no-arg version of `notifyObservers` passes a `null` Object value to the `update` method.

The example in Code E.6 illustrates these principles in action.

Code E.6   An Observer-Observer pairing to illustrate the model-view pattern (`ModelViewMain.java`)

```
import java.util.*;

    // Illustrate the model-view pattern with an Observable-Observer pair.
class ModelViewMain {
    public static void main(String[] args){
        Model model = new Model();
        Observer view = new View(model);

        new Thread(model).start();
    }
}

class View implements Observer {
    public View(Observable o){
        // Register for notifications.
        o.addObserver(this);
    }
```

(Continued)

Code E.6   *(Continued)*

```java
    public void update(Observable model, Object arg){
        if(arg == null){
            System.out.println("Goodbye from the view.");
        }
        else{
            System.out.println(arg);
        }
    }
}


        // Simulate a model changing over time by generating
        // random numbers.
class Model extends Observable implements Runnable {
    // Generate max random numbers for any observer.
    public void run(){
        final int max = 100;
        final Random rand = new Random();
        for(int i = 0; i < max; i++){
            try{
                Integer num = new Integer(rand.nextInt());
                // Notify the observers of the number.
                setChanged();
                notifyObservers(num);
                Thread.sleep(100);
            }
            catch(InterruptedException e){
            }
        }
        // Tell the observers we have finished.
        setChanged();
        notifyObservers();
        System.out.println("Goodbye from the model.");
    }
}
```

The `Model` class operates as an independent thread generating a random number from time to time.[1] After generating each number, the model sets its changed-status and notifies its observers. Notice that it is often not necessary for a sub class of Observable to override any of its super class's methods.

Many of the Swing classes demonstrate separation of model from view. The `JScrollPane` and `JTable` classes are two particular examples.

E.4   The Factory Pattern

Sometimes it is necessary to obtain an object whose exact implementation class is platform- or locale-specific. On many of these occasions, you are really only interested in the object for the methods defined in a standard abstract class or interface,

---

[1] The fact that it implements Runnable is not a requirement of extending Observable, however.

but necessarily implemented by a particular concrete class. It might not be possible to know the name of the concrete class, or the name might be different on different platforms. Such circumstances are suited to the *Factory pattern*. This has some similarities to the singleton pattern in that responsibility for creating an appropriate instance is delegated to a factory class, rather than handled directly by the client that needs the instance. The Swing `BorderFactory` class is a particular example of this approach. It is responsible for returning appropriate implementations of the `Border` interface to clients. Clients are not interested in the exact dynamic type of the instances they receive, only in the fact that they implement the Border interface in a particular style. The `FuelFactory` class (described in Section 21.6.8) provides another example. In that particular case, clients are only interested in receiving an instance of the abstract `FuelType` class and they do not need to be aware exactly how it has been implemented.

Stylistic Conventions

F.1 Introduction

Stylistic conventions are important for readers of your programs. In this appendix, we outline some guidelines that we think are worth adopting.

F.2 Comments

All programs should be properly commented. The Javadoc tool (see Appendix H) facilitates the automatic generation of program documentation where its conventions have been used. In particular, each class and method should be prefaced by a comment describing its overall purpose. For constructors and major methods, you should consider including the following items as part of their *specification*:

- purpose
- argument descriptions
- result descriptions
- constraints
- exceptions thrown

Code F.1 shows an example. Statement comments should precede the statements to which they refer and not be appended to the ends of lines. It is preferable to comment a block of statements rather than each individually. Try to get into the habit of commenting as you write, rather than after the event. In the real world, there will not be time to comment once the program is "finished".

Both single-line comments (using //) and multi-line comment forms (using /* ... */) are equally acceptable. When the multi-line comment form is used, ensure that the closing comment symbol can be easily spotted, preferably by indenting it to the same level as the opening symbol, for instance,

```
/* This comment
   is a multi-line comment
   that spans several lines.
*/
```

Code F.1   An example of method header commenting

```
    /** Locate the minimum value in the elements
     *  data[lower .. upper].
     *  Lower must be <= upper, and both must be within the
     *  range 0 .. data.length-1.
     *  @param data The data to be searched.
     *  @param lower The lowest index for the range to be searched.
     *  @param upper The highest index for the range to be searched.
     *  @return The minimum value.
     *  @throws IllegalRangeException if lower > upper, or either
     *          lower or upper is outside the bounds of data.
     */
public int locateMin(int[] data,int lower,int upper)
                    throws IllegalRangeException {
    ...
}
```

Some authors like to emphasize comments with further adornments such as:

```
/* This comment
 * is a multi-line comment
 * that spans several lines.
 */
```

This is perfectly acceptable.

F.3   Identifiers

There is no right or wrong style of choice of identifiers, except that they should be accurately descriptive. The most important point is to be consistent. A variable should have a single purpose rather than being used for several different tasks, and its name should reflect that purpose. For instance: `accountNumber`, `valueFound`, `studentName`, etc. Avoid examples like

```
    if(list.point() == -1)
```

when

```
    if(list.getNumberOfItems() == 0)
```

is much clearer.

A common style is that names of methods, attributes, method variables, and formal arguments should have an initial lowercase letter, but a single uppercase letter at word boundaries (as in the examples). Class names should start with an upper-case letter and follow a similar convention at word boundaries, e.g., `Ship`, `TemperatureController`, `PortAuthority`. Public final class variables (`public static final`) should either be all uppercase names, or they should have an initial uppercase letter.

The names for accessor and mutator methods should be based directly upon the name of the attribute to which they apply. They should have either a `get` or `set` prefix, followed by the name of the attribute with its first letter capitalized.

It is hard for a single-character variable name to convey much information about its purpose so, in general, these should be avoided, with the following exceptions:

- Loop-control variables in for loops used to systematically iterate over a fixed range.
- The formal argument name of a simple `set` mutator method. The name will typically be the first letter of the attribute being mutated.

In general, define method variables close to where they are first used, rather than bunching them all together at the start of a method. Make use of the fact that variables may be defined within nested blocks to ensure that a method variable's scope is closely related to the part of a method in which it is used.

F.4   Final Variables

As far as possible, avoid the use of *magic numbers* in your programs. Instead, create a final variable for values of significance, e.g.,

```
final int endOfList = -1;
final int meaning = 42;
final double MAXMARK = 100.0;
```

The only exceptions to this rule are the use of 0 and 1 as initializers and 1 as a simple step, although `++` and `--` are more convenient. Where final variables could be of use to objects other than the one in which they are defined, they may be defined as `public static final`, for instance,

```
class Date {
    public static final int January = 0,...;
    ...
}
```

Some authors prefer to use completely uppercase names for final variables.

Use the `final` specifier for variables whose value will remain unchanged after initialization. Final attributes may be set directly in their declaration, in every constructor, or in an instance initializer. This can avoid the need to define a mutator for such an attribute. However, omitting a mutator could make it harder to check the validity of the attribute's value when it is set at instance construction time—validity checks will need to be included at each initialization point. In such circumstances, therefore, it might be worth not using a final designation and including a validity checking mutator. The mutator will be able to prevent the attribute's value being changed once set if the attribute is an object reference, by checking whether the attribute is already non-null.

Fields defined within interfaces are always `public static final`. We recommend that these access modifiers are explicitly included in their definition.

F.5   Indentation and Layout

Try to keep lines no longer than 80 characters. Even though this limit dates from the ancient days of punch cards, longer lines often do not display well within some programs or windows. Use four spaces for each level of indentation, and use single blank lines freely in order to emphasize blocks of code, as in Code F.2. Define methods before instance variables, and public methods before those with lesser visibility. Final static variables with public visibility may be defined at the beginning of the class.

Break long lines immediately after operators in expressions and commas in argument lists. Indent the remaining part of the statement somewhat deeper than the current indentation level. Where practicable, indent to a level that relates the broken part to where it belongs on the previous line, as follows:

```
VeryLongClassName evenLongerVariableName =
                        new VeryLongClassName("Say hello to auntie.");
Greeting introduction = new Greeting("Good morning,",32,'x',
                                new Point(8,105),
                                new Point(458,47));
```

F.5.1   Initializers and Anonymous Classes

Long array initializers should be split over multiple lines, for instance,

```
int[] values = {
    3, 56, 23, 999, 101, -8, 3443, 23234, -9900,
    45, -349730, 783,
};
```

Code F.2   An example of indentation

```
class ExampleClass {
    public static final int LOW = -20, MEDIUM = 0, HIGH = 20;
    public static final int DEFAULT = MEDIUM;

    public ExampleClass(int initialValue){
        if(howMany > DEFAULT){
            setNumber(initialValue);
        }
        else{
            setNumber(DEFAULT);
        }
    }

    ...

    private void setNumber(int number){
        this.number = number;
    }

    private int number;
}
```

It is common practice to include a trailing comma after the final value, as this makes it easier to add items at a later date.

A typical layout for anonymous class definitions is as follows:

```
button.addActionListener(new ActionListener(){
    public void actionPerformed(ActionEvent e){
        ...
    }
});
```

Note the way in which the closing curly bracket is kept together with the closing parenthesis of the argument list.

F.6   Curly Brackets

Place the opening curly bracket at the end of class and method headers. A curly bracket following a class header is often separated from it by a single space. Indent the closing curly bracket of class and method bodies to the same level as the initial reserved word of the construct.

```
class ExampleClass {
    public void method(){
        ...
    }
}
```

Always use a pair of curly brackets with statements such as if, while and for, even when the body of the construct contains a single statement,

```
if(x > largest){
    largest = x;
}
```

Place the opening curly bracket immediately following the condition of an if-statement, while loop and for loop. You might need to break a long condition over more than one line—do so after an operator and indent the broken line so that it starts beneath the expression that is broken, and further to the right than the statement immediately following.

```
if((month < rainfall.length) &&
        (rainfall[month] > greatest)){
    statement;
}
```

F.7   Increment and Decrement Operators

Use the post-increment and post-decrement forms of the increment (x++) and decrement (x--) operators. Wherever possible, avoid using these operators where you are also using the value of the variable being modified. Instead, use separate statements in order to avoid possible confusion. For example, rather than writing

```
arr[index++] = reader.nextInt();
```

write:

```
arr[index] = reader.nextInt();
index++;
```

In the first example, it is easy to miss the fact that `index` is being incremented in addition to the assignment being made.

F.8   Switch Statement

Use a switch statement in preference to a cascading if-else statement, where an arithmetic expression is to be checked against multiple constant values. The compiler is usually able to create a more efficient selection of the appropriate statements with a switch statement.

Avoid overuse of omitting `break` from cases to provide a fall through to the next case. When it is omitted, always include a comment to make clear that this is not an error.

F.9   Exceptions

- Use *checked exceptions* whenever possible.
- Include a throws clause for *unchecked exceptions*, even though this is not mandatory.
- Take the opportunity to create sub classes of the basic Exception classes in order to give meaningful names to the types of errors that arise. These do not need to add additional attributes or behavior to their super class. Where such new exception classes are closing tied to a single throwing class, consider defining them as static nested classes within the throwing class.
- Use exceptions for impossible routes through methods. These will often be thrown in a final else-part of a validity-checking cascading if-else statement, or at the end of a result-returning method that should be unreachable in normal circumstances.

These rules increase both the compiler's and the programmer's opportunities to ensure that exceptional circumstances are identified and recovery mechanisms put in place.

F.10   Access Control

Use the following forms of access control, outlined in Section 14.7.4:

- An object's attributes should always be declared as private, rather than public, package, or protected, even if the class is to be extended.
- Access to private attributes of primitive type may safely be granted via accessors with public access. Greater care should be taken when returning references to private attributes of object types since this could potentially allow circumvention of validating mutators via an alias. Use either public or protected access as appropriate.

- Use protected access mutators as a general rule, unless public access is required. Public access mutators should take particular care over validation of their arguments to ensure that an object is not left in an inconsistent state.
- Methods intended purely for internal use by a class should be protected, to make possible future extension by classes in other packages easier than with package access.
- General methods intended for the receipt of messages from other classes should be public.
- Constructors should normally provide either package or public access. If the class has package access, then no harm is done in providing public constructors.
- Classes and interfaces should have either package or public access, depending upon a program's requirement.

These rules make it slightly easier to extend classes than it would be if the choice of access was simply between public and private, even when it has not been envisaged that a class might be extended in the future. Using at least protected access for its methods means that a package access class can be made extensible by classes in other packages relatively easily, by amending its constructors to at least protected level and giving public access to the class.

F.11   The Main Method

As little functionality as possible should be placed in the class holding the main method. The main method should mainly contain statements that create the initial objects that are going to interact to achieve the purposes of the overall program. It is acceptable to place major functionality here if the program is so simple that it does not justify the creation of one or more classes. Only other `static` methods should appear in the class along with the main method. You should note that this minimalist approach is *not* taken by most other Java authors.

F.12   Threads

Avoid use of the `volatile` reserved word. It is only really needed to indicate potentially undisciplined access by multiple threads to an instance variable. Avoid this by defining such a variable as `private`, and provide `synchronized` accessor and mutator methods in the usual way.

Do not overuse the `synchronized` modifier as it can result in unnecessary deadlock. Use it only where there is a clear need to lock an object against multiple thread access.

The Java 2 SDK

G.1 Introduction

The Java 2 SDK[1] is a complete implementation of the Java 2 Platform. It may be downloaded, free of charge, from the JavaSoft web site:

```
http://www.javasoft.com
```

It is this implementation that we have used to develop all of the examples in this book. Its main advantages are that it is free, authoritative, and kept up-to-date. Its main disadvantage is that it provides only command-line style development tools, rather than a graphical visual programming environment. The platform includes a comprehensive set of documentation on all of its classes and tools, so in this appendix we give a brief overview of the essentials to get started with it. We provide important information to help you with the day-to-day usage of the development tools. For full details of the topics discussed in this appendix, you should refer to the documentation supplied with the Java platform.

G.2 Directory Structure

The platform is distributed in a nested hierarchy beneath a top-level `jdk1.2` directory. You are not committed to storing the distribution beneath a directory with that exact name, but we will use it for convenience in the following descriptions. Here we introduce the main files and sub-directories of interest:

- `jdk1.2`—The top-level directory for the platform. It includes the file `src.jar`, a Java Archive (JAR) file containing the source of the core API classes.
- `jdk1.2/bin`—The location of the development tools, such as `javac` (the compiler), `java` (the runtime interpreter), `javadoc` (a documentation tool), and `jar` (the JAR archiver).
- `jdk1.2/lib/tools.jar`—A JAR file containing `.class` files used by the development tools.
- `jdk1.2/jre`—A directory for the items related to the Java Runtime Environment (JRE).

---

[1] Formerly known as the Java Development Kit (JDK)

- jdk1.2/jre/bin—The directory containing the Java launcher tool, java.
- jdk1.2/jre/lib/rt.jar—The JAR file containing .class files for the bootstrap classes. These are the classes that make up the core API that we use throughout this book—classes in the java.lang, java.io, and java.util packages, for instance. The runtime environment will automatically pick these classes up without the need for you to include them in your *CLASSPATH* environment variable (see Section G.4).
- jdk1.2/jre/lib/ext—The directory for extensions to the standard runtime environment (see Section G.4).

G.3   The PATH Environment Variable

You will need to make sure that there is a reference to the jdk1.2/bin directory on the *PATH* environment variable on the system you use, otherwise the system will not know what you mean when you try to run commands such as javac and java. On UNIX and Linux systems this refers to your shell's *search path*—$path or $PATH—which is often set up in a file called .cshrc or .bashrc, for instance,

```
# Include the path to the development tools just before the end
set path = ( ~/bin /bin /usr/bin /usr/local/jdk1.2/bin . )
```

On MS-DOS® based systems, your path environment variable %PATH is usually set in the autoexec.bat file, with a line such as:

```
rem Include the path to the development tools at the end.
set path=%path%;c:\jdk1.2\bin;
```

G.4   Classpath

Classes to be used by a program must appear on the *classpath* of the compiler and runtime interpreter, otherwise you will get a message such as:

```
Exception in thread "main" java.lang.NoClassDefFoundError: Strung
```

Classes will be searched for first in the platform library (in jdk1.2/jre/lib), then in any library extensions (in jdk1.2/jre/lib/ext), and finally in any set class path. If no explicit class path has been set, the current directory will be searched. This means that, if you are only using standard classes and all the remaining classes you are using are in your current working directory, you do not need to define an explicit classpath.[2] When it is necessary to set an explicit classpath, there are two alternatives:

- Use the -classpath command-line argument to the tool you are using, for instance on an MS-DOS system

```
java -classpath path1;path2;path3 ...
```

---

[2] This practice is different for earlier versions of the Java SDK; see the platform documentation for details.

or on a UNIX system.

```
java -classpath path1:path2:path3 ...
```

Notice that different separators are used in each case.

- Set the *CLASSPATH* environment variable for your system. This can be done in the `autoexec.bat` file on an MS-DOS system:

```
set classpath=path1;path2;path3
```

Do not include spaces around the ' = ' symbol. On a UNIX system

```
setenv CLASSPATH "path1:path2:path3 ..."
```

can be included in a `.cshrc` file, or something similar for a different shell. Notice that different separators are used in each case.

Each element of the path may be one of three things:

- The name of a `.jar` or `.zip` file.
- The name of a directory containing `.class` files in the *unnamed package*.
- The name of the directory immediately above a package directory containing `.class` files for that package.

Where an explicit classpath has been set, the current directory will not be searched by default if it does not appear on the classpath. Most operating systems use ' . ' as shorthand for the current directory, so this can easily be included as one component of a classpath. As an example:

```
java -classpath /home/djb/bundle.jar:/home/djb/Java:. package.Example
```

In addition to looking in the platform and extension libraries, the runtime system will look in `bundle.jar` for the file `package/Example.class`; in the directory `/home/djb/Java/package` for the file `Example.class`; and finally in the `package` sub-directory beneath the current directory for the file `Example.class`. Notice that the name of the package directory should *not* be included in the class path.

Many of the examples in this book make use of the `SimpleInput` class. You might like to place a copy of the file `SimpleInput.class` in a particular directory and include that directory in your classpath so that you do not need to keep a copy in every directory containing a program that needs it. If you were to place it in the directory

```
c:\java\utils
```

for instance, then you might compile a program that requires it, as follows:

```
javac -classpath .;c:\java\utils Prog.java
```

Javadoc

H.1   Introduction

Javadoc is a tool supplied as part of the Java platform (see Appendix G). It is an extremely useful means of generating documentation directly from a program source. A further advantage of such a tool is that Java documentation tends to have a consistent appearance, which makes it easier for a human reader to scan effectively. The tool extracts information both from the program text and the text of specially formatted comments and creates a set of documents using the *HyperText Markup Language (HTML)*[Word]. A Javadoc comment is introduced by the sequence `'/**'`. This is simply the ordinary multi-line comment symbol with the immediate addition of a second asterisk. Javadoc comments should precede class, interface, method, and field definitions that you wish to be documented. Section 12.15 contains a practical example, documenting the `SimpleInput` class.

In the next few sections, we give a brief introduction to the tools facilities. For full details, you should refer to the documentation supplied with the Java platform.

H.1.1   Javadoc Tags

The text of a Javadoc comment can simply be plain text. Any leading spaces or asterisks will be ignored when the text is transferred to the documentation file. However, javadoc will process a number of *javadoc tag* strings in a special way. Tags are distinguished by their inclusion of an *at* character (`@`). The current set is:

- `@author author-name`—Name the author. Multiple `@author` tags are allowed.
- `@deprecated deprecation-reason`—Include a note that this feature of a class or package is deprecated and should no longer be used.
- `@exception class description`—preferable is to use `@throws`.
- `@link name label`—produce an in-line hyper-link to name, using label as the text for the link. Similar in syntax to `@see`.
- `@param name description`—a description of a method argument (parameter).
- `@return description`—a description of the return type and value.

- `@see reference`—adds a description to a See Also section of the generated document. There are several variations of the `@see` tag, illustrated as follows:

```
@see "How Computers Play Chess, for more details"
@see java.util.StringTokenizer
@see Math
@see #tokenizer
@see #setDelimiters(String)
@see java.lang.Math#PI
```

All but the first of these creates a hyper-link to the referenced item. As a result, they can take an additional free-text label to be used as the text of the link, such as:

```
@see #setDelimiters(String) Setting the delimiters
```

- `@serial description`—a description of a serializable field.
- `@serialData description`—a description of optional serialized data.
- `@serialField name type description`—A description of an `Object-StreamField`, which is a class that documents a Serializable field.
- `@since description`—the description often refers to the version of the class being documented in which this feature was introduced.
- `@throws class description`—a description of an exception thrown by this method. A method throwing multiple exceptions should have multiple `@throws` tags. This tag is a synonym for the `@exception` tag.
- `@version description`—a description of the current version.

H.1.2   HTML Markup

The text of Javadoc comments can, in fact, be any HTML markup (although headings should not be used). Because the documentation is produced as an HTML document, the markup is transferred directly to it. Within the scope of this book, it is not possible to present more than a basic introduction to simple HTML markup. Some further examples may be found in Chapter 20. Markup usually consists of pairs of tags. Tags are delimited by a pair of angle-bracket characters (< and >). The closing tag includes a forward-slash character (/) immediately after its opening angle-bracket. Here is an example:

```
<b>This text will be in bold.</b>
```

The following example tags are used commonly:

- `<b>This text will be in bold.</b>`
- `<code>This text will use a program-text font.</code>`
- `<i>This text will be in italic.</i>`

- ```
  <pre>
        This text will be
           formatted
               literally.
     With ragged edges.
  </pre>
  ```
  ```

Several tags occur singly, rather than in pairs:

- `<br>`—produce a line break.
- `<hr>`—produce a ruled line.
- `<p>`—produce a paragraph break.

The fact that angled brackets are used to denote tags means that these characters must be escaped when they must appear literally in text. The following are common escape sequences:

- `&amp;`—an ampersand (&).
- `&lt;`—a left angled-bracket (<).
- `&gt;`—a right angled-bracket (>).

H.1.3 Javadoc Command Line Options

The Javadoc tool takes several command line options. Among them are the following:

- `-author`—Include `@author` tags, omitted by default.
- `-classpath pathlist`—Look for referenced classes on the pathlist.
- `-package`—Only show package, protected, and public items.
- `-private`—Show items at all access levels.
- `-protected`—Only show protected and public items (the default).
- `-public`—Only show public items.
- `-sourcepath pathlist`—Look for documented packages on pathlist. This option is used when the packages to be documented, rather than individual source files, are named on the command line.
- `-version`—Include `@version` tags, omitted by default.

Glossary

absolute filename: A filename whose full path is unambiguously given starting from the top (root) of a *file system* tree. For instance,

```
c:\Java\bin\javac.exe
```

See *relative filename*.

abstract class: A class with the `abstract` reserved word in its header. Abstract classes are distinguished by the fact that you may not *directly* construct objects from them using the `new` operator. An abstract class may have zero or more *abstract methods*.

abstract method: A method with the `abstract` reserved word in its header. An abstract method has no *method body*. Methods defined in an *interface* are always abstract. The body of an abstract method must be defined in a *sub class* of an *abstract class*, or the body of a class implementing an interface.

Abstract Windowing Toolkit: The Abstract Windowing Toolkit (AWT) provides a collection of classes that simplify the creation of applications with graphical user interfaces. These are to be found in the `java.awt` *packages*. Included are classes for windows, frames, buttons, menus, text areas, and so on. See Chapter 16. Related to the AWT classes are those for the *Swing* packages, described in Chapter 17.

abstraction: A simplified representation of something that is potentially quite complex. It is often not necessary to know the exact details of how something works, is represented, or is implemented, because we can still make use of it in its simplified form. Object-oriented design often involves finding the right level of abstraction at which to work when modeling real-life objects. If the level is too high, then not enough detail will be captured. If the level is too low, then a program could be more complex and difficult to create and understand than it needs to be.

accessor method: A method specifically designed to provide access to a `private` attribute of a class. By convention, we name accessors with a `get` prefix followed by the name of the attribute being accessed. For instance, the accessor for an attribute named `speed` would be `getSpeed`. By making an attribute private, we prevent objects of other classes from altering its value other than through a *mutator method*. Accessors are used both to grant safe access to the value of a private attribute and to protect attributes from inspection by objects of other classes. The latter goal is achieved by choosing an appropriate visibility for the accessor.

actor: See *client*.

actual argument: The value of an argument passed to a method from outside the method. When a method is called, the *actual argument* values are copied into the corresponding *formal arguments*. The types of the actual arguments must be compatible with those of the formal arguments.

actual parameter: See *actual argument*.

address space: The area of *virtual memory* in which a *process* is run.

agent: See *server*.

aggregation: A relationship in which an object contains one or more other subordinate objects as part of its state. The subordinate objects typically have no independent existence separate from their containing object. When the containing object has no further useful existence, neither do the subordinate objects. For instance, a gas station object might contain several pump objects. These pumps will only exist as long as the station does. Aggregation is also referred to as the *has-a relationship*, to distinguish it from the *is-a relationship*, which refers to *inheritance*.

aliases: Multiple references to a single object. Messages may be sent to the object via any of its aliases. A resulting state change will be detectable via all.

anonymous array: An array created without an *identifier*. An anonymous array is often created as an *actual argument*, for instance,

```
// Create an anonymous array of integers.
YearlyRainfall y2k = new YearlyRainfall(
               new int[]{10,10,8,8,6,4,4,0,4,4,7,10,});
```

An anonymous array may also be returned as a method result.

anonymous class: A class created without a class name. Such a class will be a *sub class*, or an implementation of an *interface*, and is usually created as an *actual argument* or returned as a method result. For instance,

```
quitButton.addActionListener(new ActionListener(){
    public void actionPerformed(ActionEvent e){
        System.exit(0);
    }
});
```

anonymous object: An object created without an *identifier*. They are usually created as array elements, *actual arguments*, or method results. For instance,

```
private Point[] vertices = {
    new Point(0,0),
    new Point(0,1),
    new Point(1,1),
    new Point(1,0),
};
```

See *anonymous class*, as these often result in the creation of anonymous objects.

append mode: A file writing mode, in which the existing contents of a file are retained when the file is opened. New contents are appended to the existing.

applet: Applets are Java programs based around the `Applet` or `JApplet` classes. They are most closely associated with the ability to provide active content within Web pages. They have several features which distinguish them from ordinary Java graphical *applications*, such as their lack of a user-defined main method, and the security restrictions that limit their abilities to perform some normal tasks. See Chapter 20.

application: Often used simply as a synonym for *program*. However, in Java, the term is particularly used of programs with a *Graphical User Interface (GUI)* that are not *applets*.

argument: Information passed to a *method*. Arguments are also sometimes called parameters. A method expecting to receive arguments must contain a *formal argument* declaration for each as part of its *method header*. When a method is called, the *actual argument* values are copied into the corresponding formal arguments.

arithmetic expression: An expression involving numerical values of integer or floating point types. For instance, operators such as +, -, *, /, and % take arithmetic expressions as their operands and produce arithmetic values as their results.

arithmetic operator: Operators, such as +, -, *, /, and %, that produce a numerical result, as part of an *arithmetic expression*.

Arpanet: A network that was a forerunner of the global Internet.

array: A fixed-size object that can hold zero or more items of the array's declared type.

array initializer: An initializer for an array. The initializer takes the place of separate creation and initialization steps. For instance, the initializer

```
int[] pair = {4, 2, };
```

is equivalent to the following four statements:

```
int[] pair;
pair = new int[2];
pair[0] = 4;
pair[1] = 2;
```

assembler: The program used to translate a program written in assembly language into the binary form of a particular *instruction set*.

assembly language: A symbolic language corresponding closely to the *instruction set* of a *Central Processing Unit*. The program used to translate a program written in assembly language is called an *assembler*.

assignment operator: The operator (=) used to store the value of an expression into a *variable*, for instance,

```
variable = expression;
```

The right-hand side is completely evaluated before the assignment is made. An assignment may, itself, be used as part of an expression. The following *assignment statement* stores zero into both variables:

```
x = y = 0;
```

assignment statement: A statement using an *assignment operator*.

attribute: A particular usage of an *instance variable*. The set of attribute values held in a particular *instance* of a class define the current *state* of that instance. A class definition may impose particular constraints on the valid states of its instances by requiring that a particular attribute, or set of attributes, do not take on particular values. For instance, attributes holding coursework marks for a class should not hold negative values. Attributes should be manipulated by *accessor* and *mutator* methods.

base case: A non-recursive route through a recursive method.

base type: The type of items which may be stored in an *array*—the array's defined type. For instance, in

```
int[] numbers;
```

the base type of numbers is int. Where the base type is a class type, it indicates the lowest *super type* of objects that may be stored in the array. For instance, in

```
Ship[] berths;
```

only *instances* of the Ship class may be stored in berths. If the base type of an array is Object, instances of any class may be stored in it.

behavior: The *methods* of a class implement its behavior. A particular object's behavior is a combination of the method definitions of its class and the current *state* of the object.

big-endian: A common difference between machines is the order in which they store the individual bytes of multi-byte numerical data. A big-endian machine stores the higher-order bytes before the lower-order bytes. See *little-endian*.

binary: Number representation in base 2. In base 2, only the digits 0 and 1 are used. Digit positions represent successive powers of 2. See *bit*.

binary operator: An *operator* taking two operands. Java has many binary operators, such as the arithmetic operators, +, -, *, /, and %, and the Boolean operators &&, | |, and ^, amongst others.

binary search: A search of sorted data, in which the middle position is examined first. Search continues with either the left or the right portion of the data, thus eliminating half the remaining search space. This process is repeated at each step, until either the required item is found, or there is no more data to search.

bit: A binary digit, which can take on two possible values: 0 and 1. Bits are the fundamental building block of both programs and data. Computers regularly move data around in multiples of 8-bit units (*bytes* for the sake of efficiency).

bit manipulation operator: Operators, such as &, |, and ∧, that are used to examine and manipulate individual *bits* within the bytes of a data item. The shift operators, <<, >>, and >>>, are also bit manipulation operators.

blank final variable: A *final variable* that is not initialized as part of its declaration. Such a variable must be initialized in either an instance initialization block or all of the constructors for its class before it is used. A static blank final variable must be initialized in a static initialization block.

block: Statements and declarations enclosed between a matching pair of curly brackets ('{' and '}'). For instance, a *class body* is a block, as is a *method body*. A block encloses a nested *scope* level.

bookmark: Used by a Web browser to remember details of a *Uniform Resource Locator (URL)*.

boolean: One of Java's *primitive types*. The boolean type has only two values: true and false.

Boolean expression: An expression whose result is of type boolean, i.e., gives a value of either true or false. Operators such as && and | | take Boolean operands and produce a Boolean result. The relational operators take operands of different types and produce Boolean results.

boot: When a computer is switched on it is said to boot up. This term comes from the phrase, "Pulling yourself up by your bootstraps." Before a computer is ready to be used, it must load the programs that it needs from its disks, but this means that it must have a program of some sort available in order to be able to load the programs it needs! The loading program is called a bootstrap.

bootstrap classes: Classes that make up the *Java Platform Core Application Programming Interface (API)*, such as those found in the java.lang, java.io, and java.util packages.

boundary error: Errors that arise from programming mistakes made at the edges of a problem—indexing off the edge of an array, dealing with no items of data, loop termination, and so on. Boundary errors are a very common type of logical error.

bounded repetition: Repetition where the statements within a loop's body are performed a fixed number of times and the number of times is established when the loop is started. There is no *control structure* in Java that guarantees bounded repetition. See *unbounded repetition*.

bounds: The limits of an *array* or collection. In Java, the lower limit is always zero. In the case of an array, the upper bound is one less than the length of the array, and is fixed. Indexing outside the bounds of an array or collection will result in an IndexOutOfBoundsException *exception* being thrown.

branch instruction: Stores a new instruction address into the program counter. The effect of this is that the next instruction to be fetched will not usually be the one immediately following the branch instruction. Hence, the normal sequential execution of instructions is disrupted. This allows both repetition and conditional execution of instructions to be effected.

break statement: A statement used to break out of a loop, switch statement, or labeled block. In all cases, control continues with the statement immediately following the containing block.

bridging method: A *method* that provides a bridge between the methods of a class's public interface and its private implementation. Bridging methods will typically have non-public visibility.

byte: In general computing, this refers to 8 *bits* of data. In Java, it is also the name of one of the primitive data types, who size is 8 bits.

bytecode: Java source files are translated by a *compiler* into bytecodes—the *instruction set* of the *Java Virtual Machine (JVM)*. Bytecodes are stored in `.class` files.

call-by-value: A semantics of passing an *argument* to a method in which a *copy* of the *actual argument* value is taken and placed in a separate memory location, represented by the corresponding *formal argument*. As a result, assignment to a formal argument within a method can have no effect on the value stored in the actual argument. This principle is often misunderstood in Java. It does *not* mean that an object referred to by an actual argument cannot be modified via the formal argument. Consider the following example of sorting the array referred to by the variable `numbers`:

```
Arrays.sort(numbers);
```

The `sort` method *will* change the order of the values stored in the object referred to by `numbers`. However, it is impossible for the `sort` method to change which array `numbers` refers to—a sorted copy, for instance.

Some languages provide an argument passing semantics known as *call-by-reference*, in which an actual argument's value may be changed. Java does not provide this, however.

carriage return: The `'\r'` character. Also used as a synonym for the Return or Enter key used to terminate a line of text. The name derives from the carriage on a mechanical typewriter.

cascading if-else statement: A form of *if-else statement* in which each else-part (except the last) consists of a further nested if-else statement. Used to overcome the problem of textual drift often associated with nested if statements.

case label: The value used to select a particular case in a *switch statement*.

case sensitive: A test that is sensitive to whether a character is uppercase (e.g., `'A'`) or lowercase (e.g., `'a'`).

cast: Where Java does not permit the use of a source value of one type, it is necessary to use a cast to force the compiler to accept the use for the target type. Care should be taken with casting values of primitive types, because this often involves loss of information. Casts on object references are checked at runtime for legality. A `ClassCastException` *exception* will be thrown for illegal ones.

catch clause: The part of a *try statement* responsible for handling a caught *exception*.

catching exceptions: Exceptions are caught within the *catch clause* of a *try statement*. Catching an exception gives the program an opportunity to recover from the problem or attempt a repair for whatever caused it.

Central Processing Unit: The Central Processing Unit (CPU) is the heart of a computer as it is the part that contains the computer's ability to obey instructions. Each type of CPU has its own *instruction set*.

character set encoding: The set of values assigned to characters in a character set. Related characters are often grouped with consecutive values, such as the alphabetic characters and digits.

checked exception: An *exception* that must be caught locally in a *try statement*, or propagated via a *throws clause* defined in the *method header*. See *unchecked exception*.

class: A programming language concept that allows data and *methods* to be grouped together. The class concept is fundamental to the notion of an *object-oriented programming language*. The methods of a class define the set of permitted operations on the class's data (its *attributes*). This close tie between data and operations means that an *instance* of a class—an *object*—is responsible for responding to messages received via its defining class's methods.

class body: The body of a *class* definition. The body groups the definitions of a class's *members*—*fields*, *methods*, and *nested classes*.

class constant: A variable defined as both `final` and `static`.

class header: The header of a *class* definition. The header gives a name to the class and defines its *access*. It also describes whether the class `extends` a *super class* or `implements` any *interfaces*.

class inheritance: When a *super class* is extended by a *sub class*, a class inheritance relationship exists between them. The sub class inherits the methods and attributes of its super class. In Java, class inheritance is *single inheritance*. See *interface inheritance* for an alternative form of inheritance.

class method: A synonym for *static method*.

class scope: Private *variables* defined outside the *methods* within a class have class scope. They are accessible from all methods within the class, regardless of the order in which they are defined. Private methods also have class scope. Variables and methods may have a wider *scope* if they do not use the `private` access modifier.

class variable: A synonym for *static variable*.

classpath: The path searched by the *compiler* and *interpreter* for class definitions. The class path may be set by a *command-line argument* to either, or via an environment variable.

client: The user of a *service*. A Web client requests resources from a Web server, for instance. When the client is an object, it is the sender of messages to its object servers.

command-line argument: Arguments passed to a program when it is run. A Java program receives these in the single formal argument to its *main method*:

```
public static void main(String[] args)
```

The arguments are stored as individual strings.

comment: A piece of text intended for the human reader of a program. Compilers ignore their contents.

Common Gateway Interface: The Common Gateway Interface (CGI) is a standard that allows Web clients to interact with programs on a Web server. A CGI script on the server is able to process input or arguments from a client, and respond accordingly.

compilation: The process of translating a programming language. This often involves translating a *high level programming language* into a *low level programming language*, or the binary form of a particular *instruction set*. The translation is performed by a program called a *compiler*. A Java compiler translates programs into *bytecodes*.

compiler: A program which performs a process of *compilation* on a program written in a *high level programming language*.

complement operator: The complement operator, ~, is used to invert the value of each *bit* in a *binary* pattern. For instance, the complement of 1010010 is 0101101.

concurrency: A feature of *parallel programming*. Parts of a program whose executions overlap in time are said to execute concurrently. Java's *thread* features support concurrency.

condition: A *Boolean expression* controlling a conditional statement or loop.

conditional operator: An *operator* taking three operands—a ternary operator. The conditional operator (?:) is used in the form

```
bexpr ? expr1 : expr2
```

where bexpr is a *Boolean expression*. If the Boolean expression has the value true, then the result of the operation is the value of expr1, otherwise it is the value of expr2.

connection handshake: An exchange of messages between two processes in an attempt to establish a connection between them.

constant: A *variable* whose value may not be changed. In Java, these are implemented by *final variables*.

constructor: A constructor is automatically called when an *instance* of its class is created. A constructor always has the same name as its class, and has no return type. For instance,

```
public class Ship {
    public Ship(String name){
        ...
    }
    ...
}
```

A class with no explicit constructor has an implicit *no-arg constructor*, which takes no arguments and has an empty body.

continue statement: A statement that may only be used inside the body of a loop. In the case of a while loop or do loop, control passes immediately to the loop's terminating test. In the case of a for loop, control passes to the post-body update expression.

continuous simulation: In a continuous simulation, time ticks past at a regular rate that is applicable to the particular simulation scenario. At each tick, all the objects in the simulation are informed of the passage of time and updated accordingly. See *discrete simulation* for an alternative form of simulation.

control structure: A statement that affects the *flow of control* within a method. Typical control structures are loops and if statements.

copy constructor: A *constructor* taking a single argument of the same class. For instance,

```
public class Point {
        // Use p's attributes to initialize this object.
    public Point(Point p){
        ...
    }
    ...
}
```

The argument is used to define the initial values of the new object's *attributes*.

coupling: Coupling arises when classes are aware of each other because their instances must interact. Linkage between two classes may be either strong or weak. Stronger coupling arises when one class has a detailed knowledge of the internal implementation of another, and is written to take advantage of that knowledge. So anything that has the potential to reduce the amount of inside knowledge will tend to weaken coupling. Hence, *information hiding* and *encapsulation*.

Java's visibility levels—private, package, protected, public—progressively reveal detail to other classes, and so increase the potential for stronger coupling. Interfaces are one way to reduce coupling—because they promote interaction with a class via an abstract definition, rather than a concrete implementation.

critical section: A section of code in which there is potential for a *race hazard*. Critical sections make use of the synchronized methods or statements.

curly brackets: See *block*.

cursor: A visual representation of the current position of the mouse on the user's *virtual desktop*. Cursor shapes are often set to represent the current state of a program—using an hourglass shape to indicate that the user should wait—or to suggest the actions that are possible by clicking the mouse over some part of a user interface.

daemon thread: Daemon threads are non-user threads. They are typically used to carry out low-priority tasks that should not take priority over the main task of the program. They can be used to do useful work when all other user threads are blocked. The *garbage collector* is one example of a daemon thread.

data type: There are eight primitive data types in Java; five of these represent numerical types of varying range and precision—double, float, int, long, and short. The remaining three are used to representing single-bit values (boolean), single byte values (byte), and 2-byte characters from the ISO Unicode character set (char).

datagram: A packet of information passed between two communicating processes across a network. Both the *Transmission Control Protocol (TCP)* and the *User Datagram Protocol (UDP)* are indirectly involved in sending datagrams to provide reliable or unreliable communication, respectively.

De Morgan's Theorem: Two rules that can help to simplify *Boolean expressions* involving multiple *logical-not operators* in combination with other *Boolean operators*.

deadlock: A situation that arises when two *threads* each acquires the lock to one of a set of resources that they both need.

decimal: Number representation in base 10. In base 10, the digits 0 to 9 are used. Digit positions represent successive powers of 10.

declaration and initialization: A statement in which a variable is declared and immediately given its initial value. Three examples of declaration and initialization are:

```
int numStudents = 23;
Ship argo = new Ship();
Student[] students = new Student[numStudents];
```

Instance variables that are not explicitly initialized when they are declared have a *default initial value* that is appropriate to their type. Uninitialized *method variables* have an undefined initial value.

decrement operator: An operator (--) that adds one to its operand. It has two forms: pre-decrement (--x) and post-decrement (x--). In its pre-decrement form, the result of the expression is the value of its argument *after* the decrement. In its post-decrement form, the result is the value of its argument *before* the decrement is performed. After the following,

```
int a = 5, b = 5;
int y,z;
y = --a;
z = b--;
```

y has the value 4 and z has the value 5. Both a and b have the value 4.

deep copy: A copy of an object in which copies of all the original object's sub-components are also made. The resulting object might, in effect, be a *clone* of the original. See *shallow copy* for an alternative.

default initial value: The default value of any variable not explicitly initialized when it is declared. Fields of numeric primitive types have the value zero by default, boolean variables have the value false, char variables have the value '\u0000', and object references have the value null. The initial values of method variables are undefined, unless explicitly initialized.

default label: The destination for all values used in a *switch statement* expression that do not have explicit *case labels*. A default label is optional.

delegation: The process by which an object passes on a message it has received to a subordinate object. If *inheritance* is not available in a programming language, delegation is the most viable alternative for avoiding code duplication and promoting code re-use.

deprecated: Something that has been made obsolete by later versions of the API. Deprecated methods should not be used because there is no guarantee that they will continue to exist in future versions.

direct recursion: Recursion that results from a method calling itself.

discrete simulation: In a discrete simulation, time passes at an irregular rate that is determined by the primary events of interest in the simulation. See *continuous simulation* for an alternative form of simulation.

disk drive: A *hardware* device used to store data. They come in many forms, such as compact disks, floppy disks, and hard disks.

divide and conquer: An approach to problem solving that attempts to reduce an overall single large problem into multiple simpler problems.

do loop: One of Java's three *control structures* used for looping. The other two are the *while loop* and *for loop*. A do loop consists of a loop body and a *Boolean expression*. The condition is tested after the loop body has been completed for the first time and re-tested each time the end of the body is completed. The loop terminates when the condition gives the value `false`. The statements in the loop body will always be executed at least once.

dotted decimal notation: The notation used to represent the four byte values of an *IP address*. Each byte is represented as a value between 0 and 255, for instance 129.12.0.1. The most significant byte is written first.

double buffering: A graphics technique used to smooth animation. The next version of an image is drawn behind the scenes and then displayed in its entirety when the drawing is complete. The assumption is that it will be relatively quick to display the fully drawn image, compared to the time it takes to compute and draw it.

downcast: A *cast* towards an object's dynamic type—that is, down the *inheritance hierarchy*. For instance,

```
// Downcast from Object to String
String s = (String) o;
```

See *upcast*.

dynamic type: The dynamic type of an object is the name of the class used to construct it. See *static type*.

edit-compile-run cycle: A common part of the program development process. A source file is created initially and compiled. Syntax errors must be corrected in the editor before compiling it again. Once the program has been successfully compiled, it can be run. The program's execution might reveal logical errors, or the need for enhancements. A further edit-compile-run iteration is the result.

encapsulation: Safeguarding the state of an object by defining its attributes as `private` and channeling access to them through *accessor* and *mutator* methods.

enumerated type: A data type—not directly available in Java—in which symbolic names are used for a sequence of constant numeric values. They facilitate the avoidance of *magic numbers*. They can be simulated in Java with fields in an interface, for instance,

```
public interface States {
    public static final int Stop = 0, Go = 1;
}
```

However, the compiler type checking usually available with enumerated types is not available with this form.

exception: An object representing the occurrence of an exceptional circumstance—typically, something that has gone wrong in the smooth running of a program. Exception objects are created from *classes* that extend the `Throwable` class. See *checked exception* and *unchecked exception*.

exception handler: The *try statement* acts as an exception handler—a place where *exception* objects are caught and dealt with.

exclusive-or operator: The exclusive-or operator (∧) is both a *Boolean operator* and a *bit manipulation operator*. The Boolean version gives the value `true` if only one of its operands is `true`, otherwise it gives the value `false`. Similarly, the bit manipulation version produces a 1 bit wherever the corresponding bits in its operands are different.

expression: A combination of *operands* and *operators* that produces a resulting value. Expressions have a resulting type, that affects the context in which they may be used. See *Boolean expression* and *arithmetic expression*, for instance.

factory pattern: A *pattern* of class definition that is used as a generator of *instances* of other classes. Often used to create platform- or locale-specific implementations of *abstract classes* or *interfaces*. This reduces *coupling* between classes as it frees the factory's client from a need to know about particular implementations.

fetch-execute cycle: The simple set of steps that are endlessly repeated by a computer's *Central Processing Unit* for each program instruction: "Fetch the next instruction referenced by the program counter," "Update the program counter to refer to the next instruction," "Execute the instruction just fetched."

field: *Variables* defined inside a class or interface, outside of the methods. Fields are *members* of a class.

file system: An *operating system* makes it possible to use space on a computer's *disk drives* by imposing a structured file system on the disk storage. Each file system has its own conventions for the way in which files are named, folders and directories are structured, and large files are split into smaller pieces, for instance. It is not usually possible to transfer data directly from the file system of one operating system to that of a different operating system, because their conventions are likely to be incompatible.

File Transfer Protocol: The File Transfer Protocol (FTP) defines a standard set of rules that make it possible to transfer a file from one *file system* to another.

filter stream: An input-output class that filters or manipulates its stream of input- or output-data in some way. Two examples are `DataInputStream` and `DataOutputStream`.

final class: A class with the `final` reserved word in its header. A final class may not be extended by another class.

final method: A method with the `final` reserved word in its header. A final method may not be overridden by a method defined in a sub class.

final variable: A variable with the `final` reserved word in its declaration. A final variable may not be assigned to once it has been initialized. Initialization often takes place as part of its declaration. However, the initialization of an uninitialized final *field* (known as a *blank final variable*) may be deferred to the class's *constructor*, or an *initializer*.

finalization: Immediately before an object is garbage collected, its `finalize` method is called. This gives it the opportunity to free any resources it might be holding on to.

finally clause: Part of a *try statement* that is always executed, either following the handling a caught *exception*, or normal termination of the *protected statements*.

first in, first out: The (FIFO) semantics of a *queue* data structure. Items are removed in the order in which they arrived in the queue, so older items are always removed before newer ones. See *last in, first out*.

floating point number: See *real number*.

for loop: One of Java's three *control structures* used for looping. The other two are the *while loop* and *do loop*. A for loop consists of a loop header and a loop body. The header consists of three expressions separated by two semicolons and one or more of these may be omitted. The first expression is only evaluated once, at the point the loop is entered. The middle expression is a *Boolean expression* representing the loop's termination test. An empty expression represents the value `true`. The third expression is evaluated after each completion of the loop's body. The loop terminates when the termination test gives the value `false`. The statements in the loop body might be executed zero or more times.

formal argument: The definition of a method's argument which is part of a *method header*. Each formal argument has an associated type. When a method is called, the *actual argument* values are copied into the corresponding formal arguments. The types of the actual arguments must be compatible with those of the formal arguments.

formal parameter: See *formal argument*.

fully-evaluating operator: An operator that evaluates all of its arguments to produce a result. Standard *arithmetic operators*, such as +, are fully evaluating. In contrast, some *Boolean operators*, such as &&, are *short-circuit operators*.

fully qualified class name: The name of a class, including any *package* name and enclosing class name. Given the following class outline:

```
package oddments;

class Outer {
    public class Inner {
        ...
    }
    ...
}
```

The fully qualified name of `Inner` is:

```
oddments.Outer.Inner
```

functional programming: A style of programming associated with languages such as Haskell. Functional programming languages are more closely tied to a mathematical concept of function than *imperative programming languages*. This makes it easier to apply program-proving techniques and logical reasoning to functional programs. In particular, functional programs do not use the concept of *variables* in the traditional sense, i.e., a memory location whose contents might be changed from time to time as a program executes.

garbage collector: A *daemon thread* that recycles objects to which there are no extant references within a program.

global variable: A phenomenon that is more usually regarded as being a problem in *structured programming languages* than in *object-oriented languages*. In a structured programming language, such as *Pascal* or *C*, a global variable is one defined outside the procedures and functions of a program. It is difficult to keep track of the usage of such a variable as it is readable and writable by the whole program or module in which it is defined. This makes such variables a common source of logical errors. In fact, *instance* *variables* pose a similar problem within class definitions, since Java's *scope rules* make them accessible to all methods defined within a class. This is one of the reasons why we prefer to channel access to instance variables through *accessor* and *mutator* methods even within a class.

Graphical User Interface: A Graphical User Interface (GUI) is part of a program that allows user interaction via graphical components, such as menus, buttons, text areas, etc. Interaction often involves use of a mouse.

hardware: The physical devices of a computer system, such as its *micro-chips*, *disk drives*, keyboard, printer, *sound card*, and so on. It is called hardware in contrast to programs, which are called *software*.

has-a relationship: See *aggregation*.

hash code: A value returned by a *hash function*. A hash code can be used as an index into a random-access data structure, providing an efficient mapping between an object and its location. Used by classes such as HashMap.

hash function: A function used to produce a *hash code* from the arbitrary contents of an object. Classes can override the hashCode method, inherited from the Object class, to define their own hash function.

heterogeneous collection: A collection of objects with different *dynamic types*. See *homogeneous collection*.

hexadecimal: Number representation in base 16. In base 16, the digits 0 to 9 and the letters A to F are used. A represents 10 (base 10), B represents 11 (base 10), and so on. Digit positions represent successive powers of 16.

high level programming language: Languages such as Java, C++, Ada, etc., which provide programmers with features such as control structures, methods, classes, packages, etc. These features are largely independent of any particular *instruction set*, and hence programs written in these languages tend to be more *portable* than those written in *low level programming languages*.

homogeneous collection: A collection of objects with the same *dynamic type*. Arrays are the most common homogeneous collection objects. See *heterogeneous collection*.

host system: A computer system on which a *process* is run.

hostname: The name of a *host system*.

hot spot: An area in an *image map* with a particular significance. A program typically monitors movements of the mouse, and responds according to the actions associated with the hot spots over which it passes. This might include displaying different status information, for instance. Often, clicking the mouse on a hot spot is used to indicate that the program should activate an associated action.

The term *hot spot* is also used to signify a computationally intensive part of a program, such as an inner loop. Such places are often a potential target for program optimization.

HSB Color Model: A color model based upon representing a color as three components: hue, saturation, and brightness. This is sometimes known as the HSV color model—hue, saturation, and value. See *RGB Color Model*.

HyperText Markup Language: The HyperText Markup Language (HTML) is a simple presentation language used to markup the content of Web pages. Its *tags* often appear in pairs to mark sections of text that should be represented in different colors of fonts.

HyperText Transfer Protocol: The HyperText Transfer Protocol (HTTP) is a set of rules defined to enable a Web client (browser) to interact with a Web server.

icon: An image intended to communicate a language- or culturally-independent meaning.

identifier: A programmer-defined name for a *variable*, *method*, *class*, or *interface*.

IEEE 754: Standard 754-1985 issued by the Institute of Electrical and Electronic Engineers for binary floating point arithmetic. This is the standard to which Java's arithmetic conforms.

if-statement: A *control structure* used to choose between performing or not performing further actions.

```
if(boolean-expression){
    // Statements performed if expression is true.
    ...
}
```

It is controlled by a *Boolean expression*. See *if-else statement*.

if-else statement: A *control structure* used to choose between performing one of two alternative actions.

```
if(boolean-expression){
    // Statements performed if expression is true.
    ...
}
else{
    // Statements performed if expression is false.
    ...
}
```

It is controlled by a *Boolean expression*. See *if statement*.

image map: An image divided into logical areas, each of which has a *hot spot*.

immutable object: An object whose *state* may not be changed. Objects of the `String` class are immutable, for instance—their length and contents are fixed once created.

imperative programming: The style of programming usually associated with languages such as C, Fortran, Pascal, and so on. Imperative programming is distinguished from *functional programming* in that the former is strongly tied to the concept of variables and memory locations. A variable is associated with a memory location and the contents of that memory location may be changed, via the variable, over the course of time. The meaning or effect of a program fragment at a particular point can only be understood by reference to the *current* contents of the set of relevant variables, therefore. In contrast, functional programs do not allow the contents of a variable to be changed once set (in simplified terms), hence making them easier to reason about. While languages such as C++ and Java are also imperative programming languages, strictly speaking, they are more commonly referred to as object-oriented programming languages.

implements clause: That part of a *class header* that indicates which interfaces are implemented by the class. A class may implement more than one interface. See *multiple inheritance*.

implicit type conversion: Type conversion that does not require a *cast*. Implicit type conversions typically do not involve any loss of information. For instance, combining an integer operand with a floating point operand in an *arithmetic expression* will result in an implicit type conversion of the integer to an equivalent floating point value.

import statement: A statement that makes the names of one or more classes or interfaces available in a different *package* from the one in which they are defined. Import statements follow any *package declaration*, and precede any class or interface definitions.

inconsistent state: A *state* that an object should not be in. A class needs to be carefully designed in order to ensure that none of its *instances* can get into an inconsistent state. An example of an inconsistent state might be a football team with too many players on the field.

increment operator: An operator (++) that adds one to its operand. It has two forms: pre-increment (++x) and post-increment (x++). In its pre-increment form, the result of the expression is the value of its argument *after* the increment. In its post-increment form, the result is the value of its argument *before* the increment is performed. After the following,

```
int a = 5, b = 5;
int y,z;
y = ++a;
z = b++;
```

y has the value 6 and z has the value 5. Both a and b have the value 6.

indirect recursion: Recursion that results from method Y calling method X, when an existing call from X to Y is still in progress.

infinite loop: A loop whose termination test never evaluates to `false`. Sometimes this is a deliberate act on the part of the programmer, using a construct such as

```
while(true) ...
```

or

```
for( ; ; ) ...
```

but it can sometimes be the result of a logical error in the programming of a normal loop condition or the statements in the body of the loop.

infinite recursion: Recursion that does not terminate. This can result from any of *direct recursion*, *indirect recursion*, or *mutual recursion*. It is usually the result of a logical error, and can result in *stack overflow*.

information hiding: The practice of ensuring that only as much information is revealed about the implementation of a class as is strictly required. Hiding unnecessary knowledge of implementation makes it less likely that other classes will rely on that knowledge for their own implementation. This tends to reduce the strength of *coupling* between classes. It also reduces the chance that a change of the underlying implementation will break another class. Ensuring that all *fields* of a class are defined as `private`, is one of the ways that we seek to promote information hiding.

inheritance: A feature of *object-oriented programming languages* in which a *sub type* inherits *methods* and *variables* from its *super type*. Inheritance is most commonly used as a synonym for *class inheritance*, but *interface inheritance* is also a feature of some languages, including Java.

inheritance hierarchy: The relationship between *super classes* and *sub classes* is known as an inheritance hierarchy. *Single inheritance* of classes means that each class has only a single parent class and that the `Object` class is the ultimate ancestor of all classes—at the top of the hierarchy. Two classes that have the same immediate super class can be thought of as *sibling sub classes*.

Multiple inheritance of interfaces gives the hierarchy a more complex structure than that resulting from simple *class inheritance*.

initializer: A *block* defined at the outer-most level of a class—similar to a method without a header. Initializer blocks are executed, in order, when an *instance* is created. They are executed before the *constructor* of the defining class, but after any *super class* constructor. They are one of the places in which *blank final variables* may be initialized.

inner class: A class defined inside an enclosing class or method. We use the term to refer to non-static *nested classes*.

instance: A synonym for *object*. Objects of a class are *instantiated* when a class *constructor* is invoked via the *new operator*.

instance variable: A non-static *field* of a *class*. Each individual object of a class has its own copy of such a field. This is in contrast to a *class variable* which is shared by all instances of the class. Instance variables are used to model the *attributes* of a class.

instantiation: The creation of an *instance* of a class—that is, an *object*.

instruction set: The set of instructions that characterize a particular *Central Processing Unit*. Programs written in the instruction set of one type of CPU cannot typically be run on any other type of CPU.

integer: A positive or negative whole number. The *primitive types* `byte`, `short`, `int`, and `long` are used to hold integer values within narrower or wider ranges.

interface inheritance: When a *class* implements an *interface*, an interface *inheritance* relationship exists between them. The class inherits no implementation from the interface, only method signatures and *static variables*. It is also possible for one interface to extend one or more interfaces. In Java, interface inheritance is the only form of *multiple inheritance*. See *class inheritance* for an alternative form of inheritance.

Internet: A global network of many interconnected networks.

Internet Service Provider: An Internet Service Provider (ISP) provides connections to the *Internet* for users who do not have their own network. The ISP provides such users with their own *IP address* that enables them to interact with other computers attached to the Internet.

interpretational inner class: An *inner class* whose role is to provide a view or interpretation of data belong to its enclosing class, but independent of the data's actual representation.

interpreter: A program which executes a translated version of a source program by implementing a *virtual machine*. Interpreters typically simulate the actions of an idealized *Central Processing Unit*. An interpreter for Java must implement the *Java Virtual Machine (JVM)* and executes the *bytecodes* produced by a Java *compiler*. The advantage of using an interpreter for Java is that it makes the language more *portable* than if it were a fully compiled language. The bytecode version of a program produced by a Java compiler may be run on any interpreter implementing the JVM.

interprocess communication: The ability of two or more separate *processes* to communicate with one another.

interrupt: An asynchronous message sent to a *process* or *thread* that interrupts what it is currently doing. This usually results in an `InterruptedException` object being received by the interrupted thread. Waiting for an interrupt is an alternative to *polling*.

IP address: An Internet Protocol (IP) address for a networked computer. Currently, IP addresses consist of four byte values, written in *dotted decimal notation*, such as 129.12.0.1. In the future, IP addresses will be sixteen bytes long to accommodate the expansion in the number of networked computers.

is-a relationship: See *inheritance*.

iteration: Repetition of a set of statements, usually using a looping *control structure*, such as a *while loop*, *for loop*, or *do loop*.

iterator pattern: A common *pattern* in which the contents of a collection are iterated over in order. The Iterator pattern frees a client of the data from needing details of the how the data is stored. This pattern is supported by the `Iterator` and `ListIterator` interfaces.

Java: A *portable high level programming language* released by Sun Microsystems.[TM]

Java 2 SDK: A particular implementation of the abstract functionality described in Sun's specification of the Java 2 Platform.

Java Archive file: A Java Archive (JAR) file makes it possible to store multiple *bytecode* files in a single file.

Java Virtual Machine (JVM): An idealized machine whose *instruction set* consists of *bytecodes*. A Java program is *compiled* to an equivalent bytecode form and executed on an *interpreter* which implements the JVM.

key value: The object used to generate an associated *hash code* for lookup in an associative data structure.

last in, first out: The (LIFO) semantics of a *stack* data structure. Items are removed in the opposite order to which they arrived in the stack, so newer items are always removed before older ones. See *first in, first out*.

layout manager: An object responsible for sharing the available space between multiple components within a graphical container.

left shift operator: The left shift operator ($<<$) is a *bit manipulation operator*. It moves the bits in its left operand zero or more places to the left, according to the value of its right operand. Zero bits are added to the right of the result.

lexicographic ordering: The ordering of words as they would be found in a dictionary. It should be noted that different *locales* order similar looking words according to their own conventions—this applies, in particular, to accented characters.

lightweight process: See *thread*.

little-endian: A common difference between machines is the order in which they store the individual bytes of multi-byte numerical data. A little-endian machine stores the lower-order bytes before the higher-order bytes. See *big-endian*.

livelock: A situation in which a *thread* waits to be notified of a condition, but, on waking, finds that another thread has inverted the condition again. The first thread is forced to wait again. When this happens indefinitely, the thread is in livelock.

local inner class: An *inner class* defined within a method.

locale: Details which are dependent upon conventions and customs adopted by a particular country or culture. Within programs, this affects issues such as number and date formatting, for instance. Designers of classes should be sensitive to the locale-specific issues that might apply to users.

logical error: An error in the logic of a method or class. Such an error might not lead to an immediate *runtime error*, but could have a significant impact on overall program correctness.

logical operators: Operators, such as &&, | |, &, |, and ∧ that take two Boolean operands and produce a Boolean result. Used as part of a *Boolean expression*, often in the condition of a *control structure*.

look-and-feel: The visual impression and interaction style provided by a user interface. This is predominantly the responsibility of the *window manager* (in collaboration with the underlying *operating system*) running on a particular computer. It refers to the style of such things as window title bars, how windows are moved and resized, how different operations are performed via a mouse, and so on. It is preferable to have a consistent look-and-feel within a single user environment. However, some window managers do allow individual programs to present a different look-and-feel from the predominant style of the host environment. Java's Swing components support this idea by allowing an application to select a pluggable look-and-feel from those provided by a user interface manager. An application running in a Microsoft Windows environment could be made to look like one that normally runs in an X Windows environment, for instance. This allows an application to look similar on different platforms, but it can also lead to confusion for users.

loop variable: A *variable* used to control the operation of a loop, such as a *for loop*. Typically, a loop variable will be given an initial value and it is then incremented after each *iteration* until it reaches or passes a terminating value.

low level programming languages: Often known as assembly languages, these provide little more than the basic instruction set of a particular *Central Processing Unit*. Hence, programs written in low level programming languages tend to be less *portable* than those written in *high level languages*.

magic number: A constant value with a significance within a particular context. For instance, the value 12 could mean many different things—the number of hours you have worked today, the number of dollars you are owed by a friend, and so on. As far as possible, such values should be associated with an *identifier* that clearly expresses their meaning:

```
final int maxSpeed = 50;
```

If stored in a *final variable*, it is unlikely that any execution overhead will be incurred by doing so.

main method: The starting point for program execution:

```
public static void main(String[] args)
```

manifest file: A file held in a *Java Archive (JAR) file*, detailing the contents of the archive.

marking interface: An *interface* with no *methods*.

member: The members of a class are *fields*, *methods*, and *nested classes*.

memory leak: A situation in which memory that is no longer being used has not been returned to the pool of free memory. A *garbage collector* is designed to return unreferenced objects to the free memory pool in order to avoid memory leaks.

message passing: We characterize object interactions as message passing. A *client* object sends a message to a *server* object by invoking a method from the server's class. Arguments may be passed with the message, and a result returned by the server.

method: The part of a *class definition* that implements some of the behavior of objects of the class. The body of the method contains *declarations* of *method variables* and *statements* to implement the behavior. A method receives input via its *arguments*, if any, and may return a result if it has not been declared as `void`.

method body: The body of a method: everything inside the outermost *block* of a method.

method header: The header of a method, consisting of the method name, its result type, formal arguments, and any exceptions thrown. Also known as a *method signature*.

method overloading: Two or more methods with the same name defined within a class are said to be overloaded. This applies to both constructors and other methods. Overloading applies through a class hierarchy, so a sub class might overload a method defined in one of its super classes. It is important to distinguish between an overloaded method and an *overridden method*. Overloaded methods must be distinguishable in some way from each other; either by having different numbers of arguments, or by the types of those arguments being different. Overridden methods have identical formal arguments.

method overriding: A method defined in a *super class* may be overridden by a method of the same name defined in a *sub class*. The two methods must have the same name and number and types of formal arguments. Any checked exception thrown by the sub class version must match the type of one thrown by the super class version, or be a sub class of such an exception. However, the sub class version does not have to throw any exceptions that are thrown by the super class version. It is important to distinguish between method overriding and *method overloading*. Overloaded methods have the same names, but differ in their formal arguments. See *overriding for breadth*, *overriding for chaining*, and *overriding for restriction*.

method result: The value returned from a method via a *return statement*. The type of the expression in the return statement must match the return type declared in the *method header*.

method signature: A synonym for *method header*.

method variable: A variable defined inside a *method body*.

micro-chip: A small electronic device used to build computers and other electronic equipment. Chips are commonly used to supply the memory and processing components of a computer. See *Central Processing Unit*.

MIME: Multipurpose Internet Mail Extensions (MIME) are rules that make it possible to use electronic mail to send content other than simple text.

modal: A dialog is modal if its parent application is blocked from further activity until the dialog has completed. See *non-modal*.

model-view pattern: A *pattern* in which the representation of data (the model) is kept separate from its visualization (the view). Such decoupling makes it easier to change the underlying data representation, or provide multiple views, for instance. Quite often a third element is added to create the Model-View-Controller (MVC) pattern. In the MVC pattern, those elements of the system which are able to control or modify the data (the model) are also defined separately.

modem: A *mo*dulator-*dem*odulator. A *hardware* device used to connect a digital computer to an analogue telephone network by turning analogue signals into digital signals, and vice versa.

module: A group of program components, typically with restricted visibility to program components in other modules. Java uses *packages* to implement this concept.

monitor: An object with one or more synchronized methods.

multiple inheritance: The ability of a class or interface to extend more than one class or interface. In Java, multiple inheritance is only available in the following circumstances:

- An interface may extend more than one interface.
- A class may implement more than one interface.

Only *single inheritance* is possible for a class extending another class.

multiple-boot options: The hardware configurations of some computers are able to run different *operating system* and *window manager* combinations. Some systems allow a user to choose which combination they wish to use during a particular session when the computer is started, or *booted*.

multiprogramming system: An operating system that is able to run multiple programs concurrently.

mutator method: A method specifically designed to allow controlled modification of a `private` attribute of a class. By convention, we name mutators with a `set` prefix followed by the name of the attribute being modified. For instance, the mutator for an attribute named `speed` would be `setSpeed`. By making an attribute private, we prevent objects of other classes from altering its value other than through its mutator. The mutator is able to check the value being used to modify the attribute and reject the modification if necessary. In addition, modification of one attribute might require others to be modified in order to keep the object in a consistent state. A mutator method can undertake this role. Mutators are used both to grant safe access to the value of a private attribute and to protect attributes from modification by objects of other classes. The latter goal is achieved by choosing an appropriate visibility for the mutator.

mutual recursion: Recursion that results from two methods calling each other recursively.

namespace: The area of a program in which particular *identifiers* are visible. Java uses *packages* to provide namespaces, and its visibility rules—private, package, protected, public—variously contain identifiers within namespaces.

native method: A method written in a language other than Java, but accessible to a Java program. Native methods are beyond the scope of this book.

nested class: A class defined inside an enclosing class. See *inner class*.

new operator: The operator used to create *instances* of a class.

newline: The `'\n'` character.

no-arg constructor: A constructor that takes no arguments. By default, all classes without an explicit constructor have a default no-arg constructor with `public` access. Its role is purely to invoke the no-arg constructor of the immediate super class.

non-modal: A dialog is non-modal if its parent application is not blocked from further activity while the dialog is being shown. See *modal*.

non-static nested class: See *inner class*.

null character: The `'\u0000'` character. Care should be taken not to confuse this with the *null reference*.

null reference: A value used to mean, "no object". Used when an object reference variable is not referring to an object.

number base: The base used to interpret numerical characters. *Decimal notation* is base 10 and *binary notation* is base 2, for instance.

object: An *instance* of a particular *class*. In general, any number of objects may be constructed from a class definition (see *singleton*, however). The class to which an object belongs defines the general characteristics of all instances of that class. Within those characteristics, an object will behave according to the current state of its *attributes* and environment.

object construction: The creation of an `object`, usually via the `new` operator. When an object is created, an appropriate *constructor* from its class is invoked.

object reference: A reference to an object. Languages other than Java use terms such as *address* or *pointer*. It is important to keep the distinction clear between an object and its reference. A variable such as `argo`

```
Ship argo;
```

is capable of holding an object reference, but is not, itself, an object. It can refer to only a single object at a time, but it is able to hold different object references from time to time.

object serialization: The writing of an object's contents in such a way that its *state* can be restored, either at a later time, or within a different *process*. This can be used to store objects between runs of a program, or to transfer objects across a network, for instance.

object-oriented language: Programming languages such as C++ and Java that allow the solution to a problem to be expressed in terms of objects which belong to classes.

octal: Number representation in base 8. In base 8, only the digits 0 to 7 are used. Digit positions represent successive powers of 8.

octal character constant: A character constant in the form `'\ddd'`, where each *d* is an *octal* digit. This may be used for characters with a Unicode value in the range 0-255.

operand: An operand is an argument of an *operator*. Expressions involve combinations of operators and operands. The value of an expression is determined by applying the operation defined by each operator to the value of its operands.

operating system: The operating system allows a computer's hardware devices to be accessed by programs. For instance, it allows data to be organized on a computer's disks in the form of a *file system* and it delivers the coordinate positions of a mouse to programs as the mouse is moved. Operating systems also make it possible for multiple programs to be run concurrently, or multiple users to share a single machine. See *concurrency*.

operator: A symbol, such as -, == or ? : , taking one, two, or three operands and yielding a result. Operators are used in both *arithmetic expressions* and *Boolean expressions*.

operator precedence: See *precedence rules*

out-of-bounds value: A *redundant value* used to indicate that a different action from the norm is required at some point. The `read` method of `InputStream` returns -1 to indicate that the end of a stream has been reached, for instance, instead of the normal positive byte-range value.

out of scope: A *variable* is in *scope* as long as the program's *flow of control* is within the variable's defining *block*. Otherwise, it is out of scope.

overriding for breadth: A form of *method overriding* in which the sub class version of a method implements its own behavior within the context of the attributes and behavior of the sub class and then calls the super class version so that it can perform a similar task within the super class context.

overriding for chaining: A form of *method overriding* in which the sub class version of a method checks to see whether it can respond to the message on its own and only calls the super class version of the method.

overriding for restriction: A form of *method overriding* in which the sub class version of a method calls the super class version first of all and then uses or manipulates the result or effects of that call in some way.

package: A named grouping of classes and interfaces that provides a package *namespace*. Classes, interfaces, and class members without an explicit `public`, `protected`, or `private` *access modifier* have *package visibility*. Public classes and interfaces may be imported into other packages via an *import statement*.

package access: See *package.*

package declaration: A declaration used to name a *package*. This must be the first item in a source file, preceding any *import statements*. For instance,

```
package java.lang;
```

parallel programming: A style of programming in which statements are not necessarily executed in an ordered sequence but in parallel. Parallel programming languages make it easier to create programs that are designed to be run on multi-processor hardware, for instance. Java's *thread* features support a degree of parallel programming.

parameter: See *argument.*

parsing: Usually applied to the action of a *compiler* in analyzing a program source file for *syntax errors*. It is also used more widely to mean the analysis of the structure of input.

pattern: A recurring theme in class design or usage. Interfaces such as `Iterator` encapsulate a pattern of access to the items in a collection, while freeing the client from the need to know details of the way in which the collection is implemented. See Appendix E.

peer: A term used of the *Abstract Windowing Toolkit (AWT)* to refer to the underlying classes that provide the platform-specific implementation of component classes.

peripheral devices: Devices attached to a computer, such as printers, disk drives, mice, etc.

pipe: A linkage between two program components. One component acts as a source of data and writes into the pipe. A second component acts as a receiver (sink) for the data and reads from the pipe. See `PipedInputStream` and `PipedOutputStream`.

pixel: A picture element—typically a colored dot on a screen.

polling: The process of repeatedly testing until a condition becomes true. Polling can be inefficient if the time between tests is short compared with the time it will take for the condition to become true. A polling *thread* should sleep between consecutive tests in order to give other threads a chance to run. An alternative approach to polling is to arrange for an *interrupt* to be sent when the condition is true, or to use the `wait` and `notify` mechanism associated with threads.

polymorphism: The ability of an object reference to be used as if it referred to an object with different forms. Polymorphism in Java results from both *class inheritance* and *interface inheritance*. The apparently different forms often result from the *static type* of the variable in which the reference is stored. Given the following class header

```
class Rectangle extends Polygon implements Comparable
```

an object whose *dynamic type* is Rectangle can behave as all of the following types: Rectangle, Polygon, Comparable, Object.

popup menu: A menu of actions that is normally not visible on the screen until a mouse button is clicked. Popup menus help to keep a user interface from becoming cluttered.

port: A number used by a *process* to communicate with another process across a network, using the *Transmission Control Protocol (TCP)* or *User Datagram Protocol (UDP)*, for instance. See *TCP endpoint.*

portable: Portability is the quality of a program that makes it possible to run it on different types of computers. Programs written in *low level languages* are typically not very portable because they are usually closely tied to a specific instruction set or characteristics of a particular type of *Central Processing Unit*. Programs written in *high level languages* tend to be more portable, but might still make non-portable assumptions about a computer's underlying *file system*, for instance. Java programs are highly portable because a lot of machine- and file-system specific details are hidden from the programmer.

post-decrement operator: See *decrement operator.*

post-increment operator: See *increment operator.*

precedence rules: The rules that determine the order of evaluation of an expression involving more than one *operator*. Operators of higher precedence are evaluated before those of lower precedence. For instance, in the expression `x+y*z`, the multiplication is performed before the addition because `*` has a higher precedence than `-`.

pre-decrement operator: See *decrement operator.*

preempt: The currently executing *thread* may be preempted, or forced to yield control, by a higher priority thread that becomes eligible to run during its *timeslice*.

pre-increment operator: See *increment operator*.

primitive type: Java's eight standard non-class types are primitive types: `boolean`, `byte`, `char`, `double`, `float`, `int`, `long`, and `short`.

priority level: Each *thread* has a priority level, which indicates to the *scheduler* where it should be placed in the pecking order for being run. An eligible unblocked thread with a particular priority will *always* be run before an eligible thread with a lower priority.

process: An individual thread-of-control to which an execution *timeslice* is allocated by an *operating system*.

program counter: A program counter is an integral part of a computer's *Central Processing Unit*. It contains a reference to the memory address of the next instruction to be fetched, ready to be executed during the next fetch-execute cycle. Immediately following an instruction fetch, the program counter is moved on to refer to the next instruction, before the current instruction is executed. The normal sequential execution of a series of instructions may be changed by executing a *branch instruction*, which stores a new instruction address into the program counter.

propagation: If an *exception* is thrown within a method, and there is no appropriate *exception handler* within the method, the exception may be propagated to the caller of the method. For a *checked exception*, the method must contain a *throws clause* in its header. A throws clause is not necessary for an *unchecked exception* to be propagated.

protected access: Protected access is available to a class *member* prefixed with the `protected` access modifier. Such a member is accessible to all classes defined within the enclosing *package*, and any *sub classes* extending the enclosing class.

protected statement: A statement within the *try clause* of a *try statement*.

protocol: A set of rules for interaction between two *processes*. A protocol is usually specified in a *Uniform Resource Locator (URL)* to indicate how a particular *resource* should be transferred from a Web server to the requesting client.

public interface: The *members* of a class prefixed with the `public` access modifier. All such members are visible to every class within a program.

punctuation: Symbols such as commas and semicolons, which a *compiler* uses to understand the structure of a program.

quantum: See *timeslice*.

queue: See *first in, first out (FIFO) queue*.

quotient: When integer division is performed, the result consists of a quotient and a remainder. The quotient represents the integer number of times that the divisor divides into the dividend. For instance, in $5/3$, 5 is the dividend and 3 is the divisor. This gives a quotient of 1 and a remainder of 2.

race condition: See *race hazard*.

race hazard: A situation that arises between multiple threads sharing a resource. A race hazard arises when one thread's assumptions about the state of a resource are invalidated by the actions of another thread.

radio buttons: A group of selectable components in which only one component may be selected. Selection of one of the group causes the previously selected component to be deselected.

Random Access Memory: Random access memory, or RAM, is memory whose contents are easily accessible to the processing components of a computer. In particular, the time it takes to read and write to a particular part of the memory does not depend on the address of the location to be read or written. This is in contrast to something like videotape which is accessed serially and, hence, the time it takes to read or write to any part of it depends on how far away the location is.

Reader class: A *sub class* of the `Reader` *abstract class*, defined in the `java.io` *package*. Reader classes translate input from a host-dependent *character set encoding* into *Unicode*. See *Writer class*.

real number: A number with an integer and a fractional part. The *primitive types* `double` and `float` are used to represent real numbers.

recursion: Recursion results from a method being invoked when an existing call to the same method has not yet returned. For instance,

```
public static void countDown(int n){
    if(n >= 0){
        System.out.println(n);
        countDown(n-1);
    }
    // else - base case. End of recursion.
}
```

See *direct recursion*, *indirect recursion*, and *mutual recursion* for the different forms this can take.

redundant value: The value of a data type that has no use or meaning within a particular context. For instance, negative values would be redundant in a class using integer attributes to model assignment marks. In some applications, redundant patterns serve a useful purpose in that they can be used explicitly as *out-of-bounds values* or *escape values*.

reflection: The ability to find out what methods, fields, constructors, and so on, are defined for a class or object. Reflection is supported by the `Class` class, and other classes in the `java.lang.reflect` *package*. Reflection makes it possible, among other things, to create dynamic programs.

relational operators: Operators, such as <, >, <=, >=, ==, and ! =, that produce a Boolean result, as part of a *Boolean expression*.

relative filename: A filename whose full path is relative to some point within a *file system* tree—often the current working folder (directory). For instance,

```
..\bin\javac.exe
```

A relative filename could refer to different files at different times, depending upon the context in which it is being used. See *absolute filename*.

repetition: See *iteration*.

reserved word: A word reserved for a particular purpose in Java, such as `class`, `int`, `public`, etc. Such words may not be used as ordinary *identifiers*. See Appendix D.

resource: See *Uniform Resource Locator (URL)*.

return statement: A statement used to terminate the execution of a method. A method with `void` *return type* may only have return statements of the following form:

```
return;
```

A method with any other return type must have at least one return statement of the form

```
return expression;
```

where the type of `expression` must match the return type of the method.

return type: The declared type of a method, appearing immediately before the method name, such as `void` in

```
public static void main(String[] args)
```

or `Point[]` in

```
public Point[] getPoints()
```

return value: The value of the *expression* used in a *return statement*.

RGB Color Model: A color model based upon representing a color as three components: red, green, and blue. See *HSB Color Model*.

right shift operator: The right shift operator (>>) is a *bit manipulation operator*. It moves the bits in its left operand zero or more places to the right, according to the value of its right operand. The most significant bit from before the shift is replicated in the left-most position—this is called *sign extension*. An alternative right shift operator (>>>) replaces the lost bits with zeros at the left.

round robin allocation: An allocation of *timeslices* that repeatedly cycles around a set of eligible *threads* in a fixed order.

runtime error: An error that causes a program to terminate when it is being run.

runtime stack: A stack structure maintained by the Java Virtual Machine that records which methods are currently being executed. The most recently entered method will be at the top of the stack and the main method of an application will be near the bottom.

scheduler: The part of the *Java Virtual Machine (JVM)* that is responsible for managing *threads*.

scheme: See *protocol*.

scope: A language's scope rules determine how widely variables, methods, and classes are visible within a class or program. Method variables have a scope limited to the *block* in which they are defined, for instance. Private methods and variables have *class scope*, limiting their accessibility to their defining class. Java provides private, package, protected, and public visibility.

search path: A list of folders (directories) to be searched—for a program or class, for instance.

security policy: A policy used to limit access by an *applet* to the resources of a *host system*.

semantic error: An error in the meaning of program. A statement may have no *syntax errors*, but might still break the rules of the Java language. For instance, if `ivar` is an `int` variable, the following statement is syntactically correct:

```
ivar = true;
```

However, it is semantically incorrect, because it is illegal to assign a `boolean` value to an integer variable.

server: Something that provides a service. A Web server delivers resources to its *clients*, for instance. When the server is an object, it is the recipient of messages from its object clients.

shallow copy: A copy of an object in which copies of all the original object's sub-components are not also made. For instance, a shallow copy of an array of objects would result in two separate array objects, each containing references to the same set of objects as were stored in the original. See *deep copy* for an alternative.

shift operator: See *left shift operator* and *right shift operator*.

short-circuit operator: An *operator* in which only as many *operands* are evaluated as are needed to determine the final result of the operation. The logical-and (`&&`) and logical-or (`||`) operators are the most common examples, although the *conditional operator* (`?:`) also only ever evaluates two of its three operands. See *fully evaluating operator*.

shortcut key: A key-press associated with a component in a *Graphical User Interface (GUI)* that provides an alternative to selecting the component's operation with a mouse.

sibling sub classes: Classes that have the same immediate super class. See *inheritance hierarchy*.

sign bit: In *twos-complement notation*, the most significant bit in an integer is used to determine the sign of the value. A `1` bit indicates a negative number, and a `0` bit indicates a positive number.

sign extension: When an integer value from a type with a particular range is stored in a variable with a bigger range, Java uses sign extension to determine the resulting value. The most significant *bit* in the original value is used to fill the extra bits of the new value. For instance, suppose a `byte` variable contains the bit pattern, `10000000`. If this is stored in a `short` variable, the resulting bit pattern will be `1111111110000000`. If the original value is `01000000`, the resulting bit pattern will be `0000000001000000`.

single inheritance: In Java, a class may not extend more than one class. This means that Java has a single inheritance model for *class inheritance*. See *multiple inheritance* for the alternative.

single line comment: A *comment* in the form:

```
// This line will be ignored by the compiler.
```

singleton pattern: A *pattern* that allows us to ensure that only a single instance of a particular class exists at any one time. Such an instance is called a singleton. The pattern can also be used when instances would have no unique state and would behave identically.

software: Programs written to run on a computer.

software engineering: The system of applying an engineering discipline to the design, implementation, and maintenance of software systems.

software re-use: The ability to re-use software components in different contexts. Object-oriented languages help to promote re-use by their support of *encapsulation*.

sound card: A *hardware* device used to turn digital data into sound.

stack: See *last in, first out (LIFO) stack*.

stack overflow: Stack overflow occurs when too many items are pushed onto a *stack* with a finite capacity.

stack trace: A display of the *runtime stack*.

state: Objects are said to possess state. The current state of an object is represented by the combined values of its attributes. Protecting the state of an object from inappropriate inspection or modification is an important aspect of class design and we recommend the use of *accessor methods* and *mutator methods* to facilitate attribute protection and integrity. The design of a class is often an attempt to model the states of objects in the real world. Unless there is a good match between the data types available in the language and the states to be modeled, class design may be complex. An important principle in class design is to ensure that an object is never put into an *inconsistent state* by responding to a message.

statement: The basic building block of a Java method. There are many different types of statements in Java, for instance, the *assignment statement*, *if statement*, *return statement*, and *while loop*.

statement terminator: The semicolon (`;`) is used to indicate the end of a statement.

static initializer: An *initializer* prefixed with the `static` reserved word. A static initializer is defined outside the methods of its enclosing class, and may only access the static fields and methods of its enclosing class.

static method: A static method (also known as a *class method*) is one with the `static` reserved word in its header. Static methods differ from all other methods in that they are not associated with any particular instance of the class to which they belong. They are usually accessed directly via the name of the class in which they are defined.

static nested class: A nested class with the `static` reserved word in its header. Unlike *inner classes*, objects of static nested classes have no enclosing object. They are also known as nested top-level classes.

static type: The static type of an object is the declared type of the variable used to refer to it. See *dynamic type*.

static variable: A `static` variable is defined inside a *class body*. Such a variable belongs to the class as a whole, and is, therefore, shared by all objects of the class. A class variable might be used to define the default value of an *instance variable*, for example, and would probably also be defined as `final`, too. They are also used to contain dynamic information that is shared between all instances of a class. For instance, the next account number to be allocated in a bank account class. Care must be taken to ensure that access to shared information, such as this, is `synchronized` where multiple threads could be involved. Class variables are also used to give names to application-wide values or objects since they may be accessed directly via their containing class name rather than an instance of the class.

stepwise refinement: A *divide and conquer* approach to programming, in which a complex problem is recursively divided into smaller, more manageable, sub-problems. This approach to program design is often used with *structured programming* languages.

stream class: An input stream class is one that delivers data from its source (often the *file system*) as a sequence of bytes. Similarly, an output stream class will write byte-level data. Stream classes should be contrasted with the operation of *reader* and *writer* classes.

string: An instance of the `String` class. Strings consist of zero or more *Unicode* characters, and they are *immutable*, once created. A literal string is written between a pair of string delimiters ("), as in:

```
"hello, world"
```

structured programming: A style of programming usually associated with languages such as C, Fortran, Pascal, and so on. Using structured programming techniques, a problem is often solved using a *divide and conquer* approach such as *stepwise refinement*. An initially large problem is broken into several smaller sub-problems. Each of these is then progressively broken into even smaller sub-problems, until the level of difficulty is considered to be manageable. At the lowest level, a solution is implemented in terms of data structures and procedures. This approach is often used with *imperative programming* languages that are not *object-oriented languages*, i.e., the data structures and procedures are not implemented as classes.

sub class: A class that `extends` its *super class*. A sub class *inherits* all of the members of its super class. All Java classes are sub classes of the `Object` class, which is at the root of the *inheritance hierarchy*. See *sub type*.

sub type: A type with a parent *super type*. The sub-type/super-type relationship is more general than the sub-class/super-class relationship. A class that implements an *interface* is a sub type of the interface. An interface that extends another interface is also a sub type.

subordinate inner class: An *inner class* that performs well-defined subordinate tasks on behalf of its *enclosing class*.

super class: A class that is extended by one or more *sub classes*. All Java classes have the `Object` class as a super class. See *super type*.

super type: A type with a child *sub type*. The sub-type/super-type relationship is more general than the sub-class/super-class relationship. An interface that is implemented by a class is a super type of the class. An interface that is extended by another interface is also a super type.

swapping: An operating system is often able to run programs that require more memory than is physically available on the *host system*. In order to do this, the full memory required is broken into smaller pieces, which are swapped in when required, and swapped out to disk when the space they occupy is required.

Swing: The Swing classes are part of a wider collection known as the *Java Foundation Classes (JFC)*. Swing classes are defined in the `javax.swing` packages. They provide a further set of components that extend the capabilities of the *Abstract Windowing Toolkit (AWT)*. Of particular significance is the greater control they provide over an application's *look-and-feel*.

switch statement: A selection statement in which the value of an *arithmetic expression* is compared for a match against different *case labels*. If no match is found, the optional *default label* is selected. For instance,

```
switch(choice){
    case 'q':
        quit();
        break;
    case 'h':
        help();
        break;
    ...
    default:
        System.out.println("Unknown command: "+choice);
        break;
}
```

swizzling: The process of recursively writing the contents of an object via *object serialization*.

synchronized statement: A statement in which an object-lock must be obtained for the target object before the body of the statement can be entered. Used to enclose a *critical section* in order to prevent a *race hazard*.

syntax error: An error detected by the *compiler* during its *parsing* of a program. Syntax errors usually result from mis-ordering symbols within expressions and statements. Missing curly brackets and semicolons are common examples of syntax errors.

TCP endpoint: The combination of an *IP address* and *Transmission Control Protocol (TCP) port* number.

ternary operator: See *conditional operator*

thread: A lightweight *process* that is managed by the *Java Virtual Machine (JVM)*. Support for threads is provided by the `Thread` class in the `java.lang` package.

thread starvation: A condition that applies to a *thread* that is prevented from running by other threads that do not yield or become blocked.

throw an exception: When an exceptional circumstance arises in a program—often as a result of a *logical error*—an *exception* object is created and thrown. If the exception is not caught by an *exception handler*, the program will terminate with a *runtime error*.

throw statement: A statement used to *throw an exception*. For instance,

```
throw new IndexOutOfBoundsException(i+" is too large.");
```

throws clause: A clause in a *method header* indicating that one or more *exceptions* will be *propagated* from this method. For instance,

```
public int find(String s) throws NotFoundException
```

timesharing system: An operating system that shares processor time between multiple processes by allocating each a *timeslice*. Once a process's timeslice has expired, another process is given a chance to run.

timeslice: The amount of running time allocated to a *process* or *thread* before the *scheduler* considers another to be run. A process or thread will not be able to use its full allocation of time if it becomes blocked or *preempted* during this period.

toggle: To alternate between two values, such as `true` and `false`, on and off, or 1 and 0.

top-level class: A class defined either at the outer-most level of a *package* or a *static nested class*.

Transmission Control Protocol: The Transmission Control Protocol (TCP) is a set of rules that allows reliable communication between two *processes* across a network. See *User Datagram Protocol (UDP)* for an alternative unreliable protocol.

trusted applet: An *applet* with more privileges than an ordinary (untrusted) applet.

try clause: See *try statement*.

try statement: The try statement acts as an *exception handler*—a place where *exception* objects are caught and dealt with. In its most general form, it consists of a *try clause*, one or more *catch clauses* and a *finally clause*.

```
try{
    statement;
    ...
}
catch(Exception e){
    statement;
    ...
}
finally{
    statement;
    ...
}
```

Either of the catch clause and finally clause may be omitted, but not both.

twos-complement notation: In twos-complement notation, the most significant bit in an integer value is used as the *sign bit*. A 1 bit indicates a negative number, and a 0 bit indicates a positive number. A positive number can be converted to its negative value by *complementing* the bit pattern and adding 1. The same operation is used to convert a negative value to its positive equivalent.

unary operator: An *operator* taking a single operand. Java's unary operators are -, +, !, ~, ++, and --.

unbounded repetition: Repetition where the statements within a loop's body are performed an arbitrary number of times, according to the effects of the statements within the loop's body. All of the loop *control structures* in Java provide for unbounded repetition. See *bounded repetition*.

unchecked exception: An *exception* for which it is not required to provide a local *try statement*, or to propagate via a *throws clause* defined in the *method header*. An exception that is not handled will cause program termination if it is thrown. See *checked exception*.

Unicode: A 16-bit character set designed to make it easier to exchange and display information that makes use of a wide range of different languages and symbols.

Uniform Resource Locator: A Uniform Resource Locator (URL) extends the concept of file access from a purely local context to one in which resources are named uniformly, irrespective of where they might be physically located. A URL encodes a location (e.g., `www.javasoft.com`), a name (e.g., `index.html`), and a scheme (e.g., `http`).

uninitialized variable: A method variable that has been declared, but has had no value assigned to it. The compiler will warn of variables which are used before being initialized.

unnamed package: All classes defined in files without a *package declaration* are placed in the unnamed package.

upcast: A cast towards an object's ultimate super type—that is, up the inheritance hierarchy towards the Object class, for instance,

```
// Upcast from VariableController to HeaterController
VariableController v;
...
HeaterController c = v;
```

See *downcast*. Java's rules of *polymorphism* mean that an explicit upcast is not usually required.

User Datagram Protocol: The User Datagram Protocol (UDP) is a set of rules that allows communication between two *processes* across a network. The protocol is unreliable, which means that information is not guaranteed to be transferred correctly between the two processes. See *Transmission Control Protocol (TCP)* for an alternative reliable protocol.

UTF: Universal Character Set (UCS) Transformation Format. A format for representing multi-byte characters that is compatible with programs and *file systems* that were only designed to handle single byte characters.

variable declaration: The association of a variable with a particular type. It is important to make a distinction between the declaration of variables of primitive types and those of class types. A variable of primitive type acts as a container for a single value of its declared type. Declaration of a variable of a class type does not automatically cause an object of that type to be constructed and, by default, a field variable will contain the value `null`. A variable of a class type acts as a holder for a reference to an object that is compatible with the variable's class type. Java's rules of *polymorphism* allow a variable of a class type to hold a reference to any object of its declared type or any of its sub types. A variable with a declared type of `Object`, therefore, may hold a reference to an object of any class.

virtual desktop: The name used to describe a user's graphical working area within a *window manager*. The name arose in the early days of graphical user interfaces when it was thought that these would lead to paperless offices. It was anticipated that the computer screen would become a user's desktop, in which virtual documents, as opposed to paper documents, would be created, read, and manipulated in various ways.

virtual machine: See *Java Virtual Machine (JVM)*.

virtual memory: A computer will have a limited amount of real memory available to it. Programs often require more memory than the amount of real memory. Furthermore, in a *multiprogramming system*, different *processes* will be competing for the same limited supply of real memory. An *operating system* overcomes these conflicts by allocating an amount of virtual memory to each process, which might be larger than the total amount of real memory. This is possible by storing unused parts of a process's *address space* on disk, until such time as it is required. When required, it is *swapped in* to part of the real memory, whose previous contents are *swapped out* to disk.

well-known port: A *port* number at which a *server* offers a familiar service. For instance, 80 is the well-known port number for servers using the *HyperText Transfer Protocol (HTTP)*.

while loop: One of Java's three *control structures* used for looping. The other two are the *do loop* and *for loop*. A while loop consists of a *Boolean expression* and a loop body. The condition is tested before the loop body is entered for the first time and re-tested each time the end of the body is completed. The loop terminates when the condition gives the value `false`. The statements in the loop body might be executed zero or more times.

white space: Characters used to create visual spacing within a program. White spaces include space, tab, carriage return, and line feed characters.

window manager: A window manager provides a computer user with a *virtual desktop* containing one or more windows and working areas in which individual programs may be run. Window managers allow the contents of a user's desktop to be arranged as required through resizing and arranging windows, and provide for *drag-and-drop* operations in collaboration with the *operating system*. They also monitor mouse movements to popup menus, for instance.

wrapper classes: Java's *primitive types* are not object types. The wrapper classes are defined in the `java.lang` *package*. They consist of a class for each primitive type: Boolean, Byte, Character,

Double, Float, Integer, Long, and Short. These classes provide methods to parse strings containing primitive values, and turn primitive values into strings. The Double and Float classes also provide methods to detect special bit patterns for floating point numbers, representing values such as NaN, $+\infty$, and $-\infty$.

Writer class: A *sub class* of the Writer *abstract class*, defined in the java.io *package*. Writer classes translate output from *Unicode* to a host-dependent *character set encoding*. See *Reader class*.

zip file: A file used to store compressed versions of files. In connection with Java *bytecode* files, these have largely been superseded by *Java Archive (JAR) files*.

Bibliography

[AIS+77] Alexander, Christopher, Sara Ishikawa, Murray Silverstein, Max Jacobson, Ingrid Fiksdahl-King, and Shlomo Angel. *A Pattern Language.* New York: Oxford University Press, 1977.

[BDMN79] Birtwhistle, Graham M., Ole-Johan Dahl, Bjørn Myhrhaug, and Kristen Nygaard. *Simula Begin.* Bromley: Chartwell-Bratt, 1979.

[BH75] Brinch Hansen, Per. "The Programming Language Concurrent Pascal." *IEEE Transactions on Software Engineering* 1 (June 1975): 199–207.

[Boo94] Booch, Grady. *Object-Oriented Analysis and Design with Applications.* 2d ed. Reading, MA: Addison-Wesley, 1994.

[Bud97] Budd, Timothy. *Object-Oriented Programming.* 2d ed. Reading, MA: Addison-Wesley, 1997.

[CES71] Coffman, E.G., M.J. Elphick, and A. Shoshani. "System Deadlocks." *Computing Surveys* 3 (June 1971): 67–78.

[Col78] Colin, Andrew J.T. *Programming and Problem-solving in Algol 68.* London and Basingstoke: Macmillan, 1978.

[Com95] Comer, Douglas E. *Internetworking with TCP/TP—Volume 1, Principles, Protocols and Architecture.* 3rd ed. Englewood Cliffs, NJ: Prentice-Hall, 1995.

[Con96] Unicode Consortium. *The Unicode Standard, Version 2.0.* Reading, MA: Addison-Wesley, 1996.

[Cou98] Courtois, Todd. *Java Networking and Communications.* Upper Saddle River, NJ: Prentice-Hall, 1998.

[Cul96] Culwin, Fintan. *Ada: A Developmental Approach.* 2d ed. Upper Saddle River, NJ: Prentice-Hall, 1996.

[FVFH90] Foley, James D., Andries van Dam, Steven K. Feiner, and John F. Hughes, *Computer Graphics—Principles and Practice.* 2d ed. Reading, MA: Addison-Wesley, 1990.

[Gal96] Galletly, John. *occam2—including occam2.1.* London: UCL Press, 1996.

[GHJV95] Gamma, Erich, Richard Helm, Ralph Johnson, and John Vlissides. *Design Patterns—Elements of Reusable Software.* Reading, MA: Addison-Wesley, 1995.

[Gra98] Grauer, Robert. *COBOL: From Micro to Mainframe.* 3rd ed. Upper Saddle River, NJ: Prentice-Hall, 1998.

[Hoa74] Hoare, C.A.R. "Monitors, An Operating System Structuring Concept." *Communications of the ACM* 17 (October 1974): 549–57. With an *erratum* in volume 18, p95, Feb. 1975.

[Ins85] Institute of Electrical and Electronic Engineers. *IEEE/ANSI Standard for Binary Floating Point Arithmetic*, 1985. IEEE Standard 754–1985.

[JW78] Jensen, Kathleen, and Niklaus Wirth. *Pascal User Manual and Report.* 2d ed. New York: Springer-Verlag, 1978.

[KK67] Kemeny, J.G., and T.E. Kurz. *Basic Programming.* New York: Wiley, 1967.

[KR78] Kernighan, Brian W., and Dennis M. Ritchie. *The C Programming Language.* Englewood Cliffs, NJ: Prentice-Hall, 1978.

[NL98] Nyhoff, Larry R., and Stanford C. Leestma, *Introduction to Fortran 90.* 2d ed. Upper Saddle River, NJ: Prentice-Hall, 1998.

[SKT96] Skublics, Suzanne, Edward Klimas, and David Thomas. *Smalltalk with Style.* Upper Saddle River, NJ: Prentice-Hall, 1996.

[Str97] Stroustrup, Bjarne. *The C++ Programming Language.* 3rd ed. Reading, MA: Addison-Wesley, 1997.

[Tan96] Tanenbaum, Andrew S. *Computer Networks.* 3rd ed. Upper Saddle River, NJ: Prentice-Hall, 1996.

[TG98] Tanenbaum, Andrew S., and James R. Goodman. *Structured Computer Organization.* 4th ed. Upper Saddle River, NJ: Prentice-Hall, 1998.

[Tho99] Thompson, Simon. *Haskell: The Craft of Functional Programming.* 2d ed. Reading MA: Addison-Wesley, 1999.

[Top98] Topley, Kim. *CORE Java Foundation Classes.* Upper Saddle River, NJ: Prentice-Hall, 1998.

[TW97] Tanenbaum, Andrew S., and Albert S. Woodhull. *Operating Systems: Design and Implementation.* 2d ed. Upper Saddle River, NJ: Prentice-Hall, 1997.

[Wel98] Welch, Peter H. Java Threads in the Light of occam/CSP. In P.H. Welch and A.W.P. Bakkers, editors, *Architectures, Languages and Patterns.* Amsterdam: IOS Press, 1998.

[Wir71] Wirth, Niklaus. "Program Development by Stepwise Refinement." *Communications of the ACM* 14 (April 1971): 221–27.

[Wora] World Wide Web Consortium. *CGI: Common Gateway Interface.* www.w3.org

[Word] World Wide Web Consortium. *HyperText Markup Language.* www.w3.org

Index